THE 1990
INFORMATION PLEASE®
SPORTS
ALMANAC

D0064521

EDITED BY
Mike Meserole

With research assistance by Howie Schwab,
Edward R. Pete and Jason Diamos.

HOUGHTON MIFFLIN COMPANY   BOSTON

The Information Please Sports Almanac invites comments and suggestion from readers. Because of the many letters received, however, it is not possible to respond personally to every correspondent. Nevertheless, all suggestions are most welcome, and the editor will consider them carefully. (The Information Please Sports Almanac does not rule on bets or wagers.)

ISSN: 1046–4980

Copies of The Information Please Sports Almanac may be ordered directly by mail from:
Customer Service Department
Houghton Mifflin Company
Burlington, MA 01803
Phone toll-free (800) 225-3362 for price and shipping information. In Massachusetts phone: 272-1500.

INFORMATION PLEASE SPORTS ALMANAC©
Editorial Office
Houghton Mifflin Company
1 Beacon Street
Boston, MA 02108

Information Please is a registered trademark of Houghton Mifflin Company.

Printed in the United States of America

wp 10 9 8 7 6 5 4 3 2 1

CONTENTS

For my parents, Barbara and Clint.

I seem to recall that when I was 11 or 12, I had a photographic memory for sports facts and figures. Unfortunately, this gift didn't lend itself to the schoolhouse rigors of math and Latin, but once out of class I could figure ERAs in my head and conjugate the starting line-ups of any major league team you wanted.

These days I have to look everything up. Luckily, I have a lot of reference books. From 1983-88, when I was working at ESPN, I had about 40 of them lined up at attention on my desk ready to jump start my failing memory at a moment's notice. Encyclopedias, almanacs, yearbooks, record books, guides, registers, directories. But a surprising number of times they weren't enough. One reference book was missing. One that would give a detailed account of the sports year just passed and also provide the winners, losers and other vital statistics of years gone by.

Enter **The 1990 Information Please Sports Almanac.** Weighing in at slightly over 550 pages, this is the missing reference book. The year in review, from Nov.1, 1988 to Oct.31, 1989, and the century on record. Sport by sport and year by year. Plus 18 essays by many of the top sportswriters in the country on sports or topics they cover closely.

Thumbing through these pages you'll notice information on everything from the just completed 1989 Bay Area World Series to the upcoming 1990 World Cup in Italy. The membership rolls of 15 Halls of Fame are in here along with a listing of every ballfield, basketball court and hockey rink any current team in the AL, NL, NFL, NBA or NHL has ever called home. There are even two special chapters that review the outstanding sports personalities of this century and recount every Division I college football season since 1936.

Like its big brother **The Information Please Almanac,** the **Sports Almanac** is for looking things up. I hope what you're looking for is in here.

—Mike Meserole

Wolcott, Conn.
October, 1989

First of all, this almanac would never have been possible without the experience, patience and tireless efforts of Michael Michaud of Unicorn Production Services in Marblehead, Mass. Mike and his wife Lynn invited me into their home in October to work on the book around the clock and I'm in their debt. I also appreciate the willingness of their daughters Annie and Molly to share their Oreos and Cheerios with me.

Another game ball goes to everybody at CopyRight Typesetting in Bedford, Mass. We pretty much invented this almanac as we went along and they had to put up with a lot of grief from me.

My telephone and fax bills over the last 10 months attest to the number of places I've called and the kind folks who have helped provide needed information. From the Iditarod Trail Committee in Wasilla, Alaska, to the New England Sports Museum in Boston, and all the major league public relations offices and college sports information departments in between.

Regrettably, there isn't room enough here to list everyone who participated in this project, but there are a few people who deserve to be mentioned: Peter Gammons; Tom Hart; Jon Latimer and everyone attached to the reference wing at Houghton Mifflin; Charley and Marcia Monagan; Lucy Pierpont; Nat Andriani of Wide World Photos; Dawn Longo; Gordon Brumm; Brian and Cathy Leary; Bill Shanahan, Chuck Pagano, Kirk Varner and all my former playmates at the ESPN SportsCenter; Wayne Patterson, Joe Horrigan, Pat Harmon and James Duplacey of the Basketball, Pro Football, College Football and Hockey Halls of Fame; John Heisler of the Notre Dame sports information office; Steve Boda and Jim Van Valkenburg of the NCAA statistics office; WHA hockey historian Jack Lautier; Dan Mearns and Steve Thomas of *The Blood-Horse* magazine; and Mike DeLeo of the Waterbury Public Library.

And finally, my thanks to the 18 sportswriters who agreed to throw in with me for modest wages back in April and whose essays have given this almanac added credibility.

—M.M.

In addition to this index, please refer to Updates (pp. 1-7) and the Review Calendar (pp. 16-27).

Updates

The following news items ocurred after chapter deadlines, but before Nov. 1, 1989.

Wide World Photos

Attorney **Paul Tagliabue** (left) was elected by NFL owners on Oct. 26 to succeed **Pete Rozelle** as commissioner.

Pro Football

The NFL finally elected a new commissioner on Oct.26, elevating league attorney **Paul Tagliabue**, 48. **Pete Rozelle** announced in March that he was stepping down as commissioner after 29 years, but would stay on for as long as it took to find a successor. The search took seven months and turned ugly on July 6 when 11 dissident "young turk" owners banded together in Chicago to block the election of New Orleans GM Jim Finks. Finks was the "old guard" choice and the only candidate nominated by the selection committee.

Backed by the so-called "Chicago 11," Tagliabue emerged as Finks' principal rival at subsequent owners' meetings at Dallas and Cleveland in October, but didn't win the job until a five-man committee was named (Oct.25) by Rozelle to resolve the impasse. The committee, made up of dissidents and old guards, recommended Tagliabue and he was elected by the 28 owners (although not unanimously).

At the halfway mark in the 1989 NFL season (Oct.30), the **San Francisco 49ers** and **New York Giants** were the only teams with 7-1 records. Buffalo, Denver and Philadelphia were at 6-2. The Los Angeles Raiders were 4-4 after a 1-3 start that cost second-year head coach **Mike Shanahan** his job. His replacement was offensive line coach **Art Shell**, 42, who became the NFL's first black head coach since Fritz Pollard coached the Hammond (Ind.) Pros in the 1920s.

Dallas (0-8) was the league's only winless team at mid-season. Desperate for future draft picks, new Cowboys' owner Jerry Jones traded the team's only star player, **Herschel Walker**, to Minnesota (Oct.12) for five Vikings and up to six 1st-, 2nd-, and 3rd-round draft picks over the next five years.

1

College Football

Notre Dame, Colorado, Nebraska, and **Alabama** were the only Division I-A teams to make it through October with undefeated records. The Buffaloes and Cornhuskers were scheduled to meet at Boulder on Nov.4, but Notre Dame's eagerly-awaited rematch with Miami of Florida on Nov. 25 would not be a showdown between No.1 and No.2. Florida State knocked Miami from the unbeaten ranks, 24-10, on Oct. 28. In 1989's only One vs Two match-up so far, the (then) No.2 Irish beat No.1 Michigan, 24-19 on Sept.16.

Elsewhere, tailback **Johnny Bailey** of Division II Texas A&I broke Tony Dorsett's career rushing record (6,082 yards) on Oct.14; while Indiana running back **Anthony Thompson** tied the NCAA career regular season touchdown record of 59 shared by Dorsett and Army's Glenn Davis.

SMU returned from two years' inactivity (due to the NCAA death penalty) and was 2-5 through October, including a humiliating 95-21 loss to Houston (Oct.21). The Cougars ran over the Mustangs for an NCAA-record 1,021 total yards.

Florida headed into November ranked 19th with a 6-1 record, but could be the NCAA's next condemned program. Last penalized by the NCAA in 1985, Florida football was in danger of being found guilty of major violations for the second time in five years (if so, it's the gallows for the Gators). Head coach Galen Hall quit Oct.8 after admitting he made unauthorized payments to two assistant coaches and arranged transportation for a player. Meanwhile, starting quarterback Kyle Morris was thrown off the team on Oct.15 for betting on college football games (although, not Florida games). But more ominous was the news that the NCAA had been investigating both the school's football and basketball programs since June (see page 3).

AP Top 25
(as of Oct.30, 1989)

The Associated Press writers' poll was expanded to 25 teams this season. This poll includes games through Oct.28, 1989. First place votes in parentheses, followed by record, total votes and ranking in preseason poll.

	Record	Pts	Preseason Poll		Record	Pts	Preseason Poll
1. Notre Dame (58)	8-0-0	1,498	2nd	14. Pittsburgh	5-1-1	653	20th
2. Colorado (2)	8-0-0	1,432	14th	15. Arizona	6-2-0	638	18th
3. Nebraska	8-0-0	1,366	3rd	16. Penn St	5-2-0	525	11th
4. Michigan	6-1-0	1,312	1st	17. Houston	5-2-0	460	21st
5. Alabama	7-0-0	1,260	16th	18. N.C.State	7-1-0	457	24th
6. Florida St	6-2-0	1,159	6th	19. Florida	6-1-0	449	30th
7. Miami, FL	6-1-0	1,114	4th	20. Texas A&M	6-2-0	437	27th
8. Illinois	6-1-0	1,083	22nd	21. Clemson	7-2-0	412	12th
9. Southern Cal	6-2-0	1,038	5th	22. Texas	4-2-0	286	31st
10. Tennessee	6-1-0	927	33rd	23. BYU	6-2-0	113	19th
11. Arkansas	6-1-0	912	10th	24. Virginia	7-2-0	112	32nd
12. Auburn	5-2-0	711	8th	25. Fresno St	6-2-0	91	42nd
13. West Virginia	6-1-1	694	17th				

Pro Basketball

The NBA, now 27 teams strong with the additon of expansion franchises in Minnesota and Orlando, was not scheduled to begin its 1989-90 season until Nov.3, but there were some interesting arrivals and departures during the off-season.

Arriving were four European players: 6-5 Soviet guard **Sharunas Marchulenis** (Golden St.); 7-1 center **Vlade Divac** of Yugoslavia (Lakers); 6-9 forward **Alexander Volkov** of the USSR (Atlanta); and 6-8 forward **Zarko Paspalj** of Yugoslavia (San Antonio). Boston signed 6-11 Yugoslavian forward **Dino Radja**, but he will not be free to play for the Celtics until next season.

Departing were **Danny Ferry**, the second overall pick of last Spring's NBA Draft (by the L.A.Clippers), and Boston guard **Brian Shaw**. Both signed in August to play with II Messaggero Roma of the Italian League. Another player threatening flight to Italy was **Rick Mahorn**, but a trade to Philadelphia from the expansion Minnesota Timberwolves should keep the former Detroit Piston in the States.

Hockey

The NHL opened its 73rd season, Oct.5, with nine former Soviet national team players in the fold: defensemen **Viacheslav Fetisov** and **Sergei Starikov** in New Jersey; forwards **Vladimir Krutov** and **Igor Larionov** in Vancouver; forwards **Sergei Makarov** and **Sergei Priakin** in Calgary; forward **Helmut Balderis** in Minnesota; forward **Alexandr Mogilny** in Buffalo; and goalie **Sergei Mylnikov** in Quebec.

Ten days later, L.A. Kings' captain **Wayne Gretzky**, 28, scored two goals and assisted on another against his former team, the Oilers, in Edmonton to break **Gordie Howe's** all-time NHL scoring record of 1,850 points. It took Howe 26 seasons to set the record, but Gretzky needed just a little over 10 to break it. The Kings, by the way, won the game, 5-4, in overtime on a goal by Gretzky.

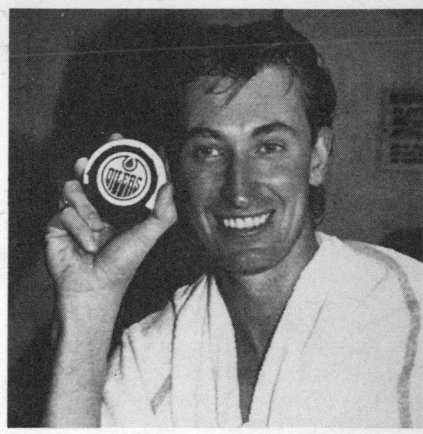

Wide World Photos

Wayne Gretzky
Breaks Howe's record.

Colleges

The head coaches of football and basketball at the **University of Florida** were both forced to resign within 24 days of each other in October. Football coach, **Galen Hall** quit Oct. 8, admitting he had made unauthorized payments to two assistant coaches. Basketall coach **Norm Sloan** stepped down Oct. 31, but maintained he was innocent of unspecified charges of NCAA infractions. The resignations were demanded by University president Robert Bryan and athletic director Bill Arnsparger.

Also, the following schools were placed on probation by the NCAA from June 15 through Oct. 15, 1989:

Adelphi — men's basketball; 3 years for recruiting violations, payments to student-athletes, and academic irregularities.

Eastern Kentucky — women's basketball; 1 year for recruiting violations and payments to student-athletes.

Memphis St. — football; 3 years for illegal payments by boosters and ethical misconduct of coach.

Grambling — men's basketball; 2 years for recruiting violations and payments to student athletes.

SE Louisiana — men's basketball; 5 years for recruiting violations, illegal employing of students, and no supervision of athletic department.

Bowling

Robin Romeo won the Rockford (Ill.) Classic, Oct.11, enabling her to break Lisa Wagner's LPBT single season earnings record. The first prize of $10,000 boosted Romeo's 1989 total to $107,970, bettering Wagner's 1988 mark by $2,470.

In other LPBT tournaments, **Donna Adamek, Lisa Wagner, Aleta Sill, Carol Gianotti, Leila Wagner** and **Nikki Gianulias** all posted Fall Tour wins through October.

The PBA Men's Tour resumed in Rochester, N.Y. with **Joe Berardi** beating Marshall Holman by a pin (210-209) to win the Budweiser Challenge (Oct.28).

Business & Media

Three and a half months after announcing they had bought the NBA's Denver Nuggets (July 10), businessmen **Bertram Lee** and **Peter Bynoe** finally closed the deal on Oct.21, becoming the first black owners of a major league sports franchise.

Nuggets' owner **Sidney Schlenker** had called the original sale off on Oct.10 when Lee and Bynoe failed to meet their final deadline for raising the $65 million purchase price. NBA commissioner David Stern then stepped in, got Lee and Bynoe together with Comsat Video Enterprises president **Robert Wussler** (former CBS president and TBS executive vice-president), and Wussler agreed to put up $17 million in exchange for 62.5 percent of the team. Lee and Bynoe, who will be the Nuggets' managing partners, and their Chicago investors will invest $8 million and control 37.5 percent. The balance of the payment will be financed.

The deal between the **United States Soccer Federation** (USSF) and **NBC Sports** to televise the 1994 World Cup (to be held in the U.S.) may be off. It was vetoed on Sept. 19 by the Federation Internationale de Football Association (FIFA) after several American TV networks complained that there had been no competitive bidding on the '94 Cup.

"We have been asked by the other television networks that they also be offered the opportunity for a bid for the 1994 rights," said FIFA general secretary Joseph (Sepp) Blattner. "That is why we have stopped the USSF from signing with NBC. The rights for 1994 are still in our hands."

A decision is expected Dec.8.

Horse Racing

Secretariat died at 19 on Oct.4 in Paris, Ky. (see "Deaths").

Triple Crown rivals **Sunday Silence** and **Easy Goer** prepped for their final meeting of the year at the Breeders' Cup on Nov. 5 by winning early Fall races. Sunday Silence won the Louisiana Super Derby (Sept.24), while Easy Goer took both the Woodward Stakes (Sept.16) and the Jockey Club Gold Cup (Oct.7) in New York. Jockey **Pat Valenzuela**, who rode Sunday Silence to victory in the Kentucky Derby and Preakness, flunked a drug test (Oct.20) and was suspended 60 days by California stewards (ruling him out of the Breeders' Cup).

In other major races: **Prized** won the Molson Challenge (Sept.10), **The Caretaker** won the Cartier Million (Oct.7), **Carroll House** won the Arc de Triomphe (Oct.8), and **Caltech** won the Bud International (Oct.22).

Nashwan, Europe's top three-year-old, was retired on Oct.17, after coming down with a high fever before the Champion Stakes in England. Nashwan was 6-0 in races in England, but lost to Golden Pheasant Sept. 17 in the Prix Neil in France.

In harness racing, **Sandman Hanover** won the Messenger Stake (Sept.9), **Goalie Jeff** won the Little Brown Jug (Sept.21), and **Peace Corps** won the Kentucky Futurity (Oct.5).

Soccer

By the end of October, 13 of 24 teams had qualified for the 1990 World Cup in Italy. Automatic qualifiers **Argentina** (defending champion) and **Italy** (the host country) were joined by **Belgium, England, Spain, Sweden** and **Yugoslavia** from Europe; **Brazil, Colombia** and **Uruguay** from South America; **Costa Rica** from Concacaf; and **South Korea** and the **United Arab Emirates** from Asia.

Left to qualify in November were eight teams from Europe, one from Concacaf and two from Africa.

The **United States** was still in the running for the remaining Concacaf berth, but had to gain at least a win and a tie in its last two matches with El Salvador (Nov.5) and Trinadad/Tobago (Nov.19). The Americans were held to a scoreless tie by Guatemala (Oct.8) in their one game so far this fall.

Golf

Tom Kite defeated Payne Stewart with a par 4 on the second hole of sudden death to win the Nabisco Championship in Hilton Head, S.C.(Oct.29). The victory gave Kite his first PGA Player of the Year award and his second title as the Tour's leading money winner. In fact, Kite's Nabisco haul of $625,000 ($450,000 first prize plus a $175,000 bonus) pushed his season's total to a record $1,395,298 and made him the PGA's all-time money winner with earnings of $5,600,691.

Gary Player, whose best year on the PGA Tour in 1978 earned him a total of $177,336, won the RJR Seniors Championship (Oct.8) and a check for $202,500. Other Seniors Tour winners were **George Archer** in his Seniors debut at the Gatlin Brothers' Southwest Classic (Oct 15), and **Billy Casper** at the Transamerica Championship (Oct 22).

Elsewhere, **Kite**, **Mark Calcavecchia**, and **Curtis Strange** teamed up to lead the U.S. over Japan, 3½ to 2½, in the final of the Dunhill Cup at St. Andrews Scotland (Oct.1); **Donnie Hammond** captured the PGA Texas Open (Oct.8); **Nick Faldo** beat Ian Woosnam 1-up over 36 holes (Oct.15) in the final of the World Matchplay Championship in England; **Tim Simpson** won the Disney Classic (Oct.22); and **Colleen Walker** defeated Hiromi Kobayashi after six holes of sudden death to win the LPGA Nichirei Cup at Ina, Japan (Oct.29).

Wide World Photos

Tom Kite
PGA Player of the Year.

Boxing

Mark Breland knocked out Mauro Martelli in the 2nd round to retain the WBA welterweight title (Geneva, Switz., Oct.13).

Juan Polo scored a unanimous 12-round decision over champion Elly Pical to win the IBF junior bantamweight title (Roanoke, Va., Oct.18).

Lusita Espinosa knocked out champion Kaokor Galaxy in the 1st round to win the WBA bantamweight title (Bangkok, Oct.18).

Virgil Hill knocked out James Kinchen in the 1st round to retain the WBA light heavyweight title (Bismarck, N.D., Oct.24).

Jeff Harding stopped Tom Collins after two rounds (Collins quit in his corner) to retain the WBC light heavyweight title (Brisbane, Australia, Oct.24).

In amateur boxing: a young U.S. squad won only one gold medal at the World Championships in Moscow. The lone American champion was **Eric Griffin** of Houston, who beat Cuba's Rogelio Marcelo, 17-13, in the 106-lb division (Sept.30). The Soviet Union won five gold medals and Cuba four.

Tennis

On the Men's Tour in October: **Brad Gilbert** defeated Anders Jarryd, 7-5,6-2 to win the Volvo of San Francisco (Oct.1); **Andre Agassi** won his first tournament in 14 months (Oct.8), beating Gilbert, 6-2,6-1, in the Prudential-Bache Classic; 19-year-old **Jim Courier** upset Stefan Edberg, 7-6,2-6,3-6,6-0,7-5, to win the Swiss Indoor in Basel (Oct.8); **Jimmy Connors** beat John McEnroe, 6-3,6-3, in the final of the Toulouse Grand Prix in France (Oct.15); **Miloslav Mecir** knocked off Michael Chang, 4-6,6-3,6-3,6-2, winning the Hong Kong Marlboro Championships (Oct.15); **Ivan Lendl** won the Australian Indoor, disposing of Lars Wahlgren 6-2,6-2,6-1 in the final (Oct.15); **Aaron Krickstein** beat Carl-Uwe Steeb 6-2,6-2, to win the Seiko Super Tournament in Tokyo (Oct.22); and **Lendl** beat Mecir 6-2,6-2,1-6,6-4 to win the European Community Championship in Antwerp (Oct.29)

There were five principal championships on the Women's Tour in October: on Oct.15 **Gabriela Sabatini** defeated Mary Joe Fernandez, 7-6,6-4, to win the Porsche Tennis Cup in Filderstadt, West Germany and **Gretchen Magers** defeated hometown favorite Natalia Zvereva of the Soviet Union, 6-3,6-4 to win the Virginia Slims of Moscow; on Oct.23, **Steffi Graf** beat Jana Novotna, 6-1,7-6, in the final of the European Indoor and **Katerina Maleeva** beat Conchita Martinez, 6-2,6-2, to win a tournament in Bayonne, France; and on Oct.29, **Graf** downed Monica Seles, 7-5,6-4 to win her 13th title of the year, in Brighton, England.

Auto Racing

The NASCAR driving championship remained in doubt going into November. Only 128 points separated **Rusty Wallace** (3,938), **Dale Earnhardt** (3,829) and **Mark Martin** (3,810) with two Winston Cup races left. In October: **Ken Schrader** won the All-Pro Auto Parts 500 (Oct.8); **Geoff Bodine** won the Holly Farms 400 (Oct.15) when Earnhardt and Ricky Rudd collided on the last lap; and **Mark Martin** won the AC Delco 500 (Oct.22) with Wallace placing second and Earnhardt 20th.

Rick Mears won the final race of the CART season, the Champion Spark Plug 300k (Oct.15), but the major Indy car news came on Oct.24 when **Emerson Fittipaldi**, the 1989 Indianapolis 500 winner and CART champion, officially joined **Mears** and **Danny Sullivan** as a member of the Penske Racing Team. Final Top 5 CART point standings: Fittipaldi, 196; Mears, 186; Michael Andretti, 150; Teo Fabi, 141; and Al Unser Jr., 136.

In Formula One, **Alessandro Nannini** of Italy was awarded first place in the Japanese Grand Prix (Oct.22) when winner **Ayrton Senna** was disqualified by race stewards for crossing the track illegally after colliding with teammate (and arch-rival) **Alain Prost** seven laps from the finish. Senna's ouster enabled Prost to clinch his third Formula One world driving championship. Senna appealed the decision to FIA, Formula One's racing tribunal. FIA not only rejected the appeal, but fined Senna $100,000 and placed him on suspension.

On the IMSA circuit, **Geoff Brabham** finished second in the Camel Grand Prix of Southern California (Oct.22) to clinch his second straight driving championship in the final race of he season.

Baseball

Baseball's senior circuit, the Florida-based Senior Professional Baseball Association, was set to begin its first 72-game season on Nov.1. The SPBA, which is open to ballplayers 35 and older (nearly all of them ex-major leaguers), will use the DH and field eight teams in two divisions. The regular season will end Jan.31, 1990, and be followed by playoffs.

North Division: Bradenton Explorers (Clete Boyer, manager); Orlando Juice (Gates Brown); St.Petersburg Pelicans (Bobby Tolan); Winter Haven Super Sox (Bill Lee).
South Division: Ft.Myers Sun Sox (Pat Dobson, manager); Gold Coast Suns (Earl Weaver); St.Lucie Legends (Graig Nettles); West Palm Beach Tropics (Dick Williams). Gold Coast will split its games between Miami and Pompano Beach.

Commissioners & Presidents

Chief executives of established major sports organizations since 1876. Five names were added in 1989.

Major League Baseball

Tenure	Commissioner
1920-44	Kenesaw Mountain Landis*
1945-51	Albert B.(Happy) Chandler
1951-65	Ford Frick
1965-68	William Eckert
1969-84	Bowie Kuhn
1984-89	Peter Ueberroth
1989	A.Bartlett Giamatti**
1989-	Fay Vincent

*Died in office.
**Died in office after 5 months (Apr.1 thru Sept.1, 1989).

National League

Tenure	President
1876	Morgan G.Bulkeley
1877-82	William A.Hulbart*
1883-84	A.G.Mills
1885-1902	Nicholas Young
1903-09	Henry Pulliam*
1910-13	Thomas J.Lynch
1914-18	John K.Tener
1918-34	John A.Heydler
1935-51	Ford Frick
1951-69	Warren Giles
1970-86	Charles (Chub) Feeney
1987-89	A.Bartlett Giamatti
1989-	Bill White

*Died in office.

American League

Tenure	President
1901-27	Bancroft (Ban) Johnson
1927-31	Ernest S.Barnard*
1931-59	William Harridge
1959-73	Joe Cronin
1974-83	Lee MacPhail
1984-	Bobby Brown

*Died in office.

National Basketball Association

Tenure	Commissioner
1949-63	Maurice Podoloff
1963-75	J.Walter Kennedy
1975-84	Larry O'Brien
1984-	David Stern

National Football League

Tenure	President
1920	Jim Thorpe
1921-39	Joe Carr
1939-41	Carl Storck

Tenure	Commissioner
1941-46	Elmer Layden
1946-59	Bert Bell*
1959-60	Austin Gunsel†
1960-89	Pete Rozelle
1989-	Paul Tagliabue

*Died in office.
†Acting Commissioner.

Canadian Football League

Tenure	Commissioner
1958-66	G.Sydney Halter
1967	Allan McEachem, Ted Workman and Keith Davey
1968-83	J.G.(Jake) Gaudaur
1984-88	Douglas Mitchell
1989-	Roy McMurtry

National Hockey League

Tenure	President
1917-43	Frank Calder*
1943-46	Mervyn (Red) Dutton
1946-77	Clarence Campbell
1977-	John Ziegler

*Died in office.

National Collegiate Athletic Assn.

Tenure	Executive Director
1951-88	Walter Byers
1988-	Richard (Dick) Schultz

International Olympic Committee

Tenure	President
1894-96	Demetrius Vikelas, Greece
1896-1925	Baron Pierre de Coubertin, France
1925-42	Count Henri de Baillet-Latour, Belgium
1942-46	Vacant
1946-52	J.Sigfried Edstrom, Sweden
1952-72	Avery Brundage, USA
1972-80	Lord Michael Killanin, Ireland
1980-	Juan Antonio Samaranch, Spain

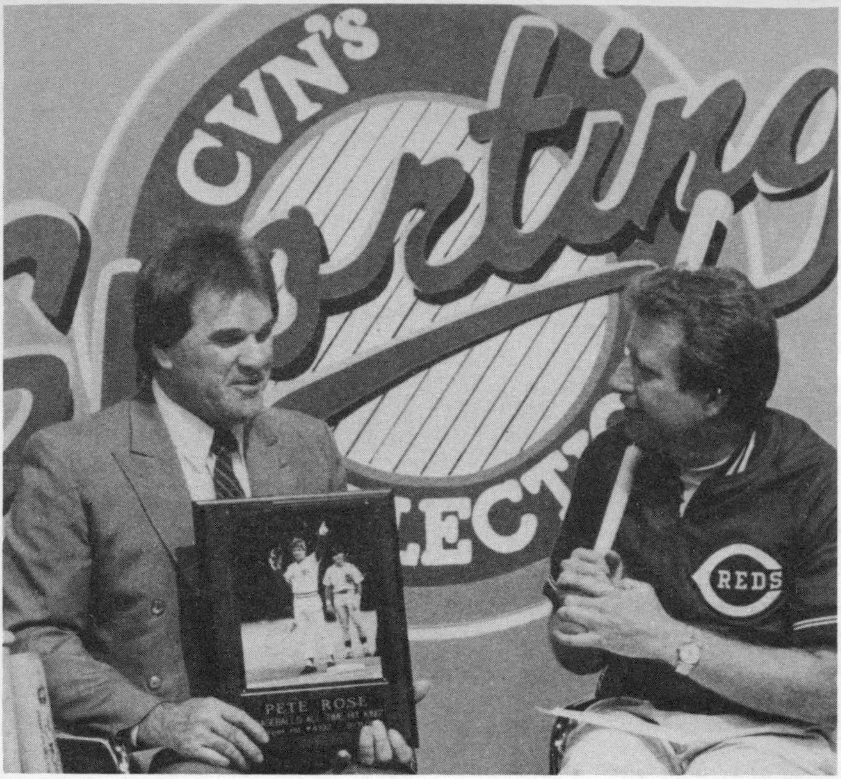

Wide World Photos

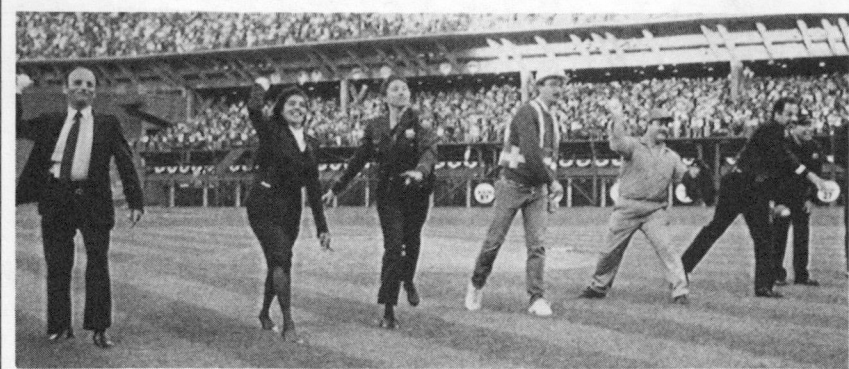

Only hours after being banned from baseball for life by commissioner A. Bartlett Giamatti, **Pete Rose** showed up on cable TV selling memories of a career in ruins.

Wide World Photos

Ten days after the Oct. 17 earthquake rocked Northern California and postponed the World Series, a cross-section of heroes in the Bay Area's rescue efforts threw out ceremonial first balls before Game 3 at Candlestick Park.

Sportsmanship took it on the chin, but 1989 had a few redeeming moments.

A Year of Living Dangerously

by Scott Ostler

Pete Rose. Need we say anything more about 1989? (*Editor's note:* Yes you do.)

OK, then, let's talk about Pete Rose, because he was the embodiment of 1989, a year in which the sports world found itself up You-Know-What Creek without a snorkel, a year in which sports went morally bankrupt yet kept writing checks.

Oh, there were wonderful and inspiring people and events, particularly in the wake of the Bay Area earthquake. But never in recent memory have the ideals, ethics and assorted elements of sportsmanship taken such a beating. They went down like the chilled sides of beef that masqueraded as Mike Tyson's opponents.

Speaking of Tyson, what can you say about a year in which the heavyweight champ was busted twice for speeding, pushed a reporter, broke a TV camera and was portrayed by his biographer and former good pal as a violent wife-beater, and then was awarded an honorary doctorate in humane letters for "his influence on the young people."

What can you say about a year in which the Most Improved Image award goes to Shoeless Joe Jackson?

But back to Rose. Was there a more pathetic scene than Pete Rose appearing live on a Cable Value Network home shopping program only hours after being suspended from baseball for life? No.

There he was, giving a whole new meaning to the nickname Charlie Hustle, proving that he loves his fans so much he will sell them the shirts off his back.

Pete, Pete, Pete. You've just been thrown out of baseball, babe. Bounced, banned, banished, blemished, disgraced, discarded, dog-housed, disowned. Can we get a tiny bit of contrition, Pete? Can we see an ounce of remorse?

No? Well then, can we get that personally-autographed (we'll take your word for it) uniform shirt for $399.92, plus COD charges?

Scott Ostler is a columnist for The National, the new sports daily newspaper. Before that he was a nationally-syndicated columnist for six years at the Los Angeles Times.

Rose's fall from grace was spectacular. But lonely? It was lonely as a lemming leap. Even among stumpy, future Hall of Fame line-drive hitters who once played third base, Rose had company in the mire. Wade Boggs and Steve Garvey starred in separate mini-dramas of third-rate romance and unsafe sex.

Boggs was sued for the equivalent of back wages by his former road mistress, Margo Adams. Boggs pleaded guilty to philandering, with a clinical explanation—he is addicted to sex. Margo bared her soul and assorted body parts in a men's magazine. She told of Wade insisting she wear no underwear to the ballpark, for luck; of Wade taking compromising Polaroids of teammates to prevent them from snitching on him.

"I hope I can still be a role model," Boggs said.

For whom? Hugh Hefner?

Garvey, who never missed a signal in his baseball career, missed at least two in bed. Two women charged that they were pregnant by the Garv, which threw a slight pall over his wedding to a third woman. Political experts speculated that the scandal would prevent Garvey from being elected to public office, at least until all his children reach voting age.

But why dwell on the titillating tabloid stories when we had some hard-core crime? This was the year of the criminal/athlete (crimelete?). Clang-clang-clang went the jail doors behind Bruce Kimball, Chip Banks, Dana Kirk, Norby Walters and Lloyd Bloom, Chuck Muncie, Bob Probert, Carlos Monzon and many more. If you weren't arrested, subpoenaed, indicted, implicated, accused or flat-out flung in the slammer, you just weren't where it was at.

College sports sank to a new low, with major scandals at Kentucky, North Carolina State, Oklahoma and Oklahoma State, and at a university or high school near you.

Oklahoma quarterback Charles Thompson was arrested for allegedly selling cocaine to a cop. Three other Sooners were busted on gang-rape charges, and redshirt Jerry Parks did 2½ months in jail for shooting a teammate in the chest. Who said Oklahoma gridders aren't straight shooters?

North Carolina State basketball coach Jim Valvano was scandalized in a book as a corrupter of young men. The book was sloppy—too many errors and anonymous witnesses—but an NC State official and school records backed up the book's central claim: Among Wolfpack hoopsters, any actual exposure to academia is purely accidental.

All my trials, Lord . . . After running out of lame denials, Ben Johnson confessed to steroid abuse . . . Baseball's team owners once again were ruled guilty of collusion . . . The NFL banned Bengal RB Stanley Wilson for life for coke abuse, then the league was embarrassed by revelations of abuses in its drug-testing program . . . Chris Washburn was suspended for life from the NBA . . . Notre Dame LB Steve Stonebreaker and Raider DB Stacey Toran were drunk drivers. Stonebreaker's passenger was badly injured; Toran was killed . . . Luis Polonia was locked up for having sex with a 15-year-old girl. And so on.

What happened? Did our heroes go mad with greed and power and lust and drugs? Did we suffer a massive meltdown of the collective athletic conscience? Or was 1989 merely a typical year, the misdeeds blown out of proportion by the increasingly snoopy and snarly media?

Surely it's not the latter. Only an incredibly myopic and faint-hearted press could have ignored the tidal wave of crime and grime. Sports people, it would seem, simply rose to a new level of arrogance. Do unto others until you get caught, then deny it.

Was there no hero in shining armor to ride up on his white horse and save the year?

OK then, how about a hero in Spandex and a plastic hat, riding a red bicycle?

On a sunny July afternoon, American son Greg LeMond went for a 27-kilometer bicycle ride through the streets of Paris. It was the 23rd and final day of the Tour de France and the day dawned with LeMond so far behind leader Laurent Fignon that even Pete Rose wouldn't have bet a franc on him.

But LeMond had heroic visions. As if living out a movie script, he brazenly cut himself off from his support crew. He wanted no outside input—no time splits, no reports of Fignon's progress. LeMond would simply ride his heart out, damn the torpedoes. In one of those moments when sport becomes simple and pure, he lit up the City of Light, beating Fignon by eight seconds.

A month later at the World Cycling Championships, as if to prove the Tour win was no one-shot fairy tale, LeMond won again with another dramatic final-day comeback, this time in driving rain.

There were other miracles. What other word would describe Joe Montana's beat-the-clock, 92-yard scoring drive to give the 49ers a 20–16 Super Bowl win over the Bengals? The press gave the MVP award to Jerry Rice—who snagged 11 Montana passes for 215 yards—perhaps because Montana's heroics have become almost routine.

Speaking of routine miracles, did you catch Michael Jordan on any given night? Neither did his defenders. The Chicago Bulls guard seemed to climb to a new rung on basketball's evolutionary ladder. Words fail. Roll the video.

Every sport should have an Air Jordan. Football got to work developing its own prototype, and named it Randall Cunningham. Until last season, Cunningham was a novelty act in Philadelphia, a second-string quarterback who made up his own plays on the fly. In a year's time he has become football's most exciting performer. Although let's not forget part-time Raider employee Bo Jackson, who is proving that the best training for football is baseball, and vice versa.

How about a miracle on ice? And is it too early to vote for the Athlete of the Decade? The nominees are: Wayne Gretzky.

The Great One was traded to the perennially forlorn and woebegone L.A. Kings. Would he become The Average One? No, Gretzky led the Kings to a playoff upset of his former Edmonton club, and converted millions—OK, thousands—of sun-baked L.A. fans to the new sport of ice hockey.

Then this fall, six games into the new season, he became the National Hockey League's all-time leading scorer at age 28. Gordie Howe needed 26 years to score 1,850 points. Gretzky required only 11 to reach 1,851.

Wide World Photos

Greg LeMond
Damn the torpedoes.

Baseball was replete with miracles, foremost among them the survival of 60,000 fans at Candlestick Park on the evening of the Big Quake, Oct. 17. As Bay Area bridges and roadways collapsed and buildings bounced off their foundations, America's most maligned sports stadium shook and swayed like a storm-tossed rowboat. Candlestick was designed and engineered to be earthquake proof, but it was also designed and engineered to be windproof and cold-proof. This time, the drab old lady lived up to her promise and held her ground. All is forgiven.

Lesser miracles marked the baseball season. The Cubs won a division championship, the Giants hummed into the

Texas pitcher **Nolan Ryan** acknowledges a cheering crowd in Anaheim, Sept. 30, after coming within five outs of his first perfect game. Ryan went on to 3-hit the Angels, 2-0, with 13 strikeouts. It was his 289th win and his 57th shutout.

Six-time U.S. Open champion **Chris Evert** (right) hugs **Zina Garrison** after losing their quarterfinal match, 7-6, 6-2, in September. Evert, winner of 18 Grand Slam singles titles since 1974, announced in August that she would be quitting the Women's Tour after the Open.

World Series for the first time since 1962, the Orioles almost won the A.L. East and Tom Lasorda lost 40 pounds.

Unfortunately for Lasorda, he also lost 83 ballgames and sparked mean-spirited theorizing that he is smarter fatter. That weighty theory gained credence when Cubs manager Don Zimmer, another Oprah Winfrey-class dieter, creatively managed the Cubs into the playoffs then immediately managed them out of it.

(The publicity overkill and commercialization of the Lasorda and Zimmer diets turned many of us into Nate Newton fans. Newton, the Dallas Cowboy guard, would have earned a $50,000 bonus by reporting to training camp at 315 pounds. He waddled in at 325 and sniffed, ''I don't need the money.'')

The Cubs once again were Destiny's Dingbats. Chicago mourned (again) but the nation breathed a sigh of relief. A tradition was preserved. If the coyote ever catches the roadrunner, a great cartoon series dies. America needs the Cubs as an enduring standard of futility.

The Orioles, meanwhile, came at us with two new wrinkles—an ornithologically correct bird on their caps and an athletically correct ballclub on their diamond. Frank Robinson's *Icteridae oriolus* faded in the end, but not before an exciting beak-to-beak stretch run with Cito Gaston's Toronto Blue Jays.

Another surprise: Many experts (ever notice how often those guys are wrong?) said it would be a miracle if Angel draftee Jim Abbott, the one-handed pitcher, ever made the big leagues. Abbott, whose pluck is exceeded only by his boyish charm, made it on his first try, winning 12 games for the Angels.

And one miracle to tug at your heart: Giants pitcher Dave Dravecky, 10 months after surgery to remove a malignant tumor (and a large hunk of muscle) from his pitching arm, returned to the big leagues and beat the Reds, 4–3. Grown men wept.

Some miracles have a lousy shelf life. Dravecky's lasted five days. In his next start, in midpitch, the bone in Dave's upper arm snapped like a dry twig. Grown men wept.

There were other tearful moments in '89, because it was a big year for the

Dave Dravecky
Inspirational comeback.

changing of the guard. And the center. Kareem Abdul-Jabbar went on his farewell tour of NBA cities, collecting a warehouse of gifts, including a $10,000 sculpture of an elephant. The elephant symbolizes dignity, longevity and strength. It also symbolizes a non-leaping beast-of-burden, long in the tooth.

In Dallas, the Cowboys were purchased by Jerry Jones, a graduate of the Atilla the Hun School of Housecleaning. Jerry immediately swept out coach Tom Landry and his fellow Cowboy founding fathers Tex Schramm and Gil Brandt. Next to go was Herschel Walker. When last seen, Jones was trying to trade the team's revered lone star symbol for a TV satellite dish and a Milky Way candy bar.

The only sloppier changing of the guard occurred at Michigan, where hoops coach Bill Frieder signed a contract with Arizona State two days before the NCAA playoffs. Nice timing, Bill.

Michigan athletic-director/tyrant Bo Schembechler immediately fired Frieder and elevated assistant Steve Fisher, who coached the Wolverines to the NCAA title. A full week later, after a thorough check to make sure John Wooden was not available, Bo signed Fisher as head coach.

Some great performers bowed out gracefully. Mike Schmidt hung 'em up, as did Ron Guidry, and Randy White and Florence Griffith-Joyner, although FloJo's retirement was tainted by steroid accusations.

Nolan Ryan would have quit but his right arm wouldn't let him. That magnificent and mystifying starboard appendage gunned down 301 American League batters. Only one other big league pitcher, Roger Clemens (230) struck out more than 201. The ravages of old age and the long season eventually took their toll on Ryan. In his final start, The Express could manage only a three-hit, 13-strikeout shutout.

John McEnroe didn't retire, but he struggled. At Wimbledon he threw a tantrum because the courtside ball refrigerator was too noisy. Growing old is hell.

It was tennis that gave us our most dramatic changes of the guard. At the French Open, the champs were 17-year-olds Michael Chang and Arantxa Sanchez. What next? A U.S. Open sponsored by Fisher-Price?

Those two teenie-bombers were for real, but just for old times' sake West German veterans Boris Becker and Steffi Graf made a lovely nostalgia tour of Wimbledon and the U.S. Open, sweeping the singles. Even in their dotage (Becker was 21, Graf 20), Boris and Steffi can still get it up for the big ones.

The most graceful performance of tennis, however, was turned in by Chris Evert. Upon losing to Zina Garrison at the U.S. Open, Evert packed up her racquets, her 20 Grand Slam titles, her 157 tournament victories, her 20 years of memories, and all that class and style that made hers one of the all-time great athletic careers, and proudly walked away from tennis.

Pete Rozelle tried to walk away from the NFL after a 29-year commissionership, but the team owners tied his shoelaces together. Pete retired in March, but discovered that the machinery by which the owners select a new commissioner was invented by Rube Goldberg. It wasn't until late October that the owners finally agreed to anoint attorney Paul Tagliabue as Rozelle's successor.

And then there were those who simply would not call it quits. Repeated blows to the head, apparently, cause damage to the area of the brain that controls retirement. Boxing's so-called Seniors Tour picked up wheezing momentum as Hitman, Sugar Ray, Hands of Stone, Boom Boom and Macho flailed away at one another in highly lucrative parodies of their once-glorious selves. George Foreman waddled through a series of cardboard cutouts disguised as opponents, thus bringing on our worst

Wide World Photos

Kareem Abdul-Jabbar

Wide World Photos

Florence Griffith Joyner

Among the year's tearful exits.

George Foreman vs. Gerry Cooney
Next stop on boxing's Seniors Tour.

nightmare—Gerry Cooney announced a ring comeback.

On a much sadder note, a moment of silence, please, for Bart Giamatti and Sal Aneuse, struck down too young by natural causes. And also for John Matuszak, Stacey Toran, Ricky Berry and Donnie Moore, whose deaths were, in varying degrees, self-inflicted.

Moore shot his wife then killed himself. His personal decline—possibly set in motion by a 1986 gopher ball—and fall reminded us that there is a side of sport that is darker than most of us can imagine.

As for Secretariat, may his final resting place be 31 lengths in front of the field.

Along with heightened cynicism and pessimism, and a handful of heroes, what did 1989 give us? It gave us glimpses of the future. It gave us:

Modern communication—Jose Canseco made himself available to the press and public via tape-recorded messages on a 900 phone line. For a nominal fee, you could listen to Jose complain about lousy room service.

Modern stadia—Toronto's SkyDome had its grand opening. Ah, baseball! The whirr of the roof-retracting motor, the aroma of sizzling McDonald's burgers and fries, the roar of the fans as they drive into the parking lot and get hit up for a $27 parking fee. Take me out to the ballgame; it's in there somewhere.

Modern breakthroughs—The NFL, finally convinced by the NBA's 23-year experiment that the presence of a black man as head coach would not destroy a league, welcomed its first—Art Shell of the Raiders.

Modern cemetery plots—A mobster claimed that Jimmy Hoffa was chopped up and buried in the Meadowlands under what is now the West end zone of Giants Stadium. That would make Jimmy the only gangster who is pushing up AstroTurf.

Hoffa wasn't alone. The year in sports left many of us feeling a little low and disconnected. Too often it left us feeling the same way about sports that Wade Boggs felt about a pretrial hearing for the Margo Adams lawsuit.

Sighed Boggs, "It wasn't something you'd want to take your family to."

Sun	Mon	Tue	Wed	Thu	Fri	Sat
		1	2	3	4	5
6	7	8	9	10	11	12
13	14	15	16	17	18	19
20	21	22	23	24	25	26
27	28	29	30			

Wide World Photos

Greta Waitz
Wins 9th NYC Marathon

1 Kansas University's basketball program is placed on three years' probation by the NCAA for recruiting violations in 1986.

2 Chicago Bears head coach Mike Ditka suffers a mild heart attack after daily workout. (Defensive coordinator Vince Tobin will take over as game coach until Ditka's return Nov.20.)

The Association of Tennis Professionals breaks off negotiations with the Men's Tennis Council, announces it will form its own tour in 1990.

4 The National Basketball Association begins its 43rd season with expansion teams in Charlotte and Miami.

5 Alysheba wins the Breeders' Cup Classic at Churchill Downs to become the richest racehorse of all time. **Personal Ensign** takes the Breeders' Cup Distaff and is the first American horse in 80 years to retire undefeated.

6 Norway's Greta Waitz (2:28:07) wins her 9th New York Marathon, while Steve Jones of Great Britain (2:08:20) is the men's champion.

7 Sugar Ray Leonard knocks out Donny Lalonde in Las Vegas to win both the WBC light heavyweight and super middleweight titles. He joins Thomas Hearns as the only two boxers to hold five separate world crowns in their careers.

9 Laffit Pincay Jr. rides two winners at Hollywood Park in California to become just the second jockey to surpass 7,000 victories. Bill Shoemaker was the first (in 1976).

11 Danny Manning, who led Kansas to the NCAA Division I basketball championship in April, ends holdout and signs with the NBA's L.A. Clippers for five years and $10.5 million.

14 Curtis Strange defeats Tom Kite on the second hole of sudden death to win the Nabisco Championships and clinch his first PGA Player of the Year award.

15 University of Kentucky athletic director Cliff Hagan resigns in the midst of an NCAA investigation into the school's basketball program.

16 Baseball writers name Oakland A's OF Jose Canseco as the Most Valuable Player in the American League. Earlier in the month, Kirk Gibson (MVP) and Orel Hershiser (NL Cy Young) of the L.A. Dodgers, and Frank Viola (AL Cy Young) of Minnesota were also honored.

17 Jack Ramsay quits as coach of the NBA's Indiana Pacers after the team's 0-7 start. He leaves with 908 career wins (including playoffs) in the league, second only to Red Auerbach's 1,037.

19 Three-time NBA MVP Larry Bird undergoes surgery to remove bone spurs from both feet. Doctors say the operation will sideline the Boston forward from three to four months.

20 Gabriela Sabatini defeats Pam Shriver in three sets to win the Virginia Slims Championship at Madison Square Garden. Shriver upset 1988 Grand Slam winner Steffi Graf in the semifinals.

Bill Elliott clinches his first NASCAR Winston Cup Championship with an 11th place finish in the Atlanta Journal 500. The race also marks the retirement of three-time Winston Cup winner Cale Yarborough.

26 No.1 Notre Dame defeats No.2 Southern Cal, 27-10, at the L.A. Coliseum to end college football's regular season at 11-0.

Vince Dooley becomes only the 10th coach in Division I-A history to win 200 games as Georgia beats Georgia Tech.

27 The Winnipeg Blue Bombers upset the B.C. Lions, 22-21, in Ottawa to capture the Canadian Football League's 76th Grey Cup.

Sun	Mon	Tue	Wed	Thu	Fri	Sat
				1	2	3
4	5	6	7	8	9	10
11	12	13	14	15	16	17
18	19	20	21	22	23	24
25	26	27	28	29	30	31

Wide World Photos

Vince Dooley
Top 'Dawg steps down

1 **NBC Sports** beats out favored CBS with a record $401 million bid to televise the 1992 Summer Olympics in Barcelona.

3 **Junior RB Barry Sanders** of Oklahoma State wins the Heisman Trophy as the nation's outstanding college football player.

Army beats Navy, 20-15, to even 89-year-old college football series at 41-41-7.

The Athletics Congress adopts a proposal calling for year-round drug testing instead of just during track season. TAC is the first governing body of the U.S. Olympic Committee to embrace out-of-competition testing.

4 **Baltimore 1B Eddie Murray** is traded to the L.A. Dodgers for three players.

Indiana beats Howard, 1-0, to capture NCAA Division I soccer championship in Bloomington, Ind. Title is the Hoosiers' third of the decade.

5 **Boris Becker** defeats Ivan Lendl in five sets to win the year-end Nabisco Masters Championship at Madison Square Garden. It is their fourth Masters final and Becker's first title.

Chicago Cubs trade of Rafael Palmeiro and pitchers Jamie Mayer and Drew Hall of the Texas Rangers for reliever Mitch Williams, starters Paul Kilgus and Steve Wilson and infielder Curtis Wilkerson.

6 **The Baltimore Orioles are sold** for $70 million to team president Larry Lucchino and three investors. Late owner Edward Bennett Williams bought the club for $12 million in 1979.

9 **Frank Layden** becomes the second NBA coach to resign in less than a month, leaving the Utah Jazz bench for the front office despite his team's 11-6 start.

The N.Y. Yankees sell exclusive local cable TV rights through the year 2000 to Madison Square Garden Network for $500 million.

12 **The United States Supreme Court** rules the NCAA did not violate UNLV basketball coach Jerry Tarkanian's constitutional rights when it suspended him for two years in 1977.

Jackie Sherrill resigns as athletic director and head football coach at Texas A&M in the wake of accusations that he paid "hush money" to a former A&M player during an NCAA investigation.

14 **Vince Dooley,** head football coach at Georgia for 25 years, announces he'll retire after the Bulldogs' Gator Bowl game with Michigan Jan. 2.

CBS Sports wrests Major League Baseball away from NBC and ABC by agreeing to pay a record $1.1 billion over four years for exclusive broadcast TV rights to the regular season, All-Star Game, league playoffs and World Series starting in 1990.

The Miami Heat finally win their first regular season game, beating the L.A. Clippers, 89-88, after an NBA record 17 straight losses to start the season.

16 **The University of Houston's** football program is put on three years' probation by the NCAA for recruiting violations and illegal payments to players from 1978-86.

17 **West Germany clinches Davis Cup,** taking a 3-0 lead against defending champion Sweden in Gothenburg. Wins by Boris Becker and Carl-Uwe Steeb in singles and Becker with partner Eric Jelen in doubles bring the Germans their first Davis Cup ever.

19 **NFL regular season ends** with neither Washington or Denver, the most recent Super Bowl finalists, making the playoffs.

The University of Oklahoma's football program is put on three years' probation by the NCAA for recruiting violations and illegal payments to players from 1981-86.

22 **West Texas State University's** basketball program is placed on three years' probation by the NCAA for violations from 1984-86. Former head coach Gary Moss, now at Sam Houston State, is banned from coaching through 1990.

27 **Marty Schottenheimer** quits as head coach of the Cleveland Browns in a dispute with owner Art Modell.

Sun	Mon	Tue	Wed	Thu	Fri	Sat
1	2	3	4	5	6	7
8	9	10	11	12	13	14
15	16	17	18	19	20	21
22	23	24	25	26	27	28
29	30	31				

Wide World Photos

Teresa Weatherspoon
Athlete of the Year

2 No. 1 Notre Dame defeats No. 3 West Virginia, 34-21, in Fiesta Bowl to clinch its first national football championship since 1977. Miami finishes at No. 2 with 23-3 win over Nebraska in Orange Bowl.

Ray Goff, 33, is promoted from assistant to head football coach at Georgia, replacing Vince Dooley.

5 Kansas City Chiefs fire head coach Frank Gansz after two years and an 8-22-1 record.

ESPN wins bidding for cable TV's Major League Baseball package, agreeing to pay out $400 million over four years beginning in 1990.

Dick Versace leaves assistant's job with the Detroit Pistons to become head coach of the Indiana Pacers. Hiring ends 7-week search to replace Jack Ramsay.

6 Oklahoma State's football program is placed on four years' probation by the NCAA for recruiting violations and illegal payments to players.

9 Johnny Bench and Carl Yastrzemski are voted into Baseball Hall of Fame in their first year of eligibility, becoming the 18th and 19th players so honored.

A revised America's Cup boat size, bigger and lighter than 12-meter yachts, is approved by 25 challengers from 11 countries. The new boat will be a 75-foot sloop with a 102-foot mast and 3,000 square feet of sail.

10 Basketball star Teresa Weatherspoon of Louisiana Tech wins Broderick Award as the nation's top collegiate woman athlete of 1988.

83rd NCAA Convention, meeting in San Francisco, narrowly approves controversial Proposition 42 by 163-154 vote. Denounced as discriminatory by many black coaches and administrators, Prop 42 would deny scholarships and even partial aid to freshmen who do not meet minimum academic standards.

14 Georgetown basketball coach John Thompson walks off court before Hoyas-Boston College game in Landover, Md., to protest Proposition 42. Thompson says his boycott will last indefinitely (he ended it Jan. 21 citing the NCAA's "sincere commitment" to reevaluate Prop 42).

15 Gene Shue is fired as head coach of L.A. Clippers after the team's 10-28 start. Shue leaves with 814 wins (including playoffs), fourth on the all-time list. He is replaced by assistant Don Casey.

22 The San Francisco 49ers beat the Cincinnati Bengals, 20-16, to win Super Bowl XXIII in Miami. The title is the 49ers' third of the decade.

23 C.M. Newton is named the new athletic director at the University of Kentucky. Newton, currently the basketball coach at Vanderbilt, will assume his new duties April 1.

Marty Schottenheimer is named new head coach of Kansas City Chiefs.

Pro Football Hall of Fame elects four new members: Terry Bradshaw, Mel Blount, Willie Wood and Art Shell.

26 Bill Walsh resigns as head coach of the San Francisco 49ers but will stay on as executive vice president. S.F. native George Seifert is named new head coach.

27 Bud Carson is named new head coach of Cleveland Browns. Carson was defensive coordinator for Pittsburgh (1972-77) and N.Y. Jets (1983-88) among others.

28 Alysheba wins Eclipse Award as thoroughbred Horse of the Year, outpolling undefeated filly Personal Ensign.

29 NFC defeats AFC, 34-3, in NFL Pro Bowl game in Hawaii. Randall Cunningham (72 yds pass, 49 yds run) is named MVP.

30 Former Olympic diver Bruce Kimball is sentenced to 17 years in prison for killing two teenagers and injuring four others in a drunk driving accident last summer.

31 Loyola-Marymount (Calif.) defeats U.S. International, 181-150, to set new NCAA record for total points in regulation game.

Sun	Mon	Tue	Wed	Thu	Fri	Sat
			1	2	3	4
5	6	7	8	9	10	11
12	13	14	15	16	17	18
19	20	21	22	23	24	25
26	27	28				

Wide World Photos

Bill White
From All-Star to President

3 Former All-Star 1B Bill White, 55, is named to succeed A.Bartlett Giamatti as NL president on April 1 when Giamatti becomes baseball commissioner. The appointment makes White the first black to head a major pro sports league.

4 Two welterweight championships are decided on same Las Vegas card—Marlon Starling knocks out WBC champion Lloyd Honeyghan in the 9th round and Mark Breland KOs South Korean Lee Seung Soon in the 1st to win vacant WBA title.

Soviet pole vaulter Radion Gataullin breaks indoor world record with vault of 19 feet, 9 inches in Gomel, Byelorussia. New mark is ¾ of an inch higher than old record Gataullin set Jan. 22.

5 South Carolina football coach Joe Morrison, 51, dies of a heart attack in Columbia, S.C. Morrison had a 101-72-7 record in 16 seasons at three colleges.

7 Campbell Conference beats Wales, 9-5, to win NHL All-Star game in Edmonton. Former Oiler Wayne Gretzky (1 goal, 2 assists) is named MVP.

Winnipeg Jets fire head coach Dan Maloney, replace him with minor league coach Rick Bowness.

9 San Diego Chargers pick Washington assistant Dan Henning as new head coach. Henning was head coach in Atlanta from 1983-86.

10 Basketball Hall of Fame elects K.C. Jones, Lenny Wilkens and William "Pop" Gates.

Former Memphis St. basketball coach Dana Kirk is sentenced to one year in jail and fined $20,000 for tax evasion and obstruction of justice.

11 Soviet pole vaulter Sergei Bubka sets new indoor world record with vault of 19 feet, 9½ inches at meet in Osaka, Japan.

12 West Conference beats East, 143-134, to win NBA All-Star game before record crowd of 44,735 at the Astrodome in Houston. Karl Malone (28 points, 9 rebounds) is named MVP.

13 FBI arrests Oklahoma QB Charles Thompson in Norman, Okla., for selling cocaine.

15 The Detroit Pistons trade F Adrian Dantley to the Dallas Mavericks for F Mark Aguirre.

16 World Series MVP Orel Hershiser of Los Angeles signs new 3-year contract for $7.9 million, closing an expensive week of baseball pitcher signings. Also inked were Roger Clemens of Boston ($7.5 million on Feb.15) and Dwight Gooden of the N.Y.Mets ($6.7 million on Feb.8).

18 The Portland Trail Blazers fire head coach Mike Schuler despite a record of 25-22 and replace him with assistant Rick Adelman.

Pernell Whitaker wins IBF lightweight title by scoring a unanimous 12-round decision over champion Greg Haugen.

19 After 17 tries, NASCAR driver Darrell Waltrip finally wins the Daytona 500, beating runner-up and teammate Ken Schrader by 7.6 seconds.

WHA pioneer Bobby Hull's No.9 jersey is retired by the Winnipeg Jets.

22 The Seattle Seahawks name former Oakland-L.A. Raiders head coach Tom Flores team president and general manager.

23 The Boston Celtics trade G Danny Ainge and F Brad Lohaus to the Sacramento Kings for F Ed Pinckney and C Joe Kleine.

The N.Y. Knicks acquire F Kiki Vandeweghe from Portland for the Knicks' 1st round pick in 1989 college draft.

24 Thirty-seven year-old Roberto Duran defeats WBC middleweight champion Iran Barkley in a unanimous 12-round decision at Atlantic City.

25 Heavyweight champion Mike Tyson TKOs Frank Bruno in 5 rounds in Las Vegas to retain title.

Florence Griffith Joyner, who set world records in the Women's 100 and 220 meter dashes and won three Olympic gold medals at the 1988 Seoul Olympics, retires from competitive track and field.

Arkansas oilman Jerry Jones buys the Dallas Cowboys and the rights to Texas Stadium for $180 million, then announces that University of Miami coach Jimmy Johnson will replace Tom Landry.

Sun	Mon	Tue	Wed	Thu	Fri	Sat
			1	2	3	4
5	6	7	8	9	10	11
12	13	14	15	16	17	18
19	20	21	22	23	24	25
26	27	28	29	30	31	

4 Detroit Red Wings F Bob Probert is banned for life by NHL president John Ziegler for attempting to smuggle cocaine across the U.S.-Canadian border (he was arrested March 2).

5 The University of Miami names Dennis Erickson, 41, new head football coach. Erickson leaves Washington St. after two seasons to succeed Jimmy Johnson.

6 Florence Griffith Joyner is named winner of the AAU's 59th Sullivan Award as the nation's top amateur athlete in 1988. Other nominees: kayaker Greg Barton, swimmers Matt Biondi and Janet Evans, speed skater Bonnie Blair, figure skater Brian Boitano, boxer Roy Jones, volleyballer Karch Kiraly, baseketball player Katrina McClain and wrestler John Smith.

The International Tennis Hall of Fame elects former Wimbledon champions Virginia Wade of Britain and Gerald Patterson of Australia.

10 Alpine skier Ingemar Stenmark of Sweden retires after his final race in Japan with an all-time record 86 World Cup victories.

11 Alpine skier Vreni Schneider of Switzerland ends 1988-89 with a record 14 victories, surpassing Stenmark's old single season mark of 12, set in 1978.

12 The Athletics Congress announces a program for random, year-round short-notice testing of track and field athletes beginning July 1.

14 Michigan basketball coach Bill Frieder signs a 4-year contract at Arizona St. two days before his 24-7 Wolverines are scheduled to play their first round game in the NCAA tournament. Michigan athletic director Bo Schembechler declines Frieder's offer to stay on and appoints assistant Steve Fisher to take over.

15 Musher Joe Runyan wins 1,160-mile, Anchorage-to-Nome Iditarod Sled Dog Race. Three-time champion Susan Butcher is second.

18 World Figure Skating Championships end in Paris with Midori Ito of Japan and Kurt Browning of Canada winning the women's and men's singles titles.

Oklahoma St wins its 27th NCAA wrestling championship, but first since 1971, in front of home state fans in Oklahoma City. Defending national champion Arizona St. is second.

Ingemar Stenmark
Hangs up his bindings

Bowler Pete Weber wins PBA National tournament in Toledo, Ohio to become only the third bowler to win each of the PBA's Triple Crown events (the US Open and Firestone Tournament of Champions are the other two).

22 NFL Commissioner Pete Rozelle announces at owners' meeting in Palm Springs, Calif. that he will retire after 29 years as soon as a successor is found.

25 Michael Nunn wins IBF middleweight title, knocking out champion Sumbu Kalambay at 1:28 in first round in Las Vegas.

26 Final Four teams set in NCAA basketball: Michigan and Seton Hall win regionals on Saturday, Duke and Illinois on Sunday.

28 New York State Supreme Court Judge Carmen B. Ciparick orders the San Diego Yacht Club to forfeit the America's Cup to New Zealand, finding that the SDYC violated the spirit of the Cup's Deed of Gift when it defended in a catamaran against New Zealand's monohull last September. San Diego will appeal.

29 Sergei Priakin, 25, receives permission from Moscow to sign 2-year contract with Calgary Flames making him first one-time Soviet national team member to play in NHL.

30 Heisman Trophy winner Barry Sanders of Oklahoma St. announces that he will pass up his final year of college eligibility and enter the NFL Draft in April.

Sun	Mon	Tue	Wed	Thu	Fri	Sat
						1
2	3	4	5	6	7	8
9	10	11	12	13	14	15
16	17	18	19	20	21	22
23	24	25	26	27	28	29
30						

Duane Black

Steve Fisher
Wins title and a job

1 Harvard University wins NCAA hockey championship in overtime, defeating Minnesota, 4-3, in St.Paul, Minn.

Seton Hall and Michigan advance to NCAA basketball finals, beating Duke and Illinois, respectively, in semifinal games at the Kingdome in Seattle.

New York Rangers coach Michel Bergeron is fired with just two games left in regular season and replaced by general manager Phil Esposito.

2 Tennessee Lady Vols gain second NCAA women's basketball championship in three years, beating Auburn, 76-60, in Tacoma, Wash.

3 Michigan wins NCAA men's basketball title, beating Seton Hall, 80-79, in overtime. Forward Glen Rice (184 points in six games) is named tournament MVP.

President George Bush throws out first ball as the 1989 baseball season opens in Baltimore and six other cities. The Orioles, baseball's worst team in 1988, beat Boston, 5-4, in 11 innings.

7 The Houston Oilers sign quarterback Warren Moon to a five-year contract worth $10 million, making Moon the highest-paid player in the league.

8 Jim Abbott, the California Angels' one-handed pitcher, becomes only the 15th rookie since 1965 to play in the major leagues without minor league experience. A home crowd of 46,847 shows up, but Abbott loses his first start to Seattle, 7-0.

9 Britain's Nick Faldo wins the Masters on the second playoff hole against Scott Hoch and Greg Norman. Faldo, tied for 9th after three rounds, shot a final round 65.

Montreal defenseman Larry Robinson sets new NHL record by appearing in his 186th Stanley Cup playoff game.

10 Finally, Steve Fisher is officially named head basketball coach at Michigan after guiding the Wolverines to the national title.

11 The Philadelphia Flyers' Ron Hextall becomes the first goalie in Stanley Cup history to score a goal when he tallies into an empty net at 18:58 of the third period against Washington in Game 5 of the Patrick Division semifinals. Hextall is also the only goalie to ever shoot and score a regular season goal.

12 Sugar Ray Robinson dies in Culver City, Calif. The former world middleweight and welterweight champion, who fought across four decades, was 67.

13 Sports agents Norby Walters and Lloyd Bloom are convicted by a federal jury in Chicago on five counts of racketeering, conspiracy and mail fraud. Both will appeal.

14 The Quebec Nordiques replace head coach Jean Perron with Michel Bergeron. Bergeron coached the Nordiques once before, from 1981-87.

17 The 93rd Boston Marathon is won by Abebe Mekonnen of Ethiopia (2:09:06) and Norway's Ingrid Kristiansen (2:24:33).

18 After 29 years as Dallas president and GM, Tex Schramm leaves the Cowboys to put together a new springtime football league for the NFL.

20 The Dallas Cowboys, who have the first choice in the NFL Draft, sign UCLA quarterback Troy Aikman to a 6-year, $11.2 million contract, making him the highest-paid NFL rookie ever.

23 At the NFL Draft in New York, OT Tony Mandarich (Green Bay) and RB Barry Sanders (Detroit) are the No.2 and No.3 overall picks.

25 Pittsburgh Penguins center Mario Lemieux ties five Stanley Cup records scoring five goals and assisting on three others as the Pens beat Philadelphia, 10-7.

Sun	Mon	Tue	Wed	Thu	Fri	Sat
	1	2	3	4	5	6
7	8	9	10	11	12	13
14	15	16	17	18	19	20
21	22	23	24	25	26	27
28	29	30	31			

1 **Boston Bruins** head coach Terry O'Reilly resigns after three seasons and guiding Bruins to Stanley Cup finals in 1988.

2 **The L.A. Kings** fire Robbie Ftorek as head coach. Kings had 42-31-7 regular season record and made Smythe Division finals, but were swept by Calgary.

4 **NBA Players Assn.** founder and former general counsel Larry Fleisher dies of a heart attack in New York. He was 58.
Soviet hockey star Alexander Mogilny defects to join the Buffalo Sabres of the NHL.

5 **Washington Redskins GM** Bobby Beathard resigns, effective May 31. Beathard helped build two Super Bowl championship teams in Washington and two in Miami.

6 **Sunday Silence** beats favorite Easy Goer by 2½ lengths to win the 115th Kentucky Derby at Churchill Downs in Louisville.

9 **New NBC Sports** president Dick Ebersol fires executive producer Michael Weisman and replaces him with former ABC Sports colleague Terry O'Neil. Weisman's production of the 1988 Seoul Olympics won six Emmy Awards, but did not achieve anticipated ratings.

14 **Norwegian cyclist** Dag Otto Lauritzen wins inaugural Albany-to-Atlantic City Tour de Trump road race. Former Tour de France winner Greg LeMond of the U.S. finishes a distant 27th.

15 **The Toronto Blue Jays** fire Jimy Williams after a 12-24 start, name batting coach Cito Gaston as interim manager.
Cincinnati Bengals RB Stanley Wilson is banned for life by NFL commissioner Pete Rozelle for continual drug use, including the night before the Super Bowl in January.

16 **In the Adams Division** of the NHL, Boston names former Bruin defenseman Mike Milbury as head coach, while Hartford fires Larry Pleau.

19 **The University of Kentucky** basketball program is placed on three years' probation by the NCAA for recruiting and academic rules violations. The Wildcats are also banned from post-season play for the next two years.
Detroit Tigers manager Sparky Anderson is sent home to California because of physical exhaustion (he will return June 5). The Tigers are last in the AL East with a 13-24 record.

20 **Sunday Silence** holds off late charge by Easy Goer to win 114th Preakness Stakes by a nose at Pimlico, Md.

Mike Schmidt
Phillie says farewell

22 **Philadelphia Flyers** goalie Ron Hextall is suspended for 12 games at the start of the 1989-90 regular season for attacking Montreal defenseman Chris Chelios in the last game of the Wales Conference finals.

24 **The New York Rangers** fire GM-coach Phil Esposito.

25 **The Calgary Flames** win their first Stanley Cup with a 4-2 victory over Montreal in Game 6 of the finals at the Forum. Defenseman Al MacInnis is named MVP.

26 **Bob Murdoch is named** head coach in Winnipeg, the Jets' 9th head coach since joining the NHL in 1979.

27 **The Seattle Mariners trade** LHP Mark Langston to Montreal for pitchers Gene Harris, Brian Holman and Randy Johnson.

28 **Emerson Fittipaldi** wins the Indianapolis 500 for the first time and is the first foreigner to win the race since Graham Hill in 1966.
The Milwaukee Bucks trade F Terry Cummings to the San Antonio Spurs for G Alvin Robertson and F Greg Anderson.

29 **Philadelphia Phillies** 3B Mike Schmidt announces his retirement, citing "deterioration" of the skills that enabled him to hit 548 home runs and win 3 MVP awards and 10 gold gloves in 17 years.

31 **The L.A. Kings** name Tom Webster as new head coach.

Sun	Mon	Tue	Wed	Thu	Fri	Sat
				1	2	3
4	5	6	7	8	9	10
11	12	13	14	15	16	17
18	19	20	21	22	23	24
25	26	27	28	29	30	

Wide World Photos

Sugar Ray Leonard
Hearns rematch a draw

1 **Rick Pitino is named** new basketball coach at the University of Kentucky (the N.Y.Knicks released Pitino from his contract, May 30, freeing him to accept the Wildcats' offer).

5 **SkyDome opens** in Toronto, but Blue Jays lose opener, 5-3, to Milwaukee. Crowd of 48,378 turns out for first game in the $400 million stadium with the retractable roof.

7 **Hartford Whalers** name former captain Rick Ley as new head coach.

9 **Race horse owner** Gene Klein, who won three straight Eclipse Awards as thoroughbred owner of the year (1985-87) says he will sell all his racing and breeding stock in November and get on with the rest of his life.

10 **Easy Goer** wins the Belmont by 8 lengths over Kentucky Derby and Preakness winner Sunday Silence.

Seventeen-year-old Arantxa Sanchez of Spain upsets Steffi Graf in French Open final, winning 7-6,3-6,7-5. The loss halts Graf's grand slam singles streak at five.

Wichita St. beats Texas, 5-3, to capture College World Series championship in Omaha, Neb. Shockers' RHP Greg Brummett (3 wins) named tournament MVP.

11 **Seventeen-year-old** Michael Chang wins the French Open in five sets over Stefan Edberg, becoming the first American to win the event since 1955 and the youngest player ever to win a Grand Slam title.

12 **Sugar Ray Leonard** and **Thomas Hearns** battle to a 12-round draw in Las Vegas. The fight is for Leonard's WBC super middleweight title and the first go-round between the two since Leonard KO'd Hearns in the 14th on Sept.16, 1981.

Edmonton Oilers president and general manager Glen Sather steps down as head coach after 11 NHL seasons and 4 Stanley Cups, names assistant John Muckler coach.

13 **Detroit Pistons** sweep LA Lakers in four games to win first NBA championship ever. Guard Joe Dumars (27.3 points a game) named MVP.

Sprinter Ben Johnson admits he lied when he denied using steroids to enhance his performance at the 1988 Olympics. Confession comes during Canadian government drug inquiry in Toronto.

16 **On the second day** of the U.S.Open in Rochester, N.Y., four golfers—Doug Weaver, Mark Wiebe, Jerry Pate and Nick Price—shoot holes-in-one on the 6th hole of Oak Hill C.C.

Buffalo Sabres name Rick Dudley as head coach one day after firing Ted Sator.

18 **Curtis Strange** wins the U.S.Open, the first time an Open champion has successfully defended his title since Ben Hogan did it in 1951.

19 **Beleaguered Oklahoma** football coach Barry Switzer quits after 16 years, 157 wins and three national championships, saying the job is no fun anymore.

Former Soviet hockey goalie Vladislav Tretiak becomes first European player elected to the Hockey Hall of Fame. He is joined by former NHL forwards Darryl Sittler and Herbie Lewis.

20 **Oklahoma names** defensive coordinator Gary Gibbs, 36, as new head football coach.

21 **The New York Yankees** trade OF Rickey Henderson to Oakland for pitchers Eric Plunk and Greg Cadaret and OF Luis Polonia.

24 **Sharunas Marchulenis** becomes the first Soviet basketball player to join the NBA as Golden State signs the 6-5 guard to a 3-year contract.

The N.J.Nets deal F Buck Williams to Portland for C Sam Bowie and the Blazers' 1st round pick in the upcoming NBA Draft.

26 **At the NBA Draft** in New York, Louisville C Pervis Ellison is the first player picked (by Sacramento), while Duke F Danny Ferry (L.A. Clippers) goes second.

Sun	Mon	Tue	Wed	Thu	Fri	Sat
						1
2	3	4	5	6	7	8
9	10	11	12	13	14	15
16	17	18	19	20	21	22
23	24	25	26	27	28	29
30	31					

Wide World Photos

Bo Jackson
All-Star Game MVP

2 **Orville Moody** wins U.S.Senior Open by 2 shots, becomes fourth player to win both U.S. Open and Senior Open (Billy Casper, Arnold Palmer and Gary Player are the others).

Milwaukee OF Robin Yount, 33, collects his 2,500th major league base hit against New York. All-time hit leader Pete Rose was 34 when he got # 2,500.

3 **Tom Browning** of the Cincinnati Reds falls three outs short of becoming the first pitcher in baseball history to throw two perfect games. Dickie Thon of Philadelphia breaks up the bid with a lead-off double in the bottom of the 9th.

6 **NFL owners**, meeting in Chicago, fail to agree on a new commissioner when 11 dissidents block the election of New Orleans GM Jim Finks.

The Chicago Bulls, citing "philosophical differences," fire head coach Doug Collins. Bulls were 47-35 in 1988-89 and reached the Eastern Conference finals before losing to Detroit.

7 **Wade Boggs** signs 3-year contract with Boston Red Sox for $7.3 million.

9 **West Germans** Steffi Graf and Boris Becker both win Wimbledon singles titles in three sets. Graf defeats Martina Navratilova and Becker downs Stefan Edberg.

10 **Two Jacksons** signed as first-time NBA coaches—Phil by the Chicago Bulls and Stu by the New York Knicks. At 33, Stu Jackson is the youngest head coach in the league.

Denver Nuggets announce sale of club for $65 million to black businessmen Bertram Lee and Peter Bynoe. Once the deal is completed, the Nuggets will be the first minority-owned franchise in major league sports history.

11 **American League** beats National, 5-3, to win baseball's All-Star Game in Anaheim. Bo Jackson (1 HR, 2 RBI and a stolen base) is named MVP.

16 **Betsy King** captures U.S. Women's Open by 4 strokes over Nancy Lopez. Winner's check of $80,000 enables King to become the first LPGA player to earn over $500,000 in a single season.

New York Rangers name Neil Smith to replace Phil Esposito as general manager.

21 **Heavyweight champion** Mike Tyson knocks out Carl "The Truth" Williams at 1:33 in the first round at Atlantic City.

22 **The Cleveland Plain-Dealer** reports that Browns QB Bernie Kosar recently negotiated an extension to his contract that calls for $15 million over six years, making him the highest paid player in NFL history.

23 **Greg LeMond** wins his second Tour de France by overtaking Frenchman Laurent Fignon in the race's final stage. Behind by 50 seconds with only a 15-mile time trial left, LeMond wins by eight seconds.

Mark Calcavecchia comes from behind to win the British Open, besting Greg Norman and Wayne Grady in a four-hole playoff at Royal Troon. An American golfer hadn't won the Open since 1983.

29 **Javier Sotomayor** becomes first high jumper to clear 8-feet with world record leap in San Juan, Puerto Rico.

31 **New York Mets** acquire 1988 AL Cy Young Award winner Frank Viola from Minnesota for five pitchers. A day later, they send OF Mookie Wilson to Toronto.

Sun	Mon	Tue	Wed	Thu	Fri	Sat
		1	2	3	4	5
6	7	8	9	10	11	12
13	14	15	16	17	18	19
20	21	22	23	24	25	26
27	28	29	30	31		

Wide World Photos

Roger Kingdom
Lowers high hurdles mark

1 **Danny Ferry** passes up a chance to play for the LA Clippers of the NBA and signs instead with Il Messaggero Roma of the Italian League.

3 **Swimmer Mike Barrowman** sets new world record in 200-meter breaststroke (2:12.90) at US National Championships in Los Angeles.

5 **First dead heat** in the 64-year history of the Hambletonian comes about when stewards at Meadowlands Race Track in New Jersey cannot separate Park Avenue Joe and Probe at the finish of their final race-off. Park Avenue Joe is declared the winner because of better showings in earlier heats.

10 **NBA loses another player** to the Italian League as guard Brian Shaw of the Boston Celtics joins Danny Ferry with Il Messaggero.

13 **Payne Stewart** birdies four of last five holes to win PGA Championship in Hawthorn Woods, Ill. Victory is the knickered Stewart's first major title.

Sacramento Kings F Ricky Berry, 24, commits suicide after having an argument with his wife.

Roger Neilson is hired to coach the N.Y. Rangers, his 6th head coaching job in the NHL.

16 **Roger Kingdom** sets a new world record in the 110-meter high hurdles (12.92) at a meet in Zurich. The old mark of 12.93 was set by Renaldo Nehemiah on the same track in 1981.

18 **The Chicago Bears** trade QB Jim McMahon to the San Diego Chargers for a conditional draft pick.

The N.Y. Yankees fire manager Dallas Green and replace him with minor league manager Bucky Dent.

19 **Four US swimmers** break world records at the Pan Pacific meet in Tokyo—Mike Barrowman in the 200-meter breaststroke (2:12.89), Dave Wharton in the 200 individual medley (2:00.11), Tom Jager in the 50 freestyle (22.12) and Janet Evans in the women's 800-meter free (8:16.22).

Said Aouita of Morocco sets new world record in 3,000-meter run (7:29.45) at a meet in Cologne, West Germany. Aouita now holds records in the 1500, 2000, 3000 and 5000 meter runs.

20 **The New Jersey Nets** name Bill Fitch as new head coach, replacing Willis Reed who resigned Aug. 11 to take a front office job with the club.

22 **Nolan Ryan**, 42, fans Rickey Henderson of Oakland to record his 5,000th career strikeout in Arlington, Tex.

The Seattle Mariners are sold to Indianapolis broadcasting executives Jeff Smulyan and Michael Browning for $76 million.

Mario Lemieux signs 5-year, $12 million contract with Pittsburgh Penguins, second in the NHL only to Wayne Gretzky's 8-year, $20 million deal with the LA Kings.

23 **Exclusive U.S.** television rights to the 1994 Winter Olympics in Lillehammer, Norway are bought by CBS for $300 million.

24 **Pete Rose is banned** from baseball for life by Commissioner A.Bartlett Giamatti, who concludes that the Cincinnati Reds manager bet on baseball games. Rose denies the charge but does not contest the ban. Tommy Helms takes over as interim manager of the Reds.

26 **Trumbull, Conn.** defeats Kaohsiung, Taiwan, 5-2, to win the Little League World Series in Williamsport, Pa. First US champion since 1983.

28 **The Philadelphia 76ers** trade guards Maurice Cheeks and David Wingate and C Chris Welp to San Antonio for G Johnny Dawkins and F Jay Vincent.

NFL suspends 13 players 30 days each for steroid use. No big names are involved.

30 **Juan Antonio Samaranch** is reelected by acclamation to a third term as president of the International Olympic Committee, which is meeting in San Juan, Puerto Rico.

31 **Arbitrator Thomas Roberts** finds baseball guilty of collusion on free agent bidding in 1985 and directs owners to pay players $10.5 million.

Sun	Mon	Tue	Wed	Thu	Fri	Sat
					1	2
3	4	5	6	7	8	9
10	11	12	13	14	15	16
17	18	19	20	21	22	23
24	25	26	27	28	29	30

Wide World Photos

Bart Giamatti
Commissioner only 5 months

1 Baseball commissioner A.Bartlett Giamatti, 51, dies of a heart attack while vacationing at Martha's Vineyard, Mass. The former president of Yale and the National League had only been commissioner since April 1.

The Atlanta Hawks sign 7-foot reserve forward and free agent Jon Koncak to a 6-year contract worth $13.2 million.

2 Deputy commissioner Fay Vincent is named acting commissioner of baseball.

3 Steinlen wins 1¼-mile Arlington Million turf race at Arlington (Ill.) International.

5 Chris Evert loses U.S. Open quarterfinal match to Zina Garrison and retires from major tournament play at age 34.

Ben Johnson stripped of world records at 100, 60, and 50 meters as International Amateur Athletics Federation votes to void any records set by admitted users of performance-enhancing drugs. Carl Lewis inherits 100-meter record (9.92).

The Green Bay Packers sign rookie offensive tackle Tony Mandarich to a 4-year, $4.4 million contract.

8 Kansas City 1B George Brett, 36, gets his 2,500th major league hit at home against Minnesota.

9 Steffi Graf beats Martina Navratilova in three sets to win the U.S.Open and her seventh Grand Slam singles title in two years.

10 Boris Becker defeats top-seeded Ivan Lendl in four sets in U.S.Open men's final, giving West Germany another singles sweep.

The Dallas Cowboys are shut out, 28-0, by New Orleans in Jimmy Johnson's debut as an NFL head coach.

12 The Cleveland Indians fire manager Doc Edwards and name scout John Hart as interim pilot. The 6th place Tribe is 65-78 and 14½ games out.

13 Baseball owners, meeting in Milwaukee, elect Fay Vincent commissioner in a unanimous vote.

16 No.2 Notre Dame beats No.1 Michigan, 24-19, at Ann Arbor as Raghib "Rocket" Ismail runs back two kickoffs for Irish touchdowns.

19 America's Cup is returned to San Diego Yacht Club as New York Appellate Court votes 4-1 to overturn lower court ruling (in March) that the SDYC must forfeit the Cup to New Zealand.

20 Former U.S. sprinter Darrell Robinson accuses U.S. track stars Florence Griffith Joyner and Carl Lewis of using steroids to enhance performances. Both Griffith Joyner and Lewis deny the charges printed in West German magazine **Stern**.

24 Europe keeps possession of the Ryder Cup by holding the U.S. to a 14-14 tie after three days of golf at The Belfry in England. The US last won the Cup in 1983.

Emerson Fittipaldi clinches his first CART Indy Car championship by winning Bosch Spark Plug Grand Prix in Nazareth, Pa.

25 Sunday Silence, returning after a 2-month layoff, wins $1 million Super Derby at Louisiana Downs by 6 lengths over Big Earl.

Yogi Berra says it's over, will retire as a Houston Astros coach at the end of the season after 42 years in the majors.

26 Chicago Cubs beat Expos, 3-2, in Montreal to clinch National League East.

27 Oakland and San Francisco wrap up AL and NL western titles as Athletics beat Texas, 5-0, and Giants clinch on a San Diego loss to Cincinnati.

The Golden State Warriors trade C-F Ralph Sampson to Sacramento for C-F Jim Petersen.

29 Beer baron and St.Louis Cardinals owner August "Gussie" Busch, 90, dies in suburban St.Louis. Busch bought the Cardinals in 1953.

Chris Mullin passes up free agency to sign 9-year contract with Golden State for a reported $20 million.

30 Toronto Blue Jays beat 2nd place Baltimore, 4-3, to clinch first place in AL East on the next to last day of the regular season.

Sun	Mon	Tue	Wed	Thu	Fri	Sat
1	2	3	4	5	6	7
8	9	10	11	12	13	14
15	16	17	18	19	20	21
22	23	24	25	26	27	28
29	30	31				

Wide World Photos

Art Shell
New Raiders head coach

3 **The L.A.Raiders** fire Mike Shanahan and name assistant Art Shell as new coach. Shell becomes the first black NFL head coach since Fritz Pollard in the 1920s.

4 **Secretariat**, 19, is destroyed in Paris, Ky. The 1973 Triple Crown winner had laminitis, a painful and incurable hoof infection.

5 **The National Hockey League** opens its 73rd season in nine cities with nine former Soviet national team players in uniform.

8 **Oakland wins AL pennant**, beating Toronto 4 games to 1. Athletics' OF Rickey Henderson (8 SB, 2 HR) is named MVP.

University of Florida head football coach Galen Hall admits making unauthorized payments to two assistant coaches and resigns after 6 seasons and a 40-18-1 record.

9 **San Francisco wins NL pennant**, eliminating Chicago in 5 games. Giants' 1B Will Clark (13 hits, 8 RBI) is named MVP.

United States defeats Spain, 3-0, in Tokyo to win the Federation Cup for the 13th time. Chris Evert, playing in her final match as a touring pro, and Martina Navratilova clinch victory with singles wins.

12 **Dallas RB Herschel Walker** is traded to Minnesota for five Viking players and up to six 1st-, 2nd- and 3rd-round draft picks over the next five years.

14 **World Series opens** in Oakland between the A's and their Bay Area rivals, the San Francisco Giants.

15 **Wayne Gretzky** becomes the NHL's new all-time leading scorer, breaking Gordie Howe's old record of 1,850 points with two goals and an assist against the Oilers in Edmonton. Gretzky's goals enable the LA Kings to win the game in OT, 5-4.

17 **Major earthquake** hits Bay Area of California. Many dead, many more homeless, damage in the billion-dollar range. Game 3 of the World Series postponed indefinitely.

21 **Sale of Denver Nuggets** to black businessmen Bertram Lee and Peter Bynoe finally completed. Short of funds to meet $65 million purchase price, Lee and Bynoe invite Comsat Video Enterprises in as a partner to close the deal.

22 **Brandy Johnson captures** second place in women's vault for the only American medal at the World Gymnastics Championships in Stuttgart, West Germany. The Soviet men and women dominate team and individual competition. U.S. women finish a surprising 4th, U.S. men 8th.

Harvey Schiller is named Executive Director of the U.S. Olympic Committee for the second time. He resigned as commissioner of the Southeastern Conference earlier in the month.

The Super Bowl champion S.F.49ers, having moved their NFL game from Candlestick Park to Stanford Stadium in Palo Alto, beat New England, 37-20, before 70,000.

26 **NFL attorney Paul Tagliabue** is named commissioner at owners' meeting in Cleveland. Election comes seven months, 11 ballots and three owners' meetings after Pete Rozelle announced his retirement March 22.

27 **The World Series resumes** at Candlestick Park in San Francisco. A's win, 13-7, to take 3-games to none lead.

28 **Oakland wins** World Series, sweeping the Giants in four games. A's pitcher and Oakland native Dave Stewart (2-0, 1.69 ERA) is named MVP.

29 **Tom Kite defeats Payne Stewart** in second hole of sudden death to win the Nabisco Championship in Hilton Head, S.C. and also clinch his first PGA Player of the Year award.

31 **Florida basketball coach** Norm Sloan is forced to resign amid charges of NCAA infractions. Sloan's ouster follows by three weeks the resignation of Gators' football coach Galen Hall, who quit after admitting he violated NCAA rules. Sloan has a career record of 627-395, including a 235-194 mark in 15 years at Florida.

DECEMBER, 1989

2 National Finals Rodeo (Las Vegas).
7 WBC Super Middleweight Title Fight: Sugar Ray Leonard vs Roberto Duran (Las Vegas).
9 Army-Navy Game (E.Rutherford, N.J.); California Bowl (Fresno, Calif.); Heisman Trophy winner announced (New York).
15 Davis Cup Final (Sweden at West Germany).
16 Independence Bowl (Shreveport, La.).
25 NFL regular season closes (Cincinnati at Minnesota); Aloha Bowl (Honolulu).
28 All-American Bowl (Birmingham, Ala.).
29 Bowl games: Freedom (Anaheim, Calif.), Holiday (San Diego), Liberty (Memphis).
30 Bowl games: Copper (Tucson, Ariz.); Gator (Jacksonville, Fla.); John Hancock (formerly the Sun Bowl, El Paso); Peach Bowl (Atlanta).
31 NFL Playoffs begin with conference wild card games.

JANUARY, 1990

1 Bowl games: Cotton (Dallas); Fiesta (Tempe, Ariz.); Citrus (Orlando, Fla.); Hall of Fame (Tampa); Rose (Pasadena), Sugar (New Orleans), Orange (Miami).
6 NFL Playoffs: AFC and NFC divisional games.
14 NFL Playoffs: AFC and NFC Championship games.
15 Australian Open Tennis begins (Melbourne).
21 NHL All-Star Game (Civic Arena, Pittsburgh).
28 Super Bowl XXIV (Superdome, New Orleans).

FEBRUARY, 1990

3 24 Hours of Daytona (Daytona Beach, Fla.).
4 NFL Pro Bowl (Aloha Stadium, Honolulu).
4 U.S. Figure Skating National Championships (Salt Lake City).
11 NBA All-Star Game (Miami Arena, Miami).
15 Pitchers and catchers begin reporting to Spring Training camps in Florida and Arizona.
18 Daytona 500 (Daytona Beach).

MARCH, 1990

3 Iditarod Sled Dog Race begins (Anchorage to Nome, Alaska).
6 World Figure Skating Championships (Halifax, Nova Scotia).
11 United States Grand Prix Formula One auto race (Phoenix).
11 PBA Bowling National Championship (Toledo, Ohio).
12 NFL Annual Meeting (Orlando, Fla.).
15 The Players Championship Golf (Ponte Vedra, Fla.).
16 Lipton International Tennis Championships (Key Biscayne, Fla.).
18 U.S.Indoor Diving National Championships (Portland, Ore.).
19 U.S.Short Course Swimming Championships (Nashville).
25 NCAA Division I Basketball Tournament seeds announced.
22 NCAA Division I Wrestling Championships (College Park, Md.).
29 NCAA Division I Hockey Final Four (Detroit).
30 NCAA Div.I Women's Basketball Final Four (Knoxville, Tenn.).
31 NCAA Div.I Men's Basketball Final Four (Denver).

APRIL, 1990

1 NHL regular season ends.
1 U.S. Men's Open Bowling (Indianapolis).
2 Baseball Opening Day.
4 NHL Stanley Cup Playoffs begin.

5 Masters Golf (Augusta, Ga.)
16 Boston Marathon.
22 NBA regular season ends.
22 NFL Draft (New York).
23 Firestone Tournament of Champions Bowling (Akron, Ohio)
26 NBA Playoffs begin.

MAY, 1990

1 ABC Masters Bowling (Reno, Nev.).
5 Kentucky Derby (Churchill Downs, Louisville).
19 Preakness Stakes (Pimlico Race Course, Baltimore).
27 Indianapolis 500.
28 French Open Tennis begins (Paris).

JUNE, 1990

1 College Baseball World Series (Omaha, Neb.).
8 World Cup Soccer tournament begins (Italy, through July 8).
8 U.S. Gymnastics Championships (Denver).
9 Belmont Stakes (Belmont Park, Elmont, N.Y.).
14 U.S. Men's Open Golf (Medinah, Ill.).
17 U.S. Pro Cycling Road Championships (Philadelphia).
25 Wimbledon Tennis Championships begin.
26 NBA Draft (New York)
28 U.S. Senior Open Golf (Ridgewood, N.J.).
30 Tour de France Cycling race begins (through July 26).

JULY, 1990

6 U.S.Olympic Festival begins (Minneapolis).
8 World Cup Soccer Final (Rome).
10 Baseball All-Star Game (Wrigley Field, Chicago).
12 U.S. Women's Open Golf (Duluth, Ga.).
19 British Open Golf (St.Andrews, Scotland).
20 Goodwill Games begin (Seattle).
29 U.S. Swimming Long Course Championships (Austin, Tex.).

AUGUST, 1990

4 Hambletonian harness race (E.Rutherford, N.J.); NFL Hall of Fame Game (Canton, Ohio).
6 U.S. Women's Amateur Golf (Summit, N.J.).
9 PGA Golf Championship (Birmingham, Ala.).
11 All-American Soap Box Derby (Akron, Ohio).
14 U.S. Outdoor Diving Championships (Dallas).
21 Little League Baseball World Series (Williamsport, Pa.).
21 U.S. Amateur Golf (Englewood, Colo.).
27 U.S. Open Tennis begins (Flushing, N.Y.).

SEPTEMBER, 1990

9 NFL regular season begins.
30 Baseball regular season ends.

OCTOBER, 1990

2 Baseball League Championship Series begin.
6 Ironman Triathlon (Kailua-Kona, Hawaii).
13 World Series begins (in city of NL champion).
27 Breeders' Cup Day (Belmont Park, Elmont, N.Y.

NOVEMBER, 1990

4 New York City Marathon.
12 ATP Tennis Men's Singles Finals (Frankfurt, West Germany).

DECEMBER, 1990

8 Army-Navy Game (Philadelphia).
24 NFL regular season ends.
30 NFL Playoffs begin with wild card games.

Wide World Photos

Oakland reliever **Dennis Eckersley** (left, facing camera) is mobbed by teammates after recording last out of World Series.

BASEBALL

INSIDE

The National Pastime proves just how resilient it can be surviving the banishment of Rose, Giamatti's death, and the 'Quake.

BASEBALL

1989 YEAR IN REVIEW

by Tim Kurkjian

Commissioner Fay Vincent has called baseball "America's most resilient institution." It had to be in 1989. The year began with the most prolific hit-maker of the last six seasons, Wade Boggs, embroiled in an embarrassing sex scandal with his former mistress, Margo Adams. That, however, turned out to be relatively tame fare. In March, allegations came out that the most prolific hit-maker of all time, Pete Rose, had bet on baseball games. It took five ugly months of investigations, hearings and denials before Rose, the manager of the Cincinnati Reds, was suspended from the game for one year, but there is no doubt it will be forever.

The man who suspended him, baseball commissioner A. Bartlett Giamatti, died of a heart attack Sept. 1—only eight days after the Rose decision.

Former California Angels reliever Don-nie Moore shot and killed himself in July. Friends said he could never forget the home run he gave up to Dave Henderson in the 1986 American League playoffs.

In August another pitcher, Dave Dravecky of the San Francisco Giants, made an inspirational comeback from cancer to pitch again—and effectively—in the major leagues. But in his second game back, his left arm snapped during a pitch, putting his career in jeopardy again.

But all the tragedy was put aside when October rolled around. The Giants and Oakland Athletics tore through their League Championship Series in five games each, and hooked up in the first "Battle of the Bay" World Series.

But 31 minutes before the start of Game 3, an earthquake measuring 7.0 on the Richter scale rocked the Bay Area destroying bridges and highways, killing at least 55 people, and leaving thousands homeless. Least importantly, it postponed the World Series—which Vincent sensitively called "our modest little game"—for 11 days.

Tim Kurkjian has covered major league baseball since 1982. He has been the baseball writer at **The Baltimore Sun** since 1986 and is a regular columnist for **Baseball America**.

and 9-6 and did not trail at any time in the Series—the first team since the 1966 Baltimore Orioles to manage that.

In 1988, Oakland reached the World Series, but fell to the underdog Los Angeles Dodgers when it could score only 11 runs in five games. Against the Giants, the A's scored 32 times in four games and set a Series record by getting home runs from eight different starters. It was the loss to the Dodgers in '88 that motivated the A's in '89. "Losing to L.A.," said DH Dave Parker, "turned this team into man-eating tigers."

Having an appetite helped the A's win 99 games and repeat as champions of the A.L. West despite the loss of three key players during the regular season: Jose Canseco (Mr. 40-40) for half the year, shortstop Walt Weiss for two months, and ace reliever Dennis Eckersley for 40 games. Acquiring left fielder Rickey Henderson in a June trade with the New York Yankees (for pitchers Eric Plunk and Greg Cadaret and outfielder Luis Polonia) helped even more.

In the postseason, Henderson batted .441, stole 11 bases, hit three homers, drove in eight runs and scored 12 times to lead the A's past Toronto in five games and the Giants in four. Henderson so intimidated Toronto early in the League Championship Series—he won Game 1 by breaking up a double play and stole four bases in Game 2—that the Blue Jays claimed he was trying to show them up. Whatever the case, Henderson was named MVP of the LCS. "He's the best ballplayer that I've ever seen, ever!" said A's pitcher Dave Stewart.

Stewart, a two-game winner in the LCS, turned in two wins, a complete game, and an ERA of 1.69 in the World Series to nail down MVP. His closest rival for the award was Henderson, who improved his .400 LCS batting average to .474.

After the Athletics had won the first two games of the Series in Oakland, UPI sportswriter Mike Tully wrote that they were so strong, only an earthquake could stop them. One did before Game 3, but only temporarily. Ten days later, on Oct. 27, the A's picked up where they left off and the Series was over by the 28th.

When the final out was made in Game 4, the A's mobbed each other around first

A's postseason hitting star **Rickey Henderson** gestures to crowd after leading off Game 4 of the World Series with an HR.

Many wanted to cancel the Series, but Vincent chose not to for a variety of reasons. One reason, he said, was that it wouldn't be fair for the teams who have come so far to be denied the game's showcase.

As it turned out, the A's ripped through the Giants in four games to become the 1989 World Champions. But this was no ordinary sweep, this was an annihilation. The A's won by scores of 5-0, 5-1, 13-7

"That was a pretty good one."

I had absolutely no idea what was going on.

It was my first earthquake, so I didn't know what to think when the tables in the main press box at Candlestick Park began to shake, pens flipped into the air, books and phones moved and I got a sick, sinking feeling that we were going to tumble into the lower deck.

Oct. 17, 1989, 5:04 p.m. They say it took only 15 seconds, but it seemed like 15 minutes. Scary? You bet. At least 15 grown men—some Californians, no less—were racing for the press box exit. Some were screaming "Don't Panic!" which, of course, made this confused, career Easterner panic more.

When it was over, Gordie Verrell, a writer from Long Beach and a life-time Californian, said "That was a pretty good one," but didn't seem impressed. Ten minutes later, a man walked in and announced that it was a 6.9 on the Richter scale, to which Giants' announcer Hank Greenwald said, "How did the East German judge score it?"

People had no idea of the severity. Verrell said "There's no way that's a 6.9, but if it is, we got trouble."

It was a 7.0. Minutes later, reports came in that the Bay Bridge had collapsed. A section of highway in Oakland had crumbled. All of a sudden, what looked to be a neat lead note for the next day's paper turned into the lead story for the next two weeks, at least.

That night's World Series game was postponed. We ran down to the field to talk with the players. Giants' pitcher Mike Krukow, clutching his young son, said the dugouts moved. Giants catcher Terry Kennedy said the dirt behind home plate spun in one direction and the warning track gyrated in another. Giants' infielder Chris Speier said he was talking with singer Larry Gatlin on the field at the time. Speier remembered Gatlin saying "What's that?" "I told him 'Don't worry, it's an earthquake, enjoy it.' Then the ground started bubbling. I knew it was big."

Every 15 minutes, horrifying reports of deaths came in. The World Series, suddenly insignificant, was postponed 11 days, causing many to question whether it should continue at all. A's outfielder Dave Henderson said "Cancel the Series. You can't fight concrete."

—Tim Kurkjian

base while manager Tony LaRussa and his coaches hugged in the dugout. With the earthquake still very much on everyone's mind the clubhouse celebration was subdued, but the media's praise of the A's was not. Some said Oakland had the makings of a dynasty to rival the A's of 1972-74.

"I think it's a dynasty right now," said Canseco. "I see us going at least to the playoffs for the next five years."

The Giants, meanwhile, came unglued in the Series because they had no pitching. In 1988, Orel Hershiser and the Dodger staff limited the A's to just two runs a game. San Francisco pitching, however, had a combined ERA of 8.21. Even Giants' ace Scott Garrelts, the N.L. ERA champion, was shelled for nine runs in two starts.

Another reason may have been that first baseman Will Clark didn't hit .650 and drive in eight runs as he did against Chicago in the National League Championship Series. Clark had been the playoff MVP, winning the deciding game with a bases-loaded single off Cubs' reliever Mitch Williams and sending the Giants to their first World Series since 1962. In the Series, however, Clark hit only .250 and failed to knock in any runs.

It was a strange year. The Baltimore Orioles, baseball's laughing-stock in 1988 with their record-smashing 0-21 start, led the American League East for 98 days, and were not eliminated until the final weekend of the season by the serene Toronto Blue Jays.

The Chicago Cubs, led by reliever Williams who said he pitched "like my hair's on fire," astounded the experts by shaking off a horrendous spring training show and winning the NL East.

The Hum-Baby San Francisco Giants found Willie Mays in Kevin Mitchell's body. He and Will Clark socked their way through the NL West, winning easily over the Padres. The Dodgers, the 1988 champions, lost 85 games.

It was a season of great and noteworthy individual performances. Nolan Ryan, 42, of the Texas Rangers, struck out 15 in his first AL start in 10 years—which also gave him 15-strikeout performances 19 years apart. Ryan took five no-hitters into the seventh inning, while becoming

Wide World Photos

Three-time 20-game winner
Dave Stewart was World Series MVP.

the oldest pitcher ever to strike out 300 hitters and the only man to strike out 5,000 in a career (together, Sandy Koufax and Bob Feller didn't strike out 5,000).

Ryne Sandberg, the Cubs elegant second baseman, broke a major league record with 90 straight errorless games, and more impressive, hit 20 homers between errors. Blue Jays shortstop Tony Fernandez set a major league record for highest fielding percentage by a shortstop. The Orioles set a major league record for the highest fielding percentage in one season.

Mitchell hit 47 homers to lead the majors (he also led in RBIs with 125), and set a major league record for intentional walks in a season by a right-handed hitter with 32. He also made an unbelievable bare-handed catch of a drive to deep left field early in the season at Busch Stadium in St. Louis.

Kirby Puckett of the Twins became the first righthanded hitter to win the AL batting title in a full season since Alex Johnson in 1970. Puckett edged Carney Lansford, and soundly beat out Wade Boggs, whose string of .350+ seasons ended at four—seven short of the streak by Ty Cobbs. Boggs did, however, become the first player to amass 200 hits and 100 walks five straight seasons.

The Padres' Tony Gwynn won his third straight NL batting title—the first man to do that since Stan Musial (1950-52). Gwynn won it on the final day, beating out the Giants' Clark, who, at his current rate, might end up better than Musial.

The A's Dave Stewart became the first pitcher to win 20 games in three straight years since Jim Palmer won 20 in four straight (1975-78). The Twins Jeff Reardon became the first reliever ever to save 30 games in five straight seasons. And Orel Hershiser's won–loss record went from 23-8 to 15-15, although his ERA was only slightly higher (2.31 from 2.26).

A look at the divisions.

AL East

Before the season, a national magazine polled 186 writers on the divisional races —170 picked the Orioles to finish last. None had them higher than fifth. Even Frank Robinson, the manager, said late in the season, ''If you had told me in spring training that we'd be playing for the division title the final week of the year, I'd have told you 'Be serious, Hollywood wouldn't even touch that script. They already made *Field of Dreams.*' ''

But it was *Field of Dreams.* The Orioles won Opening Day, and never stopped

Wide World Photos

The Pacific Sock Exchange: **Will Clark** and **Kevin Mitchell** of the Giants.

pumping. They tied the 1966-67 Cubs for the most victories (87) the year following a 100-loss season. They set a record for the most days (113) spent in first place the year after a last-place finish. They made the fourth greatest improvement from one year to the next and they were the only team in league history not to spend a day in last place after spending every day in last place the year before.

It all came down to a gripping final weekend at the SkyDome in Toronto.

Gregg Olson, who set an AL mark for saves by a rookie (27), bounced his now famous curveball, allowing Toronto to tie the score in the eighth inning of Game No. 160. The Blue Jays won that one, 2-1, in the 11th, to open a two-game lead. They wrapped it up the next day, winning, 4-3, with three in the eighth. It took a victory away from Orioles starter Dave (Magic) Johnson, the man who lives in a trailer park, a career minor leaguer who came from nowhere to win four games in August.

Managers **Cito Gaston** (left) of Toronto and **Frank Robinson** of Baltimore had the Blue Jays and Orioles battling for first place in the AL East right up to the final weekend of the regular season.

But the Blue Jays had their own story. They were lugging around a 12-24 record and serious attitude problems when their frenetic manager, Jimy Williams, was mercifully fired May 15 and replaced by hitting coach Cito Gaston, who had to be talked into taking the job. Gaston, the second black manager in baseball, "gave us peace," said Blue Jays pitcher Mike Flanagan. A new ballpark, the SkyDome, the latest eighth wonder of the world, gave them dignity. Fred McGriff gave them the league home run title with 36. And Mookie Wilson, acquired from the New York Mets in August, gave them the spark they desperately needed. The Jays played .612 baseball under Gaston's calm reign.

It was a two-team race at the end because the Brewers had too many injuries, the Red Sox went down in flames during a late-season west coast road trip, the Yankees self-destructed, the Indians were doomed to their 30th straight year finishing at least 10 games from first place, and the Tigers were awful. Detroit was so bad, manager Sparky Anderson had to leave the team for almost a month to go home and rest. Manager Dallas Green of the Yankees and Doc Edwards of the Indians were fired. Green was New York owner George Steinbrenner's 17th pilot in 17 years. Bucky Dent became No. 18.

AL West

The A's were touted as the team to beat, mainly because they were on a mission to avenge the loss to that Triple-A lineup the Dodgers started in the 1988 World Series. But, on the way to the divisional title, Canseco picked up a slew of traffic tickets, got caught with an unregistered gun in his bright red sports car and hurt his wrist so badly, he didn't play until after the All-Star break.

Still, the A's, under the brilliant handling of manager Tony LaRussa, survived despite scoring 88 fewer runs than in 1988. Stewart led a foursome of starters who won at least 17 games each—the first team that could say that since the 1971 Orioles. Eckersley missed 40 games (the A's went 20-20 in those games), but did pitch enough to record 33 saves (while walking only three batters all season).

Mitch Williams had 36 saves for the Cubs and led them to an NL East title.

Kansas City made a late run behind Bret Saberhagen (23-6), but an often punchless attack did them in. The California Angels had the best pitching in baseball for four months as Bert Blyleven (17-5) found the fountain of youth, but too many injuries and not enough hitting down the stretch killed them.

Texas traded for three team batting leaders from the previous year (Julio Franco, Rafael Palmeiro and Harold Baines) and they signed Ryan as a free agent. The Rangers got off to a 17-5 start, but played under .500 the rest of the way. The Twins, Mariners and White Sox were never in the hunt.

NL East
The Cubs could hardly win a game in spring training. General manager Jim Frey was being roasted for trading Palmeiro in a huge deal with Texas that brought very erratic reliever Mitch Williams. They were supposed to finish fifth.

"I don't understand," said Cubs outfielder Andre Dawson. "Three years ago, I came here and thought we were going to win it all. This season, I didn't think we had a chance, and we win the division."

How? Williams took the game's worst bullpen and turned it into one of the best, saving 36 games. Sandberg had a marvelous season, and rookies Jerome Walton and Dwight Smith became terrific fast.

"Cubs win! Cubs win!," shouted Harry Caray.

"Mets lose! Mets lose!," shouted everyone else. Supposedly loaded with unbeatable talent, the Mets never got going. They fought, they bickered and they didn't hit, especially for new pitcher Frank Viola, who was acquired from the Twins at mid-season. Manager Dave Johnson was rumored to get fired (he wasn't) despite averaging 96.7 victories over the last six seasons. The Mets won 87 games, same as the Orioles.

St. Louis kept it close until the end, but their decimated pitching staff, plus a popgun offense outside of Pedro Guerrero and Tom Brunansky, kept them from winning. Montreal acquired pitcher Mark Langston in May, led the division by four games in early August, then won two series the rest of the way to finish with an 81-81 record. The Phillies and Pirates went along for the ride.

NL West
You knew it was the Giants year when Mitchell made that running, bare-handed catch against the Cardinals in April. But that didn't match the home run binge he went on, piling up 31 by the All-Star break. He and Clark, who led the league in almost everything that Mitchell didn't, became the Pacific Sock Exchange. When it began to falter at the end of the year, Matt Williams returned from Phoenix and hit 16 homers in the last two months.

All this hitting made up for sporadic Giants pitching, even from their mid-season acquisition, closer Steve Bedrosian. The best pitcher on the Giants staff was Dave Dravecky, who won only two games, but came back from a cancerous tumor in his left arm in 1988 to pitch in the major leagues. The arm broke in his second start, but he inspired his team— and everyone else in baseball.

San Diego made its usual late—but always too late—charge, losing out by three games. Houston stayed in the race a lot longer than anyone expected and Los Angeles fell a lot quicker than anyone thought possible. The Dodgers traded for slugger Eddie Murray in the offseason, but despite leading the league in ERA by an overwhelming margin, they scored 30 fewer runs than any NL team and finished 14 games out of first.

It was a strange year.

Say It Ain't So, Pete.

Right to the end, Pete Rose didn't know, or didn't realize, the trouble he was in. Even on the day he was kicked out of baseball, he was hawking memorabilia on the Cable Value Network.

The all-time major league hit leader, the man of whom Peter Ueberroth once said, "Pete Rose *is* baseball," was banned from the game by Commissioner A. Bartlett Giamatti for a minimum of one year—and undoubtedly for life—for alleged betting on games while he played for, and managed, the Reds.

Yet despite 225 pages of evidence to the contrary in an investigative report by baseball's special counsel, John Dowd, Rose maintains to this day that he did not bet on baseball games. Yet Rose was caught many times contradicting his story concerning his association with Ron Peters,

Wide World Photos

Pete Rose meets the press the day he was banished from baseball.

Tommy Gioiosa and Paul Janszen, all of whom admittedly aided Rose in the placing of bets.

If nothing else, the company that Rose kept wasn't the kind that baseball encouraged. Buddy Bell, one of Rose's former players, said sitting in the clubhouse watching friends of Rose go in and out of his office was like watching an episode of "The Untouchables."

But through the entire affair, which began in February, Rose kept the attitude that he was, after all, the great Pete Rose, and therefore no one could touch him. Judge Norbert Nadel of the Hamilton County Common Pleas Court—located two miles from Cincinnati's Riverfront Stadium, which is located on Pete Rose Way—issued a stunning challenge to Giamatti's authority by granting Rose a temporary restraining order that blocked baseball from holding a hearing on the allegations facing Rose.

For a while, Rose won.

But in the end, baseball seized control, and on Aug. 24, Giamatti, in a wonderfully elegant, but forceful speech, banned Rose, citing beyond all else that no player is bigger than the game.

Rose was replaced by his close friend Tommy Helms—the first man to congratulate him after his record-setting 4,192nd hit—as the Reds manager. Rose made one final speech before going into hiding. He made three points perfectly clear: He did not have a gambling problem, he planned to be reinstated after one year and he didn't expect the ban to keep him out of the Hall of Fame. Many agreed, many disagreed. Outfielder Jim Dwyer of the Minnesota Twins said "The Hall of Fame is for baseball, heaven is for good people."

There were few better than Giamatti, many said. He had done an admirable job in the grueling job of sentencing Rose, but did what he had to do. Yet only a week later on Sept. 1, Giamatti died of a massive heart attack while vacationing on Martha's Vineyard.

The former president of Yale, a remarkably learned man, had spent his first five months on the job wrestling with the Rose affair. With that finally over, this would be his chance to sit in the stands at Fenway Park as he had so many times growing up a devout Red Sox fan. This would be his chance to be with the fans he cherished and serve the game he loved so very dearly.

He never got the chance. Fay Vincent, the deputy commissioner hired by Giamatti, was named the new commissioner. With tears in his eyes, Vincent talked of carrying out the plans set by Giamatti. One of them was keeping Rose out of the game for a long time.

National League
Final Standings
(1988 final standing in parentheses)

East Division

	W	L	Pct	GB	Home	Away
Chicago (4)	93	69	.574	—	48-33	45-36
New York (1)	87	75	.537	6	51-30	36-45
St.Louis (5)	86	76	.531	7	46-35	40-41
Montreal (3)	81	81	.500	12	44-37	37-44
Pittsburgh (2)	74	88	.457	19	39-42	35-46
Philadelphia (6)	67	95	.414	26	38-42	29-53

Managers: Chi—Don Zimmer (2nd season); NY—Davey Johnson (6th); StL—Whitey Herzog (10th); Mon—Buck Rodgers (5th); Pitt—Jim Leyland (4th); Phila—Nick Leyva (1st).

West Division

	W	L	Pct	GB	Home	Away
San Francisco (4)	92	70	.568	—	53-28	39-42
San Diego (3)	89	73	.549	3	46-35	43-38
Houston (5)	86	76	.531	6	47-35	39-41
Los Angeles (1)	77	83	.481	14	44-37	33-46
Cincinnati (2)	75	87	.463	17	38-43	37-44
Atlanta (6)	63	97	.394	28	33-46	30-51

Managers: SF—Roger Craig (5th season); SD—Jack McKeon (2nd); Hou—Art Howe (1st); Cinn—Reds were 61-66 when 6th year manager Pete Rose was banned from baseball Aug.24 and replaced by Tommy Helms; LA—Tom Lasorda (14th); Atl—Russ Nixon (2nd).

League Leaders

Batting
(Minimum of 502 plate appearances.)

	Avg	AB	R	H	HR	RBI
Tony Gwynn, SD	.336	604	82	203	4	62
Will Clark, SF	.333	588	104	196	23	111
Lonnie Smith, Atl	.315	482	.89	152	21	79
Mark Grace, Chi	.314	510	74	160	13	79
Pedro Guerrero, St.L	.311	570	60	177	17	117
Roberto Alomar, SD	.295	623	82	184	7	56
Jerome Walton, Chi	.293	475	64	139	5	46
Kevin Mitchell, SF	.291	543	100	158	47	125
Jose Oquendo, St.L	.291	556	59	162	1	48
Milt Thompson, St.L	.290	545	60	158	4	68
Ryne Sandberg, Chi	.290	606	104	176	30	76
Tom Herr, Phila	.287	561	65	161	2	37
Howard Johnson, NY	.287	571	104	164	36	101

Home Runs

Mitchell, SF	47
Johnson, NY	36
Davis, Cinn	34
Davis, Hou	34
Sandberg, Chi	30
Strawberry, NY	29
Ja.Clark, SD	26
V.Hayes, Phila	26
Bonilla, Pit	24

Triples

Thompson, SF	11
Bonilla, Pit	10
Clark, SF	9
Coleman, StL	9
Van Slyke, Pit	9

Doubles

Wallach, Mon	42
Guerrero, St.L	42
Johnson, NY	41
Clark, SF	38
Bonilla, Pit	37

Total Bases

Mitchell, SF	345
Clark, SF	321
Johnson, NY	319
Bonilla, Pit	302
Sandberg, Chi	301

Times Walked

Ja.Clark, SD	132
V.Hayes, Phila	101
Bonds, Pit	93
Raines, Mon	93
Murray, LA	87
Mitchell, SF	87

Runs Batted In

Mitchell, SF	125
Guerrero, St.L	117
Clark, SF	111
Davis, Cinn	101
Johnson, NY	101
Ja.Clark, SD	94
Davis, Hou	89
Murray, LA	88
Bonilla, Pit	86

Runs

Clark, SF	104
Sandberg, Chi	104
Johnson, NY	104
Mitchell, SF	100
Butler, SF	100

Stolen Bases

	SB	CS
Coleman, St.L	65	10
R.Alomar, SD	42	17
Samuel, NY	42	12
Johnson, NY	41	8
Raines, Mon	41	9

Slugging Pct.

Mitchell, SF	.635
Johnson, NY	.559
Clark, SF	.546
Davis, Cinn	.541
L.Smith, Atl	.533

Times Struck Out

Galarraga, Mon	158
Ja.Clark, SD	145
Murphy, Atl	142
Thompson, SF	133
Johnson, NY	126
Davis, Hou	123

Pitching
(Minimum of 162 innings pitched)

	ERA	W-L	IP	H	SO
Scott Garrelts, SF	2.28	14-5	193.1	149	119
Orel Hershiser, LA	2.31	15-15	256.2	226	178
Mark Langston, Mon	2.39	12-9	176.2	138	175
Ed Whitson, SD	2.66	16-11	227.0	198	117
Bruce Hurst, SD	2.69	15-11	244.2	214	179
Doug Drabek, Pit	2.80	14-12	244.1	215	123
John Smiley, Pit	2.81	12-8	205.1	174	123
Tim Belcher, LA	2.82	15-12	230.0	182	200
Sid Fernandez, NY	2.83	14-5	219.1	157	198
Bryn Smith, Mon	2.84	10-11	215.2	177	129
Joe Magrane, St.L	2.91	18-9	234.2	219	127
Jim Deshaies, Hou	2.91	15-10	225.2	180	153

Wins

Scott, Hou	20-10
Maddux, Chi	19-12
Bielecki, Chi	18-7
Magrane, St.L	18-9
Reuschel, SF	17-8
De.Martinez, Mon	16-7
Sutcliffe, Chi	16-11
Whitson, SD	16-11
DeLeon, St.L	16-12

Games

Williams, Chi	76
Dibble, Cinn	74
Parrett, Phila	72
Agosto, Hou	71
Dayley, St.L	71

Complete Games

Hurst, SD	10
Belcher, LA	10
Browning, Cinn	9
Magrane, St.L	9
Scott, Hou	9

Strikeouts

DeLeon, St.L	201
Belcher, LA	200
Fernandez, NY	198
Cone, NY	190
Hurst, SD	179
Hershiser, LA	178

Losses

Carman, Phila	5-15
Hill, St.L	7-15
Hershiser, LA	15-15
Four tied with 14.	

Saves

Davis, SD	44
Williams, Chi	36
Franco, Cinn	32
Burke, Mon	28
Howell, LA	28
Landrum, Pit	26
Smith, Hou	25
Myers, NY	24
Bedrosian, SF	23
McDowell, Pit	23

Innings Pitched

Hershiser, LA	256.2
Browning, Cinn	249.2
DeLeon, St.L	244.2
Hurst, SD	244.2
Drabek, Pit	244.1

Shutouts

Belcher, LA	8
Drabek, Pitt	5
Glavine, Atl	4
Hershiser, LA	4
Langston, Mon	4

Walks

Hill, St.L	99
Valenzuela, LA	98
Langston, Mon	93
Gross, Mon	88
Carman, Phila	86
Howell, Phila	86

HRs Given Up

Browning, Cinn	31
Scott, Hou	23
Robinson, SF	22
Smiley, Pit	22
Whitson, SD	22

Team by Team Statistics

Players included either had 150 official at bats or pitched 50 innings during the regular season. *Denotes rookie.

Atlanta Braves

Batting (150 AB)	Avg	AB	R	H	HR	RBI	SB
Lonnie Smith	.315	482	89	152	21	79	25
Oddibe McDowell	.304	280	56	85	7	24	15
Jeff Treadway	.277	473	58	131	8	40	3
Jeff Blauser	.270	456	63	123	12	46	5
Dion James	.259	170	15	44	1	11	1
Gerald Perry	.252	266	24	67	4	21	10
Tommy Gregg	.243	276	24	67	6	23	3
Dale Murphy	.228	574	60	131	20	84	3
Andres Thomas	.213	554	41	118	13	57	3
Darrell Evans	.207	276	31	57	11	39	0
Bruce Benedict	.194	160	12	31	1	6	0
John Russell	.182	159	14	29	2	9	0
Ron Gant	.177	260	26	46	9	25	9
Jody Davis	.169	231	12	39	4	19	0

Pitching (50 IP)	W-L	ERA	Gm	IP	BB	SO
Jim Acker	0-6	2.67	59	97.2	20	68
Jose Alvarez	3-3	2.86	30	50.1	24	45
John Smoltz	12-11	2.94	29	208.0	72	168
Marty Clary*	4-3	3.15	18	108.2	31	30
Tom Glavine	14-8	3.68	29	186.0	40	90
Joe Boever	4-11	3.94	66	82.1	34	68
Derek Lilliquist*	8-10	3.97	32	165.2	34	79
Mark Eichhorn	5-5	4.35	45	68.1	19	49
Pete Smith	5-14	4.75	28	142.0	57	115

Saves: Boever (21), Mike Stanton (3), Acker (2), Alvarez (2).

Cincinnati Reds

Batting (150 AB)	Avg	AB	R	H	HR	RBI	SB
Barry Larkin	.342	325	47	111	4	36	10
Eric Davis	.281	462	42	130	34	101	21
Paul O'Neill	.276	428	49	118	15	74	20
Joe Oliver*	.272	151	13	41	3	23	0
Rolando Roomes*	.263	315	36	83	7	34	12
Ken Griffey	.263	236	26	62	8	30	4
Chris Sabo	.260	304	40	79	6	29	14
Herm Winningham	.251	251	40	63	3	13	14
Mariano Duncan	.248	258	32	64	3	21	9
Ron Oester	.246	305	23	75	1	14	1
Todd Benzinger	.245	628	79	154	17	76	3
Luis Quinones	.244	340	43	83	12	34	2
Jeff Reed	.223	287	16	64	3	23	0

Pitching (50 IP)	W-L	ERA	Gm	IP	BB	SO
Rob Dibble	10-5	2.09	74	99.0	39	141
Jose Rijo	7-6	2.84	19	111.0	48	86
Norm Charlton	8-3	2.93	69	95.1	40	98
John Franco	4-8	3.12	60	80.2	36	60
Ron Robinson	5-3	3.35	15	83.1	28	36
Tom Browning	15-12	3.39	37	249.2	64	118
Tim Leary	8-14	3.52	33	207.0	68	123
Tim Birtsas	2-2	3.75	42	69.2	27	57
Rick Mahler	9-13	3.83	40	220.2	51	102
Scott Scudder*	4-9	4.49	23	100.1	61	66
Kent Tekulve	0-3	5.02	37	52.0	23	31
Bob Sebra	2-3	5.20	21	55.1	28	35
Danny Jackson	6-11	5.60	20	115.2	57	70

Saves: Franco (32), Dibble (2), Birtsas (1), Tekulve (1), Sebra (1).

Chicago Cubs

Batting (150 AB)	Avg	AB	R	H	HR	RBI	SB
Dwight Williams*	.324	343	52	111	9	52	9
Mark Grace	.314	510	74	160	13	79	14
Jerome Walton*	.293	475	64	139	5	46	24
Ryne Sandberg	.290	606	104	176	30	76	15
Lloyd McClendon	.286	259	47	74	12	40	6
Luis Salazar	.282	326	34	92	9	34	1
Shawon Dunston	.278	471	52	131	9	60	19
Domingo Ramos	.263	179	18	47	1	19	1
Damon Berryhill	.257	334	37	86	5	41	1
Mitch Webster	.257	272	40	70	3	19	14
Andre Dawson	.252	416	62	105	21	77	8
Joe Girardi*	.248	157	15	39	1	14	2
Curt Wilkerson	.244	160	18	39	1	10	4
Marvell Wynne	.243	342	27	83	7	39	6
Vance Law	.235	408	38	96	7	42	2

Pitching (50 IP)	W-L	ERA	Gm	IP	BB	SO
Les Lancaster	4-2	1.36	42	72.2	15	56
Mitch Williams	4-4	2.76	76	81.2	52	67
Greg Maddux	19-12	2.95	35	238.1	82	135
Mike Bielecki	18-7	3.14	33	212.1	81	147
Rick Sutcliffe	16-11	3.66	35	229.0	69	153
Jeff Pico	3-1	3.77	53	90.2	31	38
Scott Sanderson	11-9	3.94	37	146.1	31	86
Paul Assenmacher	3-4	3.99	63	76.2	28	79
Steve Wilson*	6-4	4.20	53	85.2	31	65
Paul Kilgus	6-10	4.39	35	145.2	49	61

Saves: Williams (36), Lancaster (8), Pico (2), Wilson (2), Kilgus (2).

Houston Astros

Batting (150 AB)	Avg	AB	R	H	HR	RBI	SB
Kevin Bass	.300	313	42	94	5	44	11
Terry Puhl	.271	354	41	96	0	27	9
Glenn Davis	.269	581	87	156	34	89	4
Glenn Wilson	.266	432	50	115	11	64	1
Craig Biggio	.257	443	64	114	13	70	21
Ken Caminiti	.255	585	71	149	10	72	4
Rafael Ramirez	.246	537	46	132	6	54	3
Gerald Young	.233	533	71	124	0	38	34
Bill Doran	.219	507	65	111	8	58	22
Craig Reynolds	.201	189	16	38	2	14	1

Pitching (50 IP)	W-L	ERA	Gm	IP	BB	SO
Larry Andersen	4-4	1.54	60	87.2	24	85
Danny Darwin	11-4	2.36	68	122.0	33	104
Dave Smith	3-4	2.64	52	58.0	19	31
Mark Portugal	7-1	2.75	20	108.0	37	86
Jim Deshaies	15-10	2.91	34	225.2	79	153
Juan Agosto	4-5	2.93	71	83.0	32	46
Mike Scott	20-10	3.10	33	229.0	62	172
Rick Rhoden	2-6	4.28	20	96.2	41	41
Dan Schatzeder	4-1	4.45	36	56.2	28	46
Jim Clancy	7-14	5.08	33	147.0	66	91
Bob Forsch	4-5	5.32	37	108.1	46	40

Saves: Smith (25), Darwin (7), Andersen (3), Agosto (1), Schatzeder (1).

Los Angeles Dodgers

Batting (150 AB)	Avg	AB	R	H	HR	RBI	SB
Mickey Hatcher	.295	224	18	66	2	25	1
Willie Randolph	.282	549	62	155	2	36	7
Jose Gonzalez	.268	261	31	70	3	18	9
Mike Marshall	.260	377	41	98	11	42	2
Mike Scioscia	.250	408	40	102	10	44	0
Mike Davis	.249	173	21	43	5	19	6
Eddie Murray	.247	594	66	147	20	88	7
Alfredo Griffin	.247	506	49	125	0	29	10
Kal Daniels	.246	171	33	42	4	17	9
Jeff Hamilton	.245	548	45	134	12	56	0
Lenny Harris*	.236	335	36	79	3	26	14
Kirk Gibson	.213	253	35	54	9	28	12
John Shelby	.183	345	28	63	1	12	10
Rick Dempsey	.179	151	16	27	4	16	1

Pitching (50 IP)	W-L	ERA	Gm	IP	BB	SO
Jay Howell	5-3	1.58	56	79.2	22	55
Alejandro Pena	4-3	2.13	53	76.0	18	75
Orel Hershiser	15-15	2.31	35	256.2	77	178
Mike Morgan	8-11	2.53	40	152.2	33	72
Tim Belcher	15-12	2.82	39	230.0	80	200
Ramon Martinez*	6-4	3.19	15	98.2	41	89
Tim Crews	0-1	3.21	44	61.2	23	56
Fernando Valenzuela	10-13	3.43	31	196.2	98	116
John Wetteland*	5-8	3.77	31	102.2	34	96

Saves: Howell (28), Pena (5), Belcher (1), Wetteland (1), Crews (1).

New York Mets

Batting (150 AB)	Avg	AB	R	H	HR	RBI	SB
Mackey Sasser	.291	182	17	53	1	22	0
Howard Johnson	.287	571	104	164	36	101	41
Dave Magadan	.286	374	47	107	4	41	1
Kevin McReynolds	.272	545	74	148	22	85	15
Gregg Jefferies*	.258	508	72	131	12	56	21
Tim Teufel	.256	219	27	56	2	15	1
Barry Lyons	.247	235	15	58	3	27	0
Juan Samuel	.235	532	69	125	11	48	42
Keith Hernandez	.233	215	18	50	4	19	0
Kevin Elster	.231	458	52	106	10	55	4
Darryl Strawberry	.225	476	69	107	29	77	11
Mookie Wilson	.205	249	22	51	3	18	7
Gary Carter	.183	153	14	28	2	15	0

Pitching (50 IP)	W-L	ERA	Gm	IP	BB	SO
Rick Aguilera	6-6	2.34	36	69.1	21	80
Randy Myers	7-4	2.35	65	84.1	40	88
Sid Fernandez	14-5	2.83	35	219.1	75	198
Dwight Gooden	9-4	2.89	19	118.1	47	101
Frank Viola	5-5	3.38	12	85.1	27	73
Bob Ojeda	13-11	3.47	31	192.0	78	95
Ron Darling	14-14	3.52	33	217.1	70	153
David Cone	14-8	3.52	34	219.2	74	190
Don Aase	1-5	3.94	49	59.1	26	34

Saves: Myers (24), Aguilera (7), Aase (2), Gooden (1).

Montreal Expos

Batting (150 AB)	Avg	AB	R	H	HR	RBI	SB
Tim Raines	.286	517	76	148	9	60	41
Tim Wallach	.277	573	76	159	13	77	3
Dave Martinez	.274	361	41	99	3	27	23
Damaso Garcia	.271	203	26	55	3	18	5
Hubie Brooks	.268	542	56	145	14	70	6
Andres Galarraga	.257	572	76	147	23	85	12
Nelson Santovenia	.250	304	30	76	5	31	2
Rex Hudler	.245	155	21	38	6	13	15
Mike Fitzgerald	.238	290	33	69	7	42	3
Spike Owen	.233	437	52	102	6	41	3
Tom Foley	.229	375	34	86	7	39	2
Otis Nixon	.217	258	41	56	0	21	37

Pitching (50 IP)	W-L	ERA	Gm	IP	BB	SO
Mark Langston	12-9	2.39	24	176.2	93	175
Tim Burke	9-3	2.55	68	84.2	22	54
Bryn Smith	10-11	2.84	33	215.2	54	129
Dennis Martinez	16-7	3.18	34	232.0	49	142
Pascual Perez	9-13	3.31	33	198.1	45	152
Zane Smith	1-13	3.49	48	147.0	52	93
Kevin Gross	11-12	4.38	31	201.1	88	158
Andy McGaffigan	3-5	4.68	57	75.0	30	40
Joe Hesketh	6-4	5.77	43	48.1	26	44

Saves: Burke (28), Hesketh (3), McGaffigan (2), Z.Smith (2).

Philadelphia Phillies

Batting (150 AB)	Avg	AB	R	H	HR	RBI	SB
John Kruk	.300	357	53	107	8	44	3
Tom Herr	.287	561	65	161	2	37	10
Ricky Jordan	.285	523	63	149	12	75	4
Dickie Thon	.271	435	45	118	15	60	6
Randy Ready	.264	254	37	67	8	26	4
Von Hayes	.259	540	93	140	26	78	28
Charlie Hayes*	.257	304	26	78	8	43	3
Steve Lake	.252	155	9	39	2	14	0
Steve Jeltz	.243	263	28	64	4	25	4
Lenny Dykstra	.237	511	66	121	7	32	30
Dwayne Murphy	.218	156	20	34	9	27	0
Mike Schmidt	.203	148	19	30	6	28	0
Darren Daulton	.201	368	29	74	8	44	2
Bob Dernier	.171	187	26	32	1	13	4

Pitching (50 IP)	W-L	ERA	Gm	IP	BB	SO
Roger McDowell	4-8	1.96	69	92.0	38	47
Jeff Parrett	12-6	2.98	72	105.2	44	98
Ken Howell	12-12	3.44	33	204.0	86	164
Greg Harris	2-2	3.58	44	75.1	43	51
Todd Frohwirth*	1-0	3.59	45	62.2	18	39
Dennis Cook*	7-8	3.72	23	121.0	38	67
Larry McWilliams	2-11	4.10	40	120.2	49	54
Bruce Ruffin	6-10	4.44	24	125.2	62	70
Terry Mulholland	4-7	4.92	25	115.1	36	66
Don Carman	5-15	5.24	49	149.1	86	81

Saves: McDowell (23), Parrett (6), Harris (1).

Pittsburgh Pirates

Batting (150 AB)

	Avg	AB	R	H	HR	RBI	SB
Mike LaValliere	.316	190	15	60	2	23	0
Gary Redus	.283	279	42	79	6	33	25
Bobby Bonilla	.281	616	96	173	24	86	8
R.J.Reynolds	.270	363	45	98	6	48	22
Jay Bell	.258	271	33	70	2	27	5
Barry Bonds	.248	580	96	144	19	58	32
Benny Distefano	.247	154	12	38	2	15	1
Andy Van Slyke	.237	476	64	113	9	53	16
Jose Lind	.232	578	52	134	2	48	15
Billy Hatcher	.231	481	59	111	4	51	24
John Cangelosi	.219	160	18	35	0	9	11
Junior Ortiz	.217	230	16	50	1	22	2
Rafael Belliard	.214	154	T0	33	0	8	5
Rey Quinones	.209	225	21	47	3	29	0
Jeff King*	.195	215	31	42	5	19	4

Pitching (50 IP)

	W-L	ERA	Gm	IP	BB	SO
Bill Landrum	2-3	1.67	56	81.0	28	51
Doug Bair	2-3	2.27	44	67.1	28	56
Doug Drabek.....	14-12	2.80	35	244.1	69	123
John Smiley	12-8	2.81	28	205.1	49	123
Bob Kipper	3-4	2.93	52	83.0	33	58
Neal Heaton	6-7	3.05	42	147.1	55	67
Randy Kramer* ...	5-9	3.96	35	111.1	61	52
Bob Walk	13-10	4.41	33	196.0	65	83
Jeff Robinson	7-13	4.58	50	141.1	59	95
Rick Reed	1-4	5.60	15	54.2	11	34

Saves: Landrum (26), Robinson (4), Kipper (4), Bair (1), Kramer (1).

St. Louis Cardinals

Batting (150 AB)

	Avg	AB	R	H	HR	RBI	SB
Pedro Guerrero....	.311	570	60	177	17	117	2
Jose Oquendo......	.291	556	59	162	1	48	3
Milt Thompson	.290	545	60	158	4	68	27
Ozzie Smith	.273	593	82	162	2	50	29
Terry Pendelton	.264	613	83	162	13	74	9
Tony Pena	.259	424	36	110	4	37	5
Vince Coleman	.254	563	94	143	2	28	65
Tom Brunansky	.239	556	67	133	20	85	5
Willie McGee	.236	199	23	47	3	17	8

Pitching (50 IP)

	W-L	ERA	Gm	IP	BB	SO
Frank DiPino	9-0	2.45	67	88.1	20	44
Dan Quisenberry..	3-1	2.64	63	78.1	14	37
Ken Dayley	4-3	2.87	71	75.1	30	40
Joe Magrane	18-9	2.91	34	234.2	72	127
Todd Worrell.....	3-5	2.96	47	51.2	26	41
Jose DeLeon	16-12	3.05	36	244.2	80	201
Cris Carpenter* ..	4-4	3.18	36	68.0	26	35
John Costello.....	5-4	3.32	48	62.1	20	40
Scott Terry	8-10	3.57	31	148.2	43	69
Ted Power	7-7	3.71	23	97.0	21	43
Ken Hill*	7-15	3.80	33	196.2	99	112
Ricky Horton	0-3	4.85	34	72.1	21	26

Saves: Worrell (20), Dayley (12), Quisenberry (6), Costello (3), Terry (2).

San Diego Padres

Batting (150 AB)

	Avg	AB	R	H	HR	RBI	SB
Tony Gwynn	.336	604	82	203	4	62	40
Bip Roberts	.301	329	81	99	3	25	21
Roberto Alomar ...	.295	623	82	184	7	56	42
Garry Templeton ...	.255	506	43	129	6	40	1
Chris James	.243	482	55	117	13	65	5
Jack Clark	.242	455	76	110	26	94	6
Benito Santiago ...	.236	462	50	109	16	62	11
Carmelo Martinez ...	.221	267	23	59	6	39	0
Darrin Jackson	.218	170	17	37	4	20	1

Pitching (50 IP)

	W-L	ERA	Gm	IP	BB	SO
Mark Davis	4-3	1.85	70	92.2	31	92
Greg Harris*.....	⅛-9	2.60	56	135.0	52	106
Ed Whitson	16-11	2.66	33	227.0	48	117
Bruce Hurst	15-11	2.69	33	244.2	66	179
Mark Grant	8-2	3.33	50	116.1	32	69
Calvin Schiraldi ...	6-7	3.51	59	100.0	63	71
Andy Benes*	6-3	3.51	10	66.2	31	66
Walt Terrell	5-13	4.01	19	123.1	26	63
Eric Show........	8-6	4.23	16	106.1	39	66
Dennis Rasmussen .	10-10	4.26	33	183.2	72	87

Saves: Davis (44), Harris (6), Schiraldi (4), Grant (2).

San Francisco Giants

Batting (150 AB)

	Avg	AB	R	H	HR	RBI	SB
Will Clark	.333	588	104	196	23	111	8
Kevin Mitchell	.291	543	100	158	47	125	3
Brett Butler	.283	594	100	168	4	36	31
Ernest Riles	.278	302	43	84	7	40	0
Ken Oberkfell	.269	156	19	42	2	17	0
Donell Nixon	.265	166	23	44	1	15	10
Greg Litton	.252	143	12	36	4	17	0
Robby Thompson ...	.241	547	91	132	13	50	12
Terry Kennedy	.239	355	19	85	5	34	1
Jose Uribe	.221	453	34	100	1	30	6
Candy Maldonado ..	.217	345	39	75	9	41	4
Kirt Manwaring	.210	200	14	42	0	18	2
Pat Sheridan	.205	161	20	33	3	14	4
Matt Williams	.202	292	31	59	18	50	1

Pitching (50 IP)

	W-L	ERA	Gm	IP	BB	SO
Scott Garrelts	14-5	2.28	30	193.1	46	119
Craig Lefferts....	2-4	2.69	70	107.0	22	71
Steve Bedrosian...	3-7	2.87	68	84.2	39	58
Rick Reuschel	17-8	2.94	32	208.1	54	111
Mike LaCoss	10-10	3.17	45	150.1	65	78
Don Robinson	12-11	3.43	34	197.0	37	96
Atlee Hammaker ..	6-6	3.76	28	76.2	23	30
Jeff Brantley*	7-1	4.07	59	97.1	37	69
Kelly Downs......	4-8	4.79	18	82.2	26	49
Bob Knepper	7-12	5.13	35	165.0	75	64

Saves: Bedrosian (23), Lefferts (20), Bedrosian (20), LaCoss (6), Goose Gossage (4).

Team Batting & Pitching

National League

Team Batting

	Avg	AB	R	H	HR	RBI	SB
Chicago	.261	5513	702	1438	124	653	136
St. Louis	.258	5492	632	1418	73	587	155
San Diego	.251	5422	642	1360	120	598	136
San Francisco	.250	5469	699	1365	141	647	87
Montreal	.247	5482	632	1353	100	587	160
Cincinnati	.247	5520	632	1362	128	588	128
New York	.246	5489	683	1351	147	633	158
Philadelphia	.243	5447	629	1324	123	594	106
Pittsburgh	.241	5539	637	1334	95	584	155
Los Angeles	.240	5465	554	1313	89	513	81
Houston	.239	5516	647	1316	97	598	144
Atlanta	.234	5463	584	1281	128	544	83

Team Pitching

	ERA	W	Sv	CG	ShO	HR	BB	SO
Los Angeles	2.95	77	36	25	19		95	504	1052
New York	3.29	87	38	24	12	115	532	1108
San Francisco	3.30	92	47	12	16	120	471	802
St. Louis	3.36	86	43	18	18	84	482	844
San Deigo	3.38	89	52	21	11	133	481	933
Chicago	3.43	93	55	18	10	106	532	918
Montreal	3.48	81	35	20	13	120	519	1059
Pittsburgh	3.64	74	40	20	9	121	539	827
Houston	3.64	86	38	19	12	105	551	965
Atlanta	3.70	63	33	15	8	114	468	966
Cincinnati	3.73	75	37	16	9	125	559	981
Philadelphia	4.04	67	33	10	10	127	613	899

American League

Team Batting

	Avg	AB	R	H	HR	RBI	SB
Boston	.277	5666	774	1571	108	716	56
Minnesota	.276	5581	740	1542	117	691	111
Chicago	.271	5504	693	1493	94	661	97
New York	.269	5458	698	1470	130	657	137
Texas	.263	5458	695	1433	122	654	101
Oakland	.261	5416	712	1414	127	659	157
Kansas City	.261	5475	690	1428	101	653	154
Toronto	.260	5581	731	1449	142	685	144
Milwaukee	.259	5473	707	1415	126	660	165
Seattle	.257	5512	694	1417	134	653	81
California	.256	5545	669	1422	145	624	89
Baltimore	.252	5440	708	1369	129	659	118
Cleveland	.245	5463	604	1340	127	567	74
Detroit	.242	5432	617	1315	116	564	103

Team Pitching

	ERA	W	Sv	CG	ShO	HR	BB	SO
Oakland	3.09	99	57	17	20	103	510	930
California	3.28	91	38	32	20	113	465	897
Kansas City	3.55	92	38	27	13	86	455	978
Toronto	3.58	89	38	12	12	99	478	849
Cleveland	3.65	73	38	23	13	107	452	844
Milwaukee	3.80	81	45	16	8	129	457	812
Texas	3.91	83	44	26	7	119	654	1112
Seattle	4.00	73	44	15	10	114	560	897
Baltimore	4.00	87	44	16	7	134	486	676
Boston	4.01	83	42	14	9	131	548	1054
Chicago	4.23	69	46	9	5	144	539	778
Minnesota	4.28	80	38	19	8	139	500	851
New York	4.50	74	44	15	9	150	521	787
Detroit	4.53	59	26	24	4	150	652	831

Home Attendance

National League

Based on turnstile count.

		Attendance	Dates	Average
1	St. Louis	3,082,000	82	37,585
2	Los Angeles	2,944,653	1	36,354
3	New York	2,918,710	79	36,946
4	Chicago	2,491,942	81	30,765
5	San Francisco	2,059,829	79	26,074
6	San Diego	2,009,032	80	25,113
7	Cincinnati	1,979,320	79	25,055
8	Philadelphia	1,861,985	74	25,162
9	Houston	1,834,908	81	22,653
10	Montreal	1,783,533	81	22019
11	Pittsburgh	1,374,121	78	17,617
12	Atlanta	984,930	77	12,791
	Totals	25,324,963	952	26,602

American League

Based on tickets sold.

		Attendance	Dates	Average
1	Toronto	3,375,573	80	42,195
2	Oakland	2,667,225	81	32,929
3	California	2,647,291	81	32,683
4	Baltimore	2,534,875	78	32,498
5	Boston	2,510,162	79	31,774
6	Kansas City	2,477,700	80	30,971
7	Minnesota	2,277,438	81	28,117
8	New York	2,170,485	75	28,490
9	Texas	2,043,993	79	25,873
10	Milwaukee	1,970,735	80	24,634
11	Detroit	1,543,656	79	19,540
12	Seattle	1,298,456	81	16,030
13	Cleveland	1,285,542	77	16,695
14	Chicago	1,045,651	78	13,406
	Totals	29,848,782	1,109	26,915

American League
Final Standings
(1988 final standing in parentheses)

East Division	W	L	Pct	GB	Home	Away
Toronto (3)	89	73	.549	—	46-35	43-38
Baltimore (7)	87	75	.537	2	47-34	40-41
Boston (1)	83	79	.512	6	46-35	37-44
Milwaukee (3)	81	81	.500	8	45-36	36-45
New York (5)	74	87	.460	14½	41-40	33-47
Cleveland (6)	73	89	.451	16	41-40	32-49
Detroit (2)	59	103	.364	30	38-43	21-60

West Division	W	L	Pct	GB	Home	Away
Oakland (1)	99	63	.611	—	54-27	45-36
Kansas City (3)	92	70	.568	7	55-26	37-44
California (4)	91	71	.562	8	52-29	38-42
Texas (6)	83	79	.512	16	45-36	38-43
Minnesota (2)	80	82	.494	19	45-36	35-46
Seattle (7)	73	89	.451	26	40-41	33-48
Chicago (5)	69	92	.429	29	35-45	34-47

Managers: Tor—Blue Jays were 12-24 when 4th year manager Jimy Williams was replaced May 15 by Cito Gaston; **Balt**—Frank Robinson (2nd year); **Milw**—Tom Trebelhorn (4th); **Bos**—Joe Morgan (2nd); **Clev**—Indians were 65-78 when 3rd year manager Doc Edwards was replaced Sept.12 by John Hart; **NY**—Yankees were 56-65 when 1st year manager Dallas Green was replaced Aug.18 by Bucky Dent; **Det**—Sparky Anderson (11th).

Managers: Oak—Tony LaRussa (4th season); **Cal**—Doug Rader (1st); **KC**—John Wathan (3rd); **Minn**—Tom Kelly (4th); **Tex**—Bobby Valentine (5th); **Sea**—Jim Lefebvre (1st); **Chi**—Jeff Torborg (1st).

League Leaders

Batting
(Minimum of 502 plate appearances.)

	Avg	AB	R	H	HR	RBI
Kirby Puckett, Minn	**.339**	635	75	215	9	85
Carney Lansford, Oak	**.336**	551	81	185	2	52
Wade Boggs, Bos	**.330**	621	113	205	3	54
Robin Yount, Milw	**.318**	614	101	195	21	103
Julio Franco, Tex	**.316**	548	80	173	13	92
Paul Molitor, Milw	**.315**	615	84	194	11	56
Steve Sax, NY	**.315**	651	88	205	5	63
Harold Baines, Tex	**.309**	505	73	156	16	72
Mike Greenwell, Bos	**.308**	578	87	178	14	95
Ruben Sierra, Tex	**.306**	634	101	194	29	119
Alvin Davis, Sea	**.305**	498	84	152	21	95
Don Mattingly, NY	**.303**	631	79	191	23	113

Pitching
(Minimum of 162 innings pitched)

	ERA	W-L	IP	H	SO
Bret Saberhagen, KC	**2.16**	23-6	262.1	209	193
Chuck Finley, Cal	**2.57**	16-9	199.2	171	156
Mike Moore, Oak	**2.61**	19-11	241.2	193	172
Bert Blyleven, Cal	**2.73**	17-5	241.0	225	131
Kirk McCaskill, Cal	**2.93**	15-10	212.0	202	107
Chris Bosio, Milw	**2.95**	15-10	234.2	225	173
Bob Welch, Oak	**3.00**	17-8	209.2	191	137
Mark Gubicza, Cal	**3.04**	15-11	255.0	252	173
John Cerutti, Tor	**3.07**	11-11	205.1	214	69
Tom Candiotti, Clev	**3.10**	13-10	206.0	188	124
Roger Clemens, Bos	**3.13**	17-11	253.1	215	230
Nolan Ryan, Tex	**3.20**	16-10	239.1	162	301

Home Runs

McGriff, Tor	36
Carter, Clev	35
McGwire, Oak	33
Jackson, KC	32
Esasky, Bos	30
Sierra, Tex	29
Whitaker, Det	28
Deer, Milw	26
Tettleton, Balt	26
Hrbek, Minn	25

Runs Batted In

Sierra, Tex	119
Mattingly, NY	113
Esasky, Bos	108
Carter, Clev	105
Jackson, KC	105
Bell, Tor	104
Yount, Milw	103
Evans, Bos	100
Parker, Oak	97

Wins

Saberhagen, KC	23-6
Stewart, Oak	21-9
Davis, Oak	19-7
Moore, Oak	19-11
Ballard, Balt	18-8
Blyleven, Cal	17-5
Welch, Oak	17-8
Stieb, Tor	17-8
Gordon, KC	17-9
Anderson, Minn	17-10
Clemens, Bos	17-11

Saves

Russell, Tex	38
Thigpen, Chi	34
Plesac, Milw	33
Eckersley, Oak	33
Schooler, Sea	33
Jones, Clev	32
Reardon, Minn	31
Olson, Balt	27
Harvey, Cal	26
Righetti, NY	26
Smith, Bos	26

Triples

Sierra, Tex	14
White, Cal	13
Bradley, Balt	10
Four tied with 9	

Runs

R.Henderson, Oak	113
Boggs, Bos	113
Yount, Milw	101
Sierra, Tex	101
McGriff, Tor	98

Games

Crim, Milw	76
Murphy, Bos	74
Rogers, Tex	73
Russell, Tex	71
Guetterman, NY	70

Innings Pitched

Saberhagen, KC	262.1
Stewart, Oak	257.2
Gubicza, KC	255.0
Clemens, Bos	253.1
Milacki, Bal	243.0

Doubles

Boggs, Bos	51
Puckett, Minn	45
Reed, Bos	42
Bell, Tor	41
Yount, Milw	38
Mattingly, NY	37

Stolen Bases

	SB	CS
R.Henderson, Oak	77	14
Espy, Tex	45	20
White, Cal	44	16
Pettis, Det	43	15
Sax, NY	43	17

Complete Games

Saberhagen, KC	12
Morris, Det	10
Finley, Cal	9
Five tied with 8.	

Shutouts

Blyleven, Cal	5
McCaskill, Cal	4
Saberhagen, KC	4
Three tied with 3.	

Total Bases

Sierra, Tex	344
Yount, Milw	314
Carter, Clev	303
Mattingly, NY	301
Puckett, Minn	295
McGriff, Tor	289

Slugging Pct.

Sierra, Tex	.543
McGriff, Tor	.525
Yount, Milw	.511
Esasky, Bos	.500
Davis, Sea	.496
Jackson, KC	.495

Strikeouts

Ryan, Tex	301
Clemens, Bos	230
Saberhagen, KC	193
Bosio, Milw	173
Gubicza, KC	173
Moore, Oak	172

Walks

Witt, Tex	114
Hough, Tex	95
Clemens, Bos	93
Ryan, Tex	98
Perez, Chi	90
Milacki, Bal	88

Times Walked

R.Henderson, Oak	126
McGriff, Tor	119
Boggs, Bos	107
Seitzer, KC	102
Davis, Sea	101

Times Struck Out

Jackson, KC	172
Deer, Milw	158
Barfield, NY	150
Snyder, Clev	134
Incaviglia, Tex	136

Losses

Alexander, Det	6-18
Witt, Cal	9-15
Hawkins, NY	15-15
Six tied with 14.	

HRs Given Up

Hough, Tex	28
Alexander, Det	28
Witt, Cal	26
Schmidt, Bal	24

B A S E B A L L

Team by Team Statistics

Players included either had 150 official at bats or pitched 50 innings during the regular season. *Denotes rookie.

Baltimore Orioles

Batting (150 AB)	Avg	AB	R	H	HR	RBI	SB
Joe Orsulak........	**.285**	390	59	111	7	55	5
Keith Moreland....	**.278**	425	45	118	6	45	3
Phil Bradley........	**.277**	545	83	151	11	55	20
Randy Milligan.....	**.268**	365	56	98	12	45	9
Mike Devereaux*....	**.266**	391	55	104	8	46	22
Mickey Tettleton....	**.258**	411	72	106	26	65	3
Cal Ripken.........	**.257**	646	80	166	21	93	3
Steve Finley.......	**.249**	217	35	54	2	25	17
Craig Worthington*	**.247**	497	57	123	15	70	1
Larry Sheets.......	**.243**	304	33	74	7	33	1
Bob Melvin........	**.241**	278	22	67	1	32	1
Bill Ripken.........	**.239**	318	31	76	2	26	1
Rene Gonzales.....	**.217**	166	16	36	1	11	5
Jim Traber........	**.209**	234	14	.49	4	26	4
Brady Anderson....	**.207**	266	44	55	4	16	16

Pitching (50 IP)	W-L	ERA	Gm	IP	BB	SO
Gregg Olson*....	5-2	**1.69**	64	85.0	46	90
Jay Tibbs........	5-0	**2.82**	10	54.1	20	30
Mark Williamson..	10-5	**2.93**	65	107.1	30	55
Jeff Ballard......	18-8	**3.43**	35	215.1	57	62
Bob Milacki*.....	14-12	**3.74**	37	243.0	88	113
Mark Thurmond...	2-4	**3.90**	49	90.0	17	34
Brian Holton.....	5-7	**4.02**	39	116.1	39	51
Dave Johnson*..	4-7	**4.23**	14	89.1	28	26
Pete Harnisch*...	5-9	**4.62**	18	103.1	64	70
Jose Bautista....	3-4	**5.31**	15	78.0	15	30
Dave Schmidt....	10-13	**5.69**	38	156.2	36	46

Saves: Olson(27), Williamson(9), Thurmond(4), Kevin Hickey(2).

California Angels

Batting (150 AB)	Avg	AB	R	H	HR	RBI	SB
Johnny Ray........	**.289**	530	52	153	5	62	6
Brian Downing.....	**.283**	544	59	154	14	59	0
Wally Joyner......	**.282**	593	78	167	16	79	3
Claudell Washington	**.273**	418	53	114	13	42	13
Chili Davis........	**.271**	560	81	152	22	90	3
Tony Armas........	**.257**	202	22	52	11	30	0
Devon White.......	**.245**	636	86	156	12	56	44
Lance Parrish......	**.238**	433	48	103	17	50	1
Kent Anderson*....	**.229**	223	27	51	0	17	1
Dick Schofield.....	**.228**	302	42	69	4	26	9
Jack Howell.......	**.228**	474	56	108	20	52	0

Pitching (50 IP)	W-L	ERA	Gm	IP	BB	SO
Bob McClure....	6-1	**1.55**	48	52.1	15	36
Greg Minton....	4-3	**2.20**	62	90.0	37	42
Chuck Finley.....	16-9	**2.57**	29	199.2	82	156
Bert Blyleven....	17-5	**2.73**	33	241.0	44	131
Kirk McCaskill...	15-10	**2.93**	32	212.0	59	107
Willie Fraser.....	4-7	**3.24**	44	91.2	23	46
Bryan Harvey.....	3-3	**3.44**	51	55.0	41	78
Jim Abbott*.....	12-12	**3.92**	29	181.1	74	115
Mike Witt.......	9-15	**4.54**	33	220.0	48	123
Dan Petry.......	3-2	**5.47**	19	51.0	23	21

Saves: Harvey (25), Minton (8), McClure (3), Fraser (2).

Boston Red Sox

Batting (150 AB)	Avg	AB	R	H	HR	RBI	SB
Wade Boggs.......	**.330**	621	113	205	3	54	2
Mike Greenwell.....	**.308**	578	87	178	14	95	13
Ellis Burks.........	**.303**	399	73	121	12	61	21
Danny Heep.......	**.300**	320	36	96	5	49	0
Jody Reed........	**.288**	524	76	151	3	40	4
Dwight Evans......	**.285**	520	82	148	20	100	3
Nick Esasky.......	**.277**	564	79	156	30	108	1
Kevin Romine.....	**.274**	274	30	75	1	23	1
Luis Rivera........	**.257**	323	35	83	5	29	2
Marty Barrett.....	**.256**	336	31	86	1	27	4
Rick Cerone......	**.243**	296	28	72	4	48	0
Jim Rice..........	**.234**	209	22	49	3	28	1
Randy Kutcher.....	**.225**	160	28	36	2	18	3
Rich Gedman......	**.212**	260	24	55	4	16	0

Pitching (50 IP)	W-L	ERA	Gm	IP	BB	SO
Dennis Lamp......	4-2	**2.32**	42	112.1	27	61
Rob Murphy......	5-7	**2.74**	74	105.0	41	107
Roger Clemens....	17-11	**3.13**	35	253.1	93	230
Lee Smith........	6-1	**3.57**	64	70.2	33	96
John Dopson....	12-8	**3.99**	29	169.1	69	95
Mike Boddicker...	15-11	**4.00**	34	211.2	71	145
Joe Price........	2-5	**4.35**	31	70.1	30	52
Oil Can Boyd....	3-2	**4.42**	10	59.0	19	26
Bob Stanley.....	5-2	**4.88**	43	79.1	26	32
Mike Smithson...	7-14	**4.95**	40	143.2	35	61
Wes Gardner....	3-7	**5.97**	22	86.0	47	81
Eric Hetzel*.....	2-3	**6.26**	12	50.1	28	33

Saves: Smith(25), Murphy(9), Stanley(4), Lamp(2), Smithson(2).

Chicago White Sox

Batting (150 AB)	Avg	AB	R	H	HR	RBI	SB
Ron Kittle.........	**.302**	169	26	51	11	37	0
Lance Johnson......	**.300**	180	28	54	0	16	16
Carlos Martinez*....	**.300**	350	44	105	5	32	4
Carlton Fisk.......	**.293**	375	47	110	13	68	1
Ivan Calderon.....	**.286**	622	83	178	14	87	7
Eddie Williams......	**.274**	201	25	55	3	10	1
Dave Gallagher.....	**.266**	601	74	160	1	46	5
Steve Lyons.......	**.264**	443	51	117	2	50	9
Ron Karkovice.....	**.264**	182	21	48	3	24	0
Sammy Sosa*.....	**.257**	183	27	47	4	13	7
Ozzie Guillen......	**.253**	597	63	151	1	54	36
Scott Fletcher......	**.253**	546	77	138	1	43	2
Daryl Boston......	**.252**	218	35	55	5	23	7
Dan Pasqua.......	**.248**	246	26	61	11	47	1
Greg Walker.......	**.210**	233	25	49	5	26	0

Pitching (50 IP)	W-L	ERA	Gm	IP	BB	SO
Greg Hibbard*..	6-7	**3.21**	23	137.1	41	55
Donn Pall*......	4-5	**3.31**	53	87.0	19	58
Eric King........	9-10	**3.39**	25	159.1	64	72
Tom McCarthy*..	1-2	**3.51**	31	66.2	20	27
Bobby Thigpen...	2-6	**3.76**	61	79.0	40	47
Bill Long........	5-5	**3.92**	30	98.2	37	51
Richard Dotson...	5-12	**4.46**	28	151.1	58	69
Ken Patterson*...	6-1	**4.52**	50	65.2	28	43
Shawn Hillegas..	7-11	**4.74**	50	119.2	51	76
Steve Rosenberg .	4-13	**4.94**	38	142.0	58	77
Melido Perez	11-14	**5.01**	31	183.1	90	141

Saves: Thigpen (34), Pall (6), Hillegas (3), Long (1).

Cleveland Indians

Batting (150 AB)

	Avg	AB	R	H	HR	RBI	SB
Dion James	.306	245	26	75	4	29	1
Jerry Browne	.299	598	83	179	5	45	14
Brook Jacoby	.272	519	49	141	13	64	2
Pete O'Brien	.259	555	75	144	12	55	3
Joe Carter	.243	651	84	158	35	105	13
Felix Fermin	.238	484	50	115	0	21	6
Brad Komminsk	.237	198	27	47	8	33	8
David Clark	.237	253	21	60	8	29	0
Andy Allanson	.232	323	30	75	3	17	4
Joel Skinner	.230	178	10	41	1	13	1
Joey Belle*	.225	218	22	49	7	37	2
Oddibe McDowell	.222	239	33	53	3	22	12
Cory Snyder	.215	489	49	105	18	59	6

Pitching (50 IP)

	W-L	ERA	Gm	IP	BB	SO
Jesse Orosco	3-4	2.08	69	78.0	26	79
Doug Jones	7-10	2.34	59	80.2	13	65
Tom Candiotti	13-10	3.10	31	206.0	55	124
Bud Black	12-11	3.36	33	222.1	52	88
Greg Swindell	13-6	3.37	28	184.1	51	129
John Farrell	9-14	3.63	31	208.0	71	132
Scott Bailes	5-9	4.28	34	113.2	29	47
Rod Nichols	4-6	4.40	15	71.2	24	42
Rich Yett	5-6	5.00	32	99.0	47	47

Saves: Jones (32), Orosco (3), Keith Atherton.

Kansas City Royals

Batting (150 AB)

	Avg	AB	R	H	HR	RBI	SB
Jim Eisenreich	.293	475	64	139	9	59	27
George Brett	.282	457	67	129	12	80	14
Kevin Seitzer	.281	597	78	168	4	48	17
Bob Boone	.274	405	33	111	1	43	3
Danny Tartabull	.268	441	54	118	18	62	4
Kurt Stillwell	.261	463	52	121	7	54	9
Pat Tabler	.259	390	36	101	2	42	0
Bo Jackson	.256	515	86	132	32	105	26
Frank White	.256	418	34	107	2	36	3
Willie Wilson	.253	383	58	97	3	43	24
Brad Wellman	.230	178	30	41	2	12	5
Mike Macfarlane	.223	157	13	35	2	19	0
Bill Buckner	.216	176	7	38	1	16	1

Pitching (50 IP)

	W-L	ERA	Gm	IP	BB	SO
Jeff Montgomery	7-3	1.37	63	92.0	25	94
Bret Saberhagen	23-6	2.16	36	262.1	43	193
Steve Crawford	3-1	2.83	25	54.0	19	33
Mark Gubicza	15-11	3.04	36	255.0	63	173
Luis Aquino	6-8	3.50	34	141.1	35	68
Tom Gordon*	17-9	3.64	49	163.0	86	153
Steve Farr	2-5	4.12	51	63.1	22	56
Terry Leach	5-6	4.15	30	73.2	36	34
Floyd Bannister	4-1	4.66	14	75.1	18	35
Charlie Leibrandt	5-11	5.14	33	161.0	54	73

Saves: Montgomery (18), Farr (18), Gordon (1).

Detroit Tigers

Batting (150 AB)

	Avg	AB	R	H	HR	RBI	SB
Dave Bergman	.268	385	38	103	7	37	1
Mike Heath	.263	396	38	104	10	43	7
Tracy Jones	.259	158	17	41	3	26	1
Gary Pettis	.257	444	77	114	1	18	43
Gary Ward	.253	292	27	74	9	30	1
Lou Whitaker	.251	509	77	128	28	85	6
Matt Nokes	.250	268	15	67	9	39	1
Alan Trammell	.243	449	54	109	5	43	10
Fred Lynn	.241	353	44	85	11	46	1
Chet Lemon	.237	414	45	98	7	47	1
Rick Schu	.214	266	25	57	7	21	1
Doug Strange*	.214	196	16	42	1	14	3
Kenny Williams	.205	258	29	53	6	23	9
Mike Brumley*	.198	212	33	42	1	11	8

Pitching (50 IP)

	W-L	ERA	Gm	IP	BB	SO
Frank Tanana	10-14	3.58	33	223.2	74	147
Frank Williams	3-3	3.64	42	71.2	46	33
Mike Henneman	11-4	3.70	60	90.0	51	69
Edwin Nunez	3-4	4.17	27	54.0	36	41
Kevin Ritz*	4-6	4.38	12	74.0	44	56
Doyle Alexander	6-18	4.44	33	223.0	76	95
Paul Gibson	4-8	4.64	45	132.0	57	77
Jeff Robinson	4-5	4.73	16	78.0	46	40
Jack Morris	6-14	4.86	24	170.1	59	115
Charles Hudson	1-5	6.35	18	66.2	31	23

Saves: Guillermo Hernandez (15), Henneman (7), Nunez (1), F.Williams (1).

Milwaukee Brewers

Batting (150 AB)

	Avg	AB	R	H	HR	RBI	SB
Robin Yount	.318	614	101	195	21	103	19
Paul Molitor	.315	615	84	194	11	56	27
Jim Gantner	.274	409	51	112	0	34	20
Greg Brock	.265	373	40	99	12	52	6
Bill Spiers*	.255	345	44	88	4	33	10
B.J.Surhoff	.248	436	42	108	5	55	14
Gary Sheffield*	.247	368	34	91	5	32	10
Glenn Braggs	.247	514	77	127	15	66	17
Mike Felder	.241	315	50	76	3	23	26
Charlie O'Brien	.234	188	22	44	6	35	0
Terry Francona	.232	233	26	54	3	23	2
Rob Deer	.210	466	72	98	26	65	4
Ed Romero	.209	163	17	34	0	9	0
Gus Polidor	.194	175	15	34	0	14	3

Pitching (50 IP)

	W-L	ERA	Gm	IP	BB	SO
Dan Plesac	3-4	2.35	52	61.1	17	52
Chuck Crim	9-7	2.83	76	117.2	36	59
Chris Bosio	15-10	2.95	33	234.2	48	173
Jamie Navarro*	7-8	3.12	19	109.2	32	56
Mark Knudson	8-5	3.35	40	123.2	29	47
Ted Higuera	9-6	3.46	22	135.1	48	91
Tony Fossas*	2-2	3.54	51	61.0	22	42
Tom Filer	7-3	3.61	13	72.1	23	20
Bill Krueger	3-2	3.84	34	93.2	33	72
Bryan Clutterbuck	2-5	4.14	14	67.1	16	29
Jerry Reuss	9-9	5.13	30	140.1	34	40
Don August	12-12	5.31	31	142.1	58	51
Bill Wegman	2-6	6.71	11	51.0	21	27

Saves: Plesac (33), Crim (7), Krueger (3), Fosses (1).

Minnesota Twins

Batting (150 AB)

	Avg	AB	R	H	HR	RBI	SB
Kirby Puckett	.339	635	75	215	9	85	11
Brian Harper	.325	385	43	125	8	57	2
Dan Gladden	.295	461	69	136	8	46	23
John Moses	.281	242	33	68	1	31	14
Kent Hrbek	.272	375	59	102	25	84	3
Greg Gagne	.272	460	69	125	9	48	11
Gene Larkin.......	.267	446	61	119	6	46	5
Randy Bush	.263	391	60	103	14	54	5
Carmen Castillo	.257	218	23	56	8	33	1
Al Newman	.253	446	62	113	0	38	25
Gary Gaetti.......	.251	498	63	125	19	75	6
Wally Backman	.231	299	33	69	1	26	1
Tim Laudner	.222	239	24	53	6	27	1

Pitching (50 IP)

	W-L	ERA	Gm	IP	BB	SO
Rick Aguilera	3-5	3.21	11	75.2	17	57
Gary Wayne* ...	3-4	3.30	60	71.0	36	41
Juan Berenguer ..	9-3	3.48	56	106.0	47	93
Frank Viola......	8-12	3.79	24	175.2	47	138
Allan Anderson ..	17-10	3.80	33	196.2	53	69
Roy Smith	10-6	3.92	32	172.1	51	92
Jeff Reardon	5-4	4.07	65	73.0	12	46
Francisco Oliveras*	3-4	4.53	12	55.2	15	24
Mark Guthrie* ...	2-4	4.55	13	57.1	21	38
Mike Dyer*	4-7	4.82	16	71.0	37	37
Shane Rawley....	5-12	5.21	27	145.0	60	68

Saves: Reardon (31), Berenguer (3), Wayne (1), Smith (1).

Oakland Athletics

Batting (150 AB)

	Avg	AB	R	H	HR	RBI	SB
Carney Lansford ...	.336	551	81	185	2	52	37
Rickey Henderson ...	.274	541	113	148	12	57	77
Terry Steinbach ...	.273	454	37	124	7	42	1
Jose Canseco......	.269	227	40	61	17	57	6
Dave Parker	.264	553	56	146	22	97	0
Tony Phillips	.262	451	48	118	4	47	3
Mike Gallego......	.252	357	45	90	3	30	7
Dave Henderson	.250	579	77	145	15	80	8
Stan Javier......	.248	310	42	77	1	28	12
Ken Phelps........	.242	194	26	47	7	29	0
Walt Weiss	.233	236	30	55	3	21	6
Mark McGwire	.231	490	74	113	33	95	1
Ron Hassey	.228	268	29	61	5	23	1

Pitching (50 IP)

	W-L	ERA	Gm	IP	BB	SO
Dennis Eckersley..	4-0	1.56	51	57.2	3	55
Todd Burns	6-5	2.24	50	96.1	28	49
Rick Honeycutt ...	2-2	2.35	64	76.2	26	52
Mike Moore	19-11	2.61	35	241.2	83	172
Bob Welch	17-8	3.00	33	209.2	78	137
Gene Nelson	3-5	3.26	50	80.0	30	70
Dave Stewart	21-9	3.32	36	257.2	69	155
Curt Young......	5-9	3.73	25	111.0	47	55
Storm Davis	19-7	4.36	31	169.1	68	91

Saves: Eckersley (33), Honeycutt (12), Burns (8), Nelson (3).

New York Yankees

Batting (150 AB)

	Avg	AB	R	H	HR	RBI	SB
Steve Sax..........	.315	651	88	205	5	63	43
Don Mattingly	.303	631	79	191	23	113	3
Roberto Kelly.......	.302	441	65	133	9	48	35
Luis Polonia	.300	433	70	130	3	46	22
Bob Geren*.......	.288	205	26	59	9	27	0
Alvaro Espinoza	.282	503	51	142	0	41	3
Mel Hall	.260	361	54	94	17	58	0
Don Slaught.......	.251	350	34	88	5	38	1
Steve Balboni......	.237	300	33	71	17	59	0
Jesse Barfield	.234	521	79	122	23	67	5
Tom Brookens	.226	168	14	38	4	14	1
Mike Pagliarulo	.197	223	19	44	4	16	1

Pitching (50 IP)

	W-L	ERA	Gm	IP	BB	SO
Lee Guetterman ..	5-5	2.45	70	103.0	26	51
Dave Righetti	2-6	3.00	55	69.0	26	51
Chuck Cary	4-4	3.26	22	99.1	29	79
Eric Plunk	8-6	3.28	50	104.1	64	85
Clay Parker*	4-5	3.68	22	120.0	31	53
Greg Cadaret ...	5-5	4.05	46	120.0	57	80
Lance McCullers ..	4-3	4.57	52	84.2	37	82
Andy Hawkins ..	15-15	4.80	34	208.1	76	98
Dale Mohorcic ...	2-1	4.99	32	57.2	18	24
Walt Terrell	6-5	5.20	13	83.0	24	30
Dave LaPoint	6-9	5.62	20	113.2	45	51
Tommy John.....	2-7	5.80	10	63.2	22	18

Saves: Righetti (25), Guetterman (13), McCullers (3), Mohorcic (2), Plunk (1).

Seattle Mariners

Batting (150 AB)

	Avg	AB	R	H	HR	RBI	SB
Alvin Davis	.305	498	84	152	21	95	0
Harold Reynolds ...	.300	613	87	184	0	43	25
Jay Buhner	.275	204	27	56	9	33	1
Scott Bradley	.274	270	21	74	3	37	1
Greg Briley*	.266	394	52	105	13	52	11
Henry Cotto......	.264	295	44	78	9	33	10
Ken Griffey,Jr* ...	.264	455	61	120	16	61	16
Jeffrey Leonard	.254	566	69	144	24	93	6
Darnell Coles	.252	535	54	135	10	59	5
Edgar Martinez*	.240	171	20	41	2	20	2
Dave Valle........	.237	316	32	75	7	34	0
Jim Presley.......	.236	390	42	92	12	41	0
Omar Vizquel*	.220	387	45	85	1	20	1

Pitching (50 IP)

	W-L	ERA	Gm	IP	BB	SO
Mike Schooler ...	1-7	2.81	67	77.0	19	69
Mike Jackson	4-6	3.17	65	99.1	54	94
Erik Hanson* ...	9-5	3.18	17	113.1	32	75
Jerry Reed	7-7	3.19	52	101.2	43	50
Scott Bankhead ..	14-6	3.34	33	210.1	63	140
Brian Holman	8-10	3.44	23	159.2	62	82
Mark Langston ...	4-5	3.56	10	73.1	19	60
Randy Johnson*..	7-9	4.40	22	131.0	70	104
Bill Swift	7-3	4.43	37	130.0	38	45
Clint Zavaras* ...	1-6	5.19	10	52.0	30	31
Mike Dunne	2-9	5.27	15	85.1	37	38

Saves: Schooler (33), Jackson (7), Dennis Powell (2), Swift (1).

Texas Rangers

Batting (150 AB)

	Avg	AB	R	H	HR	RBI	SB
Julio Franco.......	.316	548	80	173	13	92	21
Harold Baines	.309	505	73	156	16	72	0
Ruben Sierra	.306	634	101	194	29	119	8
Geno Petralli	.304	184	18	56	4	23	0
Fred Manrique	.294	378	46	111	4	52	4
Rafael Palmeiro ...	.275	559	76	154	8	64	4
Rick Leach	.272	239	32	65	1	23	2
Jeff Kunkel........	.270	293	39	79	8	29	3
Cecil Espy	.257	475	65	122	3	31	45
Pete Incaviglia	.236	453	48	107	21	81	5
Steve Buechele	.235	486	60	114	16	59	1
Chad Kreuter*.....	.152	158	16	24	5	9	0

Pitching (50 IP)

	W-L	ERA	Gm	IP	BB	SO
Jeff Russell	6-4	1.98	71	72.2	24	77
Kenny Rogers*.....	3-4	2.93	73	73.2	42	63
Nolan Ryan	16-10	3.20	32	239.1	98	301
Kevin Brown*.....	12-9	3.35	28	191.0	70	104
Mike Jeffcoat	9-6	3.58	22	130.2	33	64
Drew Hall.......	2-1	3.70	38	58.1	33	45
Cecilio Guante ...	6-6	3.91	50	69.0	36	69
Charlie Hough ...	10-13	4.35	30	182.0	95	94
Jamie Moyer	4-9	4.86	15	76.0	33	44
Bobby Witt.......	12-13	5.14	31	194.1	114	166

Saves: Russell (38), Rogers (2), Guante (2).

Toronto Blue Jays

Batting (150 AB)

	Avg	AB	R	H	HR	RBI	SB
Mookie Wilson	.298	238	32	71	2	17	12
George Bell	.297	613	88	182	18	104	4
Kelly Gruber	.290	545	83	158	18	73	10
Fred McGriff	.269	551	98	148	36	92	7
Nelson Liriano	.263	418	51	110	5	53	16
Ernie Whitt	.262	385	42	101	11	53	5
Manny Lee	.260	300	27	78	3	34	4
Junior Felix*	.258	415	62	107	9	46	18
Pat Borders	.257	241	22	62	3	29	2
Tony Fernandez...	.257	573	64	147	11	64	22
Rance Mulliniks ...	.238	273	25	65	3	29	0
Lloyd Moseby	.221	502	72	111	11	43	24

Pitching (50 IP)

	W-L	ERA	Gm	IP	BB	SO
Tom Henke	8-3	1.92	64	89.0	25	116
David Wells	7-4	2.40	54	86.1	28	78
John Cerutti	11-11	3.07	33	205.1	53	69
Dave Stieb	17-8	3.35	33	206.2	76	101
Frank Wills	3-1	3.66	24	71.1	30	41
Duane Ward	4-10	3.77	66	114.2	58	122
Jimmy Key	13-14	3.88	33	216.0	27	118
Todd Stottlemyre .	7-7	3.88	27	127.2	44	63
Mike Flanagan ...	8-10	3.93	30	171.2	47	47

Saves: Henke (20), Ward (15), Wells (2).

1989 All-Star Game

Date: July 11 at Anaheim Stadium in Anaheim, CA; **Managers:** Tony LaRussa (AL), Tom Lasorda (NL); **Most Valuable Player:** Bo Jackson, Kansas City.

National League

	ab	r	h	bi
Ozzie Smith, St.Louis, ss	4	0	1	0
Tony Gwynn, San Diego, rf	2	1	1	0
Andre Dawson, Chicago, rf...........	1	0	0	0
Will Clark, San Francisco, 1b	2	0	1	0
Glenn Davis, Houston, 1b	1	1	1	0
Kevin Mitchell, San Francisco, lf	4	1	2	1
Vince Coleman, St.Louis, lf	0	0	0	0
Eric Davis, Cincinnati, cf	2	0	0	0
Von Hayes, Philadelphia, cf........	1	0	1	1
Howard Johnson, New York, 3b	3	0	1	1
Tim Wallach, Montreal, 3b	1	0	0	0
Pedro Guerrero, St.Louis, dh	2	0	0	0
Bobby Bonilla, Pittsburgh, dh	2	0	2	0
Ryne Sandberg, Chicago, 2b	3	0	0	0
Willie Randolph, Los Angeles, 2b	1	0	0	0
Benito Santiago, San Diego, c	1	0	0	0
Mike Scioscia, Los Angeles, c	1	0	0	0
Tony Pena, St.Louis, c	2	0	0	0
Totals	**33**	**3**	**9**	**3**

American League

	ab	r	h	bi
Bo Jackson, Kansas City, lf	4	1	2	2
Mike Greenwell, Boston, lf	0	0	0	0
Wade Boggs, Boston, 3b	3	1	1	1
Gary Gaetti, Minnesota, 3b	1	0	0	0
Kirby Puckett, Minnesota, cf	3	1	1	0
Devon White, California, cf	1	0	0	0
Harold Baines, Chicago, dh	3	1	1	1
Jeffrey Leonard, Seattle, ph	1	0	0	0
Julio Franco, Texas, 2b	3	0	1	0
Don Mattingly, New York, 1b	1	0	1	0
Cal Ripken, Baltimore, ss	3	0	1	0
Tony Fernandez, Toronto, ss	1	0	0	0
Ruben Sierra, Texas, rf	3	1	2	1
Mark McGwire, Oakland, 1b	3	0	1	0
Steve Sax, New York, 2b	1	0	0	0
Terry Steinbach, Oakland, c	3	0	1	0
Mickey Tettleton, Baltimore, c	1	0	0	0
Totals	**35**	**5**	**12**	**5**

	123	456	789		R	H	E
National League	200	000	010	—	3	9	1
American League	212	000	00x	—	5	12	0

E — Santiago. **DP** — American (2). **LOB** — National (6), American (7). **2B** — Ripken, Mattingly. **HR** — Jackson, Boggs, Jackson. **SB** — E.Davis, Johnson, Gwynn, Jackson.

NL Pitching

	IP	H	R	ER	BB	SO	HR
Rick Reuschel, SF	1.0	3	2	2	0	0	2
John Smoltz, ATL (Loss) ..	1.0	2	1	1	0	0	0
Rick Sutcliffe, CHI	1.0	4	2	2	0	0	0
Tim Burke, MON	2.0	2	0	0	0	1	0
Mark Davis, SD..........	1.0	0	0	0	2	0	0
Jay Howell, LA	1.0	1	0	0	1	0	0
Mitch Williams, CHI	1.0	0	0	0	1	1	0
Totals	**8.0**	**12**	**5**	**5**	**5**	**2**	

NL Pitching

	IP	H	R	ER	BB	SO	HR
Dave Stewart, OAK	1.0	3	2	2	2	0	0
Nolan Ryan, TEX (Win) ..	2.0	1	0	0	0	3	0
Mark Gubicza, KC	1.0	0	0	0	0	1	0
Mike Moore, OAK	1.0	0	0	0	0	1	0
Greg Swindell, CLE......	1.2	2	0	0	0	3	0
Jeff Russell, TEX	1.0	1	1	1	0	0	0
Dan Plesac, MIL	0.0	1	0	0	0	0	0
Doug Jones, CLE (Save) ..	1.1	1	0	0	1	0	0
Totals	**9.0**	**9**	**3**	**3**	**3**	**8**	**0**

Plesac pitched to one batter in the 8th. **WP** — Sutcliffe. **Umpires** — Evans (AL), Engel (NL), Cooney (AL), Crawford (NL), Hirschbeck (NL), Davis (AL). **Attendance** — 64,036. **Time** — 2:46.

1989 League Championship Series

National League Composite Box Score

San Francisco Giants Batting (1 AB)	Avg	AB	R	H	HR	RBI	SB
Greg Litton	1.000	1	0	1	0	0	0
Will Clark	.650	20	8	13	2	8	0
Kevin Mitchell	.353	17	5	6	2	7	0
Matt Williams	.300	20	2	6	2	9	0
Robby Thompson	.278	18	5	5	2	3	0
Jose Uribe	.235	17	2	4	0	1	1
Brett Butler	.211	19	6	4	0	0	0
Terry Kennedy	.188	16	0	3	0	0	0
Pat Sheridan	.154	13	1	2	0	0	0
Candy Maldonado	.000	3	1	0	0	1	0
Donell Nixon	.000	3	0	0	0	0	1
Ken Oberkfell	.000	4	0	0	0	0	0
Kirt Manwaring	.000	2	0	0	0	0	0
Bill Bathe	.000	1	0	0	0	0	0
Scott Garrelts	.000	4	0	0	0	0	0
Kelly Downs	.000	3	0	0	0	0	0
Rick Reuschel	.000	2	0	0	0	0	0
Mike LaCoss	.000	1	0	0	0	0	0
Ernest Riles	.000	1	0	0	0	0	0
TOTALS	.267	165	30	44	8	29	2

Chicago Cubs Batting (1 AB)	Avg	AB	R	H	HR	RBI	SB
Lloyd McClendon	.667	3	0	2	0	0	0
Mark Grace	.647	17	3	11	1	8	1
Curt Wilkerson	.500	2	1	1	0	0	0
Rick Sutcliffe	.500	2	0	1	0	0	0
Ryne Sandberg	.400	20	6	8	1	4	0
Luis Salazar	.368	19	2	7	1	2	0
Jerome Walton	.364	22	4	8	0	2	0
Mitch Webster	.333	3	0	1	0	0	0
Shawon Dunston	.316	19	2	6	0	0	1
Dwight Smith	.200	15	2	3	0	0	1
Mike Bielecki	.200	5	0	1	0	2	0
Marvell Wynne	.167	6	0	1	0	0	0
Andre Dawson	.105	19	0	2	0	3	0
Joe Girardi	.100	10	1	1	0	0	0
Rick Wrona	.000	5	0	0	0	0	0
Greg Maddux	.000	3	1	0	0	0	0
Vance Law	.000	3	0	0	0	0	0
Les Lancaster	.000	1	0	0	0	0	0
Domingo Ramos	.000	1	0	0	0	0	0
TOTALS	.303	175	22	53	3	21	3

San Francisco Pitching	W-L	ERA	Gm	IP	H	BB	SO
Jeff Brantley	0-0	0.00	3	5.0	1	2	3
Don Robinson	1-0	0.00	1	1.2	3	0	0
Atlee Hammaker	0-0	0.00	1	1.0	1	0	0
Steve Bedrosian	0-0	2.70	4	3.1	4	2	2
Kelly Downs	1-0	3.12	2	8.2	8	6	6
Rick Reuschel	1-1	5.19	2	8.2	12	2	5
Scott Garrelts	1-0	5.40	2	11.2	16	2	8
Mike LaCoss	0-0	9.00	1	3.0	7	0	2
Craig Lefferts	0-0	9.00	2	1.0	1	2	1
TOTALS	4-1	4.09	5	44.0	53	16	27

Saves: Bedrosian (3).

Chicago Pitching	W-L	ERA	Gm	IP	H	BB	SO
Paul Kilgus	0-0	0.00	1	3.0	4	1	1
Scott Sanderson	0-0	0.00	1	2.0	2	0	1
Mitch Williams	0-0	0.00	2	1.0	1	0	2
Mike Bielecki	0-1	3.65	2	12.1	7	6	11
Rick Sutcliffe	0-0	4.50	1	6.0	5	4	2
Steve Wilson	0-1	4.91	3	3.2	3	1	4
Les Lancaster	1-1	6.35	2	6.0	6	1	3
Greg Maddux	0-1	13.50	2	7.1	13	4	5
Paul Assenmacher	0-0	13.50	2	0.2	3	0	0
TOTALS	1-4	5.57	5	42.0	44	17	29

Saves: None.

GAME 1
Wednesday, Oct.4 at Chicago

	1 2 3 4 5 6 7 8 9	R	H	E
San Fran	3 0 1 4 0 0 3 0 —	11	13	0
Chicago	2 0 1 0 0 0 0 0 —	3	10	1

Win — Garrelts, SF (1-0); **Loss** — Maddux, Chi.(0-1). **HR:** San Fran—Clark 2, Mitchell; Chicago—Grace, Sandberg. **RBI:** San Fran—Clark 6, Mitchell 3, Williams 2; Chicago—Grace 2, Sandberg. **SB:** San Fran—Uribe; Chicago—Grace. **Attendance** — 39,195. **Time** — 2:51.

GAME 2
Thursday, Oct.5 at Chicago

	1 2 3 4 5 6 7 8 9	R	H	E
San Fran	0 0 0 2 0 0 2 1 —	5	10	0
Chicago	6 0 0 0 0 3 0 0 x —	9	11	0

Win — Lancaster, Chi.(1-0); **Loss** — Reuschel, SF (0-1). **HR:** SF—Mitchell (2), Williams, Thompson. **RBI:** SF—Mitchell 2, Williams 2, Thompson; Chicago—Grace 4, Bielecki 2, Walton, Sandberg, Salazar. **SB:** Chicago—Dunston. **Attendance** — 39,195. **Time** — 3:08.

GAME 3
Saturday, Oct.7, at San Fran.

	1 2 3 4 5 6 7 8 9	R	H	E
Chicago	2 0 0 1 0 0 1 0 0 —	4	10	0
San Fran	3 0 0 0 0 0 2 0 x —	5	8	3

Win — Robinson, SF (1-0); **Loss** — Lancaster (1-1); **Save** — Bedrosian (2). **HR:** San Fran—Thompson (2). **RBI:** Chicago—Dawson 2, Sandberg 2; San Fran—Thompson 2, Williams, Maldonado, Uribe. **SB:** None. **Attendance** — 62,065. **Time** — 2:58.

GAME 4
Sunday, Oct.8 at San Fran.

	1 2 3 4 5 6 7 8 9	R	H	E
Chicago	1 1 0 0 2 0 0 0 —	4	12	1
San Fran	1 0 2 1 2 0 0 0 x —	6	9	1

Win — Downs, SF (1-0); **Loss** — Wilson, Chi.(0-1); **Save** — Bedrosian, SF (2). **HR:** Chicago—Salazar; San Fran—Williams (2). **RBI:** Chicago—Grace 2, Dawson, Salazar; San Fran—Williams 4, Mitchell. **SB:** Chicago—Smith; San Fran—Nixon. **Attendance** — 62,078. **Time** — 3:13.

GAME 5
Monday, Oct.9 at San Fran.

	1 2 3 4 5 6 7 8 9	R	H	E
Chicago	0 0 1 0 0 0 0 0 1 —	2	10	1
San Fran	0 0 0 0 0 0 1 2 x —	3	4	1

Win — Reuschel, SF (1-1); **Loss** — Bielecki, Chi.(0-1); **Save** — Bedrosian, SF (3). **HR:** None. **RBI:** Chicago—Walton, Sandberg; San Fran—Clark 2, Mitchell. **SB:** None. **Attendance** — 62,084. **Time** — 2:47.

Score by Innings

	1 2 3 4 5 6 7 8 9	Runs
Chicago	1 1 1 2 1 3 1 0 1 —	22
San Fran	7 0 3 7 2 0 3 7 1 —	30

DP: Chicago 1, San Fran 7. **LOB:** Chicago 43, San Fran 30. **Caught stealing:** San Fran—Sheridan. **S:** Chicago—Sutcliffe, Girardi, Sandberg; San Fran—Thompson, Downs. **SF:** Chicago—Sandberg, Grace; San Fran—Mitchell. **HBP:** M.Williams by Maddux; Dawson by Reuschel. **WP:** Chicago—Wilson, Maddux; San Fran—LaCoss, Brantley, Garrelts. **Balk:** Chicago—Sutcliffe. **PB:** Chicago—Wrona, Girardi; San Fran—Manwaring. **Umpires:** Harvey, Froemming, Tata, Quick, Williams and March.

American League Composite Box Score

Oakland Athletics

Batting (1 AB)	Avg	AB	R	H	HR	RBI	SB
Ken Phelps	1.000	1	0	1	0	0	0
Carney Lansford	.455	11	2	5	0	4	2
Rickey Henderson	.400	15	8	6	2	5	8
Mark McGwire	.389	18	3	7	1	3	0
Jose Canseco	.294	17	1	5	1	3	0
Mike Gallego	.273	11	3	3	0	1	0
Dave Henderson	.263	19	4	5	1	1	0
Terry Steinbach	.200	15	0	3	0	1	0
Dave Parker	.188	16	2	3	2	3	0
Tony Phillips	.167	18	1	3	0	1	2
Ron Hassey	.167	6	0	1	0	1	0
Walt Weiss	.111	9	2	1	0	0	1
Stan Javier	.000	2	0	0	0	0	0
TOTALS	.272	158	26	43	7	23	13

Pitching	W-L	ERA	Gm	IP	H	BB	SO
Mike Moore	1-0	0.00	1	7.0	3	2	3
Gene Nelson	0-0	0.00	1	1.1	1	0	2
Matt Young	0-0	0.00	1	0.1	0	2	0
Dennis Eckersley	0-0	1.59	4	5.2	4	0	2
Dave Stewart	2-0	2.81	2	16.0	13	3	9
Bob Welch	1-0	3.18	1	5.2	8	1	4
Storm Davis	0-0	7.11	1	6.1	5	2	3
Rick Honeycutt	0-0	32.40	3	1.2	6	5	1
TOTALS	4-1	3.89	5	44.0	40	15	24

Saves: Eckersley (3).

Toronto Blue Jays

Batting (1 AB)	Avg	AB	R	H	HR	RBI	SB
Pat Borders	1.000	1	0	1	0	1	0
Nelson Liriano	.429	7	1	3	0	1	3
Tony Fernandez	.350	20	6	7	0	1	5
Lloyd Moseby	.313	16	4	5	1	2	1
Kelly Gruber	.294	17	2	5	0	1	1
Junior Felix	.273	11	0	3	0	3	0
Mookie Wilson	.263	19	2	5	0	2	1
Manny Lee	.250	8	2	2	0	0	0
George Bell	.200	20	2	4	1	2	0
Fred McGriff	.143	21	3	3	0	3	0
Ernie Whitt	.125	16	1	2	1	3	0
Lee Mazzilli	.000	8	0	0	0	0	0
Rance Mulliniks	.000	1	0	0	0	0	0
TOTALS	.242	165	21	40	3	19	11

Pitching	W-L	ERA	Gm	IP	H	BB	SO
John Cerutti	0-0	0.00	2	2.2	0	3	1
Tom Henke	0-0	0.00	3	2.2	0	0	3
David Wells	0-0	0.00	1	1.0	0	2	1
Jin Acker	0-0	1.42	5	6.1	4	1	4
Jimmy Key	1-0	4.50	1	6.0	7	2	2
Dave Stieb	0-2	6.35	2	11.1	12	6	10
Todd Stottlemyre	0-1	7.20	1	5.0	7	2	3
Duane Ward	0-0	7.36	2	3.2	6	3	5
Mike Flanagan	0-1	10.39	1	4.1	7	1	3
TOTALS	1-4	5.02	5	43.0	43	20	32

Saves: None

GAME 1
Tuesday, Oct.3 at Oakland

	1 2 3 4 5 6 7 8 9	R	H	E
Toronto	0 2 0 1 0 0 0 0 0 —	3	5	1
Oakland	0 1 0 0 1 3 0 2 x —	7	11	0

Win — Stewart, Oak.(1-0); **Loss** — Stieb, Tor.(0-1); **Save** — Eckersley, Oak.(1). **HR:** Toronto—Whitt; Oakland—D.Henderson, McGwire. **RBI:** Toronto—Whitt 2, Liriano; Oakland—Lansford 2, Parker, D.Henderson, McGwire. **SB:** Toronto—Fernandez, Liriano, Wilson; Oakland—R.Henderson 2, Lansford, Phillips. **Attendance** — 49,425. **Time** — 2:52.

GAME 2
Wednesday, Oct.4 at Oakland

	1 2 3 4 5 6 7 8 9	R	H	E
Toronto	0 0 1 0 0 0 0 2 0 —	3	5	1
Oakland	0 0 0 2 0 3 1 0 x —	6	9	1

Win — Moore, Oak.(1-0); **Loss** — Stottlemyre, Tor.(0-1); **Save** — Eckersley, Oak.(2). **HR:** Oakland—Parker. **RBI:** Toronto—McGriff 2, Lansford; Oakland—Lansford, Parker, McGwire, Hassey, Phillips. **SB:** Toronto—Fernandez, Liriano; Oakland—R.Henderson 4, Phillips, Lansford. **Attendance** — 49,444. **Time** — 3:20.

GAME 3
Friday, Oct.6 at Toronto

	1 2 3 4 5 6 7 8 9	R	H	E
Oakland	1 0 1 1 0 0 0 0 0 —	3	8	1
Toronto	0 0 0 4 0 0 3 0 x —	7	8	0

Win — Key, Tor.(1-0); **Loss** — Davis, Oak.(0-1). **HR:** Oakland—Parker (2). **RBI:** Oakland—Lansford, McGwire, Parker; Toronto—Moseby, Wilson, Bell, Fernandez, Whitt, Felix. **SB:** Oakland—R.Henderson. **Attendance** — 50,268. **Time** — 2:54.

GAME 4
Saturday, Oct.7 at Toronto

	1 2 3 4 5 6 7 8 9	R	H	E
Oakland	0 0 3 0 2 0 1 0 0 —	6	11	1
Toronto	0 0 0 1 0 1 1 2 0 —	5	13	0

Win — Welch, Oak.(1-0); **Loss** — Flanagan, Tor.(0-1); **Save** — Eckersley, Oak.(3). **HR:** Oakland—R.Henderson 2, Canseco. **RBI:** Oakland—R.Henderson 4, Canseco 2; Toronto—Felix 2, Wilson, McGriff, Borders. **SB:** Oakland—Weiss; Toronto—Moseby, Gruber, Fernandez. **Attendance** — 50,076. **Time** — 3:20.

GAME 5
Sunday, Oct.8 at Toronto

	1 2 3 4 5 6 7 8 9	R	H	E
Oakland	1 0 1 0 0 2 0 0 —	4	4	0
Toronto	0 0 0 0 0 0 1 2 —	3	9	0

Win — Stewart, Oak.(2-0); **Loss** — Stieb, Tor.(0-2); **Save** — Eckersley, Oak.(3). **HR:** Oakland—Henderson, Canseco, Steinbach Gallego; Toronto—Moseby, Bell, Gruber. **RBI:** Oakland—Henderson, Canseco, Steinbach Gallego; Toronto—Moseby, Bell, Gruber. **Attendance** — 50,024. **Time** — 2:44.

Score by Innings

	1 2 3 4 5 6 7 8 9	Runs
Oakland	2 1 5 3 3 6 4 2 0 —	26
Toronto	0 2 1 6 0 1 4 5 2 —	21

DP: Oakland 4, Toronto 5. **LOB:** Oakland 29, Toronto 30. **Caught stealing:** Oakland—Canseco 2. **S:** Oakland—Gallego 2, Weiss. **SF:** Oakland—Hassey, McGwire; Toronto—Whitt, Bell, Gallego. **HBP:** R.Henderson by Acker. **WP:** Oakland—Honeycutt; Toronto—Ward. **PB:** Oakland—Hassey; Toronto—Whitt. **Umpires:** Phillips, Morrison, Ford, Cousins, Reed, and Palermo.

1989 World Series

Composite Box Score

Oakland Athletics

Batting (1 AB)	Avg	AB	R	H	HR	RBI	SB
Lance Blankenship . .	.500	2	1	1	0	0	0
Rickey Henderson . . .	.474	19	4	9	1	3	3
Carney Lansford	.438	16	5	7	1	4	0
Jose Canseco	.357	14	5	5	1	3	1
Mike Moore	.333	3	1	1	0	2	0
Dave Henderson	.308	13	6	4	2	4	0
Mark McGwire	.294	17	0	5	0	1	0
Terry Steinbach	.250	16	3	4	1	7	0
Tony Phillips	.235	17	2	4	1	3	0
Dave Parker	.222	9	2	2	1	0	0
Walt Weiss	.133	15	3	2	1	1	0
Dave Stewart	.000	3	0	0	0	0	0
Mike Gallego	.000	1	0	0	0	0	0
Ken Phelps	.000	1	0	0	0	0	0
TOTALS	.301	146	32	44	9	30	4

Pitching	W-L	ERA	Gm	IP	H	BB	SO
Dennis Eckersley . .	0-0	0.00	2	1.2	0	0	0
Todd Burns	0-0	0.00	2	1.2	1	1	0
Dave Stewart	2-0	1.69	2	16.0	10	2	14
Mike Moore	2-0	2.08	2	13.0	9	3	10
Rick Honeycutt . . .	0-0	6.75	3	2.2	4	0	2
Gene Nelson	0-0	54.00	1	1.0	4	2	1
TOTALS	4-0	3.50	4	36.0	28	8	27

Complete Games: Stewart (1); **Saves:** Eckersley (1).

San Francisco Giants

Batting (1 AB)	Avg	AB	R	H	HR	RBI	SB
Kirt Manwaring . . .	1.000	1	1	1	0	0	0
Greg Litton	.500	6	1	3	1	3	0
Bill Bathe	.500	2	1	1	1	3	0
Ken Oberkfell	.333	6	1	2	0	0	0
Kevin Mitchell	.294	17	2	5	1	2	0
Brett Butler	.286	14	1	4	0	1	2
Will Clark	.250	16	2	4	0	0	0
Donell Nixon	.200	5	1	1	0	0	0
Jose Uribe	.200	5	1	1	0	0	0
Terry Kennedy	.167	12	1	2	0	2	0
Matt Williams	.125	16	1	2	1	1	0
Robby Thompson . .	.091	11	0	1	0	2	0
Candy Maldonado .	.091	11	1	1	0	0	0
Scott Garrelts	.000	1	0	0	0	0	0
Mike LaCoss	.000	1	0	0	0	0	0
Pat Sheridan	.000	2	0	0	0	0	0
Ernest Riles	.000	8	0	0	0	0	0
TOTALS	.209	134	14	28	4	14	2

Pitching	W-L	ERA	Gm	IP	H	BB	SO
Steve Bedrosian . .	0-0	0.00	2	2.2	0	2	2
Craig Lefferts	0-0	3.38	3	2.2	2	2	1
Jeff Brantley	0-0	4.15	3	4.1	5	3	1
Mike LaCoss	0-0	6.23	2	3.1	4	3	2
Kelly Downs	0-0	7.71	3	4.2	3	2	4
Scott Garrelts	0-2	9.82	2	7.1	13	1	8
Rick Reuschel	0-1	11.25	1	4.0	5	4	2
Atlee Hammaker . .	0-0	15.43	2	2.1	8	0	2
Don Robinson	0-1	21.60	1	1.2	4	1	0
TOTALS	0-4	8.21	4	34.0	44	18	22

Complete Games: none; **Saves:** none.

GAME 1
Saturday, Oct.14 at Oakland

	1 2 3 4 5 6 7 8 9	R	H	E
San Fran	0 0 0 0 0 0 0 0 0 —	0	5	1
Oakland	0 3 1 1 0 0 0 0 x —	5	11	1

Win — Stewart, Oak.(1-0); **Loss** — Garrelts, SF (0-1). **HR:** Oakland—Parker (1), Weiss (1). **RBI:** Oakland—R.Henderson, Parker, Phillips, Weiss. **SB:** None. **Attendance** — 49,385. **Time** — 2:45.

GAME 2
Sunday, Oct.15 at Oakland

	1 2 3 4 5 6 7 8 9	R	H	E
San Fran	0 0 1 0 0 0 0 0 0 —	1	4	0
Oakland	1 0 0 4 0 0 0 0 x —	5	7	0

Win — Moore, Oak.(1-0); **Loss** — Reuschel, SF (0-1). **HR:** Oakland—Steinbach (1). **RBI:** San Fran—Thompson; Oakland—Steinbach 3, Lansford, Parker. **SB:** San Fran—Butler 2; Oakland—R.Henderson. **Attendance** — 49,388. **Time** — 2:47.

GAME 3
Friday, Oct.27 at San Francisco
(Delayed 10 days following Oct.17 earthquake.)

	1 2 3 4 5 6 7 8 9	R	H	E
Oakland	2 0 0 2 4 1 0 4 0 —	13	14	0
San Fran	0 1 0 2 0 0 0 0 4 —	7	10	3

Win — Stewart, Oak (2-0); **Loss** — Garrelts, SF (0-2). **HR:** Oakland—D.Henderson 2 (2), Phillips (1), Canseco (1), Lansford (1); San Fran—Williams (1), Bathe (1). **RBI:** Oakland—D.Henderson 4, Canseco 3, Lansford 2, McGwire, Steinbach, Phillips; San Fran—Bathe 3, Kennedy 2, Litton, Williams. **SB:** Oakland—R.Henderson 2 (3). **Attendance** — 62,038. **Time** — 3:03.

GAME 4
Saturday, Oct.28 at San Francisco

	1 2 3 4 5 6 7 8 9	R	H	E
Oakland	1 3 0 0 3 1 0 0 —	9	12	0
San Fran	0 0 0 0 2 4 0 0 —	6	9	0

Win — Moore, Oak (2-0); **Loss** — Robinson, SF (0-1); **Save** — Eckersley, Oak (1). **HR:** Oakland—R.Henderson (1); San Fran—Mitchell (1), Litton (1). **RBI:** Oakland—Steinbach 3, R.Henderson 2, Moore 2, Lansford, Phillips; San Fran—Mitchell 2, Litton 2, Butler, Thompson. **SB:** Oakland—Canseco (1). **Attendance** — 62,032. **Time** — 3:07.

Score by Innings

	1 2 3 4 5 6 7 8 9	Runs
Oakland	0 1 1 2 0 2 4 0 4 —	14
San Fran	4 6 1 7 7 2 0 5 0 —	32

DP: Oakland 1, San Fran 3. **LOB:** Oakland 31, San Fran 21. **Caught stealing:** Oakland—R.Henderson; San Fran—Butler. **SF:** San Fran—Thompson. **HBP:** Oakland—D.Henderson by Hammaker. **WP:** Oakland—Moore 2. **Balk:** San Fran—Brantley. **PB:** Oakland—Steinbach. **Umpires:** Runge (NL), Voltaggio (AL), Rennert (AL), Clark (AL), Gregg (NL), Garcia (AL). **Series shares:** Oakland—$5,879,252.38 ($159,620.76 per player); San Fran—$4,409,440.28 ($119,407.90 per player).

World Series, 1903-89

The World Series was started in 1903 when Pittsburgh of the older National League (founded in 1876) invited Boston of the American League (founded in 1901) to play a best-of-9 game series to determine which of the two league champions was the best. Boston was the surprise winner of the competition, 5 games to 3.

The 1904 NL champion New York Giants refused to play Boston the following year, so there was no series. Giants' owner John T. Brush hated AL president Ban Johnson and considered the junior circuit to be a minor league. By the following year, however, Brush and Johnson had smoothed over their differences and the Giants agreed to play Philadelphia in a best-of-7 game series.

Since then the World Series has been best-of-7 format, except from 1919-21 when it returned to best-of-9.

In the chart below, the National League teams are listed in capital LETTERS. Also, each World Series champion's wins and loses are noted in parentheses after the series score.

Year	Winner	Manager	Series	Loser	Manager
1903	Boston Red Sox	Jimmy Collins	5-3 (LWLLWWWW)	PITTSBURGH	Fred Clarke
1904	No Series				
1905	NY GIANTS	John McGraw	4-1 (WLWWW)	Philadelphia A's	Connie Mack
1906	Chi.White Sox	Fielder Jones	4-2 (WLWLWW)	CHICAGO CUBS	Frank Chance
1907	CHICAGO CUBS	Frank Chance	4-0-1 (TWWWW)	Detroit	Hugh Jennings
1908	CHICAGO CUBS	Frank Chance	4-1 (WWLWW)	Detroit	Hugh Jennings
1909	PITTSBURGH	Fred Clarke	4-3 (WLWLWLW)	Detroit	Hugh Jennings
1910	Philadelphia A's	Connie Mack	4-1 (WWWLW)	CHICAGO CUBS	Frank Chance
1911	Philadelphia A's	Connie Mack	4-2 (LWWWLW)	NY GIANTS	John McGraw
1912	Boston Red Sox	Jake Stahl	4-3-1 (WTLWWLLW)	NY GIANTS	John McGraw
1913	Philadelphia A's	Connie Mack	4-1 (WWLWW)	NY GIANTS	John McGraw
1914	BOSTON BRAVES	George Stallings	4-0	Philadelphia A's	Connie Mack
1915	Boston Red Sox	Bill Carrinton	4-1 (LWWWW)	PHILA.PHILLIES	Pat Moran
1916	Boston Red Sox	Bill Carrinton	4-1 (WWLWW)	BKLN.DODGERS	Wilbert Robinson
1917	Chi.White Sox	Pants Rowland	4-2 (WWLLWW)	NY GIANTS	John McGraw
1918	Boston Red Sox	Ed Barrow	4-2 (WWLWLW)	CHICAGO CUBS	Fred Mitchell
1919	CINCINNATI	Pat Moran	5-3 (WWLWWLLW)	Chi.White Sox	Kid Gleason
1920	Cleveland	Tris Speaker	4-3 (WLLWWWW)	BKLN.DODGERS	Wilbert Robinson
1921	NY GIANTS	John McGraw	5-3 (LLWLWWW)	NY Yankees	Miller Huggins
1922	NY GIANTS	John McGraw	4-0-1 (WTWWW)	NY Yankees	Miller Huggins
1923	NY Yankees	Miller Huggins	4-2 (LWLWWW)	NY GIANTS	John McGraw
1924	Washington	Bucky Harris	4-3 (LWLWLWW)	NY GIANTS	John McGraw
1925	PITTSBURGH	Bill McKechnie	4-3 (LWLLWWW)	Washington	Bucky Harris
1926	ST.L.CARDINALS	Rogers Hornsby	4-3 (LWWLLWW)	NY Yankees	Miller Huggins
1927	NY Yankees	Miller Huggins	4-0	PITTSBURGH	Donie Bush
1928	NY Yankees	Miller Huggins	4-0	ST.L.CARDINALS	Bill McKechnie
1929	Philadelphia A's	Connie Mack	4-1 (WWLWW)	CHICAGO CUBS	Joe McCarthy
1930	Philadelphia A's	Connie Mack	4-2 (WWLLWW)	ST.L.CARDINALS	Gabby Street
1931	ST.L.CARDINALS	Gabby Street	4-3 (LWWLWLW)	Philadelphia A's	Connie Mack
1932	NY Yankees	Joe McCarthy	4-0	CHICAGO CUBS	Charlie Grimm
1933	NY GIANTS	Bill Terry	4-1 (WWLWW)	Washington	Joe Cronin
1934	ST.L.CARDINALS	Frankie Frisch	4-3 (WLWLLWW)	Detroit	Mickey Cochrane
1935	Detroit	Mickey Cochrane	4-2 (LWWWLW)	CHICAGO CUBS	Charlie Grimm
1936	NY Yankees	Joe McCarthy	4-2 (LWWWLW)	NY GIANTS	Bill Terry
1937	NY Yankees	Joe McCarthy	4-1 (WWWLW)	NY GIANTS	Bill Terry
1938	NY Yankees	Joe McCarthy	4-0	CHICAGO CUBS	Gabby Hartnett
1939	NY Yankees	Joe McCarthy	4-0	CINCINNATI	Bill McKechnie
1940	CINCINNATI	Bill McKechnie	4-3 (LWLWLWW)	Detroit	Del Baker
1941	NY Yankees	Joe McCarthy	4-1 (WLWWW)	BKLN.DODGERS	Leo Durocher
1942	ST.L.CARDINALS	Billy Southworth	4-1 (LWWWW)	NY Yankees	Joe McCarthy
1943	NY Yankees	Joe McCarthy	4-1 (WLWWW)	ST.L.CARDINALS	Billy Southworth
1944	ST.L.CARDINALS	Billy Southworth	4-2 (LWLWWW)	St.Louis Browns	Luke Sewell
1945	Detroit	Steve O'Neill	4-3 (LWLWWLW)	CHICAGO CUBS	Charlie Grimm
1946	ST.L.CARDINALS	Eddie Dyer	4-3 (LWLWLWW)	Boston Red Sox	Joe Cronin
1947	NY Yankees	Bucky Harris	4-3 (WWLLWLW)	BKLN.DODGERS	Burt Shotton
1948	Cleveland	Lou Boudreau	4-2 (LWWWLW)	BOS.BRAVES	Billy Southworth
1949	NY Yankees	Casey Stengel	4-1 (WLWWW)	BKLN.DODGERS	Burt Shotton
1950	NY Yankees	Casey Stengel	4-0	PHILA.PHILLIES	Eddie Sawyer
1951	NY Yankees	Casey Stengel	4-2 (LWLWWW)	NY GIANTS	Leo Durocher
1952	NY Yankees	Casey Stengel	4-3 (LWLWLWW)	BKLN.DODGERS	Charlie Dressen
1953	NY Yankees	Casey Stengel	4-2 (WWLLWW)	BKLN.DODGERS	Charlie Dressen
1954	NY GIANTS	Leo Durocher	4-0	Cleveland	Al Lopez
1955	BKLN.DODGERS	Walter Alston	4-3 (LLWWWLW)	NY Yankees	Casey Stengel
1956	NY Yankees	Casey Stengel	4-3 (LLWWWLW)	BKLN.DODGERS	Walter Alston
1957	MILW.BRAVES	Fred Haney	4-3 (LWLWWLW)	NY Yankees	Casey Stengel
1958	NY Yankees	Casey Stengel	4-3 (LLWLWWW)	MILW.BRAVES	Fred Haney
1959	LA DODGERS	Walter Alston	4-2 (LWWWLW)	Chi.White Sox	Al Lopez

Year	Winner	Manager	Series	Loser	Manager
1960	PITTSBURGH	Danny Murtaugh	4-3 (WLLWWLW)	NY Yankees	Casey Stengel
1961	NY Yankees	Ralph Houk	4-1 (WLWWW)	CINCINNATI	Fred Hutchinson
1962	NY Yankees	Ralph Houk	4-3 (WLWLWLW)	SF GIANTS	Al Dark
1963	LA DODGERS	Walter Alston	4-0	NY Yankees	Ralph Houk
1964	ST.L.CARDINALS	Johnny Keane	4-3 (WLLWWLW)	NY Yankees	Yogi Berra
1965	LA DODGERS	Walter Alston	4-3 (LLWWWLW)	Minnesota	Sam Mele
1966	Baltimore	Hank Bauer	4-0	LA DODGERS	Walter Alston
1967	ST.L.CARDINALS	Red Schoendienst	4-3 (WLWWLLW)	Boston Red Sox	Dick Williams
1968	Detroit	Mayo Smith	4-3 (LWLLWWW)	ST.L.CARDINALS	Red Schoendienst
1969	NY METS	Gil Hodges	4-1 (LWWWW)	Baltimore	Earl Weaver
1970	Baltimore	Earl Weaver	4-1 (WWWLW)	CINCINNATI	Sparky Anderson
1971	PITTSBURGH	Danny Murtaugh	4-3 (LLWWWLW)	Baltimore	Earl Weaver
1972	Oakland A's	Dick Williams	4-3 (WWLWLLW)	CINCINNATI	Sparky Anderson
1973	Oakland A's	Dick Williams	4-3 (WLWLLWW)	NY Mets	Yogi Berra
1974	Oakland A's	Al Dark	4-1 (WLWWW)	LA DODGERS	Walter Alston
1975	CINCINNATI	Sparky Anderson	4-3 (LWWLWLW)	Boston Red Sox	Darrell Johnson
1976	CINCINNATI	Sparky Anderson	4-0	NY Yankees	Billy Martin
1977	NY Yankees	Billy Martin	4-2 (WLWLW)	LA DODGERS	Tom Lasorda
1978	NY Yankees	Bob Lemon	4-2 (LLWWWW)	LA DODGERS	Tom Lasorda
1979	PITTSBURGH	Chuck Tanner	4-3 (LWLLWWW)	Baltimore	Earl Weaver
1980	PHILA.PHILLIES	Dallas Green	4-2 (WWLLWW)	Kansas City	Jim Frey
1981	LA DODGERS	Tom Lasorda	4-2 (LLWWWW)	NY Yankees	Bob Lemon
1982	ST.L.CARDINALS	Whitey Herzog	4-3 (LWWLLWW)	Milw.Brewers	Harvey Kuenn
1983	Baltimore	Joe Altobelli	4-1 (LWWWW)	PHILA.PHILLIES	Paul Owens
1984	Detroit	Sparky Anderson	4-1 (WLWWW)	SAN DIEGO	Dick Williams
1985	Kansas City	Dick Howser	4-3 (LLWLWWW)	ST.L.CARDINALS	Whitey Herzog
1986	NY METS	Davey Johnson	4-3 (LLWLLWW)	Boston Red Sox	John McNamara
1987	Minnesota	Tom Kelly	4-3 (WWLLLWW)	ST.L.CARDINALS	Whitey Herzog
1988	LA DODGERS	Tom Lasorda	4-1 (WWLWW)	Oakland A's	Tony LaRussa
1989	Oakland A's	Tony LaRussa	4-0	SF GIANTS	Roger Craig

World Series MVPs

Year Most Valuable Player

1955 Johnny Podres, Brooklyn, P
1956 Don Larsen, NY Yankees, P
1957 Lew Burdette, Milwaukee, P
1958 Bob Turley, NY Yankees, P
1959 Larry Sherry, Los Angeles, P

1960 Bobby Richardson, NY Yankees, 2B
1961 Whitey Ford, NY Yankees, P
1962 Ralph Terry, NY Yankees, P
1963 Sandy Koufax, Los Angeles, P
1964 Bob Gibson, St.Louis, P
1965 Sandy Koufax, Los Angeles, P
1966 Frank Robinson, Baltimore, OF
1967 Bob Gibson, St.Louis, P
1968 Mickey Lolich, Detroit, P
1969 Donn Clendenon, NY Mets, 1B

1970 Brooks Robinson, Baltimore, 3B
1971 Roberto Clemente, Pittsburgh, OF
1972 Gene Tenace, Oakland, C
1973 Reggie Jackson, Oakland, OF
1974 Rollie Fingers, Oakland, P
1975 Pete Rose, Cincinnati, 3B
1976 Johnny Bench, Cincinnati, C
1977 Reggie Jackson, New York, OF
1978 Bucky Dent, New York, SS
1979 Willie Stargell, Pittsburgh, 1B

1980 Mike Schmidt, Philadelphia, 3B
1981 Pedro Guerrero, Los Angeles, OF;
     Ron Cey, LA, 3B; & Steve Yeager, LA, C
1982 Darrell Porter, St.Louis, C
1983 Rick Dempsey, Baltimore, C
1984 Alan Trammell, Detroit, SS
1985 Bret Saberhagen, Kansas City, P
1986 Ray Knight, NY Mets, 3B
1987 Frank Viola, Minnesota, P
1988 Orel Hershiser, Los Angeles, P
1989 Dave Stewart, Oakland, P

World Series Appearances

In the 88 years that the World Series has been contested, American League teams have won 48 championships while National League teams have won 36 times.

The New York Yankees, winners of 22 World Series, have appeared in the Fall Classic 33 times. The Brooklyn and Los Angeles Dodgers have appeared in 18 Series and won six. Since their first meeting in 1941, the Yankees and Dodgers have played each other 11 times with the Yanks winning eight championships.

Teams on the following list are ranked by number of Series appearances. Note that (*) indicates American League teams.

	App	W	L	Pct.	Last Series	Last Title
New York Yankees*	33	22	11	.667	1981	1978
Bklyn/LA Dodgers..	18	6	12	.333	1988	1988
NY/SF Giants	16	5	11	.313	1989	1954
St.Louis Cardinals ..	15	9	6	.600	1987	1982
Phila/KC/Oak.A's* .	13	9	4	.692	1989	1989
Chicago Cubs	10	2	8	.200	1945	1908
Boston Red Sox* ..	9	5	4	.550	1986	1918
Detroit Tigers*	9	4	5	.444	1984	1984
Cincinnati Reds....	8	4	4	.500	1976	1976
Pittsburgh Pirates ..	7	5	2	.714	1979	1979
St.L/Balt.Orioles* ..	7	3	4	.429	1983	1983
Wash/Minn.Twins* .	5	2	3	.400	1987	1987
Chicago White Sox*	4	2	2	.500	1959	1917
Bos/Milw/Atl.Braves	4	2	2	.500	1958	1957
Phila.Phillies	4	1	3	.250	1983	1980
Cleveland Indians* .	3	2	1	.667	1954	1948
New York Mets ...	3	2	1	.667	1986	1986
Kansas City Royals*	2	1	1	.500	1985	1985
Sea/Milw.Brewers* .	1	0	1	.000	1982	—
San Diego Padres .	1	0	1	.000	1984	—

League Championship Series, 1969-89

Division play came to the major leagues in 1969 when both the American and National Leagues expanded to 12 teams. With an East and West Division in each league, League Championship Series (LCS) became necessary to determine the NL and AL pennant winners.

In the charts below, the East Division champions are noted by the letter E and the West Division champions by the letter W. Also, each playoff winner's wins and losses are noted in parentheses after the series score. Note that the LCS changed from best-of-5 to best-of-seven in 1985.

National League

Year	Winner	Manager	Series	Loser	Manager
1969	E- New York	Gil Hodges	3-0	W- Atlanta	Lum Harris
1970	W- Cincinnati	Sparky Anderson	3-0	E- Pittsburgh	Danny Murtaugh
1971	E- Pittsburgh	Danny Murtaugh	3-1 (LWWW)	W- San Francisco	Charlie Fox
1972	W- Cincinnati	Sparky Anderson	3-2 (LWLWW)	E- Pittsburgh	Bill Virdon
1973	E- New York	Yogi Berra	3-2 (LWWLW)	W- Cincinnati	Sparky Anderson
1974	W- Los Angeles	Walter Alston	3-1 (WWLW)	E- Pittsburgh	Danny Murtaugh
1975	W- Cincinnati	Sparky Anderson	3-0	E- Pittsburgh	Danny Murtaugh
1976	W- Cincinnati	Sparky Anderson	3-0	E- Philadelphia	Danny Ozark
1977	W- Los Angeles	Tom Lasorda	3-1 (LWWW)	E- Philadelphia	Danny Ozark
1978	W- Los Angeles	Tom Lasorda	3-1 (WWLW)	E- Philadelphia	Danny Ozark
1979	E- Pittsburgh	Chuck Tanner	3-0	W- Cincinnati	John McNamara
1980	E- Philadelphia	Dallas Green	3-2 (WLLWW)	W- Houston	Bill Virdon
1981	W- Los Angeles	Tom Lasorda	3-2 (WLLWW)	E- Montreal	Jim Fanning
1982	E- St. Louis	Whitey Herzog	3-0	W- Atlanta	Joe Torre
1983	E- Philadelphia	Paul Owens	3-1 (WLWW)	W- Los Angeles	Tom Lasorda
1984	W- San Diego	Dick Williams	3-2 (LLWWW)	E- Chicago	Jim Frey
1985	E- St. Louis	Whitey Herzog	4-2 (LLWWWW)	W- Los Angeles	Tom Lasorda
1986	E- New York	Davey Johnson	4-2 (LWWLWW)	W- Houston	Hal Lanier
1987	E- St. Louis	Whitey Herzog	4-3 (WLWLLWW)	W- San Francisco	Roger Craig
1988	W- Los Angeles	Tom Lasorda	4-3 (LWLWLWW)	E- New York	Davey Johnson
1989	W- San Francisco	Roger Craig	4-1 (WLWWW)	E- Chicago	Don Zimmer

Playoff MVPs

Year	Most Valuable Player	Year	Most Valuable Player	Year	Most Valuable Player
1977	Dusty Baker, Los Ang., OF	1980	Manny Trillo, Phila., 2B	1985	Ozzie Smith, St.Louis, SS
1978	Steve Garvey, Los Ang., 1B	1981	Burt Hooton, Los Ang., P	1986	Mike Scott, Houston, P
1979	Willie Stargell, Pitt., 1B	1982	Darrell Porter, St.Louis, C	1987	Jeff Leonard, San Fran., OF
		1983	Gary Matthews, Phila., OF	1988	Orel Hershiser, Los Ang., P
		1984	Steve Garvey, San Diego, 1B	1989	Will Clark, San Fran., 1B

American League

Year	Winner	Manager	Series	Loser	Manager
1969	E- Baltimore	Earl Weaver	3-0	W- Minnesota	Billy Martin
1970	E- Baltimore	Earl Weaver	3-0	W- Minnesota	Bill Rigney
1971	E- Baltimore	Earl Weaver	3-0	W- Oakland	Dick Williams
1972	W- Oakland	Dick Williams	3-2 (WWLLW)	E- Detroit	Billy Martin
1973	W- Oakland	Dick Williams	3-2 (LWWLW)	E- Baltimore	Earl Weaver
1974	W- Oakland	Al Dark	3-1 (LWWW)	E- Baltimore	Earl Weaver
1975	E- Boston	Darrell Johnson	3-0	W- Oakland	Al Dark
1976	E- New York	Billy Martin	3-2 (WLWLW)	W- Kansas City	Whitey Herzog
1977	E- New York	Billy Martin	3-2 (LWLWW)	W- Kansas City	Whitey Herzog
1978	E- New York	Bob Lemon	3-1 (WLWW)	W- Kansas City	Whitey Herzog
1979	E- Baltimore	Earl Weaver	3-1 (WWLW)	W- California	Jim Fregosi
1980	W- Kansas City	Jim Frey	3-0	E- New York	Dick Howser
1981	E- New York	Bob Lemon	3-0	W- Oakland	Billy Martin
1982	E- Milwaukee	Harvey Kuenn	3-2 (LLWWW)	W- California	Gene Mauch
1983	E- Baltimore	Joe Altobelli	3-1 (LWWW)	W- Chicago	Tony LaRussa
1984	E- Detroit	Sparky Anderson	3-0	W- Kansas City	Dick Howser
1985	W- Kansas City	Dick Howser	4-3 (LLWLWWW)	E- Toronto	Bobby Cox
1986	E- Boston	John McNamara	4-3 (LWLLWWW)	W- California	Gene Mauch
1987	W- Minnesota	Tom Kelly	4-1 (WWLWW)	E- Detroit	Sparky Anderson
1988	W- Oakland	Tony LaRussa	4-0	E- Boston	Joe Morgan
1989	W- Oakland	Tony LaRussa	4-1 (WWLWW)	E- Toronto	Cito Gaston

Playoff MVPs

Year	Most Valuable Player	Year	Most Valuable Player	Year	Most Valuable Player
1980	Frank White, Kansas City, 2B	1984	Kirk Gibson, Detroit, OF	1987	Gary Gaetti, Minnesota, 3B
1981	Graig Nettles, New York, 3B	1985	George Brett, Kansas City 3B	1988	Dennis Eckersley, Oakland, P
1982	Fred Lynn, California, OF	1986	Marty Barrett, Boston, 2B	1989	Rickey Henderson, Oak., OF
1983	Mike Boddicker, Baltimore, P				

Other Playoffs

Before divisional play in 1969, there were five playoffs (one in the AL and four in the NL) between teams that tied for first place on the final day of the season. Since divisional play, deadlocks at the end of the season have happened once in each league. That's not counting the strike year of 1981, when both leagues had best-of-five game playoffs between the 1st and 2nd half season winners.

National League

Year	NL	W	L	Manager
1946	Brooklyn	96	58	Leo Durocher
	St.Louis	96	58	Eddie Dyer
	Playoff: (Best-of-3) St.Louis, 2-0			
	NL	**W**	**L**	**Manager**
1951	Brooklyn	96	58	Charlie Dressen
	New York	96	58	Leo Durocher
	Playoff: (Best-of-3) New York, 2-1 (WLW)			
	NL	**W**	**L**	**Manager**
1959	Milwaukee	86	68	Fred Haney
	Los Angeles	86	68	Walter Alston
	Playoff: (Best-of-3) Los Angeles, 2-0			

Year	NL	W	L	Manager
1962	Los Angeles	101	61	Walter Alston
	San Francisco	101	61	Al Dark
	Playoff: (Best-of-3) San Francisco, 2-1 (WLW)			
	NL West	**W**	**L**	**Manager**
1980	Houston..........	101	61	Bill Virdon
	Los Angeles	101	61	Tom Lasorda
	Playoff: (1 game) Houston, 7-1 (at LA)			
	NL East	**W**	**L**	**Manager**
1981	(1st Half) Phila ...	34	21	Dallas Green
	(2nd Half) Montreal	30	23	Jim Fanning
	Playoff: (Best-of-5) Montreal, 3-2 (WWLLW)			
	NL West	**W**	**L**	**Manager**
	(1st Half) Los Ang .	36	21	Tom Lasorda
	(2nd Half) Houston	33	20	Bill Virdon
	Playoff: (Best-of-5) Los Angeles, 3-2 (LLWWW)			

American League

Year	AL	W	L	Manager
1948	Boston	96	58	Joe McCarthy
	Cleveland	96	58	Lou Boudreau
	Playoff: (1 game) Cleveland, 8-3 (at Boston)			
	AL East	**W**	**L**	**Manager**
1978	Boston	99	63	Don Zimmer
	New York	99	63	Bob Lemon
	Playoff: (1 game) New York, 5-4 (at Boston)			

Year	AL East	W	L	Manager
1981	(1st Half) N.Y. ...	34	22	Bob Lemon
	(2nd Half) Milw. ..	31	22	Buck Rodgers
	Playoff: (Best-of-5) New York, 3-2 (WWLLW)			
	AL West	**W**	**L**	**Manager**
	(1st Half) Oakland	37	23	Billy Martin
	(2nd Half) Kan.City	30	23	Jim Frey
	Playoff: (Best-of-5), Oakland, 3-0			

Before the World Series

The NL-American Assn. Series, 1882-90

When the National League met the American League for the first time in the 1903 World Series, it was not the N.L.'s first venture into post-season play.

From 1882-90, the N.L. pennant winner engaged in a championship series with the champion of the American Association. The Nationals won four of the eight series, lost once and tied three times.

Year	Champion	Loser	Series	Year	Champion	Loser	Series
1882	Chicago (NL)	—		1886	St.Louis (AA)	Chicago (NL)	4-2
	& Cincinnati (AA)		1-1	1887	Detroit (NL)	St.Louis (AA)	10-5
1883	No series			1888	New York (NL)	St.Louis (AA)	6-4
1884	Providence (NL)	New York (AA)	3-0	1889	New York (NL)	Brooklyn (AA)	6-3
1885	Chicago (NL)	—		1890	Brooklyn (NL)	—	
	& St.Louis (AA)		3-3-1		& Louisville (AA)		3-3-1

Early NL and AL Pennant Winners

The National League had been around 27 years before the 1903 World Series. The AL, however, was only in its third season when the two leagues met. The following lists account for the pennant winners in those pre-World Series years and in 1904 when the NL champion New York Giants refused to play Boston.

NL Pennant Winners, 1876-1902,'04

Year	Winner	Manager	Year	Winner	Manager	Year	Winner	Manager
1876	Chicago	Al Spalding	1885	Chicago	Cap Anson	1895	Baltimore	Ned Hanlon
1877	Boston	Harry Wright	1886	Chicago	Cap Anson	1896	Baltimore	Ned Hanlon
1878	Boston	Harry Wright	1887	Detroit	Bill Watkins	1897	Boston	Frank Selee
1879	Providence	George Wright	1888	New York	Jim Mutrie	1898	Boston	Frank Selee
1880	Chicago	Cap Anson	1889	New York	Jim Mutrie	1899	Brooklyn	Ned Hanlon
1881	Chicago	Cap Anson	1890	Brooklyn	Bill McGunnigle	1900	Brooklyn	Ned Hanlon
1882	Chicago	Cap Anson	1891	Boston	Frank Selee	1901	Pittsburgh	Fred Clarke
1883	Boston	John Morrill	1892	Boston	Frank Selee	1902	Pittsburgh	Fred Clarke
1884	Providence	Frank Bancroft	1893	Boston	Frank Selee	1904	New York	John McGraw
			1894	Baltimore	Ned Hanlon			

AL Pennant Winners, 1901-02,'04

Year	Winner	Manager	Year	Winner	Manager	Year	Winner	Manager
1901	Chicago	Clark Griffith	1902	Philadelphia	Connie Mack	1904	Boston	Jimmy Collins

Champions of Leagues That Didn't Make It

A Special Baseball Records Committee appointed by the commissioner found in 1968 that four extinct leagues qualified for major League status—the American Association (1882-91), the Union Association (1884), the Players' League (1890) and the Federal League (1914-15). The first years of the American League (1900) and Federal League (1913) were not recognized.
The champions of the rival major leagues and their managers are listed below.

American Association

Year	Champion	Manager
1882	Cincinnati	Pop Snyder
1883	Philadelphia	Lew Simmons
1884	New York	Jim Mutrie
1885	St.Louis	Chas.Comiskey
1886	St.Louis	Chas.Comiskey
1887	St.Louis	Chas.Comiskey
1888	St.Louis	Chas.Comiskey
1889	Brooklyn	Bill McGunnigle
1890	Louisville	Jack Chapman
1891	Boston	Arthur Irwin

Union Association

Year	Champion	Manager
1884	St.Louis	Henry Lucas

Players' League

Year	Champion	Manager
1890	Boston	King Kelly

Federal League

Year	Champion	Manager
1914	Indianapolis	Bill Phillips
1915	Chicago	Joe Tinker

Major League Managers

All-Time Regular Season

Thirteen managers have led Major League ballclubs to at least 1,500 regular season wins. Active managers are in **bold** type. Note that **Pen** indicates number of pennants won.

		Yrs	Won	Lost	Pct	Pen
1	Connie Mack	53	**3,776**	4,025	.484	9
2	John McGraw	33	**2,840**	1,984	.589	10
3	Bucky Harris	29	**2,159**	2,219	.493	3
4	Joe McCarthy	24	**2,126**	1,335	.614	9
5	Walter Alston	23	**2,040**	1,613	.558	7
6	Leo Durocher	24	**2,010**	1,710	.540	3
7	Casey Stengel	25	**1,926**	1,867	.508	10
8	Gene Mauch	26	**1,901**	2,037	.483	0
9	Bill McKechnie	25	**1,898**	1,724	.524	4
10	**Sparky Anderson**	20	**1,758**	1,362	.563	5
11	Ralph Houk	20	**1,619**	1,531	.514	3
12	Fred Clarke	19	**1,602**	1,179	.576	4
13	Dick Williams	21	**1,572**	1,451	.520	4

Note: McKechnie's one season (1915) as manager of Newark (NJ) in the Federal League is included in his record.

Where They Managed

Mack—Pittsburgh NL (1894-96), Philadelphia AL (1901-50), Philadelphia AL (1901-02), New York NL (1902-32); **Harris**—Washington AL (1924-28,35-42,50-54), Detroit AL (1929-33, 55-56), Boston AL (1934), Philadelphia AL (1943), New York AL (1947-48); **McCarthy**—Chicago NL (1926-30), New York AL (1931-46), Boston AL (1948-50); **Alston**—Brooklyn/Los Angeles NL (1954-76); **Durocher**—Brooklyn NL (1939-46,48), New York NL (1948-55), Chicago NL (1966-72), Houston NL (1972-73).

Stengel—Brooklyn NL (1934-36), Boston NL (1938-43), New York AL (1949-60), NY Mets NL (1962-65); **Mauch**—Philadelphia NL (1960-68), Montreal NL (1969-75), Minnesota AL (1976-80), California AL (1981-82,85-87); **McKechnie**—Newark FL (1915), Pittsburgh NL (1922-26), St.Louis NL (1928-29), Boston NL (1930-37), Cincinnati NL (1938-46); **Anderson**—Cincinnati NL (1970-78), Detroit AL (1979-); **Houk**—New York AL (1961-63,66-73), Detroit AL (1974-78), Boston AL (1981-84); **Clarke**—Louisville NL (1897-99), Pittsburgh NL (1900-15); **Williams**—Boston AL (1967-69), Oakland AL (1971-73), California AL (1974-76), Montreal NL (1977-81), San Diego NL (1982-85), Seattle AL (1986-88).

All-Time World Series Appearances

Fifteen managers have led their ballclubs into at least 20 World Series games. Active managers are in **bold** type.

		App	Gms	W	L	Pct	Titles
1	Casey Stengel	10	**63**	37	26	.587	7
2	John McGraw	9*	**55**	26	28	.589	2
3	Joe McCarthy	9	**43**	30	13	.698	7
	Connie Mack	8*	**43**	24	19	.558	5
5	Walter Alston	7	**40**	20	20	500	4
6	Miller Huggins	6	**34**	18	15	.545	3
7	**Sparky Anderson**	5	**28**	16	12	.571	3
8	Dick Williams	4	**26**	12	14	.462	2
9	Earl Weaver	4	**24**	11	13	.458	1
10	**Tom Lasorda**	4	**23**	12	11	.522	2
11	Billy Southworth	4	**22**	11	11	.500	2
	Bill McKechnie	4	**22**	8	14	.364	2
13	Frank Chance	4	**21**	11	9	.550	2
	Bucky Harris	3	**21**	11	10	.524	2
	Whitey Herzog	3	**21**	10	11	.476	1

Note: McGraw won 10 pennants and Mack won nine, but there was no World Series in either 1902 (when Mack's Athletics won the AL) or 1904 (when McGraw's Giants won the NL).

Pennant Winners They Managed

Stengel—New York AL (1949-53,55-58,60); **McGraw**—New York NL (1904-05,1911-13,17,21-24); **McCarthy**—Chicago NL (1929); **New York AL (1932,36-39,41-43)**; **Mack**—Philadelphia AL (1905,10-11,13-14,29-31); **Alston**—Brooklyn/Los Angeles NL (1955-56,59,63,65-66,74); **Huggins**—New York AL (1921-23,26-28); **Anderson**—Cincinnati NL (1970,72,75-76), Detroit AL (1984).

Williams—Boston AL (1967), Oakland AL (1972-73), San Diego NL (1984); **Weaver**—Baltimore AL (1969-71,79); **Lasorda**—Los Angeles NL (1977-78, 81,88); **Southworth**—St.Louis NL (1942-44), Boston NL (1948); **McKechnie**—Pittsburgh NL (1925); **St.Louis NL (1928); Cincinnati NL (1939-40)**; **Chance**—Chicago NL (1906-08,10); **Harris-Washington AL (1924-25), New York AL (1947)**; **Herzog**—St.Louis NL (1982,85,87).

Active Managers
Most Wins

Records through 1989 regular season, not including League Championship Series or World Series.

National League

		Yrs	Won	Lost	Pct
1	Whitey Herzog, St.Louis ..	17	1248	1078	.537
2	Tom Lasorda, Los Angeles	14	1099	957	.535
3	Don Zimmer, Chicago....	11	790	754	.512
4	Dave Johnson, New York.	6	575	395	.593
5	Buck Rodgers, Montreal ..	8	539	495	.521
6	Roger Craig, San Francisco	7	506	483	.512
7	Jack McKeon, San Diego .	7	442	431	.506
8	Jim Leyland, Pittsburgh...	4	303	343	.469
9	Russ Nixon, Atlanta	4	206	307	.402
10	Art Howe, Houston.......	1	86	76	.531
11	Nick Leyva, Philadelphia .	1	67	95	.414
12	Tommy Helms, Cincinnati .	2*	26	36	.419

Note: Helms managed Cincinnati for 27 games in 1988 while Pete Rose was on suspension.

American League

		Yrs	Won	Lost	Pct
1	Sparky Anderson, Detroit .	20	1758	1362	.563
2	Tony LaRussa, Oakland ..	11	851	746	.533
3	Frank Robinson, Baltimore	9	591	642	.479
4	Bobby Valentine, Texas ..	5	368	408	.474
5	Tom Kelly, Minnesota	4	268	241	.527
6	Tom Trebelhorn, Milwaukee	4	265	230	.535
7	Doug Rader, California ..	5	247	272	.476
8	Jeff Torborg, Chicago....	3	226	293	.435
9	John Wathan, Kansas City	3	197	162	.549
10	Joe Morgan, Boston	2	129	110	.540
11	Cito Gaston, Toronto	1	77	49	.611
12	Jim Lefebvre, Seattle.....	1	73	89	.451
13	Bucky Dent, New York ...	1	18	22	.450
14	John Hart, Cleveland	1	8	11	.421

Manager of the Year Award

Given by **The Sporting News**. One award was presented from 1936-85. Two awards (one for each league) have been presented since 1986. Note than (*) indicates a league pennant (1936-68) or division championship (since 1969).

AL and NL Combined

Year		Improvement
1936	Joe McCarthy, NY (AL) ..	89-60 to 102-51*
1937	Bill McKechnie, Bos.(NL)..	71-83 to 79-73
1938	Joe McCarthy, NY (AL) ..	102-52* to 99-53*
1939	Leo Durocher, Bklyn.(NL).	69-80 to 84-69
1940	Bill McKechnie, Cinn.	97-57* to 100-53*
1941	Billy Southworth, St.L.(NL)	84-69 to 97-56
1942	Billy Southworth, St.L.(NL)	97-56 to 106-48*
1943	Joe McCarthy, NY (AL) ..	103-51* to 98-56*
1944	Luke Sewell, St.L.(AL)....	72-80 to 89-65*
1945	Ossie Bluege, Wash.	64-90 to 87-67
1946	Eddie Dyer, St.L.(NL)....	95-59 to 98-58*
1947	Bucky Harris, NY (AL) ..	87-67 to 97-57*
1948	Bill Meyer, Pitt.	62-92 to 83-71
1949	Casey Stengel, NY (AL) ..	94-60 to 97-57*
1950	Red Rolfe, Detroit	87-67 to 95-59
1951	Leo Durocher, NY (NL) ..	86-68 to 98-59*
1952	Eddie Stanky, St.L.	81-73 to 88-66
1953	Casey Stengel, NY (AL) ..	95-59* to 99-52*
1954	Leo Durocher, NY (NL) ..	70-84 to 97-57*
1955	Walter Alston, Bklyn.	92-62 to 98-55*
1956	Birdie Tebbetts, Cinn.	75-79 to 91-63
1957	Fred Hutchinson, St.L.....	76-78 to 87-67
1958	Casey Stengel, NY (AL) ..	98-56* to 92-62*
1959	Walter Alston, LA	71-83 to 88-68*

Year		Improvement
1960	Danny Murtaugh, Pitt. ...	78-76 to 95-59*
1961	Ralph Houk, NY (AL)	97-57* to 109-53*
1962	Bill Rigney, LA (AL).....	70-91 to 86-76
1963	Walter Alston, LA	102-63 to 99-63*
1964	Johnny Keane, St.L.	93-69 to 93-69*
1965	Sam Mele, Minnesota	79-83 to 102-60*
1966	Hank Bauer, Baltimore ..	94-68 to 97-63*
1967	Dick Williams, Boston ...	72-90 to 92-70*
1968	Mayo Smith, Detroit	91-71 to 103-59*
1969	Gil Hodges, New York (NL)	73-89 to 100-62*
1970	Danny Murtaugh, Pitts....	88-74 to 89-73*
1971	Charlie Fox, San Fran. ..	86-76 to 90-72*
1972	Chuck Tanner, Chicago (AL)	79-83 to 87-67
1973	Gene Mauch, Montreal ..	70-86 to 79-83
1974	Bill Virdon, New York (AL)	80-82 to 89-73
1975	Darrell Johnson, Bos.	84-78 to 95-65*
1976	Danny Ozark, Phila......	86-76 to 101-61*
1977	Earl Weaver, Balt.	88-74 to 97-64
1978	George Bamberger, Milw .	67-95 to 93-69
1979	Earl Weaver, Balt.	90-71 to 102-57*
1980	Bill Virdon, Houston	89-73 to 93-70*
1981	Billy Martin, Oakland ...	83-79 to 64-45*
1982	Whitey Herzog, St.L.	59-43 to 92-70*
1983	Tony LaRussa, Chicago (AL)	87-75 to 99-63*
1984	Jim Frey, Chicago (NL)...	71-91 to 96-75*
1985	Bobby Cox, Toronto	89-73 to 99-62*

Note: In 1981, both league seasons were reduced to 110 games or less due to a players strike.

National League

Year		Improvement
1986	Hal Lanier, Houston	83-79 to 96-66*
1987	Buck Rodgers, Montreal	78-83 to 91-71
1988	Tom Lasorda, Los Angeles..	73-89 to 94-67*
	& Jim Leyland, Pittsburgh ..	80-82 to 85-75

American League

Year		Improvement
1986	John McNamara, Boston ...	81-81 to 95-66*
1987	Sparky Anderson, Detroit...	87-75 to 98-64*
1988	Tony LaRussa, Oakland	81-81 to 104-58*

Player Awards

Most Valuable Player

There have been three different Most Valuable Player Awards in baseball since 1911: the Chalmers Award (1911-14) was presented by the Detroit automobile company; the League Awards (1922-29) were presented by the American and National leagues; and the Baseball Writers Assn. of America Awards (since 1931). MVP winners who also won Cy Young Award are in **bold** type. Frank Robinson is the only player who has won the award in both leagues.

Three-time winners: NL—Stan Musial, Roy Campanella, Mike Schmidt; **AL**—Jimmie Foxx, Joe DiMaggio, Yogi Berra, Mickey Mantle.

Two-time winners: NL—Rogers Hornsby; Carl Hubbell, Willie Mays, Ernie Banks, Johnny Bench, Joe Morgan, Dale Murphy; **AL**—Walter Johnson, Lou Gehrig, Mickey Cochrane, Hank Greenberg, Hal Newhouser, Ted Williams, Roger Maris.

Chalmers Award

Year	National League	Pos	Year	American League	Pos
1911	Wildfire Schulte, Chi	OF	1911	Ty Cobb, Detroit	OF
1912	Larry Doyle, New York	2B	1912	Tris Speaker, Boston	OF
1913	Jake Daubert, Brooklyn	1B	1913	Walter Johnson, Wash	P
1914	Johnny Evers, Boston	2B	1914	Eddie Collins, Phila	2B

League Award

Year	National League	Pos	Year	American League	Pos
1922	No selection		1922	George Sisler, St.L	1B
1923	No selection		1923	Babe Ruth, New York	OF
1924	Dazzy Vance, Brooklyn	P	1924	Walter Johnson, Wash	P
1925	Rogers Hornsby, St.L	2B	1925	Roger Peckinpaugh, Wash	SS
1926	Bob O'Farrell, St.L	C	1926	George Burns, Clev	1B
1927	Paul Waner, Pittsburgh	OF	1927	Lou Gehrig, New York	1B
1928	Jim Bottomley, St.L	1B	1928	Mickey Cochrane, Phila	C
1929	Rogers Hornsby, Chicago	2B	1929	No selection	

Baseball Writers' Award

Year	National League	Pos	Year	American League	Pos
1931	Frankie Frisch, St.L	2B	1931	Lefty Grove, Phila	P
1932	Chuck Klein, Phila	OF	1932	Jimmie Foxx, Phila	1B
1933	Carl Hubbell, New York	P	1933	Jimmie Foxx, Phila	1B
1934	Dizzy Dean, St.Louis	P	1934	Mickey Cochrane, Detroit	C
1935	Gabby Hartnett, Chicago	C	1935	Hank Greenberg, Detroit	1B
1936	Carl Hubbell, New York	P	1936	Lou Gehrig, New York	1B
1937	Joe Medwick, St.Louis	OF	1937	Charlie Gehringer, Det	2B
1938	Ernie Lombardi, Cinn	C	1938	Jimmie Foxx, Boston	1B
1939	Bucky Walters, Cinn	P	1939	Joe DiMaggio, New York	OF
1940	Frank McCormick, Cinn	1B	1940	Hank Greenberg, Detroit	OF
1941	Dolf Camilli, Brooklyn	1B	1941	Joe DiMaggio, New York	OF
1942	Mort Cooper, St.Louis	P	1942	Joe Gordon, New York	2B
1943	Stan Musial, St.Louis	OF	1943	Spud Chandler, New York	P
1944	Marty Marion, St.Louis	SS	1944	Hal Newhouser, Detroit	P
1945	Phil Cavarretta, Chi	1B	1945	Hal Newhouser, Detroit	P
1946	Stan Musial, St.L	1B-OF	1946	Ted Williams, Boston	OF
1947	Bob Elliott, Boston	3B	1947	Joe DiMaggio, New York	OF
1948	Stan Musial, St.Louis	OF	1948	Lou Boudreau, Cleveland	SS
1949	Jackie Robinson, Bklyn	2B	1949	Ted Williams, Boston	OF
1950	Jim Konstanty, Phila	P	1950	Phil Rizzuto, New York	SS
1951	Roy Campanella, Brooklyn	C	1951	Yogi Berra, New York	C
1952	Hank Sauer, Chicago	OF	1952	Bobby Shantz, Phila	P
1953	Roy Campanella, Brooklyn	C	1953	Al Rosen, Cleveland	3B
1954	Willie Mays, New York	OF	1954	Yogi Berra, New York	C
1955	Roy Campanella, Brooklyn	C	1955	Yogi Berra, New York	C
1956	**Don Newcombe**, Brooklyn	P	1956	Mickey Mantle, New York	OF
1957	Hank Aaron, Milwaukee	OF	1957	Mickey Mantle, New York	OF
1958	Ernie Banks, Chicago	SS	1958	Jackie Jensen, Boston	OF
1959	Ernie Banks, Chicago	SS	1959	Nellie Fox, Chicago	2B

MVP Awards (Continued)

Year	National League	Pos
1960	Dick Groat, Pittsburgh	SS
1961	Frank Robinson, Cinn	OF
1962	Maury Wills, Los Ang	SS
1963	**Sandy Koufax**, Los Ang	P
1964	Ken Boyer, St.Louis	3B
1965	Willie Mays, San Fran	OF
1966	Roberto Clemente, Pitt	OF
1967	Orlando Cepeda, St.L	1B
1968	**Bob Gibson**, St.Louis	P
1969	Willie McCovey, SF	1B
1970	Johnny Bench, Cincinnati	C
1971	Joe Torre, St.Louis	3B
1972	Johnny Bench, Cincinnati	C
1973	Pete Rose, Cincinnati	OF
1974	Steve Garvey, Los Ang	1B
1975	Joe Morgan, Cincinnati	2B
1976	Joe Morgan, Cincinnati	2B
1977	George Foster, Cinn	OF
1978	Dave Parker, Pittsburgh	OF
1979	Willie Stargell, Pitt	1B
	& Keith Hernandez, St.L	1B
1980	Mike Schmidt, Phila	3B
1981	Mike Schmidt, Phila	3B
1982	Dale Murphy, Atlanta	OF
1983	Dale Murphy, Atlanta	OF
1984	Ryne Sandberg, Chicago	2B
1985	Willie McGee, St.Louis	OF
1986	Mike Schmidt, Phila	3B
1987	Andre Dawson, Chi	OF
1988	Kirk Gibson, Los Ang	OF

Year	American League	Pos
1960	Roger Maris, New York	OF
1961	Roger Maris, New York	OF
1962	Mickey Mantle, New York	OF
1963	Elston Howard, New York	C
1964	Brooks Robinson, Balt	3B
1965	Zoilo Versalles, Minn	SS
1966	Frank Robinson, Balt	OF
1967	Carl Yastrzemski, Bos	OF
1968	**Denny McLain**, Detroit	P
1969	Harmon Killebrew, Minn	3-1B
1970	Boog Powell, Baltimore	1B
1971	**Vida Blue**, Oakland	P
1972	Dick Allen, Chicago	1B
1973	Reggie Jackson, Oakland	OF
1974	Jeff Burroughs, Texas	OF
1975	Fred Lynn, Boston	OF
1976	Thurman Munson, New York	C
1977	Rod Carew, Minnesota	1B
1978	Jim Rice, Boston	OF-DH
1979	Don Baylor, Calif	OF-DH
1980	George Brett, KC	3B
1981	**Rollie Fingers**, Milw	P
1982	Robin Yount, Milwaukee	SS
1983	Cal Ripken, Baltimore	SS
1984	**Willie Hernandez**, Det	P
1985	Don Mattingly, New York	1B
1986	**Roger Clemens**, Boston	P
1987	George Bell, Toronto	OF
1988	Jose Canseco, Oakland	OF

Cy Young Award

Voted on by the Baseball Writers Assn. of America. One award was presented from 1956-66. Two awards (one for each league) have been presented since 1967. Cy Young winners who also won the MVP Award are in **bold** type. **Four-time winner:** Steve Carlton. **Three-time winners:** Sandy Koufax, Tom Seaver and Jim Palmer.

AL and NL Combined

Year		Arm
1956	**Don Newcombe**, Bklyn, NL	R
1957	Warren Spahn, Milw, NL	L
1958	Bob Turley, New York, AL	R
1959	Early Wynn, Chicago, AL	R
1960	Vernon Law, Pitt, NL	R

Year		Arm
1961	Whitey Ford, New York, AL	L
1962	Don Drysdale, Los Ang, NL	R
1963	**Sandy Koufax**, Los Ang, NL	L
1964	Dean Chance, Los Ang, AL	R
1965	Sandy Koufax, Los Ang, NL	L
1966	Sandy Koufax, Los Ang, NL	L

National League

Year		Arm
1967	Mike McCormick, San Fran	L
1968	**Bob Gibson**, St.Louis	R
1969	Tom Seaver, New York	R
1970	Bob Gibson, St.Louis	R
1971	Ferguson Jenkins, Chi	R
1972	Steve Carlton, Phila	L
1973	Tom Seaver, New York	R
1974	Mike Marshall, Los Ang	R
1975	Tom Seaver, New York	R
1976	Randy Jones, San Diego	L
1977	Steve Carlton, Phila	L
1978	Gaylord Perry, San Diego	R
1979	Bruce Sutter, Chicago	R
1980	Steve Carlton, Phila	L
1981	Fernando Valenzuela, LA	L
1982	Steve Carlton, Phila	L
1983	John Denny, Phila	R
1984	Rick Sutcliffe, Chicago	R
1985	Dwight Gooden, New York	R
1986	Mike Scott, Houston	R
1987	Steve Bedrosian, Phila	R
1988	Orel Hershiser, Los Ang	R

Relief pitchers: Marshall (1974), Sutter (1979), Bedrosian (1979).

American League

Year		Arm
1967	Jim Lonborg, Boston	R
1968	**Denny McLain**, Detroit	R
1969	Denny McLain, Detroit	R
	& Mike Cuellar, Balt	L
1970	Jim Perry, Minnesota	R
1971	**Vida Blue**, Oakland	L
1972	Gaylord Perry, Cleve	R
1973	Jim Palmer, Baltimore	R
1974	Catfish Hunter, Oakland	R
1975	Jim Palmer, Baltimore	R
1976	Jim Palmer, Baltimore	R
1977	Sparky Lyle, New York	L
1978	Ron Guidry, New York	L
1979	Mike Flanagan, Baltimore	L
1980	Steve Stone, Baltimore	R
1981	**Rollie Fingers**, Milw	R
1982	Pete Vuckovich, Milw	R
1983	LaMarr Hoyt, Chicago	R
1984	**Willie Hernandez**, Det	L
1985	Bret Saberhagen, KC	R
1986	**Roger Clemens**, Boston	R
1987	Roger Clemens, Boston	R
1988	Frank Viola, Minnesota	L

Relief pitchers: Lyle (1977), Fingers (1981), Hernandez (1948).

Rookie of the Year Award

Voted on by the Baseball Writers Assn. of America. One award was presented from 1947-48. Two awards (one for each league) have been presented since 1949.

AL and NL Combined

Year		Pos	Year		Pos
1947	Jackie Robinson, Bklyn	1B	1948	Al Dark, Boston, NL	SS

National League	American League

Year		Pos	Year		Pos
1949	Don Newcombe, Brooklyn	P	1949	Roy Sievers, St.Louis	OF
1950	Sam Jethroe, Boston	OF	1950	Walt Dropo, Boston	1B
1951	Willie Mays, New York	OF	1951	Gil McDougald, New York	3B
1952	Joe Black, Brooklyn	P	1952	Harry Byrd, Philadelphia	P
1953	Jim Gilliam, Brooklyn	2B	1953	Harvey Kuenn, Detroit	SS
1954	Wally Moon, St.Louis	OF	1954	Bob Grim, New York	P
1955	Bill Virdon, Pittsburgh	OF	1955	Herb Score, Cleveland	P
1956	Frank Robinson, Cinn	OF	1956	Luis Aparicio, Chicago	SS
1957	Jack Sanford, Phila	P	1957	Tony Kubek, NY	INF-OF
1958	Orlando Cepeda, SF	1B	1958	Albie Pearson, Wash	OF
1959	Willie McCovey, SF	1B	1959	Bob Allison, Washington	OF
1960	Frank Howard, Los Ang	OF	1960	Ron Hansen, Baltimore	SS
1961	Billy Williams, Chicago	OF	1961	Don Schwall, Boston	P
1962	Ken Hubbs, Chicago	2B	1962	Tom Tresh, New York	SS-OF
1963	Pete Rose, Cincinnati	2B	1963	Gary Peters, Chicago	P
1964	Richie Allen, Phila	3B	1964	Tony Oliva, Minnesota	OF
1965	Jim Lefebvre, Los Ang	2B	1965	Curt Blefary, Baltimore	OF
1966	Tommy Helms, Cincinnati	3B	1966	Tommie Agee, Chicago	OF
1967	Tom Seaver, New York	P	1967	Rod Carew, Minnesota	2B
1968	Johnny Bench, Cinn	C	1968	Stan Bahnsen, New York	P
1969	Ted Sizemore, Los Ang	2B	1969	Lou Piniella, KC	OF
1970	Carl Morton, Montreal	P	1970	Thurman Munson, New York	C
1971	Earl Williams, Atlanta	C	1971	Chris Chambliss, Clev	1B
1972	Jon Matlack, New York	P	1972	Carlton Fisk, Boston	C
1973	Gary Matthews, San Fran	OF	1973	Al Bumbry, Baltimore	OF
1974	Jake McBride, St.Louis	OF	1974	Mike Hargrove, Texas	1B
1975	John Montefusco, SF	P	1975	Fred Lynn, Boston	OF
1976	Butch Metzger, San Diego	P	1976	Mark Fidrych, Detroit	P
	& Pat Zachry, Cincinnati	P	1977	Eddie Murray, Balt	DH-1B
1977	Andre Dawson, Montreal	OF	1978	Lou Whitaker, Detroit	2B
1978	Bob Horner, Atlanta	3B	1979	John Castino, Minnesota	3B
1979	Rick Sutcliffe, Los Ang	P		& Alfredo Griffin, Tor	SS
1980	Steve Howe, Los Angeles	P	1980	Joe Charboneau, Clev	OF-DH
1981	Fernando Valenzuela, LA	P	1981	Dave Righetti, New York	P
1982	Steve Sax, Los Angles	2B	1982	Cal Ripken, Balt	SS-3B
1983	Darryl Strawberry, NY	OF	1983	Ron Kittle, Chicago	OF
1984	Dwight Gooden, New York	P	1984	Alvin Davis, Seattle	1B
1985	Vince Coleman, St.Louis	OF	1985	Ozzie Guillen, Chicago	SS
1986	Todd Warrell, St.Louis	P	1986	Jose Canseco, Oakland	OF
1987	Benito Santiago, S.Diego	C	1987	Mark McGwire, Oakland	1B
1988	Chris Sabo, Cincinnati	3B	1988	Walt Weiss, Oakland	SS

Note: Fred Lynn is the only player in either league to be named MVP in his rookie year (1975).

The All-Star Game, 1933-89

Baseball's first All-Star Game was held on July 6, 1933, before 47,595 at Comiskey Park in Chicago. From that year on, the All-Star game has matched the best players in the American League against the best in the National. From 1959-62, two All-Star Games were played and in 1945, World War II travel restrictions made it necessary to call the All-Star Game off. The NL leads the series, 37-22-1.

In the chart below, the American League is listed in **bold** type.

Year	Result	Host (Ballpark)	AL Manager	NL Manager
1933	**American,** 4-2	Chicago (Comiskey Park)	Connie Mack	John McGraw
1934	**American,** 9-7	New York (Polo Grounds)	Joe Cronin	Bill Terry
1935	**American,** 4-1	Cleveland (Cleveland Stadium)	Mickey Cochrane	Frankie Frisch
1936	National, 4-3	Boston (Braves Field)	Joe McCarthy	Charlie Grimm
1937	**American,** 8-3	Washington (Griffith Stadium)	Joe McCarthy	Bill Terry
1938	National, 4-1	Cincinnati (Crosley Field)	Joe McCarthy	Bill Terry
1939	**American,** 3-1	New York (Yankee Stadium)	Joe McCarthy	Gabby Hartnett

Year	Result	Host (Ballpark)	AL Manager	NL Manager
1940	National, 4-0	St.Louis (Sportsman's Park)	Joe Cronin	Bill McKechnie
1941	**American,** 7-5	Detroit (Briggs Stadium)	Del Baker	Bill McKechnie
1942	**American,** 3-1	New York (Polo Grounds)	Joe McCarthy	Leo Durocher
1943	**American,** 5-3	Philadelphia (Shibe Park)	Joe McCarthy	Billy Southworth
1944	National, 7-1	Pittsburgh (Forbes Field)	Joe McCarthy	Billy Southworth
1945	No Game			
1946	**American,** 12-0	Boston (Fenway Park)	Steve O'Neill	Charlie Grimm
1947	**American,** 2-1	Chicago (Wrigley Field)	Joe Cronin	Eddie Dyer
1948	**American,** 5-2	St.Louis (Sportsman's Park)	Bucky Harris	Leo Durocher
1949	**American,** 11-7	Brooklyn (Ebbets Field)	Lou Boudreau	Billy Southworth
1950	National, 4-3 (14)	Chicago (Comiskey Park)	Casey Stengel	Burt Shotton
1951	National, 8-3	Detroit (Briggs Stadium)	Casey Stengel	Eddie Sawyer
1952	National, 3-2	Philadelphia (Shibe Park)	Casey Stengel	Leo Durocher
1953	National, 5-1	Cincinnati (Crosley Field)	Casey Stengel	Charlie Dressen
1954	**American,** 11-9	Cleveland (Cleveland Stadium)	Casey Stengel	Walter Alston
1955	National, 6-5 (12)	Milwaukee (County Stadium)	Al Lopez	Leo Durocher
1956	National, 7-3	Washington (Griffith Stadium)	Casey Stengel	Walter Alston
1957	**American,** 6-5	St.Louis (Busch Stadium)	Casey Stengel	Walter Alston
1958	**American,** 4-3	Baltimore (Memorial Stadium)	Casey Stengel	Fred Haney
1959	National, 5-4	Pittsburgh (Forbes Field)	Casey Stengel	Fred Haney
	American, 5-3	Los Angeles (Memorial Coliseum)	Casey Stengel	Fred Haney
1960	National, 5-3	Kansas City (Municipal Stadium)	Al Lopez	Walter Alston
	National, 6-0	New York (Yankee Stadium)	Al Lopez	Walter Alston
1961	National, 5-4 (10)	San Francisco (Candlestick Park)	Paul Richards	Danny Murtaugh
	TIE, 1-1 (9,rain)	Boston (Fenway Park)	Paul Richards	Danny Murtaugh
1962	National, 3-1	Washington (D.C.Stadium)	Ralph Houk	Fred Hutchinson
	American, 9-4	Chicago (Wrigley Field)	Ralph Houk	Fred Hutchinson
1963	National, 5-3	Cleveland (Cleveland Stadium)	Ralph Houk	Al Dark
1964	National, 7-4	New York (Shea Stadium)	Al Lopez	Walter Alston
1965	National, 6-5	Minnesota (Metropolitan Stadium)	Al Lopez	Gene Mauch
1966	National, 2-1 (10)	St.Louis (Busch Memorial Stadium)	Sam Mele	Walter Alston
1967	National, 2-1 (15)	California (Anaheim Stadium)	Hank Bauer	Walter Alston
1968	National, 1-0	Houston (The Astrodome)	Dick Williams	Red Schoendienst
1969	National, 9-3	Washington (RFK Stadium)	Mayo Smith	Red Schoendienst
1970	National, 5-4	Cincinnati (Riverfront Stadium)	Earl Weaver	Gil Hodges
1971	**American,** 6-4	Detroit (Tiger Stadium)	Earl Weaver	Sparky Anderson
1972	National, 4-3	Atlanta (Atlanta Stadium)	Earl Weaver	Danny Murtaugh
1973	National, 7-1	Kansas City (Royals Stadium)	Dick Williams	Sparky Anderson
1974	National, 7-2	Pittsburgh (Three Rivers Stadium)	Dick Williams	Yogi Berra
1975	National, 6-3	Milwaukee (County Stadium)	Al Dark	Walter Alston
1976	National, 7-1	Philadelphia (Veterans Stadium)	Darrell Johnson	Sparky Anderson
1977	National, 7-5	New York (Yankee Stadium)	Billy Martin	Sparky Anderson
1978	National, 7-3	San Diego (San Diego Stadium)	Billy Martin	Tom Lasorda
1979	National, 7-6	Seattle (The Kingdome)	Bob Lemon	Tom Lasorda
1980	National, 4-2	Los Angeles (Dodger Stadium)	Earl Weaver	Chuck Tanner
1981	National, 5-4	Cleveland (Cleveland Stadium)	Jim Frey	Dallas Green
1982	National, 4-1	Montreal (Olympic Stadium)	Billy Martin	Tom Lasorda
1983	**American,** 13-3	Chicago (Comiskey Park)	Harvey Kuenn	Whitey Herzog
1984	National, 3-1	San Francisco (Candlestick Park)	Joe Altobelli	Paul Owens
1985	National, 6-1	Minnesota (HHH Metrodome)	Sparky Anderson	Dick Williams
1986	**American,** 3-2	Houston (The Astrodome)	Dick Howser	Whitey Herzog
1987	National, 2-0 (13)	Oakland (Oakland Coliseum)	John McNamara	Davey Johnson
1988	**American,** 2-1	Cincinnati (Riverfront Stadium)	Tom Kelly	Whitey Herzog
1989	**American,** 5-3	California (Anaheim Stadium)	Tony LaRussa	Tom Lasorda

All-Star Game MVPs

Year	Most Valuable Player	Year	Most Valuable Player	Year	Most Valuable Player
1970	Carl Yastrzemski, Bos., CF-1B	1976	George Foster, Cinn., CF-RF	1983	Fred Lynn, California, CF
1971	Frank Robinson, Balt., RF	1977	Don Sutton, Los Ang., P	1984	Gary Carter, Montreal, C
1972	Joe Morgan, Cincinnati, 2B	1978	Steve Garvey, Los Ang., 1B	1985	LaMarr Hoyt, San Diego, P
1973	Bobby Bonds, San Fran., RF	1979	Dave Parker, Pitts., RF	1986	Roger Clemens, Boston, P
1974	Steve Garvey, Los Ang., 1B			1987	Tim Raines, Montreal, LF
1975	Bill Madlock, Chi.Cubs, 3B	1980	Ken Griffey, Cincinnati, LF	1988	Terry Steinbach, Oakland, C
	& Jon Matlack, NY Mets, P	1981	Gary Carter, Montreal, C	1989	Bo Jackson, Kansas City, LF
		1982	Dave Concepcion, Cinn., SS		

Major League Franchise Origins

Here is what the current 26 teams in Major League Baseball have to show for the years they have put in as members of the National League (NL) and American League (AL).

National League

	1st Year	Pennants & World Series	Franchise Stops
Atlanta Braves	1876	4 NL (1914,48,57-58) 2 WS (1914,57)	Boston (1876-1952) Milwaukee (1953-65) Atlanta (1966-)
Chicago Cubs	1876	10 NL (1906-08,10,18,29,32,35,38,45) 2 WS (1907-08)	Chicago (1876-)
Cincinnati Reds	1876	8 NL (1919,39-40,61,70,72,75-76) 4 WS (1919,40,75-76)	Cincinnati (1876-80) Cincinnati (1890-)
Houston Astros	1962	None	Houston (1962-)
Los Angeles Dodgers	1890	18 NL (1916,20,41,47,49,52-53,55-56,59,63, 65-66,74,77-78, 81,88) 6 WS (1955,59,63,65,81,88)	Brooklyn (1890-1957) Los Angeles (1958-)
Montreal Expos	1969	None	Montreal (1969-)
New York Mets	1962	3 NL (1969,73,86) 2 WS (1969,86)	New York (1962-)
Philadelphia Phillies	1880	4 NL (1915,50,80,83) 1 WS (1980)	Philadelphia (1883-)
Pittsburgh Pirates	1887	7 NL (1903,09,25,27,60,71,79) 5 WS (1909,25,60,71,79)	Pittsburgh (1887-)
St.Louis Cardinals	1892	15 NL (1926,28,30-31,34,42-44,46,64, 67-68,82,85,87) 9 WS (1926,31,34,42,44,46,64,67,82)	St.Louis (1892-)
San Diego Padres	1969	1 NL (1984)	San Diego (1969-)
San Francisco Giants	1883	15 NL (1905,11-13,17,21-24,33,36-37,51, 54,62,89) 5 WS (1905,21-22,33,54)	New York (1883-1957) San Francisco (1958-)

American League

	1st Year	Pennants & World Series	Franchise Stops
Baltimore Orioles	1902	7 AL (1944,66,69-71,79,83) 3 WS (1966,70,83)	Milwaukee (1901) St.Louis (1902-53) Baltimore (1954-)
Boston Red Sox	1901	9 AL (1903,12,15-16,18,46,67,75,86) 5 WS (1903,12,15-16,18)	Boston (1901-)
California Angels	1961	None	Los Angeles (1961-65) Anaheim, CA (1966-)
Chicago White Sox	1901	4 AL (1906,17,19,59) 2 WS (1906,17)	Chicago (1901-)
Cleveland Indians	1901	3 AL (1920,48,54) 2 WS (1920,48)	Cleveland (1901-)
Detroit Tigers	1901	9 AL (1907-09,34-35,40,45,68,84) 4 WS (1935,45,68,84)	Detroit (1901-)
Kansas City Royals	1969	2 AL (1980,85) 1 WS (1985)	Kansas City (1969-)
Milwaukee Brewers	1969	1 AL (1982)	Seattle (1969) Milwaukee (1970-)
Minnesota Twins	1901	5 AL (1924-25,33,65,87) 2 WS (1924,87)	Washington, DC (1901-60) Bloomington, MN(1961-81) Minneapolis (1982-)
New York Yankees	1901	33 AL (1921-23,26-28,32,36-39,41-43,47, 49-53,55-58,60-64,76-78,81) 22 WS (1923,27-28,32,36-39,41,43,47,49-53, 56,58,61-62,77-78)	Baltimore (1901-02) New York (1903-)
Oakland Athletics	1901	12 AL (1905,10-11,13-14,29-31,72-74,88,89) 8 WS (1910-11,13,29-30,72-74,89)	Philadelphia (1901-54) Kansas City (1955-67) Oakland (1968-)
Seattle Mariners	1977	None	Seattle (1977-)
Texas Rangers	1961	None	Washington, DC (1961-71) Arlington, TX (1972-)
Toronto Blue Jays	1977	None	Toronto (1977-)

Yearly Batting Leaders, Since 1900
Batting
National League

Year	Champion	Avg	Year	Champion	Avg	Year	Champion	Avg
1900	Honus Wagner, Pit	.381	1930	Bill Terry, NY	.401	1960	Dick Groat, Pit	.325
1901	Jesse Burkett, St.L	.382	1931	Chick Hafey, St.L	.349	1961	Roberto Clemente, Pit	.351
1902	Ginger Beaumont, Pit	.357	1932	Lefty O'Doul, Bklyn	.368	1962	Tommy Davis, LA	.346
1903	Honus Wagner, Pit	.355	1933	Chuck Klein, Phi	.368	1963	Tommy Davis, LA	.326
1904	Honus Wagner, Pit	.349	1934	Paul Waner, Pit	.362	1964	Roberto Clemente, Pit	.339
1905	Cy Seymour, Cinn	.377	1935	Arkie Vaughan, Pit	.385	1965	Roberto Clemente, Pit	.329
1906	Honus Wagner, Pit	.339	1936	Paul Waner, Pit	.373	1966	Matty Alou, Pit	.342
1907	Honus Wagner, Pit	.350	1937	Joe Medwick, St.L	.374	1967	Roberto Clemente, Pit	.357
1908	Honus Wagner, Pit	.354	1938	Ernie Lombardi, Cinn	.342	1968	Pete Rose, Cinn	.335
1909	Honus Wagner, Pit	.339	1939	Johnny Mize, St.L	.349	1969	Pete Rose, Cinn	.348
1910	Sherry Magee, Phi	.331	1940	Debs Garms, Pit	.355	1970	Rico Carty, Atl	.366
1911	Honus Wagner, Pit	.334	1941	Pete Reiser, Bklyn	.343	1971	Joe Torre, St.L	.363
1912	Heinie Zimmerman, Chi	.372	1942	Ernie Lombardi, Bos	.330	1972	Billy Williams, Chi	.333
1913	Jake Daubert, Bklyn	.350	1943	Stan Musial, St.L	.357	1973	Pete Rose, Cinn	.338
1914	Jake Daubert, Bklyn	.329	1944	Dixie Walker, Chi	.357	1974	Ralph Garr, Atl	.353
1915	Larry Doyle, NY	.320	1945	Phil Cavarretta, Chi	.355	1975	Bill Madlock, Chi	.354
1916	Hal Chase, Cinn	.339	1946	Stan Musial, St.L	.365	1976	Bill Madlock, Chi	.339
1917	Edd Roush, Cinn	.341	1947	Harry Walker, St.L-Phi	.363	1977	Dave Parker, Pit	.338
1918	Zack Wheat, Bklyn	.335	1948	Stan Musial, St.L	.376	1978	Dave Parker, Pit	.334
1919	Edd Roush, Cinn	.321	1949	Jackie Robinson, Bklyn	.342	1979	Keith Hernandez, St.L	.344
1920	Rogers Hornsby, St.L	.370	1950	Stan Musial, St.L	.346	1980	Bill Buckner, Chi	.324
1921	Rogers Hornsby, St.L	.397	1951	Stan Musial, St.L	.355	1981	Bill Madlock, Pit	.341
1922	Rogers Hornsby, St.L	.401	1952	Stan Musial, St.L	.336	1982	Al Oliver, Mon	.331
1923	Rogers Hornsby, St.L	.384	1953	Carl Furillo, Bklyn	.344	1983	Bill Madlock, Pit	.323
1924	Rogers Hornsby, St.L	.424	1954	Willie Mays, NY	.345	1984	Tony Gwynn, SD	.351
1925	Rogers Hornsby, St.L	.403	1955	Richie Ashburn, Phi	.338	1985	Willie McGee, St.L	.353
1926	Bubbles Hargrave, Cinn	.353	1956	Hank Aaron, Milw	.328	1986	Tim Raines, Mon	.334
1927	Paul Waner, Pit	.380	1957	Stan Musial, St.L	.351	1987	Tony Gwynn, SD	.370
1928	Rogers Hornsby, Bos	.387	1958	Richie Ashburn, Phi	.350	1988	Tony Gwynn, SD	.313
1929	Lefty O'Doul, Phi	.398	1959	Hank Aaron, Milw	.355	1989	Tony Gwynn, SD	.336

American League

Year	Champion	Avg	Year	Champion	Avg	Year	Champion	Avg
1901	Nap Lajoie, Phi	.422	1930	Al Simmons, Phi	.381	1960	Pete Runnels, Bos	.320
1902	Ed Delahanty, Wash	.376	1931	Al Simmons, Phi	.390	1961	Norm Cash, Det	.361
1903	Nap Lajoie, Clev	.355	1932	Dale Alexander, Det-Bos	.367	1962	Pete Runnels, Bos	.326
1904	Nap Lajoie, Clev	.381	1933	Jimmie Foxx, Phi	.356	1963	Carl Yastrzemski, Bos	.321
1905	Elmer Flick, Clev	.306	1934	Lou Gehrig, NY	.363	1964	Tony Oliva, Minn	.323
1906	George Stone, St.L	.358	1935	Buddy Myer, Wash	.349	1965	Tony Oliva, Minn	.321
1907	Ty Cobb, Det	.350	1936	Luke Appling, Chi	.388	1966	Frank Robinson, Balt	.316
1908	Ty Cobb, Det	.324	1937	Charlie Gehringer, Det	.371	1967	Carl Yastrzemski, Bos	.326
1909	Ty Cobb, Det	.377	1938	Jimmie Foxx, Bos	.349	1968	Carl Yastrzemski, Bos	.301
1910	Ty Cobb, Det	.385	1939	Joe DiMaggio, NY	.381	1969	Rod Carew, Minn	.332
1911	Ty Cobb, Det	.420	1940	Joe DiMaggio, NY	.352	1970	Alex Johnson, Cal	.329
1912	Ty Cobb, Det	.410	1941	Ted Williams, Bos	.406	1971	Tony Oliva, Minn	.337
1913	Ty Cobb, Det	.390	1942	Ted Williams, Bos	.356	1972	Rod Carew, Minn	.318
1914	Ty Cobb, Det	.368	1943	Luke Appling, Chi	.328	1973	Rod Carew, Minn	.350
1915	Ty Cobb, Det	.369	1944	Lou Boudreau, Clev	.327	1974	Rod Carew, Minn	.364
1916	Tris Speaker, Clev	.386	1945	Snuffy Stirnweiss, NY	.309	1975	Rod Carew, Minn	.359
1917	Ty Cobb, Det	.383	1946	Mickey Vernon, Wash	.353	1976	George Brett, KC	.333
1918	Ty Cobb, Det	.382	1947	Ted Williams, Bos	.343	1977	Rod Carew, Minn	.388
1919	Ty Cobb, Det	.384	1948	Ted Williams, Bos	.369	1978	Rod Carew, Minn	.333
1920	George Sisler, St.L	.407	1949	George Kell, Det	.343	1979	Fred Lynn, Bos	.333
1921	Harry Hellmann, Det	.394	1950	Billy Goodman, Bos	.354	1980	George Brett, KC	.390
1922	George Sisler, St.L	.420	1951	Ferris Fain, Phi	.344	1981	Carney Lansford, Bos	.336
1923	Harry Hellmann, Det	.403	1952	Ferris Fain, Phi	.327	1982	Willie Wilson, KC	.332
1924	Babe Ruth, NY	.378	1953	Mickey Vernon, Wash	.337	1983	Wade Boggs, Bos	.361
1925	Harry Hellmann, Det	.393	1954	Bobby Avila, Clev	.341	1984	Don Mattingly, NY	.343
1926	Heine Manush, Det	.378	1955	Al Kaline, Det	.340	1985	Wade Boggs, Bos	.368
1927	Harry Hellmann, Det	.398	1956	Mickey Mantle, NY	.353	1986	Wade Boggs, Bos	.357
1928	Goose Goslin, Wash	.379	1957	Ted Williams, Bos	.388	1987	Wade Boggs, Bos	.363
1929	Lew Fonseca, Clev	.369	1958	Ted Williams, Bos	.328	1988	Wade Boggs, Bos	.366
			1959	Harvey Kuenn, Det	.353	1989	Kirby Puckett, Minn	.339

Home Runs

National League

Year	Champion	HR
1900	Herman Long, Bos	12
1901	Sam Crawford, Cinn	16
1902	Tommy Leach, Pit	6
1903	Jimmy Sheckard, Bklyn	9
1904	Harry Lumley, Bklyn	9
1905	Fred Odwell, Cinn	9
1906	Tim Jordan, Bklyn	12
1907	Dave Brain, Bos	10
1908	Tim Jordan, Bklyn	12
1909	Red Murray, NY	7
1910	Fred Beck, Bos	10
	& Wildfire Schulte, Chi	10
1911	Wildfire Schulte, Chi	21
1912	Heinie Zimmerman, Chi	14
1913	Gavvy Cravath, Phi	19
1914	Gavvy Cravath, Phi	19
1915	Gavvy Cravath, Phi	24
1916	Dave Robertson, NY	12
	& Cy Williams, Chi	12
1917	Dave Robertson, NY	12
	& Gavvy Cravath, Phi	12
1918	Gavvy Cravath, Phi	8
1919	Gavvy Cravath, Phi	12
1920	Cy Williams, Phi	15
1921	George Kelly, NY	23
1922	Rogers Hornsby, St.L	42
1923	Cy Williams, Phi	41
1924	Jack Fournier, Bklyn	27
1925	Rogers Hornsby, St.L	39
1926	Hack Wilson, Chi	21
1927	Cy Williams, Phi	30
	& Hack Wilson, Chi	30
1928	Jim Bottomley, St.L	31
	& Hack Wilson, Chi	31
1929	Chuck Klein, Phi	43

Year	Champion	HR
1930	Hack Wilson, Chi	56
1931	Chuck Klein, Phi	31
1932	Chuck Klein, Phi	38
	& Mel Ott, NY	38
1933	Chuck Klein, Phi	28
1934	Rip Collins, St.L	35
	& Mel Ott, NY	35
1935	Wally Berger, Bos	34
1936	Mel Ott, NY	33
1937	Joe Medwick, St.L	31
	Mel Ott, NY	31
1938	Mel Ott, NY	36
1939	Johnny Mize, St.L	28
1940	Johnny Mize, St.L	43
1941	Dolf Camilli, Bklyn	34
1942	Mel Ott, NY	30
1943	Bill Nicholson, Chi	29
1944	Bill Nicholson, Chi	33
1945	Tommy Holmes, Bos	28
1946	Ralph Kiner, Pit	23
1947	Ralph Kiner, Pit	51
	& Johnny Mize, NY	51
1948	Ralph Kiner, Pit	40
	& Johnny Mize, NY	40
1949	Ralph Kiner, Pit	54
1950	Ralph Kiner, Pit	47
1951	Ralph Kiner, Pit	42
1952	Ralph Kiner, Pit	37
	& Hank Sauer, Chi	37
1953	Eddie Mathews, Milw	47
1954	Ted Kluszewski, Cinn	49
1955	Willie Mays, NY	51
1956	Duke Snider, Bklyn	43
1957	Hank Aaron, Milw	44
1958	Ernie Banks, Chi	47

Year	Champion	HR
1959	Eddie Mathews, Milw	46
1960	Ernie Banks, Chi	41
1961	Orlando Cepeda, SF	46
1962	Willie Mays, SF	49
1963	Hank Aaron, Milw	44
	& Willie McCovey, SF	44
1964	Willie Mays, SF	47
1965	Willie Mays, SF	52
1966	Hank Aaron, Atl	44
1967	Hank Aaron, Atl	39
1968	Willie McCovey, SF	36
1969	Willie McCovey, SF	45
1970	Johnny Bench, Cinn	45
1971	Willie Stargell, Pit	48
1972	Johnny Bench, Cinn	40
1973	Willie Stargell, Pit	44
1974	Mike Schmidt, Phi	36
1975	Mike Schmidt, Phi	38
1976	Mike Schmidt, Phi	38
1977	George Foster, Cinn	52
1978	George Foster, Cinn	40
1979	Dave Kingman, Chi	48
1980	Mike Schmidt, Phi	48
1981	Mike Schmidt, Phi	31
1982	Dave Kingman, NY	37
1983	Mike Schmidt, Phi	40
1984	Dale Murphy, Atl	36
	& Mike Schmidt, Phi	36
1985	Dale Murphy, Atl	37
1986	Mike Schmidt, Phi	37
1987	Andre Dawson, Chi	49
1988	Darryl Strawberry, NY	39
1989	Kevin Mitchell, SF	47

American League

Year	Champion	HR
1901	Nap Lajoie, Phi	13
1902	Socks Seybold, Phi	16
1903	Buck Freeman, Bos	13
1904	Harry Davis, Phi	10
1905	Harry Davis, Phi	8
1906	Harry Davis, Phi	12
1907	Harry Davis, Phi	8
1908	Sam Crawford, Det	7
1909	Ty Cobb, Det	9
1910	Jake Stahl, Bos	10
1911	Home Run Baker, Phi	11
1912	Home Run Baker, Phi	10
	& Tris Speaker, Bos	10
1913	Home Run Baker, Phi	12
1914	Home Run Baker, Phi	9
1915	Braggo Roth, Chi-Clev	7
1916	Wally Pipp, NY	12
1917	Wally Pipp, NY	9
1918	Babe Ruth, Bos	11
	Tilly Walker, Phi	11
1919	Babe Ruth, Bos	29
1920	Babe Ruth, NY	54
1921	Babe Ruth, NY	59
1922	Ken Williams, St.L	39
1923	Babe Ruth, NY	41
1924	Babe Ruth, NY	46
1925	Bob Meusel, NY	33
1926	Babe Ruth, NY	47
1927	Babe Ruth, NY	60
1928	Babe Ruth, NY	54
1929	Babe Ruth, NY	46
1930	Babe Ruth, NY	49
1931	Lou Gehrig, NY	46
	& Babe Ruth, NY	46

Year	Champion	HR
1932	Jimmie Foxx, Phi	58
1933	Jimmie Foxx, Phi	48
1934	Lou Gehrig, NY	49
1935	Jimmie Foxx, Phi	36
	& Hank Greenberg, Det	36
1936	Lou Gehrig, NY	49
1937	Joe DiMaggio, NY	46
1938	Hank Greenberg, Det	58
1939	Jimmie Foxx, Bos	35
1940	Hank Greenberg, Det	41
1941	Ted Williams, Bos	37
1942	Ted Williams, Bos	36
1943	Rudy York, Det	34
1944	Nick Etten, NY	22
1945	Vern Stephens, St.L	24
1946	Hank Greenberg, Det	44
1947	Ted Williams, Bos	32
1948	Joe DiMaggio, NY	39
1949	Ted Williams, Bos	43
1950	Al Rosen, Clev	37
1951	Gus Zernial, Chi-Phi	33
1952	Larry Doby, Clev	32
1953	Al Rosen, Clev	43
1954	Larry Doby, Clev	32
1955	Mickey Mantle, NY	37
1956	Mickey Mantle, NY	52
1957	Roy Sievers, Wash	42
1958	Mickey Mantle, NY	42
1959	Harmon Killebrew, Wash	42
	& Rocky Colavito, Clev	42
1960	Mickey Mantle, NY	40
1961	Roger Maris, NY	61
1962	Harmon Killebrew, Minn	48
1963	Harmon Killebrew, Minn	45

Year	Champion	HR
1964	Harmon Killebrew, Minn	49
1965	Tony Conigliaro, Bos	32
1966	Frank Robinson, Balt	49
1967	Harmon Killebrew, Minn	44
	& Carl Yastrzemski, Bos	44
1968	Frank Howard, Wash	44
1969	Harmon Killebrew, Minn	49
1970	Frank Howard, Wash	44
1971	Bill Melton, Chi	33
1972	Dick Allen, Chi	37
1973	Reggie Jackson, Oak	32
1974	Dick Allen, Chi	32
1975	Reggie Jackson, Oak	36
	& George Scott, Milw	36
1976	Graig Nettles, NY	32
1977	Jim Rice, Bos	39
1978	Jim Rice, Bos	46
1979	Gorman Thomas, Milw	45
1980	Reggie Jackson, NY	41
	& Ben Ogilvie, Milw	41
1981	Tony Armas, Bos	22
	Dwight Evans, Bos	22
	Bobby Grich, Cal	22
	& Eddie Murray, Balt	22
1982	Reggie Jackson, Cal	39
	& Gorman Thomas, Milw	39
1983	Jim Rice, Bos	39
1984	Tony Armas, Bos	43
1985	Darrell Evans, Det	40
1986	Jesse Barfield, Tor	40
1987	Mark McGwire, Oak	49
1988	Jose Canseco, Oak	42
1989	Fred McGriff, Tor	36

Runs Batted In
National League

Year	Champion	RBI
1900	Elmer Flick, Phi	110
1901	Honus Wagner, Pit	126
1902	Honus Wagner, Pit	91
1903	Sam Mertes, NY	104
1904	Bill Dahlen, NY	80
1905	Cy Seymour, Cinn	121
1906	Jim Nealon, Pit	83
1907	Sherry Magee, Phi	85
1908	Honus Wagner, Pit	109
1909	Honus Wagner, Pit	100
1910	Sherry Magee, Phi	123
1911	Wildfire Schulte, Chi	121
1912	Heinie Zimmerman, Chi	103
1913	Gavvy Cravath, Phi	128
1914	Sherry Magee, Phi	103
1915	Gavvy Cravath, Phi	115
1916	Heinie Zimmerman, Chi-NY	83
1917	Heinie Zimmerman, NY	102
1918	Sherry Magee, Cinn	76
1919	Hy Myers, Bklyn	73
1920	George Kelly, NY	94
	& Rogers Hornsby, St.L	94
1921	Rogers Hornsby, St.L	126
1922	Rogers Hornsby, St.L	152
1923	Irish Meusel, NY	125
1924	George Kelly, NY	136
1925	Rogers Hornsby, St.L	143
1926	Jim Bottomley, St.L	120
1927	Paul Waner, Pit	131
1928	Jim Bottomley, St.L	136
1929	Hack Wilson, Chi	159
1930	Hack Wilson, Chi	190
1931	Chuck Klein, Phil	121
1932	Don Hurst, Phil	143
1933	Chuck Klein, Phil	120
1934	Mel Ott, NY	135
1935	Wally Berger, Bos	130
1936	Joe Medwick, St.L	138
1937	Joe Medwick, St.L	154
1938	Joe Medwick, St.L	122
1939	Frank McCormick, Cinn	128
1940	Johnny Mize, St.L	137
1941	Dolph Camilli, Bklyn	120
1942	Johnny Mize, NY	110
1943	Bill Nicholson, Chi	128
1944	Bill Nicholson, Chi	122
1945	Dixie Walker, Bklyn	124
1946	Enos Slaughter, St.L	130
1947	Johnny Mize, NY	138
1948	Stan Musial, St.L	131
1949	Ralph Kiner, Pit	127
1950	Del Ennis, Phi	126
1951	Monty Irvin, NY	121
1952	Hank Sauer, Chi	121
1953	Roy Campanella, Bklyn	142
1954	Ted Kluszewski, Cinn	141
1955	Duke Snider, Bklyn	136
1956	Stan Musial, St.L	109
1957	Hank Aaron, Milw	132
1958	Ernie Banks, Chi	129
1959	Ernie Banks, Chi	143
1960	Hank Aaron, Milw	126
1961	Orlando Cepeda, SF	142
1962	Tommy Davis, LA	153
1963	Hank Aaron, Milw	130
1964	Ken Boyer, St.L	119
1965	Deron Johnson, Cinn	130
1966	Hank Aaron, Atl	127
1967	Orlando Cepeda, St.L	111
1968	Willie McCovey, SF	105
1969	Willie McCovey, SF	126
1970	Johnny Bench, Cinn	148
1971	Joe Torre, St.L	137
1972	Johnny Bench, Cinn	125
1973	Willie Stargell, Pit	119
1974	Johnny Bench, Cinn	129
1975	Greg Luzinski, Phi	120
1976	George Foster, Cinn	121
1977	George Foster, Cinn	149
1978	George Foster, Cinn	120
1979	Dave Winfield, SD	118
1980	Mike Schmidt, Phi	121
1981	Mike Schmidt, Phi	91
1982	Dale Murphy, Atl	109
	& Al Oliver, Mon	109
1983	Dale Murphy, Atl	121
1984	Gary Carter, Mon	106
	& Mike Schmidt, Phi	106
1985	Dave Parker, Cinn	125
1986	Mike Schmidt, Phi	119
1987	Andre Dawson, Chi	137
1988	Will Clark, SF	109
1989	Kevin Mitchell, SF	125

American League

Year	Champion	RBI
1901	Nap Lajoie, Phi	125
1902	Buck Freeman, Bos	121
1903	Buck Freeman, Bos	104
1904	Nap Lajoie, Clev	102
1905	Harry Davis, Phi	83
1906	Harry Davis, Phi	96
1907	Ty Cobb, Det	116
1908	Ty Cobb, Det	108
1909	Ty Cobb, Det	107
1910	Sam Crawford, Det	120
1911	Ty Cobb, Det	144
1912	Home Run Baker, Phi	133
1913	Home Run Baker, Phi	126
1914	Sam Crawford, Det	104
1915	Sam Crawford, Det	112
1916	Del Pratt, St.L	103
1917	Bobby Veach, Det	103
1918	Bobby Veach, Det	78
1919	Babe Ruth, Bos	114
1920	Babe Ruth, NY	137
1921	Babe Ruth, NY	171
1922	Ken Williams, St.L	155
1923	Babe Ruth, NY	131
1924	Goose Goslin, Wash	129
1925	Bob Meusel, NY	138
1926	Babe Ruth, NY	145
1927	Lou Gehrig, NY	175
1928	Lou Gehrig, NY	142
	& Babe Ruth, NY	142
1929	Al Simmons, Phi	157
1930	Lou Gehrig, NY	174
1931	Lou Gehrig, NY	184
1932	Jimmie Foxx, Phi	169
1933	Jimmie Foxx, Phi	163
1934	Lou Gehrig, NY	165
1935	Hank Greenberg, Det	170
1936	Hal Trosky, Clev	162
1937	Hank Greenberg, Det	183
1938	Jimmie Foxx, Bos	175
1939	Ted Williams, Bos	145
1940	Hank Greenberg, Det	150
1941	Joe DiMaggio, NY	125
1942	Ted Williams, Bos	137
1943	Rudy York, Det	118
1944	Vern Stephens, St.L	109
1945	Nick Etten, NY	111
1946	Hank Greenberg, Det	127
1947	Ted Williams, Bos	114
1948	Joe DiMaggio, NY	155
1949	Ted Williams, Bos	159
	& Vern Stephens, Bos	159
1950	Walt Dropo, Bos	144
	Vern Stephens, Bos	144
1951	Gus Zernial, Chi-Phi	129
1952	Al Rosen, Clev	105
1953	Al Rosen, Clev	145
1954	Larry Doby, Clev	126
1955	Ray Boone, Det	116
	& Jackie Jensen, Bos	116
1956	Mickey Mantle, NY	130
1957	Roy Sievers, Wash	114
1958	Jackie Jensen, Bos	122
1959	Jackie Jensen, Bos	112
1960	Roger Maris, NY	112
1961	Roger Maris, NY	142
1962	Harmon Killebrew, Minn	126
1963	Dick Stuart, Bos	118
1964	Brooks Robinson, Balt	118
1965	Rocky Colavito, Clev	108
1966	Frank Robinson, Balt	122
1967	Carl Yastrzemski, Bos	121
1968	Ken Harrelson, Bos	109
1969	Harmon Killebrew, Minn	140
1970	Frank Howard, Wash	126
1971	Harmon Killebrew, Minn	119
1972	Dick Allen, Chi	113
1973	Reggie Jackson, Oak	117
1974	Jeff Burroughs, Tex	118
1975	George Scott, Milw	109
1976	Lee May, Balt	109
1977	Larry Hisle, Minn	119
1978	Jim Rice, Bos	139
1979	Don Baylor, Cal	139
1980	Cecil Cooper, Milw	122
1981	Eddie Murray, Balt	78
1982	Hal McRae, KC	133
1983	Cecil Cooper, Milw	126
	& Jim Rice, Bos	126
1984	Tony Armas, Bos	123
1985	Don Mattingly, NY	145
1986	Joe Carter, Clev	121
1987	George Bell, Tor	134
1988	Jose Canseco, Oak	124
1989	Ruben Sierra, Tex	119

Stolen Bases

National League

Year	Champion	SB	Year	Champion	SB	Year	Champion	SB
1900	George Van Haltren, NY	45	1930	Kiki Cuyler, Chi	37	1960	Maury Wills, LA	50
	& Patsy Donovan, St.L..	45	1931	Frankie Frisch, St.L.	28	1961	Maury Wills, LA	35
1901	Honus Wagner, Pit	49	1932	Chuck Klein, Phi	20	1962	Maury Wills, LA	104
1902	Honus Wagner, Pit	42	1933	Pepper Martin, St.L.	26	1963	Maury Wills, LA	40
1903	Jimmy Sheckard, Bklyn .	67	1934	Pepper Martin, St.L	23	1964	Maury Wills, LA	53
	& Frank Chance, Chi	67	1935	Augie Galan, Chi	22	1965	Maury Wills, LA	94
1904	Honus Wagner, Pit	53	1936	Pepper Martin, St.L	23	1966	Lou Brock, St.L	74
1905	Art Devlin, NY	59	1937	Augie Galan, Chi	23	1967	Lou Brock, St.L	52
	& Billy Maloney, Chi	59	1938	Stan Hack, Chi	16	1968	Lou Brock, St.L	62
1906	Frank Chance, Chi	57	1939	Stan Hack, Chi	17	1969	Lou Brock, St.L	53
1907	Honus Wagner, Pit	61		& Lee Handley, Pit	17			
1908	Honus Wagner, Pit	53				1970	Bobby Tolan, Cinn	57
1909	Bob Bescher, Cinn	54	1940	Lonny Frey, Cinn	22	1971	Lou Brock, St.L	64
			1941	Danny Murtaugh, Phi	18	1972	Lou Brock, St.L	63
1910	Bob Bescher, Cinn	70	1942	Pete Reiser, Bklyn	20	1973	Lou Brock, St.L	70
1911	Bob Bescher, Cinn	81	1943	Arky Vaughan, Bklyn	20	1974	Lou Brock, St.L	118
1912	Bob Bescher, Cinn	67	1944	Johnny Barrett, Pit	28	1975	Davey Lopes, LA	77
1913	Max Carey, Pit	61	1945	Red Schoendienst, St.L.	26	1976	Davey Lopes, LA	63
1914	George Burns, NY	62	1946	Pete Reiser, Bklyn	34	1977	Frank Tavares, Pit	70
1915	Max Carey, Pit	36	1947	Jackie Robinson, Bklyn.	29	1978	Omar Moreno, Pit	71
1916	Max Carey, Pit	63	1948	Richie Ashburn, Phi	32	1979	Omar Moreno, Pit	77
1917	Max Carey, Pit	46	1949	Jackie Robinson, Bklyn.	37			
1918	Max Carey, Pit	58	1950	Sam Jethroe, Bos	35	1980	Ron LeFlore, Mon	97
1919	George Burns, NY	40	1951	Sam Jethroe, Bos	35	1981	Tim Raines, Mon	71
1920	Max Carey, Pit	52	1952	Pee Wee Reese, Bklyn	30	1982	Tim Raines, Mon	78
1921	Frankie Frisch, NY	49	1953	Bill Bruton, Milw	26	1983	Tim Raines, Mon	90
1922	Max Carey, Pit	51	1954	Bill Bruton, Milw	34	1984	Tim Raines, Mon	75
1923	Max Carey, Pit	51	1955	Bill Bruton, Milw	35	1985	Vince Coleman, St.L.	110
1924	Max Carey, Pit	49	1956	Willie Mays, NY	40	1986	Vince Coleman, St.L.	107
1925	Max Carey, Pit	46	1957	Willie Mays, NY	38	1987	Vince Coleman, St.L.	109
1926	Kiki Cuyler, Pit	35	1958	Willie Mays, SF	31	1988	Vince Coleman, St.L.	81
1927	Frank Frisch, St. L	48	1959	Willie Mays, SF	27	1989	Vince Coleman, St.L.	65
1928	Kiki Cuyler, Chi	37						
1929	Kiki Cuyler, Chi	43						

American League

Year	Champion	SB	Year	Champion	SB	Year	Champion	SB
1901	Frank Isbell, Chi	52	1930	Marty McManus, Det	23	1960	Luis Aparicio, Chi	51
1902	Topsy Hartsel, Phi	47	1931	Ben Chapman, NY	61	1961	Luis Aparicio, Chi	53
1903	Harry Bay, Clev	45	1932	Ben Chapman, NY	38	1962	Luis Aparicio, Chi	31
1904	Elmer Flick, Clev	42	1933	Ben Chapman, NY	27	1963	Luis Aparicio, Balt	40
1905	Danny Hoffman, Phi	46	1934	Bill Werber, Bos	40	1964	Luis Aparicio, Balt	57
1906	Elmer Flick, Clev	39	1935	Bill Werber, Bos	29	1965	Bert Campaneris, KC	51
	& John Anderson, Wash	39	1936	Lyn Lary, St.L.	37	1966	Bert Campaneris, KC	52
1907	Ty Cobb, Det	49	1937	Ben Chapman, Wash-Bos	35	1967	Bert Campaneris, KC	55
1908	Patsy Dougherty, Chi	47		& Bill Werber, Phi	35	1968	Bert Campaneris, Oak	62
1909	Ty Cobb, Det	76	1938	Frank Crosetti, NY	27	1969	Tommy Harper, Sea	73
1910	Eddie Collins, Phi	81	1939	George Case, Wash	51	1970	Bert Campaneris, Oak	42
1911	Ty Cobb, Det	83	1940	George Case, Wash	35	1971	Amos Otis, KC	52
1912	Clyde Milan, Wash	88	1941	George Case, Wash	33	1972	Bert Campaneris, Oak	52
1913	Clyde Milan, Wash	75	1942	George Case, Wash	44	1973	Tommy Harper, Bos	54
1914	Fritz Maisel, NY	74	1943	George Case, Wash	61	1974	Bill North, Oak	54
1915	Ty Cobb, Det	96	1944	Snuffy Stirnweiss, NY	55	1975	Mickey Rivers, CA	70
1916	Ty Cobb, Det	68	1945	Snuffy Stirnweiss, NY	33	1976	Bill North, Oak	75
1917	Ty Cobb, Det	55	1946	George Case, Clev	28	1977	Freddie Patek, KC	53
1918	George Sisler, St.L	45	1947	Bob Dillinger, St.L	34	1978	Ron LeFlore, Det	68
1919	Eddie Collins, Chi	33	1948	Bob Dillinger, St.L	28	1979	Willie Wilson, KC	83
1920	Sam Rice, Wash	63	1949	Bob Dillinger, St.L	20	1980	Rickey Henderson, Oak	100
1921	George Sisler, St.L	35	1950	Dom DiMaggio, Bos	15	1981	Rickey Henderson, Oak	56
1922	George Sisler, St.L	51	1951	Minnie Minoso, Clev-Chi	31	1982	Rickey Henderson, Oak	130
1923	Eddie Collins, Chi	47	1952	Minnie Minoso, Chi	22	1983	Rickey Henderson, Oak	108
1924	Eddie Collins, Chi	42	1953	Minnie Minoso, Chi	25	1984	Rickey Henderson, Oak	66
1925	Johnny Mostil, Chi	43	1954	Jackie Jensen, Bos	22	1985	Rickey Henderson, NY.	80
1926	Johnny Mostil, Chi	35	1955	Jim Rivera, Chi	25	1986	Rickey Henderson, NY.	87
1927	George Sisler, St.L	27	1956	Luis Aparicio, Chi	21	1987	Harold Reynolds, Sea .	60
1928	Buddy Myer, Bos	30	1957	Luis Aparicio, Chi	28	1988	Rickey Henderson, NY.	93
1929	Charlie Gehringer, Det .	28	1958	Luis Aparicio, Chi	29	1989	R.Henderson, NY-Oak.	77
			1959	Luis Aparicio, Chi	56			

Yearly Pitching Leaders, Since 1900

Winning Percentage

At least 15 wins, except in strike year of 1981 when the minimum was 10 wins.

National League

Year		W-L	Pct	Year		W-L	Pct
1900	Jesse Tannehill, Pittsburgh	20-6	.769	1945	Harry Brecheen, St. Louis	15-4	.789
1901	Jack Chesbro, Pittsburgh	21-10	.677	1946	Murray Dickson, St. Louis	15-6	.714
1902	Jack Chesbro, Pittsburgh	28-6	.824	1947	Larry Jansen, New York	21-5	.808
1903	Sam Leever, Pittsburgh	25-7	.781	1948	Harry Brecheen, St. Louis	20-7	.741
1904	Joe McGinnity, New York	35-8	.814	1949	Preacher Roe, Brooklyn	15-6	.714
1905	Christy Mathewson, NY	31-8	.795				
1906	Ed Reulbach, Chicago	19-4	.826	1950	Sal Maglie, New York	18-4	.818
1907	Ed Reulbach, Chicago	17-4	.810	1951	Preacher Roe, Brooklyn	22-3	.880
1908	Ed Reulbach, Chicago	24-7	.774	1952	Hoyt Wilhelm, New York	15-3	.833
1909	Christy Mathewson, New York	25-6	.806	1953	Carl Erskine, Brooklyn	20-6	.769
	& Howie Camnitz, Pittsburgh	25-6	.806	1954	Johnny Antonelli, New York	21-7	.750
				1955	Don Newcombe, Brooklyn	20-5	.800
1910	King Cole, Chicago	20-4	.833	1956	Don Newcombe, Brooklyn	27-7	.794
1911	Rube Marquard, New York	24-7	.774	1957	Bob Buhl, Milwaukee	18-7	.720
1912	Claude Hendrix, Pittsburgh	24-9	.727	1958	Warren Spahn, Milwaukee	22-11	.667
1913	Bert Humphries, Chicago	16-4	.800		& Lew Burdette, Milwaukee	20-10	.667
1914	Bill James, Boston	26-7	.788	1959	Roy Face, Pittsburgh	18-1	.947
1915	Grover Alexander, Phila.	31-10	.756				
1916	Tom Hughes, Boston	16-3	.842	1960	Ernie Broglio, St Louis	21-9	.700
1917	Ferdie Schupp, New York	21-7	.750	1961	Johnny Podres, Los Angeles	18-5	.783
1918	Claude Hendrix, Chicago	19-7	.731	1962	Bob Purkey, Cincinnati	23-5	.821
1919	Dutch Ruether, Cincinnati	19-6	.760	1963	Ron Perranoski, Los Angeles	16-3	.842
				1964	Sandy Koufax, Los Angeles	19-5	.792
1920	Burleigh Grimes, Brooklyn	23-11	.676	1965	Sandy Koufax, Los Angeles	26-8	.765
1921	Bill Doak, St.Louis	15-6	.714	1966	Juan Marichal, San Francisco	25-6	.806
1922	Pete Donohue, Cincinnati	18-9	.667	1967	Dick Hughes, St. Louis	16-6	.727
1923	Dolf Luque, Cincinnati	27-8	.771	1968	Steve Blass, Pittsburgh	18-6	.750
1924	Emil Yde, Pittsburgh	16-3	.842	1969	Tom Seaver, New York	25-7	.781
1925	Bill Sherdel, St.Louis	15-6	.714				
1926	Ray Kremer, Pittsburgh	20-6	.769	1970	Bob Gibson, St. Louis	23-7	.767
1927	Larry Benton, Boston-NY	17-7	.708	1971	Don Gullett, Cincinnati	16-6	.727
1928	Larry Benton, New York	25-9	.735	1972	Gary Nolan, Cincinnati	15-5	.750
1929	Charlie Root, Chicago	19-6	.760	1973	Tommy John, Los Angeles	16-7	.696
				1974	Andy Messersmith, Los Ang.	20-6	.769
1930	Freddie Fitzsimmons, NY	19-7	.731	1975	Don Gullett, Cincinnati	15-4	.789
1931	Paul Derringer, St.Louis	18-8	.692	1976	Steve Carlton, Philadelphia	20-7	.741
1932	Lon Warneke, Chicago	22-6	.786	1977	John Candelaria, Pittsburgh	20-5	.800
1933	Ben Cantwell, Boston	20-10	.667	1978	Gaylord Perry, San Diego	21-6	.778
1934	Dizzy Dean, St.Louis	30-7	.811	1979	Tom Seaver, Cincinnati	16-6	.727
1935	Bill Lee, Chicago	20-6	.769				
1936	Carl Hubbell, New York	26-6	.813	1980	Jim Bibby, Pittsburgh	19-6	.760
1937	Carl Hubbell, New York	22-8	.733	1981	Tom Seaver, Cincinnati	14-2	.875
1938	Bill Lee, Chicago	22-9	.710	1982	Phil Niekro, Atlanta	17-4	.810
1939	Paul Derringer, Cincinnati	25-7	.781	1983	John Denny, Philadelphia	19-6	.760
				1984	Rick Sutcliffe, Chicago	16-1	.941
1940	Freddie Fitzsimmons, Bklyn	16-2	.889	1985	Orel Hershiser, Los Angeles	19-3	.864
1941	Elmer Riddle, Cincinnati	19-4	.826	1986	Bob Ojeda, New York	18-5	.783
1942	Larry French, Brooklyn	15-4	.789	1987	Dwight Gooden, New York	15-7	.682
1943	Mort Cooper, St. Louis	21-8	.724	1988	David Cone, New York	20-3	.870
1944	Ted Wilks, St. Louis	17-4	.810	1989	Scott Garrelts, San Francisco	14-5	.737
					& Sid Fernandez, New York	14-5	.737

Note: In 1984, Sutcliffe was also 4-5 with Clev.(AL) for a combined record of 20-6 (.769).

American League

Year		W-L	Pct	Year		W-L	Pct
1901	Clark Griffith, Chicago	24-7	.774	1910	Chief Bender, Philadelphia	23-5	.821
1902	Bill Bernhard, Phila-Cleve	18-5	.783	1911	Chief Bender, Philadelphia	17-5	.773
1903	Cy Young, Boston	28-9	.757	1912	Smokey Joe Wood, Boston	34-5	.872
1904	Jack Chesbro, New York	41-12	.774	1913	Walter Johnson, Washington	36-7	.837
1905	Andy Coakley, Philadelphia	20-7	.741	1914	Chief Bender, Philadelphia	17-3	.850
1906	Eddie Plank, Philadelphia	19-6	.760	1915	Smokey Joe Wood, Boston	15-5	.750
1907	Wild Bill Donovan, Detroit	25-4	.862	1916	Eddie Cicotte, Chicago	15-7	.682
1908	Ed Walsh, Chicago	40-15	.727	1917	Reb Russell, Chicago	15-5	.750
1909	George Mullin, Detroit	29-8	.784	1918	Sad Sam Jones, Boston	16-5	.762
				1919	Eddie Cicotte, Chicago	29-7	.806

American League

Year		W-L	Pct	Year		W-L	Pct
1920	Jim Bagby, Cleveland	31-12	.721	1956	Whitey Ford, New York	19-6	.760
1921	Carl Mays, New York	27-9	.750	1957	Dick Donovan, Chicago	16-6	.727
1922	Joe Bush, New York	26-7	.788		& Tom Sturdivant, New York	16-6	.727
1923	Herb Pennock, New York	19-6	.760	1958	Bob Turley, New York	21-7	.750
1924	Walter Johnson, Washington	23-7	.767	1959	Bob Shaw, Chicago	18-6	.750
1925	Stan Coveleski, Washington	20-5	.800				
1926	George Uhle, Cleveland	27-11	.711	1960	Jim Perry, Cleveland	18-10	.643
1927	Waite Hoyt, New York	22-7	.759	1961	Whitey Ford, New York	25-4	.862
1928	General Crowder, St. Louis	21-5	.808	1962	Ray Herbert, Chicago	20-9	.690
1929	Lefty Grove, Philadelphia	20-6	.769	1963	Whitey Ford, New York	24-7	.774
				1964	Wally Bunker, Baltimore	19-5	.792
1930	Lefty Grove, Philadelphia	28-5	.848	1965	Mudcat Grant, Minnesota	21-7	.750
1931	Lefty Grove, Philadelphia	31-4	.886	1966	Sonny Siebert, Cleveland	16-8	.667
1932	Johnny Allen, New York	17-4	.810	1967	Joe Horlen, Chicago	19-7	.731
1933	Lefty Grove, Philadelphia	24-8	.750	1968	Denny McLain, Detroit	31-6	.838
1934	Lefty Gomez, New York	26-5	.839	1969	Jim Palmer, Baltimore	16-4	.800
1935	Eldon Auker, Detroit	18-7	.720				
1936	Monte Pearson, New York	19-7	.731	1970	Mike Cuellar, Baltimore	24-8	.750
1937	Johnny Allen, Cleveland	15-1	.938	1971	Dave McNally, Baltimore	21-5	.808
1938	Red Ruffing, New York	21-7	.750	1972	Catfish Hunter, Oakland	21-7	.750
1939	Lefty Grove, Boston	15-4	.789	1973	Catfish Hunter, Oakland	21-5	.808
				1974	Mike Cuellar, Baltimore	22-10	.688
1940	Schoolboy Rowe, Detroit	16-3	.842	1975	Mike Torrez, Baltimore	20-9	.690
1941	Lefty Gomez, New York	15-5	.750	1976	Bill Campbell, Minnesota	17-5	.773
1942	Ernie Bonham, New York	21-5	.808	1977	Paul Splittorff, Kansas City	16-6	.727
1943	Spud Chandler, New York	20-4	.833	1978	Ron Guidry, New York	25-3	.893
1944	Tex Hughson, Boston	18-5	.783	1979	Mike Caldwell, Milwaukee	16-6	.727
1945	Hal Newhouser, Detroit	25-9	.735				
1946	Boo Ferriss, Boston	25-6	.806	1980	Steve Stone, Baltimore	25-7	.781
1947	Allie Reynolds, New York	19-8	.704	1981	Pete Vuckovich, Milwaukee	14-4	.778
1948	Jack Kramer, Boston	18-5	.783	1982	Pete Vuckovich, Milwaukee	18-6	.750
1949	Ellis Kinder, Boston	23-6	.793		& Jim Palmer, Baltimore	15-3	.750
				1983	Rich Dotson, Chicago	22-7	.759
1950	Vic Raschi, New York	21-8	.724	1984	Doyle Alexander, Toronto	17-6	.739
1951	Bob Feller, Cleveland	22-8	.733	1985	Ron Guidry, New York	22-6	.786
1952	Bobby Shantz, Philadelphia	24-7	.774	1986	Roger Clemens, Boston	24-4	.857
1953	Ed Lopat, New York	16-4	.800	1987	Roger Clemens, Boston	20-9	.690
1954	Sandy Consuegra, Chicago	16-3	.842	1988	Frank Viola, Minnesota	24-7	.774
1955	Tommy Byrne, New York	16-5	.762	1989	Bret Saberhagen, Kansas City	23-6	.793

Perfect Games

Fourteen pitchers have thrown perfect games (27 up, 27 down) in major league history.

National League

Pitcher	Game	Date	Score
Lee Richmond	Wor. vs Clev.	6/12/1880	1-0
Monte Ward	Prov. vs Bos.	6/17/1880	5-0
Harvey Haddix	Pit. at Milw.	5/26/1959	0-1*
Jim Bunning	Phi. at NY	6/21/64	6-0
Sandy Koufax	LA vs Chi	9/9/65	1-0
Tom Browning	Cin. vs LA	9/16/88	1-0

*Haddix pitched 12 perfect innings before losing in the 13th. Braves' lead-off batter Felix Mantilla reached on a throwing error by Pirates 3B Don Hoak, Eddie Mathews sacrificed Mantilla to 2nd, Hank Aaron was walked intentionally, and Joe Adcock doubled in Mantilla to win the game.

American League

Pitcher	Game	Date	Score
Cy Young	Bos. vs Phi.	5/5/1904	3-0
Adrian Joss	Clev. vs Chi.	10/2/08	1-0
Ernie Shore	Bos. vs Wash.	6/23/17	4-0*
Charlie Robertson	Chi. at Det.	4/30/22	2-0
Catfish Hunter	Oak. vs Minn	5/8/68	4-0
Len Barker	Clev. vs Tor	5/15/81	3-0
Mike Witt	Cal. at Tex	9/30/84	1-0

*Babe Ruth started for Boston, walking Senators' lead-off batter Ray Morgan then getting thrown out of the game for punching umpire Brick Owens while arguing the call. Shore came on in relief. Morgan was caught stealing and Shore retired the next 26 batters in a row.

World Series

Pitcher	Game	Date	Score
Don Larson	NY vs Bklyn	10/8/56	2-0

Earned Run Average

Earned Run Averages were based on at least 10 complete games pitched (1900-50), at least 154 innings pitched (1950-60), and at least 162 innings pitched since 1961 in the AL and 1962 in the NL. In the strike year of 1981, qualifiers had to pitch at least as many innings as the total number of games their team played that season.

National League

Year		ERA	Year		ERA	Year		ERA
1900	Rube Waddell, Pit	2.37	1930	Dazzy Vance, Bklyn	2.61	1960	Mike McCormick, SF	2.70
1901	Jesse Tannehill, Pit	2.18	1931	Bill Walker, NY	2.26	1961	Warren Spahn, Milw	3.01
1902	Jack Taylor, Chi	1.33	1932	Lon Warneke, Chi	2.37	1962	Sandy Koufax, LA	2.54
1903	Sam Leever, Pit	2.06	1933	Carl Hubbell, NY	1.66	1963	Sandy Koufax, LA	1.88
1904	Joe McGinnity, NY	1.61	1934	Carl Hubbell, NY	2.30	1964	Sandy Koufax, LA	1.74
1905	Christy Mathewson,NY	1.27	1935	Cy Blanton, Pit	2.59	1965	Sandy Koufax, LA	2.04
1906	Three Finger Brown,Chi	1.04	1936	Carl Hubbell, NY	2.31	1966	Sandy Koufax, LA	1.73
1907	Jack Pfiester, Chi	1.15	1937	Jim Turner, Bos	2.38	1967	Phil Niekro, Atl	1.87
1908	Christy Mathewson,NY	1.43	1938	Bill Lee, Chi	2.66	1968	Bob Gibson, St.L	1.12
1909	Christy Mathewson,NY	1.14	1939	Bucky Walters, Cinn	2.29	1969	Juan Marichal, SF	2.10
1910	George McQuillan,Phi	1.60	1940	Bucky Walters, Cinn	2.48	1970	Tom Seaver, NY	2.81
1911	Christy Mathewson,NY	1.99	1941	Elmer Riddle, Cinn	2.24	1971	Tom Seaver, NY	1.76
1912	Jeff Tesreau, NY	1.96	1942	Mort Cooper, St.L	1.77	1972	Steve Carlton, Phi	1.98
1913	Christy Mathewson,NY	2.06	1943	Howie Pollet, St.L	1.75	1973	Tom Seaver, NY	2.08
1914	Bill Doak, St.L	1.72	1944	Ed Heusser, Cinn	2.38	1974	Buzz Capra, Atl	2.28
1915	Grover Alexander,Phi	1.22	1945	Hank Borowy, Chi	2.14	1975	Randy Jones, SD	2.24
1916	Grover Alexander,Phi	1.55	1946	Howie Pollet, St.L	2.10	1976	John Denny, St.L	2.52
1917	Grover Alexander,Phi	1.86	1947	Warren Spahn, Bos	2.33	1977	John Candelaria, Pit	2.34
1918	Hippo Vaughn, Chi	1.74	1948	Harry Brecheen, St.L	2.24	1978	Craig Swan, NY	2.43
1919	Grover Alexander,Chi	1.72	1949	Dave Koslo, NY	2.50	1979	J.R. Richard, Hou	2.71
1920	Grover Alexander,Chi	1.91	1950	Jim Hearn, St.L-NY	2.49	1980	Don Sutton, LA	2.21
1921	Bill Doak, St.L	2.59	1951	Chet Nichols, Bos	2.88	1981	Nolan Ryan, Hou	1.69
1922	Rosy Ryan, NY	3.01	1952	Hoyt Wilhelm, NY	2.43	1982	Steve Rogers, Mon	2.40
1923	Dolf Luque, Cinn	1.93	1953	Warren Spahn, Milw	2.10	1983	Atlee Hammaker, SF	2.25
1924	Dazzy Vance, Bklyn	2.16	1954	Johnny Antonelli, NY	2.29	1984	Alejandro Pena, LA	2.48
1925	Dolf Luque, Cinn	2.63	1955	Bob Friend, Pit	2.84	1985	Dwight Gooden, NY	1.53
1926	Ray Kremer, Pit	2.61	1956	Lew Burdette, Milw	2.71	1986	Mike Scott, Hou	2.22
1927	Ray Kremer, Pit	2.47	1957	Johnny Podres, Bklyn	2.66	1987	Nolan Ryan, Hou	2.76
1928	Dazzy Vance, Bklyn	2.09	1958	Stu Miller, SF	2.47	1988	Joe Magrane, St.L	2.18
1929	Bill Walker, NY	3.08	1959	Sam Jones, SF	2.82	1989	Scott Garrelts, SF	2.28

Note: In 1945, Borowy had a 3.13 ERA in 18 games with New York (AL) for a combined ERA of 2.65.

American League

Year		ERA	Year		ERA	Year		ERA
1901	Cy Young, Bos	1.62	1930	Lefty Grove, Phi	2.54	1960	Frank Baumann, Chi	2.67
1902	Ed Siever, Det	1.91	1931	Lefty Grove, Phi	2.06	1961	Dick Donovan, Wash	2.40
1903	Earl Moore, Clev	1.77	1932	Lefty Grove, Phi	2.84	1962	Hank Aguirre, Det	2.21
1904	Addie Joss, Clev	1.59	1933	Monte Pearson, Clev	2.33	1963	Gary Peters, Chi	2.33
1905	Rube Waddell, Phi	1.48	1934	Lefty Gomez, NY	2.33	1964	Dean Chance, LA	1.65
1906	Doc White, Chi	1.52	1935	Lefty Grove, Bos	2.70	1965	Sam McDowell, Clev	2.18
1907	Ed Walsh, Chi	1.60	1936	Lefty Grove, Bos	2.81	1966	Gary Peters, Chi	1.98
1908	Addie Joss, Clev	1.16	1937	Lefty Gomez, NY	2.33	1967	Joe Horlen, Chi	2.06
1909	Harry Krause, Phi	1.39	1938	Lefty Grove, Bos	3.08	1968	Luis Tiant, Clev	1.60
1910	Ed Walsh, Chi	1.27	1939	Lefty Grove, Bos	2.54	1969	Dick Bosman, Wash	2.19
1911	Vean Gregg, Clev	1.81	1940	Bob Feller, Clev	2.61	1970	Diego Segui, Oak	2.56
1912	Walter Johnson,Wash	1.39	1941	Thorton Lee, Chi	2.37	1971	Vida Blue, Oak	1.82
1913	Walter Johnson,Wash	1.09	1942	Ted Lyons, Chi	2.10	1972	Luis Tiant, Bos	1.91
1914	Dutch Leonard, Bos	1.01	1943	Spud Chandler, NY	1.64	1973	Jim Palmer, Balt	2.40
1915	Smokey Joe Wood,Bos	1.49	1944	Dizzy Trout, Det	2.12	1974	Catfish Hunter, Oak	2.49
1916	Babe Ruth, Bos	1.75	1945	Hal Newhouser, Det	1.81	1975	Jim Palmer, Balt	2.09
1917	Eddie Cicotte, Chi	1.53	1946	Hal Newhouser, Det	1.94	1976	Mark Fidrych, Det	2.34
1918	Walter Johnson,Wash	1.27	1947	Spud Chandler, NY	2.46	1977	Frank Tanana, Cal	2.54
1919	Walter Johnson,Wash	1.49	1948	Gene Bearden, Clev	2.43	1978	Ron Guidry, NY	1.74
			1949	Mel Parnell, Bos	2.77	1979	Ron Guidry, NY	2.78
1920	Bob Shawkey, NY	2.45	1950	Early Wynn, Clev	3.20	1980	Rudy May, NY	2.47
1921	Red Faber, Chi	2.48	1951	Saul Rogovin,Det-Chi	2.78	1981	Steve McCatty, Oak	2.32
1922	Red Faber, Chi	2.80	1952	Allie Reynolds, NY	2.06	1982	Rick Sutcliffe, Clev	2.96
1923	Stan Coveleski, Clev	2.76	1953	Ed Lopat, NY	2.42	1983	Rick Honeycutt, Texas	2.42
1924	Walter Johnson, Wash	2.72	1954	Mike Garcia, Clev	2.64	1984	Mike Boddicker, Balt	2.79
1925	Stan Coveleski, Wash	2.84	1955	Billy Pierce, Chi	1.97	1985	Dave Stieb, Tor	2.48
1926	Lefty Grove, Phi	2.51	1956	Whitey Ford, NY	2.47	1986	Roger Clemens, Bos	2.48
1927	Wilcy Moore, NY	2.28	1957	Bobby Shantz, NY	2.45	1987	Jimmy Key, Tor	2.76
1928	Garland Braxton,Wash	2.51	1958	Whitey Ford, NY	2.01	1988	Allen Anderson, Minn	2.45
1929	Lefty Grove, Phi	2.81	1959	Hoyt Wilhelm, Balt	2.19	1989	Bret Saberhagen, KC	2.16

Note #1: In 1927, Moore pitched only six complete games, but led the league anyway with 213 innings pitched.
Note #2: In 1940, Ernie Bonham of New York had an 1.90 ERA and 10 complete games, but appeared in only a total of 12 games and 99 innings.

Strikeouts
National League

Year		K's	Year		K's	Year		K's
1900	Rube Waddell, Pit	130	1930	Bill Hallahan, St.L	177	1960	Don Drysdale, LA	246
1901	Noodles Hahn, Cinn	239	1931	Bill Hallahan, St.L	159	1961	Sandy Koufax, LA	269
1902	Vic Willis, Bos	225	1932	Dizzy Dean, St.L	191	1962	Don Drysdale, LA	232
1903	Christy Mathewson, NY	267	1933	Dizzy Dean, St.L	199	1963	Sandy Koufax, LA	306
1904	Christy Mathewson, NY	212	1934	Dizzy Dean, St.L	195	1964	Bob Veale, Pit	250
1905	Christy Mathewson, NY	206	1935	Dizzy Dean, St.L	182	1965	Sandy Koufax, LA	382
1906	Fred Beebe, Chi-St.L	171	1936	Van Lingle Mungo,Bklyn	238	1966	Sandy Koufax, LA	317
1907	Christy Mathewson, NY	178	1937	Carl Hubbell, NY	159	1967	Jim Bunning, Phi	253
1908	Christy Mathewson, NY	259	1938	Clay Bryant, Chi	135	1968	Bob Gibson, St.L	268
1909	Orval Overall, Chi	205	1939	Claude Passeau,Phi-Chi	137	1969	Ferguson Jenkins, Chi	273
				& Bucky Walters, Cinn	137			
1910	Earl Moore, Phi	185				1970	Tom Seaver, NY	283
1911	Rube Marquard, NY	237	1940	Kirby Higbe, Phi	137	1971	Tom Seaver, NY	289
1912	Grover Alexander, Phi	195	1941	John Vander Meer,Cinn	202	1972	Steve Carlton, Phi	310
1913	Tom Seaton, Phi	168	1942	John Vander Meer,Cinn	186	1973	Tom Seaver, NY	251
1914	Grover Alexander, Phi	214	1943	John Vander Meer,Cinn	174	1974	Steve Carlton, Phi	240
1915	Grover Alexander, Phi	241	1944	Bill Voiselle, NY	161	1975	Tom Seaver, NY	243
1916	Grover Alexander, Phi	167	1945	Preacher Roe, Pitt	148	1976	Tom Seaver, NY	235
1917	Grover Alexander, Phi	201	1946	Johnny Schmitz, Chi	135	1977	Phil Niekro, Atl	262
1918	Hippo Vaughn, Chi	148	1947	Ewell Blackwell, Cinn	193	1978	J.R. Richard, Hou	303
1919	Hippo Vaughn, Chi	141	1948	Harry Brecheen, St.L	149	1979	J.R. Richard, Hou	313
			1949	Warren Spahn, Bos	151			
1920	Grover Alexander, Chi	173				1980	Steve Carlton, Phi	286
1921	Burleigh Grimes, Bklyn	136	1950	Warren Spahn, Bos	191	1981	Fernando Valenzuela,LA	180
1922	Dazzy Vance, Bklyn	134	1951	Don Newcombe, Bklyn	164	1982	Steve Carlton, Phi	286
1923	Dazzy Vance, Bklyn	197		& Warren Spahn, Bos	164	1983	Steve Carlton, Phi	275
1924	Dazzy Vance, Bklyn	262	1952	Warren Spahn, Bos	183	1984	Dwight Gooden, NY	276
1925	Dazzy Vance, Bklyn	221	1953	Robin Roberts, Phi	198	1985	Dwight Gooden, NY	268
1926	Dazzy Vance, Bklyn	140	1954	Robin Roberts, Phi	185	1986	Mike Scott, Hou	306
1927	Dazzy Vance, Bklyn	184	1955	Sam Jones, Chi	198	1987	Nolan Ryan, Hou	270
1928	Dazzy Vance, Bklyn	200	1956	Sam Jones, Chi	176	1988	Nolan Ryan, Hou	228
1929	Pat Malone, Chi	166	1957	Jack Sanford, Phi	188	1989	Jose DeLeon, St.L	201
			1958	Sam Jones, St.L	225			
			1959	Don Drydale, LA	242			

American League

Year		K's	Year		K's	Year		K's
1901	Cy Young, Bos	158	1930	Lefty Grove, Phi	209	1960	Jim Bunning, Det	201
1902	Rube Waddell, Phi	210	1931	Lefty Grove, Phi	175	1961	Camilo Pascual, Minn	221
1903	Rube Waddell, Phi	302	1932	Red Ruffing, NY	190	1962	Camilo Pascual, Minn	206
1904	Rube Waddell, Phi	349	1933	Lefty Gomez, NY	163	1963	Camilo Pascual, Minn	202
1905	Rube Waddell, Phi	287	1934	Lefty Gomez, NY	158	1964	Al Downing, NY	217
1906	Rube Waddell, Phi	196	1935	Tommy Bridges, Det	163	1965	Sam McDowell, Clev	325
1907	Rube Waddell, Phi	232	1936	Tommy Bridges, Det	175	1966	Sam McDowell, Clev	225
1908	Ed Walsh, Chi	269	1937	Lefty Gomez, NY	194	1967	Jim Lonborg, Bos	246
1909	Frank Smith, Chi	177	1938	Bob Feller, Clev	240	1968	Sam McDowell, Clev	283
			1939	Bob Feller, Clev	246	1969	Sam McDowell, Clev	279
1910	Walter Johnson, Wash	313						
1911	Ed Walsh, Chi	255	1940	Bob Feller, Clev	261	1970	Sam McDowell, Clev	304
1912	Walter Johnson, Wash	303	1941	Bob Feller, Clev	260	1971	Mike Lolich, Det	308
1913	Walter Johnson, Wash	243	1942	Tex Hughson, Bos	113	1972	Nolan Ryan, Cal	329
1914	Walter Johnson, Wash	225		& Bobo Newsom,Wash	113	1973	Nolan Ryan, Cal	383
1915	Walter Johnson, Wash	203	1943	Allie Reynolds, Clev	151	1974	Nolan Ryan, Cal	367
1916	Walter Johnson, Wash	228	1944	Hal Newhouser, Det	187	1975	Frank Tanana, Cal	269
1917	Walter Johnson, Wash	188	1945	Hal Newhouser, Det	212	1976	Nolan Ryan, Cal	327
1918	Walter Johnson, Wash	162	1946	Bob Feller, Clev	348	1977	Nolan Ryan, Cal	341
1919	Walter Johnson, Wash	147	1947	Bob Feller, Clev	196	1978	Nolan Ryan, Cal	260
			1948	Bob Feller, Clev	164	1979	Nolan Ryan, Cal	223
1920	Stan Coveleski, Clev	133	1949	Virgil Trucks, Det	153			
1921	Walter Johnson, Wash	143				1980	Len Barker, Clev	187
1922	Urban Shocker, St.L	149	1950	Bob Lemon, Clev	170	1981	Len Barker, Clev	127
1923	Walter Johnson, Wash	130	1951	Vic Raschi, NY	164	1982	Floyd Bannister, Sea	209
1924	Walter Johnson, Wash	158	1952	Allie Reynolds, NY	160	1983	Jack Morris, Det	232
1925	Lefty Grove, Phi	116	1953	Billy Pierce Chi	186	1984	Mark Langston, Sea	204
1926	Lefty Grove, Phi	194	1954	Bob Turley, Balt	185	1985	Bert Blyleven,Clev-Minn	206
1927	Lefty Grove, Phi	174	1955	Herb Score, Clev	245	1986	Mark Langston, Sea	245
1928	Lefty Grove, Phi	183	1956	Herb Score, Clev	263	1987	Mark Langston, Sea	262
1929	Lefty Grove, Phi	170	1957	Early Wynn, Clev	184	1988	Roger Clemens, Bos	291
			1958	Early Wynn, Chi	179	1989	Nolan Ryan, Texas	301
			1959	Jim Bunning, Det	201			

All-Time Single Season Leaders

BATTING

Average

Top 10 (1900-49)

	Year	AB	H	Avg
1 Rogers Hornsby, StL.(NL)	.1924	536	227	**.424**
2 Nap Lajoie, Phi.(AL)	.1901	543	229	**.422**
3 Ty Cobb, Detroit	.1911	591	248	**.420**
George Sisler, St.L (AL)	.1922	586	246	**.420**
5 Ty Cobb, Detroit	.1912	533	227	**.410**
6 Joe Jackson, Cleveland	.1911	571	233	**.408**
7 George Sisler, StL.(AL)	.1920	631	257	**.407**
8 Ted Williams, Bos.(AL)	.1941	456	185	**.406**
9 Rogers Hornsby, StL.(NL)	1925	504	203	**.403**
10 Harry Heilmann, Detroit	.1923	524	211	**.403**

Top 10 (Since 1950)

	Year	AB	H	Avg
1 George Brett, KC	.1980	449	175	**.390**
2 Rod Carew, Minnesota	.1977	616	239	**.388**
Ted Williams, Boston	.1957	420	163	**.388**
3 Tony Gwynn, San Diego	.1987	589	218	**.370**
4 Wade Boggs, Boston	.1985	653	240	**.368**
5 Wade Boggs, Boston	.1988	584	214	**.366**
Rico Carty, Atlanta	.1970	478	175	**.366**
7 Mickey Mantle, NY (AL)	.1957	474	173	**.365**
8 Rod Carew, Minnesota	.1974	599	218	**.364**
9 Joe Torre, St.Louis	.1971	634	230	**.363**
Wade Boggs, Boston	.1987	551	200	**.363**

Hits

Players who have made at least 237 base hits in a single season through the 1989 regular season.

	Year	AB	H	Avg
1 George Sisler, StL.(AL)	.1920	631	**257**	.407
2 Bill Terry, NY (NL)	.1930	633	**254**	.401
Lefty O'Doul, Phi.(NL)	.1929	638	**254**	.398
4 Al Simmons, Phi.(AL)	.1925	658	**253**	.384
5 Rogers Hornsby, StL.(NL)	.1922	623	**250**	.401
6 Chuck Klein, Phi.(NL)	.1930	648	**250**	.386
7 Ty Cobb, Detroit	.1911	591	**248**	.420
8 George Sisler, StL.(AL)	.1922	586	**246**	.420
9 Babe Herman, Brooklyn	.1930	614	**241**	.393
Heinie Manush, StL.(AL)	.1928	638	**241**	.378
11 Wade Boggs, Boston	.1985	653	**240**	.368
12 Rod Carew, Minnesota	.1977	616	**239**	.388
13 Don Mattingly, NY (AL)	.1986	677	**238**	.352
14 Harry Heilmann, Detroit	.1921	602	**237**	.394
Paul Waner, Pittsburgh	.1927	623	**237**	.380
Joe Medwick, StL.(NL)	.1937	633	**237**	.374

Home Runs

Players who have hit at least 50 HRs in a single season through the 1989 regular season.

	Year	Gm	AB	HR
1 Roger Maris, N.Y. (AL)	.1961	162	590	**61**
2 Babe Ruth, N.Y. (AL)	.1927	151	540	**60**
3 Babe Ruth, N.Y. (AL)	.1921	152	540	**59**
4 Hank Greenberg, Det.	.1938	155	556	**58**
Jimmie Foxx, Phi.(AL)	.1932	154	585	**58**
6 Hack Wilson, Chi. (NL)	.1930	155	585	**56**
7 Babe Ruth, N.Y. (AL)	.1920	142	458	**54**
Mickey Mantle, N.Y. (AL)	.1961	153	514	**54**
Babe Ruth, N.Y. (AL)	.1928	154	536	**54**
Ralph Kiner, Pittsburgh	.1949	152	549	**54**
11 Mickey Mantle, N.Y. (AL)	.1956	150	533	**52**
Willie Mays, SF Giants	.1965	157	558	**52**
George Foster, Cinn.	.1977	158	615	**52**
14 Ralph Kiner, Pittsburgh	.1947	152	565	**51**
15 Willie Mays, NY Giants	.1955	152	580	**51**
Johnny Mize, NY Giants	.1947	154	586	**51**
17 Jimmie Foxx, Boston (AL)	.1938	149	565	**50**

Runs Batted In

Top 10 (1900-49)

	Year	Avg	HR	RBI
1 Hack Wilson, Chi. (NL)	.1930	.356	56	**190**
2 Lou Gehrig, NY (AL)	.1931	.341	46	**184**
3 Hank Greenberg, Det.	.1937	.337	40	**183**
4 Lou Gehrig, NY (AL)	.1927	.373	47	**175**
Jimmie Foxx, Boston (AL)	.1938	.349	50	**175**
6 Lou Gehrig, NY (AL)	.1930	.379	41	**174**
7 Babe Ruth, NY (AL)	.1921	.378	59	**171**
8 Chuck Klein, Phi. (NL)	.1930	.386	40	**170**
Hank Greenberg, Det.	.1935	.328	36	**170**
10 Jimmie Foxx, Phi. (AL)	.1932	.364	58	**169**

Top 10 (1950-89)

	Year	Avg	HR	RBI
1 Tommy Davis, LA (NL)	.1962	.346	27	**153**
2 George Foster, Cinn.	.1977	.320	52	**149**
3 Johnny Bench, Cinn.	.1970	.293	45	**148**
4 Al Rosen, Cleve.	.1953	.336	43	**145**
Don Mattingly, NY (AL)	.1985	.324	35	**145**
6 Walt Dropo, Bos. (AL)	.1950	.322	34	**144**
Vern Stephens, Bos. (AL)	.1950	.295	30	**144**
8 Ernie Banks, Chi. (NL)	.1959	.304	45	**143**
9 Roy Campanella, Bklyn	.1953	.312	41	**142**
Orlando Cepeda, S.Fran	.1961	.311	46	**142**
Roger Maris, NY (AL)	.1961	.269	61	**142**

Total Bases

Top 10 (1900-49)

	Year	TB
1 Babe Ruth, NY (AL)	.1921	**457**
2 Rogers Hornsby, St.L.(NL)	.1922	**450**
3 Lou Gehrig, NY (AL)	.1927	**447**
4 Chuck Klein, Phi.(NL)	.1930	**445**
5 Jimmie Foxx, Phi.(AL)	.1932	**438**
6 Stan Musial, St.L.(NL)	.1948	**429**
7 Hack Wilson, Chi.(NL)	.1930	**423**
8 Chuck Klein, Phi.(NL)	.1932	**420**
9 Lou Gehrig, NY (AL)	.1930	**419**
10 Joe DiMaggio, NY (AL)	.1937	**418**

Top 10 (1950-89)

	Year	TB
1 Jim Rice, Boston	.1978	**406**
2 Hank Aaron, Milw.	.1959	**400**
3 George Foster, Cincinnati	.1977	**388**
Don Mattingly, NY (AL)	.1986	**388**
5 Willie Mays, NY (NL)	.1955	**382**
Willie Mays, San Francisco	.1962	**382**
Jim Rice, Boston	.1977	**382**
8 Frank Robinson, Cincinnati	.1962	**380**
9 Ernie Banks, Chicago (NL)	.1958	**379**
10 Duke Snider, Brooklyn	.1954	**378**

Runs

Players who have scored at least 151 runs in a single season through the 1989 regular season.

		Year	Runs
1	Babe Ruth, New York (AL)	1921	177
2	Lou Gehrig, New York (AL)	1936	167
3	Babe Ruth, New York (AL)	1928	163
	Lou Gehrig, New York (AL)	1931	163
5	Babe Ruth, New York (AL)	1920	158
	Babe Ruth, New York (AL)	1927	158
	Chuck Klein, Philadelphia (NL)	1930	158
8	Rogers Hornsby, Chicago (NL)	1929	156
9	Kiki Cuyler, Chicago (NL)	1930	155
10	Lefty O'Doul, Philadelphia (NL)	1929	152
	Woody English, Chicago (NL)	1930	152
	Al Simmons, Philadelphia (AL)	1930	152
	Chuck Klein, Philadelphia (NL)	1932	152
14	Babe Ruth, New York (AL)	1923	151
	Jimmie Foxx, Philadelphia (AL)	1932	151
	Joe DiMaggio, New York (AL)	1937	151

Walks

		Year	BB
1	Babe Ruth, New York (AL)	1923	170
2	Ted Williams, Boston (AL)	1947	162
	Ted Williams, Boston (AL)	1949	162
4	Ted Williams, Boston (AL)	1946	156
5	Eddie Yost, Washington	1956	151
6	Eddie Joost, Philadelphia (AL)	1949	149
7	Babe Ruth, New York, (AL)	1920	148
	Eddie Stanky, Brooklyn	1945	148
	Jimmy Wynn, Houston	1969	148
10	Jimmy Sheckard, Chicago (AL)	1911	147
11	Mickey Mantle, New York (AL)	1957	146
12	Ted Williams, Boston (AL)	1941	145
	Ted Williams, Boston (AL)	1942	145
	Harmon Killebrew, Minnesota	1969	145

Strikeouts

Players who have struck out at least 172 times in a single season through the 1989 regular season.

		Year	Ks
1	Bobby Bonds, San Francisco	1970	189
2	Bobby Bonds, San Francisco	1969	187
3	Rob Deer, Milwaukee	1987	186
4	Pete Incaviglia, Texas	1986	185
5	Mike Schmidt, Philadelphia	1975	180
6	Rob Deer, Milwaukee	1986	179
7	Dave Nicholson, Chicago (AL)	1963	175
	Gorman Thomas, Milwaukee	1979	175
	Jose Canseco, Oakland	1986	175
10	Jim Presley, Seattle	1986	172
	Bo Jackson, Kansas City	1989	172

Stolen Bases

Players who have stolen at least 85 bases in a single season through the 1989 regular season.

		Year	SB	CS
1	Rickey Henderson, Oakland	1982	130	42
2	Lou Brock, St.Louis	1974	118	33
3	Vince Coleman, St.Louis	1985	110	25
4	Vince Coleman, St.Louis	1987	109	22
5	Rickey Henderson, Oakland	1983	108	19
6	Vince Coleman, St.Louis	1986	107	14
7	Maury Wills, Los Angeles (NL)	1962	104	13
8	Rickey Henderson, Oakland	1980	100	26
9	Ron LeFlore, Montreal	1980	97	19
10	Ty Cobb, Detroit	1915	96	38
	Omar Moreno, Pittsburgh	1980	96	33
12	Maury Wills, Los Angeles	1965	94	31
13	Rickey Henderson, NY (AL)	1988	93	13
14	Tim Raines, Montreal	1983	90	14
15	Clyde Milan, Washington	1912	88	—
16	Rickey Henderson, NY (AL)	1986	87	18

Slugging Average

Top 10 (1900-49)

		Year	S.Avg
1	Babe Ruth, New York (AL)	1920	.847
2	Babe Ruth, New York (AL)	1921	.846
3	Babe Ruth, New York (AL)	1927	.772
4	Lou Gehrig, New York (AL)	1927	.765
5	Babe Ruth, New York (AL)	1923	.764
6	Rogers Hornsby, St.Louis (NL)	1925	.756
7	Jimmie Foxx, Philadelphia (AL)	1932	.749
8	Babe Ruth, New York (AL)	1924	.739
9	Babe Ruth, New York (AL)	1926	.737
10	Ted Williams, Boston (AL)	1941	.735

Top 10 (1950-89)

		Year	S.Avg
1	Ted Williams, Boston	1957	.731
2	Mickey Mantle, New York (AL)	1956	.705
3	Mickey Mantle, New York	1961	.687
4	Hank Aaron, Atlanta	1971	.669
5	Willie Mays, New York (NL)	1954	.667
6	Mickey Mantle, New York (AL)	1957	.665
7	George Brett, Kansas City	1980	.664
8	Norm Cash, Detroit	1961	.662
9	Willie Mays, New York (NL)	1955	.659
10	Willie McCovey, San Francisco	1969	.656

Pitching

Wins

Top 10 (1900-49)

		Year	W	L	Pct
1	Jack Chesbro, NY (AL)	1904	41	12	.774
2	Ed Walsh, Chicago (AL)	1908	40	15	.727
3	Christy Mathewson, NY (NL)	1908	37	11	.771
4	Walter Johnson, Washington	1913	36	7	.837
5	Joe McGinnity, NY (NL)	1904	35	8	.814
6	Smokey Joe Wood, Bos.(AL)	1912	34	5	.872
7	Cy Young, Boston (AL)	1901	33	10	.767
8	Grover Alexander, Phi.(NL)	1916	33	12	.733
9	Christy Mathewson, NY (NL)	1904	33	12	.733
10	Cy Young, Boston (AL)	1902	32	11	.744
10	Walter Johnson, Washington	1912	32	12	.727

Top 10 (1950-89)

		Year	W	L	Pct
1	Denny McLain, Detroit	1968	31	6	.838
2	Robin Roberts, Phila.(NL)	1952	28	7	.800
3	Don Newcombe, Brooklyn	1956	27	7	.794
	Sandy Koufax, Los Angeles	1966	27	9	.750
5	Steve Carlton, Philadelphia	1972	27	10	.730
6	Sandy Koufax, Los Angeles	1965	26	8	.765
	Juan Marichal, San Fran	1968	26	9	.743
8	Eleven pitchers tied with 25 wins				

Single Season Pitching Leaders

Winning Percentage

Pitchers with a single season winning percentage of at least .864 through the 1989 regular season.

	Year	W-L	Pct
1 Roy Face, Pittsburgh	1959	18-1	**.947**
2 Johnny Allen, Cleveland	1937	15-1	**.938**
3 Ron Guidry, New York (AL)	1978	25-3	**.893**
4 Freddie Fitzsimmons, Bklyn	1940	16-2	**.889**
5 Lefty Grove, Phila.(AL)	1931	31-4	**.886**
6 Bob Stanley, Boston	1978	15-2	**.882**
7 Preacher Roe, Brooklyn	1951	22-3	**.880**
8 Tom Seaver, Cincinnati	1981	14-2	**.875**
8 Smokey Joe Wood, Bos.(AL)	1912	34-5	**.872**
9 David Cone, New York (NL)	1988	20-3	**.870**
10 Orel Hershiser, Los Angeles	1985	19-3	**.864**

Games

Pitchers with at least 87 appearances in a single season through the 1989 regular season.

	Year	Gm
1 Mike Marshall, Los Angeles	1974	106
2 Kent Tekulve, Pittsburgh	1979	94
3 Mike Marshall, Montreal	1973	92
4 Kent Tekulve, Pittsburgh	1978	91
5 Wayne Granger, Cincinnati	1969	90
6 Mike Marshall, Minnesota	1979	90
7 Kent Tekulve, Philadelphia	1987	90
8 Mark Eichhorn, Toronto	1987	89
9 Wilbur Wood, Chicago (AL)	1968	88
10 Rob Murphy, Cincinnati	1987	87

Strikeouts

Pitchers with at least 315 strikeouts in a single season, through the 1989 regular season.

	Year	SO	P/G
1 Nolan Ryan, California	1973	383	10.57
2 Sandy Koufax, Los Angeles	1965	382	10.24
3 Nolan Ryan, California	1974	367	9.92
4 Rube Waddell, Phila.(AL)	1904	349	8.12
5 Bob Feller, Cleveland	1946	348	8.45
6 Nolan Ryan, California	1977	341	10.26
7 Nolan Ryan, California	1972	329	10.43
8 Nolan Ryan, California	1976	327	10.36
9 Sam McDowell, Cleveland	1965	325	10.71
10 Sandy Koufax, Los Angeles	1966	317	8.8

Earned Run Average

Pitchers with ERAs of 1.26 or less for a single season through the 1989 regular season.

	Year	ERA
1 Dutch Leonard, Boston (AL)	1914	**0.96**
2 Three Finger Brown, Chicago (NL)	1906	**1.04**
3 Walter Johnson, Washington	1913	**1.09**
4 Bob Gibson, St.Louis	1968	**1.12**
5 Christy Mathewson, NY (NL)	1909	**1.14**
6 Jack Pfiester, Chicago (NL)	1907	**1.15**
7 Addie Joss, Cleveland	1908	**1.16**
8 Carl Lundgren, Chicago (NL)	1907	**1.17**
9 Grover Alexander, Phila.(NL)	1915	**1.22**
10 Cy Young, Boston (AL)	1908	**1.26**

Shutouts

Pitchers with at least 11 shutouts in a single season through the 1989 regular season.

	Year	ShO
1 Grover Alexander, Phila.(NL)	1916	16
2 Jack Coombs, Philadelphia (AL)	1910	13
Bob Gibson, St.Louis	1968	13
4 Christy Mathewson, NY (NL)	1908	12
Grover Alexander, Phila.(NL)	1915	12
6 Ed Walsh, Chicago (AL)	1908	11
Walter Johnson, Washington	1913	11
Sandy Koufax, Los Angeles (NL)	1963	11
Dean Chance, Los Angeles (AL)	1964	11
10 Eleven pitchers tied with 10		

Saves

Pitchers with at least 39 saves in a single season through the 1989 regular season.

	Year	Saves
1 Dave Righetti, New York (AL)	1986	46
2 Dan Quisenberry, Kansas City	1983	45
Bruce Sutter, St.Louis	1984	45
Dennis Eckersley, Oakland	1988	45
5 Dan Quisenberry, Kansas City	1984	44
Mark Davis, San Diego	1989	44
7 Jeff Reardon, Minnesota	1988	42
8 Jeff Reardon, Montreal	1985	41
9 Steve Bedrosian, Philadelphia	1987	40
10 John Franco, Cincinnati	1988	39

Home Runs Allowed

Pitchers who have given up at least 41 HRs in a single season through the 1989 regular season.

	Year	HRs
1 Bert Blyleven, Minnesota	1986	50
2 Bert Blyleven, Minnesota	1987	46
Robin Roberts, Philadelphia	1956	46
4 Pedro Ramos, Washington	1957	43
5 Denny McLain, Detroit	1966	42
6 Robin Roberts, Philadelphia	1955	41
Phil Niekro, Atlanta	1979	41
8 Seven pitchers tied with 40		

Walks Allowed

Pitchers who have walked at least 175 batters in a single season through the 1989 regular season.

	Year	BB
1 Bob Feller, Cleveland	1938	208
2 Nolan Ryan, California	1977	204
3 Nolan Ryan, California	1974	202
4 Bob Feller, Cleveland	1941	194
5 Bobo Newsom, St.Louis (AL)	1938	192
6 Sam Jones, Chicago (NL)	1955	185
7 Nolan Ryan, California	1976	183
8 Bob Harmon, St.Louis (NL)	1911	181
Bob Turley, Baltimore	1954	181
10 Tommy Byrne, New York (AL)	1949	179
11 Bob Turley, New York (AL)	1955	177

Triple Crown Winners
Batting

Players who led either league in Batting Average, Home Runs and Runs Batted In over a single season.

National League

	Year	Avg	HR	RBI
Paul Hines, Prov	1878	.358	4	50
Hugh Duffy, Boston	1894	.438	18	145
Heinie Zimmerman, Chi	1912	.372	14	103
Rogers Hornsby, St.Louis	1922	.401	42	152
Rogers Hornsby, St.Louis	1925	.403	39	143
Chuck Klein, Phila	1933	.368	28	120
Joe Medwick, St.Louis	1937	.374	31*	154

Tied for league lead in HRs with Mel Ott, NY.

American League

	Year	Avg	HR	RBI
Nap Lajoie, Philadelphia	1901	.422	14	125
Ty Cobb, Detroit	1909	.377	9	115
Jimmie Foxx, Philadelphia	1933	.356	48	163
Lou Gehrig, New York	1934	.363	49	165
Ted Williams, Boston	1942	.356	36	137
Ted Williams, Boston	1947	.343	32	114
Mickey Mantle, New York	1956	.353	52	130
Frank Robinson, Baltimore	1966	.316	49	122
Carl Yastrzemski, Boston	1967	.326	44*	121

Tied for league lead in HRs with Harmon Killebrew, Minn.

Pitching

Pitchers who led either league in Earned Run Average, Wins and Strikeouts over a single season.

National League

	Year	ERA	W-L	SO
Tommy Bond, Boston	1877	2.11	40-17	170
Old Hoss Radbourn, Prov	1884	1.38	60-12	441
Tim Keefe, New York	1888	1.74	35-12	333
John Clarkson, Boston	1889	2.73	49-19	284
Amos Rusie, New York	1894	2.78	36-13	195
Christy Mathewson, NY	1905	1.27	31-8	206
Christy Mathewson, NY	1908	1.43	37-11	259
Grover Alexander, Phila	1915	1.22	31-10	241
Grover Alexander, Phila	1916	1.55	33-12	167
Grover Alexander, Phila	1917	1.86	30-13	201
Hippo Vaugh, Chicago	1918	1.74	22-10	148
Grover Alexander, Chi	1920	1.91	27-14	173
Dazzy Vance, Brooklyn	1924	2.16	28-6	262
Bucky Walters, Cinn	1939	2.29	27-11	137
Sandy Koufax, Los Ang	1963	1.88	25-5	306
Sandy Koufax, Los Ang	1965	2.04	26-8	382
Sandy Koufax, Los Ang	1966	1.73	27-9	317
Steve Carlton, Phila	1972	1.97	27-10	310
Dwight Gooden, New York	1985	1.53	24-4	268

Ties: in 1894, Rusie tied for league lead in wins with Jouett Meekin, NY (36-10); in 1939, Walters tied for league lead in strikeouts with Claude Passeau, Phi-Chi; in 1963, Koufax tied for the league lead in wins with Juan Marichal, SF.

American League

	Year	ERA	W-L	SO
Cy Young, Boston	1901	1.62	33-10	158
Rube Waddell, Phila	1905	1.48	26-11	287
Walter Johnson, Wash	1913	1.09	36-7	243
Walter Johnson, Wash	1918	1.27	23-13	162
Walter Johnson, Wash	1924	2.72	23-7	158
Lefty Grove, Phila	1930	2.54	28-5	209
Lefty Grove, Phila	1931	2.06	31-4	175
Lefty Gomez, New York	1934	2.33	26-5	158
Lefty Gomez, New York	1937	2.33	21-11	194
Hal Newhouser, Detroit	1945	1.81	25-9	212

Consecutive Game Streaks
Games Played

Players who have played in at least 650 consecutive regular season games through 1989. Active streak in **bold** type.

		Games
1.	Lou Gehrig	2,130
2.	Everett Scott	1,307
3.	**Cal Ripken**	**1,250**
4.	Steve Garvey	1,207
5.	Billy Williams	1,117
6.	Joe Sewell	1,103
7.	Stan Musial	895
8.	Eddie Yost	829
9.	Gus Suhr	822
10.	Nellie Fox	798
11.	Pete Rose	745
12.	Dale Murphy	740
13.	Richie Ashburn	730
14.	Ernie Banks	717
15.	Pete Rose	678
16.	Earl Averill	673
17.	Frank McCormick	652

Hitting

Players with hits in at least 31 consecutive games.

National League

	Gm	Year
Willie Keeler, Baltimore	44	1897
Pete Rose, Cincinnati	44	1978
Bill Dahlen, Chicago	42	1894
Tommy Holmes, Boston	37	1945
Billy Hamilton, Philadelphia	36	1894
Fred Clarke, Louisville	35	1895
George Davis, New York	33	1893
Rogers Hornsby, St.Louis	32	1922
Ed Delahanty, Philadelphia	31	1899
Rico Carty, Atlanta	31	1970

American League

	Gm	Year
Joe DiMaggio, New York	56	1941
George Sisler, St.Louis	41	1922
Ty Cobb, Detroit	40	1911
Paul Molitor, Milwaukee	39	1987
Ty Cobb, Detroit	35	1917
George Sisler, St.Louis	34	1925
John Stone, Detroit	34	1930
George McQuinn, St.Louis	34	1938
Dom DiMaggio, Boston	34	1949
Heinie Manush, Washington	33	1933
Sam Rice, Washington	31	1924
Ken Landreaux, Minnesota	31	1980

Four Home Runs in One Game
National League

	Date	H/A	Inn
Bobby Lowe, Boston	5/30/1894	H	9
Ed Delahanty, Philadelphia	7/13/96	A	9
Chuck Klein, Philadelphia	7/10/1936	A	10
Gil Hodges, Brooklyn	8/31/50	H	9
Joe Adcock, Milwaukee	7/31/54	A	9
Willie Mays, San Francisco	4/30/61	A	9
Mike Schmidt, Philadelphia	4/17/76	A	10
Bob Horner, Atlanta	7/6/86	H	9

American League

	Date	H/A	Inn
Lou Gehrig, New York	6/3/1932	A	9
Pat Seerey, Chicago	7/18/48	A	11
Rocky Colavito, Cleveland	6/10/59	A	9

Major League All-Time Leaders
CAREER
Batting

Average

Players with at least a .335 batting average through the 1989 regular season. Active players in **bold** type.

		Yrs	Bat	AB	Hits	Avg
1	Ty Cobb	24	L	11,429	4,191	**.366**
2	Rogers Hornsby	23	R	8,137	2,930	**.358**
3	Joe Jackson	13	L	4,981	1,774	**.356**
4	**Wade Boggs**	8	L	4,534	1,597	**.352**
5	Willie Keeler	19	L	8,591	2,962	**.345**
	Ed Delahanty	16	R	7,502	2,591	**.345**
7	Tris Speaker	22	L	10,208	3,515	**.344**
	Ted Williams	19	L	7,706	2,654	**.344**
	Billy Hamilton	14	L	6,284	2,163	**.344**
10	Dan Brouthers	19	L	6,716	2,304	**.343**
	Pete Browning	13	R	4,829	1,654	**.343**
12	Babe Ruth	22	L	8,399	2,873	**.342**
	Harry Heilmann	17	R	7,787	2,660	**.342**
14	Jesse Burkett	16	L	8,430	2,873	**.341**
	Bill Terry	14	L	6,428	2,193	**.341**
16	George Sisler	15	L	8,267	2,812	**.340**
17	Lou Gehrig	17	L	8,001	2,721	**.340**
18	Nap Lajoie	21	R	9,589	3,251	**.339**
19	Riggs Stephenson	14	R	4,508	1,515	**.336**

Home Runs

Players with at least 380 HRs through the 1989 regular season. Active players in **bold** type.

		Yrs	Bat	At Bats	HRs	Pct
1	Hank Aaron	23	R	12,364	**755**	6.1
2	Babe Ruth	22	L	8,399	**714**	8.5
3	Willie Mays	22	R	10,881	**660**	6.1
4	Frank Robinson	21	R	10,006	**586**	5.9
5	Harmon Killebrew	22	R	8,147	**573**	7.0
6	Reggie Jackson	21	L	9,864	**563**	5.7
7	Mike Schmidt	18	R	8,352	**548**	6.6
8	Mickey Mantle	18	B	8,102	**536**	6.6
9	Jimmie Foxx	20	R	8,134	**534**	6.6
10	Ted Williams	19	L	7,706	**521**	6.8
	Willie McCovey	22	L	8,197	**521**	6.4
12	Eddie Mathews	17	L	8,537	**512**	6.0
	Ernie Banks	19	R	9,421	**512**	5.4
14	Mel Ott	22	L	9,456	**511**	5.4
15	Lou Gehrig	17	L	8,001	**493**	6.2
16	Willie Stargell	21	L	7,927	**475**	6.0
	Stan Musial	22	L	10,972	**475**	4.3
18	Carl Yastrzemski	23	L	11,988	**452**	3.8
19	Dave Kingman	16	R	6,677	**442**	6.6
20	Billy Williams	18	L	9,350	**426**	4.6
21	**Darrell Evans**	21	L	8,973	**414**	4.6
22	Duke Snider	18	L	7,161	**407**	5.7
23	Al Kaline	22	R	10,116	**399**	3.9
24	Graig Nettles	22	L	8,986	**390**	4.3
25	Johnny Bench	17	R	7,658	**389**	5.1
26	Frank Howard	16	R	6,488	**382**	5.9
	Jim Rice	16	R	8,225	**382**	4.6

Hits

Players with at least 2,940 hits through the 1989 regular season.

		Yrs	Bat	AB	Hits	Avg
1	Pete Rose	24	B	14,053	**4,256**	.303
2	Ty Cobb	24	L	11,429	**4,191**	.367
3	Hank Aaron	23	R	12,364	**3,771**	.305
4	Stan Musial	22	L	10,972	**3,630**	.331
5	Tris Speaker	22	L	10,208	**3,515**	.344
6	Honus Wagner	21	R	10,427	**3,430**	.329
7	Carl Yastrzemski	23	L	11,988	**3,419**	.285
8	Eddie Collins	25	L	9,949	**3,311**	.333
9	Willie Mays	22	R	10,881	**3,283**	.302
10	Nap Lajoie	21	R	9,589	**3,251**	.339
11	Paul Waner	20	L	9,459	**3,152**	.333
12	Rod Carew	19	L	9,315	**3,053**	.328
13	Cap Anson	22	R	9,108	**3,041**	.334
14	Lou Brock	19	L	10,332	**3,023**	.293
15	Al Kaline	22	R	10,116	**3,007**	.297
16	Roberto Clemente	18	R	9,454	**3,000**	.317
17	Sam Rice	20	L	9,269	**2,987**	.322
18	Sam Crawford	19	L	9,580	**2,964**	.309
19	Willie Keeler	19	L	8,591	**2,962**	.345
20	Frank Robinson	21	R	10,006	**2,943**	.294

Active Hitters

Active players with at least 2,500 hits through the 1989 regular season.

		Yrs	Bat	AB	Hits	Avg
1	Bill Buckner	21	L	9,354	**2,707**	.289
2	Robin Yount	16	R	8,907	**2,602**	.292
3	George Brett	17	L	8,148	**2,528**	.310

Runs Batted In

Players with at least 1,600 RBIs through the 1989 regular season.

		Yrs	Bat	Games	RBIs	P/G
1	Hank Aaron	23	R	3,298	**2,297**	.70
2	Babe Ruth	22	L	2,503	**2,209**	.88
3	Lou Gehrig	17	L	2,164	**1,990**	.92
4	Ty Cobb	24	L	3,034	**1,961**	.65
5	Stan Musial	22	L	3,026	**1,951**	.64
6	Jimmie Foxx	20	R	2,317	**1,921**	.83
7	Willie Mays	22	R	2,992	**1,903**	.64
8	Mel Ott	22	L	2,732	**1,860**	.68
9	Carl Yastrzemski	23	L	3,308	**1,844**	.56
10	Ted Williams	19	L	2,292	**1,839**	.80
11	Al Simmons	20	R	2,215	**1,827**	.65
12	Frank Robinson	21	R	2,808	**1,812**	.65
13	Honus Wagner	21	R	2,786	**1,732**	.62
14	Cap Anson	22	R	2,276	**1,715**	.75
15	Reggie Jackson	21	L	2,820	**1,702**	.60
16	Tony Perez	23	R	2,777	**1,652**	.59
17	Ernie Banks	19	R	2,528	**1,636**	.65
18	Goose Goslin	18	L	2,287	**1,609**	.70

Games Played

Players with at least 2,825 games through the 1989 regular season.

		Games
1	Pete Rose	**3,562**
2	Carl Yastrzemski	**3,308**
3	Hank Aaron	**3,298**
4	Ty Cobb	**3,034**
5	Stan Musial	**3,026**
6	Willie Mays	**2,992**
7	Rusty Staub	**2,951**
8	Brooks Robinson	**2,896**
9	Al Kaline	**2,834**
10	Eddie Collins	**2,826**

At Bats

Players with at least 10,225 at bats through the 1989 regular season.

		At Bats
1	Pete Rose	**14,053**
2	Hank Aaron	**12,364**
3	Carl Yastrzemski	**11,988**
4	Ty Cobb	**11,429**
5	Stan Musial	**10,972**
6	Willie Mays	**10,881**
7	Brooke Robinson	**10,654**
8	Honus Wagner	**10,427**
9	Lou Brock	**10,332**
10	Luis Aparicio	**10,230**

Runs

Players with at least 1,825 runs scored through the 1989 regular season.

		Runs
1	Ty Cobb	**2,245**
2	Babe Ruth	**2,174**
	Hank Aaron	**2,174**
4	Pete Rose	**2,165**
5	Willie Mays	**2,062**
6	Stan Musial	**1,949**
7	Lou Gehrig	**1,888**
8	Tris Speaker	**1,881**
9	Mel Ott	**1,859**
10	Frank Robinson	**1,829**

Total Bases

Players with at least 5,000 total bases through the 1989 regular season.

		TBs
1	Hank Aaron	6,856
2	Stan Musial	6,134
3	Willie Mays	6,066
4	Ty Cobb	5,863
5	Babe Ruth	5,793
6	Pete Rose	5,752
7	Carl Yastrzemski	5,539
8	Frank Robinson	5,373
9	Tris Speaker	5,105
10	Lou Gehrig	5,059
11	Mel Ott	5,041

Walks

Players who have walked at least 1,500 times through the 1989 regular season. Active players in **bold** type.

		Walks
1	Babe Ruth	2,056
2	Ted Williams	2,019
3	Joe Morgan	1,865
4	Carl Yastrzemski	1,845
5	Mickey Mantle	1,734
6	Mel Ott	1,708
7	Eddie Yost	1,614
8	**Darrell Evans**	1,605
9	Stan Musial	1,599
10	Pete Rose	1,566
11	Harmon Killebrew	1,559
12	Lou Gehrig	1,508

Strikeouts

Players who have struck out at least 1,570 times through the 1989 regular season. Active players in **bold** type.

		K's
1	Reggie Jackson	2,597
2	Willie Stargell	1,936
3	Mike Schmidt	1,883
4	Tony Perez	1,867
5	Dave Kingman	1,816
6	Bobby Bonds	1,757
7	Lou Brock	1,730
8	Mickey Mantle	1,710
9	Harmon Killebrew	1,699
10	Lee May	1,570
	Dwight Evans	1,570

Stolen Bases

Players with at least 600 stolen bases through the 1989 regular season. Active players in **bold** type.

		Steals
1	Lou Brock	938
2	Billy Hamilton	937
3	Ty Cobb	892
4	**Rickey Henderson**	871
5	Eddie Collins	743
6	Max Carey	738
7	Honus Wagner	703
8	Joe Morgan	689
9	Arlie Latham	679
10	Bert Campaneris	649
11	Tom Brown	627
12	George Davis	615

Extra Base Hits

Players with at least 1,070 extra base hits through the 1989 regular season.

		Extra BH
1	Hank Aaron	1,477
2	Stan Musial	1,377
3	Babe Ruth	1,356
4	Willie Mays	1,323
5	Lou Gehrig	1,190
6	Frank Robinson	1,186
7	Carl Yastrzemski	1,157
8	Ty Cobb	1,139
9	Tris Speaker	1,133
10	Ted Williams	1,117
	Jimmie Foxx	1,117
12	Reggie Jackson	1,075
13	Mel Ott	1,071

Slugging Average

Players with at least a .550 slugging average through the 1989 regular season.

		S.Avg
1	Babe Ruth	.690
2	Ted Williams	.634
3	Lou Gehrig	.632
4	Jimmie Foxx	.609
5	Hank Greenberg	.605
6	Joe DiMaggio	.579
7	Rogers Hornsby	.577
8	Johnny Mize	.562
9	Stan Musial	.559
10	Willie Mays	.557
	Mickey Mantle	.557
12	Hank Aaron	.555

Pitching

Wins

Pitchers with at least 270 wins through the 1989 regular season. Active players in **bold** type.

		Yrs	Arm	GS	W	L	Pct
1	Cy Young	22	R	815	511	313	.620
2	Walter Johnson	21	R	666	416	279	.599
3	Christy Mathewson	17	R	552	373	188	.665
	Grover Alexander	20	R	598	373	208	.642
5	Warren Spahn	21	L	665	363	245	.597
6	Pud Galvin	14	R	682	361	310	.538
7	Kid Nichols	15	R	562	360	203	.639
8	Tim Keefe	14	R	595	344	225	.605
9	Steve Carlton	24	L	709	329	244	.574
10	Eddie Plank	17	L	527	327	193	.629
11	John Clarkson	12	R	518	326	177	.648
12	Don Sutton	23	R	756	324	256	.559
13	Phil Niekro	24	R	716	318	274	.537
14	Gaylord Perry	22	R	690	314	265	.542
15	Tom Seaver	20	R	647	311	205	.603
	Mickey Welch	13	R	549	311	207	.600
17	Old Hoss Radbourn	12	R	503	308	191	.617
18	Lefty Grove	17	L	456	300	141	.680
19	Early Wynn	23	R	612	300	244	.551
20	**Nolan Ryan**	23	R	676	289	263	.524
21	Tommy John	26	L	700	288	231	.555
22	Robin Roberts	19	R	609	286	245	.539
23	Tony Mullane	13	B	505	285	215	.570
24	Ferguson Jenkins	19	R	594	284	226	.557
25	Jim Kaat	25	L	625	283	237	.544
26	Red Ruffing	22	R	536	273	225	.548
27	**Bert Blyleven**	20	R	638	271	231	.540
28	Burleigh Grimes	19	R	495	270	212	.560

Strikeouts

Pitchers with at least 2,300 strikeouts through the 1989 regular season. Active players in **bold** type.

		Yrs	Arm	IP	SO	P/G
1	**Nolan Ryan**	23	R	4,787	5,076	9.54
2	Steve Carlton	24	L	5,217	4,136	7.13
3	Tom Seaver	20	R	4,783	3,640	6.85
4	Don Sutton	23	R	5,280	3,574	6.09
5	**Bert Blyleven**	20	R	4,703	3,562	6.81
6	Gaylord Perry	22	R	5,351	3,534	5.94
7	Walter Johnson	21	R	5,924	3,508	5.33
8	Phil Niekro	24	R	5,403	3,342	5.57
9	Ferguson Jenkins	19	R	4,500	3,192	6.38
10	Bob Gibson	17	R	3,885	3,117	7.22
11	Jim Bunning	17	R	3,760	2,855	6.83
12	Mickey Lolich	16	L	3,639	2,832	7.00
13	Cy Young	22	R	7,356	2,799	3.43
14	Warren Spahn	21	L	5,244	2,583	4.43
15	Bob Feller	18	R	3,827	2,581	6.07
16	Jerry Koosman	19	L	3,839	2,556	5.99
17	Tim Keefe	14	R	5,072	2,533	4.49
18	Christy Mathewson	17	R	4,782	2,502	4.71
19	Don Drysdale	14	R	3,432	2,486	6.52
20	Jim Kaat	25	L	4,528	2,461	4.89
21	Sam McDowell	15	L	2,493	2,453	8.86
22	Luis Tiant	19	R	3,486	2,416	6.24
23	Sandy Koufax	12	L	2,324	2,396	9.29
24	Robin Roberts	19	R	4,689	2,357	4.52
25	**Frank Tanana**	17	L	3,405	2,345	6.20
26	Early Wynn	23	R	4,564	2,334	4.60
27	Rube Waddell	13	L	2,961	2,316	7.04
28	Juan Marichal	16	R	3,509	2,303	5.91

Major League All-Time Leaders (Continued)

Games

Pitchers with at least 800 games (starts and relief appearances) through the 1989 regular season. Active players in **bold** type.

		Games
1	Hoyt Wilhelm	1,070
2	Kent Tekulve	1,050
3	Lindy McDaniel	987
4	Rollie Fingers	944
5	Gene Garber	931
6	Cy Young	906
7	Sparky Lyle	899
8	Jim Kaat	898
9	Don McMahon	874
10	Phil Niekro	864
11	**Goose Gossage**	853
12	Roy Face	848
13	Tug McGraw	824
14	Walter Johnson	802

Saves

Pitchers with at least 175 career saves through the 1989 regular season. Games listed are relief appearances only. Active players in **bold** type.

		Gm	Saves
1	Rollie Fingers	907	341
2	**Rich Gossage**	816	307
3	Bruce Sutter	661	300
4	**Jeff Reardon**	584	266
5	**Dan Quisenberry**	616	244
6	Sparky Lyle	899	238
7	**Lee Smith**	580	234
8	Hoyt Wilhelm	1,018	227
9	Gene Garber	722	218
10	Roy Face	821	193
11	**Dave Righetti**	393	188
	Mike Marshall	699	188
13	Kent Tekulve	1,050	184
14	Tug McGraw	785	180
15	Ron Perranoski	736	179
16	**Dave Smith**	513	176

Shutouts

Pitchers with at least 50 shutouts through the 1989 regular season. Active players in **bold** type.

		ShO
1	Walter Johnson	110
2	Grover Alexander	90
3	Christy Mathewson	80
4	Cy Young	76
5	Eddie Plank	69
6	Warren Spahn	63
7	Tom Seaver	61
8	**Bert Blyleven**	60
9	Don Sutton	58
10	Ed Walsh	57
	Three Finger Brown	57
	Nolan Ryan	57
	Pud Galvin	57
14	Bob Gibson	56
15	Steve Carlton	55
16	Jim Palmer	53
	Gaylord Perry	53
18	Juan Marichal	52
19	Rube Waddell	50
20	Vic Willis	50

Innings Pitched

Pitchers with at least 5,000 innings pitched through the 1989 regular season.

		Innings
1	Cy Young	7,356
2	Pud Galvin	5,941
3	Walter Johnson	5,924
4	Phil Niekro	5,403
5	Gaylord Perry	5,351
6	Don Sutton	5,280
7	Warren Spahn	5,244
8	Steve Carlton	5,217
9	Grover Alexander	5,189
10	Kid Nichols	5,084
11	Tim Keefe	5,072

Walks Allowed

Pitchers who have walked at least 1,500 batters through the 1989 regular season. Active players in **bold** type.

		Walks
1	**Nolan Ryan**	2,540
2	Steve Carlton	1,833
3	Phil Niekro	1,809
4	Early Wynn	1,775
5	Bob Feller	1,764
6	Bobo Newsom	1,732
7	Amos Rusie	1,716
8	Gus Weyhing	1,566
9	Red Ruffing	1,541

Home Runs Allowed

Pitchers who have given up at least 375 HRs through the 1989 regular season. Active players in **bold** type.

		HRs
1	Robin Roberts	505
2	Ferguson Jenkins	484
3	Phil Niekro	482
4	Don Sutton	472
5	Warren Spahn	434
6	Steve Carlton	414
7	Gaylord Perry	399
8	**Bert Blyleven**	398
9	Jim Kaat	395
10	Tom Seaver	380

College Baseball

NCAA Division I Champions, 1947-89

Year	Winner	Coach	Score	Loser
1947	California	Clint Evans	8-7	Yale
1948	Southern Cal	Sam Barry	9-2	Yale
1949	Texas	Bibb Falk	10-3	W.Forest
1950	Texas	Bibb Falk	3-0	Wash.St.
1951	Oklahoma	Jack Baer	3-2	Tennessee
1952	Holy Cross	Jack Barry	8-4	Missouri
1953	Michigan	Ray Fisher	7-5	Texas
1954	Missouri	Hi Simmons	4-1	Rollins
1955	Wake Forest	Taylor Sanford	7-6	W.Mich.
1956	Minnesota	Dick Siebert	12-1	Arizona
1957	California	Geo.Wolfman	1-0	Penn St.
1958	Southern Cal	Rod Dedeaux	8-7	Missouri
1959	Oklahoma St.	Toby Greene	5-3	Arizona
1960	Minnesota	Dick Siebert	2-1	USC
1961	Southern Cal	Rod Dedeaux	1-0	Okla.St.
1962	Michigan	Don Lund	5-4	S.Clara
1963	Southern Cal	Rod Dedeaux	5-2	Arizona
1964	Minnesota	Dick Siebert	5-1	Missouri
1965	Arizona	Bobby Winkles	2-1	Ohio St.
1966	Ohio St.	Marty Karow	8-2	Okla.St.
1967	Arizona St.	Bobby Winkles	11-2	Houston
1968	Southern Cal	Rod Dedeaux	4-3	So.Ill.
1969	Arizona St.	Bobby Winkles	10-1	Tulsa
1970	Southern Cal	Rod Dedeaux	2-1	Fla.St.
1971	Southern Cal	Rod Dedeaux	7-2	So.Ill.
1972	Southern Cal	Rod Dedeaux	1-0	Ariz.St.
1973	Southern Cal	Rod Dedeaux	4-3	Ariz.St.
1974	Southern Cal	Rod Dedeaux	7-3	Miami,FL
1975	Texas	Cliff Gustafson	5-1	S.Carolina
1976	Arizona	Jerry Kindall	7-1	E.Michigan
1977	Arizona	Jim Brock	2-1	S.Carolina
1978	Southern Cal	Rod Dedeaux	10-3	Ariz.St.
1979	CS Fullerton	Augie Garrido	2-1	Arkansas
1980	Arizona	Jerry Kindall	5-3	Hawaii
1981	Arizona	Jim Brock	7-4	Okla.St.
1982	Miami,FL	Ron Fraser	9-3	Wichita St.
1983	Texas	Cliff Gustafson	4-3	Alabama
1984	CS Fullerton	Augie Garrido	3-1	Texas
1985	Miami,FL	Ron Fraser	10-6	Texas
1986	Arizona	Jerry Kindall	10-2	Fla.St.
1987	Stanford	M.Marquess	9-5	Okla.St.
1988	Stanford	M.Marquess	9-4	Ariz.St.
1989	Wichita St.	G.Stephenson	5-3	Texas

Ronald Reagan rears back for the last pass of his presidency in January while entertaining **Lou Holtz** and the Notre Dame football team at the White House.

COLLEGE FOOTBALL

INSIDE

Elsewhere in Almanac
For related information refer to the following chapters: Arenas & Ballparks, Halls of Fame & Awards, and Colleges.

*H*oltz latest to win national title in
third season at Notre Dame;
Heisman to Sanders without hype;
and six programs put on probation.

COLLEGE FOOTBALL

1988
YEAR IN
REVIEW

by Bill Connors

It figured that 1988, Lou Holtz' third season at South Bend, would produce Notre Dame's eighth national championship.

Preseason form charts may not have suggested as much, but history did. The Irish often hit the jackpot as a new coach hits his third year.

Notre Dame won the first of four championships under Frank Leahy in his third season, 1943. The first of two titles under Ara Parseghian occurred in his third season, 1966. And Dan Devine won his only championship in his third season, 1977.

The one exception to this three-year formula was Knute Rockne. He won the first of his six pre-wire service national championships in his **second** season, 1919.

None of Notre Dame's modern era champions rose up from such murky depths as the 1988 Irish. Notre Dame

Bill Connors is the Sports Editor of **The Tulsa** (Okla.) **World** and has been covering college football since 1952.

had not finished a season ranked in the Top 10 since 1980 and was coming off a sour conclusion to 1987, when three straight losses dropped its final record to 8–4.

But Holtz' creative offense, featuring big passing plays from option quarterback Tony Rice, who was not known as a big passer, and an impressive defense, anchored by linebacker Michael Stonebreaker and end Frank Stams, combined to generate peak performances in pivotal games.

After riding Reggie Ho's clutch place kicking to a 5–0 start, the Irish were able to reach the top of the polls and stay there by winning the three most important games of 1988:

- Oct. 15— No. 4 Notre Dame beats No. 1 Miami, 31–30 in South Bend;
- Nov. 26— No. 1 Notre Dame beats No. 2 Southern Cal, 27–10 in Los Angeles;
- Jan. 1— No. 1 Notre Dame beats No. 3 West Virginia, 34–21 at the Fiesta Bowl in Tempe.

The Miami and USC victories proved that Notre Dame was a big-play team.

Against Miami, free safety Pat Terrell intercepted a Steve Walsh pass and returned it 60 yards for a touchdown giving ND a 21–7 lead in the second quarter. Later, after Miami had rallied to pull within 31–30 with 45 seconds left to play, Terrell broke up a Walsh 2-point conversion attempt to save the game.

Against Southern Cal, Rice broke a 65-yard TD run on the third play from scrimmage and cornerback Stan Smagala picked off a Rodney Peete pass and went 64 yards for a score. It was the first time in their 60-year rivalry that both Notre Dame and USC were undefeated when they met, but this game was over early.

Rice then saved the best for last. Against West Virginia, he rushed for 75 yards and passed for 213 more and two scores. It was a performance that earned him not only offensive MVP of the Fiesta Bowl, but an unprecedented third cover of **Sports Illustrated** in one season.

When it was all over, the game that decided the national championship was the one with Miami.

Hurricanes' coach Jimmy Johnson thought that his team, which had outgained Notre Dame 481 yards to 331 and was the victim of an apparent officiating mistake at the one-yard line late in the game, deserved to hold on to its No.1 ranking.

Johnson lobbied accordingly, much to the annoyance of Holtz (see box p.80). One of Miami's supporters was that old football fan Richard Nixon, who expressed his opinion in a letter to Johnson. But Holtz had the last laugh in the presidential poll, too. After winning the Fiesta Bowl, the Notre Dame team was invited to the White House by none other than the Gipper, Ronald Reagan.

• • • •

While 1988 found tradition regained on the team front, the rise to prominence of the season's top individual performer was anything but traditional. A junior running back, without fanfare and starting for the first time at an overshadowed school, was the runaway winner of the Heisman Trophy.

Barry Sanders of Oklahoma State had a year many would gladly call a career.

In the only No. 1 vs No. 2 showdown of the season, Notre Dame cornerback **Stan Smagala** runs back an intercepted pass 64 yards for a TD to help the Irish beat Southern Cal, 27-10.

Dlugolecki Photography

Mike Bennett

The Johnson-Holtz Feud

The Notre Dame-Miami rivalry, blazing ever since Jimmy Johnson was accused of running up the score (58–7) in Gerry Faust's last game as Irish coach in 1985, may have lost some of its passion when Johnson left Miami in February to coach the Dallas Cowboys.

The bitterness was demonstrated in Johnson's farewell speech to the Hurricanes when he urged them to beat Notre Dame in their Nov. 25 game in Miami.

What relationship there was between Johnson and Lou Holtz, the present Notre Dame coach, was first strained 13 years ago when Holtz was selected to succeed Frank Broyles at Arkansas. Johnson, Broyles' defensive coordinator, wanted the job. Holtz offered Johnson an opportunity to remain in that capacity, but he declined.

Shortly after Johnson was named head coach at Oklahoma State in 1979, Arkansas terminated a longstanding series with the Cowboys. The schools were at odds over OSU's desire to discontinue playing all or most of the games in Little Rock. But Johnson suspected Holtz forced the issue after OSU signed a quarterback coveted by Arkansas.

Last season, their dislike for each other surfaced after Notre Dame upset Miami, 31–30 in South Bend. Johnson complained that Miami was denied a touchdown by an officiating mistake on a play at the Irish goal line. He lobbied for a rematch in a bowl game and needled Notre Dame for declining.

Holtz bristled. Referring to reporters who suggested Miami was the stronger team, Holtz said, "I am amazed how gullible you guys are when something controversial occurs and you only listen to the guy who complains. There were five controversial calls in that game and four went against Notre Dame. But all you guys write about is the one that went against Miami."

He cited the disallowing of two recoveries by Notre Dame of fumbled receptions that were followed by Miami touchdowns.

When Johnson said, after beating Nebraska in the Orange Bowl, that one bad call against Notre Dame cost Miami the national championship, Holtz replied, "If they had scored, we would have come back and won, because we were the better team."

In just 11 regular season games, he set new NCAA records for rushing (2,628 yards), all-purpose running (3,250 yards) and touchdowns (39). The all-purpose running mark had been the oldest in the NCAA record book, set in 1937 by Colorado's Byron "Whizzer" White, now a Supreme Court justice. Speaking of Byrons—Byron Sanders, Barry's older brother, also made the family proud, rushing for 1,062 yards at Northwestern.

Back to Barry Sanders, who, at 5-8 and 195 pounds, combined uncommon strength and explosive speed. He rushed for over 300 yards four times in 1988 (no major college back ever had done it more than once in a career) and his 234 points amounted to more than were scored by 41 teams in Division I-A.

Sanders won the Heisman easily, beating out the pre-season hype leaders — quarterbacks Peete of Southern California and Troy Aikman of UCLA. In what proved to be his last college game on Dec. 30, Sanders gained 222 yards and scored five touchdowns in the 61–14 slaughter of Wyoming in the Holiday Bowl.

Ignored by most recruiters and confined to reserve duty and kick returns as a freshman and sophomore, Sanders became the first third-year junior to be granted permission to enter the NFL draft. He cited the financial hardship of his parents and Oklahoma State going on NCAA probation as reasons for bypassing his senior season of eligibility. The Detroit Lions selected Sanders as the third overall pick in the draft. Aikman (by Dallas) and Michigan State offensive tackle Tony Mandarich (by Green Bay) were the first two choices.

Of the other major postseason awards; tackle Tracy Rocker of Auburn won both the Outland Trophy and Lombardi Award as the nation's top lineman, while Holtz and West Virginia's Don Nehlen shared Coach of the Year honors.

Prior to the start of the '88 season, few expected Nehlen's Mountaineers to be in the race for the national championship right up to New Year's Day. But after a 6–6 record in 1987, West Virginia had 26 seniors returning—including the entire offensive line—and a favorable schedule.

Led by junior quarterback Major Har-

ris, the Mounties didn't lose a regular season game. They outscored the opposition by an average of 27 points, routed the only two Top 20 opponents they faced—Pittsburgh (31–10) and Syracuse (31–9)—and creamed long-time rival Penn State, 51–30.

West Virginia went to the Fiesta Bowl ranked third with an outside shot at the title. The subsequent loss to Notre Dame dropped the Mountaineers to fifth.

The team that replaced West Virginia at No.3 in the final polls was Florida State. The Seminoles seemed to be everybody's preseason No.1 pick in August, coming off their No.2 finish in 1987. But on Sept. 3, FSU had to open against defending national champion Miami at the Orange Bowl and the Hurricanes won big, 31–0.

Two weeks later at Clemson, coach Bobby Bowden's team needed a 78-yard run off a fake punt and a 19-yard field goal after a touchdown was called back—all in the last minute—to win 24–21. Florida State sailed through its schedule after that, beat Auburn 13–7 in the Sugar Bowl and ended up 11–1.

A 7–6 loss to LSU on Oct. 8 in Baton Rouge was all that separated Auburn

Get Me Rewrite!

Oklahoma State junior Barry Sanders didn't just break the NCAA record book's four principal single season running back records in 1988, he obliterated them.

Rushing Yards
Old: 2,342 yds by Marcus Allen, USC (1981)
New: 2,628 yds by Barry Sanders (1988)
Difference: 286 yds (59 fewer carries)

All-Purpose Yards Per Game
Old: 246.3 ypg by Whizzer White, Colo. (1937)
New: 295.5 ypg by Barry Sanders (1988)
Difference: 49.2 ypg

Touchdowns
Old: 29 by Mike Rozier, Nebraska (1983)
New: 39 by Barry Sanders (1988)
Difference: 10 touchdowns (1 less game)

Points Scored
Old: 174 pts by Mike Rozier, Nebraska (1983)
New: 234 pts by Barry Sanders (1988)
Difference: 60 points (1 less game)

Wide World Photos

Oklahoma State tailback **Barry Sanders**
with Heisman Trophy (inset) and in action against Kansas.

from an undefeated regular season. When both Tiger teams tied for the Southeastern Conference championship, Auburn was selected to defend the honor of the SEC in the Sugar Bowl because of a better overall record and a defense that gave up only 7.2 points a game.

• • • •

Elsewhere, the collegiate landscape was littered with shame in 1988. Six programs—at Oklahoma, Oklahoma State, Texas A&M, Houston, Illinois and Cincinnati—were placed on probation by the NCAA for recruiting violations and other infractions.

Jackie Sherrill, who had guided Texas A&M to three consecutive Cotton Bowl appearances, was pressured to resign in December in the wake of revelations regarding his alleged role in providing hush money to a player being investigated by the NCAA.

And Barry Switzer, the nation's winningest coach, came under fire this past February following a four week period in which three Oklahoma players were charged in a gang rape, a fourth wounded a teammate in a dormitory shooting and a fifth, quarterback Charles Thompson, was arrested for selling cocaine to an undercover FBI agent.

On Feb.5, South Carolina head coach Joe Morrison died of a heart attack at age 51. Morrison was 39–28–2 in six seasons with the Gamecocks and 101–72–7 over 16 years. His program had been the subject of a **Sports Illustrated** article (Oct. 24, 1988) on steroid use by former South Carolina lineman Tommy Chaikin and others.

Back on the field, some perennial winners took it on the chin in 1988. Oklahoma, 33–3 from 1985–87, lost three games **in one season** and was dethroned in the Big Eight by arch-rival Nebraska. Ohio State, which fired Earle Bruce in 1987 for managing only a 6–4–1 record, experienced its first losing season in 21 years under new coach John Cooper. Texas and Tennessee lost more games than they won. And even Joe Paterno suffered through his first losing campaign (5–6) in 23 years at Penn State.

On the brighter side, Columbia won a game for the first time in five years, ending its record Division I losing streak at 44. The lowly Lions beat Princeton 16–13 on Oct. 8 then topped themselves by walloping Brown 31–13 in the final game of the year to escape the Ivy League cellar.

Bo Schembechler won back-to-back bowl games for the first time in 20 years as head coach at Michigan as possibly his best Wolverine team ever beat Southern Cal, 22–14, in the Rose Bowl. And the Army-Navy Game reached absolute parity when the Cadets beat the Middies, 20–15, to even their series at 41–41–7.

• • • •

It was an unsettling year for coaches, particularly at the citadels of the Southeastern Conference. Vince Dooley retired at Georgia after 25 seasons following his 201st victory in the Gator Bowl. After scuttling plans to enter politics, Dooley stayed on as athletic director. Despite speculation that North Carolina State's Dick Sheridan or Ken Hatfield of Arkansas would be moving to Athens, Georgia promoted assistant Ray Goff to succeed Dooley.

Johnny Majors survived an 0–6 start when Tennessee won its last five games. And Bill Curry withstood bad luck, off-field misfortune and alumni grumbling at Alabama to win nine games and the Sun Bowl.

Among those coaches who did not survive were Jack Elway at Stanford, Woody Widenhofer at Missouri, Denny Stoltz at San Diego State, and Stan Parrish, who became the latest to fail at Kansas State.

A surviving coach who was in trouble despite a 10–2 record and an antiseptic reputation with the NCAA (no small consideration in the Southwest Conference) was Arkansas' Hatfield. Hatfield and athletic director Frank Broyles feuded after he rejected Broyles' advice to fire some of his assistant coaches in 1987. Not until the Razorbacks won their first undisputed SWC championship since 1965 was Hatfield's job secure.

Two other coaches made some waves by taking new jobs in the off-season: former Cleveland Browns coach Sam Rutigliano became Rev. Jerry Falwell's choice to lead Liberty College into the big time, and ex-Ohio State coach Earle Bruce left Northern Iowa after one year for Colorado State and a return to Division I-A.

The most stunning move of the year, however, was Jimmy Johnson's decision to leave Miami and replace Tom Landry as coach of the Dallas Cowboys.

Johnson, whose Hurricanes posted a 52–9 record in five years, resigned in February and received a 10-year contract to rebuild a fallen NFL dynasty that had been purchased by his former Arkansas roommate Jerry Jones.

Dennis Erickson left Washington State to replace Johnson and figured he had inherited a national championship contender. But Miami's outlook eroded somewhat when quarterback Steve Walsh, who guided the Hurricanes to No.1 in 1987 and No.2 in '88, followed the example of Erickson's quarterback at Washington State, Timm Rosenbach, and bypassed his senior year to enter the NFL's special supplemental draft.

Tailback Tim Worley of Georgia also chose to bypass his senior year. Worley, Walsh and Rosenbach were all fourth-year juniors.

Finally, there was one other coaching change of note: Rice head coach and athletic director Jerry Berndt resigned after three losing seasons to take the head job at Temple. With Columbia winning in 1988, the Owls ended the season with the longest losing streak (18 games) among Division I schools.

Fred Goldsmith, the defensive coordinator at Arkansas, became the new man in the lifeboat at Rice. Goldsmith took a hopeful approach by pointing out the improvement made in recent years by private institutions and of the many unsung schoolboys who have become major college stars.

Critics said he was dreaming, but the two top stories of 1988 supported his argument. After all, Notre Dame was a private school and who had heard of Barry Sanders a year ago?

Final 1988 AP Top 20 Poll

The sportswriters & broadcasters poll: first place votes in parentheses, records, total points (based on 20 for 1st, 19 for 2nd, etc.) bowl game result, head coach and career record, preseason rank and final regular season rank.

	Final Record	Points	Bowl Game	Head Coach (career record)	Aug.26 Rank	Dec.5 Rank
1 **N.Dame** (58½)	12–0–0	1,198½	Won Fiesta	Lou Holtz (19 yrs: 141–75–5)	13	1
2 **Miami,FL** (1½)	11–1–0	1,141½	Won Orange	Jimmy Johnson (10 yrs: 82–34–2)	8	2
3 **Florida St.**	11–1–0	1,073	Won Sugar	Bobby Bowden (23 yrs: 185–70–3)	1	4
4 **Michigan**	9–2–1	926	Won Rose	Bo Schembechler (26 yrs: 224–63–8)	11	11
5 **West Virginia**	11–1–0	917	Lost Fiesta	Don Nehlen (18 yrs: 122–71–5)	16	3
6 **UCLA**	10–2–0	864	Won Cotton	Terry Donahue (13 yrs: 108–38–7)	5	9
7 **Southern Cal**	10–2–0	803	Lost Rose	Larry Smith (13 yrs: 84–61–3)	6	5
8 **Auburn**	10–2–0	801	Lost Sugar	Pat Dye (15 yrs: 125–46–3)	7	7
9 **Clemson**	10–2–0	708	Won Citrus	Danny Ford (11 yrs: 86–27–4)	4	13
10 **Nebraska**	11–2–0	704	Lost Orange	Tom Osborne (16 yrs: 158–36–2)	2	6
11 **Oklahoma St.**	10–2–0	671	Won Holiday	Pat Jones (5 yrs: 44–15–0)	24	12
12 **Arkansas**	10–2–0	489	Lost Cotton	Ken Hatfield (10 yrs: 71–47–2)	25	8
13 **Syracuse**	10–2–0	469	Won Hall/Fame	Dick MacPherson (15 yrs: 96–65–3)	23	17
14 **Oklahoma**	9–3–0	438	Lost Citrus	Barry Switzer (16 yrs: 157–29–4)	3	10
15 **Georgia**	9–3–0	333	Won Gator	Vince Dooley (25 yrs: 201–77–10)	12	19
16 **Washington St.**	9–3–0	330	Won Aloha	Dennis Erickson (7 yrs: 50–31–1)	—	18
17 **Alabama**	9–3–0	213	Won Sun	Bill Curry (9 yrs: 47–51–4)	14	20
18 **Houston**	9–3–0	147	Lost Aloha	Jack Pardee (2 yrs: 13–9–1)	—	14
19 **LSU**	8–4–0	92	Lost Hall/Fame	Mike Archer (2 yrs: 18–5–1)	18	16
20 **Indiana**	8–3–1	75	Won Liberty	Bill Mallory (19 yrs: 125–83–2)	28	—

Others: 21. **Wyoming** (11–2,58 pts); 22. **N.C.State** (8–3)1,57 pts) 23. **Southern Miss** (10–2,41 pts); 24. **BYU** (9–4,17 pts) 25. **Colorado** (8–4,9 pts); 26. **Fresno St.** (10–2,7 pts) and **Michigan St.** (6–5)1,7 pts); 28. **Army** (9–3,4 pts); 29. **UTEP** (10–3,3 pts); 30. **Hawaii** (9–3,2 pts); 31. **Louisville** (8–3,1 pt) and **Florida** (7–5,1 pt).

1988–89 Bowl Results

Date	Bowl	Result	Date	Bowl	Result
12/10/88	**California**	Fresno St. 35, W.Mich. 30	1/2/89	**Cotton**	UCLA 17, Arkansas 3
12/23/88	**Indepen**	So.Miss. 38, UTEP 18	1/2/89	**Fiesta**	N.Dame 34, West Va. 21
12/24/88	**Sun**	Alabama 29, Army 28	1/2/89	**Fla.Citrus**	Clemson 13, Oklahoma 6
12/25/88	**Aloha**	Wash.St. 24, Houston 22	1/1/89	**Gator**	Georgia 34, Mich.St. 27
12/28/88	**Liberty**	Indiana 34, S.Carolina 10	1/2/89	**Hall/Fame**	Syracuse 23, LSU 10
12/29/88	**All-Amer**	Florida 14, Illinois 10	1/2/89	**Orange**	Miami,FL 23, Nebraska 3
12/29/88	**Freedom**	BYU 20, Colorado 17	1/2/89	**Rose**	Michigan 22, USC 14
12/30/88	**Holiday**	Okla.St. 62, Wyoming 14	1/2/89	**Sugar**	Florida St. 13, Auburn 7
12/31/88	**Peach**	N.C.State 28, Iowa 23			

35 Top Rivalries

Series records include games through 1988.

Boston College and Holy Cross ended their series after the 1986 season. The Florida–Miami,FL series is on hiatus from 1988 through 1991, but will pick up again in 1992 under an every-other-year format.

	Games	Series Leader		Games	Series Leader
Alabama–Auburn	53	Alabama (30–22–1)	**Kansas–Missouri**	97	Missouri (46–42–9)
Alabama–Tennessee	71	Alabama (37–27–7)	**Lafayette–Lehigh**	129	Lafayette (68–51–10)
Arkansas–Texas	70	Texas (52–18–0)	**LSU–Tulane**	86	LSU (57–22–7)
Army–Navy	89	TIED (41–41–7)			
Auburn–Georgia	92	Auburn (43–42–7)	**Michigan–Michigan St.**	81	Michigan (53–23–5)
			Michigan–Ohio St.	85	Michigan (47–33–5)
Baylor–TCU	95	TCU (46–42–7)	**Minnesota–Wisconsin**	98	Minnesota (53–37–8)
Boston Col–Holy Cross	79	BC (48–31–0)	**Mississippi–Miss. St.**	85	Mississippi (49–30–6)
California–Stanford	91	Stanford (43–37–11)	**Nebraska–Oklahoma**	69	Oklahoma (38–28–3)
Clemson–S. Carolina	86	Clemson (50–32–4)			
Duke–North Carolina	74	N. Carolina (36–34–4)	**N. Carolina–N.C. State**	78	N. Carolina (52–20–6)
			Notre Dame–USC	60	Notre Dame (33–23–4)
Florida–Florida St.	31	Florida (22–8–1)	**Oklahoma–Texas**	83	Texas (47–32–4)
Florida–Miami, FL	49	Florida (25–24–0)	**Oregon–Oregon St.**	92	Oregon (44–38–10)
Florida St.–Miami, FL	32	Miami (19–13–0)	**Penn St.–Pittsburgh**	88	Penn St. (43–41–4)
Georgia–Florida	66	Georgia (42–22–2)			
Georgia–Georgia Tech	83	Georgia (45–33–5)	**Richmond–Wm & Mary**	98	Richmond (47–46–5)
			Tennessee–Vanderbilt	82	Tennessee (51–26–5)
			Texas–Texas A&M	95	Texas (63–27–5)
Harvard–Yale	105	Yale (57–40–8)	**UCLA–USC**	58	USC (33–19–6)
Indiana–Purdue	91	Purdue (56–29–6)	**Washington–Wash. St.**	81	Washington (51–24–6)

1988 Final Conference Standings
NCAA Division I-A

Atlantic Coast Conference

	Conference					Overall				
	W	L	T	PF	PA	W	L	T	PF	PA
Clemson* ...	6	1	0	216	107	9	2	0	329	151
Virginia	5	2	0	162	139	7	4	0	251	244
N.C. State* ..	4	2	1	169	110	7	3	1	284	142
Wake Forest .	4	3	0	173	174	6	4	1	282	238
Maryland ...	4	3	0	190	196	5	6	0	260	304
Duke	3	3	1	204	245	7	3	1	324	324
N.Carolina ..	1	6	0	152	247	1	10	0	217	391
Georgia Tech.	0	7	0	105	153	3	8	0	200	194

Bowls: Clemson (won Fla.Citrus); N.C.State (won Peach).

Big Eight Conference

	Conference					Overall				
	W	L	T	PF	PA	W	L	T	PF	PA
Nebraska* ..	7	0	0	265	92	11	1	0	474	182
Oklahoma* .	6	1	0	235	101	9	2	0	326	147
Okla.St* ...	5	2	0	317	215	9	2	0	522	327
Colorado* ..	4	3	0	181	108	8	3	0	305	176
Iowa St	3	4	0	142	183	5	6	0	195	258
Missouri	2	5	0	164	195	3	7	1	234	330
Kansas	1	6	0	118	319	1	10	0	189	496
Kansas St ...	0	7	0	108	317	0	11	0	171	448

Bowls: Nebraska (lost Orange); Oklahoma (lost Fla.Citrus); Oklahoma St.(won Holiday); Colorado (lost Freedom).

Big Ten Conference

	Conference					Overall				
	W	L	T	PF	PA	W	L	T	PF	PA
Michigan* ...	7	0	1	273	94	8	2	1	339	153
Michigan St* .	6	1	1	219	76	6	4	1	242	143
Iowa*	4	1	3	213	141	6	3	3	313	205
Illinois*	5	2	1	177	140	6	4	1	235	229
Indiana*	5	3	0	257	168	7	3	1	362	225
Purdue	3	5	0	78	221	4	7	0	124	303
Ohio St	2	5	1	157	199	4	6	1	229	283
Northwestern.	2	5	1	137	234	2	8	1	192	350
Minnesota ...	0	6	2	120	182	2	7	2	195	246
Wisconsin ...	1	7	0	72	248	1	10	0	106	314

Bowls: Michigan (won Rose); Michigan St.(lost Gator); Iowa (lost Peach); Illinois (lost All-American); Indiana (won Liberty).

Big West Conference

	Conference					Overall				
	W	L	T	PF	PA	W	L	T	PF	PA
Fresno St* ...	7	0	0	228	52	9	2	0	358	139
CS-Fullerton .	5	2	0	170	96	5	6	0	219	215
Utah St	4	3	0	157	184	4	7	0	215	362
San Jose St ..	4	3	0	205	157	4	8	0	316	334
UNLV	3	4	0	134	187	4	7	0	176	313
L.Beach St ...	3	4	0	157	177	3	9	0	201	385
Pacific	2	5	0	106	165	2	9	0	174	324
N.Mexico St .	0	7	0	79	218	1	10	0	171	377

Bowl: Fresno St.(won California).

Mid-American Conference

	Conference					Overall				
	W	L	T	PF	PA	W	L	T	PF	PA
Western Mich*	7	1	0	249	159	9	2	0	324	202
Eastern Mich .	5	2	1	156	133	6	3	1	173	200
Ball St	5	3	0	200	126	8	3	0	286	170
Central Mich .	5	3	0	205	132	7	4	0	287	176
Ohio Univ ...	4	3	1	153	198	4	6	1	195	288
Toledo	4	4	0	154	141	6	5	0	244	221
Kent St	3	5	0	176	197	5	6	0	256	250
Bowl.Green..	1	6	1	113	206	2	8	1	159	333
Miami,OH ...	0	7	1	126	240	0	10	1	167	361

Bowl: Western Michigan (lost California).

Pacific-10 Conference

	Conference					Overall				
	W	L	T	PF	PA	W	L	T	PF	PA
USC*	8	0	0	289	121	10	1	0	356	162
UCLA*	6	2	0	219	150	9	2	0	375	187
Wash.St* ...	5	3	0	254	241	8	3	0	391	281
Arizona	5	3	0	179	171	7	4	0	279	218
Arizona St ..	3	4	0	103	184	6	5	0	192	277
Washington .	3	5	0	168	169	6	5	0	254	223
Oregon	3	5	0	144	186	6	6	0	296	247
Oregon St ..	2	5	1	163	215	4	6	1	246	280
Stanford....	1	5	2	149	152	3	6	2	238	216
California ...	1	5	1	109	188	5	5	1	243	244

Bowls: Southern Cal (lost Rose); UCLA (won Cotton); Washington St.(won Aloha).

Southeastern Conference (SEC)

	Conference					Overall				
	W	L	T	PF	PA	W	L	T	PF	PA
Auburn*	6	1	0	148	43	10	1	0	331	79
LSU*	6	1	0	132	87	8	3	0	239	181
Georgia* ...	5	2	0	193	125	8	3	0	324	185
Alabama* ..	4	3	0	196	147	8	3	0	288	160
Florida*	4	3	0	99	106	6	5	0	254	175
Mississippi ..	3	4	0	150	160	5	6	0	221	223
Tennessee...	3	4	0	114	171	5	6	0	212	286
Kentucky ...	2	5	0	122	141	5	6	0	217	208
Vanderbilt ..	2	5	0	128	178	3	8	0	202	277
Miss.St	0	7	0	98	222	1	10	0	172	332

Bowls: Auburn (lost Sugar); LSU (lost Hall of Fame); Georgia (won Gator); Alabama (won Sun); Florida (won All-American). **Note:** LSU beat Auburn, 7–6 (Oct.8), but Auburn was chosen to represent the SEC in the Sugar Bowl.

Southwest Athletic Conference (SWC)

	Conference					Overall				
	W	L	T	PF	PA	W	L	T	PF	PA
Arkansas* ...	7	0	0	216	102	10	1	0	346	173
Texas A&M ..	6	1	0	198	104	7	5	0	293	253
Houston* ...	5	2	0	245	150	9	2	0	452	195
Texas Tech .	4	3	0	184	195	5	6	0	328	332
Baylor	2	5	0	98	172	6	5	0	232	196
Texas	2	5	0	159	205	4	7	0	252	304
TCU	2	5	0	98	188	4	7	0	206	286
Rice	0	7	0	107	189	0	11	0	165	358
SMU	–	–	–	–	–	–	–	–	–	–

Bowls: Arkansas (lost Cotton); Houston (lost Aloha). **Note:** Texas A&M was on NCAA probation and ineligible for postseason play, while SMU sat out the second year of a two-year suspension.

Division I-A Standings (Continued)

Western Athletic Conference (WAC)

	Conference					Overall				
	W	L	T	PF	PA	W	L	T	PF	PA
Wyoming* . .	8	0	0	370	153	11	1	0	497	218
UTEP*	6	2	0	273	180	10	2	0	427	237
Hawaii	5	3	0	245	184	9	3	0	383	283
BYU	5	3	0	268	196	8	4	0	401	264
Utah	4	4	0	292	285	6	5	0	399	357
Air Force . . .	3	5	0	298	272	5	7	0	422	392
San Diego St.	3	5	0	175	260	3	8	0	204	384
New Mexico .	1	7	0	85	339	2	10	0	170	518
Colorado St .	1	7	0	124	261	1	10	0	192	348

*Bowls: Wyoming (lost Holiday); UTEP (lost Independence).

Hail, Columbia!

On Oct. 8, 1988, Columbia ended the longest losing streak ever (44 games) in Division I, beating Princeton 16–14.

The all-time bottom five:

No	Seasons	Broken vs	Score
44 Columbia . . .	1983–88	Princeton	16–14
34 Northwestern	1979–82	No. Illinois	31–6
28 Virginia	1958–60	Wm. & Mary	21–6*
28 Kansas St. . . .	1945–48	Arkansas St.	37–6
27 E. Mich	1980–82	Kent St.	9–7

*Note: Virginia ended its streak in opening game of 1961 season.

Major Independents

	W	L	T	PF	PA
Notre Dame*	11	0	0	359	135
West Virginia*	11	0	0	472	174
Florida St*	10	1	0	442	165
Miami,FL*	10	1	0	395	113
Army*	9	2	0	308	197
Southern Miss*	9	2	0	315	266
Syracuse*	9	2	0	318	179
Louisville	8	3	0	261	245
South Carolina*	8	3	0	222	190
Northern Illinois	7	4	0	155	185
Memphis St	6	5	0	226	205
Pittsburgh	6	5	0	300	183
SW Louisiana	6	5	0	296	224
Akron	5	6	0	233	214
Penn St	5	6	0	231	201
Rutgers	5	6	0	273	255
Tulane	5	6	0	251	334
Temple	4	7	0	207	317
Tulsa	4	7	0	254	318
Boston College	3	8	0	237	326
Cincinnati	3	8	0	201	379
East Carolina	3	8	0	281	325
Navy	3	8	0	221	274
Virginia Tech	3	8	0	176	264

*Bowls: Notre Dame (won Fiesta); West Virginia (lost Fiesta); Florida St.(won Sugar); Miami (won Orange); Army (lost Sun); Southern Miss.(won Independence); Syracuse (won Hall of Fame); South Carolina (lost Liberty).

1988 Final Conference Standings
NCAA Division I-AA

Big Sky Conference

	Conference					Overall				
	W	L	T	PF	PA	W	L	T	PF	PA
Idaho*	8	1	0	284	193	10	1	0	347	237
Montana* . .	6	3	0	231	169	8	4	0	307	212
Boise St* . .	5	3	0	212	225	8	3	0	267	252
Nevada-Reno	4	4	0	232	182	7	4	0	323	242
Northern Ariz	4	4	0	211	188	5	5	0	271	224
Weber St . . .	4	4	0	267	235	5	6	0	360	341
Montana St .	4	4	0	227	216	4	7	0	244	374
Eastern Wash	2	6	0	176	232	2	8	1	217	362
Idaho St	0	8	0	97	297	0	11	0	143	424

*Playoff Records: Idaho (2–1,lost Semifinals); Montana (0–1,lost 1st Round); Boise St.(0–1,lost 1st Round).

Colonial League

	Conference					Overall				
	W	L	T	PF	PA	W	L	T	PF	PA
Lafayette . . .	5	0	0	212	147	8	2	1	420	251
Holy Cross . .	3	1	0	113	59	9	2	0	334	182
Lehigh	2	3	0	168	174	6	5	0	351	300
Bucknell	2	3	0	111	149	3	7	0	229	323
Colgate	2	3	0	88	86	2	9	0	169	271
Davidson . . .	0	4	0	46	123	0	10	0	125	274

*Playoffs: league does not play postseason games.
Note: Davidson quit league and dropped from Div.I-AA to Div.III after completion of season.

Gateway Athletic Conference

	Conference					Overall				
	W	L	T	PF	PA	W	L	T	PF	PA
Western Ill.*	6	0	0	162	110	10	2	0	376	216
SW Mo.St . .	4	2	0	171	126	5	5	0	252	200
Indiana St . .	4	2	0	129	94	5	6	0	205	258
No.Iowa . . .	3	3	0	117	121	5	5	0	280	214
Eastern Ill. . .	2	4	0	106	137	5	6	0	204	209
Southern Ill. .	2	4	0	95	133	4	7	0	201	262
Illinois St . . .	0	6	0	75	134	1	10	0	135	272

*Playoff Record: Western Ill.(0–1,lost 1st Round).

Ivy League

	Conference					Overall				
	W	L	T	PF	PA	W	L	T	PF	PA
Pennsylvania	6	1	0	166	95	9	1	0	268	169
Cornell	6	1	0	182	75	7	2	1	234	137
Princeton . . .	4	3	0	157	130	6	4	0	269	208
Dartmouth . .	4	3	0	166	137	5	5	0	209	198
Yale	3	3	1	106	124	3	6	1	131	239
Harvard	2	5	0	131	168	2	8	0	202	272
Columbia . . .	2	5	0	103	177	2	8	0	140	303
Brown	0	6	1	91	196	0	9	1	125	285

*Playoffs: league does not play postseason games.
Note: Cornell beat Penn, 19–6 (Nov.19).

Mid-Eastern Athletic Conference

	Conference					Overall				
	W	L	T	PF	PA	W	L	T	PF	PA
Beth-Cook ..	4	2	0	129	90	5	6	0	241	207
Florida A&M	4	2	0	185	110	6	4	1	300	213
Delaware St.	4	2	0	154	90	5	5	0	235	189
Howard	3	3	0	164	130	7	4	0	357	223
S.Carolina St	3	3	0	123	112	4	7	0	178	277
N.Caro. A&T	2	4	0	87	187	2	9	0	111	357
Morgan St ..	0	6	0	63	158	1	10	0	137	317

*Playoffs: no teams from league were chosen to play.
Note: Bethune-Cookman, a winner over both Florida A&M and Delaware St. during the season, took the league title. Delaware State's 2–0 victory over Florida A&M (Sep.3) was forfeit when both teams were found playing ineligible players.

Ohio Valley Conference

	Conference					Overall				
	W	L	T	PF	PA	W	L	T	PF	PA
Eastern Ky ..	6	0	0	177	72	10	2	0	366	191
Mid. Tenn.St	4	2	0	186	57	7	4	0	294	115
Murray St ..	4	2	0	130	101	4	6	0	206	205
Austin Peay .	2	4	0	45	172	3	8	0	89	348
Morehead St	2	4	0	116	155	3	8	0	188	283
Tennessee St	2	5	0	88	122	3	7	1	167	199
Tenn.Tech . .	1	5	0	55	135	1	10	0	114	291

*Playoff Record: Eastern Ky.(2–1, lost Semifinals).

Southern Conference

	Conference					Overall				
	W	L	T	PF	PA	W	L	T	PF	PA
Marshall* ...	6	1	0	221	143	11	1	0	361	221
Furman* ...	6	1	0	167	84	10	2	0	292	114
Citadel*	5	2	0	180	150	8	4	0	318	286
Appalach.St .	4	3	0	225	140	6	4	1	324	233
Tenn-Chatt ..	3	3	0	111	119	4	7	0	213	220
VMI	1	5	0	107	166	2	9	0	152	298
E.Tenn.St ...	1	6	0	111	256	3	8	0	180	363
W.Carolina .	1	6	0	154	218	2	9	0	219	343

*Playoff Records: Marshall (1–1, lost Quarterfinals); Furman (4–0, won Final); Citadel (0–1, lost 1st Round).
Note: Marshall beat Furman, 24–10 (Oct.8), then Furman beat Marshall, 13–9 (Dec.3), in the playoffs.

Southland Conference

	Conference					Overall				
	W	L	T	PF	PA	W	L	T	PF	PA
N'western St*	6	0	0	195	104	9	2	0	329	193
S.F.Austin St*	5	1	0	118	56	10	2	0	291	111
North Texas*	4	2	0	144	78	8	4	0	330	174
McNeese St .	3	3	0	107	103	6	5	0	196	213
NE Louisiana	2	4	0	87	126	5	6	0	161	214
SW Texas St .	1	5	0	99	162	4	7	0	222	281
S.Houston St	0	6	0	33	154	3	8	0	109	225

*Playoff Records: Northwestern St.(1–1, lost Quarterfinals); S.F. Austin St.(1–1, lost Quarterfinals); North Texas (0–1, lost 1st Round).

Southwestern Athletic Conference

	Conference					Overall				
	W	L	T	PF	PA	W	L	T	PF	PA
Jackson St* .	7	0	0	169	48	8	1	2	226	124
Grambling ..	5	2	0	197	85	7	3	0	269	169
Alabama St .	4	3	0	136	94	7	3	0	176	104
Alcorn St ...	4	3	0	124	87	6	4	0	185	154
Southern-BR .	4	3	0	123	108	6	5	0	173	197
Prairie View .	3	4	0	104	175	5	5	0	137	228
Miss.Valley ..	1	6	0	72	205	3	8	0	156	292
Tex.Southern	0	7	0	61	184	0	11	0	94	321

*Playoff Record: Jackson St.(0–1, lost 1st Round).

Yankee Conference

	Conference					Overall				
	W	L	T	PF	PA	W	L	T	PF	PA
Delaware* ..	.6	2	0	191	120	7	5	0	252	239
UMass*	5	2	0	226	179	8	4	0	343	291
Villanova ...	4	2	0	131	126	5	5	1	209	225
Connecticut .	4	4	0	187	156	7	4	0	298	180
N.Hampshire	4	4	0	246	207	6	5	0	313	257
Maine	3	4	0	175	175	7	4	0	319	229
Boston Univ.	3	5	0	180	215	4	7	0	230	285
Rhode Island	3	5	0	118	178	4	7	0	161	261
Richmond ...	2	6	0	100	198	4	7	0	151	255

*Playoff Records: Delaware (0–1, lost 1st Round); Massachusetts (0–1, lost 1st Round).

I-AA Independents

	W	L	T	PF	PA
Georgia Southern*	10	2	0	409	174
Western Kentucky*	9	3	0	287	179
Liberty	8	3	0	316	180
Nicholls St	7	4	0	215	198
William & Mary	6	4	1	260	230
Towson St	5	5	0	269	244
Arkansas St..........	5	6	0	261	245
James Madison.......	5	6	0	201	209
Louisiana Tech	4	7	0	185	352
Northeastern	4	7	0	269	289
Youngstown St	4	7	0	190	267
Lamar	3	8	0	227	254

*Playoff Records: Georgia Southern (3–1, lost Final); Western Ky. (1–1, lost Quarterfinals).

1988 NCAA Playoffs
Division I-AA

First Round

Idaho 38 . . . . Montana 19
Northwestern St.,LA 22 . . . . Boise St.,ID 13
Furman,SC 21 . . . . Delaware 7
Marshall,WV 7 . . . . North Texas 0
Georgia Southern 38 . . . . Citadel, SC 20
Stephen F.Austin St. 24 . . . . Jackson St.,MS 0
Western Ky. 35 . . . . Western Ill. 32
Eastern Ky. 28 . . . . Massachusetts 17

Quarterfinals

Idaho 38 . . . . Northwestern St. 30
Furman 13 . . . . Marshall 9
Georgia Southern 27 . . . . S.F.Austin St. 6
Eastern Ky. 41 . . . . Western Ky. 24

Semifinals

Furman 38 . . . . Idaho 7
Georgia Southern 21 . . . . Eastern Ky. 17

Championship Game
(at Pocatello, Idaho)

Furman 17 . . . . Georgia Southern 12
(W–L: 13–2) (W–L: 12–3)

1988 NCAA Playoffs

Division II

First Round

North Dakota St. 49 . . . . Augustana,SD 7
Millersville, PA 27 . . . . Indiana,PA 24
Cal St.Sacramento 35 . . . . UC-Davis 14
N.C.Central 31 . . . . Winston-Salem,NC 16
Texas A&I 39 . . . . Mississippi Col. 15
Tennessee-Martin 23 . . . . Butler,IN 6
Portland St.,OR 34 . . . . Bowie St.,MD 17
Jacksonville St.,AL 63 . . . . West Chester,PA 24

Quarterfinals

North Dakota St. 36 . . . . Millersville 26
Cal St.Sacramento 56 . . . . N.C.Central 7
Texas A&I 34 . . . . Tennessee-Martin 0
Portland St. 20 . . . . Jacksonville St. 13

Semifinals

North Dakota St. 42 . . . . Cal St.Sacramento 20
Portland St. 35 . . . . Texas A&I 27

Championship Game
(at Florence, Ala.)

North Dakota St. 35 . . . . Portland St. 21
(W–L: 14–0)   (W–L: 11–3–1)

Division III

Regionals

Cortland St.,NY 32 . . . . Hofstra,NY 27
Ithaca,NY 34 . . . . **OT** . . . . Wagner,NY 31
Ferrum,VA 34 . . . . Rhodes,TN 10
Moravian,PA 17 . . . . Widener,PA 7
Wittenberg,OH 35 . . . **2 OT** . . . . . . Dayton,OH 28
Augustana,IL 25 . . . . Adrian,MI 7
Central Iowa 7 . . . . Concordia,MN 0
Wisconsin-Whitewater 29 . . . . Simpson,IA 27

Quarterfinals

Ithaca 24 . . . . Cortland St. 17
Ferrum 49 . . . . Moravian 28
Augustana 28 . . . . Wittenberg 14
Central Iowa 16 . . . . Wisc-Whitewater 13

Semifinals

Ithaca 62 . . . . Ferrum 28
Central Iowa 23 . . . . . . **2 OT** . . . . Augustana 17

Championship Game
Amos Alonzo Stagg Bowl (at Phenix City, Ala.)

Ithaca 39 . . . . Central Iowa 24
(W–L: 13–1)   (W–L: 11–2)

1988 NAIA Playoffs

Division I

First Round

Moorhead St.,MN 26 . . . . Mesa,CO 16
Adams St.,CO 14 . . . . Emporia St.,KS 10
Pittsburg St.,KS 38 . . . . Northern St.,SD 14
SE Oklahoma St. 21 . . . . **OT** . . . . Central Arkansas 14
Hillsdale,MI 42 . . . . Fairmont St.,WV 7
Carson-Newman,TN 62 . . . . Concord,WV 29
Central St.,OH 24 . . . . Catawba,NC 10
Arkansas-Monticello 20 . . . . Washburn, KS 13

Quarterfinals

Adams St. 38 . . . . SE Oklahoma St. 7
Pittsburg St. 23 . . . . Ark-Monticello 7
Carson-Newman 42 . . . . Moorhead St. 6
Central St. 14 . . . . Hillside 7

Semifinals

Carson-Newman 13 . . . . Central St. 0
Adams St. 13 . . . . Pittsburg St 10

Championship Game
(at Jefferson City, Tenn.)

Carson-Newman 56 . . . . Adams St. 21
(W–L: 12–2)   (W–L: 10–3–1)

Division II

First Round

Bluffton,OH 30 . . . . Cumberland,KY 14
Westminster,PA 34 . . . . Austin Col.,TX 12
Northwestern,IA 14 . . . . Sioux Falls,SD 9
Wisconsin-La Crosse 31 . . . . Valley City St.,ND 6
Evangel,MO 45 . . . . Nebraska Wesleyan 14
Bethany,KS 21 . . . . Baker,KS 19
Carroll,MT 28 . . . . Central Washington 7
Oregon Tech 56 . . . . Pacific Lutheran,WA 35

Quarterfinals

Westminster 40 . . . . Bluffton 7
Evangel 22 . . . . Bethany 10
Wisc.-La Crosse 45 . . . . Northwestern 33
Oregon Tech 70 . . . . Carroll 35

Semifinals

Westminster 26 . . . . Evangel 9
Wisc.-La Crosse 37 . . . . Oregon Tech 24

Championship Game
(at New Wilmington, Pa.)

Westminster 21 . . . . Wisc.-La Crosse 14
(W–L: 13–0)   (W–L: 11–3)

1988 Heisman Trophy

Presented since 1935 by the Downtown Athletic Club of New York City and named after former college coach and DAC athletic director John W.Heisman. Voting done by 1,050 members of national media. Each ballot allows for three names (points based on 3 for 1st, 2 for 2nd and 1 for 3rd).

Top 10 Vote-Getters

	Yr	Pos	Points
1 Barry Sanders, Oklahoma St . .	Jr.	RB	1,878
2 Rodney Peete, Southern Cal . . .	Sr.	QB	912
3 Troy Aikman, UCLA	Sr.	QB	582
4 Steve Walsh, Miami,FL	Jr.	QB	341
5 Major Harris, West Va	Jr.	QB	280
6 Tony Mandarich, Mich.St	Sr.	OT	52
7 Timm Rosenbach, Wash.St	Jr.	QB	44
8 Deion Sanders, Florida St	Sr.	DB	22
9 Anthony Thompson, Indiana . . .	Jr.	RB	21
10 Derrick Thomas, Alabama	Sr.	LB	20

1st place votes: B.Sanders (559), Peete (70), Aikman (31), Walsh (16), Harris (27), Mandarich (3), Rosenbach (6), D.Sanders (none), Thompson (none), D.Thomas (3).

1989 NFL College Draft

First Round Picks

First round picks at the 59th annual NFL Draft held Sunday, April 23, 1989 in New York City.

NFL Team	Selection
1 Dallas	**Troy Aikman**, QB, UCLA
2 Green Bay .	**Tony Mandarich**, T, Michigan St.
3 Detroit . . .	**Barry Sanders**, RB, Oklahoma St.
4 Kansas City	**Derrick Thomas**, LB, Alabama
5 Atlanta. . . .	**Deion Sanders**, DB, Florida St.
6 Tampa Bay .	**Broderick Thomas**, LB, Nebraska
7 Pittsburgh . .	**Tim Worley**, RB, Georgia
8 San Diego .	**Burt Grossman**, DE, Pittsburgh
9 Miami	**Sammie Smith**, RB, Florida St.
10 Phoenix . .	**Eric Hill**, LB, LSU
11 Chicago* . .	**Donnell Woolford**, DB, Clemson
12 Chicago* . .	**Trace Armstrong**, DE, Florida
13 Cleveland* .	**Eric Metcalf**, RB, Texas
14 N.Y.Jets . .	**Jeff Lageman**, LB, Virginia
15 Seattle* . . .	**Andy Heck**, T, Notre Dame
16 New Eng. .	**Hart Lee Dykes**, WR, Oklahoma St.
17 Phoenix* . .	**Joe Wolf**, G, Boston College
18 N.Y.Giants .	**Brian Williams**, G, Minnesota
19 New Orl. . .	**Wayne Martin**, DE, Arkansas
20 Denver* . . .	**Steve Atwater**, DB, Arkansas
21 L.A.Rams . .	**Bill Hawkins**, DE, Miami, FL
22 Ind'polis* . .	**Andre Rison**, WR, Michigan St.
23 Houston . . .	**David Williams**, T, Florida
24 Pittsburgh* .	**Tom Ricketts**, T, Pittsburgh
25 Miami* . . .	**Louis Oliver**, DB, Florida
26 L.A.Rams* .	**Cleveland Gary**, RB, Miami,FL
27 Atlanta* . . .	**Shawn Collins**, WR, No.Arizona
28 San Fran . .	**Keith DeLong**, LB, Tennessee

*Note: the following No.1 picks were traded away—**#11** by the L.A.Raiders; **#12** by Washington; **#13** by Denver; **#15** by Indianapolis; **#17** by Seattle; **#20** by Cleveland; **#22** by Philadelphia; **#24** by Minnesota; **#25** by Chicago; **#26** by Buffalo; **#27** by Cincinnati.

Other Major Award Winners

Offensive Players of the Year

Maxwell Award (Top Player) . . . . . Barry Sanders
Camp Award (Top Back) . . . . Barry Sanders
O'Brien Award (Top QB) . . . . Troy Aikman
UPI Lineman of Year . . . . Tony Mandarich
Payton Award (Div.I-AA Top Player)
David Meggett,Towson St., RB
Hill Trophy (Div.II Top Player)
Johnny Bailey, Texas A&I, RB

Defensive Players of the Year

Rockne Award (Top Lineman)
Tracy Rocker, Auburn
Lombardi Award (Top Lineman) . . . . Tracy Rocker
Outland Trophy (Interior Lineman) . . Tracy Rocker
Butkus Award (Top LB) . . . . Derrick Thomas
Thorpe Award (Top DB) . . . . Deion Sanders

Coaches of the Year

FWAA	Div.I-A	Lou Holtz, Notre Dame
AFCA	Div.I-A	Don Nehlen, West Virginia
	Div.I-AA	Jimmy Satterfield, Furman
	Div.II	Rocky Hager, N.Dakota St.
	Div.III	Jim Butterfield, Ithaca

"Coaches Choice" Players of the Year
(Chosen by AFCA)

NCAA	Div.I-A	Barry Sanders
NCAA	Div.I-AA	Mike Barber, Marshall, WR
College	Div.I	Johnny Bailey, Texas A&I, RB
College	Div.II	Terry Underwood, Wagner, RB

1988 Consensus All-America Team

NCAA Division I-A players cited most frequently by the following seven selectors: AFCA, AP, *The Football News*, FWAA, *The Sporting News*, UPI and Walter Camp Foundation.

Offense

	Cl	Hgt	Wgt
WR—**Hart Lee Dykes,** Oklahoma St	Sr.	6-4	220
WR—**Jason Phillips,** Houston	Sr.	5-9	175
TE—**Marv Cook,** Iowa	Sr.	6-4	232
L—**Andy Heck,** Notre Dame	Sr.	6-7	277
L—**Tony Mandarich,** Michigan St . .	Sr.	6-6	315
L—**Anthony Phillips,** Oklahoma . .	Sr.	6-3	286
L—**Mark Stepnoski,** Pittsburgh . . .	Sr.	6-3	265
L—**Mike Utley,** Washington St . . .	Sr.	6-6	290
QB—**Troy Aikman,** UCLA	Sr.	6-3	217
RB—**Barry Sanders,** Oklahoma St. .	Jr.	5-8	195
RB—**Anthony Thompson,** Indiana .	Jr.	6-0	205
K—**Kendall Trainor,** Arkansas	Sr.	6-2	205

Defense

	Cl	Hgt	Wgt
L—**Wayne Martin,** Arkansas	Sr.	6-3	270
L—**Mark Messner,** Michigan	Sr.	6-3	244
L—**Tracy Rocker,** Auburn.	Sr.	6-3	278
L—**Frank Stams,** Notre Dame	Sr.	6-4	237
LB—**Keith DeLong,** Tennessee	Sr.	6-2	220
LB—**Mike Stonebreaker,** N.Dame . .	Sr.	6-1	226
LB—**Broderick Thomas,** Nebraska . .	Sr.	6-3	235
LB—**Derrick Thomas,** Alabama . . .	Sr.	6-4	230
B—**Darryl Henley,** UCLA.	Sr.	5-10	165
B—**Markus Paul,** Syracuse	Sr.	6-2	200
B—**Deion Sanders,** Florida St	Sr.	6-1	195
B—**Donnell Woolford,** Clemson	Sr.	5-10	195
P—**Keith English,** Colorado	Sr.	6-3	215

1988 NCAA Division I-A
Individual Leaders

Total Offense

Player, School	Rushing				Passing		Total Offense				
	Car	Gain	Loss	Net	Att	Yds	Plays	Yds	YdsPP	TDR	YdsPG
Scott Michell, Utah	56	127	150	−23	533	4322	589	4299	7.30	29	390.82
Anthony Dilweg, Duke.....	55	77	188	−111	484	3824	539	3713	6.89	26	337.55
Timm Rosenbach, Wash.St..	115	551	187	+364	302	2791	417	3155	7.57	32	286.82
Brent Snyder, Utah St.....	87	251	327	−76	448	3218	535	3142	5.87	23	285.64
Steve Walsh, Miami,FL	15	18	51	−33	390	3115	405	3082	7.61	29	280.18
Erik Wilhelm, Oregon St...	70	162	132	+30	442	2896	512	2926	5.71	20	266.00
Tony Kimbrough, W.Mich ..	91	293	148	+145	324	2465	415	2610	6.29	24	261.00
Eric Jones, Vanderbilt	144	505	200	+305	360	2548	504	2853	5.66	16	259.36
Chuck Hartlieb, Iowa......	54	58	298	−240	409	3310	463	3070	6.63	15	255.83
Randy Welniak, Wyoming..	136	661	243	+418	324	2627	460	3045	6.62	35	253.75

All Purpose Runners

Player, School	Gm	Rush	Rec	PR	KOR	Total Yards	YdsPG
Barry Sanders, Oklahoma St	11	2628	106	95	421	3250	295.45
Johnny Johnson, San Jose St....	12	1219	668	0	315	2202	183.50
Eric Wilkerson, Kent St	11	1325	73	0	502	1900	172.73
Tony Boles, Michigan...........	10	1359	64	0	302	1725	172.50
Kendal Smith, Utah St	11	25	1196	141	525	1887	171.55
Michael Pierce, Tulane	10	345	534	0	765	1644	164.40
Andrew Greer, Ohio Univ	11	863	114	0	810	1787	162.45
Anthony Thompson, Indiana	11	1546	219	0	0	1765	160.45
Eric Metcalf, Texas	10	932	333	192	117	1574	157.40
Darren Lewis, Texas A&M	11	1692	13	0	0	1705	155.00

Passing Efficiency
(At least 15 attempts per game)

Player, School	Gm	Att	Cmp	Cmp Pct	Int	Int Pct	Yds	Yds/ Att	TD	TD Pct	Rating Points
Timm Rosenbach, Wash.St...	11	302	199	65.89	10	3.31	2791	9.24	23	7.62	162.0
Mike Gundy, Oklahoma St ...	11	236	153	64.83	12	5.04	2163	9.37	19	7.98	158.2
Chip Ferguson, Florida St	10	194	122	62.89	11	5.67	1714	8.84	16	8.25	153.0
Troy Aikman, UCLA...........	11	327	209	63.91	8	2.45	2599	7.95	23	7.03	149.0
Todd Philcox, Syracuse	11	234	141	60.26	11	4.70	2076	8.87	16	6.84	147.9
Steve Walsh, Miami,FL	11	390	233	59.74	12	3.08	3115	7.99	29	7.44	145.2
Warren Jones, Hawaii.........	12	259	138	53.28	11	4.25	2268	8.76	19	7.34	142.6
Scott Mitchell, Utah	11	533	323	60.60	15	2.81	4322	8.11	29	5.44	141.0
Randy Welniak, Wyoming.....	12	324	184	56.79	9	2.78	2627	8.11	21	6.48	140.7
Rodney Peete, Southern Cal ...	11	338	208	61.54	10	2.96	2654	7.85	18	5.33	139.2

Abbreviation Key

Att—Attempted Passes; **Avg**—Average; **C**—Catches; **Car**—Carries; **Cl**—Class; **Cmp**—Completions; **CPG**—Catches Per Game; **FG**—Field Goals; **FGA**—Field Goal Attempts; **FGPG**—Field Goals Per Game; **Gain**—Yards Gained; **Gm**—Games; **Int**—Interceptions; **IPG**—Interceptions Per Game; **KOR**—Kickoff Return Yards; **Loss**—Yards Lost; **Net**—Yards Gained minus Yards Lost; **No**—Number; **Pct**—Percentage; **Plays**—Plays from Scrimmage; **PR**—Punt Return Yards; **Pts**—Points; **PtsPG**—points Per Game; **Rec**—Receiving Yards; **Rush**—Rushing Yards; **TD**—Touchdowns; **TDR**—Touchdowns Responsible For; **XP**—Extra Points; **Yds**-Yards; **Yds/Att**—Yards Per Attempt; **YdsPG**—Yards Per Game.

Scoring

Non-Kickers

Player, School	Gm	TD	Pts	PtsPG
Barry Sanders, Okla.St.....	11	39	234	21.27
Anthony Thompson, Ind ...	11	24	144	13.09
Tim Worley, Georgia	11	18	108	9.82
Johnny Johnson, S.Jose St .	12	19	116*	9.67
Greg Johnson, Air Force ...	12	17	106*	8.83

*Note: J.Johnson had also had 2 Extra Points and G.Johnson had 4 Extra Points.

Kickers

Player, School	Gm	FG	XP	Pts	PtsPG
Chris Jacke, UTEP	12	48	25	123	10.25
Charlie Baumann, W.Va ...	11	58	18	112	10.18
Roman Anderson, Houston	11	51	19	108	9.82
Carlos Huerta, Miami,FL ..	11	44	21	107	9.73
Kendall Trainor, Ark	11	30	24	102	9.27

Rushing

Player, School	Car	Yds	TD	YdsPG
Barry Sanders, Okla.St. ...	344	2628	39	238.91
Darren Lewis, Texas A&M ..	306	1692	7	153.82
Anthony Thompson, Ind ...	329	1546	24	140.55
Tony Boles, Michigan	248	1359	9	135.90
Ken Clark, Nebraska	232	1497	12	124.75
Eric Bieniemy, Colorado ...	219	1243	10	124.30
Blake Ezor, Michigan St ...	290	1358	10	123.45
Eric Wilkerson, Kent St	247	1325	14	120.45
Steve Broussard, Wash.St..	189	1141	11	114.10
Don Riley, Central Mich ...	215	1238	7	112.55

Receiving

Player, School	C	Yds	TD	CPG
Jason Phillips, Houston	108	1444	15	9.82
James Dixon, Houston	102	1103	11	9.27
Boo Mitchell, Vanderbilt ...	78	1213	5	7.09
Hart Lee Dykes, Okla.St ...	74	1278	14	6.73
Roger Boone, Duke	73	630	2	6.64
Tom Waddle, Boston Col..	70	902	5	6.36
Greg Washington, Kan.St..	69	928	9	6.27
Clarkston Hines, Duke	68	1067	10	6.18
Marv Cook, Iowa	55	645	3	6.11
Kevin Evans, San Jose St ..	61	887	4	6.10

Field Goals

Player, School	FGA	FG	Pct	FGPG
Kendall Trainor, Ark.......	27	24	.889	2.18
Chris Jacke, UTEP	27	25	.926	2.08
Rob Keen, California	25	21	.840	1.91
Carlos Huerta, Miami,FL...	27	21	.778	1.91
David Browndyke, LSU	23	19	.826	1.73
John Hopkins, Stanford	24	19	.792	1.73
Roman Anderson, Houston .	25	19	.760	1.73
Philip Doyle, Alabama.....	31	19	.613	1.73
Kenny Stucker, Ball St	23	18	.783	1.64
Pat O'Morrow, Ohio St	23	18	.783	1.64

Interceptions

Player, School	Int	Yds	TD	IPG
Kurt Larson, Michigan St......	8	78	1	.73
Andy Logan, Kent St.........	8	54	0	.73
Todd Sandroni, Mississippi	7	33	1	.70
Greg Jackson, LSU	7	221	2	.64
Eddie Moore, Memphis St.....	7	51	0	.64
Tony McCorvey, Bowl.Green ...	7	33	0	.64

Punting
(At least 3.6 punts per game)

Player, School	No	Avg
Keith English, Colorado	51	45.04
Pat Thompson, BYU	49	44.80
Ken Elmore, Tennessee	41	44.34
Tony Rhynes, UNLV	66	44.02
Martin Bailey, Wake Forest	46	43.74

Punt Returns

Player, School	No	Yds	TD	Avg
Deion Sanders, Florida St ..	33	503	1	15.24
Marcus Cherry, Boston Col .	15	206	1	13.73
James Henry, S.Miss	23	309	1	13.43
Ricky Watters, N.Dame....	19	253	2	13.32
Darryl Henley, UCLA......	21	279	2	13.29

Kickoff Returns

Player, School	No	Yds	TD	Avg
Raghib Ismail, N.Dame......	12	433	2	36.08
Chris Oldham, Oregon	26	764	1	29.38
E.Mortensen, BYU	14	398	1	28.43
Carlos Snow, Ohio St	19	513	1	27.00
Larry Khan-Smith, Hawaii	32	852	1	26.63

1988 NCAA Division I-A Team Leaders

Scoring Offense

	Gm	W–L–T	Pts	Avg
Oklahoma St 11		9 – 2 – 0	522	47.5
West Virginia 11		11 – 0 – 0	472	42.9
Wyoming 12		11 – 1 – 0	497	41.4
Houston 11		9 – 2 – 0	452	41.1
Florida St 11		10 – 1 – 0	442	40.2
Nebraska 12		11 – 1 – 0	474	39.5
Utah 11		6 – 5 – 0	399	36.3
Miami,FL 11		10 – 1 – 0	395	35.9
UTEP 12		10 – 2 – 0	427	35.6
Washington St 11		8 – 3 – 0	391	35.5

Scoring Defense

	Gm	W–L–T	Pts	Avg
Auburn 11		10 – 1 – 0	79	7.2
Miami,FL 11		10 – 1 – 0	113	10.3
Notre Dame............11		11 – 0 – 0	135	12.3
Fresno St 11		9 – 2 – 0	139	12.6
North Carolina St 11		7 – 3 – 1	142	12.9
Michigan St 11		6 – 4 – 1	143	13.0
Oklahoma 11		9 – 2 – 0	147	13.4
Clemson 11		9 – 2 – 0	151	13.7
Michigan 11		8 – 2 – 1	153	13.9
Alabama 11		8 – 3 – 0	160	14.5

Total Offense

	Gm	Plays	Yds	Avg	TD	YdsPG
Utah	11	901	5795	6.4	48	526.82
Oklahoma St...	11	803	5667	7.1	66	515.18
Washington St..	11	854	5439	6.4	49	494.45
Houston	11	832	5331	6.4	55	484.64
West Virginia .	11	816	5310	6.5	56	482.73
Wyoming	12	922	5741	6.2	62	478.42
Nebraska	12	898	5735	6.4	59	477.92
Duke	11	868	5111	5.9	39	464.64
Southern Cal...	11	911	5077	5.6	45	461.55
BYU	12	909	5483	6.0	47	456.92

Total Defense

	Gm	Plays	Yds	Avg	TD	YdsPG
Auburn	11	666	2399	3.6	9	218.1
Miami,FL.....	11	726	2662	3.7	11	242.0
Florida	11	710	2726	3.8	18	247.8
Pittsburgh	11	697	2796	4.0	20	254.2
Baylor	11	686	2835	4.1	24	257.7
Ball St	11	664	2887	4.3	18	262.5
Nebraska	12	743	3153	4.2	20	262.8
N.C.State	11	783	2907	3.7	11	264.3
Fresno St	1	738	2909	3.9	17	264.5
Southern Cal...	11	655	2958	4.5	19	268.9

National Champions, 1924–88

"Who's Number One?" Two of the primary selectors since 1924 have been the Dickinson mathematical system (1924–40) and the Associated Press sportswriters and broadcasters poll (1936–present).

The Dickinson ratings were developed by late Illinois economics professor Frank Dickinson. The writers' poll was started by AP sports editor Alan Gould. AP was joined in wire service ratings by the United Press (now UPI) coaches' poll in 1950.

Dickinson and AP agreed on their selections the five years their ratings overlapped. AP and UPI, however, have chosen different champions seven times (1954, '57, '65, '70, '73, '74, and '78).

Year	Champion	Record	Bowl Game	Head Coach	Outstanding Player
1924	Notre Dame	10–0–0	Won Rose	Knute Rockne	"The Four Horsemen"*
1925	Dartmouth	10–0–0	No bowl	Jesse Hawley	Swede Oberlander, HB
1926	Stanford	10–0–1	Tied Rose	Pop Warner	Ted Shipkey, E
1927	Illinois	7–0–1	No bowl	Bob Zuppke	Russ Crane, G
1928	Southern Cal	9–0–1	No bowl	Howard Jones	Jesse Hibbs, T–K
1929	Notre Dame	9–0–0	No bowl	Knute Rockne	Frank Carideo, QB
1930	Notre Dame	10–0–0	No bowl	Knute Rockne	Marchy Schwartz, HB
1931	Southern Cal	10–1–0	Won Rose	Howard Jones	Erny Pinckert, HB
1932	Michigan	8–0–0	No bowl	Harry Kipke	Harry Newman, QB
1933	Michigan	7–0–1	No bowl	Harry Kipke	Frank Wistert, T
1934	Minnesota	8–0–0	No bowl	Bernie Bierman	Pug Lund, HB–P
1935	SMU	12–1–0	Lost Rose	Matty Bell	Bobby Wilson, HB
1936	Minnesota	7–1–0	No bowl	Bernie Bierman	Ed Widseth, T
1937	Pittsburgh	9–0–1	No bowl	Jock Sutherland	Marshall Goldberg, HB
1938	TCU	11–0–0	Won Sugar	Dutch Meyer	Davey O'Brien, QB
1939	Texas A&M	11–0–0	Won Sugar	Homer Norton	John Kimbrough, FB
1940	Minnesota	8–0–0	No Bowl	Bernie Bierman	George Franck, FB
1941	Minnesota	8–0–0	No bowl	Bernie Bierman	Bruce Smith, HB
1942	Ohio St.	9–1–0	No bowl	Paul Brown	Gene Fekete, FB
1943	Notre Dame	9–1–0	No bowl	Frank Leahy	Angelo Bertelli, QB
1944	Army	9–0–0	No bowl	Red Blaik	Glenn Davis, HB
1945	Army	9–0–0	No bowl	Red Blaik	Doc Blanchard, FB
1946	Notre Dame	8–0–1	No bowl	Frank Leahy	Johnny Lujack, QB
1947	Notre Dame	9–0–0	No bowl	Frank Leahy	Johnny Lujack, QB
1948	Michigan	9–0–0	No bowl	Bennie Oosterbaan	Dick Rifenburg, E
1949	Notre Dame	10–0–0	No bowl	Frank Leahy	Leon Hart, E
1950	Oklahoma	10–1–0	Lost Sugar	Bud Wilkinson	Leon Heath, FB
1951	Tennessee	10–0–0	Lost Sugar	Bob Neyland	Hank Lauricella, QB
1952	Michigan St.	9–0–0	No bowl	Biggie Munn	Don McAuliffe, HB
1953	Maryland	10–1–0	Lost Orange	Jim Tatum	Bernie Faloney, QB
1954	Ohio St.	10–0–0	Won Rose	Woody Hayes	Howard Cassady, HB
	UCLA (UPI)	9–0–0	No bowl	Red Sanders	Bob Davenport, FB
1955	Oklahoma	11–0–0	Won Orange	Bud Wilkinson	Jerry Tubbs, C
1956	Oklahoma	10–0–0	No bowl	Bud Wilkinson	Tommy McDonald, HB
1957	Auburn	10–0–0	No bowl	Shug Jordan	Jimmy Phillips, E
	Ohio St. (UPI)	9–1–0	Won Rose	Woody Hayes	Bob White, FB
1958	LSU	11–0–0	Won Sugar	Paul Dietzel	Billy Cannon, HB
1959	Syracuse	11–0–0	Won Cotton	Ben Schwartzwalder	Ernie Davis, HB
1960	Minnesota	8–2–0	Lost Rose	Murray Warmath	Tom Brown, G
1961	Alabama	11–0–0	Won Sugar	Bear Bryant	Billy Neighbors, T
1962	Southern Cal	11–0–0	Won Rose	John McKay	Hal Bedsole, E
1963	Texas	11–0–0	Won Cotton	Darrell Royal	Scott Appleton, T
1964	Alabama	10–1–0	Lost Orange	Bear Bryant	Joe Namath, QB
1965	Alabama	9–1–1	Won Orange	Bear Bryant	Paul Crane, C
	Mich. St. (UPI)	10–1–0	Lost Rose	Duffy Daugherty	George Webster, DB
1966	Notre Dame	9–0–1	No bowl	Ara Parseghian	Jim Lynch, LB
1967	Southern Cal	10–1–0	Won Rose	John McKay	O.J. Simpson, HB
1968	Ohio St.	10–0–0	Won Rose	Woody Hayes	Rex Kern, QB
1969	Texas	11–0–0	Won Cotton	Darrell Royal	James Street, QB
1970	Nebraska	11–0–1	Won Orange	Bob Devaney	Jerry Tagge, QB
	Texas (UPI)	10–1–0	Lost Cotton	Darrell Royal	Steve Worster, RB
1971	Nebraska	13–0–0	Won Orange	Bob Devaney	Johnny Rodgers, WR
1972	Southern Cal	12–0–0	Won Rose	John McKay	Anthony Davis, RB
1973	Notre Dame	11–0–0	Won Sugar	Ara Parseghian	Mike Townsend, DB
	Alabama (UPI)	11–1–0	Lost Sugar	Bear Bryant	Buddy Brown, OT

National Champions, 1924–88 (Continued)

Year	Champion	Record	Bowl Game	Head Coach	Outstanding Player
1974	Oklahoma	11-0-0	No bowl		
	Southern Cal (UPI)	10-1-1	Won Rose	Barry Switzer	Joe Washington, RB
1975	Oklahoma	11-1-0	Won Orange	John McKay	Anthony Davis, RB
1976	Pittsburgh	12-0-0	Won Sugar	Barry Switzer	Lee Roy Selmon, DT
1977	Notre Dame	11-1-0	Won Cotton	Johnny Majors	Tony Dorsett, RB
1978	Alabama	11-1-0	Won Sugar	Dan Devine	Ross Browner, DE
	Southern Cal (UPI)	12-1-0	Won Rose	Bear Bryant	Marty Lyons, DT
1979	Alabama	12-0-0	Won Sugar	John Robinson	Charles White, RB
				Bear Bryant	Steadman Shealy, QB
1980	Georgia	12-0-0	Won Sugar	Vince Dooley	Herschel Walker, RB
1981	Clemson	12-0-0	Won Orange	Danny Ford	Jeff Davis, LB
1982	Penn St.	11-1-0	Won Sugar	Joe Paterno	Todd Blackledge, QB
1983	Miami, FL	11-1-0	Won Orange	H. Schnellenberger	Bernie Kosar, QB
1984	BYU	13-0-0	Won Holiday	LaVell Edwards	Robbie Bosco, QB
1985	Oklahoma	11-1-0	Won Orange	Barry Switzer	Brian Bosworth, LB
1986	Penn St.	12-0-0	Won Fiesta	Joe Paterno	D.J. Dozier, RB
1987	Miami, FL	12-0-0	Won Orange	Jimmy Johnson	Steve Walsh, QB
1988	Notre Dame	12-0-0	Won Fiesta	Lou Holtz	Tony Rice, QB

*Notre Dame's **Four Horsemen** were Harry Stuhldreher (QB), Jim Crowley (HB), Don Miller (HB–P) and Elmer Layden (FB).
Note: The Dickinson system based its selection solely on regular season results.
  AP took its final vote following the regular season from 1936–64 and from 1966–67. In 1965 and ever since 1968, AP has voted after the bowl games.
  UPI named its choice after the bowls beginning in 1974.

Number 1 vs Number 2

Since the Associated Press writers poll started keeping track of such things in 1936, the No.1 and No.2 ranked teams in the country have met 24 times through 1988; 16 times during the regular season and eight times in bowl games. Notre Dame has been involved in seven of these games, one more than Oklahoma.
  Stadiums in capital LETTERS denote postseason bowl games.

Date	Match–up		Stadium
10/9/43	#1Notre Dame (2–0)	35	Michigan
	#2Michigan (3–0)	12	(Ann Arbor)
11/20/43	#1Notre Dame (8–0)	14	Notre Dame
	#2Iowa Pre-Flight (8–0)	13	(South Bend)
12/2/44	#1Army (8–0)	23	Municipal
	#2Navy (6–2)	7	(Baltimore)
11/10/45	#1Army (6–0)	48	Yankee
	#2Notre Dame (5–0–1)	0	(New York)
12/1/45	#1Army (8–0)	32	Municipal
	#2Navy (7–0–1)	13	(Phila.)
11/9/46	#1Army (7–0)	0	Yankee
	#2Notre Dame (5–0)	0	(New York)

• • • •

Date	Match–up		Stadium
1/1/63	#1USC (10–0)	42	ROSE BOWL
	#2Wisconsin (8–1)	37	(Pasadena)
10/12/63	#2Texas (3–0)	28	Cotton Bowl
	#1Oklahoma (2–0)	7	(Dallas)
1/1/64	#1Texas (10–0)	28	COTTON BOWL
	#2Navy (9–1)	6	(Dallas)
11/19/66	#1Notre Dame (8–0)	10	Spartan
	#2Michigan St. (9–0)	10	(E. Lansing)
9/28/68	#1Purdue (1–0)	37	Notre Dame
	#2Notre Dame (1–0)	22	(South Bend)
1/1/69	#1Ohio St. (9–0)	27	ROSE BOWL
	#2USC (9–0–1)	16	(Pasadena)
12/6/69	#1Texas (9–0)	15	Razorback
	#2Arkansas (9–0)	14	(Fayetteville)

Date	Match–up		Stadium
11/25/71	#1Nebraska (10–0)	35	Owen Field
	#2Oklahoma (9–0)	31	(Norman)
1/1/72	#1Nebraska (12–0)	38	ORANGE BOWL
	#2Alabama (11–0)	6	(Miami)
1/1/79	#2Alabama (10–1)	14	SUGAR BOWL
	#1Penn St. (11–0)	7	(New Orleans)

• • • •

Date	Match–up		Stadium
9/26/81	#1USC (2–0)	28	Coliseum
	#2Oklahoma (1–0)	24	(Los Angeles)
1/1/83	#2Penn St. (10–1)	27	SUGAR BOWL
	#1Georgia (11–0)	23	(New Orleans)
10/19/85	#1Iowa (5–0)	12	Kinnick
	#2Michigan (5–0)	10	(Iowa City)
9/27/86	#2Miami, FL (3–0)	28	Orange Bowl
	#1Oklahoma (2–0)	16	(Miami)
1/2/87	#2Penn St. (11–0)	14	FIESTA BOWL
	#1Miami, FL (11–0)	10	(Tempe)
11/21/87	#2Oklahoma (10–0)	17	Memorial
	#1Nebraska (10–0)	7	(Lincoln)
1/1/88	#2Miami, FL (11–0)	20	ORANGE BOWL
	#1Oklahoma (11–0)	14	(Miami)
11/26/88	#1Notre Dame (10–0)	27	Coliseum
	#2USC (10–0)	10	(Los Angeles)

Bowl Results, 1902–Jan,1989

Rose Bowl

City: Pasadena, CA; **Stadium:** Rose Bowl; **Capacity:** 104,091; **Playing surface:** grass; **Automatic berths:** Pac-10 champion vs Big 10 champion (since 1947).

First year: 1902; **Playing sites:** Tournament Park (1902, 1916–22), Rose Bowl (1923–41), Duke Stadium, Durham, NC (1942); Rose Bowl (1943–present).

Year	Result	Year	Result	Year	Result
1902*	Michigan 49, Stanford 0	1940	USC 14, Tennessee 0	1965	Michigan 34, Oregon St. 7
1916	Washington St. 14, Brown 0	1941	Stanford 21, Nebraska 13	1966	UCLA 14, Michigan St. 12
1917	Oregon 14, Penn 0	1942	Oregon St. 20, Duke 16	1967	Purdue 14, USC 13
1918	Mare Island 19, Camp Lewis 7	1943	Georgia 9, UCLA 0	1968	USC 14, Indiana 3
1919	Great Lakes 17, Mare Is. 0	1944	USC 29, Washington 0	1969	Ohio St. 27, USC 16
		1945	USC 25, Tennessee 0		
1920	Harvard 7, Oregon 6	1946	Alabama 34, USC 14	1970	USC 10, Michigan 3
1921	California 28, Ohio St. 0	1947	Illinois 45, UCLA 14	1971	Stanford 27, Ohio St. 17
1922	0–0, Calif. vs Wash.& Jeff.	1948	Michigan 49, USC 0	1972	Stanford 13, Michigan 12
1923	USC 14, Penn St. 0	1949	N'western 20, Calif. 14	1973	USC 42, Ohio St. 17
1924	14–14, Navy vs Washington			1974	Ohio St. 42, USC 21
1925	Notre Dame 27, Stanford 10	1950	Ohio St. 17, California 14	1975	USC 18, Ohio St. 17
1926	Alabama 20, Washington 19	1951	Michigan 14, California 6	1976	UCLA 23, Ohio St. 10
1927	7–7, Alabama vs Stanford	1952	Illinois 40, Stanford 7	1977	USC 14, Michigan 6
1928	Stanford 7, Pittsburgh 6	1953	USC 7, Wisconsin 0	1978	Washington 27, Michigan 20
1929	Ga.Tech 8, California 7	1954	Michigan St. 28, UCLA 20	1979	USC 17, Michigan 10
		1955	Ohio St. 20, USC 7		
1930	USC 47, Pittsburgh 14	1956	Michigan St. 17, UCLA 14	1980	USC 17, Ohio St. 16
1931	Alabama 24, Wash.St. 0	1957	Iowa 35, Oregon St. 19	1981	Michigan 23, Washington 6
1932	USC 21, Tulane 12	1958	Ohio St. 10, Oregon 7	1982	Washington 28, Iowa 0
1933	USC 35, Pittsburgh 0	1959	Iowa 38, California 12	1983	UCLA 24, Michigan 14
1934	Columbia 7, Stanford 0			1984	UCLA 45, Illinois 9
1935	Alabama 29, Stanford 13	1960	Washington 44, Wisconsin 8	1985	USC 20, Ohio St. 17
1936	Stanford 7, SMU 0	1961	Washington 17, Minnesota 7	1986	UCLA 45, Iowa 28
1937	Pitt 21, Washington 0	1962	Minnesota 21, UCLA 3	1987	Arizona St. 22, Michigan 15
1938	California 13, Alabama 0	1963	USC 42, Wisconsin 37	1988	Michigan St. 20, USC 17
1939	USC 7, Duke 3	1964	Illinois 17, Washington 7	1989	Michigan 22, USC 14

*January game from 1902–present.

Orange Bowl

City: Miami, FL; **Stadium:** Orange Bowl; **Capacity:** 75,500; **Playing surface:** grass; **Automatic berths:** Big 8 champion (1954–64 and 1976–present).

First year: 1935; **Playing sites:** Orange Bowl (1935–present).

Year	Result	Year	Result	Year	Result
1935*	Bucknell 26, Miami,FL 0	1954	Oklahoma 7, Maryland 0	1973	Nebraska 40, Notre Dame 6
1936	Catholic U. 20, Mississippi 19	1955	Duke 34, Nebraska 7	1974	Penn St. 16, LSU 9
1937	Duquesne 13, Miss.St. 12	1956	Oklahoma 20, Maryland 6	1975	Notre Dame 13, Alabama 11
1938	Auburn 6, Michigan St. 0	1957	Colorado 27, Clemson 21	1976	Oklahoma 14, Michigan 6
1939	Tennessee 17, Oklahoma 0	1958	Oklahoma 48, Duke 21	1977	Ohio St. 27, Colorado 10
		1959	Oklahoma 21, Syracuse 6	1978	Arkansas 31, Oklahoma 6
1940	Georgia Tech 21, Missouri 7	1960*	Georgia 14, Missouri 0	1979	Oklahoma 31, Nebraska 24
1941	Miss.St. 14, Georgetown 7	1961	Missouri 21, Navy 14		
1942	Georgia 40, TCU 26	1962	LSU 25, Colorado 7	1980	Oklahoma 24, Fla.St. 7
1943	Alabama 37, Boston Col. 21	1963	Alabama 17, Oklahoma 0	1981	Oklahoma 18, Fla.St. 17
1944	LSU 19, Texas A&M 14	1964	Nebraska 13, Auburn 7	1982	Clemson 22, Nebraska 15
1945	Tulsa 26, Georgia Tech 12	1965‡	Texas 21, Alabama 17	1983	Nebraska 21, LSU 20
1946	Miami,FL 13, Holy Cross 6	1966	Alabama 39, Nebraska 28	1984	Miami,FL 31, Nebraska 30
1947	Rice 8, Tennessee 0	1967	Florida 27, Ga.Tech 12	1985	Washington 28, Oklahoma 17
1948	Georgia Tech 20, Kansas 14	1968	Oklahoma 26, Tennessee 24	1986	Oklahoma 25, Penn St. 10
1949	Texas 41, Georgia 28	1969	Penn St. 15, Kansas 14	1987	Oklahoma 42, Arkansas 8
				1988	Miami,FL 20, Oklahoma 14
1950	Santa Clara 21, Kentucky 13	1970	Penn St. 10, Missouri 3	1989	Miami,FL 23, Nebraska 3
1951	Clemson 15, Miami,FL 14	1971	Nebraska 17, LSU 12		
1952	Georgia Tech 17, Baylor 14	1972	Nebraska 38, Alabama 6		
1953	Alabama 61, Syracuse 6				

*January game from 1937–present.
‡Night game from 1965–present.

Sugar Bowl

City: New Orleans, LA; **Stadium:** Louisiana Superdome; **Capacity:** 69,548; **Playing surface:** AstroTurf; **Automatic berths:** Southeastern Conference champion (since 1977).

First year: 1935; **Playing sites:** Tulane Stadium (1935–74), Superdome (1974–present).

Year	Result	Year	Result	Year	Result
1935*	Tulane 20, Temple 14	1954	Ga.Tech 42, West Va. 19	1972‡	Oklahoma 14, Penn St. 0
1936	TCU 3, LSU 2	1955	Navy 21, Mississippi 0	1973	Notre Dame 24, Alabama 23
1937	Santa Clara 21, LSU 14	1956	Ga.Tech 7, Pittsburgh 0	1974	Nebraska 13, Florida 10
1938	Santa Clara 6, LSU 0	1957	Baylor 13, Tennessee 7	1975	Alabama 13, Penn St. 6
1939	TCU 15, Carnegie Tech 7	1958	Mississippi 39, Texas 7	1977*	Pittsburgh 27, Georgia 3
		1959	LSU 7, Clemson 0	1978	Alabama 35, Ohio St. 6
1940	Texas A&M 14, Tulane 13			1979	Alabama 14, Penn St. 7
1941	Boston Col. 19, Tenn. 13	1960	Mississippi 21, LSU 0		
1942	Fordham 2, Missouri 0	1961	Mississippi 14, Rice 6	1980	Alabama 24, Arkansas 9
1943	Tennessee 14, Tulsa 7	1962	Alabama 10, Arkansas 3	1981	Georgia 17, Notre Dame 10
1944	Georgia Tech 20, Tulsa 18	1963	Mississippi 17, Arkansas 13	1982	Pittsburgh 24, Georgia 20
1945	Duke 29, Alabama 26	1964	Alabama 12, Mississippi 7	1983	Penn St. 27, Georgia 23
1946	Okla.A&M 33, St.Mary's 13	1965	LSU 13, Syracuse 10	1984	Auburn 9, Michigan 7
1947	Georgia 20, N.Carolina 10	1966	Missouri 20, Florida 18	1985	Nebraska 28, LSU 10
1948	Texas 27, Alabama 7	1967	Alabama 34, Nebraska 7	1986	Tennessee 35, Miami,FL 7
1949	Oklahoma 14, N.Carolina 6	1968	LSU 20, Wyoming 13	1987	Nebraska 30, LSU 15
		1969	Arkansas 16, Georgia 2	1988	16–16, Syracuse vs Auburn
1950	Oklahoma 35, LSU 0			1989	Florida St. 13, Auburn 7
1951	Kentucky 13, Oklahoma 7	1970	Mississippi 27, Arkansas 22		
1952	Maryland 28, Tennessee 13	1971	Tennessee 34, Air Force 13		
1953	Ga.Tech 24, Mississippi 7	1972	Oklahoma 40, Auburn 22		

*January game from 1935–72 and 1977–present.
‡Game played Dec.31, 1972–75.

Cotton Bowl

City: Dallas, TX; **Stadium:** Cotton Bowl; **Capacity:** 72,032; **Playing surface:** AstroTurf; **Automatic berths:** Southwest Athletic Conference champion (since 1942).

First year: 1937; **Playing sites:** Fair Park Stadium (1937); Cotton Bowl (1938–present).

Year	Result	Year	Result	Year	Result
1937*	TCU 16, Marquette 6	1955	Ga.Tech 14, Arkansas 6	1973	Texas 17, Alabama 13
1938	Rice 28, Colorado 14	1956	Mississippi 14, TCU 13	1974	Nebraska 19, Texas 3
1939	St.Mary's 20, Texas Tech 13	1957	TCU 28, Syracuse 17	1975	Penn St. 41, Baylor 20
		1958	Navy 20, Rice 7	1976	Arkansas 31, Georgia 10
1940	Clemson 6, Boston Col. 3	1959	0–0, TCU vs Air Force	1977	Houston 30, Maryland 21
1941	Texas A&M 13, Fordham 12			1978	Notre Dame 38, Texas 10
1942	Alabama 29, Texas A&M 21	1960	Syracuse 23, Texas 14	1979	Notre Dame 35, Houston 34
1943	Texas 14, Georgia Tech 7	1961	Duke 7, Arkansas 6		
1944	7–7, Texas vs Randolph Field	1962	Texas 12, Mississippi 7	1980	Houston 17, Nebraska 14
1945	Oklahoma A&M 34, TCU 0	1963	LSU 13, Texas 0	1981	Alabama 30, Baylor 2
1946	Texas 40, Missouri 27	1964	Texas 28, Navy 6	1982	Texas 14, Alabama 12
1947	0–0, Arkansas vs LSU	1965	Arkansas 10, Nebraska 7	1983	SMU 7, Pittsburgh 3
1948	13–13, SMU vs Penn St.	1966	LSU 14, Arkansas 7	1984	Georgia 10, Texas 9
1949	SMU 21, Oregon 13	1966‡	Georgia 24, SMU 9	1985	Boston Col. 45, Houston 28
		1968*	Texas A&M 20, Alabama 16	1986	Texas A&M 36, Auburn 16
1950	Rice 27, N.Carolina 13	1969	Texas 36, Tennessee 13	1987	Ohio St. 28, Texas A&M 12
1951	Tennessee 20, Texas 14			1988	Texas A&M 35, N.Dame 10
1952	Kentucky 20, TCU 7	1970	Texas 21, Notre Dame 17	1989	UCLA 17, Arkansas 3
1953	Texas 16, Tennessee 0	1971	Notre Dame 24, Texas 11		
1954	Rice 28, Alabama 6	1972	Penn St. 30, Texas 6		

*January game from 1935–66 and 1967–present.
‡Game played Dec.31, 1966.

Fiesta Bowl

City: Tempe, AZ; **Stadium:** Sun Devil Stadium; **Capacity:** 74,000; **Playing surface:** grass; **Automatic berths:** none.

First year: 1971; **Playing sites:** Sun Devil Stadium (1971–present).

Year	Result	Year	Result	Year	Result
1971*	Ariz.St. 45, Florida St. 38	1977	Penn St. 42, Ariz.St. 30	1984	Ohio St. 28, Pittsburgh 23
1972	Ariz.St. 49, Missouri 35	1978	10–10, Arkansas vs UCLA	1985	UCLA 39, Miami,FL 37
1973	Ariz.St. 28, Pittsburgh 7	1979	Pittsburgh 16, Arizona 10	1986	Michigan 27, Nebraska 23
1974	Oklahoma St. 16, BYU 6	1980	Penn St. 31, Ohio St. 19	1987	Penn St. 14, Miami,FL 10
1975	Ariz.St. 17, Nebraska 14	1982‡	Penn St. 26, USC 10	1988	Florida St. 31, Nebraska 28
1976	Oklahoma 41, Wyoming 7	1983	Ariz.St. 32, Oklahoma 21	1989	Notre Dame 34, West Va. 21

*December game from 1971–80.
‡January game from 1982–present.

Gator Bowl

City: Jacksonville, FL; **Stadium:** Gator Bowl; **Capacity:** 82,000; **Playing surface:** grass; **Automatic berths:** none.

First year: 1946; **Playing sites:** Gator Bowl (1946–present).

Year	Result	Year	Result	Year	Result
1946*	W.Forest 26, S.Carolina 14	1960*	Arkansas 14, Ga.Tech 7	1974	Auburn 27, Texas 3
1947	Oklahoma 34, N.C.State 13	1960‡	Florida 13, Baylor 12	1975	Maryland 13, Florida 0
1948	20–20, Maryland vs Georgia	1961	Penn St. 30, Ga.Tech 15	1976	Notre Dame 20, Penn St. 9
1949	Clemson 24, Missouri 23	1962	Florida 17, Penn St. 7	1977	Pittsburgh 34, Clemson 3
		1963	N.Carolina 35, Air Force 0	1978	Clemson 17, Ohio St. 15
1950	Maryland 20, Missouri 7	1965*	Fla.St. 36, Oklahoma 19	1979	N.Carolina 17, Michigan 15
1951	Wyoming 20, Wash.& Lee 7	1965‡	Ga.Tech 31, Texas Tech 21		
1952	Miami,FL 14, Clemson 0	1966	Tennessee 18, Syracuse 12	1980	Pittsburgh 37, S.Carolina 9
1953	Florida 14, Tulsa 13	1967	17–17, Fla.St. vs Penn St.	1981	N.Carolina 31, Arkansas 27
1954	Texas Tech 35, Auburn 13	1968	Missouri 35, Alabama 10	1982	Florida St. 31, West Va. 12
1954‡	Auburn 33, Baylor 13	1969	Florida 14, Tennessee 13	1983	Florida 14, Iowa 6
1955	Vanderbilt 25, Auburn 13			1984	Okla.St. 21, S.Carolina 14
1956	Ga.Tech 21, Pittsburgh 14	1971*	Auburn 35, Mississippi 28	1985	Florida St. 34, Okla.St. 23
1957	Tennessee 3, Texas A&M 0	1971‡	Georgia 7, N.Carolina 3	1986	Clemson 27, Stanford 21
1958	Mississippi 7, Florida 3	1972	Auburn 24, Colorado 3	1987	LSU 30, S.Carolina 13
		1973	Texas Tech 28, Tennessee 19	1989*	Georgia 34, Michigan St. 27

*January game from 1946–54, 1960, 1965, 1971 and 1989.
‡December game from 1954–58, 1960–63, 1965–69 and 1971–88.

Florida Citrus Bowl

City: Orlando, FL; **Name change:** Tangerine Bowl (1947–82), Florida Citrus Bowl (1983–present); **Stadium:** Florida Citrus Bowl-Orlando; **Capacity:** 52,300; **Playing surface:** grass; **Automatic berths:** none.

First year: 1947; **Playing sites:** Tangerine Bowl (1947–72), Florida Field, Gainesville (1973), Tangerine Bowl (1974–82), Orlando Stadium (1983–85), Florida Citrus Bowl-Orlando (1986–present). The Tangerine Bowl, Orlando Stadium and Citrus Bowl are all the same stadium.

Note: No major college teams played in the Tangerine Bowl from 1947–61 or 1963–67.

Year	Result	Year	Result	Year	Result
1947*	Catawba 31, Maryville 6	1960*	Middle Tenn. 21, Presbyterian 12	1974	Miami,OH 21, Georgia 10
1948	Catawba 7, Marshall 0			1975	Miami,OH 20, S.Carolina 7
1949	21–21, Murray St. vs Sul Ross St.	1960‡	Citadel 27, Tenn. Tech 0	1976	Oklahoma 49, BYU 21
		1961	Lamar 21, Middle Tenn. 14	1977	Fla.St. 40, Texas Tech 17
1950	St.Vincent 7, Em.& Henry 6	1962	Houston 49, Miami,OH 21	1978	N.C.State 30, Pitt 17
		1963	West.Ky. 27, Coast Guard 0	1979	LSU 34, Wake Forest 10
1951	M.Harvey 35, Em.& Henry 14	1964	E.Carolina 14, Mass. 13		
		1965	E.Carolina 31, Maine 0	1980	Florida 35, Maryland 20
1952	Stetson 35, Arkansas St. 20	1966	Morgan St. 14, W.Chester 6	1981	Missouri 19, So.Miss. 17
1953	E.Texas St. 33, Tenn. Tech 0	1967	Tenn.Martin 25, W.Chester 8	1982	Auburn 33, Boston Col. 26
1954	7–7, E.Texas St. vs Ark.St.	1968	Richmond 49, Ohio U. 42	1983	Tennessee 30, Maryland 23
1955	Neb.-Omaha 7, Eastern Ky. 6	1969	Toledo 56, Davidson 33	1984	17–17, Fla.St. vs Georgia
1956	6–6, Juniata vs Mo.Valley			1985	Ohio St. 10, BYU 7
1957	W.Texas St. 20, So.Miss. 13	1970	Toledo 40, Wm.& Mary 12	1987*	Auburn 16, USC 7
1958	E.Texas St. 10, So.Miss. 9	1971	Toledo 28, Richmond 3	1988	Clemson 35, Penn St. 10
1958‡	E.Texas St. 26, Mo.Valley 7	1972	Tampa 21, Kent St. 18	1989	Clemson 13, Oklahoma 6
		1973	Miami,OH 16, Florida 7		

*January game from 1947–58, 1960, 1987–present.
‡December game from 1958, 1960–85.

Sun Bowl
(name changed to John Hancock Bowl, June 19, 1989)

City: El Paso, TX; **Stadium:** Sun Bowl; **Capacity:** 52,000; **Playing surface:** AstroTurf; **Automatic berths:** none.

First year: 1936; **Playing sites:** Kidd Field (1936–62), Sun Bowl (1963–present).

Year	Result	Year	Result	Year	Result
1936*	14–14, Hardin-Simmons vs New Mexico St.	1953	Pacific 26, So.Miss. 7	1970	Ga.Tech 17, Texas Tech 9
1937	Hardin-Simmons 34, Texas Mines 6	1954	Tex.Western 37, So.Miss. 14	1971	LSU 33, Iowa St. 15
		1955	Tex.Western 47, Fla.St. 20	1972	N.Carolina 32, Tex.Tech 28
1938	West Va. 7, Texas Tech 6	1956	Wyoming 21, Texas Tech 14	1973	Missouri 34, Auburn 17
1939	Utah 26, New Mexico 0	1957	Geo.Wash. 13, Tex.Western 0	1974	Miss.St. 26, N.Carolina 24
		1958	Louisville 34, Drake 20	1975	Pittsburgh 33, Kansas 19
1940	0–0, Catholic U. vs Ariz.St.	1958*	Wyoming 14, Hard.-Simmons 6	1977*	Texas A&M 37, Florida 14
1941	W.Reserve 26, Ariz.St. 13	1959	New Mex.St. 28, N.Texas 8	1977‡	Stanford 24, LSU 14
1942	Tulsa 6, Texas Tech 0			1978	Texas 42, Maryland 0
1943	2nd Air Force 13, Hardin Simmons 7	1960	New Mex.St. 20, Utah St. 13	1979	Washington 14, Texas 7
		1961	Villanova 17, Wichita 9		
1944	SW Texas 7, New Mexico 0	1962	West Texas 15, Ohio U. 14	1980	Nebraska 31, Miss.St. 17
1945	SW Texas 35, U.of Mexico 0	1963	Oregon 21, SMU 14	1981	Oklahoma 40, Houston 14
1946	New Mexico 34, Denver 24	1964	Georgia 7, Gergia Tech 0	1982	N.Carolina 26, Texas 10
1947	Cincinnati 18, Va.Tech 6	1965	Texas Western 13, TCU 12	1983	Alabama 28, SMU 7
1948	Miami,OH 13, Texas Tech 12	1966	Wyoming 28, Fla.St. 20	1984	Maryland 27, Tennessee 26
1949	West Va. 21, Texas Mines 12	1967	UTEP 14, Mississippi 7	1985	13–13, Georgia vs Arizona
		1968	Auburn 34, Arizona 10	1986	Alabama 28, Washington 6
1950	Tex.Western 33, Geo'town 20	1969	Nebraska 45, Georgia 6	1987	Okla.St. 35, West Va. 33
1951	West Texas 14, Cincinnati 13			1988	Alabama 29, Army 28
1952	Texas Tech 25, Pacific 14				

*January game from 1936–58 and 1977.   ‡December game from 1958–75 and 1977–present.

Liberty Bowl

City: Memphis, TN; **Stadium:** Liberty Bowl Memorial Stadium; **Capacity:** 63,000; **Playing surface:** grass; **Automatic berths:** Starting in 1989, winner of Commander in Chief's Trophy (Army, Navy or Air Force)—if Air Force is also WAC champion, it is obligated to play in Holiday Bowl, in which case Liberty Bowl decides between Army and Navy.

First year: 1959; **Playing sites:** Philadelphia, PA (Municipal Stadium, 1959–63); Atlantic City, NJ (Convention Hall, 1964); Memphis (1965–present).

Year	Result	Year	Result	Year	Result
1959*	Penn St. 7, Alabama 0	1970	Tulane 17, Colorado 3	1980	Purdue 28, Missouri 25
		1971	Tennessee 14, Arkansas 13	1981	Ohio St. 31, Navy 28
1960	Penn St. 41, Oregon 12	1972	Ga.Tech 31, Iowa St. 30	1982	Alabama 21, Illinois 15
1961	Syracuse 15, Miami,FL 14	1973	N.C.State 31, Kansas 18	1983	N.Dame 19, Boston Col. 18
1962	Oregon St. 6, Villanova 0	1974	Tennessee 7, Maryland 3	1984	Auburn 21, Arkansas 15
1963	Miss.St. 16, N.C.State 12	1975	USC 20, Texas A&M 0	1985	Baylor 21, LSU 7
1964	Utah 32, West Virgina 6	1976	Alabama 36, UCLA 6	1986	Tennessee 21, Minnesota 14
1965	Mississippi 13, Auburn 7	1977	Nebraska 21, N.Carolina 17	1987	Georgia 20, Arkansas 17
1966	Miami,FL 14, Va.Tech 7	1978	Missouri 20, LSU 15	1988	Indiana 34, S.Carolina 10
1967	N.C.State 14, Georgia 7	1979	Penn St. 9, Tulane 6		
1968	Mississippi 34, Va.Tech 17				
1969	Colorado 47, Alabama 33				

*December game from 1959–present.

Peach Bowl

City: Atlanta, GA; **Stadium:** Atlanta Fulton County Stadium; **Capacity:** 59,800; **Playing surface:** grass; **Automatic berths:** none.

First year: 1968; **Playing sites:** Grant Field (1968–70), Atlanta Stadium (1971–present).

Year	Result	Year	Result	Year	Result
1968*	LSU 31, Florida St. 27	1975	West Va. 13, N.C.State 10	1982	Iowa 28, Tennessee 22
1969	West Va. 14, S.Carolina 3	1976	Kentucky 21, N.Carolina 0	1983	Fla.St. 28, N.Carolina 3
		1977	N.C.State 24, Iowa St. 14	1984	Virginia 27, Purdue 24
1970	Ariz.St. 48, N.Carolina 26	1978	Purdue 41, Ga.Tech 21	1985	Army 31, Illinois 29
1971	Mississippi 41, Ga.Tech 18	1979	Baylor 24, Clemson 18	1986	Va.Tech 25, N.C.State 24
1972	N.C.State 49, West Va. 13			1988‡	Tennessee 27, Indiana 22
1973	Georgia 17, Maryland 16	1981‡	Miami,FL 20, Va.Tech 10	1988*	N.C.State 28, Iowa 23
1974	6–6, Vanderbilt vs Tex.Tech	1981*	West Va. 26, Florida 6		

*December game from 1968–79, 1981–86, and 1988.   ‡January game in 1981 and 1988.

Independence Bowl

City: Shreveport, LA; **Stadium:** Independence Stadium; **Capacity:** 50,560; **Playing surface:** grass; **Automatic berths:** none.

First year: 1976; **Playing sites:** Independence Stadium (1976–present).

Year	Result	Year	Result	Year	Result
1976*	McNeese St. 20, Tulsa 16	1980	So.Miss 16, McNeese St. 14	1985	Minnesota 20, Clemson 13
1977	La.Tech 24, Louisville 14	1981	Texas A&M 33, Okla.St. 16	1986	Mississippi 20, Tex.Tech 17
1978	E.Carolina 35, La.Tech 13	1982	Wisconsin 14, Kansas St. 3	1987	Washington 24, Tulane 12
1979	Syracuse 31, McNeese St. 7	1983	Air Force 9, Mississippi 3	1988	So.Miss 38, UTEP 18
		1984	Air Force 23, Va.Tech 7		

*December game from 1976–present.

All-American Bowl

City: Birmingham, AL; **Stadium:** Legion Field; **Capacity:** 75,808; **Playing surface:** AstroTurf; **Automatic berths:** none.

First year: 1977; **Name change:** Hall of Fame Classic (1977–84), All-American Bowl (1985–present); **Playing sites:** Legion Field (1977–present).

Year	Result	Year	Result	Year	Result
1977*	Maryland 17, Minnesota 7	1980	Arkansas 34, Tulane 15	1985	Ga.Tech 17, Mich.St. 14
1978	Texas A&M 28, Iowa St. 12	1981	Miss.St. 10, Kansas 0	1986	Florida St. 27, Indiana 13
1979	Missouri 24, S.Carolina 14	1982	Air Force 36, Vanderbilt 28	1987	Virginia 22, BYU 16
		1983	West Va. 20, Kentucky 16	1988	Florida 14, Illinois 10
		1984	Kentucky 20, Wisconsin 19		

*December game from 1977–present.

Holiday Bowl

City: San Diego, CA; **Stadium:** San Diego Jack Murphy Stadium; **Capacity:** 60,750; **Playing surface:** grass; **Automatic berths:** Western Athletic Conference champion (except 1985).

First year: 1978; **Playing sites:** Jack Murphy Stadium (1978–present).

Year	Result	Year	Result	Year	Result
1978*	Navy 23, BYU 16	1981	BYU 38, Wash.St. 36	1985	Arkansas 18, Ariz.St. 17
1979	Indiana 38, BYU 37	1982	Ohio St. 47, BYU 17	1986	Iowa 39, S.Diego St. 38
		1983	BYU 21, Missouri 17	1987	Iowa 20, Wyoming 19
1980	BYU 46, SMU 45	1984	BYU 24, Michigan 17	1988	Okla.St. 62, Wyoming 14

*December game from 1978–present.

California Bowl

City: Fresno, CA; **Stadium:** Bulldog Stadium; **Capacity:** 30,000; **Playing surface:** grass; **Automatic berths:** Mid-American Conference and Big West champions (since 1981).

First year: 1981; **Playing sites:** Bulldog Stadium (1981–present).

Year	Result	Year	Result	Year	Result
1981*	Toledo 27, San Jose St. 25	1984	UNLV 30, Toledo 13	1987	E.Michigan 30, S.Jose St. 27
1982	Fresno St. 29, Bowl.Green 28	1985	Fresno St. 51, Bowl.Green 7	1988	Fresno St. 35, W.Michigan 30
1983	Northern Ill. 20, Cal St.-Fullerton 13	1986	San Jose St. 37, Miami,OH 7		

*December game from 1981–present.
Note: Toledo ruled winner of 1984 game by forfeit when UNLV was found to have used ineligible players.

Aloha Bowl

City: Honolulu, HI; **Stadium:** Aloha Stadium; **Capacity:** 50,000; **Playing surface:** AstroTurf; **Automatic berths:** none.

First year: 1982; **Playing sites:** Aloha Stadium (1982–present).

Year	Result	Year	Result	Year	Result
1982*	Washington 21, Maryland 20	1985	Alabama 24, USC 3	1987	UCLA 20, Florida 16
1983	Penn St. 13, Washington 10	1986	Arizona 30, N.Carolina 21	1988	Wash.St. 24, Houston 22
1984	SMU 27, Notre Dame 20				

*December game from 1982–present.

Freedom Bowl

City: Anaheim, CA; **Stadium:** Anaheim Stadium; **Capacity:** 70,500; **Playing surface:** grass; **Automatic berths:** none.

First year: 1984; **Playing sites:** Anaheim Stadium (1984–present).

Year	Result	Year	Result	Year	Result
1984*	Iowa 55, Texas 17	1986	UCLA 31, BYU 10	1988	BYU 20, Colorado 17
1985	Washington 20, Colorado 17	1987	Ariz.St. 33, Air Force 28		

*December game from 1984–present.

Hall of Fame Bowl

City: Tampa, FL; **Stadium:** Tampa Stadium; **Capacity:** 74,315; **Playing surface:** grass; **Automatic berths:** none.

First year: 1986; **Playing sites:** Tampa Stadium (1986–present).

Year	Result	Year	Result	Year	Result
1986*	Boston Col. 27, Georgia 24	1987‡	Michigan 28, Alabama 24	1988	Syracuse 23, LSU 10

*December game in 1986.
‡January game from 1987–present.

Bowls Discontinued in the 1980s

Bluebonnet (Houston)

Years: 1959–87; **Name change:** Astro-Bluebonnet Bowl (1968–76); **Playing sites:** Rice Stadium (1959–67, 1985–86), Astrodome (1968–84, 1987).

Year	Result	Year	Result	Year	Result
1959*	Clemson 23, TCU 7	1970	24–24, Alabama vs Oklahoma	1980	N.Carolina 16, Texas 7
1960	3–3, Texas vs Alabama	1971	Colorado 29, Houston 17	1981	Michigan 33, UCLA 14
1961	Kansas 33, Rice 7	1972	Tennessee 24, LSU 17	1982	Arkansas 28, Florida 24
1962	Missouri 14, Ga.Tech 10	1973	Houston 47, Tulane 7	1983	Okla.St. 24, Baylor 14
1963	Baylor 14, LSU 7	1974	31–31, N.C.State vs Houston	1984	West Va. 31, TCU 14
1964	Tulsa 14, Mississippi 7	1975	Texas 38, Colorado 21	1985	Air Force 24, Texas 16
1965	Tennessee 27, Tulsa 6	1976	Nebraska 27, Texas Tech 24	1986	Baylor 21, Colorado 9
1966	Texas 19, Mississippi 0	1977	USC 47, Texas A&M 28	1987	Texas 32, Pittsburgh 27
1967	Colorado 31, Miami,FL 21	1978	Stanford 25, Georgia 22		
1968	SMU 28, Oklahoma 27	1979	Purdue 27, Tennessee 22		
1969	Houston 36, Auburn 7				

*December game every year.

Cherry (Pontiac, MI)

Years: 1984–85; **Playing site:** Pontiac Silverdome (1984–85).

Year	Result
1984*	Army 10, Michigan St. 6
1985	Maryland 35, Syracuse 18

*December game both years.

Garden State (E.Rutherford, NJ)

Years: 1978–81; **Playing site:** Giants Stadium (1984–85).

Year*	Result	Year*	Result
1978*	Ariz.St. 34, Rutgers 18	1980	Houston 35, Navy 0
1979	Temple 28, California 17	1981	Tennessee 28, Wisconsin 21

*December game every year.

Winningest Division I-A Teams

All-Time Winning Pct.

Division I-A schools with best winning percentages through 1988 (regular season and bowl games included).

		Yrs	W	L	T	Pct	Bowl Record
1	Notre Dame	100	671	202	40	.757	9–5–0
2	Michigan	109	693	231	33	.741	9–11–0
3	Alabama	94	641	226	43	.728	23–15–3
4	Oklahoma	94	621	223	50	.723	18–10–1
5	Texas	96	656	249	31	.717	16–15–2
6	Southern Cal.	96	596	230	49	.709	21–11–0
7	Ohio St.	99	618	249	50	.701	11–10–0
8	Penn St.	102	629	276	40	.687	15–8–2
9	Nebraska	99	625	279	39	.683	14–13–0
10	Tennessee	92	589	265	50	.679	15–14–0
11	Central Mich.	88	450	234	30	.651	0–0–0
12	LSU	95	552	291	46	.647	11–16–1
13	Miami,OH	100	523	280	38	.645	5–2–0
14	Army	99	561	299	50	.644	2–1–0
15	Arizona St.	76	416	229	23	.640	9–5–1
16	Georgia	95	555	309	53	.634	13–12–3
17	Washington	99	516	297	49	.627	9–7–1
18	Minnesota	105	529	324	42	.615	2–3–0
19	Michigan St.	92	491	301	42	.614	3–5–0
20	UNLV	21	141	88	4	.614	1–0–0
21	Auburn	96	519	319	44	.613	10–9–2
22	UCLA	70	406	255	36	.608	9–7–1
23	Arkansas	95	523	333	38	.606	9–13–3
24	Florida St.	42	262	168	16	.605	8–7–2
25	Pittsburgh	99	544	351	40	.603	7–10–0

All-Time Victories

Division I-A schools with most victories through 1988 (regular season and bowl games included).

	Wins		Wins		Wins
1 Michigan	693	11 Army	561	21 Georgia Tech	518
2 Notre Dame	671	12 Georgia	555	22 Auburn	519
3 Texas	656	13 LSU	552	23 Washington	516
4 Alabama	641	14 Pittsburgh	544	24 North Carolina	515
5 Penn St.	629	15 Syracuse	542	25 Colorado	510
6 Nebraska	625	16 Navy	532	26 Rutgers	508
7 Oklahoma	621	17 Minnesota	529	27 Texas A&M	500
8 Ohio St	618	18 Arkansas	523	28 California	496
9 Southern Cal	596	West Virginia	523	29 Missouri	492
10 Tennessee	589	Miami, OH	523	30 Michigan St.	491

Note: Division I-AA schools with over 600 wins through 1988—Yale (746), Harvard (681), Princeton (672), and Penn (668).

Schools With 20 or More Bowl Appearances

	Bowls	Overall W L T			Big Four W L T				Bowls	Bowls W L T			Big Four W L T		
1 Alabama	41	23	15	3	17	11	1	9 Penn St	25	15	8	2	6	5	1
2 Texas	33	16	15	2	12	9	1	Arkansas	25	9	13	3	4	9	1
3 Southern Cal	32	21	11	0	18	8	0	11 Georgia Tech	23	15	8	0	9	3	0
4 Oklahoma	29	18	10	1	15	6	0	12 Mississippi	22	12	10	0	6	5	0
Tennessee	29	15	14	0	5	9	0	13 Ohio St	21	11	10	0	7	8	0
6 Georgia	28	13	12	3	7	6	0	14 Auburn	21	10	9	2	2	4	1
LSU	28	11	16	1	7	10	1	15 Michigan	20	9	11	0	6	9	0
8 Nebraska	27	14	13	0	9	10	0								

Note: The Big Four bowls are the Rose, Orange, Sugar and Cotton. Only Alabama, Georgia, Georgia Tech and Notre Dame have won all four.

Longest Division I Streaks

Winning Streaks

Division I-A and I-AA schools with most consecutive victories (including regular season and bowl games).

No		Seasons	Broken by	Score
47	Oklahoma . . .	1953–57	Notre Dame	7–0
39	Washington . .	1908–14	Oregon St.	0–0
37	Yale	1890–93	Princeton	6–0
37	Yale	1887–89	Princeton	10–0
35	Toledo	1969–71	Tampa	21–0
34	Penn	1894–96	Lafayette	6–4
31	Oklahoma . . .	1948–50	Kentucky	13–7*
31	Pittsburgh . . .	1914–18	Cleve. Naval	10–9
31	Penn	1896–98	Harvard	10–0
30	Texas	1968–70	Notre Dame	24–11*

*Note: Kentucky beat Oklahoma in 1951 Sugar Bowl and Notre Dame beat Texas in 1971 Cotton Bowl.

Unbeaten Streaks

Division I-A and I-AA schools with most consecutive games without a defeat (including regular season and bowl games).

No		Record	Seasons	Broken by	Score
63	Washington	59–0–4	1907–17	California	27–0
56	Michigan . .	55–0–1	1901–05	Chicago	2–0
50	California . .	46–0–4	1920–25	Olympic	15–0
48	Oklahoma .	47–0–1	1953–57	N. Dame	7–0
48	Yale	47–0–1	1885–89	Princeton	10–0
47	Yale	42–0–5	1879–85	Princeton	6–5
44	Yale	42–0–2	1894–96	Princeton	24–6
42	Yale	39–0–3	1904–08	Harvard	4–0
39	N. Dame . .	36–0–1	1972–75	Kansas	23–3
37	Oklahoma .	37–0–2	1946–50	Purdue	28–14

Winningest Division I-A Coaches

All-Time Victories

Division I-A coaches with most victories (regular season and bowl games included). Active coaches are in **bold** type.

		Yrs	Wins
1	Bear Bryant	38	323
2	Amos Alonzo Stagg	57	314
3	Pop Warner	44	313
4	Woody Hayes	33	238
5	**Bo Schembechler**	26	224
6	**Joe Paterno**	23	212
7	Jess Neely	40	207
8	Warren Woodson	31	203
9	Eddie Anderson	39	201
	Vince Dooley	25	201
11	Dana X. Bible	33	198
12	Dan McGugin	30	197
13	Fielding Yost	29	196
14	Howard Jones	29	194
15	Johnny Vaught	25	190

Note: Eddie Robinson of Division I-AA Grambling (1941–42, 1945–present) is the all-time leader in coaching victories with 349 wins through 1988.

All-Time Winning Pct.

Division I-A coaches with best winning percentage (regular season and bowl games included). Active coaches are in **bold** type.

		Yrs	W	L	T	Pct
1	Knute Rockne	13	105	12	5	.881
2	Frank Leahy	13	107	13	9	.864
3	George Woodruff . .	12	142	25	2	.846
4	Barry Switzer	16	157	29	4	.837
5	Percy Haughton . . .	13	96	17	6	.832
6	Bob Neyland	21	173	31	12	.829
7	Fielding Yost	29	196	36	12	.828
8	Bud Wilkinson	17	145	29	4	.826
9	Jock Sutherland	20	144	28	14	.812
10	**Tom Osborne**	16	158	36	2	.811
11	Bob Devaney	16	136	30	7	.806
12	Frank Thomas	19	141	33	9	.795
	Joe Paterno	23	212	54	2	.795
14	Henry Williams	23	139	34	10	.787
15	Gil Dobie	33	180	45	15	.781

Where They Coached

Bryant—Maryland (1945), Kentucky (1946–53), Texas A&M (1954–57), Alabama (1958–82); **Stagg**—Springfield (1890–91), Chicago (1892–1932), Pacific (1933–46); **Warner**—Georgia (1895–96), Cornell (1897–98), Carlisle (1899–1903), Cornell (1904–06), Carlisle (1907–14), Pittsburgh (1915–23), Stanford (1924–32), Temple (1933–38); **Hayes**—Denison (1946–48), Miami, OH (1949–50), Ohio St. (1951–78); **Schembechler**—Miami, OH (1963–68), Michigan (1969—).

Paterno—Penn St. (1966—); **Neely**—Southwestern, TN (1924–27), Clemson (1931–39), Rice (1940–66); **Woodson**—Conway St. (1935–40), Hardin-Simmons (1941–42 and 1946–51), Arizona (1952–56), New Mexico St. (1958–67), Trinity, TX (1972–73); **Anderson**—Loras (1922–24), DePaul (1925–31), Holy Cross (1933–38), Iowa (1939–42), Holy Cross (1950–64); **Dooley**—Georgia (1964–88).

Bible—Mississippi Col. (1913–15), LSU (1916), Texas A&M (1917 and 1919–28), Nebraska (1929–36), Texas (1937–46); **McGugin**—Vanderbilt (1904–17 and 1919–34); **Yost**—Ohio Wesleyan (1897), Nebraska (1898), Kansas (1899), Stanford (1900), Michigan (1901–23, 1925–26); **Jones**—Syracuse (1908), Yale (1909), Ohio St. (1910), Yale (1913), Iowa (1916–23), Duke (1924), USC (1925–40); **Vaught**—Mississippi (1945–70 and 1973).

Where They Coached

Rockne—Notre Dame (1918–30); **Leahy**—Boston College (1939–40), Notre Dame (1941–43, 1946–53); **Woodruff**—Penn (1892–1901), Illinois (1903), Carlisle (1905); **Switzer**—Oklahoma (1973–88); **Haughton**—Cornell (1899–1900), Harvard (1908–16), Columbia (1923–24).

Neyland—Tennessee (1926–34, 1936–40, 1946–52); **Yost**—Ohio Wesleyan (1897), Nebraska (1898), Kansas (1899), Stanford (1900), Michigan (1901–23, 1925–26); **Wilkinson**—Oklahoma (1947–63); **Sutherland**—Lafayette (1919–23), Pittsburgh (1924–38); **Osborne**—Nebraska (1973–present).

Devaney—Wyoming (1957–61), Nebraska (1962–72); **Thomas**—Chattanooga (1925–28), Alabama (1931–42, 1944–46); **Paterno**—Penn St. (1966–present); **Williams**—Army (1891), Minnesota (1900–21); **Dobie**—North Dakota St. (1906–07), Washington (1908–16), Navy (1917–19), Cornell (1920–35), Boston College (1936–38).

Active Coaches' Victories

Active Division I-A coaches with most victories through 1988 (regular season and bowl games included).

	Yrs	Wins
Bo Schembechler, Mich.	26	224
Joe Paterno, Penn St.	23	212
Bobby Bowden, Fla. St.	23	185
Jerry Claiborne, Ky.	27	173
Hayden Fry, Iowa	27	166
Tom Osborne, Nebraska	16	158
LaVell Edwards, BYU	17	155
Bill Dooley, W. Forest	22	145
Grant Teaff, Baylor	26	144
Lou Holtz, Notre Dame	19	141
Jim Sweeney, Fresno St.	24	140
Johnny Majors, Tennessee	21	139
Don James, Washington	18	137
Jim Wacker, TCU	18	128
Pat Dye, Auburn	15	125
Bill Mallory, Indiana	19	125

Coaches With 12 or More Bowl Appearances

Active coaches in **bold type**.

	Bowls	W	L	T
Bear Bryant	29	15	12	2
Vince Dooley	20	8	10	2
Joe Paterno	19	12	6	1
Johnny Vaught	18	10	8	0
Darrell Royal	16	8	7	1
Bo Schembechler	16	5	11	0
Tom Osborne	16	8	8	0
Bobby Dodd	13	9	4	0
Barry Switzer	13	8	5	0
Johnny Majors	13	7	6	0
Charlie McClendon	13	7	6	0
Lou Holtz	13	6	5	2
LaVell Edwards	13	5	8	0
Bobby Bowden	12	8	3	1
Woody Hayes	12	6	6	0
Shug Jordan	12	5	7	0

AFCA Coach of the Year

First presented in 1935 by the American Football Coaches Association. Numbers in parentheses indicate number of times multiple winners have won award.

Year	Coach, school
1935	Pappy Waldorf, N'western
1936	Dick Harlow, Harvard
1937	Hooks Mylin, Lafayette
1938	Bill Kern, Carnegie Tech
1939	Eddie Anderson, Iowa
1940	Clark Shaughnessy, Stanford
1941	Frank Leahy, Notre Dame
1942	Bill Alexander, Ga.Tech
1943	Amos Alonzo Stagg, Pacific
1944	Carroll Widdoes, Ohio St.
1945	Bo McMillin, Indiana
1946	Red Blaik, Army
1947	Fritz Crisler, Michigan
1948	Bennie Oosterbaan, Michigan
1949	Bud Wilkinson, Oklahoma

Year	Coach, school
1950	Charlie Caldwell, Princeton
1951	Chuck Taylor, Stanford
1952	Biggie Munn, Michigan St.
1953	Jim Tatum, Maryland
1954	Red Sanders, UCLA
1955	Duffy Daugherty, Mich.St.
1956	Bowden Wyatt, Tennessee
1957	Woody Hayes, Ohio St.
1958	Paul Dietzel, LSU
1959	Ben Schwartzwalder, Syracuse
1960	Marray Warmath, Minnesota
1961	Bear Bryant, Alabama
1962	John McKay, Southern Cal
1963	Darrell Royal, Texas
1964	Frank Broyles, Arkansas
	Ara Parseghian, N.Dame
1965	Tommy Prothro, UCLA
1966	Tom Cahill, Army
1967	John Pont, Indiana
1968	Joe Paterno, Penn St.
1969	Bo Schembechler, Michigan

Year	Coach, school
1970	Charlie McClendon, LSU
	Darrell Royal, Texas (2)
1971	Bear Bryant (2)
1972	John McKay (2)
1973	Bear Bryant (3)
1974	Grant Teaff, Baylor
1975	Frank Kush, Arizona St.
1976	Johnny Majors, Pittsburgh
1977	Don James, Washington
1978	Joe Paterno, Penn St.(2)
1979	Earle Bruce, Ohio St.
1980	Vince Dooley, Georgia
1981	Danny Ford, Clemson
1982	Joe Paterno, Penn St. (3)
1983	Ken Hatfield, Air Force
1984	LaVell Edwards, BYU
1985	Fisher DeBerry, Air Force
1986	Joe Paterno, Penn St. (4)
1987	Dick MacPherson, Syracuse
1988	Don Nehlen, West Virginia

FWAA Coach of the Year

First presented in 1957 by the Football Writers Association of America. Numbers in parentheses indicate number of times a coach has won the FWAA award.

The FWAA and AFCA awards have both gone to the same coach in the same season 22 times. Those double winners are preceded by (#).

Year	Coach, school
1957	#Woody Hayes, Ohio St.
1958	#Paul Dietzel, LSU
1959	#B.Schwatzwalder, Syracuse
1960	#Murray Warmath, Minnesota
1961	Darrell Royal, Texas
1962	#John McKay, Southern Cal
1963	#Darrell Royal, Texas (2)
1964	#Ara Parseghian, Notre Dame
1965	Duffy Daugherty, Mich.St.
1966	#Tom Cahill, Army
1967	#John Pont, Indiana
1968	Woody Hayes, Ohio St.(2)
1969	#Bo Schembechler, Michigan

Year	Coach, school
1970	Alex Agase, Northwestern
1971	Bob Devaney, Nebraska
1972	#John McKay, USC (2)
1973	Johnny Majors, Pittsburgh
1974	#Grant Teaff, Baylor
1975	Woody Hayes, Ohio St.(3)
1976	#Johnny Majors, Pitt. (2)
1977	Lou Holtz, Arkansas
1978	#Joe Paterno, Penn St.
1979	#Earle Bruce, Ohio St.

Year	Coach, school
1980	#Vince Dooley, Georgia
1981	#Danny Ford, Clemson
1982	#Joe Paterno, Penn St.(2)
1983	H.Schnellenberger, Miami,FL
1984	#LaVell Edwards, BYU
1985	#Fisher DeBerry, Air Force
1986	#Joe Paterno, Penn St.(3)
1987	#Dick MacPherson, Syracuse
1988	Lou Holtz, Notre Dame (2)

Player Awards
Heisman Trophy

Originally presented in 1935 as the DAC Trophy by the Downtown Athletic Club of New York City to the best college football player east of the Mississippi. In 1936, players across the country were eligible and the award was renamed the Heisman Trophy following the death of former college coach and DAC athletic director John W. Heisman.

Players who won the Heisman in their junior years are preceded by an asterisk (*), while players listed in **bold type** helped lead their team to a national championship (according to AP).

Year	Player, school	Year	Player, school
1935	Jay Berwanger, Chicago, HB	1962	Terry Baker, Oregon St., QB
1936	Larry Kelley, Yale, E	1963	*Roger Staubach, Navy, QB
1937	Clint Frank, Yale, HB	1964	John Huarte, Notre Dame, QB
1938	**Davey O'Brien, TCU, QB**	1965	Mike Garrett, USC, HB
1939	Nile Kinnick, Iowa, HB	1966	Steve Spurrier, Florida, QB
1940	Tom Harmon, Michigan, HB	1967	Gary Beban, UCLA, QB
1941	**Bruce Smith, Minnesota, HB**	1968	O.J.Simpson, USC, HB
1942	Frank Sinkwich, Georgia, TB	1969	Steve Owens, Oklahoma, HB
1943	**Angelo Bertelli, Notre Dame, QB**	1970	Jim Plunkett, Stanford, QB
1944	Les Horvath, Ohio St., TB-QB	1971	Pat Sullivan, Auburn, QB
1945	***Doc Blanchard, Army, FB**	1972	Johnny Rodgers, Nebraska, FL
1946	Glenn Davis, Army, HB	1973	John Cappelletti, Penn St., RB
1947	**Johnny Lujack, Notre Dame, QB**	1974	*Archie Griffin, Ohio St., RB
1948	*Doak Walker, SMU, HB	1975	Archie Griffin, Ohio St., RB
1949	**Leon Hart, Notre Dame, E**	1976	**Tony Dorsett, Pittsburgh, RB**
1950	*Vic Janowicz, Ohio St., HB	1977	Earl Campbell, Texas, RB
1951	Dick Kazmaier, Princeton, TB	1978	*Billy Sims, Oklahoma, RB
1952	Billy Vessels, Oklahoma, HB	1979	Charles White, USC, RB
1953	Johnny Lattner, Notre Dame, HB	1980	George Rogers, S.Carolina, RB
1954	Alan Ameche, Wisconsin, FB	1981	Marcus Allen, USC, RB
1955	Howard Cassady, Ohio St., HB	1982	*Herschel Walker, Georgia, RB
1956	Paul Hornung, Notre Dame, QB	1983	Mike Rozier, Nebraska, RB
1957	John David Crow, Texas A&M, HB	1984	Doug Flutie, Boston Col., QB
1958	Pete Dawkins, Army, HB	1985	Bo Jackson, Auburn, RB
1959	Billy Cannon, LSU, HB	1986	Vinny Testaverde, Miami,FL, QB
1960	Joe Bellino, Navy, HB	1987	Tim Brown, Notre Dame, WR
1961	Ernie Davis, Syracuse, HB	1988	*Barry Sanders, Okla.St., RB

Maxwell Award

First presented in 1937 by the Maxwell Memorial Football Club of Philadelphia, the award is named after Robert "Tiny" Maxwell, a standout lineman at the University of Chicago and Swarthmore and later Sports Editor of the *Philadelphia Public Ledger* (now the *Inquirer*) from 1916–27.

Like the Heisman, the Maxwell is given to the outstanding college player in the nation. Both awards have gone to the same player in the same season 26 times. Those players are preceded by a (#). Glenn Davis of Army and Doak Walker of SMU also won both awards, but in different years.

Year	Player, school	Year	Player, school
1937	#Clint Frank, Yale, HB	1963	#Roger Staubach, Navy, QB
1938	#Davey O'Brien, TCU, QB	1964	Glenn Ressler, Penn St., G
1939	#Nile Kinnick, Iowa, HB	1965	Tommy Nobis, Texas, LB
1940	#Tom Harmon, Michigan, HB	1966	Jim Lynch, Notre Dame, LB
1941	Bill Dudley, Virginia, HB	1967	#Gary Beban, UCLA, QB
1942	Paul Governali, Columbia, QB	1968	#O.J.Simpson, USC, HB
1943	Bob Odell, Penn, HB	1969	Mike Reid, Penn St., DT
1944	Glenn Davis, Army, HB	1970	#Jim Plunkett, Stanford, QB
1945	#Doc Blanchard, Army, FB	1971	Ed Marinaro, Cornell, RB
1946	Charley Trippi, Georgia, HB	1972	Brad VanPelt, Mich.St., DB
1947	Doak Walker, SMU, HB	1973	#J.Cappelletti, Penn St., RB
1948	Chuck Bednarik, Penn, C	1974	Steve Joachim, Temple, QB
1949	#Leon Hart, Notre Dame, E	1975	*Archie Griffin, Ohio St., RB
1950	Reds Bagnell, Penn, HB	1976	#Tony Dorsett, Pittsburgh, RB
1951	#Dick Kazmaier, Princeton, TB	1977	Ross Browner, Notre Dame, DE
1952	Johnny Lattner, N.Dame, HB	1978	Chuck Fusina, Penn St., QB
1953	#Johnny Lattner, N.Dame, HB	1979	#Charles White, USC, RB
1954	Ron Beagle, Navy, E	1980	Hugh Green, Pittsburgh, DE
1955	#Howard Cassady, Ohio St., HB	1981	#Marcus Allen, USC, RB
1956	Tommy McDonald, Oklahoma, HB	1982	#Herschel Walker, Georgia, RB
1957	Bob Reifsnyder, Navy, T	1983	#Mike Rozier, Nebraska, RB
1958	#Pete Dawkins, Army, HB	1984	#Doug Flutie, Boston Col., QB
1959	Rich Lucas, Penn St., QB	1985	Chuck Long, Iowa, QB
1960	#Joe Bellino, Navy, HB	1986	#V.Testaverde, Miami,FL, QB
1961	Bob Ferguson, Ohio St., HB	1987	Don McPherson, Syracuse, QB
1962	#Terry Baker, Oregon St., QB	1988	#Barry Sanders, Okla.St., RB

The Camp and Rockne Awards

Besides the Heisman Trophy and Maxwell Award, the Touchdown Club of Washington, DC, initiated two other player-of-the-year prizes in the late 1930s: the Walter Camp Award for the nation's best back, and the Knute Rockne Award for best lineman.

The Camp Award is named after the football innovator who chose the original college All-America Team. The Rockne Award is named after the Notre Dame All-America end (1913) and football coach (1918–30).

Camp Award

Year	Player, school
1937	Marshall Goldberg, Pitt, HB
1938	Davey O'Brien, TCU, QB
1939	Nile Kinnick, Iowa, HB
1940	Tom Harmon, Michigan, HB
1941	Bill Dudley, Virginia, HB
1942	Frank Sinkwich, Georgia, HB
1943	Angelo Bertelli, N.Dame, QB
1944	Glenn Davis, Army, HB
1945	Doc Blanchard, Army, FB
1946	Charley Trippi, Georgia, HB
1947	Johnny Lujack, N.Dame, QB
1948	Charlie Justice, N.Caro., HB
1949	Emil Sitko, Notre Dame, HB
1950	Babe Parilli, Kentucky, QB
1951	Dick Kazmaier, Princeton, TB
1952	Don McAuliffe, Mich.St., HB
1953	Alan Ameche, Wisconsin, FB
	Bernie Faloney, Maryland, QB
	Paul Giel, Minnesota, HB
	Johnny Lattner, N.Dame, HB
1954	Ralph Guglielmi, N.Dame, QB
1955	Howard Cassady, Ohio St., HB
1956	Paul Hornung, Notre Dame, QB
1957	John David Crow, Texas A&M
1958	Randy Duncan, Iowa, QB
1959	Billy Cannon, LSU, HB

Year	Player, school
1960	Joe Bellino, Navy, HB
1961	Ernie Davis, Syracuse, HB
1962	Jerry Stovall, LSU, HB
1963	Roger Staubach, Navy, QB
1964	Jerry Rhome, Tulsa, QB
1965	Jim Grabowski, Illinois, FB
1966	Steve Spurrier, Florida, QB
1967	Gary Beban, UCLA, QB
1968	O.J.Simpson, USC, HB
1969	Archie Manning, Miss., QB
1970	Ed Marinaro, Cornell, RB
1971	Ed Marinaro, Cornell, RB
1972	Greg Pruitt, Oklahoma, RB
1973	J.Cappelletti, Penn St., RB
1974	Anthony Davis, USC, HB
1975	Chuck Muncie, California, RB
1976	Tony Dorsett, Pittsburgh, RB
1977	Earl Campbell, Texas, RB
1978	Chuck Fusina, Penn St., QB
1979	Charles White, USC, RB
1980	Herschel Walker, Georgia, RB
1981	Art Schlichter, Ohio St. QB
1982	John Elway, Stanford, QB
1983	Mike Rozier, Nebraska, RB
1984	Keith Byars, Ohio St., RB
1985	Lorenzo White, Mich.St., RB
1986	Paul Palmer, Temple, RB
1987	Tim Brown, Notre Dame, WR
1988	Barry Sanders, Okla.St., RB

Rockne Award

Year	Player, school
1939	Ken Kavanaugh, LSU, E
1940	Bob Suffridge, Tennessee, G
1941	Chub Peabody, Harvard, G
1942	Bob Dove, Notre Dame, E
1943	Cas Myslinski, Army, C
1944	Don Whitmire, Navy, T
1945	Dick Duden, Navy, E
1946	Burr Baldwin, UCLA, E
1947	Chuck Bednarik, Penn, C
1948	Bill Fischer, Notre Dame, G
1949	Leon Hart, Notre Dame, E
1950	Bud McFadin, Texas, G
1951	Bob Ward, Maryland, G
1952	Dick Modzelewski, Md, T
1953	Stan Jones, Maryland, T
1954	Max Boydston, Oklahoma, E
1955	Bob Pellegrini, Maryland, C
1956	Jerry Tubbs, Oklahoma, C
1957	Lou Michaels, Kentucky, T
1958	Bob Novogratz, Army, G
1959	Roger Davis, Syracuse, G

Year	Player, school
1960	Tom Brown, Minnesota, G
1961	Joe Romig, Colorado, G
1962	Pat Richter, Wisconsin, E
1963	Dick Butkus, Illinois, C
1964	Dick Butkus, Illinois, C
1965	Tommy Nobis, Texas, LB
1966	Jim Lynch, Notre Dame, LB
1967	Ron Yary, Southern Cal, OT
1968	Ted Hendricks, Miami,FL, DE
1969	Mike Reid, Penn St., DT
1970	Jim Stillwagon, Ohio St., MG
1971	Larry Jacobson, Nebraska, DT
1972	John Hannah, Alabama, OG
1973	Ed Jones, Tennessee St., DE
1974	Randy White, Maryland, DT
1975	Lee Roy Selmon, Oklahoma, DT
1976	Wilson Whitley, Houston, DT
1977	Ken MacAfee, Notre Dame, TE
1978	Greg Roberts, Oklahoma, OG
1979	Bruce Clark, Penn St., DT
1980	Hugh Green, Pittsburgh, DE
1981	Kenneth Sims, Texas, DT
1982	Billy Ray Smith, Ark., DE
1983	Bill Fralic, Pittsburgh, OT
1984	Bruce Smith, Va.Tech, DT
1985	Tony Casillas, Oklahoma, NG
1986	Gordie Lockbaum, H.Cross, E
1987	Chad Hennings, Air Force, DT
1988	Tracy Rocker, Auburn, DT

Smith Memorial Trophy

Presented in 1943 and '44 by the Touchdown Club of Washington, DC, to the outstanding player on an armed forces team. The award was named after Lt. Robert Smith, who was the first TD Club member killed in World War II.

Year	Player, camp	Year	Player, camp
1943	Dick Todd, Iowa Pre-Flight, HB, (college: Texas A&M)	1944	Bill Dudley, Randolph Field, HB, (college: Virginia)

Outland Trophy

First presented in 1946 by the Football Writers Association of America, honoring the nation's outstanding interior lineman. The award is named after its benefactor Dr. John H.Outland (Kansas, Class of 1898).

Players who won the Outland in their junior years are preceded by an asterisk (*), while players listed in **bold** type helped lead their team to a national championship (according to AP).

Year	Player, school	Year	Player, school
1946	**George Connor, N.Dame, T**	1968	Bill Stanfill, Georgia, T
1947	Joe Steffy, Army, G	1969	Mike Reid, Penn St., DT
1948	Bill Fischer, N.Dame, G		
1949	Ed Bagdon, Mich.St., G	1970	Jim Stillwagon, Ohio St., MG
		1971	**Larry Jacobson, Neb., DT**
1950	Bob Gain, Kentucky, T	1972	Rich Glover, Nebraska, MG
1951	Jim Weatherall, Okla., T	1973	John Hicks, Ohio St., OT
1952	Dick Modzelewski, Md., T	1974	Randy White, Maryland, DT
1953	J.D.Roberts, Oklahoma, G	1975	**Lee Roy Selmon, Oklahoma, DT**
1954	Bill Brooks, Arkansas, G	1976	*Ross Browner, Notre Dame, DE
1955	Calvin Jones, Iowa, G	1977	Brad Shearer, Texas, DT
1956	Jim Parker, Ohio St., G	1978	Greg Roberts, Oklahoma, OG
1957	Alex Karras, Iowa, T	1979	Jim Richter, N.C.State, C
1958	Zeke Smith, Auburn, G		
1959	Mike McGee, Duke, T	1980	Mark May, Pittsburgh, OT
		1981	*Dave Rimington, Nebraska, C
1960	**Tom Brown, Minnesota, G**	1982	Dave Rimington, Nebraska, C
1961	Merlin Olsen, Utah St., T	1983	Dean Steinkuhler, Neb., OG
1962	Bobby Bell, Minnesota, T	1984	Bruce Smith, Va.Tech, DT
1963	**Scott Appleton, Texas, T**	1985	Mike Ruth, Boston Col., NG
1964	Steve DeLong, Tennessee, T	1986	Jason Buck, BYU, DT
1965	Tommy Nobis, Texas, G	1987	Chad Hennings, Air Force, DT
1966	Loyd Phillips, Arkansas, T	1988	Tracy Rocker, Auburn, DT
1967	**Ron Yary, Southern Cal, T**		

Lombardi Award

First presented in 1970 by the Rotary Club of Houston, honoring the nation's best lineman. The award is named after pro football coach Vince Lombardi, who, as a college guard, was a member of the famous ''Seven Blocks of Granite'' at Fordham in the 1930s.

The Lombardi and Outland awards have gone to the same player in the same year eight times. Those players are preceded by (#). Ross Browner of Notre Dame won both, but in different years.

Year	Player, school	Year	Player, school
1970	#Jim Stillwagon, Ohio St, MG	1980	Hugh Green, Pittsburgh, DE
1971	Walt Patulski, N.Dame, DE	1981	Kenneth Sims, Texas, DT
1972	#Rich Glover, Nebraska, MG	1982	#Dave Rimington, Nebraska, C
1973	#John Hicks, Ohio St., OT	1983	#Dean Steinkuhler, Neb., OG
1974	#Randy White, Maryland, DT	1984	Tony Degrate, Texas, DT
1975	#Lee Roy Selmon, Okla., DT	1985	Tony Casillas, Oklahoma, NG
1976	Wilson Whitley, Houston, DT	1986	Cornelius Bennett, Ala., LB
1977	Ross Browner, N.Dame, DE	1987	Chris Spielman, Ohio St, LB
1978	Bruce Clark, Penn St., DT	1988	#Tracy Rocker, Auburn, DT
1979	Brad Budde, USC, OG		

O'Brien Quarterback Award

First presented in 1977 as the O'Brien Memorial Trophy, the award went to the outstanding player in the Southwest. In 1981, however, the Davey O'Brien Educational and Charitable Trust of Ft. Worth, Texas, renamed the prize the O'Brien National Quarterback Award and now honors the nation's best quarterback.

The award is named after 1938 Heisman Trophy winner Davey O'Brien of Texas Christian.

Year	Player, school	Year	Player, school
1977	Earl Campbell, Texas, RB	1983	Steve Young, BYU
1978	Billy Sims, Oklahoma, RB	1984	Doug Flutie, Boston College
1979	Mike Singletary, Baylor, LB	1985	Chuck Long, Iowa
1980	Mike Singletary, Baylor, LB	1986	Vinny Testaverde, Miami,FL
1981	Jim McMahon, BYU	1987	Don McPherson, Syracuse
1982	Todd Blackledge, Penn St.	1988	Troy Aikman, UCLA

Butkus Award

First presented in 1985 by the Downtown Athletic Club of Orlando, Fla., to honor the nation's outstanding linebacker.

The award is named after Dick Butkus, two-time consensus All-America at Illinois and six-time All-Pro with the Chicago Bears.

Year	Player, school
1985	Brian Bosworth, Oklahoma
1986	Brian Bosworth, Oklahoma
1987	Paul McGowan, Florida St.
1988	Derrick Thomas, Alabama

Thorpe Award

First presented in 1986 by the Jim Thorpe Athletic Club of Oklahoma City to honor the nation's outstanding defensive back.

The award is named after Jim Thorpe, the 1912 Olympic champion, two-time consensus All-America halfback at Carlisle, and pro football pioneer.

Year	Player, school
1986	Thomas Everett, Baylor
1987	Bennie Blades, Miami,FL
	Rickey Dixon, Oklahoma
1988	Deion Sanders, Florida St.

NCAA All-Time Leaders
Division I-A (through 1988)
CAREER

Total Offense

Yards Gained

Player	Years	Yards
Doug Flutie, Boston College	1981-84	11,317
Todd Santos, San Diego St	1984-87	10,513
Kevin Sweeney, Fresno St	1983-86	10,252
Brian McClure, Bowling Green	1982-85	9,774
Jim McMahon, BYU	1977-78,80-81	9,723

Yards Per Game

Player	Years	Yards	PerGm
Mike Perez, San Jose St	1986-87	6,182	309.1
Doug Gaynor, L.Beach St	1984-85	6,710	305.0
Tony Eason, Illinois	1981-82	6,589	299.5
Steve Young, BYU	1981-83	8,817	284.4
Doug Flutie, Boston Col.	1981-84	11,317	269.5

Rushing

Yards Gained

Player	Years	Yards
Tony Dorsett, Pittsburgh	1973-76	6,082
Charles White, Southern Cal	1976-79	5,598
Herschel Walker, Georgia	1980-82	5,259
Archie Griffin, Ohio St	1972-75	5,177
George Rogers, S.Carolina	1977-80	4,958

Yards Per Game

Player	Years	Yards	PerGm
Ed Marinaro, Cornell	1969-71	4,715	174.6
O.J.Simpson, Southern Cal	1967-68	3,124	164.4
Herschel Walker, Georgia	1980-82	5,259	159.4
Tony Dorsett, Pittsburgh	1973-76	6,082	141.4
Mike Rozier, Nebraska	1981-83	4,780	136.6

All-Purpose Running

Yards Gained

Player	Years	Yards
Napoleon McCallum, Navy	1981-85	7,172
Darrin Nelson, Stanford	1977-78,80-81	6,885
Tony Dorsett, Pittsburgh	1973-76	6,615
Paul Palmer, Temple	1983-86	6,609
Charles White, Southern Cal	1976-79	6,545

Yards Per Game

Player	Years	Yards	PerGm
Howard Stevens, Louisville	1971-72	3,873	193.7
O.J.Simpson, Southern Cal	1967-68	3,666	192.9
Ed Marinaro, Cornell	1969-71	4,940	183.0
Herschel Walker, Georgia	1980-82	5,749	174.2
Louie Giammona, Utah St	1973-75	5,203	173.4

Passing
(Minimum 500 Completions)

Passing Efficiency

Player	Years	Rating
Jim McMahon, BYU	1977-78,80-81	156.9
Steve Young, BYU	1982,84-86	149.8
Troy Aikman, Okla-UCLA	1984-85,87-88	149.7
Robbie Bosco, BYU	1981-83	149.4
Chuck Hartlieb, Iowa	1985-88	148.9

Yards Gained

Player	Years	Yards
Todd Santos, San Diego St	1984-87	11,425
Kevin Sweeney, Fresno St	1983-86	10,623
Doug Flutie, Boston College	1981-84	10,579
Brian McClure, Bowling Green	1982-85	10,280
Ben Bennett, Duke	1980-83	9,614

Completions

Player	Years	No
Todd Santos, San Diego St	1984-87	910
Brian McClure, Bowling Green	1982-85	900
Ben Bennett, Duke	1980-83	820
John Elway, Stanford	1979-82	774
Jack Trudeau, Illinois	1981,83-85	736

Receiving

Catches

Player	Years	No
Mark Templeton, Long Beach St	1983-86	262
Howard Twilley, Tulsa	1963-65	261
David Williams, Illinois	1983-85	245
Marc Zeno, Tulane	1984-87	236
Darrin Nelson, Stanford	1977-78,80-81	214

Catches Per Game

Player	Years	No	PerGm
Howard Twilley, Tulsa	1963-65	261	10.0
Jason Phillips, Houston	1987-88	207	9.4
Neal Sweeney, Tulsa	1965-66	134	7.4
David Williams, Illinois	1983-85	245	7.4
James Dixon, Houston	1987-88	161	7.3

Yards Gained

Player	Years	No	Yards
Marc Zeno, Tulane	1984-87	236	3,725
Ron Sellers, Florida St	1966-68	212	3,598
Elmo Wright, Houston	1968-70	153	3,347
Howard Twilley, Tulsa	1963-65	261	3,343
Gerald Harp, W.Carolina	1977-80	197	3,305

CAREER (Continued)

Scoring

Points (Kickers)	Years	FG	XP	Pts
Derek Schmidt, Fla.St	1984-87	73	174	393
Luis Zendejas, Ariz.St	1981-84	78	134	368
Jeff Jaeger, Washington	1983-86	80	118	358
John Lee, UCLA	1982-85	79	116	353
Max Zendejas, Arizona	1982-85	77	122	353
Kevin Butler, Georgia	1981-84	77	122	353

Field Goals	Years	No
Jeff Jaeger, Washington	1983-86	80
John Lee, UCLA	1982-85	79
Luis Zendejas, Arizona St	1981-84	78
Kevin Butler, Georgia	1981-84	77
Max Zendejas, Arizona	1982-85	77

Points (Non-Kickers)	Years	TD	Xpt	FG	Pts
Tony Dorsett, Pitt	1973-76	59	2	0	356
Glenn Davis, Army	1943-46	59	0	0	354
Art Luppino, Arizona	1953-56	48	49	0	337
Steve Owens, Okla.	1967-69	56	0	0	336
Wilford White, Ariz.St	1947-50	48	27	4	327

Miscellaneous

Interceptions	Years	No
Al Brosky, Illinois	1950-52	29
John Provost, Holy Cross	1972-74	27
Martin Bayless, Bowling Green	1980-83	27
Tom Curtis, Michigan	1967-69	25
Tony Thurman, Boston College	1981-84	25

Pts Per Game (Non-Kickers)	Years	Pts	PerGm
Bob Gaiters, N. Mexico St.	1959-60	203	11.9
Ed Marinaro, Cornell	1969-71	318	11.8
Bill Burnett, Arkansas	1968-70	294	11.3
Steve Owens, Oklahoma	1967-69	336	11.2
Eddie Talboom, Wyoming	1948-50	303	10.8

Punting Average*	Years	Avg
Reggie Roby, Iowa	1979-82	45.6
Greg Montgomery, Michigan St	1985-87	45.4
Tom Tupa, Ohio St	1984-87	45.2
Barry Helton, Colorado	1984-87	44.9
Ray Guy, Southern Mississippi	1970-72	44.7
*At least 150 punts kicked		

Touchdowns Rushing	Years	No
Steve Owens, Oklahoma	1967-69	56
Tony Dorsett, Pittsburgh	1973-76	55
Ed Marinaro, Cornell	1969-71	50
Mike Rozier, Nebraska	1981-83	50
Herschel Walker, Georgia	1980-82	49

Punt Return Average*	Years	Avg
Jack Mitchell, Oklahoma	1946-48	23.6
Gene Gibson, Cincinnati	1949-50	20.5
Eddie Macon, Pacific	1949-51	18.9
Jackie Robinson, UCLA	1939-40	18.8
Mike Fuller, Auburn	1972-74	17.7
Bobby Dillon, Texas	1949-51	17.7
*At least 1.2 punt returns per game		

Touchdowns Passing	Years	No
Jim McMahon, BYU	1977-78,80-81	84
Joe Adams, Tennessee St	1977-80	81
John Elway, Stanford	1979-82	77
Dan Marino, Pittsburgh	1979-82	74
Todd Santos, San Diego St	1984-87	70

Kickoff Return Average*	Years	Avg
Forrest Hall, San Francisco	1946-47	36.2
Anthony Davis, Southern Cal	1972-74	35.1
Overton Curtis, Utah St	1957-58	31.0
Altie Taylor, Utah St	1966-68	29.3
Stan Brown, Purdue	1968-70	28.8
Henry White, Colgate	1974-77	28.8
Donald Dennis, West Texas St	1964-65	28.8
*At least 1.2 kickoff returns per game		

Touchdown Catches	Years	No
Elmo Wright, Houston	1968-70	34
Howard Twilley, Tulsa	1963-65	32
Gerald Harp, Western Carolina	1977-80	26
Phil Odle, BYU	1965-67	25
Emanuel Tolbert, SMU	1976-79	25
Marc Zeno, Tulane	1984-87	25

SINGLE SEASON

Total Offense

Yards Gained	Year	Gm	Plays	Yards
Jim McMahon, BYU	1980	12	540	4,627
Steve Young, BYU	1983	11	531	4,346
Scott Mitchell, Utah	1988	11	589	4,299
Robbie Bosco, BYU	1985	13	578	4,141
Robbie Bosco, BYU	1984	12	543	3,932

Yards Per Game	Year	Gm	Yards	YdsPG
Steve Young, BYU	1983	11	4,346	395.1
Scott Mitchell, Utah	1988	11	4,299	390.8
Jim McMahon, BYU	1980	12	4,627	385.6
Jim McMahon, BYU	1981	10	3,458	345.8
Anthony Dilweg, Duke	1988	11	3,713	337.6

Rushing

Yards Gained	Year	Gm	Car	Yards
Barry Sanders, Okla.St	1988	11	344	2,628
Marcus Allen, USC	1981	11	403	2,342
Mike Rozier, Nebraska	1983	12	275	2,148
Tony Dorsett, Pittsburgh	1976	11	338	1,948
Lorenzo White, Mich.St	1985	11	386	1,908

Yards Per Game	Year	Gm	Yards	PerGm
Barry Sanders, Okla.St	1988	11	2,628	238.9
Marcus Allen, USC	1981	11	2,342	212.9
Ed Marinaro, Cornell	1971	9	1,881	209.0
Charles White, USC	1979	10	1,803	180.3
Mike Rozier, Nebraska	1983	12	2,148	179.0

SINGLE SEASON (Continued)

All-Purpose Running

Yards Gained

	Year	Yards
Barry Sanders, Oklahoma St	1988	3,250
Paul Palmer, Temple	1986	2,633
Marcus Allen, USC	1981	2,559
Mike Rozier, Nebraska	1983	2,486
Napoleon McCallum, Navy	1983	2,385

Yards Per Game

	Year	Yards	PerGm
Barry Sanders, Oklahoma St.	1988	3,250	295.5
Byron "Whizzer" White, Colo	1937	1,970	246.3
Paul Palmer, Temple	1986	2,633	239.4
Marcus Allen, USC	1981	2,559	232.6
Ollie Matson, San Francisco	1951	2,037	226.3

Passing
(Minimum 15 Attempts Per Game)

Passing Efficiency

	Year	Rating
Jim McMahon, BYU	1980	176.9
Jerry Rhome, Tulsa	1964	172.6
Steve Young, BYU	1983	168.5
Vinny Testaverde, Miami,FL	1986	165.8
Brian Dowling, Yale	1968	165.8

Yards Gained

	Year	Yards
Jim McMahon, BYU	1980	4,571
Scott Mitchell, Utah	1988	4,322
Robbie Bosco, BYU	1985	4,273
Todd Santos, San Diego St	1987	3,932
Steve Young, BYU	1983	3,902

Completions

	Year	Att	No
Robbie Bosco, BYU	1985	511	338
Scott Mitchell, Utah	1988	533	323
Doug Gaynor, Long Beach St	1985	452	321
Steve Young, BYU	1983	429	306
Todd Santos, San Diego St	1987	492	306

Miscellaneous

Interceptions

	Year	No
Al Worley, Washington	1968	14
George Shaw, Oregon	1951	13
Five tied at 12		

Punting Average*

	Year	Avg
Reggie Roby, Iowa	1981	49.8
Kirk Wilson, UCLA	1956	49.3
Zack Jordan, Colorado	1950	48.2
Ricky Anderson, Vanderbilt	1984	48.2
Marv Bateman, Utah	1971	48.1
Reggie Roby, Iowa	1982	48.1

*Qualifies for championship

Punt Return Average*

	Year	Avg
Bill Blackstock, Tennessee	1951	25.9
George Sims, Baylor	1948	25.0
Gene Derricotte, Michigan	1947	24.8
Erroll Tucker, Utah	1985	24.3
George Hoey, Michigan	1967	24.3

*At least 1.2 returns per game

Kickoff Return Average*

	Year	Avg
Forrest Hall, San Francisco	1946	38.2
Tony Ball, Tenn-Chattanooga	1977	36.4
Raghib Ismail, Notre Dame	1988	36.1
George Marinkov, N.Carolina St	1954	35.8
Bob Baker, Cornell	1964	35.1

*At least 1.2 kickoff returns per game

Receiving

Catches

	Year	Gm	No
Howard Twilley, Tulsa	1965	10	134
Jason Phillips, Houston	1988	11	108
James Dixon, Houston	1988	11	102
David Williams, Illinois	1984	11	101
Jay Miller, BYU	1973	11	100

Catches Per Game

	Year	No	PerGm
Howard Twilley, Tulsa	1965	134	13.4
Jason Phillips, Houston	1988	108	9.8
Jerry Hendren, Idaho	1969	95	9.5
Howard Twilley, Tulsa	1964	95	9.5
James Dixon, Houston	1988	102	9.3

Yards Gained

	Year	No	Yards
Howard Twilley, Tulsa	1965	134	1,779
Chuck Hughes, Texas Western*	1965	80	1,519
Henry Ellard, Fresno St	1982	62	1,510
Ron Sellers, Florida St	1968	86	1,496
Jerry Hendren, Idaho	1969	95	1,452

*Now UTEP.

Scoring

Points

	Year	TD	Xpt	FG	Pts
Barry Sanders, Okla.St	1988	39	0	0	234
Mike Rozier, Nebraska	1983	29	0	0	174
Lydell Mitchell, Penn St	1971	29	0	0	174
Art Luppino, Arizona	1954	24	22	0	166
Bobby Reynolds, Nebraska	1950	22	25	0	157

Points Per Game

	Year	Pts	PerGm
Barry Sanders, Okla.St	1988	234	21.3
Bobby Reynolds, Nebraska	1950	157	17.4
Art Luppino, Arizona	1954	166	16.6
Ed Marinaro, Cornell	1971	148	16.4
Lydell Mitchell, Penn St	1971	174	15.8

Touchdowns Rushing

	Year	No
Barry Sanders, Oklahoma St	1988	37
Mike Rozier, Nebraska	1983	29
Ed Marinaro, Cornell	1971	24
Anthony Thompson, Indiana	1988	24
O.J.Simpson, Southern Cal	1968	22
Marcus Allen, Southern Cal	1981	22

Touchdowns Passing

	Year	No
Jim McMahon, BYU	1980	47
Dennis Shaw, San Diego St	1969	39
Doug Williams, Grambling	1977	38
Steve Young, BYU	1983	33
Robbie Bosco, BYU	1984	33

Touchdown Catches

	Year	No
Tom Reynolds, San Diego St	1969	18
Howard Twilley, Tulsa	1965	16
Clay Brown, BYU	1980	15
Henry Ellard, Fresno St	1982	15
Jason Phillips, Houston	1988	15

Field Goals

	Year	No
John Lee, UCLA	1984	29
Paul Woodside, West Virginia	1982	28
Luis Zendejas, Arizona St	1983	28
Fuad Reveiz, Tennessee	1982	27
Three tied at 25		

BEST GAMES

Total Offense

Yards Gained	Opponent	Year	Yds
Scott Mitchell, Utah	Air Force	1988	625
Virgil Carter, BYU	UTEP	1966	599
Dave Wilson, Illinois	Ohio St.	1980	585
Marc Wilson, BYU	Utah	1977	582
Jim McMahon, BYU	Utah	1981	552

Passing

Yards Gained	Opponent	Year	Yds
Scott Mitchell, Utah	Air Force	1988	631
Dave Wilson, Illinois	Ohio St.	1980	621
Robbie Bosco, BYU	New Mex.	1985	585
Marc Wilson, BYU	Utah	1977	571
Jim McMahon, BYU	Utah	1981	565

Completions	Opponent	Year	No
Sandy Schwab, N'western	Michigan	1982	45
Chuck Hartlieb, Iowa	Indiana	1988	44
Jim McMahon, BYU	Colo.St.	1981	44
Gary Schofield, W.Forest .	Maryland	1981	43
Dave Wilson, Illinois	Ohio St.	1980	43
Rich Campbell, Cal......	Florida	1980	43

Scoring

Points	Opponent	Year	Pts
Jim Brown, Syracuse	Colgate	1956	43
Showboat Boykin, Miss...	Miss.St.	1951	42
Fred Wendt, UTEP*	N.Mex.St.	1948	42
Dick Bass, Pacific	S.Diego St.	1958	38
Jimmy Nutter, Wichita St.*	North.St.	1949	37

Note: Brown's 43 points (6 TDs, 7 extra points).
*UTEP was Texas Mines in 1948 and Wichita St. was Wichita Univ. in 1949.

Touchdowns Rushing	Opponent	Year	No
Showboat Boykin, Miss...	Miss.St.	1951	7

Note: Boykin's TD runs (21-14-12-14-85-1-5).

Touchdowns Passing	Opponent	Year	No
Dennis Shaw, S.Diego St..	N.Mex.St.	1969	9

Note: Shaw's TD passes (14-2-22-34-31-32-7-30-9).

Touchdown Catches	Opponent	Year	No
Tim Delaney, S.Diego St .	N.Mex.St.	1969	6

Note: Delaney TD catches (2-22-34-31-30-9).

Field Goals	Opponent	Year	No
Dale Klein, Nebraska....	Missouri	1985	7
Mike Prindle, W.Mich	Marshall	1984	7

Note: Klein (32-22-43-44-29-43-43); Prindle (32-44-42-23-48-41-27).

Extra Points (Kick)	Opponent	Year	No
Terry Leiweke, Houston...	Tulsa	1968	13

Extra Points (2-Pts)	Opponent	Year	No
Jim Pilot, N.Mexico St ...	H-Simmons	1961	6

Rushing

Yards Gained	Opponent	Year	Yds
Rueben Mayes, Wash.St .	Oregon	1984	357
Eddie Lee Ivery, Ga.Tech .	Air Force	1978	356
Eric Allen, Mich.St	Purdue	1971	350
Paul Palmer, Temple.....	E.Caro.	1986	349
Ricky Bell, USC	Wash.St.	1976	347
Ron Johnson, Michigan ..	Wisconsin	1968	347

Receiving

Catches	Opponent	Year	No
Jay Miller, BYU	New Mexico	1973	22
Rick Eber, Tulsa	Idaho St.	1967	20
Howard Twilley, Tulsa.....	Colo.St.	1965	19
Mark Templeton, L.Beach St.	Utah St.	1986	18
Howard Twilley, Tulsa.....	So.Ill.	1965	18

Yards Gained	Opponent	Year	Yds
Chuck Hughes, UTEP*....	N.Texas St	1965	349
Rick Eber, Tulsa	Idaho St.	1967	322
Harry Wood, Tulsa	Idaho St.	1967	318
Jeff Evans, N.Mexico St ..	So.Ill.	1978	316
Tom Reynolds, S.Diego St .	Utah St.	1971	290

*UTEP was Texas Western in 1965.

Longest Plays (since 1941)

Rushing	Opponent	Year	Yds
Gale Sayers, Kansas........	Nebraska	1963	99
Max Anderson, Ariz.St	Wyoming	1967	99
Ralph Thompson, W.Texas St .	Wich.St.	1970	99
Kelsey Finch, Tennessee	Florida	1977	99

Passing	Opponent	Year	Yds
Fred Owens			
to Jack Ford, Portland......	St.Mary's	1947	99
Bo Burris			
to Warren McVea, Houston..	Wash.St.	1966	99
Colin Clapton			
to Eddie Jenkins, H.Cross ...	Boston U.	1970	99
Terry Peel			
to Robert Ford, Houston	Syracuse	1970	99
Terry Peel			
to Robert Ford, Houston	S.Diego St.	1972	99
Cris Collinsworth			
to Derrick Gaffney, Fla	Rice	1977	99
Scott Ankrom			
to James Maness, TCU	Rice	1984	99

Field Goals	Opponent	Year	Yds
Steve Little, Arkansas	Texas	1977	67
Russell Erxleben, Texas	Rice	1977	67
Joe Williams, Wichita St	So.Ill.	1978	67

Punts	Opponent	Year	Yds
Pat Brady, Nevada-Reno	Loyola,CA	1950	99
George O'Brien, Wisconsin ..	Iowa	1952	98

Punt Returns	Opponent	Year	Yds
100-yd punt returns since 1941: 7 players.			

Kickoff Returns	Opponent	Year	Yds
100-yd kickoff returns since 1941: 160 players.			

Interception Returns	Opponent	Year	Yds
100-yd interception returns since 1941: 56 players.			

Divisional Playoffs

The NCAA has decided its Division I-AA champion with a postseason playoff since 1978. Divisions II and III have had playoffs since 1973.

The NAIA has used playoffs since 1956 for Division I and since 1970 for Division II.

NCAA Championship Games

Division I-AA, 1978-88

Year	Winner	Score	Loser
1978	Florida A&M	35-28	Massachusetts
1979	Eastern Kentucky	30-7	Lehigh,PA
1980	Boise St.,ID	31-29	Eastern Kentucky
1981	Idaho St.	34-23	Eastern Kentucky
1982	Eastern Kentucky	17-14	Delaware
1983	Southern Illinois	43-7	Western Carolina
1984	Montana St.	19-6	Louisiana Tech
1985	Georgia Southern	44-42	Furman,SC
1986	Georgia Southern	48-21	Arkansas St.
1987	NE Louisiana	43-42	Marshall,WV
1988	Furman,SC	17-12	Georgia Southern

Division II, 1973-88

Year	Winner	Score	Loser
1973	Louisiana Tech	34-0	Western Kentucky
1974	Central Michigan	54-14	Delaware
1975	Northern Michigan	16-14	Western Kentucky
1976	Montana St.	24-13	Akron,OH
1977	Lehigh,PA	33-0	Jacksonville,AL
1978	Eastern Illinois	10-9	Delaware
1979	Delaware	38-21	Youngstown St,OH
1980	Cal. Poly-SLO	21-13	Eastern Illinois
1981	SW Texas St.	42-13	North Dakota St.
1982	SW Texas St.	34-9	UC-Davis
1983	North Dakota St.	41-21	Central St.,OH
1984	Troy St.,AL	18-17	North Dakota St.
1985	North Dakota St.	35-7	North Alabama
1986	North Dakota St.	27-7	South Dakota
1987	Troy St.,AL	31-17	Portland St.,OR
1988	North Dakota St.	35-21	Portland St.,OR

Division III, 1973-88

Year	Winner	Score	Loser
1973	Wittenberg,OH	41-0	Juniata,PA
1974	Central, IA	10-8	Ithaca,NY
1975	Wittenberg,OH	28-0	Ithaca,NY
1976	St.John's,MN	31-28	Towson St.,MD
1977	Widener,PA	39-36	Wabash,IN
1978	Baldwin-Wallace	24-10	Wittenberg,OH
1979	Ithaca,NY	14-10	Wittenberg,OH
1980	Dayton,OH	63-0	Ithaca,NY
1981	Widener,PA	17-10	Dayton,OH
1982	West Georgia	14-0	Augustana,IL
1983	Augustana,IL	21-17	Union,NY
1984	Augustana,IL	21-12	Central,IA
1985	Augustana,IL	20-7	Ithaca,NY
1986	Augustana,IL	31-3	Salisbury St.,MD
1987	Wagner,NY	19-3	Dayton,OH
1988	Ithaca,NY	39-24	Central,IA

NAIA Championship Games

Division I, 1956-88

Year	Winner	Score	Loser
1956	Montana St. St.Joseph's,IN	0-0	--
1957	Pittsburg St.,KS	27-26	Hillsdale,MI
1958	NE Oklahoma	19-13	Northern Arizona
1959	Texas A&I	20-7	Lenoir-Rhyne,NC
1960	Lenoir-Rhyne,NC	15-14	Humboldt St.,CA
1961	Pittsburg St.,KS	12-7	Linfield,OR
1962	Central St.,OK	28-13	Lenoir-Rhyne,NC
1963	St.John's,MN	33-27	Prairie View,TX
1964	Concordia,MN Sam Houston,TX	7-7	--
1965	St.John's,MN	33-0	Linfield,OR
1966	Waynesburg,PA	42-21	Wisc.-Whitewater
1967	Fairmont St.,WV	28-21	Eastern Wash.
1968	Troy St.,AL	43-35	Texas A&I
1969	Texas A&I	32-7	Concordia,MN
1970	Texas A&I	48-7	Wofford,SC
1971	Livingston,AL	14-12	Arkansas Tech
1972	East Texas St.	21-18	Carson-Newman,TN
1973	Abilene Christian	42-14	Elon,NC
1974	Texas A&I	34-23	Henderson St.,AR
1975	Texas A&I	37-0	Salem, WV
1976	Texas A&I	26-0	Central Arkansas
1977	Abilene Christian	24-7	SW Oklahoma
1978	Angelo St., TX	24-14	Elon,NC
1979	Texas A&I	20-14	Central St.,OK
1980	Elon,NC	17-10	NE Oklahoma
1981	Elon,NC	3-0	Pittsburg St.,KS
1982	Central St.,OK	14-11	Mesa,CO
1983	Carson-Newman,TN	36-28	Mesa,CO
1984	Carson-Newman,TN Central Arkansas	19-19	--
1985	Hillsdale,MI Central Arkansas	10-10	--
1986	Carson-Newman,TN	17-0	Cameron,OK
1987	Cameron,OK	30-2	Carson-Newman,TN
1988	Carson-Newman,TN	56-21	Adams St.,CO

Division II, 1970-88

Year	Winner	Score	Loser
1970	Westminster,PA	21-16	Anderson,IN
1971	Calif.Lutheran	30-14	Westminster,PA
1972	Missouri Southern	21-14	Northwestern,IA
1973	Northwestern,IA	10-3	Glenville St.,WV
1974	Texas Lutheran	42-0	Missouri Valley
1975	Texas Lutheran	34-8	Calif.Lutheran
1976	Westminster,PA	20-13	Redlands,CA
1977	Westminster,PA	17-9	Calif.Lutheran
1978	Concordia,MN	7-0	Findlay,OH
1979	Findlay,OH	51-6	Northwestern,IA
1980	Pacific Lutheran	38-10	Wilmington,OH
1981	Austin College,TX Concordia,MN	24-24	--
1982	Linfield,OR	33-15	William Jewell,MO
1983	Northwestern,IA	25-21	Pacific Lutheran
1984	Linfield, OR	33-22	Northwestern,IA
1985	Wisc-La Crosse	24-7	Pacific Lutheran
1986	Linfield,OR	17-0	Baker,KS
1987	Pacific Lutheran Wisc.-Stevens Pt.*	16-16	--
1988	Westminster,PA	21-14	Wisc-La Crosse

*Wisconsin-Stevens Point forfeited its entire 1987 schedule due to its use of an ineligible player.

Notre Dame's **Frank Leahy** is the only coach ever to win four national championships in one decade. Before leading the Irish to the title in 1949, he contemplated the task at hand with players Emil Sitko, Bob Williams, Paul Burns and Del Gander.

YEAR BY YEAR

COLLEGE FOOTBALL

The two most discussed topics in any college football season are "Who's No. 1?" and "Who for the Heisman?" Both questions began to attract serious national interest in 1936 when the Associated Press introduced its weekly Top 20 poll and the Downtown Athletic Club of New York City renamed its player of the year trophy in memory of John W. Heisman and made it a national award.

But there is more to a review of the last 53 years than listing AP's national champions and the DAC's Heisman Trophy winners. This section chronicles each year providing a brief summary of the season, the final AP Top 20 (with head coaches, regular season and overall records), major bowl games, major conference champions, the leading Heisman vote-getters, other major award winners, and the consensus All-America team.

1936

The first national champion chosen by the Associated Press sportswriters' poll was a controversial one. Minnesota, winner in seven of eight regular season games, was named No.1 but AP ranked Northwestern, the only team to beat the Gophers, a distant seventh. The Wildcats, who also went 7–1, ended Minnesota's 28-game unbeaten streak in late October and won the Western Conference (Big Ten) championship. They moved up to the top of the poll but three weeks later were trounced, 26–6, by No.11 Notre Dame.

LSU and Pittsburgh placed second and third in the voting. The Tigers were 9–0–1 through the regular season, but lost to Santa Clara by a touchdown in the Sugar Bowl. Pitt went 7–1–1 then shut out Washington, 21–0, for its first Rose Bowl victory in four attempts. Arkansas won the Southwest Conference, but Texas Christian was invited to the first Cotton Bowl. Why? It was Horned Frog quarterback Sammy Baugh's final college game. Baugh went out a winner, beating Marquette, 16–6.

In New York, Yale end Larry Kelley was named the outstanding player in the nation and given the second Downtown Athletic Club Trophy. The DAC renamed the award the "Heisman Trophy" in October following the death of former college coach and club athletic director John W. Heisman.

Final AP Top 20
Writers' poll taken before bowl games.

	Regular Season	Head Coach	After Bowls
1 Minnesota	7–1–0	Bernie Bierman	same
2 LSU	9–0–1	Bernie Moore	9–1–1
3 Pittsburgh	7–1–1	Jock Sutherland	8–1–1
4 Alabama	8–0–1	Frank Thomas	same
5 Washington	7–1–1	Jimmy Phelan	7–2–1
6 Santa Clara	7–1–0	Buck Shaw	8–1–0
7 Northwestern	7–1–0	Pappy Waldorf	same
8 Notre Dame	6–2–1	Elmer Layden	same
9 Nebraska	7–2–0	Dana X. Bible	same
10 Pennsylvania	7–1–0	Harvey Harman	same
11 Duke	9–1–0	Wallace Wade	same
12 Yale	7–1–0	Ducky Pond	same
13 Dartmouth	7–1–1	Red Blaik	same
14 Duquesne	7–2–0	John Smith	8–2–0
15 Fordham	5–1–2	Jim Crowley	same
16 TCU	8–2–2	Dutch Meyer	9–2–2
17 Tennessee	6–2–2	Bob Neyland	same
18 Arkansas	7–3–0	Fred Thomsen	same
19 Navy	6–3–0	Tom Hamilton	same
20 Marquette	7–1–0	Frank Murray	7–2–0

Bowl Games with Top 20 Teams

Date	Bowl	Result
1/1/37	Cotton	TCU 16, Marquette 6
1/1/37	Orange	Duquesne 13, Miss.St. 12
1/1/37	Rose	Pittsburgh 21, Washington 0
1/1/37	Sugar	Santa Clara 21, LSU 14

Major Conference Champions

Big Six	Nebraska	5–0
Ivy League*	Dartmouth	5–0–1
Missouri Valley	Tulsa/Creighton	3–0
Pacific Coast	Washington	6–0–1
Southeastern	LSU	6–0
Southern	Duke	7–0
Southwest	Arkansas	5–1
Western	Northwestern	6–0

*Not a formal league until 1956.

Heisman Trophy Voting

		Yr	Pos.	Votes
1	Larry Kelley, Yale	Sr.	E	219
2	Sam Francis, Nebraska	Sr.	FB	47
3	Ray Buivid, Marquette	Sr.	HB	43
4	Sammy Baugh, TCU	Sr.	QB	39
5	Clint Frank, Yale	Jr.	HB	33

Other Major Award Winners

AFCA Coach of the Year
Dick Harlow, Harvard (3–4–1)

Consensus All-America Team
(By position, in alphabetical order)

Ends	Larry Kelley, Yale
	Gaynell Tinsley, LSU
Tackles	Averell Daniell, Pittsburgh
	Ed Widseth, Minnesota
Guards	Steve Reid, Northwestern
	Max Starcevich, Washington
Centers	Mike Basrak, Duquesne
	Alex Wojciechowicz, Fordham
Backs	Sammy Baugh, TCU
	Ray Buivid, Marquette
	Sam Francis, Nebraska
	Ace Parker, Duke

1937

Defending national champion Minnesota lost two games in 1937, to Nebraska and Notre Dame, and fell to fifth in the final AP poll.

Pittsburgh beat both the Cornhuskers and Irish on the way to an undefeated season and succeeded the Gophers as the country's top team. The one blemish on the Panthers' record was a scoreless tie with No.3 Fordham in October. It was hardly a surprise, however, considering it was the third year in a row the two had shut each other out.

Second-ranked California had the same 9–0–1 record as Pitt and its tie game was also scoreless. Playing at home, the Bears fought unranked Washington to a standstill in November. Later, they became the country's only 10-game winner, wrapping up the season with a 13–0 victory over No.4 Alabama in the Rose Bowl. The loss was the first for the Crimson Tide in five trips to Pasadena.

Halfback Clint Frank of Yale won the Heisman Trophy as the country's outstanding player, but runner-up Whizzer White of Colorado, a Rhodes Scholar and future Supreme Court Justice, turned in the season's most impressive stats. White led the nation in scoring, rushing, all-purpose running and total offense. The unbeaten Buffaloes, the first Rocky Mountain team to crack the Top 20, were invited to the Cotton Bowl but lost to Rice, 28–14.

Meanwhile, it was an outstanding season for Top 20 head coaches' nicknames.

Final AP Top 20
Writers' poll taken before bowl games.

	Regular Season	Head Coach	After Bowls
1 Pittsburgh	9–0–1	Jock Sutherland	same
2 California	9–0–1	Stub Allison	10–0–1
3 Fordham	7–0–1	Jim Crowley	same
4 Alabama	9–0–0	Frank Thomas	9–1–0
5 Minnesota	6–2–0	Bernie Bierman	same
6 Villanova	8–0–1	Clipper Smith	same
7 Dartmouth	7–0–2	Red Blaik	same
8 LSU	9–1–0	Bernie Moore	9–2–0
9 Notre Dame	6–2–1	Elmer Layden	same
Santa Clara	8–0–0	Buck Shaw	9–0–0
11 Nebraska	6–1–2	Biff Jones	same
12 Yale	6–1–1	Ducky Pond	same
13 Ohio St.	6–2–0	Francis Schmidt	same
14 Holy Cross	8–0–2	Eddie Anderson	same
Arkansas	6–2–2	Fred Thomsen	same
16 TCU	4–2–2	Dutch Meyer	same
17 Colorado	8–0–0	Bunnie Oakes	8–1–0
18 Rice	5–3–2	Jimmy Kitts	6–3–2
19 N.Carolina	7–1–1	Ray Wolf	same
20 Duke	7–2–1	Wallace Wade	same

Bowl Games with Top 20 Teams

Date	Bowl	Result
1/1/38	Cotton	Rice 28, Colorado 14
1/1/38	Orange	Auburn 6, Michigan St. 0
1/1/38	Rose	California 13, Alabama 0
1/1/38	Sugar	Santa Clara 6, LSU 0

Major Conference Champions

Big Six	Nebraska	3–0–2
Ivy League*	Dartmouth	4–0–2
Missouri Valley	Tulsa	3–0
Pacific Coast	California	6–0–1
Southeastern	Alabama	6–0
Southern	North Carolina	4–0–1
	and Maryland	2–0
Southwest	Rice	4–1–1
Western	Minnesota	5–0

*Not a formal league until 1956.

Heisman Trophy Voting

	Yr	Pos.	Votes
1 Clint Frank, Yale	Sr.	HB	524
2 Byron (Whizzer) White, Colo.	Sr.	HB	264
3 Marshall Goldberg, Pitt	Jr.	HB	211
4 Alex Wojciechowicz, Fordham	Sr.	C	85
5 Joe Kilgrow, Alabama	Sr.	HB	78

Other Major Award Winners

Maxwell (Player)	Clint Frank, Yale
Camp (Back)	Marshall Goldberg, Pitt

AFCA Coach of the Year
Hooks Mylin, Lafayette (8–0)

Consensus All-America Team
(By position, in alphabetical order)

Ends	Andy Bershak, North Carolina
	Chuck Sweeney, Notre Dame
Tackles	Ed Franco, Fordham
	Tony Matisi, Pittsburgh
Guards	Leroy Monsky, Alabama
	Joe Routt, Texas A&M
Center	Alex Wojciechowicz, Fordham
Backs	Sam Chapman, California
	Clint Frank, Yale
	Marshall Goldberg, Pittsburgh
	Byron (Whizzer) White, Colorado

1938

Texas Christian won both the national championship and the Heisman Trophy in 1938. The Horned Frogs were undefeated and untied through 10 regular season games and they had little Davey O'Brien at quarterback.

At just 5-foot-7 and 150 lbs., O'Brien didn't look anything like predecessor Sammy Baugh. But he threw the football like Baugh, leading the nation in passing yardage for the second year in a row. O'Brien capped the season with a second half touchdown pass and field goal to spark the TCU to a come-from-behind 15–7 victory over 6th ranked Carnegie Tech in the Sugar Bowl.

Although bowl games would not count in AP's final Top 20 selections until 1965, the Orange and Rose bowls featured four of 1938's top seven teams in two of the more memorable frays of the season.

Tennessee and Oklahoma were both 11–0 and ranked 2nd and 4th, respectively, when they collided in Miami. The Vols won, 17–0, but play was so rough and penalties so numerous (a combined 220 yards stepped off against both sides) that it became known as the '39 "Orange Brawl."

No.3 Duke faced No.7 Southern Cal in the Rose Bowl. The Blue Devils were undefeated, untied and unscored upon in nine games. USC was 8–2. The Trojans won, 7–3, with less than a minute to play when reserve quarterback Doyle Nave and reserve end Al Krueger combined for 14-yard touchdown pass.

Final AP Top 20

Writers' poll taken before bowl games.

	Regular Season	Head Coach	After Bowls
1 TCU	10–0–0	Dutch Meyer	11–0–0
2 Tennessee	10–0–0	Bob Neyland	11–0–0
3 Duke	9–0–0	Wallace Wade	9–1–0
4 Oklahoma	10–0–0	Tom Stidham	10–1–0
5 Notre Dame	8–1–0	Elmer Layden	same
6 Carnegie Tech	7–1–0	Bill Kern	7–2–0
7 Southern Cal	8–2–0	Howard Jones	9–2–0
8 Pittsburgh	8–2–0	Jock Sutherland	same
9 Holy Cross	8–1–0	Eddie Anderson	same
10 Minnesota	6–2–0	Bernie Bierman	same
11 Texas Tech	10–0–0	Pete Cawthon	10–1–0
12 Cornell	5–1–1	Carl Snavely	same
13 Alabama	7–1–1	Frank Thomas	same
14 California	10–1–0	Stub Allison	same
15 Fordham	6–1–2	Jim Crowley	same
16 Michigan	6–1–1	Fritz Crisler	same
17 Northwestern	4–2–2	Pappy Waldorf	same
18 Villanova	8–0–1	Clipper Smith	same
19 Tulane	7–2–1	Red Dawson	same
20 Dartmouth	7–2–0	Red Blaik	same

Bowl Games with Top 20 Teams

Date	Bowl	Result
1/2/39	Cotton	St.Mary's 20, Texas Tech 13
1/2/39	Orange	Tennessee 17, Oklahoma 0
1/2/39	Rose	USC 7, Duke 3
1/2/39	Sugar	TCU 15, Carnegie Tech 7

Major Conference Champions

Big Six	Oklahoma	5–0
Ivy League*	Cornell	3–0–1
Missouri Valley	Tulsa	3–1
Pacific Coast	USC/California	6–1
Skyline	Utah	4–0–2
Southeastern	Tennessee	7–0
Southern	Duke	5–0
Southwest	TCU	6–0
Western	Minnesota	4–1

*Not a formal league until 1956.

Heisman Trophy Voting

	Yr	Pos.	Votes
1 Davey O'Brien, TCU	Sr.	QB	519
2 Marshall Goldberg, Pitt	Sr.	HB	294
3 Sid Luckman, Columbia	Sr.	QB	154
4 Bob MacLeod, Dartmouth	Sr.	HB	78
5 Vic Bottari, California	Sr.	HB	67

Other Major Award Winners

Maxwell (Player)	Davey O'Brien, TCU
Camp (Back)	Davey O'Brien, TCU

AFCA Coach of the Year
Bill Kern, Carnegie Tech

Consensus All-America Team

(By position, in alphabetical order)

Ends	Brud Holland, Cornell
	Bowden Wyatt, Tennessee
	Waddy Young, Oklahoma
Tackles	Ed Beinor, Notre Dame
	Alvord Wolff, Santa Clara
Guards	Ed Bock, Iowa St.
	Ralph Heikkinen, Michigan
Center	Ki Aldrich, TCU.
Backs	Vic Bottari, California
	Marshall Goldberg, Pittsburgh
	Bob MacLeod, Dartmouth
	Davey O'Brien, TCU

1939

The national championship changed hands in 1939 but stayed in the Lone Star state as Texas A&M followed Texas Christian to the top of the AP heap. A&M won all 10 of its regular season games, including a 20–6 drubbing of TCU, whose record dropped to 3–7.

Led by halfback Jim Kimbrough and a defense that held opponents to less than two points a game, the Aggies nipped No.5 Tulane, 14–13, in the Sugar Bowl to finish the campaign unbeaten and untied.

For the second straight year a team that went through the regular season undefeated, untied and unscored upon fell to Southern Cal in the Rose Bowl. This time, the 4th-ranked Trojans turned the tables on No.2 Tennessee, shutting the Vols out, 14–0, to snap a 23-game winning streak.

In the Midwest, halfbacks Nile Kinnick of Iowa and Tom Harmon of Michigan led their teams to Top 20 finishes and placed 1–2 in the Heisman vote. Kinnick won, but Harmon, a junior, would get the trophy in 1940.

The decade ended with six-time Western Conference (Big 10) champion Chicago giving up football. The Maroons had been coached for 41 years (1892–1932) by living legend Amos Alonzo Stagg and boasted the first Heisman winner—halfback Jay Berwanger—as recently as 1935. But those days seemed like distant memories by '39 when Chicago found itself getting clobbered by Illinois (46–0), Ohio State (61–0) and Michigan (85–0).

Final AP Top 20

Writers' poll taken before bowl games.

	Regular Season	Head Coach	After Bowls
1 Texas A&M	10–0–0	Homer Norton	11–0–0
2 Tennessee	10–0–0	Bob Neyland	10–1–0
3 Southern Cal	7–0–2	Howard Jones	8–0–2
4 Cornell	8–0–0	Carl Snavely	same
5 Tulane	8–0–1	Red Dawson	8–1–1
6 Missouri	8–1–0	Don Faurot	8–2–0
7 UCLA	6–0–4	Babe Horrell	same
8 Duke	8–1–0	Wallace Wade	same
9 Iowa	6–1–1	Eddie Anderson	same
10 Duquesne	8–0–1	Buff Donelli	same
11 Boston College	9–1–0	Frank Leahy	9–2–0
12 Clemson	8–1–0	Jess Neely	9–1–0
13 Notre Dame	7–2–0	Elmer Layden	same
14 Santa Clara	5–1–3	Buck Shaw	same
15 Ohio St.	6–2–0	Francis Schmidt	same
16 Georgia Tech	7–2–0	Bill Alexander	8–2–0
17 Fordham	6–2–0	Jim Crowley	same
18 Nebraska	7–1–1	Biff Jones	same
19 Oklahoma	6–2–1	Tom Stidham	same
20 Michigan	6–2–0	Fritz Crisler	same

Bowl Games with Top 20 Teams

Date	Bowl	Result
1/1/40	Cotton	Clemson 6, Boston College 3
1/1/40	Orange	Georgia Tech 21, Missouri 7
1/1/40	Rose	USC 14, Tennessee 0
1/1/40	Sugar	Texas A&M 14, Tulane 13

Major Conference Champions

Big Six	Missouri	5–0
Ivy League*	Cornell	4–0
Missouri Valley	Washington,MO	4–1
Pacific Coast	USC	5–0–2
	and UCLA	5–0–3
Skyline	Colorado	5–1
Southeastern	Tenn./Georgia Tech	6–0
	and Tulane	5–0
Southern	Duke	5–0
Southwest	Texas A&M	6–0
Western	Ohio St.	5–1

*Not a formal league until 1956.

Heisman Trophy Voting

	Yr	Pos.	Votes
1 Nile Kinnick, Iowa	Sr.	HB	651
2 Tom Harmon, Michigan	Jr.	HB	405
3 Paul Christman, Missouri	Jr.	QB	391
4 George Cafego, Tennessee	Sr.	FB	296
5 John Kimbrough, Texas A&M	Jr.	HB	268

Other Major Award Winners

AP Athlete of Year	Nile Kinnick, Iowa
Maxwell (Player)	Nile Kinnick, Iowa
Camp (Back)	Nile Kinnick, Iowa
Rockne (Lineman)	Ken Kavanaugh, LSU, E

AFCA Coach of the Year
Eddie Anderson, Iowa

Consensus All-America Team

(By position, in alphabetical order)

Ends—Ken Kavanaugh, LSU; Esco Sarkkinen, Ohio St. **Tackles**—Nick Drahos, Cornell; Harley McCollum, Tulane. **Guards**—Ed Molinski, Tennessee; Harry Smith, Southern Cal. **Center**—John Schiechl, Santa Clara. **Backs**—George Cafego, Tennessee; Tom Harmon, Michigan; John Kimbrough, Texas A&M; Nile Kinnick, Iowa.

1940

Minnesota became the first school in the five years of the AP poll to win the championship a second time. The Gophers won the pivotal game of the year against Michigan, stopping Tom Harmon and the visiting Wolverines, 7–6, in the mud on the first Saturday in November. It settled both the national and Big Nine championships.

Harmon ran wild against everyone else, particularly California. In the season opener, which also happened to be his birthday, Harmon accounted for five touchdowns against the Bears: a 96-yard kickoff return, a 72-yard punt return, runs of 86 and 8 yards from scrimmage, and a TD pass. Harmon went on to lead the nation in scoring and all-purpose running and sweep the post–season Player of the Year awards.

The most significant development of the year was Stanford's turn-around from a 1–7–1 loser in 1939 to an undefeated juggernaut under first year coach Clark Shaughnessy. The second-ranked Indians did it using Shaughnessy's revolutionary T-formation with junior quarterback Frankie Albert directly behind center and men in motion.

Elsewhere, Tennessee turned in its third consecutive 10–0 regular season under coach Bob Neyland. The 4th-ranked Vols met another unbeaten team, No.5 Boston College, in the Sugar Bowl. BC won, 19–13, in coach Frank Leahy's last game before moving on to Notre Dame.

Final AP Top 20
Writers' poll taken before bowl games.

	Regular Season	Head Coach	After Bowls
1 Minnesota	8–0–0	Bernie Bierman	same
2 Stanford	9–0–0	C.Shaughnessy	10–0–0
3 Michigan	7–1–0	Fritz Crisler	same
4 Tennessee	10–0–0	Bob Neyland	10–1–0
5 Boston Col.	10–0–0	Frank Leahy	11–0–0
6 Texas A&M	8–1–0	Homer Norton	9–1–0
7 Nebraska	8–1–0	Biff Jones	8–2–0
8 Northwestern	6–2–0	Pappy Waldorf	same
9 Miss.St.	9–0–1	Allyn McKeen	10–0–1
10 Washington	7–2–0	Jimmy Phelan	same
11 Santa Clara	6–1–1	Buck Shaw	same
12 Fordham	7–1–0	Jim Crowley	7–2–0
13 Georgetown	8–1–0	Jack Hagerty	8–2–0
14 Pennsylvania	6–1–1	George Munger	same
15 Cornell	6–2–0	Carl Snavely	same
16 SMU	8–1–1	Matty Bell	same
17 Hard.-Simmons	9–0–0	Abe Woodson	same
18 Duke	7–2–0	Wallace Wade	same
19 Lafayette	9–0–0	Hooks Mylin	9–0–0
20 —			

Bowl Games with Top 20 Teams

Date	Bowl	Result
1/1/41	Cotton	Texas A&M 13, Fordham 12
1/1/41	Orange	Miss.St. 14, Georgetown 7
1/1/41	Rose	Stanford 21, Nebraska 13
1/1/41	Sugar	Boston Col. 19, Tennessee 13

Major Conference Champions

Big Nine	Minnesota	6–0
Big Six	Nebraska	5–0
Ivy League*	Pennsylvania	5–0–1
Missouri Valley	Tulsa	4–0
Pacific Coast	Stanford	7–0
Skyline	Utah	5–1
Southeastern	Tennessee	5–0
Southern	Clemson	4–0
Southwest	Texas A&M/SMU	5–1

*Not a formal league until 1956.

Heisman Trophy Voting

	Yr	Pos.	Votes
1 Tom Harmon, Michigan	Sr.	HB	1,303
2 John Kimbrough, Texas A&M	Sr.	FB	841
3 George Franck, Minnesota	Sr.	HB	102
4 Frankie Albert, Stanford	Jr.	QB	90
5 Paul Christman, Missouri	Sr.	QB	66

Other Major Award Winners

AP Athlete of Year	Tom Harmon, Michigan
Maxwell (Player)	Tom Harmon, Michigan
Camp (Back)	Tom Harmon, Michigan
Rockne (Lineman)	Bob Suffridge, Tenn., G

AFCA Coach of Year
Clark Shaughnessy, Stanford

Consensus All-America Team

(By position, in alphabetical order)

Ends—Gene Goodreault, Boston College; Dave Rankin, Purdue. **Tackles**—Alf Bauman, Northwestern; Nick Drahos, Cornell; Urban Odson, Minnesota. **Guards**—Marshall Robnett, Texas A&M; Bob Suffridge, Tennessee. **Center**—Rudy Mucha, Washington. **Backs**—Frankie Albert, Stanford; George Franck, Minnesota; Tom Harmon, Michigan; John Kimbrough, Texas A&M.

1941

Texas appeared to have the national championship locked up when it crushed its first six opponents by an average score of 38–5. Then, on consecutive Saturday afternoons in early November, the "Immortal 13" fell from grace. First, Baylor surprised the Longhorns with a 7–7 tie, then TCU shocked them with a 14–7 beating. The week of the TCU game, the Longhorns were on the cover of *Life* magazine.

Defending national champion Minnesota replaced Texas at No.1 and stayed there. Led by Heisman–winning halfback Bruce Smith, the Gophers were unbeaten again but unable to accept a bowl invitation, given the Big Nine's ban on postseason play.

The arrival of World War II on Dec.7 resulted in moving the Rose Bowl game out of Pasadena for the only time in its history. Mindful that Japan might follow up Pearl Harbor with a bombing raid on the West Coast, the U.S.Army cancelled all large gatherings, including the Tournament of Roses Parade and Rose Bowl match between No.2 Duke and Pacific Coast Conference champ Oregon State.

Duke coach Wallace Wade, who had taken three teams to the Rose Bowl as a coach and participated in a fourth as a player, offered to host the game in Durham. Oregon State agreed, took the train east, then beat the previously undefeated Blue Devils, 20–16.

Notre Dame, 8–0–1 in its first year under Frank Leahy, ranked third. The tie was a scoreless one with Army in New York (not the last time that would happen).

Final AP Top 20

Writers' poll taken before bowl games.

	Regular Season	Head Coach	After Bowls
1 Minnesota	8–0–0	Bernie Bierman	same
2 Duke	9–0–0	Wallace Wade	9–1–0
3 Notre Dame	8–0–1	Frank Leahy	same
4 Texas	8–1–1	Dana X. Bible	same
5 Michigan	6–1–1	Fritz Crisler	same
6 Fordham	7–1–0	Jim Crowley	8–1–0
7 Missouri	8–1–0	Don Faurot	8–2–0
8 Duquesne	8–0–0	Buff Donelli	same
9 Texas A&M	9–1–0	Homer Norton	9–2–0
10 Navy	7–1–1	Swede Larson	same
11 Northwestern	5–3–0	Pappy Waldorf	same
12 Oregon St.	7–2–0	Lon Stiner	8–2–0
13 Ohio St.	6–1–1	Paul Brown	same
14 Georgia	8–1–1	Wally Butts	9–1–1
15 Pennsylvania	7–1–1	George Munger	same
16 Miss.St.	8–1–1	Allyn McKeen	same
17 Mississippi	6–2–1	Harry Mehre	same
18 Tennessee	8–2–0	John Barnhill	same
19 Washington St.	6–4–0	Babe Hollingbery	same
20 Alabama	8–2–0	Frank Thomas	9–2–0

Bowl Games with Top 20 Teams

Date	Bowl	Result
1/1/42	Cotton	Alabama 29, Texas A&M 21
1/1/42	Orange	Georgia 40, TCU 26
1/1/42	Rose	Oregon St. 20, Duke 16
		(game moved to Durham, NC)
1/1/42	Sugar	Fordham 2, Missouri 0

Major Conference Champions

Big Nine	Minnesota	5–0
Big Six	Missouri	5–0
Ivy League*	Pennsylvania	6–1
Missouri Valley	Tulsa	4–0
Pacific Coast	Oregon St.	7–2
Skyline	Utah	4–0–2
Southeastern	Mississippi St.	4–0–1
Southern	Duke	5–0
Southwest	Texas A&M	5–1

*Not a formal league until 1956.

Heisman Trophy Voting

	Yr	Pos.	Votes
1 Bruce Smith, Minnesota	Sr.	HB	554
2 Angelo Bertelli, Notre Dame	So.	QB	345
3 Frankie Albert, Stanford	Sr.	QB	336
4 Frank Sinkwich, Georgia	Jr.	HB	249
5 Bill Dudley, Virginia	Sr.	HB	237

Other Major Award Winners

Maxwell (Player)	Bill Dudley, Virginia
Camp (Back)	Bill Dudley, Virginia
Rockne (Lineman)	Chub Peabody, Harvard, G

AFCA Coach of Year
Frank Leahy, Notre Dame

Consensus All-America Team
(By position, in alphabetical order)

Ends—Bob Dove, Notre Dame; Holt Rast, Alabama. **Tackles**—Ernie Blandin, Tulane; Dick Wildung, Minnesota. **Guards**—Ray Frankowski, Washington; Chub Peabody, Harvard. **Center**—Darold Jenkins, Missouri. **Backs**—Frankie Albert, Stanford; Bill Dudley, Virginia; Frank Sinkwich, Georgia; Bruce Smith, Minnesota; Bob Westfall, Michigan.

1942

Ohio State won its first national championship in Paul Brown's second year at the helm. The 34-year-old Brown, who would later become one of pro football's greatest coaches, guided the Buckeyes to a 6–1–1 record his first season, then improved it to 9–1.

OSU's only setback was a midseason 17–7 loss to Wisconsin. The Badgers, who had last won the Big Ten championship in 1912, finished the season ranked No.3, blowing their shot at the national and conference titles by dropping a 6–0 decision to Iowa a week after beating Ohio State.

No.2 Georgia also stumbled in the stretch. The Bulldogs, led by Heisman Trophy-winning full-back Frank Sinkwich, were 9–0 and heavily favored when they met 4–4–1 Auburn in their next to last game of the regular season. Auburn stunned the SEC champs, 27–13, but Georgia came back to finish with two shutouts, wrecking No.5 Georgia Tech, 34–0, then besting UCLA, 9–0, in the Rose Bowl.

Upset of the year? Holy Cross throttling Boston College, 55–12, on Thanksgiving at Fenway Park. BC, the best team in the East, entered the game with an 8–0 record. The Eagles finished at No.8, then lost the Orange Bowl to No.10 Alabama.

Fourth-ranked Tulsa, the Missouri Valley champion, was the only Top 20 team to go undefeated over the regular season, but fell to No.7 Tennessee in the Sugar Bowl.

Bowl Games with Top 20 Teams

Date	Bowl	Result
1/1/43	Cotton	Texas 14, Georgia Tech 7
1/1/43	Orange	Alabama 37, Boston Col. 21
1/1/43	Rose	Georgia 9, UCLA 0
1/1/43	Sugar	Tennessee 14, Tulsa 7

Major Conference Champions

Big Nine	Ohio St.	5–1
Big Six	Missouri	4–0–1
Ivy League*	Navy	4–1
Missouri Valley	Tulsa	5–0
Pacific Coast	UCLA	6–1
Skyline	Colorado	5–1
Southeastern	Georgia	6–1
Southern	Wm.& Mary	4–0
Southwest	Texas	5–1

*Not a formal league until 1956.

Heisman Trophy Voting

		Yr	Pos.	Votes
1 Frank Sinkwich, Georgia		Sr.	HB	1,059
2 Paul Governali, Columbia		Sr.	QB	218
3 Clint Castleberry, Ga.Tech		Sr.	HB	99
4 Mike Holovak, Boston Col.		Sr.	FB	95
5 Billy Hillenbrand, Indiana		Sr.	HB	86
6 Angelo Bertelli, Notre Dame		Jr.	QB	75

Final AP Top 20

Writers' poll taken before bowl games.

		Regular Season	Head Coach	After Bowls
1	Ohio St.	9–1–0	Paul Brown	same
2	Georgia	10–1–0	Wally Butts	11–1–0
3	Wisconsin	8–1–1	H.Stuhldreher	same
4	Tulsa	10–1–0	Henry Frnka	10–1–0
5	Georgia Tech	9–1–0	Bill Alexander	9–2–0
6	Notre Dame	7–2–2	Frank Leahy	same
7	Tennessee	8–1–1	John Barnhill	9–1–1
8	Boston Col.	8–1–0	Denny Myers	8–2–0
9	Michigan	7–3–0	Fritz Crisler	same
10	Alabama	7–3–0	Frank Thomas	8–3–0
11	Texas	8–2–0	Dana X. Bible	9–2–0
12	Stanford	6–4–0	Marchie Schwartz	same
13	UCLA	7–3–0	Babe Horrell	7–4–0
14	Wm.& Mary	9–1–1	Carl Voyles	same
15	Santa Clara	7–2–0	Buck Shaw	same
16	Auburn	6–4–1	Jack Meagher	same
17	Wash. St.	6–2–2	Babe Hollingbery	same
18	Miss.St.	8–2–0	Allyn McKeen	same
19	Minnesota	5–4–0	George Hauser	same
	Holy Cross	5–4–0	Ank Scanlon	same
	Penn St.	6–1–1	Bob Higgins	same

Other Major Award Winners

AP Athlete of Year	Frank Sinkwich, Georgia
Maxwell (Player)	Paul Governali, Columbia
Camp (Back)	Frank Sinkwich, Georgia
Rockne (Lineman)	Bob Dove, Notre Dame, E

AFCA Coach of Year
Bill Alexander, Georgia Tech

Consensus All-America Team

(By position, in alphabetical order)

Ends—Bob Dove, Notre Dame; Dave Schreiner, Wisconsin. **Tackles**—Dick Wildung, Minnesota; Albert Wistert, Michigan. **Guards**—Julie Franks, Michigan; Harvey Hardy, Georgia Tech; Chuck Taylor, Stanford. **Center**—Joe Domnanovich, Alabama. **Backs**—Paul Governali, Columbia; Billy Hillenbrand, Indiana; Mike Holovak, Boston College; Frank Sinkwich, Georgia.

1943

Service teams dominated the AP Top 20 in 1943.

Not only were six of the top dozen squads organized by the military, but three schools—Michigan, Purdue and Duke—benefited from on-campus Navy training programs that attracted college and pro athletes from all over the region and let them play ball. Michigan, for example, took the field with an All-Big Ten backfield that included Wisconsin's Elroy "Crazy Legs" Hirsch and Minnesota's Bill Daley.

Notre Dame was everybody's choice for national champion, playing a 10-game schedule that featured seven opponents who would end up ranked among the first 13 teams in AP's final poll. The Irish became the No.1 team in early October and twice defeated AP's weekly No.2 team—first Michigan (35–12), then Iowa Pre-Flight (14–13). Army and Navy were ranked third when they each played Notre Dame and lost.

An undefeated season eluded the Irish in the last 33 seconds of their final game when Great Lakes (Ill.)Naval Station beat them 19–14 on a 46-yard Steve Lach to Paul Anderson TD pass. Nevertheless, Notre Dame remained No.1 and quarterback Angelo Bertelli, who only played the first six games before being called to boot camp by the Marines, won the Heisman.

Finally, the coach of the year was 81-year-old Amos Alonzo Stagg, whose College of the Pacific team went 7–2 and ranked 19th.

Bowl Games with Top 20 Teams

Date	Bowl	Result
1/1/44	Cotton	7–7, Texas vs Randolph Field
1/1/44	Orange	LSU 19, Texas A&M 14
1/1/44	Rose	USC 29, Washington 0
1/1/44	Sugar	Georgia Tech 20, Tulsa 18

Major Conference Champions

Big Nine	Michigan/Purdue	6–0
Big Six	Oklahoma	5–0
Ivy League*	Navy	4–0
Missouri Valley	Tulsa	1–0
Pacific Coast	USC	5–0
Skyline	Vacant (not enough teams)	
Southeastern	Georgia Tech	3–0
Southern	Duke	4–0
Southwest	Texas	5–0

*Not a formal league until 1956.

Heisman Trophy Voting

	Yr	Pos.	Votes
1 Angelo Bertelli, Notre Dame	Sr.	QB	648
2 Bob Odell, Penn	Sr.	HB	177
3 Otto Graham, Northwestern	Sr.	QB	140
4 Creighton Miller, N.Dame	Sr.	HB	134
5 Eddie Prokop, Ga.Tech	Sr.	HB	85

Final AP Top 20
Writers' poll taken before bowl games.

	Regular Season	Head Coach	After Bowls
1 Notre Dame	9–1–0	Frank Leahy	same
2 Iowa Pre-Flight	9–1–0	Don Faurot	same
3 Michigan	8–1–0	Fritz Crisler	same
4 Navy	8–1–0	Billick Whelchel	same
5 Purdue	9–0–0	Elmer Burnham	same
6 Great Lakes	10–2–0	Tony Hinkle	same
7 Duke	8–1–0	Eddie Cameron	same
8 Del Monte P-F	7–1–0	Bill Kern	same
9 Northwestern	6–2–0	Pappy Waldorf	same
10 March Field	9–1–0	Paul Schissler	same
11 Army	7–2–1	Red Blaik	same
12 Washington	4–0–0	Ralph Welch	4–1–0
13 Georgia Tech	7–3–0	Bill Alexander	8–3–0
14 Texas	7–1–0	Dana X. Bible	7–1–1
15 Tulsa	6–0–1	Henry Frnka	6–1–1
16 Dartmouth	6–1–0	Earl Brown	same
17 Bainbridge NTS	7–0–0	Joe Maniaci	same
18 Colorado Col.	7–0–0	Hal White	same
19 Pacific	7–2–0	Amos A.Stagg	same
20 Pennsylvania	6–2–1	George Munger	same

Note: March Field beat Pacific, 19–0, on Dec.11 after final poll was released.

Other Major Award Winners

Maxwell (Player)	Bob Odell, Penn
Camp (Back)	Angelo Bertelli, N.Dame
Rockne (Lineman)	Cas Myslinski, Army
Smith (GI Player)	Dick Todd, Iowa P-F, HB

AFCA Coach of Year
Amos Alonzo Stagg, Pacific

Consensus All-America Team
(By position, in alphabetical order)

Ends—Ralph Heywood, Southern Cal; John Yonakor, Notre Dame. **Tackles**—Jim White, Notre Dame; Don Whitmire, Navy. **Guards**—Alex Agase, Purdue; Pat Filley, Notre Dame. **Center**—Cas Myslinski, Army. **Backs**—Angelo Bertelli, Notre Dame; Bill Daley, Michigan; Creighton Miller, Notre Dame; Bob Odell, Pennsylvania.

1944

Army rolled through the 1944 season like Patton through France. Over the course of their 9-game schedule, the Cadets beat the opposition by an average score of 56–4. Defending national champion Notre Dame fared even worse, losing 59–0 in the most lopsided Irish defeat ever.

No college coach had ever experienced the depth that Army's Red Blaik enjoyed during the war. No other coach ever had the likes of Doc Blanchard and Glenn Davis in the same backfield, either. Only sophomores, the celebrated "Mr. Inside" (fullback Blanchard) and "Mr. Outside" (halfback Davis) double-teamed the Heisman voting for three years. They finished second and third in 1944 then each won the prize in '45 and '46.

The Army-Navy game was played in Baltimore where the Middies gave the Cadets their closest game of the year. Army came in 8-0 and No.1. Navy was 6–2 and No.2. Army won, 23–7.

Elsewhere, new Ohio State coach Carroll Widdoes did something Paul Brown couldn't do in his three years in Columbus: he guided the Buckeyes to an undefeated season and was named Coach of the Year. It didn't hurt that he had Heisman winner Les Horvath in his backfield as tailback in the single wing and quarterback for the T-formation.

No.7 Southern Cal was the only team in the Top 10 to play in a bowl game. The unbeaten Trojans played unbeaten Tennessee in the Rose Bowl and blanked the Vols, 25–0.

Bowl Games with Top 20 Teams

Date	Bowl	Result
1/2/45	Cotton	Oklahoma A&M 34, TCU 0
1/2/45	Orange	Tulsa 26, Georgia Tech 12
1/2/45	Rose	USC 25, Tennessee 0
1/2/45	Sugar	Duke 29, Alabama 26

Major Conference Champions

Big Nine	Ohio St.	6–0
Big Six	Oklahoma	4–0–1
Ivy League*	Army	3–0
Missouri Valley	Oklahoma A&M	1–0
Pacific Coast	USC	3–0–2
Skyline	Vacant (WWII)	
Southeastern	Georgia Tech	4–0
Southern	Duke	4–0
Southwest	TCU	3–1–1

*Not a formal league until 1956.

Heisman Trophy Voting

	Yr	Pos.	Votes
1 Les Horvath, Ohio St.	Sr.	HB	412
2 Glenn Davis, Army	So.	HB	287
3 Doc Blanchard, Army	So.	FB	237
4 Don Whitmire, Navy	Sr.	T	115
5 Buddy Young, Illinois	Sr.	HB	105

Final AP Top 20

Writers' poll taken before bowl games.

		Regular Season	Head Coach	After Bowls
1	Army	9–0–0	Red Blaik	same
2	Ohio St	9–0–0	Carroll Widdoes	same
3	Randolph Field	11–0–0	Frank Tritico	same
4	Navy	6–3–0	Oscar Hagberg	same
5	Bainbridge NTS	9–0–0	Joe Maniaci	same
6	Iowa Pre-Flight	10–1–0	Jack Meagher	same
7	Southern Cal	7–0–2	Jeff Cravath	8–0–2
8	Michigan	8–2–0	Fritz Crisler	same
9	Notre Dame	8–2–0	Ed McKeever	same
10	March Field	7–1–2	Paul Schissler	same
11	Duke	5–4–0	Eddie Cameron	6–4–0
12	Tennessee	8–0–1	John Barnhill	8–1–1
13	Georgia Tech	8–2–0	Bill Alexander	8–3–0
	Norman P-F	6–0–0	John Gregg	same
15	Illinois	5–4–1	Ray Eliot	same
16	El Toro Marines	8–1–0	Dick Hanley	same
17	Great Lakes	9–2–1	Paul Brown	same
18	Fort Pierce	9–0–0	Hamp Pool	same
19	St.Mary's P-F	4–4–0	Jules Sikes	same
20	2nd Air Force	7–2–1	Bill Reese	same

Other Major Award Winners

Maxwell (Player)	Glenn Davis, Army
Camp (Back)	Glenn Davis, Army
Rockne (Lineman)	Don Whitmire, Navy
Smith (GI Player)	Bill Dudley, Rand.Field, HB

AFCA Coach of Year
Carroll Widdoes, Ohio St.

Consensus All-America Team

(By position, in alphabetical order)

Ends—Jack Dugger, Ohio St.; Phil Tinsley, Georgia Tech; Paul Walker, Yale. **Tackles**—John Ferraro, Southern Cal; Don Whitmire, Navy. **Guards**—Ben Chase, Navy; Bill Hackett, Ohio St. **Center**—John Tavener, Indiana. **Backs**—Doc Blanchard, Army; Glenn Davis, Army; Les Horvath, Ohio St.; Bob Jenkins, Navy.

1945

The war was over by autumn, but Army kept up its football offensive with a second straight unbeaten season.

Each time the Cadets snapped the ball in 1945 they gained eight yards. The average score of their nine wins slipped a bit to 46–5, but again they treated Notre Dame harshly. Facing the No.2 Irish at Yankee Stadium on Nov.9, Army crushed them, 48–0.

A thousand miles from West Point, the talent pool wasn't quite so predictable. The war effort had wiped out Alabama's roster in 1943 and forced coach Frank Thomas to cancel the season. A year later, the Crimson Tide returned to go 5–1–2 and reach the Sugar Bowl. In '45, with sophomore Harry Gilmer at quarterback, they beat everyone they played, including Southern Cal by 20 points in the Rose Bowl. The loss was USC's first in the Rose Bowl after eight wins.

In the Midwest, Indiana won its first Big Ten championship and finished the season unbeaten. The Hoosiers placed 4th in the final AP poll and Bo McMillan was named Coach of the Year. Oklahoma A&M was the 5th-ranked team. Sparked by junior halfback Bob Fenimore, the nation's leader in total offense for the second year in a row, the Cowboys went undefeated and won the Sugar Bowl.

The Cotton Bowl, however, belonged to Texas' sophomore quarterback Bobby Layne. Layne ran for four touchdowns, passed for two others and kicked four extra points as the No.10 Longhorns showed Missouri, 40–27.

Bowl Games with Top 20 Teams

Date	Bowl	Result
1/1/46	Cotton	Texas 40, Missouri 27
1/1/46	Gator	Wake Forest 26, S.Carolina 14
1/1/46	Oil	Georgia 20, Tulsa 6
1/1/46	Orange	Miami,FL 13, Holy Cross 6
1/1/46	Rose	Alabama 34, USC 14
1/1/46	Sugar	Okla.A&M 33, St.Mary's 13

Major Conference Champions

Big Nine	Indiana	5–0–1
Big Six	Missouri	5–0
Ivy League*	Army	2–0
Missouri Valley	Oklahoma A&M	1–0
Pacific Coast	USC	5–1
Skyline	Vacant (not enough teams)	
Southeastern	Alabama	6–0
Southern	Duke	4–0
Southwest	Texas	5–1

*Not a formal league until 1956.

Heisman Trophy Voting

		Yr.	Pos.	Votes
1	Doc Blanchard, Army	Jr.	FB	860
2	Glenn Davis, Army	Jr.	HB	638
3	Bob Fenimore, Oklahoma A&M	Jr.	HB	187
4	Herman Wedemeyer, St.Mary's	Jr.	HB	152
5	Harry Gilmer, Alabama	So.	QB	132

Final AP Top 20

Writers' poll taken before bowl games.

	Regular Season	Head Coach	After Bowls
1 Army	9–0–0	Red Blaik	same
2 Alabama	9–0–0	Frank Thomas	10–0–0
3 Navy	7–1–1	Oscar Hagberg	same
4 Indiana	9–0–1	Bo McMillan	same
5 Oklahoma A&M	8–0–0	Jim Lookabaugh	9–0–0
6 Michigan	7–3–0	Fritz Crisler	same
7 St. Mary's	7–1–0	Jimmy Phelan	7–2–0
8 Pennsylvania	6–2–0	George Munger	same
9 Notre Dame	7–2–1	Hugh Devore	same
10 Texas	9–1–0	Dana X. Bible	10–1–0
11 Southern Cal.	7–3–0	Jeff Cravath	7–4–0
12 Ohio St	7–2–0	Carroll Widdoes	same
13 Duke	6–2–0	Eddie Cameron	same
14 Tennessee	8–1–0	John Barnhill	same
15 LSU	7–2–0	Bernie Moore	same
16 Holy Cross	8–1–0	John DeGrosa	8–2–0
17 Tulsa	8–2–0	Henry Frnka	8–3–0
18 Georgia	8–2–0	Wally Butts	9–2–0
19 Wake Forest	4–3–1	Peahead Walker	5–3–1
20 Columbia	8–1–0	Lou Little	same

Other Major Award Winners

Sullivan (Amateur Athlete)	Doc Blanchard, Army
Maxwell (Player)	Doc Blanchard, Army
Camp (Back)	Doc Blanchard, Army
Rockne (Lineman)	Dick Duden, Navy, E

AFCA Coach of Year
Bo McMillan, Indiana

Consensus All-America Team
(By position, in alphabetical order)

Ends—Hub Bechtol, Texas; Dick Duden, Navy; Max Morris, Northwestern; Bob Ravensberg, Indiana. **Tackles**—Tex Coulter, Army; George Savitsky, Pennsylvania. **Guards**—Warren Amling, Ohio St.; John Green, Army. **Center**—Vaughn Mancha, Alabama. **Backs**—Doc Blanchard, Army; Glenn Davis, Army; Bob Fenimore, Oklahoma A&M; Herman Wedemeyer, St.Mary's,CA.

1946

Army entered the 1946 season favored to win its third straight national title. The Cadets were riding an 18-game winning streak and they still had Blanchard and Davis. Clearly, coach Red Blaik's squad would have to be beaten to lose its status as the No.1 team in the nation.

Not necessarily.

Frank Leahy had coached Notre Dame to a national championship in 1943, then left South Bend for the South Pacific and two years with the Navy. He returned to his old job in '46 and was joined by a crowd of lettermen-turned-soldiers who still had eligibility remaining. The Irish were loaded and determined. Not only did they want their No.1 ranking back, but they were eager to avenge the 59–0 and 48–0 losses to Army in 1944 and '45.

Army was 7–0 and Notre Dame was 5–0 when the two teams met at Yankee Stadium on Nov.9. The No.1 Cadets came in averaging 30 points a game while the No.2 Irish averaged 35. Final score: 0–0.

Army's 25-game winning streak was over but the Cadets were still unbeaten. They won their last two games, but had to struggle past Navy. Meanwhile, Notre Dame shut out Northwestern and Tulane and beat Southern Cal by 20. A week later, the final AP poll gave the championship to the Irish.

Elsewhere, the Big Ten and Pacific Coast Conference signed an agreement to play each other in the Rose Bowl each New Year's Day. No.5 Illinois beat No.4 UCLA, 45–14, in the inaugural.

Bowl Games with Top 20 Teams

Date	Bowl	Result
1/1/47	Cigar	Delaware 21, Rollins 7
1/1/47	Cotton	0–0, LSU vs Arkansas
1/1/47	Gator	Oklahoma 34, N.C.State 13
1/1/47	Oil	Ga.Tech 41, St.Mary's 19
1/1/47	Orange	Rice 8, Tennessee 0
1/1/47	Rose	Illinois 45, UCLA 14
1/1/47	Sugar	Georgia 20, N.Carolina 10

Major Conference Champions

Big Nine	Illinois	6–1
Big Six	Oklahoma/Kansas	4–1
Ivy League*	Yale	4–1–1
Missouri Valley	Tulsa	3–0
Pacific Coast	UCLA	7–0
Skyline	Utah St./Denver	4–1–1
Southeastern	Georgia/Tennessee	5–0
Southern	N.Carolina	4–0–1
Southwest	Rice/Arkansas	5–1

*Not a formal league until 1956.

Heisman Trophy Voting

	Yr	Pos.	Votes
1 Glenn Davis, Army	Sr.	HB	792
2 Charley Trippi, Georgia	Sr.	HB	435
3 Johnny Lujack, Notre Dame	Jr.	QB	379
4 Doc Blanchard, Army	Sr.	FB	267
5 Arnold Tucker, Army	Sr.	QB	257
8 Bobby Layne, Texas	Jr.	QB	45

Final AP Top 20

Writers' poll taken before bowl games.

	Regular Season	Head Coach	After Bowls
1 Notre Dame	8–0–1	Frank Leahy	same
2 Army	9–0–1	Red Blaik	same
3 Georgia	10–0–0	Wally Butts	11–0–0
4 UCLA	10–0–0	B.LaBrucherie	10–1–0
5 Illinois	7–2–0	Ray Eliot	8–2–0
6 Michigan	6–2–1	Fritz Crisler	same
7 Tennessee	9–1–0	Bob Neyland	9–2–0
8 LSU	9–1–0	Bernie Moore	9–1–1
9 N.Carolina	8–1–1	Carl Snavely	8–2–1
10 Rice	8–2–0	Jess Neely	9–2–0
11 Georgia Tech	8–2–0	Bobby Dodd	9–2–0
12 Yale	7–1–1	Howard Odell	same
13 Pennsylvania	6–2–0	George Munger	same
14 Oklahoma	7–3–0	Jim Tatum	8–3–0
15 Texas	8–2–0	Dana X. Bible	same
16 Arkansas	6–3–1	John Barnhill	6–3–2
17 Tulsa	9–1–0	J.O.Brothers	same
18 N.C.State	8–2–0	Beattie Feathers	8–3–0
19 Delaware	9–0–0	Bill Murray	10–0–0
20 Indiana	6–3–0	Bo McMillan	same

Other Major Award Winners

AP Athlete of Year	Glenn Davis, Army
Sullivan (Amateur Athlete)	Arnold Tucker, Army
Maxwell (Player)	Charley Trippi, Georgia
Camp (Back)	Charley Trippi, Georgia
Rockne (Lineman)	Burr Baldwin, UCLA, E
Outland (Interior)	Geo.Connor, N.Dame, T

AFCA Coach of Year
Red Blaik, Army

Consensus All-America Team

(By position, in alphabetical order)

Ends—Burr Baldwin, UCLA; Hub Bechtol, Texas; Hank Foldberg, Army. **Tackles**—Warren Amling, Ohio St.; George Connor, Notre Dame; Dick Huffman, Tennessee. **Guards**—Alex Agase, Illinois; Weldon Humble, Rice. **Center**—Paul Duke, Georgia Tech. **Backs**—Doc Blanchard, Army; Glenn Davis, Army; Johnny Lujack, Notre Dame; Charley Trippi, Georgia.

1947

Michigan replaced Army as Notre Dame's primary competition for the national championship in 1947. The two undefeated teams didn't play each other but they traded the No.1 ranking back and forth three times.

The Irish and Wolverines had two common opponents during the regular season: Pittsburgh and Northwestern. Notre Dame beat both teams 40–6 and 26–19, respectively. Michigan beat them in the same order, 69–0 and 49–21.

Notre Dame won the final AP poll at the close of the regular season, but after Michigan trounced USC, 49–0, in the Rose Bowl there was such an outcry for another vote that AP gave in. Michigan carried the unprecedented ''Who's No.1?'' ballot, 226–119, but AP ruled that the earlier poll would be the vote of record.

The Heisman Trophy also came down to picking between Michigan and Notre Dame. This time the Irish won as QB Johnny Lujack outpointed Wolverine HB Bob Chappuis. Lujack, who served two years in the Navy during the war, quarterbacked the Irish to three national titles (1943–46–47).

Both the Cotton and Sugar Bowls had strong match-ups. No.3 Southern Methodist and No.4 Penn State brought their unbeaten records to Dallas and tied 13–all. In New Orleans, however, No.5 Texas and Bobby Layne whipped No.6 Alabama, 27–7.

Finally, Columbia ended Army's three-year unbeaten streak at 32. The Cadets lost 21–20, ended up at 5–2–2 and ranked 11th.

Final AP Top 20

Writers' poll taken before bowl games.

	Regular Season	Head Coach	After Bowls
1 Notre Dame	9–0–0	Frank Leahy	same
2 Michigan	9–0–0	Fritz Crisler	10–0–0
3 SMU	9–0–1	Matty Bell	9–0–2
4 Penn St.	9–0–0	Bob Higgins	9–0–1
5 Texas	9–1–0	Blair Cherry	10–1–0
6 Alabama	8–2–0	Red Drew	8–3–0
7 Pennsylvania	7–0–1	George Munger	same
8 Southern Cal	7–1–1	Jeff Cravath	7–2–1
9 N.Carolina	8–2–0	Carl Snavely	8–2–0
10 Georgia Tech	9–1–0	Bobby Dodd	10–1–0
11 Army	5–2–2	Red Blaik	same
12 Kansas	8–0–2	George Sauer	8–1–2
13 Mississippi	8–2–0	Johnny Vaught	same
14 Wm.& Mary	9–1–0	Rube McCray	9–2–0
15 California	9–1–0	Pappy Waldorf	same
16 Oklahoma	7–2–1	Bud Wilkinson	same
17 N.C.State	5–3–1	Beattie Feathers	same
18 Rice	6–3–1	Jess Neely	same
19 Duke	4–3–2	Wallace Wade	same
20 Columbia	7–2–0	Lou Little	same

Bowl Games with Top 20 Teams

Date	Bowl	Result
1/1/48	Cotton	13–13, SMU vs Penn St.
1/1/48	Delta	Mississippi 13, TCU 9
1/1/48	Dixie	Arkansas 21, Wm.& Mary 19
1/1/48	Orange	Ga.Tech 20, Kansas 14
1/1/48	Rose	Michigan 49, USC 0
1/1/48	Sugar	Texas 27, Alabama 7

Major Conference Champions

Big Nine	Michigan	6–0
Big Six	Kansas/Oklahoma	4–0–1
Ivy League*	Pennsylvania	4–0
Mid-American	Cincinnati	3–1
Missouri Valley	Tulsa	3–0
Pacific Coast	USC	6–0
Skyline	Utah	6–0
Southeastern	Mississippi	6–1
Southern	Wm.& Mary	7–1
Southwest	SMU	5–0–1

*Not a formal league until 1956.

Heisman Trophy Voting

	Yr	Pos.	Votes
1 Johnny Lujack, Notre Dame	Sr.	QB	742
2 Bob Chappuis, Michigan	Sr.	HB	555
3 Doak Walker, SMU	So.	HB	196
4 Charlie Conerly, Miss.	Sr.	QB	196
5 Harry Gilmer, Alabama	Sr.	QB	115
6 Bobby Layne, Texas	Sr.	QB	74
7 Chuck Bednarik, Penn	Jr.	C	65

Other Major Award Winners

AP Athlete of Year	Johnny Lujack, Notre Dame
Maxwell (Player)	Doak Walker, SMU
Camp (Back)	Johnny Lujack, Notre Dame
Rockne (Lineman)	Chuck Bednarik, Penn
Outland (Interior)	Joe Steffy, Army, G

AFCA Coach of Year
Fritz Crisler, Michigan

Consensus All-America Team

(By position, in alphabetical order)

Ends—Paul Cleary, Southern Cal; Bill Swiacki, Columbia. **Tackles**—George Connor, Notre Dame; Bob Davis, Georgia Tech. **Guards**—Bill Fischer, Notre Dame; Joe Steffy, Army. **Center**—Chuck Bednarik, Pennsylvania. **Backs**—Bob Chappuis, Michigan; Charlie Conerly, Mississippi; Bobby Layne, Texas; Johnny Lujack, Notre Dame; Doak Walker, SMU.

1948

Michigan and Notre Dame renewed their duel at the top of the AP poll in 1948.

Both went undefeated again, but close calls at the beginning and end of the season cost the Irish their title. In the home opener against Purdue, Notre Dame could only manage a 28–27 win (Michigan beat the Boilermakers two weeks later, 40–0). In the closer, the Irish had to rally in the last 35 seconds to tie Southern Cal, 14-all.

Michigan, on the other hand, won all nine of its games by at least a touchdown. When the season ended, the Wolverines were the unanimous choice of all the pollsters. And for the second straight year they had the country's top coach: Fritz Crisler in 1947 and now his successor, Bennie Oosterbaan.

Juniors Doak Walker of SMU and Charlie Justice of North Carolina finished 1–2 in the Heisman vote. Walker led the Mustangs to the SWC title and a Cotton Bowl win over Oregon. Justice, the aptly named "Choo-Choo," tailbacked the 3rd-ranked Tar Heel single wing to a 9–0–1 regular season mark but Carolina fell to No.5 Oklahoma in the Sugar Bowl.

Michigan was prevented from playing in its second consecutive Rose Bowl by the Big Ten's "no-repeat" rule. Conference runner-up Northwestern, the 7th-ranked team in the country, went instead and defeated No.4 California, 20–14.

Final AP Top 20

Writers' poll taken before bowl games.

	Regular Season	Head Coach	After Bowls
1 Michigan	9–0–0	Bennie Oosterbaan	same
2 Notre Dame	9–0–1	Frank Leahy	same
3 N.Carolina	9–0–1	Carl Snavely	9–1–1
4 California	10–0–0	Pappy Waldorf	10–1–0
5 Oklahoma	9–1–0	Bud Wilkinson	10–1–0
6 Army	8–0–1	Red Blaik	same
7 Northwestern	7–2–0	Bob Voigts	8–2–0
8 Georgia	9–1–0	Wally Butts	9–2–0
9 Oregon	9–1–0	Jim Aiken	9–2–0
10 SMU	8–1–1	Matty Bell	9–1–1
11 Clemson	10–0–0	Frank Howard	11–0–0
12 Vanderbilt	8–2–1	Red Sanders	same
13 Tulane	9–1–0	Henry Frnka	same
14 Michigan St.	6–2–2	Biggie Munn	same
15 Mississippi	8–1–0	Johnny Vaught	9–1–0
16 Minnesota	7–2–0	Bernie Bierman	same
17 Wm.& Mary	6–2–2	Rube McCray	7–2–2
18 Penn St.	7–1–1	Bob Higgins	same
19 Cornell	8–1–0	Lefty James	8–1–0
20 Wake Forest	6–3–0	Peahead Walker	6–4–0

Bowl Games with Top 20 Teams

Date	Bowl	Result
1/1/4	Cotton	SMU 21, Oregon 13
1/1/4	Delta	Wm.& Mary 20, Okla.A&M 0
1/1/4	Dixie	Baylor 20, Wake Forest 7
1/1/4	Gator	Clemson 24, Missouri 23
1/1/4	Orange	Texas 41, Georgia 28
1/1/4	Rose	N'western 20, California 14
1/1/4	Sugar	Oklahoma 14, N.Carolina 6

Major Conference Champions

Big Nine	Michigan‡	6–0
Big Seven	Oklahoma	5–0
Ivy League*	Cornell	5–1
Mid-American	Miami,OH	4–0
Missouri Valley	Oklahoma A&M	2–0
Pacific Coast	California/Oregon	6–0
Skyline	Utah	5–0
Southeastern	Georgia	6–0
Southern	Clemson	5–0
Southwest	SMU	5–0–1

*Not a formal league until 1956.
‡Michigan was ineligible for Big Nine berth in Rose Bowl because of "no repeat" rule.

Heisman Trophy Voting

		Yr	Pos.	Votes
1 Doak Walker, SMU		Jr.	HB	778
2 Charlie Justice, N.Carolina		Jr	HB	443
3 Chuck Bednarik, Penn		Sr.	C	336
4 Jackie Jensen, California		Sr.	HB	143
5 Stan Heath, Nevada		Sr.	QB	113
6 Norm Van Brocklin, Oregon		Sr.	QB	83

Other Major Award Winners

Maxwell (Player)	Chuck Bednarik, Penn
Camp (Back)	Charlie Justice, N.Carolina
Rockne (Lineman)	Bill Fischer, Notre Dame, G
Outland (Interior)	Bill Fischer, Notre Dame

AFCA Coach of Year
Bennie Oosterbaan, Michigan

Consensus All-America Team

(By position, in alphabetical order)

Ends—Leon Hart, Notre Dame; Dick Rifenberg, Michigan. **Tackles**—Leo Nomellini, Minnesota; Alvin Wistert, Michigan. **Guards**—Buddy Burris, Oklahoma; Bill Fischer, Notre Dame. **Center**—Chuck Bednarik, Penn. **Backs**—Jackie Jensen, California; Charlie Justice, North Carolina; Clyde Scott, Arkansas; Emil Sitko, Notre Dame; Doak Walker, SMU.

1949

The 1940s came to a close with Notre Dame winning its third national title in four years. If coach Frank Leahy still wasn't being mentioned in the same breath with Knute Rockne, he was getting mighty close. ND hadn't lost a game since Leahy's return from the war in 1946.

The Irish reclaimed the summit of the AP poll in early October and were challenged only by unranked SMU in the last game of the season. Trailing 13–0 at the half, the Mustangs' junior halfback Kyle Rote thrilled the home fans in the fourth quarter with a pair of touchdowns to tie the score at 20-all. Notre Dame responded with a 57-yard scoring drive to win 27–20 and extend its unbeaten string to 38 games.

Irish end Leon Hart received nearly all of the postseason player awards, including ND's third Heisman of the decade (Hart was only the second lineman in 15 years to win the prize).

Bud Wilkinson, whose teams would dominate the 1950s much as Leahy's Irish ruled the '40s, directed 2nd-ranked Oklahoma to 10 straight regular season wins and a Sugar Bowl rout of No.9 LSU.

No.3 California went 10–0 for the second season in a row, but lost its second consecutive Rose Bowl. Army (9–0) and College of the Pacific (11–0) were the other major undefeated teams. Pacific, with 5-foot 8-inch Eddie LeBaron at quarterback, outscored its opponents 575–66.

Final AP Top 20

Writers' poll taken before bowl games.

	Regular Season	Head Coach	After Bowls
1 Notre Dame	10–0–0	Frank Leahy	same
2 Oklahoma	10–0–0	Bud Wilkinson	11–0–0
3 California	10–0–0	Pappy Waldorf	10–1–0
4 Army	9–0–0	Red Blaik	same
5 Rice	9–1–0	Jess Neely	10–1–0
6 Ohio St.	6–1–2	Wes Fesler	7–1–2
7 Michigan	6–2–1	Bennie Oosterbaan	same
8 Minnesota	7–2–0	Bernie Bierman	same
9 LSU	8–2–0	Gaynell Tinsley	8–3–0
10 Pacific	11–0–0	Larry Siemering	same
11 Kentucky	9–2–0	Bear Bryant	9–3–0
12 Cornell	8–1–0	Lefty James	same
13 Villanova	8–1–0	Jim Leonard	same
14 Maryland	8–1–0	Jim Tatum	9–1–0
15 Santa Clara	7–2–1	Len Casanova	8–2–1
16 N.Carolina	7–3–0	Carl Snavely	7–4–0
17 Tennessee	7–2–1	Bob Neyland	same
18 Princeton	6–3–0	Charlie Caldwell	same
19 Michigan St.	6–3–0	Biggie Munn	same
20 Missouri	7–3–0	Don Faurot	7–4–0
Baylor	8–2–0	Bob Woodruff	same

Bowl Games with Top 20 Teams

Date	Bowl	Result
1/2/50	Cotton	Rice 27, N.Carolina 13
1/2/50	Gator	Maryland 20, Missouri 7
1/2/50	Orange	Santa Clara 21, Kentucky 13
1/2/50	Rose	Ohio St. 17, California 14
1/2/50	Sugar	Oklahoma 35, LSU 0

Major Conference Champions

Big Nine	Ohio St./Michigan	4–1–1
Big Seven	Oklahoma	5–0
Ivy League*	Cornell	5–1
Mid-American	Cincinnati	4–0
Missouri Valley	Detroit	4–0
Pacific Coast	California	7–0
Skyline	Wyoming	5–0
Southeastern	Tulane	5–1
Southern	North Carolina	5–0
Southwest	Rice	6–0

*Not a formal league until 1956.

Heisman Trophy Voting

	Yr	Pos.	Votes
1 Leon Hart, Notre Dame	Sr.	E	995
2 Charlie Justice, N.Carolina	Sr.	HB	272
3 Doak Walker, SMU	Sr.	HB	229
4 Arnold Galiffa, Army	Sr.	QB	196
5 Bob Williams, Notre Dame	Jr.	QB	189
6 Eddie LeBaron, Pacific	Sr.	QB	122

Other Major Award Winners

AP Athlete of Year	Leon Hart, Notre Dame
Maxwell (Player)	Leon Hart, Notre Dame
Camp (Back)	Emil Sitko, Notre Dame, HB
Rockne (Lineman)	Leon Hart, Notre Dame
Outland (Interior)	Ed Bagdon, Mich.St., G

AFCA Coach of Year
Bud Wilkinson, Oklahoma

Consensus All-America Team

(By position, in alphabetical order)

Ends—Leon Hart, Notre Dame; James Williams, Rice. **Tackles**—Leo Nomellini, Minnesota; Alvin Wistert, Michigan. **Guards**—Ed Bagdon, Michigan St.; Rod Franz, California. **Center**—Clayton Tonnemaker, Minnesota. **Backs**—Arnold Galiffa, Army; Emil Sitko, Notre Dame; Doak Walker, SMU; Bob Williams, Notre Dame.

1950

Notre Dame began the 1950s as the nation's number one team and owner of a 38-game unbeaten streak.

The Irish labored to beat North Carolina in their opener, then lost for the first time in five years to visiting Purdue 28–14. The streak lasted from Sept.28, 1946, to Oct.7, 1950. Notre Dame's record over that span was 37–0–2, the ties coming against Army in '46 and Southern Cal in '48. ND lost three more times before the end of the season, finished at 4–4–1 and failed to make the final Top 20 for the first time in 10 years.

Two other lengthy streaks were snapped, but they belonged to the two best teams in the country: Oklahoma and Army. Top-ranked Oklahoma swept through the regular season with 10 wins to run its unbeaten string to 31. The Sooners then met Bear Bryant's No.7 Kentucky team in the Sugar Bowl. The Wildcats took a 13–0 halftime lead and held on for the 13–7 upset.

Army's unbeaten streak of 28 games also came to an abrupt halt against Navy in Philadelphia. The Cadets entered the game with an average winning score of 33–3. Navy was unimpressed, building a 14–0 lead by the half and winning 14–2.

No.3 Texas and 4th-ranked Tennessee squared off in the Cotton Bowl, where the Vols came from behind to win 20–14 in the last three minutes. Out in Pasadena, No.5 California, undefeated for the third regular season in a row (overall record: 29–0–1), lost its third straight Rose Bowl.

Final AP Top 20

Writers' poll taken before bowl games.

	Regular Season	Head Coach	After Bowls
1 Oklahoma	10–0–0	Bud Wilkinson	10–1–0
2 Army	8–1–0	Red Blaik	same
3 Texas	9–1–0	Blair Cherry	9–2–1
4 Tennessee	10–1–0	Bob Neyland	11–1–0
5 California	9–0–1	Pappy Waldorf	9–1–1
6 Princeton	9–0–0	Charlie Caldwell	same
7 Kentucky	10–1–0	Bear Bryant	11–1–0
8 Michigan St.	8–1–0	Biggie Munn	same
9 Michigan	5–3–1	Bennie Oosterbaan	6–3–1
10 Clemson	8–0–1	Frank Howard	9–0–1
11 Washington	8–2–0	Howard Odell	same
12 Wyoming	9–0–0	Bowden Wyatt	10–0–0
13 Illinois	7–2–0	Ray Eliot	same
14 Ohio St.	6–3–0	Wes Fesler	same
15 Miami,FL	9–0–1	Andy Gustafson	9–1–1
16 Alabama	9–2–0	Red Drew	same
17 Nebraska	6–2–1	Bill Glassford	same
18 Wash.& Lee	8–2–0	George Barclay	8–3–0
19 Tulsa	9–1–1	J.O.Brothers	same
20 Tulane	6–2–1	Henry Frnka	same

Bowl Games with Top 20 Teams

Date	Bowl	Result
1/1/51	Cotton	Tennessee 20, Texas 14
1/1/51	Gator	Wyoming 20, Wash.& Lee 7
1/1/51	Orange	Clemson 15, Miami,FL 14
1/1/51	Rose	Michigan 14, California 6
1/1/51	Sugar	Kentucky 13, Oklahoma 7

Major Conference Champions

Big Nine	Michigan	4–1–1
Big Seven	Oklahoma	6–0
Ivy League*	Princeton	5–0
Mid-American	Miami,OH	4–0
Missouri Valley	Tulsa	3–0–1
Pacific Coast	California	5–0–1
Skyline	Wyoming	5–0
Southeastern	Kentucky	5–1
Southern	Washington & Lee	6–0
Southwest	Texas	6–0

*Not a formal league until 1956.

Heisman Trophy Voting

	Yr	Pos.	Votes
1 Vic Janowicz, Ohio St.	Sr.	HB	633
2 Kyle Rote, SMU	Sr.	HB	280
3 Reds Bagnell, Penn	Sr.	HB	231
4 Babe Parilli, Kentucky	Jr.	QB	214
5 Bobby Reynolds, Nebraska	So.	HB	174

Other Major Award Winners

Maxwell (Player)	Reds Bagnell, Penn
Camp (Back)	Babe Parilli, Kentucky
Rockne (Lineman)	Bud McFadin, Texas, G
Outland (Interior)	Bob Gain, Kentucky, T

AFCA Coach of Year
Charlie Caldwell, Princeton

Consensus All-America Team

(By position, in alphabetical order)

Tackles—Bob Gain, Kentucky; Jim Weatherall, Oklahoma. **Guards**—Bud McFadin, Texas; Les Richter, California. **Center**—Jerry Groom, Notre Dame. **Backs**—Leon Heath, Oklahoma; Vic Janowicz, Ohio St.; Babe Parilli, Kentucky; Kyle Rote, SMU

1951

Any shot Army might have had at regaining the top spot in the AP rankings disappeared on Aug.3, 1951 when 90 Cadets (37 of them football players) were dismissed from West Point in the wake of a cheating scandal. Coach Red Blaik's depleted troops went 2-7, but would return to the Top 20 in '53.

Defending national champ Oklahoma slipped to 8-2 and Texas to 7-3, leaving the way clear for unbeaten Tennessee to move up and claim the title. In 1950, the Vols had ranked 4th in the final AP poll (taken, as usual, in December). Coach Bob Neyland's bunch had been the only team in the Top 5 to win a bowl game, however, so they felt deserving of the national title. This year the opposite happened. Tennessee got the nod from AP in December then lost the Sugar Bowl to No.3 Maryland.

Despite the nearly wholesale changeover to the T-formation in college ball, it was a good year for the single wing. The top two vote-getters in the Heisman balloting, Dick Kazmaier of Princeton and Hank Lauricella of Tennessee, were single wing tailbacks.

Michigan State, Illinois and Georgia Tech all went unbeaten with the Illini and the Wreck winning their bowl games. The Spartans had been admitted to the Big Ten in 1950, but were still two years away from officially competing for the Rose Bowl.

Finally, Ollie Matson led the nation in rushing and scoring for the San Francisco Dons. USF gave up football for financial reasons in 1952.

Final AP Top 20

Writers' poll taken before bowl games.

	Regular Season	Head Coach	After Bowls
1 Tennessee	10-0-0	Bob Neyland	10-1-0
2 Michigan St.	9-0-0	Biggie Munn	same
3 Maryland	9-0-0	Jim Tatum	10-0-0
4 Illinois	8-0-1	Ray Eliot	9-0-1
5 Ga.Tech	10-0-1	Bobby Dodd	11-0-1
6 Princeton	9-0-0	Charlie Caldwell	same
7 Stanford	9-1-0	Chuck Taylor	9-2-0
8 Wisconsin	7-1-1	Ivy Williamson	same
9 Baylor	8-1-1	George Sauer	8-2-1
10 Oklahoma	8-2-0	Bud Wilkinson	same
11 TCU	6-4-0	Dutch Meyer	6-5-0
12 California	8-2-0	Pappy Waldorf	same
13 Virginia	8-1-0	Art Guepe	same
14 San Fran	9-0-0	Joe Kuharich	same
15 Kentucky	7-4-0	Bear Bryant	8-4-0
16 Boston Univ.	6-4-0	Buff Donelli	same
17 UCLA	5-3-1	Red Sanders	same
18 Wash.St.	7-3-0	Forest Evashevski	same
19 Holy Cross	8-2-0	Eddie Anderson	same
20 Clemson	7-2-0	Frank Howard	7-3-0

Bowl Games with Top 20 Teams

Date	Bowl	Result
1/1/52	Cotton	Kentucky 20, TCU 7
1/1/52	Gator	Miami,FL 14, Clemson 0
1/1/52	Orange	Ga.Tech 17, Baylor 14
1/1/52	Rose	Illinois 40, Stanford 7
1/1/52	Sugar	Maryland 28, Tennessee 13

Major Conference Champions

Big Nine	Illinois	5-0-1
Big Seven	Oklahoma	6-0
Ivy League*	Princeton	6-0
Mid-American	Cincinnati	3-0
Missouri Valley	Tulsa	4-0
Pacific Coast	Stanford	6-1
Skyline	Utah	4-1
Southeastern	Georgia Tech	7-0
	and Tennessee	5-0
Southern	Maryland/VMI	5-0
Southwest	TCU	5-1

*Not a formal league until 1956.

Heisman Trophy Voting

	Yr	Pos.	Votes
1 Dick Kazmaier, Princeton	Sr.	HB	1,777
2 Hank Lauricella, Tennessee	Sr.	HB	424
3 Babe Parilli, Kentucky	Sr.	QB	344
4 Bill McColl, Stanford	Sr.	E	313
5 Johnny Bright, Drake	Sr.	HB	230
8 Hugh McElhenny, Washington	Sr.	HB	103
9 Ollie Matson, San Fran	Sr.	HB	95

Other Major Award Winners

AP Athlete of Year	Dick Kazmaier, Princeton
Maxwell (Player)	Dick Kazmaier, Princeton
Camp (Back)	Dick Kazmaier, Princeton
Rockne (Lineman)	Bob Ward, Maryland, G
Outland (Interior)	Jim Weatherall, Okla., T

AFCA Coach of Year
Chuck Taylor, Stanford

Consensus All-America Team
(By position, in alphabetical order)

Ends—Bob Carey, Michigan St.; Bill McColl, Stanford. **Tackles**—Don Coleman, Michigan St.; Jim Weatherall, Oklahoma. **Guards**—Les Richter, California; Bob Ward, Maryland. **Center**—Dick Hightower, SMU. **Backs**—Johnny Karras, Illinois; Dick Kazmaier, Hank Lauricella, Tennessee; Babe Parilli, Kentucky.

1952

Still a year away from participation in the Big Ten, Michigan State rose to the top of the final AP poll by turning in its second unbeaten season in a row.

Georgia Tech was also unbeaten again, raising its record to 12–0 after beating Mississippi in the first All-SEC Sugar Bowl.

Notre Dame returned to the Top 20 after an absence of two years and placed third. In the last month of the season the Irish played three other Top 5 teams and beat two of them. They upset Oklahoma 27–21, lost to Michigan St. 21–3, and then in the final game of the year knocked off unbeaten Southern Cal 9–0.

Oklahoma halfback Billy Vessels gained over 1,500 yards in all-purpose running and ran off with the Heisman Trophy. Despite all the success the Sooners would enjoy this decade, Vessels would be Bud Wilkinson's only Heisman winner.

Southern Cal and UCLA were both unbeaten when they met to decide who would represent the Pacific Coast Conference in the Rose Bowl. The Bruins led 12–7 at the half, but USC won the game 14–12. After losing to Notre Dame a week later, the Trojans came back to beat Wisconsin 7–0 on New Year's and give the PCC its first win over the Big Ten in seven Rose Bowls.

Tennessee and Alabama gave the SEC four teams in the Top 10. The No.8 Vols were shut out 16–0 by 10th-ranked Texas in the Cotton Bowl, while No.9 Bama scored a postseason record 61 points routing Syracuse in the Orange Bowl.

Final AP Top 20

Writers' poll taken before bowl games.

	Regular Season	Head Coach	After Bowls
1 Michigan St.	9–0–0	Biggie Munn	same
2 Ga.Tech	11–0–0	Bobby Dodd	12–0–0
3 Notre Dame	7–2–1	Frank Leahy	same
4 Oklahoma	8–1–1	Bud Wilkinson	same
5 Southern Cal.	9–1–0	Jess Hill	10–1–0
6 UCLA	8–1–0	Red Sanders	same
7 Mississippi	8–0–2	Johnny Vaught	8–1–2
8 Tennessee	8–1–1	Bob Neyland	8–2–1
9 Alabama	.9–2–0	Red Drew	10–2–0
10 Texas	8–2–0	Ed Price	9–2–0
11 Wisconsin	6–2–1	Ivy Williamson	6–3–1
12 Tulsa	8–1–1	J.O.Brothers	8–2–1
13 Maryland	7–2–0	Jim Tatum	same
14 Syracuse	7–2–0	Ben Schwartzwalder	7–3–0
15 Florida	7–3–0	Bob Woodruff	8–3–0
16 Duke	8–2–0	Bill Murray	same
17 Ohio St.	6–3–0	Woody Hayes	same
18 Purdue	4–3–2	Stu Holcomb	same
19 Princeton	8–1–0	Charlie Caldwell	same
20 Kentucky	5–4–2	Bear Bryant	same

Bowl Games with Top 20 Teams

Date	Bowl	Result
1/1/53	Cotton	Texas 16, Tennessee 0
1/1/53	Gator	Florida 14, Tulsa 13
1/1/53	Orange	Alabama 61, Syracuse 6
1/1/53	Rose	USC 7, Wisconsin 0
1/1/53	Sugar	Ga.Tech 24, Mississippi 7

Major Conference Champions

Big Nine	Wisconsin/Purdue	4–1–1
Big Seven	Oklahoma	5–0–1
Ivy League*	Pennsylvania	4–0
Mid-American	Cincinnati	3–0
Missouri Valley	Houston	3–0
Pacific Coast	Southern Cal.	6–0
Skyline	Utah	5–0
Southeastern	Georgia Tech	6–0
Southern	Duke	5–0
Southwest	Texas	6–0

*Not a formal league until 1956.

Heisman Trophy Voting

	Yr	Pos.	Votes
1 Billy Vessels, Oklahoma	Sr.	HB	525
2 Jack Scarbath, Maryland	Sr.	QB	367
3 Paul Giel, Minnesota	Jr.	HB	329
4 Donn Moomaw, UCLA	Sr.	C	257
5 Johnny Lattner, Notre Dame	Jr.	QB	253

Other Major Award Winners

Maxwell (Player)	Johnny Lattner, Notre Dame
Camp (Back)	Don McAuliffe, Mich.St., HB
Rockne (Lineman)	Dick Modzelewski, Maryland, T
Outland (Interior)	Dick Modzelewski, Maryland

AFCA Coach of Year
Biggie Munn, Michigan St.

Consensus All-America Team

(By position, in alphabetical order)

Ends—Bernie Flowers, Purdue; Frank McPhee, Princeton. **Tackles**—Hal Miller, Georgia Tech; Dick Modzelewski, Maryland. **Guards**—John Michels, Tennessee; Elmer Wilhoite, Southern Cal. **Center**—Donn Moomaw, UCLA. **Backs**—Johnny Lattner, Notre Dame; Jack Scarbath, Maryland; Jim Sears, Southern Cal; Billy Vessels, Oklahoma.

1953

For the third time in four years, AP's national champion swooned in a bowl game. At the end of the regular season, Maryland, champion of the brand new Atlantic Coast Conference, was the only unbeaten and untied major college team in the land. The Terps played No. 4 Oklahoma in the Orange Bowl and lost 7–0.

Notre Dame was AP's number one team until a stubborn Iowa squad tied the Irish 14–14 on Nov. 21. Earlier in the season, the Irish snapped Georgia Tech's 31-game unbeaten streak, but coach Frank Leahy collapsed during halftime. He decided to retire at the end of the year and took his leave with a record of 107–13–9 and a career winning percentage second only to that of Knute Rockne.

Two-way back Johnny Lattner became the fourth Notre Dame player to win the Heisman Trophy in Leahy's 11 years at South Bend. Lattner edged Minnesota HB Paul Giel by just 56 votes.

Michigan State had its winning streak stilled by Iowa after 28 games, but the Spartans finally made it to the Rose Bowl where they rallied from 14 points back to beat UCLA 28–20.

In a year that saw the NCAA implement rules to cut back on two-platoon football, the most memorable play involved a player coming off the bench in the Cotton Bowl. The player was Alabama's Tommy Lewis and he left the sideline to tackle Rice halfback Dicky Maegle in the middle of what would have been a 95-yard touchdown run. Maegle was given the TD (one of three he had that day) and Rice won 28–6.

Final AP Top 20

Writers' poll taken before bowl games.

	Regular Season	Head Coach	After Bowls
1 Maryland	10–0–0	Jim Tatum	10–1–0
2 Notre Dame	9–0–1	Frank Leahy	same
3 Michigan St.	8–1–0	Biggie Munn	9–1–0
4 Oklahoma	8–1–1	Bud Wilkinson	9–1–1
5 UCLA	8–1–0	Red Sanders	8–2–0
6 Rice	8–2–0	Jess Neely	9–2–0
7 Illinois	7–1–1	Ray Eliot	same
8 Georgia Tech	8–2–1	Bobby Dodd	9–2–1
9 Iowa	5–3–1	Forest Evashevski	same
10 West Va.	8–1–0	Art Lewis	8–2–0
11 Texas	7–3–0	Ed Price	same
12 Texas Tech	10–1–0	DeWitt Weaver	11–1–0
13 Alabama	6–2–3	Red Drew	6–3–3
14 Army	7–1–1	Red Blaik	same
15 Wisconsin	6–2–1	Ivy Williamson	same
16 Kentucky	7–2–1	Bear Bryant	same
17 Auburn	7–2–1	Shug Jordan	7–3–1
18 Duke	7–2–1	Bill Murray	same
19 Stanford	6–3–1	Chuck Taylor	same
20 Michigan	6–3–0	Bennie Oosterbaan	same

Bowl Games with Top 20 Teams

Date	Bowl	Result
1/1/54	Cotton	Rice 28, Alabama 6
1/1/54	Gator	Texas Tech 35, Auburn 13
1/1/54	Orange	Oklahoma 7, Maryland 0
1/1/54	Rose	Michigan St. 28, UCLA 20
1/1/54	Sugar	Ga.Tech 42, West Va. 19

Major Conference Champions

Atlantic Coast	Duke	4–0
	and Maryland	3–0
Big Seven	Oklahoma	6–0
Big Ten	Mich.St./Illinois	5–1
Ivy League*	Cornell	3–1–2
Mid-American	Ohio Univ.	5–0–1
Missouri Valley	Oklahoma A&M	3–1
Pacific Coast	UCLA	6–1
Skyline	Utah	5–0
Southeastern	Alabama	4–0–3
Southern	West Virginia	4–0
Southwest	Rice/Texas	5–1

*Not a formal league until 1956.

Heisman Trophy Voting

	Yr	Pos.	Votes
1 Johnny Lattner, Notre Dame	Sr.	QB	1,850
2 Paul Giel, Minnesota	Sr.	HB	1,794
3 Paul Cameron, UCLA	Sr.	HB	444
4 Bernie Faloney, Maryland	Sr.	QB	258
5 Bob Garrett, Stanford	Sr.	QB	231
6 Alan Ameche, Wisconsin	Jr.	FB	211

Other Major Award Winners

Maxwell (Player)	Johnny Lattner, N.Dame
Camp (Backs)	Alan Ameche, Wisconsin
	Bernie Faloney, Maryland
	Paul Giel, Minnesota
	Johnny Lattner, N.Dame
Rockne (Lineman)	Stan Jones, Maryland, T
Outland (Interior)	J.D.Roberts, Oklahoma, G

AFCA Coach of Year
Jim Tatum, Maryland

Consensus All-America Team

(By position, in alphabetical order)

Ends—Don Dohoney, Michigan St.; Carlton Massey, Texas. **Tackles**—Art Hunter, Notre Dame; Stan Jones, Maryland. **Guards**—Crawford Mims, Mississippi; J.D.Roberts, Oklahoma. **Center**—Larry Morris, Georgia Tech. **Backs**—Paul Cameron, UCLA; J.C.Caroline, Illinois; Paul Giel, Minnesota; Johnny Lattner, Notre Dame.

1954

The game of the year should have been a No.1 vs No.1 battle in the Rose Bowl, but it never happened.

In 1950, United Press had joined rival Associated Press in the Top 20 business, using coaches instead of sportswriters. For four years both wire services agreed on who the national champion should be. In 1954, however, they didn't. AP picked the Big Ten's Ohio State, while UP crowned UCLA of the Pacific Coast Conference.

The Big Ten and PCC had agreed to make the Rose Bowl an exclusive rivalry back in 1946. Nine years later, it would have been the perfect setting for this dream game. Unfortunately, both conferences also had a "no repeat" rule that prevented teams from making two consecutive trips to Pasadena.

UCLA had played in the most recent Rose Bowl (losing to Michigan State), so the Bruins couldn't return. Instead, Ohio State faced PCC runner-up Southern Cal and won handily, 20–7.

Oklahoma, ranked third by both polls, won its seventh straight Big Seven championship, but like UCLA was prevented from a return to the Orange Bowl by a conference "no repeat" rule.

Twenty-five-year-old Terry Brennan succeeded Frank Leahy at Notre Dame and brought the Irish in fourth. Ranked No.1 in September, ND suffered its only loss when upset by Purdue on Oct.2.

Navy beat Army for the fourth time in five years then shut out Mississippi in the Sugar Bowl (the Middies first bowl appearance since 1924).

Final AP Top 20

Writers' poll taken before bowl games.

	Regular Season	Head Coach	After Bowls
1 Ohio St.	9–0–0	Woody Hayes	10–0–0
2 UCLA	9–0–0	Red Sanders	same
3 Oklahoma	10–0–0	Bud Wilkinson	same
4 Notre Dame	9–1–0	Terry Brennan	same
5 Navy	7–2–0	Eddie Erdelatz	8–2–0
6 Mississippi	9–1–0	Johnny Vaught	9–2–0
7 Army	7–2–0	Red Blaik	same
8 Maryland	7–2–1	Jim Tatum	same
9 Wisconsin	7–2–0	Ivy Williamson	same
10 Arkansas	8–2–0	Bowden Wyatt	8–3–0
11 Miami,FL	8–1–0	Andy Gustafson	same
12 West Va.	8–1–0	Art Lewis	same
13 Auburn	7–3–0	Shug Jordan	8–3–0
14 Duke	7–2–1	Bill Murray	8–2–1
15 Michigan	6–3–0	Bennie Oosterbaan	same
16 Va.Tech	8–0–1	Frank Moseley	same
17 Southern Cal.	8–3–0	Jess Hill	8–4–0
18 Baylor	7–3–0	George Sauer	7–4–0
19 Rice	7–3–0	Jess Neely	same
20 Penn St.	7–2–0	Rip Engle	same

Bowl Games with Top 20 Teams

Date	Bowl	Result
12/31/54	Gator	Auburn 33, Baylor 13
1/1/55	Cotton	Ga.Tech 14, Arkansas 6
1/1/55	Orange	Duke 34, Nebraska 7
1/1/55	Rose	Ohio St. 20, USC 7
1/1/55	Sugar	Navy 21, Mississippi 0

Major Conference Champions

Atlantic Coast	Duke	4–0
Big Seven	Oklahoma‡	6–0
Big Ten	Ohio St.	7–0
Ivy League*	Yale/Cornell	4–2
Mid-American	Miami,OH	4–0
Missouri Valley	Wichita	4–0
Pacific Coast	UCLA‡	6–0
Skyline	Denver	6–1
Southeastern	Mississippi	5–1
Southern	West Virginia	3–0
Southwest	Arkansas	5–1

*Not a formal league until 1956.

‡Both Oklahoma (Orange Bowl) and UCLA (Rose Bowl) were ineligible for conference bowl game berths because of "no repeat" rules.

Heisman Trophy Voting

	Yr	Pos.	Votes
1 Alan Ameche, Wisconsin	Sr.	FB	1,068
2 Kurt Burris, Oklahoma	Sr.	C	838
3 Howard Cassady, Ohio St.	Jr.	HB	810
4 Ralph Guglielmi, Notre Dame	Sr.	QB	691
5 Paul Larson, California	Sr.	QB	271
6 Dicky Maegle, Rice	Sr.	HB	258

Other Major Award Winners

Maxwell (Player)	Ron Beagle, Navy, E
Camp (Back)	Ralph Guglielmi, N.Dame
Rockne (Lineman)	Max Boydston, Oklahoma, E
Outland (Interior)	Bud Brooks, Arkansas, G

AFCA Coach of Year
Red Sanders, UCLA

Consensus All-America Team

(By position, in alphabetical order)

Ends—Ron Beagle, Navy; Max Boydston, Oklahoma. **Tackles**—Jack Ellena, UCLA; Sid Fournet, LSU. **Guards**—Bud Brooks, Arkansas; Calvin Jones, Iowa. **Center**—Kurt Burris, Oklahoma. **Backs**—Alan Ameche, Wisconsin; Howard Cassady, Ohio St.; Ralph Guglielmi, Notre Dame; Dicky Maegle, Rice.

1955

Oklahoma won its second national championship of the decade in 1955, going 10-0 and pushing its three-year winning streak to 30, two victories short of a modern college record.

Maryland was the only other undefeated and untied team in the Top 10 and finished the regular season ranked third in both the writers' and coaches' polls.

No.1 and No.3 met in the Orange Bowl where Maryland hoped to avenge a 7-0 Oklahoma win two years ago that ruined the Terps' bid for an undefeated season. Maryland lost again, 20-6.

Despite an early loss to Michigan, Michigan State won all nine of its other games to rank second in both polls. With Big Ten champ Ohio State unable to attend a second straight Rose Bowl, the Spartans took the Buckeyes' place and beat UCLA on a last second field goal.

Halfback Jim Swink of Texas Christian and quarterback George Walsh of Navy posted some of the year's gaudiest statistics, but Ohio State halfback Howard "Hopalong" Cassady was the overwhelming choice for the Heisman Trophy. That gave the Bucks two Heisman winners in six years. Vic Janowicz won the prize in 1950.

Sixth-ranked TCU won the SWC title but blew a 13-0 lead and lost the Cotton Bowl to Mississippi by a point. No.7 Georgia Tech blanked No.11 Pittsburgh 7-0 in the Sugar Bowl, giving coach Bobby Dodd five major bowl victories (3 Sugar, 1 Orange, 1 Cotton) in as many years.

Bowl Games with Top 20 Teams

Date	Bowl	Result
12/31/55	Gator	Vanderbilt 25, Auburn 13
1/2/56	Cotton	Mississippi 14, TCU 13
1/2/56	Orange	Oklahoma 20, Maryland 6
1/2/56	Rose	Michigan St. 17, UCLA 14
1/2/56	Sugar	Ga.Tech 7, Pittsburgh 0

Major Conference Champions

Atlantic Coast	Maryland/Duke	4-0
Big Seven	Oklahoma	6-0
Big Ten	Ohio St.‡	6-0
Ivy League*	Princeton	6-1
Mid-American	Miami,OH	5-0
Missouri Valley	Wichita/Detroit	3-1
Pacific Coast	UCLA	6-0
Skyline	Colorado A&M	6-1
Southeastern	Mississippi	5-1
Southern	West Virginia	4-0
Southwest	TCU	5-1

*Not a formal league until 1956.
‡Ohio St. was ineligible for Big Ten berth in Rose Bowl because of "no repeat" rule.

Heisman Trophy Voting

	Yr	Pos.	Votes
1 Howard Cassady, Ohio St.	Sr.	HB	2,219
2 Jim Swink, TCU	Jr.	HB	742
3 George Welsh, Navy	Sr.	QB	383
4 Earl Morrall, Michigan St.	Sr.	QB	323
5 Paul Hornung, Notre Dame	Jr.	QB	321

Other Major Award Winners

AP Athlete of Year	Howard Cassady, Ohio St.
Maxwell (Player)	Howard Cassady, Ohio St.
Camp (Back)	Howard Cassady, Ohio St.
Rockne (Lineman)	Bob Pellegrini, Maryland, C
Outland (Interior)	Calvin Jones, Iowa, G

AFCA Coach of Year
Duffy Daugherty, Michigan St.

Final AP Top 20

Writers' poll taken before bowl games.

		Regular Season	Head Coach	After Bowls
1	Oklahoma	10-0-0	Bud Wilkinson	11-0-0
2	Michigan St.	8-1-0	Duffy Daugherty	9-1-0
3	Maryland	10-0-0	Jim Tatum	10-1-0
4	UCLA	9-1-0	Red Sanders	9-2-0
5	Ohio St.	7-2-0	Woody Hayes	same
6	TCU	9-1-0	Abe Martin	9-2-0
7	Georgia Tech	8-1-1	Bobby Dodd	9-1-1
8	Auburn	8-1-1	Shug Jordan	8-2-1
9	Notre Dame	8-2-0	Terry Brennan	same
10	Mississippi	9-1-0	Johnny Vaught	10-1-0
11	Pittsburgh	7-3-0	John Michelosen	7-4-0
12	Michigan	7-2-0	Bennie Oosterbaan	same
13	Southern Cal.	6-4-0	Jess Hill	same
14	Miami,FL	6-3-0	Andy Gustafson	same
15	Miami,OH	9-0-0	Ara Parseghian	same
16	Stanford	6-3-1	Chuck Taylor	same
17	Texas A&M	7-2-1	Bear Bryant	same
18	Navy	6-2-1	Eddie Erdelatz	same
19	West Va.	8-2-0	Art Lewis	same
20	Army	6-3-0	Red Blaik	same

Consensus All-America Team

(By position, in alphabetical order)

Ends—Ron Beagle, Navy; Ron Kramer, Michigan. **Tackles**—Bruce Bosley, West Virginia; Norman Masters, Michigan St. **Guards**—Bo Bolinger, Oklahoma; Hardiman Cureton, UCLA; Calvin Jones, Iowa. **Center**—Bob Pellegrini, Maryland. **Backs**—Howard Cassady, Ohio St.; Paul Hornung, Notre Dame; Earl Morrall, Michigan St.; Jim Swink, TCU.

1956

How good was Oklahoma in 1956? The Sooners were good enough to hand Texas its worst beating (45–0) since 1908, pound Notre Dame 40–0 in South Bend, and beat up on the membership of the Big Seven by an average score of 49–8. They also extended their winning streak to an all-time record 40 games over four seasons.

How good a coach was Bud Wilkinson? In just 10 years at Oklahoma, Wilkinson had a record of 94-8-3, a winning percentage of .910, and three national championships.

The players were pretty good, too. Clendon Thomas led the nation in scoring with 18 touchdowns, while halfback Tommy McDonald and center Jerry Tubbs placed third and fourth in the Heisman Trophy voting.

Speaking of the Heisman, for the first time in 21 years the award went to a player on a losing team—quarterback Paul Hornung of 2–8 Notre Dame. Hornung edged Tennessee halfback Johnny Majors by 72 points. Jim Brown of Syracuse came in fifth.

Majors led No. 2 Tennessee to an SEC title and an unbeaten regular season. He didn't win the Heisman, but the Vols' Bowden Wyatt was named Coach of the Year. Unfortunately, Tennessee lost its perfect record in the Sugar Bowl, bowing to Baylor, 13–7.

No.3 Iowa and No.5 Texas A&M made it back to the AP Top 10 after long absences. The Hawkeyes had been away since 1939, the Aggies since '41.

Final AP Top 20

Writers' poll taken before bowl games.

	Regular Season	Head Coach	After Bowls
1 Oklahoma	10-0-0	Bud Wilkinson	same
2 Tennessee	10-0-0	Bowden Wyatt	10-1-0
3 Iowa	8-1-0	Forest Evashevski	9-1-0
4 Georgia Tech	9-1-0	Bobby Dodd	10-1-0
5 Texas A&M	9-0-1	Bear Bryant	same
6 Miami, FL	8-1-1	Andy Gustafson	same
7 Michigan	7-2-0	Bennie Oosterbaan	same
8 Syracuse	7-1-0	Ben Schwartzwalder	7-2-0
9 Michigan St.	7-2-0	Duffy Daugherty	same
10 Oregon St.	7-2-1	Tommy Prothro	7-3-1
11 Baylor	8-2-0	Sam Boyd	9-2-0
12 Minnesota	6-1-2	Murray Warmath	same
13 Pittsburgh	7-2-1	John Michelosen	7-3-1
14 TCU	7-3-0	Abe Martin	8-3-0
15 Ohio St.	6-3-0	Woody Hayes	same
16 Navy	6-1-2	Eddie Erdelatz	same
17 G.Washington	7-1-1	Gene Sherman	8-1-1
18 Southern Cal.	8-2-0	Jess Hill	same
19 Clemson	7-1-2	Frank Howard	7-2-2
20 Colorado	7-2-1	Dallas Ward	8-2-1
Penn St.	6-2-1	Rip Engle	same

Bowl Games with Top 20 Teams

Date	Bowl	Result
12/29/56	Gator	Ga.Tech 21, Pittsburgh 14
1/1/57	Cotton	TCU 28, Syracuse 27
1/1/57	Orange	Colorado 27, Clemson 21
1/1/57	Rose	Iowa 35, Oregon St. 19
1/1/57	Sugar	Baylor 13, Tennessee 7
1/1/57	Sun	Geo.Wash. 13, Tex.Western 0

Major Conference Champions

Atlantic Coast	Clemson	4-0-1
Big Seven	Oklahoma‡	6-0
Big Ten	Iowa	5-1
Ivy League	Yale	7-0
Mid-American	Bowling Green	5-0-1
Missouri Valley	Houston	4-0
Pacific Coast	Oregon St.	6-1-1
Skyline	Wyoming	7-0
Southeastern	Tennessee	6-0
Southern	West Virginia	5-0
Southwest	Texas A&M	6-0

‡Oklahoma was ineligible for Big Seven berth in Orange Bowl because of "no repeat" rule.

Heisman Trophy Voting

	Yr	Pos.	Votes
1 Paul Hornung, Notre Dame	Sr.	QB	1,066
2 Johnny Majors, Tennessee	Sr.	HB	994
3 Tommy McDonald, Oklahoma	Sr.	HB	973
4 Jerry Tubbs, Oklahoma	Sr.	C	724
5 Jim Brown, Syracuse	Sr.	HB	561
6 Ron Kramer, Michigan	Sr	E	518
7 John Brodie, Stanford	Sr.	QB	281
8 Jim Parker, Ohio St.	Sr.	G	248

Other Major Award Winners

Maxwell (Player)   Tommy McDonald, Oklahoma
Camp (Back)   Paul Hornung, Notre Dame
Rockne (Lineman)   Jerry Tubbs, Oklahoma
Outland (Interior)   Jim Parker, Ohio St.

AFCA Coach of Year
Bowden Wyatt, Tennessee

Consensus All-America Team

(By position, in alphabetical order)

Ends—Ron Kramer, Michigan; Joe Walton, Pittsburgh. **Tackles**—Lou Michaels, Kentucky; John Witte, Oregon St. **Guards**—Bill Glass, Baylor; Jim Parker, Ohio St. **Center**—Jerry Tubbs, Oklahoma. **Backs**—John Brodie, Stanford; Jim Brown, Syracuse; Johnny Majors, Tennessee; Tommy McDonald, Oklahoma.

1957

After 46 consecutive victories, Oklahoma's record-setting win streak came to an end on Nov.16, 1957.

A year after the Sooners had handed Notre Dame its worst-ever defeat at home (40–0), the Irish paid them back with a 7–0 shutout at Owen Field in Norman. The lone touchdown was scored by Dick Lynch with 3:50 left in the game.

The defeat was Oklahoma's only loss in 10 regular season games, but it was enough to prevent a third straight national title. The Sooners did win the Orange Bowl, however, beating Duke 48–21.

AP and UP disagreed on who the new Number One team should be. AP selected Auburn (10–0) but UP liked Ohio State (8–1). Michigan State (also 8–1) placed third in both polls.

Auburn began the decade by going 0–10. Shug Jordan became coach in 1951 and had the Tigers in the Gator Bowl by '53. Four years later, they not only won their first national championship, but their first SEC title as well. Unfortunately, the program was on probation and the team was ineligible for the Sugar Bowl.

Ohio State lost its opening game to TCU then won eight straight, including a come-from-behind, 17–13 win over No.6 Iowa for the Big Ten title. Coach of the Year Woody Hayes sent his Buckeyes into the Rose Bowl as heavy favorites, but they were lucky to beat Oregon, 10–7.

Bowl Games with Top 20 Teams

Date	Bowl	Result
12/28/57	Gator	Tennessee 3, Texas A&M 0
1/1/58	Cotton	Navy 20, Rice 7
1/1/58	Orange	Oklahoma 48, Duke 21
1/1/58	Rose	Ohio St. 10, Oregon 7
1/1/58	Sugar	Mississippi 39, Texas 7

Major Conference Champions

Atlantic Coast	North Carolina St.	5–0–1
Big Seven	Oklahoma	6–0
Big Ten	Ohio St.	7–0
Ivy League	Princeton	6–1
Mid-American	Miami,OH	5–0
Missouri Valley	Houston	3–0–1
Pacific Coast	Oregon/Oregon St.	6–2
Skyline	Utah	5–1
Southeastern	Auburn‡	7–0
Southern	VMI	6–0
Southwest	Rice	5–1

‡On probation, ineligible for bowl game.

Heisman Trophy Voting

	Yr	Pos.	Votes
1 John David Crow, Texas A&M	Sr.	HB	1,183
2 Alex Karras, Iowa	Sr.	T	693
3 Walt Kowalczyk, Mich.St	Sr	HB	630
4 Lou Michaels, Kentucky	Sr.	T	330
5 Tom Forrestal, Navy	Sr.	QB	232

Other Major Award Winners

Maxwell (Player)	Bob Reifsnyder, Navy, T
Camp (Back)	John David Crow, Texas A&M
Rockne (Lineman)	Lou Michaels, Kentucky
Outland (Interior)	Alex Karras, Iowa
AFCA Coach of Year	Woody Hayes, Ohio St.
FWAA Coach of Year	Woody Hayes, Ohio St.

Final AP Top 20

Writers' poll taken before bowl games.

	Regular Season	Head Coach	After Bowls
1 Auburn	10–0–0	Shug Jordan	same
2 Ohio St.	8–1–0	Woody Hayes	9–1–0
3 Michigan St.	8–1–0	Duffy Daugherty	same
4 Oklahoma	9–1–0	Bud Wilkinson	10–1–0
5 Navy	8–1–1	Eddie Erdelatz	9–1–1
6 Iowa	7–1–1	Forest Evashevski	same
7 Mississippi	8–1–1	Johnny Vaught	9–1–1
8 Rice	7–3–0	Jess Neely	7–4–0
9 Texas A&M	8–2–0	Bear Bryant	8–3–0
10 Notre Dame	7–3–0	Terry Brennan	same
11 Texas	6–3–1	Darrell Royal	6–4–1
12 Arizona St.	10–0–0	Dan Devine	same
13 Tennessee	7–3–0	Bowden Wyatt	8–3–0
14 Miss.St.	6–2–1	Wade Walker	same
15 N.C.State	7–1–2	Earle Edwards	same
16 Duke	6–2–2	Bill Murray	6–3–2
17 Florida	6–2–1	Bob Woodruff	same
18 Army	7–2–0	Red Blaik	same
19 Wisconsin	6–3–0	Milt Bruhn	same
20 VMI	9–0–1	John McKenna	same

Consensus All-America Team

(By position, in alphabetical order)

Ends—Jimmy Phillips, Auburn; Dick Wallen, UCLA. **Tackles**—Alex Karras, Iowa; Lou Michaels, Kentucky. **Guards**—Al Ecuyer, Notre Dame; Bill Krisher, Oklahoma. **Center**—Dan Currie, Michigan St. **Backs**—Bob Anderson, Army; John David Crow, Texas A&M; Walt Kowalczyk, Michigan St.; Clendon Thomas, Oklahoma.

1958

Missing from the final AP Top 20 since 1949, LSU not only returned to the ranks in 1958 but finished on top.

Just a .500 club the year before, coach Paul Dietzel got the most out of his bench by capitalizing on a new substitution rule that allowed any player, not just starters, to come off the field and go back in again once each quarter. The rule stopped short of permitting a return to two-platoon football, so Dietzel went with the next best thing—three platoons: a two-way unit of his best players, an offensive second team, and a defensive second team.

The defensive subs were known as the "Chinese Bandits" and their inspired play (they didn't give up a touchdown all season) symbolized LSU's remarkable 11–0 campaign. The Tigers reached No.1 the seventh week of the season and went on to win their first Sugar Bowl in five tries.

Another innovation was Army's "Lonely End" formation. Posting Bill Carpenter 15 yards off the strong side tackle and excusing him from huddles enabled the Cadets to spread the field and get their plays off faster. It not only improved the passing game but opened a lot of holes for halfback Pete Dawkins, who ran off with the Heisman Trophy as No.3 Army went unbeaten in Red Blaik's final season as coach.

Iowa, the 6th-ranked team in 1957, led the nation in total offense and moved up to No.2. The Hawkeyes tied No.6 Air Force and lost to No.8 Ohio State, but routed California to win their second Rose Bowl in three years.

Final AP Top 20

Writers' poll taken before bowl games.

	Regular Season	Head Coach	After Bowls
1 LSU	10-0-0	Paul Dietzel	11-0-0
2 Iowa	7-1-1	Forest Evashevski	8-1-1
3 Army	8-0-1	Red Blaik	same
4 Auburn	9-0-1	Shug Jordan	same
5 Oklahoma	9-1-0	Bud Wilkinson	10-1-0
6 Air Force	9-0-1	Ben Martin	9-0-2
7 Wisconsin	7-1-1	Milt Bruhn	same
8 Ohio St.	6-1-2	Woody Hayes	same
9 Syracuse	8-1-0	Ben Schwartzwalder	8-2-0
10 TCU	8-2-0	Abe Martin	8-2-1
11 Mississippi	8-2-0	Johnny Vaught	9-2-0
12 Clemson	8-2-0	Frank Howard	8-3-0
13 Purdue	6-1-2	Jack Mollenkopf	same
14 Florida	6-3-1	Bob Woodruff	6-4-1
15 S.Carolina	7-3-0	Warren Giese	same
16 California	7-3-0	Pete Elliott	7-4-0
17 Notre Dame	6-4-0	Terry Brennan	same
18 SMU	6-4-0	Bill Meek	same
19 Oklahoma St.	7-3-0	Cliff Speegle	8-3-0
20 Rutgers	8-1-0	John Stiegman	same

Bowl Games with Top 20 Teams

Date	Bowl	Result
12/13/58	Bluegrass	Okla.St. 15, Fla.St. 6
12/27/58	Gator	Mississippi 7, Florida 3
1/1/59	Cotton	0–0, Air Force vs TCU
1/1/59	Orange	Oklahoma 21, Syracuse 6
1/1/59	Rose	Iowa 38, California 12
1/1/59	Sugar	LSU 7, Clemson 0

Major Conference Champions

Atlantic Coast	Clemson	5–1
Big Eight	Oklahoma	6–0
Big Ten	Iowa	5–1
Ivy League	Dartmouth	6–1
Mid-American	Miami,OH	5–0
Missouri Valley	North Texas	2–1–1
Skyline	Wyoming	6–1
Pacific Coast	California	6–1
Southeastern	LSU	6–0
Southern	West Virginia	4–0
Southwest	TCU	5–1

Heisman Trophy Voting

	Yr	Pos.	Votes
1 Pete Dawkins, Army	Sr.	HB	1,394
2 Randy Duncan, Iowa	Sr.	QB	1,021
3 Billy Cannon, LSU	Jr.	HB	975
4 Bob White, Ohio St.	Sr.	HB	365
5 Joe Kapp, California	Sr.	QB	227
8 Dick Bass, Pacific	Jr.	HB	96

Other Major Award Winners

Maxwell (Player)	Pete Dawkins, Army
Camp (Back)	Randy Duncan, Iowa
Rockne (Lineman)	Bob Novogratz, Army, G
Outland (Interior)	Zeke Smith, Auburn, G
AFCA Coach of Year	Paul Dietzel, LSU
FWAA Coach of Year	Paul Dietzel, LSU

Consensus All-America Team

(By position, in alphabetical order)

Ends—Buddy Dial, Rice; Sam Williams, Michigan St. **Tackles**—Ted Bates, Oregon St.; Brock Strom, Air Force. **Guards**—George Deiderich, Vanderbilt; John Guzik, Pittsburgh; Zeke Smith, Auburn. **Center**—Bob Harrison, Oklahoma. **Backs**—Billy Cannon, LSU; Pete Dawkins, Army; Randy Duncan, Iowa; Bob White, Ohio St.

1959

Syracuse was the only unbeaten and untied major college team in the nation in 1959. As such, the Orangemen became the first eastern team outside the military to win the national championship since Pittsburgh did it in 1939.

Number one in both total offense and defense, and winning each week by an average score of 39–6, Syracuse rolled through 10 regular season games and then beat No. 4 Texas by nine in the Cotton Bowl.

Ole Miss (10–1) and LSU (9–2) were ranked second and third in the final AP poll. They also played each other in the year's most memorable game.

On Halloween, defending national champ LSU was ranked No. 1 and Ole Miss was No. 3. The visiting Rebels led 3–0 at halftime, but the Tigers won the game late on an electrifying 89-yard punt return by Billy Cannon, who would later win the Heisman Trophy. Visions of a second straight national title were dashed the next weekend, however, when LSU was upset 14–13 by Tennessee.

Mississippi and LSU were matched up again in the Sugar Bowl, but it was an anticlimax as the Rebels won easily, 21–0.

For the second year in a row, the NCAA introduced a rule to help promote scoring. Last season it was the two-point conversion option after a touchdown. This year the goalposts were widened from 18-feet 6-inches to 23-feet 4-inches. Place kickers on major college teams responded with 192 field goals in 390 attempts.

Final AP Top 20
Writers' poll taken before bowl games.

	Regular Season	Head Coach	After Bowls
1 Syracuse	10–0–0	Ben Schwartzwalder	11–0–0
2 Mississippi	9–1–0	Johnny Vaught	10–1–0
3 LSU	9–1–0	Paul Dietzel	9–2–0
4 Texas	9–1–0	Darrell Royal	9–2–0
5 Georgia	9–1–0	Wally Butts	10–1–0
6 Wisconsin	7–2–0	Milt Bruhn	7–3–0
7 TCU	8–2–0	Abe Martin	8–3–0
8 Washington	9–1–0	Jim Owens	10–1–0
9 Arkansas	8–2–0	Frank Broyles	9–2–0
10 Alabama	7–1–2	Bear Bryant	7–2–2
11 Clemson	8–2–0	Frank Howard	9–2–0
12 Penn St.	8–2–0	Rip Engle	9–2–0
13 Illinois	5–3–1	Ray Eliot	same
14 Southern Cal.	8–2–0	Don Clark	same
15 Oklahoma	7–3–0	Bud Wilkinson	same
16 Wyoming	9–1–0	Bob Devaney	same
17 Notre Dame	5–5–0	Joe Kuharich	same
18 Missouri	6–4–0	Dan Devine	6–5–0
19 Florida	5–4–1	Bob Woodruff	same
20 Pittsburgh	6–4–0	John Michelosen	same

Bowl Games with Top 20 Teams

Date	Bowl	Result
12/19/59	Bluebonnet	Clemson 23, TCU 7
12/19/59	Liberty	Penn St. 7, Alabama 0
1/1/60	Cotton	Syracuse 23, Texas 14
1/1/60	Orange	Georgia 14, Missouri 0
1/1/60	Rose	Washington 44, Wisconsin 8
1/1/60	Sugar	Mississippi 21, LSU 0
1/2/60	Gator	Arkansas 14, Ga.Tech 7

Major Conference Champions

AAWU*	Washington/USC/UCLA	3–1
Atlantic Coast	Clemson	6–1
Big Eight	Oklahoma‡	5–1
Big Ten	Wisconsin	5–2
Ivy League	Pennsylvania	6–1
Mid-American	Bowling Green	6–0
Missouri Valley	Houston/North Texas	3–1
Skyline	Wyoming	7–0
Southeastern	Georgia	7–0
Southern	VMI	6–0–1
Southwest	Texas/TCU/Arkansas	5–1

*Athletic Assn of Western Universities.
‡Oklahoma was ineligible for Big Eight berth in Orange Bowl because of "no repeat" rule.

Heisman Trophy Voting

		Yr	Pos.	Votes
1	Billy Cannon, LSU	Sr.	HB	1,929
2	Richie Lucas, Penn St.	Sr.	QB	613
3	Don Meredith, SMU	Sr.	QB	286
4	Bill Burrell, Illinois	Sr.	G	196
5	Charlie Flowers, Miss.	Sr.	FB	193

Other Major Award Winners

Maxwell (Player)	Richie Lucas, Penn St.
Camp (Back)	Billy Cannon, LSU
Rockne (Lineman)	Roger Davis, Syracuse, G
Outland (Interior)	Mike McGee, Duke, G

AFCA Coach of Year and
FWAA Coach of Year
Ben Schwartzwalder, Syracuse

Consensus All-America Team
(By position, in alphabetical order)

Ends—Bill Carpenter, Army; Monty Stickles, Notre Dame. **Tackles**—Don Floyd, TCU; Dan Lanphear, Wisconsin. **Guards**—Bill Burrell, Illinois; Roger Davis, Syracuse. **Center**—Maxie Baughan, Georgia Tech. **Backs**—Ron Burton, Northwestern; Billy Cannon, LSU; Charlie Flowers, Mississippi; Richie Lucas, Penn St.

1960

For the second time in three seasons, a former Red Blaik assistant led his team to the national championship.

In 1958 it had been Paul Dietzel at LSU. In '60 it was Murray Warmath at Minnesota. Meanwhile, Blaik had retired in '58 after guiding the Cadets to a record of 8–0–1 and a No.3 ranking.

Minnesota's upset of Big Ten rival Iowa was the year's pivotal game. When the two teams played in early November, Iowa was No.1, Minnesota was No.3 and both sides were 6–0. The Gophers scored three touchdowns in the second half to win, 27–10, but then lost to Purdue the following week. Nevertheless, when the regular season was over Minnesota was on top.

Mississippi went undefeated in 10 games, winning nine and tying LSU, 6–6, on two field goals. On New Year's, Ole Miss had a better day than Minnesota, beating Rice in the Cotton Bowl while the Gophers, playing in their first postseason game ever, lost to Washington in the Rose Bowl. In light of those results, the Football Writers Association of America, voting after the bowls, made the Rebels their national champion.

No.5 Missouri beat No.4 Navy by a touchdown in the Orange Bowl despite the presence of Heisman winner Joe Bellino in the Middie backfield.

Arkansas, one of three teams to tie for the SWC championship in 1959, won the conference outright in '60. However, the Hogs lost the Cotton Bowl 7–6 to Duke in the last three minutes.

Bowl Games with Top 20 Teams

Date	Bowl	Result
12/17/60	Bluebonnet	3–3, Texas vs Alabama
12/17/60	Liberty	Penn St. 41, Oregon 12
12/31/60	Gator	Florida 13, Baylor 12
12/31/60	Sun	N.Mexico St. 20, Utah St. 13
1/2/61	Cotton	Duke 7, Arkansas 6
1/2/61	Orange	Missouri 21, Navy 14
1/2/61	Rose	Washington 17, Minnesota 7
1/2/61	Sugar	Mississippi 14, Rice 6

Major Conference Champions

AAWU*	Washington	4–0
Atlantic Coast	Duke	5–0
Big Eight	Missouri	7–0
Big Ten	Minnesota/Iowa	5–1
Ivy League	Yale	7–0
Mid-American	Ohio Univ.	6–0
Missouri Valley	Wichita	3–0
Skyline	Utah St./Wyoming	6–1
Southeastern	Mississippi	5–0–1
Southern	VMI	4–1
Southwest	Arkansas	6–1

*Athletic Assn of Western Universities.

Heisman Trophy Voting

	Yr	Pos.	Votes
1 Joe Bellino, Navy	Sr.	HB	1,793
2 Tom Brown, Minnesota	Sr.	G	731
3 Jake Gibbs, Mississippi	Sr.	QB	453
4 Ed Dyas, Auburn	Sr.	HB	319
5 Billy Kilmer, UCLA	Sr.	QB	280
6 Mike Ditka, Pittsburgh	Sr.	E	223

Final AP Top 20
Writers' poll taken before bowl games.

		Regular Season	Head Coach	After Bowls
1	Minnesota	8–1–0	Murray Warmath	8–2–0
2	Mississippi	9–0–1	Johnny Vaught	10–0–1
3	Iowa	8–1–0	Forest Evashevski	same
4	Navy	9–1–0	Wayne Hardin	9–2–0
5	Missouri	9–1–0	Dan Devine	10–1–0
6	Washington	9–1–0	Jim Owens	10–1–0
7	Arkansas	8–2–0	Frank Broyles	8–3–0
8	Ohio St.	7–2–0	Woody Hayes	same
9	Alabama	8–1–1	Bear Bryant	8–1–2
10	Duke	7–3–0	Bill Murray	8–3–0
11	Kansas	7–2–1	Jack Mitchell	same
12	Baylor	8–2–0	John Bridgers	8–3–0
13	Auburn	8–2–0	Shug Jordan	same
14	Yale	9–0–0	Jordan Olivar	same
15	Michigan St.	6–2–1	Duffy Daugherty	same
16	Penn St.	6–3–0	Rip Engle	7–3–0
17	New Mex. St.	10–0–0	Warren Woodson	11–0–0
18	Florida	8–2–0	Ray Graves	9–2–0
19	Syracuse	7–2–0	Ben Schwartzwalder	same
	Purdue	4–4–1	Jack Mollenkopf	same

Other Major Award Winners

Maxwell (Player)	Joe Bellino, Navy
Camp (Back)	Joe Bellino, Navy
Rockne (Lineman)	Tom Brown, Minnesota
Outland (Interior)	Tom Brown, Minnesota
AFCA Coach of Year	Murray Warmath, Minn.
FWAA Coach of Year	Murray Warmath, Minn.

Consensus All-America Team
(By position, in alphabetical order)

Ends—Mike Ditka, Pittsburgh; Danny LaRose, Missouri. **Tackles**—Bob Lilly, TCU; Ken Rice, Auburn. **Guards**—Tom Brown, Minnesota; Joe Romig, Colorado. **Center**—E.J.Holub, Texas Tech. **Backs**—Joe Bellino, Navy; Ernie Davis, Syracuse; Bob Ferguson, Ohio St.; Jake Gibbs, Mississippi.

1961

In 1950, Bear Bryant's Kentucky team ranked 7th in the final AP poll. Six years later, his Texas A&M team placed 5th. This year, his Alabama team was Number One.

Bryant moved around and the programs he took over turned around. The year before he took the Kentucky job the Wildcats were 2–8. The year before he went to A&M the Aggies were 4–5–1. And the year before he moved to Alabama the Crimson Tide was 2–7–1.

The Bear was a winner, but he had never had an undefeated team before this. The Tide went 10–0 during the regular season then beat Arkansas 10–3 in the Sugar Bowl.

Elsewhere, TCU was the spoiler of the year. The Horned Frogs only managed a 3–5–2 record, but they tied No.2 Ohio State, 7–7, and beat No.3 Texas 6–0 to ruin otherwise perfect seasons.

From 1961–62, the Big Ten didn't automatically send a representative to the Rose Bowl, a team from the conference was invited by the bowl's selection committee. Ohio State was invited in 1961, but the school's faculty council voted 28–25 to turn the offer down, citing its discomfort with OSU's overemphasis on sports.

Two-time All-America halfbacks Ernie Davis of Syracuse and Bob Ferguson of Ohio State finished only 53 points apart in the vote for the Heisman. Davis won, becoming the first black player to gain the prize. Ferguson was also black.

Bowl Games with Top 20 Teams

Date	Bowl	Result
12/9/61	Gotham	Baylor 24, Utah St. 9
12/16/61	Bluebonnet	Kansas 33, Rice 7
12/16/61	Liberty	Syracuse 15, Miami,FL 14
12/30/61	Gator	Penn St. 30, Ga.Tech 15
1/1/62	Cotton	Texas 12, Mississippi 7
1/1/62	Orange	LSU 25, Colorado 7
1/1/62	Rose	Minnesota 21, UCLA 3
1/1/62	Sugar	Alabama 10, Arkansas 3

Major Conference Champions

AAWU*	UCLA	3–1
Atlantic Coast	Duke	5–1
Big Eight	Colorado	7–0
Big Ten	Ohio St.‡	6–0
Ivy League	Columbia/Harvard	6–1
Mid-American	Bowling Green	5–1
Missouri Valley	Wichita	3–0
Skyline	Utah St./Wyoming	5–0–1
Southeastern	Alabama	7–0
	and LSU	6–0
Southern	Citadel	5–1
Southwest	Texas/Arkansas	6–1

*Athletic Association of Western Universities.
‡Ohio St. turned down Rose Bowl invitation.

Heisman Trophy Voting

		Yr	Pos.	Votes
1	Ernie Davis, Syracuse	Sr.	HB	824
2	Bob Ferguson, Ohio St.	Sr.	HB	771
3	Jimmy Saxton, Texas	Sr.	HB	551
4	Sandy Stephens, Minnesota	Sr.	QB	543
5	Pat Trammel, Alabama	Sr.	QB	362
10	Merlin Olsen, Utah St	Sr.	T	93

Other Major Award Winners

Maxwell (Player)	Bob Ferguson, Ohio St.
Camp (Back)	Ernie Davis, Syracuse
Rockne (Lineman)	Joe Romig, Colorado, G
Outland (Interior)	Merlin Olsen, Utah St.
AFCA Coach of Year	Bear Bryant, Alabama
FWAA Coach of Year	Darrell Royal, Texas

Final AP Top 20
Writers' poll taken before bowl games.

		Regular Season	Head Coach	After Bowls
1	Alabama	10–0–0	Bear Bryant	11–0–0
2	Ohio St.	8–0–1	Woody Hayes	same
3	Texas	9–1–0	Darrell Royal	10–1–0
4	LSU	9–1–0	Paul Dietzel	10–1–0
5	Mississippi	9–1–0	Johnny Vaught	9–2–0
6	Minnesota	7–2–0	Murray Warmath	8–2–0
7	Colorado	9–1–0	Sonny Grandelius	9–2–0
8	Michigan St.	7–2–0	Duffy Daugherty	same
9	Arkansas	8–2–0	Frank Broyles	8–3–0
10	Utah St.	9–0–1	John Ralston	9–1–1
11	Missouri	7–2–1	Dan Devine	same
12	Purdue	6–3–0	Jack Mollenkopf	same
13	Georgia Tech	7–3–0	Bobby Dodd	7–4–0
14	Syracuse	7–3–0	Ben Schwartzwalder	8–3–0
15	Rutgers	9–0–0	John Bateman	same
16	UCLA	7–3–0	Bill Barnes	7–4–0
17	Rice	7–3–0	Jess Neely	7–4–0
	Penn St.	7–3–0	Rip Engle	8–3–0
	Arizona	8–1–1	Jim LaRue	same
20	Duke	7–3–0	Bill Murray	same

Consensus All-America Team
(By position, in alphabetical order)

Ends—Gary Collins, Maryland; Bill Miller, Miami,FL. **Tackles**—Billy Neighbors, Alabama; Merlin Olsen, Utah St. **Guards**—Joe Romig, Colorado; Roy Winston, LSU. **Center**—Alex Kroll, Rutgers. **Backs**—Ernie Davis, Syracuse; Bob Ferguson, Ohio St.; Jimmy Saxton, Texas; Sandy Stephens, Minnesota.

1962

For the first time since the AP poll began in 1936, the two highest-ranked teams had a date on New Year's Day: No.1 Southern Cal and No.2 Wisconsin in the Rose Bowl.

Many consider it the most exciting bowl game ever. It certainly had the wildest second half. Wisconsin, the nation's most prolific team on offense (31 points per game), trailed 42–14 after three quarters. Quarterback Ron VanderKelen got the Badgers back in the hunt in the fourth frame, directing three TD drives while the defense picked up a safety. With a minute to go, Wisconsin had rallied to within 42–37, but time ran out.

After going 9–1, 9–0–1 and 9–1 over the last three regular seasons, Mississippi finally went unbeaten and untied. But perfection only landed coach Johnny Vaught's team in third place. The Rebels beat Arkansas in the Sugar Bowl.

Texas and Alabama each held No.1 briefly during the regular season. The Longhorns were on top for two weeks in October until a 14–14 tie with Rice changed voters' minds. Bama had its moment in November but it only lasted a week, ending with a 7–6 loss to Georgia Tech.

Longest run of the season? Heisman winner Terry Baker's 99-yard romp in the Liberty Bowl as Oregon State downed Villanova, 6–0.

Biggest cutback? The AP poll was reduced from a Top 20 to Top 10 and would stay that way until 1968.

Final AP Top 10
Writers' poll taken before bowl games.
From 1962–67, AP ranked only 10 teams.

	Regular Season	Head Coach	After Bowls
1 Southern Cal.	10–0–0	John McKay	11–0–0
2 Wisconsin	8–1–0	Milt Bruhn	8–2–0
3 Mississippi	9–0–0	Johnny Vaught	10–0–0
4 Texas	9–0–1	Darrell Royal	9–1–1
5 Alabama	9–1–0	Bear Bryant	10–1–0
6 Arkansas	9–1–0	Frank Broyles	9–2–0
7 LSU	8–1–1	Charlie McClendon	9–1–1
8 Oklahoma	8–2–0	Bud Wilkinson	8–3–0
9 Penn St.	9–1–0	Rip Engle	9–2–0
10 Minnesota	6–2–1	Murray Warmath	same

Final UPI, 11–20
Coaches' poll taken before bowl games.

	Regular Season	Head Coach	After Bowls
11 Georgia Tech	7–2–1	Bobby Dodd	7–3–1
12 Missouri	7–1–2	Dan Devine	8–1–2
13 Ohio St.	6–3–0	Woody Hayes	same
14 Duke	8–2–0	Bill Murray	same
Washington	7–1–2	Jim Owens	same
16 Northwestern	7–2–0	Ara Parseghian	same
Oregon St.	8–2–0	Tommy Prothro	9–2–0
18 Arizona St.	7–2–1	Frank Kush	same
Miami,FL	7–3–0	Andy Gustafson	7–4–0
Illinois*	2–7–0	Pete Elliott	same

*Yes, 2–7–0. All three teams received one vote.

Bowl Games with Top 20 Teams

Date	Bowl	Result
12/15/62	Gotham	Nebraska 36, Miami,FL 34
12/15/62	Liberty	Oregon St. 6, Villanova 0
12/22/62	Bluebonnet	Missouri 14, Ga.Tech 10
12/29/62	Gator	Florida 17, Penn St. 7
1/1/63	Cotton	LSU 13, Texas 0
1/1/63	Orange	Alabama 17, Oklahoma 0
1/1/63	Rose	USC 42, Wisc. 37
1/1/63	Sugar	Miss. 17, Arkansas 13

Major Conference Champions

AAWU*	Southern Cal	4–0
Atlantic Coast	Duke	6–0
Big Eight	Oklahoma	7–0
Big Ten	Wisconsin	6–1
Ivy League	Dartmouth	7–0
Mid-American	Bowling Green	5–0–1
Missouri Valley	Tulsa	3–0
Southeastern	Mississippi	6–0
Southern	VMI	6–0
Southwest	Texas	6–0–1
Western Athletic	New Mexico	2–1–1

*Athletic Assn of Western Universities.

Heisman Trophy Voting

	Yr	Pos.	Votes
1 Terry Baker, Oregon St.	Sr.	QB	707
2 Jerry Stovall, LSU	Sr.	HB	618
3 Bobby Bell, Minnesota	Sr.	T	429
4 Lee Roy Jordan, Alabama	Sr.	C	321
5 George Mira, Miami,FL	Jr.	QB	284
6 Pat Richter, Wisconsin	Sr.	E	276

Other Major Award Winners

S.I.Sportsman of Year	Terry Baker, Ore.St.
Maxwell (Player)	Terry Baker, Ore.St.
Camp (Back)	Jerry Stovall, LSU
Rockne (Lineman)	Pat Richter, Wisconsin
Outland (Interior)	Bobby Bell, Minnesota
AFCA Coach of Year	John McKay, USC
FWAA Coach of Year	John McKay, USC

Consensus All-America Team
(By position, in alphabetical order)

Ends—Hal Bedsole, Southern Cal; Pat Richter, Wisconsin. **Tackles**—Bobby Bell, Minnesota; Jim Dunaway, Mississippi. **Guards**—Jack Cvercko, Northwestern; Johnny Treadwell, Texas. **Center**—Lee Roy Jordan, Alabama. **Backs**—Terry Baker, Oregon St.; Mel Renfro, Oregon; George Saimes, Michigan St.; Jerry Stovall, LSU.

1963

For the second year in a row, No.1 and No.2 squared off in a bowl game: Texas and Navy in the Cotton Bowl.

The top-ranked Longhorns entered the game unbeaten and untied for the first time since 1918. Navy would be their second No.1-No.2 confrontation on the Cotton Bowl field. In October, they upset top-ranked Oklahoma 28-7 in Dallas.

Challenger Navy had Heisman-winning junior quarterback Roger Staubach. The Cotton Bowl, however, was not a safe haven for the Middies. Earlier in the year they suffered their only regular season loss there, 32-28 to SMU. The postseason was more of the same: Texas, 28-6.

The assassination of President Kennedy on Friday, Nov.22, resulted in the postponement or cancellation of many games the next day. The Army-Navy game was one of those delayed a week. When it was finally played, Navy won 21-15.

Pittsburgh also lost to the Middies, but it was the Panthers only setback of the season as they reached the final AP Top 5 for the first time since their national championship year in 1939. Big Ten champ Illinois returned to the Rose Bowl for the first time in 12 years and beat Washington 17-7.

Finally, Oklahoma's Bud Wilkinson retired after 17 years. The Sooners ranked 8th for Wilkinson's final season and he left Norman with three national titles, a 145-29-4 record and a winning percentage of .826.

Final AP Top 10

Writers' poll taken before bowl games.
From 1962-67, AP ranked only 10 teams.

	Regular Season	Head Coach	After Bowls
1 Texas	10-0-0	Darrell Royal	11-0-0
2 Navy	9-1-0	Wayne Hardin	9-2-0
3 Illinois	7-1-1	Pete Elliott	8-1-1
4 Pittsburgh	9-1-0	John Michelosen	same
5 Auburn	9-1-0	Shug Jordan	9-2-0
6 Nebraska	9-1-0	Bob Devaney	10-1-0
7 Mississippi	7-0-2	Johnny Vaught	7-1-2
8 Alabama	8-2-0	Bear Bryant	9-2-0
9 Oklahoma	8-2-0	Bud Wilkinson	same
10 Michigan St.	6-2-1	Duffy Daugherty	same

Final UPI, 11-20

Coaches' poll taken before bowl games.

	Regular Season	Head Coach	After Bowls
11 Miss.St.	6-2-2	Paul Davis	7-2-2
12 Syracuse	8-2-0	Ben Schwartzwalder	same
13 Arizona St.	8-1-0	Frank Kush	same
14 Memphis St.	9-0-1	Billy J.Murphy	same
15 Washington	6-4-0	Jim Owens	6-5-0
16 Penn St.	7-3-0	Rip Engle	same
Southern Cal.	7-3-0	John McKay	same
Missouri	7-3-0	Dan Devine	same
19 N.Carolina	8-2-0	Jim Hickey	9-2-0
20 Baylor	7-3-0	John Bridgers	8-3-0

Bowl Games with Top 20 Teams

Date	Bowl	Result
12/21/63	Bluebonnet	Baylor 14, LSU 7
12/21/63	Liberty	Miss.St. 16, N.C.State 12
12/28/63	Gator	N.Carolina 35, Air Force 0
1/1/64	Cotton	Texas 28, Navy 6
1/1/64	Orange	Nebraska 13, Auburn 7
1/1/64	Rose	Illinois 17, Washington 7
1/1/64	Sugar	Alabama 12, Mississippi 7

Major Conference Champions

AAWU*	Washington	4-1
Atlantic Coast	N.Carolina/N.C.State	6-1
Big Eight	Nebraska	7-0
Big Ten	Illinois	5-1-1
Ivy League	Dartmouth/Princeton	5-2
Mid-American	Ohio Univ.	5-1
Missouri Valley	Cincinnati/Wichita St.	3-1
Southeastern	Mississippi	5-0-1
Southern	Virginia Tech	5-0
Southwest	Texas	7-0
Western Athletic	New Mexico	3-1

*Athletic Assn of Western Universities.

Heisman Trophy Voting

	Yr	Pos.	Votes
1 Roger Staubach, Navy	Jr.	QB	1,860
2 Billy Lothridge, Ga.Tech	Sr.	QB	504
3 Sherman Lewis, Michigan St	Sr.	HB	369
4 Don Trull, Baylor	Sr.	QB	253
5 Scott Appleton, Texas	Sr.	T	194
6 Dick Butkus, Illinois	Jr.	C	172

Other Major Award Winners

Maxwell (Player)	Roger Staubach, Navy
Camp (Back)	Roger Staubach, Navy
Rockne (Lineman)	Dick Butkus, Illinois
Outland (Interior)	Scott Appleton, Texas
AFCA Coach of Year	Darrell Royal, Texas
FWAA Coach of Year	Darrell Royal, Texas

Consensus All-America Team

(By position, in alphabetical order)

Ends—Vern Burke, Oregon St.; Lawrence Elkins, Baylor. **Tackles**—Scott Appleton, Texas; Carl Eller, Minnesota. **Guards**—Bob Brown, Nebraska; Rick Redman, Washington. **Center**—Dick Butkus, Illinois. **Backs**—Jim Grisham, Oklahoma; Sherman Lewis, Michigan St.; Paul Martha, Pittsburgh; Gale Sayers, Kansas; Roger Staubach, Navy.

1964

At the end of the regular season Alabama and Arkansas were each undefeated and untied after 10 games. AP and UPI picked the Crimson Tide as the national champion, but the bowl games would prove both wire services wrong.

On New Year's Day, Arkansas rallied in the fourth quarter to beat No.6 Nebraska 10–7 in the Cotton Bowl. That night, in the first Orange Bowl played under the lights, 5th-ranked Texas jumped out to a 21–7 halftime lead over Alabama and hung on to win 21–17.

Notre Dame's bid for its first perfect season since 1949 also evaporated in the final game. With a 9–0 record, four straight weeks at No.1 and new coach Ara Parseghian on the cover of *Time*, the Irish needed only to beat Southern Cal at the L.A.Coliseum to make their first national championship in 15 years official. Ahead 17–0 at halftime, ND collapsed in the second half and lost on a USC touchdown in the last 95 seconds, 20–17.

Only a point separated both Big Ten champion Michigan and Southwest Conference runner-up Texas from perfect seasons. The Wolverines lost 21–20 to Purdue, but qualified for the Rose Bowl and beat Oregon State by 27. The Longhorns dropped a 14–13 decision to Arkansas, but upset Alabama in the Orange Bowl.

Notre Dame quarterback John Huarte, who didn't play enough to earn a letter his junior year, won the school's sixth Heisman Trophy by just 74 points over Tulsa QB Jerry Rhome.

Final AP Top 10

Writers' poll taken before bowl games.
From 1962–67, AP ranked only 10 teams.

		Regular Season	Head Coach	After Bowls
1	Alabama	10–0–0	Bear Bryant	10–1–0
2	Arkansas	10–0–0	Frank Broyles	11–0–0
3	Notre Dame	9–1–0	Ara Parseghian	same
4	Michigan	8–1–0	Bump Elliott	9–1–0
5	Texas	9–1–0	Darrell Royal	10–1–0
6	Nebraska	9–1–0	Bob Devaney	9–2–0
7	LSU	7–2–1	Charlie McClendon	8–2–1
8	Oregon St.	7–2–0	Tommy Prothro	8–3–0
9	Ohio St.	7–2–0	Woody Hayes	same
10	Southern Cal.	7–3–0	John McKay	same

Final UPI, 11–20

Coaches' poll taken before bowl games.

		Regular Season	Head Coach	After Bowls
11	Florida St	8–1–1	Bill Peterson	9–1–1
12	Syracuse	7–3–0	Ben Schwartzwalder	7–4–0
13	Princeton	9–0–0	Dick Colman	same
14	Penn St.	6–4–0	Rip Engle	same
	Utah	8–2–0	Ray Nagel	9–2–0
16	Illinois	6–3–0	Pete Elliott	same
	New Mexico	9–2–0	Bill Weeks	same
18	Tulsa	8–2–0	Glenn Dobbs	9–2–0
19	Missouri	6–3–1	Dan Devine	same
20	Mississippi	5–4–1	Johnny Vaught	5–5–1
	Michigan St.	4–5–1	Duffy Daugherty	same

Bowl Games with Top 20 Teams

Date	Bowl	Result
12/19/64	Bluebonnet	Tulsa 14, Mississippi 7
12/19/64	Liberty	Utah 32, West Virginia 6
1/1/65	Cotton	Arkansas 10, Nebraska 7
1/1/65	Orange	Texas 21, Alabama 17
1/1/65	Rose	Michigan 34, Oregon St. 7
1/1/65	Sugar	LSU 13, Syracuse 10
1/2/65	Gator	Fla.St. 36, Oklahoma 19

Major Conference Champions

AAWU*	Oregon St./USC	3–1
Atlantic Coast	N.Carolina St.	5–2
Big Eight	Nebraska	6–1
Big Ten	Michigan	6–1
Ivy League	Princeton	7–0
Mid-American	Bowling Green	5–1
Missouri Valley	Cincinnati	4–0
Southeastern	Alabama	8–0
Southern	West Virginia	5–0
Southwest	Arkansas	7–0
Western Athletic	Utah/New Mex./Ariz.	3–1

*Athletic Assn of Western Universities.

Heisman Trophy Voting

		Yr	Pos.	Votes
1	John Huarte, Notre Dame	Sr.	QB	1,026
2	Jerry Rhome, Tulsa	Sr.	QB	952
3	Dick Butkus, Illinois	Sr.	C	505
4	Bob Timberlake, Michigan	Sr.	QB	361
5	Jack Snow, Notre Dame	Sr.	E	187
11	Joe Namath, Alabama	Sr.	QB	112

Other Major Award Winners

Maxwell (Player)	Glenn Ressler, Penn St., G
Camp (Back)	Jerry Rhome, Tulsa
Rockne (Lineman)	Dick Butkus, Illinois
Outland (Interior)	Steve DeLong, Tenn., G
AFCA Coaches of Year	Frank Broyles, Arkansas & Ara Parseghian, N.Dame
FWAA Coach of Year	Ara Parseghian, N.Dame

Consensus All-America Team

(By position, in alphabetical order)

Ends—Fred Biletnikoff, Florida St.; Jack Snow, Notre Dame. **Tackles**—Larry Kramer, Nebraska; Ralph Neely, Oklahoma. **Guards**—Rick Redman, Washington; Glenn Ressler, Penn St. **Center**—Dick Butkus, Illinois. **Backs**—Lawrence Elkins, Baylor; Tucker Frederickson, Auburn; John Huarte, Notre Dame; Gale Sayers, Kansas.

1965

Anxious to avoid the uproar that followed its regular season final poll last year, AP waited until after New Year's to crown the 1965 national champion.

Good move. At the end of the regular season Michigan State, Arkansas and Nebraska were all 10-0, with Alabama at 8-1-1 (the Tide lost their opener to Georgia and tied Tennessee). The bowl match-ups had Arkansas playing LSU in the Cotton, Michigan State vs UCLA in the Rose, and Nebraska vs Alabama in the Orange. Each game followed the other on TV.

The three top-ranked teams all lost. Arkansas, denied the '64 national title it deserved, had its 22-game winning streak snapped in Dallas. LSU took a 14-7 lead in the second quarter then shut the Razorbacks out in the second half.

Michigan State, UPI's national champ, had opened the regular season with a 13-3 win over UCLA. The Spartans hoped to close the year on the same note, but couldn't overcome the Bruins' 14-0 halftime lead. The victory was UCLA's first Rose Bowl win ever.

So the Orange Bowl, in its second year at night, became the national championship game. Underdog Alabama built up a 24-7 lead by halftime then held off a Nebraska comeback to win 39-28.

Bama's Bear Bryant joined Minnesota's Bernie Bierman (1940-41), Army's Red Blaik (1944-45), Notre Dame's Frank Leahy (1946-47) and Oklahoma's Bud Wilkinson (1955-56) as the only coaches to win back-to-back national titles.

Final AP Top 10

For the first time, the complete writers' poll was taken after the bowl games. From 1962-67, AP ranked only 10 teams.

	After Bowls	Head Coach	Regular Season
1 Alabama	9-1-1	Bear Bryant	8-1-1
2 Michigan St.	10-1-0	Duffy Daugherty	10-0-0
3 Arkansas	10-1-0	Frank Broyles	10-0-0
4 UCLA	8-2-1	Tommy Prothro	7-2-1
5 Nebraska	10-1-0	Bob Devaney	10-0-0
6 Missouri	8-2-1	Dan Devine	7-2-1
7 Tennessee	8-1-2	Doug Dickey	7-1-2
8 LSU	8-3-0	Charlie McClendon	7-3-0
9 Notre Dame	7-2-1	Ara Parseghian	same
10 Southern Cal.	7-2-1	John McKay	same

Final UPI, 11-20

Coaches' poll taken before bowl games.
Note: UPI ranked LSU 14th.

	Regular Season	Head Coach	After Bowls
10 Texas Tech	8-2-0	JT King	8-3-0
11 Ohio St.	7-2-0	Woody Hayes	same
12 Florida	7-3-0	Ray Graves	7-4-0
13 Purdue	7-2-1	Jack Mollenkopf	same
14 Georgia	6-4-0	Vince Dooley	same
16 Tulsa	8-2-0	Glenn Dobbs	8-3-0
17 Mississippi	6-4-0	Johnny Vaught	7-4-0
18 Kentucky	6-4-0	Charlie Bradshaw	6-4-0
19 Syracuse	7-3-0	Ben Schwartzwalder	same
20 Colorado	6-2-2	Eddie Crowder	same

Bowl Games with Top 20 Teams

Date	Bowl	Result
12/18/65	Bluebonnet	Tennessee 27, Tulsa 6
12/18/65	Liberty	Mississippi 13, Auburn 7
12/31/65	Gator	Ga.Tech 31, Texas Tech 21
1/1/66	Cotton	LSU 14, Arkansas 7
1/1/66	Orange	Alabama 39, Nebraska 28
1/1/66	Rose	UCLA 14, Michigan St. 12
1/1/66	Sugar	Missouri 20, Florida 18

Major Conference Champions

AAWU*	UCLA	4-0
Atlantic Coast	Clemson/N.C.State	5-2
Big Eight	Nebraska	7-0
Big Ten	Michigan St.	7-0
Ivy League	Dartmouth	7-0
Mid-American	Bowling Green/Miami,OH	5-1
Missouri Valley	Tulsa	4-0
Southeastern	Alabama	6-1-1
Southern	West Virginia	4-0
Southwest	Arkansas	7-0
Western Athletic	BYU	4-1

*Athletic Assn of Western Universities.

Heisman Trophy Voting

	Yr	Pos.	Votes
1 Mike Garrett, Southern Cal.	Sr.	HB	926
2 Howard Twilley, Tulsa	Sr.	E	528
3 Jim Grabowski, Illinois	Sr.	FB	481
4 Donny Anderson, Texas Tech	Sr.	HB	408
5 Floyd Little, Syracuse	Jr.	HB	287
6 Steve Juday, Michigan St.	Sr.	QB	281
7 Tommy Nobis, Texas	Sr.	LB	205
8 Bob Griese, Purdue	Jr.	QB	193
9 Steve Spurrier, Florida	Jr.	QB	93

Other Major Award Winners

Maxwell (Player)	Tommy Nobis, Texas
Camp (Back)	Jim Grabowski, Illinois
Rockne (Lineman)	Tommy Nobis, Texas
Outland (Interior)	Tommy Nobis, Texas
AFCA Coach of Year	Tommy Prothro, UCLA
FWAA Coach of Year	Duffy Daugherty, Mich.St.

Consensus All-America Team

(By position, in alphabetical order)

Offense

E—Howard Twilley, Tulsa; Freeman White, Nebraska. T—Sam Ball, Kentucky; Glen Ray Hines, Arkansas. G—Dick Arrington, Notre Dame; Stas Maliszewski, Princeton; C—Paul Crane, Alabama. QB—Bob Griese, Purdue. RB—Donny Anderson, Texas Tech; Mike Garrett, Southern Cal; Jim Grabowski, Illinois.

Defense

E—Aaron Brown, Minnesota; Bubba Smith, Michigan St. T—Walt Barnes, Nebraska; Loyd Phillips, Arkansas; Bill Yearby, Michigan. LB—Frank Emanuel, Tennessee; Carl McAdams, Oklahoma; Tommy Nobis, Texas. DB—Nick Rassas, Notre Dame; Johnny Roland, Missouri; George Webster, Michigan St.

1966

It may have been the most ballyhooed regular season college football game ever. Notre Dame and Michigan State, in lock step at No.1 and No.2 for five weeks, met in East Lansing on Nov.19, 1966 to settle the national championship.

That both sides were hungry was not questioned. Two years earlier, Notre Dame had the title snatched from them in the last 1:33 of their final game. Last year, Michigan State had a chance to be the undisputed national champ, but was upset in the Rose Bowl. Many of the starters from both those teams were now seniors.

Notre Dame was 8–0 and beating the opposition by an average score of 38–4. Michigan State was 9–0 and winning games at a 31–10 clip. Going in, it was the "Game of the Decade." Coming out, it was the day Notre Dame, according to Dan Jenkins of *Sports Illustrated*, "tied one for the Gipper."

Trailing 10–0 in a very hard-hitting and error-filled game, Notre Dame rallied to pull even early in the fourth quarter. Later, with the ball on his own 30 and a minute and a half left, Ara Parseghian elected to run the clock out and settle for the tie.

Everyone seemed to disagree with Parseghian except the people who counted most: the AP writers and the UPI coaches. They voted to keep Notre Dame on top. The Irish clinched the title, crushing Southern Cal, 51–0, a week later in L.A.

Meanwhile, Alabama, the two-time defending national champ, was undefeated and untied and came in third.

Final AP Top 10

After waiting until the bowl games were played last year, the writers' poll returned to a final vote before the bowl games in 1966. From 1962–67, AP ranked only 10 teams.

		Regular Season	Head Coach	After Bowls
1	Notre Dame	9–0–1	Ara Parseghian	same
2	Michigan St.	9–0–1	Duffy Daugherty	same
3	Alabama	10–0–0	Bear Bryant	11–0–0
4	Georgia	9–1–0	Vince Dooley	10–1–0
5	UCLA	9–1–0	Tommy Prothro	same
6	Nebraska	9–1–0	Bob Devaney	9–2–0
7	Purdue	8–2–0	Jack Mollenkopf	9–2–0
8	Georgia Tech	9–1–0	Bobby Dodd	9–2–0
9	Miami,FL	7–2–1	Charlie Tate	8–2–1
10	SMU	8–2–0	Hayden Fry	8–3–0

Final UPI, 11–20

Coaches' poll taken before bowl games.

		Regular Season	Head Coach	After Bowls
11	Florida	8–2–0	Ray Graves	9–2–0
12	Mississippi	8–2–0	Johnny Vaught	8–3–0
13	Arkansas	8–2–0	Frank Broyles	same
14	Tennessee	7–3–0	Doug Dickey	8–3–0
15	Wyoming	9–1–0	Lloyd Eaton	10–1–0
16	Syracuse	8–2–0	Ben Schwartzwalder	8–3–0
17	Houston	8–2–0	Bill Yeoman	same
18	Southern Cal	7–3–0	John McKay	7–4–0
19	Oregon St.	7–3–0	Dee Andros	same
20	Va.Tech	8–1–1	Jerry Claiborne	8–2–1

Bowl Games with Top 20 Teams

Date	Bowl	Result
12/10/66	Liberty	Miami,FL 14, Va.Tech 7
12/17/66	Bluebonnet	Texas 19, Mississippi 0
12/24/66	Sun	Wyoming 28, Fla.St. 20
12/31/66	Gator	Tennessee 18, Syracuse 12
12/31/66	Cotton	Georgia 24, SMU 9
1/2/67	Orange	Florida 27, Ga.Tech 12
1/2/67	Rose	Purdue 14, USC 13
1/2/67	Sugar	Alabama 34, Nebraska 7

Major Conference Champions

AAWU*	Southern Cal	4–1
Atlantic Coast	Clemson	6–1
Big Eight	Nebraska	6–1
Big Ten	Michigan St.‡	7–0
Ivy League	Harv./Dart./Prin.	6–1
Mid-American	Miami,OH/W.Michigan	5–1
Missouri Valley	Tulsa/North Texas St.	3–1
Southeastern	Alabama/Georgia	6–0
Southern	E.Carolina/Wm.& Mary	4–1–1
Southwest	SMU	6–1
Western Athletic	Wyoming	5–0

*Athletic Assn of Western Universities.
‡Michigan St. ineligible for Big 10 berth in Rose Bowl because of "no repeat" rule.

Heisman Trophy Voting

		Yr.	Pos.	Votes
1 Steve Spurrier, Florida		Sr.	QB	1,679
2 Bob Griese, Purdue		Sr.	QB	816
3 Nick Eddy, Notre Dame		Sr.	HB	456
4 Gary Beban, UCLA		Jr.	QB	318
5 Floyd Little, Syracuse		Sr.	HB	296
6 Clint Jones, Michigan St.		Sr.	HB	204

Other Major Award Winners

Maxwell (Player)	Jim Lynch, N.Dame, LB
Camp (Back)	Steve Spurrier, Florida
Rockne (Lineman)	Jim Lynch, Notre Dame
Outland (Interior)	Loyd Phillips, Ark., DT
AFCA Coach of Year	Tom Cahill, Army (8–2)
FWAA Coach of Year	Tom Cahill, Army

Consensus All-America Team

(By position, in alphabetical order)

Offense

E—Jack Clancy, Michigan; Ray Perkins, Alabama. T—Cecil Dowdy, Alabama; Ron Yary, Southern Cal. G—LaVerne Allers, Nebraska; Tom Regner, Notre Dame. C—Jim Breland, Georgia Tech. QB—Steve Spurrier, Florida. RB—Nick Eddy, Notre Dame; Mel Farr, UCLA; Clint Jones; Michigan St.

Defense

E—Alan Page, Notre Dame; Bubba Smith, Michigan St. T—Tom Greenlee, Washington; Loyd Phillips, Arkansas. MG—John LaGrone, SMU; Wayne Meylin, Nebraska. LB—Jim Lynch, Notre Dame; Paul Naumoff, Tennessee. DB—Tom Beier, Miami,FL; Nate Shaw, Southern Cal; George Webster, Michigan St.

1967

The showdown of the 1967 season was between UCLA quarterback Gary Beban and Southern Cal halfback O.J.Simpson.

Meeting on the final day of the regular season with a Rose Bowl trip and the Heisman Trophy on the line, the two All-Americas put on quite a show. Playing with badly bruised ribs, Beban passed for 301 yards and two touchdowns, while Simpson had a 64-yard touchdown run in the fourth quarter to win the game 21–20.

Simpson, a junior, got to the Rose Bowl. Beban, a senior, got the Heisman.

For Southern Cal and coach John McKay it was the second national championship in six years. USC beat No.4 Indiana in Pasadena to end the season at 10–1. The only blemish was a 3–0 loss to No.7 Oregon State.

Tennessee and Oklahoma, ranked just behind USC in the final AP and UPI polls, faced each other in the Orange Bowl. The Vols lost their opener to UCLA then won nine straight, including a 24–13 decision over Alabama that ended Bama's three-year unbeaten streak at 25. The Sooners were also 9–1, losing only to Texas. In Miami, Tennessee trailed 19–0 at the half, pulled to within 19–17 then 26–24, but lost when a last second field goal try sailed wide.

SWC champ Texas A&M returned the Cotton Bowl after a 26-year absence and upset Alabama, 20–16. Bear Bryant helped carry Aggie coach Gene Stallings off the field. Stallings played for Bryant at A&M.

Final AP Top 10

Writers' poll taken before bowl games.
From 1962–67, AP ranked only 10 teams.

	Regular Season	Head Coach	After Bowls
1 Southern Cal	9–1–0	John McKay	10–1–0
2 Tennessee	9–1–0	Doug Dickey	9–2–0
3 Oklahoma	9–1–0	Chuck Fairbanks	10–1–0
4 Indiana	9–1–0	John Pont	9–2–0
5 Notre Dame	8–2–0	Ara Parseghian	same
6 Wyoming	10–0–0	Lloyd Eaton	10–1–0
7 Oregon St.	7–2–1	Dee Andros	7–2–1
8 Alabama	8–1–1	Bear Bryant	8–2–1
9 Purdue	8–2–0	Jack Mollenkopf	same
10 Penn St.	8–2–0	Joe Paterno	8–2–1

Final UPI, 11–20

Coaches' poll taken before bowl games.
Note: UPI ranked Penn St. 11th and did not rank Alabama (on probation).

	Regular Season	Head Coach	After Bowls
10 UCLA	7–2–1	Tommy Prothro	same
12 Syracuse	8–2–0	Ben Schwartzwalder	same
13 Colorado	8–2–0	Eddie Crowder	9–2–0
14 Minnesota	8–2–0	Murray Warmath	same
15 Florida St.	7–2–1	Bill Peterson	7–2–2
16 Miami,FL	7–3–0	Charlie Tate	7–4–0
17 N.C.State	8–2–0	Earle Edwards	9–2–0
18 Georgia	7–3–0	Vince Dooley	7–4–0
19 Houston	9–2–0	Bill Yeoman	same
20 Arizona St.	8–2–0	Frank Kush	same

Bowl Games with Top 20 Teams

Date	Bowl	Result
12/16/67	Liberty	N.C.State 14, Georgia 7
12/23/67	Bluebonnet	Colorado 31, Miami,FL 21
12/30/67	Gator	17–17, Fla.St. vs Penn St.
1/1/68	Cotton	Texas A&M 20, Alabama 16
1/1/68	Orange	Oklahoma 26, Tennessee 24
1/1/68	Rose	USC 14, Indiana 3
1/1/68	Sugar	LSU 20, Wyoming 13

Major Conference Champions

AAWU*	Southern Cal	6–1
Atlantic Coast	Clemson	6–0
Big Eight	Oklahoma	7–0
Big Ten	Indiana/Purdue/Minn.	6–1
Ivy League	Yale	7–0
Mid-American	Ohio Univ./Toledo	5–1
Missouri Valley	North Texas St.	4–0
Southeastern	Tennessee	6–0
Southern	West Virginia	4–0–1
Southwest	Texas A&M	6–1
Western Athletic	Wyoming	5–0

*Athletic Assn. of Western Universities.

Heisman Trophy Voting

	Yr	Pos.	Votes
1 Gary Beban, UCLA	Sr.	QB	1,968
2 O.J. Simpson, Southern Cal.	Jr.	HB	1,722
3 Leroy Keyes, Purdue	Jr.	HB	1,366
4 Larry Csonka, Syracuse	Sr.	FB	136
5 Kim Hammond, Florida St.	Sr.	QB	90

Other Major Award Winners

Maxwell (Player)	Gary Beban, UCLA
Camp (Back)	Gary Beban, UCLA
Rockne (Lineman)	Ron Yary, USC, OT
Outland (Interior)	Ron Yary, USC
AFCA Coach of Year	John Pont, Indiana
FWAA Coach of Year	John Pont, Indiana

Consensus All-America Team

(By position, in alphabetical order)

Offense

E—Dennis Homan, Alabama; Ron Sellers, Florida. T—Ed Chandler, Georgia; Ron Yary, Southern Cal. G—Harry Olszewski, Clemson; Rich Stotter, Houston. C—Bob Johnson, Tennessee. QB—Gary Beban, UCLA. RB—Larry Csonka, Syracuse; Leroy Keyes, Purdue; O.J.Simpson, Southern Cal.

Defense

E—Ted Hendricks, Miami,FL; Tim Rossovich, Southern Cal. T—Dennis Byrd, North Carolina St. MG—Granville Liggins, Oklahoma; Wayne Meylin, Nebraska. LB—Don Manning, UCLA; Adrian Young, Southern Cal. DB—Dick Anderson, Colorado; Bobby Johns, Alabama; Frank Loria, Virginia Tech; Tom Schoen, Notre Dame.

1968

The Associated Press returned to a Top 20 poll in 1968 and decreed that from now on its national champion would be selected after New Year's. AP waited until after the bowl games in 1965, then went back to making its final decision in mid-December from 1966–67.

On Sept.28, Purdue and Notre Dame played in the first of the season's two No.1 vs No.2 showdowns. It was only the second game for both teams and the Boilermakers won 37–22.

The national title was on the line three months later when No.1 Ohio St. met No.2 Southern Cal in the Rose Bowl. The Buckeyes were 9–0 and the Trojans 9–0–1. USC also had Heisman Trophy winner O.J.Simpson, who had led the nation in rushing and all–purpose running for the second year in a row. No matter, Ohio St. spotted USC a 10–0 lead then came back to win 27–16.

Penn State, under third year coach Joe Paterno, was the only other major unbeaten team, finishing the year 11–0 with a one–point win over Kansas in the Orange Bowl. Down 14–7 with 1:16 left, the Lions rallied to score as time ran out. Kansas stopped the subsequent two-point conversion try but was called for having 12 men on the field. Given a second chance, Penn State converted and won, 15–14.

The headline of the year followed the annual Harvard-Yale game in Cambridge where undefeated and untied Harvard scored 16 points in the last minute to tie undefeated and untied Yale. Next day, the *Harvard Crimson* crowed: "HARVARD BEATS YALE, 29–29."

Final AP Top 20
Writers' poll taken after bowl games.

	Final Record	Head Coach	Before Bowls
1 Ohio St.	10–0–0	Woody Hayes	9–0–0
2 Penn St.	11–0–0	Joe Paterno	10–0–0
3 Texas	9–1–1	Darrell Royal	8–1–1
4 Southern Cal	9–1–1	John McKay	9–0–1
5 Notre Dame	7–2–1	Ara Parseghian	same
6 Arkansas	10–1–0	Frank Broyles	9–1–0
7 Kansas	9–2–0	Pepper Rodgers	9–1–0
8 Georgia	8–1–2	Vince Dooley	8–0–2
9 Missouri	8–3–0	Dan Devine	7–3–0
10 Purdue	8–2–0	Jack Mollenkopf	same
11 Oklahoma	7–4–0	Chuck Fairbanks	7–3–0
12 Michigan	8–2–0	Bump Elliott	same
13 Tennessee	8–2–1	Doug Dickey	8–1–1
14 SMU	8–3–0	Hayden Fry	7–3–0
15 Oregon St.	7–3–0	Dee Andros	same
16 Auburn	7–4–0	Shug Jordan	6–4–0
17 Alabama	8–3–0	Bear Bryant	8–2–0
18 Houston	6–2–2	Bill Yeoman	same
19 LSU	8–3–0	Charlie McClendon	7–3–0
20 Ohio Univ.	10–1–0	Bill Hess	10–0–0

Bowl Games with Top 20 Teams

Date	Bowl	Result
12/27/68	Tangerine	Richmond 49, Ohio U. 42
12/28/68	Gator	Missouri 35, Alabama 10
12/28/68	Sun	Auburn 34, Arizona 10
12/30/68	Peach	LSU 31, Florida St. 27
12/31/68	Bluebonnet	SMU 28, Oklahoma 27
1/1/69	Cotton	Texas 36, Tennessee 13
1/1/69	Orange	Penn St. 15, Kansas 14
1/1/69	Rose	Ohio St. 27, USC 16
1/1/69	Sugar	Arkansas 16, Georgia 2

Major Conference Champions

Atlantic Coast	North Carolina St.	6–1
Big Eight	Kansas/Oklahoma	6–1
Big Ten	Ohio St.	7–0
Ivy League	Harvard/Yale	6–0–1
Mid-American	Ohio Univ.	6–0
Missouri Valley	Memphis St.	5–0
Pacific–8	Southern Cal	6–0
Southeastern	Georgia	5–0–1
Southern	Richmond	6–0
Southwest	Texas/Arkansas	6–1
Western Athletic	Wyoming	6–1

Heisman Trophy Voting

	Yr	Pos.	Votes
1 O.J.Simpson, Southern Cal	Sr.	HB	2,853
2 Leroy Keyes, Purdue	Sr.	HB	1,103
3 Terry Hanratty, Notre Dame	Sr.	QB	387
4 Ted Kwalick, Penn St	Sr.	TE	254
5 Ted Hendricks, Miami,FL	Sr.	DE	174

Other Major Award Winners

Maxwell (Player)	O.J.Simpson, Southern Cal
Camp (Back)	O.J.Simpson, Southern Cal
Rockne (Lineman)	Ted Hendricks, Miami,FL
Outland (Interior)	Bill Stanfill, Georgia, DT
AFCA Coach of Year	Joe Paterno, Penn St.
FWAA Coach of Year	Woody Hayes, Ohio St.

Consensus All-America Team
(By position, in alphabetical order)

Offense
E—Ted Kwalick, Penn St.; Jerry LeVias, SMU. T—Dave Foley, Ohio St.; George Kunz, Notre Dame. G—Jim Barnes, Arkansas; Mike Montler, Colorado; Charley Rosenfelder, Tennessee. C—John Didion, Oregon St. QB—Terry Hanratty, Notre Dame. RB—Chris Gilbert, Texas; Leroy Keyes, Purdue; O.J.Simpson, Southern Cal.

Defense
E—Ted Hendricks, Miami,FL; John Zook, Kansas. T—Joe Greene, North Texas St.; Bill Stanfill, Georgia. MG—Chuck Kyle, Purdue; Ed White, California. LB—Steve Kiner, Tennessee; Dennis Onkotz, Penn St. DB—Jake Scott, Georgia; Roger Wehrli, Missouri; Al Worley, Washington.

1969

In college football's centennial year, the seventh and final No.1 vs No.2 duel of the 1960s was waged on Dec.6.

Both top–ranked Texas and Arkansas came in at 9–0. The Longhorns were averaging 44 points a game and had won 18 in a row, but the Razorbacks had a 14–0 lead after three quarters. In the fourth, though, Texas rallied behind quarterback James Street and pulled out a 15–14 victory.

President Nixon was one of the 44,000 fans squeezed into tiny Razorback Stadium and after the game he declared Texas the national champion and gave Darrell Royal a plaque that said so.

The Longhorns clinched the title by coming from behind again in the Cotton Bowl to beat Notre Dame, 21–17. It was the first bowl appearance by the Irish since Knute Rockne and the Four Horseman defeated Pop Warner's Stanford Indians in the 1925 Rose Bowl.

Arkansas, meanwhile, went to the Sugar Bowl and lost to Mississippi. It was a frustrating end to a frustrating decade for coach Frank Broyles. His Hogs won 80 regular season games, went 10–0 twice and 9–1 three times, yet the national championship escaped them.

Penn State, a 10–3 winner over Missouri in the Orange Bowl, was unbeaten and untied again and finished second again in both polls. Southern Cal placed third at 10–0–1. USC was tied by Stanford during the regular season but won the Rose Bowl for the second time in four consecutive appearances.

Final AP Top 20

Writers' poll taken after bowl games.

	Final Record	Head Coach	Before Bowls
1 Texas	11–0–0	Darrell Royal	10–0–0
2 Penn St.	11–0–0	Joe Paterno	10–0–0
3 Southern Cal.	10–0–1	John McKay	9–0–1
4 Ohio St.	8–1–0	Woody Hayes	same
5 Notre Dame	8–2–1	Ara Parseghian	8–1–1
6 Missouri	9–2–0	Dan Devine	9–1–0
7 Arkansas	9–2–0	Frank Broyles	9–1–0
8 Mississippi	8–3–0	Johnny Vaught	7–3–0
9 Michigan	8–3–0	Bo Schembechler	8–2–0
10 LSU	9–1–0	Charlie McClendon	same
11 Nebraska	9–2–0	Bob Devaney	8–2–0
12 Houston	9–2–0	Bill Yeoman	8–2–0
13 UCLA	8–1–1	Tommy Prothro	same
14 Florida	9–1–1	Ray Graves	8–1–1
15 Tennessee	9–2–0	Doug Dickey	9–1–0
16 Colorado	8–3–0	Eddie Crowder	7–3–0
17 W.Virginia	10–0–1	Jim Carlen	9–1–0
18 Purdue	8–2–0	Jack Mollenkopf	same
19 Stanford	7–2–1	John Ralston	same
20 Auburn	8–3–0	Shug Jordan	8–2–0

Bowl Games with Top 20 Teams

Date	Bowl	Result
12/13/69	Liberty	Colorado 47, Alabama 33
12/20/69	Sun	Nebraska 45, Georgia 6
12/27/69	Gator	Florida 14, Tennessee 13
12/30/69	Peach	West Va. 14, S.Carolina 3
12/31/69	Bluebonnet	Houston 36, Auburn 7
1/1/70	Cotton	Texas 21, Notre Dame 17
1/1/70	Orange	Penn St. 10, Missouri 3
1/1/70	Rose	USC 10, Michigan 3
1/1/70	Sugar	Miss. 27, Arkansas 22

Major Conference Champions

Atlantic Coast	South Carolina	6–0
Big Eight	Missouri/Nebraska	6–1
Big Ten	Michigan/Ohio St.	6–1
Ivy League	Dart./Yale/Prin.	6–1
Mid-American	Toledo	5–0
Missouri Valley	Memphis St.	5–0
Pacific Coast AA	San Diego St.	6–0
Pacific-8	Southern Cal	6–0
Southeastern	Tennessee	5–1
Southern	Davidson/Richmond	5–1
Southwest	Texas	7–0
Western Athletic	Arizona St.	6–1

Heisman Trophy Voting

		Yr	Pos.	Votes
1	Steve Owens, Oklahoma	Sr.	HB	1,488
2	Mike Phipps, Purdue	Sr.	QB	1,344
3	Rex Kern, Ohio St.	Jr.	QB	856
4	Archie Manning, Mississippi	Jr.	QB	582
5	Mike Reid, Penn St.	Sr.	DT	297
8	Jim Plunkett, Stanford	Jr.	QB	120

Other Major Award Winners

Maxwell (Player)	Mike Reid, Penn St.
Camp (Back)	Archie Manning, Miss.
Rockne (Lineman)	Mike Reid, Penn St.
Outland (Interior)	Mike Reid, Penn St.
AFCA Coach of Year	Bo Schembechler, Mich.
FWAA Coach of Year	Bo Schembechler, Mich.

Consensus All-America Team

(By position, in alphabetical order)

Offense

E—Carlos Alvarez, Florida; Walker Gillette, Richmond; Jim Mandich, Michigan. T—Bob McKay, Texas, John Ward, Oklahoma St. G—Bill Bridges, Houston; Chip Kell, Tennessee. C—Rodney Brand, Arkansas. QB—Mike Phipps, Purdue. RB—Bob Anderson, Colorado; Jim Otis, Ohio St.; Steve Owens, Oklahoma.

Defense

E—Jim Gunn, Southern Cal; Phil Olsen, Utah St. T—Mike McCoy, Notre Dame; Mike Reid, Penn St. MG—Jim Stillwagon, Ohio St. LB—Mike Ballou, UCLA; Steve Kiner, Tennessee; Dennis Onkotz, Penn St. DB—Tom Curtis, Michigan; Buddy McClinton, Auburn; Jack Tatum, Ohio St.

1970

Before Bob Devaney arrived in 1962, Nebraska had been among the Top 10 teams of the final AP poll exactly twice: No.9 in 1936 and No.7 in 1940.

Devaney's Cornhuskers made it to No.6 in 1963, No.5 two years later, then all the way to No.1 in 1970. Along the way, Nebraska replaced Oklahoma as the Big Deal in the Big Eight by winning six conference titles in nine years.

In 1970, the Huskers were tied 21–21 by Southern Cal in their second game then won 10 straight. At the end of the regular season AP ranked them third behind Texas (10–0) and Ohio State (9–0). UPI, still taking its final vote before the bowl games, named the Longhorns as national champs.

On New Year's Day both Texas and Ohio State lost, giving Nebraska a chance to take it all with a win over LSU in the Orange Bowl. The Huskers posted an early 10–0 lead, lost it in the third quarter, but came back to win in the fourth, 17–12.

Earlier in the day, Texas put its 30-game winning streak on the line against No.6 Notre Dame in the Cotton Bowl. The Irish, who lost by four points to the Longhorns in last year's Cotton showdown, won this time by 13.

In the Rose Bowl, Heisman Trophy winner Jim Plunkett quarterbacked Stanford past Ohio State with two touchdown passes in the fourth quarter.

Final AP Top 20

Writers' poll taken after bowl games.

	Final Record	Head Coach	Before Bowls
1 Nebraska	11–0–1	Bob Devaney	10–0–1
2 Notre Dame	10–1–0	Ara Parseghian	9–0–1
3 Texas	10–1–0	Darrell Royal	10–0–0
4 Tennessee	11–1–0	Bill Battle	10–1–0
5 Ohio St.	9–1–0	Woody Hayes	9–0–0
6 Arizona St.	11–0–0	Frank Kush	10–0–0
7 LSU	9–3–0	Charlie McClendon	9–2–0
8 Stanford	9–3–0	John Ralston	8–3–0
9 Michigan	9–1–0	Bo Schembechler	same
10 Auburn	9–2–0	Shug Jordan	8–2–0
11 Arkansas	9–2–0	Frank Broyles	same
12 Toledo	12–0–0	Frank Lauterbur	11–0–0
13 Georgia Tech	9–3–0	Bud Carson	8–3–0
14 Dartmouth	9–0–0	Bob Blackman	same
15 Southern Cal	6–4–1	John McKay	same
16 Air Force	9–3–0	Ben Martin	9–2–0
17 Tulane	8–4–0	Jim Pittman	7–4–0
18 Penn St.	7–3–0	Joe Paterno	same
19 Houston	8–3–0	Bill Yeoman	same
20 Oklahoma	7–4–1	Chuck Fairbanks	7–4–0
Mississippi	7–4–0	Johnny Vaught	7–3–0

Bowl Games with Top 20 Teams

Date	Bowl	Result
12/12/70	Liberty	Tulane 17, Colorado 3
12/19/70	Sun	Ga.Tech 17, Texas Tech 9
12/28/70	Tangerine	Toledo 40, Wm. & Mary 12
12/30/70	Peach	Ariz.St. 48, N.Carolina 26
12/31/70	Bluebonnet	24–24, Alabama vs Okla.
1/1/71	Cotton	Notre Dame 24, Texas 11
1/1/71	Orange	Nebraska 17, LSU 12
1/1/71	Rose	Stanford 27, Ohio St. 17
1/1/71	Sugar	Tennessee 34, Air Force 13
1/2/71	Gator	Auburn 35, Mississippi 28

Major Conference Champions

Atlantic Coast	Wake Forest	5–1
Big Eight	Nebraska	7–0
Big Ten	Ohio St.	7–0
Ivy League	Dartmouth	7–0
Mid-American	Toledo	5–0
Missouri Valley	Louisville	4–0
Pacific Coast AA	Long Beach St./S.Diego St.	5–1
Pacific-8	Stanford	6–1
Southeastern	LSU	5–0
Southern	William & Mary	3–1
Southwest	Texas	7–0
Western Athletic	Arizona St.	7–0

Heisman Trophy Voting

	Yr	Pos.	Votes
1 Jim Plunkett, Stanford	Sr.	QB	2,229
2 Joe Theismann, Notre Dame	Sr.	QB	1,410
3 Archie Manning, Mississippi	Sr.	QB	849
4 Steve Worster, Texas	Sr.	RB	398
5 Rex Kern, Ohio St.	Sr.	QB	188
6 Pat Sullivan, Auburn	Jr.	QB	180

Other Major Award Winners

Maxwell (Player)	Jim Plunkett, Stanford
Camp (Back)	Ed Marinaro, Cornell, RB
Rockne (Lineman)	Jim Stillwagon, Ohio St.
Lombardi (Lineman)	Jim Stillwagon, Ohio St.
Outland (Interior)	Jim Stillwagon, Ohio St.
AFCA Coaches of Year	Charlie McClendon, LSU & Darrell Royal, Texas
FWAA Coach of Year	Alex Agase, N'western

Consensus All-America Team

(By position, in alphabetical order)

Offense

E—Tom Gatewood, Notre Dame; Ernie Jennings, Air Force; Elmo Wright, Houston. T—Dan Dierdorf, Michigan; Bob Newton, Nebraska; Bobby Wuensch; Texas. G—Larry DiNardo, Notre Dame; Chip Kell, Tennessee. C—Don Popplewell, Colorado. QB—Jim Plunkett, Stanford. RB—Don McCauley, North Carolina; Steve Worster, Texas.

Defense

E—Bill Atessis, Texas; Charlie Weaver, Southern Cal. T—Dick Bumpas, Arkansas; Rock Perdoni, Georgia Tech. MG—Jim Stillwagon, Ohio St. LB—Mike Anderson, LSU; Jack Ham, Penn St. DB—Tommy Casanova, LSU; Dave Elmendorf, Texas A&M; Jack Tatum, Ohio St.; Larry Willingham, Auburn.

1971

In 1971, Nebraska became only the sixth team since '36 to repeat as national champions.

A year ago, the Huskers were lucky to claim their first title after the two teams ranked above them lost their bowl games. This time Bob Devaney's defenders were No.1 from the start and obliged to repel all comers, all 13 of them.

The pivotal games were two No.1 vs No.2 holiday showdowns with Oklahoma (10–0) on Thanksgiving and Alabama (11–0) on New Year's.

With the Big Eight title at stake against the Sooners, Nebraska led early, fell behind late 31–28, then rallied to win 35–31. In the Orange Bowl, Bama fumbled early and often and the Huskers won easily, extending their three-year unbeaten string to 32.

Oklahoma routed Auburn in the Sugar Bowl and Colorado beat Houston by 12 in the Bluebonnet to give the Big Eight a unique Win, Place & Show in the final AP poll. The SEC had the next best conference showing with Alabama, Georgia and Tennessee coming in 4th, 7th and 9th, respectively.

Michigan went to the Rose Bowl unbeaten and untied after shading Ohio State 10–7. In Pasadena, however, the Wolverines fell to Stanford on a last second field goal.

The Heisman Trophy was decided in another close contest. Cornell running back Ed Marinaro, who averaged an NCAA record 174.6 yards a game during his career, lost out to Auburn QB Pat Sullivan by 152 points.

Final AP Top 20

Writers' poll taken after bowl games.

	Final Record	Head Coach	Before Bowls
1 Nebraska	13–0–0	Bob Devaney	12–0–0
2 Oklahoma	11–1–0	Chuck Fairbanks	10–1–0
3 Colorado	10–2–0	Eddie Crowder	9–2–0
4 Alabama	11–1–0	Bear Bryant	11–0–0
5 Penn St.	11–1–0	Joe Paterno	10–1–0
6 Michigan	11–1–0	Bo Schembechler	11–0–0
7 Georgia	11–1–0	Vince Dooley	10–1–0
8 Arizona St.	11–1–0	Frank Kush	10–1–0
9 Tennessee	10–2–0	Bill Battle	9–2–0
10 Stanford	9–3–0	John Ralston	8–3–0
11 LSU	9–3–0	Charlie McClendon	8–3–0
12 Auburn	9–2–0	Shug Jordan	9–1–0
13 Notre Dame	8–2–0	Ara Parseghian	same
14 Toledo	12–0–0	John Murphy	11–0–0
15 Mississippi	10–2–0	Billy Kinard	9–2–0
16 Arkansas	8–3–1	Frank Broyles	8–2–1
17 Houston	9–3–0	Bill Yeoman	9–2–0
18 Texas	8–3–0	Darrell Royal	8–2–0
19 Washington	8–3–0	Jim Owens	same
20 Southern Cal	6–4–1	John McKay	same

Bowl Games with Top 20 Teams

Date	Bowl	Result
12/18/71	Sun	LSU 33, Iowa St. 15
12/20/71	Liberty	Tennessee 14, Arkansas 13
12/27/71	Fiesta	Ariz.St. 45, Fla.St. 38
12/28/71	Tangerine	Toledo 28, Richmond 3
12/30/71	Peach	Miss. 41, Ga.Tech 18
12/31/71	Bluebonnet	Colorado 29, Houston 17
12/31/71	Gator	Georgia 7, N.Carolina 3
1/1/72	Cotton	Penn St. 30, Texas 6
1/1/72	Orange	Nebraska 38, Alabama 6
1/1/72	Rose	Stanford 13, Michigan 12
1/1/72	Sugar	Oklahoma 40, Auburn 22

Major Conference Champions

Atlantic Coast	North Carolina	6–0
Big Eight	Nebraska	7–0
Big Ten	Michigan	8–0
Ivy League	Dartmouth/Cornell	6–1
Mid-American	Toledo	5–0
Missouri Valley	Memphis St.	4–1
Pacific Coast AA	Long Beach St.	5–1
Pacific-8	Stanford	6–1
Southeastern	Alabama	7–0
Southern	Richmond	5–1
Southwest	Texas	6–1
Western Athletic	Arizona St.	7–0

Heisman Trophy Voting

	Yr.	Pos.	Votes
1 Pat Sullivan, Auburn	Sr.	QB	1,597
2 Ed Marinaro, Cornell	Sr.	RB	1,445
3 Greg Pruitt, Oklahoma	Jr.	RB	586
4 Johnny Musso, Alabama	Sr.	RB	365
5 Lydell Mitchell, Penn St.	Sr.	RB	251

Other Major Award Winners

Maxwell (Player)	Ed Marinaro, Cornell
Camp (Back)	Ed Marinaro, Cornell
Rockne (Lineman)	Larry Jacobson, Neb., DT
Lombardi (Lineman)	Walt Patulski, N.Dame, DE
Outland (Interior)	Larry Jacobson, Nebraska
AFCA Coach of Year	Bear Bryant, Alabama
FWAA Coach of Year	Bob Devaney, Nebraska

Consensus All-America Team

(By position, in alphabetical order)

Offense

E—Terry Beasley, Auburn; Johnny Rodgers, Nebraska. T—Dave Joyner, Penn St.; Jerry Sisemore, Texas. G—Reggie McKenzie, Michigan; Royce Smith, Georgia. C—Tom Brahaney, Oklahoma. QB—Pat Sullivan, Auburn. RB—Ed Marinaro, Cornell; Johnny Musso, Alabama; Greg Pruitt, Oklahoma.

Defense

E—Willie Harper, Nebraska; Walt Patulski, Notre Dame. T—Larry Jacobson, Nebraska; Mel Long, Toledo; Sherman White, Stanford. LB—Jeff Siemon, Stanford; Mike Taylor, Michigan. DB—Tommy Casanova, LSU; Clarence Ellis, Notre Dame; Ernie Jackson, Duke; Bobby Majors, Tennessee.

1972

Nebraska's hopes for a third straight national championship received a jolt in the very first game. Opening the season on the road, the Huskers had their 32-game unbeaten streak snapped by UCLA, 20–17.

But it was the other Los Angeles team—Southern Cal—that succeeded Nebraska as No.1 in the final poll. The Trojans were the only major college squad to make it through the regular season without a loss. Only two-time Rose Bowl champ Stanford came within 10 points of USC and that margin was nine (30–21).

USC ended the season with a flourish, blowing Notre Dame out of the Coliseum (45–23) and Ohio State out of the Rose Bowl (42-17). Tailback Anthony Davis scored six touchdowns against the Irish (two kickoff returns went 97 and 96 yards), and fullback Sam Cunningham scored four times against the Buckeyes.

Oklahoma lost to Colorado but beat everyone else including Penn State in the Sugar Bowl. When the season was over the Sooners were placed on two-years' probation by the NCAA for using an ineligible player in three games.

Texas was blanked by Oklahoma early in the season but finished at 10–1, beating Alabama in the Cotton Bowl to place third.

Finally, Nebraska flanker Johnny Rodgers (5-ft 9) won the Heisman, Louisville running back Howard Stevens (5-ft 6) led the nation in all-purpose running, and freshmen became eligible.

Final AP Top 20

Writers' poll taken after bowl games.

	Final Record	Head Coach	Before Bowls
1 Southern Cal	12–0–0	John McKay	11–0–0
2 Oklahoma	11–1–0	Chuck Fairbanks	10–1–0
3 Texas	10–1–0	Darrell Royal	9–1–0
4 Nebraska	9–2–1	Bob Devaney	8–2–1
5 Auburn	10–1–0	Shug Jordan	9–1–0
6 Michigan	10–1–0	Bo Schembechler	same
7 Alabama	10–2–0	Bear Bryant	10–1–0
8 Tennessee	10–2–0	Bill Battle	9–2–0
9 Ohio St.	9–2–0	Woody Hayes	9–1–0
10 Penn St.	10–2–0	Joe Paterno	10–1–0
11 LSU	9–2–1	Charlie McClendon	9–1–1
12 N.Carolina	11–1–0	Bill Dooley	10–1–0
13 Arizona St.	10–2–0	Frank Kush	9–2–0
14 Notre Dame	8–3–0	Ara Parseghian	8–2–0
15 UCLA	8–3–0	Pepper Rodgers	same
16 Colorado	8–4–0	Eddie Crowder	8–3–0
17 N.C.State	8–3–1	Lou Holtz	7–3–1
18 Louisville	9–1–0	Lee Corso	same
19 Wash.St.	7–4–0	Jim Sweeney	same
20 Georgia Tech	7–4–1	Bill Fulcher	6–4–1

Bowl Games with Top 20 Teams

Date	Bowl	Result
12/18/72	Liberty	Ga.Tech 31, Iowa St. 30
12/23/72	Fiesta	Ariz.St. 49, Missouri 35
12/29/72	Peach	N.C.State 49, West Va. 13
12/30/72	Bluebonnet	Tennessee 24, LSU 17
12/30/72	Gator	Auburn 24, Colorado 3
12/30/72	Sun	N.Carolina 32, Tex.Tech 28
12/31/72	Sugar	Oklahoma 14, Penn St. 0
1/1/73	Cotton	Texas 17, Alabama 13
1/1/73	Orange	Nebraska 40, Notre Dame 6
1/1/73	Rose	USC 42, Ohio St. 17

Major Conference Champions

Atlantic Coast	North Carolina	6–0
Big Eight	Nebraska‡	5–1–1
Big Ten	Ohio St./Michigan	7–1
Ivy League	Dartmouth	5–1–1
Mid-American	Kent St.	4–1
Missouri Valley	L'ville/Drake/W.Texas	4–1
Pacific Coast AA	San Diego St.	4–0
Pacific-8	Southern Cal	7–0
Southeastern	Alabama	7–1
Southern	East Carolina	7–0
Southwest	Texas	7–0
Western Athletic	Arizona St.	5–1

‡Oklahoma was 6–1 in the Big Eight, but after the season had to forfeit three wins for using an ineligible player.

Heisman Trophy Voting

	Yr	Pos.	Votes
1 Johnny Rodgers, Nebraska	Sr.	FL	1,310
2 Greg Pruitt, Oklahoma	Sr.	RB	966
3 Rich Glover, Nebraska	Sr.	MG	652
4 Bert Jones, LSU	Sr.	QB	351
5 Terry Davis, Alabama	Sr.	QB	338

Other Major Award Winners

Maxwell (Player)	Brad VanPelt, Mich.St., DB
Camp (Back)	Greg Pruitt, Oklahoma
Rockne (Lineman)	John Hannah, Alabama, G
Lombardi (Lineman)	Rich Glover, Nebraska
Outland (Interior)	Rich Glover, Nebraska
AFCA Coach of Year	John McKay, USC
FWAA Coach of Year	John McKay, USCC

Consensus All-America Team

(By position, in alphabetical order)

Offense

E—Johnny Rodgers, Nebraska; Charles Young, Southern Cal. T—Paul Seymour, Michigan; Jerry Sisemore, Texas. G—John Hannah, Alabama; Ron Rusnak, North Carolina. C—Tom Brahaney, Oklahoma. QB—Bert Jones, LSU. RB—Otis Armstrong, Purdue; Woody Green, Arizona St.; Greg Pruitt, Oklahoma.

Defense

E—Bruce Bannon, Penn St.; Willie Harper, Nebraska; T—Dave Butz, Purdue; Greg Marx, Notre Dame. MG—Rich Glover, Nebraska. LB—Randy Gradishar, Ohio St.; John Skorupan, Penn St. DB—Cullen Bryant, Colorado; Randy Logan, Michigan; Robert Popelka, SMU; Brad VanPelt, Michigan St.

1973

A year ago, Notre Dame gave up 85 points in the last two games of the season. In 1973, it took 11 games for the new and improved Irish to yield 89 points and they won the national championship.

Ranked third at the close of the regular season, Notre Dame faced No.1 Alabama in the Sugar Bowl on New Year's Eve. In a battle that saw the lead change hands six times, the Irish came from behind to win 24–23 on a late field goal.

Notre Dame and Alabama were two of six undefeated teams at the end of the regular season. Ohio State, Michigan, Oklahoma and Penn State were the others.

Ohio State and Michigan were each 10–0 when they met in Ann Arbor to decide the Big Ten championship. The Buckeyes led at halftime, but the Wolverines rallied to tie. The conference chose OSU for the Rose Bowl and the Bucks justified their appointment by scoring 28 points in the second half to rout USC, 42–21.

Oklahoma (Barry Switzer) and Nebraska (Tom Osborne) had new coaches in 1973. They met for the first time in Norman and Switzer won, 27–0. The Sooners finished the regular season at 10–0–1, didn't play a bowl game (probation) and ranked 3rd. Nebraska (8–2–1) went to the Cotton Bowl, beat Texas and ranked 7th.

Penn State was 12–0 overall and beat LSU in the Orange Bowl, but the Lions only made it to No.5 behind Alabama. One consolation was that senior John Cappelletti became the first Eastern back in 10 years to win the Heisman.

Final AP Top 20

Writers' poll taken after bowl games.

	Final Record	Head Coach	Before Bowls
1 Notre Dame	11–0–0	Ara Parseghian	10–0–0
2 Ohio St.	10–0–1	Woody Hayes	9–0–1
3 Oklahoma	10–0–1	Barry Switzer	same
4 Alabama	11–1–0	Bear Bryant	11–0–0
5 Penn St.	12–0–0	Joe Paterno	11–0–0
6 Michigan	10–0–1	Bo Schembechler	same
7 Nebraska	9–2–1	Tom Osborne	8–2–1
8 Southern Cal	9–2–1	John McKay	9–1–1
9 Arizona St.	11–1–0	Frank Kush	10–1–0
Houston	11–1–0	Bill Yeoman	10–1–0
11 Texas Tech	11–1–0	Jim Carlen	10–1–0
12 UCLA	9–2–0	Pepper Rodgers	same
13 LSU	9–3–0	Charlie McClendon	9–2–0
14 Texas	8–3–0	Darrell Royal	8–2–0
15 Miami,OH	11–0–0	Bill Mallory	10–0–0
16 N.C.State	9–3–0	Lou Holtz	8–3–0
17 Missouri	8–4–0	Al Onofrio	7–4–0
18 Kansas	7–4–1	Don Fambrough	7–3–1
19 Tennessee	8–4–0	Bill Battle	8–3–0
20 Maryland	8–4–0	Jerry Claiborne	8–3–0
Tulane	9–3–0	Bennie Ellender	9–2–0

Bowl Games with Top 20 Teams

Date	Bowl	Result
12/17/73	Liberty	N.C.State 31, Kansas 18
12/21/73	Fiesta	Ariz.St. 28, Pittsburgh 7
12/22/73	Tangerine	Miami,OH 16, Florida 7
12/28/73	Peach	Georgia 17, Maryland 16
12/29/73	Bluebonnet	Houston 47, Tulane 7
12/29/73	Gator	Texas Tech 28, Tenn. 19
12/29/73	Sun	Missouri 34, Auburn 17
12/31/73	Sugar	Notre Dame 24, Alabama 23
1/1/74	Cotton	Nebraska 19, Texas 3
1/1/74	Orange	Penn St. 16, LSU 9
1/1/74	Rose	Ohio St. 42, USC 21

Major Conference Champions

Atlantic Coast	N.Carolina St.	6–0
Big Eight	Oklahoma‡	7–0
Big Ten	Ohio St./Michigan	7–0–1
Ivy League	Dartmouth	6–1
Mid-American	Miami,OH	5–0
Missouri Valley	N.Texas St./Tulsa	5–1
Pacific Coast AA	San Diego St.	3–0–1
Pacific-8	Southern Cal	7–0
Southeastern	Alabama	8–0
Southern	East Carolina	7–0
Southwest	Texas	7–0
Western Athletic	Arizona St./Arizona	6–1

‡On probation, ineligible for bowl game.

Heisman Trophy Voting

	Yr	Pos.	Votes
1 John Cappelletti, Penn St.	Sr.	RB	1,057
2 John Hicks, Ohio St.	Sr.	OT	524
3 Roosevelt Leaks, Texas	Sr.	RB	482
4 David Jaynes, Kansas	Sr.	QB	394
5 Archie Griffin, Ohio St.	So.	RB	326
6 Randy Gradishar, Ohio St.	Sr.	LB	282

Other Major Award Winners

Maxwell (Player)	John Cappelletti, Penn St.
Camp (Back)	John Cappelletti, Penn St.
Rockne (Lineman)	Ed Jones, Tenn.St., DE
Lombardi (Lineman)	John Hicks, Ohio St.
Outland (Interior)	John Hicks, Ohio St.
AFCA Coach of Year	Bear Bryant, Alabama
FWAA Coach of Year	Johnny Majors, Pitt (6–5–1)

Consensus All-America Team

(By position, in alphabetical order)

Offense

E—Dave Casper, Notre Dame; Lynn Swann, Southern Cal. T—Booker Brown, Southern Cal; John Hicks, Ohio St. G—Buddy Brown, Alabama; Bill Yoest, North Carolina St. C—Bill Wyman, Texas. QB—Dave Jaynes, Kansas. RB—John Cappelletti, Penn St.; Woody Green, Arizona St.; Kermit Johnson, UCLA; Roosevelt Leaks, Texas.

Defense

Line—Tony Cristiani, Miami,FL; John Dutton, Nebraska; Dave Gallagher, Michigan; Lucious Selmon, Oklahoma. LB—Randy Gradishar, Ohio St.; Rod Shoate, Oklahoma; Richard Wood, Southern Cal. DB—Dave Brown, Michigan; Artimus Parker, Southern Cal; Randy Rhino, Georgia Tech; Mike Townsend, Notre Dame.

1974

After three seasons at either No.2 or No.3, Oklahoma broke through in 1974 to win its first national championship in 18 years.

The Sooners rolled through their 11-game schedule averaging 508 yards in total offense and a final score of 43–8. Only Texas gave them a fight before losing 16–13.

Actually, UPI gave Oklahoma a fight, too. At the beginning of the season the UPI coaches board decreed that any team on NCAA probation (as Oklahoma was) was not worthy of their consideration. AP's writers went for the Sooners but UPI's coaches, voting after the bowl games for the first time, selected AP runner-up Southern Cal.

USC finished up at 10–1–1 with impressive wins over Notre Dame and Ohio State. Trailing the Irish 24–0 at the half, the Trojans came storming back behind Anthony Davis (4 TDs) to score 55 points in 17 minutes and win 55–24. In the Rose Bowl, quarterback Pat Haden passed for a touchdown and a two-point conversion in the last two minutes to beat the Buckeyes, 18–17.

Hard luck continued to stalk Michigan and Alabama. The Wolverines lost 12–10 to arch-rival Ohio State and missed out on another trip to the Rose Bowl despite another regular season with 10 wins. And the Crimson Tide failed to win a bowl game for the eighth straight year, losing 13–11 to Notre Dame and retiring coach Ara Parseghian in the Orange Bowl.

Final AP Top 20
Writers' poll taken after bowl games.

	Final Record	Head Coach	Before Bowls
1 Oklahoma	11–0–0	Barry Switzer	same
2 Southern Cal	10–1–1	John McKay	9–1–1
3 Michigan	10–1–0	Bo Schembechler	same
4 Ohio St.	10–2–0	Woody Hayes	10–1–0
5 Alabama	11–1–0	Bear Bryant	11–0–0
6 Notre Dame	10–2–0	Ara Parseghian	9–2–0
7 Penn St.	10–2–0	Joe Paterno	9–2–0
8 Auburn	10–2–0	Shug Jordan	9–2–0
9 Nebraska	9–3–0	Tom Osborne	8–3–0
10 Miami,OH	10–0–1	Dick Crum	9–0–1
11 N.C.State	9–2–1	Lou Holtz	9–2–0
12 Michigan St.	7–3–1	Denny Stolz	same
13 Maryland	8–4–0	Jerry Claiborne	8–3–0
14 Baylor	8–4–0	Grant Teaff	8–3–0
15 Florida	8–4–0	Doug Dickey	8–3–0
16 Texas A&M	8–3–0	Emory Ballard	same
17 Miss.St.	9–3–0	Bob Tyler	8–3–0
Texas	8–4–0	Darrell Royal	8–3–0
19 Houston	8–3–1	Bill Yeoman	8–3–0
20 Tennessee	7–3–2	Bill Battle	6–3–2

Bowl Games with Top 20 Teams

Date	Bowl	Result
12/16/74	Liberty	Tennessee 7, Maryland 3
12/21/74	Tangerine	Miami,OH 21, Georgia 10
12/23/74	Bluebonnet	31–31, N.C.St. vs Houston
12/28/74	Fiesta	Oklahoma St. 16, BYU 6
12/28/74	Peach	6–6, Vandy vs Tex.Tech
12/28/74	Sun	Miss.St. 26, N.Carolina 24
12/30/74	Gator	Auburn 27, Texas 3
12/31/74	Sugar	Nebraska 13, Florida 10
1/1/75	Cotton	Penn St. 41, Baylor 20
1/1/75	Orange	Notre Dame 13, Alabama 11
1/1/75	Rose	USC 18, Ohio St. 17

Major Conference Champions

Atlantic Coast	Maryland	6–0
Big Eight	Oklahoma‡	7–0
Big Ten	Ohio St./Michigan	7–1
Ivy League	Harvard/Yale	6–1
Mid-American	Miami,OH	5–0
Missouri Valley	Tulsa	6–0
Pacific Coast AA	San Diego St.	4–0
Pacific-8	Southern Cal	6–0–1
Southeastern	Alabama	6–0
Southern	VMI	5–1
Southwest	Baylor	6–1
Western Athletic	BYU	6–0–1

‡On probation, ineligible for bowl game.

Heisman Trophy Voting

	Yr	Pos.	Votes
1 Archie Griffin, Ohio St.	Jr.	RB	1,920
2 Anthony Davis, Southern Cal	Sr.	RB	819
3 Joe Washington, Oklahoma	Jr.	RB	661
4 Tom Clements, Notre Dame	Sr.	QB	244
5 David Humm, Nebraska	Sr.	QB	210
9 Randy White, Maryland	Sr.	DT	85

Other Major Award Winners

Maxwell (Player)	Steve Joachim, Temple, QB
Camp (Back)	Anthony Davis, USC
Rockne (Lineman)	Randy White, Maryland
Lombardi (Lineman)	Randy White, Maryland
Outland (Interior)	Randy White, Maryland
AFCA Coach of Year	Grant Teaff, Baylor
FWAA Coach of Year	Grant Teaff, Baylor

Consensus All-America Team
(By position, in alphabetical order)

Offense
WR—Pete Demmerle, Notre Dame. TE—Bennie Cunningham, Clemson. T—Marvin Crenshaw, Nebraska; Kurt Schumacher, Ohio St. G—Ken Huff, North Carolina; Gerry DiNardo, Notre Dame; John Roush, Oklahoma. C—Steve Myers, Ohio St. QB—Steve Bartkowski, California. RB—Anthony Davis, Southern Cal; Archie Griffin, Ohio St.; Joe Washington, Oklahoma.

Defense
Line—Leroy Cook, Alabama; Pat Donovan, Stanford; Mike Hartenstine, Penn St.; Jimmy Webb, Mississippi St.; Randy White, Maryland. MG—Rubin Carter, Miami, FL; Louie Kelcher, SMU. LB—Ken Bernich, Auburn; Woodrow Lowe, Alabama; Rod Shoate, Oklahoma; Richard Wood, Southern Cal. DB—Dave Brown, Michigan; John Provost, Holy Cross; Pat Thomas, Texas A&M.

1975

Off probation, defending national champion Oklahoma was embraced by UPI as well as AP in 1975.

Unbeaten in 30 games under Switzer and winners of 28 in a row, the Sooners were stopped cold by Kansas, 23–3, in early November. They had to rally the next weekend to beat Missouri 28–27, but then routed Nebraska 35–10 to reach the Orange Bowl.

Oklahoma's date with Michigan New Year's Night became a game for the championship when No.1 Ohio State gave up three second half touchdowns and lost the Rose Bowl to UCLA. The Sooners seized their opportunity and beat Michigan 14–6 to keep their title.

Arizona State, the Top 20's only undefeated team, edged Nebraska, 17–14, in the Fiesta Bowl to place second. The margin of victory was a 27-yard field goal by the coach's son, Dan Kush.

Alabama came on to finish third, finally winning a bowl for Bear Bryant after going 0–7–1 in the postseason since New Year's Day,1968. The Tide beat Penn State in the Sugar Bowl.

Ohio State may have lost the Rose Bowl for the second year in a row, but running back Archie Griffin became the first player to win two Heisman Trophies. In the Buckeye backfield since his freshman year, Griffin ended his career with 5,177 yards rushing and 33 games with 100 yards or more, both NCAA records. During the Griffin Era, OSU went 40–5–1, won four Big Ten titles and played in four Rose Bowls.

Final AP Top 20

Writers' poll taken after bowl games.

		Final Record	Head Coach	Before Bowls
1	Oklahoma	11–1–0	Barry Switzer	10–1–0
2	Arizona St.	12–0–0	Frank Kush	11–0–0
3	Alabama	11–1–0	Bear Bryant	10–1–0
4	Ohio St.	11–1–0	Woody Hayes	11–0–0
5	UCLA	9–2–1	Dick Vermeil	8–2–1
6	Texas	10–2–0	Darrell Royal	9–2–0
7	Arkansas	10–2–0	Frank Broyles	9–2–0
8	Michigan	8–2–2	Bo Schembechler	8–1–2
9	Nebraska	10–2–0	Tom Osborne	10–1–0
10	Penn St.	9–3–0	Joe Paterno	9–2–0
11	Texas A&M	10–2–0	Emory Bellard	10–1–0
12	Miami,OH	11–1–0	Dick Crum	10–1–0
13	Maryland	9–2–1	Jerry Claiborne	8–2–1
14	California	8–3–0	Mike White	same
15	Pittsburgh	8–4–0	Johnny Majors	7–4–0
16	Colorado	9–3–0	Bill Mallory	9–2–0
17	Southern Cal	8–4–0	John McKay	7–4–0
18	Arizona	9–2–0	Jim Young	same
19	Georgia	9–3–0	Vince Dooley	9–2–0
20	West Virginia	9–3–0	Bobby Bowden	8–3–0

Bowl Games with Top 20 Teams

Date	Bowl	Result
12/20/75	Tangerine	Miami,OH 20, S.Carolina 7
12/22/75	Liberty	USC 20, Texas A&M 0
12/26/75	Fiesta	Ariz.St. 17, Nebraska 14
12/26/75	Sun	Pittsburgh 33, Kansas 19
12/27/75	Bluebonnet	Texas 38, Colorado 21
12/29/75	Gator	Maryland 13, Florida 0
12/31/75	Peach	West Va. 13, N.C.State 10
12/31/75	Sugar	Alabama 13, Penn St. 6
1/1/76	Cotton	Arkansas 31, Georgia 10
1/1/76	Orange	Oklahoma 14, Michigan 6
1/1/76	Rose	UCLA 23, Ohio St. 10

Major Conference Champions

Atlantic Coast	Maryland	5–0
Big Eight	Oklahoma/Nebraska	6–1
Big Ten	Ohio St.	8–0
Ivy League	Harvard	6–1
Mid-American	Miami,OH	6–0
Missouri Valley	Tulsa	4–0
Pacific Coast AA	San Jose St.	5–0
Pacific-8	UCLA/California	6–1
Southeastern	Alabama	6–0
Southern	Richmond	5–1
Southwest	Ark./Texas/Tex.A&M	6–1
Western Athletic	Arizona St.	7–0

Heisman Trophy Voting

		Yr	Pos.	Votes
1	Archie Griffin, Ohio St.	Sr.	RB	1,800
2	Chuck Muncie, California	Sr.	RB	730
3	Ricky Bell, Southern Cal	Jr.	RB	708
4	Tony Dorsett, Pittsburgh	Jr.	RB	616
5	Joe Washington, Oklahoma	Sr.	RB	250

Other Major Award Winners

Maxwell (Player)	Archie Griffin, Ohio St.
Camp (Back)	Chuck Muncie, California
Rockne (Lineman)	Lee Roy Selmon, Okla., DT
Lombardi (Lineman)	Lee Roy Selmon, Oklahoma
Outland (Interior)	Lee Roy Selmon, Oklahoma
AFCA Coach of Year	Frank Kush, Arizona St.
FWAA Coach of Year	Woody Hayes, Ohio St.

Consensus All-America Team

(By position, in alphabetical order)

Offense

E—Larry Seivers, Tennessee; Steve Rivera, California. **T**—Dennis Lick, Wisconsin; Bob Simmons, Texas. **G**—Randy Johnson, Georgia; Ted Smith, Ohio St. **C**—Rik Bonness, Nebraska. **QB**—John Sciarra, UCLA. **RB**—Ricky Bell, Southern Cal; Archie Griffin, Ohio St.; Chuck Muncie, California.

Defense

Line—Leroy Cook, Alabama; Jimbo Elrod, Oklahoma; Steve Niehaus, Notre Dame; Lee Roy Selmon, Oklahoma. **MG**—Dewey Selmon, Oklahoma. **LB**—Greg Buttle, Penn St.; Sammy Green, Florida; Ed Simonini, Texas A&M. **DB**—Tim Fox, Ohio St.; Chet Moeller, Navy; Pat Thomas, Texas A&M.

1976

In the 40-odd years of the Heisman Trophy, the AFCA Coach of the Year award and the AP Top 20, no one team had won all three in the same season until Pittsburgh did it in 1976.

Led by record-breaking running back Tony Dorsett and coach Johnny Majors, Pitt was 11–0 during the regular season and a 27–3 victor over Georgia in the Sugar Bowl. It was the Panthers' first major bowl appearance since 1955, their first national championship since 1937, and their first unbeaten and untied season since 1917.

Dorsett had a remarkable season, rushing for 1,948 yards and scoring 22 touchdowns. He ended his four years with 6,082 yards and 356 points, both NCAA records. Coach Majors also worked some magic over four years, inheriting a program that had gone 1–10 in 1972 and guiding it to a 33–13–1 record.

Michigan's spirit was tested in '76. A solid No.1 choice in the polls through October, the Wolverines were upset 16–14 by Purdue in early November. They recovered to beat Ohio State for the Big Ten championship, went back to the Rose Bowl for the first time in five years, then lost to Southern Cal, 14–6.

In the Southwest Conference, Houston won a trip to the Cotton Bowl in its first year as a league member. The Cougars tied for the title with Texas Tech, but had beaten the Red Raiders during the season. On New Year's Day, Houston was in Dallas to complete its improbable year in with a 30–21 victory over unbeaten Maryland.

Final AP Top 20

Writers' poll taken after bowl games.

	Final Record	Head Coach	Before Bowls
1 Pittsburgh	12–0–0	Johnny Majors	11–0–0
2 Southern Cal	11–1–0	John Robinson	10–1–0
3 Michigan	10–2–0	Bo Schembechler	10–1–0
4 Houston	10–2–0	Bill Yeoman	9–2–0
5 Oklahoma	9–2–1	Barry Switzer	8–2–1
6 Ohio St.	9–2–1	Woody Hayes	8–2–1
7 Texas A&M	10–2–0	Emory Bellard	9–2–0
8 Maryland	11–1–0	Jerry Claiborne	11–0–0
9 Nebraska	9–3–1	Tom Osborne	8–3–1
10 Georgia	10–2–0	Vince Dooley	10–1–0
11 Alabama	9–3–0	Bear Bryant	8–3–0
12 Notre Dame	9–3–0	Dan Devine	8–3–0
13 Texas Tech	10–2–0	Steve Sloan	10–1–0
14 Oklahoma St.	9–3–0	Jim Stanley	8–3–0
15 UCLA	9–2–1	Terry Donahue	9–1–1
16 Colorado	8–4–0	Bill Mallory	8–3–0
17 Rutgers	11–0–0	Frank Burns	same
18 Kentucky	9–3–0	Fran Curci	8–3–0
19 Iowa St.	8–3–0	Earle Bruce	same
20 Miss.St.	9–2–0	Bob Tyler	same

Bowl Games with Top 20 Teams

Date	Bowl	Result
12/18/76	Tangerine	Oklahoma St. 49, BYU 21
12/20/76	Liberty	Alabama 36, UCLA 6
12/25/76	Fiesta	Oklahoma 41, Wyoming 7
12/27/76	Gator	Notre Dame 20, Penn St. 9
12/31/76	Bluebonnet	Nebraska 27, Tex.Tech 24
12/31/76	Peach	Kentucky 21, N.Carolina 0
1/1/77	Cotton	Houston 30, Maryland 21
1/1/77	Orange	Ohio St. 27, Colorado 10
1/1/77	Rose	USC 14, Michigan 6
1/1/77	Sugar	Pittsburgh 27, Georgia 3
1/2/77	Sun	Texas A&M 37, Florida 14

Major Conference Champions

Atlantic Coast	Maryland	5–0
Big Eight	Colo./Okla./Okla.St.	5–2
Big Ten	Michigan/Ohio St.	7–1
Ivy League	Brown/Yale	6–1
Mid-American	Ball St.	4–1
Missouri Valley	N.Mexico St./Tulsa	2–1–1
Pacific Coast AA	San Jose St.	4–0
Pacific-8	Southern Cal	7–0
Southeastern	Georgia/Kentucky	5–1
Southern	East Carolina	4–1
Southwest	Houston/Texas Tech	7–1
Western Athletic	BYU/Wyoming	6–1

Heisman Trophy Voting

	Yr	Pos.	Votes
1 Tony Dorsett, Pittsburgh	Sr.	RB	2,357
2 Ricky Bell, Southern Cal	Sr.	RB	1,346
3 Rob Lytle, Michigan	Sr.	RB	413
4 Terry Miller, Oklahoma St.	Jr.	RB	197
5 Tommy Kramer, Rice	Sr.	QB	63

Other Major Award Winners

Maxwell (Player)	Tony Dorsett, Pittsburgh
Camp (Back)	Tony Dorsett, Pittsburgh
Rockne (Lineman)	Wilson Whitley, Houston, DT
Lombardi (Lineman)	Wilson Whitley, Houston, DT
Outland (Interior)	Ross Browner, N.Dame, DE
AFCA Coach of Year	Johnny Majors, Pittsburgh
FWAA Coach of Year	Johnny Majors, Pittsburgh

Consensus All-America Team

(By position, in alphabetical order)

Offense

SE—Larry Seivers, Tennessee. **TE**—Ken MacAfee, Notre Dame. **T**—Mike Vaughan, Oklahoma; Chris Ward, Ohio St. **G**—Mark Donahue, Michigan; Joel Parrish, Georgia. **C**—Derrel Gofourth, Oklahoma St. **QB**—Tommy Kramer, Rice. **RB**—Ricky Bell, Southern Cal; Tony Dorsett, Pittsburgh; Rob Lytle, Michigan. **PK**—Tony Franklin, Texas A&M.

Defense

Line—Ross Browner, Notre Dame; Bob Brudzinski, Ohio St.; Joe Campbell, Maryland; Gary Jeter, Southern Cal; Wilson Whitley, Houston. **MG**—Al Romano, Pittsburgh. **LB**—Robert Jackson, Texas A&M; Jerry Robinson, UCLA. **DB**—Bill Armstrong, Wake Forest; Dave Butterfield, Nebraska; Gary Green, Baylor; Dennis Thurman, Southern Cal.

1977

For the third time in nine years, Notre Dame opened the new calendar year in the Cotton Bowl against a No.1 team from Texas.

The first time, on Jan.1, 1970, the Longhorns won 21–17 and clinched the national championship. A year later, the Irish returned to deny Texas a second straight title, winning 24–11.

This time around on Jan.2, 1978, No.5 Notre Dame jumped out to a 24–10 lead in the first half and won easily 38–10. When the dust settled, the two teams had traded places and the Irish were national champs for the seventh time in the 42 years of the AP poll.

Notre Dame was able to leapfrog the other three teams in front of it when the following happened on New Year's Day: No.2 Oklahoma lost the Orange Bowl to Arkansas, No.3 Alabama won the Sugar Bowl but against a lower ranked team (Ohio State), and No.4 Michigan lost the Rose Bowl (again).

Two bold coaching moves also marked the season. Dan Devine of Notre Dame decided to put green jerseys on his team when Southern Cal came to South Bend on Oct.22. The switch worked as the Irish beat USC for the first time in four years. Lou Holtz of Arkansas made his move right before the Orange Bowl when he suspended three key players then went out and beat Oklahoma anyway, 31–6.

Finally, Texas running back Earl Campbell won the Heisman, marking the trophy's return to the SWC after a 20-year absence.

Final AP Top 20

Writers' poll taken after bowl games.

		Final Record	Head Coach	Before Bowls
1	Notre Dame	11–1–0	Dan Devine	10–1–0
2	Alabama	11–1–0	Bear Bryant	10–1–0
3	Arkansas	11–1–0	Lou Holtz	10–1–0
4	Texas	11–1–0	Fred Akers	11–0–0
5	Penn St.	11–1–0	Joe Paterno	10–1–0
6	Kentucky	10–1–0	Fran Curci	same
7	Oklahoma	10–2–0	Barry Switzer	10–1–0
8	Pittsburgh	9–2–1	Jackie Sherrill	8–2–1
9	Michigan	10–2–0	Bo Schembechler	10–1–0
10	Washington	10–2–0	Don James	9–2–0
11	Ohio St.	9–3–0	Woody Hayes	9–2–0
12	Nebraska	9–3–0	Tom Osborne	8–3–0
13	Southern Cal	8–4–0	John Robinson	7–4–0
14	Florida St.	10–2–0	Bobby Bowden	9–2–0
15	Stanford	9–3–0	Bill Walsh	8–3–0
16	S.Diego St.	10–1–0	Claude Gilbert	same
17	N.Carolina	8–3–1	Bill Dooley	8–2–1
18	Arizona St.	9–3–0	Frank Kush	9–2–0
19	Clemson	8–3–1	Charley Pell	8–2–1
20	BYU	9–2–0	LaVell Edwards	same

Bowl Games with Top 20 Teams

Date	Bowl	Result
12/19/77	Liberty	Nebraska 21, N.Carolina 17
12/23/77	Tangerine	Fla.St. 40, Texas Tech 17
12/25/77	Fiesta	Penn St. 42, Ariz.St. 30
12/30/77	Gator	Pittsburgh 34, Clemson 3
12/31/77	Bluebonnet	USC 47, Tex.A&M 28
12/31/77	Sun	Stanford 24, LSU 14
1/2/78	Cotton	Notre Dame 38, Texas 10
1/2/78	Orange	Arkansas 31, Oklahoma 6
1/2/78	Rose	Washington 27, Michigan 20
1/2/78	Sugar	Alabama 35, Ohio St. 6

Major Conference Champions

Atlantic Coast	North Carolina	5–0–1
Big Eight	Oklahoma	7–0
Big Ten	Michigan/Ohio St.	7–1
Ivy League	Yale	6–1
Mid-American	Miami,OH	5–0
Missouri Valley	West Texas St.	5–1
Pacific Coast AA	Fresno St.	4–0
Pacific-8	Washington	6–1
Southeastern	Alabama	7–0
	Kentucky	6–0
Southern	Tennessee–Chat/VMI	4–1
Southwest	Texas	8–0
Western Athletic	Arizona St./BYU	6–1

Heisman Trophy Voting

		Yr.	Pos.	Votes
1	Earl Campbell, Texas	Sr.	RB	1,547
2	Terry Miller, Oklahoma St.	Sr.	RB	812
3	Ken MacAfee, Notre Dame	Sr.	TE	343
4	Doug Williams, Grambling	Sr.	QB	266
5	Ross Browner, Notre Dame	Sr.	DE	213

Other Major Award Winners

Maxwell (Player)	Ross Browner, Notre Dame
Camp (Back)	Earl Campbell, Texas
Rockne (Lineman)	Ken MacAfee, Notre Dame
Lombardi (Lineman)	Ross Browner, Notre Dame
Outland (Interior)	Brad Shearer, Texas, DT
AFCA Coach of Year	Don James, Washington
FWAA Coach of Year	Lou Holtz, Arkansas

Consensus All-America Team

(By position, in alphabetical order)

Offense

WR—John Jefferson, Arizona St.; Ozzie Newsome, Alabama. **TE**—Ken MacAfee, Notre Dame. **T**—Dan Irons, Texas Tech; Chris Ward, Ohio St. **G**—Mark Donahue, Michigan; Leotis Harris, Arkansas. **C**—Tom Brzoza, Pittsburgh. **QB**—Guy Benjamin, Stanford. **RB**—Charles Alexander, LSU; Earl Campbell, Texas; Terry Miller, Oklahoma St. **PK**—Steve Little, Arkansas.

Defense

Line—Ross Browner, Notre Dame; Dee Hardison, North Carolina; Randy Holloway, Pittsburgh; Brad Shearer, Texas; Art Still, Kentucky. **LB**—Tom Cousineau, Ohio St.; Jerry Robinson, UCLA; Gary Spani, Kansas St. **DB**—Luther Bradley, Notre Dame; Zac Henderson, Oklahoma; Bob Jury, Pittsburgh; Dennis Thurman, Southern Cal.

1978

Thirteen years removed from its last national championship, Alabama climbed back to the top of the final AP poll in 1978.

No.1 played No.2 for only the third time in the 1970s when the Crimson Tide upset top-ranked Penn State, 14–7, in the Sugar Bowl.

However, UPI's coaches disagreed with AP's writers and picked Southern Cal as the best team, citing USC's 24–14 victory over Bama during the regular season. Both teams had one defeat, the Trojans losing early in the year to new Pac-10 member Arizona State.

Oklahoma got the third place nod from both wire services. In the annual "brawl for it all" in the Big Eight, OU lost to Nebraska 17–14, giving Husker coach Tom Osborne his first win over Barry Switzer. The next week, however, Nebraska lost to Missouri while the Sooners were clobbering Oklahoma State. A Sooner-Husker rematch was called for and arranged in the Orange Bowl where the Switzers beat the Osbornes, 31–24.

Defending champion Notre Dame dropped its first two games of the season to Missouri and Michigan, won eight straight, then lost to Southern Cal 27–25 on a last second field goal. The Irish rebounded in an icy Cotton Bowl game, however, and scored 23 points in the fourth quarter to catch Houston, 35–34.

In the Big Ten, Michigan beat Ohio State and lost the Rose Bowl for the third year in a row, while Buckeye coach Woody Hayes was forced to retire after hitting a Clemson player in the Gator Bowl. Hayes walked away with 238 career wins and two national titles.

Final AP Top 20

Writers' poll taken after bowl games.

	Final Record	Head Coach	Before Bowls
1 Alabama	11–1–0	Bear Bryant	10–1–0
2 Southern Cal	12–1–0	John Robinson	11–1–0
3 Oklahoma	11–1–0	Barry Switzer	10–1–0
4 Penn St.	11–1–0	Joe Paterno	11–0–0
5 Michigan	10–2–0	Bo Schembechler	10–1–0
6 Clemson	11–1–0	Charley Pell	10–1–0
7 Notre Dame	9–3–0	Dan Devine	8–3–0
8 Nebraska	9–3–0	Tom Osborne	9–2–0
9 Texas	9–3–0	Fred Akers	8–3–0
10 Houston	9–3–0	Bill Yeoman	9–2–0
11 Arkansas	9–2–1	Lou Holtz	9–2–0
12 Michigan St.	8–3–0	Darryl Rogers	same
13 Purdue	9–2–1	Jim Young	8–2–1
14 UCLA	8–3–1	Terry Donahue	8–3–0
15 Missouri	8–4–0	Warren Powers	7–4–0
16 Georgia	9–2–1	Vince Dooley	9–1–1
17 Stanford	8–4–0	Bill Walsh	7–4–0
18 N.C.State	9–3–0	Bo Rein	8–3–0
19 Texas A&M	8–4–0	Emory Bellard (4–2) Tom Wilson (4–2)	7–4–0
20 Maryland	9–3–0	Jerry Claiborne	9–2–0

Bowl Games with Top 20 Teams

Date	Bowl	Result
12/20/78	All-Amer	Texas A&M 28, Iowa St. 12
12/23/78	Liberty	Missouri 20, LSU 15
12/23/78	Sun	Texas 42, Maryland 0
12/23/78	Tangerine	N.C.State 30, Pitt 17
12/25/78	Fiesta	10–10, Arkansas vs UCLA
12/29/78	Gator	Clemson 17, Ohio St. 15
12/31/78	Bluebonnet	Stanford 25, Georgia 22
1/1/79	Cotton	Notre Dame 35, Houston 34
1/1/79	Orange	Oklahoma 31, Nebraska 24
1/1/79	Rose	USC 17 Michigan 10
1/1/79	Sugar	Alabama 14, Penn St. 7

Div. I-A Conference Champs

Atlantic Coast	Clemson	6–0
Big Eight	Nebraska/Oklahoma	6–1
Big Ten	Michigan/Mich.St.	7–1
Mid-American	Ball St.	8–0
Pacific Coast AA	San Jose St./Utah St.	4–1
Pacific-10	Southern Cal	6–1
Southeastern	Alabama	6–0
Southwest	Houston	7–1
Western Athletic	BYU	5–1

Heisman Trophy Voting

	Yr	Pos.	Votes
1 Billy Sims, Oklahoma	Jr.	RB	827
2 Chuck Fusina, Penn St.	Sr.	QB	750
3 Rick Leach, Michigan	Sr.	QB	435
4 Charles White, Southern Cal	Jr.	RB	354
5 Charles Alexander, LSU	Sr.	RB	282

Other Major Award Winners

Maxwell (Player)	Chuck Fusina, Penn St.
Camp (Back)	Chuck Fusina, Penn St.
Rockne (Lineman)	Greg Roberts, Oklahoma, G
Lombardi (Lineman)	Bruce Clark, Penn St., DT
Outland (Interior)	Greg Roberts, Oklahoma
AFCA Coach of Year	Joe Paterno, Penn St.
FWAA Coach of Year	Joe Paterno, Penn St.

Consensus All-America Team

(By position, in alphabetical order)

Offense

WR—Emanuel Tolbert, SMU. **TE**—Kellen Winslow, Missouri. **T**—Kelvin Clark, Nebraska; Keith Dorney, Penn St. **G**—Pat Howell, Southern Cal; Greg Roberts, Oklahoma. **C**—Dave Huffman, Notre Dame; Jim Ritcher, North Carolina St. **QB**—Chuck Fusina, Penn St. **RB**—Charles Alexander, LSU; Ted Brown, North Carolina St; Billy Sims, Oklahoma; Charles White, Southern Cal.

Defense

Line—Mike Bell, Colorado St.; Bruce Clark, Penn St.; Hugh Green, Pittsburgh; Al Harris, Arizona St.; Marty Lyons, Alabama. **LB**—Tom Cousineau, Ohio St.; Bob Golic, Notre Dame; Jerry Robinson, UCLA. **DB**—Kenny Easley, UCLA; Johnnie Johnson, Texas; Jeff Nixon, Richmond.

1979

Alabama successfully defended its national championship in 1979, the seventh time that's been done in the 44 years of the AP poll. But Bama, Southern Cal and Oklahoma ranking 1–2–3 for the second year in a row was a first.

Except for a troublesome 3–0 squeaker against LSU, Alabama faced little resistance in piling up 11 regular season wins and a third straight SEC title. The Tide met SWC co-champ Arkansas in the Sugar Bowl and won 24–9.

Earle Bruce succeeded Woody Hayes at Ohio State and brought the Buckeyes through the regular season undefeated and untied. After beating Michigan for the first time in four years, the Bucks lost to Southern Cal in the Rose Bowl, 17–16. The defeat was the 10th in 11 years for the Big Two (OSU and Michigan) in Pasadena.

USC's Rose Bowl victory was the third in four years for coach John Robinson, who replaced John McKay in 1976. The Trojans also won the Heisman Trophy, their first since O.J. Simpson, when running back Charles White outpolled the incumbent, Billy Sims of Oklahoma.

Houston won a piece of its third SWC title since joining the conference in 1976. The Cougars then beat Nebraska 17–14 for its second Cotton Bowl victory.

Bowl game of the Year? Unbeaten BYU lost to Indiana, 38–37, as the lead changed hands eight times in the Holiday Bowl.

Bowl Games with Top 20 Teams

Date	Bowl	Result
12/15/79	Garden St.	Temple 28, California 17
12/21/79	Holiday	Indiana 38, BYU 37
12/22/79	Liberty	Penn St. 9, Tulane 6
12/22/79	Sun	Washington 14, Texas 7
12/25/79	Fiesta	Pitt 16, Arizona 10
12/28/79	Gator	N.Carolina 17, Mich. 15
12/31/79	Bluebonnet	Purdue 27, Tennessee 22
1/1/80	Cotton	Houston 17, Nebraska 14
1/1/80	Orange	Oklahoma 24, Fla.St. 7
1/1/80	Rose	USC 17, Ohio St. 16
1/1/80	Sugar	Alabama 24, Arkansas 9

Div. I-A Conference Champs

Atlantic Coast	North Carolina St.	5–1
Big Eight	Oklahoma	7–0
Big Ten	Ohio St.	8–0
Mid-American	Central Michigan	8–0–1
Pacific Coast AA	Utah St.	5–0
Pacific-10	Southern Cal	6–0–1
Southeastern	Alabama	6–0
Southwest	Houston/Arkansas	7–1
Western Athletic	BYU	7–0

Heisman Trophy Voting

		Yr	Pos.	Votes
1	Charles White, Southern Cal	Sr.	RB	1,695
2	Billy Sims, Oklahoma	Sr.	RB	773
3	Marc Wilson, BYU	Sr.	QB	589
4	Art Schlichter, Ohio St.	So.	QB	251
5	Vagas Ferguson, Notre Dame	Sr.	RB	162

Other Major Award Winners

Maxwell (Player)	Charles White, USC
Camp (Back)	Charles White, USC
Rockne (Lineman)	Bruce Clark, Penn St., DT
Lombardi (Lineman)	Brad Budde, USC, G
Outland (Interior)	Jim Ritcher, N.C.State, C
AFCA Coach of Year	Earle Bruce, Ohio St.
FWAA Coach of Year	Earle Bruce, Ohio St.

Final AP Top 20

Writers' poll taken after bowl games.

		Final Record	Head Coach	Before Bowls
1	Alabama	12–0–0	Bear Bryant	11–0–0
2	Southern Cal	11–0–1	John Robinson	10–0–1
3	Oklahoma	11–1–0	Barry Switzer	10–1–0
4	Ohio St.	11–1–0	Earle Bruce	11–0–0
5	Houston	11–1–0	Bill Yeoman	10–1–0
6	Florida St.	11–1–0	Bobby Bowden	11–0–0
7	Pittsburgh	11–1–0	Jackie Sherrill	10–1–0
8	Arkansas	10–2–0	Lou Holtz	10–1–0
9	Nebraska	10–2–0	Tom Osborne	10–1–0
10	Purdue	10–2–0	Jim Young	9–2–0
11	Washington	10–1–0	Don James	9–2–0
12	Texas	9–3–0	Fred Akers	9–2–0
13	BYU	11–1–0	LaVell Edwards	11–0–0
14	Baylor	8–4–0	Grant Teaff	7–4–0
15	N.Carolina	8–3–1	Dick Crum	7–3–1
16	Auburn	8–3–0	Doug Barfield	same
17	Temple	10–2–0	Wayne Hardin	9–2–0
18	Michigan	8–4–0	Bo Schembechler	8–3–0
19	Indiana	8–4–0	Lee Corso	7–4–0
20	Penn St.	8–4–0	Joe Paterno	7–4–0

Consensus All-America Team

(By position, in alphabetical order)

Offense

WR—Ken Margerum, Stanford. **TE**—Junior Miller, Nebraska. **T**—Jim Bunch, Alabama; Greg Kolenda, Arkansas. **G**—Brad Budde, Southern Cal; Ken Fritz, Ohio St. **C**—Jim Ritcher, North Carolina St. **QB**—Marc Wilson, BYU. **RB**—Vagas Ferguson, Notre Dame; Billy Sims, Oklahoma; Charles White, Southern Cal. **PK**—Dale Castro, Maryland.

Defense

Line—Bruce Clark, Penn St.; Hugh Green, Pittsburgh; Steve McMichael, Texas; Jim Stuckey, Clemson. **MG**—Ron Simmons, Florida St. **LB**—George Cumby, Oklahoma; Ron Simpkins, Michigan; Mike Singletary, Baylor. **DB**—Kenny Easley, UCLA; Roland James, Tennessee; Johnnie Johnson, Texas; Jeff Nixon, Richmond. **P**—Jim Miller, Mississippi.

1980

Before 1980, Georgia finished in the Top 3 of the final AP poll twice—No.2 in 1942 and No.3 in 1946. Those were also the only two years the Bulldogs had a consensus All-America running back—first Heisman winner Frank Sinkwich, then Heisman runner-up Charlie Trippi.

Thirty-four years later, along came Herschel Walker and Georgia ran all the way to Number One. With Walker rushing for a NCAA freshman record 1,616 yards, the Dawgs went undefeated and untied and clinched their first national title ever in the Sugar Bowl with a 17–10 victory over Notre Dame.

Important as Walker was, the play that saved Georgia's perfect season was a 93-yard TD pass from quarterback Buck Belue to split end Lindsay Scott in the last two minutes to beat Florida, 26–21.

Pittsburgh, led by defensive end Hugh Green, was the nation's second-ranked team. The Panthers won 11 of 12, losing a regular season game to Florida State. FSU was undefeated everywhere but in the Orange Bowl where it lost two games by a point. The Seminoles were beaten 10–9 by Miami early in the season, then lost 18–17 to Oklahoma on New Year's.

Alabama's attempt to win an unprecedented third straight national title fell short with two November losses to Mississippi State and Notre Dame. The Tide did, however, get Bear Bryant his 300th career victory. And Michigan finally won a Rose Bowl for Bo Schembechler, his first in six attempts.

Final AP Top 20

Writers' poll taken after bowl games.

	Final Record	Head Coach	Before Bowls
1 Georgia	12–0–0	Vince Dooley	11–0–0
2 Pittsburgh	11–1–0	Jackie Sherrill	10–1–0
3 Oklahoma	10–2–0	Barry Switzer	9–2–0
4 Michigan	10–2–0	Bo Schembechler	9–2–0
5 Florida St.	10–2–0	Bobby Bowden	10–1–0
6 Alabama	10–2–0	Bear Bryant	9–2–0
7 Nebraska	10–2–0	Tom Osborne	9–2–0
8 Penn St.	10–2–0	Joe Paterno	9–2–0
9 Notre Dame	9–2–1	Dan Devine	9–1–1
10 N.Carolina	11–1–0	Dick Crum	10–1–0
11 Southern Cal	8–2–1	John Robinson	same
12 BYU	12–1–0	LaVell Edwards	11–1–0
13 UCLA	9–2–0	Terry Donahue	same
14 Baylor	10–2–0	Grant Teaff	10–1–0
15 Ohio St.	9–3–0	Earle Bruce	9–2–0
16 Washington	9–3–0	Don James	9–2–0
17 Purdue	9–3–0	Jim Young	8–3–0
18 Miami,FL	9–3–0	H.Schnellenberger	8–3–0
19 Miss.St.	9–3–0	Emory Bellard	9–2–0
20 SMU	8–4–0	Ron Meyer	8–3–0

Bowl Games with Top 20 Teams

Date	Bowl	Result
12/19/80	Holiday	BYU 46, SMU 45
12/26/80	Fiesta	Penn St. 31, Ohio St. 19
12/27/80	Liberty	Purdue 28, Missouri 25
12/27/80	Sun	Nebraska 31, Miss.St. 17
12/29/80	Gator	Pitt 37, S.Carolina 9
12/31/80	Bluebonnet	N.Carolina 16, Texas 7
1/1/81	Cotton	Alabama 30, Baylor 2
1/1/81	Orange	Oklahoma 18, Fla.St. 17
1/1/81	Rose	Michigan 23, Washington 6
1/1/81	Sugar	Georgia 17, Notre Dame 10
1/2/81	Peach	Miami,FL 20, Va.Tech 10

Div. I-A Conference Champs

Atlantic Coast	North Carolina	6–0
Big Eight	Oklahoma	7–0
Big Ten	Michigan	8–0
Mid-American	Central Michigan	7–2
Pacific Coast AA	Long Beach St.	5–0
Pacific-10	Washington	6–1
Southeastern	Georgia	6–0
Southwest	Baylor	8–0
Western Athletic	BYU	6–1

Heisman Trophy Voting

	Yr	Pos.	Votes
1 George Rogers, S.Carolina	Sr.	RB	1,128
2 Hugh Green, Pittsburgh	Sr.	DE	861
3 Herschel Walker, Georgia	Fr.	RB	683
4 Mark Herrmann, Purdue	Sr.	QB	405
5 Jim McMahon, BYU	Jr.	QB	189

Other Major Award Winners

Maxwell (Player)	Hugh Green, Pittsburgh
Camp (Back)	Herschel Walker, Georgia
Rockne (Lineman)	Hugh Green, Pittsburgh
Lombardi (Lineman)	Hugh Green, Pittsburgh
Outland (Interior)	Mark May, Pittsburgh, OT
AFCA Coach of Year	Vince Dooley, Georgia
FWAA Coach of Year	Vince Dooley, Georgia

Consensus All-America Team

(By position, in alphabetical order)

Offense

WR—Ken Margerum, Stanford. **TE**—Dave Young, Purdue. **Line**—Nick Eyre, BYU; Mark May, Pittsburgh; Louis Oubre, Oklahoma; Randy Schleusener, Nebraska; Keith Van Horne, Southern Cal. **C**—John Scully, Notre Dame. **QB**—Mark Herrmann, Purdue. **RB**—Jarvis Redwine, Nebraska; George Rogers, South Carolina; Herschel Walker, Georgia.

Defense

Line—Hugh Green, Pittsburgh; E.J.Junior, Alabama; Leonard Mitchell, Houston; Kenneth Sims, Texas. **MG**—Ron Simmons, Florida St. **LB**—Bob Crable, Notre Dame; David Little, Florida; Mike Singletary, Baylor; Lawrence Taylor, North Carolina. **DB**—Kenny Easley, UCLA; Ronnie Lott, Southern Cal; John Simmons, SMU.

1981

At one time or another during the 1981 season, six different teams were able to say they were Number One. After the bowl games only Clemson could say so.

The Tigers improved their 1980 record of 6–5 to 11–0 then beat Nebraska in the Orange Bowl, giving the ACC its first national champion in 28 years. Thirty-three year-old Danny Ford became the youngest coach to ever win the title and he did it in only his third full year in charge.

Until Clemson held its own in the postseason, being named No.1 by AP was a curse. Michigan was the preseason pick but lost its opening game to Wisconsin. Notre Dame moved up but lost to Michigan. Southern Cal got the call and lost to Arizona. Texas took over and lost (by 31) to Arkansas. Penn State was next and lost to Miami. Then Pittsburgh was promoted and lost (by 34) to Penn State.

Alabama didn't get a chance at No.1, but the Crimson Tide did go 9–1–1 during the regular season. Their 28–17 victory over state rival Auburn was not only their ninth straight against the Tigers but gave Bear Bryant his 315th career win, one more than Amos Alonzo Stagg and a new major college record.

Texas beat Bama in the Cotton Bowl to finish behind Clemson in the final AP poll. Penn State and Pitt placed 3rd and 4th.

Southern Cal's Marcus Allen became the first running back to gain over 2,000 yards in one season, a feat that enabled him to outpoll Georgia sophomore Herschel Walker for the Heisman.

Final AP Top 20
Writers' poll taken after bowl games.

	Final Record	Head Coach	Before Bowls
1 Clemson	12–0–0	Danny Ford	11–0–0
2 Texas	10–1–1	Fred Akers	9–1–1
3 Penn St.	10–2–0	Joe Paterno	9–2–0
4 Pittsburgh	11–1–0	Jackie Sherrill	10–1–0
5 SMU	10–1–0	Ron Meyer	same
6 Georgia	10–2–0	Vince Dooley	10–1–0
7 Alabama	9–2–1	Bear Bryant	9–1–1
8 Miami, FL	9–2–0	H.Schnellenberger	same
9 N.Carolina	10–2–0	Dick Crum	9–2–0
10 Washington	10–2–0	Don James	9–2–0
11 Nebraska	9–3–0	Tom Osborne	9–2–0
12 Michigan	9–3–0	Bo Schembechler	8–3–0
13 BYU	11–2–0	LaVell Edwards	10–2–0
14 Southern Cal	9–3–0	John Robinson	9–2–0
15 Ohio St.	9–3–0	Earle Bruce	8–3–0
16 Arizona St.	9–2–0	Darryl Rogers	same
17 W.Virginia	9–3–0	Don Nehlen	8–3–0
18 Iowa	8–4–0	Hayden Fry	8–3–0
19 Missouri	8–4–0	Warren Powers	7–4–0
20 Oklahoma	7–4–1	Barry Switzer	6–4–1

Bowl Games with Top 20 Teams

Date	Bowl	Result
12/18/81	Holiday	BYU 38, Washington St. 36
12/19/81	Tangerine	Missouri 19, So.Miss. 17
12/26/81	Sun	Oklahoma 40, Houston 14
12/28/81	Gator	N.Carolina 31, Arkansas 27
12/30/81	Liberty	Ohio St. 31, Navy 28
12/31/81	Bluebonnet	Michigan 33, UCLA 14
12/31/81	Peach	W.Virginia 26, Florida 6
1/1/82	Cotton	Texas 14, Alabama 12
1/1/82	Fiesta	Penn St. 26, USC 10
1/1/82	Orange	Clemson 22, Nebraska 15
1/1/82	Rose	Washington 28, Iowa 0
1/1/82	Sugar	Pittsburgh 24, Georgia 20

Div. I-A Conference Champs

Atlantic Coast	Clemson	6–0
Big Eight	Nebraska	7–0
Big Ten	Iowa/Ohio St.	6–2
Mid-American	Toledo	8–1
Pacific Coast AA	San Jose St.	5–0
Pacific-10	Washington	6–2
Southeastern	Georgia/Alabama	6–0
Southwest	SMU‡	7–1
Western Athletic	BYU	7–1

‡On probation, ineligible for bowl game.

Heisman Trophy Voting

	Yr	Pos.	Votes
1 Marcus Allen, Southern Cal	Sr.	RB	1,797
2 Herschel Walker, Georgia	So.	RB	1,199
3 Jim McMahon, BYU	Sr.	QB	706
4 Dan Marino, Pittsburgh	Jr.	QB	256
5 Art Schlichter, Ohio St.	Sr.	QB	149

Other Major Award Winners

Maxwell (Player)	Marcus Allen, USC
Camp (Back)	Art Schlichter, Ohio St.
Rockne (Lineman)	Kenneth Sims, Texas, DT
Lombardi (Lineman)	Kenneth Sims, Texas
Outland (Interior)	Dave Rimington, Neb., C
AFCA Coach of Year	Danny Ford, Clemson
FWAA Coach of Year	Danny Ford, Clemson

Consensus All-America Team
(By position, in alphabetical order)

Offense
WR—Anthony Carter, Michigan. **TE**—Tim Wrightman, UCLA. **Line**—Kurt Becker, Michigan; Terry Crouch, Oklahoma; Sean Farrell, Penn St.; Ray Foster, Southern Cal; Ed Muransky, Michigan; Terry Tausch, Texas; **C**—Dave Rimington, Nebraska. **QB**—Jim McMahon, BYU. **RB**—Marcus Allen, Southern Cal; Herschel Walker, Georgia.

Defense
Line—Tim Krumrie, Wisconsin; Kenneth Sims, Texas; Billy Ray Smith, Arkansas; Andre Tippett, Iowa. **LB**—Bob Crable, Notre Dame; Jeff Davis, Clemson; Sal Sunseri, Pittsburgh. **CB**—Terry Kinard, Clemson; Fred Marion, Miami,FL; Mike Richardson, Arizona St.; Tommy Wilcox, Alabama. **P**—Reggie Roby, Iowa.

1982

Penn State finally got a shot at a "winner take all" game for the national championship in 1982 and won it.

Facing top-ranked and undefeated Georgia in a No.1 vs No.2 Sugar Bowl match-up, the Lions led from the start and upset the Dawgs, 27–23.

A loser to only Alabama (42–21) during the regular season, PSU's climb to the top came after 17 years and 162 victories under Joe Paterno. It was a frustrating wait. Three times, in 1968–69–73, the Lions had been undefeated and unloved by the pollsters. Three other years they had gone 11–1 and nobody seemed to notice. This year, they stopped Heisman–winner Herschel Walker & Co. and everybody noticed.

Southern Methodist was the only undefeated team in the Top 20 and ranked second. The Mustangs won their second straight SWC championship, returned to the Cotton Bowl for the first time in 16 years, and beat Pitt. Nebraska won 12 games, the Big Eight and the Orange Bowl to place third. The Huskers' only loss came on a last second field goal against Penn State.

The Play of the Year? Easy: California's last second, "kickoff return to beat the band" against Stanford. Bears won 25–20.

Meanwhile, Alabama (8–4) finished out of the Top 20 for the first time in 11 seasons, but won the Liberty Bowl. The victory pushed Bear Bryant's 38-year record to 323–85–17. He died less than a month later.

Final AP Top 20
Writers' poll taken after bowl games.

		Final Record	Head Coach	Before Bowls
1	Penn St.	11–1–0	Joe Paterno	10–1–0
2	SMU	11–0–1	Bobby Collins	10–0–1
3	Nebraska	12–1–0	Tom Osborne	11–1–0
4	Georgia	11–1–0	Vince Dooley	11–0–0
5	UCLA	10–1–1	Terry Donahue	9–1–1
6	Arizona St.	10–2–0	Darryl Rogers	9–2–0
7	Washington	10–2–0	Don James	9–2–0
8	Clemson	9–1–1	Danny Ford	same
9	Arkansas	9–2–1	Lou Holtz	8–2–1
10	Pittsburgh	9–3–0	Foge Fazio	9–2–0
11	LSU	8–3–1	Jerry Stovall	8–2–1
12	Ohio St.	9–3–0	Earle Bruce	8–3–0
13	Florida St.	9–3–0	Bobby Bowden	8–3–0
14	Auburn	9–3–0	Pat Dye	8–3–0
15	Southern Cal	8–3–0	John Robinson	same
16	Oklahoma	8–4–0	Barry Switzer	8–3–0
17	Texas	9–3–0	Fred Akers	9–2–0
18	N.Carolina	8–4–0	Dick Crum	7–4–0
19	W.Virginia	9–3–0	Don Nehlen	9–2–0
20	Maryland	8–4–0	Bobby Ross	8–3–0

Bowl Games with Top 20 Teams

Date	Bowl	Result
12/17/82	Holiday	Ohio St. 47, BYU 17
12/18/82	Tangerine	Auburn 33, Boston Col. 26
12/25/82	Aloha	Washington 21, Maryland 20
12/25/82	Sun	N.Carolina 26, Texas 10
12/30/82	Gator	Fla.St. 31, W.Virginia 12
12/31/82	Bluebonnet	Arkansas 28, Florida 24
1/1/83	Cotton	SMU 7, Pittsburgh 3
1/1/83	Fiesta	Ariz.St. 32, Oklahoma 21
1/1/83	Orange	Nebraska 21, LSU 20
1/1/83	Rose	UCLA 24, Michigan 14
1/1/83	Sugar	Penn St. 27, Georgia 23

Div. I-A Conference Champs

Atlantic Coast	Clemson‡	6–0
Big Eight	Nebraska	7–0
Big Ten	Michigan	8–1
Mid-American	Bowling Green	7–2
Pacific Coast AA	Fresno St.	6–0
Pacific-10	UCLA	5–1–1
Southeastern	Georgia	6–0
Southwest	SMU	7–0–1
Western Athletic	BYU	7–1

‡On probation, ineligible for bowl games.

Heisman Trophy Voting

		Yr	Pos.	Votes
1	Herschel Walker, Georgia	Jr.	RB	1,926
2	John Elway, Stanford	Sr.	QB	1,231
3	Eric Dickerson, SMU	Sr.	RB	465
4	Anthony Carter, Michigan	Sr.	WR	142
5	Dave Rimington, Nebraska	Sr.	C	137
9	Dan Marino, Pittsburgh	Sr.	QB	47
10	Mike Rozier, Nebraska	Jr.	RB	40

Other Major Award Winners

Maxwell (Player)	Herschel Walker, Georgia
Camp (Back)	John Elway, Stanford
Rockne (Lineman)	Billy Ray Smith, Ark., DE
Lombardi (Lineman)	Dave Rimington, Nebraska
Outland (Interior)	Dave Rimington, Nebraska
AFCA Coach of Year	Joe Paterno, Penn St.
FWAA Coach of Year	Joe Paterno, Penn St.

Consensus All-America Team
(By position, in alphabetical order)

Offense
WR—Anthony Carter, Michigan. **TE**—Gordon Hudson, BYU. **Line**—Jimbo Covert, Pittsburgh; Steve Korte, Arkansas; Bruce Matthews, Southern Cal; Don Mosebar, Southern Cal. **C**—Dave Rimington, Nebraska. **QB**—John Elway, Stanford. **RB**—Eric Dickerson, SMU; Mike Rozier, Nebraska; Herschel Walker, Georgia. **PK**—Chuck Nelson, Washington.

Defense
Line—Rick Bryan, Oklahoma; Wilber Marshall, Florida; Vernon Maxwell, Arizona St.; Mike Pitts, Alabama; Gabriel Rivera, Texas Tech; Billy Ray Smith, Arkansas. **MG**—George Achica, Southern Cal. **LB**—Ricky Hunley, Arizona; Marcus Marek, Ohio St.; Darryl Talley, West Virginia. **CB**—Terry Hoage, Georgia; Terry Kinard, Clemson; Mike Richardson, Arizona St. **P**—Jim Arnold, Vanderbilt.

1983

During the regular season, Nebraska was undefeated, untied and unmerciful. The Huskers beat the teams on their 12-game schedule to a pulp. They piled up 624 points and won by an average score of 52–16. Were they tough? Ask Minnesota, an 84–13 victim.

Nebraska in 1983 reminded folks of Army in 1944. Not the football team, the Normandy invasion force. Led by Heisman-winning back Mike Rozier and Outland winner Dean Steinkuhler, the Big Eight champs had won 24 games in two years. They had been the preseason choice for No.1 and nothing had changed.

In the Orange Bowl, the Huskers met a cocky, young Miami team that was ranked fifth and playing in its first major bowl game in 33 years. The Hurricanes were 10–1, but a fortunate 10–1, winning their last two regular season games by a total of six points.

At game time, Miami had a theoretical shot at No.1. Second-ranked Texas had lost the Cotton Bowl, No.4 Illinois had lost the Rose Bowl and No.3 Auburn had been very unimpressive in winning the Sugar Bowl. All the Canes had to do was beat Nebraska.

Playing on its home field, Miami scored the first 17 points of the game, led 31–17 after three quarters, then barely survived a furious Nebraska comeback in the fourth. The Huskers scored to make it 31–30 with 0:48 left, went for the win with a two-point conversion attempt, and failed.

Finally, defending Heisman Trophy winner Herschel Walker passed up his senior year at Georgia to play in the USFL.

Final AP Top 20
Writers' poll taken after bowl games.

	Final Record	Head Coach	Before Bowls
1 Miami, FL	11–1–0	H.Schnellenberger	10–1–0
2 Nebraska	12–1–0	Tom Osborne	12–0–0
3 Auburn	11–1–0	Pat Dye	10–1–0
4 Georgia	10–1–1	Vince Dooley	9–1–1
5 Texas	11–1–0	Fred Akers	11–0–0
6 Florida	9–2–1	Charley Pell	8–2–1
7 BYU	11–1–0	LaVell Edwards	10–1–0
8 Michigan	9–3–0	Bo Schembechler	9–2–0
9 Ohio St.	9–3–0	Earle Bruce	8–3–0
10 Illinois	10–2–0	Mike White	10–1–0
11 Clemson	9–1–1	Danny Ford	same
12 SMU	10–2–0	Bobby Collins	10–1–0
13 Air Force	10–2–0	Ken Hatfield	9–2–0
14 Iowa	9–3–0	Hayden Fry	9–2–0
15 Alabama	8–4–0	Ray Perkins	7–4–0
16 W.Virginia	9–3–0	Don Nehlen	8–3–0
17 UCLA	7–4–1	Terry Donahue	6–4–1
18 Pittsburgh	8–3–1	Foge Fazio	8–2–1
19 Boston Col.	9–3–0	Jack Bicknell	9–2–0
20 E.Carolina	8–3–0	Ed Emory	same

Bowl Games with Top 20 Teams

Date	Bowl	Result
12/10/83	Indepen	Air Force 9, Mississippi 3
12/22/83	All-Amer	West Va. 20, Kentucky 16
12/23/83	Holiday	BYU 21, Missouri 17
12/24/83	Sun	Alabama 28, SMU 7
12/29/83	Liberty	Notre Dame 19, Boston Col. 18
12/30/83	Gator	Florida 14, Iowa 6
1/2/84	Cotton	Georgia 10, Texas 9
1/2/84	Fiesta	Ohio St. 28, Pittsburgh 23
1/2/84	Orange	Miami, FL 31, Nebraska 30
1/2/84	Rose	UCLA 45, Illinois 9
1/2/84	Sugar	Auburn 9, Michigan 7

Div. I-A Conference Champs

Atlantic Coast	Maryland‡	5–0
Big Eight	Nebraska	7–0
Big Ten	Illinois	9–0
Mid-American	Northern Illinois	8–1
Pacific Coast AA	Cal St.-Fullerton	5–1
Pacific-10	UCLA	6–1–1
Southeastern	Auburn	6–0
Southwest	Texas	8–0
Western Athletic	BYU	7–0

‡Clemson (7–0) on probation, ineligible for both ACC championship and bowl game.

Heisman Trophy Voting

	Yr	Pos.	Votes
1 Mike Rozier, Nebraska	Sr.	RB	1,801
2 Steve Young, BYU	Sr.	QB	1,172
3 Doug Flutie, Boston Col.	Jr.	QB	253
4 Turner Gill, Nebraska	Sr.	QB	190
5 Terry Hoage, Georgia	Sr.	DB	112
10 Boomer Esiason, Maryland	Sr.	QB	57

Other Major Award Winners

Maxwell (Player)	Mike Rozier, Nebraska
Camp (Back)	Mike Rozier, Nebraska
Rockne (Lineman)	Bill Fralic, Pitt, OT
Lombardi (Lineman)	Dean Steinkuhler, Neb., G
Outland (Interior)	Dean Steinkuhler, Neb.
AFCA Coach of Year	Ken Hatfield, Air Force
FWAA Coach of Year	Howard Schnellenberger, Miami, FL

Consensus All-America Team
(By position, in alphabetical order)

Offense
WR—Irving Fryar, Nebraska. **TE**—Gordon Hudson, BYU. **Line**—Doug Dawson, Texas; Bill Fralic, Pittsburgh; Terry Long, East Carolina; Dean Steinkuhler, Nebraska. **C**—Tony Slaton, Southern Cal. **QB**—Steve Young, BYU. **RB**—Greg Allen, Florida St.; Bo Jackson, Auburn; Napoleon McCallum, Navy; Mike Rozier, Nebraska. **PK**—Luis Zendejas, Arizona St.

Defense
Line—Rick Bryan, Oklahoma; William Fuller, North Carolina; William Perry, Clemson; Reggie White, Tennessee; **LB**—Ricky Hunley, Arizona; Jeff Leiding, Texas; Wilber Marshall, Florida; Ron Rivera, California. **CB**—Russell Carter, SMU; Jerry Gray, Texas; Terry Hoage, Georgia; Don Rogers, UCLA. **P**—Jack Weil, Wyoming.

1984

Halfway into the 1980s, it was obvious that parity had overtaken Division I-A college football. For the fifth consecutive year the national champion was a first-time winner.

Georgia, Clemson, Penn State, Miami, and now Brigham Young. Of the five, only BYU's credentials were suspect. Critics accused the high-scoring WAC champion of having a quarterback (Robbie Bosco) with a strong arm and a schedule with a weak heart. Real weak. None of the teams on it would make the final AP Top 20.

Still, the Cougars were the only major college team to win all their games, so they were national champions by default. The way to the top was cleared on Nov.17th. BYU, ranked third behind Nebraska and South Carolina, rose to No.1 that afternoon when Oklahoma beat the Huskers and the Gamecocks lost to Navy.

A 6-5 Michigan team that finished sixth in the Big Ten gave the Cougars a scare in the Holiday Bowl, but BYU won by a touchdown to wrap up the title before Christmas.

Washington, a winner over Oklahoma in the Orange Bowl, and first-time SEC champ Florida ranked 2nd and 3rd. On probation, Florida had to vacate its title.

BC quarterback Doug Flutie, the first player to pass for 10,000 yards, won the Heisman. He also engineered the most memorable play in the year's most exciting game: a 65-yard pass to end Gerard Phelan for the winning touchdown in a wild, 47-45 victory over Miami.

Final AP Top 20

Writers' poll taken after bowl games.

	Final Record	Head Coach	Before Bowls
1 BYU	13-0-0	LaVell Edwards	12-0-0
2 Washington	11-1-0	Don James	10-1-0
3 Florida	9-1-1	Chas. Pell (0-1-1) same Galen Hall (9-0)	
4 Nebraska	10-2-0	Tom Osborne	9-2-0
5 Boston Col.	10-2-0	Jack Bicknell	9-2-0
6 Oklahoma	9-2-1	Barry Switzer	9-1-1
7 Oklahoma St.	10-2-0	Pat Jones	9-2-0
8 SMU	10-2-0	Bobby Collins	9-2-0
9 UCLA	9-3-0	Terry Donahue	8-3-0
10 Southern Cal	10-3-0	Ted Tollner	8-3-0
11 S.Carolina	10-2-0	Joe Morrison	10-1-0
12 Maryland	9-3-0	Bobby Ross	8-3-0
13 Ohio St.	9-3-0	Earle Bruce	9-2-0
14 Auburn	9-4-0	Pat Dye	8-4-0
15 LSU	8-3-1	Bill Arnsparger	8-2-1
16 Iowa	8-4-1	Hayden Fry	7-4-1
17 Florida St.	7-3-2	Bobby Bowden	7-3-1
18 Miami,FL	8-5-0	Jimmy Johnson	8-4-0
19 Kentucky	9-3-0	Jerry Claiborne	8-3-0
20 Virginia	8-2-2	George Welsh	7-2-2

Bowl Games with Top 20 Teams

Date	Bowl	Result
12/21/84	Holiday	BYU 24, Michigan 17
12/22/84	Fla.Citrus	17-17, Fla.St. vs Georgia
12/22/84	Sun	Maryland 27, Tennessee 26
12/26/84	Freedom	Iowa 55, Texas 17
12/27/84	Liberty	Auburn 21, Arkansas 15
12/28/84	Gator	Okla.St. 21, S.Carolina 14
12/29/84	All-Amer	Kentucky 20, Wisconsin 19
12/29/84	Aloha	SMU 27, Notre Dame 20
12/31/84	Peach	Virginia 27, Purdue 24
1/1/85	Cotton	Boston Col. 45, Houston 28
1/1/85	Fiesta	UCLA 39, Miami,FL 37
1/1/85	Orange	Washington 28, Oklahoma 17
1/1/85	Rose	USC 20, Ohio St. 17
1/1/85	Sugar	Nebraska 28, LSU 10

Div. I-A Conference Champs

Atlantic Coast	Maryland	5-0
Big Eight	Oklahoma/Nebraska	6-1
Big Ten	Ohio St.	7-2
Mid-American	Toledo	7-1-1
Pacific Coast AA	Cal St.Fullerton*	6-1
Pacific-10	Southern Cal	7-1
Southeastern	Florida‡	5-0-1
Southwest	Houston/SMU	6-2
Western Athletic	BYU	8-0

*After the PCAA season, champion UNLV (7-0) forfeited all its wins due to an ineligible player.
‡Florida was put on probation and had to vacate SEC title.

Heisman Trophy Voting

		Yr	Pos.	Votes
1 Doug Flutie, Boston Col.		Sr.	QB	2,240
2 Keith Byers, Ohio St.		Sr.	RB	1,251
3 Robbie Bosco, BYU		Jr.	QB	443
4 Bernie Kosar, Miami,FL		Jr.	QB	320
5 Ken Davis, TCU		Jr.	RB	86
6 Bill Fralic, Pittsburgh		Sr.	T	81
8 Jerry Rice, Miss.Valley St.		Sr.	WR	36

Other Major Award Winners

Maxwell (Player)	Doug Flutie, Boston Col.
Camp (Back)	Keith Byers, Ohio St.
Rockne (Lineman)	Bruce Smith, Va.Tech, DT
Lombardi (Lineman)	Tony Degrate, Texas, DT
Outland (Interior)	Bruce Smith, Va.Tech
AFCA Coach of Year	LaVell Edwards, BYU
FWAA Coach of Year	LaVell Edwards, BYU

Consensus All-America Team

(By position, in alphabetical order)

Offense

WR—Eddie Brown, Miami,FL; David Williams, Illinois. **TE**—Jay Novacek, Wyoming. Line—Lomas Brown, Florida; Bill Fralic, Pittsburgh; Jim Lachey, Ohio St.; Bill Mayo, Tennessee; Del Wilkes, South Carolina. **C**—Mark Traynowicz, Nebraska. **QB**—Doug Flutie, Boston College. **RB**—Keith Byers, Ohio St.; Kenneth Davis, TCU; Rueben Mayes, Washington St. **PK**—Kevin Butler, Georgia.

Defense

Line—Tony Casillas, Oklahoma; Tony Degrate, Texas; Ron Holmes, Washington; Bruce Smith, Virginia Tech. **LB**—Gregg Carr, Auburn; Jack Del Rio, Southern Cal; Larry Station, Iowa. **CB**—Rod Brown, Oklahoma St.; David Fulcher, Arizona St.; Jeff Sanchez, Georgia; Tony Thurman, Boston College. **P**—Ricky Anderson, Vanderbilt.

1985

The parade of first-timers to the national championship ended in 1985 as Oklahoma claimed its sixth AP title (one less than Notre Dame).

Like Georgia in 1980, Oklahoma was led by a freshman back—quarterback Jamelle Holieway, who took over for injured starter Troy Aikman (broken ankle) four games into the season. Aikman went down in OU's only loss, a 27–14 beating at Miami.

Under Holieway, the Sooners climbed to No.3 in the polls by winning seven straight games and reaching the Orange Bowl. In Miami, they met No.1 Penn State for the championship. The Lions scored first, but Oklahoma had the lead by halftime and won 25–10.

Miami went into the Sugar Bowl ranked second and needing a convincing win over SEC champ Tennessee to keep its title hopes alive should Penn State lose. Instead, the Hurricanes suffered their worst defeat of the year, 35–7.

Back on Oct.19, Iowa and Michigan met in Iowa City for the season's only No.1 vs No.2 showdown. The largest crowd ever to see a sporting event in Iowa (66,350) saw the top-ranked Hawkeyes win, 12–10, in the last two seconds on Rob Houghtlin's fourth field goal. Two weeks later, Iowa lost to Ohio State.

Auburn running back Bo Jackson beat out well-named Iowa QB Chuck Long by 45 points in the closest Heisman vote to date. And Grambling's Eddie Robinson passed Bear Bryant as the winningest coach of all time with 329 victories.

Final AP Top 20

Writers' poll taken after bowl games.

	Final Record	Head Coach	Before Bowls
1 Oklahoma	11–1–0	Barry Switzer	10–1–0
2 Michigan	10–1–1	Bo Schembechler	9–1–1
3 Penn St.	11–1–0	Joe Paterno	11–0–0
4 Tennessee	9–1–2	Johnny Majors	8–1–2
5 Florida	9–1–1	Galen Hall	same
6 Texas A&M	10–2–0	Jackie Sherrill	9–2–0
7 UCLA	9–2–1	Terry Donahue	8–2–1
8 Air Force	12–1–0	Fisher DeBerry	11–1–0
9 Miami,FL	10–2–0	Jimmy Johnson	10–1–0
10 Iowa	10–2–0	Hayden Fry	10–1–0
11 Nebraska	9–3–0	Tom Osborne	9–2–0
12 Arkansas	10–2–0	Ken Hatfield	9–2–0
13 Alabama	9–2–1	Ray Perkins	8–2–1
14 Ohio St.	9–3–0	Earle Bruce	8–3–0
15 Florida St.	9–3–0	Bobby Bowden	8–3–0
16 BYU	11–3–0	LaVell Edwards	11–2–0
17 Baylor	9–3–0	Grant Teaff	8–3–0
18 Maryland	9–3–0	Bobby Ross	8–3–0
19 Georgia Tech	9–2–1	Bill Curry	8–2–1
20 LSU	9–2–1	Bill Arnsparger	9–1–1

Bowl Games with Top 20 Teams

Date	Bowl	Result
12/22/85	Holiday	Arkansas 18, Ariz.St. 17
12/27/85	Liberty	Baylor 21, LSU 7
12/28/85	Aloha	Alabama 24, USC 3
12/28/85	Fla.Citrus	Ohio St. 10, BYU 7
12/30/85	Gator	Fla.St. 34, Okla.St. 23
12/31/85	All-Amer.	Ga.Tech 17, Mich.St. 14
12/31/85	Bluebonnet	Air Force 24, Texas 16
1/1/86	Cotton	Texas A&M 36, Auburn 16
1/1/86	Fiesta	Michigan 27, Nebraska 23
1/1/86	Orange	Oklahoma 25, Penn St. 10
1/1/86	Rose	UCLA 45, Iowa 28
1/1/86	Sugar	Tennessee 35, Miami,FL 7

Div. I-A Conference Champs

Atlantic Coast	Maryland	6–0
Big Eight	Oklahoma	7–0
Big Ten	Iowa	7–1
Mid-American	Bowling Green	9–0
Pacific Coast AA	Fresno St.	7–0
Pacific-10	UCLA	6–2
Southeastern	Tennessee‡	5–1
Southwest	Texas A&M	7–1
Western Athletic	Air Force/BYU	7–1

‡Florida (also 5–1) on probation, ineligible for SEC title and bowl game.

Heisman Trophy Voting

		Yr	Pos.	Votes
1	Bo Jackson, Auburn	Sr.	RB	1,509
2	Chuck Long, Iowa	Sr.	QB	1,464
3	Robbie Bosco, BYU	Sr.	QB	459
4	Lorenzo White, Michigan St.	So.	RB	391
5	Vinny Testaverde, Miami,FL	Jr.	QB	249

Other Major Award Winners

Maxwell (Player)	Chuck Long, Iowa
Camp (Back)	Lorenzo White, Mich.St.
Rockne (Lineman)	Tony Casillas, Okla. NT
Lombardi (Lineman)	Tony Casillas, Oklahoma
Outland (Interior)	Mike Ruth, Boston Col., NG
AFCA Coach of Year	Fisher DeBerry, Air Force
FWAA Coach of Year	Fisher DeBerry, Air Force

Consensus All-America Team

(By position, in alphabetical order)

Offense

WR—Tim McGee, Tennessee; David Williams, Illinois. **TE**—Willie Smith, Miami,FL. **Line**—Jeff Bregel, Southern Cal; Jim Dombrowski, Virginia; Jamie Dukes, Florida St.; Brian Jozwiak, West Virginia; J.D.Maarleveld, Maryland; John Reinstra, Temple. **C**—Pete Anderson, Georgia. **RB**—Reggie Dupard, SMU; Bo Jackson, Auburn; Napoleon McCallum, Navy; Thurman Thomas, Oklahoma St.; Lorenzo White, Michigan St. **PK**—John Lee, UCLA.

Defense

Line—Tony Casillas, Oklahoma; Tim Green, Syracuse; Mike Hammerstein, Michigan; Leslie O'Neal, Oklahoma St.; Mike Ruth, Boston College. **LB**—Brian Bosworth, Oklahoma; Johnny Holland, Texas A&M; Larry Station, Iowa. **CB**—Brad Cochran, Michigan; David Fulcher, Arizona St.; Scott Thomas, Air Force. **P**—Barry Helton, Colorado.

1986

Miami and Penn State each finished the regular season at 11–0 and met in the Fiesta Bowl for the national championship. It was the first No.1 vs No.2 clash between two independents since the last Army-Notre Dame showdown in 1946.

With neither team obligated to a particular bowl, bidding for the game among the lesser bowl committees was frenzied. The Fiesta Bowl (and NBC Sports) won by agreeing to double its payment to both teams (to $2.4 million each) and moving the game from New Year's Day afternoon to prime time on Jan.2.

On paper, No.1 Miami was the clear favorite. The Hurricanes had beaten defending national champ Oklahoma for the second time in two years and had Heisman-winner Vinny Testaverde at quarterback. In the hype that preceded the game, No.2 Penn State came off as being more bland than their uniforms.

No matter, the Lions' defense intercepted five Testaverde passes, held the Canes' 38-points-per-game offense to a touchdown and a field goal, and won 14–10.

Oklahoma, a 34-point winner over Arkansas in the Orange Bowl, placed third in the AP poll. The Sooners' 28–16 upset loss to Miami back in September was the season's other battle between No.1 and No.2.

Testaverde was a landslide winner in the Heisman vote, but gridiron throwback Gordie Lockbaum, a two-way junior at Division I-AA Holy Cross, received enough support to come in fifth.

Final AP Top 20

Writers' poll taken after bowl games.

	Final Record	Head Coach	Before Bowls
1 Penn St.	12–0–0	Joe Paterno	11–0–0
2 Miami,FL	11–1–0	Jimmy Johnson	11–0–0
3 Oklahoma	11–1–0	Barry Switzer	10–1–0
4 Arizona St.	10–1–1	John Cooper	9–1–1
5 Nebraska	10–2–0	Tom Osborne	9–2–0
6 Auburn	10–2–0	Pat Dye	9–2–0
7 Ohio St.	10–3–0	Earle Bruce	9–3–0
8 Michigan	11–2–0	Bo Schembechler	11–1–0
9 Alabama	10–3–0	Ray Perkins	9–3–0
10 LSU	9–3–0	Bill Arnsparger	9–2–0
11 Arizona	9–3–0	Larry Smith	8–3–0
12 Baylor	9–3–0	Grant Teaff	8–3–0
13 Texas A&M	9–3–0	Jackie Sherrill	9–2–0
14 UCLA	8–3–1	Terry Donahue	7–3–1
15 Arkansas	9–3–0	Ken Hatfield	9–2–0
16 Iowa	9–3–0	Hayden Fry	8–3–0
17 Clemson	8–2–2	Danny Ford	7–2–2
18 Washington	8–3–1	Don James	8–2–1
19 Boston Col.	9–3–0	Jack Bicknell	8–2–1
20 Va.Tech	9–2–1	Bill Dooley	8–2–1

Bowl Games with Top 20 Teams

Date	Bowl	Result
12/23/86	Hall of Fame	Boston Col.27, Georgia 24
12/25/86	Sun	Alabama 28, Washington 6
12/27/86	Aloha	Arizona 30, N.Carolina 21
12/27/86	Gator	Clemson 27, Stanford 21
12/30/86	Freedom	UCLA 31, BYU 10
12/30/86	Holiday	Iowa 39, S.Diego St. 38
12/31/86	Bluebonnet	Baylor 21, Colorado 9
12/31/86	Peach	Va.Tech 25, N.C.State 24
1/1/87	Cotton	Ohio St. 28, Texas A&M 12
1/1/87	Fla.Citrus	Auburn 16, USC 7
1/1/87	Orange	Oklahoma 42, Arkansas 8
1/1/87	Rose	Ariz.St. 22, Michigan 15
1/1/87	Sugar	Nebraska 30, LSU 15
1/2/87	Fiesta	Penn St. 14, Miami,FL 10

Div. I-A Conference Champs

Atlantic Coast	Clemson	5–1–1
Big Eight	Oklahoma	7–0
Big Ten	Michigan/Ohio St.	7–1
Mid-American	Miami,OH	6–2
Pacific Coast AA	San Jose St.	7–0
Pacific-10	Arizona St.	5–1–1
Southeastern	LSU	5–1
Southwest	Texas A&M	7–1
Western Athletic	San Diego St.	7–1

Heisman Trophy Voting

	Yr	Pos.	Votes
1 Vinny Testaverde, Miami,FL	Sr.	QB	2,213
2 Paul Palmer, Temple	Sr.	RB	672
3 Jim Harbaugh, Michigan	Sr.	QB	458
4 Brian Bosworth, Oklahoma	Jr.	LB	395
5 Gordie Lockbaum, H.Cross	Jr.	WR-DB	242

Other Major Award Winners

Maxwell (Player)	Vinny Testaverde, Miami,FL
Camp (Back)	Paul Palmer, Temple
Rockne (Lineman)	Gordie Lockbaum, Holy Cross
Lombardi (Lineman)	Cornelius Bennett, Ala., LB
Outland (Interior)	Jason Buck, BYU, DT
AFCA Coach of Year	Joe Paterno, Penn St.
FWAA Coach of Year	Joe Paterno, Penn St.

Consensus All-America Team

(By position, in alphabetical order)

Offense

WR—Cris Carter, Ohio St. TE—Keith Jackson, Oklahoma. Line—Jeff Bregel, Southern Cal; John Clay, Missouri; Randy Dixon, Pittsburgh; Danny Villa, Arizona St. C—Ben Tamburello, Auburn. QB—Vinny Testaverde, Miami,FL. RB—D.J.Dozier, Penn St.; Terrence Flagler, Clemson; Brent Fullwood, Auburn; Brad Muster, Stanford; Paul Palmer, Temple. PK—Jeff Jaeger, Washington.

Defense

Line—Jerome Brown, Miami,FL; Jason Buck, BYU; Danny Noonan, Nebraska; Reggie Rogers, Washington; Tony Woods, Pittsburgh. LB—Cornelius Bennett, Alabama; Brian Bosworth, Oklahoma; Shane Conlan, Penn St.; Chris Spielman, Ohio St. DB—Bennie Blades, Miami,FL; Tim McDonald, Southern Cal; Garland Rivers, Michigan; Rod Woodson, Purdue. P—Barry Helton, Colorado.

1987

For the second year in a row it was No.1 vs No.2 in a bowl game, this time the Orange Bowl.

Miami, the upset loser to Penn State in the championship game a year ago, returned as the underdog. Oklahoma was the favorite and had a 17–7 victory over former No.1 Nebraska to merit such support. But this was also the third meeting between the Hurricanes and Sooners in three years and the Canes had won the first two.

In a driving rain New Year's Night, Miami made it three in a row, surprising the Sooners 20–14 for their second national title in five years.

But the game of the year was the Miami–Florida State thriller in Tallahassee Oct.3. In that one, the Canes rallied from a 19–3 deficit late in the third quarter to overtake the Seminoles, 26–19, then held on as FSU scored in the last minute and missed a two-point conversion try.

It was the only game Florida State lost all year and when the final polls came out Miami and FSU were ranked 1–2, a first for two teams from the same state.

In February, the NCAA cancelled Southern Methodist's football season citing repeated rules violations. Other sanctions led SMU to forgo its '88 season as well saying it couldn't be competitive.

And Columbia set a new NCAA Division I record for futility as its five-year losing streak reached 41 and counting. The old losing streak low water mark had been 34, set by Northwestern (1979–82).

Final AP Top 20
Writers' poll taken after bowl games.

	Final Record	Head Coach	Before Bowls
1 Miami,FL	12–0–0	Jimmy Johnson	11–0–0
2 Florida St.	11–1–0	Bobby Bowden	10–1–0
3 Oklahoma	11–1–0	Barry Switzer	11–0–0
4 Syracuse	11–0–1	Dick MacPherson	11–0–0
5 LSU	10–1–1	Mike Archer	9–1–1
6 Nebraska	10–2–0	Tom Osborne	10–1–0
7 Auburn	9–1–2	Pat Dye	9–1–1
8 Michigan St.	9–2–1	George Perles	8–2–1
9 UCLA	10–2–0	Terry Donahue	9–2–0
10 Texas A&M	10–2–0	Jackie Sherrill	9–2–0
11 Oklahoma St.	10–2–0	Pat Jones	9–2–0
12 Clemson	10–2–0	Danny Ford	9–2–0
13 Georgia	9–3–0	Vince Dooley	8–3–0
14 Tennessee	10–2–1	Johnny Majors	9–2–1
15 S.Carolina	8–4–0	Joe Morrison	8–3–0
16 Iowa	10–3–0	Hayden Fry	9–3–0
17 Notre Dame	8–4–0	Lou Holtz	8–3–0
18 Southern Cal	8–4–0	Larry Smith	8–3–0
19 Michigan	8–4–0	Bo Schembechler	7–4–0
20 Arizona St.	7–4–1	John Cooper	6–4–1

Bowl Games with Top 20 Teams

Date	Bowl	Result
12/25/87	Aloha	UCLA 20, Florida 16
12/25/87	Sun	Okla.St. 35, West Va. 33
12/29/87	Liberty	Georgia 20, Arkansas 17
12/30/87	Freedom	Ariz.St. 33, A.Force 28
12/30/87	Holiday	Iowa 20, Wyoming 19
12/31/87	Gator	LSU 30, S.Carolina 13
1/1/88	Cotton	Texas A&M 35, N.Dame 10
1/1/88	Fiesta	Fla.St. 31, Nebraska 28
1/1/88	Fla.Citrus	Clemson 35, Penn St. 10
1/1/88	Orange	Miami,FL 20, Oklahoma 14
1/1/88	Rose	Michigan St. 20, USC 17
1/1/88	Sugar	16–16, Syracuse vs Auburn
1/2/88	Hall of Fame	Michigan 28, Alabama 24
1/2/88	Peach	Tennessee 27, Indiana 22

Div. I-A Conference Champs

Atlantic Coast	Clemson	6–1
Big Eight	Oklahoma	7–0
Big Ten	Michigan St.	7–0–1
Mid-American	Eastern Michigan	7–1
Pacific Coast	San Jose St.	7–0
Pac-10	Southern Cal/UCLA	7–1
Southeastern	Auburn	5–0–1
Southwest	Texas A&M	6–1
Western Athletic	Wyoming	8–0

Heisman Trophy Voting

	Yr	Pos.	Votes
1 Tim Brown, Notre Dame	Sr.	FL	1,442
2 Don McPherson, Syracuse	Sr.	QB	831
3 Gordie Lockbaum, Holy Cross	Sr.	WR-DB	657
4 Lorenzo White, Michigan St.	Sr.	RB	632
5 Craig Heyward, Pittsburgh	Jr.	RB	170

Other Major Award Winners

Maxwell (Player)	Don McPherson, Syracuse
Camp (Back)	Tim Brown, Notre Dame
Rockne (Lineman)	Chad Hennings, Air Force, DT
Lombardi (Lineman)	Chris Spielman, Ohio St., LB
Outland (Interior)	Chad Hennings, Air Force
AFCA Coach of Year	Dick MacPherson, Syracuse
FWAA Coach of Year	Dick MacPherson, Syracuse

Consensus All-America Team
(By position, in alphabetical order)

Offense
WR—Tim Brown, Notre Dame; Wendell Davis, LSU. **TE**—Keith Jackson, Oklahoma. **Line**—Dave Cadigan, Southern Cal; John Elliott, Michigan; Mark Hutson, Oklahoma; Randall McDaniel, Arizona St. **C**—Nacho Albergamo, LSU. **QB**—Don McPherson, Syracuse. **RB**—Craig Heyward, Pittsburgh; Lorenzo, White, Michigan St. **PK**—David Treadwell, Clemson.

Defense
Line—Ted Gregory, Syracuse; Chad Hennings, Air Force; Tracy Rocker, Auburn; John Roper, Texas A&M; Daniel Stubbs, Miami,FL. **LB**—Aundray Bruce, Auburn; Dante Jones, Oklahoma; Chris Spielman, Ohio St. **DB**—Bennie Blades, Miami,FL; Chuck Cecil, Arizona; Rickey Dixon, Oklahoma; Deion Sanders, Florida St. **P**—Tom Tupa, Ohio St.

1988 .

Notre Dame returned to the top of the heap after 11 years in 1988, going 12–0 to claim the national championship for a record eighth time since the AP Poll began in 1936.

The Irish clinched the title by beating No.3 West Virginia in the Fiesta Bowl, but it was regular season victories over defending champ Miami and Southern Cal that made them the top-ranked team.

Miami was No.1 and Notre Dame No.4 when they met in South Bend on Oct.15. The Irish held a 31–21 lead in the third quarter, but the Hurricanes rallied to within 31–30 on a touchdown with 45 seconds left in the game. The Canes went for the two-point conversion and missed.

Six weeks later, No.1 Notre Dame visited No.2 USC at the L.A.Coliseum (burial ground for many highly-regarded Irish teams). This time, however, it was N.D. that did the burying, 27–10.

Miami and Florida State, last year's Top Two, both finished at 11–1 to place second and third. In the season opener for both, the Hurricanes crushed the Seminoles 31–0, despite the fact that FSU was nearly everyone's preseason favorite for No.1.

The star of the year was Oklahoma State running back Barry Sanders, who came out of nowhere and with no fanfare to shatter the NCAA single season records for rushing yards (2,628) and touchdowns (39) and run away with the Heisman Trophy.

Finally, Columbia snapped its record Division I losing streak at 44, beating Princeton, 16–13, on Oct.8.

Final AP Top 20

Writers' poll taken after bowl games.

	Final Record	Head Coach	Before Bowls
1 Notre Dame	12–0–0	Lou Holtz	11–0–0
2 Miami,FL	11–1–0	Jimmy Johnson	10–1–0
3 Florida St.	11–1–0	Bobby Bowden	10–1–0
4 Michigan	9–2–1	Bo Schembechler	8–2–1
5 W.Virginia	11–1–0	Don Nehlen	11–0–0
6 UCLA	10–2–0	Terry Donahue	9–2–0
7 Southern Cal	10–2–0	Larry Smith	10–1–0
8 Auburn	10–2–0	Pat Dye	10–1–0
9 Clemson	10–2–0	Danny Ford	9–2–0
10 Nebraska	11–2–0	Tom Osborne	11–1–0
11 Oklahoma St.	10–2–0	Pat Jones	9–2–0
12 Arkansas	10–2–0	Ken Hatfield	10–1–0
13 Syracuse	10–2–0	Dick MacPherson	9–2–0
14 Oklahoma	9–3–0	Barry Switzer	9–2–0
15 Georgia	9–3–0	Vince Dooley	8–3–0
16 Wash.St.	9–3–0	Dennis Erickson	8–3–0
17 Alabama	9–3–0	Bill Curry	7–3–0
18 Houston	9–3–0	Jack Pardee	9–2–0
19 LSU	8–4–0	Mike Archer	8–3–0
20 Indiana	8–3–1	Bill Mallory	7–3–1

Bowl Games with Top 20 Teams

Date	Bowl	Result
12/24/88	Sun	Alabama 29, Army 28
12/25/88	Aloha	Wash.St. 24, Houston 22
12/28/88	Liberty	Indiana 34, S.Carolina 10
12/30/88	Holiday	Okla.St. 62, Wyoming 14
1/1/89	Gator	Georgia 34, Mich.St. 27
1/2/89	Cotton	UCLA 17, Arkansas 3
1/2/89	Fiesta	N.Dame 34, West Va. 21
1/2/89	Fla.Citrus	Clemson 13, Oklahoma 6
1/2/89	Hall of Fame	Syracuse 23, LSU 10
1/2/89	Orange	Miami,FL 23, Nebraska 3
1/2/89	Rose	Michigan 22, USC 14
1/2/89	Sugar	Florida St. 13, Auburn 7

Div. I-A Conference Champs

Atlantic Coast	Clemson	6–1
Big Eight	Nebraska	7–0
Big Ten	Michigan	7–0–1
Big West	Fresno St.	7–0
Mid-American	Western Michigan	7–1
Pac-10	Southern Cal	8–0
Southeastern	Auburn/LSU	6–1
Southwest	Arkansas	7–0
Western Athletic	Wyoming	8–0

Heisman Trophy Voting

	Yr	Pos.	Votes
1 Barry Sanders, Oklahoma St.	Jr.	RB	1,878
2 Rodney Peete, Southern Cal	Sr.	QB	912
3 Troy Aikman, UCLA	Sr.	QB	582
4 Steve Walsh, Miami,FL	Jr.	QB	341
5 Major Harris, West Virginia	Jr.	QB	280

Other Major Award Winners

Maxwell (Player)	Barry Sanders, Okla.St.
Camp (Back)	Barry Sanders, Okla.St.
Rockne (Lineman)	Tracy Rocker, Auburn, DT
Lombardi (Lineman)	Trady Rocker, Auburn
Outland (Interior)	Tracy Rocker, Auburn
AFCA Coach of Year	Don Nehlen, West Va.
FWAA Coach of Year	Lou Holtz, Notre Dame

Consensus All-America Team

(By position, in alphabetical order)

Offense

WR—Hart Lee Dykes, Oklahoma St.; Jason Phillips, Houston. **TE**—Marv Cook, Iowa. **Line**—Andy Heck, Notre Dame; Tony Mandarich, Michigan St.; Anthony Phillips, Oklahoma; Mark Stepnoski, Pittsburgh; Mike Utley, Washington St. **QB**—Troy Aikman, UCLA. **RB**—Barry Sanders, Oklahoma St.; Anthony Thompson, Indiana. **PK**—Kendall Trainor, Arkansas.

Defense

Line—Wayne Martin, Arkansas; Mark Messner, Michigan; Tracy Rocker, Auburn; Frank Stams, Notre Dame. **LB**—Keith DeLong, Tennessee; Mike Stonebreaker, Notre Dame; Broderick Thomas, Nebraska; Derrick Thomas, Alabama. **DB**—Darryl Henley, UCLA; Markus Paul, Syracuse; Deion Sanders, Florida St.; Donnell Woolford, Clemson. **P**—Keith English, Colorado.

S.F. Chronicle: Brant Ward

Retiring head coach **Bill Walsh** holds up his third Super Bowl trophy as he shares a ride with San Francisco Mayor **Art Agnos** (center) and 49ers' owner **Eddie DeBartolo** during the team's victory parade Jan. 23rd.

PRO FOOTBALL

INSIDE

Elsewhere in Almanac
For related information refer to the following chapters: Arenas & Ballparks, Halls of Fame & Awards, and Sports Organizations.

*Tale of two franchises: 49ers clean up
and Cowboys clean house.
Meanwhile, Rozelle steps down
after 29 years as NFL commissioner.*

1988 YEAR IN REVIEW

by Gary Myers

Fifty-seven seconds left on the clock. January 10, 1982. What was to transpire in the next six seconds would help shape the National Football League in the 1980s. It was to mark the beginning of one era and the end of another.

San Francisco quarterback Joe Montana rolled to his right. Closing in on him was the frightening hulk of Dallas' 6-9 defensive end Ed Jones. Just as Jones was about to pounce, Montana lofted a pass toward the back of the end zone in the general direction of Dwight Clark. Inspired by the moment, Clark soared into the late afternoon sky and pulled down Montana's pass, ending a miracle 89-yard drive. Final score: San Francisco 28, Dallas 27.

That NFC Championship game at Candlestick Park inspired the 49ers to great things in the 1980s—and started the slide

of the once-mighty Cowboys. Two weeks later, the Niners defeated the Cincinnati Bengals in Super Bowl XVI, the first of their three league championships during the decade. Three years later, they went on to hammer Miami in Super Bowl XIX, and this past January, Montana engineered another memorable drive in the final minutes to beat Cincinnati once again.

For Dallas, meanwhile, the loss to the 49ers marked the beginning of the Depression years. The Cowboys have not won a playoff game since 1982. Worse, they have endured three straight losing seasons, missed the playoffs four of the last five years, and, in February, lost legendary coach Tom Landry when the team was sold for the second time since 1985.

The 1988 season will be remembered for the magnificence of Montana and the move to the front office by coach Bill Walsh after the Super Bowl. It was a strange year for Montana. Back and forth he went with backup Steve Young, a mobile, young quarterback with whom

Gary Myers is in his first season as pro football columnist for the **N.Y. Daily News.** He previously covered the Dallas Cowboys and NFL for eight years at the **Dallas Morning News.**

San Francisco quarterback **Joe Montana** (16) gets the protection he needs while directing the 49ers' dramatic, last minute victory over Cincinnati in the Super Bowl.

Walsh seemed to be infatuated. Would Montana start? No, Walsh would say, he was tired, or couldn't throw hard enough to cut through the San Francisco wind, or the weather was too hot or too cold. But when the season was on the line and the 49ers were on the verge of losing, Walsh forgot about Young and called on Montana.

And it was fitting that in what turned out to be Walsh's final game, Montana pulled off a drive (this time covering 92 yards) strikingly similar to the beauty he executed against Dallas in '82. When NFL commissioner Pete Rozelle handed the championship trophy to Walsh, the speculation was strong that Walsh had coached his last game. And four days later he quit, replaced by his defensive coordinator, George Seifert.

But nobody had any warning that it was the final Super Bowl presentation Rozelle would make, or the last game that Landry, seated in a luxury box in Miami's Joe Robbie Stadium, would be watching as the coach of the Cowboys. In the next two months, Landry would be fired and Rozelle would stun NFL owners

by announcing he was stepping down after 29 years.

First, Landry. "This is like Lombardi's

"The Drive"

Trailing 16–13 with 3:10 left in Super Bowl XXIII, San Francisco began the game's pivotal scoring drive on its own 8-yard line. Quarterback Joe Montana led the 49ers 92 yards in 11 plays and used up 2:46 on the clock. MVP Jerry Rice, who caught 11 passes in the game for 215 yards, caught three on the drive for 51 yards. Here's how it happened:

No.	Ball on	Down	Play
1	SF	8	1st–10	Montana to Craig, 8 yds
2	SF	16	2nd–2	Montana to Frank, 7 yds
3	SF	23	1st–10	Montana to Rice, 7 yds
4	SF	30	2nd–3	Craig run, 1 yd
			—Two-Minute Warning—	
5	SF	31	3rd–2	Craig run, 4 yds
			—San Francisco Timeout—	
6	SF	35	1st–10	Montana to Rice, 17 yds
7	Cin	48	1st–10	Montana to Craig, 13 yds
8	Cin	35	1st–10	Montana incomplete to Rice
9	Cin	35	2nd–10	Montana to Craig, 4 yds (Flag: ineligible receiver downfield, play called back, 10-yd penalty)
9	Cin	45	2nd–20	Montana to Rice, 27 yds
10	Cin	18	1st–10	Montana to Craig, 8 yds
			—San Francisco Timeout—	
11	Cin	10	2nd–2	Montana to Taylor, 10 yds Touchdown (Cofer kick) 49ers lead, 20–16, with 0:24 left.

death," Rozelle said in the most poignant tribute to Landry's 29-year contribution to the Cowboys, which included five Super Bowl appearances, two championships and a string of 20 consecutive winning seasons that is unlikely to be equalled.

The Cowboys hit bottom in 1988, their 3-13 record being their worst since 1960, when they joined the league. Most importantly, however, the Texas economy had fallen further than the Cowboys, and Bum Bright, a hands-off owner, was forced to sell.

Up stepped Arkansas oilman Jerry Jones, a fast-talking former college player who spent $140 million for the privilege of owning the sport's most recognizable team and Texas Stadium. And for that kind of money, Jones bought the right to run the show and bring along his own coach. So Jones came as a package deal with his University of Arkansas college buddy, Jimmy Johnson, the University of Miami's incredibly successful coach.

The time had come for Landry to step down anyway. The shock: Nobody thought the guy who wears the funny hats would ever be fired. Not long after, president and general manager Tex Schramm left, too, to start up the NFL's international venture. And Jones then gave the pink slip to Gil Brandt, the team's vice president. Landry, Schramm and Brandt had been together for 30 years.

Less than a month later, on March 22, Rozelle, who was named commissioner in 1960 one day before the Cowboys were officially voted into the NFL, broke down and cried as he told the owners he was retiring and moving to Rancho Sante Fe, a San Diego suburb. "We must replace the irreplaceable man," said New York Giants owner Wellington Mara, the co-chairman of the search committee.

Rozelle's sense of timing and ability to look into the future propelled the NFL into the forefront of the nation's consciousness. He had built a powerhouse league: the multi-million dollar television contracts, the Super Bowl extravaganza, the packed stadiums. The NFL will miss Rozelle. He will miss it, too, but the idea of travelling, tennis and fishing held greater appeal. "I may be proven wrong, but I don't think, in trying to analyze myself honestly, that the idea of power is meaningful to me," Rozelle said. "Some people may think otherwise, but that's the way I analyze myself. The other part, the excitement and love of the game, I'm sure I will miss that. It's silly to say you won't. But I'm virtually certain I'll never say it was the wrong decision."

Rozelle's retirement was the exclamation point to a busy 1988 season and even more tumultuous offseason.

The life of Chicago coach Mike Ditka had its ups and downs, to say the least. In July, he was inducted into the Pro Football Hall of Fame as a player, then in January, he was named NFL Coach of the Year for leading the Bears to their fifth straight NFC Central Division title in what was supposed to be a transitional year. But the most stunning news concerning Ditka came in November when he suffered a mild heart attack. True to his Iron Mike nickname, he missed just one game.

Power struggles brought about big changes in Cleveland and Washington. Browns coach Marty Schottenheimer, who had his team in four consecutive playoffs, quit Dec. 27 following a disagreement over offensive responsibilities with owner Art Modell. A month later, Schottenheimer was named as Kansas City's new head coach by the Chiefs' new president and general manager Carl Peterson. Peterson, who assembled the two-time USFL champion Philadelphia-Baltimore Stars, was hired after K.C. owner Lamar Hunt purged his front office. New York Jets defensive coordinator Bud Carson replaced Schottenheimer in Cleveland.

Meanwhile, Washington general manager Bobby Beathard resigned in favor of returning home to Southern California. Beathard, architect of the Redskins' two Super Bowl championship teams, wanted to rebuild the club with young players. Head Coach Joe Gibbs preferred veterans. Gibbs had owner Jack Kent Cooke's ear, so Beathard hit the beach.

The most surprising non-change of the year actually came following the 1987 season, when Cincinnati Owner-GM Paul Brown elected to disregard public pressure and keep Sam Wyche on as head coach despite a dissension- and

New Cowboys owner **Jerry Jones** (right) addresses Dallas news conference with general manager **Tex Schramm** (left) and former owner **Bum Bright** in background.

strike-filled 4-11 season. Brown's patience was rewarded as Wyche and quarterback Boomer Esiason, the NFL's Most Valuable Player, took the Bengals to the Super Bowl.

Cincinnati's resurgence was also helped by one of the many legacies of the departing Rozelle: parity.

The NFL is designed to create all teams equal. The draft, the waiver system, the formula scheduling. Long ago, Rozelle made the determination, along with the owners, that it was not in the best interests of the league for one team to dominate. Nobody has repeated as Super Bowl champion since the 1978-79 Pittsburgh Steelers. San Francisco's three Super Bowls in the 1980s are truly remarkable considering how the NFL legislates against domination.

This year's draft will likely be the one many point to when the Cowboys turn things around in the next few years. As reward for being the league's worst team last season, the Cowboys earned the No. 1 pick in the draft. And who was sitting there? UCLA quarterback Troy Aikman, considered the best prospect at his position since John Elway in 1983. And consider-

ing that Steve Pelluer, the incumbent, is an ugly 7–20 as a starter, it's pretty obvious that the Cowboys were quarterback poor.

There were three other very interesting players in this draft. Tony Mandarich of Michigan State, Barry Sanders of Oklahoma State and Deion Sanders of Florida State.

Mandarich, selected second overall by Green Bay, was rated by scouts as the best offensive lineman to come into the league—ever. Running back Barry Sanders, who won the Heisman Trophy as a third-year junior, declared himself eligible for the draft in March not long after his school had been put on probation by the NCAA. Anxious to avoid a lawsuit, the NFL decided to OK his entry and Detroit made him the third pick.

Atlanta chose cornerback Deion Sanders (no relation to Barry) fifth overall. The best pure athlete available since Bo Jackson, Sanders made no secret of his intention to follow Bo's example and go major league in both football and baseball. By June he had been called up from the minors to play center field for the New York Yankees.

Parity played a part in the rise of teams

169

like Buffalo, Philadelphia and Houston and the demise of Dallas, Miami and Pittsburgh. The Bills and Eagles, doormats of the 1980s, each won its division last season with good, young players developed through the NFL farm system: the colleges. The Bills were particularly adept at using every avenue available in accumulating talent. They signed quarterback Jim Kelly, their No. 1 pick in 1983, after the USFL folded. General manager Bill Polian gambled in 1987, giving up two No. 1s and a No. 2 in a three-way trade that sent linebacker Cornelius Bennett to Buffalo. And the Bills used conventional means to find defensive end Bruce Smith in 1985, making him the No. 1 pick in the draft. Smith and Philadelphia's Reggie White are the two best pass rushers in the league.

Smith, however, was one of 23 players, suspended by Rozelle last season for a second violation of the league's substance abuse policy. Smith had to sit down for 30 days after he came up positive in a drug test. So did Giants linebacker Lawrence Taylor, who true to his book title, is certainly living on the edge. These two-time offenders are just one strike away from being sat down for a minimum of one year.

Indianapolis' Tony Collins is the only three-time loser in the program that went into effect in 1986. Cincinnati's Stanley Wilson got into even deeper trouble. Rozelle warned him in 1988 that one more slipup and Wilson was gone for good with no promise of reinstatement. Wilson held out until the night before the biggest game of his life: Super Bowl XXIII. He was found in a drug-induced condition in his Miami hotel room, was suspended for the game and then banned for life in May.

In March, Rozelle introduced his new steroid policy. All players would continue to be tested in training camp, but now the first offense results in a 30-day suspension and the second one costs one year.

Steroids cost Ben Johnson his 1988 Olympic gold medal and could cost several players their NFL careers. There is major concern around the league that the use of steroids not only develops an unfair competitive advantage, but develops health risks in players using them.

Wide World Photos

After 29 years as NFL commissioner, **Pete Rozelle** announced in March that he was stepping down.

Once the summer tests are conducted, a player who tested clean can get back on the juice without fear of being tested until the next training camp. It's a major loophole, but the new policy is certainly a positive step in the attempt to eliminate steroids from the league.

As the NFL winds down this decade, we've witnessed a dramatic growth in the popularity of the game. But other areas need to be worked on. A black quarterback, Doug Williams, not only started a Super Bowl, but was the MVP. Yet, the NFL is still without its first black head coach. The league continues to recycle coaches, but nobody has stepped forward to hire a black. It shouldn't be too far into the 1990s before that changes. Rozelle has urged owners to give blacks every consideration.

And the NFL will continue to grow in the 1990s. Two more teams will be added as soon as there is a new collective bargaining agreement. If the Worldwide American Football League is a success in the spring, the NFL could expand to Europe by the year 2000. There will be more cable involvement in the television contracts.

And now there will be a new commissioner to run the show.

The Rozelle Era in the NFL

1960—Rozelle, the 33-year old GM of the LA Rams, elected commissioner (Jan. 26) as compromise choice on the 23rd ballot. . . .12-team NFL votes to expand to Dallas in 1960 and Minnesota in 1961. . . .Chicago Cardinals move to St. Louis. . . .8-team AFL begins first season.

1962—Rozelle re-elected. . . .US District Court judge in Baltimore rules against AFL in its two-year antitrust suit against NFL. The AFL had charged monopoly and conspiracy in areas of TV, expansion and player signings. . . .Courts also uphold legality of NFL's TV blackout rule within 75-mile radius of home teams.

1963—Rozelle suspends Green Bay HB Paul Hornung and Detroit DT Alex Karras for betting on their own games.

1964—Hornung and Karras reinstated.

1965—NFL votes to expand to Atlanta in 1966.

1966—Rozelle announces merger agreement between NFL and AFL. World championship game and common draft will take place after '66 season with inter-league play by 1970. . . .Congress approves of merger. . . .NFL votes to expand to New Orleans in 1967.

1967—Green Bay (NFL) defeats Kansas City (AFL), 35–10, at LA Coliseum in first NFL-AFL World Championship Game. . . .Baltimore selects Michigan State DE Bubba Smith as No. 1 pick in first common draft. . . .AFL votes to expand to Cincinnati in 1968.

1969—NY Jets upset Baltimore, 16–7, as AFL wins first World Championship game (now known officially as the Super Bowl). . . Baltimore, Cleveland and Pittsburgh agree to join AFL teams in new AFC as league finalizes plans to realign into two 13-team conferences of three divisions each in 1970. . . .Two wild card entries created for 1970 playoffs. . . .ABC-TV signs three-year deal to televise "Monday Night Football."

1971—Boston Patriots move to Foxboro, Mass., become New England Patriots. . . .Dallas Cowboys move to Irving, Texas.

1972—Baltimore owner Carroll Rosenbloom and LA Rams owner Robert Irsay trade franchises (owners move, teams stay put).

1973—Jersey numbering system adopted: 1–19 for quarterbacks and specialists; 20–49 for running backs; 50–59 for centers and linebackers; 60–79 for defensive linemen, interior offensive linemen and other centers; 80–89 for wide receivers and tight ends (players with NFL or AFL experience before '73 could keep old numbers). . . .Congress adopts experimental legislation requiring any NFL game sold out 72 hours before kickoff be made available for local televising.

1974—NFL votes to expand to Tampa Bay and Seattle in 1976. . . .One sudden death overtime period added for regular season games. . . .Goal posts moved back from goal line to end line. . . .World Football League begins first season. . . .NFL Players Assn. goes on strike July 1, returns Aug. 29 in time for opening of regular season.

1975—Detroit Lions move to Pontiac, Mich. . . .WFL folds after 1½ seasons.

1976—NY Giants move to East Rutherford, N.J. . . .In Tokyo, St. Louis defeats San Diego in preseason game, first NFL game held outside North America.

1978—Regular season increased from 14 to 16 games for 1978 and two more wild card teams added to playoffs. . . .Some prime time regular season games added on Sunday and Thursday nights.

1980—LA Rams move to Anaheim, Calif. . . . Oakland Raiders, barred from moving to LA Coliseum, bring antitrust suit against NFL.

1981—ABC (21.7) and CBS (17.5) set all-time highs for NFL-TV ratings (NBC slips a little to 13.9). . . .Average league attendance tops 60,000 per game for first time ever (NFL operating at 93.8 of total stadium capacity).

1982—NFL signs five-year, $2.1 billion contract with the three TV networks through 1986. . . .Raiders win antitrust case against NFL, move to LA Coliseum, become LA Raiders. . . .NFLPA goes on strike Sept. 20, and stays out 57 days. New contract runs through 1986 season. Play resumes Nov. 21, but regular season is shortened to nine games and playoffs are opened to 16 teams.

1983—United States Football League begins play as Spring league. . . .Rozelle suspends Baltimore quarterback Art Schlichter for gambling.

1984—Baltimore Colts move to Indianapolis, become Indianapolis Colts. . . .NY Jets move to East Rutherford, N.J.

1985—Rozelle elected to Pro Football Hall of Fame.

1986—Super Bowl XX (Chicago 46, New England 10) draws TV audience of 127 million, replaces final episode of "M*A*S*H" (1983) as all-time most-viewed TV show. . . .Owners adopt limited use of instant replay for aid in officiating. . . .After an 11-week trial, USFL wins $1.7 billion antitrust suit against the NFL, but is awarded only one dollar by jury. . . .USFL essentially out of business.

1987—NFL signs three-year, $1.428 billion contract with the three TV networks through 1989. . . .Three-year cable TV deal with ESPN also signed. . . .NFLPA goes on strike Sept. 22. . . .NFL continues schedule with replacement players. . . .Strike ends after 24 days, players return but with no new agreement reached.

1988—St. Louis Cardinals move to Phoenix, become Phoenix Cardinals (play home games in Tempe, Ariz.). . . .Rozelle suspends 25 players 30 days each for drug abuse.

1989—Rozelle announces retirement (March 22) after 29 years.

1988 Final NFL Standings

American Football Conference

Eastern Division

	W	L	T	Pct	PF	PA	vs Div
*Buffalo	12	4	0	.750	329	237	7-0-1
Indianapolis	9	7	0	.563	354	315	5-3-0
New England	9	7	0	.563	250	284	5-3-0
NY Jets	8	7	1	.531	372	354	3-5-0
Miami	6	10	0	.375	319	380	0-8-0

Tiebreaker: Indianapolis (7-5) had better record against common opponents than New England (6-6).

Head Coaches: Buf—Marv Levy (3rd season); **Ind**—Ron Meyer (3rd); **NE**—Raymond Berry (5th); **Jets**—Joe Walton (6th); **Miami**—Don Shula (19th).

Central Division

	W	L	T	Pct	PF	PA	vs Div
*Cincinnati	12	4	0	.750	448	329	4-2-0
**Cleveland	10	6	0	.625	304	288	4-2-0
**Houston	10	6	0	.625	424	365	3-3-0
Pittsburgh	5	11	0	.313	336	421	1-5-0

Tiebreaker: Cleveland had better division record than Houston.

Head Coaches: Cinn—Sam Wyche (5th season); **Clev**—Marty Schottenheimer (5th); **Hou**—Jerry Glanville (4th); **Pitt**—Chuck Noll (20th).

Western Division

	W	L	T	Pct	PF	PA	vs Div
*Seattle	9	7	0	.563	339	329	6-2-0
Denver	8	8	0	.500	327	352	3-5-0
LA Raiders	7	9	0	.438	325	369	4-4-0
San Diego	6	10	0	.375	231	332	3-5-0
Kansas City	4	11	1	.281	254	320	2-6-0

Head Coaches: Sea—Chuck Knox (6th season); **Den**—Dan Reeves (8th); **Raiders**—Mike Shanahan (1st); **SD**—Al Saunders (3rd); **KC**—Frank Gansz (2nd).

*Division champion
**Playoff Wild Card

National Football Conference

Eastern Division

	W	L	T	Pct	PF	PA	vs Div
*Philadelphia	10	6	0	.625	379	319	6-2-0
NY Giants	10	6	0	.625	359	304	5-3-0
Washington	7	9	0	.438	345	387	4-4-0
Phoenix	7	9	0	.438	344	398	3-5-0
Dallas	3	13	0	.188	265	381	2-6-0

Tiebreakers: Philadelphia beat NY Giants twice head-to-head, and Washington had better division record than Phoenix.

Head Coaches: Phila—Buddy Ryan (3rd season); **Giants**—Bill Parcells (6th); **Wash**—Joe Gibbs (8th); **Phoe**—Gene Stallings (3rd); **Dal**—Tom Landry (29th).

Central Division

	W	L	T	Pct	PF	PA	vs Div
*Chicago	12	4	0	.750	312	215	6-2-0
**Minnesota	11	5	0	.688	406	233	6-2-0
Tampa Bay	5	11	0	.313	261	350	4-4-0
Detroit	4	12	0	.250	220	313	2-6-0
Green Bay	4	12	0	.250	240	315	2-6-0

Tiebreaker: Detroit beat Green Bay twice head-to-head.

Head Coaches: Chi—Mike Ditka (7th season); **Minn**—Jerry Burns (3rd); **TB**—Ray Perkins (2nd); **Det**—Lions were 2-9 when they fired 4th year coach Darryl Rogers on Nov.14 and named defensive coordinator Wayne Fontes; **GB**—Lindy Infante (1st).

Western Division

	W	L	T	Pct	PF	PA	vs Div
*San Francisco	10	6	0	.625	369	294	4-2-0
**LA Rams	10	6	0	.625	407	293	4-2-0
New Orleans	10	6	0	.625	312	283	3-3-0
Atlanta	5	11	0	.313	244	315	1-5-0

Tiebreakers: San Francisco (3-1) had better head-to-head record over LA Rams (2-2) and New Orleans (1-3); LA Rams had better division record than New Orleans and beat NY Giants head-to-head.

Head Coaches: SF—Bill Walsh (10th season); **Rams**—John Robinson (6th); **NO**—Jim Mora (3rd); **Atl**—Marion Campbell (2nd).

*Division champion
**Playoff Wild Card

1988 Paid Attendance Breakdown

Regular Season	Games	Attendance	Average
AFC	86	5,348,592	62,193
NFC	86	5,037,684	58,578
AFC vs NFC	52	3,153,572	60,646
Regular Season Total	224	13,539,848	60,446

Postseason	Attendance
AFC Wildcard:	Houston at Cleve. 75,896
Divisional:	Houston at Buffalo ... 79,523
	Seattle at Cincinnati .. 59,501
Championship:	Buffalo at Cincinnati .. 60,003

Postseason	Attendance
NFC Wildcard:	LA Rams at Minn. 61,204
Divisional:	Minn. at SF 63,598
	Phil. at Chicago 66,442
Championship:	SF at Chicago 66,908

Super Bowl XXIII: Cinn vs SF at Miami 75,129

Pro Bowl: AFC vs NFC at Honolulu 50,113

Postseason Total 658,317
Postseason Average.................... 65,832

Overall NFC Total (292 Games) 17,024,426
Overall NFL Average 58,303

Super Bowl Playoffs
Home teams noted in capital LETTERS.

American Conference

Wild Cards: Houston 24, CLEVELAND 23
Divisional: BUFFALO 17, Houston 10
CINCINNATI 21, Seattle 13
AFC Championship: CINCINNATI 21, Buffalo 10

National Conference

Wild Cards: MINNESOTA 28, LA Rams 17
Divisional: SAN FRANCISCO 34, Minnesota 9
CHICAGO 20, Philadelphia 12
NFC Championship: San Francisco 28, CHICAGO 3

Super Bowl XXIII
at Joe Robbie Stadium, Miami

Cincinnati (17-1)	0	3	10	3-**16**
San Francisco (14-5)	3	0	3	14-**20**

Scoring

SF—FG Mike Cofer 41
Cinn—FG Jim Breech 34
Cinn—FG Breech 43
SF—FG Cofer 32
Cinn—Stanford Jennings 93 kickoff return (Breech kick)
SF—Jerry Rice 14 pass from Joe Montana (Cofer kick)
Cinn—FG Breech 40
SF—John Taylor 10 pass from Montana (Cofer kick)

Date: Jan.22, 1989   **Favorite:** 49ers by 7

Attendance: 75,179   **TV Rating:** 43.5 (NBC)

Weather: Pt.Cloudy, 76 **Shares:** Winners—$36,000

Field: Grass   Losers—$18,000

Officials: Jerry Seeman (Referee); Gordon Wells (Umpire); Jerry Bergman (Head Linesman); Bob Beeks (Line Judge); Paul Baetz (Back Judge); Gary Lane (Side Judge); Bobby Skelton (Field Judge); Chuck Heberling (Replay).

Team Statistics

	Cinn	SF
First Downs	13	23
Rushing	7	6
Passing	6	16
Penalties	0	1
Third Down Efficiency	4-13	4-13
Penalties-Yards	7-65	4-32
Field Goals-Attempts	3-3	2-4
Punts-Average	5-44	4-36
Total Net Yards	229	454
Rushes-Yards	28-106	28-111
Passing Yards	123	343
Pass Completions-Attempts	11-25	23-36
Times Intercepted	1	0
Times Sacked-Yards	5-21	3-14
Fumbles-Lost	1-0	4-1
Time of Possession	32:43	27:17

Individual Statistics

Rushing

Cincinnati: Ickey Woods, 20 for 79 yds; James Brooks, 6 for 24 yds; Stanford Jennings, 1 for 3 yds; Boomer Esiason, 1 for 0 yds.
San Francisco: Roger Craig, 17 for 74 yds; Tom Rathman, 5 for 23 yds; Joe Montana, 5 for 9 yds; Jerry Rice, 1 for 5 yds.

Passing

Cincinnati: Boomer Esiason, 11 of 25 for 144 yds, 1 Int.
San Francisco: Joe Montana, 23 of 36 for 357 yds, 2 TD.

Receiving

Cincinnati: Eddie Brown, 4 for 44 yds; Cris Collinsworth, 3 for 40 yds; Tim McGee, 2 for 23 yds; James Brooks, 1 for 20 yds; Ira Hillary, 1 for 17 yds.
San Francisco: Jerry Rice, 11 for 215 yds, 1 TD; Roger Craig, 8 for 101 yds; John Frank, 2 for 15 yds; Tom Rathman, 1 for 16 yds; John Taylor, 1 for 10 yds, 1 TD.

Field Goals

Cincinnati: Jim Breech, 3 of 3, (made 34, 43, 40 yds).
San Francisco: Mike Cofer, 2 of 4 (made 41, 32 yds; missed 19, 49 yds).

Punting

Cincinnati: Lee Johnson, 5 for 223 yds, 44.6 avg.
San Francisco: Barry Helton, 4 for 148 yds, 37.0 avg.

Punt Returns

Cincinnati: Ray Horton, 1 for 5 yds; Ira Hillary, 1 for 0 yds.
San Francisco: John Taylor, 3 for 56 yds.

Kickoff Returns

Cincinnati: Stanford Jennings, 2 for 117 yds, 1 TD; James Brooks, 1 for 15 yds.
San Francisco: Del Rodgers, 3 for 53 yds; John Taylor, 1 for 13 yds; Harry Sydney, 1 for 11 yds.

Interceptions

Cincinnati: None.
San Francisco: Bill Romanowski, 1 for 0 yds.

Fumble Recoveries

Cincinnati: Jim Skow, 1.
San Francisco: Darryl Pollard, 1.

Sacks

Cincinnati: Jason Buck, 1; David Fulcher, 1; Reggie Williams, 1.
San Francisco: Charles Haley, 2; Michael Carter, 1; Kevin Fagan, 1; Daniel Stubbs, 1.

1988 Regular Season Individual Leaders

Passing

Based on rating points and a minimum of 224 attempts.

AFC	Att	Cmp	Cmp %	Yards	Avg	TD	TD %	Long	Int	Int %	Rating
Boomer Esiason, Cincinnati	388	233	57.5	3,572	9.21	28	7.2	86-TD	14	3.6	97.4
Dave Krieg, Seattle	228	134	58.8	1,741	7.64	18	7.9	75-TD	8	3.5	94.6
Warren Moon, Houston	294	160	54.4	2,327	7.91	17	5.8	57-TD	8	2.7	88.4
Bernie Kosar, Cleveland	259	156	60.2	1,890	7.30	10	3.9	77-TD	7	2.7	84.3
Dan Marino, Miami	606	354	58.4	4,434	7.32	28	4.6	80-TD	23	3.8	80.8
Ken O'Brien, NY Jets	424	236	55.7	2,567	6.05	15	3.5	50-TD	7	1.7	78.6
Jim Kelly, Buffalo	452	269	59.5	3,380	7.48	15	3.3	66-TD	17	3.8	78.2
Steve DeBerg, Kansas City	414	224	54.1	2,935	7.09	16	3.9	80-TD	16	3.9	73.5
John Elway, Denver	496	274	55.2	3,309	6.67	17	3.4	86	19	3.8	71.4
Chris Chandler, Ind'polis	233	129	55.4	1,619	6.95	8	3.4	54	12	5.2	67.2

NFC	Att	Cmp	Cmp %	Yards	Avg	TD	TD %	Long	Int	Int %	Rating
Wade Wilson, Minnesota	332	204	61.4	2,746	8.27	15	4.5	68-TD	9	2.7	91.5
Jim Everett, LA Rams	517	308	59.6	3,964	7.67	31	6.0	69-TD	18	3.5	89.2
Joe Montana, San Francisco	397	238	59.9	2,981	7.51	18	4.5	96-TD	10	2.5	87.9
Neil Lomax, Phoenix	443	255	57.6	3,395	7.66	20	4.5	93-TD	11	2.5	86.7
Phil Simms, NY Giants	479	263	54.9	3,359	7.01	21	4.4	62-TD	11	2.3	82.1
Bobby Hebert, N.Orleans	478	280	58.6	3,156	6.60	20	4.2	40-TD	15	3.1	79.3
Randall Cunningham, Phila	560	301	53.8	3,808	6.80	24	4.3	80-TD	16	2.9	77.6
Doug Williams, Washington	380	213	56.1	2,609	6.87	15	3.9	58	12	3.2	77.4
Steve Pelluer, Dallas	435	245	56.3	3,139	7.22	17	3.9	61-TD	19	4.4	73.9
Don Majkowski, Green Bay	336	178	53.0	2,119	6.31	9	2.7	56	11	3.3	67.8

Receiving

AFC	No	Yards	Avg	TD
Al Toon, NY Jets	93	1,067	11.5	5
Mark Clayton, Miami	86	1,129	13.1	14
Drew Hill, Houston	72	1,141	15.8	10
Andre Reed, Buffalo	71	968	13.6	6
Mickey Shuler, NY Jets	70	805	11.5	5
Vance Johnson, Denver	68	896	13.2	5
Stephone Paige, Kansas City	61	902	14.8	7
Ernest Givins, Houston	60	976	16.3	5
Earnest Byner, Cleveland	59	576	9.8	2
Jim Jensen, Miami	58	652	11.2	5
John L.Williams, Seattle	58	651	11.2	3

NFC	No	Yards	Avg	TD
Henry Ellard, LA Rams	86	1,414	16.4	10
Eric Martin, New Orleans	85	1,083	12.7	5
J.T.Smith, Phoenix	83	986	11.9	5
Keith Jackson, Philadelphia	81	869	10.7	6
Roger Craig, San Francisco	76	534	7.0	1
Ricky Sanders, Washington	73	1,148	15.7	12
Anthony Carter, Minnesota	72	1,225	17.0	6
Art Monk, Washington	72	946	13.1	5
Keith Byars, Philadelphia	72	705	9.8	4
Roy Green, Phoenix	68	1,097	16.1	7
John Settle, Atlanta	68	570	8.4	1

Rushing

AFC	Att	Yards	Avg	TD
Eric Dickerson, Ind'polis	388	1,659	4.3	14
John Stephens, New England	297	1,168	3.9	4
Gary Anderson, San Diego	225	1,119	5.0	3
Ickey Woods, Cincinnati	203	1,066	5.3	15
Curt Warner, Seattle	266	1,025	3.9	10
Mike Rozier, Houston	251	1,002	4.0	10
Freeman McNeil, NY Jets	219	944	4.3	6
James Brooks, Cincinnati	182	931	5.1	8
Thurman Thomas, Buffalo	207	881	4.3	2
John L.Williams, Seattle	189	877	4.6	4

NFC	Att	Yards	Avg	TD
Herschel Walker, Dallas	361	1,514	4.1	5
Roger Craig, San Francisco	310	1,502	4.8	9
Greg Bell, LA Rams	288	1,212	4.2	16
Neal Anderson, Chicago	249	1,106	4.4	12
Joe Morris, NY Giants	307	1,083	3.5	5
John Settle, Atlanta	232	1,024	4.4	7
Earl Ferrell, Phoenix	202	924	4.6	7
Dalton Hilliard, N.Orleans	204	823	4.0	5
Stump Mitchell, Phoenix	164	726	4.4	4
Rueben Mayes, N.Orleans	170	628	3.7	3

Punting

AFC	No	Yards	Long	Avg
Harry Newsome, Pittsburgh	65	2,950	62	45.4
Ralf Mojsiejenko, San Diego	85	3,745	62	44.1
Mike Horan, Denver	65	2,861	70	44.0
Rohn Stark, Indianapolis	64	2,784	65	43.5
Reggie Roby, Miami	64	2,754	64	43.0

NFC	No	Yards	Long	Avg
Jim Arnold, Detroit	97	4,110	69	42.4
Bryan Wagner, Chicago	79	3,282	70	41.5
Maury Buford, NY Giants	73	3,012	66	41.3
Mike Saxon, Dallas	80	3,271	55	40.9
Greg Horne, Phoenix	79	3,228	66	40.9

Punt Returns

AFC	No	Yards	Avg	TD
JoJo Townsell, NY Jets	35	409	11.7	1
Clarence Verdin, Indianapolis	22	239	10.9	1
Irving Fryar, New England	38	398	10.5	0
Lionel James, San Diego	28	278	9.9	0
Bobby Joe Edmonds, Seattle	35	340	9.7	0

NFC	No	Yards	Avg	TD
John Taylor, San Francisco	44	556	12.6	2
Mel Gray, New Orleans	25	305	12.2	1
Bobby Futrell, Tampa Bay	27	283	10.5	0
Vai Sikahema, Phoenix	33	341	10.3	0
Leo Lewis, Minnesota	58	550	9.5	0

Scoring

Kickers

AFC	PAT	FG	Long	Pts
Scott Norwood, Buffalo	33/33	32/37	49	129
Gary Anderson, Pitt.	34/35	28/36	52	118
Dean Biasucci, Ind'polis	39/40	25/32	53	114
Tony Zendejas, Houston	48/50	22/34	52	114
Pat Leahy, NY Jets	43/43	23/28	48	112
Norm Johnson, Seattle	39/39	22/28	47	105
Rich Karlis, Denver	36/37	23/36	51	105
Matt Bahr, Cleveland	32/33	24/29	47	104
Nick Lowery, Kansas City	23/23	27/32	51	104
Chris Bahr, LA Raiders	37/39	18/29	50	91

NFC	PAT	FG	Long	Pts
Mike Cofer, San Fran.	40/41	27/38	52	121
Mike Lansford, LA Rams	45/48	24/32	49	117
Morten Andersen, NO	32/33	26/36	51	110
Chuck Nelson, Minn.	48/49	20/25	49	108
Chip Lohmiller, Wash.	40/41	19/26	46	97
Luis Zendejas, Dal-Phila	35/36	20/27	50	95
Kevin Butler, Chicago	37/38	15/19	45	82
Greg Davis, Atlanta	25/27	19/30	52	82
Eddie Murray, Detroit	22/23	20/21	48	82
Al Del Greco, Phoenix	42/44	12/21	51	78
Donald Igwebuike, T.Bay	21/21	19/25	53	78

Touchdowns

AFC	TD	Rush	Rec	Ret	Pts
Eric Dickerson, Ind'polis	15	14	1	0	90
Ickey Woods, Cincinnati	15	15	0	0	90
James Brooks, Cincinnati	14	8	6	0	84
Mark Clayton, Miami	14	0	14	0	84
Robb Riddick, Buffalo	14	12	1	1	84
Lorenzo Hampton, Miami	12	9	3	0	72
Curt Warner, Seattle	12	10	2	0	72
Mike Rozier, Houston	11	10	1	0	66
Johnny Hector, NY Jets	10	10	0	0	60
Drew Hill, Houston	10	0	10	0	60

NFC	TD	Rush	Rec	Ret	Pts
Greg Bell, LA Rams	18	16	2	0	108
Neal Anderson, Chicago	12	12	0	0	72
Ricky Sanders, Wash.	12	0	12	0	72
Keith Byars, Philadelphia	10	6	4	0	60
Roger Craig, San Fran	10	9	1	0	60
Henry Ellard, LA Rams	10	0	10	0	60
Jerry Rice, San Fran.	10	1	9	0	60
Earl Ferrell, Phoenix	9	7	2	0	54
Bruce Hill, Tampa Bay	9	0	9	0	54

Five players tied with eight TDs (48 pts).

Interceptions

AFC	No	Yards	Avg	TD
Erik McMillan, NY Jets	8	168	21.0	2
Mark Kelso, Buffalo	7	180	25.7	1
Gill Byrd, San Diego	7	82	11.7	0
Eric Thomas, Cincinnati	7	61	8.7	0
Deron Cherry, Kansas City	7	51	7.3	0

NFC	No	Yards	Avg	TD
Scott Case, Atlanta	10	47	4.7	0
Carl Lee, Minnesota	8	118	14.8	2
Terry Hoage, Philadelphia	8	116	14.5	0
Vestee Jackson, Chicago	8	94	11.8	0
Tim McKyer, San Francisco	7	11	1.6	0

Sacks

AFC	No
Greg Townsend, LA Raiders	11½
Bruce Smith, Buffalo	11
Lee Williams, San Diego	11
Cornelius Bennett, Buffalo	9½
Jim Skow, Cincinnati	9½

NFC	No
Reggie White, Philadelphia	18
Kevin Greene, LA Rams	16½
Lawrence Taylor, NY Giants	15½
Freddie Joe Nunn, Phoenix	14
Tim Harris, Green Bay	13½

1988 NFL Team Leaders
Takeaways/Giveaways

AFC	Takeaways Int	Fum	Tot	Giveaways Int	Fum	Tot	Net Diff
NY Jets	24	16	40	11	16	27	+ 13
Cincinnati	22	14	36	14	13	27	+ 9
Houston	22	20	42	18	17	35	+ 7
Seattle	22	18	40	20	14	34	+ 6
Indianapolis	15	20	35	22	8	30	+ 5
LA Raiders	17	17	34	20	13	33	+ 1
Buffalo	15	17	32	17	16	33	− 1
Cleveland	20	11	31	17	16	33	− 2
Kansas City	18	13	31	21	12	33	− 2
New England	20	15	35	28	10	38	− 3
Miami	16	15	31	23	12	35	− 4
Denver	16	13	29	22	12	34	− 5
Pittsburgh	20	13	33	20	19	39	− 6
San Diego	16	10	26	20	12	32	− 6

NFC	Takeaways Int	Fum	Tot	Giveaways Int	Fum	Tot	Net Diff
Minnesota	36	17	53	18	12	30	+ 23
Philadelphia	32	12	44	17	9	26	+ 18
San Francisco	22	16	38	14	12	26	+ 12
NY Giants	15	18	33	14	13	27	+ 6
Detroit	15	21	36	18	15	33	+ 3
LA Rams	22	15	37	18	16	34	+ 3
Atlanta	24	14	38	19	18	37	+ 1
Chicago	26	9	35	15	19	34	+ 1
New Orleans	17	15	32	16	16	32	0
Phoenix	16	13	29	19	16	35	− 6
Green Bay	20	21	41	24	26	50	− 9
Tampa Bay	21	12	33	36	16	52	− 19
Dallas	10	9	19	27	13	40	− 21
Washington	14	8	22	25	21	46	− 24

1988 NFL Team Leaders (Continued)

Offense

AFC	Points For	Avg	Rush	Pass	Total	Avg
Cincinnati	448	28.0	2,710	3,347	**6,057**	378.6
Miami	319	19.9	1,205	4,516	**5,721**	357.6
Denver	327	20.4	1,815	3,691	**5,506**	344.1
Buffalo	329	20.6	2,133	3,182	**5,315**	332.2
NY Jets......	372	23.3	2,132	3,083	**5,215**	325.9
Houston	424	26.5	2,249	2,956	**5,205**	325.3
Pittsburgh	336	21.0	2,228	2,976	**5,204**	325.3
Cleveland	304	19.0	1,525	3,436	**5,011**	313.2
LA Raiders ..	325	20.3	1,852	3,109	**4,961**	310.1
Indianapolis ..	354	22.1	2,249	2,621	**4,870**	304.4
Kansas City ..	254	15.9	1,713	3,131	**4,844**	302.8
Seattle.......	339	21.2	2,086	2,756	**4,842**	302.6
San Diego....	231	14.4	2,041	2,388	**4,429**	276.8
New England .	250	15.6	2,120	2,173	**4,293**	268.3

Defense

AFC	Points Opp	Avg	Rush	Pass	Total	Avg
Buffalo	237	14.8	1,854	2,724	**4,578**	286.1
New England .	284	17.8	2,099	2,582	**4,681**	292.6
Cleveland	288	18.0	1,920	2,847	**4,767**	297.9
Houston	365	22.8	1,592	3,266	**4,858**	303.6
Kansas City ..	320	20.0	2,592	2,434	**5,026**	314.1
Cincinnati	329	20.6	2,048	3,134	**5,182**	323.9
Indianapolis ..	315	19.7	1,694	3,602	**5,296**	331.0
LA Raiders ...	369	23.1	2,208	3,171	**5,379**	336.2
San Diego....	332	20.8	2,133	3,285	**5,418**	338.6
Denver	352	22.0	2,538	2,933	**5,471**	341.9
NY Jets......	354	22.1	2,124	3,509	**5,633**	352.1
Seattle.......	329	20.6	2,286	3,353	**5,639**	352.4
Miami	380	23.8	2,506	3,275	**5,781**	361.3
Pittsburgh	421	26.3	1,864	3,941	**5,805**	362.8

NFC	Points For	Avg	Rush	Pass	Total	Avg
San Fran.....	369	23.1	2,523	3,377	**5,900**	368.8
LA Rams	407	25.4	2,003	3,805	**5,808**	363.0
Phoenix......	344	21.5	2,027	3,780	**5,807**	362.9
Washington ..	345	21.6	1,543	4,136	**5,679**	354.9
Minnesota....	406	25.4	1,806	3,789	**5,595**	349.7
Dallas	265	16.6	1,995	3,488	**5,483**	342.7
Philadelphia ..	379	23.7	1,945	3,485	**5,430**	339.4
Chicago	312	19.5	2,319	2,998	**5,317**	332.3
New Orleans .	312	19.5	2,046	3,085	**5,131**	320.7
Tampa Bay ...	261	16.3	1,753	3,308	**5,061**	316.3
NY Giants ...	359	22.4	1,689	3,266	**4,955**	309.7
Green Bay ...	240	15.0	1,379	3,285	**4,664**	291.5
Atlanta	244	15.3	2,016	2,566	**4,582**	286.4
Detroit	220	13.8	1,243	2,162	**3,405**	212.8

NFC	Points Opp	Avg	Rush	Pass	Total	Avg
Minnesota....	233	14.6	1,602	2,489	**4,091**	255.7
Chicago	215	13.4	1,326	3,034	**4,360**	272.5
San Fran.....	294	18.4	1,588	2,987	**4,575**	285.9
Green Bay ...	315	19.7	2,110	2,733	**4,843**	302.7
LA Rams	293	18.3	1,686	3,300	**4,986**	311.6
NY Giants ...	304	19.0	1,759	3,327	**5,086**	317.9
New Orleans .	283	17.7	1,779	3,327	**5,106**	319.1
Tampa Bay ...	350	21.9	1,551	3,604	**5,155**	322.2
Phoenix......	398	24.9	1,925	3,244	**5,169**	323.1
Washington ..	387	24.2	1,745	3,439	**5,184**	324.0
Detroit	313	19.6	2,037	3,279	**5,316**	332.3
Dallas	381	23.8	1,858	3,556	**5,414**	338.4
Atlanta	315	19.7	2,319	3,373	**5,692**	355.8
Philadelphia ..	319	19.9	1,652	4,147	**5,799**	362.4

1988 NFL Award Winners

The NFL does not sanction any postseason Player or Coach of the Year awards, but many are given out. Among the presenters are AP, UPI, *The Sporting News* and the Professional Football Writers of America. MVP awards are also given out by the Maxwell Club of Philadelphia (Bert Bell Trophy) and the NFL Players Association (Jim Thorpe Trophy).

NFL Players of the Year   **Selectors**
Boomer Esiason, Cincinnati, QB ..... AP,PFWA,TSN
Randall Cunningham, Phila, QB ..... Maxwell Club
Roger Craig, San Francisco, RB .... NFLPA

Offensive Players of the Year
NFL   Roger Craig, San Francisco, RB .... AP
AFC   Boomer Esiason, Cincinnati, QB .... UPI
NFC   Roger Craig, San Francisco, RB .... UPI

Defensive Players of the Year
NFL   Mike Singletary, Chicago, LB .... AP
AFC   Bruce Smith, Buffalo, DE .... UPI
          Cornelius Bennett, Buffalo, LB .... UPI
NFC   Mike Singletary, Chicago, LB .... UPI

Rookies of the Year
NFL   John Stephens, New England, RB .. PFWA
              Keith Jackson, Philadelphia, TE ..... TSN
Offense   John Stephens, New England, RB .... AP
Defense   Erik McMillan, NY Jets, S .... AP

Coaches of the Year
NFL   Mike Ditka, Chicago .... AP
          Marv Levy, Buffalo .... TSN
AFC   Marv Levy, Buffalo .... UPI
          Sam Wyche, Cincinnati .... PFWA
NFC   Mike Ditka, Chicago .... PFWA,UPI

1988 NFL All-Pro Team

The 1988 NFL All-Pro Team, combining the selections of AP and the Professional Football Writers of America (AP did not choose kick and punt return specialists in 1988). Holdovers from the 1987 All-Pro Team are in **bold type**. (R) denotes rookies.

Offense

Pos		Selectors
WR	**Jerry Rice**, San Francisco	AP, PFWA
WR	Henry Ellard, LA Rams	AP, PFWA
TE	Keith Jackson, Philadelphia (R)	AP, PFWA
T	**Anthony Munoz**, Cincinnati	AP, PFWA
T	**Gary Zimmerman**, Minnesota	AP, PFWA
G	Bruce Matthews, Houston	AP, PFWA
G	Tom Newberry, LA Rams	AP, PFWA
C	Jay Hilgenberg, Chicago	AP, PFWA
QB	Boomer Esiason, Cincinnati	AP, PFWA
RB	**Eric Dickerson**, Indianapolis	AP, PFWA
RB	Roger Craig, San Francisco	AP, PFWA

Defense

Pos		Selectors
DE	**Reggie White**, Philadelphia	AP,PFWA
DE	**Bruce Smith**, Buffalo	AP,PFWA
DT	Keith Millard, Minnesota	AP,PFWA
NT	Tim Krumrie, Cincinnati	AP,PFWA
OLB	Cornelius Bennett, Buffalo	AP,PFWA
OLB	Lawrence Taylor, NY Giants	AP,PFWA
ILB	**Mike Singletary**, Chicago	AP,PFWA
ILB	Shane Conlan, Buffalo	PFWA
CB	Carl Lee, Minnesota	AP,PFWA
CB	**Frank Minnifield**, Cleveland	AP,PFWA
S	Deron Cherry, Kansas City	AP,PFWA
S	**Joey Browner**, Minnesota	AP,PFWA

Specialists

Pos		Selectors
K	Scott Norwood, Buffalo	AP,PFWA
P	Mike Horan, Denver	AP,PFWA-tie
P	Jim Arnold, Detroit	PFWA-tie
KR	Tim Brown, LA Raiders (R)	PFWA
PR	John Taylor, San Francisco	PFWA

1989 NFL College Draft
First Round Picks

First round picks at the 59th annual NFL Draft held April 23, 1989 in New York City.

	Team	Player Selected
1	Dallas	Troy Aikman, UCLA, QB
2	Green Bay	Tony Mandarich, Mich.St., T
3	Detroit	Barry Sanders, Oklahoma St., RB
4	Kansas City	Derrick Thomas, Alabama, LB
5	Atlanta	Deion Sanders, Florida St., DB
6	Tampa Bay	Broderick Thomas, Nebraska, LB
7	Pittsburgh	Tim Worley, Georgia, RB
8	San Diego	Burt Grossman, Pittsburgh, DE
9	Miami	Sammie Smith, Florida St., RB
10	Phoenix	Eric Hill, LSU, LB
11	Chicago*	Donnell Woolford, Clemson, DB
12	Chicago*	Trace Armstrong, Florida, DE
13	Cleveland*	Eric Metcalf, Texas, RB
14	N.Y.Jets	Jeff Lageman, Virginia, LB
15	Seattle*	Andy Heck, Notre Dame, T
16	New England	Hart Lee Dykes, Okla.St., WR
17	Phoenix*	Joe Wolf, Boston College, G
18	N.Y.Giants	Brian Williams, Minnesota, G
19	New Orleans	Wayne Martin, Arkansas, DE
20	Denver*	Steve Atwater, Arkansas, DB
21	L.A.Rams	Bill Hawkins, Miami,FL, DE
22	Indianapolis*	Andre Rison, Michigan St., WR
23	Houston	David Williams, Florida, T
24	Pittsburgh*	Tom Ricketts, Pittsburgh, T
25	Miami*	Louis Oliver, Florida, DB
26	L.A.Rams*	Cleveland Gary, Miami,FL, RB
27	Atlanta*	Shawn Collins, No.Arizona, WR
28	San Francisco	Keith DeLong, Tennessee, LB

*Note: the following No.1 picks were traded away—11 by the L.A.Raiders; #12 by Washington; #13 by Denver; #15 by Indianapolis; #17 by Seattle; #20 by Cleveland; #22 by Philadelphia; #24 by Minnesota; #25 by Chicago #26 by Buffalo; #27 by Cincinnati.

Canadian Football League

Final 1988 Standings

Eastern Division	W	L	T	Pct	Pts	PF	PA
Toronto Argonauts	14	4	0	.778	28	571	326
Winnipeg Blue Bombers	9	9	0	.500	18	407	458
Hamilton Tiger-Cats	9	9	0	.500	18	478	465
Ottawa Rough Riders	2	16	0	.111	4	278	618

Western Division	W	L	T	Pct	Pts	PF	PA
Edmonton Eskimos	11	7	0	.611	22	477	408
Saskatch. Roughriders	11	7	0	.611	22	525	452
Brit. Columbia Lions	10	8	0	.556	20	489	417
Calgary Stampeders	6	12	0	.333	12	395	476

CFL Playoffs

Eastern Semifinal: WINNIPEG 35, Hamilton 28
Western Semifinal: BC Lions 42, SASKATCHEWAN 18

Eastern Final: Winnipeg 27, TORONTO 11
Western Final: BC Lions 37, EDMONTON 19

Grey Cup Championship
Nov. 27, 1988
at Lansdowne Park, Ottawa

Winnipeg (11-9)	4	10	5	3–22
BC Lions (12-8)	7	8	4	2–21

CFL Award Winners
Regular Season

Player of the Year .. David Williams, BC Lions, WR
Canadian Player .. Ray Elgaard, Saskatch., SB
Defensive Player .... Grover Covington, Hamil., DE
Offensive Lineman .. Roger Aldag, Saskatch., G
Rookie of the Year .. Orville Lee, Ottawa, RB
Coach of the Year .. Mike Riley, Winnipeg

Grey Cup

Offensive Player .... James Murphy, Winn., WR
Defensive Player .... Mike Gray, Winnipeg, DT
Canadian Player ... Bob Cameron, Winnipeg, P

The Super Bowl

The first AFL-NFL World Championship Game, as it was originally called, was played seven months after the two leagues agreed to merge in June of 1966. It became the Super Bowl (complete with roman numerals) by the third game in 1969. The Super Bowl winner has been presented the Vince Lombardi Trophy since 1971. Lombardi, whose Green Bay teams won the first two title games, died in 1970.

NFL champions (1966-69) and NFC champions (since 1970) are listed in capital LETTERS.

Season	Bowl	Date	Winner	Head Coach	Score	Loser	Head Coach	Site
1966	I	1/15/67	GREEN BAY	Vince Lombardi	35-10	Kansas City	Hank Stram	Los Angeles
1967	II	1/14/68	GREEN BAY	Vince Lombardi	33-14	Oakland	John Rauch	Miami
1968	III	1/12/69	NY Jets	Weeb Ewbank	16- 7	BALTIMORE	Don Shula	Miami
1969	IV	1/11/70	Kansas City	Hank Stram	23- 7	MINNESOTA	Bud Grant	New Orleans
1970	V	1/17/71	Baltimore	Don McCafferty	16-13	DALLAS	Tom Landry	Miami
1971	VI	1/16/72	DALLAS	Tom Landry	24- 3	Miami	Don Shula	New Orleans
1972	VII	1/14/73	Miami	Don Shula	14- 7	WASH.	George Allen	Los Angeles
1973	VIII	1/13/74	Miami	Don Shula	24- 7	MINNESOTA	Bud Grant	Houston
1974	IX	1/12/75	Pittsburgh	Chuck Noll	16- 6	MINNESOTA	Bud Grant	New Orleans
1975	X	1/18/76	Pittsburgh	Chuck Noll	21-17	DALLAS	Tom Landry	Miami
1976	XI	1/9/77	Oakland	John Madden	32-14	MINNESOTA	Bud Grant	Pasadena
1977	XII	1/15/78	DALLAS	Tom Landry	27-10	Denver	Red Miller	New Orleans
1978	XIII	1/21/79	Pittsburgh	Chuck Noll	35-31	DALLAS	Tom Landry	Miami
1979	XIV	1/20/80	Pittsburgh	Chuck Noll	31-19	LA RAMS	Ray Malavasi	Pasadena
1980	XV	1/25/81	Oakland	Tom Flores	27-10	PHILA.	Dick Vermeil	New Orleans
1981	XVI	1/24/82	SAN FRAN.	Bill Walsh	26-21	Cincinnati	Forrest Gregg	Pontiac, MI
1982	XVII	1/30/83	WASHINGTON	Joe Gibbs	27-17	Miami	Don Shula	Pasadena
1983	XVIII	1/22/84	LA Raiders	Tom Flores	38- 9	WASH.	Joe Gibbs	Tampa
1984	XIX	1/20/85	SAN FRAN.	Bill Walsh	38-16	Miami	Don Shula	Stanford
1985	XX	1/26/86	CHICAGO	Mike Ditka	46-10	New England	Raymond Berry	New Orleans
1986	XXI	1/25/87	NY GIANTS	Bill Parcells	39-20	Denver	Dan Reeves	Pasadena
1987	XXII	1/31/88	WASHINGTON	Joe Gibbs	42-10	Denver	Dan Reeves	San Diego
1988	XXIII	1/22/89	SAN FRAN.	Bill Walsh	20-16	Cincinnati	Sam Wyche	Miami

Super Bowl MVPs

Season	Bowl	Most Valuable Player
1966	I	QB Bart Starr, Green Bay
1967	II	QB Bart Starr, Green Bay
1968	III	QB Joe Namath, NY Jets
1969	IV	QB Len Dawson, Kansas City
1970	V	LB Chuck Howley, Dallas
1971	VI	QB Roger Staubach, Dallas
1972	VII	Safety Jake Scott, Miami
1973	VIII	RB Larry Csonka, Miami
1974	IX	RB Franco Harris, Pitts.
1975	X	WR Lynn Swann, Pitts.
1976	XI	WR Fred Biletnikoff, Oakl.
1977	XII	DE Harvey Martin, Dallas
		DT Randy White, Dallas
1978	XIII	QB Terry Bradshaw, Pitts.
1979	XIV	QB Terry Bradshaw, Pitts.
1980	XV	QB Jim Plunkett, Oakland
1981	XVI	QB Joe Montana, San Fran.
1982	XVII	RB John Riggins, Washington
1983	XVIII	RB Marcus Allen, LA Raiders
1984	XIX	QB Joe Montana, San Fran.
1985	XX	DE Richard Dent, Chicago
1986	XXI	QB Phil Simms, NY Giants
1987	XXII	QB Doug Williams, Wash.
1988	XXIII	WR Jerry Rice, San Fran.

Super Bowl Appearances

Through Super Bowl XXIII (1989), 10 NFL teams have yet to play for the Vince Lombardi Trophy. In alphabetical order: Atlanta, Buffalo, Cleveland, Detroit, Houston, New Orleans, Phoenix, San Diego, Seattle and Tampa Bay. Of the 18 teams that have made it, Dallas and Miami have the most appearances (5) and Pittsburgh has the most Lombardi Trophies (4).

	App	W	L	Pct	PF	PA
Dallas Cowboys	5	2	3	.400	112	85
Miami Dolphins	5	2	3	.400	74	103
Pittsburgh Steelers	4	4	0	1.000	103	73
Oakland/LA Raiders	4	3	1	.750	111	66
Washington Redskins	4	2	2	.500	85	79
Minnesota Vikings	4	0	4	.000	34	95
San Francisco 49ers	3	3	0	1.000	84	53
Denver Broncos	3	0	3	.000	40	108
Green Bay Packers	2	2	0	1.000	68	24
Baltimore Colts	2	1	1	.500	23	29
Kansas City Chiefs	2	1	1	.500	33	42
Cincinnati Bengals	2	0	2	.000	37	46
Chicago Bears	1	1	0	1.000	46	10
New York Giants	1	1	0	1.000	39	20
New York Jets	1	1	0	1.000	16	7
Los Angeles Rams	1	0	1	.000	19	31
New England Patriots	1	0	1	.000	10	46
Philadelphia Eagles	1	0	1	.000	10	27

Super Bowl Playoffs, 1966–88

The Super Bowl created pro football's first guaranteed multiple-game playoff format. Only four teams qualified for the playoffs in 1966, but by the time the 10 AFL teams joined the NFL in 1970, the field had doubled. Since 1978, 10 teams (out of 28) have made the postseason cut.

In the strike year of 1982, when the regular season was shortened to just nine games, playoff berths were extended to 16 teams and a 15-game tournament was played.

Throughout the following year-by-year playoff summary, home teams are noted in capital LETTERS and records of Super Bowl finalists include all games leading up to the Super Bowl.

1966 Season

NFL Playoffs

NFL Championship: Green Bay 34, DALLAS 27

AFL Playoffs

AFL Championship: Kansas City 31, BUFFALO 7

Super Bowl I
Memorial Coliseum, Los Angeles

Kansas City (12-2-1)	0	10	0	0-**10**
Green Bay (13-2)	7	7	14	7-**35**

MVP: Green Bay QB Bart Starr
(16 for 23, 250 yds, 2 TD, 1 Int)

1967 Season

NFL Playoffs

Eastern Conference: DALLAS 52, Cleveland 14
Western Conference: GREEN BAY 28, LA Rams 7
NFL Championship: GREEN BAY 21, Dallas 17

AFL Playoffs

AFL Championship: OAKLAND 40, Houston 7

Super Bowl II
Orange Bowl, Miami

Green Bay (11-4-1)	3	13	10	7-**33**
Oakland (14-1)	0	7	0	7-**14**

MVP: Green Bay QB Bart Starr
(13 for 24, 202 yds, 1 TD)

1968 Season

NFL Playoffs

Eastern Conference: CLEVELAND 31, Dallas 20
Western Conference: BALTIMORE 24, Minnesota 14
NFL Championship: Baltimore 34, CLEVELAND 0

AFL Playoffs

Western Division Tiebreaker: OAKLAND 41, Kan.City 6
AFL Championship: NY JETS 27, Oakland 23

Super Bowl III
Orange Bowl, Miami

NY Jets (12-3)	0	7	6	3-**16**
Baltimore (15-1)	0	0	0	7- **7**

MVP: NY Jets QB Joe Namath
(17 for 28, 206 yds)

1969 Season

NFL Playoffs

Eastern Conference: Cleveland 38, DALLAS 14
Western Conference: MINNESOTA 23, LA Rams 20
NFL Championship: MINNESOTA 27, Cleveland 7

AFL Playoffs

Divisional: Kansas City 13, NY JETS 6
OAKLAND 56, Houston 7
AFL Championship: Kansas City 17, OAKLAND 7

Super Bowl IV
Tulane Stadium, New Orleans

Minnesota (14-2)	0	0	7	0- **7**
Kansas City (13-3)	3	13	7	0-**23**

MVP: Kansas City QB Len Dawson
(12 for 17, 142 yds, 1 TD, 1 Int)

1970 Season

AFC Playoffs
(*denotes Wild Card qualifier)
Divisional: BALTIMORE 17, Cincinnati 0
OAKLAND 21, *Miami 14
AFC Championship: BALTIMORE 27, Oakland 17

NFC Playoffs
(*denotes Wild Card qualifier)
Divisional: DALLAS 5, *Detroit 0
San Francisco 17, MINNESOTA 14
NFC Championship: Dallas 17, SAN FRANCISCO 10

Super Bowl V
Orange Bowl, Miami

Baltimore (13-2-1)	0	6	0	10-**16**
Dallas (12-4)	3	10	0	0-**13**

MVP: Dallas LB Chuck Howley
(2 Interceptions for 22 yds)

1971 Season

AFC Playoffs
(*denotes Wild Card qualifier)
Divisional: Miami 27, KANSAS CITY 24 (OT)
*Baltimore 20, CLEVELAND 3
AFC Championship: MIAMI 21, Baltimore 0

NFC Playoffs
(*denotes Wild Card qualifier)
Divisional: Dallas 20, MINNESOTA 12
SAN FRANCISCO 24, *Washington 20
NFC Championship: DALLAS 14, San Francisco 3

Super Bowl VI
Tulane Stadium, New Orleans

Dallas (13-3-1)	3	7	7	7-**24**
Miami (12-3-1)	0	3	0	0- **3**

MVP: Dallas QB Roger Staubach
(12 for 19, 119 yds, 2 TD)

1972 Season

AFC Playoffs
(*denotes Wild Card qualifier)
Divisional: PITTSBURGH 13, Oakland 7
MIAMI 20, *Cleveland 14
AFC Championship: Miami 21, PITTSBURGH 17

NFC Playoffs
(*denotes Wild Card qualifier)
Divisional: *Dallas 30, SAN FRANCISCO 28
WASHINGTON 16, Green Bay 3
NFC Championship: WASHINGTON 26, Dallas 3

Super Bowl VII
Memorial Coliseum, Los Angeles

Miami (16-0) 7   7   0   0-**14**
Washington (13-3) 0   0   0   7- **7**
MVP: Miami safety Jake Scott
(2 Interceptions for 63 yds)

1973 Season

AFC Playoffs
(*denotes Wild Card qualifier)
Divisional: OAKLAND 33, *Pittsburgh 14
MIAMI 34, Cincinnati 16
AFC Championship: MIAMI 27, Oakland 10

NFC Playoffs
(*denotes Wild Card qualifier)
Divisional: MINNESOTA 27, *Washington 20
DALLAS 27, LA Rams 16
NFC Championship: Minnesota 27, DALLAS 10

Super Bowl VIII
Rice Stadium, Houston

Minnesota (14-2) 0   0   0   7- **7**
Miami (12-4) 14   3   7   0-**24**
MVP: Miami FB Larry Csonka
(33 carries, 145 yds, 2 TD)

1974 Season

AFC Playoffs
(*denotes Wild Card qualifier)
Divisional: OAKLAND 28, Miami 26
PITTSBURGH 32, *Buffalo 14
AFC Championship: Pittsburgh 24, OAKLAND 13

NFC Playoffs
(*denotes Wild Card qualifier)
Divisional: MINNESOTA 30, St.Louis 14
LA RAMS 19, *Washington 10
NFC Championship: MINNESOTA 14, LA Rams 10

Super Bowl IX
Tulane Stadium, New Orleans

Pittsburgh (12-3-1) 0   2   7   7-**16**
Minnesota (12-4) 0   0   0   6- **6**
MVP: Pittsburgh RB Franco Harris
(34 carries, 158 yds, 1 TD)

1975 Season

AFC Playoffs
(*denotes Wild Card qualifier)
Divisional: PITTSBURGH 28, Baltimore 10
OAKLAND 31, *Cincinnati 28
AFC Championship: PITTSBURGH 16, Oakland 10

NFC Playoffs
(*denotes Wild Card qualifier)
Divisional: LA RAMS 35, St.Louis 23
Dallas 17, MINNESOTA 14
NFC Championship: Dallas 37, LA RAMS 7

Super Bowl X
Orange Bowl, Miami

Dallas (12-4) 7   3   0   7-**17**
Pittsburgh (14-2) 7   0   0   14-**21**
MVP: Pittsburgh WR Lynn Swann
(4 catches, 161 yds, 1 TD)

1976 Season

AFC Playoffs
(*denotes Wild Card qualifier)
Divisional: OAKLAND 24, *New England 21
Pittsburgh 40, BALTIMORE 14
AFC Championship: OAKLAND 24, Pittsburgh 7

NFC Playoffs
(*denotes Wild Card qualifier)
Divisional: MINNESOTA 35, *Washington 20
LA Rams 14, DALLAS 12
NFC Championship: MINNESOTA 24, LA Rams 13

Super Bowl XI
Rose Bowl, Pasadena

Oakland (15-1) 0   16   3   13-**32**
Minnesota (13-2-1) 0   0   7   7-**14**
MVP: Oakland WR Fred Biletnikoff
(4 catches, 79 yds)

1977 Season

AFC Playoffs
(*denotes Wild Card qualifier)
Divisional: DENVER 34, Pittsburgh 21
*Oakland 37, BALTIMORE 31 (OT)
AFC Championship: DENVER 20, Oakland 17

NFC Playoffs
(*denotes Wild Card qualifier)
Divisional: DALLAS 37, *Chicago 7
Minnesota 14, LA RAMS 7
NFC Championship: DALLAS 23, Minnesota 6

Super Bowl XII
Louisiana Superdome, New Orleans

Dallas (14-2) 10   3   7   7-**27**
Denver (14-2) 0   0   10   0-**10**
MVP: Dallas DE Harvey Martin and DT Randy White
(Cowboys' defense forced 8 turnovers)

1978 Season

AFC Playoffs

Wild Cards: Houston 17, MIAMI 9
Divisional: Houston 31, NEW ENGLAND 14
PITTSBURGH 33, Denver 10
AFC Championship: PITTSBURGH 34, Houston 5

NFC Playoffs

Wild Cards: ATLANTA 14, Philadelphia 13
Divisional: DALLAS 27, Atlanta 20
LA RAMS 34, Minnesota 10
NFC Championship: Dallas 28, LA RAMS 0

Super Bowl XIII
Orange Bowl, Miami

Pittsburgh (16-2) 7 14   0 14-**35**
Dallas (14-4) 7   7   3 14-**31**
MVP: Pittsburgh QB Terry Bradshaw
(17 for 30, 318 yds, 4 TD, 1 Int)

1979 Season

AFC Playoffs

Wild Cards: HOUSTON 13, Denver 7
Divisional: Houston 17, SAN DIEGO 14
PITTSBURGH 34, Miami 14
AFC Championship: PITTSBURGH 27, Houston 13

NFC Playoffs

Wild Cards: PHILADELPHIA 27, Chicago 17
Divisional: TAMPA BAY 24, Philadelphia 17
LA Rams 21, DALLAS 19
NFC Championship: LA Rams 9, TAMPA BAY 0

Super Bowl XIV
Rose Bowl, Pasadena

LA Rams (11-7) 7   6   6   0-**19**
Pittsburgh (14-4) 3   7   7 14-**31**
MVP: Pittsburgh QB Terry Bradshaw
(14 for 21, 309 yds, 2 TD, 3 Int)

1980 Season

AFC Playoffs

Wild Cards: OAKLAND 27, Houston 7
Divisional: SAN DIEGO 20, Buffalo 14
Oakland 14, CLEVELAND 12
AFC Championship: Oakland 34, SAN DIEGO 27

NFC Playoffs

Wild Cards: DALLAS 34, LA Rams 13
Divisional: PHILADELPHIA 31, Minnesota 16
Dallas 30, ATLANTA 27
NFC Championship: PHILADELPHIA 20, Dallas 7

Super Bowl XV
Superdome, New Orleans

Oakland (14-5) 14   0 10   3-**27**
Philadelphia (14-4) 0   3   0   7-**10**
MVP: Oakland QB Jim Plunkett
(13 for 21, 261 yds, 3 TD)

1981 Season

AFC Playoffs

Wild Cards: Buffalo 31, NY JETS 27
Divisional: San Diego 41, MIAMI 38 (OT)
CINCINNATI 28, Buffalo 21
AFC Championship: CINCINNATI 27, San Diego 7

NFC Playoffs

Wild Cards: NY Giants 27, PHILADELPHIA 21
Divisional: DALLAS 38, Tampa Bay 0
FRANCISCO 38, NY Giants 24
NFC Championship: SAN FRANCISCO 28, Dallas 27

Super Bowl XVI
Pontiac Silverdome, Pontiac,MI

San Francisco (15-3) 7 13   0   6-**26**
Cincinnati (14-4) 0   0   7 14-**21**
MVP: San Francisco QB Joe Montana
(14 for 22, 157 yds, 1 TD;
6 carries, 18 yds, 1 TD)

1982 Season

A 57-day players' strike shortened the regular season from 16 games to nine. The playoff format was changed to a 16-team tournament open to the top eight teams in each conference.

AFC Playoffs

1st Round: LA RAIDERS 27, Cleveland 10
MIAMI 28, New England 3
NY Jets 44, CINCINNATI 17
San Diego 31, PITTSBURGH 28
2nd Round: NY Jets 17, LA RAIDERS 14
MIAMI 34, San Diego 13
AFC Championship: MIAMI 14, NY Jets 0

NFC Playoffs

1st Round: WASHINGTON 31, Detroit 7
DALLAS 30, Tampa Bay 17
GREEN BAY 41, St.Louis 16
MINNESOTA 30, Atlanta 24
2nd Round: WASHINGTON 21, Minnesota 7
DALLAS 37, Green Bay 26
NFC Championship: WASHINGTON 31, Dallas 17

Super Bowl XVII
Rose Bowl, Pasadena

Miami (10-2) 7 10   0   0-**17**
Washington (11-1) 0 10   3 14-**27**
MVP: Washington RB John Riggins
(38 carries, 166 yds, 1 TD; 1 catch, 15 yds)

1983 Season

AFC Playoffs

Wild Cards: SEATTLE 31, Denver 7
Divisional: Seattle 27, MIAMI 20
LA RAIDERS 38, Pittsburgh 10
AFC Championship: LA RAIDERS 30, Seattle 14

NFC Playoffs

Wild Cards: LA Rams 24, DALLAS 17
Divisional: SAN FRANCISCO 24, Detroit 23
WASHINGTON 51, LA Rams 7
NFC Championship: WASHINGTON 24,
San Francisco 21

Super Bowl XVIII
Tampa Stadium, Tampa

Washington (16-2) 0	3	6	0-	**9**
LA Raiders (14-4) 7	14	14	3-	**38**

MVP: LA Raiders RB Marcus Allen
(20 carries, 191 yds, 2 TD; 2 catches, 18 yds)

1984 Season

AFC Playoffs

Wild Cards: SEATTLE 13, LA Raiders 7
Divisional: MIAMI 31, Seattle 10
Pittsburgh 24, DENVER 17
AFC Championship: MIAMI 45, Pittsburgh 28

NFC Playoffs

Wild Cards: NY Giants 16, LA RAMS 13
Divisional: SAN FRANCISCO 21, NY Giants 10
Chicago 23, WASHINGTON 19
NFC Championship: SAN FRANCISCO 23, Chicago 0

Super Bowl XIX
Stanford Stadium, Stanford,CA

Miami (16-2) 10	6	0	0-	**16**
San Francisco (17-1) 7	21	10	0-	**38**

MVP: San Francisco QB Joe Montana
(24 for 35, 331 yds, 2 TD;
5 carries, 59 yards, 1 TD)

1985 Season

AFC Playoffs

Wild Cards: New England 26, NY JETS 14
Divisional: MIAMI 24, Cleveland 21
New England 27, LA RAIDERS 20
AFC Championship: New England 31, MIAMI 14

NFC Playoffs

Wild Cards: NY GIANTS 17, San Francisco 3
Divisional: LA RAMS 20, Dallas 0
CHICAGO 21, NY Giants 0
NFC Championship: CHICAGO 24, LA Rams 0

Super Bowl XX
Louisiana Superdome, New Orleans

Chicago Bears (17-1) 13	10	21	2-	**46**
New England (14-5) 3	0	0	7-	**10**

MVP: Chicago DE Richard Dent
(Bears defense: 7 sacks, 6 turnovers, 1 safety
and gave up just 123 total yards)

1986 Season

AFC Playoffs

Wild Cards: NY JETS 35, Kansas City 15
Divisional: CLEVELAND 23, NY Jets 20 (OT)
DENVER 22, New England 17
AFC Championship: Denver 23, CLEVELAND 20 (OT)

NFC Playoffs

Wild Cards: WASHINGTON 19, LA Rams 7
Divisional: Washington 27, CHICAGO 13
NY GIANTS 49, San Francisco 3
NFC Championship: NY GIANTS 17, Washington 0

Super Bowl XXI
Rose Bowl, Pasadena

Denver (13-5) 10	0	0	10-	**20**
NY Giants (16-2) 7	2	17	13-	**39**

MVP: NY Giants QB Phil Simms
(22 for 25, 268 yds, 3 TD; 3 carries, 25 yds)

1987 Season

A 24-day players' strike shortened the regular season
from 16 games to 15 with replacement teams playing
for three weeks. The playoffs proceeded as usual.

AFC Playoffs

Wild Cards: HOUSTON 23, Seattle 20 (OT)
Divisional: CLEVELAND 38, Indianapolis 21
DENVER 34, Houston 10
AFC Championship: DENVER 38, Cleveland 33

NFC Playoffs

Wild Cards: Minnesota 44, NEW ORLEANS 10
Divisional: Minnesota 36, SAN FRANCISCO 24
Washington 21, CHICAGO 17
NFC Championship: WASHINGTON 17, Minnesota 10

Super Bowl XXII
San Diego Jack Murphy Stadium

Washington (13-4) 0	35	0	7-	**42**
Denver (12-4-1) 10	0	0	0-	**10**

MVP: Washington QB Doug Williams
(18 for 29, 340 yds, 4 TD, 1 Int)

1988 Season

AFC Playoffs

Wild Cards: Houston 24, CLEVELAND 23
Divisional: BUFFALO 17, Houston 10
CINCINNATI 21, Seattle 13
AFC Championship: CINCINNATI 21, Buffalo 10

NFC Playoffs

Wild Cards: MINNESOTA 28, LA Rams 17
Divisional: SAN FRANCISCO 34, Minnesota 9
CHICAGO 20, Philadelphia 12
NFC Championship: San Francisco 28, CHICAGO 3

Super Bowl XXIII
Joe Robbie Stadium, Miami

Cincinnati (17-1) 0	3	10	3-	**16**
San Francisco (14-5) 3	0	3	14-	**20**

MVP: San Francisco WR Jerry Rice
(11 catches, 215 yds, 1 TD;
1 carry, 5 yds)

Before the Super Bowl

Time did not begin with the Super Bowl, it only seems that way. The first NFL champion was the Akron Pros in 1920, when the title went to the team with the best regular season record.

The first playoff game with the championship at stake came in 1932, followed by 33 championship games in the NFL and six in the AFL before Super Bowl I.

Finally, the NFL staged a consolation game between its conference runners-up from the 1960 season through 1969. Called the Bert Bell Benefit Bowl (after the late league commissioner) and referred to as the Playoff Bowl, it gave the winner of the game the bragging rights to third place in the NFL. All 10 Playoff Bowls were played in Miami.

Home teams in championship games are noted in capital LETTERS.

NFL Champions, 1920-31

Year	Champion	Head Coach, Pos.
1920	Akron (8-0-3)	Fritz Pollard, HB & Elgie Tobin, QB
1921	Chicago Staleys (9-1-1) (Renamed Bears in 1922)	George Halas, E
1922	Canton Bulldogs (10-0-2)	Guy Chamberlin, E
1923	Canton Bulldogs (11-0-1)	Guy Chamberlin, E
1924	Cleve.Bulldogs (7-1-1)	Guy Chamberlin, E
1925	Chi.Cardinals (11-2-1)	Norm Barry
1926	Frankford, PA (14-1-1)	Guy Chamberlin, E
1927	NY Giants (11-1-1)	Earl Potteiger, QB
1928	Providence, RI (8-2-1)	Jimmy Conzelman, HB
1929	Green Bay (12-0-1)	Curly Lambeau, QB
1930	Green Bay (10-3-1)	Curly Lambeau
1931	Green Bay (12-2)	Curly Lambeau

NFL Championship Game, 1932-65

Season	Tied for 1st place after regular season		Championship Game	Date	Winning Coach
1932	Portsmouth,OH (6-1-4) & Chicago Bears (6-1-6)		CHICAGO BEARS, 9-0	12/18/32	Ralph Jones

	Eastern Champion	**Western Champion**	**Championship Game**	**Date**	**Winning Coach**
1933	NY Giants (11-3)	Chicago Bears (10-2-1)	CHICAGO BEARS, 23-21	12/17/33	George Halas
1934	NY Giants (8-5)	Chicago Bears (13-0)	NY GIANTS, 30-13	12/9/34	Steve Owen
1935	NY Giants (9-3)	Detroit (7-3-2)	DETROIT, 26-7,	12/15/35	Potsy Clark
1936	Boston Redskins (7-5)	Green Bay (10-1-1)	Green Bay, 21-6 (Game played in New York)	12/13/36	Curly Lambeau
1937	Wash.Redskins (8-3)	Chicago Bears (9-1-1)	Washington, 28-21	12/12/37	Ray Flaherty
1938	NY Giants (8-2-1)	Green Bay (8-3)	NY GIANTS, 23-17	12/11/38	Steve Owen
1939	NY Giants (9-1-1)	Green Bay (9-2)	GREEN BAY, 27-0	12/10/39	Curly Lambeau
1940	Washington (9-2)	Chicago Bears (8-3)	Chicago Bears, 73-0	12/8/40	George Halas
1941	NY Giants (8-3)	Chicago Bears (11-1)*	CHICAGO BEARS, 37-9	12/21/41	George Halas
1942	Washington (10-1)	Chicago Bears (11-0)	WASHINGTON, 14-6	12/13/42	Ray Flaherty
1943	Washington (7-3-1)*	Chicago Bears (8-1-1)	CHICAGO BEARS, 41-21	12/26/43	Hunk Anderson & Luke Johnsos
1944	NY Giants (8-1-1)	Green Bay (8-2)	Green Bay, 14-7	12/17/44	Curly Lambeau
1945	Washington (8-2)	Cleveland Rams (9-1)	CLEVE.RAMS, 15-14	12/16/45	Adam Walsh
1946	NY Giants (7-3-1)	Chicago Bears (8-2-1)	Chicago Bears, 24-14	12/15/46	George Halas
1947	Philadelphia (9-4)*	Chicago Cards (9-3)	CHICAGO CARDS, 28-21	12/28/47	Jimmy Conzelman
1948	Philadelphia (9-2-1)	Chicago Cards (11-1)	PHILADELPHIA, 7-0	12/19/48	Greasy Neale
1949	Philadelphia (11-1)	LA Rams (8-2-2)	Philadelphia, 14-0	12/18/49	Greasy Neale

	American Conference	**National Conference**	**Championship Game**	**Date**	**Winning Coach**
1950	Cleveland (11-2)*	LA Rams (10-3)*	CLEVELAND, 30-28	12/24/50	Paul Brown
1951	Cleveland (11-1)	LA Rams (8-4)	LA RAMS, 24-17	12/23/51	Joe Stydahar
1952	Cleveland (8-4)	Detroit (10-3)*	Detroit, 17-7	12/28/52	Buddy Parke

	Eastern Conference	**Western Conference**	**Championship Game**	**Date**	**Winning Coach**
1953	Cleveland (11-1)	Detroit (10-2)	DETROIT, 17-16	12/27/53	Buddy Parker
1954	Cleveland (9-3)	Detroit (9-2-1)	CLEVELAND, 56-10	12/26/54	Paul Brown
1955	Cleveland (9-2-1)	LA Rams (8-3-1)	CLEVELAND, 38-14	12/26/55	Paul Brown
1956	NY Giants (8-3-1)	Chicago Bears (9-2-1)	NY GIANTS, 47-7	12/30/56	Jim Lee Howell
1957	Cleveland (9-2-1)	Detroit (9-4)*	DETROIT, 59-14	12/29/57	George Wilson
1958	NY Giants (10-3)*	Baltimore (9-3)	Baltimore, 23-17 (OT)	12/28/58	Weeb Ewbank
1959	NY Giants (10-2)	Baltimore (9-3)	BALTIMORE, 31-16	12/27/59	Weeb Ewbank
1960	Philadelphia (10-2)	Green Bay (8-4)	PHILADELPHIA, 17-13	12/26/60	Buck Shaw
1961	NY Giants (10-3-1)	Green Bay (11-3)	GREEN BAY, 37-0	12/31/61	Vince Lombardi
1962	NY Giants (12-2)	Green Bay (13-1)	Green Bay, 16-7	12/30/62	Vince Lombardi
1963	NY Giants (11-3)	Chicago Bears (11-1-2)	CHICAGO, 14-10	12/29/63	George Halas
1964	Cleveland (10-3-1)	Baltimore (12-2)	CLEVELAND, 27-0	12/27/64	Blanton Collier
1965	Cleveland (11-3)	Green Bay (11-3-1)*	GREEN BAY, 23-12	1/2/66	Vince Lombardi

Since 1965: see Super Bowl Playoffs.

*Divisional playoffs: 1941—Chi.Bears 33, Green Bay 14; 1943—Washington 28, NY Giants 0; 1947—Phila. 21, Pittsburgh 0; 1949—Cleveland 8, NY Giants 3 and LA Rams 24, Chicago Bears 14; 1952—Detroit 31, LA Rams 21; 1957—Detroit 31, San Fran. 27; 1958—NY Giants 10, Cleveland 0; 1965—Green Bay 13, Baltimore 10 (OT).

AFL Championship Game, 1960-65

Season	Eastern Conference	Western Conference	Championship Game	Date	Winning Coach
1960	Houston (10-4)	LA Chargers (10-4)	HOUSTON, 24-16	1/1/61	Lou Rymkus
1961	Houston (10-3-1)	SD Chargers (12-2)	Houston, 10-3	12/24/61	Wally Lemm
1962	Houston (11-3)	Dallas Texans (11-3)	Dallas, 20-17 (2 OT)	12/23/62	Hank Stram
1963	Boston (7-6-1)*	SD Chargers (11-3)	SD CHARGERS, 51-10	1/5/64	Sid Gillman
1964	Buffalo (12-2)	SD Chargers (8-5-1)	BUFFALO, 20-7	12/26/64	Lou Saban
1965	Buffalo (10-3-1)	SD Chargers (9-2-3)	Buffalo, 23-0	12/26/65	Lou Saban

Since 1965: see Super Bowl Playoffs.

*Divisional playoffs: 1963—Boston 26, Buffalo 8.

NFL Playoff Bowl, 1961-70

Season	Eastern Runner-up	Western Runner-up	Consolation Game	Date	Winning Coach
1960	Cleveland (8-3-1)	Detroit (7-5)	Detroit, 17-16	1/7/61	George Wilson
1961	Philadelphia (10-4)	Detroit (8-5-1)	Detroit, 38-10	1/6/62	George Wilson
1962	Pittsburgh (9-5)	Detroit (11-3)	Detroit, 17-10	1/6/63	George Wilson
1963	Cleveland (10-4)	Green Bay (11-2-1)	Green Bay, 40-23	1/5/64	Vince Lombardi
1964	St.Louis (9-3-2)	Green Bay (8-5-1)	St.Louis, 24-17	1/3/65	Wally Lemm
1965	Dallas (7-7)	Baltimore (10-4-1)*	Baltimore, 35-3	1/9/66	Don Shula
1966	Philadelphia (9-5)	Baltimore (9-5)	Baltimore, 20-14	1/8/67	Don Shula
1967	Cleveland (9-6)**	LA Rams (11-2-2)**	LA Rams, 30-6	1/7/68	George Allen
1968	Dallas (12-3)**	Minnesota (8-7)**	Dallas, 17-13	1/5/69	Tom Landry
1969	Dallas (11-3-1)**	LA Rams (11-4)**	LA Rams, 31-0	1/3/70	George Allen

Discontinued after 1969 season.

*Qualified by losing divisional playoff game for first place.
**Qualified by losing Conference championship game.

Champions Of Leagues That Didn't Make It

No professional league in American sports has had to contend with more pretenders to the throne than the NFL. Seven times in as many decades a rival league has risen up to challenge the NFL and six of them went under in less than five seasons. Only the fourth American Football League (1960-69) succeeded, forcing the older league to sue for peace and a full partnership in 1966.

Of the six leagues that didn't make it, only the All-America Football Conference (1946-49) lives on—the Cleveland Browns and San Francisco 49ers joined the NFL after the AAFC folded in 1949.

The champions of leagues past are listed below. Home teams in championship games are noted in capital LETTERS.

American Football League I

Year	Champion	Head Coach
1926	Philadelphia Quakers	Bob Folwell

American Football League II

Year	Champion	Head Coach
1936	Boston Shamrocks	George Kenneally
1937	Los Angeles Bulldogs	Gus Henderson

American Football League III

Year	Champion	Head Coach
1940	Columbus Bullies	Phil Bucklew
1941	Columbus Bullies	Phil Bucklew

All-America Football Conference

Year	Champion	Head Coach
1946	CLEVELAND 14, NY Yankees 9	Paul Brown
1947	Cleve.Browns 14, NY YANKEES 3	Paul Brown
1948	CLEVELAND 49, Buffalo 7	Paul Brown
1949	CLEVELAND 21, S.F.49ers 7	Paul Brown

World Football League

Year	Champion	Head Coach
1974	BIRMINGHAM 22, Florida 21	Jack Gotta
1975	Folded mid-season	--

United States Football League

Year	Championship Game	Head Coach
1983	Michigan 24, Phila.Stars 22	Jim Stanley
1984	Phila.Stars 23. Arizona 3	Jim Mora
1985	Balt.Stars 28, Oakland 24	Jim Mora

USFL Championship Game sites: Denver (1983), Tampa (1984), East Rutherford, N.J. (1985).

NFL Franchise Origins

Here is what the current 28 teams in the National Football League have to show for the years they have put in as members of the American Professional Football Association (APFA), the NFL, the All-America Football Conference (AAFC) and the American Football League (AFL). League and Super Bowl titles are noted by season.

American Football Conference

	First Season	League Titles	Franchise Stops
Buffalo Bills	1960 (AFL)	2 AFL (1964-65)	Buffalo (1960-72) Orchard Park, NY (1973-)
Cincinnati Bengals	1968 (AFL)	None	Cincinnati (1968-)
Cleveland Browns	1946 (AAFC)	4 AAFC (1946-49) 4 NFL (1950,54-55,64)	Cleveland (1946-)
Denver Broncos	1960 (AFL)	None	Denver (1960-)
Houston Oilers	1960 (AFL)	2 AFL (1960-61)	Houston (1960-)
Indianapolis Colts	1953 (NFL)	3 NFL (1958-59,68) 1 Super Bowl (1970)	Baltimore (1953-83) Indianapolis (1984-)
Kansas City Chiefs	1960 (AFL)	3 AFL (1962,66,69) 1 Super Bowl (1969)	Dallas (1960-62) Kansas City (1963-)
Los Angeles Raiders	1960 (AFL)	1 AFL (1967) 3 Super Bowls (1976,80,83)	Oakland (1960-81) Los Angeles (1982-)
Miami Dolphins	1966 (AFL)	2 Super Bowls (1972-73)	Miami (1966-)
New England Patriots	1960 (AFL)	None	Boston (1960-70) Foxboro, MA (1971-)
New York Jets	1960 (AFL)	1 AFL (1968) 1 Super Bowl (1968)	New York (1960-83) E.Rutherford, NJ (1984-)
Pittsburgh Steelers	1933 (NFL)	4 Super Bowls (1974-75, 78-79)	Pittsburgh (1933-)
San Diego Chargers	1960 (AFL)	1 AFL (1963)	Los Angeles (1960) San Diego (1961-)
Seattle Seahawks	1976 (NFL)	None	Seattle (1976-)

National Football Conference

	First Season	League Titles	Franchise Stops
Atlanta Falcons	1966 (NFL)	None	Atlanta (1966-)
Chicago Bears	1920 (APFA)	7 NFL (1932-33,40-41,43,46,63) 1 Super Bowl (1985)	Decatur,IL (1920) Chicago (1921-)
Dallas Cowboys	1960 (NFL)	2 Super Bowls (1971,77)	Dallas (1960-70) Irving,TX (1971-)
Detroit Lions	1930 (NFL)	4 NFL (1935,52-53,57)	Portsmouth,OH (1930-33) Detroit (1934-74) Pontiac,MI (1975-)
Green Bay Packers	1921 (APFA)	8 NFL (1936,39,44,61-62,65-67) 2 Super Bowls (1966-67)	Green Bay (1921-)
Los Angeles Rams	1937 (NFL)	2 NFL (1945,51)	Cleveland (1937-45) Los Angeles (1946-79) Anaheim (1980-)
Minnesota Vikings	1961 (NFL)	1 NFL (1969)	Bloomington, MN (1961-81) Minneapolis,MN (1982-)
New Orleans Saints	1967 (NFL)	None	New Orleans (1967-)
New York Giants	1925 (NFL)	3 NFL (1934,38,56) 1 Super Bowl (1986)	New York (1925-73,75) New Haven,CT (1973-74) E.Rutherford,NJ (1976-)
Philadelphia Eagles	1933 (NFL)	3 NFL (1948-49,60)	Philadelphia (1933-)
Phoenix Cardinals	1920 (APFA)	1 NFL (1947)	Chicago (1920-59) St.Louis (1960-87) Phoenix (1988-)
San Francisco 49ers	1946 (AAFC)	3 Super Bowls (1981,84,88)	San Francisco (1946-)
Tampa Bay Buccaneers	1976 (NFL)	None	Tampa,FL (1976-)
Washington Redskins	1932 (NFL)	2 NFL (1937,42) 2 Super Bowls (1982,87)	Boston (1932-36) Washington,DC (1937-)

NFL Head Coaches

All-Time Winning Percentages

Records through 1988 season, including playoffs. Active coaches in **bold type**.

		Yrs	W	L	T	Pct	Playoff W-L
1	Vince Lombardi	10	106	36	6	.736	10-2
2	John Madden	10	112	39	7	.731	9-7
3	**Don Shula**	26	279	124	6	.689	18-13
4	George Allen	12	120	54	5	.684	4-7
5	George Halas	40	325	151	31	.672	6-3
6	Curly Lambeau	33	229	134	22	.623	3-2
7	Bill Walsh	10	102	64	1	.614	10-4
8	Paul Brown	21	170	109	6	.607	4-9
	Chuck Knox	16	155	100	1	.607	7-11
10	Bud Grant	18	168	109	5	.605	10-13
11	Tom Landry	29	271	180	6	.600	21-18
12	Steve Owen	23	153	108	17	.581	2-8
	Buddy Parker	15	107	76	9	.581	3-1
	Chuck Noll	20	183	132	1	.581	15-7
15	Hank Stram	17	136	100	10	.573	5-3
16	Don Coryell	14	114	89	1	.561	3-6
17	Sid Gillman	18	123	104	7	.541	1-5
18	Weeb Ewbank	20	134	130	7	.507	4-1

Note #1—The following coaches had the following records in the often-forgotten Playoff Bowl: Lombardi (1-1), Shula (2-0), Allen (2-0), Brown (0-1), Grant (0-1) and Landry (1-2). The Playoff Bowl was contested by NFL conference runners-up from the 1960 season through 1969.

Note #2—The NFL does not recognize records from the All-American Football Conference (1946-49). If it did, Brown (52-4-3 in four AAFC seasons) would rank 6th (between Halas and Lambeau) with the following stats: 25 Yrs; 222 Wins; 113 Losses; 9 Ties; .658 Pct; and a 9-9 playoff record.

Where They Coached

Lombardi—Green Bay (1959-67), Washington (1969); **Madden**—Oakland (1969-78); **Shula**—Baltimore (1963-69), Miami (1970--); **Allen**—Los Angeles (1966-70), Washington (1971-77); **Halas**—Chicago Bears (1920-29, 1933-42, 1946-55, 1958-67).

Lambeau—Green Bay (1921-49), Chicago Cardinals (1950-51), Washington (1952-53); **Walsh**—San Francisco (1979-88); **Brown**—Cleveland (1950-62), Cincinnati (1968-75); **Grant**—Minnesota (1967-83, 1985); **Knox**—L.A.Rams (1973-77), Buffalo (1978-82), Seattle (1983--).

Landry—Dallas (1960-88); **Noll**—Pittsburgh (1969--); **Owen**—N.Y.Giants (1931-53); **Parker**—Chicago Cardinals (1949), Detroit (1951-56), Pittsburgh (1957-64); **Stram**—Dallas-Kansas City (1960-74), New Orleans (1976-77).

Coryell—St.Louis (1973-77), San Diego (1978-86). **Gillman**—L.A.Rams (1955-59), L.A.-San Diego Chargers (1960-69), Houston (1973-74); **Ewbank**—Baltimore (1954-62); N.Y.Jets (1963-73).

All-Time Wins

Coaches with at least 100 wins through 1988 season, including playoffs. Active coaches in **bold type**.

	Wins		Wins
George Halas	325	Hank Stram	136
Don Shula	279	Weeb Ewbank	134
Tom Landry	271	Sid Gillman	123
Curly Lambeau	229	George Allen	120
Chuck Noll	183	Don Coryell	114
Paul Brown	170	John Madden	112
Bud Grant	168	Buddy Parker	107
Steve Owen	153	Vince Lombardi	106
Chuck Knox	155	Bill Walsh	102

Active Head Coaches

Most Wins

Records through 1988 season, including playoffs.

	Yrs	W	L	T	Pct
Don Shula, Miami	26	**279**	124	6	.689
Chuck Noll, Pittsburgh	20	**183**	132	1	.581
Chuck Knox, Seattle	16	**155**	100	1	.607
Joe Gibbs, Washington	8	**92**	42	0	.687
Mike Ditka, Chicago	7	**78**	35	0	.690
Dan Reeves, Denver	8	**78**	49	1	.613
John Robinson, LA Rams	6	**58**	44	0	.569
Bill Parcells, NY Giants	6	**57**	44	1	.564
Marv Levy, Buffalo	8	**53**	60	0	.469
Joe Walton, NY Jets	6	**50**	47	1	.515
Raymond Berry, New Eng	5	**46**	30	0	.605
Marty Schottenheimer, KC	5	**46**	31	0	.597
Sam Wyche, Cincinnati	5	**43**	39	0	.524
Ron Meyer, Indianapolis	6	**39**	30	0	.565
Ray Perkins, Tampa Bay	6	**33**	57	0	.367
Jerry Burns, Minnesota	3	**31**	21	0	.596
Marion Campbell, Atlanta	8	**31**	71	1	.306
Jim Mora, New Orleans	3	**29**	19	0	.604
Jerry Glanville, Houston	4	**26**	27	0	.491
Buddy Ryan, Philadelphia	3	**22**	25	1	.469
Dan Henning, San Diego	4	**22**	41	1	.352
Gene Stallings, Phoenix	3	**18**	28	1	.394
Mike Shanahan, Raiders	1	**7**	9	0	.438
Lindy Infante, Green Bay	1	**4**	12	0	.250
Wayne Fontes, Detroit	1	**2**	3	0	.400
Bud Carson, Cleveland	0	**0**	0	0	.000
Jimmy Johnson, Dallas	0	**0**	0	0	.000
George Seifert, San Fran	0	**0**	0	0	.000

Coaching Awards

NFL-NFC Coach of the Year

Presented by UPI to the top coach in the NFL (1955-69) and NFC (since 1970). Records indicate how much coach's team improved over one season.

Year	Coach, Team	Improvement
1955	Joe Kuharich, Washington	3-9 to 8-4
1956	Buddy Parker, Detroit	3-9 to 9-3
1957	Paul Brown, Cleveland	5-7 to 9-2-1
1958	Weeb Ewbank, Baltimore	7-5 to 9-3
1959	Vince Lombardi, Green Bay	1-10-1 to 7-5
1960	Buck Shaw, Philadelphia	7-5 to 10-2
1961	Allie Sherman, NY Giants	6-4-2 to 10-3-1
1962	Allie Sherman, NY Giants	10-3-1 to 12-2

Year	Coach, Team	Improvement
1963	George Halas, Chicago	9-5 to 11-1-2
1964	Don Shula, Baltimore	8-6 to 12-2
1965	George Halas, Chicago	5-9 to 9-5
1966	Tom Landry, Dallas	7-7 to 10-3-1
1967	George Allen, LA Rams	8-6 to 11-1-2
1968	Don Shula, Baltimore	11-1-2 to 13-1
1969	Bud Grant, Minnesota	8-6 to 12-2
1970	Alex Webster, NY Giants	6-8 to 9-5

NFL-NFC Coach of the Year (Continued)

Year	Coach, Team	Improvement	Year	Coach, Team	Improvement
1971	George Allen, Washington	6-8 to 9-4-1	1980	Leeman Bennett, Atlanta	6-10 to 12-4
1972	Dan Devine, Green Bay	4-8-2 to 10-4	1981	Bill Walsh, San Francisco	6-10 to 13-3
1973	Chuck Knox, LA Rams	6-7-1 to 12-2	1982	Joe Gibbs, Washington	8-8 to 8-1
1974	Don Coryell, St.Louis	4-9-1 to 10-4	1983	John Robinson, LA Rams	2-7 to 9-7
1975	Tom Landry, Dallas	8-6 to 10-4	1984	Bill Walsh, San Francisco	10-6 to 15-1
1976	Jack Pardee, Chicago	4-10 to 7-7	1985	Mike Ditka, Chicago	10-6 to 15-1
1977	Leeman Bennett, Atlanta	4-10 to 7-7	1986	Bill Parcells, NY Giants	10-6 to 14-2
1978	Dick Vermeil, Philadelphia	5-9 to 9-7	1987	Jim Mora, New Orleans	7-9 to 12-3
1979	Jack Pardee, Washington	8-8 to 10-6	1988	Mike Ditka, Chicago	11-4 to 12-4

AFL-AFC Coach of the Year

Presented by UPI to the top coach in the AFL (1960-69) and AFC (since 1970). Records indicate how much coach's team improved over one season.

Year	Coach, Team	Improvement	Year	Coach, Team	Improvement
1960	Lou Rymkus, Houston	10-4	1975	Ted Marchibroda, Baltimore	2-12 to 10-4
1961	Wally Lemm, Houston	10-4 to 10-3-1	1976	Chuck Fairbanks, New England	3-11 to 11-3
1962	Jack Faulkner, Denver	3-11 to 7-7	1977	Red Miller, Denver	9-5 to 12-2
1963	Al Davis, Oakland	1-13 to 10-4	1978	Walt Michaels, NY Jets	3-11 to 8-8
1964	Lou Saban, Buffalo	7-6-1 to 12-2	1979	Sam Rutigliano, Cleveland	8-8 to 9-7
1965	Lou Saban, Buffalo	12-2 to 10-3-1	1980	Sam Rutigliano, Cleveland	9-7 to 11-5
1966	Mike Holovak, Boston	4-8-2 to 8-4-2	1981	Forrest Gregg, Cincinnati	6-10 to 12-4
1967	John Rauch, Oakland	8-5-1 to 13-1	1982	Tom Flores, LA Raiders	7-9 to 8-1
1968	Hank Stram, Kansas City	9-5 to 12-2	1983	Chuck Knox, Seattle	4-5 to 9-7
1969	Paul Brown, Cincinnati	3-11 to 4-9-1	1984	Chuck Knox, Seattle	9-7 to 12-4
1970	Don Shula, Miami	3-10-1 to 10-4	1985	Raymond Berry, New England	9-7 to 11-5
1971	Don Shula, Miami	10-4 to 10-3-1	1986	Marty Schottenheimer, Cleve	8-8 to 12-4
1972	Chuck Noll, Pittsburgh	6-8 to 11-3	1987	Ron Meyer, Indianapolis	3-13 to 9-6
1973	John Ralston, Denver	5-9 to 7-5-2	1988	Marv Levy, Buffalo	7-8 to 12-4
1974	Sid Gillman, Houston	1-13 to 7-7			

Player Awards
NFL Player of the Year

Unlike the other major pro team sports, the NFL no longer sanctions a Most Valuable Player award. The league gave out the Joe F.Carr Trophy (Carr was NFL president from 1921-39) for nine years but discontinued it in 1947. Since then, four principal MVP awards have been given out: UPI (1953-69), The Maxwell Club of Philadelphia's Bert Bell Trophy (since 1959), AP (since 1974) and the Professional Football Writers Association (since 1976). UPI switched to AFC and NFC Player of the Year awards in 1970.

Year	Player, Team	Awards	Year	Player, Team	Awards
1938	Mel Hein, NY Giants, C	Carr	1967	Johnny Unitas, Baltimore, QB	UPI-Bell
1939	Parker Hall, Cleveland Rams, HB	Carr	1968	Earl Morrall, Baltimore, QB	UPI
1940	Ace Parker, Brooklyn, HB	Carr		Leroy Kelly, Cleveland, RB	Bell
1941	Don Hutson, Green Bay, E	Carr	1969	Roman Gabriel, LA Rams, QB	UPI-Bell
1942	Don Hutson, Green Bay, E	Carr	1970	George Blanda, Oakland, QB-PK	Bell
1943	Sid Luckman, Chicago Bears, QB	Carr	1971	Roger Staubach, Dallas, QB	Bell
1944	Frank Sinkwich, Detroit, HB	Carr	1972	Larry Brown, Washington, RB	Bell
1945	Bob Waterfield, Cleveland Rams, QB	Carr	1973	O.J.Simpson, Buffalo, RB	Bell
1946	Bill Dudley, Pittsburgh, HB	Carr	1974	Ken Stabler, Oakland, QB	AP
1947-52	No MVP chosen			Merlin Olsen, LA Rams, DT	Bell
1953	Otto Graham, Cleveland, QB	UPI	1975	Fran Tarkenton, Minnesota, QB	Bell-AP
1954	Joe Perry, San Francisco, FB	UPI	1976	Bert Jones, Baltimore, QB	AP-PFWA
1955	Otto Graham, Cleveland, QB	UPI		Ken Stabler, Oakland, QB	Bell
1956	Frank Gifford, NY Giants, HB	UPI	1977	Walter Payton, Chicago, RB	AP-PFWA
1957	Y.A.Tittle, San Francisco, QB	UPI		Bob Griese, Miami, QB	Bell
1958	Jim Brown, Cleveland, FB	UPI	1978	Terry Bradshaw, Pittsburgh, QB	Bell-AP
1959	Johnny Unitas, Baltimore, QB	UPI-Bell		Earl Campbell, Houston, RB	PFWA
1960	Norm Van Brocklin, Phila, QB	UPI-Bell	1979	Earl Campbell, Houston, RB	Bell-AP-PFWA
1961	Paul Hornung, Green Bay, HB	UPI-Bell	1980	Brian Sipe, Cleveland, QB	AP-PFWA
1962	Andy Robustelli, NY Giants, DE	Bell		Ron Jaworski, Philadelphia, QB	Bell
	Y.A.Tittle, NY Giants, QB	UPI	1981	Ken Anderson, Cinn, QB	Bell-AP-PFWA
1963	Jim Brown, Cleveland, FB	UPI-Bell	1982	Dan Fouts, San Diego, QB	PFWA
1964	Johnny Unitas, Baltimore, QB	UPI-Bell		Mark Moseley, Washington, PK	AP
1965	Jim Brown, Cleveland, FB	UPI		Joe Theismann, Washington, QB	Bell
	Pete Retzlaff, Philadelphia, TE	Bell	1983	Joe Theismann, Washington, QB	AP-PFWA
1966	Bart Starr, Green Bay, QB	UPI		John Riggins, Washington, RB	Bell
	Don Meredith, Dallas, QB	Bell	1984	Dan Marino, Miami, QB	Bell-AP-PFWA

NFL Player of the Year (Continued)

Year	Player, Team	Awards	Year	Player, Team	Awards
1985	Marcus Allen, LA Raiders, RB	AP-PFWA	1987	Jerry Rice, San Francisco, WR	Bell-PFWA
	Walter Payton, Chicago, RB	Bell		John Elway, Denver, QB	AP
1986	Lawrence Taylor, NY Giants, LB	Bell-AP-PFWA	1988	Boomer Esiason, Cinn, QB	AP-PFWA
				Randall Cunningham, Phila, QB	Bell

NFC Player of the Year

Given out by UPI since 1970. Offensive and defensive players have been honored since 1983. Rookie winners are noted in **bold type**.

Year	Player, Team	Position
1970	John Brodie, San Francisco	Quarterback
1971	Alan Page, Minnesota	Defensive Tackle
1972	Larry Brown, Washington	Running Back
1973	John Hadl, LA Rams	Quarterback
1974	Jim Hart, St.Louis	Quarterback
1975	Fran Tarkenton, Minnesota	Quarterback
1976	Chuck Foreman, Minnesota	Running Back
1977	Walter Payton, Chicago	Running Back
1978	Archie Manning, New Orleans	Quarterback
1979	**Ottis Anderson,** St.Louis	Running Back
1980	Ron Jaworski, Philadelphia	Quarterback
1981	Tony Dorsett, Dallas	Running Back

Year	Player, Team	Position
1982	Mark Moseley, Washington	Place Kicker
1983	**Off—Eric Dickerson,** LA Rams	Running Back
	Def—Lionel Taylor, NY Giants	Linebacker
1984	Off—Eric Dickerson, LA Rams	Running Back
	Def—Mike Singletary, Chicago	Linebacker
1985	Off—Walter Payton, Chicago	Running Back
	Def—Mike Singletary, Chicago	Linebacker
1986	Off—Eric Dickerson, LA Rams	Running Back
	Def—Lionel Taylor, NY Giants	Linebacker
1987	Off—Jerry Rice, San Fran	Wide Receiver
	Def—Reggie White, Phila	Defensive End
1988	Off—Roger Craig, San Fran	Running Back
	Def—Mike Singletary, Chicago	Linebacker

AFL-AFC Player of the Year

Presented by UPI to the top player in the AFL (1960-69) and AFC (since 1970). Offensive and defensive players have been honored since 1983. Rookie winners are noted in **bold type**.

Year	Player, Team	Position
1960	**Abner Haynes,** Dallas Texans	Halfback
1961	George Blanda, Houston	Quarterback
1962	Cookie Gilchrist, Buffalo	Fullback
1963	Lance Alworth, San Diego	Flanker
1964	Gino Cappelletti, Boston	Flanker-Kicker
1965	Paul Lowe, San Diego	Halfback
1966	Jim Nance, Boston	Fullback
1967	Daryl Lamonica, Oakland	Quarterback
1968	Joe Namath, NY Jets	Quarterback
1969	Daryl Lamonica, Oakland	Quarterback
1970	George Blanda, Oakland	Quarterback-Kicker
1971	Otis Taylor, Kansas City	Wide Receiver
1972	O.J.Simpson, Buffalo	Running Back
1973	O.J.Simpson, Buffalo	Running Back
1974	Ken Stabler, Oakland	Quarterback
1975	O.J.Simpson, Buffalo	Running Back
1976	Bert Jones, Baltimore	Quarterback
1977	Craig Morton, Denver	Quarterback

Year	Player, Team	Position
1978	**Earl Campbell,** Houston	Running Back
1979	Dan Fouts, San Diego	Quarterback
1980	Brian Sipe, Cleveland	Quarterback
1981	Ken Anderson, Cincinnati	Quarterback
1982	Dan Fouts, San Diego	Quarterback
1983	**Off—Curt Warner,** Seattle	Running Back
	Def—Rod Martin, LA Raiders	Linebacker
1984	Off—Dan Marino, Miami	Quarterback
	Def—Mark Gastineau, NY Jets	Defensive End
1985	Off—Marcus Allen, LA Raiders	Running Back
	Def—Andre Tippett, New Eng	Linebacker
1986	Off—Curt Warner, Seattle	Running Back
	Def—Rulon Jones, Denver	Defensive End
1987	Off—John Elway, Denver	Quarterback
	Def—Bruce Smith, Buffalo	Defensive End
1988	Off—Boomer Esiason, Cinn	Quarterback
	Def—Bruce Smith, Buffalo	Defensive End
	& Cornelius Bennett, Buff	Linebacker

NFL-NFC Rookie of the Year

Presented by UPI to the top rookie in the NFL (1955-69) and NFC (since 1970).

Year	Rookie, Team	Position
1955	Alan Ameche, Baltimore	Fullback
1956	Lenny Moore, Baltimore	Halfback
1957	Jim Brown, Cleveland	Fullback
1958	Jimmy Orr, Baltimore	Flanker
1959	Boyd Dowler, Green Bay	Flanker
1960	Gail Cogdill, Detroit	Flanker
1961	Mike Ditka, Chicago Bears	Tight End
1962	Ronnie Bull, Chicago Bears	Fullback
1963	Paul Flatley, Minnesota	Flanker
1964	Charley Taylor, Washington	Halfback
1965	Gale Sayers, Chicago	Halfback
1966	Johnny Roland, St.Louis	Halfback
1967	Mel Farr, Detroit	Running Back

Year	Rookie, Team	Position
1968	Earl McCullough, Detroit	Flanker
1969	Calvin Hill, Dallas	Running Back
1970	Bruce Taylor, San Francisco	Defensive Back
1971	John Brockington, Green Bay	Running Back
1972	Chester Marcol, Green Bay	Place Kicker
1973	Charle Young, Philadelphia	Tight End
1974	John Hicks, NY Giants	Guard
1975	Mike Thomas, Washington	Running Back
1976	Sammy White, Minnesota	Wide Receiver
1977	Tony Dorsett, Dallas	Running Back
1978	Bubba Baker, Detroit	Defensive End
1979	Ottis Anderson, St.Louis	Running Back
1980	Billy Sims, Detroit	Running Back

NFL-NFC Rookie of the Year (Continued)

Year	Rookie, Team	Position	Year	Rookie, Team	Position
1981	George Rogers, New Orleans	Running Back	1985	Jerry Rice, San Francisco	Wide Receiver
1982	Jim McMahon, Chicago	Quarterback	1986	Reuben Mayes, New Orleans	Running Back
1983	Eric Dickerson, LA Rams	Running Back	1987	Robert Awalt, St.Louis	Tight End
1984	Paul McFadden, Philadelphia	Place Kicker	1988	Keith Jackson, Philadelphia	Tight End

AFL-AFC Rookie of the Year

Presented by UPI to the top rookie in the AFL (1960-69) and AFC (since 1970).

Year	Rookie, Team	Position	Year	Rookie, Team	Position
1960	Abner Haynes, Dallas Texans	Halfback	1975	Robert Brazile, Houston	Linebacker
1961	Earl Faison, San Diego	Defensive End	1976	Mike Haynes, New England	Defensive Back
1962	Curtis McClinton, Dallas Texans	Fullback	1977	A.J.Duhe, Miami	Defensive End
1963	Billy Joe, Denver	Fullback	1978	Earl Campbell, Houston	Running Back
1964	Matt Snell, NY Jets	Fullback	1979	Jerry Butler, Buffalo	Wide Receiver
1965	Joe Namath, NY Jets	Quarterback	1980	Joe Cribbs, Buffalo	Running Back
1966	Bobby Burnett, Buffalo	Halfback	1981	Joe Delaney, Kansas City	Running Back
1967	George Webster, Houston	Linebacker	1982	Marcus Allen, LA Raiders	Running Back
1968	Paul Robinson, Cincinnati	Running Back	1983	Curt Warner, Seattle	Running Back
1969	Greg Cook, Cincinnati	Quarterback	1984	Louis Lipps, Pittsburgh	Wide Receiver
1970	Dennis Shaw, Buffalo	Quarterback	1985	Kevin Mack, Cleveland	Running Back
1971	Jim Plunkett, New England	Quarterback	1986	Leslie O'Neal, San Diego	Defensive End
1972	Franco Harris, Pittsburgh	Running Back	1987	Shane Conlan, Buffalo	Linebacker
1973	Boobie Clark, Cincinnati	Running Back	1988	John Stephens, New England	Running Back
1974	Don Woods, San Diego	Running Back			

Number One Draft Choices, 1936-89

In an effort to blunt the dominance of the Chicago Bears and New York Giants in the 1930s and distribute talent more evenly throughout the league, the NFL established the college draft in 1936.

The first player chosen in the first draft was Jay Berwanger, the first Heisman Trophy winner as college football's outstanding player. In all, 16 Heisman winners have also been a No.1 draft choice. They are noted in **bold type.**

The American Football League (formed in 1960) held its own draft from 1961-66 before agreeing to merge with the NFL.

Year	Team	Player	Year	Team	Player
1936	Philadelphia	**Jay Berwanger,** HB, Chicago	1963	NFL LA Rams	**Terry Baker,** QB, Oregon St.
1937	Philadelphia	Sam Francis, FB, Nebraska		AFL Kan.City	Buck Buchanan, DT, Grambling
1938	Cleve.Rams	Corbett Davis, FB, Indiana	1964	NFL San Fran	Dave Parks, E, Texas Tech
1939	Chi.Cards	Ki Aldrich, C, TCU		AFL Boston	Jack Concannon, QB, B.C.
1940	Chi.Cards	George Cafego, HB, Tennessee	1965	NFL Giants	Tucker Frederickson, HB, Auburn
1941	Chi.Bears	**Tom Harmon,** HB, Michigan		AFL Houston	Lawrence Elkins, E, Baylor
1942	Pittsburgh	Bill Dudley, HB, Virginia	1966	NFL Atlanta	Tommy Nobis, LB, Texas
1943	Detroit	**Frank Sinkwich,** HB, Georgia		AFL Miami	Jim Grabowski, FB, Illinois
1944	Boston Yanks	**Angelo Bertelli,** QB, N.Dame	1967	Baltimore	Bubba Smith, DT, Michigan St.
1945	Chi.Cards	Charley Trippi, HB, Georgia	1968	Minnesota	Ron Yary, T, Southern Cal
1946	Boston Yanks	Frank Dancewicz, QB, N.Dame	1969	Buffalo (AFL)	**O.J.Simpson,** RB, Southern Cal
1947	Chi.Bears	Bob Fenimore, HB, Okla. A&M	1970	Pittsburgh	Terry Bradshaw, QB, La.Tech
1948	Washington	Harry Gilmer, QB, Alabama	1971	N.England	**Jim Plunkett,** QB, Stanford
1949	Philadelphia	Chuck Bednarik, C, Penn	1972	Buffalo	Walt Patulski, DE, Notre Dame
1950	Detroit	**Leon Hart,** E, Notre Dame	1973	Houston	John Matuszak, DE, Tampa
1951	NY Giants	Kyle Rote, HB, SMU	1974	Dallas	Ed "Too Tall" Jones, Tenn.St.
1952	LA Rams	Bill Wade, QB, Vanderbilt	1975	Atlanta	Steve Bartkowski, QB, Calif.
1953	San Fran.	Harry Babcock, E, Georgia	1976	Tampa Bay	Lee Roy Selmon, DE, Oklahoma
1954	Cleveland	Bobby Garrett, QB, Stanford	1977	Tampa Bay	Ricky Bell, RB, Southern Cal
1955	Baltimore	George Shaw, QB, Oregon	1978	Houston	**Earl Campbell,** RB, Texas
1956	Pittsburgh	Gary Glick, DB, Colo. A&M	1979	Buffalo	Tom Cousineau, LB, Ohio St.
1957	Green Bay	**Paul Hornung,** QB, N.Dame	1980	Detroit	**Billy Sims,** RB, Oklahoma
1958	Chi.Cards	King Hill, QB, Rice	1981	New Orleans	**George Rogers,** RB, S.Carolina
1959	Green Bay	Randy Duncan, QB, Iowa	1982	New England	Kenneth Sims, DT, Texas
1960	NFL LA Rams	**Billy Cannon,** HB, LSU	1983	Baltimore	John Elway, QB, Stanford
	AFL No choice———		1984	New England	Irving Fryar, WR, Nebraska
1961	NFL Minn.	Tommy Mason, HB, Tulane	1985	Buffalo	Bruce Smith, DE, Va.Tech
	AFL Buffalo	Ken Rice, G, Auburn	1986	Tampa Bay	**Bo Jackson,** RB, Auburn
1962	NFL Wash.	**Ernie Davis,** HB, Syracuse	1987	Tampa Bay	**Vinny Testaverde,** QB, Miami,FL
	AFL Oakland	Roman Gabriel, QB, N.C.State	1988	Atlanta	Aundray Bruce, LB, Auburn
			1989	Dallas	Troy Aikman, QB, UCLA

NFL All-Time Leaders
Through 1988, active players in **bold type.**

CAREER

Quarterback Ratings

Ratings based on performance standards established for completion percentage, average gain, touchdown percentage, and interception percentage. Quarterbacks are allocated points according to how their statistics measure up to those standards. At least 1,500 attempts.

	Yrs	Att	Cmp	Cmp %	Yards	Avg Gain	TD	TD %	Int	Int %	Rating
Joe Montana	10	3,673	2,322	63.2	27,533	7.50	190	5.2	99	2.7	**92.0**
Dan Marino	6	3,100	1,866	60.2	23,856	7.70	196	6.3	103	3.3	**91.5**
Boomer Esiason	5	1,830	1,038	56.7	14,825	8.10	98	5.4	65	3.6	**86.2**
Dave Krieg	9	2,344	1,358	57.9	17,549	7.49	148	6.3	96	4.1	**85.5**
Ken O'Brien	5	1,990	1,183	59.4	14,243	7.16	84	4.2	50	2.5	**85.0**
Roger Staubach	11	2,958	1,685	57.0	22,700	7.67	153	5.2	109	3.7	**83.4**
Neil Lomax	8	3,153	1,817	57.6	22,771	7.22	136	4.3	90	2.9	**82.7**
Sonny Jurgensen	18	4,262	2,433	57.1	32,224	7.56	255	6.0	189	4.4	**82.6**
Len Dawson	19	3,741	2,136	57.1	28,711	7.67	239	6.4	183	4.9	**82.6**
Ken Anderson	16	4,475	2,654	59.3	32,838	7.34	197	4.4	160	3.6	**81.9**
Danny White	13	2,950	1,761	59.7	21,959	7.44	155	5.3	132	4.5	**81.7**
Bart Starr	16	3,149	1,808	57.4	24,718	7.85	152	4.8	138	4.4	**80.5**
Jim McMahon	7	1,513	874	57.8	11,203	7.40	67	4.4	56	3.7	**80.4**
Fran Tarkenton	18	6,467	3,686	57.0	47,003	7.27	342	5.3	266	4.1	**80.4**
Dan Fouts	15	5,604	3,297	58.8	43,040	7.68	254	4.5	242	4.3	**80.2**

Note: The NFL does not recognize records from the All-American Football Conference (1946-49). If it did, Otto Graham would rank 3rd (between Marino and Esiason) with the following stats: 10 Yrs; 2,626 Att; 1,464 Comp; 55.8 Cmp %; 23,584 Yards; 8.98 Avg Gain; 174 TD; 6.6 TD %; 135 Int; 5.1 Int %; and an 86.6 Rating.

Passing Yardage

	Yrs	Att	Comp	Pct	Yards
Fran Tarkenton	18	6,467	3,686	57.0	**47,003**
Dan Fouts	15	5,604	3,297	58.8	**43,040**
Johnny Unitas	18	5,186	2,830	54.6	**40,239**
Ken Anderson	16	4,475	2,654	59.3	**32,838**
Sonny Jurgensen	18	4,262	2,433	57.1	**32,224**
John Brodie	17	4,491	2,469	55.0	**31,548**
Roman Gabriel	16	4,498	2,366	52.6	**29,444**
Len Dawson	19	3,741	2,136	57.1	**28,711**
Y.A.Tittle	15	3,817	2,118	55.5	**28,339**
Ken Stabler	15	3,793	2,270	59.8	**27,938**
Joe Namath	13	3,762	1,886	50.1	**27,663**
Joe Montana	10	3,673	2,322	63.2	**27,533**
George Blanda	26	4,007	1,911	47.7	**26,920**
Bobby Layne	15	3,700	1,814	49.0	**26,768**
Joe Theismann	12	3,602	2,044	56.7	**25,206**
Bob Griese	14	3,429	1,926	56.2	**25,092**
Bart Starr	16	3,149	1,808	57.4	**24,718**
Dan Marino	6	3,100	1,866	60.2	**23,856**
Norm Van Brocklin	12	2,895	1,553	53.6	**23,611**
Roger Staubach	11	2,958	1,685	57.0	**22,700**

Note: The NFL does not recognize records from the All-American Football Conference (1946-49). If it did, Otto Graham would rank 20th (after Van Brocklin) with the following stats: 10 Yrs; 2,626 Att; 1,464 Comp; 55.8 Pct; and 23,584 Yards.

Touchdown Passes

	Yrs	TD	Int
Fran Tarkenton	18	**342**	266
Johnny Unitas	18	**290**	253
Sonny Jurgensen	18	**255**	189
Dan Fouts	15	**254**	242
Len Dawson	19	**239**	183
George Blanda	26	**236**	277
John Brodie	17	**214**	224
Y.A.Tittle	15	**212**	221
Roman Gabriel	15	**201**	149
Ken Anderson	16	**197**	160
Dan Marino	6	**196**	103
Bobby Layne	15	**196**	243
Ken Stabler	15	**194**	222
Bob Griese	14	**192**	172
Joe Montana	10	**190**	99
Sammy Baugh	16	**187**	203
Norm Van Brocklin	12	**173**	178
Joe Namath	13	**173**	220
Earl Morrall	21	**161**	148
Joe Theismann	12	**160**	138

Note: The NFL does not recognize records from the All-American Football Conference (1946-49). If it did, Otto Graham would rank 17th (after Baugh) with the following stats: 10 Yrs; 174 TD; and 135 Int.

Receiving

	Yrs	No	Yards	Avg	TD		Yrs	No	Yards	Avg	TD
Steve Largent	13	**791**	12,686	16.0	97	Art Monk	9	**576**	7,979	13.9	39
Charlie Joiner	18	**750**	12,146	16.2	65	Lionel Taylor	10	**567**	7,195	12.7	45
Charley Taylor	13	**649**	9,110	14.0	79	**Wes Chandler**	11	**559**	8,966	16.0	56
Don Maynard	15	**633**	11,834	18.7	88	Lance Alworth	11	**542**	10,266	18.9	85
Raymond Berry	13	**631**	9,275	14.7	68	Kellen Winslow	10	**541**	6,741	12.5	45
Ozzie Newsome	11	**610**	7,416	12.2	44	John Stallworth	14	**537**	8,723	16.2	63
James Lofton	11	**599**	11,085	18.5	54	Bobby Mitchell	11	**521**	7,954	15.3	65
Harold Carmichael	14	**590**	8,985	15.2	79	Nat Moore	13	**510**	7,546	14.8	74
Fred Biletnikoff	14	**589**	8,974	15.2	76	Dwight Clark	9	**506**	6,750	13.3	48
Harold Jackson	16	**579**	10,372	17.9	76	**Stanley Morgan**	12	**506**	9,866	19.5	64

Running

Rushing Yardage

	Yrs	Att	Yards	Avg	TD
Walter Payton	13	3,838	**16,726**	4.4	110
Tony Dorsett	12	2,936	**12,739**	4.3	77
Jim Brown	9	2,359	**12,312**	5.2	106
Franco Harris	13	2,949	**12,120**	4.1	91
John Riggins	14	2,916	**11,352**	3.9	104
O.J.Simpson	11	2,404	**11,236**	4.7	61
Eric Dickerson	6	2,136	**9,915**	4.6	75
Earl Campbell	8	2,187	**9,407**	4.3	74
Jim Taylor	10	1,941	**8,597**	4.4	83
Joe Perry	14	1,737	**8,378**	4.8	53
Ottis Anderson	11	1,949	**8,294**	4.3	55
Larry Csonka	11	1,891	**8,081**	4.3	64
Mike Pruitt	11	1,844	**7,378**	4.0	51
Leroy Kelly	10	1,727	**7,274**	4.2	74
George Rogers	7	1,692	**7,176**	4.2	54
Marcus Allen	7	1,712	**6,982**	4.1	61
John Henry Johnson	13	1,571	**6,803**	4.3	48
Freeman McNeil	8	1,525	**6,794**	4.5	28
Wilbert Montgomery	9	1,540	**6,789**	4.4	45
Chuck Muncie	9	1,561	**6,702**	4.3	71

Note: The NFL does not recognize records from the All-American Football Conference (1946-49). If it did, Joe Perry would rank 8th (between Dickerson and Campbell) with the following stats: 16 Yrs; 1,929 Att; 9,723 Yards; 5.0 Avg; and 71 TD.

All-Purpose Running

	Yrs	Rush	Rec	Ret	Total
Walter Payton	13	16,726	4,538	539	**21,803**
Tony Dorsett	12	12,739	3,554	33	**16,326**
Jim Brown	9	12,312	2,499	648	**15,459**
Franco Harris	13	12,120	2,287	215	**14,622**
O.J.Simpson	11	11,236	2,142	990	**14,368**
Bobby Mitchell	11	2,735	7,954	3,389	**14,078**
John Riggins	14	11,352	2,090	-7	**13,435**
Greg Pruitt	12	5,672	3,069	4,521	**13,262**
Ollie Matson	14	5,173	3,285	4,426	**12,884**
Tim Brown	10	3,862	3,399	5,423	**12,684**
Lenny Moore	12	5,174	6,039	1,238	**12,451**
Don Maynard	15	70	11,834	475	**12,379**
Charlie Joyner	18	22	12,146	199	**12,367**
Steve Largent	12	83	12,686	224	**12,993**
Leroy Kelly	10	7,274	2,281	2,775	**12,330**
Floyd Little	9	6,323	2,418	3,432	**12,173**
Abner Haynes	8	4,630	3,535	3,900	**12,065**
Bruce Harper	8	1,829	2,409	7,191	**11,429**
Hugh McElhenny	13	5,281	3,247	2,847	**11,375**
Lance Alworth	11	129	10,266	525	**10,920**

Scoring

Overall Points

Points	Yrs	TD	FG	PAT	Points
George Blanda	26	9	335	943	**2,002**
Jan Stenerud*	19	0	373	580	**1,699**
Jim Turner	16	1	304	521	**1,439**
Mark Moseley	16	0	300	482	**1,382**
Jim Bakken	17	0	282	534	**1,380**
Fred Cox	15	0	282	519	**1,365**
Lou Groza	17	1	234	641	**1,349**
Pat Leahy*	15	0	241	467	**1,190**
Chris Bahr*	13	0	224	461	**1,133**
Gino Cappelletti	11	42	176	350	**1,130‡**
Ray Wersching*	15	0	222	456	**1,122**
Don Cockroft	13	0	216	432	**1,080**
Garo Yepremian*	14	0	210	444	**1,074**
Bruce Gossett*	11	0	219	374	**1,031**
Sam Baker	15	2	179	428	**977**
Rafael Septien*	10	0	180	420	**960**
Lou Michaels	13	1	187	386	**955‡**
Nick Lowery*	10	0	201	304	**907**
Roy Gerela*	11	0	184	351	**903**
Jim Breech*	10	0	172	381	**897**

*Soccer-style kicker
‡Cappelletti's total includes four 2-point conversions, and Michaels' total includes one safety.

Note: The NFL does not recognize records from the All-American Football Conference (1946-49). If it did, Hall of Famer Lou Groza would move up from 7th to 3rd (between Stenerud and Turner) with the following stats: 21 Yrs; 1 TD; 264 FG; 810 PAT; and 1,608 Points.

Touchdowns

Touchdowns	Yrs	Rush	Rec	Ret	Total
Jim Brown	9	106	20	0	**126**
Walter Payton	13	110	15	0	**125**
John Riggins	14	104	12	0	**116**
Lenny Moore	12	63	48	2	**113**
Don Hutson	11	3	99	3	**105**
Franco Harris	13	91	9	0	**100**
Steve Largent	13	1	97	0	**98**
Jim Taylor	10	83	10	0	**93**
Bobby Mitchell	11	18	65	8	**91**
Tony Dorsett	12	77	13	1	**91**
Leroy Kelly	10	74	13	3	**90**
Charley Taylor	13	11	79	0	**90**
Don Maynard	15	0	88	0	**88**
Lance Alworth	11	2	85	0	**87**
Paul Warfield	13	1	85	0	**86**
Tommy McDonald	12	0	84	1	**85**
Pete Johnson	8	76	6	0	**82**
Art Powell	10	0	81	1	**82**
Harold Carmichael	14	0	79	0	**79**
Frank Gifford	12	34	43	1	**78**

Miscellaneous

Interceptions

	Yrs	No	Yards
Paul Krause	16	81	1,185
Emlen Tunnell	14	79	1,282
Dick "Night Train" Lane	14	68	1,207
Ken Riley	15	65	596
Dick LeBeau	13	62	762

Punt Return Average
Minimum 75 returns

	Yrs	No	Yards	Avg	TD
George McAfee	8	112	1,431	**12.8**	2
Jack Christiansen	8	85	1,084	**12.8**	8
Claude Gibson	5	110	1,381	**12.6**	3
Bill Dudley	9	124	1,515	**12.2**	3
Rick Upchurch	9	248	3,008	**12.1**	8
Henry Ellard	5	112	1,355	**12.1**	4

Punting Average
Minimum 300 points

	Yrs	No	Yards	Avg
Sammy Baugh	16	338	15,245	**45.1**
Tommy Davis	11	511	22,833	**44.7**
Rohn Stark	7	514	22,791	**44.3**
Yale Lary	11	503	22,279	**44.3**
Horace Gillom	7	385	16,872	**43.8**

Kickoff Return Average
Minimum 75 returns

	Yrs	No	Yards	Avg	TD
Gale Sayers	7	91	2,781	**30.6**	6
Lynn Chandnois	7	92	2,720	**29.6**	3
Abe Woodson	9	193	5,538	**28.7**	5
Buddy Young	6	90	2,514	**27.9**	2
Travis Williams	5	102	2,801	**27.5**	6

SINGLE SEASON

Scoring

Points

	Year	TD	PAT	FG	Pts
Paul Hornung, Green Bay	1960	15	41	15	**176**
Mark Moseley, Washington	1983	0	62	33	**161**
Gino Cappelletti, Boston	1964	7	38	25	**155**
Gino Cappelletti, Boston	1961	8	48	17	**147**
Paul Hornung, Green Bay	1961	10	41	15	**146**
Jim Turner, NY Jets	1968	0	43	34	**145**
John Riggins, Washington	1983	24	0	0	**144**
Kevin Butler, Chicago	1985	0	51	31	**144**
Tony Franklin, New Eng	1986	0	44	32	**140**
Gary Anderson, Pittsburgh	1985	0	40	33	**139**

Note: The NFL regular season schedule grew from 12 games (1947-60) to 14 (1961-77) to 16 (1978-present). The AFL regular season schedule was always 14 games (1960-69).

Field Goals

	Year	Att	No
Ali Haji-Sheikh, NY Giants*	1983	42	**35**
Jim Turner, NY Jets	1968	46	**34**
Chester Marcol, Green Bay*	1972	48	**33**
Mark Moseley, Washington	1983	47	**33**
Gary Anderson, Pittsburgh*	1985	42	**33**
Jim Turner, NY Jets	1969	47	**32**
Tony Franklin, New England*	1986	41	**32**
Scott Norwood, Buffalo*	1988	37	**32**
Morten Anderson, New Orleans*	1985	35	**31**
Kevin Butler, Chicago*	1985	37	**31**

*Soccer-style kicker

Touchdowns

	Year	Rush	Rec	Ret	Tot
John Riggins, Washington	1983	24	0	0	**24**
O.J.Simpson, Buffalo	1975	16	7	0	**23**
Jerry Rice, San Fran	1987	1	22	0	**23**
Gale Sayers, Chicago	1966	14	6	2	**22**
Chuck Foreman, Minn	1975	13	9	0	**22**
Jim Brown, Cleveland	1965	17	4	0	**21**
Joe Morris, NY Giants	1985	21	0	0	**21**
Lenny Moore, Baltimore	1964	16	3	1	**20**
Leroy Kelly, Cleveland	1968	16	4	0	**20**
Eric Dickerson, LA Rams	1983	18	2	0	**20**

Touchdowns Rushing

	Year	No
John Riggins, Washington	1983	**24**
Joe Morris, NY Giants	1985	**21**
Jim Taylor, Green Bay	1962	**19**
Earl Campbell, Houston	1979	**19**
Chuck Muncie, San Diego	1981	**19**
Eric Dickerson, LA Rams	1983	**18**
George Rogers, Washington	1986	**18**
Jim Brown, Cleveland	1958	**17**
Jim Brown, Cleveland	1965	**17**

Touchdowns Passing

	Year	No
Dan Marino, Miami	1984	**48**
Dan Marino, Miami	1986	**44**
George Blanda, Houston	1961	**36**
Y.A.Tittle, NY Giants	1963	**36**
Y.A.Tittle, NY Giants	1962	**33**
Dan Fouts, San Diego	1981	**33**
Johnny Unitas, Baltimore	1959	**32**
Sonny Jurgensen, Philadelphia	1961	**32**
Lynn Dickey, Green Bay	1983	**32**
Sonny Jurgensen, Washington	1967	**31**
Jim Everett, LA Rams	1988	**31**

Touchdown Catches

	Year	No
Jerry Rice, San Francisco	1987	**22**
Mark Clayton, Miami	1984	**18**
Don Hutson, Green Bay	1942	**17**
Elroy "Crazylegs" Hirsch, LA Rams	1951	**17**
Bill Groman, Houston	1961	**17**
Art Powell, Oakland	1963	**16**
Jerry Rice, San Francisco	1986	**15**

Rushing

Yards Gained

	Year	Att	Yards	Avg
Eric Dickerson, LA Rams	1984	379	**2,105**	5.6
O.J.Simpson, Buffalo	1973	332	**2,003**	6.0
Earl Campbell, Houston	1980	373	**1,934**	5.2
Jim Brown, Cleveland	1963	291	**1,883**	6.4
Walter Payton, Chicago	1977	339	**1,852**	5.5

Yards Gained

	Year	Att	Yards	Avg
Eric Dickerson, LA Rams	1986	404	**1,821**	4.5
O.J.Simpson, Buffalo	1975	329	**1,817**	5.5
Eric Dickerson, LA Rams	1983	390	**1,808**	4.6
Marcus Allen, LA Raiders	1985	390	**1,759**	4.6
Gerald Riggs, Atlanta	1985	397	**1,719**	4.3

Passing

Yards Gained	Year	Att	Cmp	Pct	Yards
Dan Marino, Miami	1984	564	362	64.2	**5,084**
Dan Fouts, San Diego	1981	609	360	59.1	**4,802**
Dan Marino, Miami	1986	623	378	60.7	**4,746**
Dan Fouts, San Diego	1980	589	348	59.1	**4,715**
Neil Lomax, St.Louis	1984	560	345	61.6	**4,614**

Yards Gained	Year	Att	Cmp	Pct	Yards
Lynn Dickey, Green Bay	1983	484	289	59.7	**4,458**
Dan Marino, Miami	1988	606	354	58.4	**4,434**
Bill Kenney, KC	1983	603	346	57.4	**4,348**
Dan Marino, Miami	1985	567	336	59.3	**4,137**
Brian Sipe, Cleveland	1980	554	337	60.8	**4,132**

Receiving

Catches	Year	No	Yards
Art Monk, Washington	1984	**106**	1,372
Charley Hennigan, Houston	1964	**101**	1,546
Lionel Taylor, Denver	1961	**100**	1,176
Todd Christensen, LA Raiders	1986	**95**	1,153
Johnny Morris, Chicago	1964	**93**	1,200
Al Toon, NY Jets	1988	**93**	1,067

Catches	Year	No	Yards
Lionel Taylor, Denver	1960	**92**	1,235
Todd Christensen, LA Raiders	1983	**92**	1,247
Roger Craig, San Francisco	1985	**92**	1,016
Art Monk, Washington	1985	**91**	1,226
J.T.Smith, St.Louis	1987	**91**	1,117

Miscellaneous

Interceptions	Year	No
Dick "Night Train" Lane, Detroit	1952	**14**
Dan Sandifer, Washington	1948	**13**
Spec Sanders, NY Yanks	1950	**13**
Lester Hayes, Oakland	1980	**13**

Punt Return Avg (qualifiers)	Year	Avg
Herb Rich, Baltimore	1950	**23.0**
Jack Christiansen, Detroit	1952	**21.5**
Dick Christy, NY Titans	1961	**21.3**
Bob Hayes, Dallas	1968	**20.8**

Punting Avg (qualifiers)	Year	Avg
Sammy Baugh, Washington	1940	**51.4**
Yale Lary, Detroit	1963	**48.9**
Sammy Baugh, Washington	1941	**48.7**

Kickoff Return Avg (qualifiers)	Year	Avg
Travis Williams, Green Bay	1967	**41.1**
Gale Sayers, Chicago	1967	**37.7**
Ollie Matson, Chicago Cardinals	1958	**35.5**

BEST GAMES

Rushing

Yards Gained	Date	Yds
Walter Payton, Chicago vs Minn	11/20/77	**275**
O.J.Simpson, Buffalo vs Detroit	11/25/76	**273**
O.J.Simpson, Buffalo vs New Eng	9/16/73	**250**
Willie Ellison, LA Rams vs N.Orl	12/5/71	**247**
Cookie Gilchrist, Buffalo vs NY Jets	12/8/63	**243**

Passing

Yards Gained	Date	Yds
Norm Van Brocklin, LA vs NY Yanks	9/28/51	**554**
Dan Marino, Miami vs NY Jets	10/23/88	**521**
Phil Simms, NY Giants vs Cincinnati	10/13/85	**513**
Vince Ferragamo, LA Rams vs Chicago	12/26/82	**509**
Y.A.Tittle, NY Giants vs Washington	10/28/62	**505**

Completions	Date	No
Richard Todd, NY Jets vs San Fran	9/21/80	**42**
Ken Anderson, Cinn vs San Diego	12/20/82	**40**
Phil Simms, NY Giants vs Cincinnati	10/13/85	**40**
Dan Marino, Miami vs Buffalo	11/16/86	**39**

Receiving

Catches	Date	No
Tom Fears, LA Rams vs Green Bay	12/3/50	**18**
Clark Gaines, NY Jets vs San Fran	9/21/80	**17**
Sonny Randle, St.Louis vs NY Giants	11/4/62	**16**
Rickey Young, Minnesota vs New Eng	12/16/79	**15**
William Andrews, Atlanta vs Pitts	11/15/81	**15**
Kellen Winslow, San Diego vs G.Bay	10/7/84	**15**
Steve Largent, Seattle vs Detroit	10/18/87	**15**

Yards Gained	Date	Yds
Stephone Paige, KC vs San Diego	12/22/85	**309**
Jim Benton, Cleveland vs Detroit	11/22/45	**303**
Cloyce Box, Detroit vs Baltimore	12/3/50	**302**
Charley Hennigan, Houston vs Boston	10/13/61	**272**
Del Shofner, NY Giants vs Wash	10/28/62	**269**

Scoring

Points	Date	Pts
Ernie Nevers, Chi.Cards vs Chi.Bears	11/28/29	**40**
Dub Jones, Cleveland vs Chi.Bears	11/25/51	**36**
Gale Sayers, Chi.Bears vs San Fran	12/12/65	**36**
Paul Hornung, Green Bay vs Balt	10/8/61	**33**
Bob Shaw, Chi.Cards vs Baltimore	10/2/50	**30**
Jim Brown, Cleveland vs Baltimore	11/1/59	**30**
Abner Haynes, Dal.Texans vs Oakland	11/26/61	**30**
Billy Cannon, Houston vs NY Titans	12/10/61	**30**
Cookie Gilchrist, Buffalo vs NY Jets	12/8/63	**30**
Kellen Winslow, San Diego vs Oakland	11/22/81	**30**

Note: Nevers celebrated Thanksgiving, 1929, by scoring all the Cardinals' points on six rushing TDs and four PATs. The Cards beat Red Grange and the Bears, 40-6.

Touchdowns Rushing	Date	No
Ernie Nevers, Chi.Cards vs Chi.Bears	11/28/29	**6**
Dub Jones, Cleveland vs Chi.Bears	11/25/51	**6**
Gale Sayers, Chi.Bears vs San Fran	12/12/65	**6**
7 players tied with 5 TDs		

Touchdowns Passing	Date	No
Sid Luckman, Chi.Bears vs NY Giants	11/14/43	**7**
Adrian Burk, Phildelphia vs Wash	10/17/54	**7**
George Blanda, Houston vs NY Titans	11/19/61	**7**
Y.A.Tittle, NY Giants vs Washington	10/28/62	**7**
Joe Kapp, Minnesota vs Baltimore	9/28/69	**7**

Touchdown Catches	Date	No
Bob Shaw, Chi.Cards vs Baltimore	10/2/50	**5**
Kellen Winslow, San Diego vs Oakland	11/22/81	**5**

Field Goals	Date	No
Jim Bakken, St.Louis vs Pittsburgh	9/24/67	**7**
8 players tied with 6 FGs		

Note: Bakken's FGs, in order, were from 18,24,33,29,24,32 and 23 yards out. He also missed attempts from 50 and 45 yards.

LONGEST PLAYS

Run from Scrimmage (all for TDs)	Date	Yds
Tony Dorsett, Dallas vs Minnesota.......	1/3/83	99
Andy Uram, Green Bay vs Chi.Cards	10/8/39	97
Bob Gage, Pittsburgh vs Chi.Bears	12/4/49	97

Passing (all for TDs)	Date	Yds
Frank Filchock		
to Andy Farkas, Washington vs Pitt 10/15/39		99
George Izo		
to Bobby Mitchell, Wash.vs Cleve	9/15/63	99
Karl Sweetan		
to Pat Studstill, Detroit vs Balt 10/16/66		99
Sonny Jurgensen		
to Gerry Allen, Wash.vs Chicago......	9/15/68	99
Jim Plunkett		
to Cliff Branch, LA Raiders vs Wash ...	10/2/83	99
Ron Jaworski		
to Mike Quick, Phila.vs Atlanta 11/10/85		99

Field Goals	Date	Yds
Tom Dempsey, New Orleans vs Detroit ...	11/8/70	63
Steve Cox, Cleveland vs Cincinnati 10/21/84		60
Tony Franklin, Phila.vs Dallas...........11/12/79		59

Punts	Date	Yds
Steve O'Neal, NY Jets vs Denver.......	9/21/69	98
Joe Lintzenich, C.Bears vs NY Giants 10/16/31		94
Don Chandler, Green Bay vs San Fran ...10/10/65		90

Punt Returns (all for TDs)	Date	Yds
Gil LeFebvre, Cincinnati vs Brooklyn	12/3/33	98
Charlie West, Minnesota vs Washington ..	11/3/68	98
Dennis Morgan, Dallas vs St.Louis.......10/13/74		98

Kickoff Returns (all for TDs)	Date	Yds
Al Carmichael, Green Bay vs Chi.Bears ..	10/7/56	106
Noland Smith, Kansas City vs Denver 12/17/67		106
Roy Green, St.Louis vs Dallas 10/21/79		106
7 players tied with 105-yd returns		

Interception Returns (all for TDs)	Date	Yds
Vencie Glenn, San Diego vs Denver 11/29/87		103
4 players tied with 102-yd returns		

All Star Games

NFL Pro Bowl

A postseason All-Star game between the new league champion and a team of professional all-stars was added to the NFL schedule in 1939. In the first game at Wrigley Field in Los Angeles, the NY Giants beat a team made up of players from NFL teams and two independent clubs in L.A. (the LA Bulldogs and Hollywood Stars). An all-NFL All-Star team provided the opposition over the next four seasons, but the game was cancelled in 1943.

The Pro Bowl was revived in 1951 as a contest between conference all-star teams: American vs National (1951–53), Eastern vs Western (1954–70), and AFC vs NFC (since 1971).

Date	Winner	Score	Loser	Site
1/15/39	NY Giants	13–10	All-Stars	Los Ang.
1/14/40	Green Bay	16–7	All-Stars	Los Ang.
12/29/40	Chi.Bears	28–14	All-Stars	Los Ang.
1/4/42	Chi.Bears	35–24	All-Stars	New York
12/27/42	All-Stars	17–14	Washington	Phila.
1943–50	No game			

Year	Winner		Players of the Game
1951	Amer,	28–27	Otto Graham, Cleveland
1952	Natl,	30–13	Dan Towler, LA Rams
1953	Natl,	27–7	Don Doll, Detroit
1954	East,	20–9	Chuck Bednarik, Phila.
1955	West,	26–19	Billy Wilson, San Fran.
1956	East,	31–30	Ollie Matson, Chi.Cards
1957	West,	19–10	Bert Rechichar, Balt. &
			Ernie Stautner, Pitt.
1958	West,	26–7	Hugh McElhenny, San Fran. &
			Gene Brito, Washington
1959	East,	28–21	Frank Gifford, NY Giants &
			Doug Aikins, Chi.Bears
1960	West,	38–21	Johnny Unitas, Baltimore &
			Big Daddy Lipscomb, Balt.
1961	West,	35–31	Johnny Unitas, Baltimore &
			Sam Huff, NY Giants
1962	West,	31–30	Jim Brown, Cleveland &
			Henry Jordan, Green Bay
1963	East,	30–20	Jim Brown, Cleveland &
			Big Daddy Lipscomb, Pitt.
1964	West,	31–17	Johnny Unitas, Baltimore &
			Gino Marchetti, Balt.
1965	West,	34–14	Fran Tarkenton, Minnesota &
			Terry Barr, Detroit
1966	East,	36–7	Jim Brown, Cleveland &
			Dale Meinert, St.Louis

Year	Winner		Players of the Game
1967	East,	20–10	Gale Sayers, Chicago &
			Floyd Peters, Phila.
1968	West,	38–20	Gale Sayers, Chicago &
			Dave Robinson, Green Bay
1969	West,	10–7	Roman Gabriel, LA Rams &
			Merlin Olsen, LA Rams
1970	West,	16–13	Gale Sayers, Chicago &
			George Andrie, Dallas
1971	NFC,	27–6	Mel Renfro, Dallas &
			Fred Carr, Green Bay
1972	AFC,	26–13	Jan Stenerud, KC &
			Willie Lanier, KC
1973	AFC,	33–28	O.J.Simpson, Buffalo
1974	AFC,	15–13	Garo Yepremian, Miami
1975	NFC,	17–10	James Harris, LA Rams
1976	NFC,	23–20	Billy Johnson, Houston
1977	AFC,	24–14	Mel Blount, Pittsburgh
1978	NFC,	14–13	Walter Payton, Chicago
1979	NFC,	13–7	Ahmad Rashad, Minnesota
1980	NFC,	37–27	Chuck Muncie, New Orleans
1981	NFC,	21–7	Eddie Murray, Detroit
1982	AFC,	16–13	Kellen Winslow, San Diego &
			Lee Roy Selmon, Tampa Bay
1983	NFC,	20–19	Dan Fouts, San Diego &
			John Jefferson, Green Bay
1984	NFC,	45–3	Joe Theismann, Washington
1985	AFC,	22–14	Mark Gastineau, NY Jets
1986	NFC,	28–24	Phil Simms, NY Giants
1987	AFC,	10–6	Reggie White, Philadelphia
1988	AFC,	15–6	Bruce Smith, Buffalo
1989	NFC,	34–3	Randall Cunningham, Phila.

Playing Sites (1951–89)—Memorial Coliseum in Los Angeles (1951–72); Texas Stadium in Irving,TX (1973); Arrowhead Stadium in Kansas City (1974); Orange Bowl in Miami (1975); Superdome in New Orleans (1976); Kingdome in Seattle (1977); Tampa Stadium in Tampa,FL (1978); Memorial Coliseum in Los Angeles (1979); and Aloha Stadium in Honolulu (since 1980).

AFL All-Star Game

The AFL did not play an All-Star after its first season (1960), but did stage a January post-season contest from 1962–70. All-Star teams from the Eastern and Western Divisions played each other every year but 1966, when AFL champion Buffalo met an All-Star team made up of the league's other eight clubs.

Year	Winner	Players of the Game	Year	Winner	Players of the Game
1962	West, 47–27	Cotton Davidson, Oakland	1967	East, 30–23	Babe Parilli, Boston &
1963	West, 21–14	Curtis McClinton, Dallas &			Verlon Biggs, NY Jets
		Earl Faison, S.Diego	1968	East, 25–24	Namath/Don Maynard, Jets &
1964	West, 27–24	Keith Lincoln, San Diego &			Speedy Duncan, S.Diego
		Archie Matsos, Oak.	1969	West, 38–25	Len Dawson, Kansas City &
1965	West, 38–14	Keith Lincoln, San Diego &			George Webster, Hous.
		Willie Brown, Denver			
1966	All-Stars def.	Joe Namath, NY Jets &	1970	West, 26–3	John Hadl, San Diego
	Buf., 30–19	Frank Buncom, S.Diego			

Since 1970: see NFC vs AFC.

Playing Sites (1962–70)—Balboa Stadium in San Diego (1962–64); Jeppesen Stadium in Houston (1965); Rice Stadium in Houston (1966); Oakland Coliseum (1967); Gator Bowl in Jacksonville,FL (1968–69); and Astrodome in Houston (1970).

Chicago College All-Star Game

On Aug.31, 1934, a year after sponsoring Major League Baseball's first All-Star Game, the Chicago Tribune and sports editor Arch Ward presented the first Chicago College All-Star Game at Soldier Field. A crowd of 79,432 turned out to see an all-star team of graduated college seniors battle the 1933 NFL champion Chicago Bears to a scoreless tie. The preseason game was played annually at Soldier Field until it was cancelled in 1977.

Year	Result	Year	Result	Year	Result
1934	Chi.Bears 0, All-Stars 0	1950	All-Stars 17, Philadelphia 7	1966	Green Bay 38, All-Stars 0
1935	Chi.Bears 5, All-Stars 0	1951	Cleveland 33, All-Stars 0	1967	Green Bay 27, All-Stars 0
1936	Detroit 7, All-Stars 0	1952	LA Rams 10, All-Stars 7	1968	Green Bay 34, All-Stars 17
1937	All-Stars 6, Green Bay 0	1953	Detroit 24, All-Stars 10	1969	NY Jets 26, All-Stars 24
1938	All-Stars 28, Washington 16	1954	Detroit 31, All-Stars 6		
1939	NY Giants 9, All-Stars 0	1955	All-Stars 30, Cleveland 27	1970	Kansas City 24, All-Stars 3
		1956	Cleveland 26, All-Stars 0	1971	Baltimore 24, All-Stars 17
1940	Green Bay 45, All-Stars 28	1957	NY Giants 22, All-Stars 12	1972	Dallas 20, All-Stars 7
1941	Chi.Bears 37, All-Stars 13	1958	All-Stars 35, Detroit 19	1973	Miami 14, All-Stars 3
1942	Chi.Bears 21, All-Stars 0	1959	Baltimore 29, All-Stars 0	1974	No Game (NFLPA Strike)
1943	All-Stars 27, Washington 7			1975	Pittsburgh 21, All-Stars 14
1944	Chi.Bears 24, All-Stars 21	1960	Baltimore 32, All-Stars 7	1976	Pittsburgh 24, All-Stars 0*
1945	Green Bay 19, All-Stars 7	1961	Philadelphia 28, All-Stars 14		
1946	All-Stars 16, LA Rams 0	1962	Green Bay 42, All-Stars 20	*Downpour flooded field, game called
1947	All-Stars 16, Chi.Bears 0	1963	All-Stars 20, Green Bay 17	with 1:22 left in 3rd quarter.
1948	Chi.Cards 28, All-Stars 0	1964	Chi.Bears 28, All-Stars 17		
1949	Philadelphia 38, All-Stars 0	1965	Cleveland 24, All-Stars 16		

Canadian Football League
Grey Cup Champions, 1909–88

Earl Grey, the Governor-General of Canada (1904–11) donated a trophy in 1909 for the Rugby Football Championship of Canada. The trophy, which later became known as the Grey Cup, was originally open to competition for teams registered with the Canada Rugby Union. Since 1954, the Cup has gone to the champion of the Canadian Football League (CFL).

In 1940, the Grey Cup winner was determined in a two-game, total points format that was discontinued in 1941.

Year	Winner	Score	Loser	Year	Winner	Score	Loser
1909	Univ.of Toronto	26–6	Toronto Parkdale	1925	Ottawa Senators	24–1	Winnipeg Tigers
				1926	Ottawa Senators	10–7	Univ.of Toronto
1910	Univ.of Toronto	16–7	Hamilton Tigers	1927	Tor.Balmy Beach	9–6	Hamilton Tigers
1911	Univ.of Toronto	14–7	Toronto Argonauts	1928	Hamilton Tigers	30–0	Regina Roughriders
1912	Hamilton Alerts	11–4	Toronto Argonauts	1929	Hamilton Tigers	14–3	Regina Roughriders
1913	Hamilton Tigers	44–2	Toronto Parkdale				
1914	Toronto Argonauts	14–2	Univ.of Toronto	1930	Tor.Balmy Beach	11–6	Regina Roughriders
1915	Hamilton Tigers	13–7	Toronto Rowing	1931	Montreal AAA	22–0	Regina Roughriders
1916	No Game (WW I)			1932	Hamilton Tigers	25–6	Regina Roughriders
1917	No Game (WW I)			1933	Toronto Argonauts	4–3	Sarnia Imperials
1918	No Game (WW I)			1934	Sarnia Imperials	20–12	Regina Roughriders
1919	No Game (WW I)			1935	Winn.Winnipegs	18–12	Hamilton Tigers
				1936	Sarnia Imperials	26–20	Ot'wa Rough Riders
1920	Univ.of Toronto	16–3	Toronto Argonauts	1937	Toronto Argonauts	4–3	Winn.Blue Bombers
1921	Toronto Argonauts	23–0	Edmonton Eskimos	1938	Toronto Argonauts	30–7	Winn.Blue Bombers
1922	Queen's University	13–1	Edmonton Elks	1939	Winn.Blue Bombers	8–7	Ot'wa Rough Riders
1923	Queen's University	54–0	Regina Roughriders				
1924	Queen's University	11–3	Tor.Balmy Beach				

CFL Grey Cup (Continued)

Year	Winner	Score	Loser
1940	Ot'wa Rough Riders	8–2	Tor.Balmy Beach
	Ot'wa Rough Riders	12–5	Tor.Balmy Beach
1941	Winn.Blue Bombers	18–16	Ot'wa Rough Riders
1942	Toronto RACF	8–5	Winnipeg RACF
1943	Hamilton Wildcats	23–14	Winnipeg RACF
1944	Montreal HMCS	7–6	Hamilton Wildcats
1945	Toronto Argonauts	35–0	Winn.Blue Bombers
1946	Toronto Argonauts	28–6	Winn.Blue Bombers
1947	Toronto Argonauts	10–9	Winn.Blue Bombers
1948	Calg. Stampeders	12–7	Ot'wa Rough Riders
1949	Montreal Alouettes	28–15	Calg. Stampeders
1950	Toronto Argonauts	13–0	Winn.Blue Bombers
1951	Ot'wa Rough Riders	21–14	Saskatchewan
1952	Toronto Argonauts	21–11	Edmonton Eskimos
1953	Hamilton Tiger Cats	12–6	Winn.Blue Bombers

*The first Rough Riders vs Roughriders Grey Cup final. Regina Roughriders became Saskatchewan Roughriders in 1946.

Year	Grey Cup Game (CFL)	Winning Coach
1954	Edmonton 26, Montreal 25	Pop Ivy
1955	Edmonton 34, Montreal 19	Pop Ivy
1956	Edmonton 50, Montreal 27	Pop Ivy
1957	Hamilton 32, Winnipeg 7	Jim Trimble
1958	Winnipeg 35, Hamilton 28	Bud Grant
1959	Winnipeg 21, Hamilton 7	Bud Grant

Year	Grey Cup Game (CFL)	Winning Coach
1960	Ottawa 16, Edmonton 6	Frank Clair
1961	Winn. 21, Hamilton 14 (OT)	Bud Grant
1962	Winnipeg 28, Hamilton 27	Bud Grant
1963	Hamilton 21, BC Lions 10	Ralph Sazio
1964	BC Lions 34, Hamilton 24	Dave Skrien
1965	Hamilton 22, Winnipeg 16	Ralph Sazio
1966	Saskatchewan 29, Ottawa 14	Eagle Keys
1967	Hamilton 24, Saskat. 1	Ralph Sazio
1968	Ottawa 24, Calgary 21	Frank Clair
1969	Ottawa 29, Saskatchewan 11	Frank Clair
1970	Montreal 23, Calgary 10	Sam Etcheverry
1971	Calgary 14, Toronto 11	Jim Duncan
1972	Hamilton 13, Saskat. 10	Jerry Williams
1973	Ottawa 22, Edmonton 18	Jack Gotta
1974	Montreal 20, Edmonton 7	Marv Levy
1975	Edmonton 9, Montreal 8	Ray Jauch
1976	Ottawa 23, Saskatchewan 20	George Brancato
1977	Montreal 41, Edmonton	Marv Levy
1978	Edmonton 20, Montreal 13	Hugh Campbell
1979	Edmonton 17, Montreal 9	Hugh Campbell
1980	Edmonton 48, Hamilton 10	Hugh Campbell
1981	Edmonton 26, Ottawa 23	Hugh Campbell
1982	Edmonton 32, Toronto 16	Hugh Campbell
1983	Toronto 18, B.C.Lions 17	Bob O'Billovich
1984	Winnipeg 47, Hamilton 17	Cal Murphy
1985	BC Lions 37, Hamilton 24	Don Matthews
1986	Hamilton 39, Edmonton 15	Al Bruno
1987	Edmonton 38, Toronto 36	Joe Faragalli
1988	Winnipeg 22, BC Lions 21	Mike Riley

CFL Player of the Year

CFL regular season Player of the Year from 1953–88.

Year	Player of the Year
1953	Billy Vessels, Edmonton, RB
1954	Sam Etcheverry, Montreal, RB
1955	Pat Abbruzzi, Montreal, RB
1956	Hal Patterson, Montreal, E-DB
1957	Jackie Parker, Edmonton, RB
1958	Jackie Parker, Edmonton, QB
1959	Johnny Bright, Edmonton, RB
1960	Jackie Parker, Edmonton, QB
1961	Bernie Faloney, Hamilton, QB
1962	George Dixon, Montreal, RB
1963	Russ Jackson, Ottawa, QB
1964	Lovell Coleman, Calgary, RB
1965	George Reed, Saskatchewan, RB
1966	Russ Jackson, Ottawa, QB
1967	Peter Liske, Calgary, QB
1968	Bill Symons, Toronto, RB
1969	Russ Jackson, Ottawa, QB

Year	Player of the Year
1970	Ron Lancaster, Saskatchewan, QB
1971	Don Jonas, Winnipeg, QB
1972	Garney Henley, Hamilton, WR
1973	George McGowan, Edmonton, WR
1974	Tom Wilkinson, Edmonton, QB
1975	Willie Burden, Calgary, RB
1976	Ron Lancaster, Saskatchewan, QB
1977	Jimmy Edwards, Hamilton, RB
1978	Tony Gabriel, Ottawa, TE
1979	David Green, Montreal, RB
1980	Dieter Brock, Winnipeg, QB
1981	Dieter Brock, Winnipeg, QB
1982	Condredge Holloway, Toronto, QB
1983	Warren Moon, Edmonton, QB
1984	Willard Reaves, Winnipeg, RB
1985	Merv Fernandez, BC Lions, WR
1986	James Murphy, Winnipeg, WR
1987	Tom Clements, Winnipeg, QB
1988	David Williams, BC Lions, WR

Duane Black

Michigan stalwarts **Rumeal Robinson** (left) and **Glen Rice** (center) raise the championship trophy in Seattle as the surprising Wolverines celebrate their first NCAA title.

COLLEGE BASKETBALL

INSIDE

Michigan NCAA champion in overtime,
8th different winner of the 1980's;
Kansas penalized, Kentucky investigated;
Women's title returns to Tennessee

COLLEGE BASKETBALL

1988-89 YEAR IN REVIEW

by Billy Reed

The 1988–89 college basketball season—the entire decade, really—came to a perfect climax on Monday night, April 3, before 39,187 witnesses in the Seattle Kingdome when Michigan, under interim coach Steve Fisher, and Seton Hall, unheralded before the season, needed an overtime, first in a title game since 1963, to decide the championship of the NCAA basketball tournament.

With only 0:03 left on the clocks, Seton Hall's Gerald Greene was whistled for blocking Michigan's Rumeal Robinson, who was trying to dish off on a penetration move. Robinson swished both free throws for the winning points in the 80–79 victory that gave Michigan its first basketball title and made Fisher, named to replace Bill Frieder only two days before the tournament, the first substitute head coach (and only undefeated one) to reach the game's pinnacle.

It was an ending that nobody could have predicted on the day the NCAA's tournament committee announced the 64-team field and pairings, but, then, the element of unpredictability is one reason the NCAA tournament became sports' biggest success story of the 1980s. Every year, from Louisville's 1980 championship in Indianapolis to Michigan's triumph in Seattle, the tournament's story was an upward spiral of success any way you want to measure it—attendance, revenue, TV ratings, and national interest.

The reason?

Simple.

Only occasionally do the Super Bowl, World Series, Kentucky Derby or Masters golf tournament, to name a few of the other major events, deliver the sort of drama and excitement that have become routine in the Final Four. When Robinson canned those two free throws against Seton Hall and the Pirates barely missed a subsequent last-second shot, it marked the third time in the decade that the championship has been decided inside the final five seconds. And of the 10 title

Billy Reed, who has covered the last 22 Final Fours, is a sports columnist for the Lexington (Ky.) **Herald-Leader** and a special contributor to **Sports Illustrated**.

games played since 1980, the average margin of victory was just over four points. Three were decided by a point, two by two points, and one by three.

This is the sort of consistently fine entertainment that comes from parity, which will be remembered as the college game's buzzword of the 1980s. After a 12-year period in which UCLA won 10 championships, the power started shifting and spreading in 1976. No team since has won two straight championships, although two teams did win twice in the 1980s—Louisville (1980 and '86) and Indiana (1981 and '87). In addition, Georgetown played in three title games (1982, '84 and '85), but won only in 1984. More to the point, North Carolina's 1981–82 team was the only consensus preseason No. 1 pick that also was able to deliver the championship, indicating how wide-open the game has become.

The 1988–89 season was typical. There was no consensus No. 1 pick heading into the season (the magazine picks included

Georgetown, Louisville, Duke, and Syracuse), and the top spot in the polls was tossed around like the proverbial hot potato. After early leader Duke momentarily hit the skids when Atlantic Coast Conference play began, there was a wild, giddy stretch where the nation had a new No. 1 every week. At one time or another, Georgetown, Oklahoma, Arizona, and Illinois each took its turn in the hot seat. Yet the truth was, there really wasn't a No. 1. Many teams had one outstanding player—the leading contenders for Player of the Year were Duke's Danny Ferry, Arizona's Sean Elliott, Louisville's Pervis Ellison, Oklahoma's Stacey King, and North Carolina's J.R. Reid—but each team also had flaws and weaknesses that left it vulnerable and questionable.

Besides its scramble at the top, 1988–89 will be remembered as a season of controversy and conflict. A few of the more prominent examples:

• Kansas, the defending national champion, was ineligible for the tournament because of NCAA recruiting violations revealed in the wake of coach Larry Brown's move to the pros. Nevertheless, the Jayhawks acquitted themselves well (19–12) under new coach Roy Williams, a former Dean Smith assistant at North Carolina.

• Another of the sport's great names, Kentucky, had its first losing season in more than 50 years, the result of personnel losses stemming from a widely publicized NCAA investigation. As a first big cleanup step, Kentucky announced in January that alumnus C.M. Newton, who passed the 500-win milestone during the season, had been con-

With 0:03 left in overtime, Michigan's **Rumeal Robinson** stepped to the line and won the championship.

Duane Black

Wide World Photos

Duane Black

In his first six games as a college head coach, Michigan's **Steve Fisher** went undefeated and won an NCAA title. During the regular season, **Bob Knight** of Indiana (inset) won his 500th game, the Big Ten, and was consensus Coach of the Year.

vinced to end his coaching career at Vanderbilt and return to Lexington as athletic director. Head coach Eddie Sutton resigned in March. (See Colleges chapter for further developments.)

• After 11 years, Jerry Tarkanian finally lost his battle with the NCAA in the U.S. Supreme Court, which ruled in December that the NCAA had not violated Tarkanian's constitutional rights by ordering the university to suspend him for recruiting violations.

• At Missouri, an otherwise outstanding season was disrupted when coach Norm Stewart passed out on a plane trip and had to miss the rest of the season because of cancer surgery. Under interim coach Rich Daly, the Tigers still managed to win the Big Eight tournament and reach the NCAA round of 16, even amid recruiting allegations that sparked an NCAA investigation.

• In January, after the NCAA convention passed a new measure known as Proposition 42 that would put more teeth into academic eligibility requirements, Georgetown coach John Thompson

staged a widely publicized protest by walking off the floor in Landover, Md., before a Big East game against Connecticut, touching off a national backlash against the measure. Thompson returned to the bench after a meeting with NCAA officials in which he was assured that the measure would be re-evaluated. Under the proposal, incoming freshmen declared academically ineligible would not be allowed to receive financial aid. This, said Thompson, further discriminated against players from disadvantaged backgrounds.

• In the Atlantic Coast Conference, Jim Valvano's North Carolina State program was rocked by the release of the dust jacket from an impending book that was to detail various allegations and improprieties in the Wolfpack program. Eventually, after vehement Valvano denials and various investigations, publication of the book was suspended.

Ah, but not all the news was bad. The season introduced a sensational freshman class, the most publicized of which were Georgetown's Alonzo Mourning, Syracuse's Billy Owens, Kentucky's Chris Mills, Indiana's Eric Anderson, Notre Dame's Laphonso Ellis, UCLA's Don MacLean, and, most noticeably, LSU's Chris Jackson.

Only 6-foot-1, Jackson generated more excitement than any newcomer since Pete Maravich was a sophomore, also at LSU, back in the 1968–69 season. While not quite the gunner Maravich was—Pistol Pete still owns virtually all the NCAA scoring records—Jackson nevertheless had a 30.1 scoring average that ranked only behind the 32.9 by national scoring champion Hank Gathers of Loyola-Marymount. When he and Georgetown's Mourning (the 6-11 frosh who led the nation in blocked shots) led their respective teams against each other in late January, the game drew a crowd of 54,321 to the Superdome in New Orleans. Jackson scored 23 and LSU won at the buzzer, 82–80.

While Jackson was writing his name into the game's history book, others were achieving milestones. Oregon State coach Ralph Miller retired after 38 seasons and 657 victories. Indiana coach Bob Knight, 47, became the second youngest coach to win 500 games, in addition to supplantng former Purdue coach Piggy Lambert as the winningest coach in Big Ten history. Syracuse point guard Sherman Douglas became the all-time Division I leader in assists, and Arizona's Elliott surpassed former UCLA great Lew Alcindor (now Kareem Abdul-Jabbar) as the Pac Ten's all-time scoring leader. In the Atlantic Ten, the spectrum ranged from West Virginia's 22-game winning streak to George Washington's 27 losses, both national highs.

And then there was the story of Ohio State's Jay Burson, an unprepossessing specimen of 6-1 and 158 pounds who looked more like—take your pick—the team manager, a trombone player, or a hot-dog vendor. Nevertheless, he captured the public's heart with his guts, his hustle, and his deadly shooting. Sadly, his career was ended prematurely by a neck injury that forced him to watch the Buckeyes' final games from the bench, his head encased in a weird-looking support cage.

As usual, however, the regular season was overshadowed by the events of March. Among the big winners was the Tennessee women's team, which used 27 points from Bridgette Gordon to beat fellow Southeastern Conference member Auburn 76–60 in the title game in Tacoma, Wash., giving the Lady Vols and coach Pat Summitt their second title in three years. Gordon, who also was a mainstay of the 1988 U.S. gold-medal Olympic team, hit 11 of 21 shots and had 11 rebounds in her final college game.

Back on the mens' side, Princeton won an eternal spot in the hearts of underdog lovers everywhere by coming within a play of stunning top-seeded Georgetown in the first round of the East Regional. The Hoyas barely escaped with a 50–49 victory, but only after a last-second block by Mourning, who some observers felt should have been called for a foul. If that was THE game that will be remembered the longest, the story of the tournament nevertheless was Michigan.

In nine seasons under Frieder, the Wolverines had developed the reputation as a team that always had great talent, but that also always choked in the tournament. Despite being consistently ranked among the nation's leaders, Michigan never made it past the NCAA round of 16 under Frieder, an outstanding recruiter whose bench coaching often made him the target of boos at home games. When Frieder announced—on the eve of the NCAAs—that he had accepted the Arizona State job, Wolverine athletic director Bo Schembechler, also the school's football coach, replaced him immediately rather than let him coach in the tournament.

It's Slippery at the Top

During a five-week stretch from mid-January to early February, there was a different Number One team every week in the AP Top 20 poll. Oklahoma finally broke the streak with back-to-back No.1 weeks, but could not make it three in a row.

The weekly AP Number Ones from Jan.16 through the final AP poll on March 13:

Week	Number One	But then lost to
1/16	Duke	N.Carolina, 91-71; W.Forest,75-71
1/23	Illinois	Minnesota, 69-62
1/30	Oklahoma	Oklahoma St., 77-73
2/6	Arizona	Oklahoma, 82-80
2/13	Oklahoma	Did not lose
2/20	Oklahoma	Missouri, 97-84
2/27	Arizona	Did not lose
3/6	Arizona	Did not lose
3/13	Arizona	Did not lose

Danny Ferry (35), who split Player of the Year honors with Sean Elliott of Arizona,
led Duke to its third Final Four in four years, but the Blue Devils came up short again.

The decision seemed little more than a typical Bo-dacious fit of pique—"I want a Michigan man to coach Michigan," Schembechler asserted—and tantamount to forfeiting the Wolverines' chances of making the Final Four, considering that Fisher was only a seven-year aide who had never been a head coach above the high school level. Michigan fans greeted the news with mixed feelings, considering the growing disenchantment with Frieder. The transition was smoothed by the fact that Illinois had blown out the Wolverines 89–73 in Ann Arbor in what was to be Frieder's final game.

But after Fisher assumed command, the Wolverines pulled together and only grew stronger and more confident. The catalyst was Robinson, the fine point guard from whom all good things flowed, but the star was Glen Rice, the 6–7 senior forward whose outside shooting was so sensational throughout the tournament that he was able to break the all-time tourney scoring record set by Princeton's Bill Bradley in 1965. In six tourney games, Rice had 184 points, including 31 against Seton Hall in the final game.

While Michigan was cruising its way through the Southeast Regional, Illinois was winning the Midwest to set up a third meeting between the teams in the national semifinal. The other semi matched Duke, which had regrouped after its January slump to win the East, and Seton Hall, the sleeper from the Big East that used depth and defense to shock such big-name foes as Indiana and Nevada-Las Vegas to win the West. None of the four had ever won the championship.

In the first semifinal, Seton Hall got off to a horrid start, spotting Duke a 25–8 lead in the first nine minutes, but came roaring back to blow out the favored Blue Devils, 95–78, despite 34 points by the multi-talented Ferry. In the nightcap, Illinois provided the perfect measure of how much Michigan had improved under Fisher. Although the Illini played just as hard and just as well as it had in two regular-season blowout wins over the Wolverines, Michigan hung tough this time and won in the final seconds when sophomore Sean Higgins rebounded Terry Mills' miss from the corner and put it back in over Illinois' Nick Anderson with 0:03 to go, giving the Wolverines an 83–81 win.

As charming as the Fisher story was, Seton Hall's arrival in the championship game was even more appealing. Only two years earlier, after all, the student newspaper had called for the resignation of coach P.J. Carlesimo on the grounds that he hadn't been able to make the Pirates competitive in the formidable Big East. What the critics didn't understand was that the Pirates were about ready to turn the corner, thanks to a greater financial commitment from the administration and some inspired recruiting by Carlesimo. Of Seton Hall's five starters in the championship game, three came from the playgrounds of New York City, and two were from out of the country. Indeed, after the season, Carlesimo was criticized in some quarters for using forward Andrew Gaze, a member of the Australian Olympic team who didn't report to school until October and who went back home four days after the title game.

As usual, the championship game was a classic. Early in the second half, it looked as if Michigan was on the brink of blowing it open. But after the Wolverines had stretched their lead to 12 points, here came Seton Hall, using its great defense and the scoring of John Morton, to scratch its way back into contention. The Pirates even took the lead, 67–66, with 2:01 to play in regulation, but had to settle for a 71–71 tie and the historic overtime that was finally settled by Robinson's dramatic free throws.

"I'm the happiest man alive," said Fisher only moments after the final horn. "Rumeal is such a gutty kid. You have to look back to the Wisconsin game in the regular season, when he missed a foul shot with eight seconds left and we ended up losing. For weeks, he shot 100 from the line every night after practice. I rebounded for him. He kept telling me, 'Coach, I'll make 'em next time.'"

And he did, bringing to an end the final season in what will be remembered as boom decade for college basketball.

Bridgette Gordon (30) of Tennessee had 27 points and 11 rebounds in her final college game as the Lady Vols beat SEC rival Auburn in the Women's NCAA final.

203

Final 1989 AP Top 20 Poll
Taken before NCAA tournament

The sportswriters & broadcasters poll: first place votes in parentheses, records through March 12, total points (based on 20 for 1st, 19 for 2nd, etc.), what round team lost in NCAA tournament, head coach (career years/years at present school), and preseason ranking. Records include conference tournament games. Teams in **bold type** went on to reach NCAA Final Four.

				Head Coach	Preseason Rank
1	Arizona (46)	27-3	1,219	L-3rd to UNLV	Lute Olson (16 yrs/6th)	11
2	Georgetown (13) . . .	26-4	1,155	L-4th to Duke	John Thompson (17 yrs/17th)	2
3	**Illinois** (3)	27-4	1,121	L-Semi to Michigan	Lou Henson (27 yrs/14th)	9
4	Oklahoma	28-5	989	L-3rd to Virginia	Billy Tubbs (15 yrs/9th)	5
5	North Carolina	27-7	976	L-3rd to Michigan	Dean Smith (28 yrs/28th)	6
6	Missouri	27-7	875	L-3rd to Syracuse	*Rich Daly (1 yr/1st)	14
7	Syracuse	27-7	863	L-4th to Illinois	Jim Boeheim (13 yrs/13th)	8
8	Indiana	25-7	834	L-3rd to Seton Hall	Bob Knight (24 yrs/18th)	30
9	**Duke**	24-7	808	L-Semi to Seton Hall	Mike Krzyzewski (14 yrs/9th)	1
10	**Michigan**	24-7	666	Won Championship	*Steve Fisher (1 yr/1st)	3
11	**Seton Hall**	26-6	582	L-Final to Michigan	P.J.Carlesimo (6 yrs/6th)	--
12	Louisville	22-8	518	L-3rd to Illinois	Denny Crum (18 yrs/18th)	4
13	Stanford	26-6	481	L-1st to Siena	Mike Montgomery (11 yrs/3rd)	20
14	Iowa	22-9	379	L-2nd to N.C.State	Tom Davis (18 yrs/3rd)	7
15	UNLV	26-7	338	L-4th to Seton Hall	Jerry Tarkanian (21 yrs/16th)	10
16	Florida St	22-7	328	L-1st to Mid.Tenn.St.	Pat Kennedy (9 yrs/3rd)	16
17	West Virginia	25-4	216	L-2nd to Duke	Gale Catlett (17 yrs/11th)	27
18	Ball St	28-2	143	L-2nd to Illinois	Rick Majerus (5 yrs/2nd)	--
19	N.Carolina St	20-8	115	L-3rd to Georgetown	Jim Valvano (18 yrs/9th)	18
20	Alabama	23-7	101	L-1st to South Ala.	Wimp Sanderson (9 yrs/9th)	--

Others receiving votes: 21. Arkansas (24-6,71 pts); **22. La Salle** (26-5,68); **23. St.Mary's,CA** (25-4,60); **24. Memphis St.**(21-10,33); **25. UTEP** (25-6,22); **26. Florida** (21-12,16); **27. Evansville** (24-5,7) and **LSU** (20-11,7); **29. Georgia Tech** (20-11,6) and **Oregon St.** (22-7,6); **31. Virginia** (19-10,5); **32. Arkansas-Little Rock** (23-7,4); **33. Kansas St.** (19-10,2) and **Siena** (24-4,2); **35. Colorado St.** (22-9,1), **Idaho** (25-5,1), **Pittsburgh** (17-12,1) and **Texas** (24-8,1).

*Interim coaches—Missouri assistant Rich Daly replaced Norm Stewart on Feb 9 and Michigan assistant Steve Fisher replaced Bill Frieder on March 15.

The 1989 NCAA Tournament
Men's Division I

MIDWEST
Seeds

1 **Illinois** (27-4)	9 Ball St.(28-2)
2 Syracuse (27-7)	10 Colorado St.(22-9)
3 Missouri (27-7)	11 Texas (24-8)
4 Louisville (22-8)	12 Loyola,CA (20-10)
5 Arkansas (24-6)	13 Ark-Little Rock (23-7)
6 Georgia Tech (20-11)	14 Creighton (20-10)
7 Florida (21-12)	15 Bucknell (23-7)
8 Pittsburgh (17-12)	16 McNeese St.(16-13)

First Round
Indianapolis,IN (Hoosier Dome)—ILLINOIS 77, McNeese St. 71; BALL ST. 68, Pittsburgh 64; LOUISVILLE 76, Ark-Little Rock 71; ARKANSAS 120, Loyola Marymount-CA 101.
Dallas,TX (Reunion Arena)—SYRACUSE 104, Bucknell 81; COLORADO ST. 68, Florida 46; MISSOURI 85, Creighton 69; TEXAS 76, Georgia Tech 70.

Second Round
Indianapolis—ILLINOIS 72, Ball St. 60; LOUISVILLE 93, Arkansas 84.
Dallas—SYRACUSE 65, Colorado St. 50; MISSOURI 108, Texas 89.

Regionals
Minneapolis,MN (Metrodome)
Semifinals—ILLINOIS 83, Louisville 69; SYRACUSE 83, Missouri 80.
Championship—ILLINOIS 89, Syracuse 86.

SOUTHEAST
Seeds

1 Oklahoma (28-5)	9 Louisiana Tech (22-8)
2 North Carolina (27-7)	10 Iowa St.(17-11)
3 **Michigan** (24-7)	11 South Alabama (22-8)
4 Florida St.(22-7)	12 Providence (18-10)
5 Virginia (19-10)	13 Middle Tenn St.(22-7)
6 Alabama (23-7)	14 Xavier,OH (21-11)
7 UCLA (20-9)	15 Southern Univ.(20-10)
8 La Salle (26-5)	16 East Tenn St.(20-10)

First Round
Nashville,TN (Memorial Gym)—OKLAHOMA 72, East Tenn St. 71; LOUISIANA TECH 83, La Salle 74; VIRGINIA 100, Providence 97; MIDDLE TENN ST. 97, Florida St. 83.
Atlanta,GA (The Omni)—NORTH CAROLINA 93, Southern Univ. 79; UCLA 84, Iowa St. 74; MICHIGAN 92, Xavier 87; SOUTH ALABAMA 86, Alabama 84.

Second Round
Nashville—OKLAHOMA 124, Louisiana Tech 81; VIRGINIA 104, Middle Tenn St. 83.
Atlanta—NORTH CAROLINA 88, UCLA 81; MICHIGAN 91, South Alabama 82.

Regionals
Lexington,KY (Rupp Arena)
Semifinals—VIRGINIA 86, Oklahoma 80; MICHIGAN 92, North Carolina 87.
Championship—MICHIGAN 102, Virginia 65.

EAST
Seeds

1 Georgetown (26-4)
2 **Duke** (24-7)
3 Stanford (26-6)
4 Iowa (22-9)
5 N.Carolina St.(20-8)
6 Kansas St.(19-10)
7 West Virginia (25-4)
8 Vanderbilt (19-13)

9 Notre Dame (20-8)
10 Tennessee (19-10)
11 Minnesota (17-11)
12 South Carolina (19-10)
13 Rutgers (18-12)
14 Siena (24-4)
15 S.Carolina St.(25-7)
16 Princeton (19-7)

First Round
Providence,RI (Civic Center)—GEORGETOWN 50, Princeton 49; NOTRE DAME 81, Vanderbilt 65; IOWA 87, Rutgers 73; N.C.STATE 81, South Carolina 66.
Greensboro, NC (Coliseum)—DUKE 90, S.Carolina St. 69; WEST VIRGINIA 84, Tennessee 68; SIENA 80, Stanford 78; MINNESOTA 86, Kansas St. 75.

Second Round
Providence—GEORGETOWN 81, Notre Dame 74; N.C. STATE 102, Iowa 96 (2 OT).
Greensboro—DUKE 70, West Virginia 63; MINNESOTA 80, Siena 67.

Regionals
E.Rutherford,NJ (Meadowlands Arena)
Semifinals—GEORGETOWN 69, N.C.State 61; DUKE 87, Minnesota 70.
Championship—DUKE 85, Georgetown 77

WEST
Seeds

1 Arizona (27-3)
2 Indiana (25-7)
3 **Seton Hall** (26-6)
4 UNLV (26-7)
5 Memphis St.(21-10)
6 Oregon St.(21-7)
7 UTEP (25-6)
8 St.Mary's,CA (25-4)

9 Clemson (18-10)
10 LSU (20-11)
11 Evansville (24-5)
12 DePaul (20-11)
13 Idaho (25-5)
14 SW Missouri St(21-9)
15 G.Mason (20-10)
16 Robert Morris (21-8)

First Round
Boise,ID (University Pavilion)—ARIZONA 94, Robert Morris 60; CLEMSON 83, St.Mary's 70; UNLV 68, Idaho 56; DePAUL 66, Memphis St. 63.
Tucson,AZ (McKale Center)—INDIANA 99, George Mason 85; UTEP 85, LSU 74; SETON HALL 60, SW Missouri St. 51; EVANSVILLE 94, Oregon St. 90 (OT).

Second Round
Boise—ARIZONA 94, Clemson 68; UNLV 85, DePaul 70.
Tucson—INDIANA 92, UTEP 69; SETON HALL 87, Evansville 73.

Regionals
Denver,CO (McNichols Sports Arena)
Semifinals—UNLV 68, Arizona 67; SETON HALL 78, Indiana 65.
Championship—SETON HALL 84, UNLV 61.

THE FINAL FOUR
at Seattle,WA (Kingdome)
Semifinals
Michigan 83 . . . . Illinois 81
Seton Hall 95 . . . . Duke 78

Championship
Michigan 80 . . . . OT . . . . Seton Hall 79

Final records: Michigan (30-7), Seton Hall (31-7), Illinois (31-5), Duke (28-8).

All-Tournament Team: Guards—Rumeal Robinson of Michigan, and Gerald Greene and John Morton of Seton Hall; Forwards—Glen Rice Michigan, and Danny Ferry of Duke.

Most Valuable Player: Glen Rice, Michigan

Championship
Michigan 80, Seton Hall 79 (OT)

Michigan	Min	FG M-A	FT M-A	Pts	Rb	A	F
Glen Rice	42	12-25	2- 2	**31**	11	0	2
Terry Mills	34	4- 8	0- 0	**8**	6	2	2
Loy Vaught	26	4- 8	0- 0	**8**	7	0	2
Mike Griffin	17	0- 0	0- 0	**0**	4	3	4
Rumeal Robinson . .	43	6-13	9-10	**21**	3	11	2
Sean Higgins	27	3-10	3- 4	**10**	9	2	3
Mark Hughes	25	1- 1	0- 0	**2**	2	0	2
Demetrius Calip	11	0- 2	0- 0	**0**	0	1	3
TOTALS	225	30-67	14-16	**80**	45	19	20

Three-point field goals: 6-16 (Rice 5-12, Higgins 1-4); **Blocked Shots:** 4 (Mills 3, Higgins); **Turnovers:** 14 (Robinson 5, Griffin 2, Mills 2, Rice 2, Vaught 2, Higgins); **Steals:** 3 (Mills 2, Vaught); **Technical fouls:** none.

FG Pct: Game (.448); **FT Pct:** Game (.875).

Seton Hall	Min	FG M-A	FT M-A	Pts	Rb	A	F
Andrew Gaze	39	1- 5	2- 2	**5**	3	3	3
Daryll Walker	39	5- 9	3- 4	**13**	11	1	2
Ramon Ramos	33	4- 9	1- 1	**9**	5	1	2
Gerald Greene	43	5-13	1- 3	**13**	5	5	3
John Morton	37	11-26	9-10	**35**	4	3	4
Michael Cooper	14	0- 0	0- 0	**0**	2	0	1
Anthony Avent	11	1- 2	0- 0	**2**	3	1	0
Frantz Volcy	7	0- 0	0- 2	**0**	1	0	2
Pookey Wigington . .	2	1- 1	0- 0	**2**	0	0	1
TOTALS	225	28-65	16-22	**79**	36	14	17

Three-point field goals: 7-23 (Morton 4-12, Greene 2-5, Gaze 1-5, Walker 0-1); **Blocked Shots:** 2 (Cooper, Ramos); **Turnovers:** 11 (Morton 3, Gaze 2, Greene 2, Walker 2, Cooper, Ramos); **Steals:** 4 (Greene 2, Gaze, Ramos); **Technical fouls:** none.

FG Pct: Game (.431); **FT Pct:** Game (.727).

Michigan (29-7)	37	34	9	––	80
Seton Hall (31-6)	32	39	8	––	79

Officials: Mickey Crowley, Tom Rucker and John Clougherty.
Attendance: 39,187. **TV Rating:** 21.2 (CBS)

1989 NIT
National Invitation Tournament

First three rounds played on home court of higher seeded teams. Semifinal, Championship and Third Place games played March 27 and 29 at Madison Square Garden in New York. Winning teams are noted in capital LETTERS.

First Round
CONNECTICUT 67, NC-Charlotte 62; OHIO ST. 81, Akron 71; PENN ST. 89, Murray St. 73; RICHMOND 70, Temple 56; ST.JOHN'S 70, Mississippi 67; ST.LOUIS 87, Southern Ill. 54; VILLANOVA 76, St.Peter's 56; WISCONSIN 63, New Orleans 61

ALA-BIRMINGHAM 83, Georgia Southern 74; MICHIGAN ST. 83, Kent St. 69; NEBRASKA 81, Arkansas St. 79; WICHITA ST. 70, UC-Santa Barbara 62; CALIFORNIA 73, Hawaii 57; PEPPERDINE 84, New Mexico St. 69; NEW MEXICO 91, Santa Clara 76; OKLAHOMA ST. 69, Boise St. 55.

Second Round
ALA-BIRMINGHAM 64, Richmond 61; CONNECTICUT 73, California 72; MICHIGAN ST. 79, Wichita St. 67; OHIO ST. 85, Nebraska 74; ST.LOUIS 73, Wisconsin 68; VILLANOVA 76, Penn St. 67; NEW MEXICO 86, Pepperdine 69; ST.JOHN'S 76, Oklahoma St. 64.

Quarterfinals
ALA-BIRMINGHAM 85, Connecticut 79; MICHIGAN ST. 70, Villanova 63; ST.JOHN'S 83, Ohio St. 80 (OT); ST.LOUIS 66, New Mexico 65.

Semifinals
ST.LOUIS 74, Michigan St. 64
ST.JOHN'S 76, Ala-Birmingham 65.

Championship
ST.JOHN'S 73, St.Louis 65.

Third Place
ALA-BIRMINGHAM 78, Michigan St. 76

Final records: St.John's (20-13), St. Louis (27-10); Ala-Birmingham (23-11); Michigan St. (19-14).

Tournament MVP: Center Jayson Williams of St. John's.

1989 Final Conference Standings
NCAA Division I

Conference records include regular season games only. Overall records include conference tournament results. NCAA and NIT tournament results are not counted.

American South Conference

	Conference			Overall		
	W	L	Pct	W	L	Pct
#New Orleans	7	3	.700	19	10	.655
*Louisiana Tech	6	4	.600	22	8	.733
#Arkansas St	6	4	.600	20	9	.690
SW Louisiana	4	6	.400	17	12	.586
Pan American	4	6	.400	15	13	.536
Lamar	3	7	.300	12	16	.429

Conf. Tourney Final: La.Tech 84, New Orleans 62.

*NCAA Tournament: La.Tech (1-1).

#NIT Tournament: New Orleans (0-1), Arkansas St.(0-1).

Association of Mid-Continent Universities

	Conference			Overall		
	W	L	Pct	W	L	Pct
*SW Missouri St	10	2	.833	21	9	.700
Northern Iowa	8	4	.667	19	9	.679
Eastern Illinois	7	5	.583	16	16	.500
Wisconsin-Green Bay	6	6	.500	14	14	.500
Valparaiso	4	8	.333	10	19	.345
Western Illinois	4	8	.333	9	19	.321
Illinois-Chicago	3	9	.250	13	17	.433
Cleveland St	–	–	–––	16	12	.571

Note: Cleveland St. on probation, ineligible for regular season and postseason championships.

Conf. Tourney Final: SW Mo.St. 73, Ill-Chicago 67.

*NCAA Tournament: SW Missouri St.(0-1).

Atlantic Coast Conference

	Conference			Overall		
	W	L	Pct	W	L	Pct
*North Carolina St	10	4	.714	20	8	.714
*North Carolina	9	5	.643	27	7	.794
*Duke	9	5	.643	24	7	.774
*Virginia	9	5	.643	19	10	.655
*Georgia Tech	8	6	.571	20	11	.645
*Clemson	7	7	.500	18	10	.643
Wake Forest	3	11	.214	13	15	.464
Maryland	1	13	.071	9	20	.310

Conf. Tourney Final: North Carolina 77, Duke 74.

*NCAA Tournament: Duke (4-1, lost Semifinal), Virginia (3-1), N.C.State (2-1), North Carolina (2-1), Clemson (1-1), Ga.Tech (0-1).

Atlantic 10 Conference

	Conference			Overall		
	W	L	Pct	W	L	Pct
*West Virginia	17	1	.944	25	4	.862
#Temple	15	3	.833	18	11	.621
*Rutgers	13	5	.722	18	12	.600
#Penn St	12	6	.667	19	11	.633
Rhode Island	9	9	.500	13	15	.464
St. Bonaventure	7	11	.389	13	15	.464
Duquesne	7	11	.389	13	16	.448
Massachusetts	5	13	.278	10	18	.357
St.Joseph's (PA)	4	14	.222	8	21	.276
George Washington	1	17	.056	1	27	.036

Conf. Tourney Final: Rutgers 70, Penn St. 66.

*NCAA Tournament: West Virginia (1-1), Rutgers (0-1).

#NIT Tournament: Penn St.(1-1), Temple (0-1).

Big East Conference

	Conference			Overall		
	W	L	Pct	W	L	Pct
*Georgetown	13	3	.813	26	4	.867
*Seton Hall	11	5	.688	26	6	.813
*Syracuse	10	6	.625	27	7	.794
*Pittsburgh	9	7	.563	17	12	.586
*Providence	7	9	.438	18	10	.643
#Villanova	7	9	.438	16	15	.516
#St.John's	6	10	.375	15	13	.536
#Connecticut	6	10	.375	16	12	.571
Boston College	3	13	.188	12	17	.414

Conf. Tourney Final: Georgetown 88, Syracuse 79.

***NCAA Tournament:** Seton Hall (5-1, lost Final), Georgetown (3-1), Syracuse (3-1), Pittsburgh (0-1), Providence (0-1).

#NIT Tournament: St.John's (5-0, won Final), Villanova (2-1), Connecticut (2-1).

Big Eight Conference

	Conference			Overall		
	W	L	Pct	W	L	Pct
*Oklahoma	12	2	.857	28	5	.849
*Missouri	10	4	.714	27	7	.794
*Kansas St	8	6	.571	19	10	.655
*Iowa St	7	7	.500	17	11	.607
#Oklahoma St	7	7	.500	16	13	.552
Kansas	6	8	.429	19	12	.613
#Nebraska	4	10	.286	16	15	.516
Colorado	2	12	.143	7	21	.250

Note: Kansas on probation, ineligible for NCAA tournament.

Conf. Tourney Final: Missouri 98, Oklahoma 86.

***NCAA Tournament:** Oklahoma (2-1), Missouri (2-1), Kansas St.(0-1), Iowa St.(0-1).

#NIT Tournament: Oklahoma St.(1-1), Nebraska (1-1).

Big Sky Conference

	Conference			Overall		
	W	L	Pct	W	L	Pct
#Boise St	13	3	.813	23	6	.793
*Idaho	13	3	.813	25	5	.833
Montana..............	11	5	.688	20	11	.645
Nevada-Reno	10	6	.625	16	12	.571
Weber St	9	7	.563	17	11	.607
Montana St	6	10	.375	14	15	.483
Eastern Washington	5	11	.313	8	22	.267
Idaho St	4	12	.250	9	18	.333
Northern Arizona	1	15	.063	2	25	.074

Conf. Tourney Final: Idaho 59, Boise St. 52.

***NCAA Tournament:** Idaho (0-1).

#NIT Tournament: Boise St.(0-1).

Big South Conference

	Conference			Overall		
	W	L	Pct	W	L	Pct
Coastal Carolina	9	3	.750	14	14	.500
Campbell	8	4	.667	18	12	.600
NC-Asheville...........	6	6	.500	16	14	.533
Baptist College	6	6	.500	12	16	.429
Winthrop	5	7	.417	16	13	.552
Radford	5	7	.417	15	13	.536
Augusta	3	9	.250	5	23	.179

Conf. Tourney Final: NC-Asheville 93, Campbell 78.

Big Ten Conference

	Conference			Overall		
	W	L	Pct	W	L	Pct
*Indiana.............	15	3	.833	25	7	.781
*Illinois.............	14	4	.778	27	4	.871
*Michigan	12	6	.667	24	7	.774
*Iowa	10	8	.556	22	9	.710
*Minnesota..........	9	9	.500	17	11	.607
#Wisconsin	8	10	.444	17	11	.607
Purdue	8	10	.444	15	16	.484
#Ohio St	6	12	.333	17	14	.548
#Michigan St	6	12	.333	15	13	.536
Northwestern	2	16	.111	9	19	.321

Conf. Tourney Final: Big Ten has no tournament.

***NCAA Tournament:** Michigan (6-0, won Final), Illinois (4-1, lost Semifinal), Indiana (2-1), Minnesota (2-1), Iowa (1-1).

#NIT Tournament: Michigan St.(3-1, lost Semifinal), Ohio St.(2-1), Wisconsin (1-1).

Big West Conference

	Conference			Overall		
	W	L	Pct	W	L	Pct
*UNLV	16	2	.889	26	7	.788
#New Mexico St	12	6	.667	21	10	.677
#UC Santa Barbara	11	7	.611	20	10	.667
Cal St-Fullerton	10	8	.556	16	13	.552
Long Beach	10	8	.556	13	15	.464
Utah St.............	10	8	.556	12	16	.429
Fresno St	9	9	.500	15	14	.517
UC Irvine	8	10	.444	12	17	.414
Pacific..............	3	15	.167	7	21	.250
San Jose St	1	17	.056	5	23	.179

Conf. Tourney Final: UNLV 68, New Mexico St. 62.

***NCAA Tournament:** UNLV (3-1).

#NIT Tournament: New Mexico St.(0-1), Santa Barbara (0-1).

Colonial Athletic Association

	Conference			Overall		
	W	L	Pct	W	L	Pct
#Richmond	13	1	.929	20	9	.690
*George Mason	10	4	.714	20	10	.667
American	9	5	.643	17	11	.607
NC-Wilmington	9	5	.643	16	14	.533
James Madison	6	8	.429	16	14	.533
East Carolina	6	8	.429	15	14	.517
William & Mary	2	12	.143	5	23	.179
Navy	1	13	.071	6	22	.214

Conf. Tourney Final: Geo.Mason 78, NC-Wilmington 72 (OT).

***NCAA Tournament:** George Mason (0-1).

#NIT Tournament: Richmond (1-1).

East Coast Conference

	Conference			Overall		
	W	L	Pct	W	L	Pct
*Bucknell	11	3	.786	23	7	.767
Towson St	10	4	.714	19	10	.655
Lafayette.............	8	6	.571	20	10	.667
Hofstra	7	7	.500	14	15	.483
Drexel	7	7	.500	12	16	.429
Delaware	6	8	.429	14	14	.500
Lehigh..............	5	9	.357	10	18	.357
Rider	2	12	.143	5	23	.179

Conf. Tourney Final: Bucknell 71, Lafayette 65.

***NCAA Tournament:** Bucknell (0-1).

ECAC North Atlantic

	Conference			Overall		
	W	L	Pct	W	L	Pct
*Siena	16	1	.941	24	4	.857
Boston University	14	4	.778	21	9	.700
Northeastern	12	5	.706	17	11	.607
Canisius	11	7	.611	13	15	.464
Hartford	10	7	.588	15	13	.536
Maine	7	11	.389	9	19	.321
Niagara	6	12	.333	9	19	.321
Colgate	5	13	.278	6	22	.214
Vermont	4	14	.222	6	21	.222
New Hampshire	3	14	.176	4	22	.154

Conf. Tourney Final: Siena 68, Boston Univ. 67.

*NCAA Tournament: Siena (1-1).

Ivy League

	Conference			Overall		
	W	L	Pct	W	L	Pct
*Princeton	11	3	.786	19	7	.731
Dartmouth	10	4	.714	17	9	.654
Pennsylvania	9	5	.643	13	13	.500
Harvard	7	7	.500	11	15	.423
Cornell	7	7	.500	10	16	.385
Yale	6	8	.429	11	17	.393
Columbia	4	10	.286	8	18	.308
Brown	2	12	.143	7	19	.269

Conf. Tourney Final: Ivy League has no tournament.

*NCAA Tournament: Princeton (0-1).

Metro Conference

	Conference			Overall		
	W	L	Pct	W	L	Pct
*Florida St	9	3	.750	22	7	.759
*Louisville	8	4	.667	22	8	.733
*Memphis St	8	4	.667	21	10	.677
*South Carolina	8	4	.667	19	10	.655
Cincinnati	5	7	.417	15	12	.556
Virginia Tech	2	10	.167	11	17	.393
Southern Mississippi	2	10	.167	10	17	.370

Conf. Tourney Final: Louisville 87, Florida St. 80.

*NCAA Tournament: Louisville (2-1), Florida St.(0-1), Memphis St.(0-1), South Carolina (0-1).

Metro Atlantic Conference

	Conference			Overall		
	W	L	Pct	W	L	Pct
*La Salle	13	1	.929	26	5	.839
#St.Peter's	11	3	.786	22	8	.733
Iona	8	6	.571	15	16	.484
Fordham	8	6	.571	14	15	.483
Army	6	8	.429	12	16	.429
Holy Cross	5	9	.357	13	15	.464
Manhattan	3	11	.214	7	21	.250
Fairfield	2	12	.143	7	21	.250

Conf. Tourney Final: La Salle 71, St.Peter's 58.

*NCAA Tournament: La Salle (0-1).

#NIT Tournament: St.Peter's (0-1).

Mid-American Conference

	Conference			Overall		
	W	L	Pct	W	L	Pct
*Ball St	14	2	.875	28	2	.933
#Kent St	11	5	.688	20	10	.667
Toledo	9	7	.563	16	15	.516
Miami,OH	8	8	.500	13	15	.464
Eastern Michigan	7	9	.438	16	13	.552
Bowling Green	6	10	.375	12	16	.429
Central Michigan	6	10	.375	12	16	.429
Western Michigan	6	10	.375	12	16	.429
Ohio University	5	11	.313	12	17	.414

Conf. Tourney Final: Ball St. 67, Kent St. 65.

*NCAA Tournament: Ball St.(1-1).

#NIT Tournament: Kent St.(0-1).

Mid-Eastern Athletic Conference

	Conference			Overall		
	W	L	Pct	W	L	Pct
*South Carolina St	14	2	.875	25	7	.781
Florida A&M	12	4	.750	20	10	.667
Coppin St	11	5	.688	18	11	.621
Morgan St	8	8	.500	14	15	.483
Bethune-Cookman	8	8	.500	12	16	.429
Delaware St	6	10	.375	11	17	.393
Howard	6	10	.375	10	18	.357
North Carolina A&T	6	10	.375	9	18	.333
Maryland-East.Shore	1	15	.063	1	26	.037

Conf. Tourney Final: S.Carolina St. 83, Florida A&M 79.

*NCAA Tournament: S.Carolina St.(0-1).

Midwestern Collegiate Conference

	Conference			Overall		
	W	L	Pct	W	L	Pct
*Evansville	10	2	.833	24	5	.828
#St.Louis	8	4	.667	23	9	.719
*Xavier,OH	7	5	.583	21	11	.656
Dayton	6	6	.500	12	17	.414
Loyola,IL	4	8	.333	11	17	.393
Detroit	4	8	.333	7	21	.250
Butler	3	9	.250	11	17	.393

Conf. Tourney Final: Xavier 85, Evansville 78.

*NCAA Tournament: Evansville (1-1), Xavier (0-1).

#NIT Tournament: St.Louis (4-1, lost Final).

Missouri Valley Conference

	Conference			Overall		
	W	L	Pct	W	L	Pct
*Creighton	11	3	.786	20	10	.667
#Wichita St	10	4	.714	18	10	.643
Tulsa	10	4	.714	18	13	.581
Bradley	7	7	.500	13	14	.481
#Southern Illinois	6	8	.429	20	13	.606
Illinois St	6	8	.429	13	17	.433
Drake	6	8	.429	12	17	.414
Indiana St	0	14	.000	4	24	.143

Conf. Tourney Final: Creighton 79, So.Illinois 77.

*NCAA Tournament: Creighton (0-1).

#NIT Tournament: Wichita St.(1-1), So.Illinois (0-1).

Northeast Conference

	Conference			Overall		
	W	L	Pct	W	L	Pct
*Robert Morris	12	4	.750	21	8	.724
Fairleigh Dickinson	11	5	.688	17	12	.586
Monmouth,NJ	9	7	.563	15	13	.536
Marist	9	7	.563	13	15	.464
Loyola,MD	7	9	.438	10	18	.357
Long Island	7	9	.438	9	19	.321
St.Francis,PA	6	10	.375	13	16	.448
Wagner	6	10	.375	11	16	.407
St.Francis,NY	5	11	.313	11	16	.407

Conf. Tourney Final: Robt.Morris 67, FDU 66.

NCAA Tournament: Robert Morris (0-1).

Ohio Valley Conference

	Conference			Overall		
	W	L	Pct	W	L	Pct
*Middle Tenn.St	10	2	.833	22	7	.759
#Murray St	10	2	.833	19	10	.655
Austin Peay	8	4	.667	18	12	.600
Morehead St	5	7	.417	15	16	.484
Eastern Kentucky	4	8	.333	7	22	.241
Tennessee Tech	3	9	.250	10	20	.333
Tennessee St	2	10	.167	4	24	.143

Conf. Tourney Final: Middle Tenn. 82, Austin Peay 79.

NCAA Tournament: Middle Tenn.St.(1-1).

#NIT Tournament: Murray St.(0-1).

Pacific-10 Conference

	Conference			Overall		
	W	L	Pct	W	L	Pct
*Arizona	17	1	.944	27	3	.900
*Stanford	15	3	.833	26	6	.813
*Oregon St	13	5	.722	21	7	.750
*UCLA	13	5	.722	20	9	.690
#California	10	8	.556	19	11	.633
Washington	8	10	.444	12	16	.429
Arizona St	5	13	.278	12	16	.429
Washington St	4	14	.222	10	19	.345
Oregon	3	15	.167	8	21	.276
Southern Cal	2	16	.111	10	22	.313

Conf. Tourney Final: Arizona 73, Stanford 51.

NCAA Tournament: Arizona (2-1), UCLA (1-1), Stanford (0-1), Oregon St.(0-1).

#NIT Tournament: California (1-1).

Southeastern Conference

	Conference			Overall		
	W	L	Pct	W	L	Pct
*Florida	13	5	.722	21	11	.656
*Alabama	12	6	.667	23	7	.767
*Vanderbilt	12	6	.667	18	13	.581
*Tennessee	11	7	.611	19	10	.655
*LSU	11	7	.611	20	11	.645
#Mississippi	8	10	.444	15	14	.517
Kentucky	8	10	.444	13	19	.406
Mississippi St	7	11	.389	13	15	.464
Georgia	6	12	.333	15	16	.484
Auburn	2	16	.111	9	19	.321

Conf. Tourney Final: Alabama 72, Florida 60.

NCAA Tournament: Florida (0-1), Alabama (0-1), Vanderbilt (0-1), Tennessee (0-1), LSU (0-1).

#NIT Tournament: Mississippi (0-1)

Southern Conference

	Conference			Overall		
	W	L	Pct	W	L	Pct
Tenn-Chattanooga	10	4	.714	18	12	.600
Furman	9	5	.643	17	12	.586
Appalachian St	8	6	.571	20	8	.714
*East Tennessee St	7	7	.500	20	10	.667
Citadel	7	7	.500	16	12	.571
Marshall	6	8	.429	15	15	.500
VMI	5	9	.357	11	17	.393
Western Carolina	4	10	.286	12	16	.429

Conf. Tourney Final: E.Tenn.St. 96, Marshall 73.

NCAA Tournament: East Tenn.St.(0-1).

Southland Conference

	Conference			Overall		
	W	L	Pct	W	L	Pct
North Texas	10	4	.714	14	15	.483
NE Louisiana	9	5	.643	16	12	.571
*McNeese St	9	5	.643	16	13	.552
Sam Houston St	8	6	.571	12	16	.429
Northwestern LA	7	7	.500	12	16	.429
SW Texas St	6	8	.429	13	16	.448
Texas-Arlington	4	10	.286	7	20	.259
Stephen F.Austin	3	11	.214	10	18	.357

Conf. Tourney Final: McNeese St. 85, North Texas 68.

NCAA Tournament: McNeese St.(0-1).

Southwest Conference

	Conference			Overall		
	W	L	Pct	W	L	Pct
*Arkansas	13	3	.813	24	6	.800
*Texas	12	4	.750	24	8	.750
TCU	9	7	.563	17	13	.567
Houston	8	8	.500	17	14	.548
Texas A&M	8	8	.500	16	14	.533
Texas Tech	8	8	.500	13	15	.464
SMU	7	9	.438	13	16	.448
Rice	6	10	.375	12	16	.429
Baylor	1	15	.063	5	22	.185

Conf. Tourney Final: Arkansas 100, Texas 76.

NCAA Tournament: Arkansas (1-1), Texas (1-1).

Southwestern Athletic Conference

	Conference			Overall		
	W	L	Pct	W	L	Pct
*Southern University	10	4	.714	20	10	.667
Texas Southern	10	4	.714	17	13	.567
Grambling	10	4	.714	15	14	.517
Jackson St	7	7	.500	15	13	.536
Alabama St	7	7	.500	13	16	.448
Prairie View	5	9	.357	11	16	.407
Alcorn St	4	10	.286	5	23	.179
Mississippi Valley	3	11	.214	8	20	.286

Conf. Tourney Final: Southern 86, Tex.Southern 81 (OT).

NCAA Tournament: Southern Univ.(0-1).

Sun Belt Conference

	Conference			Overall		
	W	L	Pct	W	L	Pct
*South Alabama	11	3	.786	22	8	.733
#NC-Charlotte	10	4	.714	17	11	.607
Va.Commonwealth	9	5	.643	13	15	.464
#Ala-Birmingham	8	6	.571	18	11	.621
Old Dominion	7	7	.500	15	13	.536
Jacksonville	5	9	.357	14	16	.467
Western Kentucky	4	10	.286	14	15	.483
South Florida	2	12	.143	7	21	.250

Conf. Tourney Final: S.Alabama 105, Jacksonville 59.

***NCAA Tournament:** South Alabama (1-1).

#NIT Tournament: Ala-Birmingham (3-1, lost Semifinal), NC-Charlotte (0-1).

Trans America Athletic Conference

	Conference			Overall		
	W	L	Pct	W	L	Pct
#Georgia Southern	16	2	.889	23	5	.821
*Ark-Little Rock	14	4	.778	23	7	.767
Stetson	10	8	.556	17	12	.586
Centenary	9	9	.500	16	14	.533
Georgia St	9	9	.500	14	14	.500
Mercer	9	9	.500	14	14	.500
Texas-San Antonio	8	10	.444	15	13	.536
Houston Baptist	6	12	.333	9	20	.310
Samford	5	13	.278	8	19	.296
Hardin-Simmons	4	14	.222	8	19	.296

Conf. Tourney Final: Ark-Little Rock 100, Centenary 72.

***NCAA Tournament:** Ark-Little Rock (0-1).

#NIT Tournament: Georgia Southern (0-1)

Division I Independents

	W	L	Pct
#Akron	21	7	.750
*Notre Dame	20	8	.714
*DePaul	20	11	.645
Miami,FL	19	12	.613
Maryland-Baltimore County	17	11	.607
Wright St	17	11	.607
Marquette	13	15	.464
Mount St.Mary's,MD	12	15	.444
Chicago St	12	16	.429
Nicholls St	12	16	.429
Northern Illinois	11	17	.393
U.S. International	11	17	.393
Liberty	10	17	.370
Central Connecticut	10	18	.357
Florida International	10	18	.357
Southern Utah	10	18	.357
Oral Roberts	8	20	.286
Central Florida	7	20	.259
Davidson	7	24	.226
Youngstown St	5	23	.179
Brooklyn	4	23	.148
SE Louisiana	4	23	.148

***NCAA Tournament:** Notre Dame (1-1), DePaul (1-1).

#NIT Tournament: Akron (0-1).

West Coast Athletic Conference

	Conference			Overall		
	W	L	Pct	W	L	Pct
*St.Mary's	12	2	.857	25	4	.862
*Loyola Marymount	10	4	.714	20	10	.667
#Pepperdine	10	4	.714	19	12	.613
San Francisco	8	6	.571	16	12	.571
#Santa Clara	7	7	.500	20	10	.667
Gonzaga	5	9	.357	14	14	.500
San Diego	2	12	.143	8	20	.286
Portland	2	12	.143	2	26	.071

Conf. Tourney Final: Loyola Marymount 75, Santa Clara 70.

***NCAA Tournament:** St.Mary's (0-1), Loyola Marymount (0-1).

#NIT Tournament: Pepperdine (1-1), Santa Clara (0-1).

Western Athletic Conference

	Conference			Overall		
	W	L	Pct	W	L	Pct
*Colorado St	12	4	.750	22	9	.710
*UTEP	11	5	.688	24	6	.800
#New Mexico	11	5	.688	20	9	.690
#Hawaii	9	7	.563	17	12	.586
BYU	7	9	.438	14	15	.483
Air Force	6	10	.375	14	14	.500
Utah	6	10	.375	16	17	.485
Wyoming	6	10	.375	14	17	.452
San Diego St	4	12	.250	12	17	.414

Conf. Tourney Final: UTEP 73, Colorado St. 60.

***NCAA Tournament:** Colorado St.(1-1), UTEP (1-1).

#NIT Tournament: New Mexico (2-1), Hawaii (0-1).

1989 Consensus All-America Team

The NCAA Division I players cited most frequently by the following All-America selectors: AP, US Basketball Writers, National Assn of Basketball Coaches, and UPI.

First Team

	Class	Hgt	Pos
Sean Elliott, Arizona	Sr	6-8	G/F
Danny Ferry, Duke	Sr	6-10	F
Stacey King, Oklahoma	Sr	6-10	C
Chris Jackson, LSU	Fr	6-1	G
Pervis Ellison, Louisville	Sr	6-9	F/C

Second Team

	Class	Hgt	Pos
Mookie Blaylock, Oklahoma	Sr	6-1	G
Jay Edwards, Indiana	So	6-4	G
Todd Lichti, Stanford	Sr	6-4	G
Glen Rice, Michigan	Sr	6-7	F
Lionel Simmons, La Salle	Jr	6-6	F

1989 Players of the Year

Sean Elliott of Arizona—AP, National Assn of Basketball Coaches, and the John Wooden Award.
Danny Ferry of Duke—UPI, the U.S.Basketball Writers Assn., and the James Naismith Award.

1989 Coaches of the Year

Bob Knight of Indiana—AP, UPI, and the U.S.Basketball Writers Assn.
P.J.Carlesimo of Seton Hall—the National Assn. of Basketball Coaches.
Mike Krzyzewski of Duke—the Naismith Award.

1989 NCAA Men's Division I Individual Leaders

Scoring

Player, School	Cl	FG	FT	Pts	Avg
Hank Gathers, Loyola,CA	Jr	419	177	1015	32.7
Chris Jackson, LSU	Fr	359	163	965	30.2
Lionel Simmons, La Salle	Jr	349	189	908	28.4
Gerald Glass, Miss.	Jr	326	148	841	28.0
Blue Edwards, E.Carolina	Sr	297	154	773	26.7
Raymond Dudley, A.Force	Jr	262	117	746	26.6
Bimbo Coles, Va.Tech	Jr	249	157	717	26.6
Michael Smith, BYU	Sr	286	160	765	26.4
Stacey King, Oklahoma	Sr	324	211	859	26.0
John Taft, Marshall	So	245	159	701	26.0
Jeff Martin, Murray St	Sr	266	148	745	25.7
Glen Rice, Michigan	Sr	363	124	949	25.6
Kurk Lee, Towson St	Jr	243	170	736	25.4
Tom Davis, Delaware St	So	276	154	706	25.2
Eric Brown, Miami,FL	Sr	255	246	765	24.7

Rebounding

Player, School	Cl	Gm	Reb	Avg
Hank Gathers, Loyola,CA	Jr	31	426	13.7
Tyrone Hill, Xavier	Jr	33	403	12.2
Ron Draper, American	Jr	28	336	12.0
Daryl Battles, Southern-BR	Sr	31	360	11.6
Lionel Simmons, La Salle	Jr	32	365	11.4
Derrick Coleman, Syracuse	Jr	37	422	11.4
Fred Burton, LIU-Brooklyn	Jr	28	309	11.0
Rodney Mack, S.Carolina St	Sr	33	361	10.9
Kenny Sanders, George Mason	Sr	30	326	10.9
Rico Washington, Weber St	Sr	28	303	10.8

Blocked Shots

Player, School	Cl	Gm	No	Avg
Alonzo Mourning, Georgetown	Fr	34	169	5.0
Duane Causwell, Temple	So	30	124	4.1
Alan Ogg, Ala-Birmingham	Jr	34	129	3.8
Derrick Coleman, Syracuse	Jr	37	127	3.4
Mike Butts, Bucknell	Sr	31	100	3.2
Pervis Ellison, Louisville	Sr	31	98	3.2
Monty Henderson, Siena	Sr	28	86	3.1
Kenny Green, Rhode Island	Jr	28	85	3.0
Fred West, Texas Southern	Jr	30	90	3.0
Elden Campbell, Clemson	Jr	29	87	3.0

Assists

Player, School	Cl	Gm	No	Avg
Glenn Williams, Holy Cross	Sr	28	278	9.9
Chris Corchiani, N.C.State	So	31	266	8.6
Sherman Douglas, Syracuse	Sr	38	326	8.6
Gary Payton, Oregon St	Jr	30	244	8.1
Anthony Manuel, Bradley	Sr	27	216	8.0
Jeff Timberlake, Boston Univ	Sr	30	238	7.9
Doug Overton, La Salle	So	32	244	7.6
Pooh Richardson, UCLA	Sr	31	236	7.6
Carlos Sample, Southern-BR	Sr	31	234	7.5
Darrell McGee, New Mexico	Jr	33	243	7.4

Steals

Player, School	Cl	Gm	No	Avg
Kenny Robertson, Cleveland St	Jr	28	111	4.0
Mookie Blaylock, Oklahoma	Sr	35	131	3.7
Darrion Applewhite, TX-South'n	Jr	30	105	3.5
Carlton Screen, Providence	Jr	29	101	3.5
Kurk Lee, Towson St	Jr	29	98	3.4
D'wayne Tanner, Rice	Jr	28	94	3.4

Field Goal Percentage

Player, School	Cl	Gm	FG	FGA	Pct
Dwayne Davis, Florida	So	33	179	248	72.2
Cameron Burns, Miss.St	So	28	167	249	67.1
Dale Davis, Clemson	So	29	146	218	67.0
Rodney Mack, S.Carolina St	Sr	33	204	306	66.7
Brian parker, Cleve.St	Jr	28	168	253	66.4

Free Throw Percentage

Player, School	Cl	Gm	FT	FTA	Pct
Michael Smith, BYU	Sr	29	160	173	92.5
Steve Henson, Kansas St	Jr	30	92	100	92.0
Larry Simmons, MD-Balt	Jr	28	83	92	90.2
Kai Nurnberger, So.Ill	Sr	32	129	143	90.2
Scott Haffner, Evanville	Sr	31	136	151	90.1

3-Pt Field Goal Percentage

Player, School	Cl	Gm	FG	FGA	Pct
Dave Calloway, Monm.,NJ	So	28	48	82	58.5
Joel Tribelhorn, Colo.St	Sr	33	76	135	56.3
Mike Joseph, Bucknell	Jr	31	62	115	53.9
John Bays, Towson St	Sr	29	71	132	53.8
Mark Anglavar, Marquette	So	28	53	99	53.5

3-Pt Field Goals Per Game

Player, School	Cl	Gm	FG	Pct
Timothy Pollard, Miss.Valley	Sr	28	124	4.4
Sydney Grider, SW Louisiana	Jr	29	122	4.2
Jeff Fryer, Loyola,CA	Jr	31	126	4.1
Dana Barros, Boston College	Sr	29	112	3.9
Four players tied at 3.8				

1989 NCAA Men's Division I Team Leaders

Scoring Offense

	Gm	W-L	Pts	Avg
Loyola-Marymount,CA	31	20-11	3,486	112.5
Oklahoma	36	30- 6	3,680	102.2
Southern-BR	31	20-11	3,015	97.3
Texas	34	25- 9	3,206	94.3
LSU	32	20-12	2,966	92.7
Ark-Little Rock	31	23- 8	2,851	92.0
Michigan	37	30- 7	3,393	91.7
Florida St	30	22- 8	2,739	91.3
South Alabama	32	23- 9	2,912	91.0
Middle Tennessee St	31	23- 8	2,810	90.6
Miami,FL	31	19-12	2,809	90.6

Scoring Defense

	Gm	W-L	Pts	Avg
Princeton	27	19- 8	1,430	53.0
St.Mary's,CA	30	25- 5	1,728	57.6
Boise St	30	23- 7	1,767	58.9
Colorado St	33	23-10	2,012	61.0
Idaho	31	25- 6	1,894	61.1
Ball St	32	29- 3	1,968	61.5
Fresno St	29	15-14	1,823	62.9
SW Missouri St	31	21-10	1,962	63.3
Arkansas St	30	20-10	1,901	63.4
Wisconsin-Green Bay	28	14-14	1,790	63.9

Scoring Margin

	Off	Def	Margin
St.Mary's,CA	76.1	57.6	18.5
Arizona	84.5	66.9	17.6
Michigan	91.7	74.8	16.9
Duke	86.5	69.8	16.8
Siena	85.0	69.8	15.1
Idaho	76.2	61.1	15.1
Akron	85.3	70.7	14.6
Georgetown	80.0	65.4	14.6
Arkansas	89.7	75.4	14.3
Oklahoma	102.2	88.5	13.7
Syracuse	89.7	76.1	13.7

Other NCAA Men's Tournaments

Division II

After eight regionals, the 1989 Div.II Quarterfinal pairings were as follows: Sacred Heart,CT (22-9) vs North Carolina Central (25-4); Ky.Wesleyan (24-6) vs Jacksonville St.,AL (26-4); Wisconsin-Milwaukee (24-6) vs Southeast Missouri St.(25-5); Millersville,PA (26-6) vs UC-Riverside (27-4).

Final Eight (at Springfield,MA): **Quarterfinals**—SE MISSOURI ST. 93, Wisc-Milwaukee 84; JACKSONVILLE ST. 107, Ky.Wesleyan 70; UC-RIVERSIDE 92, Millersville 86; N.C.CENTRAL 58, Sacred Heart 57. **Semifinals**— SE MISSOURI ST. 84, UC-Riverside 83 (OT); N.C.CENTRAL 90, Jacksonville St. 70. **Third Place**—UC-RIVERSIDE 90, Jacksonville St. 81. **Championship**— N.C.CENTRAL 73, SE Missouri St. 46.

Division III

After eight regionals, the 1989 Div.III Quarterfinal pairings were as follows: Franklin & Marshall,PA (27-2) at Southern Maine (22-6); Potsdam St.,NY (24-4) at Trenton St.,NJ (28-1); Otterbein,OH (21-9) at Wisconsin-Whitewater (26-2); Cal St.Stanislaus (21-7) at Centre,KY (23-5).

Quarterfinals—SOUTHERN MAINE 79, Franklin & Marshall 71; TRENTON ST. 78, Potsdam St. 62; WISC-WHITEWATER 105, Otterbein 86; CENTRE 124, CS-Stanislaus 123 (2 OT). **Final Four** (at Springfield,OH): **Semifinals**—TRENTON ST. 84, Southern Maine 62; WISC-WHITEWATER 88, Centre 81. **Third Place**—SOUTHERN MAINE 81, Centre 70. **Championship**—WISC-WHITEWATER 94, Trenton St. 86.

Women's NCAA Tournaments

Division I

MIDEAST

Seeds

1 **Auburn** (28-1)	7 Rutgers (23-6)
2 N.C.State (23-6)	8 Temple (21-9)
3 Mississippi (21-7)	9 Holy Cross (21-9)
4 Clemson (19-10)	10 Southern Miss (26-4)
5 Georgia (22-6)	11 Villanova (18-11)
6 Old Dominion (22-8)	12 Tenn-Chatt (19-11)

First Round

GEORGIA 90, Tenn-Chatt 69; OLD DOMINION 66, Villanova 41; RUTGERS 95, Southern Miss 73; TEMPLE 90, Holy Cross 80.

Second Round

AUBURN 88, Temple 54; N.C.STATE 75, Rutgers 73; MISSISSIPPI 74, Old Dominion 58; CLEMSON 78, Georgia 65.

Regionals (at Auburn, AL)

Semifinals—AUBURN 71, Clemson 60; MISSISSIPPI 68, N.C.State 63.
Championship—AUBURN 77, Mississippi 51.

EAST

Seeds

1 **Tennessee** (30-2)	7 Vanderbilt (21-7)
2 Long Beach St.(28-4)	8 Connecticut (24-5)
3 Ohio St.(23-5)	9 La Salle (27-2)
4 Virginia (20-9)	10 St.Joseph's (22-7)
5 Western Ky.(22-8)	11 Providence (22-10)
6 James Madison (25-3)	12 West Va.(22-7)

First Round

WEST VIRGINIA 66, Western Ky. 57; JAMES MADISON 94, Providence 74; ST.JOSEPH'S 82, Vanderbilt 68; LA SALLE 72, Connecticut 63.

Second Round

TENNESSEE 91, La Salle 61; LONG BEACH ST. 84, St.Joseph's 65; OHIO ST. 81, James Madison 66; VIRGINIA 81, West Virginia 68.

Regionals (at Bowling Green,KY)

Semifinals—TENNESSEE 80, Virginia 47; LONG BEACH ST. 89, Ohio St. 83.
Championship—TENNESSEE 94, Long Beach St. 80

MIDWEST

Seeds

1 **Louisiana Tech** (29-3)	7 Illinois St.(22-7)
2 Stanford (26-2)	8 Miami,FL (21-7)
3 Iowa (26-4)	9 Oklahoma St.(19-11)
4 LSU (18-10)	10 NW Louisiana (22-7)
5 Purdue (23-5)	11 Tenn.Tech (21-7)
6 South Carolina (23-6)	12 Arkansas (22-7)

First Round

PURDUE 91, Arkansas 63; TENNESSEE TECH 77, South Carolina 73; ILLINOIS ST. 100, NW Louisiana 79; OKLAHOMA ST. 93, Miami,FL 69.

Second Round

LOUISIANA TECH 103, Oklahoma St. 78; STANFORD 105, Illinois St. 77; IOWA 77, Tennessee Tech 75; LSU 54, Purdue 53.

Regionals (at Ruston, LA)

Semifinals—LOUISIANA TECH 85, LSU 68; STANFORD 98, Iowa 74.
Championship—LOUISIANA TECH 85, Stanford 75.

WEST

Seeds

1 **Maryland** (26-2)	7 CS-Fullerton (21-8)
2 Texas (25-4)	8 Cincinnati (21-8)
3 Colorado (27-3)	9 Bowling Green (25-3)
4 S.F.Austin (29-3)	10 Montana (26-3)
5 Washington (22-9)	11 Utah (24-5)
6 UNLV (25-6)	12 Hawaii (18-9)

First Round

WASHINGTON 87, Hawaii 79; UNLV 67, Utah 53; MONTANA 82, Cal St-Fullerton 67; BOWLING GREEN 69, Cincinnati 59.

Second Round

MARYLAND 78, Bowling Green 65; TEXAS 83, Montana 54; UNLV 84, Colorado 74; S.F.AUSTIN 73, Washington 63.

Regionals (at Austin,TX)

Semifinals—MARYLAND 89, S.F.Austin 54; TEXAS 88, UNLV 77.
Championship—MARYLAND 79, Texas 71

THE FINAL FOUR
at Tacoma, WA (Tacoma Dome)

Semifinals

Auburn 76 . . . . Louisiana Tech 71
Tennessee 77 . . . . Maryland 65

Championship

Tennessee 76 . . . . Auburn 60

Final records: Tennessee (35-2), Auburn (32-2), Maryland (29-3), Louisiana Tech (32-4).

All-Tournament Team: Vicki Orr of Auburn; Venus Lacy of La.Tech; Deanna Tate of Maryland; Bridgette Gordon and Sheila Frost of Tennessee.

Most Valuable Player: Bridgette Gordon, Tennessee.

Championship
Tennessee 76, Auburn 60

Auburn	Min	FG M-A	FT M-A	Pts	Rb	A	F
Jocelyn McGilberry	18	0- 2	0- 1	**0**	4	0	2
Patrena Scruggs	30	2- 9	2- 3	**6**	0	0	4
Vickie Orr	34	8-15	0- 0	**16**	11	0	1
Carolyn Jones	39	5-10	2- 2	**12**	4	2	3
Ruthie Bolton	36	5-11	0- 0	**10**	6	9	4
Linda Godby	20	5-11	3- 4	**13**	3	0	4
Chantel Tremitiere	4	1- 1	0- 0	**2**	1	0	2
Lynn Stevenson	6	0- 1	1- 2	**1**	0	0	2
Kendall Mago	6	0- 0	0- 0	**0**	0	0	0
Evelyn Thompson	6	0- 0	0- 0	**0**	1	1	2
Lisa Ciampi	1	0- 0	0- 0	**0**	0	0	0
TOTALS	200	26-60	8-12	**60**	30	12	24

Three-point field goals: 0-4 (Scruggs 0-1, Jones, 0-1; Bolton 0-1, Stevenson 0-1); **Blocked Shots:** 4 (Orr 4); **Turnovers:** 18 (Bolton 7, McGilberry 3, Orr 2, Jones 2, Scruggs, Godby, Tremitiere, Stevenson); **Steals:** 6 (Jones 2, Bolton 2, McGhee, Orr); **FG Pct—** .433; **FT Pct—** .667.

Tennessee	Min	FG M-A	FT M-A	Pts	Rb	A	F
Bridgette Gordon	36	11-21	5- 6	**27**	11	1	3
Carla McGhee	22	1- 3	1- 2	**3**	4	1	0
Sheila Frost	36	2- 8	2- 3	**6**	12	1	4
Dena Head	37	6-12	7- 9	**19**	3	2	4
Melissa McCray	35	2-10	2- 2	**6**	6	10	1
Daedra Charles	21	5- 7	3- 4	**13**	7	0	2
Debbie Scott	7	1- 4	0- 0	**2**	1	0	0
Kelli Casteel	1	0- 0	0- 0	**0**	0	0	0
Dennie Hawhee	1	0- 0	0- 0	**0**	0	0	0
Regina Clark	4	0- 1	0- 0	**0**	0	1	0
TOTALS	200	28-66	20-26	**76**	45	16	4

Three-point field goals: None; **Blocked Shots:** 7 (Frost 5, Charles 2); **Turnovers:** 15 (Charles 3, McCray 3, Head 3, McGhee 2, Clark 2, Gordon, Scott); **Steals:** 8 (Frost 3, McGhee 2, Charles 2, Gordon); **Team Rebounds:** 1; **FG Pct—** .424; **FT Pct—** .769.

Auburn (32-2)	. . . . .27 33	—80
Tennessee (35-2)	. . . . .35 41	—76

Officials: Patty Broderick and June Corteau.
Attendance: 9,758.

Other NCAA
Women's Tournaments

Division II

After eight regionals, the 1989 Div.II Quarterfinal pairings were as follows: Bloomsburg,PA (28-1) at Bentley,MA (29-2); St.Joseph's,IN (27-3) at Cal Poly Pomona (26-5); District of Columbia (22-3) at Delta St.,MS (27-4); Central Missouri St.(28-3) at St.Cloud St.,MN (21-8).

Quarterfinals—DELTA ST. 85, Distrist of Columbia 53; CENTRAL MISSOURI ST. 87, St.Cloud St. 71; BENTLEY 73, Bloomsburg 68; CAL POLY POMONA 72, St.Joseph's 63.

Final Four (at Cleveland,MS): **Semifinals—**CAL POLY POMONA 84, Bentley 83 (2 OT); DELTA ST. 94, Central Missouri St. 73. **Third Place—**BENTLEY 83, Central Missouri St. 81. **Championship—**DELTA ST. 88, Cal Poly Pomona 58.

Division III

After eight regionals, the 1989 Div.III Quarterfinal pairings were as follows: Elizabethtown,PA (26-2) at Muskingum,OH (29-1); Wisconsin-Eau Claire (24-3) at Centre,KY (21-7); Clark,MA (28-0) at Clarkson,NY (25-5); Cal St.Stanislaus (25-1) at Luther,IA (22-6).

Quarterfinals—ELIZABETHTOWN 72, Muskingum 67; CENTRE 82, Wisc-Eau Claire 62; CLARKSON 72, Clark 58; CS-STANISLAUS 70, Luther 67.

Final Four (at Danville,KY). **Semifinals—**CS-STANISLAUS 89, Clarkson 74; ELIZABETHTOWN 73, Centre 64 (OT). **Third Place—**CENTRE 106, Clarkson 78. **Championship—**ELIZABETHTOWN 66, CS-Stanislaus 65.

NAIA Tournament

Men

After two rounds in the 32-team, 1989 tournament at Kemper Arena in Kansas City,MO, the Quarterfinal pairings were as follows: East Central,OK (23-6) vs Siena Heights,MI (31-6); Central Washington (31-9) vs Wheeling Jesuit,WV (31-3); Wisconsin-Eau Claire (28-3) vs Hastings,NE (26-8); St.Mary's,TX (25-5) vs College of Idaho (24-8).

Quarterfinals—EAST CENTRAL 77, Siena Heights 67; CENTRAL WASH. 87, Wheeling Jesuit 78; WISC-EAU CLAIRE 88, Hastings 73; ST.MARY'S 81, Col.of Idaho 80.

Semifinals—EAST CENTRAL 58, Wisc-Eau Claire 56; ST.MARY'S 60, Central Wash. **Championship—**ST.MARY'S 61, East Central 58.

Women

After two rounds in the 32-team, 1989 tournament at Kemper Arena in Kansas City,MO, the Quarterfinal pairings were as follows: St.Ambrose,IA (34-1) vs Doane,NE (27-6); Claflin,SC (33-0) vs Central St.,OH (29-1); Arkansas Tech (34-1) vs Wayland Baptist,TX (30-7); Southern Nazarene,OK (33-2) vs Western Washington (29-4).

Quarterfinals—ST.AMBROSE 90, Doane 69; CLAFLIN 91, Central St. 85; ARKANSAS TECH 78, Wayland Baptist 66; SO.NAZARENE 92, Western Wash. 68.

Semifinals—CLAFLIN 90, St.Ambrose 89; SO. NAZARENE 73, Arkansas Tech 57. **Championship—**SO.NAZARENE 98, Claflin 96.

NCAA Final Four, 1939-89

The NCAA basketball championship was first sponsored in 1939 by the National Association of Basketball Coaches. The NCAA took control of the tournament in 1940. Coaches are listed with their teams. No consolation game was played from 1939-45 and since 1982.

Year	Champion	Score	Runner-Up		Third Place
1939	**Oregon** Howard Hobson	46-33	**Ohio St.** Harold Olsen	**Oklahoma** Bruce Drake	**Villanova** Alex Severance
1940	**Indiana** Branch McCracken	60-42	**Kansas** Phog Allen	**Duquesne** Chick Davies	**Southern Cal** Sam Barry
1941	**Wisconsin** Bud Foster	39-34	**Washington St.** Jack Friel	**Arkansas** Glen Rose	**Pittsburgh** Harold Carlson
1942	**Stanford** Everett Dean	53-38	**Dartmouth** Ozzie Cowles	**Colorado** Frosty Cox	**Kentucky** Adolf Rupp
1943	**Wyoming** Everett Shelton	46-34	**Georgetown** Elmer Ripley	**DePaul** Ray Meyer	**Texas** Bully Gilstrap
1944	**Utah** Vadal Peterson	42-40	**Dartmouth** Earl Brown	**Iowa St.** Louis Menze	**Ohio St.** Harold Olsen
1945	**Oklahoma A&M** Henry Iba	49-45	**NYU** Howard Cann	**Arkansas** Eugene Lambert	**Ohio St.** Harold Olsen

Year	Champion	Score	Runner-Up	Third Place	Score	Fourth Place
1946	**Oklahoma A&M** Henry Iba	43-40*	**North Carolina** Ben Carnevale	**Ohio St.** Harold Olsen	63-45	**California** Nibs Price
1947	**Holy Cross** Doggie Julian	58-47	**Oklahoma** Bruce Drake	**Texas** Jack Gray	54-50	**CCNY** Nat Holman
1948	**Kentucky** Adolf Rupp	58-42	**Baylor** Bill Henderson	**Holy Cross** Doggie Julian	60-54	**Kansas St.** Bill Henderson
1949	**Kentucky** Adolf Rupp	46-36	**Oklahoma A&M** Hank Iba	**Illinois** Harry Combes	57-53	**Oregon St.** Slats Gill
1950	**CCNY** Nat Holman	71-68	**Bradley** Forddy Anderson	**N.Carolina St.** Everett Case	53-41	**Baylor** Bill Henderson
1951	**Kentucky** Adolf Rupp	68-58	**Kansas St.** Jack Gardner	**Illinois** Harry Combes	61-46	**Oklahoma A&M** Hank Iba
1952	**Kansas** Phog Allen	80-63	**St.John's,NY** Frank McGuire	**Illinois** Harry Combes	67-64	**Santa Clara** Bob Feerick
1953	**Indiana** Branch McCracken	69-68	**Kansas** Phog Allen	**Washington** Tippy Dye	88-69	**LSU** Harry Rabenhorst
1954	**LaSalle** Ken Loeffler	92-76	**Bradley** Forddy Anderson	**Penn St.** Elmer Gross	70-61	**Southern Cal** Forrest Twogood
1955	**San Francisco** Phil Woolpert	77-63	**LaSalle** Ken Loeffler	**Colorado** Bebe Lee	75-54	**Iowa** Bucky O'Connor
1956	**San Francisco** Phil Woolpert	83-71	**Iowa** Bucky O'Connor	**Temple** Harry Litwack	90-81	**SMU** Doc Hayes
1957	**North Carolina** Frank McGuire	54-53†	**Kansas** Dick Harp	**San Francisco** Phil Woolpert	67-60	**Michigan St.** Forddy Anderson
1958	**Kentucky** Adolf Rupp	84-72	**Seattle** John Castellani	**Temple** Harry Litwack	67-57	**Kansas St.** Tex Winter
1959	**California** Pete Newell	71-70	**West Virginia** Fred Schaus	**Cincinnati** George Smith	98-85	**Louisville** Peck Hickman
1960	**Ohio St.** Fred Taylor	75-55	**California** Pete Newell	**Cincinnati** George Smith	95-71	**NYU** Lou Rossini
1961	**Cincinnati** Ed Jucker	70-65*	**Ohio St.** Fred Taylor	**St.Joseph's,PA** Jack Ramsay	127-120‡	**Utah** Jack Gardner
1962	**Cincinnati** Ed Jucker	71-59	**Ohio St.** Fred Taylor	**Wake Forest** Bones McKinney	82-80	**UCLA** John Wooden
1963	**Loyola,IL** George Ireland	60-58*	**Cincinnati** Ed Jucker	**Duke** Vic Bubas	85-63	**Oregon St.** Slats Gill
1964	**UCLA** John Wooden	98-83	**Duke** Vic Bubas	**Michigan** Dave Strack	100-90	**Kansas St.** Tex Winter
1965	**UCLA** John Wooden	91-80	**Michigan** Dave Strack	**Princeton** B.van Breda Kolff	118-82	**Wichita St.** Gary Thompson
1966	**Texas Western** Don Haskins	72-65	**Kentucky** Adolf Rupp	**Duke** Vic Bubas	79-77	**Utah** Jack Gardner
1967	**UCLA** John Wooden	79-64	**Dayton** Don Donoher	**Houston** Guy Lewis	84-62	**North Carolina** Dean Smith
1968	**UCLA** John Wooden	78-55	**North Carolina** Dean Smith	**Ohio St.** Fred Taylor	89-85	**Houston** Guy Lewis
1969	**UCLA** John Wooden	92-72	**Purdue** George King	**Drake** Maurice John	104-84	**North Carolina** Dean Smith

Year	Champion	Score	Runner-Up	Third Place	Score	Fourth Place
1970	**UCLA** John Wooden	80-69	**Jacksonville** Joe Williams	**New Mexico St.** Lou Henson	75-73	**St. Bonaventure** Larry Weise
1971	**UCLA** John Wooden	68-62	**Villanova** Jack Kraft	**Western Kentucky** Johnny Oldham	77-75	**Kansas** Ted Owens
1972	**UCLA** John Wooden	81-76	**Florida St.** Hugh Durham	**North Carolina** Dean Smith	105-91	**Louisville** Denny Crum
1973	**UCLA** John Wooden	87-66	**Memphis St.** Gene Bartow	**Indiana** Bobby Knight	97-79.	**Providence** Dave Gavitt
1974	**N. Carolina St.** Norm Sloan	76-64	**Marquette** Al McGuire	**UCLA** John Wooden	78-61	**Kansas** Ted Owens
1975	**UCLA** John Wooden	92-85	**Kentucky** Joe Hall	**Louisville** Denny Crum	96-88	**Syracuse** Roy Danforth
1976	**Indiana** Bobby Knight	86-68	**Michigan** Johnny Orr	**UCLA** Gene Bartow	106-92	**Rutgers** Tom Young
1977	**Marquette** Al McGuire	67-59	**North Carolina** Dean Smith	**UNLV** Jerry Tarkanian	106-94	**NC-Charlotte** Lee Rose
1978	**Kentucky** Joe Hall	94-88	**Duke** Bill Foster	**Arkansas** Eddie Sutton	71-69	**Notre Dame** Digger Phelps
1979	**Michigan St.** Jud Heathcote	75-64	**Indiana St.** Bill Hodges	**DePaul** Ray Meyer	96-93	**Pennsylvania** Bob Weinhauer
1980	**Louisville** Denny Crum	59-54	**UCLA** Larry Brown	**Purdue** Lee Rose	75-58	**Iowa** Lute Olson
1981	**Indiana** Bobby Knight	63-50	**North Carolina** Dean Smith	**Virginia** Terry Holland	78-74	**LSU** Dale Brown

Year	Champion	Score	Runner-Up	Third Place		
1982	**North Carolina** Dean Smith	63-62	**Georgetown** John Thompson	**Houston** Guy Lewis		**Louisville** Denny Crum
1983	**N. Carolina St.** Jim Valvano	54-52	**Houston** Guy Lewis	**Georgia** Hugh Durham		**Louisville** Denny Crum
1984	**Georgetown** John Thompson	84-75	**Houston** Guy Lewis	**Kentucky** Joe Hall		**Virginia** Terry Holland
1985	**Villanova** Rollie Massimino	66-64	**Georgetown** John Thompson	**St. John's, NY** Lou Carnesecca		**Memphis St.** Dana Kirk
1986	**Louisville** Denny Crum	72-69	**Duke** Mike Krzyzewski	**Kansas** Larry Brown		**LSU** Dale Brown
1987	**Indiana** Bob Knight	74-73	**Syracuse** Jim Boeheim	**UNLV** Jerry Tarkanian		**Providence** Rick Pitino
1988	**Kansas** Larry Brown	83-79	**Oklahoma** Billy Tubbs	**Arizona** Lute Olson		**Duke** Mike Krzyzewski
1989	**Michigan** Steve Fisher	80-79*	**Seton Hall** P.J. Carlesimo	**Illinois** Lou Henson		**Duke** Mike Krzyzewski

*Overtime   †Three overtimes   ‡Four overtimes
Note: Five teams have had their standing in the Final Four vacated for using ineligible players: **1961**—St. Joseph's, PA (3rd place); **1971**—Villanova (Runner-up) and Western Kentucky (3rd place); **1980**—UCLA (Runner-up); **1985**—Memphis St. (3rd place).

Most Outstanding Player

The Most Outstanding Players of each Final Four, including semifinal, consolation and championship games. No selection was made in 1939 or '51. Winners of the award who did not play for the tournament champion are in **bold type**.

Year	Outstanding Player	Cl	Final 4 Site	Year	Outstanding Player	Cl	Final 4 Site
1939	No Selection	—	Evanston, IL	1955	Bill Russell, San Fran.	Jr.	Kansas City
				1956	**Hal Lear, Temple**	Sr.	Evanston, IL
1940	Marv Huffman, Indiana	Sr.	Kansas City	1957	**Wilt Chamberlain, Kansas**	So.	Kansas City
1941	John Kotz, Wisconsin	So.	Kansas City	1958	**Elgin Baylor, Seattle**	Jr.	Louisville
1942	Howie Dallmar, Stanford	Jr.	Kansas City	1959	**Jerry West, West Va**	Jr.	Louisville
1943	Kenny Sailors, Wyoming	Jr.	New York				
1944	Arnie Ferrin, Utah,	Fr.	New York	1960	Jerry Lucas, Ohio St.	So.	San Fran.
1945	Bob Kurland, Okla.A&M	Jr.	New York	1961	**Jerry Lucas, Ohio St.**	Jr.	Kansas City
1946	Bob Kurland, Okla.A&M	Sr.	New York	1962	Paul Hogue, Cincinnati	Sr.	Louisville
1947	George Kaftan, H.Cross	So.	New York	1963	**Art Heyman, Duke**	Sr.	Louisville
1948	Alex Groza, Kentucky	Jr.	New York	1964	Walt Hazzard, UCLA	Sr.	Kansas City
1949	Alex Groza, Kentucky	Sr.	Seattle	1965	**Bill Bradley, Princeton**	Sr.	Portland, OR
				1966	**Jerry Chambers, Utah**	Sr.	Col. Park, MD
1950	Irwin Dambrot, CCNY	Sr.	New York	1967	Lew Alcindor, UCLA	So.	Louisville
1951	No Selection	—	Minneapolis	1968	Lew Alcindor, UCLA	Jr.	Los Angeles
1952	Clyde Lovelette, Kansas	Sr.	Seattle	1969	Lew Alcindor, UCLA	Sr.	Louisville
1953	**B.H.Born, Kansas**	Jr.	Kansas City				
1954	Tom Gola, La Salle	Jr.	Kansas City				

Most Outstanding Player (Continued)

Year	Outstanding Player	Cl	Final 4 Site
1970	Sidney Wicks, UCLA	Jr.	Col.Park,MD
1971	Howard Porter, Villanova	Sr.	Houston
1972	Bill Walton, UCLA	So.	Los Angeles
1973	Bill Walton, UCLA	Jr.	St.Louis
1974	David Thompson, N.C.St.	Jr.	Greensboro,NC
1975	Richard Washington, UCLA	Jr.	San Diego
1976	Kent Benson, Indiana	Jr.	Philadelphia
1977	Butch Lee, Marquette	Jr.	Atlanta
1978	Jack Givens, Kentucky	Sr.	St.Louis
1979	Magic Johnson, Mich.St.	So.	S.Lake City
1980	Darrell Griffith, L'ville	Sr.	Indianapolis
1981	Isiah Thomas, Indiana	So.	Philadelphia
1982	James Worthy, N.Carolina	Jr.	New Orleans
1983	Akeem Olajuwon, Houston	So.	Albuquerque
1984	Patrick Ewing, Georgetown	Jr.	Seattle
1985	Ed Pinckney, Villanova	Sr.	Lexington
1986	Pervis Ellison, L'ville	Fr.	Dallas
1987	Keith Smart, Indiana	Jr.	New Orleans
1988	Danny Manning, Kansas	Sr.	Kansas City
1989	Glen Rice, Michigan	Sr.	Seattle

Note: Howard Porter (1971) was declared ineligible after the tournament and his award was vacated.

NIT Finals, 1938-89

The National Invitation Tournament began under the sponsorship of the Metropolitan New York Basketball Writers Assn. in 1938. All championship games have been played at Madison Square Garden.

Year	Winner	Score	Loser
1938	Temple	60-36	Colorado
1939	Long Island U.	44-32	Loyola,IL
1940	Colorado	51-40	Duquesne
1941	Long Island U.	56-42	Ohio Univ.
1942	West Virginia	47-45	Western Ky.
1943	St.John's,NY	48-27	Toledo
1944	St.John's,NY	47-39	DePaul
1945	DePaul	71-54	Bowling Green
1946	Kentucky	46-45	Rhode Island
1947	Utah	49-45	Kentucky
1948	St.Louis	65-52	NYU
1949	San Francisco	48-47	Loyola,IL
1950	CCNY	69-61	Bradley
1951	BYU	62-43	Dayton
1952	La Salle	75-64	Dayton
1953	Seton Hall	58-46	St.John's,NY
1954	Holy Cross	71-62	Duquesne
1955	Duquesne	70-58	Dayton
1956	Louisville	93-80	Dayton
1957	Bradley	84-83	Memphis St.
1958	Xavier,OH	78-74*	Dayton
1959	St.John's,NY	76-71*	Bradley
1960	Bradley	88-72	Providence
1961	Providence	62-59	St.Louis
1962	Dayton	73-67	St.John's,NY
1963	Providence	81-66	Canisius
1964	Bradley	86-54	New Mexico
1965	St.John's,NY	55-51	Villanova
1966	BYU	97-84	NYU
1967	So.Illinois	71-56	Marquette
1968	Dayton	61-48	Kansas
1969	Temple	89-76	Boston College
1970	Marquette	65-53	St.John's,NY
1971	North Carolina	84-66	Georgia Tech
1972	Maryland	100-69	Niagara
1973	Virginia Tech	92-91*	Notre Dame
1974	Purdue	97-81	Utah
1975	Princeton	80-69	Providence
1976	Kentucky	71-67	NC-Charlotte
1977	St.Bonaventure	94-91	Houston
1978	Texas	101-93	N.C.State
1979	Indiana	53-52	Purdue

Year	Winner	Score	Loser
1980	Virginia	58-55	Minnesota
1981	Tulsa	86-84*	Syracuse
1982	Bradley	67-58	Purdue
1983	Fresno St.	69-60	DePaul
1984	Michigan	83-63	Notre Dame
1985	UCLA	65-62	Indiana
1986	Ohio St.	73-63	Wyoming
1987	Southern Miss.	84-80	La Salle
1988	Connecticut	72-67	Ohio St.
1989	St.John's,NY	73-65	St.Louis

*Overtime

The Red Cross Benefit Games 1943-45

For three seasons during World War II, the NCAA and NIT champions met in a benefit game at Madison Square Garden to raise money for the Red Cross. The NCAA champion won all three games.

Year	Winner	Score	Loser
1943	Wyoming (NCAA)	52-47	St.John's (NIT)
1944	Utah (NCAA)	43-36	St.John's (NIT)
1945	Okla.A&M(NCAA)	52-44	DePaul (NIT)

Teams in both NCAA and NIT

A dozen teams played in both the NCAA and NIT tournaments from 1940-52. Colorado (1940), Utah (1944), Kentucky (1949) and BYU (1951) won one of the titles, while CCNY won two in 1950, beating Bradley in both championship games.

Year		NIT	NCAA
1940	Colorado	Won Final	Lost 1st Rd
	Duquesne	Lost Final	Lost 2nd Rd
1944	Utah	Lost 1st Rd	Won Final
1949	Kentucky	Lost 2nd Rd	Won Final
1950	CCNY	Won Final	Won Final
	Bradley	Lost Final	Lost Final
1951	BYU	Won Final	Lost 2nd Rd
	N.C.State	Lost 2nd Rd	Lost 2nd Rd
	Arizona	Lost 2nd Rd	Lost 1st Rd
1952	St.John's	Lost Final	Lost 2nd Rd
	Dayton	Lost 1st Rd	Lost Final
	Duquesne	Lost 2nd Rd	Lost 2nd Rd

NCAA and NIT Tourney Fields

Older than the NCAA tournament by one year, the NIT has grown from six teams to 32 since 1938 while the NCAA has gone from eight teams to 64. The fields, year-by-year:

Year	NCAA	NIT	Year	NCAA	NIT	Year	NCAA	NIT
1938	—	6	1955	24	12	1972	25	16
1939	8	6	1956	25	12	1973	25	16
1940	8	6	1957	23	12	1974	25	16
1941	8	8	1958	24	12	1975	32	16
1942	8	8	1959	23	12	1976	32	12
1943	8	8	1960	25	12	1977	32	16
1944	8	8	1961	24	12	1978	32	16
1945	8	8	1962	25	12	1979	40	24
1946	8	8	1963	25	12	1980	48	32
1947	8	8	1964	25	12	1981	48	32
1948	8	8	1965	23	14	1982	48	32
1949	8	12	1966	22	14	1983	52	32
1950	8	12	1967	23	14	1984	53	32
1951	16	12	1968	23	16	1985	64	32
1952	16	12	1969	25	16	1986	64	32
1953	22	12	1970	25	16	1987	64	32
1954	24	12	1971	25	16	1988	64	32
						1989	64	32

Winningest Div.I Teams

All-Time Winning Pct.

Division I schools with best winning percentages through 1988-89 season (regular season and tournament games included).

	Yrs	Won	Lost	Tied	Pct
1 Kentucky	86	1,466	476	1	.755
2 North Carolina	79	1,460	526	1	.735
3 St.John's	82	1,397	594	1	.702
4 UCLA	70	1,204	542	1	.690
5 Western Kentucky	70	1,210	558	1	.684
6 Kansas	91	1,402	664	1	.679
7 DePaul	66	1,058	509	0	.675
8 Syracuse	88	1,266	612	1	.674
9 Notre Dame	84	1,307	635	1	.673
10 Weber St	27	502	257	1	.661
11 Duke	84	1,316	677	0	.660
12 Louisville	75	1,147	610	1	.653
13 N.Carolina St	77	1,196	640	1	.651
14 La Salle	59	960	522	1	.6477
15 Temple	93	1,312	714	1	.6475

All-Time Victories

Division I schools with most victories through 1988-89 (regular season and tournament games included).

	Yrs	Wins
1 Kentucky	86	1,466
2 North Carolina	79	1,460
3 Kansas	91	1,402
4 St.John's	82	1,397
5 Oregon St	87	1,350
6 Duke	84	1,316
7 Temple	93	1,312
8 Notre Dame	84	1,307
9 Pennsylvania	88	1,303
10 Washington	87	1,268
11 Syracuse	88	1,266
12 Indiana	89	1,224
13 Western Kentucky	70	1,210
14 UCLA	70	1,204
15 Bradley	85	1,199

Most NCAA Tournaments

Division I schools with 15 or more appearances in the NCAA tournament through 1989. Listed are number of appearances, overall wins and losses, times reaching the Final Four, and number of NCAA titles.

App		W-L	F4	NCAA Titles	App		W-L	F4	NCAA Titles
33	Kentucky	55-30	9	5 (1948-49,51,58,78)	17	Marquette	25-18	2	1 (1977)
25	UCLA	62-19	14	10 (1964-65,67-73,75)	17	Syracuse	24-18	2	None
23	N.Carolina	48-24	9	2 (1957,82)	16	N.C.State	26-15	3	2 (1974,83)
23	Notre Dame	25-27	1	None	16	Houston	26-21	5	None
20	Louisville	37-22	7	2 (1980,86)	16	W.Virginia	11-16	1	None
19	Villanova	34-19	3	1 (1985)	16	Ohio St	25-14	8	1 (1960)
19	Kansas St	27-23	4	None	15	San Fran	21-13	3	2 (1955-56)
19	St.John's	18-21	2	None	15	Arkansas	14-16	3	None
18	Indiana	39-13	6	5 (1940,53,76,81,87)	15	Oregon St	12-18	2	None
18	Kansas	36-18	8	2 (1952,88)	15	Princeton	11-19	1	None
18	DePaul	20-21	2	None					

Division I Winning Streaks

Full Season

Division I schools with 40 or more consecutive victories (including regular season and tournament games).

No	Team	Seasons	Broken by	Score
88	UCLA	1971-74	Notre Dame	71-70
60	San Francisco	1955-57	Illinois	62-33
47	UCLA	1966-68	Houston	71-69
44	Texas	1913-17	Rice	24-18
43	Seton Hall	1939-41	LIU-Brooklyn	49-26
43	LIU-Brooklyn	1935-37	Stanford	45-31
41	UCLA	1968-69	Southern Cal	46-44

Regular Season

Division I schools with 50 or more consecutive victories (regular season only).

No	Team	Seasons	Broken by	Score
77	UCLA	1971-74	Notre Dame	71-70
57	Indiana	1975-77	Toledo	59-57
56	Marquette	1970-72	Detroit	70-49
54	Kentucky	1952-55	Ga.Tech	59-58
51	San Francisco	1955-57	Illinois	62-33

Winningest Div.I Coaches

All-Time Victories

Division I coaches with most victories through 1988-89 season (regular season and tournament games included). Minimum of 10 seasons as Div.I head coach. Active coaches in **bold type**.

	Yrs	Wins
Adolph Rupp	41	875
Phog Allen	46	770
Henry Iba	41	767
Ed Diddle	42	759
Ray Meyer	42	724
Dean Smith	28	667
John Wooden	29	667
Ralph Miller	38	656
Marv Harshman	40	642
Norm Sloan	37	627
Cam Henderson	36	611
Slats Gill	36	599
Guy Lewis	30	592
Abe Lemons	32	579
Tony Hinkle	41	560
Frank McGuire	30	550
Don Haskins	28	541
Lefty Driesell	27	540
Lou Henson	27	535
Harry Miller	34	534

Where They Coached

Rupp—Kentucky (1931-72); **Allen**—Kansas & Baker (1908-09) & Haskell (1909), Central Mo.St.(1913-19), Kansas (1920-56) **Iba**—NW Mo.St.(1930-33), Colorado (1934), Okla.St.(1935-70) **Diddle**—Western Ky. (1923-64) **Meyer**—DePaul (1943-84) **Smith**—North Carolina (1962-) **Wooden**—Indiana St.(1947-48), UCLA (1949-75) **R.Miller**—Wichita St.(1952-64), Iowa (1965-70), Oregon St.(1971-89) **Harshman**—Pacific Lutheran (1946-58), Wash.St.(1959-71), Washington (1972-85) **Sloan**—Presbyterian (1952-55), Citadel (1957-60), Florida (1961-66), N.C.State (1967-80), Florida (1981-) **Henderson**—Muskingum (1920-22), Davis & Elkins (1923-35), Marshall (1936-55). **Gill**—Oregon St.(1929-64) **Lewis**—Houston (1957-86) **Lemons**—Okla.City (1956-73), Pan American (1974-76), Texas (1977-82), Okla.City (1984-) **Hinkle**—Butler (1927-42,46-70) **F.McGuire**—St.John's (1948-52), N. Carolina (1953-61), S.Carolina (1965-80) **Haskins**—UTEP (1962-) **Driesell**—Davidson(1961-69), Maryland (1970-86),James Madison (1989-) **Henson**—Hardin-Simmons (1963-66), New Mexico St.(1967-75), Illinois (1976-) **H.Miller**—Western St.CO (1953-58), Fresno St.(1961-65), Eastern New Mex.(1966-70), N.Texas (1971), Wichita St. (1972-78), S.F.Austin St.(1979-88).

All-Time Winning Pct.

Division I coaches with best winning percentage through 1988-89 season (regular season and tournament games included). Minimum of 10 seasons in Div.I as head coach. Active coaches in **bold type**.

		Yrs	Won	Lost	Pct
1	Clair Bee	21	410	86	.827
2	**Jerry Tarkanian**	21	530	114	.823
3	Adolph Rupp	41	875	190	.822
4	John Wooden	29	667	161	.806
5	**Dean Smith**	28	667	190	.778
6	Phog Allen	46	770	233	.768
7	George Koegan	24	385	117	.767
8	Jack Ramsay	11	231	71	.765
9	Frank Keaney	28	403	124	.765
10	Vic Bubas	10	213	67	.761
11	**Jim Boeheim**	13	317	101	.758
12	Chick Davies	21	314	106	.748
13	Denny Crum	18	436	148	.747
14	**John Thompson**	17	399	135	.747
15	Ray Mears	21	399	135	.747

Where They Coached

Bee—Rider (1929-31), LIU-Brooklyn (1932-45, 46-51); **Tarkanian**—Long Beach St.(1969-73), UNLV (1974-); **Rupp**—Kentucky (1931-72); **Wooden**—Indiana St.(1947-48), UCLA (1949-75); **Smith**—North Carolina (1962-); **Allen**—Kansas & Baker (1908-09), & Haskell (1909), Central Mo.St.(1913-19), Kansas (1920-56); **Koegan**—St.Louis (1916), Allegheny (1919), Valparaiso (1920-21), Notre Dame (1924-43). **Ramsay**—St.Joseph's PA (1956-66); **Keaney**—Rhode Island (1921-48); **Bubas**—Duke (1960-69); **Boeheim**—Syracuse (1977-); **Davies**—Duquesne (1925-43,47-48); **Crum**—Louisville (1972-); **Thompson**—Georgetown (1973-); **Mears**—Wittenberg (1957-62), Tennessee (1963-77).

Active Coaches' Victories

Active Division I coaches with 450 or more victories through 1988-89 season (regular season and tournament games included). Minimum of five seasons as Div.I head coach.

	Yrs	Wins
Dean Smith, N.Carolina	28	667
Norm Sloan, Florida	37	627
Don Haskins, UTEP	28	541
Lefty Driesell, JMU	27	540
Lou Henson, Illinois	27	535
Jerry Tarkanian, UNLV	21	530
Bob Knight, Indiana	24	514
Gene Bartow, Ala-Birm	27	514
Glenn Wilkes, Stetson	32	497
Tom Young, Old Domin	29	496
Lou Carnesecca, St.J	21	460
Davey Whitney, Alcorn St	25	450

Most NCAA Tournaments

Division I coaches with 12 or more appearances in the NCAA tournament through 1989. Listed are number of appearances, overall wins and losses, times reaching the Final Four, and number of NCAA titles. Active coaches in **bold type**.

App		W-L	F4	NCAA Titles
20	Adolph Rupp	30-18	6	4 (1948-49, 51,58)
19	**Dean Smith**	41-20	7	1 (1982)
16	John Wooden	47-10	12	10 (1964,65, 67-73,75)
15	**Lou Carnesecca**	13-17	1	None
14	**Denny Crum**	31-14	5	2 (1980,86)
14	Guy Lewis	26-18	5	None
13	**Bob Knight**	29-10	4	3 (1976,81,87)
13	**John Thompson**	25-12	3	1 (1984)
13	**Digger Phelps**	15-15	1	None
13	Ray Meyer	14-16	2	None
12	**Jim Boeheim**	16-12	1	None
12	**Don Haskins**	12-11	1	1 (1966)

Coach of the Year Awards

UPI picked the first national Division I Coach of the Year in 1955. Since then, The U.S.Basketball Writers Assn (1959), AP (1967), the National Assn of Basketball Coaches (1969), and the Atlanta Tip-Off Club (1987) have joined in.

Since 1969, the first year all four awards were given out, the same coach has won all of them in the same season five times: John Wooden of UCLA in 1970 and '72, Bob (then Bobby) Knight of Indiana in 1975, Ralph Miller of Oregon St. in 1981 and John Chaney of Temple in 1988.

United Press International

Voted on by a panel of UPI college basketball writers and first presented in 1955. Numbers in parentheses indicate repeat winners.

Year Coach, school
1955 Phil Woolpert, San Francisco
1956 Phil Woolpert, San Fran (2)
1957 Frank McGuire, N.Carolina
1958 Tex Winter, Kansas St.
1959 Adolph Rupp, Kentucky

1960 Pete Newell, California
1961 Fred Taylor, Ohio St.
1962 Fred Taylor, Ohio St.(2)
1963 Ed Jucker, Cincinnati
1964 John Wooden, UCLA
1965 Dave Strack, Michigan
1966 Adolph Rupp, Kentucky (2)
1967 John Wooden, UCLA (2)

Year Coach, school
1968 Guy Lewis, Houston
1969 John Wooden, UCLA (3)

1970 John Wooden, UCLA (4)
1971 Al McGuire, Marquette
1972 John Wooden, UCLA (5)
1973 John Wooden, UCLA (6)
1974 Digger Phelps, Notre Dame
1975 Bobby Knight, Indiana
1976 Tom Young, Rutgers
1977 Bob Gaillard, San Francisco
1978 Eddie Sutton, Arkansas
1979 Bill Hodges, Indiana St.

Year Coach, school
1980 Ray Meyer, DePaul
1981 Ralph Miller, Oregon St.
1982 Norm Stewart, Missouri
1983 Jerry Tarkanian, UNLV
1984 Ray Meyer, DePaul (2)
1985 Lou Carnesecca, St.John's
1986 Mike Krzyzewski, Duke
1987 John Thompson, Georgetown
1988 John Chaney, Temple
1989 Bob Knight, Indiana (2)

U.S. Basketball Writers Assn.

Voted on by the USBWA and first presented in 1959. Numbers in parentheses indicate repeat winners.

Year Coach, school
1959 Eddie Hickey, Marquette

1960 Pete Newell, California
1961 Fred Taylor, Ohio St.
1962 Fred Taylor, Ohio St.(2)
1963 Ed Jucker, Cincinnati
1964 John Wooden, UCLA
1965 B.van Breda Kolff, Princeton
1966 Adolph Rupp, Kentucky
1967 John Wooden, UCLA (2)
1968 Guy Lewis, Houston
1969 Maury John, Drake

Year Coach, school
1970 John Wooden, UCLA (3)
1971 Al McGuire, Marquette
1972 John Wooden, UCLA (4)
1973 John Wooden, UCLA (5)
1974 Norm Sloan, N.C.State
1975 Bobby Knight, Indiana
1976 Bobby Knight, Indiana (2)
1977 Bob Gaillard, San Francisco
1978 Eddie Sutton, Arkansas
1979 Bill Hodges, Indiana St.

Year Coach, school
1980 Ray Meyer, DePaul
1981 Ralph Miller, Oregon St.
1982 Ralph Miller, Oregon St.(2)
1983 Guy Lewis, Houston (2)
1984 Ray Meyer, DePaul (2)
1985 Bill Frieder, Michigan
1986 Eddie Sutton, Kentucky
1987 Tom Davis, Iowa
1988 John Chaney, Temple
1989 Bob Knight, Indiana (3)

Associated Press

Voted on by AP sportswriters and broadcasters and first presented in 1967. Numbers in parentheses indicate repeat winners.

Year Coach, school
1967 John Wooden, UCLA
1968 Guy Lewis, Houston
1969 John Wooden, UCLA (2)

1970 John Wooden, UCLA (3)
1971 Al McGuire, Marquette
1972 John Wooden, UCLA (4)
1973 John Wooden, UCLA (5)
1974 Norm Sloan, N.C.State

Year Coach, school
1975 Bobby Knight, Indiana
1976 Bobby Knight, Indiana
1977 Bob Gailliard, San Francisco
1978 Eddie Sutton, Arkansas
1979 Bill Hodges, Indiana St.

1980 Ray Meyer, DePaul
1981 Ralph Miller, Oregon St.
1982 Ralph Miller, Oregon St. (2)

Year Coach, school
1983 Guy Lewis, Houston (2)
1984 Ray Meyer, DePaul (2)
1985 Bill Frieder, Michigan
1986 Eddie Sutton, Kentucky
1987 Tom Davis, Iowa
1988 John Chaney, Temple
1989 Bobby Knight, Indiana (3)

Nat'l Assn. of Basketball Coaches

Voted on by NABC and first presented in 1969. Numbers in parentheses indicate repeat winners.

Year Coach, school
1969 John Wooden, UCLA

1970 John Wooden, UCLA (2)
1971 Jack Kraft, Villanova
1972 John Wooden, UCLA (3)
1973 Gene Bartow, Memphis St.
1974 Al McGuire, Marquette
1975 Bobby Knight, Indiana
1976 Johnny Orr, Michigan

Year Coach, school
1977 Dean Smith, N.Carolina
1978 Bill Foster, Duke
     & Abe Lemons, Texas
1979 Ray Meyer, DePaul

1980 Lute Olson, Iowa
1981 Ralph Miller, Oregon St.
     & Jack Hartman, Kansas St.
1982 Don Monson, Idaho

Year Coach, school
1983 Lou Carnesecca, St.John's
1984 Marv Harshman, Washington
1985 John Thompson, Georgetown
1986 Eddie Sutton, Kentucky
1987 Rick Pitino, Providence
1988 John Chaney, Temple
1989 P.J.Carlesimo, Seton Hall

Naismith Award

Voted on by a panel of coaches, sportswriters and broadcasters and first presented by the Atlanta Tip-Off Club in 1987.

Year Coach, school
1987 Bob Knight, Indiana

Year Coach, school
1988 Larry Brown, Kansas

Year Coach, school
1989 Mike Krzyzewski, Duke

Player of the Year Awards

UPI picked the first national Division I Player of the Year in 1955. Since then, The U.S.Basketball Writers Assn.(1959), the Commonwealth Athletic Club of Kentucky's Adolph Rupp Trophy (1961), the Atlanta Tip-Off Club (1969), the National Assn. of Basketball Coaches (1975), and the LA Athletic Club's John Wooden Award (1977) have joined in.

Since 1977, the first year all six awards were given out, the same player has won all of them in the same season six times: Marques Johnson of UCLA in 1977, Larry Bird of Indiana St. in 1979, Ralph Sampson of Virginia in 1982 and '83, Michael Jordan of North Carolina in 1984, and David Robinson of Navy in 1987.

United Press International

Voted on by a panel of UPI college basketball writers and first presented in 1955. Numbers in parentheses indicate repeat winners.

Year Player, school
1955 Tom Gola, La Salle
1956 Bill Russell, San Francisco
1957 Chet Forte, Columbia
1958 Oscar Robertson, Cincinnati
1959 Oscar Robertson, Cinn.(2)

1960 Oscar Robertson, Cinn.(3)
1961 Jerry Lucas, Ohio St.
1962 Jerry Lucas, Ohio St.(2)
1963 Art Heyman, Duke
1964 Gary Bradds, Ohio St.
1965 Bill Bradley, Princeton
1966 Cazzie Russell, Michigan

Year Player, school
1967 Lew Alcindor, UCLA
1968 Elvin Hayes, Houston
1969 Lew Alcindor, UCLA (2)

1970 Pete Maravich, LSU
1971 Austin Carr, Notre Dame
1972 Bill Walton, UCLA
1973 Bill Walton, UCLA (2)
1974 Bill Walton, UCLA (3)
1975 David Thompson, N.C.State
1976 Scott May, Indiana
1977 Marques Johnson, UCLA
1978 Butch Lee, Marquette
1979 Larry Bird, Indiana St.

Year Player, school
1980 Mark Aguirre, DePaul
1981 Ralph Sampson, Virginia
1982 Ralph Sampson, Virginia (2)
1983 Ralph Sampson, Virginia (3)
1984 Michael Jordan, N.Carolina
1985 Chris Mullin, St.John's
1986 Walter Berry St.John's
1987 David Robinson, Navy
1988 Hersey Hawkins, Bradley
1989 Danny Ferry, Duke

U.S. Basketball Writers Assn.

Voted on by the USBWA and first presented in 1959. Numbers in parentheses indicate repeat winners.

Year Player, school
1959 Oscar Robertson, Cincinnati
1960 Oscar Robertson, Cinn.(2)
1961 Jerry Lucas, Ohio St.
1962 Jerry Lucas, Ohio St.(2)
1963 Art Heyman, Duke
1964 Walt Hazzard, UCLA
1965 Bill Bradley, Princeton
1966 Cazzie Russell, Michigan
1967 Lew Alcindor, UCLA
1968 Elvin Hayes, Houston
1969 Lew Alcindor, UCLA (2)

Year Player, school
1970 Pete Maravich, LSU
1971 Sidney Wicks, UCLA
1972 Bill Walton, UCLA
1973 Bill Walton, UCLA (2)
1974 Bill Walton, UCLA (3)
1975 David Thompson, N.C.State
1976 Adrian Dantley, Notre Dame
1977 Marques Johnson, UCLA
1978 Phil Ford, North Carolina
1979 Larry Bird, Indiana St

Year Player, school
1980 Mark Aguirre, DePaul
1981 Ralph Sampson, Virginia
1982 Ralph Sampson, Virginia (2)
1983 Ralph Sampson, Virginia (3)
1984 Michael Jordan, N.Carolina
1985 Chris Mullin, St.John's
1986 Walter Berry St.John's
1987 David Robinson, Navy
1988 Hersey Hawkins, Bradley
1989 Danny Ferry, Duke

Rupp Trophy (AP)

Voted on by AP sportswriters and broadcasters and first presented in 1961 by the Commonwealth Athletic Club of Kentucky in the name of former Univ.of Kentucky coach Adolph Rupp. Numbers in parentheses indicate repeat winners.

Year Player, school
1961 Jerry Lucas, Ohio St.
1962 Jerry Lucas, Ohio St.(2)
1963 Art Heyman, Duke
1964 Gary Bradds, Ohio St.
1965 Bill Bradley, Princeton
1966 Cazzie Russell, Michigan
1967 Lew Alcindor, UCLA
1968 Elvin Hayes, Houston
1969 Lew Alcindor, UCLA (2)

Year Player, school
1970 Pete Maravich, LSU
1971 Austin Carr, Notre Dame
1972 Bill Walton, UCLA
1973 Bill Walton, UCLA (2)
1974 David Thompson, N.C.State
1975 David Thompson, N.C.St.(2)
1976 Scott May, Indiana
1977 Marques Johnson, UCLA
1978 Butch Lee, Marquette
1979 Larry Bird, Indiana St.

Year Player, school
1980 Mark Aguirre, DePaul
1981 Ralph Sampson, Virginia
1982 Ralph Sampson, Virginia (2)
1983 Ralph Sampson, Virginia (3)
1984 Michael Jordan, N.Carolina
1985 Patrick Ewing, Georgetown
1986 Walter Berry, St.John's
1987 David Robinson, Navy
1988 Hersey Hawkins, Bradley
1989 Sean Elliott, Arizona

Naismith Award

Voted on by a panel of coaches, sportswriters and broadcasters and first presented in 1969 by the Atlanta Tip-Off Club in 1969 in the name of the inventor of basketball, Dr.James Naismith. Numbers in parentheses indicate repeat winners.

Year Player, school
1969 Lew Alcindor, UCLA
1970 Pete Maravich, LSU
1971 Austin Carr, Notre Dame
1972 Bill Walton, UCLA
1973 Bill Walton, UCLA (2)
1974 Bill Walton, UCLA (3)
1975 David Thompson, N.C.State

Year Player, school
1976 Scott May, Indiana
1977 Marques Johnson, UCLA
1978 Butch Lee, Marquette
1979 Larry Bird, Indiana St.
1980 Mark Aguirre, DePaul
1981 Ralph Sampson, Virginia
1982 Ralph Sampson, Virginia (2)

Year Player, school
1983 Ralph Sampson, Virginia (3)
1984 Michael Jordan, N.Carolina
1985 Patrick Ewing, Georgetown
1986 Johnny Dawkins, Duke
1987 David Robinson, Navy
1988 Danny Manning, Kansas
1989 Danny Ferry, Duke

Eastman Kodak (NABC)

Voted on by the National Assn.of Basketball Coaches and first presented in 1975. Numbers in parentheses indicate repeat winners.

Year Player, school
1975 David Thompson, N.C.State
1976 Scott May, Indiana
1977 Marques Johnson, UCLA
1978 Phil Ford, North Carolina
1979 Larry Bird, Indiana St.

Year Player, school
1980 Michael Brooks, La Salle
1981 Danny Ainge, BYU
1982 Ralph Sampson, Virginia
1983 Ralph Sampson, Virginia (2)
1984 Michael Jordan, N.Carolina
1985 Patrick Ewing, Georgetown

Year Player, school
1986 Walter Berry St.John's
1987 David Robinson, Navy
1988 Danny Manning, Kansas
1989 Sean Elliott, Arizona

Wooden Award

Voted on by a panel of coaches, sportswriters and broadcasters and first presented in 1977 by the Los Angeles Athletic Club in the name of former Purdue All-America and UCLA coach John Wooden. Numbers in parentheses indicate repeat winners.

Year Player, school
1977 Marques Johnson, UCLA
1978 Phil Ford, North Carolina
1979 Larry Bird, Indiana St.
1980 Darrell Griffith, Louisville

Year Player, school
1981 Danny Ainge, BYU
1982 Ralph Sampson, Virginia
1983 Ralph Sampson, Virginia (2)
1984 Michael Jordan, N.Carolina
1985 Chris Mullin, St.John's

Year Player, school
1986 Walter Berry St.John's
1987 David Robinson, Navy
1988 Danny Manning, Kansas
1989 Sean Elliott, Arizona

NCAA Division I Records
CAREER
Scoring

Points	Years	Gm	Total		Average	Years	Pts	Avg
Pete Maravich, LSU	1968-70	83	**3,667**		Pete Maravich, LSU	1968-70	3,667	**44.2**
Freeman Williams, Portland St	1975-78	106	**3,249**		Austin Carr, Notre Dame	1969-71	2,560	**34.6**
Harry Kelly, Texas Southern	1980-83	110	**3,066**		Oscar Robertson, Cincinnati	1958-60	2,973	**33.8**
Hersey Hawkins, Bradley	1985-88	125	**3,008**		Calvin Murphy, Niagara	1968-70	2,548	**33.1**
Oscar Robertson, Cincinnati	1958-60	88	**2,973**		Dwight Lamar, SW Louisiana	1972-73	1,862	**32.7**
Danny Manning, Kansas	1985-88	147	**2,951**		Frank Selvy, Furman	1952-54	2,538	**32.5**
Alfredrick Hughes, Loyola-IL	1982-85	120	**2,914**		Rick Mount, Purdue	1968-70	2,323	**32.3**
Elvin Hayes, Houston	1966-68	93	**2,884**		Darrell Floyd, Furman	1954-56	2,281	**32.1**
Larry Bird, Indiana St	1977-79	94	**2,850**		Nick Werkman, Seton Hall	1962-64	2,273	**32.0**
Otis Birdsong, Houston	1974-77	116	**2,832**		Willie Humes, Ohio St	1970-71	1,510	**31.5**

Field Goal Pct.	Years	FG	FGA	Pct		Free Throw Pct.	Years	FT	FTA	Pct
Steve Johnson, Ore.St	1978-81	828	1,222	**67.8**		Greg Starrick, Ky/So.Ill	1969-72	341	375	**90.9**
Murray Brown, Fla.St	1977-80	566	847	**66.8**		Jack Moore, Nebraska	1979-82	446	495	**90.1**
Joe Senser, W.Chester	1976-79	476	719	**66.2**		Steve Alford, Indiana	1984-87	535	596	**89.8**
Kevin Magee, Cal-Irvine	1981-82	552	841	**65.6**		Bob Lloyd, Rutgers	1965-67	543	605	**89.8**
O.Phillips, Pepperdine	1982-83	404	618	**65.4**		Jim Barton, Dartmouth	1986-89	394	440	**89.5**
Note: Minimum 400 FGs scored.						**Note:** Minimum 250 FTs scored.				

Rebounding

Rebounds (before 1973)	Years	Gm	Total		Rebounds (since 1973)	Years	Gm	Total
Tom Gola, La Salle	1952-55	118	**2,201**		Ralph Sampson, Virginia	1980-83	132	**1,511**
Joe Holup, G.Washington	1953-56	104	**2,030**		Pete Padgett, Nevada-Reno	1973-76	104	**1,464**
Charlie Slack, Marshall	1953-56	88	**1,916**		Michael Brooks, La Salle	1977-80	114	**1,372**
Ed Conlin, Fordham	1951-55	102	**1,884**		Xavier McDaniel, Wichita St	1982-85	117	**1,359**
Dickie Hemric, Wake Forest	1952-55	104	**1,802**		John Irving, Hofstra	1974-77	103	**1,348**

2,000 Points/1,000 Rebounds

	Years	Gm	Pts	Reb			Years	Gm	Pts	Reb
Harry Kelly, Texas So	1980-83	110	3,066	**1,085**		Daren Queenan, Lehigh	1985-88	118	2,703	**1,013**
Oscar Robertson, Cinn	1958-60	88	2,973	**1,338**		David Robinson, Navy	1984-87	127	2,669	**1,314**
Danny Manning, Kansas	1985-88	147	2,951	**1,187**		Wayman Tisdale, Okla	1983-85	104	2,661	**1,048**
Elvin Hayes, Houston	1966-68	93	2,884	**1,602**		Michael Brooks, L'Salle	1977-80	114	2,628	**1,372**
Larry Bird, Indiana St	1977-79	94	2,850	**1,247**		Dickie Hemric, W.Forest	1952-55	104	2,587	**1,802**
						Danny Ferry, Duke	1986-89	143	2,155	**1,003**

SINGLE SEASON
Scoring

Points	Year	Gm	Total		3-Pt Field Goal Pct	Year	3FG	3FGA	Pct
Pete Maravich, LSU	1970	31	**1,381**		Glenn Tropf, Holy Cross	1988	52	82	**63.4**
Elvin Hayes, Houston	1968	33	**1,214**		Dave Calloway, Mon.,NJ	1989	48	82	**58.5**
Frank Selvy, Furman	1954	29	**1,209**		Steve Kerr, Arizona	1988	114	199	**57.3**
Pete Maravich, LSU	1969	26	**1,148**		Reginald Jones, Prairie	1987	64	112	**57.1**
Pete Maravich, LSU	1968	26	**1,138**		Joel Tribelhorn, Colo.St	1989	76	135	**56.3**

Average	Year	Pts	Avg		Free Throw Pct.	Year	FT	FTA	Pct
Pete Maravich, LSU	1970	1,381	**44.5**		Craig Collins, Penn St	1985	94	98	**95.9**
Pete Maravich, LSU	1969	1,148	**44.2**		Rod Foster, UCLA	1982	95	100	**95.0**
Pete Maravich, LSU	1968	1,138	**43.8**		Carlos Gibson, Marshall	1978	84	89	**94.4**
Frank Selvy, Furman	1954	1,209	**41.7**		Jim Barton, Dartmouth	1986	65	69	**94.2**
Johnny Neumann, Mississippi	1971	923	**40.1**		Jack Moore, Nebraska	1982	123	131	**93.9**

Field Goal Pct.	Year	FG	FGA	Pct
Steve Johnson, Oregon St	1981	235	315	**74.6**
Dwayne Davis, Florida	1989	179	248	**72.2**
Keith Walker, Utica,NY	1985	154	216	**71.3**
Steve Johnson, Oregon St	1980	211	297	**71.0**
Alan Williams, Princeton	1987	163	232	**70.3**

Assists

Average	Year	Gm	No	Avg
Avery Johnson, South-BR	1988	30	399	**13.3**
Anthony Manuel, Bradley	1988	31	373	**12.0**
Avery Johnson, South-BR	1987	31	333	**10.7**
Mark Wade, UNLV	1987	38	406	**10.7**
Glenn Williams, H.Cross	1989	28	278	**9.9**

Rebounding

Rebounds	Year	Gm	Total
Walter Dukes, Seton Hall	1953	33	**734**
Leroy Wright, Pacific	1959	26	**652**
Tom Gola, La Salle	1954	30	**652**
Charlie Tyra, Louisville.......	1956	29	**645**
Paul Silas, Creighton	1964	29	**631**

Average (before 1973)	Year	Rebs	Avg
Charlie Slack, Marshall	1955	538	**25.6**
Leroy Wright, Pacific	1959	652	**25.1**
Art Quimby, Connecticut	1955	611	**24.4**

Average (since 1973)	Year	Rebs	Avg
Kermit Washington, American.	1973	439	**20.0**
Marvin Barnes, Providence ...	1973	571	**19.0**
Marvin Barnes, Providence ...	1974	597	**18.7**

Blocked Shots

Average	Year	Gm	No	Avg
David Robinson, Navy	1986	35	207	**5.9**
Alonzo Mourning, Georgetown	1989	34	169	**5.0**
David Robinson, Navy	1987	32	144	**4.5**
Derrick Lewis, Maryland.....	1987	26	114	**4.4**
Duane Causwell, Temple	1989	30	124	**4.1**

Steals

Average	Year	Gm	No	Avg
Darron Bittman, Chicago St..	1986	28	139	**5.0**
Aldwin Ware, Florida A&M ..	1988	29	142	**4.9**
Jim Paguaga, St.Francis,NY..	1986	28	120	**4.3**
Marty Johnson, Towson St ...	1988	30	124	**4.1**
Tony Fairly, Baptist.........	1987	28	114	**4.1**

BEST GAMES

Scoring

Points vs Div.I Team	Year	Pts
Pete Maravich, LSU vs Alabama	1970	**69**
Calvin Murphy, Niagara vs Syracuse...	1969	**68**
Jay Handlan, Wash.& Lee vs Furman ..	1951	**66**
Pete Maravich, LSU vs Tulane	1969	**66**
Anthony Roberts, Oral Rbts vs N.C.A&T	1977	**66**
Scott Haffner, Evansville vs Dayton ...	1989	**65**
Anthony Roberts, Oral Rbts vs Oregon	1977	**65**
Pete Maravich, LSU vs Kentucky	1970	**64**
Hersey Hawkins, Bradley vs Detroit ...	1988	**63**
Johnny Neumann, Mississippi vs LSU ...	1971	**63**

Points vs Non-Div.I Team	Year	Pts
Frank Selvy, Furman vs Newberry.....	1954	**100**
Paul Arizin, Villanova vs Phila.NAMC .	1949	**85**
Freeman Williams, Port.St.vs Rocky Mt	1978	**81**
Bill Mlkvy, Temple vs Wilkes	1951	**73**
Freeman Williams, Port.St.vs S.Oregon	1977	**71**

Rebounding

Rebounds (before 1973)	Year	No
Bill Chambers, Wm.& Mary vs Virginia ...	1953	**51**
Charlie Slack, Marshall vs M.Harvey	1954	**43**
Tom Heinsohn, Holy Cross vs Boston Col .	1955	**42**
Art Quimby, Connecticut vs Boston Univ ..	1955	**40**
Maurice Stokes, St.Francis vs J.Carroll....	1955	**39**
Dave DeBusschere, Detroit vs Cent.Mich .	1960	**39**
Keith Swagerty, Pacific vs UC-S.Barbara ..	1965	**39**

Rebounds (since 1973)	Year	No
David Vaughn, Oral Roberts vs Brandeis .	1973	**34**
Robert Parish, Centenary vs So.Miss	1973	**33**
Jim Bradley, No.Ill vs Wisc-Milwaukee ...	1973	**31**
Calvin Natt, NE La. vs Ga.Southern	1976	**31**
Eddie Woods, Oral Roberts vs Lamar	1972	**30**
Eddie Woods, Oral Roberts vs La.Tech ...	1972	**30**
Brad Robinson, Kent St.vs Central Mich ...	1974	**30**

NCAA Division I Tournament Records

CAREER

Scoring

Points	Years	Gm	Total
Elvin Hayes, Houston	1966-68	13	**358**
Danny Manning, Kansas ...	1985-88	16	**328**
Oscar Robertson, Cincinnati	1958-60	10	**324**
Lew Alcindor, UCLA	1967-69	12	**304**
Bill Bradley, Princeton	1963-65	9	**303**

Average	Years	Pts	Avg
Austin Carr, Notre Dame ..	1969-71	289	**41.3**
Bill Bradley, Princeton	1963-65	303	**33.7**
Oscar Robertson, Cincinnati	1958-60	324	**32.4**
Jerry West, West Virginia ..	1958-60	275	**30.6**
Len Chappell, Wake Forest .	1961-62	221	**27.6**

Rebounding

Rebounds	Years	Gm	Tot	Avg
Elvin Hayes, Houston....	1966-68	13	222	**17.1**
Lew Alcindor, UCLA	1967-69	12	201	**16.8**
Jerry Lucas, Ohio St.....	1960-62	12	197	**16.4**
Bill Walton, UCLA	1972-74	12	159	**13.3**
Sam Lacey, New Mexico St	1968-70	11	157	**14.3**

SINGLE TOURNAMENT

Scoring

Points	Year	Gm	Total
Glen Rice, Michigan	1989	6	**184**
Bill Bradley, Princeton	1965	5	**177**
Elvin Hayes, Houston	1968	5	**167**
Danny Manning, Kansas	1988	6	**163**
Jerry West, West Virginia......	1959	5	**160**

Average	Year	Gm	Pts	Avg
Austin Carr, Notre Dame ...	1970	3	158	**50.2**
Austin Carr, Notre Dame ...	1971	3	125	**41.7**
Jerry Chambers, Utah	1966	4	143	**35.8**
Bill Bradley, Princeton	1965	5	177	**35.4**
Clyde Lovellette, Kansas.....	1952	4	141	**35.3**
Jerry West, West Virginia ...	1960	3	105	**35.0**

Other Men's Champions

NCAA Div.II Finals, 1957-89

Division II Finals held in Evansville, IN (1957-76) and Springfield, MA (since 1977).

Year	Winner	Score	Loser
1957	Wheaton, IL	89-65	Ky.Wesleyan
1958	South Dakota	75-53	St.Michaels, VT
1959	Evansville, IN	83-67	SW Missourt St.
1960	Evansville, IN	90-69	Chapman, CA
1961	Wittenberg, OH	42-38	SE Missouri St.
1962	Mt.St.Mary's, MD	58-57*	CS-Sacramento
1963	South Dakota St.	42-40	Wittenberg, OH
1964	Evansville, IN	72-59	Akron, OH
1965	Evansville, IN	85-82*	Southern Illinois
1966	Ky.Weslayan	54-51	Southern Illinois
1967	Winston-Salem, NC	77-74	SW Missouri St.
1968	Ky.Wesleyan	63-52	Indiana St.
1969	Ky.Wesleyan	75-71	SW Missouri St.
1970	Phila.Textile	76-65	Tennessee St.
1971	Evansville, IN	97-82	Old Dominion, VA
1972	Roanoke, VA	84-72	Akron, OH
1973	Ky.Wesleyan	78-76*	Tennessee St.
1974	Morgan St., MD	67-52	SW Missouri St.
1975	Old Dominion, VA	76-74	New Orleans, LA
1976	Puget Sound, WA	83-74	Tennessee-Chatt.
1977	Tennessee-Chatt.	71-62	Randolph-Macon
1978	Cheyney, PA	47-40	Wisc-Green Bay
1979	North Alabama	64-50	Wisc-Green Bay
1980	Virginia Union	80-74	New York Tech
1981	Florida Southern	73-68	Mt.St.Mary's, MD
1982	Dist.of Columbia	73-63	Florida Southern
1983	Wright St., OH	92-73	Dist.of Columbia
1984	Central Mo.St.	81-77	St.Augustine's, NC
1985	Jacksonville St.	74-73	South Dakota St.
1986	Sacred Heart, CT	93-87	SE Missouri St.
1987	Ky.Weslayan	92-74	Gannon, PA
1988	Lowell, MA	75-72	Alaska-Anchorage
1989	N.C.Central	73-46	SE Missouri St.

*Overtime

NCAA Div.III Finals, 1975-89

Division III Finals held in Reading, PA (1975-76); Rock Island, IL (1977-81); and Grand Rapids, MI (since 1982).

Year	Winner	Score	Loser
1975	LeMoyne-Owen, TN	57-54	Glassboro St., NJ
1976	Scranton, PA	60-57	Wittenberg, OH
1977	Wittenberg, OH	79-66	Oneonta St., NY
1978	North Park, IL	69-57	Widener, PA
1979	North Park, IL	66-62	Potsdam St., NY
1980	North Park, IL	83-76	Upsala, NJ
1981	Potsdam St., NY	67-65*	Augustana, IL
1982	Wabash, IN	83-62	Potsdam St., NY
1983	Scranton, PA	64-63	Wittenberg, OH
1984	Wisc-Whitewater	103-86	Clark, MA
1985	North Park, IL	72-71	Potsdam St., NY
1986	Potsdam St., NY	76-73	LeMoyne-Owen, TN
1987	North Park, IL	106-100	Clark, MA
1988	Ohio Wesleyan	92-70	Scranton, PA
1989	Wisc-Whitewater	94-86	Trenton St., NJ

*Overtime

NAIA Finals, 1937-89

NAIA tournament held in Kansas City at Municipal Auditorium (1937-74) and Kemper Arena (since 1975).

Year	Winner	Score	Loser
1937	Central Missouri	35-24	Morningside, IA
1938	Central Missouri	45-30	Roanoke, VA
1939	Southwestern, KS	32-31	San Diego St.
1940	Tarkio, MO	52-31	San Diego St.
1941	San Diego St.	36-32	Murray St., KY
1942	Hamline, MN	33-31	S'eastern Okla.
1943	SE Missouri St.	34-32	NW Missouri St.
1944	No tournament held		
1945	Loyola, LA	49-36	Pepperdine, CA
1946	Southern Illinois	49-40	Indiana St.
1947	Marshall, WV	73-59	Mankato St., MN
1948	Louisville, KY	82-70	Indiana St.
1949	Hamline, MN	57-46	Regis, CO
1950	Indiana St.	61-47	East Central, OK
1951	Hamline, MN	69-61	Millikin, IL
1952	SW Missouri St.	73-64	Murray St., KY
1953	SW Missouri St.	79-71	Hamline, MN
1954	St.Benedict's, KS	62-56	Western Illinois
1955	East Texas St.	71-54	S'eastern Okla.
1956	McNeese St., LA	60-55	Texas Southern
1957	Tennessee St.	92-73	S'eastern Okla.
1958	Tennessee St.	85-73	Western Illinois
1959	Tennessee St.	97-87	Pacific-Luth., WA
1960	SW Texas St.	66-44	Westminster, PA
1961	Grambling, LA	95-75	Georgetown, KY
1962	Prairie View, TX	62-53	Westminster, PA
1963	Pan American, TX	73-62	Western Carolina
1964	Rockhurst, MO	66-56	Pan American, TX
1965	Central St., OH	85-51	Oklahoma Baptist
1966	Oklahoma Baptist	88-59	Georgia Southern
1967	St.Benedict's, KS	71-65	Oklahoma Baptist
1968	Central St., OH	51-48	Fairmont St., WV
1969	Eastern N.Mexico	99-76	MD-Eastern Shore
1970	Kentucky St.	79-71	Central Wash.
1971	Kentucky St.	102-82	Eastern Michigan
1972	Kentucky St.	71-62	Wisc-Eau Claire
1973	Guilford, NC	99-96	MD-Eastern Shore
1974	West Georgia	97-79	Alcorn St., MS
1975	Grand Canyon, AZ	65-54	M'western St., TX
1976	Coppin St., MD	96-91	Henderson St., AR
1977	Texas Southern	71-44	Campbell, NC
1978	Grand Canyon, AZ	79-75	Kearney St., NE
1979	Drury, MO	60-54	Henderson St., AR
1980	Cameron, OK	84-77	Alabama St.
1981	Beth.Nazarene, OK	86-85*	Ala-Huntsville
1982	USC-Spartanburg	51-38	Biola, CA
1983	C.of Charleston, SC	57-53	West Va.Wesleyan
1984	Fort Hays St., KS	48-46*	Wisc-Stevens Pt.
1985	Fort Hays St., KS	82-80*	Wayland Bapt., TX
1986	David Lipscomb, TN	67-54	Ark-Monticello
1987	Washburn, KS	79-77	West Va.St.
1988	Grand Canyon, AZ	88-86*	Auburn-Montg, AL
1989	St.Mary's, TX	61-58	East Central, OK

*Overtime

Women's Basketball

Div.I Player of the Year

The Broderick Award was first given out to the women's Division I or Large School Player of the Year in 1977. Since then, the National Assn.for Girls and Women in Sports (1978) and the Atlanta Tip-Off Club (1983) have joined in.

Since 1983, the first year all three awards were given out, the same player has won all of them in the same season once: Cheryl Miller of Southern Cal in 1985.

Broderick Award

Voted on by a national panel of women's collegiate athletic directors and first presented by the late Thomas Broderick, an athletic outfitter who created the award in 1977. Numbers in parentheses indicate repeat winners.

Year	Coach, school
1977	Lusia Harris, Delta St.
1978	Ann Meyers, UCLA
1979	Nancy Lieberman, Old Dominion
1980	Nancy Lieberman, Old Dom.(2)
1981	Lynette Woodard, Kansas
1982	Pam Kelly, Louisiana Tech
1983	Anne Donovan, Old Dominion
1984	Cheryl Miller, USC
1985	Cheryl Miller, USC (2)
1986	Cheryl Miller, USC (3)
1987	Kamie Ethridge, Texas
1988	Teresa Weatherspoon, La.Tech
1989	TBA in fall

Wade Trophy

Voted on by the National Assn.for Girls and Women in Sports (NAGWS) and first presented in 1978 in the name of former Delta St. coach Margaret Wade. Numbers in parentheses indicate repeat winners.

Year	Coach, school
1978	Carol Blazejowski, Montclair St.
1979	Nancy Lieberman, Old Dominion
1980	Nancy Lieberman, Old Dom.(2)
1981	Lynette Woodard, Kansas
1982	Pam Kelly, Louisiana Tech
1983	LaTaunya Pollard, Long Beach St.
1984	Janice Lawrence, Louisiana Tech
1985	Cheryl Miller, Southern Cal
1986	Kamie Ethridge, Texas
1987	Shelly Pennefather, Villanova
1988	Teresa Weatherspoon, La.Tech
1989	Clarissa Davis, Texas

Naismith Trophy

Voted on by a panel of coaches, sportswriters and broadcasters and first presented in 1983 by the Atlanta Tip-Off Club in the name of the inventor of basketball, Dr.James Naismith. Numbers in parentheses indicate repeat winners.

Year	Player, school
1983	Anne Donovan, Old Dominion
1984	Cheryl Miller, USC
1985	Cheryl Miller, USC (2)
1986	Cheryl Miller, USC (3)
1987	Clarissa Davis, Texas
1988	Sue Wicks, Rutgers
1989	Clarissa Davis, Texas (2)

Tournaments
AIAW Finals, 1972-82

The Association of Intercollegiate Athletics for Women Large College tournament determined the women's national champion for 10 years until supplanted by the NCAA. In 1982, most Division I teams entered the first NCAA tournament rather than the last one staged by the AIAW.

Year	Winner	Score	Loser
1972	Immaculata,PA	52-48	West Chester,PA
1973	Immaculata,PA	59-52	Queens College,NY
1974	Immaculata,PA	68-53	Mississippi Col.
1975	Delta St.,MS	90-81	Immaculata,PA
1976	Delta St.,MS	69-64	Immaculata,PA
1977	Delta St.,MS	68-55	LSU
1978	UCLA	90-74	Maryland
1979	Old Dominion	75-65	Louisiana Tech
1980	Old Dominion	68-53	Tennessee
1981	Louisiana Tech	79-59	Tennessee
1982	Rutgers	83-77	Texas

NCAA Div.I Finals, 1982-89

Division I Finals held in Norfolk,VA (1982-83); Los Angeles (1984); Austin,TX, (1985,87); Lexington,KY (1986); and Tacoma,WA (since 1988).

Year	Winner	Score	Loser
1982	Louisiana Tech	76-62	Cheyney,PA
1983	Southern Cal	69-67	Louisiana Tech
1984	Southern Cal	72-61	Tennessee
1985	Old Dominion	70-65	Georgia
1986	Texas	97-81	Southern Cal
1987	Tennessee	67-44	Louisiana Tech
1988	Louisiana Tech	56-54	Auburn
1989	Tennessee	76-60	Auburn

Outstanding Players: 1982—Janice Lawrence, La. Tech; **1983**—Cheryl Miller, USC; **1984**—Cheryl Miller, USC; **1985**-Tracy Claxton, Old Dominion; **1986**—Clarissa Davis, Texas; **1987**—Tonya Edwards, Tennessee; **1988**—Erica Westbrooks, L.Tech; **1989**—Bridgette Gordon, Tennessee.

NCAA Div.II Finals, 1982-89

Division II Finals held in Springfield,MA (1982-87); Fargo,ND (1988); and Cleveland,MS (1989).

Year	Winner	Score	Loser
1982	Cal Poly Pomona	93-74	Tuskegee,AL
1983	Virginia Union	73-60	Cal Poly Pomona
1984	Central Mo.St.	80-73	Virginia Union
1985	Cal Poly Pomona	80-69	Central Mo.St.
1986	Cal Poly Pomona	70-63	North Dakota St.
1987	New Haven,CT	77-75	Cal Poly Pomona
1988	Hampton,VA	65-48	West Texas St.
1989	Delta St.,MS	88-58	Cal Poly Pomona

NCAA Div.III Finals, 1982-89

Division III Finals held in Elizabethtown,PA (1982); Worcester,MA (1983); Scranton,PA (1984,87); DePere,WI (1985); Salem,MA (1986); Moorhead,MN (1988); and Danville,KY (1989).

Year	Winner	Score	Loser
1982	Elizabethtown,PA	67-66*	NC-Greensboro
1983	North Central,IL	83-71	Elizabethtown,PA
1984	Rust College,MS	51-49	Elizabethtown,PA
1985	Scranton,PA	68-59	New Rochelle,NY
1986	Salem St.,MA	89-85	Bishop,TX
1987	Wisc-Stevens Pt.	81-74	Concordia,MN
1988	Concordia,MN	65-57	St.John Fisher,NY
1989	Elizabethtown,PA	66-65	CS-Stanislaus

*Overtime
Note: Concordia,MN is Concordia College in Moorhead,MN, not Concordia College in St.Paul,MN.

NAIA Finals, 1981-89

NAIA tournament held in Kansas City,MO (1981-83,87-89) and Cedar Rapids,IA (1984-86).

Year	Winner	Score	Loser
1981	Kentucky St.	73-67	Texas Southern
1982	S'western Okla.	80-45	Mo.Southern
1983	S'western Okla.	80-68	Ala-Huntsville
1984	NC-Asheville	72-70*	Portland,OR
1985	S'western Okla.	55-54	Saginaw Val.,MI
1986	Francis Marion,SC	75-65	Wayland Bapt.,TX
1987	S'western Okla.	60-58	North Georgia
1988	Oklahoma City	113-95	Claflin,SC
1989	So.Nazarene	98-96	Claflin,SC

*Overtime

Oklahoma athletic director **Donnie Duncan** (left) and football coach **Barry Switzer** face reporters on Dec. 20, 1988 after the NCAA put the Sooners on probation for three years

COLLEGE SPORTS

INSIDE

Elsewhere in Almanac

For related information refer to the following chapters: Arenas & Ballparks, Halls of Fame & Awards, Sports Organizations, and Miscellaneous.

*As the probations pile up,
winning at all costs
is an expense intercollegiate
athletics can no longer afford.*

COLLEGE SPORTS

1988-89 YEAR IN REVIEW

by Jeffrey Marx

Item: University of Kentucky officials say they will soon approach New York Knicks Coach Rick Pitino about the school's head basketball coaching job. A judgment on the Kentucky program from the NCAA Committee on Infractions is coming soon.

Item: Texas Gov. Bill Clements, who two years ago apologized for his role in the pay-for-play scandal that cost Southern Methodist its football program, signs a bill making it a crime to recruit student-athletes with money or gifts.

Item: Boosters say they housed Marshall University basketball players in violation of NCAA rules. Marshall declares two players, including Southern Conference player of the year John Taft, ineligible because of their involvement.

Item: Georgia professor Jan Kemp charges that some athletic department

Jeffrey Marx shared the 1986 Pulitzer Prize in investigative reporting for a series on cheating in major college basketball programs. He is a staff writer for **The National**, the new sports daily newspaper, and is currently writing a book with track and field star Carl Lewis.

tutors ''are incompetent'' and says she will not apologize for steering students away from them.

Item: Eight football bowls are fined by the NCAA for using a professional athlete in promotions or promoting the NFL. The Rose Bowl is fined the most, $11,892.

Item: Attorneys for convicted sports agents Norby Walters and Lloyd Bloom are seeking a new trial for their clients, claiming a federal judge in Chicago made errors.

What is going on here?

This is not the college-sports scandal news of a year. It is the news of a **day**, May 18, 1989. And it might as well have been the scandal news of any day during the year. We can no longer turn to the sports page, watch the evening news or flip to ESPN without seeing something about troubles in college sports.

The primary reason for that is not entirely clear. Are we bombarded with sports-scandal news because there is more cheating than ever before? Or does it only seem like there is more cheating because the news media are searching

Wide World Photos

Kentucky president **David Roselle** (left) confers with new athletic director **C.M. Newton** May 19 after the Wildcats' basketball program was put on three years' probation by the NCAA.

more than ever for such stories and playing them at the top of the news?

Either way, a new climate exists on college campuses, in the offices of the National Collegiate Athletic Association and among the public. In March, a national poll released by the Associated Press showed overwhelmingly that Americans widely doubted the integrity of top sports colleges, believing they commonly give secret payments and inflated grades to athletes. Two-thirds of the people interviewed said that colleges overemphasize sports and neglect academic standards for athletes.

The same day in May that all that sports news was breaking, a U.S. House education subcommittee conducted a hearing on college sports. Among the witnesses were NCAA Executive Director Richard Schultz and Robert Atwell, president of the American Council on Education, an umbrella organization for the nation's colleges and universities. Their views contrasted greatly.

Schultz, less than two years into his NCAA job, disputed charges that the NCAA deals only superficially with rules violations, academic problems and drug abuse in college sports. He said that colleges were making progress in dealing with athletics problems.

"In my judgment," Schultz said, "intercollegiate athletics in 1989 is under greater hands-on control by college leaders than at any time in this century."

Schultz also suggested that reports of NCAA problems, being presented as the norm, should really be treated as isolated incidents.

Not so, said Atwell, because the scandals afflicting big-time sports programs are symptoms of a "basically unhealthy" enterprise. Atwell proposed the elimination of freshman eligibility for football and basketball, shortening the seasons in both, and equal sharing of television revenues among all schools.

"First and foremost," he said, "we must try to break the insidious connection between money and winning."

Sports Illustrated called Schultz a

"Pollyanna" for declaring that college athletics were 99 percent clean. In response, Schultz conceded that there were "plenty of problems" in college sports but he rejected the Pollyanna label and said, "For every athlete making a mistake, there are a thousand who are doing things right."

But even longtime supporters of the NCAA disagreed. On April 6, upon being named commissioner of the Big Ten Conference, former NCAA official James Delany called for fresh ideas to keep sports in perspective. His words were tough.

"At this unique time in college athletics, all is not well," Delany said. "I think it's important to find a better balance. There's got to be a way to make sure education is first. And I don't think that's the case in all institutions today. . . .There has been tinkering with NCAA rules . . . but in my opinion there has not been reform."

The next month, outgoing Georgetown University President Rev. Timothy Healy tried to explain the lack of reform in the NCAA.

"It's as complex as the federal government," Healy said in an interview with the **Washington Post**. "There's such an inertial resistance to change [in the NCAA] it's frightening. You've only got so much indignation and I've about used mine up."

The names and places change, but the basic structure of the debate over the NCAA and its problems remains the same. Given the severity of some recent busts by the NCAA, and the publicity that accompanies the fall of a major program, it is no wonder that the debate rages in academic and athletic circles, on television and radio talk shows, in newspapers, magazines and neighborhood bars.

One of the most severe cases brought by the NCAA, on the eve of the 1988–89 college basketball season, resulted in heavy penalties against the Kansas Jayhawks, defending national champions. Recruiting violations that resulted in a three-year probation occurred under former Kansas coach Larry Brown, but the fact that he had already moved onto the pros did not lessen the blow.

As a result of the penalties, Kansas became the first national collegiate basketball champion to be denied, even before the season began, any chance of defending its title.

At the time, 18 intercollegiate programs—ranging from SMU football to Eastern Washington basketball—were on probation. But some NCAA observers were surprised that a program as prominent as Kansas basketball had been nailed. Arizona coach Lute Olson called

NCAA Probation List

The NCAA's roster of member institutions on probation as of June 5,1989. The number of years each school is on probation and the date that probation ends are listed in the far right column.

School	Div.	Sport	Probation Yrs (over)
Alabama A&M . .	I	Soccer	1½ (Indef.)
Arizona St	I	Men's & Women's Track	2 (11/10/90)
Cincinnati	I-A	Football	3 (11/3/91)
	I	Basketball	3 (11/3/91)
Cleveland St	I	Basketball	3 (4/21/91)
Eastern Wash . . .	I	Basketball	2 (11/24/89)
Houston	I-A	Football	3 (12/31/91)
Illinois	I-A	Football	1½ (7/1/89)
Kansas	I	Basketball	3 (11/1/91)
Kentucky	I	Basketball	3 (May,1992)
Marist	I	Basketball	2 (1/9/90)
Minnesota	I	Basketball	2 (3/10/90)
Oklahoma	I-A	Football	3 (12/27/91)
Oklahoma St. .	I-A	Football	4 (1/9/93)
SMU	I-A	Football	3½ (9/1/90)
Texas A&M . . .	I-A	Football	2 (9/20/90)
UTEP	I	Cross-Country & Track (M&W)	3 (6/13/89)
Virginia Tech . .	I-A	Football	2 (11/6/89)
	I	Basketball	2 (11/6/89)
West Texas St . .	II	Basketball	3 (1/6/92)

Banned from Post Season Play

1988-89—Arizona St. Men's & Women's track; Cincinnati football and basketball; Cleveland St. basketball; Kansas basketball; Marist basketball; Texas A&M football; Virginia Tech basketball; West Texas St. basketball.

1989-90—Cleveland St. basketball; Houston football; Kentucky basketball; Oklahoma football; Oklahoma St. football.

1990-91—Houston football; Kentucky basketball; Oklahoma football; Oklahoma St. football.

1991-92—Oklahoma St. football.

Indefinitely—Alabama A&M soccer.

An emotional **Barry Switzer** announced his resignation in June after 16 years as Oklahoma football coach.

the case "a warning signal. Either abide by the rules or get nailed."

The next major program to get punished was Oklahoma football. On December 19, 1988, the Sooners were hit with a three-year probation for widespread and numerous abuses. That was only the beginning of the end for longtime coach Barry Switzer, who took a lot of heat the next six months as criminal charges were brought against five of his players, in separate cases, for a variety of crimes.

Oklahoma football was very badly damaged, painted by the media as the ultimate example of an out-of-control college sports program. On June 19, 1989, Switzer resigned, saying that he had lost his energy and enthusiasm. Of course, in the tradition of tarnished coaches, Switzer took a parting shot at the NCAA.

"I want this resignation to stand for something," Switzer told a packed news conference in Norman, Okla. "Barry Switzer is totally frustrated working within a set of rigid rules that does not recognize the financial needs of many of our young athletes."

Oklahoma football would have been the biggest probation story of the year. if the Kentucky basketball program had

been behaving itself. But after a lengthy investigation, the NCAA determined that Kentucky, which traditionally played above its opponents, had also been playing above the rules. Kentucky was nailed, too, with a near knockout punch delivered on May 19, 1989, not long after the resignations of Athletic Director Cliff Hagan and Coach Eddie Sutton.

Among the sanctions: three years of probation including a two-year ban on post-season play, a one-year ban on live television appearances, and scholarship reductions.

In addition, the Wildcats lost two of their best players, Chris Mills, whose family, the NCAA determined, had received $1,000 in an overnight package from the Kentucky basketball office, and Eric Manuel, who committed "the most serious kind of violation" by cheating on a college entrance exam, the NCAA said.

And the penalties could have been harsher. NCAA officials had considered shutting down Kentucky basketball for one or two seasons. "It was a very real possibility," said Steve Morgan, an associate executive director of the NCAA who went to Lexington, Ky., to announce the penalties.

While the investigations of some of the biggest programs drew a lot of attention,

A cautious **Rick Pitino** left the NBA after two years to become Kentucky's new basketball coach.

Wide World Photos

Wide World Photos

Lloyd Bloom (left) and **Norby Walters** (right) were the first sports agents ever convicted by a federal jury for their dealings with college athletes.

they were not the only ways NCAA problems were publicly aired. A criminal trial of sports agents Norby Walters and Lloyd Bloom provided a vivid look into the dark side of college athletics, academics and money.

Walters and Bloom, who had signed dozens of college football and basketball players in April in violation of NCAA rules, were convicted on five of seven counts covering racketeering, mail fraud and extortion. Walters, 58, and Bloom, 30, were the first sports agents ever convicted by a federal jury for their dealings with college athletes. U.S. Attorney Anton Valukas, who prosecuted the case, called the convictions "a message" that federal laws "apply across the board" to colleges, athletes and agents.

Other messages were delivered by defense attorneys who tried to show that widespread corruption existed in college sports before the entrance of Walters and Bloom. Transcripts of some prominent athletes, including former Iowa football star Ronnie Harmon and 1986 Heisman Trophy runner-up Paul Palmer of Temple, were entered as evidence to illustrate a win-at-all costs mentality, and a number of athletes and schools were rightfully embarrassed.

Rick Telander of **Sports Illustrated**,

who has written a lot about problems in college sports, offered a nice summary of the agents' case, comparing Bloom and Walters to "rats in a basement full of garbage. It's fine that we're getting rid of the rats, but it's even more important to get rid of the garbage that attracts them."

After learning that Palmer had signed with Walters and Bloom before his senior season, Temple erased his statistics and 16 school records, and the school forfeited six victories in which he played. Palmer did not think that Temple officials treated him fairly.

"It hurts. . .bad," Palmer, then playing with the Kansas City Chiefs, told the **Philadelphia Daily News**. "For four years, I was always there for them whenever they needed me. Then I make one mistake my whole college career, and everything is just gone."

The Walters and Bloom case was only one example of the way college sports problems have moved into outside arenas. The courts, Congress and several state legislatures all got involved.

In Congress, Sen. Bill Bradley, a New Jersey Democrat and member of the Basketball Hall of Fame, introduced a bill to require colleges to make public their graduation rates, primarily so athletes would have access to such information when they are being recruited.

In Nebraska, a state bill was introduced to require sports agents to register and post bond with the Nebraska secretary of state, and another bill was written to require the NCAA to use due process in disciplinary proceedings against Nebraska schools.

Some coaches started talking about suing boosters responsible for problems in their programs. One of the most vocal proponents of the idea was new Texas A&M football coach R.C. Slocum, who replaced Jackie Sherrill. Slocum started talking about lawsuits shortly after Sherrill resigned on Dec.12, 1988, amid reports of widespread cheating in the A&M program.

There was increasing talk of other roles for lawyers and lawmakers. The more people involved in fighting the problems of college sports, the thinking seems to be, the fewer times the Kentuckys and Oklahomas will embarrass the college sports world.

Dispatches from the Front

—How about this for a sign of the times? The Southwestern Athletic Conference penalized Prairie View A&M for using ineligible football players in beating Southern University and Texas Southern. Among other penalties, Prairie View had to forfeit the Southern game. But not the Texas Southern game. Texas Southern, it was learned, had also used an ineligible player.

—Football player Hart Lee Dykes made a big name for himself and big trouble for schools that improperly recruited him. Dykes, who earned All-America honors as a wide receiver for Oklahoma State, was said to be a key to landing Illinois, Texas A&M, Oklahoma and his own school on probation. "Long after Dykes has gone to the pros," **Sports Illustrated** reported, "his name may continue to serve as a reminder to college athletic administrators of the increasingly large financial risks that come with cheating."

HART LEE DYKES

—The NCAA, often criticized for keeping athletes out of its decision-making process, voted to create a student-athlete advisory committee. "It is not planned that the committee would be authorized to put forward legislation," NCAA president Will Bailey said. "But they could certainly recommend legislation."

—A massive study on the college experiences of athletes was commissioned by the NCAA at a cost of $1.75 million. Among the findings: athletes lag academically behind students in other extracurricular activities; athletes incur more injuries than students who do not participate in sports; football and basketball players say they need more spending money. "No great surprises," said Martin Massengale, chairman of the NCAA Presidents Commission. Newsweek magazine poked fun at the report, suggesting that the NCAA deserved one of Sen. William Proxmire's Golden Fleece awards for spending large amounts of time and money to discover the obvious.

—David Berst, for years the NCAA's top enforcement official, tires of hearing rules-breaking basketball coaches complain that they were only helping athletes in need, not cheating. "I do hear occasionally the rationalization that cheating is in reality a humanitarian act," Berst says. But he did find a pattern. "Violations are tied more directly to how high someone can jump and how well they shoot."

—Large schools are not the only ones with problems. Baptist Christian College in Louisiana shut down its basketball program because eight of 11 players were academically ineligible. "Some of them don't even have grade point averages," said school president Phillip Martin. They did not have a good season either. Their record was 4–16.

1988-89 NCAA Champions

Stanford and Louisiana State (LSU) each won three NCAA Division I team championships during the 1988-89 school year. The Cardinal won Women's Swimming & Diving in the Winter and both Men's and Women's tennis in the Spring. LSU won three track titles—Women's Indoor and both Men's and Women's Outdoor.

In Division II, California Polytechnic State in San Luis Obispo was the only school to win three championships (Women's Cross Country, Men's Baseball and Women's Outdoor Track), while the University of California at San Diego won three Division III titles (Men's Soccer, Women's Volleyball and Women's Tennis).

FALL

Cross Country

Men's Division I . . . . Wisconsin
        Division II . . . . Edinboro,PA
                    & Mankato St.,MN
        Division III . . . . Wisconsin-Oshkosh

Women's Division I . . . . Kentucky
        Division II . . . . Cal Poly SLO
        Division III . . . . Wisconsin-Oshkosh

Field Hockey

Division I . . . . Old Dominion
Division III . . . . Trenton St.NJ

Football

Division I-A (unofficial) . . . . . . Notre Dame*
Division I-AA . . . . Furman
Division II . . . . North Dakota St.
Division III . . . . Ithaca,NY
*There is no NCAA Div.I-A playoff

Soccer

Men's Division I . . . . Indiana
        Division II . . . . Florida Tech
        Division III . . . . UC San Diego

Women's Division I . . . . North Carolina
        Division II . . . . Cal St.Hayward
        Division III . . . . William Smith,NY

Volleyball

Women's Division I . . . . Texas
        Division II . . . . Portland St.
        Division III . . . . UC San Diego

Water Polo

Men's Champion . . . . California

WINTER

Basketball

Men's Division I . . . . Michigan
        Division II . . . . N.Carolina Central
        Division III . . . . Wisconsin-Whitewater

Women's Division I . . . . Tennessee
        Division II . . . . Delta St.,MS
        Division III . . . . Elizabethtown,PA

Fencing

Men's Champion . . . . Columbia
Women's Champion . . . . Wayne St.,MI

Gymnastics

Men's Champion . . . . Illinois
Women's Champion . . . . Georgia

Ice Hockey

Division I . . . . Harvard
Division III . . . . Wisconsin-Stevens Pt.

Rifle

Men/Women Combined . . . . . West Virginia

Skiing

Men/Women Combined . . . . . Vermont

Swimming & Diving

Men's Division I . . . . Texas
        Division II . . . . Cal St.Bakersfield
        Division III . . . . Kenyon,OH

Women's Division I . . . . Stanford
        Division II . . . . Cal St.Northbridge
        Division III . . . . Kenyon,OH

Indoor Track

Men's Division I . . . . Arkansas
        Division II . . . . St.Augustine's,NC
        Division III . . . . North Central,IL

Women's Division I . . . . LSU
        Division II . . . . Abilene Christian,TX
        Division III . . . . Christopher
                            Newport,VA

Wrestling

Division I . . . . Oklahoma St.
Division II . . . . Portland St.
Division III . . . . Ithaca,NY

SPRING

Baseball

Division I . . . . Wichita St.
Division II . . . . Cal Poly SLO
Division III . . . . N.Carolina Wesleyan

Golf

Men's Division I . . . . Oklahoma
     Division II . . . . Columbus,GA
     Division III . . . . Cal St.Stanislaus

Women's Champion . . . . San Jose St.

Lacrosse

Men's Division I . . . . Syracuse
     Division III . . . . Hobart,NY

Women's Division I . . . . Penn St.
     Division III . . . . Ursinus,PA

Softball

Women's Division I . . . . UCLA
     Division II . . . . Cal St.Bakersfield
     Division III . . . . Trenton St.,NJ

Tennis

Men's Division I . . . . Stanford
     Division II . . . . Hampton,VA
     Division III . . . . UC Santa Cruz

Women's Division I . . . . Stanford
     Division II . . . . So.Ill.-Edwardsville
     Division III . . . . UC San Diego

Outdoor Track

Men's Division I . . . . LSU
     Division II . . . . St.Augustine's,NC
     Division III . . . . North Central,IL

Women's Division I . . . . LSU
     Division II . . . . Cal Poly SLO
     Division III . . . . . . Christopher
                      Newport,VA

Volleyball

Men's Champion . . . . UCLA

1988-89 NAIA Champions

Pacific Lutheran of Tacoma, Wash. was the only NAIA school to win two team championships in 1989-90. The Lutes won both titles (Women's Cross Country and Women's Soccer) in the Fall.

FALL

Cross Country

Men's . . . . Adams St.,CO
Women's . . . . Pacific Lutheran,WA

Football

Division I . . . . Carson-Newman,TN
Division II . . . . Westminster,PA

Soccer

Men's . . . . Sangamon St.,IL
Women's . . . . Pacific Lutheran,WA

Volleyball

Women's . . . . Hawaii-Hilo

WINTER

Basketball

Men's . . . . St.Mary's,TX
Women's . . . . Southern Nazarene,OK

Swimming & Diving

Men's . . . . Drury,MO
Women's . . . . Puget Sound,WA

Indoor Track

Men's . . . . Wayland Baptist,TX
Women's . . . . Midland Lutheran,NE

Wrestling

Men's . . . . Central St.,OK

SPRING

Baseball

Men's . . . . Lewis Clark St.,ID

Golf

Men's . . . . Guilford,NC

Softball

Women's . . . . Saginaw Valley,MI

Tennis

Men's . . . . Texas-Tyler
Women's . . . . Flagler,FL

Outdoor Track

Men's . . . . Azusa Pacific,CA
Women's . . . . Prairie View,TX

NCAA Division I-A Football Schools

School	Nickname	Conf.	Head Coach	Location	Colors
Air Force	Falcons	WAC	Fisher DeBerry	Colo.Springs,CO	Blue/Silver
Akron	Zips	Indep.	Gerry Faust	Akron,OH	Blue/Gold
Alabama	Crimson Tide	SEC	Bill Curry	Tuscaloosa,AL	Crimson/White
Arizona	Wildcats	Pac-10	Dick Tomey	Tucson,AZ	Cardinal/Navy
Arizona St.	Sun Devils	Pac-10	Larry Marmie	Tempe,AZ	Maroon/Gold
Arkansas	Razorbacks	SWC	Ken Hatfield	Fayetteville,AR	Cardinal/White
Army	Cadets	Indep.	Jim Young	West Point,NY	Black/Gold/Gray
Auburn	Tigers	SEC	Pat Dye	Auburn,AL	Orange/Blue
Ball St	Cardinals	MAC	Paul Schudel	Muncie,IN	Cardinal/White
Baylor	Bears	SWC	Grant Teaff	Waco,TX	Green/Gold
Boston College	Eagles	Indep.	Jack Bicknell	Chestnut Hill,MA	Maroon/Gold
Bowling Green	Falcons	MAC	Moe Ankney	Bowling Green,OH	Orange/Brown
Brig. Young	Cougars	WAC	LaVell Edwards	Provo,UT	Blue/White
California	Golden Bears	Pac-10	Bruce Snyder	Berkeley,CA	Blue/Gold
CS-Fullerton	Titans	Big West	Gene Murphy	Fullerton,CA	Orange/Blue/White
Central Mich.	Chippewas	MAC	Herb Deromedi	Mt.Pleasant,MI	Maroon/Gold
Cincinnati	Bearcats	Indep.	Tim Murphy	Cincinnati,OH	Red/Black
Clemson	Tigers	ACC	Danny Ford	Clemson,SC	Purple/Orange
Colorado	Buffaloes	Big 8	Bill McCartney	Boulder,CO	Silver/Gold/Black
Colorado St.	Rams	WAC	Earle Bruce	Colo.Springs,CO	Green/Gold
Duke	Blue Devils	ACC	Steve Spurrier	Durham,NC	Royal Blue/White
East Carolina	Pirates	Indep.	Bill Lewis	Greenville,NC	Purple/Gold
Eastern Mich.	Hurons	MAC	Jim Harkema	Ypsilanti,MI	Green/White
Florida	Gators	SEC	Galen Hall	Gainesville,FL	Orange/Blue
Florida St.	Seminoles	Indep.	Bobby Bowden	Tallahassee,FL	Garnet/Gold
Fresno St	Bulldogs	Big West	Jim Sweeney	Fresno,CA	Cardinal/Blue
Georgia	Bulldogs,'Dawgs	SEC	Ray Goff	Athens,GA	Red/Black
Georgia Tech	Yellow Jackets	ACC	Bobby Ross	Atlanta,GA	Old Gold/White
Hawaii	Rainbows	WAC	Bob Wagner	Honolulu,HI	Green/White
Houston	Cougars	SWC	Jack Pardee	Houston,TX	Cougar Red/White
Illinois	Fighting Illini	Big 10	John Mackovic	Champaign,IL	Orange/Blue
Indiana	Hoosiers	Big 10	Bill Mallory	Bloomington,IN	Cream/Crimson
Iowa	Hawkeyes	Big 10	Hayden Fry	Iowa City,IA	Old Gold/Black
Iowa St.	Cyclones	Big 8	Jim Walden	Ames,IA	Cardinal/Gold
Kansas	Jayhawks	Big 8	Glen Mason	Lawrence,KS	Crimson/Blue
Kansas St.	Wildcats	Big 8	Bill Snyder	Manhattan,KS	Purple/White
Kent St.	Golden Flashes	MAC	Dick Crum	Kent,OH	Navy Blue/Gold
Kentucky	Wildcats	SEC	Jerry Claiborne	Lexington,KY	Blue/White
Liberty	Flames	Indep.	Sam Rutigliano	Lynchburg,VA	Red/White/Blue
Long Beach St.	49ers	Big West	Larry Reisbig	Long Beach,CA	Brown/Gold
LSU	Fighting Tigers	SEC	Mike Archer	Baton Rouge,LA	Purple/Gold
Louisville	Cardinals	Indep.	H.Schnellenberger	Louisville,KY	Red/Black/White
Maryland	Terrapins,Terps	ACC	Joe Krivak	College Park,MD	Red/White/Black/Gold
Memphis St.	Tigers	Indep.	Chuck Stobart	Memphis,TN	Blue/Gray
Miami, FL	Hurricanes	Indep.	Dennis Erickson	Miami,FL	Orange/Green/White
Miami, OH	Redskins	MAC	Tim Rose	Oxford,OH	Red/White
Michigan	Wolverines	Big 10	Bo Schembechler	Ann Arbor,MI	Maize/Blue
Michigan St.	Spartans	Big 10	George Perles	East Lansing,MI	Green/White
Minnesota	Golden Gophers	Big 10	John Gutekunst	Minneapolis,MN	Maroon/Gold
Mississippi	Rebels,Ole Miss	SEC	Billy Brewer	University,MS	Card.Red/Navy Blue
Mississippi St.	Bulldogs	SEC	Rockey Felker	Miss.State,MS	Maroon/White
Missouri	Tigers	Big 8	Bob Stull	Columbia,MO	Old Gold/Black
Navy	Midshipmen	Indep.	Elliot Uzelac	Annapolis,MD	Navy Blue/Gold
Nebraska	Cornhuskers	Big 8	Tom Osborne	Lincoln,NE	Scarlet/Cream
New Mexico	Lobos	WAC	Mike Sheppard	Albuquerque,NM	Cherry/Silver
N.Mexico St.	Aggies	Big West	Mike Knoll	Las Cruces,NM	Crimson/White
N.Carolina	Tar Heels	ACC	Mack Brown	Chapel Hill,NC	Carolina Blue/White
N.Carolina St.	Wolfpack	ACC	Dick Sheridan	Raleigh,NC	Red/White
Northern Ill.	Huskies	Indep.	Jerry Pettibone	De Kalb,IL	Cardinal/Black
Northwestern	Wildcats	Big 10	Francis Peay	Evanston,IL	Purple/White
Notre Dame	Fighting Irish	Indep.	Lou Holtz	Notre Dame,IN	Gold/Blue

School	Nickname	Conf.	Head Coach	Location	Colors
Ohio Univ. . . . . Bobcats		MAC	Cleve Bryant	Athens,OH	Kelly Green/White
Ohio St. . . . . . . Buckeyes		Big 10	John Cooper	Columbus,OH	Scarlet/Gray
Oklahoma . . . . . Sooners		Big 8	Gary Gibbs	Norman,OK	Crimson/Cream
Oklahoma St. . . Cowboys		Big 8	Pat Jones	Stillwater,OK	Orange/Black
Oregon . . . . Ducks		Pac-10	Rich Brooks	Eugene,OR	Green/Yellow
Oregon St. . . . . Beavers		Pac-10	Dave Kragthorpe	Corvallis,OR	Orange/Black
Pacific . . . . Tigers		Big West	Walt Harris	Stockton,CA	Orange/Black
Penn St. . . . . . . Nittany Lions		Indep.	Joe Paterno	Univ.Park,PA	Blue/White
Pittsburgh . . . . . Panthers		Indep.	Mike Gottfried	Pittsburgh,PA	Blue/Gold
Purdue . . . . Boilermakers		Big 10	Fred Akers	W.Lafayette,IN	Old Gold/Black
Rice . . . . Owls		SWC	Fred Goldsmith	Houston,TX	Blue/Gray
Rutgers . . . . Scarlet Knights		Indep.	Dick Anderson	New Brunswick,NJ	Scarlet
San Diego St. . . Aztecs		WAC	Al Luginbill	San Diego,CA	Scarlet/Black
San Jose St. . . . Spartans		Big West	Claude Gilbert	San Jose,CA	Gold/White Blue
S.Carolina . . . . . Gamecocks		Indep.	Sparky Woods	Columbia,SC	Garnet/Black
Southern Cal. . . Trojans		Pac-10	Larry Smith	Los Angeles,CA	Cardinal/Gold
SMU . . . . Mustangs		SWC	Forrest Gregg	Dallas,TX	Red/Blue
Southern Miss. Golden Eagles		Indep.	Curley Hallman	Hattiesburg,MS	Black/Gold
SW Louisiana . . Ragin' Cajuns		Indep.	Nelson Stokley	Lafayette,LA	Vermilion/White
Stanford . . . . . . Cardinal		Pac-10	Dennis Green	Stanford,CA	Cardinal/White
Syracuse . . . . . . Orangemen		Indep.	Dick MacPherson	Syracuse,NY	Orange
Temple . . . . Owls		Indep.	Jerry Berndt	Philadelphia,PA	Cherry/White
Tennessee . . . . . Volunteers		SEC	Johnny Majors	Knoxville,TN	Orange/White
Texas . . . . Longhorns		SWC	Dave McWilliams	Austin,TX	Burnt Orange/White
Texas A&M . . . . Aggies		SWC	R.C.Slocum	College Station,TX	Maroon/White
TCU . . . . Horned Frogs		SWC	Jim Wacker	Ft.Worth,TX	Purple/White
Texas Tech . . . . Red Raiders		SWC	Spike Dykes	Lubbock,TX	Scarlet/Black
Toledo . . . . Rockets		MAC	Dan Simrell	Toledo,OH	Blue/Gold
Tulane . . . . Green Wave		Indep.	Greg Davis	New Orleans,LA	Olive Green/Sky Blue
Tulsa . . . . Golden Hurricane		Indep.	David Rader	Tulsa,OK	Blue/Gold
UCLA . . . . Bruins		Pac-10	Terry Donahue	Los Angeles,CA	Blue/Gold
UNLV . . . . Runnin' Rebels		Big West	Wayne Nunnely	Las Vegas,NV	Scarlet/Gray
Utah . . . . Utes		WAC	Jim Fassel	Salt Lake City,UT	Crimson/White
Utah St. . . . . . . Aggies		Big West	Chuck Shelton	Logan,UT	Navy Blue/White
UTEP . . . . Miners		WAC	David Lee	El Paso,TX	Orange/White/Blue
Vanderbilt . . . . . Commodores		SEC	Watson Brown	Nashville,TN	Black/Gold
Virginia . . . . Cavaliers		ACC	George Welsh	Charlottesville,VA	Orange/Blue
Virginia Tech . . Hokies/Gobblers		Indep.	Frank Beamer	Blacksburg,VA	Orange/Maroon
Wake Forest . . . Demon Deacons		ACC	Bill Dooley	Winston-Salem,NC	Old Gold/Black
Washington . . . Huskies		Pac-10	Don James	Seattle,WA	Purple/Gold
Wash.St. . . . . . . Cougars		Pac-10	Mike Price	Pullman,WA	Crimson/Gray
West Virginia . . Mountaineers		Indep.	Don Nehlen	Morgantown,WV	Old Gold/Blue
Western Mich. . Broncos		MAC	Al Molde	Kalamazoo,MI	Brown/Gold
Wisconsin . . . . . Badgers		Big 10	Don Morton	Madison,WI	Cardinal/White
Wyoming . . . . . Cowboys		WAC	Paul Roach	Laramie,WY	Brown/Yellow

NCAA Division I-AA Football Schools

School	Nickname	Conference	Head Coach	Location	Colors
Alabama St . . Hornets		S'western	Houston Markham	Montgomery,AL	Black/Gold
Alcorn St . . . . Braves		S'western	Theo Danzy	Lorman,MS	Purple/Gold
Appalach.St. . Mountaineers		Southern	Jerry Moore	Boone,NC	Black/Gold
Arkansas St . . Indians		Indep.	Larry Lacewell	State Univ.,AR	Scarlet/Black
Austin Peay . . Governors		Ohio Valley	Paul Brewster	Clarksville,TN	Red/White
Beth-Cookman Wildcats		Mid-Eastern	Larry Little	Daytona Beach,FL	Maroon/Gold
Boise St . . . . . Broncos		Big Sky	Skip Hall	Boise,ID	Orange/Blue
Boston Univ . . Terriers		Yankee	Chris Palmer	Boston,MA	Scarlet/White
Brown . . . . . . Bruins		Ivy	John Rosenberg	Providence,RI	Brown/Red/White
Bucknell . . . . . Bison		Colonial	Lou Maranzana	Lewisburg,PA	Orange/Blue
The Citadel . . Bulldogs		Southern	Charlie Taaffe	Charleston,SC	Blue/White
Colgate . . . . . Red Raiders		Colonial	Mike Foley	Hamilton,NY	Maroon/White
Columbia . . . . Lions		Ivy	Ray Tellier	New York,NY	Lt.Blue/White
Connecticut . . Huskies		Yankee	Tom Jackson	Storrs,CT	Blue/White
Cornell . . . . . . Big Red		Ivy	Jack Fouts	Ithaca,NY	Red/White

NCAA Division I-AA Football Schools (Continued)

School	Nickname	Conference	Head Coach	Location	Colors
Dartmouth	Big Green	Ivy	Buddy Teevens	Hanover,NH	Green/White
Delaware	Blue Hens	Yankee	Tubby Raymond	Newark,DE	Blue/Gold
Delaware St	Hornets	Mid-Eastern	William Collick	Dover,DE	Red/Blue
East Tenn.St	Buccaneers	Southern	Don Riley	Johnson City,TN	Blue/Gold
Eastern Ill	Panthers	Gateway	Bob Spoo	Charleston,IL	Blue/Gold
Eastern Ky	Colonels	Ohio Valley	Roy Kidd	Richmond,KY	Maroon/White
Eastern Wash	Eagles	Big Sky	Dick Zornes	Cheney,WA	Red/White
Florida A&M	Rattlers	Mid-Eastern	Ken Riley	Tallahassee,FL	Orange/Green
Furman	Paladins	Southern	Jim Satterfield	Greenville, SC	Purple/White
Ga.Southern	Eagles	Indep.	Erk Russell	Statesboro,GA	Blue/White
Grambling	Tigers	S'western	Eddie Robinson	Grambling,LA	Black/Gold
Harvard	Crimson	Ivy	Joe Restic	Cambridge,MA	Crimson/Black/White
Holy Cross	Crusaders	Colonial	Mark Duffner	Worcester,MA	Royal Purple
Howard	Bison	Mid-Eastern	Steve Wilson	Washington,DC	Blue/White
Idaho	Vandals	Big Sky	Keith Gilbertson	Moscow,ID	Silver/Gold
Idaho St	Bengals	Big Sky	Garth Hall	Pocatello,ID	Orange/Black
Illinois St	Redbirds	Gateway	Jim Heacock	Normal,IL	Red/White
Indiana St	Sycamores	Gateway	Dennis Raetz	Terre Haute,IN	Blue/White
Jackson St	Tigers	S'western	W.C.Gorden	Jackson,MS	Blue/White
J.Madison	Dukes	Indep.	Joe Purzycki	Harrisonburg,VA	Purple/Gold
Lafayette	Leopards	Colonial	Bill Russo	Easton, PA	Maroon/White
Lamar	Cardinals	Indep.	Ray Alborn	Beaumont, TX	Red/White
Lehigh	Brown & White	Colonial	Hank Small	Bethlehem,PA	Brown/White
Louisiana Tech	Bulldogs	Indep.	Joe Raymond Peace	Ruston,LA	Red/Blue
Maine	Black Bears	Yankee	Tom Lichtenberg	Orono,ME	Blue/White
Marshall	Thundering Herd	Southern	George Chaump	Huntington,WV	Green/White
Massachusetts	Minutemen	Yankee	Jim Reid	Amherst,MA	Maroon/White
McNeese St	Cowboys	Southland	Sonny Jackson	Lake Charles,LA	Blue/Gold
Mid.Tenn.St	Blue Raiders	Ohio Valley	Boots Donnelly	Murfreesboro,TN	Blue/White
Miss.Valley	Delta Devils	S'western	Ken Pettiford	Itta Bena,MS	Green/White
Montana	Grizzlies	Big Sky	Don Read	Missoula,MT	Copper/Silver/Gold
Montana St	Bobcats	Big Sky	Earle Solomonson	Bozeman,MT	Blue/Gold
Morehead St	Eagles	Ohio Valley	Bill Baldridge	Morehead,KY	Blue/Gold
Morgan St	Bears	Mid-Eastern	Ed Wyche	Baltimore,MD	Blue/Orange
Murray St	Racers	Ohio Valley	Mike Mahoney	Murray,KY	Blue/Gold
Nevada-Reno	Wolf Pack	Big Sky	Chris Ault	Reno,NV	Silver/Blue
New Hampshire	Wildcats	Yankee	Bill Bowes	Durham,NH	Blue/White
Nicholls St	Colonels	Indep.	Phil Greco	Thibodaux,LA	Red/Gray
N.Car.A&T	Aggies	Mid-Eastern	Bill Hayes	Greensboro,NC	Blue/Gold
North Texas	Mean Green	Southland	Corky Nelson	Denton,TX	Green/White
NE Louisiana	Indians	Southland	Dave Roberts	Monroe,LA	Maroon/Gold
Northeastern	Huskies	Indep.	Paul Pawlak	Boston,MA	Red/Black
Northern Ariz	Lumberjacks	Big Sky	Larry Kentera	Flagstaff,AZ	Blue/Gold
No.Iowa	Panthers	Gateway	Terry Allen	Cedar Falls,IA	Purple/Old Gold
N'western St	Demons	Southland	Sam Goodwin	Natchitoches,LA	Purple/White
Pennsylvania	Quakers	Ivy	Larry Steele	Philadelphia,PA	Red/Blue
Prairie View	Panthers	S'western	Haney Catchings	Prairie View,TX	Purple/Gold
Princeton	Tigers	Ivy	Steve Tosches	Princeton,NJ	Orange/Black
Rhode Island	Rams	Yankee	Bob Griffen	Kingston,RI	Blue/White
Richmond	Spiders	Yankee	Jim Marshall	Richmond,VA	Red/Blue
S.Houston St	Bearkats	Southland	Ron Randleman	Huntsville,TX	Orange/White/Blue
S.Carolina St	Bulldogs	Mid-Eastern	Willie Jeffries	Orangeburg,SC	Garnet/Blue
Southern Ill	Salukis	Gateway	Bob Smith	Carbondale,IL	Maroon/White
Southern-BR	Jaguars	SWAC	Gerald Kimble	Baton Rouge,LA	Blue/Gold
SW Mo.St	Bears	Gateway	Jesse Branch	Springfield,MO	Maroon/White
SW Texas St	Bobcats	Southland	John O'Hara	San Marcos, TX	Maroon/Gold
S.F.Austin St	Lumberjacks	Southland	Lynn Graves	Nacogdoches,TX	Purple/White
Tennessee St	Tigers	Ohio Valley	Joe Gilliam	Nashville,TN	Blue/White
Tenn.Tech	Golden Eagles	Ohio Valley	Jim Ragland	Cookeville,TN	Purple/Gold
Tenn-Chatt	Moccasins	Southern	Buddy Nix	Chattanooga,TN	Navy Blue/Gold
Tex.Southern	Tigers	SWAC	Walt Highsmith	Houston,TX	Maroon/Gray
Towson St	Tigers	Indep.	Phil Albert	Towson,MD	Gold/White

School	Nickname	Conference	Head Coach	Location	Colors
Villanova	Wildcats	Yankee	Andy Talley	Villanova,PA	Blue/White
Va.Military	Keydets	Southern	Jim Shuck	Richmond,VA Lexington,VA	Black/Gold Red/White/Yellow
Weber St	Wildcats	Big Sky	Dave Arslanian	Ogden,UT	Purple/White
W.Carolina	Catamounts	Southern	Dale Strahm	Cullowhee,NC	Purple/Gold
Western Ill	Leathernecks	Gateway	Bruce Craddock	Macomb,IL	Purple/Gold
Western Ky	Hilltoppers	Indep.	Jack Harbaugh	Bowling Green,KY	Red/White
Wm. & Mary	Indians	Indep.	Jimmye Laycock	Williamsburg,VA	Green/Gold
Yale	Bulldogs,Elis	Ivy	Carmen Cozza	New Haven,CT	Yale Blue/White
Yngstown St	Penguins	Indep.	Jim Tressel	Youngstown,OH	Scarlet/White

NCAA Division I Basketball Schools

School	Nickname	Conference	Head Coach	Location	Colors
Air Force	Falcons	WAC	Reggie Minton	Colo.Springs,CO	Blue/Silver
Akron	Zips	Indep.	Coleman Crawford	Akron,OH	Blue/Gold
Alabama	Crimson Tide	SEC	Wimp Sanderson	Tuscaloosa,AL	Crimson/White
Alabama St	Hornets	S'western	James Oliver	Montgomery,AL	Black/Gold
Alabama-Birm.	Blazers	Sun Belt	Gene Bartow	Birmingham,AL	Green/Gold
Alcorn St	Braves	S'western	Lonnie Walker	Lorman,MS	Purple/Gold
American	Eagles	Colonial	Ed Tapscott	Washington,DC	Red/White/Blue
Appalach.St	Mountaineers	Southern	Tom Apke	Boone,NC	Black/Gold
Arizona	Wildcats	Pac-10	Lute Olson	Tucson,AZ	Cardinal/Navy
Arizona St	Sun Devils	Pac-10	Bill Frieder	Tempe,AZ	Maroon/Gold
Arkansas	Razorbacks	SWC	Nolan Richardson	Fayetteville,AR	Cardinal/White
Arkansas St	Indians	Amer.South	Nelson Catalina	State Univ.,AR	Scarlet/Black
Ark-Little Rock	Trojans	Trans Amer.	Mike Newell	Little Rock,AR	Maroon/White
Army	Cadets	Metro Atl.	Les Wothke	West Point,NY	Black/Gold/Gray
Auburn	Tigers	SEC	Tommy Joe Eagles	Auburn,AL	Orange/Blue
Augusta	Jaguars	Big South	Clint Bryant	Augusta,GA	Blue/White
Austin Peay	Governors	Ohio Valley	Lake Kelly	Clarksville,TN	Red/White
Ball St	Cardinals	Mid-Amer.	Dick Hunsaker	Muncie,IN	Cardinal/White
Baptist	Buccaneers	Big South	Gary Edwards	Charleston,SC	Blue/Gold
Baylor	Bears	SWC	Gene Iba	Waco,TX	Green/Gold
Beth-Cookman	Wildcats	Mid-Eastern	Jack McLairen	Daytona Beach,FL	Maroon/Gold
Boise St	Broncos	Big Sky	Bobby Dye	Boise,ID	Orange/Blue
Boston College	Eagles	Big East	Jim O'Brien	Chestnut Hill,MA	Maroon/Gold
Boston Univ	Terriers	North Atl.	Mike Jarvis	Boston,MA	Scarlet/White
Bowling Green	Falcons	Mid-Amer.	Jim Larranaga	Bowling Green,OH	Orange/Brown
Bradley	Braves	Mo.Valley	Stan Albeck	Peoria,IL	Red/White
Brig.Young	Cougars	WAC	Roger Reid	Provo,UT	Blue/White
Brooklyn	Kingsmen	Indep.	Mark Reiner	Brooklyn,NY	Maroon/Gold
Brown	Bruins	Ivy	Mike Cingiser	Providence,RI	Brown/Red/White
Bucknell	Bison	East Coast	Charlie Woollum	Lewisburg,PA	Orange/Blue
Butler	Bulldogs	Midwestern	Barry Collier	Indianapolis,IN	Blue/White
California	Golden Bears	Pac-10	Lou Campanelli	Berkeley,CA	Blue/Gold
CS-Fullerton	Titans	Big West	John Sneed	Fullerton,CA	Orange/Blue/White
Campbell	Fighting Camels	Big South	Billy Lee	Buies Creek,NC	Orange/Black
Canisius	Golden Griffins	Metro Atl.	Marty Marbach	Buffalo,NY	Blue/Gold
Centenary	Gentlemen	Trans Amer.	Tom Canterbury	Shreveport,LA	Maroon/White
Central Conn	Blue Devils	Indep.	Mike Brown	New Britain,CT	Blue/White
Central Fla	Knights	Indep.	Joe Dean Jr.	Orlando,FL	Black/Gold
Central Mich	Chippewas	Mid-Amer.	Charlie Coles	Mt.Pleasant,MI	Maroon/Gold
Chicago St	Cougars	Indep.	Tommy Suitts	Chicago,IL	Green/White
Cincinnati	Bearcats	Metro	Bob Huggins	Cincinnati,OH	Red/Black
Citadel	Bulldogs	Southern	Randy Nesbit	Charleston,SC	Blue/White
Clemson	Tigers	ACC	Cliff Ellis	Clemson,SC	Purple/Orange
Cleveland St	Vikings	Mid-Cont.	Kevin Mackey	Cleveland,OH	Green/White
Coastal Caro	Chanticleers	Big South	Russ Bergman	Conway,SC	Red/White/Black
Colgate	Red Raiders	North Atl.	Jack Bruen	Hamilton,NY	Maroon/White
Colorado	Buffaloes	Big 8	Tom Miller	Boulder,CO	Silver/Gold/Black
Colorado St	Rams	WAC	Boyd Grant	Colo.Springs,CO	Green/Gold
Columbia	Lions	Ivy	Wally Halas	New York,NY	Lt.Blue/White
Connecticut	Huskies	Big East	Jim Calhoun	Storrs,CT	Blue/White
Coppin St	Eagles	Mid-Eastern	Ron Mitchell	Baltimore,MD	Blue/Gold
Cornell	Big Red	Ivy	Mike Dement	Ithaca,NY	Red/White
Creighton	Bluejays	Mo.Valley	Tony Barone	Omaha,NE	Blue/White

NCAA Division I Basketball Schools (Continued)

School	Nickname	Conference	Head Coach	Location	Colors
Dartmouth	Big Green	Ivy	Paul Cormier	Hanover,NH	Green/White
Davidson	Wildcats	Indepen.	Bob McKillop	Davidson,NC	Red/Black
Dayton	Flyers	Midwestern	Jim O'Brien	Dayton,OH	Red/Blue
DePaul	Blue Demons	Indep.	Joey Meyer	Chicago,IL	Scarlet/Blue
Delaware	Blue Hens	East Coast	Steve Steinwedel	Newark,DE	Blue/Gold
Delaware St	Hornets	Mid-Eastern	Jeff Jones	Dover,DE	Red/Blue
Detroit	Titans	Midwestern	Ricky Byrdsong	Detroit,MI	Cardinal/White
Drake	Bulldogs	Mo.Valley	Tom Abatemarco	Des Moines,IA	Blue/White
Drexel	Dragons	East Coast	Ed Burke	Philadelphia,PA	Navy/Gold
Duke	Blue Devils	ACC	Mike Krzyzewski	Durham,NC	Royal Blue/White
Duquesne	Dukes	Atlantic 10	John Carroll	Pittsburgh,PA	Red/Blue
East Carolina	Pirates	Colonial	Mike Steele	Greenville,NC	Purple/Gold
East Tenn.St	Buccaneers	Southern	Les Robinson	Johnson City,TN	Blue/Gold
Eastern Ill	Panthers	Mid-Cont.	Rick Samuels	Charleston,IL	Blue/Gray
Eastern Ky	Colonels	Ohio Valley	Mike Pollio	Richmond,KY	Maroon/White
Eastern Mich	Hurons	Mid-Amer.	Ben Braun	Ypsilanti,MI	Green/White
Eastern Wash	Eagles	Big Sky	Bob Hofman	Cheney,WA	Red/White
Evansville	Purple Aces	Midwestern	Jim Crews	Evansville,IN	Purple/White
Fairfield	Stags	Metro Atl.	Mitch Buonaguro	Fairfield,CT	Cardinal Red
FDU-Teaneck	Knights	Northeast	Tom Green	Teaneck,NJ	Maroon/White/Blue
Florida	Gators	SEC	Norman Sloan	Gainesville,FL	Orange/Blue
Florida A&M	Rattlers	Mid-Eastern	Willie Booker	Tallahassee,FL	Orange/Green
Florida Int'l	Golden Panthers	Indep.	Rich Walker	Miami,FL	Blue/Gold
Florida St	Seminoles	Metro	Pat Kennedy	Tallahassee,FL	Garnet/Gold
Fordham	Rams	Metro Atl.	Nick Macarchuk	Bronx,NY	Maroon/White
Fresno St	Bulldogs	Big West	Ron Adams	Fresno,CA	Cardinal/Blue
Furman	Paladins	Southern	Butch Estes	Greenville, SC	Purple/White
George Mason	Patriots	Colonial	Ernie Nestor	Fairfax,VA	Green/Gold
G.Washington	Colonials	Atlantic 10	John Kuester	Washington,DC	Buff/Blue
Georgetown	Hoyas	Big East	John Thompson	Washington,DC	Blue/Gray
Georgia	Bulldogs,'Dawgs	SEC	Hugh Durham	Athens,GA	Red/Black
Ga.Southern	Eagles	Trans Amer.	Frank Kerns	Statesboro,GA	Blue/White
Georgia St	Crimson Panthers	Trans Amer.	Bob Reinhart	Atlanta,GA	Royal Blue/Crimson
Georgia Tech	Yellow Jackets	ACC	Bobby Cremins	Atlanta,GA	Old Gold/White
Gonzaga	Bulldogs,Zags	West Coast	Dan Fitzgerald	Spokane,WA	Blue/White/Red
Grambling	Tigers	S'western	Vacant	Grambling,LA	Black/Gold
Hard.-Simmons	Cowboys	Trans Amer.	Dennis Harp	Abilene,TX	Purple/Gold
Hartford	Hawks	North Atl.	Jack Phelan	Hartford,CT	Scarlet/White
Harvard	Crimson	Ivy	Peter Roby	Cambridge,MA	Crimson/Black/White
Hawaii	Rainbows	WAC	Riley Wallace	Honolulu,HI	Green/White
Hofstra	Flying Dutchmen	East Coast	B.vanBreda Kolff	Hempstead,NY	Blue/White/Gold
Holy Cross	Crusaders	Metro Atl.	George Blaney	Worcester,MA	Royal Purple
Houston	Cougars	SWC	Pat Foster	Houston,TX	Cougar Red/White
Howard	Bison	Mid-Eastern	A.B.Williamson	Washington,DC	Blue/White
Idaho	Vandals	Big Sky	Kermit Davis	Moscow,ID	Silver/Gold
Idaho St	Bengals	Big Sky	Jim Boutin	Pocatello,ID	Orange/Black
Illinois	Fighting Illini	Big 10	Lou Henson	Champaign,IL	Orange/Blue
Ill-Chicago	Flames	Mid-Cont.	Bob Hallberg	Chicago,IL	Indigo/Flame
Illinois St	Redbirds	Mo.Valley	Bob Bender	Normal,IL	Red/White
Indiana	Hoosiers	Big 10	Bob Knight	Bloomington,IN	Cream/Crimson
Indiana St	Sycamores	Mo.Valley	Tates Locke	Terre Haute,IN	Blue/White
Iona	Gaels	Metro Atl.	Gary Brokaw	New Rochelle,NY	Maroon/Gold
Iowa	Hawkeyes	Big 10	Tom Davis	Iowa City,IA	Old Gold/Black
Iowa St	Cyclones	Big 8	Johnny Orr	Ames,IA	Cardinal/Gold
Jackson St	Tigers	S'western	John Prince	Jackson,MS	Blue/White
Jacksonville	Dolphins	Sun Belt	Rich Haddad	Jacksonville,FL	Green/Gold
J.Madison	Dukes	Colonial	Lefty Driesell	Harrisonburg,VA	Purple/Gold
Kansas	Jayhawks	Big 8	Roy Williams	Lawrence,KS	Crimson/Blue
Kansas St	Wildcats	Big 8	Lon Kruger	Manhattan,KS	Purple/White
Kent St	Golden Flashes	Mid-Amer.	Jim McDonald	Kent,OH	Navy Blue/Gold
Kentucky	Wildcats	SEC	Rick Pitino	Lexington,KY	Blue/White

School	Nickname	Conference	Head Coach	Location	Colors
La Salle	Explorers	Metro Atl.	Bill Morris	Philadelphia,PA	Blue/Gold
Lafayette	Leopards	East Coast	John Leone	Easton,PA	Maroon/White
Lamar	Cardinals	Amer.South	Tony Branch	Beaumont,TX	Red/White
Lehigh	Engineers	East Coast	Dave Duke	Bethlehem,PA	Brown/White
Liberty	Flames	Indepen.	Jeff Meyer	Lynchburg,VA	Red/White/Blue
Long Beach St	49ers	Big West	Joe Harrington	Long Beach,CA	Brown/Gold
LIU-Brooklyn	Blackbirds	Northeast	Paul Lizzo	Brooklyn,NY	Blue/White
LSU	Fighting Tigers	SEC	Dale Brown	Baton Rouge,LA	Purple/Gold
Louisiana Tech	Bulldogs	Amer.South	Jerry Loyd	Ruston,LA	Red/Blue
Louisville	Cardinals	Metro	Denny Crum	Louisville,KY	Red/Black/White
Loyola, Cal	Lions	West Coast	Paul Westhead	Los Angeles,CA	Crimson/Gray/Lt.Blue
Loyola, Ill	Ramblers	Midwestern	Will Rey	Chicago,IL	Maroon/Gold
Loyola, Md	Greyhounds	Metro Atl.	Tom Schneider	Baltimore,MD	Green/Gray
Maine	Black Bears	North Atl.	Rudy Keeling	Orono,ME	Blue/White
Manhattan	Jaspers	Metro Atl.	Steve Lappas	Riverdale,NY	Green/White
Marist	Red Foxes	Northeast	Dave Magarity	Poughkeepsie,NY	Red/White
Marquette	Warriors	Midwestern	Kevin O'Neill	Milwaukee,WI	Blue/Gold
Marshall	Thundering Herd	Southern	Dana Altman	Huntington,WV	Green/White
Maryland	Terrapins	ACC	Gary Williams	College Park,MD	Red/White/Black/Gold
Md-Balt.Cty	Retrievers	Indep.	Earl Hawkins	Baltimore,MD	Black/Old Gold
Md-East.Shore	Hawks	Mid-Eastern	Steve Williams	Princess Anne,MD	Maroon/Gray
Massachusetts	Minutemen	Atlantic 10	John Calipari	Amherst,MA	Maroon/White
McNeese St	Cowboys	Southland	Steve Welch	Lake Charles,LA	Blue/Gold
Memphis St	Tigers	Metro	Larry Finch	Memphis,TN	Blue/Gray
Mercer	Bears	Trans Amer.	Bill Bibb	Macon,GA	Orange/Black
Miami, FL	Hurricanes	Indep.	Bill Foster	Miami,FL	Orange/Green/White
Miami, OH	Redskins	Mid-Amer.	Jerry Peirson	Oxford,OH	Red/White
Michigan	Wolverines	Big 10	Steve Fisher	Ann Arbor,MI	Maize/Blue
Michigan St	Spartans	Big 10	Jud Heathcote	East Lansing,MI	Green/White
Mid.Tenn.St	Blue Raiders	Ohio Valley	Bruce Stewart	Murfreesboro,TN	Blue/White
Minnesota	Golden Gophers	Big 10	Clem Haskins	Minneapolis,MN	Maroon/White
Mississippi	Rebels,Ole Miss	SEC	Ed Murphy	Oxford,MS	Red/Blue
Mississippi St	Bulldogs	SEC	Richard Williams	Starkville,MS	Maroon/White
Miss.Valley	Delta Devils	S'western	Lafayette Stribling	Itta Bena,MS	Green/White
Missouri	Tigers	Big 8	Norm Stewart	Columbia,MO	Old Gold/Black
Monmouth	Hawks	Northeast	Terry Glasgow	W.Long Branch,NJ	Royal Blue/White
Montana	Grizzlies	Big Sky	Stew Morrill	Missoula,MT	Copper/Silver/Gold
Montana St	Bobcats	Big Sky	Stu Starner	Bozeman,MT	Blue/Gold
Morehead St	Eagles	Ohio Valley	Tommy Gaither	Morehead,KY	Blue/Gold
Morgan St	Bears	Mid-Eastern	Nat Frazier	Baltimore,MD	Blue/Orange
Mt.St.Mary's	Mountaineers	Northeast	Joe McGuinness	Emmitsburg,MD	Navy Blue/Old Gold
Murray St	Racers	Ohio Valley	Steve Newton	Murray,KY	Blue/Gold
Navy	Midshipmen	Colonial	Pete Herrmann	Annapolis,MD	Navy Blue/Gold
Nebraska	Cornhuskers	Big 8	Danny Nee	Lincoln,NE	Scarlet/Cream
Nevada-Reno	Wolf Pack	Big Sky	Len Stevens	Reno,NV	Silver/Blue
New Hamp.	Wildcats	North Atl.	Jim Boylan	Durham,NH	Blue/White
New Mexico	Lobos	WAC	Dave Bliss	Albuquerque,NM	Cherry/Silver
N.Mex.St	Aggies	Big West	Neil McCarthy	Las Cruces,NM	Crimson/White
New Orleans	Privateers	Amer.South	Tim Floyd	New Orleans,LA	Royal Blue/Silver
Niagara	Purple Eagles	Metro Alt.	Jack Armstrong	Niagara U.,NY	Purple/White/Gold
Nicholls St	Colonels	Indep.	Gordon Stauffer	Thibodaux,LA	Red/Gray
N.Carolina	Tar Heels	ACC	Dean Smith	Chapel Hill,NC	Carolina Blue/White
N.Car.A&T	Aggies	Mid-Eastern	Don Corbett	Greensboro,NC	Blue/Gold
N.Carolina St	Wolfpack	ACC	Jim Valvano	Raleigh,NC	Red/White
NC-Asheville	Bulldogs	Big South	Don Doucette	Asheville,NC	Royal Blue/White
NC-Charlotte	49ers	Sun Belt	Jeff Mullins	Charlotte,NC	Green/White
NC-Wilmington	Seahawks	Colonial	Robt. McPherson	Wilmington,NC	Green/Gold
North Texas	Mean Green	Southland	Jimmy Gales	Denton,TX	Green/White
NE Louisiana	Indians	Southland	Mike Vining	Monroe,LA	Maroon/Gold
Northeastern	Huskies	North Atl.	Karl Fogel	Boston,MA	Red/Black
Northern Ariz.	Lumberjacks	Big Sky	Pat Rafferty	Flagstaff,AZ	Blue/Gold
Northern Ill.	Huskies	Indep.	Jim Molinari	De Kalb,IL	Cardinal/Black
No.Iowa	Panthers	Mid-Cont.	Eldon Miller	Cedar Falls,IA	Purple/Old Gold
Northwestern	Wildcats	Big 10	Bill Foster	Evanston,IL	Purple/White
N'western La	Demons	Southland	Dan Bell	Natchitoches,LA	Burnt Orange/Purple
Notre Dame	Fighting Irish	Indep.	Digger Phelps	Notre Dame,IN	Gold/Blue

NCAA Division I Basketball Schools (Continued)

School	Nickname	Conference	Head Coach	Location	Colors
Ohio Univ	Bobcats	Mid-Amer.	Larry Hunter	Athens,OH	Kelly Green/White
Ohio St	Buckeyes	Big 10	Randy Ayers	Columbus,OH	Scarlet/Gray
Oklahoma	Sooners	Big 8	Billy Tubbs	Norman,OK	Crimson/Cream
Oklahoma St	Cowboys	Big 8	Leonard Hamilton	Stillwater,OK	Orange/Black
Old Dominion	Monarchs	Sun Belt	Tom Young	Norfolk,VA	Slate Blue/Silver
Oregon	Ducks	Pac-10	Don Monson	Eugene,OR	Green/Yellow
Oregon St	Beavers	Pac-10	Jim Anderson	Corvallis,OR	Orange/Black
Pacific	Tigers	Big West	Bob Thomason	Stockton,CA	Orange/Black
Pan American	Broncs	Amer.South	Kevin Wall	Edinburg,TX	Green/White
Penn St	Nittany Lions	Atlantic 10	Bruce Parkhill	Univ.Park,PA	Blue/White
Pennsylvania	Quakers	Ivy	Fran Dunphy	Philadelphia,PA	Red/Blue
Pepperdine	Waves	West Coast	Tom Asbury	Malibu,CA	Blue/Orange
Pittsburgh	Panthers	Big East	Paul Evans	Pittsburgh,PA	Gold/Blue
Portland	Pilots	West Coast	Larry Steele	Portland,OR	Purple/White
Prairie View	Panthers	S'western	Jim Duplantier	Prairie View,TX	Purple/Gold
Princeton	Tigers	Ivy	Pete Carril	Princeton,NJ	Orange/Black
Providence	Friars	Big East	Rick Barnes	Providence,RI	Black/White
Purdue	Boilermakers	Big 10	Gene Keady	W.Lafayette,IN	Old Gold/Black
Radford	Highlanders	Big South	Oliver Purnell	Radford,VA	Blue/Red/Green
Rhode Island	Rams	Atlantic 10	Al Skinner	Kingston,RI	Blue/White
Rice	Owls	SWC	Scott Thompson	Houston,TX	Blue/Gray
Richmond	Spiders	Colonial	Dick Tarrant	Richmond,VA	Red/Blue
Rider	Broncs	East Coast	Kevin Bannon	Lawrenceville,NJ	Purple/Gold
Robert Morris	Colonials	Northeast	Jarrett Durham	Coraopolis,PA	Blue/White
Rutgers	Scarlet Knights	Atlantic 10	Bob Wenzel	New Brunswick,NJ	Scarlet
S.Houston St	Bearkats	Southland	Larry Brown	Huntsville,TX	Orange/White
Samford	Bulldogs	Trans Amer.	Ed McLean	Birmingham,AL	Crimson/Blue
San Diego	Toreros	West Coast	Hank Egan	San Diego,CA	Lt.Blue/Navy/White
San Diego St	Aztecs	WAC	Jim Brandenburg	San Diego,CA	Scarlet/Black
San Francisco	Dons	West Coast	Jim Brovelli	San Francisco,CA	Green/Gold
San Jose St	Spartans	Big West	Stan Morrison	San Jose,CA	Gold/White/Blue
Santa Clara	Broncos	West Coast	Carroll Williams	Santa Clara,CA	Bronco Red/White
Seton Hall	Pirates	Big East	P.J.Carlesimo	South Orange,NJ	Blue/White
Siena	Saints	Metro-Atl.	Mike Deane	Loudonville,NY	Green/Gold
S.Alabama	Jaguars	Sun Belt	Ronnie Arrow	Mobile,AL	Red/White/Blue
S.Carolina	Gamecocks	Metro	George Felton	Columbia,SC	Garnet/Black
S.Carolina St	Bulldogs	Mid-Eastern	Cy Alexander	Orangeburg,SC	Garnet/Blue
South Florida	Bulls	Sun Belt	Bobby Paschal	Tampa,FL	Green/Gold
Southern Cal	Trojans	Pac-10	George Raveling	Los Angeles,CA	Cardinal/Gold
Southern Ill	Salukis	Mo.Valley	Rich Herrin	Carbondale,IL	Maroon/White
So.Methodist	Mustangs	Southwest	John Shumate	Dallas,TX	Red/Blue
Southern Miss	Golden Eagles	Metro	M.K.Turk	Hattiesburg,MS	Black/Gold
So.Utah St	Thunderbirds	Indepen.	Neil Roberts	Cedar City,UT	Scarlet/Royal Blue
Southern-BR	Jaguars	S'western	Ben Jobe	Baton Rouge,LA	Blue/Gold
SW Mo.St	Bears	Mid-Cont.	Charlie Spoonhour	Springfield,MO	Maroon/White
SW Texas St	Bobcats	Southern	Harry Larrabee	San Marcos, TX	Maroon/Gold
SW Louisiana	Ragin' Cajuns	Amer.South	Marty Fletcher	Lafayette,LA	Vermilion/White
St.Bonaventure	Bonnies	Atlantic 10	Tom Chapman	St.Bonaventure,NY	Brown/White
St.Francis, NY	Terriers	Northeast	Rich Zvosec	Brooklyn,NY	Red/Blue
St.Francis, PA	Red Flash	Northeast	Jim Baron	Loretto,PA	Red/White
St.John's, NY	Redmen	Big East	Lou Carnesecca	Jamaica,NY	Red/White
St.Joseph's	Hawks	Atlantic 10	Jim Boyle	Philadelphia,PA	Crimson/Gray
St.Louis	Billikens	Midwestern	Rich Grawer	St.Louis,MO	Blue/White
St.Mary's, CA	Gaels	West Coast	Paul Landreaux	Moraga,CA	Red/Blue
St.Peter's	Peacocks	Metro Atl.	Ted Fiore	Jersey City,NJ	Blue/White
Stanford	Cardinal	Pac 10	Mike Montgomery	Stanford,CA	Cardinal/White
S.F.Austin St	Lumberjacks	Southern	Mike Martin	Nacogdoches,TX	Purple/White
Stetson	Hatters	Trans Amer.	Glenn Wilkes	Deland,FL	Green/White
Syracuse	Orangemen	Big East	Jim Boeheim	Syracuse,NY	Orange

School	Nickname	Conference	Head Coach	Location	Colors
Temple	Owls	Atlantic 10	John Chaney	Philadelphia,PA	Cherry/White
Tennessee	Volunteers	SEC	Wade Houston	Knoxville,TN	Orange/White
Tennessee St	Tigers	Ohio Valley	Ron Abernathy	Nashville,TN	Blue/White
Tenn.Tech	Golden Eagles	Ohio Valley	Tom Deaton	Cookeville,TN	Purple/Gold
Tenn-Chatt	Moccasins	Southern	Mack McCarthy	Chattanooga,TN	Navy Blue/Gold
Texas	Longhorns	SWC	Tom Penders	Austin,TX	Burnt Orange/White
Texas A&M	Aggies	SWC	Shelby Metcalf	College Station,TX	Maroon/White
TCU	Horned Frogs	SWC	Moe Iba	Ft.Worth,TX	Purple/White
Texas Southern	Tigers	S'western	Robt.Moreland	Houston,TX	Maroon/Gray
Texas Tech	Red Raiders	SWC	Gerald Myers	Lubbock,TX	Scarlet/Black
Tex-Arlington	Mavericks	Southland	Mark Nixon	Arlington,TX	Royal Blue/White
Tex-San Ant	Roadrunners	Trans Amer.	Ken Burmeister	San Antonio,TX	Orange/Navy Blue
Toledo	Rockets	Mid-Amer.	Jay Eck	Toledo,OH	Blue/Gold
Towson St	Tigers	East Coast	Terry Truax	Towson,MD	Gold/White/Black
Tulane	Green Wave	Metro	Perry Clark	New Orleans, LA	Olive Green/Sky Blue
Tulsa	Golden Hurricane	Mo.Valley	J.D.Barnett	Tulsa,OK	Blue/Red/Gold
US Int'l	Gulls	Indep.	Gary Zarkecky	San Diego,CA	Lt.Blue/Sun Gold
UC-Irvine	Anteaters	Big West	Bill Mulligan	Irvine,CA	Blue/Gold
UCLA	Bruins	Pac-10	Jim Harrick	Los Angeles,CA	Blue/Gold
UC-S.Barbara	Gauchos	Big West	Jerry Pimm	Santa Barbara,CA	Blue/Gold
UNLV	Runnin' Rebels	Big West	Jerry Tarkanian	Las Vegas,NV	Scarlet/Gray
Utah	Utes	WAC	Rick Majerus	Salt Lake City,UT	Crimson/White
Utah St	Aggies	Big West	Kohn Smith	Logan,UT	Navy Blue/White
UTEP	Miners	WAC	Don Haskins	El Paso,TX	Orange/White/Blue
Valparaiso	Crusaders	Mid-Cont.	Homer Drew	Valparaiso,IN	Brown/Gold
Vanderbilt	Commodores	SEC	Eddie Fogler	Nashville,TN	Black/Gold
Vermont	Catamounts	North Atl.	Tom Brennan	Burlington,VT	Green/Gold
Villanova	Wildcats	Big East	Rollie Massimino	Villanova,PA	Blue/White
Virginia	Cavaliers	ACC	Terry Holland	Charlottesville,VA	Orange/Blue
Va.Common	Rams	Sun Belt	Sonny Smith	Richmond,VA	Black/Gold
Va.Military	Keydets	Southern	Joe Cantafio	Lexington,VA	Red/White/Yellow
Virginia Tech	Hokies,Gobblers	Metro	Frankie Allen	Blacksburg,VA	Orange/Maroon
Wagner	Seahawks	Northeast	Tim Capstraw	Staten Island,NY	Green/White
Wake Forest	Demon Deacons	ACC	Dave Odom	Winston-Salem,NC	Old Gold/Black
Washington	Huskies	Pac-10	Lynn Nance	Seattle,WA	Purple/Gold
Wash.St	Cougars	Pac-10	Kelvin Sampson	Pullman,WA	Crimson/Gray
Weber St	Wildcats	Big Sky	Denny Huston	Ogden,UT	Royal Purple/White
West Virginia	Mountaineers	Atlantic 10	Gale Catlett	Morgantown,WV	Old Gold/Blue
W.Carolina	Catamounts	Southern	Greg Blatt	Cullowhee,NC	Purple/Gold
Western Ill	Leathernecks	Mid-Cont.	Jack Margenthaler	Macomb,IL	Purple/Gold
Western Ky	Hilltoppers	Sun Belt	Murray Arnold	Bowling Green,KY	Red/White
Western Mich	Broncos	Mid-Amer.	Bob Donewald	Kalamazoo,MI	Brown/Gold
Wichita St	Shockers	Mo.Valley	Mike Cohen	Wichita,KS	Yellow/Black
Wm. & Mary	Indians	Colonial	Chuck Swenson	Williamsburg,VA	Green/Gold/Silver
Winthrop	Eagles	Big South	Steve Vacendak	Rock Hill,SC	Garnet/Gold
Wisconsin	Badgers	Big 10	Steve Yoder	Madison,WI	Cardinal/White
WI-Green Bay	Phoenix	Mid-Cont.	Dick Bennett	Green Bay,WI	Cardinal/Green
Wright St	Raiders	Indep.	Ralph Underhill	Dayton,OH	Green/Gold
Wyoming	Cowboys	WAC	Benny Dees	Laramie,WY	Brown/Yellow
Xavier	Musketeers	Midwestern	Pete Gillen	Cincinnati,OH	Blue/White
Yale	Bulldogs,Elis	Ivy	Dick Kuchen	New Haven,CT	Yale Blue/White
Yngstown St	Penguins	Ohio Valley	Jim Cleamons	Youngstown,OH	Scarlet/White

Coaching Changes

Division I-A Football

There were 18 coaching changes made at Division I-A football schools between the 1988 and 1989 seasons. Unless otherwise indicated, all outgoing coaches resigned. Head Coaches who left one school to coach at another are in **bold type**.

School	Old Coach	New Coach	School	Old Coach	New Coach
Cincinnati	Dave Currey	**Tim Murphy**	Rice	**Jerry Berndt**	Fred Goldsmith
Colorado St	Leon Fuller	**Earle Bruce**	S.Diego St	Denny Stolz*	Al Luginbill‡
E.Carolina	Art Baker	Bill Lewis	S.Carolina	Joe Morrison†	Sparky Woods
Georgia	Vince Dooley	Ray Goff‡	Stanford	Jack Elway*	Dennis Green
Kansas St	Stan Parrish	Bill Snyder	Temple	Bruce Arians	**Jerry Berndt**
Memphis St	Charlie Bailey	Chuck Stobart	Texas A&M	Jackie Sherrill	R.C.Slocum‡
Miami,FL	Jimmy Johnson	**Dennis Erickson**	UTEP	**Bob Stull**	David Lee
Missouri	Woody Widenhofer	**Bob Stull**	Wash.St	**Dennis Erickson**	**Mike Price**
Oklahoma	Barry Switzer	Gary Gibbs‡			
Pacific	Bob Cope*	Walt Harris			

*Fired; †Died; ‡ Promoted.

Head Coaches who changed schools: Tim Murphy from Maine to Cincinnati; Earle Bruce from Northern Iowa to Colorado St.; Dennis Erickson from Washington St. to Miami,FL; Bob Stull from UTEP to Missouri; Sparky Woods from Appalachian St. to South Carolina; Jerry Berndt from Rice to Temple; Mike Price from Weber St. to Washington St.

Division I Basketball

There were 48 coaching changes made at Division I basketball schools between the 1988-89 and 1989-90 seasons. Unless otherwise indicated, all outgoing coaches resigned. Head Coaches who left one school to coach at another are in **bold type**.

School	Old Coach	New Coach	School	Old Coach	New Coach
Akron	**Bob Huggins**	Coleman Crawford	Northern Ill	Jim Rosborough*	Jim Molinari
Alcorn St	Dave Whitney	Lonnie Walker‡	Ohio St	**Gary Williams**	Randy Ayers‡
Arizona St	Steve Patterson	**Bill Frieder**	Ohio Univ	Billy Hahn*	**Larry Hunter**
Auburn	**Sonny Smith**	**Tommy Joe Eagles**	Oregon St	Ralph Miller†	Jim Anderson‡
Ball St	Rick Majerus	Dick Hunsaker‡	Pennsylvania	**Tom Schneider**	Francis Dunphy‡
BYU	Ladell Anderson†	Roger Reid‡	Rider	John Carpenter	Kevin Bannon
Butler	Joe Sexton	Barry Collier	St.Bona	Ron DeCarli*	**Tom Chapman**
Central Fla	Phil Carter	**Joe Dean Jr.**	St.Mary's,CA	**Lynn Nance**	Paul Landreaux
Cincinnati	Tony Yates*	Bob Huggins	S.Houston St	Gary Moss*	Larry Brown
Colgate	Joe Baker*	Jack Bruen	San Jose St	Bill Berry*	Stan Morrison
Davidson	Bobby Hussey	Bob McKillop	SE Louisiana	Leo McClure	No Team
Dayton	Don Donoher*	Jim O'Brien	Tennessee	Don DeVoe	Wade Houston
Duquesne	Jim Satalin*	John Carroll	Tennessee St	Larry Reid	Ron Abernathy
Eastern Ky	Max Good*	**Mike Pollio**	Tulane	No team	Perry Clark
Illinois St	**Bob Donewald***	Bob Bender	Utah	Lynn Archibald*	**Rick Majerus**
Indiana St	Ron Greene	Tates Locke	Vanderbilt	C.M.Newton	**Eddie Fogler**
Kentucky	Eddie Sutton	**Rick Pitino**	VCU	**Mike Pollio**	**Sonny Smith**
La.Tech	**Tommy Joe Eagles**	Jerry Loyd	Wagner	Neil Kennett*	Tim Capstraw
Loyola,IL	Gene Sullivan	Will Rey	Wake Forest	Bob Staak	Dave Odom
Loyola,MD	Mark Amatucci	**Tom Schneider**	Washington	Andy Russo	**Lynn Nance**
Marquette	Bob Dukiet*	Kevin O'Neill	Western Caro	Dave Possinger	**Greg Blatt**
Marshall	Rick Huckabay	Dana Altman	Western Mich	Vernon Payne	**Bob Donewald**
Maryland	Bob Wade	**Gary Williams**	Wichita St	**Eddie Fogler**	Mike Cohen‡
Michigan	**Bill Frieder**	Steve Fisher‡			
New Hamp	Gerry Friel	Jim Boylan			

*Fired; †Resigned; ‡Promoted.

Interim Coaches in 1988-89: Bob Schermerhorn at Arizona St.; John Ferguson at Eastern Ky.; Bob Collins at Northern Ill.; Jeff Dittman at Sam Houston St.

Head Coaches who changed schools: Bill Frieder from Michigan to Arizona St.; Tommy Joe Eagles from Louisiana Tech to Auburn; Joe Dean Jr. from Birmingham Southern (NAIA) to Central Florida; Bob Huggins from Akron to Cincinnati; Mike Pollio from Virginia Comm. to Eastern Ky.; Rick Pitino from the New York Knicks (NBA) to Kentucky; Tom Schneider from Penn to Loyola,MD; Gary Williams from Ohio St. to Maryland; Larry Hunter from Wittenburg to Ohio Univ.; Tom Chapman from Gannon to St.Bonaventure; Rick Majerus from Ball St. to Utah; Eddie Fogler from Wichita St. to Vanderbilt; Sonny Smith from Auburn to Virginia Comm.; Lynn Nance from St.Mary's, CA to Washington; Greg Blatt from Presbyterian (NAIA) to Western Carolina; Bob Donewald from Illinois St. to Western Michigan.

Detroit owner **Bill Davidson** is the center of attention as **Isiah Thomas** (11) and the Pistons celebrate after winning the team's first NBA title.

PRO BASKETBALL

I N S I D E

Elsewhere in Almanac
For related information refer to the following chapters: Arenas & Ballparks, Halls of Fame & Awards, and Sports Organizations.

*The Pistons finally make it,
Kareem hangs up the Sky Hook,
the Suns come up in Phoenix,
and Magic outpolls Michael.*

PRO BASKETBALL

1988-89 YEAR IN REVIEW

by Bob Ryan

Say this for the Detroit Pistons: they took the hard road, paying every set of dues imaginable.

Losers in the seventh game of the Eastern Conference Finals in 1987 and losers in the seventh game of the NBA Finals in 1988—each deciding contest played on the opponents' home floor—they vowed to seize better control of their destiny this past season. "If there's a seventh game this year," declared center Bill Laimbeer before the playoffs began, "it will be played on our floor."

The Pistons didn't need any seventh games, sweeping three of their four series and losing only two of their 17 playoff games en route to the first championship in franchise history.

Much excitement was expected prior to the playoffs, but many of the expected great match-ups failed to materialize, as upsets and surprising sweeps were the rule.

Bob Ryan has covered the Celtics and the NBA for 15 of his 20 years at **The Boston Globe.** He has also written a book with Larry Bird that is due out this Christmas.

The Knicks were picked by many to be the prime challengers to Detroit, but Rick Pitino's squad was dumped by Chicago in six games. The Bulls weren't even supposed to get that far, but with Michael Jordan acting heroically in every game, they startled the Cavaliers, winning the deciding fifth game on a spectacular hang-in-the-air Jordan jumper at the buzzer.

Chicago did manage to provide the Pistons with a taste of competition, which is more than anyone else could say. Detroit swept Boston and Milwaukee, defeated Chicago in 6 and then swept the Lakers.

Golden State was the early story in the West, stunning favored Utah in four games before losing to Phoenix in five. The Suns were playing well enough to make people think they had a chance against the Lakers, but the defending champs rose to the challenge and eliminated Phoenix in four straight in the Western Finals.

LA was actually playing as well as it had all season entering the Finals, but in-

Chicago's **Michael Jordan** glides to the basket against New York. Jordan led the NBA in scoring for the third straight season.

juries to both Byron Scott and Magic Johnson were too much to overcome against a team as good as the Pistons.

Detroit's foundation was laid during the regular season, when the Pistons carved out a league-high 63 victories to earn the home court advantage in each playoff series. Detroit enhanced its reputation as a premier defensive team, holding foes to 100.8 points per game during the regular season, and then improving that figure during the post-season, when they limited Boston, Milwaukee, Chicago and Los Angeles to a paltry 92.9 points per game, a total more indicative of the old (i.e., pre-24 second clock) rules and style, than of the present day.

But if the Pistons' eventual success was expected, the play of some other top teams was not. When the season began, what brave soul would dared have forecast a banner season for Golden State, or would have projected Phoenix into the Western Finals? New York looked to be improved, but 52 victories? Could anyone have foreseen 49 wins for Del Harris' Milwaukee club? For that matter, who except for the ghost of Dr. J. expected the 76ers to ring up 46 wins?

Individually, Michael Jordan did more air, moon and water-walking, leading the league in scoring for the third year in succession, while recording new personal highs in rebounds, assists, field goal percentage and one new category—triple-doubles.

But his heroics weren't enough to bag a second consecutive Most Valuable Player Award. He was nosed out by the irrepressible Magic Johnson in one of the closest and most debated MVP votes in league history. Backers of each superstar went to the mats in defense of their man, resolving nothing, but proving beyond doubt that the NBA is very fortunate to have such a treasured pair.

The leading newcomer was Golden State guard Mitch Richmond, a powerful inside player. Danny Manning, the highly touted first pick of the draft, reported late to the Los Angeles Clippers in a salary dispute and then, just as he was flashing the form which made him a Kansas All-America, was lost for the final four months of the season when he tore up a knee in Milwaukee.

The Farewell Tour to end all Farewell Tours took place as the NBA bade adieu to Kareem Abdul-Jabbar, its all-time leading scorer. Kareem was laden with gifts of every description, as fans were given a chance to salute his unprecedented two-decade career. Unfortunately, he failed to bequeath his fabled Sky Hook to anybody.

Conspicuous by his absence was Larry Bird. The three-time MVP hobbled though six games with painful heels before submitting to an operation on November 19. Without him, the Celtics confirmed their fans' worst fears, slipping from 57 wins to 42, and struggling to the last day of the season before qualifying as the final Eastern Conference playoff entrant.

The league roster grew to 25 team with the addition of Charlotte and Miami. The former became the first expansion franchise ever to lead a pro sport in attendance, as the people of Charlotte and its environs proved conclusively that basketball in the Carolinas means more than just the ACC. Miami also filled its arena to capacity each night, proving that Florida can be a fertile NBA market.

A look at the divisional races:

Atlantic Division

With the Celtics unable to acclimate themselves to Life Without Larry, the New York Knicks were able to fill the vacuum and win their first divisional title since 1973.

They did it using the all-around skills of center Patrick Ewing, a scrappy, press-oriented defense and a bombs-away approach to offense which resulted in a record 386 successful three-point field goals. So wedded to the three-pointer were the Knicks that veteran swingman Trent Tucker actually attempted more threes than twos.

The driving personality behind the Knicks' success belonged to coach Rick Pitino, who in the space of two seasons improved the team's record by 28 victories (24 to 52) while steering the Knicks to a pair of playoff berths. He departed for the University of Kentucky at the season's end, however, leaving the Knicks vulnerable in the coming season.

A surprise second place finisher—to everybody but the outspoken Charles Barkley, that is—was Philadelphia. Barkley gave a typical Barkley performance, but the difference was that this year he had scoring aid from the likes of veteran Ron Anderson and rookie Hersey Hawkins.

The hallowed Celtics barely broke .500 (42-40), and they had the dubious distinction of being the only team in the league that couldn't manage a win on the road against a team with a .500 record or better. The individual high points for the Celtics were the improvement of second-year man Reggie Lewis and the inspirational play of center Robert Parish.

Boston needed a home court victory on the final day of the season to hold off Washington, a team that didn't figure on paper but which vastly overachieved due to the coaching of Wes Unseld, a legitimate Coach of the Year candidate. Plagued, as usual, by injuries, and held back, as usual, by minimal crowd support in the dull Brendan Byrne Arena, were the New Jersey Nets. Newcomer Charlotte got off to a nice start before reality set in. But the Hornets hustled from Day One to Day Eighty-Two for coach Dick Harter and they did manage to defeat Philadelphia three times and New York twice.

Central Division

Treachery abounded in the Central Division, where a 47-win season was only good enough to bring Chicago fifth place.

Cleveland had the early speed, going undefeated in the exhibitions and running up a five-game lead over favored Detroit before sliding in the month of March. The turning point in the Cavaliers' fortunes appeared to be a Rick Mahorn elbow to the head of valued Cleveland playmaker Mark Price. Price missed key games (including a big one against Detroit), and the Cavs' attack never appeared to be the same again.

The Pistons featured a well-balanced offense (no one over 20 points per game), a rugged defense and the league's best nine-man unit. No team in the league featured as many interchangeable parts. Their veteran unit experience was the determining factor in many games, not to mention the long haul. Whatever Cleveland's level of success, the Pistons never stopped believing they would come out on top in the end.

Buoyed by the addition of Moses Malone and Reggie Theus, the Atlanta Hawks were the choice of many to win the title. In truth, the unit never jelled, although 52 wins is not a bad season. Not having forward Kevin Willis (out all season with a foot facture) left the Hawks one brick shy of the expected load.

Milwaukee fooled most experts, as Del Harris stitched together a successful team from a variety of sources. Terry Cummings had a strong season, while center Jack Sikma became a three-point bombardier. Long considered one of the deeper teams in the league, the Bucks, like the Pistons, made good use of a strong bench.

Chicago rode Michael Jordan's nightly heroics to 47 wins, but the best part of the Bulls' season was the playoffs, when they eliminated Cleveland and New York before losing a tough six-game

Wide World Photos

MVP **Magic Johnson** led the L.A. Lakers to another Pacific Division flag.

series to eventual champion Detroit. The development of young stars Scottie Pippen and Horace Grant enabled Chicago fans to think about a championship in the near future, and that optimism expanded on draft day when the Bulls bagged Oklahoma star Stacey King and Iowa guard B.J. Armstrong, the former to give some inside scoring punch and the latter to be the long-sought point guard who can make life easier for the one-and-only Mr. Jordan.

But confusion was the dominant attitude in the end, as coach Doug Collins was mysteriously fired two weeks after the NBA Finals.

Indiana had a tumultuous season. Veteran coach Jack Ramsay departed after seven winless games, and things never really came together for the Pacers.

Midwest Division

In the Midwest Division, Utah lived up to its press clippings. Karl Malone, the only unanimous choice to the All-League

Pistons' guard **Joe Dumars** (left) drives past **Tony Campbell** of the L.A. Lakers in the NBA Finals. Dumars was named MVP of the playoffs.

team, emerged as a megastar, while guard John Stockton won both the assist and steals crowns. With massive center Mark Eaton anchoring the defense, the Jazz held foes to 43 percent shooting. Even a surprise coaching change—Frank Layden resigned in favor of Jerry Sloan in December—didn't deter the Jazz.

Competition came from Houston, led by Akeem Olajuwon, and Denver. The Nuggets had injury problems, but still came away with 44 triumphs. Houston boasted a strong 1-2 inside punch in Olajuwon and Otis Thorpe.

Dallas, a league upper echelon team for several years, had a dismal season, finishing with a 38-44 record. The Mavericks lost standout forward Roy Tarpley to drug rehab, and made a big decision to unload long-time problem child Mark Aguirre in favor of Adrian Dantley. Losing center James Donaldson to a serious knee injury was the final blow.

Nothing was expected to go right for the expansion Miami Heat and nothing did—not in the beginning, anyway. The Heat hustled and played sound defense, but lost their first 17 games due to an impotent offense which produced a mere 97 points a game. Nothing went right for Larry Brown's San Antonio squad, either. The mentor suffered through the first losing season in his long coaching career, but at least he now has David Robinson (and first round draft choice Sean Elliott) to look forward to.

Pacific Division

The Pacific Division was won, as usual, by the Lakers, but not without difficulty. The revamped Phoenix Suns, one of the great reclamation projects in league history, improved by a staggering 27 games (from 28 wins to 55) and pushed L.A. to the final days of the season. The Lakers appeared particularly vulnerable during the month of December when they lost eight road games in succession, but by the season's end reliable stars such as MVP Magic Johnson, James Worthy and Byron Scott had the team back on its accustomed perch, atop the division.

Midway through the previous season, Suns owner-General Manager Jerry Colangelo backed up the truck, as they say, and began to change over his ballclub. In the off-season he signed free agent Tom Chambers. Almost every move worked twice as well as everyone thought. Guard Kevin Johnson blossomed into a star, Chambers had the proverbial career year, all the role players fulfilled their function and the Suns became a feared team. Most of all, Cotton Fitzsimmons turned in a virtuoso coaching job.

That coaching performance was matched by Don Nelson in Oakland. The Warriors were similarly downtrodden, but Nelson made some weird pieces fit, especially when he stopped playing with a center and began winning games with a front line whose size wouldn't impress an NAIA coach. Chris Mullin, freed from an alcohol problem, became a great player, and Mitch Richmond was Rookie of the Year.

Seattle was another pesky team. The Sonics got another big season from guard Dale Ellis and another 20 points a game year from Xavier McDaniel (switched to a sixth man for most of the year). Derrick McKey became a force at the forward spot. The Sonics fell a bit shy in the bench department.

File Portland's season under "D," for Disappointment. The Trail Blazers underachieved to get coach Mike Schuler fired, but not quite enough to prevent interim coach Rick Adelman from being rehired. The offensive numbers of the principals look good enough, but the Blazers never got rolling.

That leaves Sacramento and the Los Angeles Clippers. The Kings were second only to the Knicks in their love of the bomb, throwing up 824 three-pointers. They had to, since trades ripped apart their inside game. They fared better in the postseason draft lottery, getting the first overall pick and taking Louisville center Pervis Ellison. The Clippers, beneficiaries of three first round picks for the second year in succession, had the worst possible break when Danny Manning messed up his knee in early January. They won 21 games, which, for them, is a milestone, since they had only won 29 in the two previous years combined.

Finally, attendance increased by 22% in 1988-89. Expansion helped Miami sell out all of its home games and Charlotte played to capacity 35 of 41 times.

Gone but not Forgotten

What was the mourning stripe for on everybody's uniform during the 1989 playoffs?

Every NBA player wore that black band out of respect to someone who had more to do with improving their professional lot than anyone else. They were paying respect to the late Larry Fleisher, who died of a heart attack during the playoffs.

Larry Fleisher had been the Executive Director of the NBA Players Association for 27 years until his retirement at the conclusion of the 1987-88 season. During that time he had made the NBA Players Association the most advanced athletic union in the world, giving the players clout most other athletes could only dream of.

What set Fleisher apart from other sports labor negotiators was the astonishing fact that he managed to provide salaries and benefits for his players while simultaneously earning the respect and admiration of those at the other side of the bargaining table.

But Fleisher was not the only towering figure lost to the NBA last season. The '89-'90 season will be the first in 37 years in which Jack McMahon will not be in attendance at a ballgame somewhere, and the league will never be quite the same again. As player, coach and scout, Jack McMahon may have established the NBA record for honest opinions expressed and friends made. A man of enormous good cheer, he was a gentleman (thought now to be an extinct species) and everyone's favorite traveling companion.

With these two huge personal losses, no player, coach, scout, administrator or member of the media was left untouched.

Kareem's NBA Score

In college, Lew Alcindor led UCLA to three straight NCAA championships (1967-69). He was also named the Outstanding Player in the tournament three times and Player of the Year twice.

As the NBA's first overall draft pick (by Milwaukee) in 1969, Alcindor was expected to deliver immediately and he did. He helped improve the Bucks' record by 29 games his first season and was named Rookie of the Year. His second year he led them to the NBA championship and was named Most Valuable Player of both the regular season and the playoffs.

Alcindor changed his name to Kareem Abdul-Jabbar after the 1970-71 season and when he finally retired this June after 20 seasons that name was almost everywhere you looked in the NBA record book.

Some of the highlights:

NBA Titles

1971—Milwaukee*	1985—LA Lakers*
1980—LA Lakers	1987—LA Lakers
1982—LA Lakers	1988—LA Lakers

*Playoff MVP

Honors

Rookie of the Year: 1970
Most Valuable Player: 1971 1974 1977
1972 1976 1980

All-NBA 1st Team	All-NBA 2nd Team
1971 1973 1977 1984	1970 1979 1985
1972 1974 1980 1986	1978 1983
1976 1981	

NBA All-Star Games (18)
1970 1974 1979 1983 1987
1971 1975 1980 1984 1988
1972 1976 1981 1985 1989
1973* 1977 1982 1986
*Selected, but did not play.

NBA 35th Anniversary All-Time Team
Vote taken in 1980.

Kareem Abdul-Jabbar	George Mikan
Elgin Baylor	Bob Pettit
Wilt Chamberlain	Oscar Robertson
Bob Cousy	Bill Russell
Julius Erving	Jerry West
John Havlicek	

NBA Career Records

Regular season	Playoffs
Seasons (20)	Seasons (18)
Games (1,560)	Games (237)
Minutes (57,446)	Minutes (8,851)
Points (38,387)	Points (5,762)
FG Attempts (28,301)	FG Attempts (4,422)
FG Made (15,832)	FG Made (2,356)
Blocked Shots (3,189)	Blocked Shots (476)
Personal Fouls (4,655)	Personal Fouls (797)

All-Star Games

Games (18)	Points (251)
FG Made (40)	Minutes (449)
FG Attempts (54)	Personal Fouls (57)

Wide World Photos

1988-89 Final Standings

Eastern Conference

Atlantic Division

	W	L	Pct	GB	Pts Per Game Off	Def
New York	52	30	.634	—	116.7	112.9
Philadelphia	46	36	.561	6	111.9	110.4
Boston	42	40	.512	10	109.2	108.1
Washington	40	42	.488	12	108.3	110.4
New Jersey	26	56	.317	26	103.7	110.1
Charlotte	20	62	.244	32	104.5	113.0

Head Coaches: NY—Rick Pitino (2nd season); **Phila**—Jim Lynam (2nd); **Bos**—Jim Rodgers (1st); **Wash**—Wes Unseld (2nd); **NJ**—Willis Reed (2nd); **Char**—Dick Harter (1st).

Central Division

	W	L	Pct	GB	Pts Per Game Off	Def
Detroit	63	19	.768	—	106.6	100.8
Cleveland	57	25	.695	6	108.8	101.2
Atlanta	52	30	.634	11	111.0	106.1
Milwaukee	49	33	.598	14	108.9	105.3
Chicago	47	35	.573	16	106.4	105.0
Indiana	28	54	.341	35	106.9	111.1

Head Coaches: Det—Chuck Daly (6th season); **Cleve**—Lenny Wilkens (3rd); **Atl**—Mike Fratello (6th); **Milw**—Del Harris (2nd); **Chi**—Doug Collins (3rd); **Ind**—three coaches: Jack Ramsay (3rd, 0-7), George Irvine (6-14) and Dick Versace (22-33).

Western Conference

Midwest Division

	W	L	Pct	GB	Pts Per Game Off	Def
Utah	51	31	.622	—	104.7	99.7
Houston	45	37	.549	6	108.5	107.5
Denver	44	38	.537	7	118.0	116.3
Dallas	38	44	.463	13	103.5	104.7
San Antonio	21	61	.256	30	105.5	112.8
Miami	15	67	.183	36	97.8	109.0

Head Coaches: Utah—two coaches: Frank Layden (8th season, 11-6) and Jerry Sloan (40-25); **Hous**—Don Chaney (1st); **Den**—Doug Moe (9th); **Dal**—John MacLeod (2nd); **SA**—Larry Brown (1st); **Miami**—Ron Rothstein (1st).

Pacific Division

	W	L	Pct	GB	Pts Per Game Off	Def
LA Lakers	57	25	.695	—	114.7	107.5
Phoenix	55	27	.671	2	118.6	110.9
Seattle	47	35	.573	10	112.1	109.2
Golden St	43	39	.524	14	116.6	116.9
Portland	39	43	.476	18	114.6	113.1
Sacramento	27	55	.329	30	105.5	111.0
LA Clippers	21	61	.256	36	106.2	116.2

Head Coaches: Lakers—Pat Riley (8th season); **Phoe**—Cotton Fitzsimmons (1st); **Sea**—Bernie Bickerstaff (4th); **GS**—Don Nelson (1st); **Port**—two coaches: Mike Schuler (3rd, 25-22) and Rick Adelman (14-21); **Sac**—Jerry Reynolds (3rd); **Clippers**—two coaches: Gene Shue (2nd, 10-28) and Don Casey (11-33).

Overall Conference Standings

Sixteen teams—8 from each conference—qualify for the NBA Playoffs. In each conference, berths go to the two regular season division champions and the six remaining teams with the best records. The division winners get the top two seeds.

Eastern Conference

	W	L	Home	Away	Conf
1 **Detroit***	63	19	37-4	26-15	41-15
2 **Cleveland**	57	25	37-4	20-21	38-18
3 **Atlanta**	52	30	33-8	19-22	38-18
New York*	52	30	35-6	17-24	36-20
5 **Milwaukee**	49	33	31-10	18-23	29-17
6 **Chicago**	47	35	30-11	17-24	28-28
7 **Philadelphia**	46	36	30-11	16-25	31-25
8 **Boston**	42	40	32-9	10-31	27-29
9 Washington	40	42	30-11	10-31	25-31
10 Indiana	28	54	20-21	8-33	15-41
11 New Jersey	26	56	17-24	9-32	16-40
12 Charlotte	20	62	12-29	8-33	12-44

Western Conference

	W	L	Home	Away	Conf
1 **LA Lakers***	57	25	35-6	22-19	43-15
2 **Phoenix**	55	27	35-6	20-21	41-17
3 **Utah***	51	31	34-7	17-24	37-21
4 **Seattle**	47	35	31-10	16-25	37-21
5 **Houston**	45	37	31-10	14-27	33-25
6 **Denver**	44	38	35-6	9-32	32-26
7 **Golden St**	43	39	29-12	14-27	29-29
8 **Portland**	39	43	28-13	11-30	30-28
9 Dallas	38	44	24-17	14-27	30-28
10 Sacramento	27	55	21-20	6-35	23-35
11 LA Clippers	21	61	17-24	4-37	17-41
12 San Antonio	21	61	18-23	3-38	15-43
13 Miami	15	67	12-29	3-38	10-48

Realigned NBA for 1989-90

Eastern Conference

Atlantic Division
Boston Celtics
Miami Heat
New Jersey Nets
New York Knicks
Philadelphia 76ers
Washington Bullets

Central Division
Atlanta Hawks
Chicago Bulls
Cleveland Cavaliers
Detroit Pistons
Indiana Pacers
Milwaukee Bucks
Orlando Magic

Western Conference

Midwest Division
Charlotte Hornets
Dallas Mavericks
Denver Nuggets
Houston Rockets
Minnesota Timberwolves
San Antonio Spurs
Utah Jazz

Pacific Division
Golden State Warriors
Los Angeles Clippers
Los Angeles Lakers
Phoenix Suns
Portland Trail Blazers
Sacramento Kings
Seattle SuperSonics

NBA LEADERS
Regular Season
Scoring

	Pos	GP	Pts	Avg
Michael Jordan, Chicago...	G	81	2,633	32.5
Karl Malone, Utah	F	80	2,326	29.1
Dale Ellis, Seattle	F	82	2,253	27.5
Clyde Drexler, Portland	G/F	78	2,123	27.2
Chris Mullin, Golden St	G	82	2,176	26.5
Alex English, Denver	F	82	2,175	26.5
Dominique Wilkins, Atlanta .	F	80	2,099	26.2
Charles Barkley, Phila	F	79	2,037	25.8
Tom Chambers, Phoenix ...	C/F	81	2,085	25.7
Akeem Olajuwon, Houston .	C	82	2,034	24.8
Terry Cummings, Milwaukee	F	80	1,829	22.9
Patrick Ewing, New York...	C	80	1,815	22.7
Kelly Tripucka, Charlotte ...	F	71	1,606	22.6
Kevin McHale, Boston	F	78	1,758	22.5
Magic Johnson, LA Lakers .	G	77	1,730	22.5
Mitch Richmond, Golden St .	G	79	1,741	22.0
Jeff Malone, Washington ..	G	76	1,651	21.7
Chuck Person, Indiana	.F	80	1,728	21.6
Eddie Johnson, Phoenix ...	F	70	1,504	21.5
Bernard King, Washington .	F	81	1,674	20.7
James Worthy, LA Lakers ..	F	81	1,657	20.5
Xavier McDaniel, Seattle ...	F	82	1,677	20.5
Kevin Johnson, Phoenix ...	G	81	1,652	20.4
Moses Malone, Atlanta	C	81	1,637	20.2
Lafayette Lever, Denver ...	G	71	1,409	19.8

Rebounds

	Avg
Olajuwon, Houston .	13.5
Barkley, Phila	12.5
Parish, Boston	12.5
M.Malone, Atlanta .	11.8
K.Malone, Utah ...	10.7
Oakley, New York .	10.5
Eaton, Utah	10.3
Thorpe, Houston ...	9.6
Laimbeer, Detroit ...	9.6
Cage, Seattle	9.6

Assists

	Avg
Stockton, Utah	13.6
M.Johnson, Lakers .	12.8
K.Johnson, Phoe ..	12.2
Porter, Portland ...	9.5
McMillan, Seattle ..	9.3
Floyd, Houston	8.6
Jackson, New York .	8.6
Price, Cleveland ...	8.4
Thomas, Detroit ...	8.3
Jordan, Chicago	8.0

Field Goal Pct.

	Pct
Rodman, Detroit ..	.595
Barkley, Phila	.579
Parish, Boston	.570
Ewing, New York .	.567
Worthy, Lakers ...	.548

Free Throw Pct.

	Pct
Johnson, Lakers ..	.911
Sikma, Milwaukee .	.905
Skiles, Indiana	.903
Price, Cleveland ..	.901
Mullin, Gold.St ...	.892

3-Pt Field Goals

	Pct
Sundvold, Miami ..	.522
Ellis, Seattle	.478
Price, Cleveland ..	.441
Hawkins, Phila ...	.428
Hodges, Chicago .	.417

Steals

	Avg
Stockton, Utah	3.21
Robertson, S.A ...	3.03
Jordan, Chicago ...	2.89
Lever, Denver	2.75
Drexler, Port	2.73

NBA AWARDS
Most Valuable Player Voting
(Maurice Podoloff Trophy)

Voting done by a national panel of 85 pro basketball writers and broadcasters. Each ballot has five entries. Points are awarded on a 10-7-5-3-1 basis.

		1st	Pts
1	Magic Johnson, LA Lakers, G	42½	664.5
2	Michael Jordan, Chicago, G	27½	598.8
3	Karl Malone, Utah, F	5	362.0
4	Patrick Ewing, New York, C	8	200.0
5	Akeem Olajuwon, Houston, C	2	179.3
6	Charles Barkley, Phila., F	0	94.3
7	John Stockton, Utah, G	0	28.0
8	Kevin Johnson, Phoenix, G	0	22.0
9	Tom Chambers, Phoenix, F-C	0	20.0
10	Mark Price, Cleveland, G	0	18.0
11	Brad Daugherty, Cleveland, C ...	0	4.0
12	Robert Parish, Boston, C	0	4.0
13	Mark Eaton, Utah, C...........	0	3.0
14	Moses Malone, Atlanta, C.......	0	3.0
15	Chris Mullin, Golden St., F	0	3.0
16	Larry Nance, Cleveland, F	0	3.0
17	Terry Cummings, Milwaukee, F ...	0	1.0
18	Joe Dumars, Detroit, G	0	1.0
19	Isiah Thomas, Detroit, G	0	1.0

Rookie of the Year Voting
(Eddie Gottlieb Trophy)

Voting done by a national panel of 85 pro basketball writers and broadcasters. Each ballot has one entry.

	Pos	Votes
1 Mitch Richmond, Golden St.(Kan.St.)	G	80
2 Willie Anderson, S.Antonio (Georgia)	G	4
3 Chris Morris, New Jersey (Auburn) .	F	1

Coach of the Year Voting
(Red Auerbach Trophy)

Voting done by a national panel of 85 pro basketball writers and broadcasters. Each ballot has one entry. Columns under W-L Records heading compare 1987-88 and 1988-89 regular seasons.

		W-L Records	
	Votes	87-88	88-89
1 Cotton Fitzsimmons, Phoe ..	36½	28-54	55-27
2 Don Nelson, Golden St	26½	20-62	43-39
3 Lenny Wilkens, Cleveland ..	9	42-40	57-25
4 Chuck Daly, Detroit.......	5	54-28*	63-19*
5 Wes Unseld, Washington ..	4	38-44	40-42
6 Rick Pitino, New York	2	38-44	52-30*
7 Del Harris, Milwaukee	1	42-40	49-33
8 Pat Riley, LA Lakers	1	62-20*	57-25*

*Won Division

Other Awards

Schick Award .... Michael Jordan, Chicago
  (Contributed most to team's overall success)
Sixth Man .... Eddie Johnson, Phoenix
Defensive Player of the Year .... Mark Eaton, Utah
Most Improved Player ...... Kevin Johnson, Phoenix
Good Hands Award .... John Stockton, Utah
Kennedy Citizenship Award ..... Thurl Bailey, Utah

All-NBA Teams

Voting done by a national panel of 85 pro basketball writers and broadcasters.

Pos	First Team	1st	Pts
F	Karl Malone, Utah	85	425
G	Magic Johnson, LA Lakers*	84	423
G	Michael Jordan, Chicago*	84	423
F	Charles Barkley, Philadelphia*	80	412
C	Akeem Olajuwon, Houston*	66	379

*Also on 1987-88 First Team

Pos	Second Team	1st	Pts
C	Patrick Ewing, New York	17	267
G	John Stockton, Utah	1	224
F	Tom Chambers, Phoenix	1	174
F	Chris Mullin, Golden St	0	137
G	Kevin Johnson, Phoenix	0	131

Pos	Third Team	1st	Pts
F	Dominique Wilkins, Atlanta	2	116
G	Dale Ellis, Seattle	1	83
G	Mark Price, Cleveland	0	73
F	Terry Cummings, Milwaukee	1	70
C	Robert Parish, Boston	1	70

All-Defensive Teams

Voting done by the NBA's 25 head coaches. Two points for a 1st Team vote, one point for a 2nd Team vote and coaches cannot vote for players on their own team.

Pos	First Team	1st	Pts
F	Dennis Rodman, Detroit	23	47
G	Michael Jordan, Chicago	18	39
G	Joe Dumars, Detroit	14	36
C	Mark Eaton, Utah	11	29
F	Larry Nance, Cleveland	12	28

Pos	Second Team	1st	Pts
C	Patrick Ewing, New York	10	25
G	John Stockton, Utah	4	15
G	Alvin Robertson, San Antonio	3	11
F	Kevin McHale, Boston	3	11
F	A.C.Green, LA Lakers	2	10

All-Rookie Teams

Voting done by the NBA's 25 head coaches. Two points for a 1st Team vote, one point for a 2nd Team vote and coaches cannot vote for players on their own team. Selections made without regard to position.

Pos	First Team	Pts
G	Mitch Richmond, Golden St.(Kansas St.)	48
G	Willie Anderson, San Antonio (Georgia)	45
G	Hersey Hawkins, Philadelphia (Bradley)	40
C	Rik Smits, Indiana (Marist)	38
F	Charles Smith, LA Clippers (Pitt)	31

Pos	Second Team	Pts
G	Brian Shaw, Boston (UC-Santa Barbara)	26
G	Rex Chapman, Charlotte (Kentucky)	25
F	Chris Morris, New Jersey (Auburn)	22
G	Rod Strickland, New York (DePaul)	18
G	Kevin Edwards, Miami (DePaul)	16

1989 NBA All-Star Game
West 143, East 134

Date: Feb. 12, at the Astrodome in Houston; **Coaches:** Pat Riley (West), Lenny Wilkens (East); **Most Valuable Player:** Karl Malone, Utah.

East	Min	FG M-A	FT M-A	Pts	Rb	A	F
Charles Barkley	.20	6-11	5- 8	17	8	0	0
Dominique Wilkins	15	3- 8	3- 3	9	3	0	0
Moses Malone	19	3- 9	3- 3	9	12	0	1
Michael Jordan	33	13-23	2- 4	28	3	3	1
Isiah Thomas	33	7-13	4- 6	19	3	14	2
Patrick Ewing	17	2- 8	0- 4	4	7	2	2
Terry Cummings	19	4- 9	2- 2	10	7	1	4
Larry Nance	17	5- 9	0- 0	10	9	1	1
Mark Price	20	3- 9	2- 2	9	4	1	2
Mark Jackson	16	3- 5	2- 4	9	3	4	1
Brad Daugherty	15	0- 3	0- 0	0	5	0	0
Kevin McHale	16	5- 7	0- 0	10	4	0	3
TOTALS	240	54-114	23-36	134	68	26	17

Three-point field goals: 3-9 (Jackson, 1-1, Thomas 1-3, Price 1-4, Jordan 0-1); **Blocked Shots:** 9 (Ewing 2, McHale 2, Barkley, Malone, Cummings, Nance, Jackson); **Turnovers:** 23 (Thomas 6, Jordan 4, Ewing 3, Wilkins 2, Price 2, Jackson 2, Barkley, Malone, Daugherty, McHale); **Steals:** 24 (Jordan 5, Thomas 4, Cummings 3, Wilkins 3, Barkley 2, Price 2, Malone, Ewing, Nance, Jackson, Daugherty); **FG Pct—** .474; **FT Pct—** .639.

West	Min	FG M-A	FT M-A	Pts	Rb	A	F
Alex English	29	8-13	0- 0	16	4	4	0
Karl Malone	26	12-17	4- 6	28	13	3	3
Akeem Olajuwon	25	5-12	2- 3	12	11	3	2
Dale Ellis	26	12-16	2- 2	27	9	2	2
John Stockton	32	5- 6	0- 0	11	2	17	4
Kareem Abdul-Jabbar	13	1- 6	2- 2	4	3	0	3
Clyde Drexler	25	7-19	0- 0	14	18	4	3
Tom Chambers	16	4- 8	6- 6	14	7	1	3
Chris Mullin	14	1- 4	2- 2	4	4	2	0
James Worthy	18	4- 7	0- 0	8	2	2	0
Mark Eaton	9	0- 0	0- 0	0	5	0	1
Kevin Duckworth	7	2- 5	1- 2	5	2	0	2
TOTALS	240	61-113	19-23	143	80	38	23

Three-point field goals: 2-4 (Ellis 1-1, Stockton 1-1, Abdul-Jabbar 0-1, Worth 0-1); **Blocked Shots:** 6 (Alajuwon 2, Eaton 2, Abdul-Jabbar 2); **Turnovers:** 31 (Stockton 12, Drexler 6, English 3, Olajuwon 3, Malone 2, Ellis 2, Chambers 2, Mullin); **Steals:** 16 (Stockton 5, Olajuwon 3, English 2, Malone 2, Drexler 2, Worthy 2); **FG Pct—** .540; **FT Pct—** .826.

East	31	28	37	38—134
West	47	40	24	32—143

Technical Fouls: None; **Officials:** Evans, Bavetta, Saar; **Attendance:** 44,735.

Team by Team Statistics

Players included scored at least 100 points during the 1988-89 regular season. *Denotes rookies.

Atlanta Hawks

	GP	FG%	Pts	Per Game Pts	Reb	Ast
Dominique Wilkins . .	80	.464	2099	26.2	6.9	2.6
Moses Malone	81	.491	1637	20.2	11.8	1.4
Reggie Theus	82	.466	1296	15.8	3.0	4.7
Doc Rivers	76	.455	1032	13.6	3.8	6.9
John Battle	82	.457	779	9.5	1.7	2.4
Cliff Levingston	80	.528	734	9.2	6.2	0.9
Antoine Carr	78	.481	582	7.5	3.5	1.2
Jon Koncak	74	.524	345	4.7	6.1	0.8
Spud Webb	81	.459	319	3.9	1.5	3.5
Duane Ferrell*	41	.422	100	2.4	1.0	0.2
Ray Tolbert	51	.421	103	2.0	1.7	0.3

Cleveland Cavaliers

	GP	FG%	Pts	Per Game Pts	Reb	Ast
Brad Daugherty	78	.538	1475	18.9	9.2	3.7
Mark Price	75	.526	1415	18.9	3.0	8.4
Ron Harper	82	.511	1526	18.6	5.0	5.3
Larry Nance	73	.539	1259	17.2	8.0	2.2
John Williams	82	.509	948	11.6	5.8	1.3
Mike Sanders	82	.453	764	9.3	3.7	1.6
Craig Ehlo	82	.475	608	7.4	3.6	3.2
Darnell Valentine . .	77	.426	365	4.7	1.3	2.3
Randolph Keys*	42	.433	169	4.0	1.3	0.5
Chris Dudley	61	.435	185	3.0	2.6	0.3
Tree Rollins	61	.446	136	2.2	2.3	0.3

Boston Celtics

	GP	FG%	Pts	Per Game Pts	Reb	Ast
Kevin McHale	78	.546	1759	22.6	8.2	2.2
Larry Bird	6	.471	116	19.3	6.2	4.8
Robert Parish	80	.570	1486	18.6	12.5	2.2
Reggie Lewis	81	.486	1494	18.4	4.7	2.7
Ed Pinckney	80	.513	918	11.5	5.6	1.5
Dennis Johnson	72	.434	721	10.0	2.6	6.6
Jim Paxson	57	.454	492	8.6	1.3	1.9
Brian Shaw*	82	.433	703	8.6	4.6	5.8
Kelvin Upshaw*	32	.467	219	6.8	1.5	3.7
Joe Kleine	75	.405	484	6.5	5.0	0.9
Kevin Gamble	44	.551	187	4.3	1.0	0.8
Ron Grandison*	72	.415	177	2.5	1.3	0.6
Mark Acres	62	.482	137	2.2	2.4	0.3

Dallas Mavericks

	GP	FG%	Pts	Per Game Pts	Reb	Ast
Rolando Blackman . .	78	.476	1534	19.7	3.5	3.7
Adrian Dantley	73	.493	1404	19.2	4.5	2.4
Derek Harper	81	.477	1404	17.3	2.8	7.0
Roy Tarpley	19	.541	328	17.3	11.5	0.9
Sam Perkins	78	.464	1171	15.0	8.8	1.6
Herb Williams	76	.436	777	10.2	7.8	1.6
James Donaldson . . .	53	.573	481	9.1	10.8	0.7
Brad Davis	78	.483	497	6.4	1.4	3.1
Terry Tyler	70	.469	386	5.5	3.0	0.6
Bill Wennington	65	.433	300	4.6	4.4	0.7
Morlon Wiley*	51	.404	111	2.2	0.9	1.5

Charlotte Hornets

	GP	FG%	Pts	Per Game Pts	Reb	Ast
Kelly Tripucka	71	.466	1598	22.5	3.8	3.1
Rex Chapman*	75	.414	1267	16.9	2.5	2.3
Robert Reid	82	.428	1207	14.7	3.7	1.9
Dell Curry	48	.489	569	11.9	2.2	1.0
Kurt Rambis	75	.520	840	11.2	9.3	2.1
Michael Holton	67	.427	553	8.3	1.6	6.3
Brian Rowsom	34	.494	226	6.6	4.0	0.7
Earl Cureton	82	.501	532	6.5	6.0	1.6
Dave Hoppen	77	.564	500	6.5	5.0	0.7
Tim Kempton	79	.513	486	6.2	3.8	1.3
Tyrone Bogues	79	.426	423	5.4	2.1	7.8
Ricky Green	33	.432	128	3.9	0.7	2.5
Ralph Lewis	42	.479	136	3.2	1.5	0.4
Greg Kite	70	.430	150	2.1	3.5	0.5

Denver Nuggets

	GP	FG%	Pts	Per Game Pts	Reb	Ast
Alex English	82	.491	2175	26.5	4.0	4.7
Lafayette Lever	71	.457	1409	19.8	9.3	7.9
Michael Adams	77	.433	1424	18.5	3.7	6.4
Walter Davis	81	.499	1267	15.6	1.9	2.3
Danny Schayes	77	.522	978	12.7	6.6	1.4
Darwin Cook	66	.456	507	7.7	1.6	1.9
Blair Rasmussen	77	.445	583	7.6	3.7	0.6
David Greenwood . .	67	.423	466	7.0	6.0	1.4
Wayne Cooper	78	.495	511	6.6	7.9	1.0
Bill Hanzlik	41	.437	201	4.9	2.3	2.1
Jerome Lane*	54	.426	261	4.8	3.7	1.1
Elston Turner	78	.428	337	4.3	3.7	1.8

Chicago Bulls

	GP	FG%	Pts	Per Game Pts	Reb	Ast
Michael Jordan	81	.538	2633	32.5	8.0	8.0
Scottie Pippen	73	.476	1048	14.4	6.1	3.5
Bill Cartwright	78	.475	966	12.4	6.7	1.2
Horace Grant	79	.519	950	12.0	8.6	2.1
Sam Vincent	70	.484	656	9.4	2.7	4.8
Craig Hodges	59	.472	529	9.0	1.5	2.5
John Paxson	78	.480	567	7.3	1.2	3.9
Brad Sellers	80	.485	551	6.9	2.8	1.2
Dave Corzine	81	.461	479	5.9	3.9	1.3
Charles Davis	49	.426	185	3.8	2.3	0.6
Jack Haley*	51	.474	110	2.2	1.4	0.2

Detroit Pistons

	GP	FG%	Pts	Per Game Pts	Reb	Ast
Mark Aguirre	80	.461	1511	18.9	4.8	3.5
Isiah Thomas	80	.464	1458	18.2	3.4	8.3
Joe Dumars	69	.504	1184	17.2	2.5	5.7
Vinnie Johnson	82	.464	1130	13.8	3.1	3.0
Bill Laimbeer	81	.499	1108	13.7	9.6	2.2
Dennis Rodman	82	.595	735	9.0	9.4	1.2
James Edwards	76	.500	555	7.3	3.0	0.6
Rick Mahorn	72	.517	522	7.3	6.9	0.8
John Salley	67	.497	463	6.9	4.9	1.1
John Long	68	.409	372	5.5	1.1	1.2
Michael Williams* . .	49	.364	127	2.6	0.6	1.4

Golden State Warriors

	GP	FG%	Pts	Per Pts	Game Reb	Ast
Chris Mullin	82	.512	2176	26.5	5.9	5.0
Mitch Richmond*	80	.469	1741	21.8	5.9	4.2
Terry Teagle	66	.476	1002	15.2	4.0	1.5
Winston Garland	79	.434	1145	14.5	4.2	6.3
Rod Higgins	81	.476	856	10.6	4.6	2.0
Otis Smith	80	.435	803	10.0	4.1	1.8
Ralph Sampson	61	.449	393	6.4	5.0	1.3
Larry Smith	80	.552	456	5.7	8.2	1.5
Steve Alford	66	.473	366	5.5	1.1	1.4
John Starks	36	.400	144	4.0	1.1	0.8
Manute Bol	80	.369	314	3.9	5.8	0.3
Tellis Frank	32	.385	109	3.4	1.9	0.5

Houston Rockets

	GP	FG%	Pts	Per Pts	Game Reb	Ast
Akeem Olajuwon	82	.508	2034	24.8	13.5	1.8
Otis Thorpe	82	.542	1370	16.7	9.6	2.5
Sleepy Floyd	82	.443	1162	14.2	3.7	8.6
Mike Woodson	81	.438	1046	12.9	2.4	2.5
Buck Johnson	69	.521	651	9.4	4.2	1.9
Derrick Chievous*	81	.437	750	9.3	3.2	1.0
Walter Berry	69	.507	609	8.8	3.9	1.1
Purvis Short	65	.413	482	7.4	2.8	1.6
Tim McCormick	81	.481	425	5.2	3.2	0.7
Frank Johnson	65	.448	284	4.4	1.2	2.7
Allen Leavell	55	.346	179	3.3	1.0	2.3

Indiana Pacers

	GP	FG%	Pts	Per Pts	Game Reb	Ast
Chuck Person	80	.489	1728	21.6	6.5	3.6
Reggie Miller	74	.479	1181	16.0	3.9	3.1
Vern Fleming	76	.515	1084	14.3	4.1	6.5
LaSalle Thompson	76	.489	1059	13.9	9.4	1.1
Detlef Schrempf	69	.480	828	12.0	5.7	2.6
Rik Smits*	82	.517	956	11.7	6.1	0.9
Scott Skiles	80	.448	546	6.8	1.9	4.9
Randy Wittman	64	.455	291	4.5	1.3	1.7
Anthony Frederick*	46	.504	152	3.3	1.1	0.4
Stuart Gray	72	.471	188	2.6	3.4	0.4
Greg Dreiling	53	.558	129	2.4	1.7	0.3

Los Angeles Clippers

	GP	FG%	Pts	Per Pts	Game Reb	Ast
Ken Norman	80	.502	1450	18.1	8.3	3.4
Danny Manning*	26	.494	434	16.7	6.6	3.1
Benoit Benjamin	79	.541	1299	16.4	8.8	2.0
Charles Smith*	71	.496	1155	16.3	6.5	1.4
Quintin Dailey	69	.465	1114	16.1	3.0	2.2
Gary Grant*	71	.435	846	11.9	3.4	7.1
Reggie Williams	63	.438	642	10.2	2.8	1.6
Norm Nixon	53	.414	362	6.8	1.5	6.3
Tom Garrick*	72	.490	454	6.3	2.2	3.4
Joe Wolf	66	.423	386	5.8	4.1	1.7
Kevin Williams	50	.405	209	4.2	1.4	1.1
Eric White	38	.517	158	4.2	1.8	0.4
Grant Gondrezick	27	.400	105	3.9	1.3	1.3

Los Angeles Lakers

	GP	FG%	Pts	Per Pts	Game Reb	Ast
Magic Johnson	77	.509	1730	22.5	7.9	12.8
James Worthy	81	.548	1657	20.5	6.0	3.6
Byron Scott	74	.491	1448	19.6	4.1	3.1
A.C. Green	82	.529	1088	13.3	9.0	1.3
Kareem Abdul-Jabbar	74	.475	748	10.1	4.5	1.0
Orlando Woolridge	74	.468	715	9.7	3.6	0.8
Mychal Thompson	80	.559	738	9.2	5.8	0.6
Michael Cooper	80	.431	587	7.3	2.4	3.9
Tony Campbell	63	.458	388	6.2	2.1	0.7
Mark McNamara	39	.500	113	2.9	2.6	0.3
David Rivers*	47	.402	134	2.9	0.9	2.3

Miami Heat

	GP	FG%	Pts	Per Pts	Game Reb	Ast
Kevin Edwards*	79	.425	1094	13.8	3.3	4.4
Rory Sparrow	80	.452	1000	12.5	2.7	5.4
Grant Long*	82	.486	976	11.9	6.7	1.8
Rony Seikaly*	78	.448	848	10.9	7.0	0.7
Billy Thompson	79	.487	854	10.8	7.2	2.2
Jon Sundvold	68	.455	709	10.4	1.3	2.0
Pat Cummings	53	.500	466	8.8	5.3	0.9
Sylvester Gray*	55	.420	440	8.0	5.2	2.1
Pearl Washington	54	.424	411	7.6	2.3	4.2
Anthony Taylor*	21	.397	144	6.9	1.6	2.0
John Shasky*	65	.488	357	5.5	3.6	0.3
Todd Mitchell*	22	.466	118	5.4	2.1	0.9
Scott Hastings	75	.436	386	5.1	3.1	0.8
Craig Neal*	54	.366	114	2.1	0.5	2.2

Milwaukee Bucks

	GP	FG%	Pts	Per Pts	Game Reb	Ast
Terry Cummings	80	.467	1829	22.9	8.1	2.5
Ricky Pierce	75	.518	1317	17.6	2.6	2.1
Jack Sikma	80	.431	1068	13.4	7.8	3.6
Larry Krystkowiak	80	.473	1017	12.7	7.6	1.3
Sidney Moncrief	62	.491	752	12.1	2.8	3.0
Paul Pressey	67	.474	813	12.1	3.9	6.6
Jay Humphries	73	.483	844	11.6	2.6	5.5
Fred Roberts	71	.486	417	5.9	2.9	0.9
Rickey Green	29	.550	161	5.6	1.6	3.5
Randy Breuer	48	.480	200	4.2	2.8	0.5
Mark Davis*	33	.490	130	3.9	1.1	0.4
Tony Brown*	43	.424	127	3.0	1.0	0.6
Paul Mokeski	74	.354	163	2.2	2.5	0.5

New Jersey Nets

	GP	FG%	Pts	Per Pts	Game Reb	Ast
Roy Hinson	82	.482	1308	16.0	6.4	0.9
Joe Barry Carroll	64	.448	902	14.1	7.4	1.6
Chris Morris*	76	.457	1074	14.1	5.2	1.6
Buck Williams	74	.531	959	13.0	9.4	1.1
Mike McGee	80	.473	1038	13.0	2.4	1.5
Dennis Hopson	62	.419	788	12.7	3.3	1.7
Lester Conner	82	.457	843	10.3	4.3	7.4
John Bagley	68	.416	500	7.4	2.1	5.8
Keith Lee	57	.422	271	4.8	4.5	0.7
Bill Jones*	37	.490	129	3.5	1.3	0.5
Chas. Shackleford*	60	.494	187	3.1	2.6	0.4

New York Knicks

	GP	FG%	Pts	Per Pts	Game Reb	Ast
Patrick Ewing	80	.567	1815	22.7	9.3	2.4
Mark Jackson	72	.467	1219	16.9	4.7	8.6
Johnny Newman	81	.475	1293	16.0	2.5	2.0
Gerald Wilkins	81	.452	1161	14.3	3.0	3.4
Charles Oakley	82	.510	1061	12.9	10.5	2.3
Kiki Vandeweghe	45	.469	499	11.1	1.6	1.5
Rod Strickland*	81	.467	721	8.9	2.0	3.9
Trent Tucker	81	.454	687	8.5	2.2	1.6
Sidney Green	82	.460	517	6.3	4.8	0.9
Kenny Walker	80	.489	419	5.2	2.9	0.5
Eddie Lee Wilkins	71	.465	289	4.1	2.1	0.1

Philadelphia 76ers

	GP	FG%	Pts	Per Pts	Game Reb	Ast
Charales Barkley	79	.579	2039	25.8	12.5	4.1
Mike Gminski	82	.477	1409	17.2	9.4	7.1
Ron Anderson	82	.491	1330	16.2	5.0	1.7
Hersey Hawkins*	79	.455	1194	15.1	2.8	3.0
Cliff Robinson	14	.481	212	15.1	5.4	2.3
Maurice Cheeks	71	.483	824	11.6	2.6	7.7
Derek Smith	65	.435	568	8.7	2.6	2.0
Gerald Henderson	65	.414	425	6.5	1.0	2.2
Scott Brooks*	82	.420	428	5.2	1.1	3.7
Ben Coleman	58	.485	295	5.1	3.1	0.3
Shelton Jones*	49	.441	238	4.9	2.3	0.8
David Wingate	33	.470	137	4.2	1.1	2.2
Chris Welp	72	.442	246	3.4	2.7	0.4
Bob Thornton	54	.423	127	2.4	1.7	0.3

Phoenix Suns

	GP	FG%	Pts	Per Pts	Game Reb	Ast
Tom Chambers	81	.471	2085	25.7	8.4	2.9
Eddie Johnson	70	.497	1502	21.5	4.4	2.3
Kevin Johnson	81	.505	1652	20.4	4.2	12.2
Armon Gilliam	74	.503	1176	15.9	7.3	0.7
Jeff Hornacek	78	.495	1054	13.5	3.4	6.0
Dan Majerle*	54	.419	467	8.6	3.9	2.4
Tyrone Corbin	76	.541	629	8.3	5.2	1.5
Mark West	82	.653	594	7.2	6.7	0.5
Tim Perry*	62	.529	257	4.1	2.1	0.3
Andrew Lang*	62	.513	159	2.6	2.4	0.1

Portland Trail Blazers

	GP	FG%	Pts	Per Pts	Game Reb	Ast
Clyde Drexler	78	.496	2123	27.2	7.9	5.8
Kevin Duckworth	79	.477	1432	18.1	8.0	0.8
Terry Porter	81	.471	1431	17.7	4.5	9.5
Jerome Kersey	76	.469	1330	17.5	8.3	3.2
Steve Johnson	72	.524	721	10.0	5.0	1.5
Sam Bowie	20	.451	171	8.6	5.3	1.8
Adrian Branch	67	.463	498	7.4	2.0	0.9
Danny Young	48	.460	297	6.2	1.5	2.6
Richard Anderson	72	.417	371	5.2	3.2	1.4
Mark Bryant*	56	.478	280	5.0	3.2	0.6
Jerry Sichting	25	.442	102	4.1	1.2	2.4
Brook Steppe	27	.423	103	3.8	1.2	0.6
Clint Wheeler	28	.517	105	3.8	1.1	1.9
Caldwell Jones	72	.421	202	2.8	4.2	0.8

Sacramento Kings

	GP	FG%	Pts	Per Pts	Game Reb	Ast
Danny Ainge	73	.457	1281	17.5	3.5	5.5
Wayman Tisdale	79	.514	1381	17.5	7.7	1.6
Kenny Smith	81	.462	1403	17.3	2.8	7.7
Rodney McCray	68	.466	854	12.6	7.6	4.3
Harold Pressley	80	.439	981	12.3	6.1	2.2
Ricky Berry*	64	.450	706	11.0	3.1	1.3
Jim Petersen	66	.459	671	10.2	6.3	1.2
Vinny DelNegro*	80	.475	569	7.1	2.1	2.6
Brad Lohaus	77	.432	502	6.5	3.3	0.9

San Antonio Spurs

	GP	FG%	Pts	Per Pts	Game Reb	Ast
Willie Anderson*	81	.498	1508	18.6	5.1	4.6
Alvin Robertson	65	.483	1122	17.3	5.9	6.0
Johnny Dawkins	32	.443	454	14.2	3.2	7.0
Frank Brickowski	64	.515	875	13.7	6.3	2.0
Greg Anderson	82	.503	1127	13.7	8.2	0.7
Vernon Maxwell*	79	.432	927	11.7	2.6	3.8
Anthony Bowie*	18	.500	155	8.6	3.1	1.6
Jay Vincent	29	.405	249	8.6	3.8	0.9
Albert King	46	.431	327	7.1	3.0	1.7
Dallas Comegys	67	.487	438	6.5	3.5	0.4
Calvin Natt	24	.405	151	6.3	3.3	0.8
Michael Anderson*	36	.417	204	5.7	2.5	4.3
Todd Mitchell*	24	.443	123	5.1	2.1	0.9
Mike Smrek	43	.471	193	4.5	3.0	0.3
Jerome Whitehead	58	.396	175	3.0	2.3	0.3
Scott Roth	63	.353	181	2.9	1.0	0.9

Seattle Supersonics

	GP	FG%	Pts	Per Pts	Game Reb	Ast
Dale Ellis	82	.501	2253	27.5	4.2	2.0
Xavier McDaniel	82	.489	1677	20.5	5.3	1.6
Derrick McKey*	82	.502	1305	15.9	5.7	2.7
Michael Cage	80	.498	825	10.3	9.6	1.6
Sedale Threatt	63	.494	544	8.6	1.9	3.8
Alton Lister	82	.499	657	8.0	6.6	0.7
Jerry Reynolds	56	.417	428	7.6	1.8	1.1
Nate McMillan	75	.410	532	7.1	5.2	9.3
Russ Schoene	69	.387	358	5.2	2.4	0.5
John Lucas	74	.398	310	4.2	1.1	3.5
Olden Polynice	80	.506	233	2.9	2.6	0.3

Utah Jazz

	GP	FG%	Pts	Per Pts	Game Reb	Ast
Karl Malone	81	.519	2326	28.7	10.5	2.7
Thurl Baily	82	.483	1595	19.5	5.5	1.7
John Stockton	82	.538	1400	17.1	3.0	13.6
Darrell Griffith	82	.446	1135	13.8	4.0	1.6
Bob Hansen	46	.467	341	7.4	2.8	1.1
Mark Eaton	82	.462	508	6.2	10.3	1.0
Mike Brown	66	.419	300	4.5	3.9	0.6
Eric Leckner*	75	.545	319	4.3	2.7	0.2
Jim Farmer	37	.401	152	4.1	1.5	0.8
Jose Oritiz	51	.440	141	2.8	1.1	0.2
Marc Iavaroni	77	.442	180	2.3	1.7	0.4
Jimmy Les*	82	.301	138	1.7	1.1	2.6

Washington Bullets

	GP	FG%	Pts	Per Pts	Game Reb	Ast
Jeff Malone	76	.480	1651	21.7	2.4	2.9
Bernard King	81	.477	1674	20.7	4.7	3.6
John Williams	82	.466	1120	13.7	7.0	4.3
Ladell Eackles*	80	.434	917	11.5	2.3	1.5
Terry Catledge	79	.490	822	10.4	7.2	0.9
Darrell Walker	79	.420	714	9.0	6.4	6.3
Mark Alarie	74	.479	498	6.7	3.4	0.9
Steve Colter	80	.444	534	6.7	2.3	2.8
Harvey Grant*	71	.464	396	5.6	2.3	1.1
Dave Feitl	57	.436	286	5.0	3.5	0.6
Charles Jones	58	.489	160	2.8	4.7	0.8

1989 NBA Playoffs

Eastern Conference
Game winning teams in capital LETTERS.

Western Conference
Game winning teams in capital LETTERS.

FIRST ROUND SERIES (Best of 5)

New York 3, Philadelphia 0
Apr.27 . . Philadelphia 96, at NEW YORK 102
Apr.29 . . Philadelphia 106, at NEW YORK 107
May 2 . . NEW YORK 116, at Philadelphia 115 (OT)

Detroit 3, Boston 0
Apr.28 . . Boston 91, at DETROIT 101
Apr.30 . . Boston 95, at DETROIT 102
May 2 . . DETROIT 100, at Boston 85

Chicago 3, Cleveland 2
Apr.28 . . CHICAGO 95, at Cleveland 88
Apr.30 . . Chicago 88, at CLEVELAND 96
May 3 . . Cleveland 94, at CHICAGO 101
May 5 . . CLEVELAND 108, at Chicago 105 (OT)
May 7 . . CHICAGO 101, at Cleveland 100

Milwaukee 3, Atlanta 2
Apr.27 . . Milwaukee 92, at ATLANTA 100
Apr.29 . . MILWAUKEE 108, at Atlanta 98
May 2 . . Atlanta 113, at MILWAUKEE 117 (OT)
May 5 . . ATLANTA 113, at Milwaukee 106 (OT)
May 7 . . MILWAUKEE 96, at Atlanta 92

LA Lakers 3, Portland 0
Apr.27 . . . . Portland 108, at LA LAKERS 128
Apr.30 . . . . Portland 105, at LA LAKERS 113
May 3 . . . . LA LAKERS 116, at Portland 108

Golden State 3, Utah 0
Apr.27 . . . . GOLDEN ST. 123, at Utah 119
Apr.29 . . . . GOLDEN ST. 99, at Utah 91
May 2 . . . . Utah 106, at GOLDEN ST. 120

Phoenix 3, Denver 0
Apr.28 . . . . Denver 103, at PHOENIX 104
Apr.30 . . . . Denver 114, at PHOENIX 132
May 2 . . . . PHOENIX 130, at Denver 121

Seattle 3, Houston 1
Apr.28 . . . . Houston 107, at SEATTLE 111
Apr.30 . . . . Houston 97, at SEATTLE 109
May 3 . . . . Seattle 107, at HOUSTON 126
May 5 . . . . SEATTLE 98, at Houston 96

CONFERENCE SEMIFINALS (Best of 7)

Chicago 4, New York 2
May 9 . . . . . CHICAGO 120, at New York 109 (OT)
May 11 . . . . Chicago 97, at NEW YORK 114
May 13 . . . . New York 88, at CHICAGO 111
May 14 . . . . New York 93, at CHICAGO 106
May 16 . . . . Chicago 114, at NEW YORK 121
May 19 . . . . New York 111, at CHICAGO 113

Detroit 4, Milwaukee 0
May 10 . . . . Milwaukee 80, at DETROIT 85
May 12 . . . . Milwaukee 92, at DETROIT 112
May 14 . . . . DETROIT 110, at Milwaukee 90
May 15 . . . . DETROIT 96, at Milwaukee 94

Phoenix 4, Golden State 1
May 6 . . . . Golden St. 103, at PHOENIX 130
May 9 . . . . GOLDEN ST. 127, at Phoenix 122
May 11 . . . . PHOENIX 113, at Golden St. 104
May 13 . . . . PHOENIX 135, at Golden St. 99
May 16 . . . . Golden St. 104, at PHOENIX 116

LA Lakers 4, Seattle 0
May 7 . . . . Seattle 102, at LA LAKERS 113
May 10 . . . . Seattle 108, at LA LAKERS 130
May 12 . . . . LA LAKERS 91, at Seattle 86
May 14 . . . . LA LAKERS 97, at Seattle 95

CONFERENCE FINALS (Best of 7)

Detroit 4, Chicago 2
May 21 . . . . CHICAGO 94, at Detroit 88
May 23 . . . . Chicago 91, at DETROIT 100
May 27 . . . . Detroit 97, at CHICAGO 99
May 29 . . . . DETROIT 86, at Chicago 80
May 31 . . . . Chicago 85, at DETROIT 94
June 2 . . . . . DETROIT 103, at Chicago 94

LA Lakers 4, Phoenix 0
May 20 . . . . . . Phoenix 119, at LA LAKERS 127
May 23 . . . . . . Phoenix 95, at LA LAKERS 101
May 26 . . . . . . LA LAKERS 110, at Phoenix 107
May 28 . . . . . . LA LAKERS 122, at Phoenix 117

NBA FINALS (Best of 7)

Detroit 4, LA Lakers 0
June 6 . . . . LA Lakers 97, at DETROIT 109
June 8 . . . . LA Lakers 105, at DETROIT 108
June 11 . . . . DETROIT 114, at LA Lakers 110
June 13 . . . . DETROIT 105, at LA Lakers 97

NBA Finals MVP

Joe Dumars, Detroit

Game 1—22 points, 7 assists, 2 turnovers, in 39 minutes; **Game 2**—33 points (26 in 1st half), 6 assists, no turnovers in 36 minutes; **Game 3**—31 points (21 in 3rd quarter, including 17 in a row), 5 assists, 2 steals, 3 turnovers in 35 minutes; **Game 4**—23 points (13-17 at foul line), 6 assists, 2 turnovers in 37 minutes.

NBA Finals Composite Box Scores

Detroit vs LA Lakers (4 games)

	GP	Reb	Ast	FG%	Pts	Avg
Joe Dumars........	4	7	24	.576	109	**27.3**
Isiah Thomas......	4	10	29	.485	85	**21.3**
Vinnie Johnson....	4	13	11	.600	68	**17.0**
James Edwards....	4	14	3	.444	36	**9.0**
Bill Laimbeer......	4	21	9	.545	32	**8.0**
Mark Aguirre......	4	24	6	.364	30	**7.5**
John Salley........	4	10	5	.684	30	**7.5**
Rick Mahorn......	4	21	4	.556	24	**6.0**
Dennis Rodman....	4	40	5	.467	20	**5.0**
John Long........	1	0	0	1.000	2	**2.0**
Fennis Dembo.....	1	0	0	—	0	**0.0**
Michael Williams ..	1	0	1	—	0	**0.0**

Totals	GP	Reb	Ast	FG%	Pts	Avg
Pistons...........	4	160	97	.527	436	**109.0**
LA Lakers	4	145	92	.465	409	**102.3**

LA Lakers vs Detroit (4 games)

	GP	Reb	Ast	FG%	Pts	Avg
James Worthy	4	17	14	.481	102	**25.5**
Kareem Abdul-Jabbar	4	20	7	.435	50	**12.5**
Michael Cooper ...	4	6	27	.378	48	**12.0**
Magic Johnson ...	3	11	24	.462	35	**11.7**
Tony Campbell ...	4	10	4	.625	44	**11.0**
Mychal Thompson..	4	19	3	.433	40	**10.0**
Orlando Woolridge	4	21	6	.611	38	**9.5**
A.C. Green	4	37	2	.440	35	**8.8**
David Rivers	3	3	5	.333	12	**4.0**
Jeff Lamp	4	1	0	.667	5	**1.3**
Mark McNamara ..	2	0	0	—	0	**0.0**
Unable to Play: Byron Scott (torn left harmstring)						

Totals	GP	Reb	Ast	FG%	Pts	Avg
Lakers	4	145	92	.465	409	**102.3**
Detroit...........	4	160	97	.527	436	**109.0**

1989 NBA Expansion Draft

Draft held June 15, 1989 to stock two new NBA franchises—the Orlando Magic and Minnesota Timberwolves—for the 1989-90 season.

Orlando Magic

Pick		Pos	Gm	Reb	Ast	Avg
1	Sidney Green, N.Y...	F	82	4.8	0.9	6.3
3	Reggie Theus, Atl....	G	81	3.0	4.7	15.8
5	Terry Catledge, Wash	F	79	7.2	0.9	10.4
7	Sam Vincent, Chicago	G	70	2.7	4.8	12.0
9	Otis Smith, Golden St	G	80	4.1	1.8	10.0
11	Scott Skiles, Indiana ..	G	80	1.9	4.9	6.8
13	Jerry Reynolds, Sea ..	G/F	56	1.8	1.1	7.6
15	Mark Acres, Boston ..	F/C	62	2.4	0.3	2.2
17	Morlon Wiley, Dallas..	G	51	0.9	1.5	2.2
19	Jim Farmer, Utah....	G	37	1.5	0.8	4.1
21	Keith Lee, New Jersey	F	57	4.5	0.7	4.8
23	Frank Johnson, Hous .	G	67	1.2	2.7	4.4

Minnesota Timberwolves

Pick		Pos	Gm	Reb	Ast	Avg
2	Rick Mahorn, Detroit .	F	72	6.9	0.8	7.3
4	Tyrone Corbin, Phoe ..	G/F	77	5.2	1.5	8.2
6	Steve Johnson, Port..	F/C	72	5.0	1.5	10.0
8	Brad Lohaus, Sacra .	C	77	3.3	0.9	6.5
10	David Rivers, Lakers .	G	47	0.9	2.3	2.9
12	Mark Davis, Milw*...	G	33	1.1	0.4	3.8
14	Scott Roth, San Ant ..	F	63	1.0	0.9	2.9
16	Shelton Jones, Phila..	F	49	2.3	0.8	4.9
18	Eric White, Clippers ..	F	38	1.8	0.4	4.2
20	Maurice Martin, Den .	G	Did not play			
22	Gunther Behnke, Cleve	C	Did not play			

*In addition, Minnesota received a 1989 2nd round draft pick (34th overall).

1989 NBA College Draft

First and second round picks at the 43rd annual NBA Draft held June 27, 1989 in New York City. Eligible undergraduates in **bold type**.

First Round

	Team	Player Selected
1	Sacramento	Pervis Ellison, Louisville, F
2	LA Clippers	Danny Ferry, Duke, F
3	San Antonio	Sean Elliott, Arizona, F
4	Miami	Glen Rice, Michigan, F
5	Charlotte	**J.R. Reid, North Carolina, F**
6	Chicago*	Stacey King, Oklahoma, C-F
7	Indiana	George McCloud, Florida St., G
8	Dallas	Randy White, Louisiana Tech, F
9	Washington	Tom Hammonds, Georgia Tech, F
10	Minnesota	Pooh Richardson, UCLA, G
11	Orlando	**Nick Anderson, Illinois, F**
12	New Jersey*	Mookie Blaylock, Oklahoma, G
13	Boston	Michael Smith, BYU, F
14	Golden St	Tim Hardaway, UTEP, G
15	Denver	Todd Lichti, Stanford, G
16	Seattle*	Dana Barros, Boston Col., G
17	Seattle*	**Shawn Kemp, Trinity Val.CC, F**
18	Chicago*	B.J. Armstrong, Iowa, G
19	Philadelphia*	Kenny Payne, Louisville, F
20	Chicago*	Jeff Sanders, Ga. Southern, F
21	Utah	Blue Edwards, E.Carolina, G
22	Portland*	Byron Irvin, Missouri, G
23	Atlanta	Roy Marble, Iowa, G
24	Phoenix	Anthony Cook, Arizona, F
25	Cleveland	John Morton, Seton Hall, G
26	LA Lakers	**Vlade Divac, Yugoslavia, C**
27	Detroit	Kenny Battle, Illinois, F

***Note:** the following No.1 picks were traded away—**#6** by New Jersey; **#12** by Portland; **#16** by Golden St.(acquired from Houston); **#17** by Philadelphia; **#18** by Seattle (acquired from Chicago); **#19** by Seattle; **#20** by Milwaukee; **#22** by New York.

NBA Finals, 1947-89

Although the National Basketball Association traces its first championship back to the 1946-47 season, the league was then called the Basketball Association of America (BAA). It did not become the NBA until after the 1948-49 season when the BAA and the National Basketball League (NBL) agreed to merge.

In the chart below, the Eastern finalists (representing the NBA Eastern Division from 1947-70, and the NBA Eastern Conference since 1971) are listed in capital LETTERS. Also, each NBA champion's wins and losses are noted in parentheses after the series score.

Year	Winner	Head Coach	Series	Loser	Head Coach
1947	PHILA.WARRIORS	Eddie Gottlieb	4-1 (WWWLW)	Chicago Stags	Harold Olsen
1948	Balt.Bullets	Buddy Jeannette	4-2 (LWWWLW)	PHILA.WARRIORS	Eddie Gottlieb
1949	Minn.Lakers	John Kundla	4-2 (WWWLLW)	WASH.CAPITOLS	Red Auerbach
1950	Minn.Lakers	John Kundla	4-2 (WLWWLW)	SYRACUSE	Al Cervi
1951	Rochester	Les Harrison	4-3 (WWWLLLW)	NEW YORK	Joe Lapchick
1952	Minn.Lakers	John Kundla	4-3 (WLWLWLW)	NEW YORK	Joe Lapchick
1953	Minn.Lakers	John Kundla	4-1 (LWWWW)	NEW YORK	Joe Lapchick
1954	Minn.Lakers	John Kundla	4-3 (WLWLWLW)	SYRACUSE	Al Cervi
1955	SYRACUSE	Al Cervi	4-3 (WWLLLWW)	Ft.Wayne Pistons	Charles Eckman
1956	PHILA.WARRIORS	George Senesky	4-1 (WLWWW)	Ft.Wayne Pistons	Charles Eckman
1957	BOSTON	Red Auerbach	4-3 (LWLWLWW)	St.Louis Hawks	Alex Hannum
1958	St.Louis Hawks	Alex Hannum	4-2 (WLWLWW)	BOSTON	Red Auerbach
1959	BOSTON	Red Auerbach	4-0	Minn.Lakers	John Kundla
1960	BOSTON	Red Auerbach	4-3 (WLWLWLW)	St.Louis Hawks	Ed Macauley
1961	BOSTON	Red Auerbach	4-1 (WWLW)	St.Louis Hawks	Paul Seymour
1962	BOSTON	Red Auerbach	4-3 (WLLLWLWW)	LA Lakers	Fred Schaus
1963	BOSTON	Red Auerbach	4-2 (WWLWLW)	LA Lakers	Fred Schaus
1964	BOSTON	Red Auerbach	4-1 (WWWLW)	SF Warriors	Alex Hannum
1965	BOSTON	Red Auerbach	4-1 (WWLWW)	LA Lakers	Fred Schaus
1966	BOSTON	Red Auerbach	4-3 (LWWWLLW)	LA Lakers	Fred Schaus
1967	PHILA.76ERS	Alex Hannum	4-2 (WWLWLW)	SF Warriors	Bill Sharman
1968	BOSTON	Bill Russell	4-2 (WLWLWW)	LA Lakers	B.van Breda Kolff
1969	BOSTON	Bill Russell	4-3 (LLWWLWW)	LA Lakers	B.van Breda Kolff
1970	NEW YORK	Red Holzman	4-3 (WLWLWLW)	LA Lakers	Joe Mullaney
1971	Milwaukee	Larry Costello	4-0	BALT.BULLETS	Gene Shue
1972	LA Lakers	Bill Sharman	4-1 (LWWWW)	NEW YORK	Red Holzman
1973	NEW YORK	Red Holzman	4-1 (LWWWW)	LA Lakers	Bill Sharman
1974	BOSTON	Tommy Heinsohn	4-3 (WLWLWLW)	Milwaukee	Larry Costello
1975	Gold.St.Warriors	Al Attles	4-0	WASH.BULLETS	K.C. Jones
1976	BOSTON	Tommy Heinsohn	4-2 (WWLLWW)	Phoenix	John MacLeod
1977	Portland	Jack Ramsay	4-2 (LLWWWW)	PHILA.76ERS	Gene Shue
1978	WASH.BULLETS	Dick Motta	4-3 (LWLWLWW)	Seattle	Lenny Wilkens
1979	Seattle	Lenny Wilkens	4-1 (LWWWW)	WASH.BULLETS	Dick Motta
1980	LA Lakers	Paul Westhead	4-2 (WLWLWW)	PHILA.76ERS	Billy Cunningham
1981	BOSTON	Bill Fitch	4-2 (WLWLWW)	Houston	Del Harris
1982	LA Lakers	Pat Riley	4-2 (WLWWLW)	PHILA 76ERS	Billy Cunningham
1983	PHILA.76ERS	Billy Cunningham	4-0	LA Lakers	Pat Riley
1984	BOSTON	K.C. Jones	4-3 (LWLWLWW)	LA Lakers	Pat Riley
1985	LA Lakers	Pat Riley	4-2 (LWWLWW)	BOSTON	K.C. Jones
1986	BOSTON	K.C. Jones	4-2 (WWLWLW)	Houston	Bill Fitch
1987	LA Lakers	Pat Riley	4-2 (WWLWLW)	BOSTON	K.C. Jones
1988	LA Lakers	Pat Riley	4-3 (LWWLLWW)	DETROIT PISTONS	Chuck Daly
1989	DETROIT PISTONS	Chuck Daly	4-0	LA Lakers	Pat Riley

Note: Four Finalists were led by player-coaches: **1948**—Buddy Jeannette (guard) of Baltimore; **1950**—Al Cervi (guard) of Syracuse; **1968**—Bill Russell (center) of Boston; **1969**—Bill Russell (center) of Boston.

NBA Playoff MVPs

Year	Most Valuable Player	Year	Most Valuable Player
1969	Jerry West, LA Lakers, G	1979	Dennis Johnson, Seattle, G
1970	Willis Reed, New York, C	1980	Magic Johnson, LA Lakers, G/C
1971	Kareem Abdul-Jabbar, Milwaukee, C	1981	Cedric Maxwell, Boston, F
1972	Wilt Chamberlain, LA Lakers, C	1982	Magic Johnson, LA Lakers, G
1973	Willis Reed, New York, C	1983	Moses Malone, Philadelphia, C
1974	John Havlicek, Boston, F	1984	Larry Bird, Boston, F
1975	Rick Barry, Golden State, F	1985	Kareem Abdul-Jabbar, LA Lakers, C
1976	Jo Jo White, Boston, G	1986	Larry Bird, Boston, F
1977	Bill Walton, Portland, C	1987	Magic Johnson, LA Lakers, G
1978	Wes Unseld, Washington, C	1988	James Worthy, LA Lakers, F
		1989	Joe Dumars, Detroit, G

Here is what the current 27 teams in the National Basketball Association have to show for the years they have put in as members of the National Basketball League (NBL), Basketball Association of America (BAA), the NBA, and the American Basketball Association (ABA). League titles are noted by year won.

Eastern Conference

	First Season	League Titles	Franchise Stops
Atlanta Hawks..........1946-47 (NBL)		1 NBA (1958)	Tri-Cities (1946-51)
			Milwaukee (1951-55)
			St.Louis (1955-68)
			Atlanta (1968-)
Boston Celtics ....1946-47 (BAA)		16 NBA (1957,59-66,68-69 74,76,81,84,86)	Boston (1946-)
Chicago Bulls ....1966-67 (NBA)		None	Chicago (1966-)
Cleveland Cavaliers......1970-71 (NBA)		None	Cleveland (1970-74)
Detroit Pistons..........1941-42 (NBL)		2 NBL (1944-45) 1 NBA (1989)	Ft.Wayne,IN (1941-57)
			Detroit (1957-78)
			Pontiac,MI (1978-88)
			Auburn Hills,MI (1988-)
Indiana Pacers ....1967-68 (ABA)		3 ABA (1970,72-73)	Indianapolis (1967-)
Miami Heat ....1988-89 (NBA)		None	Miami (1988-)
Milwaukee Bucks ....1968-69 (NBA)		1 NBA (1971)	Milwaukee (1968-)
New Jersey Nets ....1967-68 (ABA)		2 ABA (1974,76)	Paramus,NJ (1967-68)
			Commack,NY (1968-69)
			W.Hempstead,NY (1969-71)
			Uniondale,NY (1971-77)
			Piscataway,NJ (1977-81)
			E.Rutherford,NJ (1981-)
New York Knicks ....1946-47 (BAA)		2 NBA (1970,73)	New York (1946-)
Orlando Magic ....1989-90 (NBA)		None	Orlando,FL (1989-)
Philadelphia 76ers.......1949-50 (NBA)		3 NBA (1955,67,83)	Syracus,NY (1949-63)
			Philadelphia (1963-)
Washington Bullets ......1961-62 (NBA)		1 NBA (1978)	Chicago (1961-63)
			Baltimore (1963-73)
			Landover,MD (1973-)

Note: The Tri-Cities Blackhawks represented Moline and Rock Island, Ill., and Davenport, Iowa.

Western Conference

	First Season	League Titles	Franchise Stops
Charlotte Hornets ....1988-89 (NBA)		None	Charlotte (1988-)
Dallas Mavericks ....1980-81 (NBA)		None	Dallas (1980-)
Denver Nuggets ....1967-68 (ABA)		None	Denver (1967-)
Golden St. Warriors......1946-47 (BAA)		1 BAA (1947) 2 NBA (1956,75)	Philadelphia (1946-62)
			San Francisco (1962-71)
			Oakland (1971-)
Houston Rockets ....1967-68 (NBA)		None	San Diego (1967-71)
			Houston (1971-)
LA Clippers ....1970-71 (NBA)		None	Buffalo (1970-78)
			San Diego (1978-84)
			Los Angeles (1984-)
LA Lakers ....1947-48 (NBL)		1 NBL (1947) 1 BAA (1949) 10 NBA (1950,52-54,72, 80,82,85,87-88)	Minneapolis (1947-60)
			Los Angeles (1960-67)
			Inglewood,CA (1967-)
Minn. Timberwolves .....1989-90 (NBA)		None	Minneapolis (1989-)
Phoenix Suns............1968-69 (NBA)		None	Phoenix (1968-)
Port.Trail Blazers ....1970-71 (NBA)		1 NBA (1977)	Portland (1970-)
Sacramento Kings ....1945-46 (NBL)		1 NBL (1946) 1 NBA (1951)	Rochester,NY (1945-58)
			Cincinnati (1958-72)
			KC-Omaha (1972-75)
			Kansas City (1975-85)
			Sacramento (1985-)
San Antonio Spurs ....1967-68 (ABA)		None	Dallas (1967-73)
			San Antonio (1973-)
Seattle SuperSonics ......1967-68 (NBA)		1 NBA (1979)	Seattle (1967-)
Utah Jazz ....1974-75 (NBA)		None	New Orleans (1974-79)
			Salt Lake City (1979-)

NBA Head Coaches

All-Time Winning Percentages

NBA head coaches with at least 400 wins (including playoffs) through the 1988-89 season. Active coaches in **bold type**.

		Yrs'	W	L	Pct	Playoff W-L
1	**Pat Riley**	8	568	217	**.724**	98-42
2	Billy Cunningham . .	8	520	235	**.689**	66-39
3	K.C.Jones	8	542	247	**.687**	79-54
4	Red Auerbach	20	1037	479	**.662**	99-69
5	Tommy Heinsohn . .	9	474	296	**.616**	47-33
6	**Don Nelson**	12	629	433	**.592**	46-50
7	Larry Costello	10	467	323	**.591**	37-23
8	John Kundla	11	483	337	**.589**	60-35
9	**Doug Moe**	12	599	500	**.545**	33-47
10	Red Holzman	18	754	651	**.537**	58-47
11	Alex Hannum	12	516	446	**.536**	45-34
12	**Lenny Wilkens** . . .	16	724	645	**.529**	41-38
13	Jack Ramsay	21	908	841	**.519**	44-58
14	**John MacLeod** . . .	16	717	667	**.518**	47-51
	Al Attles	14	588	548	**.518**	31-30
16	Bill Fitch	18	811	757	**.517**	49-43
17	Dick Motta	19	864	820	**.513**	56-70
18	**Cotton Fitzsimmons**	16	663	693	**.489**	20-32
19	Gene Shue	22	814	908	**.473**	30-47

Note: The NBA does not recognize ABA coaching records. If it did, Alex Hannum would move down to 12th place with 634 wins, 580 losses, a .522 winning percentage, and a 49-42 playoff record.

Where They Coached

Riley—LA Lakers (1981-); **Cunningham**—Philadelphia (1977-85); **Jones**—Washington (1973-76), Boston (1983-88); **Auerbach**—Washington (1946-49); Tri-Cities (1949-50); Boston (1950-66); **Heinsohn**—Boston (1969-77); **Nelson**—Milwaukee (1976-87), Golden St.(1988--); **Costello**—Milwaukee (1968-76), Chicago (1978-79); **Kundla**—Minneapolis (1948-57,58-59); **Moe**—San Antonio (1976-80), Denver (1981--); **Holzman**—Milwaukee-St.Louis (1954-57), NY Knicks (1968-77,78-82).

Hannum—St.Louis (1957-58), Syracuse (1960-63), San Francisco (1963-66), Philadelphia (1966-68), Houston (1970-71); **Wilkens**—Seattle (1969-72), Portland (1974-76), Seattle (1977-85), Cleveland (1986--); **Ramsay**—Philadelphia (1968-72), Buffalo (1972-76), Portland (1976-86), Indiana (1986-88); **MacLeod**—Phoenix (1973-87), Dallas (1987--); **Attles**—Golden St.(1970-80,80-83); **Fitch**—Cleveland (1970-79), Boston (1979-83), Houston (1983-88); **Motta**—Chicago (1968-76), Washington (1976-80), Dallas (1980-87); **Fitzsimmons**—Phoenix (1970-72), Atlanta (1972-76), Buffalo (1977-78), Kansas City (1978-84), San Antonio (1984-86), Phoenix (1988--); **Shue**—Baltimore (1967-73), Philadelphia (1973-77), San Diego (1978-80), Washington (1980-86), LA Clippers (1987-89).

All-Time Wins

NBA head coaches with at least 500 overall victories through the 1988-89 season. Listed are regular season, playoff and overall wins. Active coaches in **bold type**.

		Regular	Playoffs	Total
1	Red Auerbach	938	99	**1,037**
2	Jack Ramsay	864	44	**908**
3	Dick Motta	808	56	**864**
4	Gene Shue	784	30	**814**
5	Bill Fitch	762	49	**811**
6	Red Holzman	696	58	**754**
7	**Lenny Wilkens**	683	41	**724**
8	**John MacLeod**	670	47	**717**
9	**Cotton Fitzsimmons** .	643	20	**663**
10	**Don Nelson**	583	46	**629**
11	**Doug Moe**	566	33	**599**
12	Al Attles	557	31	**588**
13	**Pat Riley**	470	98	**568**
14	K.C.Jones	463	79	**542**
15	Billy Cunningham	454	66	**520**
16	Alex Hannum	471	45	**516**

Active NBA Head Coaches
Most Wins

Current NBA head coaches' career records (including playoffs) through the 1988-89 season.

		Yrs	W	L	Pct
1	Lenny Wilkens, Cleveland . .	16	**724**	645	.529
2	John MacLeod, Dallas	16	**717**	667	.518
3	Cotton Fitzsimmons, Phoe . .	16	**663**	693	.489
4	Don Nelson, Golden St	12	**629**	433	.592
5	Doug Moe, Denver	12	**599**	500	.545
6	Pat Riley, LA Lakers	8	**568**	217	.724
7	Chuck Daly, Detroit	7	**366**	240	.604
8	Mike Fratello, Atlanta	7	**301**	234	.563
9	Del Harris, Milwaukee	6	**252**	285	.469
10	Larry Brown, San Antonio . .	6	**246**	232	.515
11	Bernie Bickerstaff, Seat	4	**173**	182	.487
12	Jerry Sloan, Utah	4	**136**	153	.464
13	Matt Guokas, Orlando	3	**127**	97	.567
14	Jim Lynam, Philadelphia . . .	5	**114**	153	.427
15	Don Chaney, Houston	4	**99**	172	.365
16	Willis Reed, New Jersey	4	**84**	128	.396
17	Wes Unseld, Washington . . .	2	**72**	70	.507
18	Jerry Reynolds, Sacra	3	**49**	93	.345
19	Jim Rodgers, Boston	1	**42**	40	.512
20	Bill Musselman, Minnesota . .	2	**27**	67	.287
21	Dick Versace, Indiana	1	**22**	33	.400
22	Dick Harter, Charlotte	1	**20**	62	.244
23	Ron Rothstein, Miami	1	**15**	67	.183
24	Rick Adelman, Portland	1	**14**	24	.368
25	Don Casey, LA Clippers	1	**11**	33	.250
26	Phil Jackson, Chicago	0	**0**	0	.000
27	Stu Jackson, New York	0	**0**	0	.000

Note: The NBA does not recognize ABA coaching records. If it did, Larry Brown would move up to 7th place with 384 wins, 288 losses, and a .572 winning percentage.

NBA Regular Season Leaders
CAREER

Scoring (NBA only)

NBA players with at least 18,000 points through the 1988-89 regular season. Active players in **bold type**.

		Yrs	Gms	Points	Avg
1	Kareem Abdul-Jabbar	20	1,560	**38,387**	24.6
2	Wilt Chamberlain	14	1,045	**31,419**	30.1
3	Elvin Hayes	16	1,303	**27,313**	21.0
4	Oscar Robertson	14	1,040	**26,710**	25.7
5	John Havlicek	16	1,270	**26,395**	20.8
6	Jerry West	14	932	**25,192**	27.0
7	**Alex English**	13	1,034	**23,417**	22.6
8	**Moses Malone**	13	1,001	**23,340**	23.3
9	Elgin Baylor	14	846	**23,149**	27.4
10	**Adrian Dantley**	13	900	**22,458**	25.0
11	Hal Greer	15	1,122	**21,586**	19.2
12	Walt Bellamy	14	1,043	**20,941**	20.1
13	Bob Pettit	11	792	**20,880**	26.4
14	George Gervin	10	791	**20,708**	26.2
15	Dolph Schayes	16	1,059	**19,249**	18.2
16	Bob Lanier	14	959	**19,248**	20.1
17	Gail Goodrich	14	1,031	**19,181**	18.6
18	Chet Walker	13	1,032	**18,831**	18.2
19	Bob McAdoo	14	852	**18,787**	22.1
20	Rick Barry	10	794	**18,395**	23.2
21	Julius Erving	11	836	**18,364**	22.0
22	Dave Bing	12	901	**18,327**	20.3

Scoring (NBA-ABA combined)

Combined list of NBA and ABA players with at least 25,000 points through the 1988-89 regular season. Active players in **bold type**.

		Yrs	Gms	Points	Avg
1	Kareem Abdul-Jabbar	20	1,560	**38,387**	24.6
2	Wilt Chamberlain	14	1,045	**31,419**	30.1
3	Julius Erving	16	1,243	**30,026**	24.2
4	Dan Issel	15	1,218	**27,482**	22.6
5	Elvin Hayes	16	1,303	**27,313**	21.0
6	Oscar Robertson	14	1,040	**26,710**	25.7
7	George Gervin	14	1,060	**26,595**	25.1
8	John Havlicek	16	1,270	**26,395**	20.8
9	**Moses Malone**	15	1,127	**25,511**	22.6
10	Rick Barry	14	1,020	**25,279**	24.8
11	Jerry West	14	932	**25,192**	27.0

Scoring Average

NBA players with a career scoring average of at least 25.0 points per game through the 1988-89 regular season. Minimum of 400 games or 10,000 points. Active players in **bold type**.

		Yrs	Gms	Points	Avg
1	**Michael Jordan**	5	345	11,263	**32.6**
2	Wilt Chamberlain	14	1,045	31,419	**30.1**
3	Elgin Baylor	14	846	23,149	**27.4**
4	Jerry West	14	932	25,192	**27.0**
5	Bob Pettit	11	792	20,880	**26.4**
6	George Gervin	10	791	20,708	**26.2**
7	**Dominique Wilkins**	7	559	14,557	**26.0**
8	Oscar Robertson	14	1,040	26,710	**25.7**
9	**Larry Bird**	10	717	17,899	**25.0**
10	**Adrian Dantley**	13	900	22,458	**25.0**

Field Goals

NBA players with at least 9,000 field goals made through the 1988-89 regular season. Active players in **bold type**.

		Yrs	FGA	FGM	Pct
1	Kareem Abdul-Jabbar	20	28,307	**15,837**	.559
2	Wilt Chamberlain	14	23,497	**12,681**	.540
3	Elvin Hayes	16	24,272	**10,976**	.452
4	John Havlicek	16	23,900	**10,513**	.440
5	**Alex English**	13	19,009	**9,702**	.510
6	Oscar Robertson	14	19,620	**9,508**	.485
7	Jerry West	14	19,032	**9,016**	.474

Free Throws

NBA players with at least 6,000 free throws made through the 1988-89 regular season. Active players in **bold type**.

		Yrs	FTA	FTM	Pct
1	Oscar Robertson	14	9,185	**7,694**	.838
2	**Moses Malone**	13	9,403	**7,197**	.765
3	Jerry West	14	8,801	**7,160**	.814
4	Dolph Schayes	16	8,273	**6,979**	.844
5	Kareem Abdul-Jabbar	20	9,304	**6,712**	.721
6	**Adrian Dantley**	13	8,071	**6,614**	.819
7	Bob Pettit	11	8,119	**6,182**	.761
7	Wilt Chamberlain	14	11,862	**6,057**	.511

Assists

NBA players with at least 6,000 assists through the 1988-89 regular season. Active players in **bold type**.

		Yrs	Gm	Asst	Avg
1	Oscar Robertson	14	1,040	**9,887**	9.5
2	**Magic Johnson**	10	716	**8,025**	11.2
3	Lenny Wilkens	15	1,077	**7,211**	6.7
4	Bob Cousy	14	924	**6,955**	7.5
5	Guy Rodgers	12	892	**6,917**	7.8
6	Nate Archibald	13	876	**6,476**	7.4
7	Norm Nixon	10	768	**6,386**	8.3
8	Jerry West	14	932	**6,238**	6.7
9	**Isiah Thomas**	8	635	**6,220**	9.8
10	**John Lucas**	13	879	**6,216**	7.1
11	**Maurice Cheeks**	11	853	**6,212**	7.3
12	John Havlicek	16	1,270	**6,114**	4.8

Rebounds

NBA players with at least 13,000 rebounds through the 1988-89 regular season. Active players in **bold type**.

		Yrs	Gm	Reb	Avg
1	Wilt Chamberlain	14	1,045	**23,924**	22.9
2	Bill Russell	13	963	**21,620**	22.5
3	Kareem Abdul-Jabbar	20	1,560	**17,440**	11.2
4	Elvin Hayes	16	1,303	**16,279**	12.5
5	Nate Thurmond	14	964	**14,464**	15.0
6	Walt Bellamy	14	1,043	**14,241**	13.7
7	Wes Unseld	13	984	**13,769**	14.0
8	**Moses Malone**	13	1,001	**13,671**	13.7

NBA Career Leaders (Continued)

Personal Fouls

NBA players with at least 3,500 personal fouls through the 1988-89 regular season.

		Yrs	Gm	Fouls	Disq
1	Kareem Abdul-Jabbar . . .	20	1,560	**4,657**	48
2	Elvin Hayes	16	1,303	**4,193**	53
3	Hal Greer	15	1,122	**3,855**	72
4	Dolph Schayes	16	1,059	**3,664**	90
5	Walt Bellamy	14	1,043	**3,536**	58

Years Played

NBA players with at least 15 years played through the 1988-89 regular season.

		Yrs	Career	Games
1	Kareem Abdul-Jabbar	**20**	1970-89	1,560
2	Dolph Schayes	**16**	1949-64	1,059
	John Havlicek	**16**	1963-78	1,270
	Paul Silas	**16**	1965-80	1,254
	Elvin Hayes	**16**	1969-84	1,303
6	Hal Greer	**15**	1959-73	1,122
	Lenny Wilkens	**15**	1961-75	1,077

SINGLE SEASON

Scoring Average

NBA players with a single season scoring average of at least 35 points per game (through the 1988-89 season).

	Season	Avg
Wilt Chamberlain, Philadelphia	1961-62	**50.4**
Wilt Chamberlain, San Francisco . .	1962-63	**44.8**
Wilt Chamberlain, Philadelphia	1960-61	**38.4**
Elgin Baylor, Los Angeles	1961-62	**38.3**
Wilt Chamberlain, Philadelphia	1959-60	**37.6**
Michael Jordan, Chicago	1986-87	**37.1**
Wilt Chamberlain, San Francisco . .	1963-64	**36.9**
Rick Barry, San Francisco	1966-67	**35.6**
Michael Jordan, Chicago	1987-88	**35.0**

Field Goal Percentage

Top 5 NBA single season field goal percentages through the 1988-89 regular season.

	Season	Pct.
Wilt Chamberlain, Los Angeles	1972-73	**.727**
Wilt Chamberlain, San Francisco . .	1966-67	**.683**
Artis Gilmore, Chicago	1980-81	**.670**
Artis Gilmore, Chicago	1981-82	**.652**
Wilt Chamberlain, Los Angeles	1971-72	**.649**

Free Throw Percentage

Top 5 NBA single season free throw percentages through the 1988-89 regular season.

	Season	Pct.
Calvin Murphy, Houston	1980-81	**.958**
Rick Barry, Houston	1978-79	**.947**
Ernie DiGregorio, Buffalo	1976-77	**.945**
Ricky Sobers, Chicago	1980-81	**.9352**
Rick Barry, Houston	1979-80	**.9346**

3-Pt Field Goal Pct.

Top 5 NBA single season 3-point field goal percentages through the 1988-89 regular season (compiled since 1979-80).

	Season	Pct.
Jon Sundvold, Miami	1988-89	**.522**
Craig Hodges, Milw-Phoenix	1987-88	**.491**
Mark Price, Cleveland	1987-88	**.486**
Kiki Vandeweghe, Portland	1986-87	**.481**
Detlef Schrempf, Dallas	1986-87	**.4782**
Dale Ellis, Seattle	1988-89	**.4778**

Assist Average

Top 5 NBA single season assists-per-game averages through the 1988-89 regular season.

	Season	Avg
Isiah Thomas, Detroit	1984-85	**13.9**
John Stockton, Utah	1987-88	**13.8**
John Stockton, Utah	1988-89	**13.6**
Kevin Porter, Detroit	1978-79	**13.4**
Magic Johnson, LA Lakers	1983-84	**13.1**

Rebound Average

Top 5 NBA single season rebounds-per-game averages through the 1988-89 regular season (compiled since 1950-51).

	Season	Avg
Wilt Chamberlain, Philadelphia . .	1960-61	**27.2**
Wilt Chamberlain, Philadelphia . .	1959-60	**27.0**
Wilt Chamberlain, Philadelphia . .	1961-62	**25.7**
Bill Russell, Boston	1963-64	**24.7**
Wilt Chamberlain, Philadelphia . .	1965-66	**24.6**

Blocked Shots Average

Top 5 NBA single season blocked shots-per-game averages through the 1988-89 regular season (compiled since 1973-74).

	Season	Avg
Mark Eaton, Utah	1984-85	**5.56**
Manute Bol, Washington	1985-86	**4.96**
Elmore Smith, LA Lakers	1973-74	**4.85**
Mark Eaton, Utah	1985-86	**4.61**
Manute Bol, Golden St	1988-89	**4.31**

Steals Average

Top 5 NBA single season steals-per-game averages through the 1988-89 regular season (compiled since 1973-74).

	Season	Avg
Alvin Robertson, San Antonio	1985-86	**3.67**
Don Buse, Indiana	1976-77	**3.47**
Magic Johnson, LA Lakers	1980-81	**3.43**
Michael Ray Richardson, New York	1979-80	**3.23**
Alvin Robertson, San Antonio	1986-87	**3.21**

BEST GAMES

Points

	Date	FG-FT—	Pts
Wilt Chamberlain, Phi.vs NY	3/2/62	36-38 —	**100**
Wilt Chamberlain, Phi.vs LA*	12/8/61	31-16 —	**78**
Wilt Chamberlain, Phi.vs Chi	1/13/62	29-15 —	**73**
Wilt Chamberlain, SF at NY	11/16/62	29-15 —	**73**
David Thompson, Den.at Det	4/9/78	28-17 —	**73**
Wilt Chamberlain, SF at LA	11/3/62	29-14 —	**72**
Elgin Baylor, LA at NY	11/15/60	28-15 —	**71**
Wilt Chamberlain, SF at Syr	3/10/63	27-16 —	**70**

*Triple overtime.

Field Goals

	Date	FGA	FGM
Wilt Chamberlain, Phi.vs NY	3/2/62	63	**36**
Wilt Chamberlain, Phi.vs LA*	12/8/61	62	**31**
Wilt Chamberlain, Phi.at Chi	12/16/67	40	**30**
Rick Barry, Golden St.vs Port	2/26/74	45	**30**
Four players tied with 29.			

*Triple overtime.

Free Throws

	Date	FTA	FTM
Wilt Chamberlain, Phila.vs NY	3/2/62	32	**28**
Adrian Dantley, Utah vs Hou.*	1/4/84	29	**28**
Adrian Dantley, Utah vs Den	11/25/83	31	**27**

3-Pt Field Goals

	Date	No
Rick Barry, Houston vs Utah	2/9/80	8
John Roche, Denver vs Seattle	1/9/82	8
Michael Adams, Denver vs Milw	1/21/89	8

Assists

	Date	No
Kevin Porter, New Jersey vs Houston	2/24/78	**29**
Bob Cousy, Boston vs Minneapolis	2/27/59	**28**
Guy Rodgers, San Fran.vs St.Louis	3/14/63	**28**
Geoff Huston, Cleveland vs Gold.St	1/27/82	**27**
John Stockton, Utah vs Portland	4/14/88	**26**

Rebounds

	Date	No
Wilt Chamberlain, Phila.vs Boston	11/24/60	**55**
Bill Russell, Boston vs Syracuse	2/5/60	**51**
Bill Russell, Boston vs Phila	11/16/57	**49**
Bill Russell, Boston vs Detroit	3/11/65	**49**

Blocked Shots

	Date	No
Elmore Smith, LA vs Portland	10/28/73	**17**
Manute Bol, Washington vs Atlanta	1/25/86	**15**
Manute Bol, Washington vs Indiana	2/26/87	**15**

Steals

	Date	No
Larry Kenon, San Antonio vs KC	2/9/80	**11**

11 players tied with 10 steals in one game, including Alvin Robertson of San Antonio (3 times).

NBA Playoff Leaders
CAREER

Scoring

NBA players with at least 2,200 points through the 1989 playoffs. Active players in **bold type.**

		Yrs	Gm	Points	Avg
1	Kareem Abdul-Jabbar	18	237	**5,762**	24.3
2	Jerry West	13	153	**4,457**	29.1
3	John Havlicek	13	172	**3,776**	22.0
4	Elgin Baylor	12	134	**3,623**	27.0
5	Wilt Chamberlain	13	160	**3,607**	22.5
6	**Larry Bird**	9	145	**3,559**	24.5
7	Julius Erving	11	141	**3,088**	21.9
8	**Dennis Johnson**	12	175	**3,047**	17.4
9	**Magic Johnson**	10	158	**2,999**	19.0
10	Sam Jones	12	154	**2,909**	18.9
11	Bill Russell	13	165	**2,673**	16.2
12	**Kevin McHale**	9	139	**2,603**	18.7
13	**Robert Parish**	10	149	**2,380**	16.0
14	**James Worthy**	6	111	**2,356**	21.2
15	Bob Pettit	9	88	**2,240**	25.5

Scoring Average

NBA players with a career scoring average of at least 25.0 points per game through the 1989 playoffs. Minimum of 25 games or 625 points. Active players in **bold type.**

		Yrs	Gms	Points	Avg
1	**Michael Jordan**	5	37	1,309	**35.4**
2	Jerry West	13	153	4,457	**29.1**
3	**Akeem Olajuwon**	5	43	1,186	**27.6**
4	**Bernard King**	4	25	679	**27.2**
5	Elgin Baylor	12	134	3,623	**27.0**
6	George Gervin	9	59	1,592	**27.0**
7	**Dominique Wilkins**	6	43	1,151	**26.8**
8	Bob Pettit	9	88	2,240	**25.5**

Field Goals

NBA players with at least 1,400 field goals made through the 1989 playoffs.

		Yrs	FGA	FGM	Pct
1	Kareem Abdul-Jabbar	18	4,422	**2,356**	.533
2	Jerry West	13	3,460	**1,622**	.469
3	John Havlicek	13	3,329	**1,451**	.436
4	Wilt Chamberlain	13	2,728	**1,425**	.522

Free Throws

NBA players with at least 800 free throws made through the 1989 playoffs. Active players in **bold type.**

		Yrs	FTA	FTM	Pct
1	Jerry West	13	1,507	**1,213**	.805
2	Kareem Abdul-Jabbar	18	1,452	**1,077**	.742
3	John Havlicek	13	1,046	**874**	.836
4	Elgin Baylor	12	1,101	**847**	.769
5	**Larry Bird**	9	925	**825**	.892
6	**Magic Johnson**	10	984	**813**	.826

Assists

NBA players with at least 900 assists through the 1989 playoffs. Active players in **bold type.**

		Yrs	Gms	Asst	Avg
1	**Magic Johnson**	10	158	**1,965**	12.4
2	**Dennis Johnson**	12	175	**978**	5.6
3	Jerry West	13	153	**970**	6.3
4	Bob Cousy	13	109	**937**	8.6
5	**Larry Bird**	9	145	**932**	6.4

Rebounds

NBA players with at least 1,700 rebounds through the 1989 playoffs.

	Yrs	Gm	Reb	Avg
1 Bill Russell	13	165	**4,104**	24.9
2 Wilt Chamberlain	13	160	**3,913**	24.5
3 Kareem Abdul-Jabbar . .	18	237	**2,481**	10.5
4 Wes Unseld	12	119	**1,777**	14.9
5 Elgin Baylor	12	134	**1,725**	12.9

Personal Fouls

NBA players with at least 520 personal fouls through the 1989 playoffs. Active players in **bold type**.

	Yrs	Gm	Fouls	Disq
1 Kareem Abdul-Jabbar . .	18	237	**797**	7
2 **Dennis Johnson**	12	175	**558**	7
3 Bill Russell	13	165	**546**	8
4 **Robert Parish**	10	149	**522**	15

Years Played

NBA players with at least 13 years' playoff experience through 1989.

	Yrs		Yrs
Kareem Abdul-Jabbar .	18	Hal Greer	13
Dolph Schayes	15	John Havlicek	13
Paul Silas	14	Bill Russell	13
Wilt Chamberlain	13	Chet Walker	13
Bob Cousy	13	Jerry West . . :	13

Games Played

NBA players with at least 150 games through the 1989 playoffs. Active players in **bold type**.

	Gms		Gms
Kareem Abdul-Jabbar	237	Wilt Chamberlain . .	160
Dennis Johnson	175	Magic Johnson	159
John Havlicek	172	Sam Jones	154
Bill Russell	165	Jerry West	153
Paul Silas	163	Don Nelson	150

BEST GAMES

Points

	Date	FG-FT—Pts
Michael Jordan, Chi.at Bos* . .	4/20/86	22 - 19— **63**
Elgin Baylor, LA at Boston	4/14/62	22 - 17— **61**
Wilt Chamberlain, Phi.vs Syr . .	3/22/62	22 - 12— **56**
Rick Barry, SF vs Phi	4/18/67	22 - 11— **55**
Michael Jordan, Chi.vs Clev . .	5/1/88	24 - 7— **55**

*Double overtime.

Field Goals

	Date	FGA	FGM
Wilt Chamberlain, Phi.vs Syr . . .	3/14/60	42	**24**
John Havlicek, Boston vs Atl . . .	4/1/73	36	**24**
Michael Jordan, Chi. vs Clev . . .	5/1/88	45	**24**

Seven players tied with 22.

Free Throws

	Date	FTA	FTM
Bob Cousy, Boston vs Syr†	3/21/53	32	**30**
Michael Jordan, Chi. vs NY	5/14/89	28	**23**
Oscar Robertson, Cinn.at Bos . .	4/10/63	22	**21**
Bob Cousy, Boston vs Syr*	3/17/54	25	**20**
Jerry West, LA at Detroit	4/3/62	23	**20**
Jerry West, LA vs Baltimore . . .	4/5/65	21	**20**

†Four overtimes. *One overtime.

3-Pt Field Goals

	Date	No
Michael Cooper, Lakers vs Boston	6/4/87	**6**
Michael Adams, Denver at Phoenix	4/30/89	**6**
Mike Bratz, Phoenix at LA	4/8/80	**5**
Brad Davis, Dallas at Utah	4/25/86	**5**
Craig Hodges, Milwaukee at Phila	5/9/86	**5**
Larry Bird, Boston at Milwaukee	5/18/86	**5**
Danny Ainge, Boston vs LA Lakers	6/11/87	**5**

Assists

	Date	No
Magic Johnson, Lakers vs Phoenix	5/15/84	**24**
John Stockton, Utah at LA Lakers	5/17/88	**24**
Magic Johnson, LA Lakers at Port	5/3/85	**23**
Doc Rivers, Atlanta vs Boston	5/16/88	**22**
Magic Johnson, Lakers vs Boston	6/3/84	**21**

Rebounds

	Date	No
Wilt Chamberlain, Phila.vs Boston	4/5/67	**41**
Bill Russell, Boston vs Phila	3/23/58	**40**
Bill Russell, Boston vs St.Louis	3/29/60	**40**
Bill Russell, Boston vs LA*	4/18/62	**40**

Three players tied with 39.

*One overtime.

Blocked Shots

	Date	No
Mark Eaton, Utah vs Houston	4/26/85	**10**
Kareem Abdul-Jabbar, LA vs Gold.St . .	4/22/77	**9**
Manute Bol, Washington at Phila	4/18/86	**9**

13 players tied with 8.

Steals

	Date	No
Rick Barry, Golden St.vs Seattle	4/14/75	**8**
Lionel Hollins, Portland at LA	5/8/77	**8**
Maurice Cheeks, Phila.vs NJ	4/11/79	**8**
Craig Hodges, Milwaukee at Phila	5/9/86	**8**

Eight players tied with 7.

NBA FINALS

Scoring

Series		Year	Pts	Avg
4-Gm	Rick Barry, G.St.vs Wash	1975	**118**	29.5
5-Gm	Jerry West, LA vs Boston	1965	**169**	33.8
6-Gm	Rick Barry, SF vs Phila	1967	**245**	40.8
7-Gm	Elgin Baylor, LA vs Boston	1962	**284**	40.6

Field Goals

Series		Year	No
4-Gm	K.Abdul-Jabbar, Milw.vs Bal	1971	**46**
5-Gm	Wilt Chamberlain, SF vs Boston	1964	**62**
6-Gm	Rick Barry, SF vs Phila	1967	**94**
7-Gm	Elgin Baylor, LA vs Boston	1962	**101**

Free Throws

Series		Year	No
4-Gm	Phil Chenier, Wash.vs Golden St	1975	**34**
5-Gm	Jerry West, LA vs Boston	1965	**51**
6-Gm	George Mikan, Minn.vs Syr.	1950	**67**
7-Gm	Elgin Baylor, LA vs Boston	1962	**82**

Assists

Series		Year	No
4-Gm	Bob Cousy, Boston vs Minn.	1959	**51**
5-Gm	Bob Cousy, Boston vs St.Louis	1961	**53**
6-Gm	Magic Johnson, LA vs Boston	1985	**84**
7-Gm	Magic Johnson, LA vs Boston	1984	**95**

Rebounds

Series		Year	No
4-Gm	Bill Russell, Boston vs Minn	1959	**118**
5-Gm	Bill Russell, Boston vs St.Louis	1961	**144**
6-Gm	Wilt Chamberlain, Phila.vs SF	1967	**171**
7-Gm	Bill Russell, Boston vs LA	1962	**189**

Blocked Shots

Series		Year	No
4-Gm	Elvin Hayes, Wash.vs Gold.St	1975	**11**
	George Johnson, G.St.vs Wash	1975	**11**
	Julius Erving, Phila.vs LA	1983	**11**
	John Salley, Detroit vs LA	1989	**11**
5-Gm	Jack Sikma, Seattle vs Wash	1979	**16**
6-Gm	K.Abdul-Jabbar, LA vs Phila	1980	**23**
7-Gm	Marvin Webster, Seattle vs Wash	1978	**18**

Steals

Series		Year	No
4-Gm	Rick Barry, Golden St.vs Wash	1975	**14**
5-Gm	Dennis Johnson, Seattle vs Wash	1979	**9**
6-Gm	Julius Erving, Phila.vs Port	1977	**16**
	Magic Johnson, LA vs Phila	1980	**16**
	Larry Bird, Boston vs Houston	1986	**16**
7-Gm	Isiah Thomas, Detroit vs LA	1988	**20**

BEST GAMES

Points

	Date	FG-FT—Pts
Elgin Baylor, LA at Boston	4/14/62	22-17 —**61**
Rick Barry, SF v Phila	4/18/67	22-11 —**55**

Assists

	Date	No
Magic Johnson, LA vs Bos	6/3/84	**21**
Magic Johnson, LA vs Bos	6/4/87	**20**

Rebounds

	Date	No
Bill Russell, Bos vs St.L	3/29/60	**40**
Bill Russell, Bos vs LA*	4/18/62	**40**

*One overtime.

Overall Standings

Standings of all teams that have reached the NBA Finals. Based on number of appearances.

	App	Titles	Defeats
LA Lakers	23	11	12
Minneapolis Lakers	6	5	1
LA Lakers	17	6	11
Boston Celtics	19	16	3
Philadelphia 76ers	8	3	5
Syracuse Nats	3	1	2
Phila.76ers	5	2	3
Golden St.Warriors	6	3	3
Phila.Warriors	3	2	1
SF Warriors	2	0	2
Golden St.Warriors	1	1	0
New York Knicks	6	2	4
Detroit Pistons	4	1	3
Ft.Wayne Pistons	2	0	2
Detroit Pistons	2	1	1
Atlanta Hawks	4	1	3
St.Louis Hawks	4	1	3
Washington Bullets	4	1	3
Baltimore Bullets	1	0	1
Washington Bullets	3	1	2
Milwaukee Bucks	2	1	1
Seattle SuperSonics	2	1	1
Houston Rockets	2	0	2
Balt.Bullets (folded)	1	1	0
Sacramento Kings	1	1	0
Rochester Royals	1	1	0
Chicago Stags (folded)	1	0	1
Wash.Capitols (folded)	1	0	1
TOTALS	86	43	43

NBA Awards

Maurice Podoloff Trophy
(Most Valuable Player)

Named after the first commissioner of the NBA. Winner selected first by the NBA players (1956-80) and then a national panel of pro basketball writers and broadcasters (since 1981). Numbers in parentheses indicate repeat winners.

Season	Most Valuable Player	Pos
1955-56	Bob Pettit, St.Louis	F
1956-57	Bob Cousy, Boston	G
1957-58	Bill Russell, Boston	C
1958-59	Bob Pettit, St.Louis (2)	F
1959-60	Wilt Chamberlain, Philadelphia	C
1960-61	Bill Russell, Boston (2)	C
1961-62	Bill Russell, Boston (3)	C
1962-63	Bill Russell, Boston (4)	C
1963-64	Oscar Robertson, Cincinnati	G
1964-65	Bill Russell, Boston (5)	C
1965-66	Wilt Chamberlain, Philadelphia (2)	C
1966-67	Wilt Chamberlain, Philadelphia (3)	C
1967-68	Wilt Chamberlain, Philadelphia (4)	C
1968-69	Wes Unseld, Baltimore	C
1969-70	Willis Reed, New York	C
1970-71	Lew Alcindor, Milwaukee*	C
1971-72	Kareem Abdul-Jabbar, Milwaukee (2)	C
1972-73	Dave Cowens, Boston	C
1973-74	Kareem Abdul-Jabbar, Milwaukee (3)	C
1974-75	Bob McAdoo, Buffalo	F
1975-76	Kareem Abdul-Jabbar, LA Lakers (4)	C
1976-77	Kareem Abdul-Jabbar, LA Lakers (5)	C
1977-78	Bill Walton, Portland	C
1978-79	Moses Malone, Houston	C
1979-80	Kareem Abdul-Jabbar, LA Lakers (6)	C
1980-81	Julius Erving, Philadelphia	F
1981-82	Moses Malone, Houston (2)	C
1982-83	Moses Malone, Philadelphia (3)	C
1983-84	Larry Bird, Boston	F
1984-85	Larry Bird, Boston (2)	F
1985-86	Larry Bird, Boston (3)	F
1986-87	Magic Johnson, LA Lakers	G
1987-88	Michael Jordan, Chicago	G
1988-89	Magic Johnson, LA Lakers (2)	G

*Lew Alcindor changed his name to Kareem Abdul-Jabbar after the 1970-71 season.
Note: Wilt Chamberlain (1959-60) and Wes Unseld (1968-69) are the only players to be named MVP in their rookie years.

Eddie Gottlieb Trophy
(Rookie of the Year)

Named after the pro basketball pioneer and owner-coach of the first NBA champion Philadelphia Warriors. Winner selected by a national panel of pro basketball writers and broadcasters (since 1953).

Season	Rookie of the Year	Pos
1952-53	Don Meineke, Ft.Wayne (Dayton)	F
1953-54	Ray Felix, Baltimore (LIU)	C
1954-55	Bob Pettit, St.Louis (LSU)	F
1955-56	Maurice Stokes, Roch.(St.Francis,PA)	F/C
1956-57	Tommy Heinsohn, Boston (Holy Cross)	F
1957-58	Woody Sauldsberry, Phila.(Texas So.)	F/C
1958-59	Elgin Baylor, Minneapolis (Seattle)	F
1959-60	Wilt Chamberlain, Phila.(Kansas)	C
1960-61	Oscar Robertson, Cinn.(U.of Cinn.)	G
1961-62	Walt Bellamy, Chicago (Indiana)	C
1962-63	Terry Dischinger, Chicago (Detroit)	F
1963-64	Jerry Lucas, Cincinnati (Ohio St.)	F/C
1964-65	Willis Reed, New York (Grambling)	C
1965-66	Rick Barry, San Francisco (Miami)	F
1966-67	Dave Bing, Detroit (Syracuse)	G
1967-68	Earl Monroe, Balt.(Winston-Salem)	G
1968-69	Wes Unseld, Baltimore (Louisville)	C
1969-70	Lew Alcindor, Milwaukee (UCLA)*	C
1970-71	Dave Cowens, Boston (Florida St.)	C
	& Geoff Petrie, Portland (Princeton)	F
1971-72	Sidney Wicks, Portland (UCLA)	F
1972-73	Bob McAdoo, Buffalo (N.Carolina)	C/F
1973-74	Ernie DiGregorio, Buffalo (Providence)	G
1974-75	Keith Wilkes, Golden St.(UCLA)	F
1975-76	Alvan Adams, Phoenix (Oklahoma)	C
1976-77	Adrian Dantley, Buffalo (Notre Dame)	F
1977-78	Walter Davis, Phoenix (N.Carolina)	G
1978-79	Phil Ford, Kansas City (N.Carolina)	G
1979-80	Larry Bird, Boston (Indiana St.)	F
1980-81	Darrell Griffith, Utah (Louisville)	G
1981-82	Buck Williams, New Jersey (Maryland)	F
1982-83	Terry Cummings, San Diego (DePaul)	F
1983-84	Ralph Sampson, Houston (Virginia)	C
1984-85	Michael Jordan, Chicago (N.Carolina)	G
1985-86	Patrick Ewing, New York (Georgetown)	C
1986-87	Chuck Person, Indiana (Auburn)	F
1987-88	Mark Jackson, New York (St.John's)	G
1988-89	Mitch Richmond, Golden St.(Kan.St.)	G

*Lew Alcindor changed his name to Kareem Abdul-Jabbar after the 1970-71 season.

Red Auerbach Trophy
(Coach of the Year)

Named after the former Boston coach who led the Celtics to nine NBA titles. Winner selected by a national panel of pro basketball writers and broadcasters (since 1963). Numbers in parentheses indicate repeat winners.

Season	Coach of the Year	W-L Improvement
1962-63	Harry Gallatin, St.L	29-51 to 48-32
1963-64	Alex Hannum, San Fran	31-49 to 48-32*
1964-65	Red Auerbach, Boston	59-21* to 62-18*
1965-66	Dolph Schayes, Phila	40-40 to 55-25*
1966-67	Johnny Kerr, Chicago	33-48 (new team)
1967-68	Richie Guerin, St.L	39-42 to 56-26*
1968-69	Gene Shue, Baltimore	36-46 to 57-25*
1969-70	Red Holzman, New York	54-28 to 60-22*
1970-71	Dick Motta, Chicago	39-43 to 51-31
1971-72	Bill Sharman, Los Ang	48-34* to 69-13*
1972-73	Tommy Heinsohn, Boston	56-26* to 68-14*
1973-74	Ray Scott, Detroit	40-42 to 52-30
1974-75	Phil Johnson, KC-Omaha	33-49 to 44-38
1975-76	Bill Fitch, Cleveland	40-42 to 49-33*
1976-77	Tom Nissalke, Houston	40-42 to 49-33*
1977-78	Hubie Brown, Atlanta	31-51 to 41-41
1978-79	Cotton Fitzsimmons, KC	31-51 to 48-34*
1979-80	Bill Fitch, Boston (2)	29-53 to 61-21*
1980-81	Jack McKinney, Indiana	37-45 to 44-38
1981-82	Gene Shue, Wash. (2)	39-43 to 43-39
1982-83	Don Nelson, Milwaukee	55-27* to 51-31*
1983-84	Frank Layden, Utah	30-52 to 45-37
1984-85	Don Nelson, Milw. (2)	50-32* to 59-23*
1985-86	Mike Fratello, Atlanta	34-48 to 50-32
1986-87	Mike Schuler, Portland	40-42 to 49-33
1987-88	Doug Moe, Denver	37-45 to 54-28*
1988-89	C.Fitzsimmons, Phoe.(2)	28-54 to 55-27

*Won Division.

NBA Scoring Leaders

Season		Gm	Pts	Avg
1946-47	Joe Fulks, Philadelphia . . .	60	1,389	23.2
1947-48	Max Zaslofsky, Chicago . .	48	1,007	21.0
1948-49	George Mikan, Minn	60	1,698	28.3
1949-50	George Mikan, Minn	68	1,865	27.4
1950-51	George Mikan, Minn	68	1,932	28.4
1951-52	Paul Arizin, Phila	66	1,674	25.4
1952-53	Neil Johnston, Phila	70	1,564	22.3
1953-54	Neil Johnston, Phila	72	1,759	24.4
1954-55	Neil Johnston, Phila	72	1,631	22.7
1955-56	Bob Pettit, St.Louis	72	1,849	25.7
1956-57	Paul Arizin, Phila	71	1,817	25.6
1957-58	George Yardley, Detroit .	72	2,001	27.8
1958-59	Bob Pettit, St.Louis	72	2,105	29.2
1959-60	Wilt Chamberlain, Phila .	72	2,707	37.6
1960-61	Wilt Chamberlain, Phila .	79	3,033	38.4
1961-62	Wilt Chamberlain, Phila .	80	4,029	50.4
1962-63	Wilt Chamberlain, SF	80	3,586	44.8
1963-64	Wilt Chamberlain, SF	80	2,948	36.9
1964-65	Wilt Chamberlain, SF-Phi .	73	2,534	34.7
1965-66	Wilt Chamberlain, Phila .	79	2,649	33.5
1966-67	Rick Barry, San Fran	78	2,775	35.6

Season		Gm	Pts	Avg
1967-68	Dave Bing, Detroit	79	2,142	27.1
1968-69	Elvin Hayes, San Diego . .	82	2,327	28.4
1969-70	Jerry West, Los Angeles . .	74	2,309	31.2
1970-71	Lew Alcindor, Milwaukee*	82	2,596	31.7
1971-72	K.Abdul-Jabbar, Milw. . . .	81	2,822	34.8
1972-73	Nate Archibald, KC-O. . . .	80	2,719	34.0
1973-74	Bob McAdoo, Buffalo . . .	74	2,261	30.6
1974-75	Bob McAdoo, Buffalo	82	2,831	34.5
1975-76	Bob McAdoo, Buffalo	78	2,427	31.1
1976-77	Pete Maravich, N.Orleans	73	2,273	31.1
1977-78	George Gervin, S.Ant. . . .	82	2,232	27.2
1978-79	George Gervin, S.Ant. . . .	80	2,365	29.6
1979-80	George Gervin, S.Ant. . . .	78	2,585	33.1
1980-81	Adrian Dantley, Utah	80	2,452	30.7
1981-82	George Gervin, S.Ant. . . .	79	2,551	32.3
1982-83	Alex English, Denver	82	2,326	28.4
1983-84	Adrian Dantley, Utah	79	2,418	30.6
1984-85	Bernard King, New York . .	55	1,809	32.9
1985-86	Dominique Wilkins, Atl . . .	78	2,366	30.3
1986-87	Michael Jordan, Chicago .	82	3,041	37.1
1987-88	Michael Jordan, Chicago .	82	2,868	35.0
1988-89	Michael Jordan, Chicago .	81	2,633	32.5

*Lew Alcindor changed his name to Kareem Abdul-Jabbar after the 1970-71 season.

No.1 Draft Picks, 1966-89

Overall first choices in the NBA Draft since the abolition of the Territorial Draft in 1966. Players who became Rookie of the Year in **bold type**.

Year	Team	Overall 1st Round Pick
1966	New York	Cazzie Russell, Michigan
1967	Detroit	Jimmy Walker, Providence
1968	Houston	Elvin Hayes, Houston
1969	Milwaukee	**Lew Alcindor, UCLA***
1970	Detroit	Bob Lanier, St.Bonaventure
1971	Cleveland	Austin Carr, Notre Dame
1972	Portland	LaRue Martin, Loyola-Chicago
1973	Philadelphia	Doug Collins, Illinois St.
1974	Portland	Bill Walton, UCLA
1975	Atlanta	David Thompson, N.C.State
		(signed with Denver of ABA)
1976	Houston	John Lucas, Maryland
1977	Milwaukee	Kent Benson, Indiana
1978	Portland	Mychal Thompson, Minnesota
1979	LA Lakers	Magic Johnson, Michigan St.
1980	Golden St	Joe Barry Carroll, Purdue
1981	Dallas	Mark Aguirre, DePaul
1982	LA Lakers	James Worthy, N.Carolina
1983	Houston	**Ralph Sampson,** Virginia
1984	Houston	Akeem Olajuwon, Houston
1985	New York	**Patrick Ewing,** Georgetown
1986	Cleveland . . .·. .	Brad Daugherty, N.Carolina
1987	San Antonio	David Robinson, Navy
1988	LA Clippers	Danny Manning, Kansas
1989	Sacramento	Pervis Ellison, Louisville

*Lew Alcindor changed his name to Kareem Abdul-Jabbar after the 1970-71 season.

Wilt Chamberlain's 100-Point Game

March 2, 1962 at Hershey, PA

Final Score:
Philadelphia Warriors, 169
New York Knicks, 147

New York	FGA	FGM	FTA	FTM	Pts
Willie Naulls	22	9	15	13	**31**
Johnny Green	7	3	0	0	**6**
Darrall Imhoff	7	3	1	1	**7**
Richie Guerin	29	13	17	13	**39**
Al Butler	13	4	0	0	**8**
Cleveland Butler	26	16	1	1	**33**
Dave Budd	8	6	1	1	**13**
Donnie Butcher	6	3	6	4	**10**
TOTALS	118	57	41	33	**147**

FG Pct.: .483, FT Pct.: .805.

Philadelphia	FGA	FGM	FTA	FTM	Pts
Paul Arizin	18	7	2	2	**16**
Tom Meschery	12	7	2	2	**16**
Wilt Chamberlain . . .	63	36	32	28	**100**
Guy Rodgers	4	1	12	9	**11**
Al Attles	8	8	1	1	**17**
York Larese	5	4	1	1	**9**
Ed Conlin	4	0	0	0	**0**
Joe Ruklick	1	0	2	0	**0**
Ted Luckenbill	0	0	0	0	**0**
TOTALS	115	63	52	43	**169**

FG Pct.: .548, FT Pct.: .827.

Score by Periods

	1st	2nd	3rd	4th	Final
New York	26	42	38	41	**147**
Philadelphia	42	37	46	44	**169**

Officials: Willie Smith and Pete D'Ambrosio.
Attendance: 4,124.

NBA All-Star Game, 1951-89

The NBA staged its first All-Star Game before 10,094 at Boston Garden on March 2, 1951. From that year on, the All-Star game has matched the best players in the East against the best in the West. Winning coaches are listed first.

Year	Result	Host	Coaches	Most Valuable Player
1951	East 111, West 94	Boston	Joe Lapchick, John Kundla	Ed Macauley, Boston
1952	East 108, West 91	Boston	Al Cervi, John Kundla	Paul Arizin, Phila.
1953	West 79, East 75	Ft.Wayne	John Kundla, Joe Lapchick	George Mikan, Minn.
1954	East 98, West 93 (OT)	New York	Joe Lapchick, John Kundla	Bob Cousy, Boston
1955	East 100, West 91	New York	Al Cervi, Charley Eckman	Bill Sharman, Boston
1956	West 108, East 94	Rochester	Charley Eckman, George Senesky	Bob Pettit, St.Louis
1957	East 109, West 97	Boston	Red Auerbach, Bobby Wanzer	Bob Cousy, Boston
1958	East 130, West 118	St.Louis	Red Auerbach, Alex Hannum	Bob Pettit, St.Louis
1959	West 124, East 108	Detroit	Ed Macauley, Red Auerbach	Bob Pettit, St.Louis & Elgin Baylor, Minn.
1960	East 125, West 115	Philadelphia	Red Auerbach, Ed Macauley	Wilt Chamberlain, Phila.
1961	West 153, East 131	Syracuse	Paul Seymour, Red Auerbach	Oscar Robertson, Cinn.
1962	West 150, East 130	St.Louis	Fred Schaus, Red Auerbach	Bob Pettit, St.Louis
1963	East 115, West 108	Los Angeles	Red Auerbach, Fred Schaus	Bill Russell, Boston
1964	East 111, West 107	Boston	Red Auerbach, Fred Schaus	Oscar Robertson, Cinn.
1965	East 124, West 123	St.Louis	Red Auerbach, Alex Hannum	Jerry Lucas, Cinn.
1966	East 137, West 94	Cincinnati	Red Auerbach, Fred Schaus	Adrian Smith, Cinn.
1967	West 135, East 120	San Francisco	Fred Schaus, Red Auerbach	Rick Barry, San Fran.
1968	East 144, West 124	New York	Alex Hannum, Bill Sharman	Hal Greer, Phila.
1969	East 123, West 112	Baltimore	Gene Shue, Richie Guerin	Oscar Robertson, Cinn.
1970	East 142, West 135	Philadelphia	Red Holzman, Richie Guerin	Willis Reed, New York
1971	West 108, East 107	San Diego	Larry Costello, Red Holzman	Lenny Wilkens, Seattle
1972	West 112, East 110	Los Angeles	Bill Sharman, Tom Heinsohn	Jerry West, Los Ang.
1973	East 104, West 84	Chicago	Tom Heinsohn, Bill Sharman	Dave Cowens, Boston
1974	West 134, East 123	Seattle	Larry Costello, Tom Heinsohn	Bob Lanier, Detroit
1975	East 108, West 102	Phoenix	K.C.Jones, Al Attles	Walt Frazier, New York
1976	East 123, West 109	Philadelphia	Tom Heinsohn, Al Attles	Dave Bing, Washington
1977	West 125, East 124	Milwaukee	Larry Brown, Gene Shue	Julius Erving, Phila.
1978	East 133, West 125	Atlanta	Billy Cunningham, Jack Ramsay	Randy Smith, Buffalo
1979	West 134, East 129	Detroit	Lenny Wilkens, Dick Motta	David Thompson, Denver
1980	East 144, West 135 (OT)	Washington	Billy Cunningham, Len Wilkens	George Gervin, S.Ant.
1981	East 123, West 120	Cleveland	Billy Cunningham, John MacLeod	Nate Archibald, Bost.
1982	East 120, West 118	New Jersey	Bill Fitch, Pat Riley	Larry Bird, Boston
1983	East 132, West 123	Los Angeles	Billy Cunningham, Pat Riley	Julius Erving, Phila.
1984	East 154, West 145 (OT)	Denver	K.C.Jones, Frank Layden	Isiah Thomas, Detroit
1985	West 140, East 129	Indiana	Pat Riley, K.C.Jones	Ralph Sampson, Houston
1986	East 139, West 132	Dallas	K.C.Jones, Pat Riley	Isiah Thomas, Detroit
1987	West 154, East 149 (OT)	Seattle	Pat Riley, K.C.Jones	Tom Chambers, Seattle
1988	East 138, West 133	Chicago	Mike Fratello, Pat Riley	Michael Jordan, Chicago
1989	West 143, East 134	Houston	Pat Riley, Lenny Wilkens	Karl Malone, Utah

American Basketball Association
ABA Finals, 1968-76

The American Basketball Assn. began play in 1967-68 as a 10-team rival of the 21 year-old NBA. The ABA, which introduced the three-point basket, a multi-colored ball and the All-Star Game Slam Dunk Contest, lasted nine seasons before folding following the 1975-76 season. Four ABA teams—Denver, Indiana, New York and San Antonio—survived to enter the NBA in 1976-77. The NBA also adopted the 3-pt basket (in 1979-80) and the All-Star Game Slam Dunk Contest. The older league, however, refused to take in the ABA ball.

In the chart below, each ABA champion's wins and losses are noted in parentheses after the series score.

Year	Winner	Head Coach	Series	Loser	Head Coach
1968	**Pittsburgh Pipers**	Vince Cazetta	4-3 (WLLWLWW)	**New Orleans Bucs**	Babe McCarthy
1969	**Oakland Oaks**	Alex Hannum	4-1 (WLWWW)	**Indiana Pacers**	Bob Leonard
1970	**Indiana Pacers**	Bob Leonard	4-2 (WWLWLW)	**Los Angeles Stars**	Bill Sharman
1971	**Utah Stars**	Bill Sharman	4-3 (WWLLWLW)	**Kentucky Colonels**	Frank Ramsey
1972	**Indiana Pacers**	Bob Leonard	4-2 (WLWLWW)	**New York Nets**	Lou Carnesecca
1973	**Indiana Pacers**	Bob Leonard	4-3 (WLLLWWW)	**Kentucky Colonels**	Joe Mullaney
1974	**New York Nets**	Kevin Loughery	4-1 (WWWLW)	**Utah Stars**	Joe Mullaney
1975	**Kentucky Colonels**	Hubie Brown	4-1 (WWWW)	**Indiana Pacers**	Bob Leonard
1976	**New York Nets**	Kevin Loughery	4-2 (WLWLWW)	**Denver Nuggets**	Larry Brown

ABA Awards

Most Valuable Player

Season		Pos
1967-68	Connie Hawkins, Pittsburgh	C
1968-69	Mel Daniels, Indiana	C
1969-70	Spencer Haywood, Denver	C
1970-71	Mel Daniels, Indiana (2)	C
1971-72	Artis Gilmore, Kentucky	C
1972-73	Billy Cunningham, Carolina	F
1973-74	Julius Erving, New York	F
1974-75	Julius Erving, New York (2)	F
	& George McGinnis, Indiana	F
1975-76	Julius Erving, New York (3)	F

Note: Spencer Haywood (1969-70) and Artis Gilmore (1971-72) were the only players to be named MVP in their rookie years.

Rookie of the Year

Season		Pos
1967-68	Mel Daniels, Minnesota (New Mexico)	C
1968-69	Warren Armstrong, Oakland (Wich.St.)	G
1969-70	Spencer Haywood, Denver (Detroit) . .	C
1970-71	Dan Issel, Kentucky (Kentucky)	C
	& Charlie Scott, Virginia (N.Caro.) . . .	G
1971-72	Artis Gilmore, Kentucky (J'ksonville) . .	C
1972-73	Brian Taylor, New York (Princeton) . .	G
1973-74	Swen Nater, San Antonio (UCLA)	C
1974-75	Marvin Barnes, St.Louis (Providence) .	C
1975-76	David Thompson, Denver (N.C.State) .	F

*Warren Armstrong changed his name to Warren Jabali after the 1970-71 season.

Coach of the Year

Season	Coach of the Year	W-L Improvement
1967-68	Vince Cazetta, Pitts	54-24* (new team)
1968-69	Alex Hannum, Oakland . .	22-56 to 60-18*
1969-70	Joe Belmont, Denver	44-34 to 51-33*
	& Bill Sharman, LA	33-45 to 43-41
1970-71	Al Bianchi, Virginia	44-40 to 55-29*
1971-72	Tom Nissalke, Dallas	30-54 to 42-42
1972-73	Larry Brown, Carolina	35-49 to 57-27*
1973-74	Babe McCarthy, Kentucky .	56-28 to 53-31
	& Joe Mullaney, Utah	55-29* to 51-33*
1974-75	Larry Brown, Denver	37-47 to 65-19*
1975-76	Larry Brown, Denver	65-19* to 60-24*

*Won Division.

ABA Scoring Leaders

Season		Gm	Pts	Avg
1967-68	Connie Hawkins, Pitts . . .	70	1,875	**26.8**
1968-69	Rick Barry, Oakland	35	1,190	**34.0**
1969-70	Spencer Haywood, Den. .	84	2,519	**30.0**
1970-71	Dan Issel, Kentucky	83	2,480	**29.9**
1971-72	Charlie Scott, Virginia . .	73	2,524	**34.6**
1972-73	Julius Erving, Virginia . . .	71	2,268	**31.9**
1973-74	Julius Erving, New York.	84	2,299	**27.4**
1974-75	George McGinnis, Indiana	79	2,353	**29.8**
1975-76	Julius Erving, New York.	84	2,462	**29.3**

ABA All-Star Game, 1968-76

The ABA All-Star Game was an Eastern Division vs Western Division contest from 1968-75. League membership had dropped to seven teams by 1976, the ABA's last season, so the team in first place at the break (Denver) played an All-Star team made up from the other six clubs.

Year	Result	Host	Coaches	Most Valuable Player
1968	East 126, West 120	Indiana	Jim Pollard, Babe McCarthy	Larry Brown, N.Orleans
1969	West 133, East 127	Louisville	Alex Hannum, Gene Rhodes	John Beasley, Dallas
1970	West 128, East 98	Indiana	Babe McCarthy, Bob Leonard	Spencer Haywood, Denver
1971	East 126, West 122	Carolina	Al Bianchi, Bill Sharman	Mel Daniels, Indiana
1972	East 142, West 115	Louisville	Joe Mullaney, Ladell Andersen	Dan Issel, Kentucky
1973	West 123, East 111	Utah	Ladell Andersen, Larry Brown	Warren Jabali, Denver
1974	East 128, West 112	Virginia	Babe McCarthy, Joe Mullaney	Artis Gilmore, Kentucky
1975	East 151, West 124	San Antonio	Kevin Loughery, Larry Brown	Freddie Lewis, St.Louis
1976	Denver 144, ABA 138	Denver	Larry Brown, Kevin Loughery	David Thompson, Denver

Wide World Photos

Calgary captain **Larry McDonald** holds the Stanley Cup high after the Flames beat Montreal at the Forum.

HOCKEY

INSIDE

*Gretzky's trade to the Kings
shifts the balance of power
from Edmonton to Calgary;
Meanwhile, the Russians are coming.*

PRO HOCKEY

1988-89 YEAR IN REVIEW

by Eric Duhatschek

History tells us that every dynasty, from Ming (1368-1644) to Edmonton Oiler (1984-88) eventually comes to an end, sometimes because of internal squabbling, sometimes because of weak leadership.

In Edmonton's case, it turned out to be a little of both.

The most significant event of the 1988-89 season took place 34 days before training camps officially opened.

The Oilers sent Wayne Gretzky, the National Hockey League's second-leading scorer of all time, to the Los Angeles Kings in a complicated deal that included cash ($15 million) and players (Jimmy Carson, teenage prospect Martin Gelinas and three No. 1 draft choices).

The deal sent shock waves of such magnitude through the NHL that ultimately it seemed to affect almost everything that happened during the season.

Nominally, Edmonton went into '88-'89 as the defending champions, but the reality was something else again. The Oilers' reign stopped on Aug. 9th, the day they traded away Gretzky, putting an end to an era characterized by four Stanley Cup championships and some of the most crowd-pleasing hockey played in the 1980s.

Oilers' owner Peter Pocklington, refusing to insert a no-trade clause in Gretzky's long-term contract, had been discreetly shopping his superstar around the league. Gretzky, aware that he could be traded anyplace, anytime, pushed for the deal, thinking there was no time like the present and no place like Hollywood.

The Gretzky deal made the Stanley Cup a possibility for a raft of challengers, signalling the beginning of parity. It also brought to an end the most enduring feature of the NHL playoff system, the repeat champion.

Unlike the three other pro sports, the NHL had a history of teams winning again and again. Until the 1988-89 season, only four teams—Philadelphia

Eric Duhatschek has covered the Flames, the NHL and international hockey for the **Calgary Herald** since 1980. He is also a correspondent for **The Hockey News**.

Wayne Gretzky skating against Detroit on Oct. 6, 1988, in his first NHL game as a Los Angeles King.

Flyers, Montreal Canadiens, New York Islanders and Edmonton—in the previous 17 years had won the Stanley Cup. Gretzky's absence brought Edmonton back to the pack.

"The Oilers dominated people," said Detroit Red Wings coach Jacques Demers. "They had a mystique. I don't think there was a team in the NHL like that this season."

In September, however, there were a lot of eager challengers, wondering if they could step up in class and supplant the defending champions.

In the furor over the Gretzky deal, the second most significant trade of the year, however, was largely overlooked. Calgary acquired center Doug Gilmour and forward Mark Hunter from St. Louis in a seven-player deal Sept. 5 that cost them only one front-liner, Mike Bullard. In Gil-

mour, the Flames received the missing piece to their puzzle. A team on the verge for five seasons (fifth, sixth, third and then two first overalls), the Flames constantly found themselves stymied by the presence of the Oilers in the ultracompetitive Smythe Division.

In Gretzky's absence, the Oilers sank, but the Kings did not rise enough to reach Calgary's class. Gilmour came in and proved again that the playoffs bring out the best in him. Gilmour also turned Joey Mullen, five times a 40-goal scorer, into a 50-goal man for the first time in his career. In the playoffs, Mullen scored 16 goals and Gilmour finished with 22 points, leading Calgary to its first-ever Stanley Cup championship in a stirring six-game series against Montreal. The overriding question facing the Flames in the playoffs was: Would their goaltending hold up?

In 1986, as a rookie, Mike Vernon played well enough to get the Flames to the Stanley Cup finals. That year, they lost to Montreal. In the next two years, Vernon's goaltending was pretty average as favored Calgary lost in the first round to Winnipeg in 1987 and in the second round to Edmonton in 1988.

Early in the season, the Flames seriously considered a deal for Tom Barrasso, the Buffalo Sabres' goalie, but decided the asking price—two of their better young players, defenseman Dana Murzyn and left winger Gary Roberts—was too high. Accordingly, they stuck with Vernon, gambling that he could return to his '86 playoff form.

Vernon responded with an exceptional playoff. The highlight: overtime in the seventh game of their opening series against the Vancouver Canucks. With the season on the line, Vernon stopped three Canucks' players—Petri Skriko, Stan Smyl, Tony Tanti—in alone during sudden death, setting the stage for Joel Otto's game-winning goal and allowing them to play another day.

In the fifth game of that series, the Canucks held Flames' defenseman Al MacInnis off the scoresheet. That would be the last time that happened in the playoffs, however. MacInnis scored a point in each of the remaining 17 playoff games, setting a consecutive games scoring record for defensemen. In the process, he earned the Conn Smythe Trophy as the playoff MVP. Considered the hardest shooter in the NHL, MacInnis did something no one else could in the first three rounds: He intimidated Canadiens' goaltender Patrick Roy with his speed-of-sound slapshot. MacInnis scored four goals in the final series, including two game-winners. By the time it ended, Roy was throwing his hands up in disgust every time MacInnis overpowered him with another shot.

That the Flames wrapped up the championship on Montreal Forum ice proved to be doubly significant. First, it has never happened before; second, the decisive goal came off the stick of 36-year-old Lanny McDonald. McDonald, the Flames' answer to Kareem Abdul-Jabbar, made his farewell tour around the NHL last season, but it had its down days as well. Forced to play on the right side loaded with talent—Joey Mullen, Hakan Loob, Mark and Tim Hunter—McDonald had been shuffled in and out of the lineup right up until the final game.

In the move partly inspired by sentiment, coach Terry Crisp reinserted McDonald on that last night—and was rewarded when McDonald scored the go-ahead goal in what would end as a Stanley-Cup winning sixth game.

McDonald, accepting the Stanley Cup from NHL president John Ziegler afterwards, held it aloft as he drifted around the Forum ice, sporting his bushy playoff beard and wrinkles around his eyes. McDonald was asked afterwards if the Stanley Cup—the Holy Grail he'd pursued throughout his career—turned out to be heavier than he thought.

"It has no weight to it," replied McDonald. "You could carry it around forever—and we probably will."

Two weeks after the Flames carried the Cup home to Calgary, Gretzky brought the season and the decade to a close with an uncanny symmetry by winning the Hart Trophy as the NHL's Most Valuable Player. It was his ninth MVP award since entering the league after the NHL-WHA merger in 1979.

Gretzky's impact in Los Angeles was impressive, exceeding the expectations of Kings' owner Bruce McNall, who never dreamed the Great One could turn the City of Angels into a hockey town. But he did. Gretzky made his debut in the Kings' new silver-and-black livery Oct. 6 against the Detroit Red Wings. He scored his first goal on his first shot, set up three others and the Kings—18th in the league the year before—knocked off one of the league's semifinalists 8-2. In the end, the Kings would vault into fourth place overall, improve to 91 points from 68 and defeat Edmonton in an emotionally charged first-round playoff series.

Gretzky said shaking hands with ex-teammates Mark Messier and Kevin Lowe afterwards was one of the most difficult moments in his life. "I didn't enjoy playing this series," he said.

Perhaps just as significantly, hockey in the United States had its best marketing opportunity since 1980's Miracle On Ice. The Kings capitalized too. They sold out 24 games; average attendance rose from

The NHL's Revolving Door

First Paul Coffey.
Then Wayne Gretzky.
Finally Glen Sather.

Sather, the architect of the Edmonton Oilers' four Stanley Cup-winning teams, chose the second week of June, 1989 to step down as the team's head coach.

The team he presided over during the glory days of the mid-eighties was showing signs of coming apart at the seams. In a move precipitated by owner Peter Pocklington, Sather decided he needed to give full-time attention to his managerial duties as GM and president.

Accordingly, he turned the reins over to his assistants, John Muckler and Ted Green, and spent the summer sorting through the debris.

In the 1988-89 season, the Oilers slipped to 84 points, their lowest total in six years. Gretzky's loss created an unhappiness in the dressing room that spurred the Oilers' all-world goaltender Grant Fuhr to announce his retirement four days before Sather stepped down.

In explaining his decision, Fuhr implied that his relationship with Sather was at the bottom of their troubles.

"Things were said that shouldn't have been said, some of them by Glen," said Fuhr, cryptically. "It wasn't just one person."

The timing of Sather's announcement suggested a last-ditch effort to smooth over the collective unhappiness that overcame the Oilers' dressing room. No one expected Fuhr to stay retired, but could he reconcile his differences with Sather?

With Sather moving his infamous smirk upstairs, maybe it didn't matter.

The only certainty was that Sather's decision signalled the end of an era.

Even Muckler acknowledged as much. Perhaps in an attempt to shield himself from unrealistic expectations—could the Oilers get back on the right path?—Muckler stated: "There's no doubt we're in transition. Our club is not ready to win a Stanley Cup at this particular time. We have some talent coming, but whether that talent is ready to step in or not, only training camp will tell."

How secure is a head coach's job in the NHL? The Oilers are one of 10 teams that

Edmonton Journal

Edmonton GM-coach **Glen Sather** kicked himself upstairs when the season was over.

made changes behind the bench from September, 1988 to July, 1989. Five teams—Toronto, N.Y. Islanders, Quebec, Winnipeg and N.Y. Rangers—replaced coaches during the regular season, while eight clubs—Winnipeg (again), Rangers (again), Quebec (again), Los Angeles, Boston, Hartford, Edmonton and Buffalo—all moved in new men after the season was over.

Here are the changes: **Toronto**—John Brophy fired, George Armstrong hired; **N.Y. Islanders**— Terry Simpson fired, Al Arbour back; **Quebec**—Ron Lapointe out (illness), assistant GM Jean Perron in, Perron resigned, Michel Bergeron back (see N.Y. Rangers); **Winnipeg**—Dan Maloney fired, Rick Bowness hired, Bowness fired, Bob Murdock hired; **N.Y. Rangers**—Bergeron fired, GM Phil Esposito named himself, Esposito fired as both coach and GM, no replacement named as of July 1st; **Los Angeles**—Robbie Ftorek fired, Tom Webster hired; **Boston**—Terry O'Reilly resigned, Mike Milbury hired; **Hartford**—Larry Pleau fired, Rick Ley hired; **Edmonton**—Sather resigned, Muckler promoted; **Buffalo**—Ted Sator fired, Rick Dudley hired.

Hall of Famer **Guy Lafleur** came out of retirement to score 18 goals for the New York Rangers.

11,667 to 14,875. In October, Gretzky predicted that to sell out, the Kings would need to be more competitive than in the past: ''There's a possibility of getting 16,000 people a game because you can put 10,000 hockey fans in here and 6,000 sports fans. If you're not winning, then the 6,000 sports fans are not coming out.''

One person who said he would like to come out was Hall of Famer Guy Lafleur, who announced his readiness to unretire at age 37 and skate on Gretzky's wing. The Kings weighed the three-time scoring champion's offer but said no thanks. The New York Rangers, however, were willing to take a chance that Lafleur could shake off four years of rust and the ex-Canadien came through with a respectable 18 goals and 27 assists in 67 games. His best game came on Feb. 4 when he returned to a cheering Montreal Forum and scored a pair of goals in a thrilling 7-5 loss to the Habs.

There were far fewer thrills in Detroit where the Red Wings won the lackluster Norris Division with a .500 record and led the league in only one category—problem children. Joey Kocur was charged with assault and Petr Klima was twice arrested for drunk driving. But the most serious charges, importing cocaine, were levelled against left winger Bob Probert. In and out of drug rehab centers all season, Probert received chance after chance to straighten out and didn't. NHL president John Ziegler responded to the cocaine bust by banning Probert for life (unless he is exonerated of the charges).

Coach Demers called it the most trying year of his career. Even the brilliance of Steve Yzerman, who recovered from a serious knee injury the previous March to give Gretzky and Mario Lemieux a serious run for MVP honors, could not keep the Wings going. They lost in the first round to a mediocre Chicago Blackhawks' team.

Individually, Pittsburgh Penguins' center Mario Lemieux dominated the league.

Proving that the 1987-88 season was no fluke, Lemieux won his second consecutive scoring championship and was chosen the all-star center. More importantly, he put the Penguins into the playoffs for the first time in his NHL career. The Penguins came within one win of the Patrick Division championship, falling to the Philadelphia Flyers in the finals.

The 1988-89 season also proved to be the year of the comeback. In addition to Lafleur, the Canucks' Paul Reinhart, Calgary's Jamie Macoun, Chicago's Doug Wilson and Philadelphia's Tim Kerr all staged brilliant comebacks from career-threatening injuries. Not only did they play, they played at a high level. Even **The Hockey News**—the only publication that names comeback players of the year—couldn't separate them and named all but Wilson co-winners of the award.

Some ugliness crept into the game as well. The Rangers' David Shaw received a 12-game suspension for a machete chop on Lemieux, prompting the Penguins Steve Dykstra to say that Shaw was "dead" the next time the two teams met. In turn, the players association's insurance company, Lloyd's of London, threatened to cancel its policy if statements like that continued. The most visible display of stupidity took place in the Flyers-Canadiens' semifinal playoff series when goaltender Ron Hextall raced out of his goal crease to attack defenseman Chris Chelios in the waning moments of the sixth game. The Flyers had made veiled threats against Chelios following an unpenalized hit on Brian Propp earlier in the series. There, on cable TV in the U.S. and national television in Canada, Hextall gave the game —trying to fight its image as WWF on blades—a black eye. That, perhaps as much as anything, resulted in Hextall's 12-game suspension, which would begin in October, 1989. Hextall's tantrum spoiled an otherwise excellent playoff for the Philadelphia goaltender, who scored his second NHL goal into an empty net earlier in the playoffs.

Finally, the NHL reinforced its image as the most cosmopolitan of the four major leagues when a member of the Soviet national team, Sergei Priakin, received permission to sign a two-year contract with Calgary and join the Flames for the final weeks of the season. Other Soviet players will join the league in 1989-90, including veteran defensemen Vyacheslav Fetisov and Sergei Starikov with the New Jersey Devils and right wing Alexandr Mogilny with the Buffalo Sabres.

Mogilny, a 20-year-old star on Moscow's Central Red Army team, defected in Sweden, on May 4 throwing future dealings between the Soviets and the NHL into doubt. By the end of June, however, both sides were talking again and Fetisov and Starikov, both thirtysomething, were allowed to relocate in New Jersey.

Wide World Photos

Russian Devils **Vyacheslav Fetisov** (left) and **Sergei Starikov** with New Jersey GM **Lou Lamoriello** after signing NHL contracts in July.

1988-89 Regular Season
Final Standings

Wales Conference
Adams Division

	W	L	T	Pts	— Goals — For	Opp	Dif
1 Montreal	53	18	9	**115**	315	218	+97
2 Boston	37	29	14	**88**	289	256	+33
3 Buffalo	38	35	7	**83**	291	299	−8
4 Hartford	37	38	5	**79**	299	290	+9
5 Quebec	27	46	7	**61**	269	342	−73

Head Coaches: Mon—Pat Burns (1st season); **Bos**—Terry O'Reilly (3rd); **Buf**—Ted Sater (3rd); **Hart**—Larry Pleau (2nd); **Que**—Nordiques were 11-20-2 when they replaced ailing 2nd year coach Ron Lapointe with Asst GM Jean Perron.

Patrick Division

	W	L	T	Pts	— Goals — For	Opp	Dif
1 Washington	41	29	10	**92**	305	259	+46
2 Pittsburgh	40	33	7	**87**	347	349	−2
3 NY Rangers	37	35	8	**82**	310	307	+3
4 Philadelphia	36	36	8	**80**	307	285	+22
5 New Jersey	27	41	12	**66**	281	325	−44
6 NY Islanders ...	28	47	5	**61**	265	325	−60

Head Coaches: Wash—Bryan Murray (8th season); **Pitt**—Gene Ubriaco (1st); **NYR**—Rangers were 37-33-8 when 2nd year coach Michel Bergeron was replaced by GM Phil Esposito; **Phila**—Paul Holmgren (1st); **NJ**—Jim Schoenfeld (2nd); **NYI**—Islanders were 7-18-2 when 3rd year coach Terry Simpson was replaced by Al Arbour.

Campbell Conference
Norris Division

	W	L	T	Pts	— Goals — For	Opp	Dif
1 Detroit	34	34	12	**80**	313	316	−3
2 St.Louis	33	35	12	**78**	275	285	−10
3 Minnesota	27	37	16	**70**	258	278	−20
4 Chicago	27	41	12	**66**	297	335	−38
5 Toronto	28	46	6	**62**	259	342	−83

Head Coaches: Det—Jacques Demers (3rd season); **St.L**—Brian Sutter (1st); **Min**—Pierre Page (1st); **Chi**—Mike Keenan (1st); **Tor**—Maple Leafs were 11-20-2 when 3rd year coach John Brophy was replaced by head scout George Armstrong.

Smythe Division

	W	L	T	Pts	——Goals—— For	Opp	Dif
1 Calgary	54	17	9	**117**	354	226	+128
2 Los Angeles....	42	31	7	**91**	376	335	+41
3 Edmonton	38	34	8	**84**	325	306	+19
4 Vancouver	33	39	8	**74**	251	253	−2
5 Winnipeg	26	42	12	**64**	300	355	−55

Head Coaches: Cal—Terry Crisp (2nd season); **LA**—Robbie Ftorek (2nd); **Edm**—Glen Sather (10th); **Van**—Bob McCammon (2nd); **Win**—Jets were 18-25-9 when 3rd year coach Dan Maloney was replaced by Rick Bowness.

Home & Away Records

Team-by-team records (wins-losses-ties) for the entire regular season, at home and away. Teams are ranked by overall points.

Wales Conference

	Pts	Overall	Home	Away
Montreal	**115**	53-18- 9	30- 6- 4	23-12- 5
Washington	**92**	41-29-10	25-12- 3	16-17- 7
Boston	**88**	37-29-14	17-15- 8	20-14- 6
Pittsburgh......	**87**	40-33- 7	24-13- 3	16-20- 4
Buffalo	**83**	38-35- 7	25-12- 3	13-23- 4
NY Rangers	**82**	37-35- 8	21-17- 2	16-18- 6
Philadelphia	**80**	36-36- 8	22-15- 3	14-21- 5
Hartford	**79**	37-38- 5	21-17- 2	16-21- 3
New Jersey	**66**	27-41-12	17-18- 5	10-23- 7
NY Islanders ...	**61**	28-47- 5	19-18- 3	9-29- 2
Quebec	**61**	27-46- 7	16-20- 4	11-26- 3

Campbell Conference

	Pts	Overall	Home	Away
Calgary	**117**	54-17- 9	32- 4- 4	22-13- 5
Los Angeles	**91**	42-31- 7	25-12- 3	17-19- 4
Edmonton	**84**	38-34- 8	21-16- 3	17-18- 5
Detroit	**80**	34-34-12	20-14- 6	14-20- 6
St.Louis	**78**	33-35-12	22-11- 7	11-24- 5
Vancouver	**74**	33-39- 8	19-15- 6	14-24- 2
Minnesota	**70**	27-37-16	17-15- 8	10-22- 8
Chicago	**66**	27-41-12	16-14-10	11-27- 2
Winnipeg.......	**64**	26-42-12	17-18- 5	9-24- 7
Toronto	**62**	28-46- 6	15-20- 5	13-26- 1

1989 NHL All-Star Game
Campbell 9, Wales 5

Date: Feb. 7, at Northlands Coliseum, Edmonton; **Coaches:** Glen Sather (Campbell), Terry O'Reilly (Wales); **Most Valuable Player:** Wayne Gretzky, Los Angeles.

Wales (East)	....	2	1	2—**5**
Campbell (West)	....	2	3	4—**9**

First Period: Scoring—1.CAMPBELL, Jari Kurri (Wayne Gretzky, Luc Robitaille), 1:07; **2.**CAMPBELL, Gretzky (Steve Duchesne), 4:33; **3.**WALES, Cam Neely (PP, Mario Lemieux, Scott Stevens); **4.**WALES, Walt Poddubny (Mike Ridley, Larry Robinson), 10:38. **Penalty**—CAMPBELL, Mark Messier (holding), 9:35.

Second Period: Scoring—5.WALES, Glen Wesley (Pat LaFontaine, Brian Mullen), 3:16, **6.**CAMPBELL, Joey Mullen (Messier, Joe Nieuwendyk), 7:57; **7.**CAMPBELL, Steve Yzerman (Duchesne, Dino Ciccarelli), 17:21; **8.**CAMPBELL, Gary Leeman (Jimmy Carson), 17:35. **Penalty**—WALES, Ray Bourque (tripping), 13:44.

Third Period: Scoring—9.WALES, Poddubny (Rick Tocchet, Robinson), 4:40; **10.**CAMPBELL, J.Mullen (Dave Mason), 6:53; **11.**WALES, Ridley (Bourque, Tocchet), 9:35; **12.**CAMPBELL, Robitaille (Kurri, Gretzky); **13.**CAMPBELL, Carson (Leeman, Brett Hull); **14.**CAMPBELL, Messier (Nieuwendyk, J.Mullen), 17:14. **Penalties**—None.

Shots on Goal

Wales	....	14	9	15—**38**
Campbell	....	13	10	14—**37**

Goalies—WALES: Sean Burke (29:58, 17 shots/14 saves) and Reggie Lemelin (30:02, 20/14); CAMPBELL: Grant Fuhr (29:58, 20/17) and Mike Vernon (30:02, 18/16); **Referee**—Ronn Hoggarth; **Linesmen**—Wayne Bonney, Ron Asselstine; **Attendance**—17,503.

1988-89 NHL Leaders

Scoring

The season's scoring leader automatically wins the Art Ross Trophy, named after the former Boston coach and general manager and first presented in 1947.

	Pos	GP	G	A	Pts	PMin
Mario Lemieux, Pitts	C	76	85	114	**199**	100
Wayne Gretzky, Los Ang	C	78	54	114	**168**	26
Steve Yzerman, Detroit	C	80	65	90	**155**	61
Bernie Nicholls, LA	C	79	70	80	**150**	96
Rob Brown, Pittsburgh	RW	68	49	66	**115**	118
Paul Coffey, Pitts	D	75	30	83	**113**	193
Joey Mullen, Calgary	C	79	51	59	**110**	16
Jari Kurri, Edmonton	RW	76	44	58	**102**	69
Jimmy Carson, Edmonton	C	80	49	51	**100**	36
Luc Robitaille, LA	LW	78	46	52	**98**	65
Dale Hawerchuk, Winn	C	75	41	55	**96**	28
Dan Quinn, Pittsburgh	C	79	34	60	**94**	102
Mark Messier, Edmonton	LW	72	33	61	**94**	130
Gerard Gallant, Det	LW	76	39	54	**93**	230
Ed Olczyk, Toronto	C	80	38	52	**90**	75
Kevin Dineen, Hartford	RW	79	45	44	**89**	167
Mike Ridley, Wash	C	80	41	48	**89**	49
Tim Kerr, Philadelphia	RW	69	48	40	**88**	73
Pat LaFontaine, NYI	C	79	45	43	**88**	26
Pierre Turgeon, Buff	C	80	34	54	**88**	26
Tomas Sandstrom, NYR	RW	79	32	56	**88**	148
Thomas Steen, Winnipeg	C	80	27	61	**88**	80

Goals

Lemieux, Pitts	85
Nicholls, Los Ang	70
Yzerman, Detroit	65
Gretzky, Los Ang	54
Mullen, Calgary	51
Nieuwendyk, Cal	51
Brown, Pittsburgh	49
Carson, Edmonton	49
Kerr, Philadelphia	48
Robitaille, LA	46

Assists

Lemieux, Pitts	114
Gretzky, Los Ang	114
Yzerman, Detroit	90
Coffey, Pittsburgh	83
Nicholls, Los Ang	80
Brown, Pittsburgh	66
Oates, Detroit	62
Messier, Edmonton	61
Steen, Winnipeg	61
Stevens, Wash	61
Quinn, Pittsburgh	60

Power Play Goals

Lemieux, Pittsburgh	31
Kerr, Philadelphia	25
Brown, Pittsburgh	24
Nicholls, Los Ang	21
Dineen, Hartford	20
McBain, Winnipeg	20

Short-Handed Goals

Lemieux, Pittsburgh	13
Graham, Chicago	10
Nicholls, Los Ang	8
Tikkanen, Edmonton	8
Messier, Edmonton	6

Plus/Minus

Mullen, Calg.	+51
Gilmour, Calg.	+45
Patterson, Calg.	+44
McCrimmon, Calg.	+43
Muni, Edmonton	+43
Lemieux, Pitt.	+41

Penalty Minutes

T.Hunter, Calg.	375
McRae, Minn.	365
Manson, Chi.	352
McSorley, Los Ang	350
Hartman, Buffalo	316
Miller, Boston-LA	301

Goaltending
(Minimum 25 games)

	GP	Min	GA	SO	Avg
Patrick Roy, Montreal	48	2,744	113	4	**2.47**
Mike Vernon, Calgary	52	2,938	130	0	**2.65**
Pete Peeters, Washington	33	1,854	88	4	**2.85**
Brian Hayward, Montreal	36	2,091	101	1	**2.90**
Rick Wamsley, Calgary	35	1,927	95	2	**2.96**
Steve Weeks, Vancouver	35	2,056	102	0	**2.98**
Reggie Lemelin, Boston	40	2,392	120	0	**3.01**
Peter Sidorkiewicz, Hart.	44	2,635	133	4	**3.03**
Jon Casey, Minnesota	55	2,961	151	1	**3.06**
Kirk McLean, Vancouver	42	2,477	127	4	**3.08**

Wins

	W- L-T
Vernon, Calgary	37- 6-5
Roy, Montreal	33- 5-6
Hextall, Phila	30-28-6
VB'brouck, NYR	28-21-4
Hrudey, NYI-LA	28-28-5

Shutouts

Millen, St.Louis	6
Roy, Montreal	4
Peeters, Washington	4
Sidorkiewicz, Hart	4
McLean,Vancouver	4

NHL Trophies

Hart Trophy
(Most Valuable Player)

Voting done by Professional Hockey Writers' Assn. Each ballot has three entries. Points are awarded on 5-3-1 basis. The Hart Trophy is named after former Montreal coach and general manager Cecil Hart and was first presented in 1924.

	1st	2nd	3rd	Pts
1 Wayne Gretzky, Los Angeles, C.	40	22	1	**267**
2 Mario Lemieux, Pittsburgh, C	18	27	16	**187**
3 Steve Yzerman, Detroit, C	5	14	42	**109**
4 Patrick Roy, Montreal, G	0	0	2	**2**
5 Joey Mullen, Calgary, RW	0	0	1	**1**
Chris Chelios, Montreal, D	0	0	1	**1**

Calder Trophy
(Rookie of the Year)

Voting done by Professional Hockey Writers' Assn. Each ballot has three entries. Points are awarded on 5-3-1 basis. The Calder Trophy is named after the NHL's first president Frank Calder and was first presented in 1933.

	1st	2nd	3rd	Pts
1 Brian Leetch, NY Rangers, D	42	19	1	**268**
2 Tevor Linden, Vancouver, C	20	33	7	**206**
3 Tony Granato, NY Rangers, RW	1	6	33	**56**
4 Peter Sidorkiewicz, Hart, G	0	1	10	**13**
5 Craig Janney, Boston, C	0	2	6	**12**

Others: 6. Daniel Marios, Tor.(4 points); **7.** Greg Hawgood, Bos.(3); **8.** Pat Elynuik, Winn.(2) and Joe Sakic, Que.(2); **10.** Jiri Hrdina, Calg.(1).

Jack Adams Trophy
(Coach of the Year)

Voting done by the NHL Broadcasters' Assn. Each ballot has three entries. Points are awarded on 5-3-1 basis. The Adams Trophy is named after the former coach and general manager of the Detroit Red Wings and was first presented in 1974.

	1st	2nd	3rd	Pts
1 Pat Burns, Montreal	24	4	3	135
2 Bob McCammon, Vancouver	4	9	12	59
3 Terry Crisp, Calgary	2	8	6	40
4 Michel Bergeron, NY Rangers	0	4	3	15
5 Pierre Page, Minnesota	1	2	3	14
Brian Murray, Washington	0	4	2	14

Selke Trophy
(Best Defensive Forward)

Voting done by Professional Hockey Writers' Assn. Each ballot has three entries. Points are awarded on 5-3-1 basis. The Selke Trophy is named after former Montreal general manager Frank Selke and was first presented in 1978.

	1st	2nd	3rd	Pts
1 Guy Carbonneau, Montreal	36	11	9	222
2 Esa Tikkanen, Edmonton	8	8	9	73
Colin Patterson, Calgary	6	11	10	73
4 Rick Meagher, St.Louis	1	6	6	29
5 Bengt Gustafsson, Washington	3	3	4	28

Vezina Trophy
(Best Goaltender)

Voting done by the 21 NHL general managers. Each ballot has three entries. Points are awarded on 5-3-1 basis. The Vezina Trophy is named after 1920's goaltender Georges Vezina of Montreal and was first presented in 1927 (a year after his death from tuberculosis).

	1st	2nd	3rd	Pts
1 Patrick Roy, Montreal	15	3	3	87
2 Mike Vernon, Calgary	5	9	2	54
3 Kirk McLean, Vancouver	0	5	2	17
4 John Vanbiesbrouck, NY Rangers	1	0	1	6
5 Grant Fuhr, Edmonton	0	1	2	5
Greg Millen, St.Louis	0	1	2	5

Norris Trophy
(Best Defenseman)

Voting done by Professional Hockey Writers' Assn. Each ballot has three entries. Points are awarded on 5-3-1 basis. The Norris Trophy is named after James Norris, the late owner and president of the Detroit Red Wings and was first presented in 1954.

	1st	2nd	3rd	Pts
1 Chris Chelios, Montreal	37	12	5	226
2 Paul Coffey, Pittsburgh	14	14	3	115
3 Al MacInnis, Calgary	3	10	12	57
4 Ray Bourque, Boston	3	8	17	56
5 Steve Duchesne, Los Angeles	2	5	5	30

Lady Byng Trophy
(Most Gentlemanly Player)

Voting done by Professional Hockey Writers' Assn. Each ballot has three entries. Points are awarded on 5-3-1 basis. The Lady Byng Trophy is named after the wife of Canada's former Governor-General (Baron Byng of Vimy) and was first presented in 1925.

	1st	2nd	3rd	Pts
1 Joey Mullen, Calgary, RW	45	9	2	254
2 Wayne Gretzky, Los Angeles, C	8	22	8	114
3 Mats Naslund, Montreal, LW	3	9	17	59
4 Jimmy Carson, Edmonton, C	0	7	10	31
5 Pat LaFontaine, NY Islanders, C	2	4	4	26

Other Awards

Lester Pearson Award (NHL Players Assn. MVP): to Steve Yzerman of Detroit; **William Jennings Trophy** (fewest goals against): to Montreal goalies Patrick Roy and Brian Hayward; **Bill Masterson Trophy** (perserverance, sportsmanship & dedication to hockey): to Tim Kerr of Philadelphia; **King Clancy Trophy** (humanitarian contribution to community): to Bryan Trottier of NY Islanders. **Man of the Year** (positive role model): to Lanny McDonald of Calgary.

All-Star Teams

Voting done by Professional Hockey Writers' Assn.

Pos First Team	1st	Pts
C Mario Lemieux, Pittsburgh*	48	277
RW Joey Mullen, Calgary	48	276
LW Luc Robitaille, Los Angeles*	40	251
D Chris Chelios, Montreal	31	267
D Paul Coffey, Pittsburgh	15	192
G Patrick Roy, Montreal	52	291

*Also on 1987-88 First Team.

Pos Second Team	1st	Pts
C Wayne Gretzky, Los Angeles	10	201
RW Jari Kurri, Edmonton	8	150
LW Gerard Gallant, Detroit	13	153
D Al MacInnis, Calgary	5	151
D Ray Bourque, Boston	5	136
G Mike Vernon, Calgary		

All-Rookie Team

Voting done by Professional Hockey Writers' Assn. **Center**—Trevor Linden, Vancouver; **Right Wing**—Tony Granato, NY Rangers; **Left Wing**—David Volek, NY Islanders; **Defense**—Brian Leetch, NY Rangers and Zarley Zalapski, Pittsburgh; **Goal**—Peter Sidorkiewicz, Hartford.

Team by Team Statistics

(R) denotes rookies   (C) denotes team captain

Boston Bruins

Top Scorers	Pos	GP	G	A	Pts	+/–	PMin
Cam Neely	RW	74	37	38	75	+14	190
Ken Linseman	C	78	27	45	72	+15	164
Craig Janney (R)	C	62	16	46	62	+20	12
Randy Burridge	RW	80	31	30	61	+19	39
Ray Bourque (C)	D	60	18	43	61	+20	52
Glen Wesley	D	77	19	35	54	+23	61
Bob Joyce (R)	LW	77	18	31	49	+8	46
Greg Hawgood (R)	D	56	16	24	40	+4	84
Bobby Carpenter	C	57	16	24	40	+7	26
Andy Brickley	LW	71	13	22	35	+4	20
Keith Crowder	RW	69	15	18	33	+6	147
Garry Galley	D	78	8	21	29	–7	80
Bob Sweeney	RW	75	14	14	28	–19	99
John Carter (R)	LW	44	12	10	22	–1	24
Greg Johnston	RW	57	11	10	21	+7	32
Michael Thelven	D	40	3	18	21	+10	71

Note: Carpenter played 39 games with LA.

Goaltending	GP	Min	Avg	SO	Record
Reggie Lemelin	40	2,392	3.01	0	19-15-6
Andy Moog	41	2,482	3.22	1	18-14-8
TOTALS	80	4,882	3.15	1	37-29-14

Assists: Lemelin (1), Moog (1).

Buffalo Sabres

Top Scorers	Pos	GP	G	A	Pts	+/–	PMin
Pierre Turgeon	C	80	34	54	88	–3	26
Phil Housley	D	72	26	44	70	+6	47
Christian Ruuttu	C	67	14	46	60	+13	98
Rick Vaive	RW	58	31	26	57	+2	124
Dave Andreychuk	LW	56	28	24	52	+1	40
Doug Bodger	D	71	8	44	52	+15	59
Mike Foligno (C)	RW	75	27	22	49	–7	156
Benoit Hogue (R)	C	69	14	30	44	–4	120
John Tucker	RW	60	13	31	44	–4	31
Ray Sheppard	RW	67	22	21	43	–7	15
Scott Arniel	LW	80	18	23	41	+10	46
Mark Napier	RW	66	11	17	28	–4	33
Grant Ledyard	D	74	4	16	20	+2	51
Jeff Parker (R)	C	57	9	9	18	+3	82
Kevin Maguire	RW	60	8	10	18	+9	241
Uwe Krupp	D	70	5	13	18	0	55

Note: Vaive played 30 games with Chicago, Bodger 10 with Pittsburgh, and Ledyard 61 with Washington.

Goaltending	GP	Min	Avg	SO	Record
Clint Malarchuk	7	326	2.39	1	3-1-1
Daren Puppa	37	1,908	3.36	1	17-10-6
Jacques Cloutier	36	1,786	3.63	0	15-14-0
Darcy Wakaluk (R)	6	214	4.21	0	1-3-0
Tom Barrasso	10	545	4.95	0	2-7-0
TOTALS	80	4,855	3.70	2	38-35-7

Assists: Puppa (4), Barrasso (3), Cloutier (2).
Note: Sabres traded Barrasso to Pittsburgh and acquired Malarchuk from Washington.

Calgary Flames

Top Scorers	Pos	GP	G	A	Pts	+/–	PMin
Joey Mullen	RW	79	51	59	110	+51	16
Hakan Loob	RW	79	27	58	85	+28	44
Doug Gilmour	C	72	26	59	85	+45	44
Joe Nieuwendyk	C	77	51	31	82	+26	40
Al MacInnis	D	79	16	58	74	+38	126
Gary Suter	D	63	13	49	62	+26	78
Jiri Hrdina (R)	C	70	22	32	54	+19	26
Joel Otto	C	72	23	30	53	+12	213
Brian MacLellan	LW	72	18	26	44	+3	118
Gary Roberts	LW	71	22	16	38	+32	250
Colin Patterson	RW	74	14	24	38	+44	56
Jim Peplinski (C)	LW	79	13	25	38	+6	241
Theo Fleury (R)	C	36	14	20	34	+5	46
Mark Hunter	RW	66	22	8	30	+4	194
Jamie Macoun	D	72	8	19	27	+40	76
Brad McCrimmon	D	72	5	17	22	+43	96
Dana Murzyn	D	63	3	19	22	+26	142
Lanny McDonald	RW	51	11	7	18	–1	26

Note: MacLellan played 60 games with Minnesota.

Goaltending	GP	Min	Avg	SO	Record
Mike Vernon	52	2,938	2.65	0	37-6-5
Rick Wamsley	35	1,927	2.96	2	17-11-4
TOTALS	80	4,871	2.78	2	54-17-9

Assists: Vernon (4), Wamsley (1).

Chicago Blackhawks

Top Scorers	Pos	GP	G	A	Pts	+/–	PMin
Steve Larmer	RW	80	43	44	87	+2	54
Denis Savard	C	58	23	59	82	–5	110
Dirk Graham (C)	LW	80	33	45	78	+8	89
Doug Wilson	D	66	15	47	62	+8	69
Dave Manson	D	79	18	36	54	+5	352
Troy Murray	C	79	21	30	51	0	113
Adam Creighton	C	67	22	24	46	–9	136
Steve Thomas	LW	45	21	19	40	–2	69
Wayne Presley	RW	72	21	19	40	–3	100
Trent Yawney (R)	D	69	5	19	24	–5	116
Mike Hudson (R)	LW	41	7	16	23	–12	20
Greg Gilbert	LW	59	8	13	21	+2	45
Bob Bassen	C	68	5	16	21	+5	83
Jeremy Roenick (R)	C	20	9	9	18	+4	4
Steve Konroyd	D	78	6	12	18	–16	42
Keith Brown	D	74	2	16	18	–5	84

Note: Creighton played 24 games with Buffalo, Gilbert 55 with NY Islanders, Bassen 19 with NY Islanders, and Konroyd 21 with NY Islanders.

Goaltending	GP	Min	Avg	SO	Record
Alain Chevrier	27	1,573	3.51	0	13-11-2
Ed Belfour (R)	23	1,148	3.87	0	4-12-3
Darren Pang	35	1,644	4.38	0	10-11-6
Jim Waite (R)	11	494	5.22	0	0-7-1
TOTALS	80	4,874	4.12	0	27-41-12

Assists: Pang (3), Belfour (1).
Note: Blackhawks acquired Chevrier from Winnipeg.

Detroit Red Wings

Top Scorers	Pos	GP	G	A	Pts	+/-	PMin
Steve Yzerman (C)	C	80	65	90	**155**	+17	61
Gerard Gallant	LW	76	39	54	**93**	+7	230
Adam Oates	C	69	16	62	**78**	-1	14
Paul MacLean	RW	76	36	35	**71**	+7	118
Dave Barr	RW	73	27	32	**59**	+12	69
Steve Chiasson	D	65	12	35	**47**	-6	149
Shawn Burr	C	79	19	27	**46**	+5	78
Lee Norwood	D	66	10	32	**42**	+6	100
Petr Klima	LW	51	25	16	**41**	+5	44
Rick Zombo	D	75	1	20	**21**	+23	106
Joe Kocur	RW	60	9	9	**18**	-4	213
Mike O'Connell	D	66	1	15	**16**	-8	41
Jim Nill	RW	71	8	7	**15**	-1	83
Tim Higgins	RW	42	5	9	**14**	0	62
Jeff Sharples	D	46	4	9	**13**	+5	26
Doug Houda	D	57	2	11	**13**	+17	67

Goaltending	GP	Min	Avg	SO	Record
Glen Hanlon	39	2,092	**3.56**	1	13-14-8
Sam St.Laurent	4	141	**3.83**	0	0-1-1
Greg Stefan	46	2,499	**4.01**	0	21-17-3
Tim Cheveldae (R)	2	122	**4.43**	0	0-2-0
TOTALS	80	4,874	**3.89**	1	34-34-12

Assists: Stefan (2), Hanlon (1).

Hartford Whalers

Top Scorers	Pos	GP	G	A	Pts	+/-	PMin
Kevin Dineen	RW	79	45	44	**89**	-6	167
Ron Francis (C)	C	69	29	48	**77**	+4	36
Ray Ferraro	C	80	41	35	**76**	+1	86
Scott Young (R)	RW	76	19	40	**59**	-21	27
Dave Babych	D	70	6	41	**47**	-5	54
Paul MacDermid	RW	74	17	27	**44**	+1	141
Brian Lawton	C	65	17	26	**43**	-11	67
Dave Tippett	LW	80	17	24	**41**	-6	45
John Anderson	LW	62	16	24	**40**	+15	28
Ulf Samuelsson	D	71	9	26	**35**	+23	181
Jody Hull (R)	RW	60	16	18	**34**	+6	10
Norm Maciver	D	63	1	32	**33**	-3	38
Sylvain Turgeon	LW	42	16	14	**30**	-11	40
Dean Evason	C	67	11	17	**28**	-9	60
Don Maloney	LW	52	7	20	**27**	+3	39

Note: Lawton played 30 games with NY Rangers, Maciver 26 with NY Rangers, and Maloney 31 with NY Rangers.

Goaltending	GP	Min	Avg	SO	Record
Peter Sidorkiewicz (R)	44	2,635	**3.03**	4	22-8-4
Kay Whitmore (R)	3	180	**3.33**	0	2-1-0
Mike Liut	35	2,006	**4.25**	1	13-19-1
TOTALS	80	4,835	**3.60**	5	37-38-5

Assists: Sidorkiewicz (3), Whitmore (2).

Edmonton Oilers

Top Scorers	Pos	GP	G	A	Pts	+/-	PMin
Jari Kurri	RW	76	44	58	**102**	+19	69
Jimmy Carson	C	80	49	51	**100**	+3	36
Mark Messier (C)	LW	72	33	61	**94**	-5	130
Esa Tikkanen	LW	67	31	47	**78**	+10	92
Craig Simpson	LW	66	35	41	**76**	-3	80
Glenn Anderson	RW	79	16	48	**64**	-16	93
Craig MacTavish	C	80	21	31	**52**	+10	55
Charlie Huddy	D	76	11	33	**44**	0	52
Tomas Jonsson	D	73	10	33	**43**	-25	56
Norm. Lacombe	RW	64	17	11	**28**	+2	57
Miroslav Frycer	LW	37	12	13	**25**	-2	65
Kevin Lowe	D	76	7	18	**25**	+26	98
Steve Smith	D	35	3	19	**22**	+5	97
Kevin McClelland	C	79	6	14	**20**	-10	161
Craig Muni	D	69	5	13	**18**	+43	71
Randy Gregg	D	57	3	15	**18**	-9	28

Note: Jonsson played 53 games with NY Islanders and Frycer 23 with Detroit.

Goaltending	GP	Min	Avg	SO	Record
Bill Radford	29	1,509	**3.50**	1	15-8-2
Grant Fuhr	59	3,341	**3.83**	1	23-26-6
TOTALS	80	4,860	**3.78**	2	38-34-8

Assists: Fuhr (1).

Los Angeles Kings

Top Scorers	Pos	GP	G	A	Pts	+/-	PMin
Wayne Gretzky	C	78	54	114	**168**	+15	26
Bernie Nicholls	C	79	70	80	**150**	+30	96
Luc Robitaille	RW	78	46	52	**98**	+5	65
Steve Duchesne	D	79	25	50	**75**	+31	92
John Tonelli	LW	77	31	33	**64**	+9	110
Dave Taylor (C)	RW	70	26	37	**63**	+10	80
Mike Krushelnyski	LW	78	26	36	**62**	+9	110
Steve Kasper	C	78	19	31	**50**	-2	63
Mike Allison	RW	55	14	22	**36**	+7	122
Dale DeGray	D	63	6	22	**28**	+3	97
Marty McSorley	RW	66	10	17	**27**	+3	350
Doug Crossman	D	74	10	15	**25**	-11	53
Igor Liba (R)	LW	37	7	18	**25**	-3	36
Ron Duguay	RW	70	7	17	**24**	+23	48
Tim Watters	D	76	3	18	**21**	+17	168

Note: Kasper played 49 games with Boston and Liba 10 with NY Rangers.

Goaltending	GP	Min	Avg	SO	Record
Kelly Hrudey	16	974	**2.90**	1	10-4-2
Mark Fitzpatrick (R)	17	957	**4.01**	0	6-7-3
Glenn Healy	48	2,699	**4.27**	0	25-19-2
Rollie Melanson	4	178	**6.40**	0	1-1-0
TOTALS	80	4,854	**4.14**	1	42-31-7

Assists: Hrudey (2), Fitzpatrick (1), Healy (1).
Note: Kings acquired Hrudey from NY Islanders and traded Fitzpatrick to NY Islanders.

Minnesota North Stars

Top Scorers	Pos	GP	G	A	Pts	+/−	PMin
Dave Gagner	C	75	35	43	78	+13	104
Mike Gartner	RW	69	33	36	69	+11	73
Neal Broten	C	68	18	38	56	+1	57
Marc Habscheid	LW	76	23	31	54	+2	40
Brian Bellows	RW	60	23	27	50	−14	55
Larry Murphy	D	78	11	35	46	0	82
Reed Larson	D	54	9	29	38	−10	68
David Archibald	LW	72	14	19	33	−11	14
Basil McRae	LW	78	12	19	31	−8	365
Stewart Gavin	LW	73	8	18	26	+3	34
Shawn Chambers (R)	D	72	5	19	24	−4	80
Frantisek Musil	D	55	1	19	20	+4	54
Craig Hartsburg (C)	D	30	4	14	18	−8	47
Bob Brooke	C	57	7	9	16	−12	57
Curt Giles	D	76	5	10	15	+2	77

Note: Gartner played 56 games with Washington, Murphy 65 with Washington, and Larson 10 with NY Islanders and 33 with Boston.

Goaltending	GP	Min	Avg	SO	Record
Don Beaupre	1	59	3.05	0	0-1-0
Jon Casey	55	2,961	3.06	1	18-17-12
Kari Takko	32	1,603	3.48	0	8-15-4
Jarmo Myllys (R)	6	238	5.55	0	1-4-0
TOTALS	80	4,882	3.42	1	27-37-16

Assists: Casey (1).

Montreal Canadiens

Top Scorers	Pos	GP	G	A	Pts	+/−	PMin
Mats Naslund	LW	77	33	51	84	+34	14
Bobby Smith	C	80	32	51	83	+25	69
Chris Chelios	D	80	15	58	73	+35	185
Stephane Richer	RW	68	25	35	60	+4	61
Guy Carbonneau	C	79	26	30	56	+37	44
Claude Lemieux	RW	69	29	22	51	+14	136
Shayne Corson	LW	80	26	24	50	−1	193
Petr Svoboda	D	71	8	37	45	+28	147
Russ Courtnall	RW	73	23	18	41	+9	19
Mike McPhee	LW	73	19	22	41	+14	74
Brian Skrudland	C	71	12	29	41	+22	84
Mike Keane (R)	RW	69	16	19	35	+9	69
Ryan Walter	LW	78	14	17	31	+23	48
Brian Gilchrist (R)	C	49	8	16	24	+9	16
Bob Gainey (C)	LW	49	10	7	17	+13	34

Note: Courtnall played 9 games with Toronto.

Goaltending	GP	Min	Avg	SO	Record
Patrick Roy	48	2,744	2.47	4	33-5-6
Brian Hayward	36	2,091	2.90	1	20-13-3
TOTALS	80	4,849	2.70	5	53-18-9

Assists: Roy (6).

New Jersey Devils

Top Scorers	Pos	GP	G	A	Pts	+/−	PMin
John MacLean	RW	74	42	45	87	+26	127
Kirk Muller (C)	C	80	31	43	74	−23	119
Patrik Sundstrom	LW	65	28	41	69	+22	36
Tom Kurvers	D	74	16	50	66	+11	38
Aaron Broten	LW	80	16	43	59	−7	81
Brendan Shanahan	LW	68	22	28	50	+2	115
Pat Verbeek	RW	77	26	21	47	−18	189
Mark Johnson	C	40	13	25	38	−1	24
Tommy Albelin	D	60	9	28	37	+12	67
Jim Korn	RW	65	15	16	31	−3	212
Jack O'Callahan	D	36	5	21	26	0	51
Doug Brown	RW	63	15	10	25	−7	15
Joe Cirella	D	80	3	19	22	−14	155
Claude Loiselle	C	74	7	14	21	−10	209
Randy Velischek	D	80	4	14	18	−2	70

Note: Albelin played 14 games with Quebec.

Goaltending	GP	Min	Avg	SO	Record
Chris Terreri (R)	8	402	2.69	0	0-4-2
Sean Burke (R)	62	3,590	3.84	3	22-31-9
Bob Sauve	15	720	4.67	0	4-5-1
Craig Billington	3	140	4.71	0	1-1-0
TOTALS	80	4,873	4.00	3	27-41-12

Assists: Burke (3).

New York Islanders

Top Scorers	Pos	GP	G	A	Pts	+/−	PMin
Pat LaFontaine	C	79	45	43	88	−8	26
Brent Sutter (C)	C	77	29	34	63	−12	77
Dave Volek (R)	RW	77	25	34	59	−11	24
Bryan Trottier	C	73	17	28	45	−7	44
Mikko Makela	RW	76	17	28	45	−16	22
Derek King	LW	60	14	29	43	+10	14
Alan Kerr	RW	71	20	18	38	−5	144
Gerald Diduck	D	65	11	21	32	+9	155
Jeff Norton (R)	D	69	1	30	31	−24	74
Randy Wood	LW	77	15	13	28	−18	44
Patrick Flatley	RW	41	10	15	25	−5	31
Brad Dalgarno	RW	55	11	10	21	−8	86
Gary Nylund	D	69	7	10	17	−19	137
Marc Bergevin	D	69	2	13	15	−1	80
Richard Pilon (R)	D	62	0	14	14	−9	242

Note: Nylund played 23 games with Chicago and Bergevin 11 with Chicago.

Goaltending	GP	Min	Avg	SO	Record
Jeff Hackett (R)	13	622	3.53	0	4-7-0
Mark Fitzpatrick (R)	11	627	3.92	0	3-5-2
Kelly Hrudey	50	2,800	3.92	0	18-24-3
Billy Smith	17	730	4.44	0	3-11-0
TOTALS	80	4,832	4.04	0	28-47-5

Assists: Hackett (1), Fitzpatrick (1), Hrudey (1).
Note: Islanders traded Hrudey to LA and acquired Fitzpatrick from LA.

New York Rangers

Top Scorers	Pos	GP	G	A	Pts	+/-	PMin
Tomas Sandstrom	RW	79	32	56	88	+5	148
Carey Wilson	C	75	32	45	77	-11	59
Brian Leetch (R)	D	68	23	48	71	+8	50
Brian Mullen	LW	78	29	35	64	+7	60
Tony Granato (R)	RW	78	36	27	63	+17	140
Kelly Kisio (C)	C	70	26	36	62	+14	91
James Patrick	D	68	11	36	47	+3	41
Guy Lafleur	RW	67	18	27	45	+1	12
Ulf Dahlen	LW	56	24	19	43	-6	50
John Ogrodnick	LW	60	13	29	42	0	14
Lucien DeBlois	C	73	9	24	33	-6	107
Michel Petit	D	69	8	25	33	-15	154
Jason Lafreniere	C	38	8	25	24	-3	6
Marcel Dionne	LW	37	7	16	23	6	20
Lindy Ruff	D	76	6	16	22	-23	117

Note: Wilson played 34 games with Hartford and Ruff 63 with Buffalo.

Goaltending	GP	Min	Avg	SO	Record
John Vanbiesbrouck	56	3,207	3.69	0	28-21-4
Bob Froese	30	1,621	3.78	1	9-14-4
TOTALS	80	4,844	3.80	1	37-35-8

Assists: Vanbiesbrouck (2), Froese (1).

Philadelphia Flyers

Top Scorers	Pos	GP	G	A	Pts	+/-	PMin
Tim Kerr	RW	69	48	40	88	-4	73
Rick Tocchet	RW	66	45	36	81	-1	183
Brian Propp	LW	77	32	46	78	+16	37
Pelle Eklund	LW	79	18	51	69	+5	23
Mike Bullard	C	74	27	38	65	+2	106
Scott Mellanby	RW	76	21	29	50	-13	183
Ron Sutter	C	55	26	22	48	+25	80
Terry Carkner	D	78	11	32	43	-6	149
Keith Acton	C	71	14	25	39	+10	111
Mark Howe	D	52	9	29	38	+7	45
Murray Craven	LW	51	9	28	37	+4	52
Dave Poulin (C)	C	69	18	17	35	+4	49
Gord Murphy (R)	D	75	4	31	35	-3	68
Derrick Smith	LW	74	16	14	30	-4	43
Jay Wells	D	67	2	19	21	-3	184

Note: Bullard played 20 games with St.Louis and Acton 46 with Edmonton.

Goaltending	GP	Min	Avg	SO	Record
Ron Hextall	64	3,756	3.23	0	30-28-6
Mark LaForest	17	933	4.12	0	5-7-2
Ken Wregget	3	130	6.00	0	1-1-0
TOTALS	80	4,854	3.52	0	36-36-8

Assists: Hextall (8), LaForest (4).
Note: Flyers acquired Wregget from Toronto.

Pittsburgh Penguins

Top Scorers	Pos	GP	G	A	Pts	+/-	PMin
Mario Lemieux (C)	C	76	85	114	199	+41	100
Rob Brown	RW	68	49	66	115	+27	118
Paul Coffey	D	75	30	83	113	-10	193
Dan Quinn	C	79	34	60	94	-37	102
Bob Errey	LW	76	26	32	58	+40	124
John Cullen (R)	C	79	12	37	49	-25	112
Zarley Zalapski (R)	D	58	12	33	45	+9	57
Randy Cunneyworth	LW	70	25	19	44	-22	156
Phil Bourque	LW	80	17	26	43	-22	97
Dave Hannan	C	72	10	20	30	-12	157
Randy Hillier	D	68	1	23	24	-4	141
Troy Loney	RW	69	10	6	16	-5	165
Jim Johnson	D	76	2	14	16	+7	163
Kevin Stevens (R)	LW	24	12	3	15	-8	19
Jock Callender	RW	30	6	5	11	-3	20

Goaltending	GP	Min	Avg	SO	Record
Frank Pietrangelo (R)	15	669	4.04	0	5-3-0
Tom Barrasso	44	2,406	4.04	0	18-15-7
Steve Guenette (R)	11	574	4.29	0	5-6-0
Wendall Young	22	1,150	4.80	0	12-9-0
TOTALS	80	4,844	4.32	0	40-33-7

Assists: Barrasso (5), Young (2), Guenette (1).
Note: Penguins acquired Barrasso from Buffalo.

Quebec Nordiques

Top Scorers	Pos	GP	G	A	Pts	+/-	PMin
Peter Stastny (C)	C	72	35	50	85	-23	117
Walt Poddubny	RW	72	38	37	75	-18	107
Jeff Brown	D	78	21	47	68	-22	62
Michel Goulet	LW	69	26	38	64	-20	67
Joe Sakic (R)	C	70	23	39	62	-36	24
Iiro Jarvi (R)	RW	75	11	30	41	-13	40
Paul Gillis	C	79	15	25	40	-14	163
Marc Fortier	LW	57	20	19	39	-18	45
Anton Stastny	RW	55	7	30	37	-19	12
Gaetan Duchesne	LW	70	8	21	29	0	56
Randy Moller	D	74	7	22	29	+2	136
Robert Picard	D	74	7	14	21	-28	61
Mike Hough	RW	46	9	10	19	-7	39
Ken McRae (R)	C	37	6	11	17	-9	68
Mario Marois	D	49	3	12	15	-21	118

Note: Marois played 7 games with Winnipeg.

Goaltending	GP	Min	Avg	SO	Record
Ron Tugnutt (R)	26	1,367	3.60	0	10-10-3
Mario Gosselin	39	2,064	4.24	0	11-19-3
Bob Mason	22	1,168	4.73	0	5-14-1
Mario Brunetta	5	226	5.04	0	1-3-0
TOTALS	80	4,841	4.24	0	27-46-7

Assists: Tugnutt (3), Gosselin (2), Mason (1).

St.Louis Blues

Top Scorers	Pos	GP	G	A	Pts	+/−	PMin
Brett Hull	RW	78	41	43	84	−17	33
Peter Zezel	C	78	21	49	70	−14	42
Bernie Federko	C	66	22	45	67	−20	54
Cliff Ronning	C	64	24	31	55	+3	18
Greg Paslawski	RW	75	26	26	52	+8	18
Tony Hrkac	C	70	17	28	45	−10	8
Gino Cavallini	LW	74	20	23	43	+2	79
Tony McKegney	LW	71	25	17	42	−1	58
Brian Benning	D	66	8	26	34	−23	102
Rick Meagher	C	78	15	14	29	+9	53
Sergio Momesso	LW	53	9	17	26	−1	139
Gordie Roberts	D	77	2	24	26	+7	90
Steve Tuttle (R)	LW	53	13	12	25	+3	6
Paul Cavallini	D	65	4	20	24	+25	128
Tom Tilley (R)	D	70	1	22	23	+1	47

Note: Zezel played 26 games with Philadelphia.

Goaltending	GP	Min	Avg	SO	Record
Greg Millen	52	3,019	3.38	6	22-20-7
Vincent Riendeau (R)	32	1,842	3.52	0	11-15-5
TOTALS	80	4,871	3.51	6	33-35-12

Assists: Riendeau (1).

Toronto Maple Leafs

Top Scorers	Pos	GP	G	A	Pts	+/−	PMin
Ed Olczyk	C	80	38	52	90	0	75
Gary Leeman	RW	61	32	43	75	+5	66
Vincent Damphousse	LW	80	26	42	68	−8	75
Tom Fergus	C	80	22	45	67	−38	48
Dan Marois (R)	RW	76	31	23	54	−4	76
Mark Osborne	LW	75	16	30	46	−5	112
Al Iafrate	D	65	13	20	33	+3	72
Dave Reid	RW	77	9	21	30	+12	22
Todd Gill	LW	59	11	14	25	−3	72
Craig Laughlin	RW	66	10	13	23	−22	41
Borje Salming	D	63	3	17	20	+7	86
Peter Ihnacak	C	26	2	16	18	+3	10
Brad Marsh	D	80	1	15	16	−16	79
Derek Laxdal (R)	RW	41	9	6	15	−11	65
Chris Kotsopoulos	D	57	1	14	15	−4	44

Goaltending	GP	Min	Avg	SO	Record
Allan Bester	43	2,460	3.80	2	17-20-3
Ken Wregget	32	1,888	4.42	0	9-20-2
Jeff Reese (R)	10	486	4.94	0	2-6-1
TOTALS	80	4,846	4.23	2	28-46-6

Assists: Wregget (3), Bester (2).
Note: Maple Leafs traded Wregget to Philadelphia.

Vancouver Canucks

Top Scorers	Pos	GP	G	A	Pts	+/−	PMin
Petri Skriko	LW	74	30	36	66	−3	57
Trevor Linden (R)	C	80	30	29	59	−10	41
Paul Reinhart	D	64	7	50	57	−4	44
Tony Tanti	RW	77	24	25	49	−10	69
Brian Bradley	C	71	18	27	45	−5	42
Barry Pederson	C	62	15	26	41	+5	22
Robert Nordmark	D	80	6	35	41	−4	97
Jim Sandlak	RW	72	20	20	40	+8	99
Steve Bozek	C	71	17	18	35	+1	64
Greg C.Adams	LW	61	19	14	33	−21	24
Rich Sutter	RW	75	17	15	32	+3	122
Stan Smyl (C)	RW	75	7	18	25	0	102
Doug Lidster	D	63	5	17	22	−4	78
Garth Butcher	D	78	0	20	20	+4	227
Dan Hodgson	C	23	4	13	17	+3	25

Goaltending	GP	Min	Avg	SO	Record
Troy Gamble (R)	5	302	2.38	0	2-3-0
Steve Weeks	35	2,056	2.98	0	11-19-5
Kirk McLean	42	2,477	3.08	4	20-17-3
TOTALS	80	4,856	3.13	4	33-39-8

Assists: McLean (1).

Washington Capitals

Top Scorers	Pos	GP	G	A	Pts	+/−	PMin
Mike Ridley	C	80	41	48	89	+17	49
Geoff Courtnall	LW	79	42	38	80	+11	112
Dino Ciccarelli	RW	76	44	30	74	−6	76
Bengt Gustafsson	C	72	18	51	69	+13	18
Scott Stevens	D	80	7	61	68	+1	225
Dave Christian	LW	80	34	31	65	+2	12
Dale Hunter	C	80	20	37	57	−3	219
Kelly Miller	RW	78	19	21	40	+13	45
Kevin Hatcher	D	62	13	27	40	+19	101
Steve Leach	RW	74	11	19	30	−4	94
Michal Pivonka	LW	52	8	19	27	+9	30
Calle Johansson	D	59	3	18	21	−6	37
Rod Langway (C)	D	76	2	19	21	+12	65
Bob Rouse	D	79	4	15	19	−3	160
Bob Gould	RW	75	5	13	18	−2	65

Note: Ciccarelli played 65 games with Minnesota, Johansson 47 with Buffalo, and Rouse 66 with Minnesota.

Goaltending	GP	Min	Avg	SO	Record
Pete Peeters	33	1,854	2.85	4	20-7-3
Don Beaupre	11	578	2.91	1	5-4-0
Clint Malarchuk	42	2,428	3.48	1	16-18-7
TOTALS	80	4,865	3.19	6	41-29-10

Assists: Peeters (1), Malarchuk (1).
Note: Caps acquired Beaupre from Minnesota and traded Malarchuk to Buffalo.

Winnipeg Jets

Top Scorers	Pos	GP	G	A	Pts	+/−	PMin
Dale Hawerchuk (C)	C	75	41	55	96	−30	28
Thomas Steen	C	80	27	61	88	+14	80
Andrew McBain	RW	80	37	40	77	−35	71
Brent Ashton	LW	75	31	37	68	−5	36
Fredrik Olausson	D	75	15	47	62	+6	32
Dave Ellett	D	75	22	34	56	−18	62
Pat Elynuik (R)	RW	56	26	25	51	+5	29
Iain Duncan	LW	57	14	30	44	−17	74
Randy Carlyle	D	78	6	38	44	−19	78
Laurie Boschman	C	70	10	26	36	−17	163
Doug Smail	LW	47	14	15	29	+12	52
Paul Fenton	LW	80	16	12	28	−16	39
Gord Donnelly	RW	73	10	10	20	−20	274
Peter Taglianetti	D	66	1	14	15	−23	226
Teppo Numminen (R)	D	69	1	14	15	−11	36

Note: Fenton played 21 games with LA; Donnelly 16 with Quebec.

Goaltending	GP	Min	Avg	SO	Record
Bob Essensa (R)	20	1,102	3.70	1	6-8-3
Pokey Reddick	41	2,109	4.10	0	11-17-7
Alain Chevrier	22	1,092	4.29	1	8-8-2
Daniel Berthiaume	9	443	5.96	0	0-8-0
Tom Draper (R)	2	120	6.00	0	1-1-0
TOTALS	80	4,880	4.36	2	26-42-12

Assists: Chevrier (4), Reddick (1).
Note: Jets traded Chevrier to Chicago.

1989 Stanley Cup Playoffs

All series in each conference Best-of-7 games. Winning teams in capital LETTERS.

Campbell Conference

NORRIS DIVISION

Semifinal: Chicago over Detroit, 4-2
Apr. 5...Chicago 2, at DETROIT 3
Apr. 6...CHICAGO 5, at Detroit 4 (OT)
Apr. 8...Detroit 2, at CHICAGO 4
Apr. 9...Detroit 2, at CHICAGO 3
Apr.11...Chicago 4, at DETROIT 6
Apr.13...Detroit 1, at CHICAGO 7

Semifinal: St.Louis over Minnesota, 4-1
Apr. 5...Minnesota 3, at ST.LOUIS 4 (OT)
Apr. 6...Minnesota 3, at ST.LOUIS 4 (OT)
Apr. 8...ST.LOUIS 5, at Minnesota 3
Apr. 9...St.Louis 4, at MINNESOTA 5
Apr.11..Minnesota 1, at ST.LOUIS 6

Final: Chicago over St.Louis, 4-1
Apr.18..CHICAGO 3, at St.Louis 1
Apr.20..Chicago 4, at ST.LOUIS 5 (OT)
Apr.22..St.Louis 2, at CHICAGO 5
Apr.24..St.Louis 2, at CHICAGO 3
Apr.26..CHICAGO 4, at St.Louis 2

SMYTHE DIVISION

Semifinal: Calgary over Vancouver, 4-3
Apr. 5...VANCOUVER 4, at Calgary 3 (OT)
Apr. 6...Vancouver 2, at CALGARY 5
Apr. 8...CALGARY 4, at Vancouver 0
Apr. 9...Calgary 3, at VANCOUVER 5
Apr.11..Vancouver 0, at CALGARY 4
Apr.13..Calgary 3, at VANCOUVER 6
Apr.15..Vancouver 3, at CALGARY 4 (OT)

Semifinal: Los Angeles over Edmonton, 4-3
Apr. 5...EDMONTON 4, at Los Angeles 3
Apr. 6...Edmonton 2, at LOS ANGELES 5
Apr. 8...Los Angeles 0, at EDMONTON 4
Apr. 9...Los Angeles 3, at EDMONTON 4
Apr.11..Edmonton 4, at LOS ANGELES 4
Apr.13..LOS ANGELES 4, at Edmonton 1
Apr.15..Edmonton 3, at LOS ANGELES 6

Final: Calgary over Los Angeles, 4-0
Apr.18..Los Angeles 3, at CALGARY 4 (OT)
Apr.20..Los Angeles 3, at CALGARY 8
Apr.22..CALGARY 5, at Los Angeles 2
Apr.24..CALGARY 5, at Los Angeles 3

CONFERENCE FINALS

Calgary over Chicago, 4-1
May 2...Chicago 0, at CALGARY 3
May 4...CHICAGO 4, at Calgary 2
May 6...CALGARY 5, at Chicago 2
May 8...CALGARY 2, at Chicago 1 (OT)
May 10..Chicago 1, at CALGARY 3

Wales Conference

ADAMS DIVISION

Semifinal: Montreal over Hartford, 4-0
Apr. 5 ...Hartford 2, at MONTREAL 6
Apr. 6 ...Hartford 2, at MONTREAL 3
Apr. 8 ...MONTREAL 5, at Hartford 4 (OT)
Apr. 9 ...MONTREAL 4, at Hartford 3 (OT)

Semifinal: Boston over Buffalo, 4-1
Apr. 5 ...BUFFALO 6, at Boston 0
Apr. 6 ...Buffalo 3, at BOSTON 5
Apr. 8 ...BOSTON 4, at Buffalo 2
Apr. 9 ...BOSTON 3, at Buffalo 2
Apr.11 ...Buffalo 1, at BOSTON 4

Final: Montreal over Boston, 4-1
Apr.18 ...Boston 2, at MONTREAL 3
Apr.20 ...Boston 2, at MONTREAL 3 (OT)
Apr.22 ...MONTREAL 5, at Boston 4
Apr.24 ...Montreal 2, at BOSTON 3
Apr.26 ...Boston 2, at MONTREAL 3

PATRICK DIVISION

Semifinal: Philadelphia over Washington, 4-2
Apr. 5 ...Philadelphia 2, at WASHINGTON 3
Apr. 6 ...PHILADELPHIA 3, at Washington 2
Apr. 8 ...WASHINGTON 4, at Philadelphia 3 (OT)
Apr. 9 ...Washington 2, at PHILADELPHIA 5
Apr.11 ...PHILADELPHIA 8, at Washington 5
Apr.13 ...Washington 3, at PHILADELPHIA 4

Semifinal: Pittsburgh over NY Rangers, 4-0
Apr. 5 ...NY Rangers 1, at PITTSBURGH 3
Apr. 6 ...NY Rangers 4, at PITTSBURGH 7
Apr. 8 ...PITTSBURGH 5, NY Rangers 3
Apr. 9 ...PITTSBURGH 4, NY Rangers 3

Final: Philadelphia over Pittsburgh, 4-3
Apr.17 ...Philadelphia 3, at PITTSBURGH 4
Apr.19 ...PHILADELPHIA 4, at Pittsburgh 2
Apr.21 ...PITTSBURGH 4, at Philadelphia 3 (OT)
Apr.23 ...Pittsburgh 1, at PHILADELPHIA 4
Apr.25 ...Philadelphia 7, at PITTSBURGH 10
Apr.27 ...Pittsburgh 2, at PHILADELPHIA 6
Apr.29 ...PHILADELPHIA 4, at Pittsburgh 1

CONFERENCE FINALS

Montreal over Philadelphia, 4-2
May 1 ...PHILADELPHIA 3, at Montreal 1
May 3 ...Philadelphia 0, at MONTREAL 3
May 5 ...MONTREAL 5, at Philadelphia 1
May 7 ...MONTREAL 3, at Philadelphia 0
May 9 ...PHILADELPHIA 2, at Montreal 1 (OT)
May 11 ..MONTREAL 4, at Philadelphia 2

STANLEY CUP FINALS

Calgary over Montreal, 4-2
May 14 . . Montreal 2, at CALGARY 3
May 17 . . MONTREAL 4, at Calgary 2
May 19 . . Calgary 3, at MONTREAL 4 (2 OT)
May 21 . . CALGARY 4, at Montreal 2
May 23 . . Montreal 2, at CALGARY 3
May 25 . . CALGARY 4, at Montreal 2

Conn Smythe Trophy (Playoffs MVP)
Al MacInnis, Calgary, D
(22 games: 7 goals, 24 assists)

Final Playoff Standings

					— Goals —		
	GP	W	L	Pts	For	Opp	Dif
Calgary	22	16	6	32	82	55	+27
Montreal	21	14	7	28	67	51	+16
Philadelphia	19	10	9	20	64	60	+4
Chicago	16	9	7	18	52	45	+7
Pittsburgh	11	7	4	14	43	42	+1
St.Louis	10	5	5	10	35	34	+1
Boston	10	5	5	10	29	30	−1
Los Angeles	11	4	7	8	36	42	−6

					— Goals —		
	GP	W	L	Pts	For	Opp	Dif
Edmonton	7	3	4	6	20	25	−5
Vancouver	7	3	4	6	20	26	−6
Washington	6	2	4	4	19	25	−6
Detroit	6	2	4	4	18	25	−7
Minnesota	5	1	4	2	15	23	−8
Buffalo	5	1	4	2	14	16	−2
Hartford	4	0	4	0	11	18	−7
NY Rangers	4	0	4	0	11	19	−8

Individual Statistics

Scoring

	Pos	GP	G	A	Pts	PMin
Al MacInnis, Calgary	D	22	7	24	31	46
Tim Kerr, Philadelphia	RW	19	14	11	25	27
Joe Mullen, Calgary	RW	21	16	8	24	4
Brian Propp, Phila	LW	18	14	9	23	14
Doug Gilmour, Calgary	C	22	11	11	22	20
Wayne Gretzky, Los Angeles	C	11	5	17	22	0
Mario Lemieux, Pitts	C	11	12	7	19	16
Bobby Smith, Montreal	C	21	11	8	19	46
Denis Savard, Chicago	C	16	8	11	19	10
Joel Otto, Calgary	C	22	6	13	19	46
Chris Chelios, Montreal	D	21	4	15	19	28
Steve Larmer, Chicago	RW	16	8	9	17	22
Hakan Loob, Calgary	RW	22	8	9	17	4
Bernie Nicholls, Los Ang	C	11	7	9	16	12
Mats Naslund, Montreal	LW	21	4	11	15	6
Paul Coffey, Pittsburgh	D	11	2	13	15	31
Mark Howe, Philadelphia	D	19	0	15	15	10
Joe Nieuwendyk, Calgary	C	22	10	4	14	10
Russ Courtnall, Mont	C	21	8	5	13	18
Craig Janney, Boston (R)	C	10	4	9	13	21
Colin Patterson, Calgary	RW	22	3	10	13	24

Goals

Goals		Assists	
Mullen, Calgary	16	MacInnis, Calgary	24
Propp, Philadelphia	14	Gretzky, Los Ang	17
Kerr, Philadelphia	14	Howe, Philadelphia	15
Lemieux, Pittsburgh	12	Chelios, Montreal	15
Smith, Montreal	11	Coffey, Pittsburgh	13
Gilmour, Calgary	11	Otto, Calgary	13

Power Play Goals		Short-Handed Goals	
Kerr, Philadelphia	8	Wayne Presley, Chi	3
Lemieux, Pittsburgh	7	Dave Poulin, Phila	2
Chris Kontos, LA	6	Derrick Smith, Phila	2
Mullen, Calgary	6	Loob, Calgary	2
Nieuwendyk, Calgary	6		

Goaltending
(10 games played)

	GP	Min	W-L	GA	SO	Avg
Patrick Roy, Mont	19	1,206	13-6	42	2	2.09
Mike Vernon, Cal	22	1,381	16-5	52	3	2.26
Alain Chevrier, Chi	16	1,013	9-7	44	0	2.61
Greg Millen, St.L	10	649	5-5	34	0	3.14
Ron Hextall, Phila	15	886	8-7	49	0	3.32
Kelly Hrudey, LA	10	566	4-6	35	0	3.71
Tom Barrasso, Pitts	11	631	7-4	40	0	3.80

The Stanley Cup

The Stanley Cup was originally donated to the Canadian Amateur Hockey Assn. by Sir Frederick Arthur Stanley, Lord Stanley of Preston and 16th Earl of Derby, who had become interested in the sport while Governor General of Canada from 1888 to 1893. Stanley wanted the trophy to be a challenge cup, contested for each year by the best amateur hockey teams in Canada.

In 1893, the Cup was presented without a challenge to the AHA champion Montreal Amateur Athletic Assn. team. Every year since, however, there has been a playoff. In 1914, Cup trustees limited the field challenging for the trophy to the champion of the eastern professional National Hockey Assn.(NHA, organized in 1910) and the western professional Pacific Coast Hockey Assn.(PCHA, organized in 1912).

The NHA became the National Hockey League (NHL) in November, 1917. From 1918 to 1926, the NHL and PCHL champions played for the Cup with the Western Canada Hockey League (WCHL) champion joining in a three-way challenge in 1923 and '24. The PCHA disbanded after the 1925-26 season and the NHL playoffs have decided the winner of the Stanley Cup ever since.

Stanley Cup Champions, 1893-1917

Year	Champion	Year	Champion	Year	Champion
1893	Montreal A.A.A.	1900	Montreal Shamrocks	1910	Montreal Wanderers
1894	Montreal A.A.A.	1901	Winnipeg Victorias	1911	Ottawa Senators
1895	Montreal Victorias	1902	Montreal A.A.A.	1912	Quebec Bulldogs
1896	(Feb.) Winn.Victorias	1903	Ottawa Silver Seven	1913	Quebec Bulldogs
	(Dec.) Mont.Victorias	1904	Ottawa Silver Seven	1914	Toronto Blueshirts (NHA)
1897	Montreal Victorias	1905	Ottawa Silver Seven	1915	Vancouver Millionaires (PCHA)
1898	Montreal Victorias	1906	Montreal Wanderers	1916	Montreal Canadiens (NHA)
1899	Montreal Shamrocks	1907	(Jan.) Kenora Thistles	1917	Seattle Metropolitans (PCHA)
			(Mar.) Mont.Wanderers		
		1908	Montreal Wanderers		
		1909	Ottawa Senators		

Stanley Cup Champions, 1918-89

Year	Winner	Head Coach	Series	Loser	Head Coach
1918	**Toronto Arenas**	Dick Carroll	3-2 (WLWLW)	**Vancouver (PCHA)**	Frank Patrick
1919	No Decision: Montreal (NHL) and Seattle (PCHA) series tied when called off (see below).				
1920	**Ottawa**	Pete Green	3-2 (WWLLW)	**Seattle (PCHA)**	Pete Muldoon
1921	**Ottawa**	Pete Green	3-2 (LWWLW)	**Vancouver (PCHA)**	Frank Patrick
1922	**Toronto St.Pats**	Eddie Powers	3-2 (LWLWW)	**Vancouver (PCHA)**	Frank Patrick
1923	**Ottawa**	Pete Green	3-1 (WLWW)	**Vancouver (PCHA)**	Frank Patrick
			2-0	**Edmonton (WCHL)**	K.C.McKenzie
1924	**Montreal**	Leo Dandurand	2-0	**Vancouver (PCHA)**	Frank Patrick
			2-0	**Calgary (WCHL)**	Eddie Oatman
1925	**Victoria (PCHA)**	Lester Patrick	3-1 (WWLW)	**Montreal**	Leo Dandurand
1926	**Montreal Maroons**	Eddie Gerard	3-1 (WWLW)	**Victoria (PCHA)**	Lester Patrick
1927	**Ottawa**	Dave Gil	2-0 (TWTW)	**Boston**	Art Ross
1928	**NY Rangers**	Lester Patrick	3-2 (LWLWW)	**Montreal**	Cecil Hart
1929	**Boston**	Art Ross	2-0	**NY Rangers**	Lester Patrick
1930	**Montreal**	Cecil Hart	2-0	**Boston**	Art Ross
1931	**Montreal**	Cecil Hart	3-2 (WLLWW)	**Chicago**	Art Duncan
1932	**Toronto**	Dick Irvin	3-0	**NY Rangers**	Lester Patrick
1933	**NY Rangers**	Lester Patrick	3-1 (WWLW)	**Toronto**	Dick Irvin
1934	**Chicago**	Tommy Gorman	3-1 (WWLW)	**Detroit**	Jack Adams
1935	**Montreal Maroons**	Lionel Conacher	3-0	**Toronto**	Dick Irvin
1936	**Detroit**	Jack Adams	3-1 (WWLW)	**Toronto**	Dick Irvin
1937	**Detroit**	Jack Adams	3-2 (LWLWW)	**NY Rangers**	Lester Patrick
1938	**Chicago**	Bill Stewart	3-1 (WLWW)	**Toronto**	Dick Irvin
1939	**Boston**	Art Ross	4-1 (WLWWW)	**Toronto**	Dick Irvin
1940	**NY Rangers**	Frank Boucher	4-2 (WWLLWW)	**Toronto**	Dick Irvin
1941	**Boston**	Cooney Weiland	4-0	**Detroit**	Jack Adams
1942	**Toronto**	Hap Day	4-3 (LLLWWWW)	**Detroit**	Jack Adams
1943	**Detroit**	Ebbie Goodfellow	4-0	**Boston**	Art Ross
1944	**Montreal**	Dick Irvin	4-0	**Chicago**	Paul Thompson
1945	**Toronto**	Hap Day	4-3 (WWWLLLW)	**Detroit**	Jack Adams
1946	**Montreal**	Dick Irvin	4-1 (WWWLW)	**Boston**	Dit Clapper
1947	**Toronto**	Hap Day	4-2 (LWWWLW)	**Montreal**	Dick Irvin
1948	**Toronto**	Hap Day	4-0	**Detroit**	Tommy Ivan
1949	**Toronto**	Hap Day	4-0	**Detroit**	Tommy Ivan

Year	Winner	Head Coach	Series	Loser	Head Coach
1950	**Detroit**	Tommy Ivan	4-3 (WLWLLWW)	**NY Rangers**	Lynn Patrick
1951	**Toronto**	Joe Primeau	4-1 (WLWWW)	**Montreal**	Dick Irvin
1952	**Detroit**	Tommy Ivan	4-0	**Montreal**	Dick Irvin
1953	**Montreal**	Dick Irvin	4-1 (WLWWW)	**Boston**	Lynn Patrick
1954	**Detroit**	Tommy Ivan	4-3 (WLWWLLW)	**Montreal**	Dick Irvin
1955	**Detroit**	Jimmy Skinner	4-3 (WWLLWLW)	**Montreal**	Dick Irvin
1956	**Montreal**	Toe Blake	4-1 (WWLWW)	**Detroit**	Jimmy Skinner
1957	**Montreal**	Toe Blake	4-1 (WWWLW)	**Boston**	Milt Schmidt
1958	**Montreal**	Toe Blake	4-2 (WLWLWW)	**Boston**	Milt Schmidt
1959	**Montreal**	Toe Blake	4-1 (WWLWW)	**Toronto**	Punch Imlach
1960	**Montreal**	Toe Blake	4-0	**Toronto**	Punch Imlach
1961	**Chicago**	Rudy Pilous	4-2 (WLWLWW)	**Detroit**	Sid Abel
1962	**Toronto**	Punch Imlach	4-2 (WWLLWW)	**Chicago**	Rudy Pilous
1963	**Toronto**	Punch Imlach	4-1 (WWLWW)	**Detroit**	Sid Abel
1964	**Toronto**	Punch Imlach	4-3 (WLLWLWW)	**Detroit**	Sid Abel
1965	**Montreal**	Toe Blake	4-3 (WWLLWLW)	**Chicago**	Billy Reay
1966	**Montreal**	Toe Blake	4-2 (LLWWWW)	**Detroit**	Sid Abel
1967	**Toronto**	Punch Imlach	4-2 (LWWLWW)	**Montreal**	Toe Blake
1968	**Montreal**	Toe Blake	4-0	**St. Louis**	Scotty Bowman
1969	**Montreal**	Claude Ruel	4-0	**St. Louis**	Scotty Bowman
1970	**Boston**	Harry Sinden	4-0	**St. Louis**	Scotty Bowman
1971	**Montreal**	Al MacNeil	4-3 (LLWWLWW)	**Chicago**	Billy Reay
1972	**Boston**	Tom Johnson	4-2 (WWLWLW)	**NY Rangers**	Emile Francis
1973	**Montreal**	Scotty Bowman	4-2 (WWLWLW)	**Chicago**	Billy Reay
1974	**Philadelphia**	Fred Shero	4-2 (LWWWLW)	**Boston**	Bep Guidolin
1975	**Philadelphia**	Fred Shero	4-2 (WWLLWW)	**Buffalo**	Floyd Smith
1976	**Montreal**	Scotty Bowman	4-0	**Philadelphia**	Fred Shero
1977	**Montreal**	Scotty Bowman	4-0	**Boston**	Don Cherry
1978	**Montreal**	Scotty Bowman	4-2 (WWLLWW)	**Boston**	Don Cherry
1979	**Montreal**	Scotty Bowman	4-1 (LWWWW)	**NY Rangers**	Fred Shero
1980	**NY Islanders**	Al Arbour	4-2 (WLWWLW)	**Philadelphia**	Pat Quinn
1981	**NY Islanders**	Al Arbour	4-1 (WWWLW)	**Minnesota**	Glen Sonmor
1982	**NY Islanders**	Al Arbour	4-0	**Vancouver**	Roger Neilson
1983	**NY Islanders**	Al Arbour	4-0	**Edmonton**	Glen Sather
1984	**Edmonton**	Glen Sather	4-1 (WLWWW)	**NY Islanders**	Al Arbour
1985	**Edmonton**	Glen Sather	4-1 (LWWWW)	**Philadelphia**	Mike Keenan
1986	**Montreal**	Jean Perron	4-1 (LWWWW)	**Calgary**	Bob Johnson
1987	**Edmonton**	Glen Sather	4-3 (WWLWLLW)	**Philadelphia**	Mike Keenan
1988	**Edmonton**	Glen Sather	4-0	**Boston**	Terry O'Reilly
1989	**Calgary**	Terry Crisp	4-2 (WLLWWW)	**Montreal**	Pat Burns

Note: 1919 Finals cancelled after five games due to influenza epidemic with Montreal and Seattle tied at 2-2-1.

Conn Smythe Trophy
(Stanley Cup Playoff MVP)

Selected by Professional Hockey Writers Assn. and presented since 1965 by Maple Leaf Gardens Limited in the name of the former Toronto coach, GM and owner. Trophy winners who did not play for the Cup champion are in **bold type**.

Year

1965 Jean Beliveau, Montreal, C
1966 **Roger Crozier,** Detroit, G
1967 Dave Keon, Toronto, C
1968 **Glenn Hall,** St.Louis, G
1969 Serge Savard, Montreal, D

1970 Bobby Orr, Boston, D
1971 Ken Dryden, Montreal, G
1972 Bobby Orr, Boston, D
1973 Yvan Cournoyer, Montreal, RW
1974 Bernie Parent, Philadelphia, G
1975 Bernie Parent, Philadelphia, G
1976 **Reggie Leach,** Philadelphia, RW

Year

1977 Guy Lafleur, Montreal, RW
1978 Larry Robinson, Montreal, D
1979 Bob Gainey, Montreal, LW

1980 Bryan Trottier, NY Islanders, C
1981 Butch Goring, NY Islanders, LW
1982 Mike Bossy, NY Islanders, RW
1983 Billy Smith, NY Islanders, G
1984 Mark Messier, Edmonton, LW
1985 Wayne Gretzky, Edmonton, C
1986 Patrick Roy, Montreal, G
1987 **Ron Hextall,** Philadelphia, G
1988 Wayne Gretzky, Edmonton, C
1989 Al MacInnis, Calgary, D

Note: Ken Dryden (1971) and Patrick Roy (1986) are the only players to win the Smythe Trophy as rookies.

NHL Head Coaches

All-Time Winning Percentages

NHL head coaches with at least 300 overall wins (including playoffs) through the 1988-89 season. Active coaches in **bold type**.

		Yrs	Gm	W	L	T	Pct
1	Scotty Bowman	.17	1462	853	399	210	**.655**
2	Toe Blake	.13	1033	582	292	159	**.640**
3	Glen Sather	.10	926	535	287	104	**.634**
4	Fred Shero	.10	842	451	272	119	**.606**
5	Al Arbour	.17	1381	728	455	197	**.598**
6	Tommy Ivan	.9	677	338	227	112	**.582**
7	**Bryan Murray**	.8	679	349	251	79	**.572**
8	Billy Reay	.16	1219	599	445	175	**.563**
9	Emile Francis	.11	871	433	326	112	**.561**
10	Hap Day	.10	626	308	237	81	**.557**
11	Dick Irvin	.26	1627	790	609	228	**.556**
12	Art Ross	.16	798	393	310	95	**.552**
13	Lester Patrick	.13	669	312	242	115	**.552**
14	Punch Imlach	.15	1051	467	421	163	**.522**
15	**Michel Bergeron**	9	780	357	326	97	**.520**
16	Jack Adams	.17	1069	465	442	164	**.512**
17	Bob Pulford	.14	838	364	344	130	**.512**
18	Bob Berry	.9	721	315	306	100	**.506**
19	Sid Abel	.15	1039	414	470	155	**.473**
20	Red Kelly	.10	804	302	368	134	**.459**

Note: The NHL does not recognize WHA coaching records. If it did, Glen Sather would have 638 overall wins, 378 losses, 111 ties and a winning percentage of .615.

All-Time Wins

NHL head coaches with at least 300 overall wins through the 1988-89 season. Listed are regular season, playoff and overall wins. Active coaches in **bold type**.

		Regular	Playoffs	Total
1	Scotty Bowman	739	114	**853**
2	Dick Irvin	690	100	**790**
3	**Al Arbour**	615	113	**728**
4	Billy Reay	542	57	**599**
5	Toe Blake	500	82	**582**
6	Glen Sather	446	89	**535**
7	Punch Imlach	423	44	**467**
8	Jack Adams	413	52	**465**
9	Fred Shero	390	61	**451**
10	Emile Francis	393	40	**433**
11	Sid Abel	382	32	**414**
12	Art Ross	361	32	**393**
13	Bob Pulford	336	28	**364**
14	**Michel Bergeron**	326	31	**357**
15	**Bryan Murray**	325	24	**349**
16	Tommy Ivan	302	36	**338**
17	Bob Berry	311	4	**315**
18	Lester Patrick	281	31	**312**
19	Hap Day	259	49	**308**
20	Red Kelly	278	24	**302**

Note: The NHL does not recognize WHA coaching records. If it did, Glen Sather would move up to 4th place with 638 wins.

Where They Coached

Bowman—St.L.(1967-71), Mont.(1971-79), Buf.(1979-87); **Blake**—Mont.(1955-68); **Sather**—Edm.(1979-89); **Shero**—Phila.(1971-78), NY Rangers (1978-81); **Arbour**—St.L.(1970-73), NY Islanders (1973-86,88—); **Ivan**—Det.(1947-54), Chi.(1956-58); **Murray**—Wash. (1982—); **Reay**—Tor.(1957-59), Chi.(1963-77); **Francis**—NY Rangers (1965-75), St.L.(1976-77,81-83); **Day**—Tor.(1940-50).

Irvin—Chi.(1930-31,55-56), Tor.(1931-40), Mont.(1940-55); **Ross**—Bos.(1924-28,29-34,36-39,41-45); **Patrick**—NY Rangers (1926-39); **Imlach**—Tor.(1958-69), Buf.(1970-72), Tor.(1979-81); **Bergeron**—Que.(1980-87), NY Rangers (1987-89), Que.(1989—); **Adams**—Det.(1927-44); **Pulford**—LA (1972-77), Chi.(1977-79,81-82,85-87); **Berry**—LA (1978-81), Mont.(1981-84), Pit.(1984-87); **Abel**—Chi.(1952-54), Det.(1957-68,69-70), St.L.(1971-72), KC (1975-76); **Kelly**—LA (1967-69), Pit.(1969-73), Tor.(1973-77).

Active Head Coaches

Most Wins

Current NHL head coaches career records (including playoffs) through the 1988-89 season.

		Yrs	W	L	T	Pct
1	Al Arbour, NY Isles	.17	**728**	455	197	.598
2	Michel Bergeron, Que.	.9	**357**	326	97	.520
3	Bryan Murray, Wash	.8	**349**	251	79	.572
4	Jacques Demers, Detroit	.7	**276**	283	72	.494
5	Mike Keenan, Chicago	.5	**258**	175	40	.588
6	Bob McCammon, Vanc.	.5	**181**	166	48	.519
7	Terry Crisp, Calgary	.2	**122**	51	18	.686
8	Jim Schoenfeld, NJ	.3	**74**	81	18	.480
9	Pat Burns, Montreal	.1	**67**	25	9	.708
10	Gene Ubriaco, Pitts	.1	**47**	37	7	.555
11	Paul Holmgren, Phila	.1	**46**	45	8	.505
12	Brian Sutter, St.Louis	.1	**38**	40	12	.489
13	Bob Murdoch, Winnipeg	1	**31**	45	9	.418
14	Pierre Page, Minnesota	.1	**28**	41	16	.424
15	George Armstrong, Tor	.1	**17**	26	4	.404
16	John Muckler, Edmonton	1	**6**	23	6	.257
17	Tom Webster, Los Ang.	.1	**5**	7	2	.429
18	Mike Milbury, Boston	.0	**0**	0	0	.000
19	Rick Ley, Hartford	.0	**0**	0	0	.000
20	Rick Dudley, Buffalo	.0	**0**	0	0	.000
21	NY Rangers job vacant as of July 31,1989.					

Note: The NHL does not recognize WHA coaching records. If it did, Jacques Demers would move up to 2nd place with 431 wins, 447 losses, 94 ties, and a winning percentage of .492.

NHL All-Time Leaders

CAREER

Scoring

Goals

NHL players with at least 420 goals through the 1988-89 regular season. Active players in **bold type**.

	Yrs	Games	Goals
1 Gordie Howe	26	1,767	801
2 **Marcel Dionne**	18	1,348	**731**
3 Phil Esposito	18	1,282	**717**
4 **Wayne Gretzky**	10	774	**637**
5 Bobby Hull	16	1,063	**610**
6 Mike Bossy	10	752	**573**
7 John Bucyk	23	1,540	**556**
8 Maurice Richard	18	978	**544**
9 Stan Mikita	22	1,394	**541**
10 **Guy Lafleur**	15	1,028	**536**
11 Frank Mahovlich	18	1,181	**533**
12 Gilbert Perreault	17	1,191	**512**
13 Jean Beliveau	18	1,125	**507**
14 Lanny McDonald	16	1,111	**500**
15 Jean Ratelle	21	1,281	**491**
16 Norm Ullman	20	1,410	**490**
17 **Bryan Trottier**	14	1,064	**487**
18 Darryl Sittler	15	1,096	**484**
19 Alex Delvecchio	24	1,549	**456**
20 Rick Middleton	14	1,005	**448**
21 **Jari Kurri**	9	676	**441**
22 **Michel Goulet**	10	756	**440**
23 Yvan Cournoyer	16	968	**428**
24 Steve Shutt	13	930	**424**
25 Bill Barber	12	903	**420**

Assists

NHL players with at least 615 assists through the 1988-89 regular season. Active players in **bold type**.

	Yrs	Games	Assists
1 **Wayne Gretzky**	10	774	**1,200**
2 Gordie Howe	26	1,767	**1,049**
3 **Marcel Dionne**	18	1,348	**1,040**
4 Stan Mikita	22	1,394	**926**
5 Phil Esposito	18	1,281	**873**
6 Bobby Clarke	15	1,144	**852**
7 **Bryan Trottier**	14	1,064	**842**
8 Alex Delvecchio	24	1,549	**825**
9 Gilbert Perreault	17	1,191	**814**
10 John Bucyk	23	1,540	**813**
11 Jean Ratelle	21	1,281	**776**
12 **Guy Lafleur**	15	1,028	**755**
13 Denis Potvin	15	1,060	**742**
14 Norm Ullman	20	1,410	**739**
15 **Bernie Federko**	13	927	**721**
16 Jean Beliveau	20	1,125	**712**
17 Henri Richard	20	1,256	**688**
18 **Larry Robinson**	16	1,202	**686**
19 Brad Park	17	1,113	**683**
20 Bobby Orr	12	657	**645**
21 Darryl Sittler	15	1,096	**637**
22 **Peter Stastny**	9	675	**630**
23 Andy Bathgate	17	1,069	**624**
24 **Borje Salming**	16	1,099	**620**
25 Rod Gilbert	18	1,065	**615**

Points

NHL players with at least 1,000 points through the 1988-89 regular season. Active players in **bold type**.

	Yrs	Gm	G	A	Pts
1 Gordie Howe	26	1,767	801	1,049	**1,850**
2 **Wayne Gretzky**	10	774	637	1,200	**1,837**
3 **Marcel Dionne**	18	1,348	731	1,040	**1,771**
4 Phil Esposito	18	1,282	717	873	**1,590**
5 Stan Mikita	22	1,394	541	926	**1,467**
6 John Bucyk	23	1,540	556	813	**1,369**
7 **Bryan Trottier**	14	1,064	487	842	**1,329**
8 Gilbert Perreault	17	1,191	512	814	**1,326**
9 **Guy Lafleur**	15	1,028	536	755	**1,291**
10 Alex Delvecchio	24	1,549	456	825	**1,281**
11 Jean Ratelle	21	1,281	491	776	**1,267**
12 Norm Ullman	20	1,410	490	739	**1,229**
13 Jean Beliveau	20	1,125	507	712	**1,219**
14 Bobby Clarke	15	1,144	358	852	**1,210**
15 Bobby Hull	16	1,063	610	560	**1,170**
16 Mike Bossy	10	752	573	553	**1,126**
17 Darryl Sittler	15	1,096	484	637	**1,121**
18 Frank Mahovlich	18	1,181	533	570	**1,103**
19 **Bernie Federko**	13	927	352	721	**1,073**
20 Denis Potvin	15	1,060	310	742	**1,052**
21 Henri Richard	20	1,256	358	688	**1,046**
22 Rod Gilbert	18	1,065	406	615	**1,021**
23 Lanny McDonald	16	1,111	500	506	**1,006**

Combined NHL-WHA Points

Combined list of NHL and WHA players with at least 1,000 points through the 1988-89 regular season. Active players in **bold type**.

	Yrs	Gm	G	A	Pts
1 Gordie Howe*	32	2,186	975	1,383	**2,358**
2 **Wayne Gretzky***	11	834	683	1,264	**1,947**
3 Bobby Hull*	23	1,474	913	895	**1,808**
4 **Marcel Dionne**	18	1,348	731	1,040	**1,771**
5 Phil Esposito	18	1,282	717	873	**1,590**
6 Stan Mikita	22	1,394	541	926	**1,467**
7 John Bucyk	23	1,540	556	813	**1,369**
8 Norm Ullman*	22	1,554	537	822	**1,359**
9 Frank Mahovlich*	22	1,418	622	713	**1,335**
10 Bryan Trottier	14	1,064	487	842	**1,329**
11 Gilbert Perreault	17	1,191	512	814	**1,326**
12 **Guy Lafleur**	15	1,028	536	755	**1,291**
13 Alex Delvecchio	24	1,549	456	825	**1,281**
14 Dave Keon*	22	1,597	498	779	**1,277**
15 Jean Ratelle	21	1,281	491	776	**1,267**
16 Jean Beliveau	20	1,125	507	712	**1,219**
17 Bobby Clarke	15	1,144	358	852	**1,210**
18 Mike Bossy	10	752	573	553	**1,126**
19 Darryl Sittler	15	1,096	484	637	**1,121**
20 **Bernie Federko**	13	927	352	721	**1,073**
21 Marc Tardif*	14	963	510	557	**1,067**
22 Denis Potvin	15	1,060	310	742	**1,052**
23 Henri Richard	20	1,256	358	688	**1,046**
24 Rod Gilbert	18	1,065	406	615	**1,021**
25 Lanny McDonald	16	1,111	500	506	**1,006**

*WHA Totals: **Howe** (6 yrs, 419 games, 174 goals-334 assists—508 points); **Gretzky** (1 yr, 60 gms, 46-64-110); **Hull** (7 yrs, 411 gms, 303-335—638); **Ullman** (2 yrs, 144 gms, 47-83—130); **Mahovlich** (4 yrs, 237 gms, 89-143—232); **Keon** (4 yrs, 301 games, 102-189—291); **Tardif** (6 yrs, 446 gms, 316-350—666).

Years Played

Players who have played at least 20 seasons in the NHL.

		Yrs
1	Gordie Howe	26
2	Alex Delvecchio	24
	Tim Horton	24
4	John Bucyk	23
5	Stan Mikita	22
	Doug Mohns	22
	Dean Prentice	22
8	Harry Howell	21
	Eric Nesterenko	21
	Jean Ratelle	21
	Terry Sawchuk	21
	Allan Stanley	21
	Ron Stewart	21
	Gump Worsley	21
15	George Armstrong	20
	Jean Beliveau	20
	Dit Clapper	20
	Bill Gadsby	20
	Red Kelly	20
	Marcel Pronovost	20
	Henri Richard	20
	Norm Ullman	20

Note: Combined NHL-WHA years played: Howe (32), Howell (24), Nesterenko and Bobby Hull (23), and Norm Ullman, Frank Mahovlich and Dave Keon (22).

Games Played

Players who have played at least 1,200 games in the NHL. Active players in **bold type**.

		Games
1	Gordie Howe	1,767
2	Alex Delvecchio	1,549
3	John Bucyk	1,540
4	Tim Horton	1,446
5	Harry Howell	1,411
6	Norm Ullman	1,410
7	Stan Mikita	1,394
8	Doug Mohns	1,390
9	Dean Prentice	1,378
10	Ron Stewart	1,353
11	**Marcel Dionne**	1,348
12	Red Kelly	1,316
13	Dave Keon	1,296
14	Phil Esposito	1,282
15	Jean Ratelle	1,281
16	Henri Richard	1,256
17	Bill Gadsby	1,248
18	Allan Stanley	1,244
19	Eddie Westfall	1,227
20	Eric Nesterenko	1,219
21	Marcel Pronovost	1,206
22	**Larry Robinson**	1,202

Note: Combined NHL-WHA games played: Howe (2,186), Keon (1,597), Howell (1,581), Ullman (1,554), Hull (1,474), Mahovlich (1,418), and Nesterenko (1,248).

Penalty Minutes

NHL players with at least 1,800 penalty minutes through the 1988-89 regular season. Active players in **bold type**.

		Yrs	Gm	PMin
1	Dave Williams	13	962	**3,966**
2	Willi Plett	12	834	**2,572**
3	**Chris Nilan**	10	566	**2,447**
4	Dave Schultz	9	535	**2,294**
5	Bryan Watson	16	878	**2,212**
6	Terry O'Reilly	14	891	**2,095**
7	Phil Russell	15	1,016	**2,038**
8	**Dale Hunter**	9	682	**2,004**
9	Andre Dupont	13	810	**1,986**
10	Al Secord	10	733	**1,962**
11	**Harold Snepsts**	15	933	**1,923**
12	Garry Howatt	12	720	**1,836**
13	**Tim Hunter**	7	414	**1,816**
14	Carol Vadnais	17	1,087	**1,813**
15	**Larry Playfair**	11	684	**1,810**
16	Ted Lindsay	17	1,068	**1,808**

Goaltending

Wins

NHL goaltenders with at least 250 wins through the 1988-89 regular season. Active players in **bold type**.

		Yrs	Gm	W	L	T	Pct
1	Terry Sawchuk	21	971	**435**	337	188	.545
2	Jacques Plante	18	837	**434**	246	137	.600
3	Tony Esposito	16	886	**423**	307	151	.563
4	Glenn Hall	18	906	**407**	327	165	.540
5	Rogie Vachon	16	795	**355**	291	115	.519
6	Gump Worsley	21	862	**335**	353	150	.476
7	Harry Lumley	16	804	**332**	324	143	.502
8	Turk Broda	12	629	**302**	224	101	.560
9	Billy Smith	18	680	**301**	216	100	.516
10	Ed Giacomin	13	610	**289**	206	97	.553
11	Dan Bouchard	14	655	**286**	232	113	.523
12	Tiny Thompson	12	553	**284**	194	75	.581
13	Bernie Parent	13	608	**270**	197	121	.544
14	Gilles Meloche	18	761	**262**	342	126	.427
15	Ken Dryden	8	397	**258**	57	74	.743
16	Frank Brimsek	10	514	**252**	182	80	.568
17	**Mike Liut**	10	571	**252**	232	68	.501
18	Johnny Bower	15	549	**251**	196	90	.539

Shutouts

NHL goaltenders with at least 50 shutouts through the 1988-89 regular season.

		Yrs	Career	Games	No
1	Terry Sawchuk	21	1949-70	971	**103**
2	George Hainsworth	11	1926-37	465	**94**
3	Glenn Hall	18	1952-71	906	**84**
4	Jacques Plante	18	1952-73	837	**82**
5	Tiny Thompson	12	1928-40	552	**81**
6	Alex Connell	12	1925-37	416	**80**
7	Tony Esposito	16	1968-84	886	**76**
8	Lorne Chabot	11	1926-37	412	**73**
9	Harry Lumley	16	1943-60	803	**71**
10	Roy Worters	12	1925-37	488	**66**
11	Turk Broda	12	1936-52	628	**62**
12	Clint Benedict	13	1917-26	360	**58**
13	John Roach	14	1921-35	492	**58**
14	Bernie Parent	13	1965-79	608	**55**
15	Ed Giacomin	13	1965-78	610	**54**
16	Dave Kerr	11	1930-41	427	**51**
17	Rogie Vachon	16	1966-82	795	**51**

Combined NHL-WHA Wins

Combined list of NHL and WHA goaltenders with at least 250 wins through the 1988-89 regular season. Active players in **bold type**.

	Yrs	Gm	W	L	T	Pct
1 Jacques Plante*	.19	868	**449**	260	138	.597
2 Terry Sawchuk	.21	971	**435**	337	188	.545
3 Tony Esposito	.16	886	**423**	307	151	.563
4 Glenn Hall	.18	906	**407**	327	165	.540
5 Rogie Vachon	.16	795	**355**	291	115	.519
6 Gump Worsley	.21	862	**353**	353	150	.476
7 Harry Lumley	.16	804	**332**	324	143	.502
8 Gerry Cheevers*	.16	609	**329**	172	83	.608
9 Bernie Parent*	.14	671	**303**	225	121	.542
10 Turk Broda	.12	629	**302**	224	101	.560
11 Billy Smith	.18	680	**301**	216	100	.516
12 Ed Giacomin	.13	610	**289**	206	97	.553
13 Dan Bouchard	.14	655	**286**	232	113	.523
14 Tiny Thompson	.12	553	**284**	194	75	.581
15 **Mike Liut***	.12	652	**283**	271	72	.489
16 Gilles Meloche	.18	761	**262**	342	126	.427
17 Ken Dryden	.8	397	**258**	57	74	.743
18 Frank Brimsek	.10	514	**252**	182	80	.568
19 Johnny Bower	.15	549	**251**	196	90	.539

*WHA Totals: **Plante** (1 yr, 31 gms, 15-14-1); **Cheevers** (4 yrs, 191 gms, 99-78-9); **Parent** (1 yr, 63 gms, 33-28-0); **Liut** (2 yrs, 81 gms, 31-39-4).

Goals Against Average
Careers Ending Before 1950

NHL goaltenders whose careers ended before 1950, with a Goals Against Average of 2.50 or less. Minimum of 300 games played.

	Gm	Mins	GA	Avg
1 George Hainsworth	.465	29,415	937	**1.91**
2 Alex Connell	.416	26,030	837	**2.01**
3 Chuck Gardiner	.316	19,687	664	**2.02**
4 Lorne Chabot	.412	25,309	861	**2.04**
5 Tiny Thompson	.552	34,174	1,183	**2.08**

Playing Since 1950

NHL goaltenders, who have played since 1950, with a Goals Against Average of 2.80 or less. Minimum of 300 games played.

	Gm	Mins	GA	Avg
1 Ken Dryden	.397	23,352	870	**2.24**
2 Jacques Plante	.837	49,633	1,965	**2.38**
3 Glenn Hall	.906	53,484	2,239	**2.512**
4 Terry Sawchuk	.971	57,205	2,401	**2.518**
5 Johnny Bower	.552	32,077	1,347	**2.52**
6 Bernie Parent	.608	35,136	1,493	**2.55**
7 Turk Broda	.628	37,680	1,605	**2.56**
8 Frank Brimsek	.515	31,210	1,404	**2.70**
Charlie Hodge	.358	20,593	927	**2.70**
9 Harry Lumley	.803	48,107	2,210	**2.76**
10 Al Rollins	.430	25,717	1,196	**2.79**

SINGLE SEASON

Goals

NHL players who have scored at least 65 goals in one season through the 1988-89 regular season.

	Season	Gm	G
1 Wayne Gretzky, Edmonton	.1981-82	80	**92**
2 Wayne Gretzky, Edmonton	.1983-84	74	**87**
3 Mario Lemieux, Pittsburgh	.1988-89	76	**85**
4 Phil Esposito, Boston	.1970-71	78	**76**
5 Wayne Gretzky, Edmonton	.1984-85	80	**73**
6 Jari Kurri, Edmonton	.1984-85	73	**71**
Wayne Gretzky, Edmonton	.1982-83	80	**71**
8 Mario Lemieux, Pittsburgh	.1987-88	77	**70**
Bernie Nicholls, Los Ang	.1988-89	79	**70**
10 Mike Bossy, NY Islanders	.1978-79	80	**69**
11 Phil Esposito, Boston	.1973-74	78	**.68**
Jari Kurri, Edmonton	.1985-86	78	**68**
Mike Bossy, NY Islanders	.1980-81	79	**68**
14 Phil Esposito, Boston	.1971-72	76	**66**
Lanny McDonald, Calgary	.1982-83	80	**66**
16 Steve Yzerman, Detroit	.1988-89	80	**65**

WHA 65 goals or more: 77—Bobby Hull, Winn.(1974-75); **75**—Real Cloutier, Que.(1978-79); **71**—Marc Tardif, Que.(1975-76); **70**—Anders Hedberg, Winn.(1976-77); **66**—Real Cloutier, Que.(1976-77); **65**—Marc Tardif, Que.(1977-78) and Morris Lukowich, Winn.(1978-79).

Assists

NHL players with at least 90 assists in one season through the 1988-89 regular season.

	Season	Gm	A
1 Wayne Gretzky, Edmonton	.1985-86	80	**163**
2 Wayne Gretzky, Edmonton	.1984-85	80	**135**
3 Wayne Gretzky, Edmonton	.1982-83	80	**125**
4 Wayne Gretzky, Edmonton	.1986-87	79	**121**
5 Wayne Gretzky, Edmonton	.1981-82	80	**120**
6 Wayne Gretzky, Edmonton	.1983-84	74	**118**
7 Mario Lemieux, Pittsburgh	.1988-89	76	**114**
Wayne Gretzky, Los Ang	.1988-89	78	**114**
8 Wayne Gretzky, Edmonton	.1987-88	64	**109**
Wayne Gretzky, Edmonton	.1980-81	80	**109**
10 Bobby Orr, Boston	.1970-71	78	**102**
11 Mario Lemieux, Pittsburgh	.1987-88	77	**98**
12 Mario Lemieux, Pittsburgh	.1985-86	79	**93**
13 Peter Stastny, Quebec	.1981-82	80	**93**
14 Bobby Orr, Boston	.1973-74	74	**90**
Paul Coffey, Edmonton	.1985-86	79	**90**
Steve Yzerman, Detroit	.1988-89	80	**90**

WHA 90 assists or more: 106—Andre Lacroix, S.Diego (1974-75); **94**—Ulf Nilsson, Winn.(1974-75).

Points

NHL players who have scored at least 150 points in one season through the 1988-89 regular season.

		Season	G	A	Pts
1	Wayne Gretzky, Edm	1985-86	52	163	**215**
2	Wayne Gretzky, Edm	1981-82	92	120	**212**
3	Wayne Gretzky, Edm	1984-85	73	135	**208**
4	Wayne Gretzky, Edm	1983-84	87	118	**205**
5	Mario Lemieux, Pitt	1988-89	85	114	**199**
6	Wayne Gretzky, Edm	1982-83	71	125	**196**
7	Wayne Gretzky, Edm	1986-87	62	121	**183**
8	Mario Lemieux, Pitt	1987-88	70	98	**168**
	Wayne Gretzky, LA	1988-89	54	114	**168**
10	Wayne Gretzky, Edm	1980-81	55	109	**164**
11	Phil Esposito, Bos	1970-71	76	76	**152**

WHA 150 points or more: 154—Marc Tardif, Que.(1977-78).

Penalty Minutes

NHL players with at least 350 penalty minutes in one season through the 1988-89 regular season.

		Season	PMin
1	Dave Schultz, Philadelphia	1974-75	**472**
2	Paul Baxter, Pittsburgh	1981-82	**407**
3	Dave Schultz, Los Angeles	1977-78	**405**
4	Basil McRae, Minnesota	1987-88	**382**
5	Tim Hunter, Calgary	1988-89	**375**
6	Steve Durbano, Pitt-KC	1975-76	**370**
7	Basil McRae, Minnesota	1988-89	**365**
8	Tim Hunter, Calgary	1986-87	**361**
9	Tiger Williams, Los Angeles	1986-87	**358**
10	Tiger Williams, Toronto	1977-78	**351**

WHA 350 minutes or more: 365—Curt Brackenbury, Minn-Que.(1975-76); **351**—Kim Clackson, Ind.(1975-76).

Goaltending

Wins

NHL goaltenders with at least 40 wins in one season through the 1988-89 regular season.

		Season	W	L	T
1	Bernie Parent, Phila	1973-74	**47**-13-12
2	Bernie Parent, Phila	1974-75	**44**-14- 9
3	Terry Sawchuk, Detroit	1950-51	**44**-13-13
4	Terry Sawchuk, Detroit	1951-52	**44**-14-12
5	Jacques Plante, Mont	1955-56	**42**-12-10
6	Jacques Plante, Mont	1961-62	**42**-14-14
7	Ken Dryden, Montreal	1975-76	**42**-10- 8

WHA 40 wins or more: 44—Richard Brodeur, Que.(1975-76); **41**—Joe Daley, Winn.(1975-76) and Dave Dryden, Edm. (1978-79).

Losses

NHL goaltenders with at least 40 losses in one season through the 1988-89 regular season.

		Season	W	L	T
1	Gary Smith, California	1970-71	19- **48**- 4
2	Al Rollins, Chicago	1953-54	12- **47**- 7
3	Harry Lumley, Chicago	1951-52	17- **44**- 9
4	Harry Lumley, Chicago	1950-51	12- **41**-10
5	Eddie Johnston, Boston	1963-64	18- **40**-12

Most WHA losses in one season: 36—Don McLeod, Van.(1974-75) and Andy Brown, Ind.(1974-75).

Shutouts

NHL goaltenders with at least 14 shutouts through the 1988-89 regular season.

		Season	Gm	No
1	George Hainsworth, Mont	1928-29	44	**22**
2	Alex Connell, Ottawa	1925-26	361	**15**
3	Alex Connell, Ottawa	1927-28	441	**15**
4	Hal Winkler, Boston	1927-28	441	**15**
5	Tony Esposito, Chicago	1969-70	631	**15**
6	George Hainsworth, Mont	1926-27	441	**14**

Most WHA shutouts in one season: 5—Jerry Cheevers, Cleve. (1972-73); Joe Daly, Winn. (1975-76).

Goals Against Average

Before 1950

NHL goaltenders with lowest Goals Against Averages through the 1949-50 regular season.

		Season	Gm	Avg
1	George Hainsworth, Mont	1928-29	44	**0.98**
2	George Hainsworth, Mont	1927-28	44	**1.09**
3	Alex Connell, Ottawa	1925-26	36	**1.17**
4	Tiny Thompson, Boston	1928-29	44	**1.18**
5	Roy Worters, NY Amer	1928-29	38	**1.21**

Since 1950

NHL goaltenders with lowest Goals Against Averages since the 1949-50 regular season.

		Season	Gm	Avg
1	Al Rollins, Toronto	1950-51	40	**1.77**
2	Tony Esposito, Chicago	1971-72	48	**1.77**
3	Harry Lumley, Toronto	1953-54	69	**1.86**
4	Jacques Plante, Montreal	1955-56	64	**1.86**
5	Jacques Plante, Toronto	1970-71	40	**1.88**

BEST GAMES

Scoring

Most Goals	Date	No
Joe Malone, Quebec vs Toronto	1/31/20	7
Newsy Lalonde, Montreal vs Toronto	1/10/20	6
Joe Malone, Quebec vs Ottawa	3/10/20	6
Corb Denneny, Toronto vs Hamilton	1/26/21	6
Cy Denneny, Ottawa vs Hamilton	3/7/21	6
Syd Howe, Detroit vs NY Rangers	2/3/44	6
Red Berenson, St.Louis at Phila	11/7/68	6
Darryl Sittler, Toronto vs Boston	2/7/76	6

Most Assists	Date	No
Billy Taylor, Detroit at Chicago	3/16/47	7
Wayne Gretzky, Edmonton at Wash	2/15/80	7
Wayne Gretzky, Edmonton at Chicago	12/11/85	7
Wayne Gretzky, Edmonton vs Quebec	2/14/86	7
15 players tied with 6 assists each.		

Most Points	Date	G-A—Pts
Darryl Sittler, Toronto vs Bos	2/7/76	6-4—10
Maurice Richard, Mont.vs Det	12/28/44	5-3— 8
Bert Olmstead, Mont.vs Chicago	1/9/54	4-4— 8
Tom Bladon, Phila.vs Cleve	12/11/77	4-4— 8
Bryan Trottier, NYI vs NYR	12/23/78	5-3— 8
Peter Stastny, Quebec at Wash	2/22/81	4-4— 8
Anton Stastny, Quebec at Wash	2/22/81	3-5— 8
Wayne Gretzky, Edm. vs NJ	11/19/83	3-5— 8
Wayne Gretzky, Edmonton vs Minn	1/4/84	4-4— 8
Paul Coffey, Edmonton vs Det	3/14/86	2-6— 8
Mario Lemieux, Pitt.vs St.L	10/15/88	2-6— 8
Bernie Nicholls, LA vs Tor	12/1/88	2-6— 8
Mario Lemieux, Pitt.vs NJ	12/31/88	5-3— 8

BEST PERIODS

Scoring

Most Goals	Date	Per	No
Busher Jackson, Tor.vs St.L	11/20/34	3rd	4
Max Bentley, Chicago vs NYR	1/28/43	3rd	4
Clint Smith, Chicago vs Montreal	3/4/45	3rd	4
Red Berenson, St.Louis at Phila	11/7/68	2nd	4
Wayne Gretzky, Edmonton vs St.L.	2/18/81	3rd	4
Grant Mulvey, Chicago vs St.L	2/3/82	1st	4
Bryan Trottier, NYI vs Phila	2/13/82	2nd	4
Al Secord, Chicago vs Toronto	1/7/87	2nd	4
Joe Nieuwendyk, Calgary vs Winn	1/11/89	2nd	4

Most Assists	Date	Per	No
Dale Hawerchuck, Winn.at LA	3/6/84	2nd	5
28 players (Gretzky 10 times) tied with 4 assists.			

Points	Date	Per	G-A—Pts
Bryan Trottier, NYI vs NYR	12/23/78	2nd	3-3— 6
Les Cunningham, Chi.vs Mon	1/28/40	3rd	2-3— 5
Max Bentley, Chi.vs NYR	1/28/43	3rd	4-1— 5
Leo Labine, Boston vs Det	11/28/54	2nd	3-2— 5
Darryl Sittler, Tor.vs Bos	2/7/76	2nd	3-2— 5
Dale Hawerchuck, Winn.at LA	3/6/84	2nd	0-5— 5
Jari Kurri, Edm.vs LA	10/26/84	2nd	2-3— 5
Pat Elynuik, Winn.vs Pitt	1/20/89	2nd	2-3— 5

Stanley Cup Playoff Leaders

CAREER

Stanley Cup Playoff leaders through 1989. Years listed indicate playoff appearances. Active players in **bold type.**

Scoring

Most Goals	Yrs	Gm	G
Wayne Gretzky	10	131	86
Mike Bossy	10	129	85
Jari Kurri	9	124	82
Maurice Richard	17	133	82
Jean Beliveau	17	162	79

Most Assists	Yrs	Gm	A
Wayne Gretzky	10	131	188
Larry Robinson	17	203	109
Denis Potvin	13	185	108
Bryan Trottier	13	171	106
Mark Messier	10	126	102

Most Points	Yrs	Gm	G	A	Pts
Wayne Gretzky	10	131	86	188	274
Jari Kurri	9	124	82	95	177
Jean Beliveau	17	162	79	97	176
Mark Messier	10	126	67	102	169
Bryan Trottier	13	171	63	106	169

Goaltending

Most Wins	Gm	Mins	W	L
Billy Smith	132	7,645	88	36
Ken Dryden	112	6,841	80	32
Jacques Plante	112	6,651	71	37
Grant Fuhr	94	5,446	66	25
Turk Broda	102	6,406	58	42

Most Shutouts	Gm	ShO
Clint Benedict	48	15
Jacques Plante	112	15
Turk Broda	102	13
Terry Sawchuck	106	12
Ken Dryden	112	10

Goals Against Avg.*	Gm	Mins	GA	Avg
George Hainsworth	52	3,486	112	1.93
Turk Broda	101	6,348	211	1.98
Jacques Plante	112	6,651	241	2.17
Ken Dryden	112	6,841	274	2.40
Bernie Parent	71	4,302	174	2.43

*At least 50 games played.

Miscellaneous

Most Championships	Yrs	Cups
Henri Richard, Montreal	18	11
Jean Beliveau, Montreal	17	10
Yvan Cournoyer, Montreal	15	10
Claude Provost, Montreal	14	9
Maurice Richard, Montreal	17	8
Red Kelly, Detroit-Toronto	19	8
Jacques Lemaire, Montreal	11	8

Most Years in Playoffs	Yrs	Gm
Gordie Howe, Detroit-Hartford	20	157
Red Kelly, Detroit-Toronto	19	164
Stan Mikita, Chicago	18	155
Henri Richard, Montreal	18	180

Most Games Played	Yrs	Gm
Larry Robinson, Montreal	17	**203**
Denis Potvin, NY Islanders	15	**185**
Bob Gainey, Montreal	16	**182**
Henri Richard, Montreal	18	**180**
Bryan Trottier, NY Islanders	13	**171**

Most Games Played in Goal	Yrs	Gm
Billy Smith, NY Islanders	13	**132**
Glenn Hall, Detroit-Chicago-St.L.	17	**115**
Jacques Plante, Mont-St.L-Tor-Bos	16	**112**
Ken Dryden, Montreal	8	**112**

Most Penalty Minutes	Yrs	Gm	PMin
Willi Plett, Atl-Cal-Min-Bos	10	83	**466**
Dave Williams, Tor-Van-LA	12	83	**455**
Dale Hunter, Que-Wash	9	87	**444**
Chris Nilan, Mont-NYR	9	81	**435**
Dave Schultz, Phila-LA-Buff	6	73	**412**

SINGLE SEASON

Scoring

Most Goals	Year	Gm	G
Reggie Leach, Philadelphia	1976	16	**19**
Jari Kurri, Edmonton	1985	18	**19**
Mike Bossy, NY Islanders	1981	18	**17**
Wayne Gretzky, Edmonton	1985	18	**17**
Steve Payne, Minnesota	1981	19	**17**
Mike Bossy, NY Islanders	1982	19	**17**
Mike Bossy, NY Islanders	1983	19	**17**

Most Assists	Year	Gm	A
Wayne Gretzky, Edmonton	1988	19	**31**
Wayne Gretzky, Edmonton	1985	18	**30**
Wayne Gretzky, Edmonton	1987	21	**29**
Wayne Gretzky, Edmonton	1983	16	**26**
Paul Coffey, Edmonton	1985	18	**25**

Most Points	Year	Gm	G	A	Pts
Wayne Gretzky, Edmonton	1985	18	17	30	**47**
Wayne Gretzky, Edmonton	1988	19	12	31	**43**
Wayne Gretzky, Edmonton	1983	16	12	26	**38**
Paul Coffey, Edmonton	1985	18	12	25	**37**
Mike Bossy, NY Islanders	1981	18	17	18	**35**
Wayne Gretzky, Edmonton	1984	19	13	22	**35**

Goaltending

Most Wins	Year	Gm	Mins	W-L
Grant Fuhr, Edmonton	1988	19	1,136	**16- 2**
Mike Vernon, Calgary	1989	22	1,381	**16- 5**
Billy Smith, NY Isles	1982	18	1,120	**15- 3**
Grant Fuhr, Edmonton	1985	18	1,064	**15- 3**
Billy Smith, NY Isles	1980	20	1,198	**15- 4**
Patrick Roy, Montreal	1986	20	1,218	**15- 5**
Ron Hextall, Phila	1987	26	1,540	**15-11**

Most Shutouts	Year	Gm	ShO
Clint Benedict, Mont.Maroons	1928	9	**4**
Dave Kerr, NY Rangers	1937	9	**4**
Frank McCool, Toronto	1945	13	**4**
Terry Sawchuck, Detroit	1952	8	**4**
Bernie Parent, Philadelphia	1975	17	**4**
Ken Dryden, Montreal	1977	14	**4**

Goals Against Avg.*	Year	Gm	Min	GA	Avg
Terry Sawchuk, Detroit	1952	8	480	5	**0.63**
Turk Broda, Toronto	1951	9	509	9	**1.06**
Dave Kerr, NY Rangers	1937	9	553	10	**1.08**
Jacques Plante, Montreal	1960	8	488	11	**1.35**
Jacques Plante, St.Louis	1969	10	589	14	**1.43**

*At least eight games played.

BEST GAMES

Scoring

Most Goals	Date	G
Maurice Richard, Montreal vs Tor	3/23/44	**5**
Darryl Sittler, Toronto vs Phila	4/22/76	**5**
Reggie Leach, Phila.vs Boston	5/6/76	**5**
Mario Lemieux, Pitt.vs Phila	4/25/89	**5**

Most Assists	Date	A
Mikko Leinonen, NYR vs Phila	4/8/82	**6**
Wayne Gretzky, Edmonton vs LA	4/9/87	**6**
Nine players tied with 5 assists.		

Most Points	Date	G-A—Pts
Patrik Sundstrom, NJ vs Wash	4/22/88	3-5 — **8**
Mario Lemieux, Pitt.vs Phila	4/25/89	5-3 — **8**
Wayne Gretzky, Edm.at Calg.	4/17/83	4-3 — **7**
Wayne Gretzky, Edm.at Winn	4/25/85	3-4 — **7**
Wayne Gretzky, Edm.vs LA	4/9/87	1-6 — **7**

NHL Awards

Art Ross Trophy
(Leading Scorer)

Given to the player who leads the league in points scored and named after the former Boston Bruins general manager-coach. First presented in 1947, names of prior leading scorers have been added retroactively. A tie for the scoring championship is broken three ways: 1. total goals; 2. fewest games played; 3. first goal scored.

Season		Gm	G	A	Pts
1917-18	Joe Malone, Montreal	20	44	—	44
1918-19	Newsy Lalonde, Mont.	17	23	9	32
1919-20	Joe Malone, Quebec	24	39	6	45
1920-21	Newsy Lalonde, Montreal	24	33	8	41
1921-22	Punch Broadbent, Ottawa	24	32	14	46
1922-23	Babe Dye, Toronto	22	26	11	37
1923-24	Cy Denneny, Ottawa	21	22	1	23
1924-25	Babe Dye, Toronto	29	38	6	44
1925-26	Nels Stewart, M.Maroons	36	34	8	42
1926-27	Bill Cook, NY Rangers	44	33	4	37
1927-28	Howie Morenz, Montreal	43	33	18	51
1928-29	Ace Bailey, Toronto	44	22	10	32
1929-30	Cooney Weiland, Boston	44	43	30	73
1930-31	Howie Morenz, Montreal	39	28	23	51
1931-32	Harvey Jackson, Toronto	48	28	25	53
1932-33	Bill Cook, NY Rangers	48	28	22	50
1933-34	Charlie Conacher, Tor	42	32	20	52
1934-35	Charlie Conacher, Tor	47	36	21	57
1935-36	Sweeney Schriner, NYAmer	48	19	26	45
1936-37	Sweeney Schriner, NYAmer	48	21	25	46
1937-38	Gordie Drillon, Toronto	48	26	26	52
1938-39	Toe Blake, Montreal	48	24	23	47
1939-40	Milt Schmidt, Boston	48	22	30	52
1940-41	Bill Cowley, Boston	46	17	45	62
1941-42	Bryan Hextall, NY Rang	48	24	32	56
1942-43	Doug Bentley, Chicago	50	33	40	73
1943-44	Herbie Cain, Boston	48	36	46	82
1944-45	Elmer Lach, Montreal	50	26	54	80
1945-46	Max Bentley, Chicago	47	31	30	61
1946-47	Max Bentley, Chicago	60	29	43	72
1947-48	Elmer Lach, Montreal	60	30	31	61
1948-49	Roy Conacher, Chicago	60	26	42	68
1949-50	Ted Lindsay, Detroit	69	23	55	78
1950-51	Gordie Howe, Detroit	70	43	43	86
1951-52	Gordie Howe, Detroit	70	47	39	86
1952-53	Gordie Howe, Detroit	70	49	46	95
1953-54	Gordie Howe, Detroit	70	33	48	81
1954-55	Bernie Geoffrion, Mont	70	38	37	75
1955-56	Jean Beliveau, Montreal	70	47	41	88
1956-57	Gordie Howe, Detroit	70	44	45	89
1957-58	Dickie Moore, Montreal	70	36	48	84
1958-59	Dickie Moore, Montreal	70	41	55	96
1959-60	Bobby Hull, Chicago	70	39	42	81
1960-61	Bernie Geoffrion, Mont	64	50	45	95
1961-62	Bobby Hull, Chicago*	70	50	34	84
1962-63	Gordie Howe, Detroit	70	38	48	86
1963-64	Stan Mikita, Chicago	70	39	50	89
1964-65	Stan Mikita, Chicago	70	28	59	87
1965-66	Bobby Hull, Chicago	65	54	43	97
1966-67	Stan Mikita, Chicago	70	35	62	97
1967-68	Stan Mikita, Chicago	72	40	47	87
1968-69	Phil Esposito, Boston	74	49	77	126
1969-70	Bobby Orr, Boston	76	33	87	120
1970-71	Phil Esposito, Boston	78	76	76	152
1971-72	Phil Esposito, Boston	76	66	67	133
1972-73	Phil Esposito, Boston	78	55	75	130
1973-74	Phil Esposito, Boston	78	68	77	145
1974-75	Bobby Orr, Boston	80	46	89	135
1975-76	Guy Lafleur, Montreal	80	56	59	125
1976-77	Guy Lafleur, Montreal	80	56	80	136
1977-78	Guy Lafleur, Montreal	79	60	72	132
1978-79	Bryan Trottier, NY Isles	76	47	87	134
1979-80	Marcel Dionne, Los Ang*	80	53	84	137
1981-82	Wayne Gretzky, Edmonton	80	55	109	164
1982-83	Wayne Gretzky, Edmonton	80	92	120	212
1983-84	Wayne Gretzky, Edmonton	80	71	125	196
1984-85	Wayne Gretzky, Edmonton	74	87	118	205
1985-86	Wayne Gretzky, Edmonton	80	73	135	208
1986-87	Wayne Gretzky, Edmonton	80	52	163	215
1987-88	Wayne Gretzky, Edmonton	79	62	121	183
1987-88	Mario Lemieux, Pitts	77	70	98	168
1988-89	Mario Lemieux, Pitts	76	85	114	199

*Note: The two times players have tied for total points in one season the player with more goals won the Ross Trophy. In 1961-62, Bobby Hull of Chicago outscored Andy Bathgate of NY Rangers 50 goals to 28. In 1979-80, Marcel Dionne of LA outscored Wayne Gretzky of Edmonton 53-51.

Hart Memorial Trophy
(Most Valuable Player)

Awarded to the player "adjudged to be the most valuable to his team" and named after Cecil Hart, the former manager-coach of the Montreal Canadiens. Winners selected by Professional Hockey Writers Assn. Numbers in parentheses indicate repeat winners.

Season	Most Valuable Player	Pos
1923-24	Frank Nighbor, Ottawa Senators	C
1924-25	Billy Burch, Hamilton Tigers	C
1925-26	Nels Stewart, Montreal Maroons	C
1926-27	Herb Gardiner, Montreal	D
1927-28	Howie Morenz, Montreal	C
1928-29	Roy Worters, NY Americans	G
1929-30	Nels Stewart, Montreal Maroons (2)	C
1930-31	Howie Morenz, Montreal (2)	C
1931-32	Howie Morenz, Montreal (3)	C
1932-33	Eddie Shore, Boston	D
1933-34	Aurel Joliat, Montreal	LW
1934-35	Eddie Shore, Boston (2)	D
1935-36	Eddie Shore, Boston (3)	D
1936-37	Babe Siebert, Montreal	D
1937-38	Eddie Shore, Boston (4)	D
1938-39	Toe Blake, Montreal	LW
1939-40	Ebbie Goodfellow, Detroit	D
1940-41	Bill Cowley, Boston	C
1941-42	Tommy Anderson, NY Americans	D
1942-43	Bill Cowley, Boston (2)	C
1943-44	Babe Pratt, Toronto	D
1944-45	Elmer Lach, Montreal	C

Season	Most Valuable Player	Pos	Season	Most Valuable Player	Pos
1945-46	Max Bentley, Chicago	C	1967-68	Stan Mikita, Chicago (2)	C
1946-47	Maurice Richard, Montreal	RW	1968-69	Phil Esposito, Boston	C
1947-48	Buddy O'Connor, NY Rangers	C	1969-70	Bobby Orr, Boston	D
1948-49	Sid Abel, Detroit	C	1970-71	Bobby Orr, Boston (2)	D
1949-50	Chuck Rayner, NY Rangers	G	1971-72	Bobby Orr, Boston (3)	D
1950-51	Milt Schmidt, Boston	C	1972-73	Bobby Clarke, Philadelphia	C
1951-52	Gordie Howe, Detroit	RW	1973-74	Phil Esposito, Boston (2)	C
1952-53	Gordie Howe, Detroit (2)	RW	1974-75	Bobby Clarke, Philadelphia (2)	C
1953-54	Al Rollins, Chicago	G	1975-76	Bobby Clarke, Philadelphia (3)	C
1954-55	Ted Kennedy, Toronto	C	1976-77	Guy Lafleur, Montreal	RW
1955-56	Jean Beliveau, Montreal	C	1977-78	Guy Lafleur, Montreal (2)	RW
1956-57	Gordie Howe, Detroit (3)	RW	1978-79	Bryan Trottier, NY Islanders	C
1957-58	Gordie Howe, Detroit (4)	RW	1979-80	Wayne Gretzky, Edmonton	C
1958-59	Andy Bathgate, NY Rangers	RW	1980-81	Wayne Gretzky, Edmonton (2)	C
1959-60	Gordie Howe, Detroit (5)	RW	1981-82	Wayne Gretzky, Edmonton (3)	C
1960-61	Bernie Geoffrion, Montreal	RW	1982-83	Wayne Gretzky, Edmonton (4)	C
1961-62	Jacques Plante, Montreal	G	1983-84	Wayne Gretzky, Edmonton (5)	C
1962-63	Gordie Howe, Detroit (6)	RW	1984-85	Wayne Gretzky, Edmonton (6)	C
1963-64	Jean Beliveau, Montreal (2)	C	1985-86	Wayne Gretzky, Edmonton (7)	C
1964-65	Bobby Hull, Chicago	LW	1986-87	Wayne Gretzky, Edmonton (8)	C
1965-66	Bobby Hull, Chicago (2)	LW	1987-88	Mario Lemieux, Pittsburgh	C
1966-67	Stan Mikita, Chicago	C	1988-89	Wayne Gretzky, Los Angeles (9)	C

Lester Pearson Award
(Outstanding Player)

Awarded to the season's most outstanding player and named after the former diplomat and Canadian prime minister. Winners selected by the NHL Players Assn. Numbers in parentheses indicate repeat winners.

Season	Most Outstanding Player	Pos	Season	Most Outstanding Player	Pos
1970-71	Phil Esposito, Boston	C	1979-80	Marcel Dionne, Los Angeles (2)	C
1971-72	Jean Ratelle, NY Rangers	C	1980-81	Mike Liut, St.Louis	G
1972-73	Phil Esposito, Boston (2)	C	1981-82	Wayne Gretzky, Edmonton	C
1973-74	Bobby Clarke, Philadelphia	C	1982-83	Wayne Gretzky, Edmonton (2)	C
1974-75	Bobby Orr, Boston	D	1983-84	Wayne Gretzky, Edmonton (3)	C
1975-76	Guy Lafleur, Montreal	RW	1984-85	Wayne Gretzky, Edmonton (4)	C
1976-77	Guy Lafleur, Montreal (2)	RW	1985-86	Mario Lemieux, Pittsburgh	C
1977-78	Guy Lafleur, Montreal (3)	RW	1986-87	Wayne Gretzky, Edmonton (5)	C
1978-79	Marcel Dionne, Los Angeles	C	1987-88	Mario Lemieux, Pittsburgh (2)	C
			1988-89	Steve Yzerman, Detroit	C

Lady Byng Memorial Trophy
(Most Gentlemanly Player)

Awarded to the player "adjudged to have exhibited the best type of sportsmanship and gentlemanly conduct combined with a high standard of playing ability" and named after the wife of former Candian Governor General (1921-26) Baron Byng of Vimy. Winners selected by Professional Hockey Writers' Assn. Defenseman who have won the award are in **bold type**. Numbers in parentheses indicate repeat winners.

Year	Winner	Year	Winner	Year	Winner
1925	Frank Nighbor, Ottawa	1947	Bobby Bauer, Boston (3)	1970	Phil Goyette, St.Louis
1926	Frank Nighbor, Ottawa	1948	Buddy O'Connor, NY Rangers	1971	John Bucyk, Boston
1927	Billy Burch, NY Americans	1949	**Bill Quackenbush,** Detroit	1972	Jean Ratelle, NY Rangers
1928	Frank Boucher, NY Rangers	1950	Edgar Laprade, NY Rangers	1973	Gilbert Perreault, Buff.
1929	Frank Boucher, NY Rang.(2)	1951		1974	John Bucyk, Boston (2)
1930	Frank Boucher, NY Rang.(3)	1952	Sid Smith, Toronto	1975	Marcel Dionne, Detroit
1931	Frank Boucher, NY Rang.(4)	1953	**Red Kelly,** Detroit (2)	1976	Jean Ratelle, NY-Bos.(2)
1932	Joe Primeau, Toronto	1954	**Red Kelly,** Detroit (3)	1977	Marcel Dionne, LA (2)
1933	Frank Boucher, NY Rang.(5)	1955	Sid Smith, Toronto (2)	1978	Butch Goring, Los Ang.
1934	Frank Boucher, NY Rang.(6)	1956	Earl Reibel, Detroit	1979	Bob MacMillan, Atlanta
1935	Frank Boucher, NY Rang.(7)	1957	Andy Hebenton, NY Rangers	1980	Wayne Gretzky, Edmonton
1936	Doc Romnes, Chicago	1958	Camille Henry, NY Rangers	1981	Rick Kehoe, Pittsburgh
1937	Marty Barry, Detroit	1959	Alex Delvecchio, Detroit	1982	Rick Middleton, Boston
1938	Gordie Drillon, Toronto	1960	Don McKenney, Boston	1983	Mike Bossy, NY Islanders
1939	Clint Smith, NY Rangers	1961	**Red Kelly,** Toronto (4)	1984	Mike Bossy, NY Isles (2)
1940	Bobby Bauer, Boston	1962	Dave Keon, Toronto	1985	Jari Kurri, Edmonton
1941	Bobby Bauer, Boston (2)	1963	Dave Keon, Toronto (2)	1986	Mike Bossy, NY Isles (3)
1942	Syl Apps, Toronto	1964	Ken Wharram, Chicago	1987	Joey Mullen, Calgary
1943	Max Bentley, Chicago	1965	Bobby Hull, Chicago	1988	Mats Naslund, Montreal
1944	Clint Smith, Chicago (2)	1966	Alex Delvecchio, Det.(2)	1989	Joey Mullen, Calgary (2)
1945	Bill Mosienko, Chicago	1967	Stan Mikita, Chicago		
1946	Toe Blake, Montreal	1968	Stan Mikita, Chicago (2)		
		1969	Alex Delvecchio, Det.(3)		

Note: 1950 and 1951 entries "Edgar Laprade, NY Rangers" and "**Red Kelly,** Detroit" are bracketed together in the original.

Norris Memorial Trophy
(Best Defenseman)

Awarded to the most outstanding defenseman of the year and named after James Norris, the late Detroit Red Wings owner-president. Winners selected by Professional Hockey Writers Assn. Numbers in parentheses indicate repeat winners.

Year	Winner	Year	Winner	Year	Winner
1954	Red Kelly, Detroit	1966	Jacques Laperriere, Mont.	1978	Denis Potvin, NY Isles (2)
1955	Doug Harvey, Montreal	1967	Harry Howell, NY Rangers	1979	Denis Potvin, NY Isles (3)
1956	Doug Harvey, Montreal (2)	1968	Bobby Orr, Boston	1980	Larry Robinson, Mont.(2)
1957	Doug Harvey, Montreal (3)	1969	Bobby Orr, Boston (2)	1981	Randy Carlyle, Pittsburgh
1958	Doug Harvey, Montreal (4)	1970	Bobby Orr, Boston (3)	1982	Doug Wilson, Chicago
1959	Tom Johnson, Montreal	1971	Bobby Orr, Boston (4)	1983	Rod Langway, Washington
1960	Doug Harvey, Montreal (5)	1972	Bobby Orr, Boston (5)	1984	Rod Langway, Wash.(2)
1961	Doug Harvey, Montreal (6)	1973	Bobby Orr, Boston (6)	1985	Paul Coffey, Edmonton
1962	Doug Harvey, NY Rang.(7)	1974	Bobby Orr, Boston (7)	1986	Paul Coffey, Edmonton (2)
1963	Pierre Pilote, Chicago	1975	Bobby Orr, Boston (8)	1987	Ray Bourque, Boston
1964	Pierre Pilote, Chicago (2)	1976	Denis Potvin, NY Islanders	1988	Ray Bourque, Boston (2)
1965	Pierre Pilote, Chicago (3)	1977	Larry Robinson, Montreal	1989	Chris Chelios, Montreal

Vezina Trophy
(Best Goaltender)

From 1926-80, given to the principal goaltender(s) on the team allowing the fewest goals during the regular season and named after 1920's goalie Georges Vezina of the Montreal Canadiens, who died of tuberculosis in 1926.

Since the 1980-81 season, the trophy has been awarded to the most outstanding goaltender of the year as selected by the league's general managers. Numbers in parentheses indicate repeat winners.

Season	Team—Goaltender(s)	Gm	GA
1926-27	Montreal—George Hainsworth	.44	67
1927-28	Montreal—Geo.Hainsworth (2)	.44	48
1928-29	Montreal—Geo.Hainsworth (3)	.44	43
1929-30	Boston—Tiny Thompson	.44	98
1930-31	NY Americans—Roy Worters	.44	74
1931-32	Chicago—Charlie Gardiner	.48	101
1932-33	Boston—Tiny Thompson (2)	.48	88
1933-34	Chicago—Charlie Gardiner (2)	.48	83
1934-35	Chicago—Lorne Chabot	.48	88
1935-36	Boston—Tiny Thompson (3)	.48	83
1936-37	Detroit—Normie Smith	.48	102
1937-38	Boston—Tiny Thompson (4)	.48	89
1938-39	Boston—Frank Brimsek	.48	76
1939-40	NY Rangers—Dave Kerr	.48	77
1940-41	Toronto—Turk Broda	.48	99
1941-42	Boston—Frank Brimsek (2)	.48	118
1942-43	Detroit—Johnny Mowers	.50	124
1943-44	Montreal—Bill Durnan	.50	109
1944-45	Montreal—Bill Durnan (2)	.50	121
1945-46	Montreal—Bill Durnan (3)	.50	134
1946-47	Montreal—Bill Durnan (4)	.60	138
1947-48	Toronto—Turk Broda (2)	.60	143
1948-49	Montreal—Bill Durnan (5)	.60	126
1949-50	Montreal—Bill Durnan (6)	.70	150
1950-51	Toronto—Al Rollins	.70	138
1951-52	Detroit—Terry Sawchuk	.70	133
1952-53	Detroit—Terry Sawchuk (2)	.70	133
1953-54	Toronto—Harry Lumley	.70	131
1954-55	Detroit—Terry Sawchuk (3)	.70	134
1955-56	Montreal—Jacques Plante	.70	131
1956-57	Montreal—Jacques Plante (2)	.70	155
1957-58	Montreal—Jacques Plante (3)	.70	158
1958-59	Montreal—Jacques Plante (4)	.70	158
1959-60	Montreal—Jacques Plante (5)	.70	178
1960-61	Toronto—Johnny Bower	.70	176
1961-62	Montreal—Jacques Plante (6)	.70	166
1962-63	Chicago—Glenn Hall	.70	178
1963-64	Montreal—Charlie Hodge	.70	167

Season	Team—Goaltender(s)	Gm	GA
1964-65	Toronto—Terry Sawchuk (4) & Johnny Bower (2)	.70	173
1965-66	Montreal—Gump Worsley & Charlie Hodge (2)	.70	173
1966-67	Chicago—Glenn Hall (2) & Denis Dejordy	.70	170
1967-68	Montreal—Gump Worsley (2) & Rogie Vachon	.74	167
1968-69	St.Louis—Jacques Plante (7) & Glenn Hall (3)	.76	157
1969-70	Chicago—Tony Esposito	.76	170
1970-71	NY Rangers—Ed Giacomin & Gilles Villemure	.78	177
1971-72	Chicago—Tony Esposito (2) & Gary Smith	.78	166
1972-73	Montreal—Ken Dryden, Montreal.	.78	184
1973-74	Philadelphia—Bernie Parent & Chicago—Tony Esposito (3)	.78 .78	164 164
1974-75	Philadelphia—Bernie Parent (2)	.80	181
1975-76	Montreal—Ken Dryden (2)	.80	174
1976-77	Montreal—Ken Dryden (3) & Bunny Larocque	.80	171
1977-78	Montreal—Ken Dryden (4) & Bunny Larocque (2)	.80	183
1978-79	Montreal—Ken Dryden (5) & Bunny Larocque (3)	.80	204
1979-80	Buffalo—Bob Sauve & Don Edwards	.80	201
1980-81	Montreal—Richard Sevigny, Denis Herron & Bunny Larocque (4)	.80	232

Season	Outstanding Goalie	Record	Avg
1981-82	Billy Smith, NY Islanders	32- 9-4	2.97
1982-83	Pete Peeters, Boston	40-11-9	2.36
1983-84	Tom Barrasso, Buffalo	26-12-3	2.84
1984-85	Pelle Lindbergh, Phila	40-17-7	3.02
1985-86	John Vanbiesbrouck, NYR	31-21-5	3.32
1986-87	Ron Hextall, Phila	37-21-6	3.00
1987-88	Grant Fuhr, Edmonton	40-24-9	3.43
1988-89	Patrick Roy, Montreal	33- 5-6	2.47

Jennings Trophy

When the Vezina Trophy switched from a team to an individual award in 1981-82, this trophy, named after the late NY Rangers president William Jennings, was created and given to the principal goaltenders on the team allowing the fewest goals during the regular season.

Season	Team—Goaltenders	Gm	GA	Season	Team—Goaltenders	Gm	GA
1981-82	Montreal—Rick Wamsley & Denis Herron	80	223	1985-86	Philadelphia—Bob Froese & Darren Jensen	80	241
1982-83	NY Islanders—Roland Melanson & Billy Smith	80	226	1986-87	Montreal—Patrick Roy & Brian Hayward	80	241
1983-84	Washington—Al Jensen & Pat Riggin	80	226	1987-88	Montreal—Patrick Roy & Brian Hayward	80	238
1984-85	Buffalo—Tom Barrasso & Bob Sauve	80	237	1988-89	Montreal—Patrick Roy & Brian Hayward	80	218

Calder Memorial Trophy
(Rookie of the Year)

Awarded to the most outstanding rookie of the year and named after Frank Calder, the late NHL president (1917-43). Winners selected by Professional Hockey Writers Assn.

Season	Rookie of the Year	Pos	Season	Rookie of the Year	Pos
1932-33	Carl Voss, Detroit	C	1959-60	Bill Hay, Chicago	C
1933-34	Russ Blinco, Montreal Maroons	C	1960-61	Dave Keon, Toronto	C
1934-35	Sweeney Schriner, NY Americans	LW	1961-62	Bobby Rousseau, Montreal	RW
1935-36	Mike Karakas, Chicago	G	1962-63	Kent Douglas, Toronto	D
1936-37	Syl Apps, Toronto	C	1963-64	Jacques Laperriere, Montreal	D
1937-38	Cully Dahlstrom, Chicago	C	1964-65	Roger Crozier, Detroit	G
1938-39	Frank Brimsek, Boston	G	1965-66	Brit Selby, Toronto	LW
1939-40	Kilby MacDonald, NY Rangers	LW	1966-67	Bobby Orr, Boston	D
1940-41	John Quilty, Montreal	C	1967-68	Derek Sanderson, Boston	C
1941-42	Knobby Warwick, NY Rangers	RW	1968-69	Danny Grant, Minnesota	LW
1942-43	Gaye Stewart, Toronto	LW	1969-70	Tony Esposito, Chicago	G
1943-44	Gus Bodnar, Toronto	C	1970-71	Gilbert Perreault, Buffalo	C
1944-45	Frank McCool, Toronto	G	1971-72	Ken Dryden, Montreal	G
1945-46	Edgar Laprade, NY Rangers	C	1972-73	Steve Vickers, NY Rangers	LW
1946-47	Howie Meeker, Toronto	RW	1973-74	Denis Potvin, NY Islanders	D
1947-48	Jim McFadden, Detroit	C	1974-75	Eric Vail, Atlanta	LW
1948-49	Penny Lund, NY Rangers	RW	1975-76	Bryan Trottier, NY Islanders	C
			1976-77	Willi Plett, Atlanta	RW
1949-50	Jack Gelineau, Boston	G	1977-78	Mike Bossy, NY Islanders	RW
1950-51	Terry Sawchuck, Detroit	G	1978-79	Bobby Smith, Minnesota	C
1951-52	Bernie Geoffrion, Montreal	RW			
1952-53	Gump Worsley, NY Rangers	G	1979-80	Ray Bourque, Boston	D
1953-54	Camille Henry, NY Rangers	LW	1980-81	Peter Stastny, Quebec	C
1954-55	Ed Litzenberger, Chicago	RW	1981-82	Dale Hawerchuk, Winnipeg	C
1955-56	Glenn Hall, Detroit	G	1982-83	Steve Larmer, Chicago	RW
1956-57	Larry Regan, Boston	RW	1983-84	Tom Barrasso, Buffalo	G
1957-58	Frank Mahovlich, Toronto	LW	1984-85	Mario Lemieux, Pittsburgh	C
1958-59	Ralph Backstrom, Montreal	C	1985-86	Gary Suter, Calgary	D
			1986-87	Luc Robitaille, Los Angeles	LW
			1987-88	Joe Nieuwendyk, Calgary	C
			1988-89	Brian Leetch, NY Rangers	D

Jack Adams Award
(Coach of the Year)

Awarded to the coach "adjudged to have contributed the most to his team's success" and named after the late Detroit Red Wings coach and general manager. Winners selected by NHL Broadcasters' Assn. Numbers in parentheses indicate repeat winners.

Year	Coach of the Year	W-L Improvement	Year	Coach of the Year	W-L Improvement
1974	Fred Shero, Phila	37-30-11 to 50-16-12*	1982	Tom Watt, Winnipeg	9-57-14 to 33-33-14
1975	Bob Pulford, Chi	41-14-23 to 37-35-8	1983	Orval Tessier, Chi	30-38-12 to 47-23-10*
1976	Don Cherry, Boston	40-26-14 to 48-15-17*	1984	Bryan Murray, Wash	39-25-16 to 48-27-5
1977	Scotty Bowman, Mont	58-11-11* to 60-8-12*	1985	Mike Keenan, Phila	44-26-10 to 53-20-7*
1978	Bobby Kromm, Detroit	16-55-9 to 32-34-14	1986	Glen Sather, Edm	49-20-11* to 56-17-7*
1979	Al Arbour, NY Isles	48-17-15* to 51-15-14*	1987	Jacques Demers, Det	17-57-6 to 34-36-10
1980	Pat Quinn, Phila	40-25-15 to 48-12-20*	1988	J.Demers, Det.(2)	34-36-10 to 41-28-11*
1981	Red Berenson, St.L	34-34-12 to 45-18-17*	1989	Pat Burns, Montreal	45-22-13* to 53-18-9*

*Won Division.

Frank Selke Trophy

Awarded to the outstanding defensive forward of the year and named after the late Montreal Canadiens general manager. Winners selected by the Professional Hockey Writers' Assn.

Year	Winner	Year	Winner	Year	Winner
1978	Bob Gainey, Montreal	1982	Steve Kasper, Boston	1986	Troy Murray, Chicago
1979	Bob Gainey, Montreal	1983	Bobby Clarke, Phila.	1987	Dave Poulin, Phila.
1980	Bob Gainey, Montreal	1984	Doug Jarvis, Wash.	1988	Guy Carbonneau, Mont.
1981	Bob Gainey, Montreal	1985	Craig Ramsay, Buffalo	1989	Guy Carbonneau, Mont.

Bill Masterton Trophy

Awarded to the player who "best exemplifies the qualities of perseverance, sportsmanship and dedication to hockey" and named after the 29-year-old rookie center of the Minnesota North Stars who died of a head injury sustained in a 1968 NHL game. Presented by the Professional Hockey Writers' Assn.

Year	Winner	Year	Winner	Year	Winner
1968	Claude Provost, Mont.	1975	Don Luce, Buffalo	1982	Chico Resch, Colo.
1969	Ted Hampson, Oakland	1976	Rod Gilbert, NYR	1983	Lanny McDonald, Calg.
1970	Pit Martin, Chicago	1977	Ed Westfall, NYI	1984	Brad Park, Detroit
1971	Jean Ratelle, NYR	1978	Butch Goring, LA	1985	Anders Hedberg, NYR
1972	Bobby Clarke, Phila.	1979	Serge Savard, Mont.	1986	Charlie Simmer, Bos.
1973	Lowell McDonald, Pitt.	1980	Al MacAdam, Minn.	1987	Doug Jarvis, Hart.
1974	Henri Richard, Mont.	1981	Blake Dunlop, St.L	1988	Bob Bourne, LA
				1989	Tim Kerr, Phila.

NHL Franchise Origins

Here is what the current 21 teams in the National Hockey League have to show for the years they have put in as members of the NHL and World Hockey Association (WHA). League titles are noted by year won.

Prince of Wales Conference

	First Season	League Titles	Franchise Stops
Boston Bruins	1924-25 (NHL)	5 NHL (1929,39,41,70,72)	Boston (1924-)
Buffalo Sabres	1970-71 (NHL)	None	Buffalo (1970-)
Hartford Whalers	1972-73 (WHA)	1 WHA (1973)	Boston (1972-74)
			W.Springfield,MA (1974-75)
			Hartford,CT (1975-78)
			Springfield,MA (1978-80)
			Hartford (1980-)
Montreal Canadiens	1917-18 (NHL)	22 NHL (1924,30-31,44,46,53, 56-60,65-66,68-69, 71,73,76-79,86)	Montreal (1917-)
New Jersey Devils	1974-75 (NHL)	None	Kansas City (1974-76)
			Denver (1976-82)
			E.Rutherford,NJ (1982-)
New York Islanders	1972-73 (NHL)	4 NHL (1980-83)	Uniondale,NY (1972-)
New York Rangers	1926-27 (NHL)	3 NHL (1928,33,40)	New York (1926-)
Philadelphia Flyers	1967-68 (NHL)	2 NHL (1974-75)	Philadelphia (1967-)
Pittsburgh Penguins	1967-68 (NHL)	None	Pittsburgh (1967-)
Quebec Nordiques	1972-73 (WHA)	1 WHA (1977)	Quebec City (1972-)
Washington Capitals	1974-75 (NHL)	None	Landover,MD (1974-)

Clarence Campbell Conference

	First Season	League Titles	Franchise Stops
Calgary Flames	1972-73 (NHL)	1 NHL (1989)	Atlanta (1972-80)
			Calgary (1980-)
Chicago Blackhawks	1926-27 (NHL)	3 NHL (1934,38,61)	Chicago (1926-)
Detroit Red Wings	1926-27 (NHL)	7 NHL (1936-37,43,50, 52,54-55)	Detroit (1926-)
Edmonton Oilers	1973-74 (WHA)	4 NHL (1984-85,87-88)	Edmonton (1972-)
Los Angeles Kings	1967-68 (NHL)	None	Los Angeles (1967-)
Minn.North Stars	1967-68 (NHL)	None	Bloomington,MN (1967-)
St.Louis Blues	1967-68 (NHL)	None	St.Louis (1967-)
Toronto Maple Leafs	1917-18 (NHL)	13 NHL (1918,22,32,42,45, 47-49,51,62-64,67)	Toronto (1917-)
Vancouver Canucks	1970-71 (NHL)	None	Vancouver (1970-)
Winnipeg Jets	1972-73 (WHA)	3 WHA (1976,78-79)	Winnipeg (1972-)

Note: The Hartford Civic Center roof caved in Jan,1978, forcing the Whalers to move home games to the Springfield,MA Civic Center for two years.

NHL All-Star Game, 1947-89

The NHL All-Star Game began at the start of the 1947-48 season as an exhibition contest between the defending league champion and a squad of star players from the other five teams. Two All-Star teams played each other in 1951 and '52, but 1953 saw a return to the original format. The game moved to mid-season in 1967, became an East Division vs West Division contest in 1969, and finally a Wales Conference vs Campbell Conference contest in 1975. Winning coaches are listed first.

Year	Result	Host	Coaches	Most Valuable Player
1947	All-Stars 4, Toronto 3	Toronto	Dick Irvin, Hap Day	No award
1948	All-Stars 3, Toronto 1	Chicago	Tommy Ivan, Hap Day	No award
1949	All-Stars 3, Toronto 1	Toronto	Tommy Ivan, Hap Day	No award
1950	Detroit 7, All-Stars 1	Detroit	Tommy Ivan, Lynn Patrick	No award
1951	1st Team 2, 2nd Team 2	Toronto	Joe Primeau, Hap Day	No award
1952	1st Team 1, 2nd Team 1	Detroit	Tommy Ivan, Dick Irvin	No award
1953	All-Stars 3, Montreal 1	Montreal	Lynn Patrick, Dick Irvin	No award
1954	All-Stars 2, Detroit 2	Detroit	King Clancy, Jim Skinner	No award
1955	Detroit 3, All-Stars 1	Detroit	Jim Skinner, Dick Irvin	No award
1956	All-Stars 1, Montreal 1	Montreal	Jim Skinner, Toe Blake	No award
1957	All-Stars 5, Montreal 3	Montreal	Milt Schmidt, Toe Blake	No award
1958	Montreal 6, All-Stars 3	Montreal	Toe Blake, Milt Schmidt	No award
1959	Montreal 6, All-Stars 1	Montreal	Toe Blake, Punch Imlach	No award
1960	All-Stars 2, Montreal 1	Montreal	Punch Imlach, Toe Blake	No award
1961	All-Stars 3, Chicago 1	Chicago	Sid Abel, Rudy Pilous	No award
1962	Toronto 4, All-Stars 1	Toronto	Punch Imlach, Rudy Pilous	Eddie Shack, Toronto
1963	All-Stars 3, Toronto 3	Toronto	Sid Abel, Punch Imlach	Frank Mahovlich, Tor.
1964	All-Stars 3, Toronto 2	Toronto	Sid Abel, Punch Imlach	Jean Beliveau, Mont.
1965	All-Stars 5, Montreal 2	Montreal	Billy Reay, Toe Blake	Gordie Howe, Detroit
1966	No Game (see below)			
1967	Montreal 3, All-Stars 0	Montreal	Toe Blake, Sid Abel	Henri Richard, Mont.
1968	Toronto 4, All-Stars 3	Toronto	Punch Imlach, Toe Blake	Bruce Gamble, Tor.
1969	West 3, East 3	Montreal	Scotty Bowman, Toe Blake	Frank Mahovlich, Det.
1970	East 4, West 1	St.Louis	Claude Ruel, Scotty Bowman	Bobby Hull, Chicago
1971	West 2, East 1	Boston	Scotty Bowman, Harry Sinden	Bobby Hull, Chicago
1972	East 3, West 2	Minnesota	Al MacNeil, Billy Reay	Bobby Orr, Boston
1973	East 5, West 4	NY Rangers	Tom Johnson, Billy Reay	Greg Polis, Pitt.
1974	West 6, East 4	Chicago	Billy Reay, Scotty Bowman	Garry Unger, St.L.
1975	Wales 7, Campbell 1	Montreal	Bep Guidolin, Fred Shero	Syl Apps,Jr.,Pitt.
1976	Wales 7, Campbell 5	Philadelphia	Floyd Smith, Fred Shero	Peter Mahovlich, Mont.
1977	Wales 4, Campbell 3	Vancouver	Scotty Bowman, Fred Shero	Rick Martin, Buffalo
1978	Wales 3, Campbell 2 (OT)	Buffalo	Scotty Bowman, Fred Shero	Billy Smith, NYI
1979	No Game (see below)			
1980	Wales 6, Campbell 3	Detroit	Scotty Bowman, Al Arbour	Reggie Leach, Phila.
1981	Campbell 4, Wales 1	Los Angeles	Pat Quinn, Scotty Bowman	Mike Liut, St.Louis
1982	Wales 4, Campbell 2	Washington	Al Arbour, Glen Sonmor	Mike Bossy, NYI
1983	Campbell 9, Wales 3	NY Islanders	Roger Neilson, Al Arbour	Wayne Gretzky, Edm.
1984	Wales 7, Campbell 6	New Jersey	Al Arbour, Glen Sather	Don Maloney, NYR
1985	Wales 6, Campbell 4	Calgary	Al Arbour, Glen Sather	Mario Lemieux, Pitt.
1986	Wales 4, Campbell 3 (OT)	Hartford	Mike Keenan, Glen Sather	Grant Fuhr, Edm.
1987	No Game (see below)			
1988	Wales 6, Campbell 5 (OT)	St.Louis	Mike Keenan, Glen Sather	Mario Lemieux, Pitt.
1989	Campbell 9, Wales 5	Edmonton	Glen Sather, Terry O'Reilly	Wayne Gretzky, LA

No All-Star Game: in 1966 (moved from start of season to mid-season); in 1979 (replaced by Challenge Cup series with USSR); in 1987 (replaced by Rendez-Vous'87 series with USSR). See "International Series" for outcome.

World Hockey Association
WHA Finals, 1973-79

The World Hockey Association began play in 1972-73 as a 12-team rival of the 56-year-old NHL. The WHA played for the Avco World Trophy in its seven playoff finals (Avco Financial Services underwrote the playoffs).

Year	Winner	Head Coach	Series	Loser	Head Coach
1973	NE Whalers	Jack Kelley	4-1 (WWLWW)	Winnipeg Jets	Bobby Hull
1974	Houston Aeros	Bill Dineen	4-0	Chicago Cougars	Pat Stapleton
1975	Houston Aeros	Bill Dineen	4-0	Que.Nordiques	Jean-Guy Gendron
1976	Winnipeg Jets	Bobby Kromm	4-0	Houston Aeros	Bill Dineen
1977	Que.Nordiques	Marc Boileau	4-3 (LWLWWLW)	Winnipeg Jets	Bobby Kromm
1978	Winnipeg Jets	Larry Hillman	4-0	NE Whalers	Harry Neale
1979	Winnipeg Jets	Larry Hillman	4-2 (WWLWLW)	Edmonton Oilers	Glen Sather

Playoff MVPs, 1973-79

1973—No award; **1974**—No award; **1975**—Ron Grahame, Houston, G; **1976**—Ulf Nilsson, Winnipeg, C; **1977**—Serg Bernier, Quebec, C; **1978**—Bobby Guindon, Winnipeg, C; **1979**—Rich Preston, Winnipeg, RW.

WHA Awards

Most Valuable Player

Year	MVP	G	A	Pts	Pos
1973	Bobby Hull, Winnipeg	51	52	**103**	LW
1974	Gordie Howe, Houston	31	69	**100**	RW
1975	Bobby Hull, Winnipeg	77	65	**142**	LW
1976	Marc Tardif, Quebec	71	77	**148**	LW
1977	Robbie Ftorek, Phoenix	46	71	**117**	C
1978	Marc Tardif, Quebec	65	89	**154**	LW
1979	Dave Dryden, Edmonton		2.89 GA Avg		G

Best Goaltender

Year		Gm	GA
1973	Cleveland—Gerry Cheevers	78	239
1974	Houston—Don MacLeod	78	219
1975	Houston—Ron Grahame	78	247
1976	Indianapolis—Michel Dion	80	247
1977	Houston—Ron Grahame	80	241
1978	New England—Al Smith	80	269
1979	Edmonton—Dave Dryden	80	266

Rookie of the Year

Year	
1973	Terry Caffery, N.Eng., C
1974	Mark Howe, Houston, D
1975	Anders Hedberg, Winn., RW
1976	Mark Napier, Toronto, RW
1977	George Lyle, N.Eng., LW
1978	Kent Nilsson, Winn., C
1979	Wayne Gretzky, Edm., C

Coach of the Year

Year		W-L Improvement
1973	Jack Kelley, New Eng	46-30-2* (new team)
1974	Billy Harris, Toronto	35-39-4 to 41-33-4
1975	Sandy Hucul, Phoenix	39-31-8 (new team)
1976	Bobby Kromm, Winnipeg	38-35-5 to 52-27-2*
1977	Bill Dineen, Houston	53-27-0* to 50-24-6*
1978	Bill Dineen, Houston	50-24-6* to 42-34-4
1979	John Brophy, Birm'gham	36-41-3 to 32-42-6

*Won Division.

Best Defenseman

Year	
1973	J.C.Tremblay, Quebec
1974	Pat Stapleton, Chicago
1975	J.C.Tremblay, Quebec
1976	Paul Shmyr, Cleveland
1977	Ron Plumb, Cincinnati
1978	Lars-Erik Sjoberg, Winn.
1979	Rick Ley, New England

WHA Scoring Leaders

Season		Gm	G	A	Pts
1972-73	Andre Lacroix, Phila	78	50	74	**124**
1973-74	Mike Walton, Minnesota	78	57	60	**117**
1974-75	Andre Lacroix, S.Diego	78	41	106	**147**
1975-76	Marc Tardif, Quebec	81	71	77	**148**
1976-77	Real Cloutier, Quebec	76	66	75	**141**
1977-78	Marc Tardif, Quebec	78	65	89	**154**
1978-79	Real Cloutier, Quebec	77	75	54	**129**

Note: In 1978-79, 18 year-old Rookie of the Year Wayne Gretzky finished third in scoring (46-64—110).

WHA All-Star Game, 1973-79

The WHA All-Star Game was an Eastern Division vs Western Division contest from 1973-75. In 1976, the league's five Canadian-based teams played the nine teams in the US. Over the final three seasons—East played West in 1977; AVCO Cup champion Quebec played a WHA All-Star team in 1978; and in 1979, a full WHA All-Star team played a three-game series with Moscow Dynamo of the Soviet Union.

Year	Result	Host	Coaches	Most Valuable Player
1973	East 6, West 2	Quebec	Jack Kelley, Bobby Hull	Wayne Carleton, Ottawa
1974	East 8, West 4	St.Paul,MN	Jack Kelley, Bobby Hull	Mike Walton, Minnesota
1975	West 6, East 4	Edmonton	Bill Dineen, Ron Ryan	Rejean Houle, Quebec
1976	Canada 6, USA 1	Cleveland	Jean-Guy Gendron, Bill Dineen	Can—Real Cloutier, Que. USA—Paul Shmyr, Cleve.
1977	East 4, West 2	Hartford	Jacques Demers, Bobby Kromm	East—L.Levasseur, Min. West—W.Lindstrom, Win.
1978	Quebec 5, WHA 4	Quebec	Marc Boileau, Bill Dineen	Quebec—Marc Tardif WHA—Mark Howe, NE
1979	WHA 4, Moscow Dynamo 2 WHA 4, Moscow Dynamo 2 WHA 4, Moscow Dynamo 3	Edmonton Edmonton Edmonton	Larry Hillman, P.Iburtovich	No awards

International Hockey
World Championships

World and Olympic champions from 1920 to the present. Olympic years and winners are indicated in **bold type**. There were no tournaments during World War II (1940-45) and 1946.

Year	Winner	Year	Winner	Year	Winner	Year	Winner
1920	**Canada**	1943	No tournament	1960	**United States**	1975	Soviet Union
1924	**Canada**	1944	No tournament	1961	Canada	**1976**	**Olym: USSR**
1928	**Canada**	1945	No tournament	1962	Sweden		World: Czech.
1930	Canada	1946	No tournament	1963	Soviet Union	1977	Czechoslovakia
1931	Canada	1947	Czechoslovakia	**1964**	**Soviet Union**	1978	Soviet Union
1932	**Canada**	**1948**	**Canada**	1965	Soviet Union	1979	Soviet Union
1933	United States	1949	Czechoslovakia	1966	Soviet Union		
1934	Canada	1950	Canada	1967	Soviet Union	**1980**	**United States**
1935	Canada	1951	Canada	**1968**	**Soviet Union**	1981	Soviet Union
1936	**Great Britain**	**1952**	**Canada**	1969	Soviet Union	1982	Soviet Union
1937	Canada	1953	Sweden			1983	Soviet Union
1938	Canada	1954	Soviet Union	1970	Soviet Union	**1984**	**Soviet Union**
1939	Canada	1955	Canada	1971	Soviet Union	1985	Czechoslovakia
		1956	**Soviet Union**	**1972**	**Olym: USSR**	1986	Soviet Union
1940	No tournament	1957	Sweden		World: Czech.	1987	Sweden
1941	No tournament	1958	Canada	1973	Soviet Union	**1988**	**Soviet Union**
1942	No tournament	1959	Canada	1974	Soviet Union	1989	Soviet Union

Canada vs USSR Summits

The first competition between the Soviet National Team and the NHL took place Sept.2-28, 1972. A team of NHL All-Stars emerged as the winner of the heralded 8-game series, but just barely—winning with a record of 4-3-1 after trailing 1-3-1.

Two years later a WHA All-Star team played the Soviet Nationals and could win only one game and tie three others in eight contests. Two other Canada vs USSR series took place during NHL All-Star breaks: the three-game Challenge Cup at New York in 1979, and the two-game Rendez-Vous '87 in Quebec City in 1987.

In additon, the six-team Canada Cup tournament was started in 1976 and continued in 1981, 1984, and 1987. The NHL All-Stars played the USSR in a three-game Challenge Cup series in 1979.

1972 Team Canada vs USSR

NHL All-Stars vs Soviet National Team.

Date	City	Score	Goaltenders
9/2	Montreal	USSR 7, Canada 3	Tretiak/Dryden
9/4	Toronto	Canada 4, USSR 1	Esposito/Tretiak
9/6	Winnipeg	USSR 4, Canada 4	Tretiak/Esposito
9/8	Vancouver	USSR 5, Canada 4	Tretiak/Dryden
9/22	Moscow	USSR 5, Canada 4	Tretiak/Esposito
9/24	Moscow	Canada 3, USSR 2	Dryden/Tretiak
9/26	Moscow	Canada 4, USSR 3	Esposito/Tretiak
9/28	Moscow	Canada 6, USSR 5	Dryden/Tretiak

Standings

	W	L	T	Pts	GF	GA
Team Canada (NHL)	4	3	1	8	32	32
Soviet Union	3	4	1	8	32	32

Leading Scorers

1. Phil Esposito, Canada, (7-6—13); **2.** Aleksandr Yakushev, USSR (7-4—11); **3.** Paul Henderson, Canada (7-2—9); **4.** Boris Shadrin, USSR (3-5—8); **5.** Valeri Kharlamov, USSR (3-4—7) and Vladimir Petrov, USSR (3-4—7); **7.** Bobby Clarke, Canada (2-4—6).

1974 Team Canada vs USSR

WHA All-Stars vs Soviet National Team.

Date	City	Score	Goaltenders
9/17	Quebec	Canada 3, USSR 3	Tretiak/Cheevers
9/19	Toronto	Canada 4, USSR 1	Cheevers/Tretiak
9/21	Winnipeg	USSR 8, Canada 5	Tretiak/McLeod
9/23	Vancouver	Canada 5, USSR 5	Tretiak/Cheevers
10/1	Moscow	USSR 3, Canada 2	Tretiak/Cheevers
10/3	Moscow	USSR 5, Canada 2	Tretiak/Cheevers
10/5	Moscow	Canada 4, USSR 4	Cheevers/Tretiak
10/6	Moscow	USSR 3, Canada 2	Sdn'kov/Cheevers

Standings

	W	L	T	Pts	GF	GA
Soviet Union	4	1	3	11	32	27
Team Canada (WHA)	1	4	3	5	27	32

Leading Scorers

1. Bobby Hull, Canada (7-2—9); **2.** Aleksandr Yakushev, USSR (6-2—8), Ralph Backstrom, Canada (4-4—8) and Valeri Kharlamov, USSR (2-6—8); **5.** Gordie Howe, Canada (3-4—7), Andre Lacroix, Canada (1-6—7) and Vladimir Petrov, USSR (1-6—7).

1979 Challenge Cup Series

NHL All-Stars vs Soviet National Team

Date	City	Score	Goaltenders
2/8	New York	NHL 4, USSR 2	K.Dryden/Tretiak
2/10	New York	USSR 5, NHL 4	Tretiak/K.Dryden
2/11	New York	USSR 6, NHL 0	Myshkin/Cheevers

Standings

	W	L	T	Pts	GF	GA
Soviet Union	2	1	0	4	13	8
Team Canada	1	2	0	2	8	13

Rendez-Vous '87

NHL All-Stars vs Soviet National Team

Date	City	Score	Goaltenders
2/11	Quebec	NHL 4, USSR 3	Fuhr/Belosheykhin
2/13	Quebec	USSR 5, NHL 3	Belosheykhin/Fuhr

Standings

	W	L	T	Pts	GF	GA
Soviet Union	1	1	0	2	8	7
Team Canada	1	1	0	2	7	8

The Canada Cup

1976

Round Robin Standings

	W	L	T	Pts	GF	GA
Canada	4	1	0	8	22	6
Czechoslovakia	3	1	1	7	19	9
Soviet Union	2	2	1	5	23	14
Sweden	2	2	1	5	16	18
United States	1	3	1	3	14	21
Finland	1	4	0	2	16	42

Finals (Best of 3 Games)

Date	City	Score
9/13	Toronto	Canada 6, Czechoslovakia 0
9/15	Montreal	Canada 5, Czechoslovakia 4 (OT)

Note: Darryl Sittler scored the winning goal for Canada at 11:33 in overtime to clinch the Cup, 2 games to none.

Team MVPs

Canada—Rogie Vachon Sweden—Borje Salming
Czech.—Milan Novy USA—Robbie Ftorek
USSR—Alexandr Maltsev Finland—Matti Hagman
Tournament MVP—Bobby Orr, Canada

1981

Round Robin Standings

	W	L	T	Pts	GF	GA
Canada	4	0	1	9	32	13
Soviet Union	3	1	1	7	20	13
Czechoslovakia	2	1	2	6	21	13
United States	2	2	1	5	17	19
Sweden	1	4	0	2	13	20
Finland	0	4	1	1	6	31

Semifinals

Date	City	Score
9/11	Ottawa	USSR 4, Czechoslovakia 1
9/15	Montreal	Canada 4, United States 1

Finals

Date	City	Score
9/13	Montreal	USSR 8, Canada 1

Leading Scorers

1. Wayne Gretzky, Canada (5-7—12); **2.** Mike Bossy, Canada (8-3—11), Bryan Trottier, Canada (3-8--11), Guy Lafleur, Canada (2-9—11), Alexei Kasatonov, USSR (1-10—11).

All-Star Team

Goal—Vladislav Tretiak, USSR; **Defense**—Arnold Kadlec, Czech. and Alexei Kasatonov, USSR; **Forwards**—Mike Bossy, Canada, Gil Perreault, Canada, and Sergei Shepelev, USSR. **Tournament MVP**—Tretiak.

1984

Round Robin Standings

	W	L	T	Pts	GF	GA
Soviet Union	5	0	0	10	22	7
United States	3	1	1	7	21	13
Sweden	3	2	0	6	15	16
Canada	2	2	1	5	23	18
West Germany	0	4	1	1	13	29
Czechoslovakia	0	4	1	1	10	21

Semifinals

Date	City	Score
9/12	Edmonton	Sweden 9, United States 2
9/15	Montreal	Canada 3, USSR 2 (OT)

Note: Mike Bossy scored the winning goal for Canada at 12:29 in overtime.

Finals (Best of 3 Games)

Date	City	Score
9/16	Calgary	Canada 5, Sweden 2
9/18	Edmonton	Canada 6, Sweden 5

Leading Scorers

1. Wayne Gretzky, Canada (5-7—12); **2.** Michel Goulet, Canada (5-6—11), Kent Nilsson, Sweden (3-8—11), Paul Coffey, Canada (3-8—11); **5.** Hakan Loob, Sweden (6-4—10).

All-Star Team

Goal—Vladimir Myshkin, USSR; **Defense**—Paul Coffey, Canada and Rod Langway, USA; **Forwards**—Wayne Gretzky, Canada, John Tonelli, Canada, and Sergei Makarov, USSR. **Tournament MVP**—Tonelli.

1987

Round Robin Standings

	W	L	T	Pts	GF	GA
Canada	3	0	2	8	19	13
Soviet Union	3	1	1	7	22	13
Sweden	3	2	0	6	17	14
Czechoslovakia	2	2	1	5	12	15
United States	2	3	0	4	13	14
Finland	0	5	0	0	9	23

Semifinals

Date	City	Score
9/8	Hamilton	USSR 4, Sweden 2
9/9	Montreal	Canada 5, Czechoslovakia 3

Finals (Best of 3 Games)

Date	City	Score
9/11	Montreal	USSR 6, Canada 5 (OT)
9/13	Hamilton	Canada 6, USSR 5 (2 OT)
9/15	Hamilton	Canada 6, USSR 5

Note: In Game 1, Alexander Semak of USSR scored at 5:33 in overtime. In Game 2, Mario Lemieux of Canada scored at 10:07 in the second overtime period. Lemieux also won Game 3 on a goal with 1:26 left in regulation time.

Leading Scorers

1. Wayne Gretzky, Canada (3-18—21); **2.** Mario Lemieux, Canada (11-7—18); **3.** Sergei Makarov, USSR (7-8—15); **4.** Vladimir Krutov, USSR (7-7—14); **5.** Viacheslav Bykov, USSR (2-7—9); **6.** Ray Bourque, Canada (2-6—8).

All-Star Team

Goal—Grant Fuhr, Canada; **Defense**—Ray Bourque, Canada and Viacheslav Fetisov, USSR; **Forwards**—Wayne Gretzky, Canada, Mario Lemieux, Canada, and Vladimir Krutov, USSR. **Tournament MVP**—Gretzky.

1989 NCAA Tournament Division I

Tournament Seeds

NCAA East
1 Maine (29-11-0)
2 Harvard (27-3-0)
3 St.Lawrence (29-5-0)
4 Boston Col.(22-9-4)
5 Providence (19-15-2)
6 St.Cloud St.(17-14-2)

NCAA West
1 Michigan St.(34-7-1)
2 Minnesota (31-10-3)
3 Lake Superior (27-9-6)
4 No.Michigan (25-15-2)
5 Bowling Green (26-16-3)
6 Wisconsin (23-14-5)

First Round (Best of 3)

WISCONSIN over St.Lawrence, 2 games to none (3-1,4-2); BOSTON COLLEGE over Bowling Green, 2 games to none (8-5,4-2); LAKE SUPERIOR ST. over St.Cloud St., 2 games to none (6-3,4-2); and PROVIDENCE over Northern Michigan, 2 games to 1 (5-9,4-2,2-0).

Quarterfinals (Best of 3)

HARVARD over Lake Superior St., 2 games to none (4-2,5-2); MINNESOTA over Wisconsin, 2 games to none (4-2,4-2); MAINE over Providence, 2 games to 1 (6-8,3-2,4-3 in double OT); and MICHIGAN ST. over Boston College, 2 games to 1 (3-6,7-2,5-4 in OT).

Final Four (Single Games) at St.Paul, MN Civic Center

Semifinals: MINNESOTA 7, Maine 4; and HARVARD 6, Michigan St. 3. **Consolation Game:** Michigan St. 7, Maine 4. **Championship Game:** HARVARD 4, Minnesota 3 (4:16 in OT).

All-Tournament Team: G—Allain Roy, Harvard; **D**—Kevin Sneddon, Harvard and Todd Richards, Minnesota; **F**—Ted Donato and Lane MacDonald of Harvard, and Jon Anderson, Minnesota. **Most Outstanding Player:** Ted Donato, Harvard (Semifinal—1 goal, 2 assists; Final—2 goals).

NCAA Division I Finals, 1948-89

Year	Winner	Winning Coach	Score	Loser	Losing Coach
1948	Michigan	Vic Heyliger	8-4	Dartmouth	Eddie Jeremiah
1949	Boston College	Snooks Kelley	4-3	Dartmouth	Eddie Jeremiah
1950	Colorado College	Cheddy Thompson	13-4	Boston Univ.	Harry Cleverly
1951	Michigan	Vic Heyliger	7-1	Brown	Wes Moulton
1952	Michigan	Vic Heyliger	4-1	Colorado College	Cheddy Thompson
1953	Michigan	Vic Heyliger	7-3	Minnesota	John Mariucci
1954	RPI	Ned Harkness	5-4 OT	Minnesota	John Mariucci
1955	Michigan	Vic Heyliger	5-3	Colorado College	Cheddy Thompson
1956	Michigan	Vic Heyliger	7-5	Michigan Tech	John MacInnes
1957	Colorado College	Tom Bedecki	13-6	Michigan	Vic Heyliger
1958	Denver	Murray Armstrong	6-2	North Dakota	Bob May
1959	North Dakota	Bob May	4-3 OT	Michigan St.	Amo Bessone
1960	Denver	Murray Armstrong	5-3	Michigan Tech	John MacInnes
1961	Denver	Murray Armstrong	12-2	St.Lawrence	George Menard
1962	Michigan Tech	John MacInnes	7-1	Clarkson	Len Ceglarski
1963	North Dakota	Barry Thorndycraft	6-5	Denver	Murray Armstrong
1964	Michigan	Allen Renfrew	6-3	Denver	Murray Armstrong
1965	Michigan Tech	John MacInnes	8-2	Boston College	Snooks Kelley
1966	Michigan St.	Amo Bessone	6-1	Clarkson	Len Ceglarski
1967	Cornell	Ned Harkness	4-1	Boston Univ.	Jack Kelley
1968	Denver	Murray Armstrong	4-0	North Dakota	Bill Selman
1969	Denver	Murray Armstrong	4-3	Cornell	Ned Harkness
1970	Cornell	Ned Harkness	6-4	Clarkson	Len Ceglarski
1971	Boston Univ.	Jack Kelley	4-2	Minnesota	Glen Sonmor
1972	Boston Univ.	Jack Kelley	4-0	Cornell	Dick Bertrand
1973	Wisconsin	Bob Johnson	4-2	Denver	Murray Armstrong
1974	Minnesota	Herb Brooks	4-2	Michigan Tech	John MacInnes
1975	Michigan Tech	John MacInnes	6-1	Minnesota	Herb Brooks
1976	Minnesota	Herb Brooks	6-4	Michigan Tech	John MacInnes
1977	Wisconsin	Bob Johnson	6-5 OT	Michigan	Dan Farrell
1978	Boston Univ.	Jack Parker	5-3	Boston College	Len Ceglarski
1979	Minnesota	Herb Brooks	4-3	North Dakota	Gino Gasparini
1980	North Dakota	Gino Gasparini	5-2	Northern Mich.	Rick Comley
1981	Wisconsin	Bob Johnson	6-3	Minnesota	Brad Buetow
1982	North Dakota	Gino Gasparini	5-2	Wisconsin	Bob Johnson
1983	Wisconsin	Jeff Sauer	6-2	Harvard	Billy Cleary
1984	Bowling Green	Jerry York	5-4 OT	Minn.-Duluth	Mike Sertich
1985	RPI	Mike Addesa	2-1	Providence	Steve Stirling
1986	Michigan St.	Ron Mason	6-5	Harvard	Billy Cleary
1987	North Dakota	Gino Gasparini	5-3	Michigan St.	Ron Mason
1988	Lake Superior St.	Frank Anzalone	4-3 OT	St.Lawrence	Joe Marsh
1989	Harvard	Billy Cleary	4-3 OT	Minnesota	Doug Woog

Overtime Goals: 1954—1:54; **1959**—4:22; **1977**—0:23; **1984**—7:11 in 4th OT; **1988**—4:46; **1989**—4:16.

Most Outstanding Player

The Most Outstanding Players of each NCAA Div.I tournament since the first one in 1948. Winners of the award who did not play for the tournament champion are in **bold type**. In 1960, three players, none on the winning team, shared the award.

Year	Outstanding Player	Finals Site
1948	**Joe Riley,** Dartmouth, F	Colo.Springs
1949	**Dick Desmond,** Dartmouth, G	Colo.Springs
1950	**Ralph Bevins,** Boston Univ., G	Colo.Springs
1951	**Ed Whiston,** Brown, G	Colo.Springs
1952	**Ken Kinsley,** Colorado Col., G	Colo.Springs
1953	John Matchefts, Michigan, F	Colo.Springs
1954	Abbie Moore, RPI, F	Colo.Springs
1955	**Phil Hilton,** Colorado Col., D	Colo.Springs
1956	Lorne Howes, Michigan, G	Colo.Springs
1957	Bob McCusker, Colorado Col., F	Colo.Springs
1958	Murray Massier, Denver, F	Minneapolis
1959	Reg Morelli, North Dakota, F	Troy,NY
1960	**Lou Angotti,** Michigan Tech, F; **Bob Marquis,** Boston Univ., F; **& Barry Urbanski,** Boston Univ., G	Boston
1961	Bill Masterton, Denver, F	Denver
1962	Lou Angotti, Michigan Tech, F	Hamilton,NY
1963	Al McLean, North Dakota, F	Boston
1964	Bob Gray, Michigan, G	Denver
1965	Gary Milroy, Michigan Tech, F	Providence,RI
1966	Gaye Cooley, Michigan St., G	Minneapolis

Year	Outstanding Player	Finales Site
1967	Walt Stanowski, Cornell, D	Syracuse, NY
1968	Gerry Powers, Denver, G	Duluth,MN
1969	Keith Magnuson, Denver, D	Colo.Springs
1970	Dan Lodboa, Cornell, D	Lake Placid,NY
1971	Dan Brady, Boston Univ., G	Syracuse, NY
1972	Tim Regan, Boston, Univ., G	Boston
1973	Dean Talafous, Wisconsin, F	Boston
1974	Brad Shelstad, Minnesota, G	Boston
1975	Jim Warden, Michigan Tech, G	St.Louis
1976	Tom Vanelli, Minnesota, F	Denver
1977	Julian Baretta, Wisconsin, G	Detroit
1978	Jack O'Callahan, Boston U., D	Providence,RI
1979	Steve Janaszak, Minnesota, G	Detroit
1980	Doug Smail, North Dakota, F	Providence,RI
1981	Marc Behrend, Wisconsin, G	Duluth,MN
1982	Phil Sykes, North Dakota, F	Providence,RI
1983	Marc Behrend, Wisconsin, G	Grand Forks,ND
1984	Gary Kruzich, Bowl.Green, G	Lake Placid,NY
1985	**Chris Terreri,** Providence G	Detroit
1986	Mike Donnelly, Mich.St., F	Providence,RI
1987	Tony Hrkac, North Dakota, F	Detroit
1988	Bruce Hoffort, Lk.Superior, G	Lake Placid,NY
1989	Ted Donato, Harvard, F	St.Paul,MN

Other NCAA Champions

Division II-III, 1978-83

NCAA College Division tournament was discontinued in 1984 in favor of separate playoffs for Divisions II and III.

Year	Winner	Score	Loser
1978	Merrimack,MA	12-2	Lake Forest,IL
1979	Lowell,MA	6-4	Mankato St.,MN
1980	Mankato St.,MN	5-2	Elmira,NY
1981	Lowell,MA	5-4	Plattsburgh St.,NY
1982	Lowell, MA	6-1	Plattsburgh St.,NY
1983	Rochester Inst.,NY	4-2	Bemidji St.,MN

Division III, 1984-89

In effect, the old NCAA Division II-III tournament.

Year	Winner	Score	Loser
1984	Babson,MA	8-0	Union,NY
1985	Rochester Inst.,NY	5-1	Bemidji St.,MN
1986	Bemidji St.,MN	8-5	Plattsburgh St,NY
1987	Plattsburgh St., NY	8-3	Oswego St.,NY
1988	Wisc.-River Falls	3-0†	Elmira,NY
1989	Wisc.-Stevens Pt.	1-0†	Rochester Inst.,NY

†Two-Game Series
1988: Game 1—River Falls, 7-1; Game 2—Elmira, 5-3; Mini-Game (15 min.)—River Falls, 3-0. **1989:** Game 1—3-3 tie; Game 2—Stevens Pt., 1-0.

1988-89 Hobey Baker Award
(Player of the Year)

National coaches' vote determines 10 finalists. Winner then selected by 13-member panel of writers, broadcasters, coaches and pro scouts. First presented in 1981 by the Decathlon Athletic Club of Bloomington,MN, in the name of the late Princeton collegiate hockey and football star.

Winner: Lane McDonald, Harvard, Sr., LW.

Finalists (in order of finish, vote totals not released): **2.** Robb Stauber, Minnesota, Jr., G; **3.** Greg Brown, Boston College, So., D; **4.** Bruce Hoffort, Lake Superior St, So., G; **5.** David Capuano, Maine, Jr., RW; **6.** Bobby Reynolds, Mich.St., Sr., LW; **7.** Kip Miller, Mich.St., Jr., C; **8.** Tim Sweeney, Boston College, Sr., LW; **9.** (tie) Allen Bourbeau, Harvard, Sr., C, and Nelson Emerson, Bowling Green, Jr., C.

Hobey Baker Winners, 1981-89

Year		Class
1981	Neal Broten, Minnesota, F	So.
1982	George McPhee, Bowling Green, F	Sr.
1983	Mark Fusco, Harvard, D	Sr.
1984	Tom Kurvers, Minnesota-Duluth, D	Sr.
1985	Bill Watson, Minnesota-Duluth, F	Jr.
1986	Scott Fusco, Harvard, F	Sr.
1987	Tony Hrkac, North Dakota, F	So.
1988	Robb Stauber, Minnesota, G	So.
1989	Lane MacDonald, Harvard, F	Sr.

Three of the century's outstanding sports personalities have been baseball's **Babe Ruth** (above, with broadcaster Graham McNamee); boxing's **Muhammad Ali**; and football's **George Halas** (below, with Vince Lombardi).

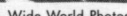

*T*hanks to money and personalities
sports has been America's
favorite growth industry
for the last 90 years.

20th
Century
Unlimited

by Dave Anderson

With the energetic ego that symbolized his three-time reign as
world heavyweight champion,
Muhammad Ali once surveyed the future
of boxing without him.

"When I go," he proclaimed with a
smile, "they'll take the game to the
graveyard."

But when Ali went, boxing didn't die.
Instead, its lifeblood and the lifeblood of
every sport, money, flowed more freely
than ever. Mike Tyson knows. In his first
three years as heavyweight champion,
Tyson's earnings easily surpassed the $60
million that Ali had earned in the ring
over two decades.

And as the '90s arrived, money dominated Sports in Amerca as never before.

Money for athlete's salaries. Money for
television contracts. Money for new
stadiums and arenas. Money for tickets.
Money for endorsements and commer-

cials. Money for advertising. Money,
money, money.

If Sports in America were to commission a coat of arms for the '90s, it should
be a dollar sign on a field of television
antennas atop a domed stadium.

To the marketeers, this is progress. But
much of the romance of sports has been
forgotten, if not lost. In baseball too
many domed stadiums have replaced the
old ballparks. In football too many arti-
ficial surfaces have all but eliminated
grass stains, much less muddy fields. In
basketball and hockey too many bad
teams are permitted in the NBA and NHL
playoffs. In boxing too many champions
reign in too many divisions. In college
athletics too many so-called student-
athletes seldom go to class. And in
almost every sport too many athletes
aren't worth too many million-dollar
contracts.

Even so, Sports in America continue to
flourish. Partly as an escape from the
reality of a harsh world, but also as a
reflection of the small, small world that
television has created.

Dave Anderson has been a sports columnist for
the **N.Y. Times** since 1976. He won the Pulitzer
Prize for commentary in 1981.

If a sports event deserves a world audience now, its television coverage is bounced off satellites to viewers just about everywhere waiting to see it: the Olympics, the World Cup soccer tournament, a heavyweight title fight, the Super Bowl, the World Series, the NBA playoffs, the Stanley Cup playoffs, the Wimbledon tennis championships, the Masters golf tournament, the World Track and Field championships, the Kentucky Derby, the Indianpolis 500, the Tour de France.

Nearly a century ago people in America waited on streetcorners for inning-by-inning scores of the World Series to be posted outside a newspaper office after a Western Union operator had deciphered the dots and dashes of Morse code. In later years they listened to radio descriptions. Then they turned on their TV sets. And someday they will decide if a sports event is worth the pay-per-view price on cable television.

As the '90s begin, the evolution of Sports in America has revolved around the most important personalities of each era. And not all those personalities were athletes.

In the '80s, the dominant personality of Sports in America was a businessman: Peter Ueberroth, the architect of the 1984 Summer Olympics in Los Angeles and later the Commissioner of Baseball who negotiated its current billion-dollar television contract. Nobody had ever succeeded in putting the Olympics on a bottom-line basis before. But this one-time California travel impressario organized the Summer Games as no nation or city ever had. And in his 4½-year tenure as Commissioner, he produced the television income that enabled baseball's clubowners to afford all those million-dollar contracts.

For whatever reason, in the story of 20th century sports, baseball has provided most of the key personalities, beginning with Babe Ruth, the loudest roar in the Roaring Twenties.

At the time Sports in America was in jeopardy. Even before eight members of the 1919 Chicago White Sox were banned from baseball for life by the first Commissioner, Judge Kenesaw Mountain Landis, for their involvement in the fixing of that year's World Series, baseball had an unsavory image. For years other players had been suspected of fixing games for gambling purposes. Baseball was considered a game for rowdies in a time that preferred gentlemen sports: golf and tennis.

But with his home runs, the Babe changed all that. For all his escapades

Peter Ueberroth (left) and International Olympic Committee president **Juan Antonio Samaranch** inspect Olympic Village before 1984 Summer Games in Los Angeles.

Wide World Photos

as a carouser, this fun-loving orphan from Baltimore not only gave baseball respectability, he embellished it as the "national pastime." And the Babe did all this just when the nation needed it most: in the "flapper age" during the years after World War I when people relished irreverance. When the Babe was asked if he deserved to earn more money with his $80,000 salary than President Hoover did, he laughed.

"I had a better year than he did," the Babe said.

Now the yearly salary of some utility infielders is more than that of the President of the United States, and for that they can thank Marvin Miller, the labor leader who freed the baseball slaves from the reserve clause that bound them to a team forever.

In between, in the New York City borough of Brooklyn where apartment houses now rise where Ebbets Field once entertained millions, Branch Rickey changed baseball's social structure and Walter O'Malley changed how baseball as well as all professional sports is perceived. Rickey put baseball's first black player, Jackie Robinson, on the Dodgers in 1947 and a decade later O'Malley, his successor as the Dodger president, put baseball in Los Angeles.

With that move (which also included the New York Giants' transfer to San Francisco) fans realized that baseball was more a business than a game.

O'Malley had ignored Brooklyn's devotion and departed for L.A., where politicians had donated a downtown site for a luxurious stadium. O'Malley had permeated sports with a "bottom-line" philosophy. And television, whose 21-inch stare had hypnotized the nation, was an accomplice. Part of the lure for O'Malley, and the Giants' owner, Horace Stoneham, was a pay-television deal that never materialized, but only because the idea was ahead of its time. Several years and several million miles of television cable lay ahead.

Boxing, meanwhile, continues to fit television better than any other sport. In only three years as the world heavyweight champion, Mike Tyson's earnings were approaching $100 million. He owed most of it not to his left hook, but to Home Box Office, the cable-television network, and the extravagance of casino owners in Las Vegas and Atlantic City who hired him as a shill for high rollers.

As boxing buffs always do, they wondered if Tyson was as good as Jack Dempsey, Joe Louis, or Muhammad Ali. Dempsey did in boxing what Babe Ruth

Walter O'Malley (right), the man who moved the Dogers out of Brooklyn, with Los Angeles mayor **Norris Poulson** at City Hall welcoming ceremonies on Opening Day in 1958.

Wide World Photos

Two lions of the Roaring Twenties:
Knute Rockne (left) and **Jack Dempsey**.

did in baseball: established himself as a legend that endured from his reign shortly after World War I to his presence in the window of his Broadway restaurant. Louis did in boxing what Jackie Robinson later did in baseball: provide black America with a hero to worship.

But then Ali did what nobody had ever done: create a loud mouth who not only challenged the establishment, but won.

Not long after dethroning the glowering Charles (Sonny) Liston in 1964, the boxer born Cassius Marcellus Clay, already self-proclaimed as the "greatest of all times," stunned the nation with a sociological combination of punches. He took the Muslim name of Muhammad Ali and refused to be inducted into military service during the Viet Nam war.

"I got nothin' against them Viet Cong," he said.

Eventually the United States Supreme Court upheld Ali's religious rights. But at the time of his induction-refusal, boxing politicians had stripped Ali of the heavyweight title, forcing him into a 3½ year exile that enabled Joe Frazier to earn recognition as the champion and an equal

share of the unprecedented bonanza of $2.5 million each for their 1971 showdown at Madison Square Garden. When that bout's primary promoter, Jerry Perenchio, projected a gross of $20 million, Ali objected.

"Joe!" he shouted, glancing at Frazier, "They got us cheap!"

Ali lost a unanimous 15-round decision, but nobody ever got him cheap again. When he dethroned George Foreman in 1974 in Zaire, each collected $5 million. With a worldwide television market, Ali had established a multi-million dollar extravaganza in boxing. Soon it would spread to other sports, even college sports.

Knute Rockne, an end at little known Notre Dame, helped to popularize college football shortly before World War I by catching seven forward passes in a shocking 35-13 upset of Army. And as the Notre Dame coach throughout the Roaring Twenties he emerged as an American folk hero until his death in a 1931 plane crash in Kansas.

But by 1990, the image of a college football coach had changed. Drastically. Barry Switzer resigned in disgrace as the University of Oklahoma coach after some of his so-called student-athletes had been charged with crimes involving drugs, guns and sexual assault.

Not that Switzer was alone. In the grab for television's big money, too many college officials and coaches had forgotten their responsibility as educators. Paul (Bear) Bryant, the University of Alabama football coach until shortly before his death in 1983, was accorded more respect than the Governor of Alabama, an indication of how the perspective of college sports had changed. For the worse.

Pro football, meanwhile, had prospered. When the National Football League was formed in 1920 in a Hupmobile showroom in Canton, Ohio, its primary attraction was Jim Thorpe, the 1912 Olympic decathlon champion whom King Gustav V of Sweden saluted as "the greatest athlete in the world." But in 1990, the NFL's primary attraction was the Super Bowl that Commissioner Pete Rozelle had created.

No other sport had such a spectacular one-day event. Super Bowl Sunday was virtually a national holiday. And more than anyone else, Rozelle elevated the Super Bowl into a symbol of pro football.

Another symbol was the quarterback. Not so much any particular quarterback, but the position itself. Paul Brown, as the coach of the Cleveland Browns named for him, used Otto Graham to define the importance of the quarterback. And a decade later David (Sonny) Werblin, the president of the New York Jets in the aspiring American Football League, defined the worth of the quarterback by signing a rookie, Joe Namath, to a then unheard-of three-year $427,000 contract. As a rookie.

As the N.F.L. moved into 1990, the worth of a quarterback had soared. Some were earning more than $2 million a season, several others had contracts for more than $1 million. And many of those contracts had evolved from those quarterbacks' performances on Super Bowl Sunday.

Pro basketball also had come of age. In the early years of the National Basket-ball Association after World War II, the Minneapolis Lakers were the champions, their 6-9 center George Mikan the dominating player. So much so that the Madison Square Garden marquee once read:

"George Mikan vs Knicks."

Just as Mikan established the center of gravity in pro basketball, Kareem Abdul-Jabbar embellished it. When he finally took off his Los Angeles Lakers' uniform at the age 42, he held virtually all the NBA career scoring records. But of the NBA teams, the Boston Celtics have been by far the most successful: 16 championships, including eight in a row (1959-1966). Now that's a dynasty. It's also a tribute to the coaching, player selection and front-office leadership of Arnold (Red) Auerbach, who never met a Chinese restaurant he didn't like.

Off the court, Auerbach's most formidable foe was Larry Fleisher, the executive director of the NBA Players Association as well as an agent for several players. Fleisher was a New York attorney whose

New York Jets president **Sonny Werblin** (center) and coach **Week Ewbank** (left) look on as rookie quarterback **Joe Namath** signs contract in 1965.

Minneapolis Lakers' star **George Mikan** (lower left), shines up his name on the Madison Square Garden marquee before an NBA game in 1949.

collective-bargaining brilliance lifted the average NBA player's salary higher than that of any other sport. When he died in 1989, every player wore a black band on his uniform.

Hockey has never completely melted the ice with some sports fans, perhaps because of the National Hockey League's tolerance for brawling. But it produced a sports superman in Gordie Howe, at his best a rugged and record-scoring right wing for the Detroit Red Wings who continued to play effectively for the Hartford Whalers past his 50th birthday. It also displayed a genius on skates in Wayne Gretzky, a bony center who guided the Edmonton Oilers to four Stanley Cup championships before being traded in 1988 to the Los Angeles Kings in a $15 million deal.

Off the ice, Conn Smythe turned Maple Leaf Gardens into a Toronto shrine. Frank Selke and Sam Pollock collaborated on the construction of the Montreal Canadiens' dominance over more than a quarter of a century. And more than any other sport, hockey was the first to shake hands with the European athlete. Beginning in 1972, Alan Eagleson's Team Canada battled the Soviets almost annually. Before the 1989-90 season, a few Russians had even been imported by NHL teams with Soviet approval, notably the renowned defenseman Viacheslav Fetisov by the New Jersey Devils.

The mystique of the Russians also was a factor as the Olympics emerged as one of the world's most popular television events. For decades Avery Brundage tried to keep the Olympics pristine pure, but like just about everybody else in sports, the Olympics eventually turned pro. Not only in some sports, but also in its finances.

Long before Peter Ueberroth put the 1984 Summer Games in Los Angeles on

ABC Sports president **Roone Arledge** (right) and sportscaster **Howard Cosell** appear before a 1977 House communications subcommitttee hearing in Washington.

a bottom-line basis, Roone Arledge put the International Olympic Committee's television rights on a bottom-line basis. As the president of ABC Sports, Arledge's multi-million bids turned the Olympics into prime-time entertainment and big-time business. Back in 1960 the TV rights to the Winter Games at Squaw Valley, Calif., were obtained by CBS for $50,000. For the 1992 Summer Games in Barcelona, Spain, NBC will pay $401 million, a record price for a single TV event.

All that money would have baffled George Halas, who constructed and coached the Chicago Bears into pro football's Monsters of the Midway after having been one of the NFL's founding fathers.

No matter what the American economy was at the time, Depression or Big Spenders, Halas survived by pinching pennies. Mike Ditka, the Hall of Fame tight end who coached the Bears team

that won Super Bowl XX after Halas' death, once said during a contract impasse that the Papa Bear "threw nickels around like manhole covers." But he threw enough nickels around to build a franchise. And in the process, pro football.

"I'm not a legend," Vince Lombardi, the Green Bay Packers coach, once said. "George Halas is a legend."

Gary Davidson is not a legend. He formed leagues that didn't last but they left a lasting impression. The American Basketball Association produced Julius Erving, the World Hockey Association produced Wayne Gretzky, and the World Football League hijacked a few NFL players. The bidding wars elevated player salaries in the NBA, NHL, and NFL that are still ascending.

With higher salaries, agents surfaced. Some from law school, some from underneath rocks. Many athletes have been

Arnold Palmer on tour in 1967. No golfer has attracted a
larger following or amassed a larger fortune.

burned, but Arnold Palmer still prospers.

For all his success and charisma as a
golfer, Palmer accumulated his wealth in
an alliance with Mark McCormack, a
Cleveland attorney who respresented him
with a handshake agreement that has
never been formalized. McCormack also
created the International Management
Group that represents hundreds of athletes, mostly golfers and tennis players.
One of IMG's clients, Bjorn Borg, collected about $10 million annually in tour-
nament earnings and off-the-court income during his six-year reign as the
Wimbledon champion.

Multi-million dollar deals have created
a different type of clubowner, too. Tom
Yawkey once owned the Boston Red Sox
so he could take batting practice at Fenway Park when nobody was watching.
But now George Steinbrenner owns the
New York Yankees so he can take center
stage in controversies when everybody is
watching. Ted Turner owns the Atlanta
Braves and Atlanta Hawks so he can take
a prime-time slot for his teams games on
his TBS Superstation whether or not
anybody is watching.

Once upon a time most clubowners
knew sports and depended on sports as
their primary source of income. Bill Veeck
and Larry MacPhail in baseball, Art

Rooney and the Maras in pro football, Eddie Gottlieb and Lester Harrison in pro basketball. But the new breed of owner emerged after Charles O. Finley, a Chicago insurance baron, organized the Oakland Athletics into World Series winners before he self-destructed. Free agency liberated his underpaid players and they signed with the highest bidders.

Corporations pounced on sports. CBS purchased the Yankees in 1964 without realizing the team was in decline, then eventually sold it to Steinbrenner's group. Having learned CBS's lesson, other corporations cluttered the titles of sports events as sponsors, some unashamedly. College football's Sun Bowl in El Paso, Tex. is now the John Hancock Bowl, hopefully on a rainy day.

Once the epitome of blue-blooded amateurism, the America's Cup yacht race off Fremantle, Australia in 1987 was marketed by Dennis Conner into a series of spinnakers with different corporate logos that his 12-meter, Stars & Stripes, displayed after each race of its 4-0 sweep. Cynics snickered that if Sir Thomas Lipton, the English tea tycoon who underwrote several challenges nearly a century ago, were involved now, it would be known as the Lipton Tea Cup.

Competition was enough, if not all, for Babe Didrikson Zaharias—the century's other Babe—first as a 1932 track-and-field Olympian and later as a Hall of Fame golfer. Billie Jean King endured as the winner of a record 20 Wimbledon tennis titles in singles, doubles and mixed doubles. But after the 1988 Olympics in Seoul, South Korea, Florence Giffith Joyner's three gold medals weren't enough to keep her running. Several lucrative commerical deals persuaded her to stop competing.

Money and technology also changed sports media. Once upon a time "The Sporting News" struggled as a baseball weekly. But now ESPN thrives as a 24-hour sports television network. In the process, bylines and voices also evolved: from Grantland Rice to Red Smith, from Graham McNamee to Red Barber, from Ronald Reagan doing simulated Cubs baseball games on an Iowa radio station to Howard Cosell doing his thing on Monday Night Football.

In another era, Bobby Jones was deified as much for remaining an amateur as he was for his 1930 Grand Slam in golf. But now Michael Jordan is considered the consummate pro, as much for his overall multi-million dollar annual income from sneakers and other endoresements as for his adventures at altitude in basketball.

But on many campuses money has vandalized what college sports is supposed to stand for. Once a college constructs a huge football stadium or basketball arena, it must fill all those seats to pay the mortgage. Filling these seats means fielding a winning team. To assure a winning team, it needs athletes who are not necessarily students. And once it compromises itself to obtain those athletes, it's not longer what college sports is supposed to be: serious students pursuing serious subjects in order to earn a serious degree. For proof, check the NCAA's probation list.

Money has always created the temptation of a gambling scandal, from the 1919 Black Sox to the 1951 college basketball fixes to Pete Rose's investigation by new Baseball Commissioner Bart Giamatti.

But big money has created new problems in sports: illegal drugs and steroids. With their million-dollar contracts, athletes can celebrate with cocaine and other illegal drugs. Dozens of baseball, football and basketball players have been treated in drug-rehab centers. And

Billie Jean King signing pro contract in 1968.

Wide World Photos

with million-dollar contracts at stake, athletes are using steroids to improve their performance. Ben Johnson, the Canadian sprinter, was stripped of his 1988 Olympic gold medal in the 100-meter dash at Seoul, for having tested positive for stanozolol, a steroid banned by the IOC.

The media attention focused on Johnson's fall from Olympic grace rivaled that generated by Jesse Owens' triumphant 4-gold medal performance at the 1936 Summer Games in Berlin.

So much has changed since then.

With only a decade left in the century, what lies ahead is anyone's guess. But one thing is for sure: there's a buck to be made. In sports, as in any other business, money reflects its reality.

Michael Jordan, the consummate pro, gets airborne during the 1989 NBA playoffs.

Noteworthy Personalities
Over 500 sports names dating back to 1900.

Hank Aaron (b.1934): Baseball OF, led NL in HRs and RBI 4 times each and batting twice, MVP in 1957, played in 24 All-Star games, all-time leader in HRs (755) and RBI (2,297), 3rd in hits (3,771).

Kareem Abdul-Jabbar (b.Lew Alcindor,1947): Basketball C, led UCLA to 3 NCAA titles (1967-69), tourney MVP 3 times, Player of Year twice; led Milwaukee (1) and LA Lakers (5) to 6 NBA titles, playoff MVP twice (1971,85), reg.season MVP 6 times (1971-72, 74,76-77, 80), retired after 20 seasons as all-time leader in over 20 categories.

Tenley Albright (b.1935): Figure skater, 2-time world champion (1953,55), won Olympic silver (1952) and gold (1956) medals.

Grover Cleveland Alexander (1887-1950): Baseball RHP, won 20 or more games 9 times, 373 career wins and 90 shutouts.

Vasily Alexeyev (b.1942): Soviet weightlifter, 8-time world champion, 2-time Olympic super-heavyweight champ (1972,76), set 80 world records between 1970-77.

Muhammad Ali (b.Cassius Clay,1942): Boxer, 1960 Olympic light-heavyweight champion; 3-time world heavyweight champ (1964-67,74-78,78-79), pro record 56-5 with 37 KOs, 19 successful title defenses.

Forrest (Phog) Allen (1885-74): Basketball, college coach 46 years, directed Kansas to NCAA title (1952), 770 career wins.

Bobby Allison (b.1937): Auto racer, 3-time winner of Daytona 500 (1978,82,88), NASCAR national champ in 1983.

Walter Alston (1911-84): Baseball, managed Brooklyn-LA Dodgers 23 years, won 7 pennants and 4 W.Series (1955,59,63,65).

Sparky Anderson (b.1934): Baseball, only manager to win World Series in each league—Cincinnati in NL (1975-76) and Detroit in AL (1984).

Mario Andretti (b.1940): Auto racer, only driver to win Daytona 500 (1967), Indy 500 (1969) and Formula 1 world championship (1978); 4-time USAC/CART national champ (1965-66,69,84).

Earl Anthony (b.1938): Bowler, 6-time PBA Bowler of Year, 41 career titles; first to earn $100,000 in 1 season (1975), first to earn $1 million in career.

Said Aouita (b.1960): Moroccan runner, world record holder in 5 events—1500m, 2000m, 3000m, 2-mile, 5000m—through Sept.,1989.

Luis Aparicio (b.1934): Baseball SS, all-time leader in most games, assists, chances and double plays by shortstop; led AL in stolen bases 9 times (1956-64), 506 career steals.

Al Arbour (b.1932): Hockey, coached NY Islanders to 4 straight Stanley Cup titles (1980-83).

Eddie Arcaro (b.1916): Jockey, 2-time Triple Crown winner (Whirlaway in 1941, Citation in '48); won Kentucky Derby 5 times, Preakness and Belmont 6 times each.

Roone Arledge (b.1931): Sports TV innovator of live events, anthology shows, Olympic coverage and "Monday Night Football;" ran ABC Sports from 1968-86.

Henry Armstrong (1912-88): Boxer, held feather-, light- and welterweight titles simultaneously in 1938; pro record 145-20-9 with 98 KOs.

Arthur Ashe (b.1943): Tennis, first black man to win US Championship (1968) and Wimbledon (1975), 1st US player to earn $100,000 in 1 year (1970), won Davis Cup as player (1968-70) and captain (1981-82).

Red Auerbach (b.1917): Basketball, winningest coach in NBA history (1,037 wins including playoffs), led Boston to 9 NBA titles, including 8 in a row (1959-66); still Celtics' GM.

Hobey Baker (1892-1918): Football and hockey star at Princeton (1911-14), member of college football and pro hockey halls of fame, college hockey Player of the Year award named after him.

Seve Ballesteros (b.1957): Spanish golfer, has won British Open 3 times (1979,84,88) and Masters twice (1980,83).

Ernie Banks (b.1931): Baseball SS-1B, led NL in home runs and RBI twice each, 2-time MVP (1958-59) with Chicago, 512 career HRs.

Roger Bannister (b.1929): British runner, first to run mile in less than 4 minutes (3:59.4 on May 6, 1954).

Rick Barry (b.1944): Basketball F, only player to lead both NBA and ABA in scoring, 5-time All-NBA 1st team; playoff MVP with Golden St. in 1975.

Sammy Baugh (b.1914): Football QB, led Washington to NFL titles in 1937 (his rookie year) and '42, led league in passing 6 times, punting 4 times and interceptions once.

Elgin Baylor (b.1934): Basketball F, MVP of NCAA tournament in 1958; led Minn.-LA Lakers to 8 NBA Finals, 10-time All-NBA 1st team (1959-65,67-69).

Bob Beamon (b.1946): Track & Field, won 1968 Olympic gold medal in long jump with world record (29 ft,2½ in.) that still stands.

Boris Becker (b.1967): West German tennis player, 3-time Wimbledon champ (1985-86,89), youngest male (17) to win Wimbledon, led country to 1st Davis Cup win in 1988.

Jean Beliveau (b.1931): Hockey C, led Montreal to 10 Stanley Cups in 17 playoffs, playoff MVP (1965), 2-time reg.season MVP (1956,64).

Johnny Bench (b.1947): Baseball C, led NL in HRs twice and RBIs 3 times, 2-time reg.season MVP (1970,72) with Cincinnati, W.Series MVP in 1976; 389 career HRs.

Patty Berg (b.1918): Golfer, 57 career pro wins including 15 Majors, 3-time AP Female Athlete of Year (1938,43,55).

Yogi Berra (b.1925): Baseball C, played on 10 W.Series winners with NY Yankees, 3-time AL MVP (1951,54-55), managed both Yankees (1964) and NY Mets (1973) to pennants.

Jay Berwanger (b.1915): Football HB, U.of Chicago star, won 1st Heisman Trophy in 1935.

Abebe Bikila (1932-1973): Ethiopian runner, 1st to win consecutive Olympic marathons (1960,64).

Matt Biondi (b.1965): Swimmer, won 5 gold medals (2 individual), 1 silver and 1 bronze in 1988 Olympics.

Larry Bird (b.1956): Basketball F, college Player of Year (1979); 9-time All-NBA 1st team, 3-time reg.season MVP (1984-86), led Boston to 3 NBA titles, playoff MVP (1984,86).

The Black Sox—8 Chicago White Sox players who were banned from baseball for life in 1921 for allegedly throwing the 1919 W.Series: RHP **Eddie Cicotte** (1884-1969), OF **Happy Felsch** (1891-1964), 1B **Chick Gandil** (1887-1970), OF **Shoeless Joe Jackson** (1887-1951), INF **Fred McMullan** (1891-1952), SS **Swede Risberg** (1894-1975), 3B-SS **Buck Weaver** (1890-1956), and LHP **Lefty Williams** (1893-1959).

Earl (Red) Blaik (1897-89): Football, coached Army to consecutive national titles in 1944-45, 166 career wins and 3 Heisman Trophy winners (Blanchard, Davis, Dawkins).

Bonnie Blair (b.1964): Speedskater, won 500m gold medal at 1988 Winter Olympics, World Sprint champion in 1989.

Toe Blake (b.1912): Hockey LW, led Montreal to 2 Stanley Cups as a player and 8 more as coach, regular season MVP in 1939.

Felix (Doc) Blanchard (b.1924): Football FB, 3-time All-America, led Army to national titles in 1944-45, Glenn Davis' running mate, won Heisman Trophy and Sullivan Award in 1945.

George Blanda (b.1927): Football QB-PK, NFL's all-time leading scorer (2,002 points), led Houston to 2 AFL titles (1960-61), played 26 pro seasons, retired at 48.

Fanny Blankers-Koen (b.1918): Dutch sprinter, 30 year-old mother of two who won 4 gold medals (100m, 200m, 800m hurdles and 4x100m relay) at 1948 Olympics.

Wade Boggs (b.1958): Baseball 3B, entered 1989 season with 5 AL batting titles (1983,85-88) at Boston and .356 career average.

Brian Boitano (b.1963): Figure skater, 2-time world champion (1986,88), won gold medal at 1988 Olympics.

Bjorn Borg (b.1956): Swedish tennis player, 2-time Player of Year (1979-80), won 6 French Opens and 5 straight Wimbledons (1976-80), led Sweden to 1st Davis Cup win in 1975.

Mike Bossy (b.1957): Hockey RW, led NY Islanders to 4 Stanley Cups, playoff MVP in 1982, scored 50 goals or more 9 straight years, 573 career goals.

Ralph Boston (b.1939): Track & Field, medaled in 3 consecutive Olympic long jumps—gold (1960), silver (1964), bronze (1968).

Jack Brabham (b.1926): Australian auto racer, 3-time Formula 1 champion (1959-60,66), 14 career wins.

Bill Bradley (b.1943): Basketball F, 3-time All-America at Princeton, Player of Year and NCAA tourney MVP in 1965, led NY Knicks to 2 NBA titles (1970,73), US Senator (D,NJ) since 1979.

Terry Bradshaw (b.1948): Football QB, led Pittsburgh to 4 Super Bowl titles (1975-76,79-80), 2-time Super Bowl MVP (1979-80).

George Brett (b.1953): Baseball 3B-1B, has led AL in batting twice (1976,80), MVP in 1980, led KC to W.Series title in 1985.

Lou Brock (b.1939): Baseball OF, all-time stolen base leader (938), led NL in steals 8 times, led St.Louis to 2 W.Series titles (1964,67), had 3,023 career hits.

Jim Brown (b.1936): Football FB, led NFL in rushing 8 times, 8-time All-Pro (1957-61,63-65), 3-time MVP (1958,63,65) with Cleveland, ran for 12,312 yards and scored 756 points in just 9 seasons.

Paul Brown (b.1908): Football innovator, coached Ohio St. to national title in 1942; in pros, directed Cleve.Browns to 4 straight AAFC titles (1946-49) and 3 NFL titles (1950,54-55), formed Cinn.Bengals in 1968 (reached playoffs in '70).

Valery Brumel (b.1942): Soviet high jumper, dominated event from 1961-64, broke world record 5 times, won silver medal in 1960 Olympics and gold in 1964, highest jump 7-5¾.

Avery Brundage (1887-1975): Amateur sports' czar for over 40 years as president of AAU (1928-35), US Olympic Committee (1929-53) and Int'l Olympic Committee (1952-72).

Paul (Bear) Bryant (1913-1983): Football, coached at 4 colleges over 38 years, directed Alabama to 5 national titles (1961,64-65,78-79), 323 career wins, 15 bowl wins including 8 Sugar Bowls.

Sergei Bubka (b.1963): Soviet pole vaulter, has set 18 world records (in & outdoor), 2-time world champion (1983,87), won gold medal at 1988 Olympics; highest vault 19-10½.

Don Budge (b.1915): Tennis, in 1938 became 1st player to win the Grand Slam—the French, Wimbledon, US and Australian titles in 1 year; led US to 2 Davis Cups (1937-38); turned pro in late '38.

Maria Bueno (b.1939): Brazilian tennis player, won 4 US Championships (1959,63-64,66) and 3 Wimbledons (1959-60,64).

Dick Butkus (b.1942): Football LB, 2-time All-America at Illinois (1963-64); All-Pro 7 of 9 NFL seasons with Chicago.

Dick Button (b.1929): Figure skater, 5-time world champion (1948-52), 2-time Olympic champ (1948,52).

Walter Byers (b.1923): College athletics, 1st executive director of NCAA, served from 1951-88.

Lee Calhoun (1933-89): Track & Field: won consecutive Olympic gold medals in the 110m Hurdles (1956,60).

Walter Camp (1859-1925): Football coach and innovator, established scrimmage line, center snap, downs, 11 players per side; named 1st All-America team (1889).

Roy Campanella (b.1921): Baseball C, 3-time NL MVP (1951,53,55), led Brooklyn to 5 pennants and 1st W.Series title (1955).

Earl Campbell (b.1955): Football RB, won Heisman Trophy in 1977, led NFL in rushing 3 times, 3-time All-Pro, 2-time MVP (1978-80) at Houston.

Milt Campbell (b.1933): Track & field, won silver medal in 1952 Olympic decathlon and gold medal in '56.

Tony Canzoneri (1908-59): Boxer, 2-time world lightweight champion (1930-33,35-36); pro record 141-24-10 with 44 KOs.

Rod Carew (b.1945): Baseball 2B-1B, led AL in batting 7 times (1969,72-75,77-78) with Minnesota, MVP in 1977, had 3,053 career hits.

Steve Carlton (b.1944): Baseball LHP, won 20 or more games 6 times, 4-time Cy Young winner (1972,77, 80,82) with Phila., 329 career wins.

JoAnn Carner (b.1939): Golfer, 5-time US Amateur champion, 2-time US Open champ, 3-time LPGA Player of Year (1974,81-82).

Don Carter (b.1926): Bowler, 6-time Bowler of Year (1953-54,57-58,60-61), voted Greatest of All-Time in 1970.

Billy Casper (b.1931): Golfer, 2-time PGA Player of Year (1966,70), has won US Open (1959,66), Masters (1970), US Sr.Open (1983).

Tracy Caulkins (b.1963): Swimmer, won 3 gold medals (2 individual) at 1984 Olympics, set 5 world records and won 48 US national titles from 1978-84.

Evonne Goolagong Cawley (b.1951): Australian tennis player, won Australian Open 4 times, Wimbledon twice (1971-79), French once.

Florence Chadwick (b.1918): Dominant distance swimmer of 1950s, set English Channel records from France to England (1950) and England to France (1951 and '55).

Wilt Chamberlain (b.1936): Basketball C, led NBA in scoring 7 times and rebounding 11 times, 7-time All-NBA first team, 4-time MVP (1960,66-68) with Phila., scored 100 pts in one game (1962), led Phila. (1967) and LA (1972) to NBA titles, playoff MVP in 1972.

Waldemar Cierpinski (b.1950): East German runner, won consecutive Olympic marathons (1976,80).

Jim Clark (1936-68): Scottish auto racer, 2-time Formula 1 world champion (1963,65), won Indy 500 in 1965, killed in car crash.

Bobby Clarke (b.1949): Hockey C, led Philadelphia to consecutive Stanley Cups in 1974-75, 3-time reg. season MVP (1973,75-76).

Ron Clarke (b.1937): Australian runner,from 1963-70 set 17 world records in races from 2 miles to 20,000 meters, never won Olympic gold medal.

Roger Clemens (b.1962): Baseball RHP, fanned record 20 batters in 9-inning game (1986), 2 Cy Young Awards (1986-87) with Boston, AL MVP in 1986.

Roberto Clemente (1934-72): Baseball OF, hit .300 or better 13 times with Pittsburgh, led NL in batting 4 times, W.Series MVP in 1971, regular season MVP in 1966, had 3,000 career hits.

Ty Cobb (1886-1961): Baseball OF, all-time highest career batting average (.367), hit .400 or better 3 times, led AL in batting 12 times and stolen bases 6 times with Detroit, MVP in 1911, had 4,191 career hits and 892 steals.

Mickey Cochrane (1903-62): Baseball C, led Phila.A's (1929-30) and Detroit (1935) to 3 W.Series titles, 2-time AL MVP (1928,34).

Sebastian Coe (b.1956): British runner, won consecutive gold medals in 800m at 1980 and '84 Olympics, held world records in 1,500m, mile and 800m in 1979.

Eddie Collins (1887-1951): Baseball 2B, led Phila.A's (1910-11) and Chi.White Sox (1917) to 3 W.Series titles, AL MVP in 1914, had 3,311 career hits and 743 stolen bases.

Nadia Comaneci (b.1961): Romanian gymnast, 1st to record perfect 10 in Olympics, won 3 indivdual gold medals at 1976 Olympics and 2 more in '80.

Lionel Conacher (1902-54): Canada's greatest all-around athlete, NHL hockey (2 Stanley Cups), CFL football (1 Grey Cup), minor league baseball, soccer, lacrosse, track, amateur boxing champion; also member of Parliament (1949-54).

Billy Conn (b.1917): Boxer, world light heavyweight champion (1939-41); pro record 63-11-1 with 14 KOs.

Dennis Connor (b.1942): Sailing, 2-time America's Cup-winning skipper (1980,87), but 1st American to lose Cup (1983).

Maureen Connolly (1934-69): Tennis, in 1953 1st women to win Grand Slam (at age 19), riding accident ended her career in '54, won both Wimbledon and US titles 3 times (1951-53); 3-time AP Female Athlete of Year (1951-53).

Jimmy Connors (1952): Tennis, No.1 player in world 5 times (1974-78), has won 5 US Opens, 2 Wimbledons and 1 Australian.

Angel Cordero, Jr. (b.1942): Jockey, winner of more than 6,000 races, won Kentucky Derby 3 times, Preakness twice and Belmont once, 2-time Eclipse winner (1982-83).

Margaret Smith Court (b.1942): Australian tennis player, won Grand Slam in both singles (1970) and mixed doubles (1963 with Ken Fletcher); 26 G.Slam singles titles—11 Australian, 7 US, 5 French and 3 Wimbledon.

Bob Cousy (b.1928): Basketball G, led NBA in assists 8 times, 10-time All-NBA 1st team (1952-61), MVP in 1957, led Boston to 6 NBA titles (1957,59-63).

Joe Cronin (1906-84): Baseball SS, hit over .300 and drove in over 100 runs 8 times each, MVP in 1930, player-manager in Washington and Boston (1933-47); AL president (1959-73).

Glenn Cunningham (1910-88): Track & Field, dominant US miler of 1930s, ran sub-4:10 mile 12 times, lost Olympic 1,500m to Jack Lovelock in 1936.

Stanley Dancer (b.1927): Harness racing, winner of 4 Hambletonians, trainer-driver of 2 Trotting Triple Crown winners (1968,72), one Pacing Triple Crown winner (1970).

Gary Davidson (b.1934): Entrepreneur, fueled boom in new sports leagues from 1967-75, 1st president of ABA, WHA and WFL.

Al Davis (b.1929): Football, GM-coach of Oakland 1963-66, helped force AFL-NFL merger as AFL commissioner (April-July,1966), returned to Oakland as GM and directed club to 3 Super Bowl wins (1977,81,84); moved Raiders to LA in 1982.

Glenn Davis (b.1924): Football HB, 3-time All-America, led Army to national titles in 1944-45, Doc Blanchard's running mate, won Heisman Trophy in 1946.

John Davis (1921-84): Weightlifting, 6-time world champion, 2-time Olympic super-heavyweight champ (1948,52), undefeated 1938-53.

Pierre de Coubertin (1862-1940): of France, father of the Modern Olympic Games, IOC president from 1896-1925.

Dizzy Dean (1911-74): Baseball RHP, led NL in strikeouts and complete games 4 times, last NL pitcher to win 30 games (30-7 in 1934), MVP in 1934 with St. Louis, 150 career wins.

Clarence Demar (1888-58): Track & Field, only 7-time winner of Boston Marathon (1911,22-24,27-28, 30), Olympic bronze in 1924.

Jack Dempsey (1895-1983): Boxer, world heavyweight champion from 1919-26, lost title and rematch to Gene Tunney, pro record 62-6-10 with 49 KOs.

Eric Dickerson (b.1960): Football RB, has led NFL in rushing 4 times (1983-84,86,88), All-Pro 5 times, traded from LA Rams to Indianapolis (Oct.31,1987).

Harrison Dillard (b.1923): Track & Field, only man to win Olympic gold medals in both sprints (100m in 1948) and hurdles (110m in 1952).

Marcel Dionne (b.1951): Hockey C, scored 50 or more goals 6 times, led NHL in scoring in 1980, ended 1989 2nd in All-Time goals (731), 3rd in assists (1,348) and 3rd in points (1,771).

Klaus Dibiasi (b.1947): Italian diver, won 3 consecutive Olympic gold medals in Platform Diving (1968,72,76).

Joe DiMaggio (b.1914): Baseball OF, hit safely in 56 straight games (1941), led AL in batting, HRs and RBI twice each, 3-time MVP (1939,41,47), led NY Yankees to 10 W.Series titles in 13 seasons.

Ken Dryden (b.1947): Hockey G, led Montreal to 6 Stanley Cup titles, playoff MVP as rookie in 1971, won or shared 5 Vezina Trophies.

Margaret Osborne du Pont (b.1918): Tennis, won 5 French, 7 Wimbledon and an unprecendented 24 US national titles in singles, doubles and mixed doubles from 1941-62.

Roberto Duran (b.1951): Panamanian boxer, world lightweight champion (1972-79), world welterweight champ (1980), pro record (thru July,1989) 85-7 with 60 KOs.

Leo Durocher (b.1905): Baseball, managed in NL 24 years, won 2,010 games, 3 pennants with Brooklyn (1941) and NY Giants (1951,54), won W.Series in 1954.

Eddie Eagan (1898-1967): Only US athlete to win gold medals in Summer and Winter Olympics (Boxing in 1920, Bobsled in 1932).

Alan Eagleson (b.1933): Hockey, executive dir. of NHL players union since 1967, arranged Team Canada vs Soviet series (1972) and Canada Cup (1976,81,84,87).

Gertrude Ederle (b.1906): Swimmer, 1st woman to swim English Channel, breaking men's record by 2 hours in 1926, won 3 medals in 1924 Olympics.

Bill Elliott (b.1955): Auto racer, 2-time winner of Daytona 500 (1985,87), NASCAR national champ in 1988, won 11 races in '85.

Herb Elliott (b.1938): Australian runner, undefeated from 1958-60, ran 17 sub-4:00 miles, 3 world records, won gold medal in 1,500m of 1960 Olympics, retired at 22.

Roy Emerson (b.1936): Australian tennis player, won 12 Majors in singles—6 Australian, 2 French, 2 Wimbledon and 2 US from 1961-67.

Kornelia Ender (b.1958): East German swimmer, 1st woman to win 4 gold medals at one Olympics (1976), all in world record time.

Julius Erving (b.1950): Basketball F, in ABA (1972-76)—3-time MVP, 2-time playoff MVP, led NY Nets to 2 titles (1974-76); in NBA (1977-87)—5-time All-NBA 1st team, MVP in 1981, led Phila.76ers to title in 1983.

Phil Esposito (b.1942): Hockey C, 1st NHL player to score 100 points in a season (126 in 1969), 6-time All-NHL 1st team with Boston, 2-time MVP (1969,74), 5-time scoring champ, star of 1972 Canada-Soviet series.

Janet Evans (b.1971): Swimmer, won 3 individual gold medals (400m & 800m freestyle, 400m IM) at 1988 Olympics, held 3 world records in 1989.

Lee Evans (b.1947): Track & Field, dominant quarter-miler in world from 1966-72, world record in 400m at 1968 Olympics stood 20 years.

Chris Evert (b.1954): Tennis, No.1 player in world 5 times (1975-77,80-81), won at least 1 Grand Slam singles title every year from 1974-86, 18 Majors in all—7 French, 6 US, 3 Wimbledon and 2 Australian.

Patrick Ewing (b.1962): Basketball C, 3-time All-America, led Georgetown to 3 NCAA Finals, tourney MVP in 1984; NBA Rookie of Year with New York in 1986.

Ray Ewry (1873-1937): Track & Field, won 8 gold medals over 3 consecutive Olympics (1900,04,08); all events he won (Standing HJ,LJ and TJ) were discontinued in 1912.

Juan Manuel Fangio (b.1911): Argentine auto racer, 5-time Formula 1 world champion (1951,54-57), 24 career wins, retired in 1958.

Bob Feller (b.1918): Baseball RHP, led AL in strikeouts 7 times and wins 6 times with Cleveland, threw 3 no-hitters and 12 one-hitters, 266 career wins.

Tom Ferguson (b.1950): Rodeo, 6-time All-Around champion (1974-79); 1st cowboy to win $100,000 in a season (1978), 1st to win $1 million in career (1986).

Herve Filion (b.1940): Harness racing, 12-time leading dashwinner, All-Time leader in races won with over 10,500.

Rollie Fingers (b.1946): Baseball RHP, all-time save leader with 341, won AL MVP and Cy Young awards in 1981 with Milwaukee, W.Series MVP in 1974 with Oakland.

Charles O.Finley (b.1918): Baseball owner, moved KC A's to Oakland in 1968, won 3 straight World Series from 1972-74; also owned teams in NHL and ABA.

Bobby Fischer (b.1943): Chess, only American to hold world championship (1972-75), resigned title in 1975.

Emerson Fittipaldi (b.1946): Brazilian auto racer, 2-time Formula 1 world champion (1972,74), won Indy 500 in 1989.

James (Sunny Jim) Fitzsimmons (1873-1966): Horse racing, trained horses that won over 2,275 races, including 2 Triple Crown winners—Gallant Fox in 1930 and Omaha in '35.

Larry Fleisher (1930-89): Basketball, led NBA players union from 1961-89; in that time, increased average yearly salary from $9,400 in 1967 to $600,000 without a strike.

Peggy Fleming (b.1948): Figure skating, 3-time world champion (1966-68), won Olympic gold medal in 1968.

Curt Flood (b.1938): Baseball OF, played 15 years (1956-71), lost challenge to MLB's reserve clause in Supreme Court in 1972 (see Peter Seitz).

Whitey Ford (b.1928): Baseball LHP, all-time leader in W.Series wins (10), led AL in wins 3 times, won both Cy Young and W.Series MVP in 1961 with NY Yankees.

George Foreman (b.1948): Boxer, 1968 Olympic heavyweight champion; world heavyweight champ (1973-74); pro record (thru July,1989) 64-2 with 60 KOs.

Dick Fosbury (b.1947): Track & Field, revolutionized high jump with "Fosbury Flop," won gold medal at 1968 Olympics.

Bob Foster (b.1938): Boxer, world light-heavyweight champion (1968-74); pro record 56-8-1 with 46 KOs.

The Four Horsemen—Senior backfield that led Notre Dame to national championship in 1924: HB **Jim Crowley** (1902-86), FB **Elmer Layden** (1903-73), HB **Don Miller** (1902-79) and QB **Harry Stuhldreher** (1901-65).

The Four Musketeers—French quartet that dominated men's world tennis in 1920s and '30s, winning 8 straight French singles titles (1925-32), 6 Wimbledons in a row (1924-29) and 6 consecutive Davis Cups (1927-32): **Jean Borotra** (b.1898), **Jacques Brugnon** (1895-1978), **Henri Cochet** (1901-1987), **Rene Lacoste** (b.1904).

Jimmie Foxx (1907-67): Baseball 1B, led AL in HRs 4 times and batting twice, won Triple Crown in 1933, 3-time MVP (1932-33,38) with Phila. and Boston, hit 30 HRs or more 12 years in a row, 534 career HRs.

A.J.Foyt (b.1935): Auto racer, 4-time Indy 500 winner (1961,64,67,77), 7-time USAC/CART national champ, only driver to win Indy 500, Daytona 500 (1972) and 24 Hours of LeMans (1967 with Dan Gurney).

Dawn Fraser (b.1937): Australian swimmer, won gold medals in 100m freestyle at 3 consecutive Olympics (1956,60,64).

Joe Frazier (b.1944): Boxer, 1964 Olympic heavyweight champion; world heavyweight champ (1970-73), fought Muhammad Ali 3 times, pro record 32-4-1 with 27 KOs.

Walt Frazier (b.1945): Basketball G, 4-time All-NBA 1st team, 7-time All-Defense 1st team, led New York to 2 NBA titles (1970,73).

Frankie Frisch (1898-1973): Baseball 2B, played on 8 NL pennant winners in 19 years with NY and St.Louis, hit .300 or better 11 years in a row (1921-31), MVP in 1931, player-manager from 1933-37.

Dan Gable (b.1948): Wrestling, 2-time NCAA champ at Iowa St., tourney MVP in 1969 (137 lbs.); won gold medal (149 lbs) at 1972 Olympics; coached Iowa to 9 straight NCAA titles (1978-86).

Eddie Gaedel (1925-61): Baseball PH, St.Louis Browns' midget whose career lasted one at bat (he walked) on Aug.19,1951.

Lou Gehrig (1903-41): Baseball 1B, played in 2,130 consecutive games from 1923-39, led AL in RBI 5 times and HRs 3 times, drove in 100 runs or more 13 years in a row, 2-time MVP (1927,36), led NY Yankees to 7 W.Series titles.

Charlie Gehringer (b.1903): Baseball 2B, hit .300 or better 13 times, AL batting champion and MVP with Detroit in 1937.

A.Bartlett Giamatti (1938-89): Scholar and 7th commissioner of baseball, banned Pete Rose for life for betting on Major League games and associating with known gamblers and drug dealers; also served as president of both Yale Univ. (1978-86) and National League (1986-89).

Althea Gibson (b. 1927): Tennis, won both Wimbledon and US championships in 1957 and '58, 1st black to play in either tourney and 1st to win each title.

Bob Gibson (b. 1935): Baseball RHP, won 20 or more games 5 times, won 2 NL Cy Young Awards (1968,70), MVP in 1968, led St. Louis to 2 W.Series titles, Series MVP twice (1964,67), 251 career wins.

Josh Gibson (1911-47): Baseball C, the "Babe Ruth of the Negro Leagues," Satchel Paige's battery mate with Pittsburgh Crawfords.

Frank Gifford (b. 1930): Football HB, 4-time All-Pro (1955-57,59), MVP in 1956, led NY Giants to 3 NL title games.

Sid Gillman (b.1911): Football innovator, coached LA Rams (1955-59) in NFL, then led LA-SD Chargers of AFL to 5 Western titles and 1 championship in the league's 1st six years.

George Gipp (1895-1920): Football FB, died of throat infection (Dec.14) 2 weeks before he made All-America (Notre Dame's 1st); rushed for 2,341 yards, scored 156 points and averaged 38 yards a punt in 4 years (1917-20).

Pancho Gonzalez (b.1928): Tennis, won consecutive US Championships in 1947-48 before turning pro at 21, dominated pro tour from 1950-61; in 1969 at age 41, played longest Wimbledon match ever (5:12) beating Charlie Pasarell 22-24,1-6,16-14,6-3,11-9.

Shane Gould (b.1956): Australian swimmer, set world records in 5 different freestyle events between July,1971 and Jan,1972; won 3 gold medals, a silver and bronze in 1972 Olympics then retired at age 16.

Steffi Graf (b.1969): West German tennis player, won Grand Slam in 1989 at age 19, No.1 player in world twice (1987-88) so far.

Gillis Grafstrom (1894-1938): Swedish figure skater, 3-time world champ, won 3 straight gold medals then a silver in 4 Olympics (1920,24,28,32).

Otto Graham (b.1921): Football QB and basketball All-America at Northwestern; in pro ball, led Cleve. Browns to 7 league titles in 10 years, winning 4 AAFC championships (1946-50) and 3 NFL (1950,54-55), 5-time All-Pro, 2-time NFL MVP (1953,55).

Red Grange (b.1903): Football HB, 3-time All-America at Illinois who brought 1st huge crowds to pro football when he signed with Chicago in 1925; formed 1st AFL with manager C.C.Pyle in 1926, but league folded and he returned to NFL.

Hank Greenberg (1911-86): Baseball 1B, led AL in HRs and RBI 4 times each, 2-time MVP (1935,40) with Detroit, 331 career HRs.

Joe Greene (b.1946): Football DT, 5-time All-Pro (1972-74,77,79), led Pittsburgh to 4 Super Bowl titles.

Wayne Gretzky (b.1961): Hockey C, 9-time regular season MVP (1979-87,89), 7-time scoring champ, has scored 200 points or more in a season 4 times, led Edmonton to 4 Stanley Cups (1984-85,87-88), 2-time playoff MVP (1985,88), traded to LA Kings (Aug.9, 1988), will overtake Gordie Howe for all-time NHL scoring lead early in 1989-90 season.

Bob Griese (b.1945): Football QB, 2-time All-Pro (1971,77), led Miami to undefeated season (17-0) in 1972 and consecutive Super Bowl titles (1973-74).

Archie Griffin (b.1954): Football RB, only college player to win two Heisman Trophies (1974-75), rushed for 5,177 yards in career at Ohio St.

Emile Griffith (b.1938): Boxer, world welterweight champion (1961,62-63,63-65), world middleweight champ (1966-67,67-68), pro record 85-24-2 with 23 KOs.

Florence Griffith Joyner (b.1959): Track & Field, set world records in 100 and 200 meters in 1988, won 3 gold medals at '88 Olympics (100m,200m,4x100 relay).

Lefty Grove (1900-75): Baseball LHP, won 20 or more games 8 times, led AL in ERA 9 times and strikeouts 7 times, 31-4 record and MVP in 1931 with Phila., 300 career wins.

Lou Groza (b.1924): Football T-PK, 6-time All-Pro, played in 13 championship games for Cleveland from 1946-67, kicked winning field goal in 1950 NFL title game, 1,608 career points (1,349 in NFL).

Tony Gwynn (b.1960): Baseball OF, entered 1989 season with 3 NL batting titles (1984,87-88) at San Diego and career average of .331.

Harvey Haddix (b.1925): Baseball LHP, pitched 12 perfect innings for Pittsburgh but lost to Milwaukee in the 13th, 1-0 (May 26,1959).

Walter Hagen (1892-1969): Pro golf pioneer, won 2 US Opens (1914,19), 4 British Opens (1922,24,28-29), 5 PGA Championships (1921,24-27) and 5 Western Opens; US Ryder Cup captain 6 times.

Marvin Hagler (b.1954): Boxer, world middleweight champion 1980-87; pro record 62-3-2 with 52 KOs.

George Halas (1895-1983): Football pioneer, MVP in 1919 Rose Bowl; player-coach-owner of Chicago Bears from 1920-83, signed Red Grange in 1925, coached Bears for 40 seasons and won 7 NFL titles (1932-33,40-41,43,46,63), all-time leader in career wins (325).

Dorothy Hamill (b.1956): Figure skater, won Olympic gold medal and world championship in 1976.

Scott Hamilton (b.1958): Figure skater, 4-time world champion (1981-84), won gold medal at 1984 Olympics.

Franco Harris (b.1950): Football RB, ran for over 1,000 yards a season 8 times, rushed for 12,120 yards in 13 years, led Pittsburgh to 4 Super Bowl titles.

Bill Hartack (b.1932): Jockey, won Kentucky Derby 5 times (1957,60,62,64,69), Preakness 3 times (1956,64,69), but the Belmont only once (1960).

Doug Harvey (b.1924): Hockey D, 10-time All-NHL 1st team, won Norris Trophy 7 times (1955-58,60-62), led Montreal to 6 Stanley Cups.

Billy Haughton (1923-86): Harness racing, 4-time winner of Hambletonian, trainer-driver of one Pacing Triple Crown winner (1968), winner of 4,910 races in career.

John Havlicek (b.1940): Basketball, played in 3 NCAA finals at Ohio St.(1960-62); led Boston to 8 NBA titles (1963-66,68-69,74,76), playoff MVP in 1974; 4-time All-NBA 1st team.

Bob Hayes (b.1942): Track & Field/Football, won gold medal in 100m at 1964 Olympics, All-Pro SE for Dallas in 1966.

Woody Hayes (1913-87): Football, coached Ohio St. to 3 national titles (1954,57,68) and 4 Rose Bowl victories, 238 career wins.

Eric Heiden (b.1958): Speed skater, 3-time overall world champion (1977-79), won all 5 men's gold medals at 1980 Olympics setting new records in each.

Mel Hein (b.1909): Football C, NFL All-Pro 8 straight years (1933-40), MVP in 1938 with NY Giants, didn't miss a game in 15 seasons.

John W.Heisman (1869-1936): Football, coached at 9 colleges from 1892-1927, won 185 games, Dir.of Athletics at Downtown Athletic Club in NYC (1928-36), DAC named Heisman Trophy after him.

Carol Heiss (b.1940): Figure skater, 5-time world champion (1956-60), won Olympic silver medal in 1956, gold in '60, married 1956 men's gold medalist Hayes Jenkins.

Rickey Henderson (b.1958): Baseball OF, set single season base stealing record of 130 in 1982, has led AL in steals 8 times, entered 1989 season with 794 thefts.

Sonja Henie (1912-69): Norwegian figure skater, 10-time world champion (1927-36), won 3 consecutive Olympic gold medals (1928,32,36).

Graham Hill (1929-75): British auto racer, 2-time Formula 1 world champion (1962,68), won Indy 500 in 1966, killed in plane crash.

Edmund Hillary (b.1919): New Zealand explorer, one of first 2 men (with Sherpa guide Tenzing Norgay) to reach the top of Mt. Everest and return (May 29,1953).

Max Hirsch (1880-1969): Horse racing, trained 1,933 winners from 1908-68, won Triple Crown with Assault in 1946.

Tommy Hitchcock (1900-44): Polo, world class player at 20, achieved 10-goal rating 18 times from 1922-40.

Ben Hogan (b.1912): Golfer, 4-time PGA Player of Year; won 4 US Opens, 2 Masters, 2 PGA and 1 British Open between 1946-53; won 3 of 4 Majors (Masters, US Open, British Open) in 1953; 62 career wins.

Eleanor Holm (b.1913): Swimmer, won gold medal in 100m backstroke at 1932 Olympics, thrown off '36 US team for drinking champagne in public and shooting craps on boat to Germany.

Nat Holman (b.1896): Basketball pioneer, played pro with Original Celtics (1920-28); coached CCNY to both NCAA and NIT titles in 1950 (a year later, several of his players were caught up in a point-shaving scandal); 423 career wins.

Larry Holmes (b.1949): Boxer, heavyweight champion (WBC or IBF) from 1978-85, defended title 21 times, pro record 48-3 with 34 KOs.

Willie Hoppe (1887-1959): Billiards, dominant player from 1904-52; won over 50 world championship matches at 18.1 balkline, 18.2 balkline and 3-cushion billiards.

Rogers Hornsby (1896-1963): Baseball 2B, hit .400 three times, including .424 in 1924, led NL in batting 7 times, 2-time MVP (1925,29) with St. Louis, hit .358 over 23 years.

Paul Hornung (b.1935): Football HB-PK, only Heisman Trophy winner to play for losing team (2-8 Notre Dame in 1956); 3-time NFL scoring leader (1959-61) at Green Bay, 176 points in 1960 all-time record, MVP in 1961.

Gordie Howe (b.1928): Hockey RW, played 32 seasons in NHL and WHA from 1946-80, led NHL in scoring 6 times, All-NHL 1st team 12 times, MVP 6 times in NHL (1952-53,57-58,60,63) with Detroit and once in WHA (1974) with Houston, retired as NHL all-time leader in goals (801), assists (1,049) and points (1,850).

Cal Hubbard (1900-77): Member of baseball, college, and pro football halls of fame; 9 years in NFL, 4-time All-Pro at end and tackle; AL umpire for 15 years (1936-51).

Carl Hubbell (1903-88): Baseball LHP, led NL in wins and ERA 3 times each, 2-time MVP (1933,36) with NY Giants; fanned Ruth, Gehrig, Foxx, Simmons and Cronin in succession in 1934 All-Star Game, 253 career wins.

Miller Huggins (1880-1929): Baseball, managed NY Yankees to 6 pennants and 3 W.Series titles from 1921-27.

Bobby Hull (b.1939): Hockey LW, led NHL in scoring 3 times, 2-time MVP (1965-66) with Chicago, All-NHL first team 10 times; jumped to WHA in 1972, 2-time MVP there (1973,75) with Winnipeg, scored 913 goals in both leagues.

Jim (Catfish) Hunter (b.1946): Baseball RHP, won 20 games or more 5 times (1971-75), played on 5 W.Series winners with Oakland, NY Yankees; threw perfect game in 1968, won Cy Young Award in '74.

Don Hutson (b.1913): Football E-PK, led NFL in receptions 8 times and interceptions once, 9-time All-Pro (1936, 38-45) for Green Bay, record 99 TD catches in career.

Henry Iba (b.1904): Basketball, coached Oklahoma A&M to 2 straight NCAA titles (1945-46), 767 career wins in 41 years; coached US Olympic team to 2 gold medals (1964,68) but lost to Soviets in controversial '72 final.

Punch Imlach (1918-1987): Hockey, directed Toronto to 4 Stanley Cups (1962-64,67) in 11 seasons as GM-coach.

Bo Jackson (b.1962): Baseball OF and Football RB, won Heisman Trophy in 1985; starter for baseball's KC Royals and NFL's LA Raiders in 1988.

Joe Jackson (1887-1951): Baseball OF, hit .300 or better 11 times, career average of .356; (see Black Sox).

Reggie Jackson (b.1946): Baseball OF, led AL in HRs 4 times, MVP in 1973, played on 5 W.Series winners with Oakland, NY Yankees; 1977 Series MVP with 5 HRs, 563 career HRs, all-time strikeout leader (2,597).

Helen Jacobs (b.1908): Tennis, 4-time winner of US Championship (1932-35), Wimbledon winner in 1936; lost 4 Wimbledon finals to arch-rival Helen Wills Moody.

Jim Jacobs (1930-88): Handball/Boxing, won 12 US Handball titles (6 singles and 6 doubles) from 1955-68; also managed 4 world champion boxers, including Mike Tyson (from 1985-88).

James J.Jeffries (1875-1953): Boxer, world heavyweight champion (1899-1905); retired undefeated but came back to fight Jack Johnson in 1910 and lost (KO,15th).

Hayes Jenkins (b.1933): Figure skater, 4-time world champion (1953-56), won gold medal at 1956 Olympics, married 1960 women's gold medalist Carol Heiss.

David Jenkins (b.1936): Figure skater, brother of Hayes, 3-time world champion (1957-59), won gold medal at 1960 Olympics.

Bruce Jenner (b.1949): Track & Field, won gold medal in 1976 Olympic decathlon.

Ben Johnson (b.1961): Canadian sprinter, set 100m world record (9.83) at 1987 World Championships; won 100m at 1988 Olympics, but flunked drug test and forfeited gold medal; 1987 world record revoked in '89 for admitted steroid use.

Jack Johnson (1878-1946): Boxer, 1st black world heavyweight champion (1908-15), pro record 78-8-12 with 45 KOs.

Earvin (Magic) Johnson (b.1959): Basketball G, led Mich.St. to NCAA title in 1979, tourney MVP; All-NBA 1st team 7 times, has led NBA in assists 4 times, 2-time MVP (1987,89), has led LA Lakers to 5 NBA titles, 3-time playoff MVP (1980,82,87).

Rafer Johnson (b.1935): Track & Field, won silver medal in 1956 Olympic decathlon and gold medal in 1960.

Walter Johnson (1887-1946): Baseball RHP, won 20 games or more 10 straight years; led AL in ERA 5 times, wins 6 times and strikeouts 12 times, twice MVP (1913, 24) with Washington; all-time leader in shutouts (113) and 2nd in wins (416).

Ben A. Jones (1882-1961): Horse racing, Calumet Farm trainer (1939-47), saddled 6 Kentucky Derby champions and 2 Triple Crown winners—Whirlaway in 1941 and Citation in '48.

Deacon Jones (b. 1938): Football DE, 5-time All-Pro (1965-69) with LA Rams.

Bobby Jones (1902-71): Won US and British Opens plus US and British Amateurs in 1930 to become golf's only Grand Slam winner ever; from 1922-30, won 4 US Opens, 5 US Amateurs, 3 British Opens, and played in 6 Walker Cups; founded Masters tournament in 1934.

Michael Jordan (b. 1963): Basketball G, College Player of Year in 1984; has led NBA in scoring 3 times (1987-89) with Chicago, 3-time All NBA 1st team, MVP in 1988.

Jackie Joyner-Kersee (b. 1962): Track & Field, entered 1989 as world record holder in heptathlon (7,291 pts); won gold medals in heptathlon and long jump at 1988 Olympics.

Alberto Juantorena (b. 1951): Cuban runner, won both 400m and 800m gold medals at 1976 Olympics.

Sonny Jurgensen (b.1934): Football QB, played 18 seasons with Phila. and Wash., led NFL in passing twice (1967,69), All-Pro in 1961, 255 career TD passes.

Duke Kahanamoku (1890-1968): Swimmer, won 3 gold medals and 2 silver over 3 Olympics (1912,20,24); also surfing pioneer.

Al Kaline (b.1934): Baseball, youngest player (20) to win batting title (led AL with .340 in 1955), had 3,007 hits, 399 HRs in 22 years with Detroit.

Anatoly Karpov (b.1951): Chess, Soviet world champion, 1975-85.

Gary Kasparov (b.1963): Chess, Soviet world champion since 1985; defeated Karpov for title.

Kip Keino (b.1940): Kenyan runner, won one gold medal in 1,500m at 1968 Olympics and another in steeplechase at 1972 Games.

Harmon Killebrew (b.1936): Baseball 3B-1B, led AL in HRs 6 times and RBI 4 times, MVP in 1969 with Minnesota, 573 career HRs.

Jean Claude Killy (b.1943): French alpine skier, 2-time World Cup champion (1967-68), won 3 gold medals 1968 Olympics.

Ralph Kiner (b.1922): Baseball OF, led NL in home runs 7 straight years (1946-52) with Pittsburgh, 369 career HRs.

Billie Jean King (b.1943): Tennis, Wimbledon singles champ 6 times, US champ 4 times, first woman athlete to earn $100,000 in one year (1971).

Bob Knight (b.1940): Basketball, has coached Indiana to 3 NCAA titles (1976,81,87); coached 1984 US Olympic team to gold.

Olga Korbut (b.1955): Soviet gymnast, 3 gold medals 1972 Olympics, first to perform back somersault on balance beam.

Sandy Koufax (b.1935): Baseball LHP, led NL in strikeouts 4 times and ERA 5 straight years, won 3 Cy Young Awards (1963,65,66) with LA Dodgers, MVP in 1963, 2-time W.Series MVP (1963,65); pitched 1 perfect game and 3 other no-hitters.

Alvin Kraenzlein (1876-1928): Track & Field, won 4 individual gold medals in 1900 Olympics (60m,long jump, and 110m & 200m hurdles).

Jack Kramer (b.1921): Tennis, Wimbledon singles champ 1947, US champ 1946-47; promoter and Open pioneer.

Ingrid Kristiansen (b.1956): Norwegian runner, 2-time Boston Marathon winner (1986,89), world record holder in 5,000m, 10,000m and marathon.

Bob Kurland (b.1924): Basketball C, 3-time All-America (1944-46), led Okla.A&M to 2 NCAA titles (1945-46) and US to 2 Olympic gold medals (1948,52), did not turn pro.

Marion Ladewig (b.1914): named Woman Bowler of the Year 9 times, (1950-54,57-59,63).

Guy Lafleur (b.1951): Hockey RW, has led NHL in scoring 3 times (1975-78), 2-time MVP (1977-78), played for 5 Stanley Cup winners in Montreal, playoff MVP in 1977.

Napoleon Lajoie (1875-1959): Baseball 2B, led AL in batting 4 times (1901-04), hit .422 in 1901, had 3,251 career hits.

Jack Lambert (b.1952): Football LB, 6-time All-Pro (1975-76,79-82), led Pittsburgh to 4 Super Bowl titles.

Kenesaw Mountain Landis (1866-1944): Baseball's first commissioner (1920-44), banned Black Sox for life.

Tom Landry (b.1924): Football, coached Dallas for 29 years (1960-88), won 2 Super Bowls (1972,78), 271 career wins.

Steve Largent (b.1954): Football WR, entered 1989 season with Seattle as all-time NFL leader in passes caught (791), second in TD passes caught (97).

Don Larson (b.1929): Baseball RHP, pitched only perfect game in W.Series history—NY Yankees 2, Brooklyn 0 (Oct.8,1956), Series MVP that year.

Larissa Latynina (b.1934): Soviet gymnast, won total of 18 medals, (9 gold) in 3 Olympics (1956,60,64).

Nikki Lauda (b.1949): Austrian auto racer, 3-time world Formula 1 champion (1975,77,84), 25 career wins from 1971-85.

Rod Laver (b.1938): Australian tennis player, only player to win Grand Slam twice (1962,69), Wimbledon champion 4 times, 1st to earn $1 million in prize money.

Andrea Mead Lawrence (b.1932): Alpine skier, won 2 gold medals at 1952 Olympics.

Bobby Layne (1926-86): Football QB, college star at Texas, led Detroit to 2 straight NFL titles (1952-53).

Frank Leahy (1908-73): Football, coached Notre Dame to four national titles (1943,46-47,49), career record of 107-13-9.

Sammy Lee (b.1920): US diver, 1st to repeat as Olympic diving champ (1948,52).

Greg LeMond (b.1962): Cyclist, 2-time Tour de France winner (1986,89), first American cyclist to win the event.

Mario Lemieux (b.1965): Hockey C, has led NHL in scoring twice (1988-89), 2-time All-NHL 1st team, MVP in 1988 with Pittsburgh.

Ivan Lendl (b.1960): Tennis, No.1 player in the world from 1985-87, has won both French and US Opens 3 times.

Suzanne Lenglen (1899-1938): French tennis player, dominated women's tennis from 1919-26, won both Wimbledon and French singles titles 6 times.

Sugar Ray Leonard (b.1956): Boxer, light welterweight Olympic champ (1976), won world welterweight title 1979, four more titles since; pro record (thru July,1989) 35-1-1 with 25 KOs.

Carl Lewis (b.1961): Track & Field, won 4 gold medals in 1984 Olympics (100m,200m,400m relay and long jump), 2 more (100m, long jump) in 1988.

Sonny Liston (1932-70): Boxer, heavyweight champ (1962-64), lost title to Muhammad Ali (then Cassius Clay) in 1964; pro record 50-4 with 39 KOs.

Vince Lombardi (1913-70): Football, coached Green Bay to 5 NFL titles, won first 2 Super Bowls (1967-68).

Johnny Longden (b.1907): Jockey, first to win 6,000 races, rode Count Fleet to Triple Crown in 1943.

Nancy Lopez (b.1957): Golfer, 4-time LPGA Player of the Year (1978-79,85,88), reached Hall of Fame by age 30.

Greg Louganis (b.1960): US diver, won platform and springboard gold medals at both 1984 and '88 Olympics.

Joe Louis (1914-81): Boxer, world heavyweight champion (1937-49); reign of 11 years, 8 months longest in division history; pro record 63-3 with 49 KOs.

Sid Luckman (b.1916): Football QB, 6-time All-Pro, led Chicago Bears to 4 NFL titles (1940-41,43,46), MVP in 1943.

Hank Luisetti (b. 1916): Basketball F, 3-time All-America at Stanford (1935-38), revolutionized game with one-handed shot.

Johnny Lujack (b.1925): Football QB, led Notre Dame to three national titles (1943,46-47), won Heisman Trophy in 1947.

Larry MacPhail (1890-1975): Baseball executive, introduced major leagues to night games at Cincinnati on May 24,1935.

Connie Mack (1862-1956): Baseball owner, managed Phila.A's until he was 87 (1901-50), won 9 AL pennants and 5 W.Series (1910-11,13,29-30).

Larry Mahan (b.1943): Rodeo, 6-time All-Around Cowboy (1966-70,73).

Phil Mahre (b.1957): Alpine skier, 3-time World Cup overall champ (1981-83), finished 1-2 with twin brother Steve in 1984 Olympic slalom.

Moses Malone (b.1955): Basketball C, has led NBA in rebounding 6 times, 4-time All-NBA 1st team, 3-time NBA MVP (1979,82-83), playoff MVP with Phila. in 1983.

Mickey Mantle (b.1931): Baseball OF, led AL in home runs 4 times, won Triple Crown in 1956, 3-time MVP (1956-57,62), 536 career HRs, played on 7 W.Series winners with NY Yankees.

Pete Maravich (1948-88): Basketball, NCAA scoring leader 3 times (1968-70), averaged 44.2 points a game over career, Player of Year in 1970; NBA scoring champ in 1977.

Alice Marble (b.1913): Tennis, 4-time US champion (1936,38-40), won Wimbledon in 1939; swept US singles, doubles and mixed doubles from 1938-40.

Gino Marchetti (b.1927): Football DE, 8-time NFL All-Pro (1957-64) with Baltimore Colts.

Rocky Marciano (1923-69): Boxer, heavyweight champion (1952-56), retired undefeated, pro record of 49-0 with 43 KOs.

Juan Marichal (b.1937): Baseball RHP, won 21 or more games 6 times with S.F. Giants, 243 career wins.

Dan Marino (b.1961): Football QB, set NFL single-season records for TD passes (48) and passing yards (5,084) in 1984.

Roger Maris (1934-85): Baseball OF, broke Babe Ruth's single season HR record with 61 in 1961, 2-time AL MVP (1960-61) with NY Yankees.

Eddie Mathews (b.1931): Baseball 3B, led NL in HRs twice (1953,59), hit 30 or more home runs 9 straight years, 512 career HRs.

Christy Mathewson (1880-1925): Baseball RHP, won 22 or more games 12 straight years (1903-14), 373 career wins, pitched 3 shutouts in 1905 W.Series.

Bob Mathias (b.1930): Track & Field, first 2-time Olympic decathlon champion (1948,52).

Willie Mays (b.1931): Baseball OF, led NL in HRs and stolen bases 4 times each, 2-time MVP (1954,65) with NY-SF Giants, played in 24 All-Star games, 660 HRs and 3,283 hits in career.

Joe McCarthy (1887-1978): Baseball, managed NY Yankees to 8 pennants and 7 W.Series titles (1931-46).

Pat McCormick (b.1930): US diver, won women's platform and springboard gold medals in both 1952 and '56 Olympics.

Willie McCovey (b.1938): led NL in HRs 3 times and RBI twice, MVP in 1969 with SF, 521 career HRs.

Terry McDermott (b.1940): Speed skater, first place in Men's 500m was only gold medal won by an American at 1964 Winter Olympics.

John McEnroe (b.1959): Tennis, No.1 player in the world from 1981-84, 4-time US Open singles champ (1979-81,84), 3-time Wimbledon champ (1981,83-84), played on 4 Davis Cup winners (1978-79,81-82).

John McGraw (1873-1934): Baseball, managed NY Giants to 10 NL pennants and 3 W.Series titles in 30 years, 4,879 career wins.

John McKay (b.1923): Football, coached Southern Cal to 3 national titles (1962,67,72), won Rose Bowl 5 times.

Tamara McKinney (b.1962): Alpine skier, only American woman to win World Cup overall title (1983).

Denny McLain (b.1944): Baseball RHP, last pitcher to win 30 games (1968), 2-time Cy Young winner (1968-69) with Detroit.

Debbie Meyer (b.1952): Swimmer, 1st swimmer to win 3 individual gold medals at one Olympics (1968).

George Mikan (b.1924): Basketball C, 3-time All-America (1944-46), led DePaul to NIT title (1945); led Minneapolis Lakers to 5 NBA titles in 6 years (1949-54).

Stan Mikita (b.1940): Hockey C, led NHL in scoring 4 times, won both MVP and Lady Byng awards in 1967 and '68 with Chicago.

Cheryl Miller (b.1964): Basketball, 3-time college Player of Year (1984-86), led USC to NCAA title and US to Olympic gold medal in 1984.

Del Miller (b.1913): Harness racing—driver, trainer, owner, breeder, seller and track owner. Drove 1,775 winners (1939-74).

Marvin Miller (b.1917): Baseball, executive dir. of Players' Assn from 1966-82, increased average salary from $19,000 to over $240,000, led 13-day strike in 1972 and 50-day walkout in '81.

Billy Mills (b.1938): Track & Field, upset winner of 10,000m gold medal at 1964 Olympics.

Joe Montana (b.1956): Football QB, led Notre Dame to national title in 1977; has since led San Francisco to 3 Super Bowl wins (1982,85,89), 2-time Super Bowl MVP.

Helen Wills Moody (b.1905): Tennis, won 8 Wimbledon singles titles, 7 US and 4 French from 1923-38.

Archie Moore (b.1913): Boxer, world light-heavyweight champion (1952-60), pro record 199-26-8 with 145 KOs.

Howie Morenz (1902-37): Hockey C, 3-time NHL MVP (1928,31-32), led Montreal Canadiens to 3 Stanley Cups, voted Outstanding Player of the Half-Century in 1950.

Joe Morgan (b.1943): Baseball 2B, led NL in walks 4 times, regular season MVP both years he led Cincinnati to W.Series titles (1975-76).

Bobby Morrow (b.1935): Track & Field, won 3 gold medals at 1956 Olympics (100m,200m and 4x400m relay).

Willie Mosconi (b.1913), Pocket Billiards, 14-time world champion from 1941-57.

Edwin Moses (b.1955): Track & Field, won 400m hurdles at 1976 and '84 Olympics, bronze medal in '88, also winner of 122 consecutive races from 1977-87.

Sterling Moss (b.1929): Auto racer, won 194 of 466 career races and 16 Formula 1 events, but was never world champion.

Marion Motley (b.1920): Football FB, all-time leading AAFC rusher, rushed for over 4,700 yards and 31 TDs for Cleve.Browns (1946-53).

Shirley Muldowney (b.1940): Drag racer, 3-time Top Fuel champion (1977,80,82), first woman to win title.

Dale Murphy (b.1956): Baseball OF, led NL in HRs and RBI twice each, 2-time MVP (1982-83) with Atlanta.

Stan Musial (b.1920): Baseball OF-1B, led NL in batting 7 times, 3-time MVP (1943,46,48) with St. Louis, played in 24 All-Star games, had 3,630 career hits and .331 average.

John Naber (b.1956): Swimmer, won 4 gold medals and a silver in 1976 Olympics.

Bronko Nagurski (b.1908): Football FB-T, All-America at Minnesota (1929), All-Pro with Chicago Bears (1932-34), charter member of both college and pro halls of fame.

James Naismith (1861-1939): Canadian physical education instructor who invented basketball in 1891 at the YMCA Training School (now Springfield College) in Springfield, Mass.

Joe Namath (b.1943): Football QB, signed for unheard of $400,000 as rookie with AFL's NY Jets in 1965, 2-time All-AFL (1968-69) and All-NFL (1972), led Jets to Super Bowl title as MVP in '69.

Ilie Nastase (b.1946): Rumanian tennis player, No.1 in the world twice (1972-73), won US (1972) and French (1973) Opens.

Martina Navratilova (b.1956): Tennis, all-time money winner, No.1 player in the world 7 times (1978-79,82-86), has won 8 Wimbledon singles titles, 4 US, 3 Australian and 2 French.

Byron Nelson (b.1912): Golfer, won Masters and PGA twice, US Open once; also won 11 consecutive tournaments (19 overall) in 1945.

Ernie Nevers (1903-76): Football FB, earned 11 letters in four sports at Stanford; played pro football, baseball and basketball, scored 40 points for Chicago Cardinals in one NFL game (1929).

John Newcombe (b.1943): Australian tennis player, No.1 player in world 3 times (1967,70-71), won Wimbledon 3 times, US twice.

Jack Nicklaus (b.1940): Golfer, winner of 20 major tournaments, including 6 Masters, 5 PGAs, 4 US Opens and 3 British Opens; PGA Player of the Year 5 times (1967,72-73,75-76).

Chuck Noll (b.1931): Football, coached Pittsburgh to 4 Super Bowl titles (1975-76,79-80), 183 career wins through 1988.

Leo Nomellini (b.1924): Football DT, played in 174 consecutive regular season games over 14 seasons with San Francisco.

Paavo Nurmi (1897-1973): Finnish runner, won 9 gold medals (6 individual) in 1920,'24 and'28 Olympics; from 1921-31 broke 23 world outdoor records in events ranging from 1,500 to 20,000 meters.

Parry O'Brien (b.1932): Track & field, in 4 consecutive Olympics, won two gold medals, a silver and placed 4th in the shot put (1952-64).

Walter O'Malley (1903-79): Baseball owner, moved Brooklyn Dodgers to Los Angeles after 1957 season.

Al Oerter (b.1936): Track & Field, won 4 consecutive Olympic gold medals in discus (1956-68).

Sadaharu Oh (b.1940): Baseball 1B, led Japan League in HRs 15 times, 9-time MVP for Tokyo Giants, hit 868 HRs in 22 years.

Barney Oldfield (1878-1946): Auto racing pioneer, drove cars built by Henry Ford, first man to drive car a mile per minute (1903).

Bobby Orr (b.1948): Hockey D, 8-time Norris Trophy winner as best defenseman, led NHL in scoring twice and assists 5 times, All-NHL 1st team 8 times, regular season MVP 3 times (1970-72), playoff MVP twice (1970,72) with Boston.

Mel Ott (1909-58): Baseball OF, joined NY Giants at age 16, led NL in HRs 6 times, had 511 HRs and 1,860 RBI in 22 years.

Kristin Otto (b.1966): East German swimmer, 1st woman to win 6 gold medals (4 individual) at one Olympics (1988).

Francis Ouimet (1893-1967): Golfer, won 1913 US Open as 20-year-old amateur playing on Brookline, Mass. course where he used to caddie; won US Amateur twice, 8-time Walker Cup player.

Jesse Owens (1913-80): Track & Field, won 4 gold medals (100m,200m,4x400 relay and long jump) at 1936 Olympics.

Satchel Paige (1906-82): Baseball RHP, pitched 55 career no-hitters in Negro Leagues, entered Major Leagues in 1948 at age 42.

Arnold Palmer (b.1929): Golfer, winner of 4 Masters, 2 British Opens and 1 US Open, PGA Player of the Year twice (1960,62), first player to earn over $1 million in career (1968).

Jim Palmer (b.1945): Baseball RHP, 3-time Cy Young Award winner (1973,75-76), won 20 or more games 8 times with Baltimore.

Bernie Parent (b.1945): Hockey G, led Philadelphia Flyers to 2 Stanley Cups as playoff MVP (1974,75), 2-time Vezina Trophy winner.

Joe Paterno (b.1926): Football, has coached Penn State to 2 national titles (1982,85) in 23 years, 212 career wins through 1988.

Lester Patrick (1883-1960): Pro hockey pioneer as player, coach and manager for 43 years, managed NY Rangers to their only Stanley Cups (1928,33,40).

Floyd Patterson (b.1935): Boxer, Olympic middleweight champ in 1952, world heavyweight champion (1956-59,60-62), 1st to regain heavyweight crown; pro record 55-8-1 with 40 KOs.

Walter Payton (b.1954): Football RB, NFL's all-time leading rusher with 16,726 yards, scored 109 TDs, All-Pro 7 times with Chicago, MVP in 1977.

Pele' (b.1940) Brazilian soccer F, given name—Edson Arantes do Nascimento; led Brazil to 3 World Cup titles (1958,62,70), came to US in 1975 to play for NY Cosmos in NASL, scored 1,281 goals in 22 years.

Willie Pep (b.1922): Boxer, 2-time world featherweight champion (1942-48,49-50); pro record 230-11-1 with 65 KOs.

Fred Perry (b.1909): British tennis player, 3-time Wimbledon champ (1934-36), last native to win All-England men's title.

Gaylord Perry (b.1938): Baseball RHP, won Cy Young Awards in each league, 314 wins and 3,534 strikeouts in 22 years.

Bob Pettit (b.1932): Basketball F, All-NBA 1st team 10 times (1955-64), 2-time MVP (1956,59) with St. Louis Hawks, first player to score 20,000 points.

Richard Petty (b.1937): Auto racer, 7-time winner of Daytona 500, 7-time NASCAR national champ (1964, 67,71-72,74-75,79), first stock car driver to win $1 million in career.

Laffit Pincay, Jr. (b.1946): Jockey, 5-time Eclipse award winner (1971,73-74,79,85), trails only Shoemaker in career wins, winner of 3 Belmonts and 1 Kentucky Derby (aboard Swale in 1984).

Nelson Piquet (b.1952): Brazilian auto racer, 3-time Formula 1 world champion (1981,83,87), 20 career wins thru 1988.

Jacques Plante (1929-86): Hockey G, led Montreal to 6 Stanley Cups (1953,56-60), won 7 Vezina Trophies, MVP in 1962, first goalie to regularly wear a mask.

Gary Player (b.1936): South African golfer, 3-time winner of Masters and British Open, also won 2 PGAs, a US Open and 2 US Senior Opens.

Jim Plunkett (b.1947): Football QB, Heisman Trophy winner in 1970, led Oakland-LA Raiders to Super Bowl wins in 1981 and '84, MVP in '81.

Sam Pollack (b.1925): Hockey GM, managed Montreal to 9 Stanley Cups in 14 years (1965-78).

Denis Potvin (b.1953): Hockey D, won Norris Trophy 3 times (1976,78-79), 5-time All-NHL 1st-team, led NY Islanders to 4 Stanley Cups.

Annemarie Moser Proell (b.1953): Austrian alpine skier, won World Cup overall title 6 times (1971-75,79), won Downhill in 1980 Olympics.

Alain Prost (b.1955): French auto racer, 2-time Formula 1 world champion (1985-86), 35 career wins thru 1988.

Willis Reed (b.1942): Basketball C, led NY Knicks to NBA titles in 1970 and '73, playoff MVP both years, regular season MVP 1970.

Mary Lou Retton (b.1968): Gymnast, won gold medal in women's All-Around at the 1984 Olympics, also won a silver and 2 bronzes.

Grantland Rice (1880-54): first celebrated American sportswriter, chronicled the Golden Age of Sport in 1920s, immortalized Notre Dame's "Four Horsemen."

Jerry Rice (b.1962): Football WR, 3-time ALL-Pro, regular season MVP in 1987 and Super Bowl MVP in 1989 with San Francisco.

Maurice Richard (b.1921): Hockey RW, 8-time NHL 1st team All-Star, MVP in 1947, 1st to score 50 goals in one season (1945), 544 career goals, played on 8 Stanley Cup winners in Montreal.

Bob Richards (b.1926): Track & Field, only 2-time Olympic gold medalist in pole vault (1952,56).

Tex Rickard (1870-1929): Promoter who handled boxing's first $1 million gate (Dempsey vs Carpentier in 1921), built Madison Square Garden in 1925.

Branch Rickey (1881-1965): In baseball 59 years as player, manager and GM, made Jackie Robinson 1st black player in Majors (1947).

Bobby Riggs (b.1918): Tennis, won Wimbledon once (1939) and US title twice (1939,41) before turning pro in 1941, beat Margaret Court Smith but lost to Billie Jean King in 1973 exhibition matches.

Pat Riley (b.1945): Basketball, coached LA Lakers to 4 of their 5 NBA titles in 1980s (1982,85,87-88).

Oscar Robertson (b.1938): Basketball G, 3-time college Player of Year (1958-60), 9-time All-NBA first team, MVP in 1964 with Cinn. Royals, record-holder for career assists (9,887).

Brooks Robinson (b.1937): Baseball 3B, led AL in fielding 12 times from 1960-72 with Baltimore, MVP in 1964, W.Series MVP in 1970.

Eddie Robinson (b.1919): Football, coaching at Grambling for over 45 years, winningest coach in college history, 349 wins thru 1988.

Frank Robinson (b.1935): Baseball OF, won MVP in both leagues (1961,66), Triple Crown and W.Series MVP in 1966 with Baltimore, 1st black manager in Major Leagues with Cleveland in 1975.

Jackie Robinson (1919-72): Baseball 2B, 4-sport athlete at UCLA; 1st black player in Majors with Brooklyn in 1947, Rookie of the Year in 1947, NL MVP in 1949.

Sugar Ray Robinson (1920-89): Boxer, world welterweight champion (1946-51), 5-time middleweight champ, retired at age 45 after 25 years in the ring; pro record 174-19-6 with 109 KOs.

Knute Rockne (1888-1931): Football, coached Notre Dame to 3 consensus national titles (1924,29,30), career record of 105-12-5 in 13 years.

Bill Rodgers (b.1947): Track & Field, won Boston and New York City marathons 4 times each from 1975-80.

Irina Rodnina (b.1953): Soviet figure skater, won 10 world championships and 3 Olympic gold medals in pairs competiton from 1971-80.

Art Rooney (1901-1988): Sportsman and pro football pioneer, owned Pittsburgh Steelers for 55 years.

Murray Rose (b.1939): Australian swimmer, won 3 gold medals at 1956 Olympics; added a gold, silver and bronze in 1960.

Mauri Rose (1906-81): Auto racer, 3-time winner of Indy 500 (1941,47-48).

Pete Rose (b.1941): Baseball OF-Inf., all-time hits leader with 4,256, led NL in batting 3 times, regular season MVP in 1973, W.Series MVP in 1975, had 44-game hitting streak in '78; managed Cincinnati (1984-89), banned for life in '89 for betting on baseball and associating with known gamblers and drug dealers.

Ken Rosewall (b.1934): Tennis, won French singles title at age 17 and Australian at 18, US champ twice, but never won Wimbledon.

Pete Rozelle (b.1926): Football, NFL Commissioner from 1960-89.

Wilma Rudolph (b.1940): Track & Field, won 3 gold medals (100m,200m and 4x400m relay) at 1960 Olympics.

Adolph Rupp (1901-77) Basketball, all-time college wins leader with 875, coached Kentucky to 4 NCAA titles (1948-49,51,58).

Bill Russell (b.1934): Basketball C, won titles in college, Olympics and pros, 5-time NBA MVP, led Boston to 11 titles, also became first big league black head coach in 1966.

Babe Ruth (1895-1948): Baseball LHP-OF, 2-time 20-game winner with Boston Red Sox, sold to NY Yankees in 1920, led AL in HRs 12 times and RBI 6 times, hit 60 HRs in 1927, ended career in 1935 with 714 HRs, 2,211 RBI and batting average of .342.

Johnny Rutherford (b.1938): Auto racer, 3-time winner of Indy 500 (1974,76,80), CART national champion in 1980.

Nolan Ryan (b.1947): Baseball RHP, all-time leader in strikeouts for a season and career, has also thrown a record 5 no-hitters through 1988 season.

Juan Antonio Samaranch (b.1920): President of International Olympic Committee since 1980.

Joan Benoit Samuelson (b.1957): Track & Field, has won Boston marathon twice (1979,83), winner of first women's Olympic marathon in 1984.

Earl Sande (1889-1968): Jockey, rode Gallant Fox to Triple Crown in 1930, won 5 Belmonts and 3 Kentucky Derbys.

Gene Sarazen (b.1901): Golfer, won Masters, British Open, 2 US Opens and 3 PGA titles between 1922-35; invented sand wedge in 1930.

Glen Sather (b.1943): Hockey, GM-coach of 4 Stanley Cup winners in Edmonton (1984-85,87-88).

Terry Sawchuk (1929-1970): Hockey G, recorded 103 shutouts in 21 NHL seasons, 4-time Vezina Trophy winner, played on 4 Stanley Cup winners at Detroit and Toronto.

Gale Sayers (b.1943): Football HB, 5-time All-Pro with Chicago, scored then-record 22 TDs in rookie year (1965).

Mike Schmidt (b.1949): Baseball 3B, led NL in HRs 8 times, 3-time MVP (1980,81,86) with Phila., 548 career HRs, 10 gold gloves.

Don Schollander (b.1946): Swimming, won 4 gold medals at 1964 Olympics, plus one gold and one silver in 1968.

Bob Seagren (b.1946): Track & Field, won gold medal in pole vault at 1968 Olympics, broke world outdoor record 5 times.

Tom Seaver (b.1944): Baseball RHP, won 3 Cy Young Awards (1969,73,75), had 311 wins and 3,640 strikeouts over 20 years.

Peter Seitz (b.1905): Baseball arbitrator, ruled in 1975 (Dec.23) that players who perform for one season without a signed contract can become free agents; decision ushered in big money era for players.

Frank Selke (1893-1985): Hockey, GM of 6 Stanley Cup champions in Montreal (1953,56-60).

Wilbur Shaw (1902-54): Auto racer, 3-time winner and 3-time runner-up of Indy 500 from 1933-1940.

Bill Shoemaker (b.1931): Jockey, all-time career wins leader, has won Belmont 5 times, Kentucky Derby 4 times and Preakness twice.

Eddie Shore (1902-85): Hockey D, only defenseman (including Orr) to win MVP trophy 4 times (1933,35-36,38), all with Boston.

Frank Shorter (b.1947): Track & Field, won gold medal in marathon at 1972 Olympics, 1st US marathoner to win in 64 years.

Jim Shoulders (b.1928): Rodeo, 5-time All-Around Cowboy (1949,56-59), won record 16 different rodeo titles.

Don Shula (b.1930): Football, coached 6 teams to Super Bowl, won twice with Miami (1973-74), 2nd to only George Halas in career wins.

Al Simmons (1902-56): Baseball OF, led AL in batting twice (1930-31) and knocked in 100 runs or more 11 straight years (1924-34).

O.J.Simpson (b.1947): Football RB, won Heisman Trophy in 1966 at Southern Cal; ran for 2,003 yards in NFL in 1973, All-Pro 5 times, MVP in 1973, rushed for 11,236 career yards.

George Sisler (1893-73): Baseball 1B, hit over .400 twice (1920,22), 257 hits in 1920 still a major league record.

Billy Smith (b.1950): Hockey G, led NY Islanders to 4 consecutive Stanley Cups (1979-83).

Ozzie Smith (b.1954): Baseball SS, entered 1989 with 9 straight gold gloves, 7-time starter for NL in All-Star Game.

Red Smith (1905-82): Sportswriter for newspapers in Philadelphia and New York from 1936-82, won Pulitzer Prize in 1976.

Conn Smythe (1895-80): Hockey pioneer, built Maple Leaf Gardens in 1931, managed Toronto to 7 Stanley Cups before retiring in 1961.

Sam Snead (b.1912): Golfer, won both Masters and PGA 3 times, British Open once, runner-up in US Open 4 times but never won, PGA Player of Year in 1949, PGA career victory leader with 84.

Peter Snell (b.1939): New Zealander who won gold medal in 800m at 1960 Olympics, then won both the 800m and 1,500m at 1964 Games.

Javier Sotomayor (b.1967): Cuban high jumper, first man to clear 8 feet (July 29,1989).

Warren Spahn (b.1921): Baseball LHP, led NL in wins 8 times, won 20 or more games 13 times, Cy Young winner in 1957, most career wins (363) by a left-hander.

Tris Speaker (1888-1958): Baseball OF, all-time leader in outfield assists (449) and doubles (793), had .344 career batting average and 3,515 hits.

Mark Spitz (b.1950): Swimmer, set 23 world and 35 US records, won record 7 gold medals (4 individual, 3 relay) at 1972 Olympics.

Amos Alonzo Stagg (1862-1965): Football innovator, coached at U.of Chicago for 41 seasons and College of the Pacific for 14 more, won 314 games, elected to both college football and basketball halls of fame.

Willie Stargell (b.1941): Baseball OF-1B, led NL in home runs twice (1971,73), 475 career HRs, regular season and W.Series MVP in 1979.

Bart Starr (b.1934): Football QB, led Green Bay to 5 NFL titles and 2 Super Bowl wins from 1961-67, reg.season MVP in 1966, 2-time Super Bowl MVP (1967,68).

Roger Staubach (b.1942): Football QB, Heisman Trophy winner as Navy junior in 1963; led NFL in passing 4 times, led Dallas to 2 Super Bowl titles (1972,78), Super Bowl MVP in 1972.

Casey Stengel (1890-1975): Baseball, player for 14 years and manager for 25, guided NY Yankees to 10 pennants and 7 W.Series titles from 1949-60.

Ingemar Stenmark (b.1956): Swedish alpine skier, 3-time World Cup overall champ (1976-78), 86 World Cup wins in 16 years, won 2 gold medals at 1980 Olympics.

Teofilo Stevenson (b.1951): Cuban boxer, won 3 consecutive gold medals as Olympic heavyweight (1972,76,80); did not turn pro.

Jackie Stewart (b.1939): Auto racer, won 27 Formula 1 races and 3 world driving titles from 1965-73.

Curtis Strange (b.1955): Golfer, won consecutive US Open titles (1988-89), first PGA player to win $1 million in one year (1988).

Louise Suggs (b.1923): Golfer, won 11 Majors and 50 LPGA events overall from 1949-62.

John L.Sullivan (1858-1918): Boxer, world heavyweight champion (1882-92), last of bare-knuckle champions.

Barry Switzer (b.1937): Football, coached Oklahoma to 3 national titles (1974-75,85), 157 career wins in 16 years.

Fran Tarkenton (b.1940): Football QB, 2-time All-Pro (1973,75), threw for 47,003 yards and 342 TDs (both NFL records) in 18 seasons.

Anatoli Tarasov (b.1918): Hockey, coached USSR to 9 straight world championships and 3 Olympic gold medals (1964,68,72).

Gustave Thoeni (b.1951): Italian alpine skier, 4-time World Cup overall champion (1971-73,75), won Giant Slalom at 1972 Olympics.

Daley Thompson (b.1958): British decathlete, won consecutive gold medals in decathlon at 1980 and '84 Olympics.

Jim Thorpe (1888-1953): 2-time All-America in football, won 2 gold medals at 1912 Olympics, played major league baseball (1913-19), and pro football (1920-26,28), chosen "Athlete of the Half Century" by AP in 1950.

Bill Tilden (1893-1953): Tennis, won 7 US and 3 Wimbledon titles in 1920s, led US to 7 straight Davis Cup victories (1920-26).

Tinker to Evers to Chance—Chicago Cubs double play combination from 1903-08; SS **Joe Tinker** (1880-1948), 2B **Johnny Evers** (1883-47) and 1B **Frank Chance**; all 3 managed the Cubs and made the Hall of Fame.

Y.A.Tittle (b.1926): Football QB, played 17 years in AFC and NFL, All-Pro 4 times, MVP with San Francisco (1957) and NY Giants (1962), passed for 28,339 career yards.

Bill Toomey (b.1939): Track & Field, won decathlon gold medal at 1968 Olympics.

Bill Torrey (b.1934): Hockey GM, managed NY Islanders to 4 Stanley Cups (1980-83).

Pie Traynor (1899-1972): Baseball 3B, hit .300 or better 10 times, led Pittsburgh to W.Series title in 1925.

Vladislav Tretiak (b.1952): Hockey G, led USSR to Olympic gold medals in 1972 and '76; starred for Soviets against Team Canada in 1972, and again in 2 Canada Cups (1976,81).

Lee Trevino (b.1939): Golfer, 2-time winner of 3 Majors—US Open (1968,71), British Open (1971-72) and PGA (1974,84).

Bryan Trottier (b.1956): Hockey C, led NY Islanders to 4 straight Stanley Cups (1980-83), reg.season MVP in 1979, playoff MVP in 1980.

Gene Tunney (b.1897-78): Boxer, world heavyweight champion (1926-28), defeated Jack Dempsey twice on points, pro record 65-2-1 with 43 KOs.

Ted Turner (b.1938): Sportsman, skippered *Courageous* to America's Cup win in 1977, owner of both Atlanta Braves and Hawks, cable TV pioneer, founder of Goodwill Games.

Mike Tyson (b.1965): Boxer, youngest (age 19) to win heavyweight title (WBC, 1986), undisputed champ since 1987; pro record (thru July,1989) 37-0 with 33 KOs.

Wyomia Tyus (b.1945): Track & Field, 1st woman or man to win consecutive Olympic gold medals in 100m (1964-68).

Peter Ueberroth (b.1937): Organizer of financially successful 1984 Summer Olympics in LA, 1984 Time Man of the Year, baseball commissioner from 1984-89.

Johnny Unitas (b.1933): Football QB, led Baltimore Colts to 2 NFL titles (1958-59) and a Super Bowl win (1971), All-Pro 5 times, 3-time MVP (1959,64,67), passed for 40,239 career yards and 290 TDs.

Al Unser, Sr. (b.1939): Auto racer, brother of Bobby, 4-time winner of Indy 500 (1970-71,78,87), 3-time USAC/CART national champ.

Bobby Unser (b.1934): Auto racer, brother of Al, 3-time winner of Indy 500 (1968,75,81), 2-time USAC-CART national champ.

Norm Van Brocklin (1926-83): Football QB, led NFL in passing 3 times and punting twice, led LA Rams (1951) and Philadelphia (1960) to NFL titles, MVP in 1960.

Steve Van Buren (b.1920): Football HB, led Philadelphia to 2 NFL titles (1948-49), league's top rusher 4 times.

Johnny Vander Meer (b.1914): Baseball LHP, only major leaguer to pitch consecutive no-hitters (June 11 & 15, 1938).

Harold S.Vanderbilt (1884-70): Sportsman, successfully defended America's Cup 3 times (1930,34,37), also invented contract bridge in 1926.

Glenna Collett Vare (1904-89): Golfer, won record 6 US Amateurs from (1922-35).

Andy Varipapa (1891-1984): Bowler, trick-shot artist, won consecutive All-Star match game titles (1947-48) at age 53.

Bill Veeck (1914-86): Maverick baseball executive, owned major league teams in Cleveland, St.Louis and Chicago from 1946-80, introduced ballpark giveaways, exploding scoreboards, and midget Eddie Gaedel.

Lasse Viren (b.1949): Finnish runner, won gold medals in 5,000m and 10,000m at both the 1972 and '76 Olympics.

Honus Wagner (1874-1955): Baseball SS, hit .300 for 17 consecutive seasons (1897-1913) with Pittsburgh, led NL in batting 8 times, had 3,430 career hits.

Grete Waitz (b.1953): Norwegian runner, 9-time winner of New York City Marathon from 1978-88.

Doak Walker (b.1927): Football HB, won Heisman Trophy as SMU junior in 1948; led Detroit to 2 NFL titles (1952-53), All-Pro 4 times in 6 years.

Bill Walsh (b.1931): Football, coached San Francisco to 3 Super Bowl titles (1982,85,89).

Bill Walton (b.1950): Basketball C, 3-time college Player of Year (1972-74), led UCLA to 2 national titles (1972-73); led Portland to NBA title as MVP in 1977, regular season MVP in 1978.

Darrell Waltrip (b.1947): Auto racer, 3-time NASCAR national champion (1981-82,85), won 1989 Daytona 500.

Arch Ward (1896-55): Promoter and sports editor of Chicago Tribune from 1930-55, founder of baseball All-Star Game (1933) and Chicago College All-Star Football Game (1934), also developed Golden Gloves boxing tournament.

Paul Waner (1903-65): Baseball OF, led NL in batting 3 times, MVP in 1927 with Pittsburgh, had 3,152 hits and .333 career average, brother of Lloyd.

Cornelius (Dutch) Warmerdam (b.1915): Track & Field, 1st pole vaulter to clear 15 feet (1940).

Glenn (Pop) Warner (1872-54): Football innovator, coached at 7 colleges over 49 years, 313 career wins; produced 47 All-Americas, including Thorpe and Nevers.

Tom Watson (b.1949): Golfer, 6-time PGA player of the Year (1977-80,82,84), has won 5 British Opens, 2 Masters and 1 US Open.

Dick Weber (b.1929): Bowler, 3-time PBA Bowler of the Year (1961,63,65), won 30 PBA titles in 4 decades.

Johnny Weismuller (1904-84): Swimmer, won 3 gold medals at 1924 Olympics and 2 more at 1928 Games, became Hollywood's most famous Tarzan.

Jerry West (b.1938): Basketball G, 2-time All-America at W.Va.; 10-time All-NBA first-team, led LA Lakers to NBA title once as player (1972) and 5 times as GM.

Kathy Whitworth (b.1939): Golf, 7-time LPGA Player of the Year (1966-69,71-73), won 6 Majors, 88 tour wins most on LPGA or PGA tour.

Bud Wilkinson (b.1916): Football, coached Oklahoma to 3 national titles (1950,55,56), 145 career wins in 17 years.

Ted Williams (b.1919): Baseball OF, led AL in batting 6 times, won Triple Crown twice (1942,47), MVP twice (1946,49), last player to hit .400 (1941), hit .344 with 521 HRs in 19 years.

Katarina Witt (b.1965): East German figure skater, 4-time world champion (1984-85,87-88), won consecutive Olympic gold medals (1984,88).

John Wooden (b.1910): Basketball, college Player of Year at Purdue in 1932, coached UCLA to 10 national titles (1964-65,67-73,75); only member of Basketball Hall of Fame inducted as player and coach.

Mickey Wright (b.1935): Golfer, won 3 of 4 Majors (LPGA, US Open, Titleholders) in 1961, 4-time winner of both US Open and LPGA titles, 82 career wins including 13 Majors.

Early Wynn (b.1920): Baseball RHP, won 20 games 5 times, Cy Young winner in 1959, 300 career wins in 23 years.

Cale Yarborough (b.1939): Auto racer, 4-time winner of Daytona 500 (1968,77,83-84), NASCAR national champ 3 times (1976-78).

Carl Yastrzemski (b.1939): Baseball OF, led AL in batting 3 times, won Triple Crown and MVP in 1967, had 3,419 hits and 452 HRs in 23 years with Boston.

Cy Young (1867-1955): Baseball RHP, won 20 games or more 16 times, holds record for career wins (511) and innings pitched (7,377).

Babe Didrikson Zaharias (1914-56): won 2 gold medals and a silver at 1932 Olympics; took up golf in 1935, won 55 pro & amateur events, helped found LPGA in 1949, won 10 Majors including 3 US Opens (1948,50,54) chosen female "Athlete of the Half Century" by AP in 1950.

Tony Zale (b.1913): Boxer, world middleweight champion (1941-47,48), pro record 67-18-2 with 44 KOs.

Emile Zatopek (b.1922): Czech runner, won total of 4 Olympic gold medals, including unprecedented triple (5,000m, 10,000m and marathon), in 1952.

Johnny Bench (left) and **Carl Yastrzemski**
at the 1983 All-Star Game in Chicago.
This year they entered Cooperstown together.

HALLS OF FAME & AWARDS

INSIDE

Indianapolis Motor Speedway Hall of Fame

Originally Auto Racing Hall of Fame. Founded by American Automobile Assn. in 1952, disbanded in 1955, revived by Indianapolis Speedway Foundation in 1962.

Members are listed with year of induction. Note that + indicates deceased members.

Drivers

+Aitken, Johnny	+Fengler, Harlan	+Moore, Lou
........1981	1983	1969
+Anderson, Gil	Foyt, A.J.	+Mulford, Ralph
.........1983	1978	...1953-54
Andretti, Mario	+Frame, Fred	+Murphy, Jimmy
......1986	1984	1964
+Baker, E.G.(Cannonball) .1981	+Goux, Jules 1989	Nalon, Dennis (Duke) ...1983
Banks, Henry 1985	+Grant, Harry 1982	
+Bergere, Cliff 1976	Gurney, Dan 1988	+Oldfield, Barney........1952
+Bettenhausen, Tony 1968	Hanks, Sam 1981	+Parsons, Johnnie 1986
+Boyer, Joe 1985	+Harroun, Ray 1952	+Resta, Dario 1953-54
+Bruce-Brown, David 1980	+Hartz, Harry 1963	+Rickenbacker, Eddie 1954
+Burman, Bob........1953-54	+Hearne, Eddie 1964	+Roberts, Floyd 1985
+Bryan, Jimmy 1973	+Hepburn, Ralph 1970	+Rose, Mauri 1967
+Chevrolet, Gaston 1964	+Horn, Ted...........1964	Rutherford, Johnny 1987
+Chevrolet, Louis 1952	Jones, Parnelli 1985	+Shaw, Wilbur 1963
+Clark, Jimmy 1988	+Keech, Ray 1984	+Snyder, Jimmy 1981
+Cooper, Earl 1953-54		+Stevens, Myron 1983
+Cummings, Bill 1970	+Lockhart, Frank 1965	+Strang, Lewis 1982
+Dawson, Joe 1976	+Mays, Rex 1963	Unser, Al 1986
+DePalma, Ralph 1953-54	+McGrath, Jack 1987	+Vukovich, Bill 1972
+DePaolo, Peter 1963	Meyer, Louis...........1963	Ward, Roger 1981
+Durant, Cliff 1983	+Milton, Tommy 1953-54	+Wilcox, Howard........1963

Contributors

+Allison, James A........1964	+Firestone, Harvey, Sr 1952	+Offenhauser, Fred 1982
Bignotti, George........1975	+Fisher, Carl...........1952	+Pillsbury, Art...........1981
+Brawner, Clint 1984	+Ford, Henry 1952	+Ricker, Chester 1989
+Christie, Walter 1980	+Gilmore, Earl 1987	+Robertson, George 1980
Cloutier, Joe...........1989	+Goossen, Leo 1978	+Sparks, Art 1987
+Dingley, Bert 1952	+Henning, Harry (Cotton) .1969	+Stutz, Henry 1963
+Duesenberg, Augie 1963	+Hulman, Tony.........1967	+Vanderbilt, William K....1952
+Duesenberg, Fred 1962	+Kurtis, Frank..........1983	+Wagner, Fred 1952
+Edenburn, Eddie 1986	+Marcenac, Jean 1968	Watson, A.J 1981
	+Miller, Harry 1963	+Welch, Lew 1986
	+Myers, T.E.(Pop) 1952	+Winfield, Ed 1983

Baseball Hall of Fame

Located in Cooperstown, N.Y. Founded by Major League Baseball to celebrate the sport's 100th anniversary in 1935.

Members are listed with year of induction. Note that + indicates deceased members.

1st Basemen

+Anson, Cap 1939	+Connor, Roger 1976	Killebrew, Harmon 1984
+Beckley, Jake 1971	+Foxx, Jimmie 1951	McCovey, Willie........1986
+Bottomley, Jim 1974	+Gehrig, Lou 1939	Mize, Johnny 1981
+Brouthers, Dan........1945	+Greenberg, Hank.......1956	+Sisler, George 1939
+Chance, Frank 1946	+Kelly, George 1973	Stargell, Willie 1988
		+Terry, Bill 1954

2nd Basemen

+Collins, Eddie 1939	+Frisch, Frankie 1947	+Hornsby, Rogers 1942
Doerr, Bobby 1986	Gehringer, Charlie 1949	+Lajoie, Nap 1937
+Evers, Johnny..........1946	Herman, Billy 1975	+Robinson, Jackie........1962
		Schoendienst, Red 1989

Shortstops

Aparicio, Luis 1984	+Cronin, Joe 1956	Sewell, Joe 1977
Appling, Luke 1964	+Jackson, Travis 1982	+Tinker, Joe 1946
+Bancroft, Dave 1971	+Jennings, Hugh 1945	+Vaughan, Arky 1985
Banks, Ernie 1977	+Maranville, Rabbit 1954	+Wagner, Honus 1936
Boudreau, Lou 1970	Reese, Pee Wee 1984	+Wallace, Bobby 1953
		+Ward, Monte 1964

3rd Basemen

+Baker, Frank...........1955	Kell, George...........1983	Mathews, Eddie........1978
+Collins, Jimmy.........1945	+Lindstrom, Fred.......1976	Robinson, Brooks.......1983
		+Traynor, Pie...........1948

Left Fielders

Brock, Lou.............1985	+Hafey, Chick..........1971	+O'Rourke, Jim.........1945
+Burkett, Jesse..........1946	+Kelley, Joe............1971	+Simmons, Al...........1953
+Clarke, Fred...........1945	Kiner, Ralph...........1975	+Wheat, Zack..........1959
+Delahanty, Ed.........1945	+Manush, Heinie........1964	Williams, Billy.........1987
+Goslin, Goose.........1968	+Medwick, Joe..........1968	Williams, Ted..........1966
	Musial, Stan..........1969	Yastrzemski, Carl.......1989

Center Fielders

+Averill, Earl..........1975	DiMaggio, Joe.........1955	+Roush, Edd...........1962
+Carey, Max...........1961	+Duffy, Hugh..........1945	Snider, Duke..........1980
+Cobb, Ty.............1936	+Hamilton, Billy........1961	+Speaker, Tris.........1937
+Combs, Earle.........1970	Mantle, Mickey.........1974	+Waner, Lloyd.........1967
	Mays, Willie..........1979	+Wilson, Hack.........1979

Right Fielders

Aaron, Hank..........1982	+Hooper, Harry........1971	+Rice, Sam...........1963
+Clemente, Roberto......1973	Kaline, Al.............1980	Robinson, Frank........1982
+Crawford, Sam........1957	+Keeler, Willie........1939	+Ruth, Babe..........1936
+Cuyler, Kiki..........1968	+Kelly, King...........1945	Slaughter, Enos.......1985
+Flick, Elmer..........1963	+Klein, Chuck.........1980	+Thompson, Sam........1974
+Heilmann, Harry.......1952	+McCarthy, Tommy......1946	+Waner, Paul..........1952
	+Ott, Mel............1951	+Youngs, Ross.........1972

Catchers

Bench, Johnny.........1989	Campanella, Roy.......1969	Ferrell, Rick..........1984
Berra, Yogi............1972	+Cochrane, Mickey......1947	+Hartnett, Gabby.......1955
+Bresnahan, Roger......1945	Dickey, Bill...........1954	+Lombardi, Ernie.......1986
	+Ewing, Buck..........1939	+Schalk, Ray..........1955

Pitchers

+Alexander, Grover......1938	+Grove, Lefty..........1947	+Nichols, Kid..........1949
+Bender, Chief.........1953	+Haines, Jess..........1970	+Pennock, Herb........1948
+Brown, Mordecai.......1949	+Hoyt, Waite..........1969	+Plank, Eddie.........1946
+Chesbro, Jack........1946	+Hubbell, Carl.........1947	+Radbourne, Old Hoss...1939
+Clarkson, John........1963	Hunter, Catfish........1987	+Rixey, Eppa..........1963
+Coveleski, Stan.......1969	+Johnson, Walter.......1936	Roberts, Robin........1976
+Dean, Dizzy..........1953	+Joss, Addie..........1978	+Ruffing, Red.........1967
Drysdale, Don.........1984	+Keefe, Tim...........1964	+Rusie, Amos.........1977
+Faber, Red...........1964	Koufax, Sandy.........1972	Spahn, Warren........1973
Feller, Bob...........1962	Lemon, Bob...........1976	+Vance, Dazzy.........1955
Ford, Whitey..........1974	+Lyons, Ted...........1955	+Waddell, Rube.........1946
+Galvin, Pud..........1965	Marichal, Juan........1983	+Walsh, Ed...........1946
Gibson, Bob..........1981	+Marquard, Rube.......1971	+Welch, Mickey.........1973
+Gomez, Lefty.........1972	+Mathewson, Christy.....1936	Wilhelm, Hoyt.........1985
+Grimes, Burleigh.......1964	+McGinnity, Joe........1946	Wynn, Early..........1972
		+Young, Cy............1937

From Negro Leagues

Bell, Cool Papa (OF)....1974	+Dihigo, Martin (P-OF)...1977	+Johnson, Judy (3B)......1975
+Charleston, Oscar (1B-OF)1976	+Foster, Rube (P-Mgr)....1981	Leonard, Buck (1B)......1972
Dandridge, Ray (3B)....1987	+Gibson, Josh (C).......1972	+Lloyd, Pop (SS)........1977
	Irvin, Monte (OF).......1973	+Paige, Satchel (P).......1971

Managers

+Alston, Walter.........1983	Lopez, Al.............1977	+McGraw, John.........1937
+Harris, Bucky.........1975	+Mack, Connie.........1937	+McKechnie, Bill.........1962
+Huggins, Miller........1964	+McCarthy, Joe.........1957	+Robinson, Wilbert.......1945
		+Stengel, Casey.........1966

Umpires

Barlick, Al............1989	+Connolly, Tom.........1953	+Hubbard, Cal.........1976
+Conlan, Jocko........1974	+Evans, Billy..........1973	+Klem, Bill............1953

Baseball Hall of Fame (Continued)

Pioneers and Executives

+ Barrow, Ed 1953
+ Bulkeley, Morgan 1937
+ Cartwright, Alexander . . . 1938
+ Chadwick, Henry 1938
  Chandler, Happy 1982
+ Comiskey, Charles 1939

+ Cummings, Candy 1939
+ Frick, Ford 1970
+ Giles, Warren 1979
+ Griffith, Clark 1946
+ Harridge, Will 1972
+ Johnson, Ban 1937
+ Landis, Kenesaw 1944

+ MacPhail, Larry 1978
+ Rickey, Branch 1967
+ Spalding, Al 1939
+ Weiss, George 1971
+ Wright, George 1937
+ Wright, Harry 1953
+ Yawkey, Tom 1980

Basketball Hall of Fame

Located in Springfield, Mass. Established by National Assn. of Basketball Coaches in memory of the sport's inventor, Dr. James Naismith. Opened in 1968.

Members are listed with year of induction. Note that + indicates deceased members.

Players

  Arizin, Paul 1977
+ Barlow, Thomas (Babe) . . 1980
  Barry, Rick 1987
  Baylor, Elgin 1976
+ Beckman, John 1972
+ Borgmann, Benny 1961
  Bradley, Bill 1982
+ Brennan, Joe 1974
  Cervi, Al 1984
  Chamberlain, Wilt 1978
+ Cooper, Charles (Tarzan) 1976
  Cousy, Bob 1970
  Cunningham, Billy 1986
  Davies, Bob 1969
+ DeBernardi, Forrest 1961
  DeBusschere, Dave 1982
+ Dehnert, Dutch 1968
  Endacott, Paul 1971
  Foster, Bud 1964
  Frazier, Walt 1987
+ Friedman, Marty 1971
+ Fulks, Joe 1977
  Gale, Laddie 1976
  Gates, William (Pop) 1989
  Gola, Tom 1975
  Greer, Hal 1981

+ Gruenig, Robert 1963
  Hagan, Cliff 1977
+ Hanson, Victor 1960
  Havlicek, John 1983
  Heinsohn, Tom 1986
  Holman, Nat 1964
  Houbregs, Bob 1987
+ Hyatt, Chuck 1959
+ Johnson, Bill (Skinny) 1976
  Jones, K. C. 1989
  Jones, Sam 1983
  Krause, Edward (Moose) . 1975
  Kurland, Bob 1961
+ Lapchick, Joe 1966
  Lovellette, Clyde 1988
  Lucas, Jerry 1979
  Luisetti, Hank 1959
  Macauley, Ed 1960
+ Maravich, Pete 1987
  Martin, Slater 1981
+ McCracken, Branch 1960
+ McCracken, Jack 1962
  McDermott, Bobby 1988
  Mikan, George 1959
  Murphy, Charles (Stretch) 1960

+ Page, Harlan (Pat) 1962
  Pettit, Bob 1970
  Phillip, Andy 1961
  Pollard, Jim 1977
  Ramsey, Frank 1981
  Reed, Willis 1981
  Robertson, Oscar 1979
+ Roosma, John 1961
+ Russell, John (Honey) 1964
  Russell, Bill 1974
  Schayes, Dolph 1972
+ Schmidt, Ernest J 1973
+ Schommer, John 1959
+ Sedran, Barney 1962
  Sharman, Bill 1975
+ Steinmetz, Christian 1961
  Thompson, John (Cat) . . . 1962
  Thurmond, Nate 1984
  Twyman, Jack 1982
  Unseld, Wes 1988
+ Vandivier, Robert (Fuzzy) 1974
+ Wachter, Ed 1961
  Wanzer, Bobby 1987
  West, Jerry 1979
  Wilkens, Lenny 1989
  Wooden, John 1960

Teams

Buffalo Germans 1961

First Team 1959

New York Renaissance 1963
Original Celtics 1959

Coaches

+ Anderson, Harold (Andy) 1984
  Auerbach, Red 1968
+ Barry, Sam 1978
+ Blood, Ernest (Prof) 1960
  Cann, Howard 1967
+ Carlson, Henry (Doc) 1959
  Carnevale, Ben 1969
+ Case, Everett 1981
  Dean, Everett 1966
+ Diddle, Ed 1971
+ Drake, Bruce 1972
  Gaines, Clarence 1981
  Gardner, Jack 1983

+ Gill, Amory (Slats) 1967
  Harshman, Marv 1984
+ Hickey, Eddie 1978
  Hobson, Howard (Hobby) 1965
  Holzman, Red 1986
  Iba, Henry 1968
+ Julian, Alvin (Doggie) . . . 1967
+ Keaney, Frank 1960
+ Keogan, George 1961
+ Lambert, Ward (Piggy) . . 1960
  Litwack, Harry 1975
+ Leoffler, Ken 1964
+ Lonborg, Dutch 1972

  McCutchan, Arad 1980
  McGuire, Frank 1976
+ Meanwell, Walter (Doc) . 1959
  Meyer, Ray 1978
  Miller, Ralph 1988
+ Rupp, Adolph 1968
+ Sachs, Leonard 1961
+ Shelton, Everett 1979
  Smith, Dean 1982
  Taylor, Fred 1985
  Wade, Margaret 1984
  Watts, Stan 1985
  Wooden, John 1972

Referees

+ Enright, Jim 1978
+ Hepbron, George 1960
+ Hoyt, George 1961

+ Kennedy, Pat 1959
+ Leith, Lloyd 1982
  Mihalik, Red 1986
  Nucatola, John 1977

+ Quigley, Ernest (Quig) . . . 1961
  Shirley, J. Dallas 1979
  Tobey, Dave 1961
+ Walsh, David 1961

Contributors

+Abbott, Senda Berenson . . 1984
+Allen, Forrest (Phog) 1959
+Bee, Clair 1967
+Brown, Walter A 1965
+Bunn, John 1964
+Douglas, Bob 1971
+Duer, Al 1981
  Fagen, Clifford B 1983
+Fisher, Harry 1973
+Gottlieb, Eddie 1971
+Gulick, Luther 1959
  Harrison, Les 1979
+Hepp, Ferenc 1980
+Hickcox, Ed 1959

  Hinkle, Tony 1965
+Irish, Ned 1964
+Jones, R. William 1964
+Kennedy, Walter 1980
+Liston, Emil (Liz) 1974
  McLendon, John 1978
+Mokray, Bill 1965
+Morgan, Ralph 1959
+Morgenweck, Frank (Pop) . 1962
+Naismith, James 1959
  Newell, Pete 1978
+O'Brien, John J. (Jack) . . . 1961
+Olsen, Harold G 1959
+Podoloff, Maurice 1973

+Porter, Henry (H.V.) 1960
+Reid, William A 1963
+Ripley, Elmer 1972
+St. John, Lynn W 1962
+Saperstein, Abe 1970
+Schabinger, Arthur 1961
+Stagg, Amos Alonzo 1959
  Steitz, Ed 1983
+Taylor, Chuck 1968
  Teague, Bertha 1984
+Tower, Oswald 1959
+Trester, Ather (A.L.) 1961
+Wells, Cliff 1971
+Wilke, Lou 1982

National Bowling Halls of Fame

Located in St. Louis, Mo. Divided into three principal wings: the American Bowling Congress, the Professional Bowlers Assn., and the Women's International Bowling Congress.
  Members are listed with year inducted. Note that + indicates deceased members.

American Bowling Congress

Performance

  Allison, Glenn 1979
  Anthony, Earl 1986
+Asplund, Harold 1978
  Baer, Gordy 1987
  Benkovic, Frank 1958
  Billick, George 1982
+Blouin, Jimmy 1953
  Bluth, Ray 1973
+Bodis, Joe 1941
  Bomar, Buddy 1966
+Brandt, Allie 1960
+Brosius, Eddie 1976
+Bujack, Fred 1967
  Bunetta, Bill 1968
  Burton, Nelson, Sr 1964
  Burton, Nelson, Jr 1981
  Campi, Lou 1968
+Carlson, Adolph 1941
  Carter, Don 1970
+Caruana, Frank 1977
  Cassio, Marty 1972
+Castellano, Graz 1976
+Clause, Frank 1980
  Cohn, Alfred 1985
  Crimmins, John 1962
+Daw, Charlie 1941
+Day, Ned 1952
+Easter, Sarge 1963
  Ellis, Don 1981
+Falcaro, Joe 1968
  Faragalli, Lindy 1968
  Fazio, Buzz 1963

  Gersonde, Russ 1968
+Gibson, Therm 1965
  Godman, Jim 1987
  Golembiewski, Billy 1979
  Hardwick, Billy 1985
  Hennessey, Tom 1976
  Hoover, Dick 1974
  Howard, George 1986
  Johnson, Don 1982
  Johnson, Earl 1987
  Joseph, Joe 1969
+Jouglard, Lee 1979
+Kartheiser, Frank 1967
+Kawolics, Ed 1968
+Kissoff, Joe 1976
  Klares, John 1982
+Knox, Billy 1954
+Koster, John 1941
+Krems, Eddie 1973
  Kristof, Joe 1968
+Krumske, Paul 1968
+Lange, Herb 1941
  Lauman, Hank 1976
  Lillard, Bill 1972
  Lindenmann, Tony 1979
+Lindsey, Mort 1941
  Lubanski, Ed 1971
  Lucci, Vince, Sr 1978
+Marino, Hank 1941
  Martino, John 1969
+McMahon, Junie 1967
+Mercurio, Skang 1967

+Meyers, Norm 1984
+Nagy, Steve 1963
  Norris, Joe 1954
  O'Donnell, Chuck 1968
+Patterson, Pat 1974
  Ritger, Dick 1984
  Salvino, Carmen 1979
+Schwoegler, Connie 1968
+Sielaff, Lou 1968
+Sinke, Joe 1977
+Sixty, Billy 1961
  Smith, Harry 1978
+Smith, Jimmy 1941
  Soutar, Dave 1985
  Sparando, Tony 1968
  Spinella, Barney 1968
+Steers, Harry 1941
  Stefanich, Jim 1983
+Stein, Otto, Jr 1971
  Strampe, Bob 1977
+Thoma, Sykes 1971
+Varipapa, Andy 1957
+Ward, Walter 1959
  Weber, Dick 1970
+Welu, Billy 1975
+Wilman, Joe 1951
+Wolf, Phil 1961
+Young, George 1959
  Zahn, Wayne 1980
  Zikes, Les 1983
+Zunker, Gil 1941

Meritorious Service

+Allen, Harold 1966
  Baker, Frank 1975
+Baumgarten, Elmer 1963
+Bellisimo, Lou 1986
  Bensinger, Bob 1969
+Chase, LeRoy 1972
+Coker, John 1980
+Collier, Chuck 1963
+Cruchon, Steve 1983
+Ditzen, Walt 1973
+Doehrman, Bill 1968

  Elias, Eddie 1985
+Hagerty, Jack 1963
+Hattstrom, H.A.(Doc) 1980
+Hermann, Cone 1968
+Howley, Pete 1941
+Kennedy, Bob 1981
+Langtry, Abe 1963
+Levine, Sam 1971
+Luby, David 1969
+Luby, Mort, Sr 1974
+McCullough, Howard 1971

+Patterson, Morehead 1985
+Petersen, Louie 1963
  Pezzano, Chuck 1982
  Raymer, Milt 1972
+Reed, Elmer 1978
  Rudo, Milt 1984
+Sweeney, Dennis 1974
+Thum, Joe 1980
  Weinstein, Sam 1970
+Whitney, Eli 1975
  Wolf, Fred 1976

Bowling Halls of Fame (Continued)

Professional Bowlers Assn.

Performance

Allen, Bill 1983	Godman, Jim 1987	Roth, Mark 1987
Allison, Glenn 1979	Guenther, John 1986	Salvino, Carmen 1975
Anthony, Earl 1986	Hardwick, Billy 1977	Smith, Harry 1975
Bluth, Ray 1975	Johnson, Don 1977	Soutar, Dave 1979
Burton, Nelson, Jr 1979	Joseph, Joe 1985	Stefanich, Jim 1980
Carter, Don 1975	Laub, Larry 1985	Strampe, Bob 1987
Davis, Dave 1978	Pappas, George 1986	Weber, Dick 1975
Fazio, Buzz 1976	Petraglia, John 1982	+Welu, Billy 1975
	Ritger, Dick 1978	Zahn, Wayne 1981

Meritorious Service

Elias, Eddie 1976	Fisher, E.A.(Bud) 1984	+Nagy, Steve 1977
Esposito, Frank 1975	Frantz, Lou 1978	Pezzano, Chuck 1975
Evans, Dick 1986	Golden, Harry 1983	+Richards, Joe 1976
Firestone, Raymond 1987	Hoffman, Ted, Jr 1985	Schenkel, Chris 1976
		Stitzlein, Lorraine 1980

Women's International Bowling

Performance

Abel, Joy 1984	Fothergill, Dotty 1980	Ladewig, Marion 1964
Bolt, Mae 1978	Garms, Shirley 1971	Martin, Sylvia Wene 1966
Bouvia, Gloria 1987	Harman, Janet 1985	Martorella, Millie 1975
Boxberger, Loa 1984	Havlish, Jean 1987	Merrick, Marge 1980
Cantaline, Anita 1979	Hoffman, Martha 1979	+Mikiel, Val 1979
Carter, LaVerne 1977	Holm, Joan 1974	Morris, Betty 1983
Coburn, Doris 1976	+Humphreys, Birdie 1979	Notaro, Phyllis 1979
Costello, Pat 1986	Jacobson, D.D 1981	Ortner, Bev 1972
Dryer, Pat 1978	Kelly, Annesse 1985	+Sablatnik, Ethel 1979
Duval, Helen 1970	Knechtges, Doris 1983	Soutar, Judy 1976
	Kuczynski, Betty 1981	Zimmerman, Donna 1982

Meritorious Service

Baetz, Helen 1977	+Kay, Nora 1964	Porter, Cora 1986
Berger, Winifred 1976	+Kelly, Ellen 1979	+Quinn, Zoe 1979
Botkin, Freda 1986	Kelone, Theresa 1978	+Rishling, Gertrude 1972
+Crowe, Alberta 1982	+Knepprath, Jeannette 1963	Sloan, Catherine 1985
+Dornblaser, Gertrude.... 1979	+Lasher, Iolia 1967	+Speck, Birdie 1966
Duffy, Agnes 1987	Marrs, Mabel 1979	+Spring, Alma 1979
+Fisk, Rae 1983	+McBride, Bertha 1968	+Switzer, Pearl 1973
+Haas, Dorothy 1977	+Menne, Catherine 1979	+Veatch, Georgia 1974
Higley, Margaret 1969	+Phaler, Emma 1965	White, Mildred 1975
		+Wood, Ann 1970

Stars of Yesteryear

Bohlen, Philena 1955	+Hatch, Grayce 1953	Ryan, Esther 1963
Burling, Catherine 1958	+Hochstadter, Bee 1967	+Schulte, Myrtle 1965
Burns, Nina Van Camp .. 1977	+Jaeger, Emma 1953	Shablis, Helen 1977
+Chapman, Emily 1957	Matthews, Merle 1974	Simon, Violet (Billy) 1960
Duffy, Agnes 1987	+McCutcheon, Floretta.... 1956	Small, Tess 1971
Fellmeth, Catherine 1970	+Miller, Dorothy 1954	+Smith, Grace 1968
+Fritz, Deane 1966	+Mraz, Jo 1959	+Stockdale, Louise 1953
Gloor, Olga 1976	Powers, Connie 1973	Toepfer, Elvira 1976
+Greenwald, Goldie 1953	+Robinson, Leona 1969	+Twyford, Sally 1964
Hartrick, Stella 1972	+Rump, Anita 1962	+Warmbier, Marie 1953
	+Ruschmeyer, Addie 1961	+Winandy, Cecelia 1975

Boxing Hall of Fame

According to **The Ring** Record Book & Encyclopedia. Members are divided into four groups: Modern fighters, Old-Timers, Pioneers and Meritorious Service. There is no actual Hall of Fame site.

Modern Group

Ali, Muhammad 1987	Foster, Bob 1983	Patterson, Floyd 1976
Ambers, Lou 1964	Frazier, Joe 1980	Pep, Willie 1963
Angott, Sammy........1973	Fullmer, Gene 1974	Perez, Pascual 1977
Apostoli, Fred........1978	Garcia, Ceferino 1977	Petrolle, Billy 1962
Armstrong, Fred.......1954	Gavilan, Kid 1966	Ortiz, Carlos 1988
Baer, Max 1968	Graziano, Rocky 1971	Robinson, Sugar Ray 1967
Basilio, Carmen 1969	Greb, Harry 1955	Rosenbloom, Maxie 1972
Berg, Jackie Kid 1975	Griffith, Emile 1981	Ross, Barney..........1956
Braddock, James J 1964	Jack, Beau 1972	Saddler, Sandy 1971
Britton, Jack 1960	Jenkins, Lew 1976	Schmeling, Max 1970
Brown, Joe 1988	Jofre, Eder 1986	Shirai, Yoshio 1977
Canzoneri, Tony 1956	Leonard, Benny 1955	Tendlaer, Lew..........1961
Cerdan, Marcel 1962	Lesnevich, Gus 1973	Tiger, Dick 1974
Charles, Ezzard 1970	Louis, Joe 1954	Tunney, Gene..........1955
Chocolate, Kid 1959	McLarnin, Jimmy 1956	Walcott, Jersey Joe 1955
Conn, Billy 1965	Marciano, Rocky 1959	Walker, Mickey 1955
Dempsey, Jack 1954	Maxim, Joey...........1975	Williams, Ike 1978
Dundee, Johny 1957	Monzon, Carlos 1983	Wright, Chalky 1976
Escobar, Sixto.........1975	Moore, Archie 1966	Zale, Tony 1958
	Napoles, Jose 1985	Zivic, Fritzie 1972

Old-Timers Group

Attell, Abe 1955	Gibbons, Tom..........1963	McVey, Sam 1986
Berlenbach, Paul 1971	Graham, Billy 1988	Maher, Peter 1978
Britt, Jimmy 1976	Griffo, Young 1981	Mitchell, Charley 1957
Brown, Panama Al 1985	Herman, Pete 1959	Moran, Owen 1965
Burley, Charley 1983	Houck, Leo 1969	Nelson, Battling 1957
Burns, Tommy.........1960	Jeanette, Joe 1967	O'Brien, Phila. Jack 1968
Carpentier, Georges ...1964	Jeffra, Harry 1982	Ortiz, Manuel 1985
Chaney, George K.D 1974	Jeffries, James J 1954	Papke, Billy...........1972
Choynski, Joe 1959	Johnson, Jack 1954	Ritchie, Willie 1962
Corbett, James J 1954	Ketchel, Stanley 1954	Root, Jack 1961
Corbett, Young II 1965	Kid, The Dixie.........1975	Ryan, Tommy 1958
Coulon, Johnny 1965	Kilbane, Johnny 1960	Sharkey, Jack 1980
Darcy, Les 1957	Klaus, Frank 1976	Sharkey, Tom 1959
Delaney, Jack.........1973	Labarba, Fidel 1972	Smith, Jeff............1969
Dempley, Jack (Non-Pareil)1954	Lamotta, Jake..........1985	Stribling, Young 1985
Dillon, Jack...........1959	Langford, Sam 1955	Sullivan, John L 1954
Dixon, George 1956	Lavigne, George (Kid) ...1959	Taylor, Charles (Bud) 1986
Driscoll, Jem..........1956	Levinsky, Battling 1966	Villa, Pancho 1961
Fields, Jackie 1977	Lewis, Ted (Kid) 1964	Walcott, Joe...........1955
Fitzsimmons, Bob 1954	Lynch, Benny 1986	Welsh, Freddie 1960
Flowers, Tiger.........1971	McAuliffe, Jack........1954	Wilde, Jimmy 1959
Gans, Joe............1954	McCoy, Charles (Kid) 1957	Willard, Jess...........1977
Genaro, Frankie........1973	McFarland, Packey......1957	Williams, Kid 1970
Gibbons, Mike 1958	McGovern, Terry 1955	Wills, Harry 1970
		Wolgast, Ad...........1958

Pioneer Group

Aaron, Barney (Young) ..1967	Goss, Joe 1969	Mendoza, Daniel 1954
Broughton, Jack 1954	Gully, John...........1959	Molineaux, Tom 1958
Burke, James (Deaf).....1966	Heenan, John C 1954	Morrissey, John 1954
Chambers, Arthur 1954	Hyer, Jacob 1968	Pearce, Henry 1987
Chandler, Tom 1972	Hyer, Tom 1954	Price, Ned 1962
Clark, Nobby 1971	Jackling,Thomas 1985	Richmond, Bill..........1956
Collyer, Sam...........1964	Jackson, Gentleman John 1954	Ryan, Paddy 1973
Cribb, Tom 1954	Jackson, Peter 1957	Sam, Young Dutch 1975
Curtis, Dick 1974	Kilrain, Jake 1965	Sayers, Tom 1954
Donnelly, Dan 1960	King, Tom 1976	Spring, Tom 1961
Donovan, Prof. Mike 1970	Langham, Nat 1986	Thompson, William 1955
Figg, James 1954	Mace, Jem 1954	Ward, Jem 1963

Meritorious Service

Arcel, Ray 1982	Daniel, Dan 1977	Kearns, Jack 1981
Chambers, John 1986	Donovan, Arthur 1981	Lonsdale, Lord 1985
D'Amato, Cus.........1988	Fleisher, Nat 1975	Rickard, Tex 1980
	Jacobs, Jimmy 1988	Taub, Sam 1978

College Football Hall of Fame

Located in King's Island, Ohio. Established by the National Football Foundation. Founded in 1955 but not opened until 1978.

Members are listed with final year they played in college. Note that + indicates deceased members.

Players

+ Abell, Earl–Colgate 1915
Agase, Alex–Purdue/Ill. . . . 1946
+ Agganis, Harry–Boston U . 1952
Albert, Frank–Stanford 1941
+ Aldrich, Ki–TCU 1938
+ Aldrich, Malcolm–Yale 1921
+ Alexander, John–Syracuse . 1920
Alworth, Lance–Arkansas . . 1961
+ Ames, Knowlton–Princeton . 1889
+ Ameche, Alan– Wisconsin . 1954
Amling, Warren–Ohio St . . 1946
Anderson, Donny–Tex.Tech 1966
+ Anderson, Hunk–N.Dame . 1921
Atkins, Doug–Tennessee . . 1952

Bacon, Everett–Wesleyan . 1912
Bagnell, Reds–Penn 1950
+ Baker, Hobey–Princeton . 1913
+ Baker, John–USC 1931
+ Baker, Moon–N'western . . 1926
Baker, Terry–Oregon St . . 1962
+ Ballin, Harold–Princeton . 1914
+ Banker, Bill–Tulane 1929
Banonis, Vince–Detroit . . . 1941
Barnes, Stanley–So. Calif . 1921
+ Barrett, Charles–Cornell . . . 1915
+ Baston, Bert–Minnesota . . . 1916
+ Battles, Cliff–WV Wesleyan 1931
Baugh, Sammy–TCU 1936
Baughan, Maxie–Ga.Tech . 1959
+ Bausch, James–Kansas . . . 1930
Beagle, Ron–Navy 1955
Beban, Gary–UCLA 1967
+ Bechett, John–Oregon . . . 1913
Bednarik, Chuck–Penn . . . 1948
Behm, Forrest–Nebraska . . 1940
Bellino, Joe–Navy 1960
Below, Marty–Wisconsin . . 1923
+ Benbrook, Al–Michigan . . . 1911
Bertelli, Angelo–N.Dame . 1943
+ Berry, Charlie–Lafayette . . 1924
Berwanger, Jay–Chicago . 1935
+ Bettencourt, L.–St.Mary's . 1927
Blanchard, Doc–Army . . . 1946
+ Blozis, Al–Georgetown . . . 1941
Bock, Ed–Iowa St 1938
Bomar, Lynn–Vanderbilt . . 1924
+ Bomeisler, Bo–Yale 1913
+ Booth, Albie–Yale 1931
+ Borries, Fred–Navy 1934
Bosely, Bruce–West Va . . . 1955
Bottari, Vic–California . . . 1939
+ Boynton, Ben–Williams . . 1920
+ Brewer, Charles–Harvard . 1895
+ Bright, Johnny–Drake . . . 1951
Brodie, John–Stanford . . . 1956
+ Brooke, George–Penn . . . 1895
Brown, Geo–Navy/S.Diego St1947
+ Brown, Gordon–Yale 1900
+ Brown, John, Jr.–Navy . . . 1913
+ Brown, Johnny Mack–Ala . 1925
Brown, Raymond–USC 1932
+ Bunker, Paul–Army 1902
Butkus, Dick–Illinois 1964
+ Butler, Robert–Wisconsin . 1912

Cafego, George–Tenn 1939
+ Cagle, Chris–SW La./Army 1929
+ Cain, John–Alabama 1932
Cameron, Ed–Wash.& Lee . 1924
+ Campbell, David–Harvard . 1901
+ Cannon, Jack–N.Dame . . . 1929
Carideo, Frank–N.Dame . . 1929
Caroline, J.C.–Illinois 1954
+ Carney, Charles–Illinois . . . 1921
Carpenter, Bill–Army 1959
+ Carpenter, Hunter–VPI . . . 1905
Carroll, Chas.–Washington 1928
+ Casey, Edward–Harvard . . 1919
Cassady, Howard–Ohio St. 1955
+ Chamberlain, Guy–Neb. . . 1915
Chapman, Sam–California . 1938
Chappuis, Bob–Michigan . 1947
+ Christman, Paul–Missouri . 1940
Cleary, Paul–USC 1947
+ Clevenger, Zora–Indiana . . 1903
+ Cochran, Gary–Princeton . 1895
+ Cody, Josh–Vanderbilt . . . 1920
Coleman, Don–Mich.St . . . 1951
Conerly, Charlie, Miss 1947
Connor, George–N.Dame . 1947
+ Corbin, William–Yale 1888
Corbus, William–Stanford . 1933
+ Cowan, Hector–Princeton . 1889
+ Coy, Edward (Tad)–Yale . 1909
+ Crawford, Fred–Duke 1933
Crow, John David–Tex.A&M1957
+ Crowley, Jim–Notre Dame 1924
Csonka, Larry–Syracuse . . 1967
Cutter, Slade–Navy 1934
+ Czarobski, Ziggie–N.Dame 1947

Dale, Carroll–Va.Tech 1959
+ Dalrymple, Gerald–Tulane . 1931
Daniell, Averell–Pitt 1936
+ Daniell, James–Ohio St . . . 1941
Dalton, John–Navy 1912
Daly, Chas.–Harvard/Army 1902
+ Davies, Tom–Pittsburgh . . . 1921
+ Davis, Ernie–Syracuse . . . 1961
Davis, Glenn–Army 1946
Davis, Robert–Ga.Tech . . . 1947
Dawkins, Pete–Army 1958
DeRogatis, Al–Duke 1940
+ DesJardien, Paul–Chicago . 1914
+ Devine, Aubrey–Iowa 1921
+ DeWitt, John–Princeton . . . 1903
Ditka, Mike–Pittsburgh 1960
Dobbs, Glenn–Tulsa 1942
+ Dodd, Bobby–Tennessee . . 1930
Donan, Holland–Princeton . 1950
+ Donchess, Joseph–Pitt 1929
+ Dougherty, Nathan–Tenn . 1909
Drahos, Nick–Cornell 1940
+ Driscoll, Paddy–N'western . 1917
+ Drury, Morley–USC 1927
Dudley, William–Virginia . . 1941

+ Eckersall, Walter–Chicago . 1906
+ Edwards, Turk–Wash.St . . . 1931
Edwards, Wm.–Princeton . . 1900

+ Eichenlaub, Ray–N.Dame . 1913
Elliott, Bump–Mich/Purdue . 1947
Evans, Ray–Kansas 1947
+ Exendine, Albert–Carlisle . . 1908

Falaschi, Nello–S.Clara . . . 1937
Fears, Tom–S.Clara/UCLA . 1947
+ Feathers, Beattie–Tenn 1933
Fenimore, Bob–Okla.St . . . 1947
+ Fenton, Doc–LSU 1909
Ferraro, John–USC 1944
Fesler, Wesley–Ohio St . . . 1930
+ Fincher, Bill–Ga.Tech 1920
Fischer, Bill–Notre Dame . . 1948
Fish, Hamilton–Harvard . . . 1909
+ Fisher, Robert–Harvard . . . 1911
+ Flowers, Allen–Ga.Tech . . . 1920
Fortmann Daniel–Colgate . 1935
Francis, Sam–Nebraska . . . 1936
Franco, Ed–Fordham 1937
Frank, Clint–Yale 1937
Franz, Rodney–California . . 1949
+ Friedman, Benny–Michigan 1926

Gabriel, Roman–N.C.State 1961
Gain, Bob–Kentucky 1950
+ Galiffa, Arnold–Army 1949
Gallarneau, Hugh–Stanford 1941
+ Garbisch, Edgar–Army . . . 1924
Garrett, Mike–USC 1965
+ Gelbert, Charles–Penn 1896
+ Geyer, Forest–Oklahoma . . 1915
Giel, Paul–Minnesota 1953
Gifford, Frank–USC 1951
+ Gilbert, Walter–Auburn . . . 1936
+ Gipp, George–N.Dame . . . 1920
+ Gladchuk, Chet–Boston Col 1940
Glass, Bill–Baylor 1956
Goldberg, Marshall–Pitt . . . 1938
Goodreault, Gene–BC 1940
+ Gordon, Walter–Calif 1918
+ Governale, Paul–Columbia 1942
Graham, Otto–N'western . 1943
Grange, Red–Illinois 1925
+ Grayson, Robert–Stanford . 1935
+ Green, Jack–Army 1945
Green, Joe–N.Texas St 1968
Griese, Bob–Purdue 1965
Griffin, Archie–Ohio St . . . 1975
+ Gulick, Merel–Hobart 1929
+ Guyon, Joe–Ga.Tech 1919

Hale, Edwin–Miss.College . 1921
Hamilton, Bob–Stanford . . . 1935
Hamilton, Tom–Navy 1925
+ Hanson, Vic–Syracuse 1926
+ Hardwick, Tack–Harvard . . 1914
+ Hare, T.Truxton–Penn 1900
+ Harley, Chick–Ohio St . . . 1919
Harmon, Tom–Michigan . . . 1940
+ Harpster, Howard–Carnegie 1928
Hart, Edward–Princeton . . . 1911
Hart, Leon–Notre Dame . . 1949
Hartman, Bill–Georgia 1937
+ Hazel, Homer–Rutgers 1924
+ Hazeltine, Matt–Calif 1954
+ Healey, Ed.–Dartmouth . . . 1916

+ Heffelfinger, Pudge–Yale . . 1891
Hein, Mel–Washington St . 1930
Heinrich, Don–Washington 1952
Hendricks, Ted–Miami 1968
+ Henry, Wilber–Wash&Jeff . 1919
+ Herschberger, C.–Chicago . 1899
+ Herwig, Robert–Calif 1937
+ Heston, Willie–Michigan . . 1904
+ Hickman, Herman–Tenn . . 1931
+ Hickey, Frank–Yale 1894
+ Hickok, William–Yale 1895
Hill, Dan–Duke 1938
+ Hillebrand, Art–Princeton . 1899
Hinkle, Carl–Vanderbilt . . 1937
Hinkle, Clark–Bucknell 1932
Hirsch, Elroy–Wisc./Mich . . 1943
+ Hitchcock, James–Auburn . 1932
Hoffman, Frank–N.Dame . . 1931
+ Hogan, James J.–Yale 1904
+ Holland, Brud–Cornell 1938
+ Holleder, Don–Army 1955
+ Hollenbeck, Bill–Penn 1908
Holovak, Mike–Boston Col . 1942
Holub, E.J.–Texas Tech . . . 1960
Hornung, Paul–N.Dame . . 1956
Horrell, Edwin–Calif 1924
Horvath, Les–Ohio St 1944
+ Howe, Arthur–Yale 1911
+ Howell, Millard–Alabama . 1934
+ Hubbard, Cal–Centenary . . 1926
+ Hubbard, John–Amherst . . 1906
+ Hubert, Allison–Alabama . . 1925
Huff, Sam–West Virginia . . 1955
Humble, Weldon–Rice 1946
+ Hunt, Joe–Texas A&M 1927
Huntington, Ellery–Colgate 1914
Hutson, Don–Alabama 1934

+ Ingram, James–Navy 1906
+ Isbell, Cecil–Purdue 1937

+ Jablonsky, J.–Army/Wash . 1933
Janowicz, Vic–Ohio St 1951
+ Jenkins, Darold–Missouri . . 1941
+ Jensen, Jackie–Calif 1948
+ Joesting, Herbert–Minn . . . 1927
Johnson, Bob–Tennessee . . 1967
+ Johnson, James–Carlisle . . 1903
+ Jones, Calvin–Iowa 1955
+ Jones, Gomer–Ohio St 1935
Jordan, Lee Roy–Alabama . 1962
+ Juhan, Frank–U.of South . . 1910
Justice, Charlie–N.Car 1949

Kaer, Mort–USC 1926
Kavanaugh, Ken–LSU 1939
+ Kaw, Edgar–Cornell 1922
Kazmaier, Dick–Princeton . . 1951
+ Keck, James–Princeton 1921
Kelley, Larry–Yale 1936
+ Kelly, William–Montana . . . 1926
Kenna, Ed–Syracuse 1966
+ Kern, George–Boston Col . . 1941
+ Ketcham, Henry–Yale 1913
+ Killinger, Glenn–Penn St . . . 1921
Kimbrough, John–TexA&M 1940
+ Kinard, Frank–Mississippi . . 1937
+ King, Phillip–Princeton 1893
+ Kinnick, Nile–Iowa 1939
+ Kipke, Harry–Michigan . . . 1923
+ Kirkpatrick, John–Yale 1910
+ Kitzmiller, John–Oregon . . . 1929
+ Koch, Barton–Baylor 1931

+ Koppisch, Walt–Columbia . 1924
+ Kitner, Malcolm–Texas . . . 1942
+ Kramer, Ron–Michigan 1956
+ Krueger, Charlie–Tex.A&M 1957
Kwalick, Ted–Penn St 1968

+ Lach, Steve–Duke 1941
+ Lane, Myles–Dartmouth . . . 1927
Lattner, Johnny–N.Dame . . 1953
Lauricella, Hank–Tenn 1952
+ Lautenschlaeger–Tulane . . . 1925
+ Layden, Elmer–N.Dame . . . 1924
+ Layne, Bobby–Texas 1947
+ Lea, Langdon–Princeton . . . 1895
LeBaron, Eddie–Pacific 1949
+ Leech, James–VMI 1920
Lester, Darrell–TCU 1935
Lilly, Bob–TCU 1960
Little, Floyd–Syracuse 1966
+ Lio, Augie–Georgetown . . . 1940
+ Locke, Gordon–Iowa 1922
Lourie, Don–Princeton 1921
Lucas, Richie–Penn St 1959
Luckman, Sid–Columbia . . . 1938
Lujack, Johnny–N.Dame . . . 1947
Lund, Pug–Minnesota 1934

+ Macomber, Bart–Illinois . . . 1915
MacLeod, Robert–Dart. 1938
Maegle, Dick–Rice 1954
+ Mahan, Ned–Harvard 1915
Majors, John–Tennessee . . . 1956
+ Mallory, William–Yale 1893
Mann, Gerald–SMU 1927
Manning, Archie–Miss 1970
Manske, Edgar–N'western . 1933
Markov, Vic–Washington . . 1937
+ Marshall, Bobb–Minnesota 1906
Matson, Ollie–San Fran . . . 1952
Matthews, Ray–TCU 1928
+ Maulbetsch, John–Mich . . . 1914
+ Mauthe, Pete–Penn St 1912
+ Maxwell, Robt.–Swarthmore 1906
McAfee, George–Duke 1939
+ McClung, Thomas–Yale . . . 1891
McColl, Bill–Stanford 1951
+ McCormick, Jim–Princeton . 1907
McDonald, Tom–Okla 1956
+ McDowall, Jack–N.C.State 1927
McElhenny, Hugh–Wash . . 1951
+ McEver, Gene–Tennessee . . 1931
+ McEwan, John–Army 1916
McFadden, Banks–Clemson 1939
McFadin, Bud–Texas 1950
+ McGinley, Edward–Penn . . 1924
+ McGovern, John–Minn 1910
McGraw, Thurman–Colo.St 1949
+ McKeever, Mike–USC 1960
+ McLaren, George–Pitt 1918
+ McMillan, Dan–USC/Calif . 1922
+ McMillin, Bo–Centre 1921
+ McWhorter, Bob–Georgia . 1913
+ Mercer, LeRoy–Penn 1912
Meredith, Don–SMU 1959
+ Metzger, Bert–N.Dame . . . 1930
Mickal, Abe–LSU 1935
Miller, Creighton–N.Dame . 1943
+ Miller, Don–Notre Dame . . 1925
Miller, Rip–Notre Dame . . . 1924
+ Miller, Eugene–Penn St . . . 1913
+ Miller, Fred–Notre Dame . . 1928
+ Milstead, C.A.–Wabash/Yale 1923
+ Minds, John–Penn 1897

Minisi, Skip–Penn/Navy . . . 1947
+ Moffatt, Alex–Princeton . . . 1884
Montgomery, Cliff–Columbia 1933
Moomaw, Donn–UCLA 1952
+ Morley, William–Columbia 1903
Morris, George–Ga.Tech . . 1952
+ Morton, Bill–Dartmouth . . . 1931
+ Moscrip, Monk–Stanford . . 1935
+ Muller, Brick–Calif 1922

Nagurski, Bronko–Minn . . . 1929
+ Nevers, Ernie–Stanford . . . 1925
+ Newell, Marshall–Harvard 1893
Newman, Harry–Michigan . 1932
Nobis, Tommy–Texas 1965
Nomellini, Leo–Minnesota . 1949

+ Oberlander, Andrew–Dart . 1925
+ O'Brien, Davey–TCU 1938
+ O'Dea, Pat–Wisconsin 1899
+ O'Hearn, Jack–Cornell 1915
Olds, Robin–Army 1942
+ Oliphant, Elmer–Army/Pur . 1917
Olsen, Merlin–Utah St 1961
Oosterbaan, Ben–Michigan 1927
O'Rourke, Charles–BC 1940
+ Orsi, John–Colgate 1931
+ Osgood, Win–Cornell 1895
Osmanski, Bill–Holy Cross . 1938
+ Owen, George–Harvard . . 1922
Owens, Jim–Oklahoma . . . 1949

Pardee, Jack–Texas A&M . 1956
Parilli, Babe–Kentucky 1951
Parker, Clarence–Duke . . . 1936
Parker, Jackie–Miss.St 1953
Parker, Jim–Ohio St 1956
+ Pazzetti, V.J.–Lehigh 1912
+ Peabody, Chub–Harvard . . 1941
+ Peck, Robert–Pittsburgh . . 1916
+ Pennock, Stan–Harvard . . . 1914
Pfann, George–Cornell . . . 1923
+ Phillips, H.D.–U.of South . . 1904
Pingel, John–Michigan St . . 1938
Pihos, Pete–Indiana 1945
+ Pinckert, Erny–USC 1931
+ Poe, Arthur–Princeton 1899
+ Pollard, Fritz–Brown 1916
Poole, B.–Miss/NC/Army . . 1947
Pregulman, Merv–Michigan 1943
+ Price, Eddie–Tulane 1949
+ Pund, Peter–Georgia Tech . 1928

Ramsey, G.–Wm&Mary . . . 1942
+ Reeds, Claude–Oklahoma . 1913
Reid, Mike–Penn St. 1970
Reid, Steve–Northwestern . 1936
+ Reid, William–Harvard 1900
Renfro, Mel–Oregon 1963
+ Rentner, Pug–N'western . . . 1932
Reynolds, Bobby–Nebraska 1952
Reynolds, Bob–Stanford . . . 1935
Richter, Les–California 1951
Riley, Jack–Northwestern . . 1931
+ Rinehart, Chas.–Lafayette . 1897
+ Rodgers, Ira–West Va 1919
+ Rogers, Edward–Minnesota 1903
Romig, Joe–Colorado 1961
+ Rosenberg, Aaron–USC . . . 1934
Rote, Kyle–SMU 1950
+ Routt, Joe–Texas A&M 1937

+ Salmon, Louis–N.Dame . . . 1904
Sauer, George–Nebraska . . 1933

College Football Hall of Fame (Continued)

Sayers, Gale–Kansas 1964
Scarbath, Jack–Maryland . . 1952
+ Scarlett, Hunter–Penn 1909
Schloredt, Bob–Wash 1960
+ Schoonover, Wear–Ark. . . 1929
+ Schreiner, Dave–Wisconsin 1942
+ Schultz, Germany–Mich . . . 1908
+ Schwab, Frank–Lafayette . . 1922
Schwartz, Marchy–N.Dame 1931
+ Schwegler, Paul–Wash . . . 1931
Scott, Clyde–Arkansas 1949
Scott, Richard–Navy 1947
Scott, Tom–Virginia 1953
+ Seibels, Henry–Sewanee . . 1899
Sellers, Ron–Florida St 1968
Selmon, Lee Roy–Okla 1975
+ Shakespeare, Bill–N.Dame . 1935
+ Shelton, Murray–Cornell . . 1915
+ Shevlin, Tom–Yale 1905
+ Shively, Bernie–Illinois 1926
+ Simons, Monk–Tulane 1934
Simpson, O.J.–USC 1968
Sington, Fred–Alabama . . . 1930
Sinkwich, Frank–Georgia . . 1942
+ Sitko, Emil–Notre Dame . . . 1949
+ Skladany, Joe–Pittsburgh . . 1933
+ Slater, Duke–Iowa 1921
+ Smith, Bruce–Minnesota . . . 1941
Smith, Bubba–Michigan St . 1966
+ Smith, Ernie–USC 1932
Smith, Harry–USC 1939
Smith, Jim Ray–Baylor 1954
+ Smith, Clipper–N.Dame . . . 1927
Smith, Riley–Alabama 1935
+ Smith, Vernon–Georgia . . . 1931
+ Snow, Neil–Michigan 1901
Sparlis, Al–UCLA 1945
+ Spears, Clarence–Dart 1915
Spears, W.D.–Vanderbilt . . 1927
+ Sprackling, Wm.–Brown . . . 1911
+ Sprague, Bud–Army/Texas . 1928
Spurrier, Steve–Florida 1966
Stafford, Harrison–Texas . . 1932
+ Stagg, Amos Alonzo–Yale . 1889
Staubach, Roger–Navy . . . 1963

+ Steffen, Walter–Chicago . . 1908
Steffy, Joe–Army 1947
+ Stein, Herbert–Pitt 1921
Steuber, Robert–Missouri . . 1943
+ Stevens, Mal–Yale 1923
+ Stinchcomb, Pete–Ohio St . 1920
+ Stevenson, Vincent–Penn . . 1905
Strom, Brock–Air Force . . . 1959
+ Strong, Ken–NYU 1928
+ Strupper, George–Ga.Tech 1917
+ Stuhldreher, Harry–N.Dame1924
+ Sturhan, Herb–Yale 1926
+ Stydahar, Joe–West Va . . . 1935
+ Suffridge, Bob–Tennessee . 1940
+ Suhey, Steve–Penn St 1947
+ Sundstrom, Frank–Cornell . 1923
+ Swanson, Clarence–Neb . 1921
+ Swiacki, Bill–Columbia/HC . 1947
Swink, Jim–TCU 1956

Taliaferro, Geo.–Indiana . . 1948
Tarkenton, Fran–Georgia . . 1960
Taylor, Chuck–Stanford . . . 1942
Thomas, Aurelius–Ohio St . 1957
+ Thompson, Joe–Pittsburgh . 1907
+ Thorne, Samuel–Yale 1906
+ Thorpe, Jim–Carlisle 1912
+ Ticknor, Ben–Harvard 1930
+ Tigert, John–Vanderbilt . . . 1904
Tinsley, Gaynell–LSU 1936
Tipton, Eric–Duke 1938
Tonnemaker, Clayton–Minn 1949
+ Torrey, Bob–Pennsylvania . 1906
+ Travis, Brick–Missouri 1920
Trippi, Charley–Georgia . . 1946
+ Tryon, Edward–Colgate . . . 1925

+ Utay, Joe–Texas A&M 1907

+ Van Brocklin, Norm–Ore . . 1948
+ Van Sickel, Dale–Florida . . 1929
+ Van Surdam, H.–Wesleyan 1905
+ Very, Dexter–Penn St 1912
Vessels, Billy–Oklahoma . . . 1952
+ Vick, Ernie–Michigan 1921

+ Wagner, Huber–Pittsburgh 1913
Walker, Doak–SMU 1949

Wallace, Bill–Rice 1935
+ Walsh, Adam–N.Dame . . . 1924
+ Warburton, Cotton, USC . . 1934
Ward, Robert–Maryland . . 1951
+ Warner, William–Cornell . . 1903
+ Washington, Kenny–UCLA . 1939
Webster, George–Mich.St . 1966
Wedemeyer, H.–St.Mary's 1947
+ Weekes, Harold–Columbia 1902
Weir, Ed–Nebraska 1925
+ Welch, Gus–Carlisle 1914
+ Weller, John–Princeton . . . 1935
+ Wendell, Percy–Harvard . . 1913
+ West, Belford–Colgate . . . 1919
+ Westfall, Bob–Michigan . . . 1941
+ Weyand, Alex–Army 1915
+ Wharton, Buck–Penn 1896
+ Wheeler, Arthur–Princeton 1894
White, Byron–Colorado . . . 1937
Whitmire, Don–Navy/Ala . 1944
+ Wickhorst, Frank–Navy . . . 1926
Widseth, Ed–Minnesota . . . 1936
+ Wildung, Dick–Minnesota . 1942
Williams, Bob–N.Dame . . . 1950
Williams, James–Rice 1949
Willis, Bill–Ohio St 1945
+ Wilson, George–Wash . . . 1925
Wilson, Mike–Lafayette . . . 1928
Wilson, Harry–Army/Penn St1923
Wistert, Albert–Michigan . . 1942
Wistert, Alvin–Michigan . . . 1949
+ Wistert, Whitey–Michigan . 1933
+ Wood, Barry–Harvard 1931
Wojciechowicz, Alex–Ford . 1936
+ Wyant, Andy–Chi/B'nell . . 1894
+ Wyatt, Bowden–Tenn 1938
+ Wyckoff, Clint–Cornell 1895

+ Yarr, Tommy–N.Dame 1931
Yary, Ron–USC 1968
+ Yoder, Lloyd–Carnegie . . . 1926
+ Young, Buddy–Illinois 1946
+ Young, Harry–Wash.& Lee 1916
+ Young, Waddy–Okla 1938

Zarnas, Gust–Ohio State . . 1937

Coaches

+ Aillet, Joe 1989
+ Alexander, Bill 1951
+ Anderson, Ed 1971
+ Armstrong, Ike 1957

+ Bachman, Charlie 1978
+ Bell, Matty 1955
+ Bezdek, Hugo 1954
+ Bible, Dana X 1951
+ Bierman, Bernie 1955
Blackman, Bob 1987
+ Blaik, Earl (Red) 1965
Broyles, Frank 1983
+ Bryant, Paul (Bear) 1986

+ Caldwell, Charlie 1961
+ Camp, Walter 1951
Casanova, Len 1977
+ Cavanaugh, Frank 1954
+ Crisler, Fritz 1954

+ Daugherty, Duffy 1984
Devaney, Bob 1981
Devine, Dan 1985
+ Dobie, Gil 1951
+ Donohue, Michael 1951

+ Dorais, Gus 1954
+ Edwards, Bill 1986
+ Engle, Rip 1973
Faurot, Don 1961
Gaither, Jake 1973
Gillman, Sid 1989
+ Godfrey, Ernest 1972
+ Gustafson, Andy 1985

+ Hall, Edward 1951
+ Harding, Jack 1980
+ Harlow, Richard 1954
+ Harman, Harvey 1981
+ Harper, Jesse 1971
+ Haughton, Percy 1951
+ Hayes, Woody 1983
+ Heisman, John W 1954
+ Higgins, Robert 1954
+ Hollingberry, Babe 1979
Howard, Frank 1989

+ Ingram, Bill 1973

+ Jennings, Morley 1973
+ Jones, Howard 1951

+ Jones, Biff 1954
+ Jones, Tad 1958
Jordan, Lloyd 1978
+ Jordan, Ralph (Shug) 1982
+ Kerr, Andy 1951
+ Leahy, Frank 1970
+ Little, George 1955
+ Little, Lou 1960
+ Madigan, Slip 1974
McClendon, Charley 1986
+ McCracken, Herb 1973
+ McGugin, Dan 1951
McKay, John 1988
+ McLaughry, Tuss 1962
+ Meyer, Dutch 1956
+ Mollenkopf, Jack 1988
+ Moore, Bernie 1954
+ Moore, Scrappy 1980
+ Morrison, Ray 1954
+ Munger, George 1976
+ Munn, Clarence (Biggie) . . . 1959
+ Murray, Bill 1974
+ Murray, Frank 1983

+ Mylin, Ed (Hooks) 1974
+ Neale, Earle (Greasy) 1967
+ Neely, Jess 1971
  Nelson, David 1987
+ Neyland, Robert.........1956
+ Norton, Homer 1971
+ O'Neill, Frank (Buck) 1951
+ Owen, Bennie...........1951
  Parseghian, Ara 1980
  Perry, Doyt.............1988
+ Phelan, Jimmy 1973
+ Robinson, E.N 1955
+ Rockne, Knute 1951

+ Romney, Dick 1954
+ Roper, Bill.............1951
  Royal, Darrell 1983
+ Sanford, George 1971
+ Schmidt, Francis 1971
  Schwartzwalder, Ben 1982
+ Shaughnessy, Clark 1968
+ Shaw, Buck 1972
+ Smith, Andy 1951
+ Snavely, Carl 1965
+ Stagg, Amos Alonzo 1951
+ Sutherland, Jock 1951
+ Tatum, Jim 1984
+ Thomas, Frank 1951

+ Vann, Thad 1987
  Vaught, John 1979
+ Wade, Wallace 1955
+ Waldorf, Lynn (Pappy) ...1966
+ Warner, Glenn (Pop) 1951
+ Wieman, E.E.(Tad).......1956
+ Wilce, John 1954
  Wilkinson, Bud 1969
+ Williams, Henry 1951
+ Woodruff, George 1963
  Woodson, Warren 1989
+ Yost, Fielding (Hurry Up)..1951
+ Zuppke, Bob 1951

Pro Football Hall of Fame

Located in Canton, Ohio. Established by the National Football League to commemorate the sport's professional origins. Opened in 1963.

Members are listed with year inducted. Note that + indicates deceased members.

Players

Adderley, Herb 1980
Alworth, Lance 1978
Atkins, Doug...........1982
Badgro, Red 1981
+ Battles, Cliff 1968
Baugh, Sammy 1963
Bednarik, Chuck 1967
Bell, Bobby 1983
Berry, Raymond 1973
Biletnikoff, Fred 1988
Blanda, George 1981
Blount, Mel 1989
Bradshaw, Terry 1989
Brown, Jim 1971
Brown, Roosevelt 1975
Brown, Willie 1984
Butkus, Dick 1979
Canadeo, Tony..........1974
+ Christiansen, Jack........1970
+ Clark, Dutch 1963
Connor, George 1975
Csonka, Larry...........1987
Davis, Willie 1981
Dawson, Len...........1987
Ditka, Mike 1988
Donovan, Art 1968
Driscoll, Paddy 1965
Dudley, Bill 1966
+ Edwards, Turk 1969
Fears, Tom 1970
Ford, Len 1976
Fortmann, Dan 1985
Gatski, Frank 1985
+ George, Bill 1974
Gifford, Frank 1977
Graham, Otto 1965
Grange, Red 1963
Greene, Joe 1987
Gregg, Forrest 1977
Groza, Lou 1974
+ Guyon, Joe 1966
Ham, Jack 1988

+ Healey, Ed 1964
Hein, Mel 1963
+ Henry, Pete 1963
+ Herber, Arnie..........1966
+ Hewitt, Bill 1971
+ Hinkle, Clarke..........1964
Hirsch, Elroy (Crazylegs) ..1968
Hornung, Paul 1986
Houston, Ken 1986
+ Hubbard, Cal 1963
Huff, Sam 1982
Hutson, Don 1963
Johnson, John Henry 1987
Jones, Deacon 1980
Jurgensen, Sonny 1983
+ Kinard, Frank (Bruiser) 1971
Lane, Dick (Night Train)...1974
Langer, Jim............1987
Lanier, Willie 1986
Lary, Yale.............1979
Lavelli, Dante 1975
+ Layne, Bobby 1967
+ Leemans, Tuffy 1978
Lilly, Bob.............1980
Luckman, Sid 1965
Lyman, Roy (Link) 1964
Marchetti, Gino 1972
Matson, Ollie 1972
Maynard, Don 1987
McAfee, George 1966
McCormack, Mike 1984
McElhenny, Hugh 1970
+ McNally, Johnny (Blood) ..1963
+ Michalske, Mike 1964
+ Millner, Wayne 1968
Mitchell, Bobby.........1983
Mix, Ron 1979
Moore, Lenny 1975
Motley, Marion 1968
Musso, George 1982
Nagurski, Bronko 1963
Namath, Joe 1985
Nevers, Ernie 1963

Nitschke, Ray 1978
Nomellini, Leo 1969
Olsen, Merlin 1982
Otto, Jim 1980
Page, Alan 1988
Parker, Clarence (Ace)....1972
Parker, Jim 1973
Perry, Joe.............1969
Pihos, Pete 1970
Ringo, Jim 1981
Robustelli 1971
Sayers, Gale...........1977
Schmidt, Joe 1973
Shell, Art 1989
Simpson, O.J 1985
Starr, Bart 1977
Staubach, Roger 1985
Stautner, Ernie 1969
+ Strong, Ken 1967
+ Stydahar, Joe 1967
Tarkenton, Fran 1986
Taylor, Charley.........1984
Taylor, Jim 1976
Thorpe, Jim 1963
Tittle, Y.A 1971
Trafton, George 1964
Trippi, Charley 1968
+ Tunnell, Emlen 1967
Turner, Clyde (Bulldog) ..1966
Unitas, Johnny 1979
Upshaw, Gene 1987
+ Van Brocklin, Norm 1971
Van Buren, Steve 1965
Walker, Doak...........1986
Warfield, Paul 1983
+ Waterfield, Paul 1965
Weinmeister, Arnie 1984
Willis, Bill 1977
Wilson, Larry 1978
Wojciechowicz, Alex 1968
Wood, Willie 1989

Pro Football Hall of Fame (Continued)

Player and Coach

+Chamberlin, Guy 1965

Flaherty, Ray 1976
+Kiesling, Walt 1966

+Owen, Steve............1966

Player, Coach and Owner

+Conzelman, Jimmy 1964

+Halas, George 1963

Coaches

Brown, Paul 1967
Ewbank, Weeb 1978

Gillman, Sid 1983
+Lambeau, Curly 1963

+Lombardi, Vince 1971
+Neale, Earle (Greasy) 1969

Contributors

+Bell, Bert..............1963
+Bidwill, Charles, Sr 1967
+Carr, Joe 1963

Hunt, Lamar 1972
+Mara, Tim.............1963
+Marshall, George Preston .1963

+Ray, Hugh (Shorty) 1966
+Reeves, Dan 1967
+Rooney, Art 1964
Rozelle, Pete...........1985

Canadian Football Hall of Fame

Located in Hamilton, Ontario. Established in 1963, the Canadian Football Hall of Fame and Museum officially opened in 1972.

Members are listed with year of induction. Note that + indicates deceased members.

Players

Atchison, Ron 1978
Bailey, Byron 1975
Barrow, John 1976
Batstone, Harry 1963
Beach, Ormond 1963
Box, Ab 1965
Breen, Joseph 1963
Bright, Johnny 1970
Brown, Tom 1984
Casey, Tom 1964
Coffey, Tommy Joe 1977
Conacher, Lionel 1963
Copeland, Royal 1988
+Cox, Ernest 1963
+Craig, Ross 1964
+Cronin, Carl 1967
+Cutler, Wes 1968
Dixon, George 1974
+Eliowitz, Abe 1969
+Emerson, Eddie 1963
Etcheverry, Sam 1969
Evanshen, Terry 1984
Faloney, Bernie 1974
+Fear, A.H. (Cap) 1967
+Ferraro, John 1966
Fieldgate, Norm 1979
Fleming, Willie 1982
Gabriel, Tony 1985
+Gall, Hugh 1963
Golab, Tony 1964
Gray, Herbert 1983
Griffing, Dean 1965
Hanson, Fritz 1963
Harris, Wayne 1976

Helton, John 1986
Henley, Garney 1979
Huffman, Dick 1987
+Isbister, Bob Sr 1965
Jackson, Russ 1973
+Jacobs, Jack 1963
+James, Eddie 1963
James, Gerry 1981
+Kabat, Greg 1966
Kapp, Joe 1984
Keeling, Jerry 1989
Krol, Joe 1963
Kwong, Normie 1969
Lancaster, Ron 1982
+Lawson, Smirle 1963
+Leadlay, Frank 1963
+Lear, Les 1974
+Lewis, Leo 1973
Lunsford, Earl 1983
Luzzi, Don 1986
McCance, Ches 1976
+McGill, Frank 1965
McQuarters, Ed 1988
Miles, Rollie 1980
+Molson, Percy 1963
Morris, Frank 1983
+Morris, Ted 1964
Mosca, Angelo 1987
Nelson, Roger 1986
Neumann, Peter 1979
O'Quinn, John Red 1981
Pajaczkowski, Tony.....1988
Parker, Jackie..........1971

Patterson, Hal 1971
Perry, Gordon 1970
+Perry, Norman 1963
Ploen, Ken 1975
Quilty, S.P.(Silver) 1966
Rebholz, Russ 1963
Reed, George.........1979
+Reeve, Ted 1963
Rigney, Frank 1985
+Rodden, Michael 1964
Rowe, Paul 1964
Ruby, Martin 1974
+Russel, Jeff 1963
Scott, Vince 1982
Shatto, Dick 1975
+Simpson, Ben 1963
Simpson, Bob 1976
+Sprague, David 1963
Stevenson, Art 1969
Stewart, Ron 1977
Stirling, Hugh (Bummer) ...1966
Thelen, Dave 1989
+Timmis, Brian 1963
Tinsley, Bud 1982
Tommy, Andy 1989
+Trawick, Herb 1975
+Tubman, Joe 1968
Urness, Ted 1989
Vaughan, Kaye 1978
Wagner, Virgil 1980
+Welch, Hawley (Huck) 1964
Wilkinson, Tom 1987
Wylie, Harvey 1980
+Zock, William 1985

Builders

+Back, Leonard 1971
+Bailey, Harold 1965
Ballard, Harold 1987
+Brook, Tom 1975
+Brown, D.Wes 1963
Chipman, Arthur 1969
Clair, Frank 1981

+Crighton, Hec.........1986
Currie, Andrew 1974
+Davies, Dr. Andrew 1969
+DeGruchy, John 1963
Dojack, Paul 1978
+Duggan, Eric 1981
+DuMoulin, Seppi 1963

+Foulds, William 1963
Gaudaur, J.G.(Jake) 1984
Grant, Bud 1983
+Grey, Lord Earl 1963
Griffith, Harry 1963
Halter, Sydney 1966
Hannibal, Frank 1963

Builders (Continued)

+Hayman, Lew 1975	+Montgomery, Ken 1970	Spring, Harry C 1976
+Hughes, W.P.(Billy) 1974	+Newton, Jack 1964	Stukus, Annis............1974
Kramer, R.A. (Bob) 1987	+Ritchie, Alvin 1963	+Taylor, N.J.(Piffles) 1963
+Lieberman, M.I.(Moe).....1973	+Ryan, Joseph 1968	Tindall, Frank 1985
+McBrien, Harry 1978	Sazio, Ralph 1988	+Warner, Clair 1965
+McCaffrey, Jimmy 1967	+Shaughnessy, Frank (Shag) .1963	+Warwick, Bert 1964
+McCann, Dave 1966	+Shouldice, W.T.(Hap)......1977	+Wilson, Seymour 1984
+McPherson, Don 1983	+Simpson, Jimmie 1986	
+Metras, Johnny 1980	Slocomb, Karl 1989	

Golf Halls of Fame

There are currently two primary golf halls of fame: the PGA/World Golf Hall of Fame in Pinehurst, N.C., and the LPGA Hall of Fame in Sugar Land, Texas. The old PGA Hall of Fame was discontinued in 1983 when the PGA took control of the World Golf Hall of Fame. All members of the PGA Hall will eventually be inducted into the PGA/World Hall.

Members are listed with year of induction. Note that + indicates deceased members.

PGA/World Golf Hall of Fame

Men

+Anderson, Willie 1975	+Guldahl, Ralph 1981	+Ouimet, Francis 1974
+Armour, Tommy 1976	+Hagen, Walter 1974	Palmer, Arnold 1974
+Ball, John, Jr 1977	+Hilton, Harold 1978	Player, Gary 1974
+Barnes, Jim.............1989	Hogan, Ben 1974	Sarazen, Gene 1974
Boros, Julius 1982	+Jones, Bobby 1974	Snead, Sam 1974
+Braid, James............1976	+Little, Lawson 1980	+Taylor, John H 1975
Casper, Billy 1978	+Locke, Bobby 1977	Thomson, Peter..........1988
+Cotton, Thomas 1980	Middlecoff, Cary 1986	+Travers, Jerry 1976
+Demaret, Jimmy 1983	+Morris, Tom, Sr 1976	+Travis, Walter 1979
DeVicenzo, Roberto 1989	+Morris, Tom, Jr 1975	Trevino, Lee 1981
+Evans, Chick............1975	Nelson, Byron 1974	+Vardon, Harry 1974
Floyd, Ray 1989	Nicklaus, Jack 1974	Watson, Tom 1988

Women

Berg, Patty 1974	Lopez, Nancy............1989	+Wethered, Joyce 1975
+Howe, Dorothy C.H 1978	Rawls, Betsy 1987	Whitworth, Kathy 1982
Carner, JoAnne 1985	Suggs, Louise 1979	Wright, Mickey..........1976
	+Vare, Glenna Collett 1975	+Zaharias, Babe Didrikson ..1974

Contributors

+Corcoran, Fred 1975	+Graffis, Herb 1977	Jones, Robert Trent 1987
+Crosby, Bing............1978	+Harlow, Robert 1988	+Roberts, Clifford 1978
Dey, Joseph 1975	Hope, Bob 1983	+Ross, Donald 1977

PGA Hall of Fame

Men

+Anderson, Willie 1940	+Farrell, Johnny 1961	Middlecoff, Cary 1974
+Armour, Tommy 1940	Ford, Doug.............1975	Nelson, Byron 1953
+Barnes, Jim............1940	+Ghezzi, Vic............1965	+Ouimet, Francis 1940
Boros, Julius 1974	+Guldahl, Ralph 1963	Palmer, Arnold 1980
+Brady, Mike 1960	+Hagen, Walter 1940	+Picard, Henry 1961
+Burke, Billy 1966	Harbert, Chick 1968	Revolta, Johnny 1963
Burke, Jack, Jr 1975	Harper, Chandler 1969	Runyan Paul 1959
Casper, Billy 1982	+Harrison, Dutch 1962	Sarazen, Gene 1940
Cooper, Harry 1959	Hogan, Ben 1953	+Shute, Denny 1957
+Cruickshank, Bobby 1967	+Hutchison, Jock, Sr.......1959	+Smith, Alex 1940
+Demaret, Jimmy 1960	+Jones, Bobby 1940	+Smith, Horton 1958
DeVicenzo, Roberto 1979	+Little, Lawson 1961	+Smith, Macdonald 1954
+Diegel, Leo 1955	Littler, Gene 1982	Snead, Sam 1953
+Dudley, Ed 1964	+McDermott, John 1940	+Travers, Jerry 1940
+Dutra, Olin 1962	+Mangrum, Lloyd 1964	+Travis, Walter 1940
+Evans, Chick............1940	+McLeod, Fred............1960	+Craig Wood 1956

Women

Berg, Patty 1978	+Zaharias, Babe Didrikson ..1976

LPGA Hall of Fame

Berg, Patty 1951	Jameson, Betty 1951	Suggs, Louise 1951
Carner, JoAnne 1982	Lopez, Nancy............1987	Whitworth, Kathy 1975
Haynie, Sandra 1977	Mann, Carol 1977	Wright, Mickey..........1964
	Rawls, Betsy 1960	+Zaharias, Babe Didrikson ..1951

Hockey Hall of Fame

Located in Toronto, Ontario. Established by the National Hockey League and opened in 1961.
Members are listed with year of induction. Note that + indicates deceased members.

Players

Abel, Sid 1969	Gilbert, Rod 1982	+Oliver, Harry 1967
+Adams, Jack 1959	+Gilmour, Billy 1962	Olmstead, Bert 1985
Apps, Syl 1961	+Goheen, Moose 1952	Orr, Bobby 1979
Armstrong, George 1975	+Goodfellow, Ebbie 1963	Park, Brad 1988
	+Grant, Mike 1950	+Patrick, Lester 1945
Bailey, Ace 1975	+Green, Wilfred 1962	+Patrick, Lynn 1980
+Bain, Donald 1945	+Griffis, Si 1950	+Phillips, Tom 1945
Baker, Hobey 1945	Hall, Joe 1975	Pilote, Pierre 1975
+Barry, Marty 1965	Harvey, Doug 1973	+Pitre, Didier 1962
Bathgate, Andy 1978	+Hay, George 1958	+Pratt, Babe 1966
Beliveau, Jean 1972	+Hextall, Bryan 1969	+Primeau, Joe 1963
+Bentley, Doug 1964	+Hooper, Tom 1962	Pronovost, Marcel 1978
+Bentley, Max 1966	Horner, Red 1965	+Pulford, Harvey 1945
Blake, Toe 1966	+Horton, Tim 1977	Quackenbush, Bill 1976
Boivin, Leo 1986	Howe, Gordie 1972	+Rankin, Frank 1961
+Boon, Richard 1952	+Howe, Syd 1965	Ratelle, Jean 1985
Bouchard, Emile 1966	Howell, Harry 1979	Reardon, Ken 1966
+Boucher, Frank 1958	Hull, Bobby 1983	Richard, Henri 1979
+Boucher, George 1960	+Hyland, Harry 1962	Richard, Maurice 1961
+Bowie, Russell 1945	+Irvin, Dick 1958	+Richardson, George 1950
+Broadbent, Punch 1962	+Jackson, Busher 1971	+Roberts, Gordie 1971
Bucyk, John 1981	+Johnson, Ching 1958	+Ross, Art 1945
Burch, Billy 1974	+Johnson, Ernie 1952	+Russell, Blair 1965
+Cameron, Harry 1962	Johnson, Tom 1970	+Russell, Ernie 1965
+Clancy, King 1958	+Joliat, Aurel 1947	+Ruttan, Jack 1962
+Clapper, Dit 1945	+Keats, Duke 1958	Savard, Serge 1986
Clarke, Bobby 1987	Kelly, Red 1969	+Scanlan, Fred 1965
+Cleghorn, Sprague 1958	Kennedy, Ted 1966	Schmidt, Milt 1961
Colville, Neil 1967	Keon, Dave 1986	Schriner, Sweeney 1962
Conacher, Charlie 1961	Lach, Elmer 1966	Seibert, Earl 1963
+Cook, Bill 1952	Lafleur, Guy 1988	+Seibert, Oliver 1961
Coulter, Art 1974	+Lalonde, Newsy 1950	+Shore, Eddie 1945
Cournoyer, Yvan 1982	Laperriere, Jacques 1987	+Siebert, Babe 1964
Cowley, Bill 1968	+Laviolette, Jack 1962	+Simpson, Joe 1962
+Crawford, Rusty 1962	Lemaire, Jacques 1984	Sittler, Darryl 1989
+Darragh, Jack 1962	Lewis, Herbie 1989	+Smith, Alf 1962
+Davidson, Scotty 1950	Lindsay, Ted 1966	+Smith, Hooley 1972
Day, Hap 1961	+MacKay, Mickey 1952	+Smith, Tommy 1973
Delvecchio, Alex 1977	Mahovlich, Frank 1981	Stanley, Allan 1981
+Denneny, Cy 1959	+Malone, Joe 1950	+Stanley, Barney 1962
+Drillon, Gordie 1975	+Mantha, Sylvio 1960	+Stewart, Jack 1964
+Drinkwater, Graham 1950	+Marshall, Jack 1965	+Stewart, Nels 1962
+Dunderdale, Tommy 1974	+Maxwell, Fred 1962	+Stuart, Bruce 1961
+Dutton, Red 1958	+McGee, Frank 1945	+Stuart, Hod 1945
+Dye, Babe 1978	+McGimsie, Billy 1962	+Taylor, Cyclone 1945
Esposito, Phil 1984	+McNamara, George 1958	+Trihey, Harry 1950
	Mikita, Stan 1983	Ullman, Norm 1982
+Farrell, Arthur 1965	Moore, Dickie 1974	+Walker, Jack 1960
+Foyston, Frank 1958	+Morenz, Howie 1945	+Walsh, Marty 1962
+Frederickson, Frank 1958	+Mosienko, Bill 1965	+Watson, Harry 1962
Gadsby, Bill 1970	+Nighbor, Frank 1945	+Weiland, Cooney 1971
+Gardiner, Herb 1958	+Noble, Reg 1962	+Westwick, Harry 1962
+Gardner, Jimmy 1962	+O'Connor, Buddy 1988	+Whitcroft, Fred 1962
Geoffrion, Bernie 1972		+Wilson, Gordon 1962
+Gerard, Eddie 1945		

Goaltenders

+Benedict, Clint 1965	+Gardiner, Chuck 1945	+Moran, Paddy 1958
Bower, Johnny 1976	Giacomin, Ed 1987	Parent, Bernie 1984
Brimsek, Frank 1966	+Hainsworth, George 1961	+Plante, Jacques 1978
+Broda, Turk 1967	Hall, Glenn 1975	Rayner, Chuck 1973
Cheevers, Gerry 1985	Hern, Riley 1962	+Sawchuk, Terry 1971
+Connell, Alex 1958	+Holmes, Harry 1972	+Thompson, Tiny 1959
Dryden, Ken 1983	+Hutton, J.B 1962	Tretiak, Vladislav 1989
+Durnan, Bill 1964	+Lehman, Hugh 1958	+Vezina, George 1945
Esposito, Tony 1988	+LeSueur, Percy 1961	Worsley, Gump 1980
	Lumley, Harry 1980	+Worters, Roy 1969

Referees & Linesmen

Ashley, John 1981
Chadwick, Bill 1964
+ Elliott, Chaucer 1961

+ Hayes, George 1988
+ Hewitson, Bobby 1963
+ Ion, Mickey 1961
Pavelich, Matt 1987

Rodden, Mike 1962
+ Smeaton, J. Cooper 1961
Storey, Red 1967
Udvari, Frank 1973

Builders

+ Adams, Charles 1960
+ Adams, Weston 1972
+ Ahearn, Frank 1962
+ Ahearn, J.F 1977
+ Allan, Montagu 1945

Ballard, Harold 1977
+ Bauer, Fr. David 1989
+ Bickell, J.P 1978
+ Brown, George 1961
+ Brown, Walter 1962
+ Buckland, Frank 1975
Butterfield, Jack 1980

+ Calder, Frank 1945
+ Campbell, Angus 1964
+ Campbell, Clarence 1966
+ Cattarinich, Joseph 1977

+ Dandurand, Leo 1963
Dilio, Frank 1964
+ Dudley, George 1958
+ Dunn, James 1968

Eagleson, Alan 1989

Francis, Emile 1982

+ Gibson, Jack 1976
+ Gorman, Tommy 1963

Hanley, Bill 1986
+ Hay, Charles 1984
+ Hendy, Jim 1968
+ Hewitt, Foster 1965
+ Hewitt, W.A 1945
+ Hume, Fred 1962

+ Imlach, Punch 1984
Ivan, Tommy 1964

+ Jennings, William 1975
Juckes, Gordon 1979

+ Kilpatrick, John 1960

+ Leader, Al 1969
LeBel, Robert 1970
+ Lockhart, Thomas 1965
+ Loicq, Paul 1961

+ Mariucci, John 1985
+ McLaughlin, Frederic 1963
+ Milford, Jake 1984
Molson, Hartland 1973

+ Nelson, Francis 1945
+ Norris, Bruce 1969
+ Norris, James D 1962
Norris, James, Sr 1958
+ Northey, William 1945

+ O'Brien, J.A 1962

+ Patrick, Frank 1958
+ Pickard, Allan 1958
Pilous, Rudy 1985
Pollock, Sam 1978

+ Raymond, Donat 1958
+ Robertson, John Ross 1945
+ Robinson, Claude 1945
+ Ross, Philip 1976

+ Selke, Frank 1960
Sinden, Harry 1983
+ Smith, Frank 1962
+ Smythe, Conn 1958
Snider, Ed 1988
+ Stanley, Lord 1945
+ Sutherland, James 1945

Tarasov, Anatoli 1974
Turner, Lloyd 1958
+ Tutt, Thayer 1978

Voss, Carl 1974

+ Waghorne, Fred 1961
+ Wirtz, Arthur 1971
Wirtz, Bill 1976

Ziegler, John 1987

U.S. Hockey Hall of Fame

Located in Eveleth, Minn. Established by the Eveleth Civic Assn. and opened in 1973.
Members are listed with year of induction. Note that + indicates deceased members.

Players

+ Abel, Clarence (Taffy) 1973
+ Baker, Hobey 1973
Bartholome, Earl 1977
Bessone, Peter 1978
Blake, Robert 1985
Brimsek, Frank 1973
+ Chaisson, Ray 1974
Chase, John P 1973
Christian, Bill 1984
Christian, Roger 1989
Cleary, Robert 1981
Cleary, William 1976
+ Conroy, Anthony 1975
Dahlstrom, Carl (Cully) 1973
DesJardins, Victor 1974
Desmond, Richard 1988

Dill, Robert 1979
Everett, Doug 1974
+ Garrison, John B 1974
Garrity, Jack 1986
+ Goheen, Frank (Moose) . . .1973
Harding, Austin (Austie) . . .1975
Iglehart, Stewart 1975
Johnson, Virgil 1974
Karakas, Mike 1973
Kirrane, Jack 1987
Lane, Myles 1973
+ Linder, Joseph 1975
+ LoPresti, Sam 1973
+ Mariucci, John 1973
Mayasich, John 1976
McCartan, Jack 1983

Moe, William 1974
Moseley, Fred 1975
+ Murray, Hugh (Muzz) Sr . .1987
+ Nelson, Hubert (Hub) 1978
Olson, Eddie 1977
+ Owen, George Jr 1973
+ Palmer, Winthrop 1973
Paradise, Bob 1989
Purpur, Clifford (Fido) 1974
Riley, William 1977
+ Romnes, Elwin (Doc) 1973
Rondeau, Richard 1985
Williams, Thomas 1981
+ Winters, Frank (Coddy) . . .1973
Yackel, Ken 1986

Coaches

+ Almquist, Oscar 1983
+ Gordon, Malcolm 1973
Heyliger, Vic 1974

+ Jeremiah, Eddie 1973
+ Kelley, John (Snooks) 1974
Riley, Jack 1979

Ross, Larry 1988
+ Thompson, Clifford 1973
+ Stewart, William 1982
+ Winsor, Alfred (Ralph) 1973

Administrators

+ Brown, George V 1973
+ Brown, Walter A 1973
Bush, Walter 1980
Clark, Donald 1978

+ Gibson, J.C. (Doc) 1973
+ Jennings, William 1981
+ Kahler, Nick 1980
+ Lockhart, Thomas 1973
Marvin, Cal 1982

Ridder, Robert 1976
Trumble, Harold 1970
+ Tutt, William Thayer 1973
Wirtz, William (Bill) 1967
+ Wright, Lyle 1973

Referee

Chadwick, Bill 1974

Lester Patrick Trophy

An annual award presented by the NHL and the New York Rangers "for outstanding service to hockey in the United States." The trophy is named after the former Rangers' coach and general manager. Note that * indicates award was presented posthumously.

Year Recipients
1966 J.J.(Jack) Adams.
1967 Gordie Howe; Charles Adams*; James Norris, Sr*.
1968 Thomas Lockhart; Walter A.Brown*; Gen.John Kilpatrick.
1969 Bobby Hull; Eddie Jeremiah.
1970 Eddie Shore; James C.V.Hendy*.
1971 William Jennings; John Sollenberger*.
1972 Clarence Campbell; John Kelly; Cooney Weiland; James D.Norris*.
1973 Walter L.Bush, Jr.
1974 Alex Delvecchio; Murray Murdoch; Weston W. Adams, Sr*; Charles L.Crovat*.
1975 Donald Clark; Bill Chadwick; Tommy Ivan.
1976 Stan Mikita; George Leader; Bruce A. Norris.
1977 John Bucyk; Murray Armstrong; John Mariucce.

Year Recipients
1978 Phil Esposito; Tom Fitzgerald; William Tutt; William W.Wirtz.
1979 Bobby Orr.
1980 Bobby Clarke; Edward Snider; Fred Shero; 1980 US Olympic Hockey Team.
1981 Charles M.Schulz.
1982 Emile Francis.
1983 Bill Torrey.
1984 John Ziegler; Arthur Howie Ross*.
1985 Jack Butterfield; Arthur M.Wirtz.
1986 John MacInnes; Jack Riley.
1987 Hobey Baker*; Frank Mathers.
1988 Keith Allen; Fred Cusick; Bob Johnson.
1989 Dan Kelly; Lou Nanne; Lynn Patrick; Bud Poile.

National Horse Racing Hall of Fame

Located in Saratoga Springs, N.Y. Established by the Saratoga Springs Racing Assn. in 1950 and opened in 1955. Members are listed with year of induction. Note that + indicates deceased members.

Jockeys

+Adams, Frank (Dooley)* ..1970	Guerin, Eric 1972	+Parke, Ivan............1978
+Adams, John 1965	Hartack, Bill 1959	+Patrick, Gil 1970
+Aitcheson, Joe Jr.*.......1978	+Johnson, Albert 1971	Pincay, Laffit Jr 1975
Arcaro, Eddie...........1958	+Knapp, Willie 1969	+Purdy, Sam 1970
Atkinson, Ted 1957	+Kummer, Clarence 1972	+Reiff, John 1956
Baeza, Braulio 1976	+Kurtsinger, Charles......1967	+Robertson, Alfred........1971
+Bassett, Carroll* 1972	+Loftus, John 1959	Rotz, John L 1983
+Blum, Walter 1987	Longden, Johnny 1958	+Sande, Earl...........1955
+Bostwick, George H.* 1968	+Maher, Danny 1955	+Schilling, Carroll 1970
+Boulmetis, Sam 1973	+McAtee, Linus..........1956	Shoemaker, Bill..........1958
+Brooks, Steve 1963	McCarron, Chris........1989	+Simms, Willie 1977
+Burns, Tommy 1983	+McCreary, Conn........1974	+Sloan, Todhunter 1955
+Butwell, Jimmy 1984	+McKinney, Rigan 1968	+Smithwick, A. Patrick* 1973
+Coltiletti, Frank 1970	+McLaughlin, James 1955	+Stout, James 1968
Cordero, Angel Jr........1988	+Miller, Walter 1955	+Taral, Fred 1955
+Crawford, Robert (Specs)* .1973	+Murphy, Isaac 1955	+Tuckman, Bayard Jr.* 1973
+Fator, Laverne 1955	+Neves, Ralph 1960	Turcotte, Ron 1979
+Ensor, Lavelle (Buddy) ...1962	+Notter, Joe.............1963	+Turner, Nash 1955
+Garner, Andrew (Mack)...1969	+Odom, George 1955	Ussery, Robert 1980
+Garrison, Snapper 1955	+O'Connor, Winnie 1956	+Woolfe, George..........1955
+Griffin, Henry...........1956	+O'Neill, Frank 1956	+Workman, Raymond 1956
		Ycaza, Manuel 1977

*Steeplechase jockey

Trainers

Barrera, Laz 1979
+ Bedwell, H.Guy 1971
+ Brown, Edward D. 1984
Burch, Elliot 1980
+ Burch, Preston M 1963
+ Burch, W.P. 1955
+ Burlew, Fred. 1973
+ Byers, J.D. (Dilly) 1967
+ Childs, Frank E 1968
Cocks, W. Burling 1985
+ Duke, William. 1956
+ Feustel, Louis 1964
+ Fitzsimmons, J.(Sunny Jim) .1958
+ Gaver, John M. 1966
+ Healey, Thomas 1955
+ Hildreth, Samuel. 1955
+ Hirsch, Max 1959
+ Hirsch, W.J.(Buddy) 1982
+ Hitchcock, Thomas Sr 1973

+ Hughes, Hollie 1973
+ Hyland, John 1956
+ Jacobs, Hirsch 1958
Jerkens, H. Allen 1975
+ Johnson, William R 1986
+ Jolley, LeRoy 1987
+ Jones, Ben A 1958
Jones, H.A.(Jimmy) 1959
+ Joyner, Andrew 1955
Laurin, Lucien 1977
+ Lewis, J. Howard 1969
Luro, Horatio 1980
+ Madden, John 1983
+ Maloney, Jim 1989
Martin, Frank (Pancho) . . .1981
+ McDaniel, Henry 1956
+ Miller, MacKenzie 1987
+ Molter, William, Jr 1960
+ Mulholland, Winbert 1967

+ Neloy, Eddie 1983
Nerud, John 1972
+ Parke, Burley 1986
Penna, Angel Sr 1988
+ Pincus, Jacob 1988
+ Rogers, John 1955
+ Rowe, James Sr 1955
+ Smith, Robert A 1976
+ Smithwick, Mike 1976
Stephens, Woody 1976
+ Thompson, H.J. 1969
+ Trotsek, Harry 1984
Van Berg, Jack 1985
+ Van Berg, Marion 1970
+ Veitch, Sylvester 1977
+ Walden, Robert 1970
+ Ward, Sherrill 1978
Whiteley, Frank Jr 1978
Whittingham, Charlie 1974
Winfrey, Carey 1971

Horses
Year foaled in parentheses.

+ Ack Ack (1966) 1986
Affectionately (1960) 1989
Affirmed (1975) 1980
+ Alsab (1939). 1976
Alydar (1975) 1989
+ American Eclipse (1814) . . .1970
+ Armed (1941). 1963
+ Artful (1902) 1956
+ Assault (1943) 1964

+ Battleship (1927) 1969
+ Bed O'Roses (1947) 1976
+ Beldame (1901) 1956
+ Ben Brush (1893) 1955
+ Bewitch (1945) 1977
+ Black Gold (1919) 1989
+ Blue Larkspur (1926) 1957
+ Bold Ruler (1954) 1973
+ Bon Nouvel (1960) 1976
+ Boston (1833). 1955
+ Broomstick (1901). 1956
+ Buckpasser (1963) 1970
+ Busher (1942) 1964
+ Bushranger (1930) 1967

+ Cafe Prince (1970) 1985
+ Carry Back (1958) 1975
+ Challendon (1936) 1977
+ Chris Evert (1988) 1971
+ Cicada (1959) 1967
+ Citation (1945) 1959
+ Coaltown (1945) 1983
+ Colin (1905) 1956
+ Commando (1898) 1956
+ Count Fleet (1940) 1961

+ Dahlia (1971) 1981
+ Damascus (1964) 1974
+ Dark Mirage (1965) 1974
+ Davona Dale (1976) 1985
+ Desert Vixen (1970) 1979
+ Devil Diver (1939) 1980
+ Discovery (1931) 1969
+ Domino (1891) 1955
+ Dr. Fager (1964) 1971

+ Elkridge (1938) 1966
+ Emperor of Norfolk (1885) 1988
+ Equipoise (1928) 1957
+ Exterminator (1915) 1957

+ Fairmount (1921) 1985
+ Fair Play (1905) 1956
+ Firenze (1885) 1981
+ Forego (1971) 1979

+ Gallant Bloom (1966) 1977
+ Gallant Fox (1927) 1957
+ Gallant Man (1954) 1987
+ Gallorette (1942) 1962
+ Gamely (1964) 1980
Genuine Risk (1977) 1986
+ Good and Plenty (1900) . . .1956
+ Grey Lag (1918) 1957

+ Hamburg (1895) 1986
+ Hanover (1884) 1955
+ Henry of Navarre (1891) .1985
+ Hindoo (1878) 1955

+ Imp (1894) 1965

+ Jay Trump (1957) 1971
+ Jolly Roger (1922) 1965

+ Kingston (1884) 1955
+ Kelso (1957) 1967
+ Kentucky (1861) 1983

+ L'Escargot (1963) 1977
+ Lexington (1850) 1955
+ Longfellow (1867) 1971
+ Luke Blackburn (1877) 1956

+ Majestic Prince (1966) . . .1988?
+ Man O'War (1917) 1957
+ Miss Woodford (1880) 1967
+ Myrtlewood (1933). 1979

+ Nashua (1952) 1965
+ Native Dancer (1950) 1963
+ Native Diver (1959) 1978
Northern Dancer (1961) . . .1976
+ Neji (1950) 1966

+ Oedipus (1941) 1978
+ Old Rosebud (1911) 1968
+ Omaha (1932) 1965

+ Pan Zareta (1910) 1972
+ Parole (1873) 1984
+ Peter Pan (1904) 1956

+ Real Delight (1949) 1987
+ Regret (1912) 1957
+ Reigh Count (1925) 1978
+ Roamer (1911) 1981
+ Roseben (1901) 1956
+ Round Table (1954) 1972
+ Ruffian (1972) 1976
+ Ruthless (1864) 1975

+ Salvator (1886) 1955
+ Sarazen (1921) 1957
+ Seabiscuit (1933) 1958
+ Searching (1952) 1978
Seattle Slew (1974) 1981
Secretariat (1970) 1974
+ Shuvee (1966) 1975
+ Silver Spoon (1956) 1978
+ Sir Archy (1805) 1955
+ Sir Barton (1916) 1957
+ Stymie (1941) 1975
+ Susan's Girl (1969) 1976
+ Swaps (1952) 1966
+ Sword Dancer (1956) 1977
+ Sysonby (1902). 1956

+ Tim Tam (1955) 1985
+ Tom Fool (1949). 1960
+ Top Flight (1929) 1966
+ Tosmah (1961) 1984
+ Twenty Grand (1928). 1957
+ Twilight Tear (1941) 1963

+ War Admiral (1934) 1958
+ Whirlaway (1938) 1959
+ Whisk Broom II (1907). . . .1979

+ Zev (1920) 1983

Exemplars of Racing

+ Hanes, John W 1982
+ Jeffords, Walter M. 1973
+ Widener, George D 1971

U.S. Olympic Hall of Fame

Established by the U.S. Olympic Committee with athletes inducted as of 1983. A building to house the Hall of Fame in Colorado Springs, Colo., is in the planning stages.
Members are listed with year of induction. Note that + indicates deceased members.

Bobsled
+ Eagan, Eddie (see Boxing) . 1983

Boxing

Clay, Cassius* 1983
+ Eagan, Eddie (see Bobsled) 1983
*Clay changed name to Muhammad Ali in 1964.

Frazier, Joe 1989
Leonard, Sugar Ray 1985

Patterson, Floyd 1987

Figure Skating

Albright, Tenley 1988

Button, Dick 1983

Fleming, Peggy..........1983

Gymnastics
Retton, Mary Lou 1985

Speed Skating
Heiden, Eric 1983

Swimming & Diving

Babashoff, Shirley 1987
+ Daniels, Charles 1988
de Varona, Donna 1987

+ Kahanamoku, Duke 1984
Louganis, Greg..........1985
McCormick, Pat 1985
Meyer, Debbie 1986

Naber, John............1984
Schollander, Don 1983
Spitz, Mark 1983
+ Weissmuller, Johnny 1983

Track & Field

Beamon, Bob 1983
Boston, Ralph 1985
Davis, Glenn 1986
+ Didrikson, Babe 1983
Dillard, Harrison 1983
Evans, Lee 1989
+ Ewry, Ray 1983
Jenner, Bruce 1986
Johnson, Rafer 1983

+ Kraenzlein, Alvin 1985
Lewis, Carl 1985
Mathias, Bob 1983
Mills, Billy 1984
Morrow, Bobby 1989
Moses, Edwin 1985
O'Brien, Parry 1984
Oerter, Al..............1983
+ Owens, Jesse 1983

Richards, Bob 1983
Rudolph, Wilma 1983
+ Sheppard, Mel 1989
Shorter, Frank 1984
+ Thorpe, Jim 1983
Toomey, Bill 1984
Tyus, Wyomia 1985
Whitfield, Mal 1988
+ Wykoff, Frank 1984

Weight Lifting
+ Davis, John.............1989

Wrestling
Gable, Dan 1985

Contributors

Arledge, Roone 1989
+ Brundage, Avery 1983

Iba, Henry 1985
Kane, Robert 1986

McKay, Jim............1988
Miller, Don 1984
Walker, Leroy 1987

Teams

1956 Basketball—Dick Boushka, Carl Cain, Chuck Darling, Bill Evans, Gib Ford, Burdy Haldorson, Bill Hougland, Bob Jeangerard, K.C.Jones, Bill Russell, Ron Tomsic, + Jim Walsh and coach Gerald Tucker.

1960 Basketball—Jay Arnette, Walt Bellamy, Bob Boozer, Terry Dischinger, Burdy Haldorson, Darrall Imhoff, Allen Kelley, + Lester Lane, Jerry Lucas, Oscar Robertson, Adrian Smith, Jerry West and coach Pete Newell.

1964 Basketball—Jim Barnes, Bill Bradley, Larry Brown, Joe Caldwell, Mel Counts, Richard Davies, Walt Hazzard, Luke Jackson, John McCaffrey, Jeff Mullins, Jerry Shipp, George Wilson and coach Henry Iba.

1960 Ice Hockey—Billy Christian, Roger Christian, Billy Cleary, Bob Cleary, Gene Grazia, Paul Johnson, Jack Kirrane, John Mayasich, Jack McCartan, Bob McKay, Dick Meredith, Weldon Olson, Ed Owen, Rod Paavola, Larry Palmer, Dick Rodenheiser, Tom Williams and coach Jack Riley.

1980 Ice Hockey—Bill Baker, Neal Broten, Dave Christian, Steve Christoff, Jim Craig, Mike Eruzione, John Harrington, Steve Janaszak, Mark Johnson, Ken Morrow, Rob McClanahan, Jack O'Callahan, Mark Pavelich, Mike Ramsey, Buzz Schneider, Dave Silk, Eric Strobel, Bob Suter, Phil Verchota, Mark Wells and coach Herb Brooks.

National Sportscasters & Sportswriters Hall of Fame

Established by the National Sportscasters and Sportswriters Assn. in 1960 and opened in 1962. A building to house the Hall of Fame in Salisbury, NC, is in the planning stages.

Members are listed with year of induction. Note that + indicates deceased members.

Sportscasters

Allen, Mel 1972	Gowdy, Curt 1981	+McNamee, Graham 1964
Barber, Walter (Red) 1973	Harwell, Ernie 1989	Nelson, Lindsey 1979
Brickhouse, Jack 1983	+Hodges, Russ 1975	+Prince, Bob 1986
Caray, Harry 1989	+Husing, Ted 1963	Schenkel, Chris 1981
+Dean, Jay Hanna (Dizzy) . . 1976	+McCarthy, Clem 1970	Scott, Ray 1982
Dunphy, Don 1986	McKay, Jim 1987	+Stern, Bill 1974

Sportswriters

Bisher, Furman 1989	+Kieran, John 1971	+Rice, Grantland 1962
Burick, Si 1985	+Lardner, Ring 1967	+Runyon, Damon 1964
+Cannon, Jimmy 1986	+Murphy, Jack 1988	Russell, Fred 1988
+Considine, Bob 1980	Murray, Jim 1978	+Smith, Walter (Red) 1977
+Daley, Arthur 1976	+Parker, Dan 1975	+Spink, J.G.Taylor 1969
+Grimsley, Will 1987	Povich, Shirley 1984	+Ward, Arch 1973
		+Woodward, Stanley 1974

Memorable Athletes

+Lou Gehrig 1980	+Jesse Owens 1978

Contributors

Ronald Reagan 1989	+John Wayne 1979

International Tennis Hall of Fame

Located in Newport, R.I. Originally the National Tennis Hall of Fame when founded in 1953. Renamed the International Tennis Hall of Fame in 1976.

Members are listed with year of induction. Note that + indicates deceased members.

Players

Addie, Pauline Betz 1965	Emerson, Roy 1982	Marble, Alice 1964
+Adee, George 1964	+Etchebaster, Pierre 1978	+McKinley, Chuck 1986
+Alexander, Fred 1961	Falkenburg, Bob 1974	+McLoughlin, Maurice 1957
+Allison, Wilmer 1963	Fraser, Neale 1984	McNeill, Don 1965
+Alonso, Manuel 1977	Fry, Shirley (Irvin) 1970	Moody, Helen Wills (Roark) 1959
Ashe, Arthur 1985	+Garland, Chuck 1969	+Moore, Elisabeth 1971
+Atkinson, Juliette 1974	Gibson, Althea 1971	Mulloy, Gardnar 1972
+Barger-Wallach, Maud . . . 1958	Godfree, Kathleen McKane 1978	+Murray, Lindley 1958
+Behr, Karl 1969	Gonzales, Pancho 1968	+Myrick, Julian 1963
Borg, Bjorn 1987	+Grant, Bryan (Bitsy) 1972	Newcombe, John 1986
Borotra, Jean 1976	+Griffin, Clarence 1970	+Nielsen, Arthur 1971
Bromwich, John 1984	+Hackett, Harold 1961	+Nuthall, Betty (Shoemaker) 1977
+Brookes, Norman 1977	+Hansell, Ellen 1965	Olmedo, Alex 1987
Brough, Louise (Clapp) . . . 1967	Hard, Darlene 1973	+Osuna, Rafael 1979
+Browne, Mary 1957	Hart, Doris 1969	Palfrey, Sarah (Danzig) . . . 1963
+Brugnon, Jacques 1976	+Heldman, Gladys 1979	Parker, Frank 1966
Budge, Don 1964	Hoad, Lew 1980	Patterson, Gerald 1989
Bueno, Maria 1978	+Hovey, Fred 1974	Patty, Budge 1977
+Cahill, Mabel 1976	+Hunt, Joe 1966	Perry, Fred 1975
+Campbell, Oliver 1955	+Hunter, Frank 1961	+Pettitt, Tom 1982
Cawley, Evonne Goolagong 1988	Jacobs, Helen Hull 1962	Peitrangeli, Nicola 1986
+Chace, Malcolm 1961	+Johnston, Bill 1958	Quist, Adrian 1984
+Clark, Clarence 1983	Jones, Ann Haydon 1985	Ralston, Dennis 1987
+Clark, Joseph 1955	+Jones, Perry 1970	+Renshaw, Ernest 1983
+Clothier, William 1956	King, Billie Jean 1987	+Renshaw, William 1983
+Cochet, Henri 1976	Kramer, Jack 1968	+Richards, Vincent 1961
+Connolly, Maureen (Brinker) 1968	Lacoste, Rene 1976	Riggs, Bobby 1967
Court, Margaret Smith . . . 1979	+Lambert Chambers, Dorothea 1981	Roche, Tony 1986
Crawford, Jack 1979	+Larned, William 1956	+Roosevelt, Ellen 1975
+Dod, Lottie 1983	Larsen, Art 1969	Rosewall, Ken 1980
+Doeg, John 1962	Laver, Rod 1981	+Round, Dorothy (Little) . . . 1986
+Doherty, Lawrence 1980	+Lenglen, Suzanne 1978	+Ryan, Elizabeth 1972
+Doherty, Reginald 1980	Lott, George 1964	Santana, Manuel 1984
Drobny, Jaroslav	Mako, Gene 1973	Savitt, Dick 1976
du Pont, Margaret Osborne 1967	+Mallory, Molla Bjurstedt . . 1958	Schroeder, Ted 1966
+Dwight, James 1955		+Sears, Eleonora 1968

International Tennis Hall of Fame (Continued)

+ Sears, Richard 1955
Sedgman, Frank 1979
Segura, Pancho 1984
Seixas, Vic 1971
+ Shields, Frank 1964
+ Slocum, Henry 1955
Smith, Stan 1987
Stolle, Fred 1985
+ Sutton, May (Bundy) 1956

Talbert, Bill 1967
+ Tilson, Bill 1959
Tinling, Ted 1986
+ Townsend, Bertha (Toulmin) 1974
Trabert, Tony 1970

Van Ryn, John 1963
Vines, Ellsworth 1962
+ von Cramm, Gottfried 1977

Wade, Virginia 1989
+ Wagner, Marie 1969
+ Ward, Holcombe 1956
+ Washburn, Watson 1965
+ Whitman, Malcolm 1955
+ Wightman, Hazel Hotchkiss 1957
+ Wilding, Anthony 1978
+ Williams, Richard II 1957
Wood, Sidney 1964
+ Wrenn, Robert 1955
+ Wright, Beals 1956

Contributors

+ Baker, Lawrence, Sr 1975
+ Danzig, Allison 1968
+ Davis, Dwight 1956
+ Gray, David 1985

+ Gustaf V (King of Sweden) 1980
Hester, Slew 1981
+ Hopman, Harry 1978
+ Laney, Al 1979
Martin, Alastair 1973

Martin, William 1982
+ Outerbridge, Mary 1981
+ Pell, Theodore 1966
Tingay, Lance 1982
Van Alen, James 1965

National Track & Field Hall of Fame

Founded in 1974 and originally located in Charleston, W.Va., the National Track and Field Hall of Fame reopened in Indianapolis, Ind., in 1986. Members are listed with year of induction. Note that + indicates deceased members.

+ Abramson, Jesse 1981
Albritton, Dave 1980
Ashenfelter, Horace 1975
+ Bakjian, Andy 1986
Baskin, Weems 1982
+ Bausch, James 1979
Beamon, Bob 1977
Beard, Percy 1981
Bell, Greg 1988
+ Boeckmann, Dee 1976
Botts, Tom 1983
Boston, Ralph 1974
Bowerman, Bill 1981
+ Brundage, Avery 1974
Bush, Jim 1987

+ Calhoun, Lee 1974
Campbell, Milt 1989
Connolly, Harold 1984
Courtney, Tom 1978
+ Cromwell, Dean 1974
+ Cunningham, Glenn 1974
+ Curtis, William 1979

Davenport, Willie 1982
Davis, Glenn 1974
Davis, Harold 1974
Dillard, Harrison 1974
Doherty, Ken 1976
Easton, Bill 1975
+ Elliott, Jumbo 1981
Evans, Lee 1983
Ewell, Barney 1986
+ Ewry, Ray 1974

Ferrell, Barbara 1988
+ Ferris, Dan 1974
+ Flanagan, John 1975
Fosbury, Dick 1981

+ Giegengack, Bob 1978
Gordien, Fortune 1979
+ Griffith, John 1979

+ Hahn, Archie 1983
+ Hamilton, Brutus 1974
+ Hardin, Glenn 1978
+ Haydon, Ted 1975
Hayes, Billy 1976
Hayes, Bob 1976
Haylett, Ward 1979
Held, Bud 1987
Higgins, Ralph 1982
+ Hillman, Harry 1976
Hines, Jim 1979
Houser, Bud 1979
+ Hubbard, DeHart 1979
Hurt, Edward 1975
+ Hutsell, Wilbur 1977

Jenner, Bruce 1980
Johnson, Rafer 1974
Jones, Hayes 1976
+ Jones, Thomas 1977
Jordan, Payton 1982
Kelley, John 1980
Kiviat, Abel 1985
+ Kraenzlein, Alvin 1974

Laird, Ron 1986
+ Littlefield, Clyde 1981

Mathias, Bob 1974
Matson, Randy 1984
Meredith, Ted 1982
+ Metcalfe, Ralph 1975
Mills, Billy 1976
+ Moakley, Jack 1988
Moore, Tom 1988
Morrow, Bobby 1975
+ Murphy, Michael 1974
Myers, Lawrence 1974
Nelson, Cordner 1988
O'Brien, Parry 1974
Oerter, Al 1974
Osborn, Harold 1974
+ Owens, Jesse 1974

+ Paddock, Charley 1976
Patton, Mel 1985
Peacock, Eulace 1987
+ Prefontaine, Steve 1976
+ Ray, Joie 1976
Rice, Greg 1977
Richards, Bob 1975
+ Rose, Ralph 1976
Ryun, Jim 1980
+ Scholz, Jackson 1977
Seagren, Bob 1986
+ Sheppard, Mel 1976
+ Sheridan, Martin 1988
Shorter, Frank 1989
Sime, Dave 1981
+ Simpson, Robert 1974
Smith, Tommie 1978
+ Snyder, Larry 1978
+ Stanfield, Andy 1977
Steers, Les 1974
+ Sullivan, James 1977

Temple, Ed 1989
+ Templeton, Dink 1976
Thomas, John 1985
+ Thomson, Earl 1977
+ Thorpe, Jim 1975
+ Tolan, Eddie 1982
Toomey, Bill 1975
Towns, Forrest 1976

Walker, Leroy 1983
Warmerdam, Cornelius ...1974
White, Willye 1981
Whitfield, Mal 1974
Wilt, Fred 1981
+ Winter, Bud 1985
Woodruff, John 1978
Wottle, Dave 1982
+ Wykoff, Frank 1977

Yancy, Joseph 1984
Young, George 1981

Women

Coachman, Alice 1975
+ Didrikson, Babe 1974
Faggs, Mae 1976
Hall, Evelyne 1988
+ Jackson, Nell 1989

Manning, Madeline 1984
McDaniel, Mildred 1983
McGuire, Edith 1979
Robinson, Betty 1977
Rudolph, Wilma 1974

Stephens, Helen 1975
Tyus, Wyomia 1980
+ Walsh, Stella 1975
Watson, Martha 1987

Retired Uniform Numbers
Major League Baseball

The NY Yankees have retired the most uniform numbers (twelve) in the Major Leagues; followed by Los Angeles and Pittsburgh (eight); the Chicago White Sox and San Francisco (six each); and St. Louis (five). Only three players and a manager have had their number retired by more than one team: Hank Aaron—#44 by Atlanta and Milwaukee; Rod Carew—#29 by Minnesota and California; Frank Robinson—#20 by Cincinnati and Baltimore; and Casey Stengel—#37 by the NY Yankees and NY Mets.

American League

Baltimore
4 Earl Weaver
5 Brooks Robinson
20 Frank Robinson
22 Jim Palmer
33 Eddie Murray

Boston Red Sox
1 Bobby Doerr
4 Joe Cronin
8 Carl Yastrzemski
9 Ted Williams

California Angels
26 Gene Autry
29 Rod Carew

Chicago White Sox
2 Nellie Fox
4 Like Appling
9 Minnie Minoso
11 Luis Aparicio
16 Ted Lyons
19 Billy Pierce

Cleveland Indians
3 Earl Averill
5 Lou Boudreau
19 Bob Feller

Detroit Tigers
2 Charlie Gehringer
5 Hank Greenberg
6 Al Kaline

Kansas City Royals
10 Dick Howser

Milwaukee Brewers
44 Hank Aaron

Minnesota Twins
3 Harmon Killebrew
29 Rod Carew

New York Yankees
1 Billy Martin
3 Babe Ruth
4 Lou Gehrig
5 Joe DiMaggio
7 Mickey Mantle
8 Yogi Berra
  & Bill Dickey

9 Roger Maris
10 Phil Rizzuto
15 Thurman Munson
16 Whitey Ford
32 Elston Howard
37 Casey Stengel

Oakland Athletics
None

Seattle Mariners
None

Texas Rangers
None

Toronto Blue Jays
None

National League

Atlanta Braves
21 Warren Spahn
35 Phil Niekro
41 Eddie Mathews
44 Hank Aaron

Chicago Cubs
14 Ernie Banks
26 Billy Williams

Cincinnati Reds
1 Fred Hutchinson
5 Johnny Bench

Houston Astros
32 Jim Umbricht
40 Don Wilson

Los Angeles Dodgers
1 Pee Wee Reese
4 Duke Snider
19 Jim Gilliam
24 Walter Alston
32 Sandy Koufax
39 Roy Campanella
42 Jackie Robinson
53 Don Drysdale

Montreal Expos
None

New York Mets
14 Gil Hodges
37 Casey Stengel
41 Tom Seaver

Philadelphia Phillies
1 Richie Ashburn
32 Steve Carlton
36 Robin Roberts

Pittsburgh Pirates
1 Billy Meyer
4 Ralph Kiner
8 Willie Stargell
9 Bill Mazeroski
20 Pie Traynor
21 Roberto Clemente
33 Honus Wagner
40 Danny Murtaugh

St. Louis Cardinals
6 Stan Musial
14 Ken Boyer

17 Dizzy Dean
20 Lou Brock
45 Bob Gibson

San Diego Padres
6 Steve Garvey

San Francisco Giants
* Christy Mathewson
* John McGraw
3 Bill Terry
4 Mel Ott
11 Carl Hubbell
24 Willie Mays
27 Juan Marichal
44 Willie McCovey

*Mathewson played and McGraw managed before numbers were worn on major league uniforms.

National Basketball Association

Boston has retired the most uniform numbers (fifteen) in the NBA; followed by Milwaukee, New York and Portland (five each); and Golden St., Philadelphia and Sacramento (four each). Three players in NBA history have had their numbers retired by more than one team: Julius Erving—#32 by New Jersey and #6 by Philadelphia; Oscar Robertson—#14 by Sacramento and #1 by Milwaukee; and Nate Thurmond—#42 by Golden St. and Cleveland.

Atlanta Hawks
9 Bob Pettit
23 Lou Hudson

Boston Celtics
1 Walter A. Brown
2 Red Auerbach
6 Bill Russell
10 Jo Jo White
14 Bob Cousy
15 Tom Heinsohn
16 Tom (Satch) Sanders
17 John Havlicek
18 Dave Cowens
19 Don Nelson
21 Bill Sharman
22 Ed Macauley
23 Frank Ramsey
24 Sam Jones
25 K.C. Jones
Loscy Jim Loscutoff

Charlotte Hornets
None

Chicago Bulls
4 Jerry Sloan

Cleveland Cavaliers
7 Bingo Smith
34 Austin Carr
42 Nate Thurmond

Dallas Mavericks
None

Denver Nuggets
40 Byron Beck
44 Dan Issel

Detroit Pistons
21 Dave Bing

Golden St. Warriors
14 Tom Meschery
16 Al Attles
24 Rick Barry
42 Nate Thurmond

Houston Rockets
23 Calvin Murphy
45 Rudy Tomjanovich

Indiana Pacers
30 George McGinnis
34 Mel Daniels
35 Roger Brown

LA Clippers
None

LA Lakers
13 Wilt Chamberlain
22 Elgin Baylor
44 Jerry West

Miami Heat
None

Minnesota Timberwolves
None

Milwaukee Bucks
1 Oscar Robertson
2 Junior Bridgeman
14 Jon McGlocklin
16 Bob Lanier
32 Brian Winters

New Jersey Nets
4 Wendell Ladner
25 Bill Melchionni
32 Julius Erving

New York Knicks
10 Walt Frazier
15 Earl Monroe
19 Willis Reed
22 Dave DeBusschere
24 Bill Bradley

Retired NBA Numbers (Continued)

Orlando Magic
None

Philadelphia 76ers
6 Julius Erving
15 Hal Greer
24 Bobby Jones
32 Billy Cunningham
Microphone Dave Zinkoff

Phoenix Suns
5 Dick Van Arsdale
33 Alvan Adams
42 Connie Hawkins
44 Paul Westphal

Portland Trail Blazers
13 Dave Twardzik
20 Maurice Lucas
36 Lloyd Neal
45 Geoff Petrie

Sacramento Kings
6 Fans ("Sixth Man")
12 Maurice Stokes
14 Oscar Robertson
27 Jack Twyman
44 Sam Lacey

San Antonio Spurs
13 James Silas
44 George Gervin

Seattle SuperSonics
19 Lenny Wilkens
32 Fred Brown

Utah Jazz
1 Frank Layden
7 Pete Maravich

Washington Bullets
11 Elvin Hayes
25 Gus Johnson
41 Wes Unseld

National Football League

Chicago has retired the most uniform numbers (ten) in the NFL; followed by Indianapolis, the NY Giants, San Francisco (seven each); Detroit (six); and Cleveland, Kansas City, and Philadelphia (five each).

No NFL player has had his uniform number retired by more than one team in the league.

American Conference

Buffalo Bills
None

Cincinnati Bengals
54 Bob Johnson

Cleveland Browns
14 Otto Graham
32 Jim Brown
45 Ernie Davis
46 Don Fleming
76 Lou Groza

Denver Broncos
18 Frank Tripucka
44 Floyd Little

Houston Oilers
34 Earl Campbell
43 Jim Norton
65 Elvin Bethea

Indianapolis Colts
19 Johnny Unitas
22 Buddy Young
24 Lenny Moore
70 Art Donovan
77 Jim Parker
82 Raymond Berry
89 Gino Marchetti

Kansas City Chiefs
16 Len Dawson
28 Abner Haynes
33 Stone Johnson
36 Mack Lee Hill
78 Bobby Bell

Los Angeles Raiders
None

Miami Dolphins
12 Bob Griese

N.England Patriots
20 Gino Cappelletti
79 Jim Hunt
89 Bob Dee

New York Jets
12 Joe Namath
13 Don Maynard

Pittsburgh Steelers
None

San Diego Chargers
14 Dan Fouts

Seattle Seahawks
12 Fans ("12th Man")

National Conference

Atlanta Falcons
31 William Andrews
60 Tommy Nobis
57 Jeff Van Note

Chicago Bears
3 Bronko Nagurski
5 George McAfee
28 Willie Galimore
34 Walter Payton
41 Brian Piccolo
42 Sid Luckman
56 Bill Hewitt
61 Bill George
66 Bulldog Turner
77 Red Grange
GSH George Halas

Dallas Cowboys
None

Detroit Lions
7 Dutch Clark
22 Bobby Layne
37 Doak Walker
56 Joe Schmidt
85 Chuck Hughes
88 Charlie Sanders

Green Bay Packers
3 Tony Canadeo
14 Don Hutson
15 Bart Starr
66 Ray Nitschke

Los Angeles Rams
7 Bob Waterfield
74 Merlin Olsen

Minnesota Vikings
10 Fran Tarkenton

New Orleans Saints
31 Jim Taylor
81 Doug Atkins

New York Giants
1 Ray Flaherty
7 Mel Hein
14 Y.A.Tittle
32 Al Blozis
40 Joe Morrison
42 Charlie Conerly
50 Ken Strong

Philadelphia Eagles
15 Steve Van Buren
40 Tom Brookshier
44 Pete Retzlaff
60 Chuck Bednarik
70 Al Wistert

Phoenix Cardinals
8 Larry Wilson
77 Stan Mauldin
88 J.V.Cain
99 Marshall Goldberg

San Francisco 49ers
12 John Brodie
34 Joe Perry
37 Jimmy Johnson
39 Hugh McElhenny
70 Charlie Krueger
73 Lou Nomellini
87 Dwight Clark

Tampa Bay Buccaneers
63 Lee Roy Selmon

Washington Redskins
33 Sammy Baugh

National Hockey League

Boston has retired the most uniform numbers (seven) in the NHL, followed by Montreal (six), Chicago (four), Hartford and Philadelphia three each).

Two players in NHL history have had their numbers retired by more than one team: Gordie Howe—#9 by Detroit and Hartford; and Bobby Hull—#9 by Chicago and Winnipeg.

Campbell Conference

Calgary Flames
None

Chicago Blackhawks
1 Glenn Hall
9 Bobby Hull
21 Stan Mikita
35 Tony Esposito

Detroit Red Wings
6 Larry Aurie
9 Gordie Howe

Edmonton Oilers
3 Al Hamilton

Los Angeles Kings
30 Rogie Vachon

Minnesota North Stars
19 Bill Masterton

St.Louis Blues
3 Bob Gassoff
8 Barclay Plager
11 Brian Sutter

Toronto Maple Leafs
5 Bill Barilko
6 Ace Bailey

Vancouver Canucks
11 Wayne Maki

Winnipeg Jets
9 Bobby Hull

Wales Conference

Boston Bruins
2 Eddie Shore
3 Lionel Hitchman
4 Bobby Orr
5 Dit Clapper
7 Phil Esposito
9 Johnny Bucyk
15 Milt Schmidt

Buffalo Sabres
2 Tim Horton

Hartford Whalers
2 Rick Ley
9 Gordie Howe
19 John McKenzie

Montreal Canadiens
2 Doug Harvey
4 Jean Beliveau
 & Aurele Joliat
7 Howie Morenz
9 Maurice Richard
10 Guy Lafleur
16 Henri Richard
 & Elmer Lach

New Jersey Devils
None

New York Islanders
5 Denis Potvin

New York Rangers
1 Eddie Giacomin
7 Rod Gilbert

Philadelphia Flyers
1 Bernie Parent
4 Barry Ashbee
16 Bobby Clarke

Pittsburgh Penguins
21 Michel Briere

Quebec Nordiques
3 J.C.Tremblay
8 Marc Tardif

Washington Capitals
7 Yvon Labre

Awards

James E. Sullivan Award, 1930-88

Presented annually by The Amateur Athletic Union since 1930. The JamesE. Sullivan Memorial Award is named after the former AAU president and given to the athlete who "by his or her performance, example and influence as an amateur, has done the most during the year to advance the cause of sportsmanship."
An athlete cannot win the award twice.

Year		Year		Year	
1930	**Bobby Jones**, golf	1950	**Fred Wilt**, track	1970	**John Kinsella**, swimming
1931	**Barney Berlinger**, track	1951	**Bob Richards**, track	1971	**Mark Spitz**, swimming
1932	**Jim Bausch**, track	1952	**Horace Ashenfelter**, track	1972	**Frank Shorter**, track
1933	**Glenn Cunningham**, track	1953	**Sammy Lee**, diving	1973	**Bill Walton**, basketball
1934	**Bill Bonthron**, track	1954	**Mal Whitfield**, track	1974	**Rich Wohlhuter**, track
1935	**Lawson Little**, golf	1955	**Harrison Dillard**, track	1975	**Tim Shaw**, swimming
1936	**Glenn Morris**, track	1956	**Pat McCormick**, diving	1976	**Bruce Jenner**, track
1937	**Don Budge**, tennis	1957	**Bobby Morrow**, track	1977	**John Naber**, swimming
1938	**Don Lash**, track	1958	**Glenn Davis**, track	1978	**Tracy Caulkins**, swimming
1939	**Joe Burk**, rowing	1959	**Parry O'Brien**, track	1979	**Kurt Thomas**, gymnastics
1940	**Greg Rice**, track	1960	**Rafer Johnson**, track	1980	**Eric Heiden**, speed skating
1941	**Leslie MacMitchell**, track	1961	**Wilma Rudolph**, track	1981	**Carl Lewis**, track
1942	**Cornelius Warmerdam**, track	1962	**Jim Beatty**, track	1982	**Mary Decker**, track
1943	**Gilbert Dodds**, track	1963	**John Pennel**, track	1983	**Edwin Moses**, track
1944	**Ann Curtis**, swimming	1964	**Don Schollander**, swimming	1984	**Greg Louganis**, diving
1945	**Doc Blanchard**, football	1965	**Bill Bradley**, basketball	1985	**Joan B. Samuelson**, track
1946	**Arnold Tucker**, football	1966	**Jim Ryun**, track	1986	**Jackie Joyner-Kersee**, track
1947	**John B. Kelly, Jr.**, rowing	1967	**Randy Matson**, track	1987	**Jim Abbott**, baseball
1948	**Bob Mathias**, track	1968	**Debbie Meyer**, swimming	1988	**Florence Griffith Joyner**, track
1949	**Dick Button**, skating	1969	**Bill Toomey**, track		

Honda Broderick Cup

To the outstanding collegiate woman athlete of the year in NCAA competition. Winner is chosen from nominees in each of the NCAA's 10 competitive sports. Final voting is done by member athletic directors. Award is named after founder and sportswear manufacturer Thomas Broderick.

Year	Winner, School	Sport	Year	Winner, School	Sport
1976-77	**Lucy Harris**, Delta St	basketball	1982-83	**Deitre Collins**, Hawaii	volleyball
1977-78	**Ann Meyers**, UCLA	basketball	1983-84	**Tracy Caulkins**, Florida (2)	swimming
1978-79	**Nancy Lieberman**, Old Dominion	basketball		& **Cheryl Miller**, USC	basketball
1979-80	**Julie Shea**, N.C.State	track & field	1984-85	**Jackie Joyner**, UCLA	track & field
1980-81	**Jill Sterkel**, Texas	swimming	1985-86	**Kamie Ethridge**, Texas	basketball
1981-82	**Tracy Caulkins**, Florida	swimming	1986-87	**Mary T.Meagher**, California	swimming
			1987-88	**Teresa Weatherspoon**, La.Tech	basketball

Awards (Continued)

Associated Press Athletes of the Year, 1931-88

Male

Year		Year		Year	
1931	Pepper Martin, baseball	1950	Jim Konstanty, baseball	1970	George Blanda, pro football
1932	Gene Sarazen, golf	1951	Dick Kazmaier, football	1971	Lee Trevino, golf
1933	Carl Hubbell, baseball	1952	Bob Mathias, track	1972	Mark Spitz, swimming
1934	Dizzy Dean, baseball	1953	Ben Hogan, golf	1973	O.J.Simpson, pro football
1935	Joe Louis, boxing	1954	Willie Mays, baseball	1974	Muhammad Ali, boxing
1936	Jesse Owens, track & field	1955	Hopalong Cassidy, football	1975	Fred Lynn, baseball
1937	Don Budge, tennis	1956	Mickey Mantle, baseball	1976	Bruce Jenner, track
1938	Don Budge, tennis	1957	Ted Williams, baseball	1977	Steve Cauthen, horse racing
1939	Nile Kinnick, football	1958	Herb Elliot, track	1978	Ron Guidry, baseball
1940	Tom Harmon, football	1959	Ingemar Johansson, boxing	1979	Willie Stargell, baseball
1941	Joe DiMaggio, baseball	1960	Rafer Johnson, track	1980	US Olympic Hockey Team
1942	Frank Sinkwich, football	1961	Roger Maris, baseball	1981	John McEnroe, tennis
1943	Gunder Haegg, track	1962	Maury Wills, baseball	1982	Wayne Gretzky, hockey
1944	Byron Nelson, golf	1963	Sandy Koufax, baseball	1983	Carl Lewis, track
1945	Byron Nelson, golf	1964	Don Schollander, swimming	1984	Carl Lewis, track
1946	Glenn Davis, football	1965	Sandy Koufax, baseball	1985	Dwight Gooden, baseball
1947	Johnny Lujack, football	1966	Frank Robinson, baseball	1986	Larry Bird, pro basketball
1948	Lou Boudreau, baseball	1967	Carl Yastrzemski, baseball	1987	Ben Johnson, track
1949	Leon Hart, football	1968	Denny McLain, baseball	1988	Orel Hershiser, baseball
		1969	Tom Seaver, baseball		

Female

Year		Year		Year	
1931	Helene Madison, swimming	1950	Babe Didrikson Zaharias, golf	1970	Chi Cheng, track
1932	Babe Didrikson, track	1951	Maureen Connolly, tennis	1971	Evonne Goolagong, tennis
1933	Helen Jacobs, tennis	1952	Maureen Connolly, tennis	1972	Olga Korbut, gymnastics
1934	Virginia Van Wie, golf	1953	Maureen Connolly, tennis	1973	Billie Jean King, tennis
1935	Helen Wills Moody, tennis	1954	Babe Didrikson Zaharias, golf	1974	Chris Evert, tennis
1936	Helen Stephens, track	1955	Patty Berg, golf	1975	Chris Evert, tennis
1937	Katherine Rawls, swimming	1956	Pat McCormick, diving	1976	Nadia Comaneci, gymnastics
1938	Patty Berg, golf	1957	Althea Gibson, tennis	1977	Chris Evert, tennis
1939	Alice Marble, tennis	1958	Althea Gibson, tennis	1978	Nancy Lopez, golf
1940	Alice Marble, tennis	1959	Maria Bueno, tennis	1979	Tracy Austin, tennis
1941	Betty Hicks Newell, golf	1960	Wilma Rudolph, track	1980	Chris Evert Lloyd, tennis
1942	Gloria Callen, swimming	1961	Wilma Rudolph, track	1981	Tracy Austin, tennis
1943	Patty Berg, golf	1962	Dawn Fraser, swimming	1982	Mary Decker Tabb, track
1944	Ann Curtis, swimming	1963	Mickey Wright, golf	1983	Martina Navratilova, tennis
1945	Babe Didrikson Zaharias, golf	1964	Mickey Wright, golf	1984	Mary Lou Retton, gymnastics
1946	Babe Didrikson Zaharias, golf	1965	Kathy Whitworth, golf	1985	Nancy Lopez, golf
1947	Babe Didrikson Zaharias, golf	1966	Kathy Whitworth, golf	1986	Martina Navratilova, tennis
1948	Fanny Blankers-Koen, track	1967	Billie Jean King, tennis	1987	Jackie Joyner-Kersee, track
1949	Marlene Bauer, golf	1968	Peggy Fleming, skating	1988	Florence Griffith Joyner, track
		1969	Debbie Meyer, swimming		

Sports Illustrated Sportsman of the Year, 1954-88

Selected annually by **Sports Illustrated** magazine since 1954.

Year		Year		Year	
1954	Roger Bannister, track	1969	Tom Seaver, baseball	1983	Mary Decker, track
1955	Johnny Podres, baseball	1970	Bobby Orr, hockey	1984	Edwin Moses, track &
1956	Bobby Morrow, track	1971	Lee Trevino, golf		Mary Lou Retton, gymnastics
1957	Stan Musial, baseball	1972	Billie Jean King, tennis	1985	K.Abdul-Jabbar, basketball
1958	Rafer Johnson, track		& John Wooden, basketball	1986	Joe Paterno, football
1959	Ingemar Johansson, boxing	1973	Jackie Stewart, auto racing	1987	''8 Athletes Who Care''
1960	Arnold Palmer, golf	1974	Muhammad Ali, boxing		Bob Bourne, hockey
1961	Jerry Lucas, basketball	1975	Pete Rose, baseball		Kip Keino, track
1962	Terry Baker, football	1976	Chris Evert, tennis		Judi Brown King, track
1963	Pete Rozelle, pro football	1977	Steve Cauthen, horse racing		Dale Murphy, baseball
1964	Ken Venturi, golf	1978	Jack Nicklaus, golf		Chip Rives, football
1965	Sandy Koufax, baseball	1979	Terry Bradshaw, football		Patty Sheehan, golf
1966	Jim Ryun, track		& Willie Stargell, baseball		Rory Sparrow, basketball
1967	Carl Yastrzemski, baseball	1980	US Olympic hockey team		Reggie Williams, football
1968	Bill Russell, basketball	1981	Sugar Ray Leonard, boxing	1988	Orel Hershiser, baseball
		1982	Wayne Gretzky, hockey		

The Sporting News Man of the Year, 1968-88

Selected annually by **The Sporting News** since 1968.

Year		Year		Year	
1968	**Denny McLain**, baseball	1975	**Archie Griffin**, football	1982	**Whitey Herzog**, baseball
1969	**Tom Seaver**, baseball	1976	**Larry O'Brien**, basketball	1983	**Bowie Kuhn**, baseball
1970	**John Wooden**, basketball	1977	**Steve Cauthen**, horse racing	1984	**Peter Ueberroth**, LA Oly.
1971	**Lee Trevino**, golf	1978	**Ron Guidry**, baseball	1985	**Pete Rose**, baseball
1972	**Charles O. Finley**, baseball	1979	**Willie Stargell**, baseball	1986	**Larry Bird**, pro basketball
1973	**O.J. Simpson**, pro football	1980	**George Brett**, baseball	1987	**No award**
1974	**Lou Brock**, baseball	1981	**Wayne Gretzky**, hockey	1988	**Jackie Joyner-Kersee**, track

The 40 Who Changed Sports From 1946-86

Selected by **Sport Magazine** for its 40th Anniversary Issue, December, 1986.

Auto Racing
Bill France, Sr.

Baseball
Hank Aaron
Curt Flood
Mickey Mantle
Willie Mays
Marvin Miller
Branch Rickey
Jackie Robinson
Pete Rose
Casey Stengel
Ted Williams

Basketball
Red Auerbach
Wilt Chamberlain
Bob Cousy
Bill Russell
John Wooden

Boxing
Muhammad Ali
Jim Norris
Sugar Ray Robinson

Football
Jim Brown
Paul Brown
Bear Bryant
Al Davis
Vince Lombardi
Joe Namath
Pete Rozelle

Golf
Jack Nicklaus
Arnold Palmer

Hockey
Wayne Gretzky
Bobby Orr

Horse Racing
Bill Shoemaker

Literature
Jim Bouton

Olympics
Abebe Bikila
Avery Brundage

Soccer
Pelé

Television
Roone Arledge
Howard Cosell

Tennis
Chris Evert
Billie Jean King
Martina Navratilova

Sportscasters & Sportswriters of the Year

Presented annually since 1959 by the National Sportscasters and Sportswriters Association, based in Salisbury, N.C. Voting is done by NSSA members and selected national media.

Sportscaster of the Year

Year		Year		Year	
1959	**Lindsey Nelson**, NBC	1970	**Chris Schenkel**, ABC	1980	**Dick Enberg**, NBC
1960	**Lindsey Nelson**, NBC	1971	**Ray Scott**, CBS		**& Al Michaels**, ABC
1961	**Lindsey Nelson**, NBC	1972	**Keith Jackson**, ABC	1981	**Dick Enberg**, NBC
1962	**Lindsey Nelson**, NBC	1973	**Keith Jackson**, ABC	1982	**Vin Scully**, LA Dodgers/NBC
1963	**Chris Schenkel**, CBS	1974	**Keith Jackson**, ABC	1983	**Al Michaels**, ABC
1964	**Chris Schenkel**, ABC	1975	**Keith Jackson**, ABC	1984	**John Madden**, CBS
1965	**Vin Scully**, LA Dodgers	1976	**Keith Jackson**, ABC	1985	**Bob Costas**, NBC
1966	**Curt Gowdy**, NBC	1977	**Pat Summerall**, CBS	1986	**Al Michaels**, ABC
1967	**Chris Schenkel**, ABC	1978	**Vin Scully**, LA Dodgers/CBS	1987	**Bob Costas**, NBC
1968	**Ray Scott**, CBS	1979	**Dick Enberg**, NBC	1988	**Bob Costas**, NBC
1969	**Curt Gowdy**, NBC				

Sportswriter of the Year

Year		Year		Year	
1959	**Red Smith**, NY Herald-Trib	1970	**Jim Murray**, LA Times	1980	**Will Grimsley**, AP
1960	**Red Smith**, NY Herald-Trib	1971	**Jim Murray**, LA Times	1981	**Will Grimsley**, AP
1961	**Red Smith**, NY Herald-Trib	1972	**Jim Murray**, LA Times	1982	**Frank Deford**, Sports Ill.
1962	**Red Smith**, NY Herald-Trib	1973	**Jim Murray**, LA Times	1983	**Will Grimsley**, AP
1963	**Arthur Daley**, NY Times	1974	**Jim Murray**, LA Times	1984	**Frank Deford**, Sports Ill.
1964	**Jim Murray**, LA Times	1975	**Jim Murray**, LA Times	1985	**Frank Deford**, Sports Ill.
1965	**Red Smith**, NY Herald-Trib	1976	**Jim Murray**, LA Times	1986	**Frank Deford**, Sports Ill.
1966	**Jim Murray**, LA Times	1977	**Jim Murray**, LA Times	1987	**Frank Deford**, Sports Ill.
1967	**Jim Murray**, LA Times	1978	**Will Grimsley**, AP	1988	**Frank Deford**, Sports Ill.
1968	**Jim Murray**, LA Times	1979	**Jim Murray**, LA Times		
1969	**Jim Murray**, LA Times				

Awards (Continued)
Pulitzer Prizes

The Pulitzer Prizes for journalism, letters and music have been presented annually since 1917 in the name of Joseph Pulitzer, the former publisher of **The World** in New York City. Prizes are awarded by the president of Columbia University on the recommendation of the board of review.

In 72 years, only five Pulitzer Prizes have been given for sports writing.

Reporting, No Edition Time
1956 **Arthur Daley**, NY Times columnist

Commentary
1976 **Red Smith**, NY Times columnist
1981 **Dave Anderson**, NY Times columnist

Specialized Reporting
1985 **Randall Savage & Jackie Crosby,** Macon (Ga.) Telegraph and News, for investigation of academics and athletics at U.of Georgia and Georgia Tech.

Investigative Reporting
1986 **Jeffrey Marx & Michael York,** Lexington (Ky.) Herald-Leader, for investigation basketball program at U.of Kentucky and other major colleges.

Peabody Awards

Presented annually since 1940 for outstanding achievement in radio and radio broadcasting. Only 10 Peabodys have been given for sports programming.

Named after Georgia banker and philanthropist George Foster Peabody, the awards are administered by the Henry W.Grady College of Journalism and Mass Communication at the University of Georgia.

Television (9)
Year Winner
1960 **CBS** for coverage of 1960 Winter and Summer Olympic Games (for Outstanding Contribution to International Understanding).
1966 ABC's **"Wide World of Sports"** (for Outstanding Achievement in Promotion of International Understanding).
1968 **ABC Sports** coverage of both the 1968 Winter and Summer Olympic Games.
1972 **ABC Sports** coverage of the 1972 Summer Olympics in Munich.
1973 **Joe Garagiola** of NBC Sports (for "The Baseball World of Joe Garagiola").
1976 **ABC Sports** coverage of both the 1976 Winter and Summer Olympic Games.
1984 **Roone Arledge,** president of ABC News & Sports (for significant contributions to television news and sports programming.
1986 **WFAA-TV**, Dallas for its investigation of the Southern Methodist University football program.
1988 **Jim McKay** of ABC Sports (for pioneering efforts and career accomplishments in the world of TV sports).

Radio (1)
Year Winner
1974 **WSB** radio in Atlanta for "Henry Aaron: A Man with a Mission."

Wide World Photos

CBS president **Laurence Tisch** (left) and baseball commissioner **Peter Ueberroth** shake hands Dec. 14, 1988 after closing deal on record $1.06 billion television contract.

BUSINESS & MEDIA

INSIDE

Elsewhere in Almanac
For related information refer to individual sports chapters, plus Arenas & Ballparks and the Year in Review calendar.

*Boom times in the sports biz—
the cost of teams, TV rights
combine to put the "gross"
in Gross National Sports Products.*

BUSINESS & MEDIA

1988-89 YEAR IN REVIEW

by John McManus

Call 1989 a year when every sports professional, competitor, and fan awakened to the somewhat grim reality that, these days, as much happens off the field as on it.

From the public fall from grace of Pete Rose to the backroom wrangling to find a successor to Pete Rozelle. From athletes who charge kids for autographs to the ever-escalating cost of exclusive TV rights. At no time has it been more clear that sports is big business. The pages of the **Wall Street Journal, Business Week** and other financial publications now devote obligatory coverage to sports franchise transactions, major television rights deals, marketing and endorsement contracts and other sports news, proving that sports is not only a business, but an industry—a complex web of individuals, organizations and operations driven by glamour, competition and money.

***

John McManus is a staff writer with **Adweek** magazine and writes frequently on sports business and media.

It's an industry that has been quantified by Richard Sandomir, who developed the Gross National Sports Product for **Sports Inc.**, a magazine that reported weekly on sports business. Sandomir studied the economics of each piece in the sports pie, ranging from leisure and participant sports, to sporting goods, to athlete endorsements, to stadium and arena construction, and he painted a fiscal tableau that shows sports to be one of the country's top 25 industries, No. 23 in fact, ahead of the auto and security and commodity brokerage sectors of the United States' $4.52- trillion national economy. The projection for the GNSP in 1989: $56.1 billion.

As Sandomir observed in **Sports Inc.**, "Nearly every sector of the sports economy is growing. More people are attending sporting events, consuming beer and hot dogs and buying magazines and books. Licensed products are flying off retail store shelves. Corporate sponsors are seeking involvement in more events. Companies are finding stadium and
(continued on page 363)

IOC vice president **Richard Pound** (left) announcing in New York, Dec. 1, 1988, that NBC Sports president **Arthur Watson** (right) had won the exclusive U.S. television rights to the 1992 Summer Olympics for $401 million.

Come to the Table with a Dog That Will Hunt.

Negotiating a TV rights deal has never been a game for the faint of heart.

Like in the spring of 1979, when an entourage of buttondown CBS executives went to Dallas and sat across the conference table from Field Stovell, the curmudgeonly grandpappy of the Cotton Bowl, and tried to cut a deal with him to renew their rights to televise the event for another three years.

Frank Smith, then CBS Sports president, was accompanied by Neal Pilson, who was CBS Sports' head of business affairs at the time, and Kevin O'Malley then director of program acquisitions and now TBS vice president for sports programming. Smith read aloud a three-page document, spelling out in perfect legalese the terms and conditions of the three-year pact. Then, after a pause, Smith read the financials of the offer.

Stovell, not missing a beat, turned to his lawyer and said, "That dog won't hunt."

Smith whispered to O'Malley, "What's he saying?"

O'Malley whispered to Smith, "He's saying, 'That dog won't hunt.' "

"I know that," said Smith, "but what's he *saying?*" O'Malley shrugged, but eventually Smith got Stovell's message. CBS upped its ante and renewed its Cotton Bown deal.

Sports television has become a picaresque game of billionaire rogues and heroic risks, and the object of the game has become clear to all players: Come to the table with a dog that will hunt. The television has, without doubt, become the electronic beacon around which the sports industry revolves. In order to gain the exposure needed to fuel its growth and revenues, each sport now plays for its portion of television's bounty. Witness, for example, the National Football League's proposed international spinoff, the World League of American Football. The WLAF would have been a go for the Spring 1990 but for one problem: the new league could not secure a television contract, so its debut has been postponed to 1991.

Indeed, evidence has begun mounting that TV sports is going haywire as he broadcast and cable network titans clash ferociously for big ticket sports programming, sending rights fees soaring to unprecedented heights.

The spiral was set in motion in May of 1988 when CBS paid $243 million for the 1992 Albertville Olympics.

In December 1988, NBC, which had sharply criticized CBS's Albertville bid, paid $401 million for the 1992 Summer Games in Barcelona, $101 million more than it had paid for the Seoul Games of 1988. A week later, Madison Square Garden Network paid $500 million for local rights to the New York Yankees through the year 2000, followed the next week by a $1.06-billion CBS offer to secure rights to Major League Baseball through 1993, a 37.5% premium over the previous network contract.

So far in 1989, two more huge deals have been struck. In January, amid fierce competition from Turner Broadcasting System (TBS) and SportsChannel America, ESPN agreed to a four-year, $400 million contract with Major League Baseball through 1993. Then in August, CBS came away with another gem for its mounting cache of TV sports treasures: the 1994 Winter Olympics in Lillehammer, Norway. The price tag this time was $300 million, a 23% increase over what the same network paid for the Albertville Winter Games just eight months earlier.

"Every time I think that the marketplace has to have peaked out, it comes back and reaches more staggering heights," said former CBS Sports chief Barry Frank, who is now senior corporate vice president at International Management Group's Trans World International. It was Barry who negotiated the Lillehammer TV rights deal on behalf of the International Olympics Committee.

As a result of this sports rights feeding frenzy, CBS has cornered the TV sports market for 1990 (see page 365). Next year, it will carry Super Bowl XXIV, the NCAA basketball tournament and Final Four, the NBA playoffs and Finals, the Daytona 500 in auto racing, the Masters in golf, the U.S. Open in tennis, and Major League Baseball's All-Star Game, league playoffs and World Series. And that's not including the Winter Olympics in 1992 and '94.

NBC and ABC, if they want to play the big ticket sports game, have to bite the bullet and try to derail CBS in its attempt to retain dominance. In the last quarter of 1989 and the first quarter of 1990, broadcast and cable television networks will ante up an estimated $2.7 billion in new contracts with the NFL, the NBA, the NCAA basketball tournament, and the College Football Association.

Only when those negotiations are over will we learn which networks had the dogs that would hunt.

Olympian Heights of TV Rights

The reported cost of securing exclusive U.S. television rights for the Olympic Games has skyrocketed over the last 30 years. In 1960, CBS acquired the Winter Olympics for $50,000. This August, CBS agreed to pay $300 million for the 1994 Winter Games—an increase of 6,000 percent. In the same time, the cost of the Summer Games has leaped from just under $400,000 to just over $400 million.

Year	Games	Location	Rights Fee	Net
1960	Winter	Squaw Valley	$50,000	CBS
	Summer	Rome	$394,000	CBS
1964	Winter	Innsbruck	$597,000	ABC
	Summer	Tokyo	$1.5 million	NBC
1968	Winter	Grenoble	$2.5 million	ABC
	Summer	Mexico City	$4.5 million	ABC
1972	Winter	Sapporo	$6.4 million	NBC
	Summer	Munich	$7.5 million	ABC
1976	Winter	Innsbruck	$10 million	ABC
	Summer	Montreal	$25 million	ABC
1980	Winter	Lake Placid	$15.5 million	ABC
	Summer	Moscow	$85 million	NBC
1984	Winter	Sarajevo	$91.5 million	ABC
	Summer	Los Angeles	$225 million	ABC
1988	Winter	Calgary	$309 million	ABC
	Summer	Seoul	$300 million	NBC
1992	Winter	Albertville	$243 million	CBS
	Summer	Barcelona	$401 million	NBC
1994	Winter	Lillehammer	$300 million	CBS

arena signage an increasingly effective buy. Consumers are paying up for better, higher-priced sporting goods even if they're not always buying more goods. New stadia and arenas are going up and more are planned. And baseball card sales almost defy logic."

In sports sponsorship alone, the numbers are staggering. Overall, 2,800 corporations had $2.1 billion earmarked for sports marketing in 1989, according to the Chicago-based Special Events Report. That represents a 20% increase in spending from last year and a 150% increase from 1985.

But two events in 1989 could throw a wrench into the sports sponsorship machinery. The $25-billion leveraged buy-out of RJR Nabisco by Kohlberg Kravis Roberts & Co., consummated in the Spring of 1989, may go down as one of the more significant events in the world of sports sponsorships. KKR, eyeing RJR Nabisco's $3 billion-a-year in debt obligations, will undoubtedly cut back from the $60 million the company annually spends on sports involvement ranging from the Winston Cup and Camel GT auto racing circuits to PGA golf, and will most likely look for a buyer for its 20% stake in ESPN.

The other ominous sign is the ban on beer advertising that NCAA executive director Richard Schultz has proposed for games during the NCAA basketball tournament. Many brewing companies fear that a beer commercial prohibition of any kind during the tournament would lead to further bans on all college sports telecasts. Such a development would not sit well with breweries that believe they are entitled to promote legal products to their strategically targeted audiences.

In baseball, commissioner Francis Vincent faces the considerable challenge of hammering out a new collective bargaining agreement to replace the present contract between teams and players, which expires on Dec. 31, 1989. Labor strife is a distinct possibility and both the owners and the Major League Players Association have set aside considerable reserve funds in the event of a strike next season. An extra ingredient in the negotiations mix is a proposed new baseball league which would bid for the

The NCAA's **Dick Schultz** wants to rid the basketball tournament of beer ads.

services of free agents and recruit new talent from an already understocked pool of potential major leaguers.

In the NFL, Pete Rozelle's decision in March to step down after 29 years as commissioner precipitated a smoldering feud between the league's old-guard owners and many of its newer and younger ones over the selection of a successor. The old-guard's candidate, New Orleans general manager Jim Finks, was voted down in July when the dissidents demanded that other candidates from outside the NFL be considered. The dispute meant that Rozelle was still commissioner when the new season kicked off in September.

NFL management will be hard-pressed to replace Rozelle, who for many years was regarded as the consummate TV sports negotiator. Twelve of the league's 28 clubs lost money in 1988 and with attendance levels holding steady, it will be the job of the man who replaces Rozelle to garner greater revenues from the networks.

Meanwhile, many sectors of the sports economy are booming, especially in the area of professional team transactions. A line forms every time a team is rumored to be up for sale, no matter what the

Wide World Photos

New Denver Nuggets owner **Bertram Lee** (left) and partner **Peter Bynoe** (right) join new team president **David Checketts** at July 10 press conference announcing their purchase of the NBA club.

sport. With such bidding, family ownership is disappearing, replaced by individual buyers and investor groups possessed of significant fortunes and diverse and profitable businesses.

In 1988, two NBA teams—the Portland Trail Blazers and San Antonio Spurs—changed hands for $70 million and $60 million, respectively. What is more, four expansion teams—the Miami Heat, Orlando Magic, Charlotte Hornets and Minnesota Timberwolves—paid $32.5 million each to join the league. That admission price is an increase of $20.5 million from what the Dallas Mavericks had to pay the last time the NBA expanded in 1980.

The NBA's 1988-89 newcomers, Miami and Charlotte, packed fans into sold-out new arenas while the NBA soared to record-breaking attendance levels for the sixth consecutive year. And in July, Bertram Lee and Peter Bynoe broke new ground by becoming professional sports' first black owners, leading a group of investors in the $65- million purchase of the Denver Nuggets.

Fourteen years ago, the Nordstrom family gained a controlling interest in the NFL's Seattle Seahawks for $8.16 million. They sold the team for $80 million in 1989. The New England Patriots also went for $80 million—to electric shaver pitch man Victor Kiam, whose TV commercials say he liked his Remington so much he bought the whole company.

The year's blockbuster sole, however, came in Dallas where Arkansas oilman Jerry Jones and a group of investors bought the Cowboys in a transaction worth as much as $150 million, including the operating rights to Texas Stadium. Jones liked the Cowboys so much he fired Tom Landry and Tex Schramm, the only head coach and general manager the team had ever known.

Elsewhere, the Hartford Whalers, who play in the NHL's smallest U.S. market, fetched $31 million only seven years after the Detroit Red Wings were bought for a mere $8 million. Hockey's biggest sale of 1988—majority control of the Los Angeles Kings to Bruce McNall for $20 million

—turned into a shrewd investment when McNall followed it up by bringing Wayne Gretzky to L.A. for $20 million more and turning the franchise around.

Finally, the Baltimore Orioles, Texas Rangers and Seattle Mariners all found new owners in the last 12 months. The Mariners, who have never had a winning season in 13 years, were snapped up for $75 million by radio moguls Jeff Smulyan and Michael Browning of Indianapolis. The new owners insisted the Mariners will not be moved but stay tuned, their lease at the Kingdome runs out in 1994. Former M's owner George Argyros cleaned up in the deal, considering his initial outlay for the team in 1981 was $13.1 million, of which only $2.6 million was his own money.

Competition to land a baseball team has driven the market value of the game's three most lucrative franchises—the Los Angeles Dodgers, New York Mets and New York Yankees—to $200 million and clubs like the Kansas City Royals and St. Louis Cardinals could find buyers at $100 million.

"Is the sports economy unstoppable?" asks writer Richard Sandomir. "Not entirely, but as viewed within the context of the Gross National Sports Product it is extremely healthy." And as U.S. sports go international and the trade barriers fall in Europe in 1992 and electronic media continue to shrink the globe, 1989 will stand as the year that sports finally recognized itself as a cohesive business marketplace.

Network TV Rights: Who Owns What

With NFL, NBA, CFA college football, and NCAA basketball tournament contracts up for renewal in late 1989 and early 1990, here is the network-by-network roster of TV rights as of Oct. 1, 1989.

ABC
NFL Football—Monday Night Football (1989)
Major League Baseball—1989 World Series
Pan Am Games—1991 (Cuba)
College Football—Big 10/Pac-10 regular season, Rose Bowl, Sugar Bowl
NCAA Basketball—regular season
Men's Golf—US Open, British Open, PGA
Bowling—PBA Tour
Horse Racing—Kentucky Derby, Preakness, Belmont Stakes
Cycling—Tour de France
Auto Racing—Indianapolis, 500 CART, NASCAR

CBS
NFL Football—NFC regular season, NFC Playoffs, Super Bowl XXIV (1990)
NBA Basketball—regular season, All-Star game, playoffs, finals (1990)
College Football—CFA regular season, Army-Navy, Cotton Bowl
NCAA Basketball—regular season, Tournament (1990)
Major League Baseball—regular season, All-Star game, playoffs, World Series (1990-93)
Golf—Masters
Tennis—US Open
Olympics—1992 and 1994 Winter Games
Auto Racing—Daytona 500, NASCAR, CART

NBC
NFL Football—AFC regular season, AFC playoffs, Super Bowl
College Football—Orange Bowl, Fiesta Bowl
Major League Baseball—1989 league playoffs
NCAA Basketball—regular season
Tennis—French Open, Wimbledon
Horse Racing—Breeders' Cup
Figure Skating—World Championships (1990-94)
Olympics—1992 Summer Games
Auto Racing—CART
World Track & Field Championships–1991 (Tokyo)

ESPN
NFL Football—Sunday Night Football, Pro Bowl (1990)
Major League Baseball—regular season (1990-93)
College Football—regular season CFA, Big 10, Pac-10
College Basketball—regular season, NCAA tournament (early rounds)
Golf—US Open, British Open, PGA (all early rounds
Tennis—Australian Open, French Open (early rounds)
Auto Racing—CART, NASCAR, Formula-One
Bowling—PBA and LPBT tours
Horse Racing—The Hambletonian

TBS/TNT
NBA Basketball—regular season, playoffs (TNT)
NBA Basketball—Atlanta Hawks (TBS)
College Football—SEC regular season (TBS)
Major League Baseball—Atlanta Braves (TBS)
Auto Racing—NASCAR (TBS)
Goodwill Games—1990 Games (TBS)
Soccer—1990 World Cup (TBS)
Olympics—cable TV 1992 Albertville, 1994 Lillehammer (TNT)

SportsChannel America
NHL Hockey—regular season, Stanley Cup playoffs
Olympics—cable TV 1992 Summer Games

HBO
Tennis—Wimbledon (early rounds)
Boxing—Mike Tyson heavyweight fights

USA Network
Golf—Masters (early rounds)
Tennis—US Open (early rounds)

Leagues, Teams & Officials
As of Oct. 1, 1989

Auto Racing

CART (Championship Auto Racing Teams)
390 Enterprise Court, Bloomfield Hills, MI 48013
313-334-8500
President   John Caponigro
Director of Public Relations   Mel Poole

Formula One
(Federation Internationale de Sport Automobile)
8 Rue de la Concorde, Paris 8E, France
331-426-599-51
President   Jean Marie Balestre
Public Relations Director   Martin Whiticker

NASCAR
(National Assn. of Stock Car Auto Racing)
1801 Volusia Ave., Daytona Beach, FL 32015
904-253-0611
President   Bill France, Jr.
Public Relations Manager   Bill Seaborn, Jr.

Major League Baseball

Office of the Commissioner
350 Park Ave., New York, NY 10022
212-371-7800
Commissioner   Francis (Fay) Vincent, Jr.
Director of Public Relations   Rich Levin

MLB Players Association
805 Third Ave., New York, NY 10022
212-826-0808
Exec. Director & Gen. Counsel   Donald Fehr
Special Assistant   Mark Belanger

AL

American League Office
350 Park Ave., 18th Floor, New York, NY 10022
212-371-7600
President   Bobby Brown
Director of Public Relations   Phyllis Merhige

Baltimore Orioles
Memorial Stadium, Baltimore, MD 21218
301-243-9800
President   Lawrence Lucchino
Vice President & Gen. Manager   Roland Hemond
Director of Public Relations   Richard Vaughn

Boston Red Sox
Fenway Park, 4 Yawkey Way, Boston, MA 02215
617-267-9440
Majority Owner-Chairwoman   Jean Yawkey
President   John Harrington
Senior V.P. and General Manager   Lou Gorman
Dir. of Public Relations   Dick Bresciani

California Angels
P.O. Box 2000, Anaheim, CA 92803
714-937-6700 or 213-625-1123
President and Chairman   Gene Autry
Executive V. P. and General Manager   Mike Port
Public Relations Director   Tim Mead

Chicago White Sox
Comiskey Park, 324 W. 35th St., Chicago, IL 60616
312-924-1000
Chairman   Jerry Reinsdorf
President   Eddie Einhorn
Senior V.P., General Manager   Larry Himes
V.P., Public Relations   Chuck Adams

Cleveland Indians
Cleveland Stadium, Cleveland, OH 44114
216-861-1200
Chairman   Richard Jacobs
President   Hank Peters
Director of Media Relations   Rick Minch

Detroit Tigers
Tiger Stadium, Detroit, MI 48216
313-962-4000
Owner-Vice Chairman   Tom Monaghan
President   Jim Campbell
Vice President and General Manager   Bill Lajoie
Dir.-Press and Public Relations   Dan Ewald

Kansas City Royals
P.O. Box 419969, Kansas City, MO 64141
816-921-2200
Co-owner and Chairman   Ewing Kauffman
Co-owner and Vice Chairman   Avron Fogelman
President   Joe Burke
Exec. V.P. and General Manager   John Schuerholz
Vice President-Public Relations   Dean Vogelaar

Milwaukee Brewers
County Stadium, 201 S. 46th St., Milwaukee, WI 53214
414-933-4114
President   Bud Selig
Exec. V.P. and General Manager   Harry Dalton
Director of Publicity   Tom Skibosh

Minnesota Twins
Hubert H. Humphrey Metrodome
501 Chicago Ave. So., Minneapolis, MN 55415
612-375-1366
Owner   Carl Pohlad
President   Jerry Bell
Exec. V.P. & General Manager   Andy MacPhail
Director of Media Relations   Tom Mee

New York Yankees
Yankee Stadium, Bronx, NY 10451
212-293-4300
Principal Owner   George Steinbrenner
V.P. of Baseball Operations   Bob Quinn
Director of Media Relations   Arthur Richman

Oakland Athletics
Oakland Alameda County Coliseum
Oakland, CA 94621
415-638-4900
Managing General Partner   Walter Haas, Jr.
V.P., Baseball Operations   Sandy Alderson
Director of Information   Jay Alves

Seattle Mariners
P.O. Box 4100, Seattle, WA 98104
206-628-3555
Owners   Jeff Smulyan
                                            Michael Browning
V.P., Baseball Operations   Woody Woodward
Director of Public Relations   Dave Aust

Texas Rangers
P.O. Box 1111 1250 Copeland Rd.
Arlington, TX 76010
817-273-5206
Co-owners   George W. Bush
                                            Edward W. Rose, III
President   Michael Stone
Vice President and General Manager   Tom Grieve
Director of Media Relations   John Blake

Toronto Blue Jays
300 The Esplanade West, Suite 3200
Toronto, Ontario M5V 3B3 CAN
416-341-1000
Chairman N.E. Hardy
President Paul Beeston
Exec. Vice President, Baseball Pat Gillick
Director of Public Relations Howard Starkman

NL

National League Office
350 Park Ave., New York, NY 10022
212-371-7300
President and Treasurer Bill White
Dir. of Media and Public Affairs Katy Feeney

Atlanta Braves
P.O. Box 4064, Atlanta, GA 30302
404-522-7630
President Stan Kasten
Vice President & General Manager Bobby Cox
Director of Public Relations Jim Schultz

Chicago Cubs
Clark and Addison Sts., Chicago, IL 60613
312-281-5050
President Donald Grenesko
General Manager Jim Frey
Director of Media Relations Ned Colletti

Cincinnati Reds
100 Riverfront Stadium, Cincinnati, OH 45202
513-421-4510
Owner-President Marge Schott
Vice President & General Manager Murray Cook
Dir. Information & Publications Jon Braude

Houston Astros
P.O. Box 288, Houston, TX 77001
713-799-9500
Chairman John McMullen
General Manager Bill Wood
Director of Public Relations Rob Matwick

Los Angeles Dodgers
1000 Elysian Park Ave., Los Angeles, CA 90012
213-224-1500
President Peter O'Malley
General Manager Fred Claire
Publicity Director Mike Williams

Montreal Expos
P.O. Box 500, Station M
Montreal, Quebec H1V 3P2
514-253-3434
Chairman Charles Broufman
President Claude Brochu
General Manager Dave Dombrowski
Public Relations Director Richard Griffin

New York Mets
126th St. & Roosevelt Ave., Flushing, NY 11368
718-507-6387   FAX: 718-565-4382
President Fred Wilpon
Exec. V.P. & General Manager Frank Cashen
Public Relations Director Jay Horwitz

Philadelphia Phillies
P.O. Box 7575, Philadelphia, PA 19101
215-463-6000
President and General Partner Bill Giles
Vice President & General Manager Lee Thomas
Publicity Director Vince Nauss

Pittsburgh Pirates
P.O. Box 7000, Pittsburgh, PA 15212
412-323-5000
President Carl Barger
Senior V.P. & General Manager Larry Doughty
Director of Media Relations Jim Lachimia

St. Louis Cardinals
250 Stadium Plaza, St. Louis, MO 63102
314-421-4040
Chairman and President August Busch, Jr.
Vice President & General Manager Dal Maxvill
Dir. of Public & Media Relations Kip Ingle

San Diego Padres
P.O. Box 2000, San Diego, CA 92120
619-283-7294
Owner-Chairman Joan Kroc
Exec. Vice President Dick Freeman
GM-Manager Jack McKeon
Media Relations Director Bill Beck

San Francisco Giants
Candlestick Park, San Francisco, CA 94124
415-468-3700
Chairman Bob Lurie
President and General Manager Al Rosen
Director of Media Relations Matt Fischer

National Basketball Association

League Office
Olympic Tower, 545 Fifth Ave.,
New York, NY 10022
212-826-7000
Commissioner David Stern
Exec. Vice President Russell Granik
Director of Public Relations Brian McIntyre

NBA Players Association
1775 Broadway, Suite 2401, New York, NY 10019
212-333-7510
Executive Director Charles Grantham

Atlanta Hawks
100 Techwood Drive NW, Atlanta, GA 30303
404-827-3800
Owner Ted Turner
President and General Manager Stan Kasten
Director of Public Relations Bill Needle

Boston Celtics
150 Causeway St., Boston, MA 02114
617-523-6050
Chairman Don Gaston
President Red Auerbach
Executive V.P. & General Manager Jan Volk
Director of Public Relations Jeff Twiss

Charlotte Hornets
Two First Union Center, Suite 2600
Charlotte, NC 28282
704-376-6430
Majority Owner and President George Shinn
Vice President & General Manager Carl Scheer
Director of Media Relations Andy Warfield

Chicago Bulls
One Magnificent Mile, 960 N. Michigan Ave.
Suite 1600, Chicago, IL 60611
312-943-5800
Chairman of General Partners Jerry Reinsdorf
V.P. of Basketball Operations Jerry Krause
Director of Media Services Tim Hallam

Cleveland Cavaliers
The Coliseum
2923 Streetsboro Road, Richfield, OH 44286
216-659-9100

Co-chairmen	George Gund III
	Gordon Gund
President	Arthur Savage
Vice President & General Manager	Wayne Embry
Director of Public Relations	Bob Price

Dallas Mavericks
Reunion Arena, 777 Sports St., Dallas, TX 75207
214-748-1808

Owner and President	Donald Carter
General Manager	Norm Sonju
Director of Media Services	Kevin Sullivan

Denver Nuggets
McNichols Sports Arena
1635 Clay St., P.O. Box 4658, Denver, CO 80204
303-893-6700

Owner	Sydney Shlenker
President & General Manager	Pete Babcock
Director of Public Relations	Bill Young

Detroit Pistons
The Palace of Auburn Hills
3777 Lapeer Road, Auburn Hills, MI 48057
313-377-0100

Managing Partner	Bill Davidson
General Manager	Jack McCloskey
Director of Public Relations	Matt Dobek

Golden State Warriors
Oakland Coliseum Arena, Oakland, CA 94621
415-638-6300

Chairman	James Fitzgerald
President	Daniel Finnane
Head Coach and General Manager	Don Nelson
Director of Public Relations	TBA

Houston Rockets
The Summit, Ten Greenway Plaza
Houston, TX 77046
713-627-0600

Chairman	Charlie Thomas
President	Ray Patterson
General Manager	Steve Patterson
Director of Media Information	Jay Goldberg

Indiana Pacers
Two West Washington, Suite 510
Indianapolis, IN 46204
317-263-2100

Owners	Melvin Simon
	Herbert Simon
Executive V.P. & General Manager	Donnie Walsh
Media Relations Director	Dale Ratermann

Los Angeles Clippers
L.A. Memorial Sports Arena
3939 S. Figueroa St., Los Angeles, CA 90037
213-748-8000

Owner	Donald Sterling
President	Alan Rothenberg
Exec. V.P. & General Manager	Elgin Baylor
Director of Public Relations	TBA

Los Angeles Lakers
The Forum, 3900 West Manchester Blvd.
P.O. Box 10, Inglewood, CA 90306
213-419-3100

Owner	Jerry Buss
General Manager	Jerry West
Director of Public Relations	Josh Rosenfeld

Miami Heat
The Miami Arena, Miami, FL 33136-4102
305-577-4328

Managing General Partner	Lewis Schaffel
Director of Public Relations	Mark Pray

Milwaukee Bucks
Bradley Center
1001 N. Fourth St., Milwaukee, WI 53203
414-227-0500

President	Herb Kohl
Director of Player Personal	Bob Zuffelato
Director of Public Relations	Bill King II

Minnesota Timberwolves
500 City Place, 730 Hennepin Ave.
Minneapolis, MN 55403
612-337-3865

Co-owners	Harvey Ratner
	Marv Wolfenson
President	Bob Stein
Director of Public Relations	Tim Bryant

New Jersey Nets
Meadowlands Arena, East Rutherford, NJ 07073
201-935-8888

Chairman	Alan Aufzien
President	Bernie Mann
Vice President & General Manager	Harry Weltman
Coordinator of Public Relations	John Mertz

New York Knickerbockers
Madison Square Garden
Four Pennsylvania Plaza, New York, NY 10001
212-563-8000

President	Richard Evans
Vice President & General Manager	Al Bianchi
Dir. of Communications	John Cirillo

Orlando Magic
Orlando Arena, 1 Magic Place, Orlando, FL 32801
407-649-3200

Owner	William du Pont III
President and General Manager	Pat Williams
Director of Media Relations	Alex Martins

Philadelphia 76ers
Veterans Stadium
P.O. Box 25040, Philadelphia, PA 19147
215-339-7600

President	Harold Katz
General Manager	John Nash
Director of Public Relations	Zack Hill

Phoenix Suns
2910 N. Central Ave., Phoenix, AZ 85012
602-266-5753

President	Jerry Colangelo
Head Coach, Dir. of Player Personnel	Cotton Fitzsimmons
Media Relations Director	Barry Ringel

Portland Trail Blazers
Suite 950 Lloyd Building
700 Multnomah St., Portland, OR 97232
503-234-9291

Chairman	Paul Allen
President	Harry Glickman
Senior V.P. and General Manager	Jon Spoelstra
Director of Media Services	John Lashway

Sacramento Kings
One Sports Parkway, Sacramento, CA 95834
916-928-0000

Managing General Partner	Gregg Lukenbill
Exec. V.P., Basketball Operations	Bill Russell
Director of Publicity	Julie Fie

San Antonio Spurs
600 East Market St., Suite 102, San Antonio, TX 78205
512-224-4611

Chairman	Red McCombs
President	Gary Woods
Public Relations Director	Wayne Witt

Seattle Supersonics
190 Queen Anne Ave. N.
Box C 900911, Seattle WA 98109-9711
206-281-5800

Chairman	Barry Ackerley
President	Bob Whitsitt
Dir. of Public and Media Relations	Jim Rupp

Utah Jazz
5 Triad Center, Suite 500
Salt Lake City, UT 84180
801-575-7800

Owner	Larry Miller
President	Frank Layden
General Manager	Tim Howells
Director of Public Relations	Kim Turner

Washington Bullets
Capital Centre, Landover, MD 20785
301-773-2255

Chairman and President	Abe Pollin
Vice President/General Manager	Bob Ferry
Director of Public Relations	Rick Moreland

Bowling

BPAA (Bowling Proprietors' Assn. of America)
P.O. Box 5802, Arlington, TX 76005
817-649-5105

President	Don Hillman
V.P., Marketing	Stuart Robinson

LPBT (Ladies Professional Bowlers Tour)
7171 Cherryvale Blvd., Rockford, IL 61112
815-332-5756

President	John Falzone
Dir. of Marketing	Bill Vint

PBA (Professional Bowlers Association)
1720 Merriman Road, P.O. Box 5118
Akron, OH 44313

Commissioner	Joseph Antenora
Dir. of Public Relations	Kevin Shippy

Boxing

IBF (International Boxing Federation)
30 Clinton Street, Newark, NJ 07102
201-621-7200

President	Bob Lee
Dir. of Public Relations	Cy Roseman

WBA (World Boxing Association)

President	Gilberto Mendoza
General Counsel	Jimmy Binns
& Spokesman in USA	300 Walnut Street
	Philadelphia, PA 19106
	215-922-4000

WBC (World Boxing Council)

President	Jose Sulaiman
Treasurer	Steve Crosson
& Spokesman in USA	5445 La Sierra Dr., Suite 400
	Dallas, TX 75231
	214-739-3388

Canadian Football League

1200 Bay St., 12th Floor
Toronto, Ontario M5R 2A5
416-928-1200

Chairman	Roy McMurtry
President	Bill Baker
Dir. of Marketing	Morrey Rae Hutnick

B.C. Lions
B.C. Place Stadium, 765 Pacific Blvd. South
Vancouver, B.C. V6B 4Y9
604-681-5466

President	Norm Fieldgate
General Manager	Joe Galat
Public Relations Director	Keith Hunt

Calgary Stampeders
McMahon Stadium, 1817 Crowchild Tr. NW
Calgary, Alberta T2M 4R6
403-289-0205

Chairman	William McKay
President-GM	Norman Kwong
Public Relations Director	Kevin Gallant

Edmonton Eskimos
9023 — 111 Ave. Edmonton, Alberta T5B 0C3
403-429-2821

President	W.E.(Bill) Gardiner
General Manager	Hugh Campbell
Public Relations Director	Allan Watt

Hamilton Tiger-Cats
P.O. Box 172 Hamilton, Ontario L8N 3A2
416-547-2418

Owner-President	David Braley
General Manager	Joe Zuger
Communications Director	Chris Dowhun

Ottawa Rough Riders
Coliseum Building, Lansdowne Park
Ottawa, Ontario K1S 3W7
613-563-4551

President	G.B.(Hap) Nicholls
General Manager	Jo-Anne Polak
Communications Director	Phil Legault

Saskatchewan Roughriders
2940 — 10th Ave., P.O. Box 1277
Regina, Saskatchewan S4P 3B8
306-569-2323

President	Tom Shepard
General Manager	Alan Ford
Public Relations Director	Jim Dorash

Toronto Argos
Exhibition Place, Toronto, Ontario M6K 3C3
416-595-9600

President-CEO	Ralph Sazio
GM-Head Coach	Bob O'Billovich
Publicity Director	Brian Snelgrove

Winnipeg Blue Bombers
1465 Maroons Road, Winnipeg, Manitoba R3G 0L6
204-786-2583
President	Ross Brown
General Manager	Cal Murphy
Public Relations Director	Kevin O'Donovan

National Football League

League Office
410 Park Ave., New York, NY 10022
212-758-1500
Commissioner	Pete Rozelle
Exec. V. P. and League Counsel	Jay Moyer
Director of Public Relations	Jim Heffernan

NFL Players Association
2021 L. Street NW, Washington, DC 20036
202-463-2200 ·
Executive Director	Gene Upshaw
Assistant Director	Doug Allen
Director of Public Relations	Frank Wofchitz

AFC

American Football Conference
President	Lamar Hunt
Assistant to the President	Roger Goodell
Director of Information	Pete Abitante

Buffalo Bills
One Bills Drive, Orchard Park, NY 14127
716-648-1800
President	Ralph Wilson,Jr.
Vice President & General Manager	Bill Polian
Vice President-Head Coach	Marv Levy
Director of Public Relations	Denny Lynch

Cincinnati Bengals
200 Riverfront Stadium, Cincinnati, OH 45202
513-621-3550
President	John Sawyer
General Manager	Paul Brown
Director of Public Relations	Al Heim

Cleveland Browns
Tower B, Cleveland Stadium, Cleveland, OH 44114
216-696-5555
Owner-President	Art Modell
Exec. V.P., Football Operations	Ernie Accorsi
Vice President, Public Relations	Kevin Byrne

Denver Broncos
5700 Logan St., Denver, CO 80216
303-296-1982
President	Pat Bowlen
Vice President-Head Coach	Dan Reeves
General Manager	John Beake
Director of Media Relations	Jim Saccomano

Houston Oilers
6910 Fannin St., Houston, TX 77030
713-797-9111
President	Bud Adams
General Manager	Mike Holovak
Director of Media Relations	Chip Namias

Indianapolis Colts
P.O. Box 535000, Indianapolis, IN 46253
317-297-2658
President and Treasurer	Robert Irsay
Vice President-General Manager	James Irsay
Director of Public Relations	Craig Kelley

Kansas City Chiefs
One Arrowhead Drive, Kansas City, MO 64129
816-924-9300
Owner	Lamar Hunt
President and General Manager	Carl Peterson
Director of Public Relations	Bob Moore

Los Angeles Raiders
332 Center St., El Segundo, CA 90245
213-322-3451
Managing General Partner	Al Davis
Executive Assistant	Al LoCasale
Director of Player Personnel	Ron Wolf

Miami Dolphins
Joe Robbie Stadium
2269 N.W. 199th Street, Miami, FL 33056
305-620-5000
President	Joe Robbie
Exec. V.P.-General Manager	Michael Robbie
Director of Media Relations	Harvey Greene

New England Patriots
Sullivan Stadium, Route 1, Foxboro, MA 02035
508-543-7911
Chairman	Victor Kiam
President	Billy Sullivan
General Manager	Pat Sullivan
Director of Public Relations	Dave Wintergrass

New York Jets
598 Madison Ave., New York, NY 10022
212-421-6600
Chairman	Leon Hess
President	Steve Gutman
Director of Player Personnel	Mike Hickey
Director of Public Relations	Frank Ramos

Pittsburgh Steelers
Three Rivers Stadium
300 Stadium Circle, Pittsburgh, PA 15212
412-323-1200
President	Dan Rooney
Director of Player Personnel	Dick Haley
Public Relations Director	Dan Edwards

San Diego Chargers
San Diego Jack Murphy Stadium
P.O. Box 20666, San Diego, CA 92120
619-280-2111
Chairman and President	Alex Spanos
Director of Football Operations	Steve Ortmayer
Director of Public Relations	Rick Smith

Seattle Seahawks
11220 N.E. 53rd Street, Kirkland, WA 98033
206-827-9777
Owner	Ken Behring
President and General Manager	Tom Flores
Vice President, Public Relations	Gary Wright

NFC

National Football Conference
President	Wellington Mara
Assistant to President	Jim Noel
Director of Information	Dick Maxwell

Atlanta Falcons
Suwanee Road at I-85, Suwanee, GA 30174
404-945-1111
Chairman	Rankin Smith, Sr.
President	Rankin Smith, Jr.
Director of Public Relations	Charlie Taylor

Chicago Bears
Halas Hall, 250 N. Washington, Lake Forest, IL 60045
312-295-6600
Chairman   Edward McCaskey
President   Mike McCaskey
Vice President of Player Personnel   Bill Tobin
Director of Public Relations   Bryan Harlan

Dallas Cowboys
Cowboys Center
One Cowboys Parkway, Irving, TX 75063
214-556-9900
Owner-President-GM   Jerry Jones
Director of Player Personnel   Bob Ackles
Public Relations Director   Greg Aiello

Detroit Lions
Pontiac Silverdome
1200 Featherstone Road, Box 4200, Pontiac, MI 48057
313-335-4131
Owner-President   William Clay Ford
Executive V.P.-General Manager   Russ Thomas
Head Coach, Dir. of Operations   Wayne Fontes
Director of Public Relations   Bill Keenist

Green Bay Packers
1265 Lombardi Ave., P.O. Box 10628
Green Bay, WI 54307
414-494-2351
Chairman   Robert Parins
President   Bob Harlan
Exec. V.P., Football Operations   Tom Braatz
Director of Public Relations   Lee Remmel

Los Angeles Rams
2327 West Lincoln Ave., Anaheim, CA 92801
714-535-7267 or 213-585-5400
President   Georgia Frontiere
Administrator, Football Operations   Jack Faulkner
Director of Public Relations   John Oswald

Minnesota Vikings
9520 Viking Drive, Eden Prairie, MN 55344
612-828-6500
Chairman   John Skoglund
President   Wheelock Whitney
General Manager   Mike Lynn
Director of Public Relations   Merrill Swanson

New Orleans Saints
1500 Poydras St., New Orleans, LA 70112
504-733-0255
Owner-General Partner   Tom Benson
President and General Manager   Jim Finks
Director of Media Relations   Rusty Kasmiersky

New York Giants
Giants Stadium, East Rutherford, NJ 07073
201-935-8111
President   Wellington Mara
Vice President-General Manager   George Young
Director of Media Services   Ed Croke

Philadelphia Eagles
Veterans Stadium, Broad St. & Pattison Ave.
Philadelphia, PA 19148
215-463-2500
Owner   Norman Braman
President   Harry Gamble
Director of Public Relations   Ron Howard

Phoenix Cardinals
P.O. Box 888, Phoenix, AZ 85001-0888
602-967-1010
President   William Bidwill
Vice President & General Manager   Larry Wilson
Public Relations Director   Paul Jensen

San Francisco 49ers
4949 Centennial Blvd., Santa Clara, CA 95054
408-562-4949
Owner and President   Edward DeBartolo, Jr.
Vice President-General Manager   John McVay
Director of Public Relations   Jerry Walker

Tampa Bay Buccaneers
One Buccaneer Place, Tampa, FL 33607
813-870-2700
Owner and President   Hugh Culverhouse
Vice President-Head Coach   Ray Perkins
Director of Public Relations   Rick Odioso

Washington Redskins
Redskin Park, P.O. Box 17247, Dulles Int'l Airport,
Washington, DC 20041
703-471-9100
Chairman   Jack Kent Cooke
Exec. Vice President   John Kent Cooke
General Manager   Charlie Casserly
Director of Public Relations   Marty Hurney

Golf

LPGA Tour
(Ladies Professional Golf Association)
2570 Volusia Ave., Daytona Beach, FL 32114
904-To be announced
Commissioner   William Blue
Vice President, Operations   Jim Webb
Dir. of Communications   Julie Gumlia

PGA Tour ·
(Professional Golfer's Association)
Sawgrass, Ponte Vedra, FL 32082
904-285-3700
Commissioner   Deane Beman
V.P., Tournament Affairs   Steve Rankin
Dr. of Information   Tom Place

USGA
(United States Golf Association)
Liberty Corner Road, Far Hills, NJ 07931
201-234-2300
Executive Director   David Fay
President   William Battle
Dir. of Communications   John Morris

National Hockey League
Chairman of the Board   William Wirtz
President   John Ziegler
Executive Vice President   Brian O'Neill
Vice President and General Counsel   Gilbert Stein
V. P., Marketing and Public Relations   Steve Ryan
Montreal Office: 1155 Metcalfe St., Suite 960
                        Montreal, Quebec H3B 2W2
                        514-871-9220
New York Office: 650 Fifth Ave., 33rd Floor,
                        New York, NY 10019
                        212-398-1100

NHL Players' Association
37 Maitland St., Toronto, Ontario M4Y 1C8
416-924-7800
Executive Director   Alan Eagleson
Dir. of Operations   Sam Simpson

Boston Bruins
Boston Garden, 150 Causeway St., Boston, MA 02114
617-227-3206
President   William Hassett, Jr.
General Manager   Harry Sinden
Dir. Public Relations & Marketing   Nate Greenberg

Buffalo Sabres
Memorial Auditorium, Buffalo, NY 14202
716-856-7300
Chairman and President   Seymour Knox, III
General Manager   Gerry Meehan
Director of Public Relations   John Gurtler

Calgary Flames
Olympic Saddledome, P.O. Box 1540 Station M,
Calgary, Alberta T2P 3B9
403-261-0475
President and General Manager   Cliff Fletcher
Director of Public Relations   Rick Skaggs

Chicago Blackhawks
Chicago Stadium, 1800 W. Madison St., Chicago,
IL 60612
312-733-5300
President   William Wirtz
General Manager   Bob Pulford
Public Relations Director   Jim DeMaria

Detroit Red Wings
Joe Louis Sports Arena
600 Civic Drive, Detroit, MI 48226
313-567-7333
Owner-President   Mike Ilitch
Vice President & General Manager   Jim Devellano
Director of Public Relations   Bill Jamieson

Edmonton Oilers
Northlands Coliseum
Edmonton, Alberta T5B 4M9
403-474-8561
Owner   Peter Pocklington
President and General Manager   Glen Sather
Director of Public Relations   Bill Tuele

Hartford Whalers
Hartford Civic Center Coliseum
One Civic Center Plaza, Hartford, CT 06103
203-728-3366
Owner-Chairman   Donald Conrad
President   Emile Francis
Vice President-General Manager   Eddie Johnston
Director of Public Relations   Phil Langan

Los Angeles Kings
The Forum, 3900 West Manchester Blvd.
Box 17013, Inglewood, CA 90306
213-419-3160
President   Bruce NcNall
General Manager   Rogie Vachon
Director of Media Relations   Nick Salata

Minnesota North Stars
Metropolitan Sports Center
7901 Cedar Ave. South, Bloomington, MN 55425
612-853-9333
Co-chairmen   George Gund III
    Gordon Gund
President   Lou Nanne
Vice President & General Manager   Jack Ferreira
Public Relations Director   Joe Janasz

Montreal Canadiens
Montreal Forum, 2313 St. Catherine Street West,
Montreal, Quebec H3H 1N2
514-932-2582
Chairman and President   Ronald Corey
General Manager   Serge Savard
Director of Public Relations   Claude Mouton

New Jersey Devils
Byre Meadowlands Arena
P.O. Box 504, East Rutherford, NJ 07073
201-935-6050
Chairman   John McMullen
President and General Manager   Lou Lamoriello
Director, Public & Media Relations   David Freed

New York Islanders
Nassau Veterans' Memorial Coliseum
Uniondale, NY 11553
516-794-4100
Chairman   John Pickett, Jr.
President and General Manager   Bill Torrey
Director of Public Relations   Greg Bouris

New York Rangers
Madison Square Garden
4 Pennsylvania Plaza, New York, NY 10001
212-563-8000
President   Richard Evans
General Manager   Neil Smith
Vice President, Communications   John Halligan

Philadelphia Flyers
The Spectrum, Pattison Place, Philadelphia, PA 19148
215-465-4500
Majority Owner   Ed Snider
President   Jay Snider
Vice President & General Manager   Bob Clarke
Director of Public Relations   Rodger Gottlieb

Pittsburgh Penguins
Civic Arena, Pittsburgh, PA 15219
412-642-1800
Chairman   Edward DeBartolo, Sr.
Vice President & General Manager   Tony Esposito
Director of Press Relations   Cindy Himes

Quebec Nordiques
Colisée de Québec, 2205 Ave. du Colisée
Quebec City, Quebec G1L 4W7
418-529-8441
President   Marcel Aubut
General Manager   Martin Madden
Public Relations Director   Nicole Bouchard

St. Louis Blues
St. Louis Arena
5700 Oakland Ave., St. Louis, MO 63110
314-781-5300
Chairman   Michael Shanahan
President   Jack Quinn
Vice-President, General Manager   Ronald Caron
V.P., Public Relations/Marketing   Susie Mathieu

Toronto Maple Leafs
Maple Leaf Gardens
60 Carlton St., Toronto, Ontario M5B 1L1
416-977-1641
President-Managing Director	Harold Ballard
General Manager	Floyd Smith
Director of Public Relations	Bob Stellick

Vancouver Canucks
Pacific Coliseum, 100 North Renfrew St.,
Vancouver, British Columbia V5K 3N7
604-254-5141
Chairman	Frank Griffiths
President and General Manager	Pat Quinn
Director of Public and Media Relations	Darcy Rota

Washington Capitals
Capital Centre, Landover, MD 20785
301-350-3400
Chairman	Abe Pollin
President	Richard Patrick
Vice-President & General Manager	Dave Poile
Director of Public Relations	Lou Corletto

Winnipeg Jets
Winnipeg Arena, 15-1430 Maroons Road,
Winnipeg, Manitoba R3G 0L5
204-583-5387
President	Barry Shenkarow
General Manager	Mike Smith
Director of Public Relations	Murray Harding

Horse Racing

TRA
(Thoroughbred Racing Assn. of N.America)
3000 Marcus Ave., Suite ZW4
Lake Success, NY 11042
516-328-2660
President	Robert Levey
Dir. of Service Bureau	Richard Schulhoff

USTA
(United States Trotting Association)
750 Michigan Ave., Columbus, OH 43215
614-224-2291
Exec. Vice President	Francis X. Ready
Dir. of Public Relations	John Pawlak

Media

DAILY NEWSPAPERS

The National
(Scheduled for publication Jan., 1990)
15 West 52nd St., New York, NY 10019
212-826-5400
Publisher	Peter Price
Editor	Frank Deford

USA Today
P.O. Box 500, Washington, DC 20044
703-276-3400
Publisher	Cathleen Black
Managing Editor/Sports	Gene Policinski

WEEKLY MAGAZINES

Sports Illustrated
Time&Life Bldg., Rockefeller Ctr.,
New York, NY 10020
212-586-1212
Publisher	Donald J. Barr
Managing Editor	Mark Mulvoy

The Sporting News
1212 N.Lindbergh Blvd., St. Louis, MO 63132
314-997-7111
Chairman	Richard Waters
Editor	Tom Barnidge

TELEVISION

ABC Sports
47 West 66th St., 13th Floor, New York, NY 10023
212-887-4867
President	Dennis Swanson
Senior V.P.-Production	Dennis Lewin
Executive Producer	Geoffrey Mason
Dir. of Public Relations	Bob Wheeler

CBS Sports
51 West 52nd St., 30th Floor, New York, NY 10019
212-975-4907
President	Neal Pilson
V.P. Programming	Jay Rosenstein
Executive Producer	Ted Shaker
Dir. of Information	Mark Carlson

CNN Sports
One CNN Center, P.O.Box 105366
Atlanta, GA 30348
404-827-1500
Vice President-Sports	Bill MacPhail
Senior Exec. Producer	Jim Walton
Dir. of Public Relations	Alyssa Levy

ESPN
ESPN Plaza, Bristol, CT 06010
203-585-2000
President	Roger Werner
Exec. V.P., Programming	Steve Bornstein
Dir. of Production	Steve Anderson
Dir. of Communications	Chris LaPlaca

HBO Sports
1100 Ave. of the Americas, New York, NY 10036
212-512-1000
Senior V.P. Sports	Seth Abraham
V.P., Sports Programming	Bob Greenway
Executive Producer	Ross Greenburg

NBC Sports
30 Rockefeller Plaza, New York, NY 10020
212-664-4444
President	Dick Ebersol
Exec. Vice President	Ken Schanzer
Executive Producer	Terry O'Neil
Dir. of Information	Kevin Monaghan

SportsChannel America
150 Crossways Park West, Woodbury, NY 11797
516-364-2222
President	Jim Greiner
Senior V.P., Exec. Producer	Jeff Ruhe
Dir. of Media Relations	Dan Martinsen

TBS Sports
One CNN Center, P.O.Box 105366
Atlanta, GA 30348
404-827-1458
President	Terry McGuirk
V.P., Exec. Producer	Don McGuire
V.P., Programming	Kevin O'Malley
Dir. of Public Relations	TBA

Olympics

**Albertville Olympic Organizing Committee
(1992 Winter Games)**
11 rue Pargoux, 73200 Albertville, France
Tel: (33.7)9379242
President   Michel Barnier

**Barcelona Olympic Organizing Committee
(1992 Summer Games)**
Edificio Hellos, C/Mejia Lequerica, S/N 08028,
Barcelona, Spain
Tel: (34.3)4321992
Chairman and President   M. Pasqual Maragall

**COA
(Canadian Olympic Association)**
1600 James Naismith Dr., Ottawa, Ontario K1B 5N4
613-748-5647
President   Roger Jackson
IOC Members (2)   James Worrall & Richard Pound
Dir. of Communications   Frank Ratcliffe

**IOC
(International Olympic Committee)**
Chateau de Vidy, CH-1007 Lausanne, Switzerland
Tel.: (41.21)253271
President   Juan Antonio Samaranch
Administrative Delegate   Raymond Gafner
Dir. of Information   Michele Verdier

**USOC
(United States Olympic Committee)**
1750 East Boulder St., Colorado Springs, CO 80909
719-632-5551
President   Robert Helmick
IOC Members (2)   Robert Helmick & Anita DeFrantz
Dir. of Information   Mike Moran

**U.S. Olympic Festival
(1990 Organizing Committee)**
World Trade Center, 12th Floor, St. Paul, MN 55101
612-291-1990
President & Exec. Director   Jack Kelly
Dir. of Media Relations   Mike Minich

Soccer

**FIFA
(Federation Internationale de Football Assn.)**
P.O. Box 85, CH-8030 Zurich, Switzerland
Tel: (01.5)55400
President   Joao Havelange
Dir. of Public Relations   Guido Tognoni

**MISL
(Major Indoor Soccer League)**
7101 College Blvd., Overland Park, KS 66210
913-339-6475
Commissioner   Earl Foreman
Dir. of Communications   John Griffin

**USSF
(United States Soccer Federation)**
1750 East Boulder St., Colorado Springs, CO 80909
719-578-4678
President   Werner Fricker
Dir. of Public Relations   John Polis

Tennis

**ATP
(Association of Tennis Professionals)**
200 Tournament Players Rd.
Ponte Vedra Beach, FL 32082
904-285-8000
Executive Director   Hamilton Jordan
Dir. of Media Services   Greg Sharko

**USTA
(United States Tennis Association)**
1212 Ave. of the Americas, 12th Floor, New York,
NY 10036
212-302-3322
Chairman and President   Gordon Jorgensen
Dir. of Public Relations   Edwin Fabricius

**WITA
(Women's International Tennis Assn.)**
2665 S.Bayshore Dr., Suite 1002, Miami, FL 33133
305-856-4030
Executive Director   Merritt Stierheim
Dir. of Public Relations   Ana Leaird

Other

**AAU
(Amateur Athletic Union)**
3400 W.86th St., Indianapolis, IN 46268
317-872-2900
President   Gussie Crawford
Executive Director   Stan Hooley
Dir. of Communications   Chip Powers

**Goodwill Games
1990 Seattle Organizing Committee**
2203 Airport Way S., Seattle, WA 98134
206-622-1990
Chairman   Fr. William Sullivan, S.J.
Dir. of Media Relations (Seattle)   Bill Sears
Dir. of Media Relations (NYC)   Donn Bernstein

**NAIA
(National Assn. of Intercollegiate Athletics)**
1221 Baltimore Ave., Kansas City, MO 64105
816-842-5050
Executive Director   Jefferson Farris
Dir. of Publications & Services   Mary Beth Brutton

**NCAA
(National Collegiate Athletic Assn.)**
6299 Nall Ave., Mission, KS 66202
913-384-3220
Executive Director   Richard Schultz
Dir. of Enforcement   David Berst
Dir. of Communications   Jim Marchiony

**TAC
(The Athletics Congress)**
200 S.Capitol Ave., Suite 140
Indianapolis, IN 46225
317-638-9155
Executive Director   Ollan Cassell
Dir. of Information   Pete Cava

Toronto's **SkyDome**, with a retractable roof and a $350 million price tag, opened in June as the home field of baseball's Blue Jays and the CFL's Argos.

ARENAS & BALLPARKS

INSIDE

Major League Baseball

National League

		Built	Capacity	—Outfield Fences—					
				LF	LCF	CF	RCF	RF	Field
Atlanta Braves	Atlanta-Fulton County Stadium	1966	52,007	330	385	402	385	330	Grass
Chicago Cubs	Wrigley Field	1916	39,012	355	368	400	368	353	Grass
Cincinnati Reds	Riverfront Stadium	1970	53,631	330	375	404	375	330	Turf
Houston Astros	The Astrodome	1965	52,000	330	378	400	378	330	Turf
Los Angeles Dodgers	Dodger Stadium	1962	56,000	330	385	400	385	330	Grass
Montreal Expos	Olympic Stadium	1977	59,975	325	375	404	375	325	Turf
New York Mets	Shea Stadium	1964	55,601	338	371	410	371	338	Grass
Philadelphia Phillies	Veterans Stadium	1971	62,382	330	371	408	371	330	Turf
Pittsburgh Pirates	Three Rivers Stadium	1970	58,729	335	375	400	375	335	Turf
St.Louis Cardinals	Busch Stadium	1966	54,224	330	383	414	383	330	Turf
San Diego Padres	San Diego/ Jack Murphy Stadium	1969	59,022	330	370	405	370	330	Grass
San Francisco Giants	Candlestick Park	1960	60,000	335	365	400	365	335	Grass

American League

		Built	Capacity	—Outfield Fences—					
				LF	LCF	CF	RCF	RF	Field
Baltimore Orioles	Memorial Stadium	1954	54,017	309	378	405	378	309	Grass
Boston Red Sox	Fenway Park	1912	34,182	315	379	390	380	302	Grass
California Angels	Anaheim Stadium	1966	64,593	333	386	404	386	333	Grass
Chicago White Sox	Comiskey Park	1910	43,931	347	382	409	382	347	Grass
Cleveland Indians	Cleveland Stadium	1932	74,483	320	382	400	382	320	Grass
Detroit Tigers	Tiger Stadium	1912	52,416	340	365	440	375	325	Grass
Kansas City Royals	Royals Stadium	1973	40,625	330	385	410	385	330	Turf
Milwaukee Brewers	County Stadium	1953	53,192	315	392	402	392	315	Grass
Minnesota Twins	Hubert H.Humphrey Metrodome	1982	55,884	343	385	408	367	327	Turf
New York Yankees	Yankee Stadium	1923	57,545	318	399	408	385	314	Grass
Oakland Athletics	Oakland Coliseum	1968	48,219	330	375	400	375	330	Grass
Seattle Mariners	The Kingdome	1977	58,150	316	357	410	357	316	Turf
Texas Rangers	Arlington Stadium	1972	43,508	330	380	400	380	330	Grass
Toronto Blue Jays	SkyDome	1989	49,500	328	375	400	375	328	Turf

Rank by Capacity

National League		American League	
Veterans	62,382	Cleveland	74,483
Candlestick	60,000	Anaheim	64,593
Olympic	59,975	Kingdome	58,150
Jack Murphy	59,022	Yankee	57,545
Three Rivers	58,729	Metrodome	55,884
Dodger	56,000	Memorial	54,017
Shea	55,601	County	53,192
Busch	54,224	Tiger	52,416
Riverfront	53,631	SkyDome	49,500
Atlanta	52,007	Oakland	48,219
Astrodome	52,000	Comiskey	43,931
Wrigley	39,012	Arlington	43,508
		Royals	40,625
		Fenway	34,182

Rank by Age

National League		American League	
Wrigley	1914	Comiskey	1910
Candlestick	1960	Fenway	1912
Dodger	1962	Tiger	1912
Shea	1964	Yankee	1923
Astrodome	1965	Cleveland	1932
Atlanta	1965	Memorial	1949
Busch	1966	County	1953
Jack Murphy	1967	Arlington	1965
Riverfront	1970	Anaheim	1966
Three Rivers	1970	Oakland	1966
Veterans	1971	Royals	1973
Olympic	1976	Kingdome	1977
		Metrodome	1982
		Skydome	1989

Home Fields

Listed below are the principal home fields used through the years by current National and American League teams. The N.L. became a major league in 1876, the A.L. in 1901.

The capacity figures in the right hand column indicate the largest seating capacity of the ballpark while the club played there. Capacity figures before 1915 (and the introduction of concrete grandstands) are sketchy at best and have been left blank.

National League

Atlanta Braves

1876-94	South End Grounds I (Boston) . . .	—
1894-1914	South End Grounds II	—
1915-52	Braves Field	40,000
1953-65	County Stadium (Milwaukee)	43,394
1966-	Atlanta-Fulton County Stadium . .	52,007
	(1966 capacity—50,000)	

Chicago Cubs

1876-77	State Street Grounds	—
1878-84	Lakefront Park	—
1885-91	West Side Park	—
1891-93	Brotherhood Park	—
1893-1915	West Side Grounds	—
1916-	Wrigley Field*	39,012
	(1916 capacity—16,000)	

Cincinnati Reds

1876-79	Avenue Grounds	—
1880	Bank Street Grounds	—
1890-1901	Redland Field I*	—
1902-11	Palace of the Fans	—
1912-70	Crosley Field*	29,603
1970-	Riverfront Stadium	53,631
	(1970 capacity—52,000)	

Houston Astros

1962-64	Colt Stadium	32,601
1965	The Astrodome*	52,000
	(1965 capacity—45,011)	

Note: Astrodome capacity will go from 45,000 to 52,000 seats in time for 1990 season.

Los Angeles Dodgers

1890	Washington Park I (Brooklyn) . . .	—
1891-97	Eastern Park	—
1898-1912	Washington Park II	—
1913-56	Ebbets Field	31,497
1957	Ebbets Field	31,497
	& Roosevelt Stadium	
	(Jersey City)	24,167
1958-61	Memorial Coliseum	
	(Los Angeles)	93,600
1962-	Dodger Stadium	56,000
	(1962 capacity—56,000)	

Montreal Expos

1969-76	Jarry Park	28,000
1977-	Olympic Stadium	59,975
	(1977 capacity—58,500)	

New York Mets

1962-63	Polo Grounds	55,987
1964-	Shea Stadium	55,601
	(1964 capacity—55,101)	

Philadelphia Phillies

1883-86	Recreation Park	—
1887-94	Huntingdon Ave.Grounds	—
1895-1938	Baker Bowl	18,800
1938-70	Shibe Park*	33,608
1971-	Veterans Stadium	62,382
	(1971 capacity—56,371)	

Pittsburgh Pirates

1887-90	Recreation Park	—
1891-1909	Exposition Park	—
1909-70	Forbes Field	35,000
1970-	Three Rivers Stadium	58,729
	(1970 capacity—50,235)	

St.Louis Cardinals

1876-77	Sportsman's Park I	—
1885-86	Vandeventer Lot	—
1892-1920	Robison Field*	18,000
1920-66	Sportsman's Park II	30,500
1966-	Busch Stadium*	54,224
	(1966 capacity—50,126)	

San Diego Padres

1969-	San Diego/Jack Murphy Stadium* .	59,022
	(1969 capacity—47,634)	

San Francisco Giants

1876	Union Grounds (Brooklyn)	—
1883-88	Polo Grounds I (New York)	—
1889-90	Manhattan Field	—
1891-1957	Polo Grounds II	55,987
1958-59	Seals Stadium (San Francisco) . . .	22,900
1960-	Candlestick Park	60,000
	(1960 capacity—42,553)	

*Ballpark Name Changes: ATLANTA—**Atlanta Fulton County Stadium** originally Atlanta Stadium (1966-1974); CHICAGO—**Wrigley Field** originally Weeghman Park (1914-17), then Cubs Park (1918-25); CINCINNATI—**Redland Field** originally League Park (1890-93) and **Crosley Field** originally Redland Field II (1912-33); HOUSTON— **Astrodome** called Harris County Domed Stadium before it opened in 1965; PHILADELPHIA—**Shibe Park** renamed Connie Mack Stadium in 1953; ST.LOUIS—**Robison Field** originally Vandeventer Lot, then League Park, then Cardinal Park all before becoming Robison Field in 1901, **Sportsman's Park** renamed Busch Stadium in 1953, and **Busch Stadium** originally Busch Memorial Stadium (1966-82); SAN DIEGO—**San Diego/Jack Murphy Stadium** originally San Diego Stadium (1967-81).

American League

Baltimore Orioles

1901	Lloyd Street Grounds (Milwaukee)	—
1902-53	Sportsman's Park II* (St.Louis) . .	30,500
1954-	Memorial Stadium (Baltimore) . . .	54,017
	(1954 capacity—47,866)	

Boston Red Sox

1901-11	Huntington Ave.Grounds	—
1912-	Fenway Park	34,182
	(1934 capacity—27,000)	

California Angels

1961	Wrigley Field (Los Angeles)	20,457
1962-65	Dodger Stadium*	56,000
1966-	Anaheim Stadium	64,593
	(1966 capacity—43,250)	

Chicago White Sox

1901-10	Southside Park	—
1910-	Comiskey Park*	43,931
	(1910 capacity—32,000)	

American League Home Fields (Continued)

Cleveland Indians

1901-09	League Park I	—
1910-46	League Park II*	21,414
1932-	Cleveland Stadium*	74,483
	(1932 capacity—77,797)	

Detroit Tigers

1901-11	Bennett Park	—
1912-	Tiger Stadium*	52,416
	(1912 capacity—23,000)	

Kansas City Royals

1969-72	Municipal Stadium	35,020
1973-	Royals Stadium	40,625
	(1973 capacity—40,762)	

Milwaukee Brewers

1969	Sick's Stadium (Seattle)	25,420
1970-	County Stadium (Milwaukee)	53,192
	(1970 capacity—46,625)	

Minnesota Twins

1901-02	American League Park (Wash.,DC)	—
1903-60	Griffith Stadium*	27,410
1960-81	Metropolitan Stad. (Bloomington,MN)	45,919
1982-	HHH Metrodome (Minneapolis)	55,884
	(1982 capacity—54,000)	

New York Yankees

1901-02	Oriole Park (Baltimore)	—
1903-12	Hilltop Park (New York)	—
1913-22	Polo Grounds II	38,000
1923-73	Yankee Stadium I	67,224
1974-75	Shea Stadium	55,101
1976-	Yankee Stadium II	57,545
	(1976 capacity—57,145)	

Oakland Athletics

1901-08	Columbia Park (Philadelphia)	—
1909-54	Shibe Park*	33,608
1955-67	Municipal Stadium (Kansas City)	35,020
1968-	Oakland Alameda County Coliseum	48,219
	(Original 1968 capacity—48,621)	

Seattle Mariners

1977-	The Kingdome	58,150
	(Original 1977 capacity—59,438)	

Texas Rangers

1961	Griffith Stadium* (Wash.,DC)	27,410
1962-71	D.C. Stadium*	45,016
1972-	Arlington (TX) Stadium	43,508
	(Original 1972 capacity—35,698)	

Toronto Blue Jays

1977-89	Exhibition Stadium	43,737
1989-	SkyDome	49,500

*Ballpark Name Changes: CHICAGO—Comiskey Park originally White Sox Park (1910-12), then Comiskey Park in 1913, then White Sox Park again in 1962, then Comiskey Park again in 1976; CLEVELAND—League Park renamed Dunn Field in 1920, then League Park again in 1928; Cleveland Stadium originally Municipal Stadium (1932-74); DETROIT—Tiger Stadium originally Navin Field (1912-37), then Briggs Stadium (1938-60); LOS ANGELES—Dodger Stadium referred to as Chavez Ravine by AL while Angels played there (1962-65); PHILADELPHIA—Shibe Park renamed Connie Mack Stadium in 1953; ST.LOUIS—Sportsman's Park renamed Busch Stadium in 1953; WASHINGTON—Griffith Stadium originally National Park (1892-20), D.C.Stadium renamed Robert F.Kennedy Stadium in 1968.

National Basketball Association

Eastern Conference

		Location	Built	Capacity
Atlanta Hawks	The Omni	Atlanta, GA	1972	16,818
Boston Celtics	Boston Garden	Boston, MA	1928	14,890
Chicago Bulls	Chicago Stadium	Chicago, IL	1929	17,500
Cleveland Cavaliers	The Coliseum	Richfield, OH	1974	20,900
Detroit Pistons	The Palace	Auburn Hills, MI	1988	21,454
Indiana Pacers	Market Square Arena	Indianapolis, IN	1974	16,912
Miami Heat	Miami Arena	Miami, FL	1988	15,362
Milwaukee Bucks	Bradley Center	Milwaukee, WI	1988	18,633
New Jersey Nets	Byrne Meadowlands Arena	East Rutherford, NJ	1981	20,089
New York Knicks	Madison Square Garden	New York, NY	1968	19,591
Orlando Magic	Orlando Arena	Orlando, FL	1989	15,500
Philadelphia 76ers	The Spectrum	Philadelphia, PA	1967	18,168
Washington Bullets	Capital Centre	Landover, MD	1973	18,643

Western Conference

		Location	Built	Capacity
Charlotte Hornets	Charlotte Coliseum	Charlotte, NC	1988	23,500
Dallas Mavericks	Reunion Arena	Dallas, TX	1980	17,007
Denver Nuggets	McNichols Arena	Denver, CO	1975	16,700
Golden St. Warriors	Oakland Coliseum Arena	Oakland, CA	1966	15,025
Houston Rockets	The Summit	Houston, TX	1975	16,611
Los Angeles Clippers	Memorial Sports Arena	Los Angeles, CA	1959	15,371
Los Angeles Lakers	Great Western Forum	Inglewood, CA	1967	17,505
Minnesota Timberwolves	Hubert H.Humphrey Metrodome	Minneapolis, MN	1982	23,000
Phoenix Suns	Veterans' Coliseum	Phoenix, AZ	1965	14,471
Portland Trail Blazers	Memorial Coliseum	Portland, OR	1960	12,880
Sacramento Kings	ARCO Arena	Sacramento, CA	1988	16,517
San Antonio Spurs	HemisFair Arena	San Antonio, TX	1968	15,770
Seattle SuperSonics	The Coliseum	Seattle, WA	1962	14,200
Utah Jazz	The Salt Palace	Salt Lake City, UT	1969	12,444

Ranked by Capacity

Eastern Conference		Western Conference	
The Palace	21,454	Charlotte Colis	23,500
Clev.Coliseum	20,900	HHH Metrodome	23,000
NJ Meadowlands	20,089	LA Forum	17,505
Mad.Sq.Garden	19,591	Reunion Arena	17,007
Capital Center	18,643	McNichols Arena	16,700
Bradley Center	18,633	The Summit	16,611
The Spectrum	18,168	ARCO Arena	16,517
Chicago Stadium	17,500	HemisFair Arena	15,770
Market Sq.Arena	16,912	LA Sports Arena	15,371
The Omni	16,818	Oakland Arena	15,025
Orlando Arena	15,500	Phoe.Coliseum	14,471
Miami Arena	15,362	Seat.Coliseum	14,200
Boston Garden	14,890	Port.Coliseum	12,880
		Salt Palace	12,444

Ranked by Age

Eastern Conference		Western Conference	
Boston Garden	1928	LA Sports Arena	1959
Chicago Stadium	1929	Portland Coliseum	1960
The Spectrum	1967	Seattle Coliseum	1962
Mad.Sq.Garden	1968	Phoenix Coliseum	1965
The Omni	1972	Oakland Coliseum	1966
Capital Centre	1973	LA Forum	1967
Cleve.Coliseum	1974	HemisFair Arena	1968
Market Sq.Arena	1974	Salt Palace	1969
NJ Meadowlands	1981	McNichols Arena	1975
Miami Arena	1988	The Summit	1975
Bradley Center	1988	Reunion Arena	1980
The Palace	1988	HHH Metrodome	1982
Orlando Arena	1989	Charlotte Colis.	1988
		ARCO Arena	1988

Home Courts

Listed below are the principal home courts used through the years by current NBA teams. The largest capacity of each arena is noted in the right hand column. ABA arenas (1972-76) are included for Denver, Indiana, New Jersey and San Antonio.

Eastern Conference

Atlanta Hawks

1949-51	Wheaton Field House (Moline,IL)	6,000
1951-55	Milwaukee Arena	11,000
1955-68	Kiel Auditorium (St.Louis)	10,000
1968-72	Alexander Mem. Coliseum (Atlanta)	7,166
1972-	The Omni (Atlanta)	16,818
	(1972 capacity—16,818)	

Boston Celtics

1946-	Boston Garden	14,890
	(1946 capacity—13,909)	

Note: Since 1975-76, the Celtics have played several regular season games at the Hartford Civic Center.

Chicago Bulls

1966-67	Chicago Amphitheater	11,002
1967-	Chicago Stadium	17,500
	(1967 capacity—17,374)	

Cleveland Cavaliers

1970-74	Cleveland Arena	11,000
1974-	The Coliseum (Richfield,OH)	20,900
	(1974 capacity—19,500)	

Detroit Pistons

1948-52	North Side H.S.Gym (Ft.Wayne,IN)	3,800
1952-57	Memorial Coliseum (Ft.Wayne)	9,306
1957-61	Olympia Stadium (Detroit)	14,000
1961-78	Cobo Arena	11,147
1978-88	Silverdome (Pontiac,MI)	22,366
1988-	The Palace (Auburn Hills, MI)	21,454

Indiana Pacers

1967-74	State Fairgrounds (Indianapolis)	9,479
1974-	Market Square Arena	16,912
	(1974 capacity—17,287)	

Miami Heat

1988-	Miami Arena	15,362

Milwaukee Bucks

1968-88	Milwaukee Arena (The Mecca)	11,052
1988-	Bradley Center	18,633

New Jersey Nets

1967-68	Teaneck,NJ Armory	3,500
1968-69	Long Island Arena (Commmack,NY)	6,500
1969-71	Island Garden	
	(West Hempstead,NY)	5,200
1971-77	Nassau Coliseum (Uniondale,NY)	15,500
1977-81	Rutgers Ath.Center (Piscataway,NJ)	9,050
1981-	Meadowlands Arena	
	(E.Rutherford,NJ)	20,089
	(1981 capacity—20,089)	

New York Knicks

1946-68	Madison Sq. Garden III (50th St)	18,496
1968-	Madison Sq. Garden IV (33rd St.)	19,591
	(1968 capacity—19,694)	

Orlando Magic

1989-	Orlando Arena	15,500

Philadelphia 76ers

1949-51	State Fair Coliseum (Syracuse,NY)	7,500
1951-63	Onondaga County (NY)	
	War Memorial	8,000
1963-67	Convention Hall (Philadelphia)	12,000
	& Philadelphia Arena	7,777
1967-	The Spectrum	18,168
	(1967 capacity—15,205)	

Washington Bullets

1961-62	Chicago Amphitheater	11,000
1962-63	Chicago Coliseum	7,100
1963-73	Baltimore Civic Center	12,289
1973-	Capital Centre (Landover,MD)	18,643
	(1973 capacity—17,500)	

NBA Home Courts (Continued)
Western Conference

Charlotte Hornets
1988- Charlotte Coliseum 23,500

Dallas Mavericks
1980- Reunion Arena 17,007
(1980 capacity—17,828)

Denver Nuggets
1967-75 Auditorium Arena 6,841
1975- McNichols Sports Arena 16,700
(1975 capacity—16,700)

Golden State Warriors
1946-52 Philadelphia Arena 7,777
1952-62 Convention Hall (Philadelphia) 9,200
& Philadelphia Arena 7,777
1962-64 Cow Palace (San Francisco) 13,862
1964-66 Civic Auditorium 7,500
& (USF Memorial Gym) 6,000
1966-67 Cow Palace, Civic Auditorium
& Oakland Coliseum Arena 15,000
1967-71 Cow Palace 14,500
1971- Oakland Coliseum Arena 15,039
(1971 capacity—12,905)

Houston Rockets
1967-71 San Diego Sports Arena 14,000
1971-72 Hofheinz Pavilion (Houston) 10,218
& six other sites
1972-73 Hofheinz Pavilion 10,218
& HemisFair Arena (San Antonio) . . 10,446
1973-75 Hofheinz Pavilion 10,218
1975- The Summit 16,611
(1975 capacity—15,600)

Note: During the 1971-72 season, the Rockets played 21 games
at Hofheinz, 8 at Astrohall and 6 at the Astrodome in Houston,
as well as 3 games in San Antonio, 2 in Waco and 1 in El Paso.
In 1972-73, they played 28 games at Hofheinz and 13 at the
HemisFair in San Antonio.

Los Angeles Clippers
1970-78 Memorial Auditorium (Buffalo) 17,300
1978-84 San Diego Sports Arena 12,167
1985- Los Angeles Sports Arena 15,371
(1985 capacity—15,371)

Los Angeles Lakers
1948-60 Minneapolis Auditorium 10,000
1960-67 Los Angeles Sports Arena 14,781
1967- The Forum (Inglewood,CA) 17,505
(1967 capacity—17,086)

Minnesota Timberwolves
1989- Hubert H.Humphrey Metrodome . 23,000

Phoenix Suns
1968- Ariz.Veterans' Memorial Coliseum 14,471
(1968 capacity—12,200)

Portland Trail Blazers
1970- Memorial Coliseum 12,880
(1970 capacity—12,366)

Sacramento Kings
1948-55 Edgarton Park Arena
(Rochester,NY) 5,000
1955-58 Rochester War Memorial 10,000
1958-72 Cincinnati Gardens 11,438
1972-74 Municipal Auditorium (Kansas City) . 9,929
& Omaha,Neb. Civic Auditorium . . 9,136
1974-78 Kemper Arena (Kansas City) 16,785
& Omaha Civic Auditorium 9,136
1978-85 Kemper Arena 16,785
1985-88 ARCO Arena I 10,333
1988- ARCO Arena II 16,517

San Antonio Spurs
1967-70 Memorial Coliseum (Dallas) 8,088
& Moody Coliseum (Dallas) 8,500
1970-71 Three courts—Moody Coliseum 8,500
Tarrant Conven.Center(Ft.Wroth) . 13,500
& Municipal Coliseum (Lubbock) . . . 10,400
1971-73 Two courts—Moody Coliseum 9,500
& Memorial Auditorium 8,088
1973- HemisFair Arena (San Antonio) 15,770
(1973 capacity—10,446)

Seattle Supersonics
1967-78 Seattle Center Coliseum 14,098
1978-85 Kingdome 40,192
1985- The Coliseum 14,200
(1985 capacity—14,000)

Utah Jazz
1974-75 Municipal Auditorium 7,853
& Louisiana Superdome 47,284
1975-79 Superdome 47,284
1979-83 Salt Palace (Salt Lake City) 12,519
1983-84 Salt Palace 12,519
& Thomas Mack Center (Las Vegas) 18,500
1985- Salt Palace 12,444
(1979 capacity—12,519)

National Football League
American Football Conference

		Location	Built	Capacity	Field
Buffalo Bills	Rich Stadium	Orchard Park, NY	1973	80,290	Turf
Cincinnati Bengals	Riverfront Stadium	Cincinnati, OH	1970	60,311	Turf
Cleveland Browns	Cleveland Stadium	Cleveland, OH	1932	80,098	Grass
Denver Broncos	Mile High Stadium	Denver, CO	1948	76,274	Grass
Houston Oilers	The Astrodome	Houston, TX	1965	62,000	Turf
Indianapolis Colts	The Hoosier Dome	Indianapolis, IN	1984	60,129	Turf
Kansas City Chiefs	Arrowhead Stadium	Kansas City, MO	1972	78,067	Turf
Los Angeles Raiders	Memorial Coliseum	Los Angeles, CA	1923	92,488	Grass
Miami Dolphins	Joe Robbie Stadium	Miami, FL	1987	74,930	Grass
New England Patriots	Sullivan Stadium	Foxboro, MA	1971	61,000	Turf
New York Jets	Giants Stadium	E.Rutherford, NJ	1976	76,891	Turf
Pittsburgh Steelers	Three Rivers Stadium	Pittsburgh, PA	1970	59,030	Turf
San Diego Chargers	San Diego/Jack Murphy Stadium	San Diego, CA	1967	60,750	Grass
Seattle Seahawks	The Kingdome	Seattle, WA	1976	64,981	Turf

National Football Conference

		Location	Built	Capacity	Field
Atlanta Falcons	Atlanta-Fulton County Stadium	Atlanta, GA	1965	59,643	Grass
Chicago Bears	Soldier Field	Chicago, IL	1924	66,946	Grass
Dallas Cowboys	Texas Stadium	Irving, TX	1971	65,024	Turf
Detroit Lions	Pontiac Silverdome	Pontiac, MI	1975	80,638	Turf
Green Bay Packers	Lambeau Field	Green Bay, WI	1957	57,095	Grass
	& County Stadium	Milwaukee, WI	1953	56,051	Grass
Los Angeles Rams	Anaheim Stadium	Anaheim, CA	1966	69,008	Grass
Minnesota Vikings	Hubert H.Humphrey Metrodome	Minneapolis, MN	1982	63,300	Turf
New Orleans Saints	Louisiana Superdome	New Orleans, LA	1975	69,065	Turf
New York Giants	Giants Stadium	E.Rutherford, NJ	1976	76,891	Turf
Philadelphia Eagles	Veterans Stadium	Philadelphia, PA	1971	66,945	Turf
Phoenix Cardinals	Sun Devil Stadium	Tempe, AZ	1958	73,500	Grass
San Francisco 49ers	Candlestick Park	San Francisco, CA	1960	66,252	Grass
Tampa Bay Buccaneers	Tampa Stadium	Tampa, FL	1967	74,314	Grass
Washington Redskins	Robert F.Kennedy Stadium	Washington, DC	1961	55,750	Grass

Ranked by Capacity

AFC		NFC	
LA Coliseum	92,488	Silverdome	80,638
Rich	80,290	Giants	76,891
Cleveland	80,098	Tampa	74,314
Arrowhead	78,067	Sun Devil	73,500
Giants	76,891	Superdome	69,065
Mile High	76,274	Anaheim	69,008
Joe Robbie	74,930	Soldier Field	66,946
Kingdome	64,981	Veterans	66,945
Astrodome	62,000	Candlestick	66,252
Sullivan	61,000	Texas	65,024
Jack Murphy	60,750	Metrodome	63,300
Riverfront	60,311	Atlanta	59,643
Hoosier Dome	60,129	Lambeau Field	57,095
Three Rivers	59,030	Milw.County	56,051
		RFK	55,750

Ranked by Age

AFC		NFC	
LA Coliseum	1923	Soldier Field	1924
Cleveland	1931	Milw.County	1953
Mile High	1948	Lambeau Field	1957
Astrodome	1965	Sun Devil	1958
Jack Murphy	1967	Candlestick	1960
Riverfront	1970	RFK	1961
Three Rivers	1970	Atlanta	1965
Sullivan	1971	Anaheim	1966
Arrowhead	1972	Tampa	1967
Rich	1973	Texas	1971
Giants	1976	Veterans	1971
Kingdome	1976	Silverdome	1975
Hoosier Dome	1984	Superdome	1975
Joe Robbie	1987	Giants	1976
		Metrodome	1982

Home Fields

Listed below are the principal home fields used through the years by current NFL teams. The largest capacity of each stadium is noted in the right hand column. All-America Football Conference stadiums (1946-49) are included for Cleveland and San Francisco; and American Football League stadiums (1960-69) are included for Buffalo, Cincinnati, Denver, Houston, Kansas City, LA (Oakland) Raiders, Miami, New England (Boston), NY Jets and San Diego.

American Conference

Buffalo Bills
1960-72	War Memorial Stadium	45,748
1973-	Rich Stadium (Orchard Park,NY)	80,290
	(1973 capacity—80,020)	

Cincinnati Bengals
1968-69	Nippert Stadium (U.of Cincinnati)	26,500
1970-	Riverfront Stadium	60,311
	(1970 capacity—56,200)	

Cleveland Browns
1946-	Cleveland Stadium*	80,098
	(1946 capacity—85,703)	

Denver Broncos
1960-	Mile High Stadium*	76,274
	(1960 capacity—34,000)	

NFL Football Home Fields (Continued)

Houston Oilers
1960-64	Jeppesen Stadium	23,500
1965-67	Rice Stadium (Rice Univ.)	70,000
1968-	Astrodome	62,000
	(1968 capacity—52,000)	

Indianapolis Colts
1953-83	Memorial Stadium (Baltimore)	60,020
1984-	Hoosier Dome (Indianapolis)	60,129
	(1984 capacity—60,127)	

Kansas City Chiefs
1960-62	Cotton Bowl (Dallas)	72,000
1963-71	Municipal Stadium (Kansas City)	47,000
1972-	Arrowhead Stadium	78,067
	(1972 capacity—78,097)	

Los Angeles Raiders
1960	Kesar Stadium (San Francisco)	59,636
1961	Candlestick Park	42,500
1962-65	Frank Youell Field (Oakland)	20,000
1966-81	Oakland-Alameda County Coliseum	54,587
1982-	Memorial Coliseum (Los Angeles)	92,488
	(1982 capacity—92,488)	

Note: Youell Field was on the campus of Laney College.

Miami Dolphins
1966-86	Orange Bowl	75,206
1987-	Joe Robbie Stadium	74,930
	(1987 capacity—75,500)	

New England Patriots
1960-62	Nickerson Field (Boston Univ.)	17,369
1963-68	Fenway Park	33,379
1969	Alumni Stadium (Boston College)	26,000
1970	Harvard Stadium	37,300
1971-	Sullivan Stadium* (Foxboro,MA)	61,000
	(1971 capacity—61,114)	

New York Jets
1960-63	Polo Grounds	55,987
1964-83	Shea Stadium	60,372
1984-	Giants Stadium (E.Rutherford,NJ)	76,891
	(1984 capacity—76,891)	

Pittsburgh Steelers
1933-57	Forbes Field	35,000
1958-63	Forbes Field	35,000
	& Pitt Stadium	54,500
1964-69	Pitt Stadium	54,500
1970-	Three Rivers Stadium	59,030
	(1970 capacity—49,000)	

San Diego Chargers
1960	Memorial Coliseum (Los Angeles)	92,604
1961-66	Balboa Stadium (San Diego)	34,000
1967-	San Diego/Jack Murphy Stadium*	60,750
	(1967 capacity—54,000)	

Seattle Seahawks
1976-	Kingdome	64,981
	(1976 capacity—65,000)	

*Ballpark Name Changes: CLEVELAND—**Cleveland Stadium** originally Municipal Stadium (1932-74); DENVER —**Mile High Stadium** originally Bears Stadium (1948-66); NEW ENGLAND—**Sullivan Stadium** originally Schaefer Stadium (1971-82); SAN DIEGO—**San Diego/Jack Murphy Stadium** originally San Diego Stadium (1967-81).

National Conference

Atlanta Falcons
1966-	Atlanta-Fulton County Stadium*	59,643
	(1966 capacity—58,850)	

Chicago Bears
1920	Staley Field (Decatur,IL)	—
1921-70	Wrigley Field* (Chicago)	37,741
1971-	Soldier Field	66,946
	(1971 capacity—55,049)	

Dallas Cowboys
1960-70	Cotton Bowl	72,132
1971-	Texas Stadium (Irving,TX)	65,024
	(1971 capacity—65,101)	

Detroit Lions
1930-33	Spartan Stadium (Portsmouth,OH)	8,200
1934-37	Univ.of Detroit Stadium	25,000
1938-74	Tiger Stadium*	54,468
1975-	Pontiac Silverdome*	80,638
	(1975 capacity—80,638)	

Green Bay Packers
1921-22	Hagemeister Brewery Park	—
1923-24	Bellevue Park	—
1925-56	City Stadium I	24,800
1957-	Lambeau Field*	57,095
	(1957 capacity—32,150)	

Note: The Packers have played some games in Milwaukee each season since 1933: at Borchert Field, State Fair Park and Marquette Stadium (1933-52), and County Stadium (56,051) since 1953.

Los Angeles Rams
1937-42	Municipal Stadium (Cleveland)	85,703
1945	Suspended operations for one year	
1944-45	Municipal Stadium	85,703
1946-79	Memorial Coliseum (Los Angeles)	92,604
1980-	Anaheim Stadium	69,008
	(1980 capacity—69,008)	

Minnesota Vikings
1961-81	Metropolitan Stadium (Bloomington)	48,446
1982-	HHH Metrodome (Minneapolis)	63,300
	(1982 capacity—62,220)	

New Orleans Saints
1967-74	Tulane Stadium	80,997
1975-	Louisiana Superdome	69,065
	(1975 capacity—74,472)	

New York Giants
1925-55	Polo Grounds II	55,200
1956-73	Yankee Stadium I	63,800
1973-74	Yale Bowl (New Haven,CT)	70,896
1975	Shea Stadium	60,372
1976-	Giants Stadium (E.Rutherford,NJ)	76,891
	(1976 capacity—76,800)	

Philadelphia Eagles

1933-35	Baker Bowl	18,800
1936-39	Municipal Stadium	73,702
1940	Shibe Park	33,608
1941	Municipal Stadium	73,702
1942	Shibe Park	33,608
1943	Forbes Field (Pittsburgh)	34,528
1944-57	Shibe Park*	33,608
1958-70	Franklin Field (Univ.of Penn.)	60,546
1971-	Veterans Stadium	66,945
	(1971 capacity—65,000)	

Phoenix Cardinals

1920-21	Normal Field (Chicago)	7,500
1922-25	Comiskey Park	28,000
1926-28	Normal Field	7,500
1929-59	Comiskey Park	52,000
1960-65	Busch Stadium (St.Louis)	34,000
1966-87	Busch Memorial Stadium*	54,392
1988-	Sun Devil Stadium (Tempe,AZ)	73,500

San Francisco 49ers

1946-70	Kezar Stadium	59,636
1971-	Candlestick Park	66,252
	(1971 capacity—45,000)	

Tampa Bay Buccaneers

1976-	Tampa Stadium	74,314
	(1976 capacity—71,951)	

Washington Redskins

1932	Braves Field (Boston)	40,000
1933-36	Fenway Park	27,000
1937-60	Griffith Stadium (Wash.,DC)	35,000
1961-	RFK Stadium*	55,750
	(1961 capacity—55,004)	

*Ballpark Name Changes: ATLANTA—**Atlanta-Fulton County Stadium** originally Atlanta Stadium (1966-74); CHICAGO—**Wrigley Field originally Cubs Park (1916-25), also, Comiskey Park** originally originally White Sox Park (1910-12); DETROIT—**Tiger Stadium** originally Navin Field (1912-37), then Briggs Stadium (1938-60), also, **Pontiac Silverdome** originally Pontiac Metropolitan Stadium (1975); GREEN BAY—**Lambeau Field** originally City Stadium II (1957-64); PHILADELPHIA—**Shibe Park** renamed Connie Mack Stadium in 1953; ST. LOUIS—**Busch Memorial Stadium** renamed Busch Stadium in 1983; WASHINGTON—**RFK Stadium** originally D.C.Stadium (1961-68).

San Francisco's **Kezar Stadium**, built in 1925 and home of the football 49ers from 1946-70, was torn down this spring.

Canadian Football League

Eastern Division

		Location	Built	Capacity	Field
Hamilton Tiger-Cats	Ivor Wynne Stadium	Hamilton, ONT.	1932	29,183	Turf
Ottawa Rough Riders	Lansdowne Park	Ottawa, ONT.	1967	30,927	Turf
Toronto Argos	Skydome	Toronto, ONT.	1989	53,595	Turf
Winnipeg Blue Bombers	Winnipeg Stadium	Winnipeg, MAN.	1953	32,694	Turf

Western Division

		Location	Built	Capacity	Field
British Columbia Lions	B.C.Place	Vancouver, BC	1983	59,478	Turf
Calgary Stampeders	McMahon Stadium	Calgary, ALB.	1960	38,400	Turf
Edmonton Eskimos	Commonwealth Stadium	Edmonton, ALB.	1978	60,081	Grass
Saskatchewan Roughriders	Taylor Field	Regina, SASK.	1948	27,637	Turf

National Hockey League

Wales Conference

		Location	Built	Capacity
Boston Bruins	Boston Garden	Boston, MA	1928	14,637
Buffalo Sabres	Memorial Auditorium	Buffalo, NY	1940	16,433
Hartford Whalers	Civic Center Coliseum	Hartford, CT	1975	15,223
Montreal Canadiens	Montreal Forum	Montreal, Que	1924	16,084
New Jersey Devils	Byrne Meadowlands Arena	E.Rutherford, NJ	1981	19,040
New York Islanders	Veterans' Mem. Coliseum	Uniondale, NY	1971	16,297
New York Rangers	Madison Square Garden	New York, NY	1968	17,500
Philadelphia Flyers	The Spectrum	Philadelphia, PA	1967	17,425
Pittsburgh Penguins	Civic Arena	Pittsburgh, PA	1961	16,025
Quebec Nordiques	Colisée de Québec	Quebec City, Que	1951	15,399
Washington Capitals	Capital Centre	Landover, MD	1973	18,130

Campell Conference

		Location	Built	Capacity
Calgary Flames	Olympic Saddledome	Calgary, Alb.	1983	20,002
Chicago Blackhawks	Chicago Stadium	Chicago, IL	1929	17,317
Detroit Red Wings	Joe Louis Sports Arena	Detroit, MI	1979	19,275
Edmonton Oilers	Northlands Coliseum	Edmonton, Alb.	1974	17,312
Los Angeles Kings	Great Western Forum	Los Angeles, CA	1967	16,005
Minnesota North Stars	Met Center	Bloomington, MN	1967	15,499
St.Louis Blues	St.Louis Arena	St.Louis, MO	1929	17,188
Toronto Maple Leafs	Maple Leaf Gardens	Toronto, Ont.	1931	16,864
Vancouver Canucks	Pacific Coliseum	Vancouver, B.C.	1968	16,160
Winnipeg Jets	Winnipeg Arena	Winnipeg, Man.	1954	15,401

Ranked by Capacity

Wales Conference	Campbell Conference
Meadowlands . . . 19,040	Saddledome 20,002
Capital Centre . . 18,130	Joe Louis 19,275
Mad.Sq.Garden . 17,500	Chicago Stadium 17,317
Spectrum 17,425	Northlands 17,312
Buffalo Aud 16,433	St.Louis 17,188
Nassau Coliseum 16,297	M.Leaf Gardens . 16,864
Montreal Forum . 16,084	Pacific Col 16,160
Pitt.Civ.Arena . . . 16,025	LA Forum 16,005
Le Colisée 15,399	Met Center 15,499
Hart.Civ.Center . 15,223	Winnipeg Arena 15,401
Boston Garden . . 14,637	

Note: Figures do not include Standing Room.

Ranked by Age

Wales Conference	Campbell Conference
Montreal Forum . . 1924	Chicago Stadium . . 1929
Boston Garden . . . 1928	St.Louis Arena 1929
Buffalo Aud 1940	M.Leaf Gardens . . 1931
Le Colisee 1951	Winnipeg Arena . . 1954
Pitt Civic Arena . . 1961	Met Center 1967
Spectrum 1967	LA Forum 1967
Mad.Sq.Garden . . 1968	Pacific Coliseum . . 1968
Nassau Coliseum . . 1971	Northlands Col . . . 1974
Capital Center 1973	Joe Louis Arena . . 1979
Hart.Civic Center . 1975	Saddledome 1983
Meadowlands 1981	

Note: The Montreal Forum was rebuilt in 1968, the Hartford Civic Center in 1980.

Home Ice

Listed below are the principal home buildings used through the years by current NHL teams. The largest capacity of each arena is noted in the right hand column. World Hockey Association arenas (1972-76) are included for Edmonton, Hartford, Quebec and Winnipeg.

Wales Conference

Boston Bruins
1924-28	Boston Arena	6,200
1928-	Boston Garden	14,637
	(1928 capacity—14,500)	

Buffalo Sabres
1970-	Memorial Auditorium	16,433
	(1970 capacity—10,429)	

Hartford Whalers
1972-73	Boston Garden	14,442
1973-74	Boston Garden (regular season)	14,442
	W.Springfield,MA Big E (playoffs)	5,513
1974-75	West Springfield Big E	5,513
	& Hartford (CT) Civic Center	10,507
1975-77	Hartford Civic Center	10,507
1977-78	Hartford Civic Center	10,507
	& Springfield (MA) Civic Center	7,725
1978-79	Springfield Civic Center	7,725
1979-80	Springfield Civic Center	7,725
	& Hartford Civic Center II	14,250
1980-	Hartford Civic Center II	15,223
	(1980 capacity—14,460)	

Note: The Hartford Civic Center roof caved in Jan,1978, forcing the Whalers to move their home games to Springfield,MA, for two years.

Montreal Canadiens
1910-20	Jubilee Arena	3,200
1913-18	Montreal Arena (Westmount)	6,000
1918-26	Mount Royal Arena	6,750
1926-68	Montreal Forum I	15,500
1968-	Montreal Forum II	16,084
	(1968 capacity—16,084)	

Note: The Forum (original capacity: 9,200) was built in 1924 for Montreal's other NHL team, the Maroons, who were its only tenant from 1924-26. The Maroons, who folded after the 1937-38 season, shared the Forum with the Canadiens from 1924-38.

New Jersey Devils
1974-76	Kemper Arena (Kansas City)	16,300
1976-82	McNichols Arena (Denver)	15,900
1982-	Meadowlands Arena	
	(E.Rutherford,NJ)	19,040
	(1982 capacity—19,023)	

New York Islanders
1972-	Nassau Veterans' Mem.Coliseum	16,297
	(1972 capacity—14,500)	

New York Rangers
1925-68	Madison Square Garden III	15,925
1968-	Madison Square Garden IV	17,500
	(1968 capacity—17,250)	

Philadelphia Flyers
1967-	The Spectrum	17,425
	(1967 capacity—14,558)	

Note: A section of Spectrum roof blew off in March,1968, forcing the Flyers to play their last seven regular season home games at Madison Sq.Garden (1 game), Maple Leaf Gardens (1) and Le Colisée in Quebec (5). The roof was fixed by the playoffs.

Pittsburgh Penguins
1967-	Civic Arena	16,025
	(1967 capacity—12,508)	

Quebec Nordiques
1972-	Le Colisée de Québec	15,399
	(1972 capacity—10,004)	

Washington Capitals
1974-	Capital Centre (Landover,MD)	18,130
	(1974 capacity—18,130)	

Campbell Conference

Calgary Flames
1972-80	The Omni (Atlanta)	15,278
1980-83	Calgary Corral	7,424
1983-	Olympic Saddledome	20,002
	(1983 capacity—16,674)	

Chicago Stadium
1926-29	Chicago Coliseum	5,000
1929-	Chicago Stadium	17,317
	(1929 capacity—16,500)	

Detroit Red Wings
1926-27	Border Cities Arena (Windsor,Ont.)	3,200
1927-79	Olympia Stadium (Detroit)	16,700
1979-	Joe Louis Arena	19,275
	(1979 capacity—19,275)	

Edmonton Oilers
1972-74	Edmonton Gardens	7,200
1974-	Northlands Coliseum	17,312
	(1974 capacity—15,513)	

Los Angeles Kings
1967-	Great Western Forum (Inglewood)	16,005
	(1967 capacity—15,651)	

Note: The Kings played 17 games at Long Beach Sports Arena and LA Sports Arena at the start of the 1967-68 season.

Minnesota North Stars
1967-	Met Center	15,499
	(1967 capacity—14,400)	

St.Louis Blues
1967-	St.Louis Arena	17,188
	(1967 capacity—14,200)	

Toronto Maple Leafs
1917-31	Mutual Street Arena	8,000
1931-	Maple Leaf Gardens	16,864
	(1931 capacity—13,542)	

Vancouver Canucks
1970-	Pacific Coliseum	16,160
	(1970 capacity—15,760)	

Winnipeg Jets
1972-	Winnipeg Arena	15,401
	(1972 capacity—10,177)	

Building Name Changes: LOS ANGELES—**Great Western Forum** originally The Forum (1967-88); MINNESOTA—**Met Center** originally Metropolitan Sports Center (1967-82); ST.LOUIS—**St.Louis Arena** renamed The Checkerdome in 1977, then St.Louis Arena again in 1982.

Major College Football Stadiums

Stadiums played in by NCAA Division I-A football teams. Teams with home games in more than one stadium are noted.

Atlantic Coast Conference

	Stadium	Built	Seating	Field
Clemson	Memorial	1942	79,853	Grass
Duke	Wallace Wade	1929	33,941	Grass
Ga.Tech	Grant Field	1914	46,000	Turf
Maryland	Byrd	1950	45,000	Grass
N.Carolina	Kenan	1927	52,000	Grass
N.C.State	Carter-Finley	1966	53,500	Grass
Virginia	Scott	1931	42,000	Turf
Wake Forest	Groves	1968	31,500	Grass

Big Eight Conference

	Stadium	Built	Seating	Field
Colorado	Folsom Field	1924	51,463	Turf
Iowa St	Trice Field	1975	50,000	Turf
Kansas	Memorial	1927	50,250	Turf
Kansas St	KSU	1968	42,000	Turf
Missouri	Faurot Field	1926	62,000	Turf
Nebraska	Memorial	1923	73,650	Turf
Oklahoma	Owen Field	1923	75,004	Turf
Oklahoma St	Lewis Field	1920	50,440	Turf

Big Ten Conference

	Stadium	Built	Seating	Field
Illinois	Memorial	1923	70,538	Turf
Indiana	Memorial	1960	52,354	Turf
Iowa	Kinnick	1929	67,700	Grass
Michigan	Michigan	1927	101,701	Turf
Michigan St	Spartan	1957	76,000	Turf
Minnesota	Metrodome	1982	63,300	Turf
Northwestern	Dyche	1926	49,256	Turf
Ohio St	Ohio	1922	85,339	Turf
Purdue	Ross-Ade	1924	67,861	Grass
Wisconsin	Camp Randall	1917	77,280	Turf

Big West Conference

	Stadium	Built	Seating	Field
Fresno St	Bulldog	1980	30,000	Grass
CS-Fullerton	Santa Ana	1963	12,000	Grass
L.Beach St	Veterans	1966	12,500	Grass
N.Mexico St	Memorial	1978	30,343	Grass
Pacific	Memorial	1950	30,153	Grass
San Jose St	Spartan	1932	31,365	Grass
UNLV	Silver Bowl	1971	32,000	Turf
Utah St	Romney	1968	30,257	Grass

Mid-American Conference

	Stadium	Built	Seating	Field
Ball St	Ball State	1967	16,319	Grass
Bowl.Green	Perry Field	1966	30,300	Grass
Central Mich	Kelly/Shorts	1972	20,086	Turf
Eastern Mich	Rynearson	1969	19,800	Grass
Kent St	Dix	1969	30,520	Grass
Miami,OH	Yager	1983	25,183	Grass
Ohio Univ	Peden	1929	20,000	Grass
Toledo	Glass Bowl	1937	18,500	Turf
Western Mich	Waldo	1939	25,000	Turf

Pac-10 Conference

	Stadium	Built	Seating	Field
Arizona	Arizona	1928	57,000	Grass
Arizona St	Sun Devil	1958	73,500	Grass
California	Memorial	1923	75,630	Turf
Oregon	Autzen	1967	41,698	Turf
Oregon St	Parker	1953	39,597	Turf
Stanford	Stanford	1921	86,011	Grass
UCLA	Rose Bowl	1922	104,091	Grass
USC	LA Coliseum	1923	92,488	Grass
Washington	Husky	1920	72,500	Turf
Wash.St	Martin	1972	40,000	Turf

Southeastern Conference

	Stadium	Built	Seating	Field
Alabama	Bryant-Denny	1929	70,123	Turf
	Legion Field	1927	75,952	Turf
Auburn	Jordan-Hare	1939	85,214	Grass
Florida	Florida Field	1929	74,000	Turf
Georgia	Sanford	1929	82,122	Grass
Kentucky	Commonwealth	1973	57,800	Grass
LSU	Tiger	1924	80,140	Grass
Mississippi	Vaught-H'way	1941	42,000	Grass
	Memorial	1953	62,529	Grass
Miss.St	Scott Field	1935	41,200	Grass
	Memorial	1953	62,529	Grass
Tennessee	Neyland	1921	91,249	Turf
Vanderbilt	Vanderbilt	1981	41,000	Turf

Note: At **Alabama**, Bryant-Denny Stadium is in Tuscaloosa and Legion Field in Birmingham; at **Mississippi**, Vaught-Hemingway Stadium is in Oxford and Memorial Stadium in Jackson; at **Mississippi St.**, Scott Field is in Starkville and Memorial Stadium in Jackson.

Southwest Athletic Conference

	Stadium	Built	Seating	Field
Arkansas	Razorback	1938	52,860	Turf
	War Memorial	1948	53,250	Turf
Baylor	Baylor	1950	48,500	Turf
Houston	Astrodome	1965	62,000	Turf
Rice	Rice	1950	70,000	Turf
SMU	Ownby	1926	24,576	Turf
Texas	Memorial	1924	80,000	Turf
	Cotton Bowl	1932	72,032	Turf
Texas A&M	Kyle Field	1925	72,387	Turf
TCU	Carter	1929	46,000	Turf
Texas Tech	Amon C. Jones	1947	47,000	Turf

Note: At **Arkansas**, Razorback Stadium is in Fayetteville and War Memorial Stadium in Little Rock; at **Texas**, Memorial Stadium is in Austin and the Cotton Bowl in Dallas.

Western Athletic Conference

	Stadium	Built	Seating	Field
Air Force	Falcon	1962	52,153	Grass
BYU	BYU	1964	65,000	Grass
Colorado St	Hughes	1968	30,000	Turf
Hawaii	Aloha	1975	50,000	Turf
New Mexico	University	1960	30,646	Grass
S.Diego St	Jack Murphy	1967	60,750	Grass
Utah	Rice	1927	35,000	Turf
UTEP	Sun Bowl	1963	52,000	Turf
Wyoming	War Memorial	1950	33,500	Grass

I-A Independents

	Stadium	Built	Seating	Field
Akron	Rubber Bowl	1940	35,482	Turf
Army	Michie	1924	39,867	Turf
Boston Col	Alumni	1957	32,000	Turf
Cincinnati	Nippert	1916	26,592	Turf
	Riverfront	1970	60,311	Turf
E.Carolina	Ficklen	1963	35,000	Grass
Florida St	Doak Campbell	1950	60,519	Grass
Louisville	Cardinal	1956	35,500	Turf
Memphis St	Liberty Bowl	1965	63,244	Grass
Miami,FL	Orange Bowl	1935	75,500	Grass
Navy	Navy-Marine Corps Memorial	1959	30,000	Grass
No.Illinois	Huskie	1965	30,998	Turf
N.Dame	Notre Dame	1930	59,075	Grass
Penn St	Beaver	1960	83,370	Grass
Pittsburgh	Pitt	1925	56,500	Turf
Rutgers	Rutgers	1938	23,000	Grass
	Giants	1976	76,891	Turf
S.Carolina	Williams-Brice	1934	72,400	Grass
SW La.	Cajun Field	1970	31,000	Grass
So.Miss	Roberts	1976	33,000	Grass
Syracuse	Carrier Dome	1980	50,000	Turf
Temple	Veterans	1971	66,945	Turf
Tulane	Superdome	1975	69,065	Turf
Tulsa	Skelly	1930	44,210	Turf
Va.Tech	Lane	1965	51,000	Grass
West Va	Mountaineer Fld	1980	63,500	Turf

Bowl Games

	Stadium	Built	Seating	Field
All-American	Legion Field	1927	75,952	Turf
Aloha	Aloha	1975	50,000	Turf
California	Bulldog	1980	30,000	Grass
Copper	Arizona	1928	57,000	Grass
Cotton	Cotton Bowl	1932	72,032	Turf
Fiesta	Sun Devil	1958	73,500	Grass
Fla.Citrus	Fla.Citrus Bowl-Orlando	1936	60,000	Grass
Freedom	Anaheim	1966	69,008	Grass
Gator	Gator Bowl	1949	82,000	Grass
Hall of Fame	Tampa	1967	74,314	Grass
Holiday	Jack Murphy	1967	60,750	Grass
John Hancock	Sun Bowl	1963	52,000	Turf
Independence	Independence	1936	50,560	Grass
Liberty	Liberty Bowl	1965	63,244	Grass
Orange	Orange Bowl	1935	75,500	Grass
Peach	Atlanta	1965	59,643	Grass
Rose	Rose Bowl	1922	104,091	Grass
Sugar	Superdome	1975	69,065	Turf

Bowl Game Sites: All-American—Birmingham,AL; **Aloha**—Honolulu; **California**—Fresno; **Copper**—Tucson,AZ; **Cotton**—Dallas; **Fiesta**—Tempe,AZ; **Florida Citrus**—Orlando; **Freedom**—Anaheim,CA; **Gator**—Jacksonville,FL; **Hall of Fame**—Tampa,FL; **Holiday**—San Diego; **John Hancock**—El Paso,TX; **Independence**—Shreveport,LA; **Liberty**—Memphis,TN; **Orange**—Miami; **Peach**—Atlanta; **Rose**—Pasadena,CA; **Sugar**—New Orleans.

The 25 Largest Stadiums

The twenty-five largest home fields in Division I-A college football. Note that (*) indicates part-time home field.

	Seating	Home Team	Conference	Built	Field
1 Rose Bowl	104,091	UCLA	Pac-10	1922	Grass
2 Michigan Stadium	101,701	Michigan	Big Ten	1927	Turf
3 LA Coliseum	92,488	USC	Pac-10	1923	Grass
4 Neyland Stadium	91,249	Tennessee	SEC	1921	Turf
5 Stanford Stadium	86,011	Stanford	Pac-10	1921	Grass
6 Ohio Stadium	85,339	Ohio St.	Big Ten	1922	Turf
7 Jordan-Hare Stadium	85,214	Auburn	SEC	1939	Grass
8 Beaver Stadium	83,370	Penn St.	Independent	1960	Grass
9 Sanford Stadium	82,122	Georgia	SEC	1929	Grass
10 Tiger Stadium	80,140	LSU	SEC	1924	Grass
11 Memorial Stadium	80,000	Texas	SWC	1924	Turf
12 Memorial Stadium	79,853	Clemson	ACC	1942	Grass
13 Camp Randall Stadium	77,280	Wisconsin	Big Ten	1917	Turf
14 Giants Stadium	76,891	Rutgers*	Independent	1976	Turf
15 Spartan Stadium	76,000	Michigan St.	Big Ten	1957	Turf
16 Legion Field	75,952	Alabama*	SEC	1927	Turf
17 Memorial Stadium	75,630	California	Pac-10	1923	Turf
18 Orange Bowl	75,500	Miami, FL	Independent	1935	Grass
19 Owen Field	75,004	Oklahoma	Big Eight	1923	Turf
20 Florida Field	74,000	Florida	SEC	1929	Turf
21 Memorial Stadium	73,650	Nebraska	Big Eight	1923	Turf
22 Sun Devil Stadium	73,500	Arizona St.	Pac-10	1958	Grass
23 Husky Stadium	72,500	Washington	Pac-10	1920	Turf
24 Williams-Brice Stadium	72,400	South Carolina	Independent	1934	Grass
25 Kyle Field	72,387	Texas A&M	SWC	1925	Turf

Major College Basketball Arenas

NCAA Division I basketball arenas that have a seating capacity of at least 12,000.

Arena	Seating	Home Team
Carrier Dome	33,000	Syracuse
Thompson-Boling Center	24,535	Tennessee
Charlotte Coliseum	23,500	NC-Charlotte & Davidson*
Marriott Center	23,000	BYU
Rupp Arena	23,000	Kentucky
Dean Smith Center	21,146	N.Carolina
Meadowlands Arena	20,039	Seton Hall*
Madison Square Garden	19,591	St.John's*
Freedom Hall	18,865	Louisville
Capital Centre	18,643	Georgetown
Bradley Center	18,633	Marquette
Thomas & Mack Center	18,500	UNLV
The Spectrum	18,168	Villanova*
Rosemont Horizon	17,500	DePaul
Assembly Hall	17,357	Indiana
The Pit	17,126	New Mexico
Birm.-Jefferson Coliseum	17,000	Ala.-Birm.*
Williams Arena	16,991	Minnesota
Memorial Auditorium	16,476	Canisius*
Pittsburgh Civic Arena	16,290	Pittsburgh*
Erwin Sp.Events Center	16,231	Texas
Assembly Hall	16,153	Illinois
Hartford Civic Center	16,016	Connecticut* & Hartford*
Allen Field House	15,800	Kansas
Greensboro Coliseum	15,753	Wake Forest*
Memorial Gymnasium	15,626	Vanderbilt
Carver-Hawkeye Arena	15,450	Iowa
LA Sports Arena	15,310	USC
Coleman Coliseum	15,043	Alabama
Arena-Auditorium	15,028	Wyoming
Hinkle Fieldhouse	15,000	Butler
Huntsman Center	15,000	Utah

Arena	Seating	Home Team
Boston Garden	14,890	Boston Col.*
Cole Field House	14,500	Maryland
Devaney Sports Center	14,478	Nebraska
Univ.Activity Center	14,287	Arizona St.
Maravich Assembly Center	14,236	LSU
Mackey Arena	14,123	Purdue
Hilton Coliseum	14,020	Iowa St.
UWV Coliseum	14,000	West Virginia
San Diego Sports Arena	13,741	San Diego St.
St.John Arena	13,681	Ohio St.
Crisler Arena	13,609	Michigan
Bramlage Coliseum	13,500	Kansas St.
U.of Dayton Arena	13,455	Dayton
Pan American Center	13,222	N.Mexico St.
Hernes Center	13,143	Missouri
McKale Center	13,124	Arizona
Convocation Center	13,080	Ohio Univ.
Providence Civic Center	13,000	Providence & Rhode Is.*
Pauley Pavilion	12,543	UCLA
Tallahassee-Leon County Civic Center	12,500	Florida St.
Carolina Coliseum	12,401	S.Carolina
Reynolds Coliseum	12,400	N.C.State
E.A.Diddle Arena	12,370	Western Ky.
Eaves Memorial Coliseum	12,231	Auburn
Special Events Center	12,222	UTEP
BSU Pavilion	12,200	Boise St.
Friel Court	12,058	Wash.St.
Cajun Dome	12,000	SW Louisiana
Chicago Ampitheater	12,000	Loyola,IL
Dee Events Center	12,000	Weber St.
O'Connell Center	12,000	Florida

*Teams that also play some home games in smaller campus gyms.

Pete Weber became only the third bowler in history to win all three men's major tournaments when he captured the PBA National in Toledo on March 18.

BOWLING

INSIDE

Through the Years

Elsewhere in Almanac

For related information refer to the following chapters: Halls of Fame & Awards, Sports Organizations and Updates.

*Bowling projects upscale image
as purses, TV ratings rise;
Aulby and Romeo win U.S. Opens,
Ballard victor in Firestone.*

BOWLING

1988-89 YEAR IN REVIEW

by Lynda Collins

According to Arbitron statistics, Super Bowl XXIII was the highest-rated sports telecast the last week of January. Second in the TV ratings was super bowling of another kind: the Professional Bowlers' Association Quaker State Open.

Buoyed by its appearance as an exhibition sport at the 1988 Summer Olympics as well as record-breaking performances by professionals Brian Voss and Lisa Wagner, bowling—a sport often relegated to second-class status by the national media—enjoyed a resurgence in popularity in 1989, particularly on television. TV numbers climbed considerably for both pro tours, and new performance standards loomed on the horizon as the fall season approached.

Money played a large role in this rebirth. Though the players would insist

---

Lynda Collins is a sportswriter for the **Las Vegas Review-Journal** and a regular contributor to **Bowlers Journal** and **Bowling Digest**.

it was only a small step in their long journey to attain financial parity with other professional athletes, the two tours welcomed increased purses that led to earnings records in 1988 and the promise of new ones in 1989.

The ballyhooed, made-for-TV "skins" shootout in November 1988 was a ratings blockbuster that offered a new approach to marketing the sport, as well as an opportunity for a few of its top stars to pick up some significant cash. Irascible and irreverent Marshall Holman, inarguably the game's most hated and loved performer, walked away with the winner's check of $80,000 and a new fishing boat.

The fact that Voss and Wagner epitomized the image the sport so desperately wants to project was another plus. The stereotyped caricature of bowlers as beer-bellied carousers or female fuddie-duddies went out a few years ago when bowling alleys became bowling centers and gutters turned into channels. The 1988 Bowlers of the Year were testament

Roaring their approval, **Marshall Holman** (left) and **Del Ballard, Jr.** react to pivotal strikes on their way to respective victories in December's $100,000 shootout and April's Firestone Tournament of Champions.

to that with their yuppie lifestyles, lean bodies and magazine-cover good looks. This year's top bowlers, Mike Aulby and Robin Romeo, also fit the desired profile.

The PBA Senior Tour grew to five tournaments this year, all on television, featuring legends like Dick Weber, Earl Anthony and Carmen Salvino. PBA Commissioner Joe Antenora envisioned 10 tournaments and a $1 million prize fund within two years, and plans were announced by Jeannette Robinson, a former president of the women's tour, for the start-up of a Golden Ladies Tour in 1990. The two tours also got together and agreed to conduct their first combined tournament in Reno, Nev., after the regular season was finished.

As good a game as the sport threw during 1988-89, it wasn't all strikes.

The PBA continued to be enmeshed in legal difficulties with a group of its players, and the Ladies Professional Bowlers Tour (LPBT) was still regrouping from a 1987 split that alienated sponsors and resulted in two tours that held competing

major events 90 miles from each other. The women's tour was also troubled by the discovery of transvestites on the circuit in 1988 (a matter the LPBT cleared up last December by adopting a new policy of unannounced sex testing).

Also on the negative-factor list was Pete Weber's six-month suspension for detrimental conduct that allegedly involved drug and alcohol abuse. The suspension lasted from Sept. 8, 1988 to Jan. 30, 1989 when PBA commissioner Antenora, not without some controversy, allowed Weber to return five weeks early. Weber quickly regained championship form, winning the PBA National tournament in March. In doing so, he joined Billy Hardwick and Johnny Petraglia as the only men to win each of bowling's Triple Crown events (the U.S. Open and the Tournament of Champions are the other two).

Meanwhile, players on both tours voiced frustration over their inability to command megabuck purses like their counterparts in golf and tennis.

On the amateur level, the Olympic excitement bowling experienced in Seoul was replaced by serious doubts that the sport would be included in the 1992 Summer Games in Barcelona. And the annual American Bowling Congress Tournament in Wichita, Kan., was marked by a rash of high scores that inflamed industry-wide debate about new equipment and lane surfaces that some insist threaten the game's integrity.

Passions also raged over classification of amateurs and professionals as male touring pros loudly protested the fact that amateurs often make more money in a single tournament than they do in a whole year. Mike Lichstein was only 19 when he won $200,000 in the 1988 High Roller at the Showboat Lanes in Las Vegas. He finished the year as the sport's second-leading money winner, earning just a few thousand dollars less than Voss' PBA-record $225,485, then said he had no plans to turn pro and join the tour.

"Why should I?" Lichstein asked. "I can make a lot more money as an amateur with far fewer expenses and a lot less hassle."

While Lichstein was regarded as a top pro prospect, the 1989 High Roller champion, New York City limousine driver Guy Stenning, wasn't even considered to be in the top half of his weekly league. He simply got hot, benefitted from the tournament's format and earned more in one day ($200,000) than many pros do in five years.

"Is it any wonder we want in?" asked former PBA President Ernie Schlegel.

Wayne Schuerman, a used car salesman who pocketed $150,000 by winning the American Dream Classic in October 1988 at Sam's Town in Las Vegas, earned more than all but a handful of PBA players during the year. His haul was also more than any player on the women's tour, including Wagner, whose $105,500 in 1988 broke the women's single season mark by nearly $25,000.

"It's an honor to be the first to win $100,000," said Wagner, whose 213.02 average was more than 2½ pins better than her closest competitor. I'd also like to be the first to hit $200,000."

Donna Adamek, who won the $25,000 first prize at the Sam's Town Invitational in November 1988, finished the year with $46,735, good for fourth on the money list behind Wagner, Jeanne Maiden ($54,670) and Robin Romeo ($49,320).

Romeo emerged as a candidate to break Wagner's record this year, winning four tournments—including May's U.S. Open in Addison, Ill.—and $88,495 through the Summer Tour.

Cheryl Daniels, another four-time winner in '89, and Carol Gianotti, who won the Women's International Bowling Congress (WIBC) Queens championship, lagged far behind with nearly $500,000 up for grabs in nine Fall Tour tournaments, including the season-ending $100,000 Sam's Town Invitational.

Wagner, who took advantage of her record-shattering 1988 season by stepping up her off-the-lanes commitments this year, was under $40,000 and needed a superb autumn to have any opportunity this year to repeat as Bowler of the Year.

With six Fall tournaments remaining on the '89 PBA calendar, it appeared likely that Aulby—the 1985 Bowler of the Year and the first player to win $200,000 in a season—would be the first to break the $300,000 barrier, too. With the Summer Tour completed, Aulby had won four tournaments—including th U.S. Open in Edmond, Okla., and the ABC Masters—and taken home $282,215. The PBA prize fund in 1989 is in excess of $7 million.

If Aulby was to be challenged for Bowler of the Year, former problem children Del Ballard Jr., and Pete Weber, along with foreign-born Amleto Monacelli, were the only contenders.

Ballard, who confessed early in the year to a one-time drinking problem, got out of the gate quickly with back-to-back victories in January at Las Vegas and Dallas. He then won the Firestone Tournament of Champions in April, beating out Walter Ray Williams, Jr., a world-class horseshoe pitcher who two weeks earlier had helped President George Bush dedicate the new White House horseshoe pit.

The Venezuelan-born Monacelli and Weber, son of PBA and ABC Hall of Famer Dick Weber, each had two victories and were separated by only $11,000 as the Fall Tour geared up.

Weber, the PBA National champion,

U.S. Open champions **Robin Romeo** (left) and **Mike Aulby** were also the LBPT and PBA tour leaders heading into the fall tournaments.

also reached the five-man finals in the other Triple Crown events and was nearly three pins ahead of the field with his 218.37 average. Monacelli was at 215.48, followed by two-time titlist Dave Ferraro, Ballard and Aulby.

Voss, meanwhile, had won two tournaments, but dropped from the Top 10 average leaders and fell to fifth on the money list—as he, like Wagner, increased his personal commitments. He also announced his engagement to a Florida woman at the Firestone when media attention was at a peak.

Another big story in 1989 was Holman's mysterious vanishing act from the Top 10 in everything. After being dubbed bowling's most consistent performer in the 1980s, the 1987 Bowler of the Year appeared to be vanquished by the PBA's new lane-dressing techniques. Lane conditions and oiling procedures have been a powder keg in a never-ending lefty-righty power struggle that reached all the way to U.S. Federal Court in Seattle, Wash., in late 1988. The

PBA fired its lane maintenance man and began spraying oil in a new way in 1989. Right-hander Holman was considered a major victim when conditions turned in favor of southpaws.

Nevertheless, Holman still joined Aulby, Weber, four-time Bowler of the Year Mark Roth and six-time Bowler of the Year Earl Anthony as the leading candidates for Bowler of the Decade, which the nation's bowling writers will choose in early 1990.

Wagner was the frontrunner for Bowler of the Decade honors among the women. Adamek and Aleta Sill, with six Bowler of the Year trophies between them, are considered her strongest competition.

Aulby and Wagner were named captains of the 51st **Bowlers Journal** All-American teams when the squads were announced in August. Ballard, Voss, Dave Ferraro and Randy Pedersen filled the remaining four slots on the men's team, while Romeo, Maiden, Daniels and Leanne Barrette rounded out the women's squad.

1989 Tournaments

PBA Tour
Through the Summer Tour, ending Aug. 16, 1989.

Event	Winner
ARC Pinole Open	Ernie Schlegel
AC-Delco Classic	Randy Pedersen
Showboat Invitational	Del Ballard, Jr.
Quaker State Open	Del Ballard, Jr.
Budweister Classic	Randy Pedersen
Bowlers Journal Florida Open	Brian Voss
Don Carter's New Orleans Classic	Brian Voss
True Value Open	Wayne Webb
Showboat Atlantic City Open	Mike Aulby
Budweiser Open	Mike Aulby
Trustcorp PBA Nat'l Championship	Pete Weber
King Louie Open	Butch Soper
Seagram's Coolers US Open	Mike Aulby
Fair Lanes Open	Ron Bell
Greater Hartford Open	Charlie Tapp
Firestone Tourn. of Champions	Del Ballard, Jr.
ABC Masters*	Mike Aulby
A&W Fair Lanes Open	Harry Sullins
Fresno Open	Marc McDowell
Showboat Doubles Classic	Mike Aulby & Steve Cook
Kessler Open	Pete Weber
Seattle Open	Jess Stayrook
Kessler Classic	Tom Crites
Miller Lite Challenge	Amleto Monacelli
El Paso Open	Tony Westlake
Columbia Open	Joe Salvemini
Wichita Open	Amleto Monacelli
LaMonde Classic	Jim Pencak
Senior/Touring Pro Doubles	Marc McDowell & Dick Weber

*The ABC Masters is not a PBA Tour event.

LPBT Tour
Through the Summer Tour, ending Aug. 24, 1989.

Event	Winner
Canoga Park Classic	Robin Romeo
Lady LaMonde Open	Lisa Wagner
San Diego Classic	Robin Romeo
San Dimas Classic	Dede Davidson
Ft. Pierce Classic	Diana Davenport
Clearwater Classic	Cheryl Daniels
Greater Atlanta Open	Leanne Barrette
Carolina Classic	Tish Johnson
Fair Lanes Capitol Classic	Robin Romeo
Seagram's Coolers US Open	Robin Romeo
WIBC Queens	Carol Gianotti
Fair Lanes Denver Classic	Cheryl Daniels
Yuma Open	Cheryl Daniels
South Bend Classic	Sandra Jo Shiery
Michigan Classic Satellite Bowl	Aleta Sill
Albuquerque Open Leisure Bowl	Leanne Barrette
LBPT Gold Rush Mixed Doubles	Nancy & Steven Fehr
LBPT National Doubles	Cheryl Daniels & Joslyn Jennings

Seniors Tour
Events through Aug. 30, 1989.

Event	Winner
Showboat Sr. Invitational	Jimmy Certain
Senior/Touring Pro Doubles	Dick Weber & Marc McDowell
Ebonite PBA Sr. Championship	Les Zikes
Hammer Sr. Open	Allan Choder

Leading 1989 Money Winners

PBA Tour
Through the Summer Tour, ending Aug. 16, 1989. Number of PBA tournament wins in parentheses.

	Earnings
1 Mike Aulby (4)	$282,215*
2 Del Ballard Jr. (3)	196,260
3 Amleto Monacelli (2)	142,215
4 Pete Weber (2)	131,278
5 Brian Voss (2)	101,230
6 Dave Ferraro	101,172
7 Jess Stayrook (1)	100,005
8 Tony Westlake (1)	93,450
9 Randy Pedersen (2)	87,225
10 Jim Pencak (1)	86,833

*Earnings include ABC Masters 1st prize of $43,600 even though Masters is not a PBA event.

LPBT Tour
Through the Summer Tour, ending Aug. 24, 1989. Number of tournament wins in parentheses.

	Earnings
1 Robin Romeo (4)	$88,495
2 Cheryl Daniels (4)	47,485
3 Leanne Barrette (2)	41,220
4 Lisa Wagner (1)	39,015
5 Aleta Sill (1)	33,200
6 Michelle Mullen	32,767
7 Nikki Gianulias	30,320
8 Jeanne Maiden	28,825
9 Tish Johnson	22,382
10 Carol Gianotti (1)	20,985

Seniors Tour
Tournaments through Aug. 30, 1989. Number of Tournament wins in parentheses.

	Earnings
1 Jimmy Certain (1)	$29,000
2 Les Zikes (1)	21,270
3 Dick Weber (1)	20,660
4 John Handegard	18,200
5 Teada Semiz	11,965

Men's Major Championships

BPAA All-Star/US Open

Started by the Bowling Proprietors' Assn. of America nearly 20 years before the founding of the PBA. Originally the BPAA All-Star Tournament, it became the US Open in 1971. There were two BPAA All-Star tournaments in 1955, in January and December.

Year	Winner	Year	Winner	Year	Winner
1941	John Crimmons	1957	Not held	1973	Mike McGrath
1942	Connie Schwoegler	1958	Don Carter	1974	Larry Laub
1943	Ned Day	1959	Billy Welu	1975	Steve Neff
1944	Buddy Bomar			1976	Paul Moser
1945	Joe Wilman	1960	Harry Smith	1977	Johnny Petraglia
1946	Andy Varipapa	1961	Bill Tucker	1978	Nelson Burton Jr.
1947	Andy Varipapa	1962	Dick Weber	1979	Joe Berardi
1948	Connie Schwoegler	1963	Dick Weber		
1949	Junie McMahon	1964	Bob Strampe	1980	Steve Martin
		1965	Dick Weber	1981	Marshall Holman
1950	Dick Hoover	1966	Dick Weber	1982	Dave Husted
1951	Junie McMahon	1967	Les Schissler	1983	Gary Dickinson
1952	Don Carter	1968	Jim Stefanich	1984	Mark Roth
1953	Not held	1969	Billy Hardwick	1985	Marshall Holman
1954	Don Carter			1986	Steve Cook
1955	Steve Nagy	1970	Bobby Cooper	1987	Del Ballard Jr.
1955	Bill Lillard	1971	Mike Lemongello	1988	Pete Weber
1956	Don Carter	1972	Don Johnson	1989	Mike Aulby

PBA National Championship

The Professional Bowlers Assn. was formed in 1958. The PBA's first national championship was held in Memphis in 1960. The tournament has been played in Toledo, Ohio, since 1981.

Year	Winner	Year	Winner	Year	Winner
1960	Don Carter	1970	Mike McGrath	1980	Johnny Petraglia
1961	Dave Soutar	1971	Mike Lemongello	1981	Earl Anthony
1962	Carmen Salvino	1972	Johnny Guenther	1982	Earl Anthony
1963	Billy Hardwick	1973	Earl Anthony	1983	Earl Anthony
1964	Bob Strampe	1974	Earl Anthony	1984	Bob Chamberlain
1965	Dave Davis	1975	Earl Anthony	1985	Mike Aulby
1966	Wayne Zahn	1976	Paul Colwell	1986	Tom Crites
1967	Dave Davis	1977	Tommy Hudson	1987	Randy Pedersen
1968	Wayne Zahn	1978	Warren Nelson	1988	Brian Voss
1969	Mike McGrath	1979	Mike Aulby	1989	Pete Weber

Firestone Tournament of Champions

The Tournament of Champions has been held in Akron, Ohio, since it began in 1965.

Year	Winner	Year	Winner	Year	Winner
1965	Billy Hardwick	1973	Jim Godman	1981	Steve Cook
1966	Wayne Zahn	1974	Earl Anthony	1982	Mike Durbin
1967	Jim Stefanich	1975	Dave Davis	1983	Joe Berardi
1968	Dave Davis	1976	Marshall Holman	1984	Mike Durbin
1969	Jim Godman	1977	Mike Berlin	1985	Mark Williams
		1978	Earl Anthony	1986	Marshall Holman
1970	Don Johnson	1979	George Pappas	1987	Pete Weber
1971	Johnny Petraglia			1988	Mark Williams
1972	Mike Durbin	1980	Wayne Webb	1989	Del Ballard, Jr.

ABC Masters Tournament

Sponsored by the American Bowling Congress, the Masters is open to qualified pros and amateurs.

Year	Winner	Year	Winner	Year	Winner
1951	Lee Jouglard	1964	Billy Welu	1977	Earl Anthony
1952	Willard Taylor	1965	Billy Welu	1978	Frank Ellenburg
1953	Rudy Habetler	1966	Bob Strampe	1979	Doug Myers
1954	Red Elkins	1967	Lou Scalia		
1955	Buzz Fazio	1968	Pete Tountas	1980	Neil Burton
1956	Dick Hoover	1969	Jim Chestney	1981	Randy Lightfoot
1957	Dick Hoover			1982	Joe Berardi
1958	Tom Hennessey	1970	Don Glover	1983	Mike Lastowski
1959	Ray Bluth	1971	Jim Godman	1984	Earl Anthony
		1972	Bill Beach	1985	Steve Wunderlich
1960	Billy Golembiewski	1973	Dave Soutar	1986	Mark Fahy
1961	Don Carter	1974	Paul Colwell	1987	Rick Steelsmith
1962	Billy Golembiewski	1975	Eddie Ressler	1988	Del Ballard, Jr.
1963	Harry Smith	1976	Nelson Burton Jr.	1989	Mike Aulby

World's Invitational
Tournament discontinued after 1964.

Year	Winner	Year	Winner	Year	Winner
1922	Jimmy Bloudin	1957	Don Carter	1960	Don Carter
		1958	Ed Lubanski	1961	Don Carter
		1959	Don Carter	1962	Don Carter
				1963	Jim St. John
				1964	Jim St. John

Women's Major Championships

BPAA All-Star/US Open

Sponsored by the Bowling Proprietors' Assn. of America, the BPAA Women's All-Star became the US Women's Open in 1971. There were two BPAA All-Star tournaments in 1955, in January and December. Note that (*) indicates amateur player.

Year	Winner	Year	Winner	Year	Winner
1949	Marion Ladewig	1962	Shirley Garms	1976	Patty Costello
		1963	Marion Ladewig	1977	Betty Morris
1950	Marion Ladewig	1964	LaVerne Carter	1978	Donna Adamek
1951	Marion Ladewig	1965	Ann Slattery	1979	Diana Silva
1952	Marion Ladewig	1966	Joy Abel		
1953	Not held	1967	Gloria Bouvia	1980	Pat Costello
1954	Marion Ladewig	1968	Dorothy Fothergill	1981	Donna Adamek
1955	Sylvia Wene	1969	Dorothy Fothergill	1982	Shinobu Saitoh
1955	Anita Cantaline			1983	Dana Miller
1956	Marion Ladewig	1970	Mary Baker	1984	Karen Ellingsworth
1957	Not held	1971	Paula Sperber*	1985	Pat Mercatanti
1958	Merle Matthews	1972	Lorrie Koch*	1986	Wendy Macpherson
1959	Marion Ladewig	1973	Millie Martorella	1987	Carol Norman
		1974	Pat Costello	1988	Lisa Wagner
1960	Sylvia Wene	1975	Paula Sperber Carter	1989	Robin Romeo
1961	Phyllis Notaro				

PWBA National Championship

The Professional Women's Bowling Assn. National Championship tournament was discontinued after 1980.

Year	Winner	Year	Winner	Year	Winner
1960	Marion Ladewig	1967	Betty Mivelaz	1974	Pat Costello
1961	Shirley Garms	1968	Dotty Fothergill	1975	Pam Buckner
1962	Stevie Balogh	1969	Dotty Fothergill	1976	Patty Costello
1963	Janet Harman			1977	Vesma Grinfelds
1964	Betty Kuczynski	1970	Bobbe North	1978	Toni Gillard
1965	Helen Duval	1971	Patty Costello	1979	Cindy Coburn
1966	Judy Lee	1972	Patty Costello	1980	Donna Adamek
		1973	Betty Morris		

WIBC Queens Tournament

Sponsored by the Women's International Bowling Congress, the Queens is open to qualified pros and amateurs.

Year	Winner	Year	Winner	Year	Winner
1961	Janet Harman	1970	Millie Martorella	1980	Donna Adamek
1962	Dorothy Wilkinson	1971	Millie Martorella	1981	Katsuko Sugimoto
1963	Irene Monterosso	1972	Dotty Fothergill	1982	Katsuko Sugimoto
1964	D.D.Jacobsen	1973	Dotty Fothergill	1983	Aleta Sill
1965	Betty Kuczynski	1974	Judy Soutar	1984	Kazue Inahashi
1966	Judy Lee	1975	Cindy Powell	1985	Aleta Sill
1967	Millie Martorella	1976	Pam Buckner	1986	Cora Fiebig
1968	Phyllis Massey	1977	Dana Stewart	1987	Cathy Almeida
1969	Ann Feigel	1978	Loa Boxberger	1988	Wendy Macpherson
		1979	Donna Adamek	1989	Carol Gianotti

Sam's Town Invitational

Originally in Milwaukee as the Pabst Tournament of Champions in 1981, the event was revived and moved to Las Vegas in 1984 as the Sam's Town TOC. Since then it has been known as the LPBT TOC (1985), the Sam's Town National Pro/Am (1986-88) and is now called the Sam's Town Invitational.

Year	Winner	Year	Winner	Year	Winner
1981	Cindy Coburn	1985	Patty Costello	1987	Debbie Bennett
1984	Aleta Sill	1986	Aleta Sill	1988	Donna Adamek

Bowling Awards
MEN

BWAA Bowler of the Year
Voting done by Bowling Writers Assn. of America.

Year		Year		Year	
1942	Johnny Crimmins	1958	Don Carter	1973	Don McCune
1943	Ned Day	1959	Ed Lubanski	1974	Earl Anthony
1944	Ned Day			1975	Earl Anthony
1945	Buddy Bomar	1960	Don Carter	1976	Earl Anthony
1946	Joe Wilman	1961	Dick Weber	1977	Mark Roth
1947	Buddy Bomar	1962	Don Carter	1978	Mark Roth
1948	Andy Varipapa	1963	Dick Weber	1979	Mark Roth
1949	Connie Schwoegler	1964	Billy Hardwick		
		1965	Dick Weber	1980	Wayne Webb
1950	Junie McMahon	1966	Wayne Zahn	1981	Earl Anthony
1951	Lee Jouglard	1967	Dave Davis	1982	Earl Anthony
1952	Steve Nagy	1968	Jim Stefanich	1983	Earl Anthony
1953	Don Carter	1969	Billy Hardwick	1984	Mark Roth
1954	Don Carter			1985	Mike Aulby
1955	Steve Nagy	1970	Nelson Burton Jr.	1986	Walter Ray Williams Jr.
1956	Bill Lillard	1971	Don Johnson	1987	Marshall Holman
1957	Don Carter	1972	Don Johnson	1988	Brian Voss

PBA Player of the Year

Year		Year		Year	
1963	Billy Hardwick	1970	Nelson Burton Jr.	1980	Wayne Webb
1964	Bob Strampe	1971	Don Johnson	1981	Earl Anthony
1965	Dick Weber	1972	Don Johnson	1982	Earl Anthony
1966	Wayne Zahn	1973	Don McCune	1983	Earl Anthony
1967	Dave Davis	1974	Earl Anthony	1984	Mark Roth
1968	Jim Stefanich	1975	Earl Anthony	1985	Mike Aulby
1969	Billy Hardwick	1976	Earl Anthony	1986	Walter Ray Williams Jr.
		1977	Mark Roth	1987	Marshall Holman
		1978	Mark Roth	1988	Brian Voss
		1979	Mark Roth		

PBA Rookie of the Year

Year		Year		Year	
1964	Jerry McCoy	1970	Denny Krick	1980	Pete Weber
1965	Jim Godman	1971	Tye Critchlow	1981	Mark Fahy
1966	Bobby Cooper	1972	Tommy Hudson	1982	Mike Steinbach
1967	Mike Durbin	1973	Steve Neff	1983	Toby Contreras
1968	Bob McGregor	1974	Cliff McNealy	1984	John Gant
1969	Larry Lichstein	1975	Guy Rowbury	1985	Tom Crites
		1976	Mike Berlin	1986	Marc McDowell
		1977	Steve Martin	1987	Ryan Shafer
		1978	Joseph Groskind	1988	Rick Steelsmith
		1979	Mike Aulby		

WOMEN

BWAA Bowler of the Year
Voting done by Bowling Writers Assn. of America.

Year		Year		Year	
1948	Val Mikiel	1961	Shirley Garms	1975	Judy Soutar
1949	Val Mikiel	1962	Shirley Garms	1976	Patty Costello
		1963	Marion Ladewig	1977	Betty Morris
1950	Marion Ladewig	1964	LaVerne Carter	1978	Donna Adamek
1951	Marion Ladewig	1965	Betty Kuczynski	1979	Donna Adamek
1952	Marion Ladewig	1966	Joy Abel		
1953	Marion Ladewig	1967	Millie Martorella	1980	Donna Adamek
1954	Marion Ladewig	1968	Dotty Fothergill	1981	Donna Adamek
1955	Sylvia Wene	1969	Dotty Fothergill	1982	Nikki Gianulias
1956	Anita Cantaline			1983	Lisa Rathgeber
1957	Marion Ladewig	1970	Mary Baker	1984	Aleta Sill
1958	Marion Ladewig	1971	Paula Sperber	1985	Aleta Sill
1959	Marion Ladewig	1972	Patty Costello	1986	Lisa Rathgeber Wagner
		1973	Judy Soutar	1987	Betty Morris
1960	Sylvia Wene	1974	Betty Morris	1988	Lisa Wagner

Awards (Continued)

LPBT Player of the Year

Year	Year	Year
1983 Lisa Rathgeber Wagner	1985 Patty Costello	1987 Betty Morris
1984 Aleta Sill	1986 Jeanne Maiden	1988 Lisa Wagner

WPBA & LPBT Rookies of the Year

Year	Year	Year
1978 Toni Gillard	1981 Cindy Mason	1985 Dede Davidson
1979 Nikki Gianulias	1982 Carol Norman	1986 Wendy Macpherson
1980 Lisa Rathgeber	1983 Anne Marie Pike	1987 Paula Drake
	1984 Paula Vidad	1988 Mary Martha Cerniglia

Yearly Tour Money Winners

MEN		WOMEN	
Year	**Earnings**	**Year**	**Earnings**
1959 Dick Weber	$ 7,672	1965 Betty Kuczynski	$ 3,792
1960 Don Carter	22,525	1966 Joy Abel	5,795
1961 Dick Weber	26,280	1967 Shirley Garms	4,920
1962 Don Carter	49,972	1968 Dotty Fothergill	16,170
1963 Dick Weber	46,333	1969 Dotty Fothergill	9,220
1964 Bob Strampe	33,592	1970 Patty Costello	9,317
1965 Dick Weber	47,675	1971 Vesma Grinfelds	4,925
1966 Wayne Zahn	54,720	1972 Patty Costello	11,350
1967 Dave Davis	54,165	1973 Judy Cook	11,200
1968 Jim Stefanich	67,375	1974 Betty Morris	30,037
1969 Billy Hardwick	64,160	1975 Judy Soutar	20,395
1970 Mike McGrath	52,049	1976 Patty Costello	39,585
1971 Johnny Petraglia	85,065	1977 Betty Morris	23,802
1972 Don Johnson	56,648	1978 Donna Adamek	31,000
1973 Don McCune	69,000	1979 Donny Adamek	26,280
1974 Earl Anthony	99,585	1980 Donna Adamek	31,907
1975 Earl Anthony	107,585	1981 Nikki Gianulias	41,335
1976 Earl Anthony	110,833	1982 Nikki Gianulias	45,875
1977 Mark Roth	105,583	1983 Aleta Sill	42,525
1978 Mark Roth	134,500	1984 Aleta Sill	81,452
1979 Mark Roth	124,517	1985 Aleta Sill	52,655
1980 Wayne Webb	116,700	1986 Aleta Sill	36,962
1981 Earl Anthony	164,735	1987 Betty Morris	63,735
1982 Earl Anthony	134,760	1988 Lisa Wagner	105,500
1983 Earl Anthony	135,605		
1984 Mark Roth	158,712		
1985 Mike Aulby	201,200		
1986 Walter R. Williams	145,550		
1987 Pete Weber	175,491		
1988 Brian Voss	225,485		

Sunday Silence, with **Pat Valenzuela** aboard, ran stride for stride and a nose in front to beat **Easy Goer** in the Preakness Stakes, May 20.

HORSE RACING

INSIDE

Elsewhere in Almanac

For related information refer to the following chapters: Halls of Fame & Awards, Sports Organizations, and Updates.

*Sunday Silence and Easy Goer
dominate the Triple Crown,
Open Mind fairest of fillies,
and a Hambletonian dead heat.*

HORSE RACING

1988-89 YEAR IN REVIEW

by Sharon B. Smith

By post time for the 1988 Breeders' Cup Classic, the rain-soaked crowd at Churchill Downs in Louisville had already experienced November weather in Kentucky at its worst. By the end of the race, it had experienced Thoroughbred racing at its best, although the fans had to peer through a cold mist and the shadows of an early nightfall to do it.

Alysheba, favored in spite of muddy footing, overcame Waquoit at the eighth pole then held off Seeking the Gold to win the $3 million Classic, earning himself Horse of the Year honors, and completing his career by coming full circle.

Eighteen months earlier at the same track, Alysheba had burst into the public consciousness with a nearly miraculous win in the Kentucky Derby after being knocked to his knees in the stretch. His courageous performance in the Classic provided both an appropriate

Sharon B. Smith is the Contributing Editor of Horse Illustrated and has been a TV commentator at the Breeders' Cup for NBC since 1984. She also anchored ESPN's "Down the Stretch," which won an Eclipse Award in 1982.

end to a brilliant career and a paycheck that pushed his lifetime earnings to $6,679,242, good enough for first place on the all-time list.

"There's no question about it," said Alysheba's jockey Chris McCarron after the Classic. "He's the best horse I've ever ridden." That was high praise indeed from the man who had ridden previous top earner John Henry during the last few years of the great gelding's career.

Another career ended on a high note on Breeders' Cup Day. Personal Ensign's win—by a nose over Winning Colors in the Breeders' Cup Distaff—allowed her to retire with 13 wins in 13 starts. She became the first fully-campaigned American race horse in 80 years to retire undefeated.

The enormity of Personal Ensign's accomplishment—combining talent with luck to remain unbeaten—was pointed up the same day by her stablemate Easy Goer. By Breeders' Cup day, there was little disagreement that he was the best two-year-old around. Three times previously, Easy Goer had beaten the

Alysheba and jockey **Chris McCarron** cross the finish line in the dark and the mud at Churchill Downs on Nov. 5, 1988, to win the Breeders' Cup Classic.

D. Wayne Lukas-trained Is It True. But a poor start, a muddy track, and a finish line that came too soon conspired to keep Easy Goer from catching Is It True in the million-dollar Juvenile.

Easy Goer's reputation was little damaged, though, and he wintered in Florida as both the two-year-old champion for 1988 and the early favorite for the 1989 Triple Crown races. His 1989 debut came in the Swale Stakes at Gulfstream Park in March, which he won easily in the fastest seven furlong clocking of the Florida winter season.

By the time Easy Goer returned north in April for his final Triple Crown preparations, "great" was used as often as "good" to describe him, and his powerful red body and breathtaking acceleration conjured up memories of Secretariat.

In Aqueduct's Gotham Mile on April 8, Easy Goer went a step beyond Secretariat, who had used the same race as a Kentucky Derby prep in 1973. Secretariat

had won his Gotham easily in 1:33⅖, a stakes and track record. Easy Goer won his by 13 lengths in 1:32⅖, a full second faster than Secretariat. It was not just a track record but also the second fastest mile in horse racing history.

The record was accomplished with extraordinary ease, with little urging from jockey Pat Day. "The last furlong, I was just along for the ride," Day said in the winners' circle. "What do you think he would have done if I'd asked him to run?" It was a question nobody was prepared to answer.

Easy Goer's victory in the Wood Memorial two weeks later was easy enough, but less quick and less dominant. Trainer Shug McGaughey shrugged off any disappointment in the race. "It was perfect," he said. "It was enough to move him forward. The Derby is two weeks away and I'm not going to get him there with an empty tank."

But as satisfied as McGaughey appeared to be, the Wood win did not scare away 14 Kentucky Derby rivals, including one with credentials almost as good as Easy Goer's. Sunday Silence's easy victory in the Santa Anita Derby would have made him the favorite in Kentucky in most other years; it did make him second choice in the 115th edition of America's most famous horse race.

Even Easy Goer's most confident supporters found it hard to overlook the equal confidence of Sunday Silence's trainer, the redoubtable 76-year-old Charlie Whittingham. Three years earlier, Whittingham had won his first Derby with Ferdinand, and his pronouncements in 1989 had earned extra weight.

"We're ready," Whittingham announced during Derby Week. By Derby Eve, his confidence had grown further. "We'll win," he said on Friday. "Sunday Silence has more ability and more speed than Ferdinand."

He also had more liking than Easy Goer for the racing surface he found at post time. May 6th was almost a carbon copy of the previous November 5th at Churchill Downs: cold, wet, even a little icy. The track was muddy, as it had been for Easy Goer's defeat on Breeders' Cup Day.

While the mud moved Easy Goer back, it did the opposite to Sunday Silence. After allowing the fast but short-winded Houston to take an early lead, Sunday Silence swept boldly past the field on the far turn. He swerved in the stretch—an act attributed variously to his spotting a marching band, reacting to urging, or tiring—but at no point did the late-running Easy Goer look like he was going to catch the winner.

The favorite managed to salvage second, but trainer McGaughey had no explanations for Easy Goer's lackluster performance, apart from the horse's presumed dislike of the mud. "I'm not making excuses," McGaughey said after the race. "The best horse won today."

Two weeks later, a different Easy Goer —one closer to the genuine article— showed up for the Preakness Stakes at Pimlico. For a few seconds, the fans thought they were seeing the Easy Goer touted so loudly in the early spring.

Houston, as he had in the Derby, again led early and again failed to last beyond six furlongs, giving up control of the race to the two top horses. Easy Goer snatched the lead in midstretch but Sunday Silence refused to be swept away. The horses kept close company—Easy Goer's rider later lodged a disallowed claim of foul— but as in the Derby, Sunday Silence was under the wire first, Easy Goer second. The race was far more thrilling, but the results were the same.

Only a couple of inches separated the two horses at the end of the Preakness, but those inches were enough to make Sunday Silence a heavy favorite to become the 12th Triple Crown winner and to make Easy Goer a disappointment of considerable magnitude. Still, there was one disquieting thought in the Sunday Silence camp. Eleven horses in the past had won the first two legs of the Triple Crown and then—for reasons ranging from bad luck to injury to lack of staying power—had failed in the Belmont Stakes.

Before the race, jockey Pat Valenzuela was expressing confidence, tempered by the realization that disappointment was possible. "Everybody's been disappointed in racing at one time," Valenzuela said, "but you have to go out there thinking you're going to win. I think I'm going to win, because I think my horse is a little better than those other eleven."

Indeed, Sunday Silence did almost everything necessary to complete his Triple Crown. He caught and passed front runner Le Voyageur. He held off stretch runner Awe Inspiring. And he won a million dollar bonus for the highest composite finish in Triple Crown races.

What Sunday Silence could not do was withstand the extraordinary stretch run of Easy Goer, who moved a step beyond his performances of the early spring. Easy Goer swept into contention on the final turn and, after a brief moment of resistance from Sunday Silence, moved ahead so quickly that Valenzuela could not prepare his horse for a fight.

Easy Goer, with no urging past the eighth pole, won the Belmont Stakes by 8 lengths over Sunday Silence. The 2:26 for the mile and a half made his Belmont the second fastest ever—only Secretariat had ever run faster.

The win provided both vindication and relief for Pat Day, whose riding had been

Jockey **Pat Day** exults after riding **Easy Goer**
to an 8-length victory over Triple Crown hopeful Sunday Silence
in the Belmont Stakes, June 10.

questioned in his Derby and Preakness losses. Day saw it as vindication for the horse, too. "I never lost confidence in this horse," Day said. "I hope this will reinforce the feelings people had about him in the spring."

The race did just that. Charlie Whittingham thought the overall Triple Crown results left the two horses nearly equal in reputation. "He beat us fair and square and he beat us easy," Whittingham said. "But he's won one of them and we've won two."

Shug McGaughey, on the other hand, thought the sheer quality of the Belmont win left Easy Goer on top. "I think that if we meet again, we'll win," he said. "I thought my horse was the best horse all along."

Summer racing solidified Easy Goer's position on top. He easily won both the Whitney Handicap and the Travers Stakes at Saratoga in August, while Sunday Silence lost the Swaps Stakes at Hollywood Park in July to the little known Prized.

Meanwhile, both colts were served

notice that a further slip by either of them could lead to a loss of Horse of the Year honors to a mere slip of a filly. A sweep of the Acorn, the Mother Goose, and the Coaching Club American Oaks at Belmont Park gave the three-year-old Open Mind the Triple Tiara for fillies. A courageous victory in the Alabama at Saratoga in August increased her credentials for Horse of the Year for 1989.

Open Mind's magnificent year provided a final fling for her owner Eugene Klein, one of the most successful buyers and campaigners of Thoughbreds during the 1980's. Klein announced in June that he would auction off all his horses late in the year.

"I just want to back off," said the 69-year-old Klein, a multiple winner to the Eclipse Award as outstanding owner. In addition to Open Mind, Klein and his wife had raced such champions as Lady's Secret, Winning Colors, and Family Style.

Several jockeys reached milestones during the year. Both 43-year-old Jorge Velasquez and 47-year-old Larry Snyder sur-

Best Kentucky-bred 3-year-old? Maybe Nashwan.

While the winner of the Easy Goer–Sunday Silence rivalry might call himself the best three-year-old in North America, he would have no automatic claim on honors as the best three-year-old in the world. He might not even be the best horse born in Kentucky during the spring of 1986.

One of the finest colts ever to set foot on a racecourse graced European racing during 1989. Nashwan, foaled within a few miles of the birthplaces of both Sunday Silence and Easy Goer, was shipped to Europe as a young horse. After being undefeated in two starts at age two, Nashwan won an unprecedented sequence of major stakes at three—the Two Thousand Guineas, the Epsom Derby, the Eclipse Stakes, and the King George VI and Queen Elizabeth Diamond Stakes, beating most of the best horses in training in Great Britain in the process.

Racing fans on both sides of the Atlantic spent their summer tantalizing themselves with speculation on how the son of the Kentucky stallion Blushing Groom might do against the top American colts. But the contrasts in racing being what they are—the classic races are conducted on dirt tracks in North America and on grass courses in Europe—fans were forced to limit themselves to speculation. It's unlikely that Nashwan will meet either Easy Goer or Sunday Silence during their racing careers.

Wide World Photos

Nashwan and jockey **Willie Carson** after winning the Epsom Derby, June 7.

passed the 6,000 win plateau in August; 34-year-old Chris McCarron notched his 5,000 win in July. McCarron, the 10th rider to reach that level, did it more quickly than any jockey in history. The previous holder, Bill Shoemaker, required three weeks longer.

For Shoemaker, 1989 was also a milestone year. The man who has won more races than any other jockey — nearly 9,000—began a farewell tour in June. By the time the tour ends—early in 1990 with a final race in Santa Anita—Shoemaker will have made final riding appearances in 20 countries and most major tracks in North America. The 58-year-old Shoemaker plans to train after his retirement from competitive riding.

When Kentucky native Steve Cauthen won the Irish Derby aboard Old Vic on July 2, he became the first jockey ever to have ridden winners of the Kentucky, English, French, and Irish Derbies. Cauthen, now one of the leading riders in Europe, is best known this side of the Atlantic as the rider of Affirmed, the Triple Crown winner of 1978.

Horse racing lost one of its great innovators with the death in August of Frank

DeFrancis, an owner of Laurel and Pimlico Race Tracks. DeFrancis deserved much of the credit for the recent revitalization of Maryland racing.

In harness racing, 1989 was a year marked by a dramatic and controversial development in the sport's most prestigious event. The Hambletonian, the showcase for three-year-old trotters, shaped up as a duel between the colt Valley Victory, unbeaten in 1989, and the filly Peace Corps, whose year had also been perfect.

But just a week before the race, Valley Victory became ill and was scratched. Peace Corps stepped out onto the track apparently healthy, but she trotted two uncharacteristically dull heats and failed to make the race-off. The race-off, required because no single horse had won the two heats, featured unexpected participants Park Avenue Joe and Probe. The two trotted to the wire as a team; the photo finish camera failed to separate them and stewards declared the first dead heat in the Hambletonian's 64-year history.

Race rules call for placing by summary in the case of ties, and, as Park Avenue Joe had a better finish in the heat he lost, he was declared the winner. But race rules also say that the winner of two heats wins the Hambletonian, so the owners of Probe challenged the placing.

Regardless of the ultimate distribution of the purse, 1989 will be remembered by harness racing fans as the year of the dead heat at the Hambletonian. In Thoroughbred racing, 1989 will be remembered as the year of Easy Goer, who rose, and fell, and then rose again.

Meadowlands Racetrack

Park Avenue Joe (top), driven by **Ron Waples**, and **Probe**, driven by **Bill Fahy**, finish in a dead heat in the race-off for the 1989 Hambletonian, Aug. 5.

Major Races, 1988-89
Major horse race results from Sept.10, 1988 through September 3, 1989.

Thoroughbreds

1988

Date	Race	Winner
Sep. 11	Molson Challenge	Ballindaggin
Sep. 25	Super Derby	Seeking the Gold
Oct. 1	Cartier Million (IRE)	Corwyn Bay
Oct. 2	Arc de Triomphe (FRA)	Tony Bin
Oct. 8	Jockey Club Gold Cup	Waquoit
Oct. 16	Rothman's Stakes	Infamy
Nov. 1	Melbourne Cup (AUS)	Empire Ruse
Nov. 5	Breeders' Cup Classic	Alysheba
Nov. 5	Breeders' Cup Distaff	Personal Ensign
Nov. 5	Breeders' Cup Juvenile	Is It True
Nov. 5	Breeders' Cup Fillies	Open Mind
Nov. 5	Breeders' Cup Mile	Miesque
Nov. 5	Breeders' Cup Sprint	Gulch
Nov. 5	Breeders' Cup Turf	Grt.Communicator
Nov. 27	Japan Cup	Pay the Butler
Dec. 18	Hollywood Futurity	King Glorious

1989

Date	Race	Winner
Mar. 4	Florida Derby	Mercedes Won
Mar. 5	Santa Anita Handicap	Martial Law
Apr. 8	Santa Anita Derby	Sunday Silence
Apr. 22	Wood Memorial	Easy Goer
May 6	Kentucky Derby	Sunday Silence
May 20	Preakness Stakes	Sunday Silence
June 7	Epsom Derby (GBR)	Nashwan
June 10	Belmont Stakes	Easy Goer
July 2	Budweiser Irish Derby	Old Vic
July 29	Haskell Invitational	King Glorious
Aug. 19	Travers Stakes	Easy Goer
Sept. 3	Arlington Million	Steinlen

Harness Racing
1989

Trotters

Date	Race	Winner
July 15	Yonkers Trot	Valley Victory
Aug. 5	Hambletonian	Park Avenue Joe
Oct. 5	Kentucky Futurity	

Pacers

Date	Race	Winner
Aug.26	Cane Pace	Dancing Master
Sept. 9	Messenger Stakes	
Sept.21	Little Brown Jug	

1989 Thoroughbred Poll
Poll of 42 sports and thoroughbred media in U.S. and Canada conducted by Thoroughbred Racing Communications (TRC) and covering performances through Sept. 4, 1989. First place votes in parentheses; A/S indicates age and sex (C-colt, G-gelding, H-horse, F-filly, M-mare); starts; 1-2-3 finishes; and total points (based on 10 pts for each 1st place vote, 9 for 2nd, etc.)

Horse	A/S	Starts	1-2-3	Pts		Horse	A/S	Starts	1-2-3	Pts
1 Easy Goer (40)	3/C	8	6-2-0	418		6 Bayakoa	5/M	8	6-1-0	136
2 Open Mind (1)	3/F	8	8-0-0	358		7 Clever Trevor	3/G	9	4-3-0	124
3 Sunday Silence (1)	3/C	7	5-2-0	399		8 Blushing John	4/C	7	4-1-0	122
4 Steinlen	6/H	9	5-3-1	205		9 Proper Reality	4/C	9	4-3-1	96
5 King Glorious	3/C	4	3-1-0	174		10 Summer Squall	2/C	5	5-0-0	64

Note: Steinlen is a British horse and Bayakoa is from Argentina.

1989 National Money Leaders
Compiled by the **Daily Racing Form** covering races through Aug. 31, 1989.

Horses	Starts	Wins	Purses
1 Sunday Silence	7	5	$2,628,454
2 Easy Goer	8	6	2,017,350
3 With Approval	10	6	1,722,150
4 Open Mind	8	8	985,140
5 Proper Reality	9	4	902,290
6 Blushing John	7	4	860,000
7 Clever Trevor	9	4	850,470
8 Awe Inspiring	9	6	778,052
9 Cryptoclearance	8	3	667,230
10 Western Playboy	10	2	665,015

Jockeys	Mounts	Wins	Purses
1 Pay Day	950	261	$8,686,571
2 Laffit Pincay, Jr.	1,119	222	7,645,841
3 Gary Stevens	1,141	193	7,500,819
4 Pat Valenzuela	842	122	6,799,349
5 Angel Cordero, Jr.	810	164	6,744,034

Jockeys	Mounts	Wins	Purses
6 Eddie Delahoussaye	955	161	6,597,142
7 Jose Santos	943	174	6,576,966
8 Chris McCarron	803	160	6,110,470
9 Kent Desormeaux	1,532	408	5,756,262
10 Chris Antley	1,057	240	5,725,643

Trainers	Starts	Wins	Purses
1 D.Wayne Lukas	940	207	$9,099,094
2 Charlie Whittingham	298	65	7,504,956
3 Shug McGaughey	128	44	4,280,484
4 Roger Attfield	212	35	2,984,137
5 Neil Drysdale	194	53	2,826,710
6 Ron McAnally	298	55	2,247,362
7 Julio Canani	208	41	1,984,477
8 Mel Stute	380	48	1,910,951
9 Dick Lundy	135	26	1,906,342
10 Gary Jones	278	52	1,856,312

Thoroughbred Racing

Triple Crown Winners

Eleven horses have won the Kentucky Derby, Preakness Stakes and Belmont Stakes in the same year. Two trainers, James "Sunny Jim" Fitzsimmons and Ben A.Jones, won it twice, while Eddie Arcaro is the only jockey to have ridden two winners.

Year	Horse	Jockey	Trainer	Owner	Sire/Dam
1919	**Sir Barton**	Johnny Loftus	H.Guy Bedwell	J.K.L.Ross	*Star Shoot/Lady Sterling
1930	**Gallant Fox**	Earle Sande	J.E. Fitzsimmons	Belair Stud	*Sir Gallahad III/Marguerite
1935	**Omaha**	Willie Saunders	J.E. Fitzsimmons	Belair Stud	Gallant Fox/Flambino
1937	**War Admiral**	Chas.Kurtsinger	George Conway	Samuel Riddle	Man O'War/Brushup
1941	**Whirlaway**	Eddie Arcaro	Ben A.Jones	Calumet Farm	*Blenheim II/Dustwhirl
1943	**Count Fleet**	Johnny Longden	Don Cameron	Mrs.J.D.Hertz	Reigh Count/Quickly
1946	**Assault**	Warren Mehrtens	Max Hirsch	King Ranch	Bold Venture/Igual
1948	**Citation**	Eddie Arcaro	Ben A.Jones	Calumet Farm	Bull Lea/*Hydroplane II
1973	**Secretariat**	Ron Turcotte	Lucien Laurin	Meadow Stable	Bold Ruler/Somethingroyal
1977	**Seattle Slew**	Jean Cruguet	Billy Turner	Karen Taylor	Bold Reasoning/My Charmer
1978	**Affirmed**	Steve Cauthen	Laz Barrera	Harbor View Farm	Exclusive Native/Won't Tell You

Note: Gallant Fox (1930) is the only Triple Crown winner to sire another Triple Crown winner, Omaha (1935). Wm.Woodward Sr. owner of Belair Stud, was breeder-owner of both horses and both were trained by James (Sunny Jim) Fitzsimmons.

Triple Crown Near Misses

Thirty-two horses have won two legs of the Triple Crown. Of those, a dozen won the Kentucky Derby (KD) and Preakness Stakes (PS) only to be beaten in the Belmont Stakes (BS). Two others, Burgoo King (1932) and Bold Venture (1936), each won the Derby and Preakness but were forced out of the Belmont with the same injury—a bowed tendon—that effectively ended their racing careers.

Year	Horse	KD	PS	BS	Year	Horse	KD	PS	BS
1877	**Cloverbrook**	DNS	won	won	1956	**Needles**	won	2nd	won
1878	**Duke of Magenta**	DNS	won	won	1958	**Tim Tam**	won	won	2nd
1880	**Grenada**	DNS	won	won	1961	**Carry Back**	won	won	7th
1881	**Saunterer**	DNS	won	won	1963	**Chateaugay**	won	2nd	won
1895	**Belmar**	DNS	won	won	1964	**Northern Dancer**	won	won	3rd
1920	**Man O'War**	DNS	won	won	1966	**Kauai King**	won	won	4th
1922	**Pillory**	DNS	won	won	1967	**Damascus**	3rd	won	won
1923	**Zev**	won	12th	won	1968	**Forward Pass**	won*	won	2nd
1931	**Twenty Grand**	won	2nd	won	1969	**Majestic Prince**	won	won	2nd
1932	**Burgoo King**	won	won	DNS	1971	**Canonero II**	won	won	4th
1936	**Bold Venture**	won	won	DNS	1972	**Riva Ridge**	won	4th	won
1939	**Johnstown**	won	5th	won	1974	**Little Current**	5th	won	won
1940	**Bimelech**	2nd	won	won	1976	**Bold Forbes**	won	3rd	won
1942	**Shut Out**	won	5th	won	1979	**Spectacular Bid**	won	won	3rd
1944	**Pensive**	won	won	2nd	1981	**Pleasant Colony**	won	won	3rd
1949	**Capot**	2nd	won	won	1984	**Swale**	won	7th	won
1950	**Middleground**	won	2nd	won	1987	**Alysheba**	won	won	4th
1953	**Native Dancer**	2nd	won	won	1988	**Risen Star**	3rd	won	won
1955	**Nashua**	2nd	won	won	1989	**Sunday Silence**	won	won	2nd

*Won on disqualification.
Note: in 1978, Affirmed and Alydar placed 1-2 in all three Triple Crown races, the only time that has happened.

Kentucky Derby, 1875-89

For three-year-olds. Held the first Saturday in May at Churchill Downs in Louisville, Ky. Inaugurated in 1987.
Originally run at 1½ miles (1985-95), shortened to present 1¼ miles in 1896.
Trainer with most wins: Ben A. Jones (6).
Jockeys with most wins: Eddie Arcaro and Bill Hartack (5).
Winning fillies: Regret (1915), Genuine Risk (1980) and Winning Colors (1988).

Year	Winner	Time	Jockey	Trainer	2nd place	3rd place
1875	**Aristides**	2:37¾	Oliver Lewis	Andy Anderson	Volcano	Verdigris
1876	**Vagrant**	2:38¼	Bobby Swim	James Williams	Creedmoor	Harry Hill
1877	**Baden-Baden**	2:38	Billy Walker	Ed Brown	Leonard	King William
1878	**Day Star**	2:37¼	Jimmy Carter	Lee Paul	Himyar	Leveler
1879	**Lord Murphy**	2:37	Charlie Shauer	George Rice	Falsetto	Strathmore
1880	**Fonso**	2:37½	George Lewis	Tice Hutsell	Kimball	Bancroft
1881	**Hindoo**	2:40	Jim McLaughlin	James Rowe,Sr.	Lelex	Alfambra
1882	**Apollo**	2:40¼	Babe Hurd	Green Morris	Runnymede	Bengal
1883	**Leonatus**	2:43	Billy Donohue	Raleigh Colston	Drake Carter	Lord Raglan
1884	**Buchanan**	2:40¼	Isaac Murphy	William Bird	Loftin	Audrain
1885	**Joe Cotton**	2:37¼	Babe Henderson	Alex Perry	Bersan	Ten Booker
1886	**Ben Ali**	2:36½	Paul Duffy	Jim Murphy	Blue Wing	Free Knight

Kentucky Derby (Continued)

Year	Winner	Time	Jockey	Trainer	2nd place	3rd place
1887	**Montrose**	2:39¼	Isaac Lewis	John McGinty	Jim Gore	Jacobin
1888	**MacBeth II**	2:38¼	Geo.Covington	John Campbell	Gallifet	White
1889	**Spokane**	2:34½	Thomas Kiley	John Rodegap	Proctor Knott	Once Again
1890	**Riley**	2:45	Isaac Murphy	Edward Corrigan	Bill Letcher	Robespierre
1891	**Kingman**	2:52¼	Isaac Murphy	Dud Allen	Balgowan	High Tariff
1892	**Azra**	2:41½	Lonnie Clayton	John Morris	Huron	Phil Dwyer
1893	**Lookout**	2:39¼	Eddie Kunze	Wm.McDaniel	Plutus	Boundless
1894	**Chant**	2:41	Frank Goodale	Eugene Leigh	Pearl Song	Sigurd
1895	**Halma**	2:37½	Soup Perkins	Byron McClelland	Basso	Laureate
1896	**Ben Brush**	2:07¼	Willie Simms	Hardy Campbell	Ben Eder	Semper Ego
1897	**Typhoon II**	2:12½	Buttons Garner	J.C.Cahn	Ornament	Dr. Catlett
1898	**Plaudit**	2:09	Willie Simms	John Madden	Lieber Karl	Isabey
1899	**Manuel**	2:12	Fred Taral	Robert Walden	Corsini	Mazo
1900	**Lieut. Gibson**	2:06¼	Jimmy Boland	Charles Hughes	Florizar	Thrive
1901	**His Eminence**	2:07¾	Jimmy Winkfield	F.B.VanMeter	Sannazarro	Driscoll
1902	**Alan-a-Dale**	2:08¾	Jimmy Winkfield	T.C.McDowell	Inventor	The Rival
1903	**Judge Himes**	2:09	Hal Booker	J.P.Mayberry	Early	Bourbon
1904	**Elwood**	2:08½	Shorty Prior	C.E.Durnell	Ed. Tierney	Brancas
1905	**Agile**	2:10¾	Jack Martin	Robert Tucker	Ram's Horn	Layson
1906	**Sir Huon**	2:08⅕	Roscoe Troxler	Pete Coyne	Lady Navarre	James Reddick
1907	**Pink Star**	2:12⅗	Andy Minder	W.H.Fizer	Zal	Ovelando
1908	**Stone Street**	2:15⅕	Arthur Pickens	J.W.Hall	Sir Cleges	Dunvegan
1909	**Wintergreen**	2:08⅕	Vincent Power	Charles Mack	Miami	Dr. Barkley
1910	**Donau**	2:06⅖	Fred Herbert	George Ham	Joe Morris	Fighting Bob
1911	**Meridian**	2:05	Geo.Archibald	Albert Ewing	Governor Gray	Colston
1912	**Worth**	2:09⅖	C.H.Shilling	Frank Taylor	Duval	Flamma
1913	**Donerail**	2:04⅘	Roscoe Goose	Thomas Hayes	Ten Point	Gowell
1914	**Old Rosebud**	2:03⅖	John McCabe	F.D.Weir	Hodge	Bronzewing
1915	**Regret**	2:05⅖	Joe Notter	James Rowe,Sr.	Pebbles	Sharpshooter
1916	**George Smith**	2:04	Johnny Loftus	Hollie Hughes	Star Hawk	Franklin
1917	**Omar Khayyam**	2:04⅗	Charles Borel	C.T.Patterson	Ticket	Midway
1918	**Exterminator**	2:10⅘	William Knapp	Henry McDaniel	Escoba	Viva America
1919	**SIR BARTON**	2:09⅘	Johnny Loftus	H.Guy Bedwell	Billy Kelly	Under Fire
1920	**Paul Jones**	2:09	Ted Rice	Billy Garth	Upset	On Watch
1921	**Behave Yourself**	2:04⅕	Chas.Thompson	H.J.Thompson	Black Servant	Prudery
1922	**Morvich**	2:04⅗	Albert Johnson	Fred Burlew	Bet Mosie	John Finn
1923	**Zev**	2:05⅖	Earl Sande	D.J.Leary	Martingale	Vigil
1924	**Black Gold**	2:05⅕	John Mooney	Hedley Webb	Chilhowee	Beau Butler
1925	**Flying Ebony**	2:07⅗	Earl Sande	William Duke	Captain Hal	Son of John
1926	**Bubbling Over**	2:03⅗	Albert Johnson	H.J.Thompson	Bagenbaggage	Rock Man
1927	**Whiskery**	2:06	Linus McAtee	Fred Hopkins	Osmond	Jock
1928	**Reigh Count**	2:10⅖	Chick Lang	Bert Michell	Misstep	Toro
1929	**Clyde Van Dusen**	2:10⅘	Linus McAtee	Clyde Van Dusen	Naishapur	Panchio
1930	**GALLANT FOX**	2:07⅗	Earl Sande	Jim Fitzsimmons	Gallant Knight	Ned O.
1931	**Twenty Grand**	2:01⅘	Chas.Kurtsinger	James Rowe,Jr.	Sweep All	Mate
1932	**Burgoo King**	2:05⅕	Eugene James	H.J.Thompson	Economic	Stepenfetchit
1933	**Brokers Tip**	2:06⅘	Don Meade	H.J.Thompson	Head Play	Charley O.
1934	**Cavalcade**	2:04	Mack Garner	Bob Smith	Discovery	Agrarian
1935	**OMAHA**	2:05	Willie Saunders	Jim Fitzsimmons	Roman Soldier	Whiskolo
1936	**Bold Venture**	2:03⅗	Ira Hanford	Max Hirsch	Brevity	Indian Brown
1937	**WAR ADMIRAL**	2:03⅕	Chas.Kurtsinger	George Conway	Pompoon	Reaping Reward
1938	**Lawrin**	2:04⅘	Eddie Arcaro	Ben Jones	Dauber	Can't Wait
1939	**Johnstown**	2:03⅗	James Stout	Jim Fitzsimmons	Challedon	Heather Broom
1940	**Gallahadion**	2:05	Carroll Bierman	Roy Waldron	Bimelech	Dit
1941	**WHIRLAWAY**	2:01⅖	Eddie Arcaro	Ben Jones	Staretor	Market Wise
1942	**Shut Out**	2:04⅖	Wayne Wright	John Gaver	Alsab	Valdina Orphan
1943	**COUNT FLEET**	2:04	Johnny Longden	Don Cameron	Blue Swords	Slide Rule
1944	**Pensive**	2:04⅕	Conn McCreary	Ben Jones	Broadcloth	Stir Up
1945	**Hoop Jr**	2:07	Eddie Arcaro	Ivan Parke	Pot o'Luck	Darby Dieppe
1946	**ASSAULT**	2:06⅗	Warren Mehrtens	Max Hirsch	Spy Song	Hampden
1947	**Jet Pilot**	2:06⅘	Eric Guerin	Tom Smith	Phalanx	Faultless
1948	**CITATION**	2:05⅖	Eddie Arcaro	Ben Jones	Coaltown	My Request
1949	**Ponder**	2:04⅕	Steve Brooks	Ben Jones	Capot	Palestinian
1950	**Middleground**	2:01⅗	William Boland	Max Hirsch	Hill Prince	Mr. Trouble
1951	**Count Turf**	2:02⅗	Conn McCreary	Sol Rutchick	Royal Mustang	Ruhe
1952	**Hill Gail**	2:01⅗	Eddie Arcaro	Ben Jones	Sub Fleet	Blue Man
1953	**Dark Star**	2:02	Hank Moreno	Eddie Hayward	Native Dancer	Invigorator

Year	Winner	Time	Jockey	Trainer	2nd place	3rd place
1954	**Determine**	2:03	Raymond York	Willie Molter	Hasty Road	Hasseyampa
1955	**Swaps**	2:01⅘	Bill Shoemaker	Mesh Tenney	Nashua	Summer Tan
1956	**Needles**	2:03⅖	David Erb	Hugh Fontaine	Fabius	Come On Red
1957	**Iron Liege**	2:02⅕	Bill Hartack	Jimmy Jones	Gallant Man	Round Table
1958	**Tim Tam**	2:05	I.Valenzuela	Jimmy Jones	Lincoln Road	Noureddin
1959	**Tomy Lee**	2:02⅕	Bill Shoemaker	Frank Childs	Sword Dancer	First Landing
1960	**Venetian Way**	2:02⅖	Bill Hartack	Victor Sovinski	Bally Ache	Victoria Park
1961	**Carry Back**	2:04	John Sellers	Jack Price	Crozier	Bass Clef
1962	**Decidedly**	2:00⅖	Bill Hartack	Horatio Luro	Roman Line	Ridan
1963	**Chateaugay**	2:01⅘	Braulio Baeza	James Conway	Never Bend	Candy Spots
1964	**Northern Dancer**	2:00	Bill Hartack	Horatio Luro	Hill Rise	The Scoundrel
1965	**Lucky Debonair**	2:01⅕	Bill Shoemaker	Frank Catrone	Dapper Dan	Tom Rolfe
1966	**Kauai King**	2:02	Don Brumfield	Henry Forrest	Advocator	Blue Skyer
1967	**Proud Clarion**	2:00⅗	Bobby Ussery	Loyd Gentry	Barbs Delight	Damascus
1968	**Forward Pass***	2:02⅕	I.Valenzuela	Henry Forrest	Francie's Hat	T.V. Commercial
1969	**Majestic Prince**	2:01⅘	Bill Hartack	Johnny Longden	Arts & Letters	Dike
1970	**DustCommander**	2:03⅖	Mike Manganello	Don Combs	My Dad George	High Echelon
1971	**Canonero II**	2:03⅕	Gustavo Avila	Juan Arias	Jim French	Bold Reason
1972	**Riva Ridge**	2:01⅘	Ron Turcotte	Lucien Laurin	No Le Hace	Hold Your Peace
1973	**SECRETARIAT**	1:59⅖	Ron Turcotte	Lucien Laurin	Sham	Our Native
1974	**Cannonade**	2:04	Angel Cordero	Woody Stephens	Hudson County	Agitate
1975	**Foolish Pleasure**	2:02	Jacinto Vasquez	LeRoy Jolley	Avatar	Diabolo
1976	**Bold Forbes**	2:01⅜	Angel Cordero	Laz Barrera	Honest Pleasure	Elocutionist
1977	**SEATTLE SLEW**	2:02⅕	Jean Cruguet	Billy Turner	Run Dusty Run	Sanhedrin
1978	**AFFIRMED**	2:01⅕	Steve Cauthen	Laz Barrera	Alydar	Believe It
1979	**Spectacular Bid**	2:02⅖	Ron Franklin	Buddy Delp	General Assembly	Golden Act
1980	**Genuine Risk**	2:02	Jacinto Vasquez	LeRoy Jolley	Rumbo	Jaklin Klugman
1981	**Pleasant Colony**	2:02	Jorge Velasquez	John Campo	Woodchopper	Partez
1982	**Gato Del Sol**	2:02⅕	E.Delahoussaye	Eddie Gregson	Laser Light	Reinvested
1983	**Sunny's Halo**	2:02⅕	E.Delahoussaye	David Cross	Desert Wine	Caveat
1984	**Swale**	2:02⅖	Laffit Pincay	Woody Stephens	Coax Me Chad	At The Threshold
1985	**Spend A Buck**	2:00⅕	Angel Cordero	Cam Gambolati	Stephan's Odyssey	Chief's Crown
1986	**Ferdinand**	2:02⅘	Bill Shoemaker	Chas.Whittingham	Bold Arrangement	Broad Brush
1987	**Alysheba**	2:03⅖	Chris McCarron	Jack Van Berg	Bet Twice	Avies Copy
1988	**Winning Colors**	2:02⅕	Gary Stevens	D.Wayne Lukas	Forty Niner	Risen Star
1989	**Sunday Silence**	2:05	Pat Valenzuela	Chas.Whittingham	Easy Goer	Awe Inspiring

*Dancer's Image finished first but was disqualified after traces of prohibited medication were found in his system.

Preakness Stakes, 1873-89

For three-year-olds. Held two weeks after the Kentucky Derby at Pimlico Race Course in Baltimore, Md. Inaugurated 1873.
Originally run at 1½ miles (1873-88), then at 1¼ miles (1889), 1½ miles (1890), 1¹⁄₁₆ miles (1894-1900), 1 mile & 70 yards (1901-07), 1¹⁄₁₆ miles (1908), 1 mile (1909-10), 1⅛ miles (1911-24), and the present 1³⁄₁₆ miles since 1925.
Trainer with most wins: Robert W.Walden (7).
Jockey with most wins: Eddie Arcaro (6).
Winning fillies: Flocarline (1903), Whimsical (1906), Rhine Maiden (1915) and Nellie Morse (1924).

Year	Winner	Time	Jockey	Trainer	2nd place	3rd place
1873	**Survivor**	2:43	G.Barbee	A.D.Pryor	John Boulger	Artist
1874	**Culpepper**	2:56½	W.Donohue	H.Gaffney	King Amadeus	Scratch
1875	**Tom Ochiltree**	2:43½	L.Hughes	R.W.Walden	Viator	Bay Final
1876	**Shirley**	2:44¾	G.Barbee	W.Brown	Rappahannock	Algerine
1877	**Cloverbrook**	2:45½	C.Holloway	J.Walden	Bombast	Lucifer
1878	**Duke of Magenta**	2:41¾	C.Holloway	R.W.Walden	Bayard	Albert
1879	**Harold**	2:40½	L.Hughes	R.W.Walden	Jericho	Rochester
1880	**Grenada**	2:40½	L.Hughes	R.W. Walden	Oden	Emily F.
1881	**Saunterer**	2:40½	T.Costello	R.W. Walden	Compensation	Baltic
1882	**Vanguard**	2:44½	T.Costello	R.W. Walden	Heck	Col. Watson
1883	**Jacobus**	2:42½	G.Barbee	R.Dwyer	Parnell	—
1884	**Knight of Ellerslie**	2:39½	S.Fisher	T.B.Doswell	Welcher	—
1885	**Tecumseh**	2:49	Jim McLaughlin	C.Littlefield	Wickham	John C.
1886	**The Bard**	2:45	S.Fisher	J.Huggins	Eurus	Elkwood
1887	**Dunboyne**	2:39½	W.Donohue	W.Jennings	Mahoney	Raymond
1888	**Refund**	2:49	F.Littlefield	R.W.Walden	Judge Murray	Glendale
1889	**Buddhist**	2:17½	W.Anderson	J.Rogers	Japhet	—
1890	**Montague**	2:36¾	W.Martin	E.Feakes	Philosophy	Barrister
1891	Not held					
1892	Not held					
1893	Not held					

Preakness Stakes (Continued)

Year	Winner	Time	Jockey	Trainer	2nd place	3rd place
1894	**Assignee**	1:49¼	F.Taral	W.Lakeland	Potentate	Ed Kearney
1895	**Belmar**	1:50½	F.Taral	E.Feakes	April Fool	Sue Kittie
1896	**Margrave**	1:51	H.Griffin	Byron McClelland	Hamilton II	Intermission
1897	**Paul Kauvar**	1:51¼	T.Thorpe	T.P.Hayes	Elkins	On Deck
1898	**Sly Fox**	1:49⅗	W.Simms	H.Campbell	The Huguenot	Nuto
1899	**Half Time**	1:47	R.Clawson	F.McCabe	Filigrane	Lackland
1900	**Hindus**	1:48⅖	H.Spencer	J.H.Morris	Sarmation	Ten Candles
1901	**The Parader**	1:47⅕	F.Landry	T.J.Healey	Sadie S.	Dr. Barlow
1902	**Old England**	1:45⅘	L.Jackson	G.B.Morris	Maj.Daingerfield	Namtor
1903	**Flocarline**	1:44⅘	W.Gannon	H.C.Riddle	Mackey Dwyer	Rightful
1904	**Bryn Mawr**	1:44⅕	E.Hildebrand	W.F.Presgrave	Wotan	Dolly Spanker
1905	**Cairngorm**	1:45⅘	W.Davis	A.J.Joyner	Kiamesha	Coy Maid
1906	**Whimsical**	1:45	Walter Miller	T.J.Gaynor	Content	Larabie
1907	**Don Enrique**	1:45⅖	G.Mountain	A.J.Joyner	Ethon	Zambesi
1908	**Royal Tourist**	1:46⅖	Eddie Dugan	A.J.Joyner	Live Wire	Robert Cooper
1909	**Effendi**	1:39⅘	Willie Doyle	F.C.Frisbie	Fashion Plate	Hilltop
1910	**Layminister**	1:40⅗	R.Estep	J.S.Healy	Dalhousie	Sager
1911	**Watervale**	1:51	Eddie Dugan	J.Whalen	Zeus	The Nigger
1912	**Colonel Holloway**	1:56⅗	C.Turner	D.Woodford	Bwana Tumbo	Tipsand
1913	**Buskin**	1:53⅖	James Butwell	J.Whalen	Kleburne	Barnegat
1914	**Holiday**	1:53⅘	A.Schuttinger	J.S.Healy	Brave Cunarder	Defendum
1915	**Rhine Maiden**	1:58	Douglas Hoffman	F.Devers	Half Rock	Runes
1916	**Damrosch**	1:54⅘	Linus McAtee	A.G.Weston	Greenwood	Achievement
1917	**Kalitan**	1:54⅖	E.Haynes	Bill Hurley	Al M. Dick	Kentucky Boy
1918	**War Cloud**	1:53⅗	Johnny Loftus	W.B.Jennings	Sunny Slope	Lanius
1918	**Jack Hare Jr**	1:53⅖	Charles Peak	F.D.Weir	The Porter	Kate Bright
1919	**SIR BARTON**	1:53	Johnny Loftus	H.Guy Bedwell	Eternal	Sweep On
1920	**Man o'War**	1:51⅗	Clarence Kummer	L.Feustel	Upset	Wildair
1921	**Broomspun**	1:54⅕	F.Coltiletti	James Rowe,Sr.	Polly Ann	Jeg
1922	**Pillory**	1:51⅗	L.Morris	Thomas Healey	Hea	June Grass
1923	**Vigil**	1:53⅗	B.Marinelli	Thomas Healey	General Thatcher	Rialto
1924	**Nellie Morse**	1:57⅕	John Merimee	A.B.Gordon	Transmute	Mad Play
1925	**Coventry**	1:59	Clarence Kummer	William Duke	Backbone	Almadel
1926	**Display**	1:59⅘	John Maiben	Thomas Healey	Blondin	Mars
1927	**Bostonian**	2:01⅗	Whitey Abel	Fred Hopkins	Sir Harry	Whiskery
1928	**Victorian**	2:00⅕	Sonny Workman	James Rowe,Jr.	Toro	Solace
1929	**Dr. Freeland**	2:01⅗	Louis Schaefer	Thomas Healey	Minotaur	African
1930	**GALLANT FOX**	2:00⅗	Earl Sande	Jim Fitzsimmons	Crack Brigade	Snowflake
1931	**Mate**	1:59	George Ellis	J.W.Healey	Twenty Grand	Ladder
1932	**Burgoo King**	1:59⅘	John Maiben	Thomas Healey	Tick On	Boatswain
1933	**Head Play**	2:02	Chas.Kurtsinger	Thomas Hayes	Ladysman	Utopian
1934	**High Quest**	1:58⅕	Robert Jones	Bob Smith	Cavalcade	Discovery
1935	**OMAHA**	1:58⅖	Willie Saunders	Jim Fitzsimmons	Firethorn	Psychic Bid
1936	**Bold Venture**	1:59	George Woolf	Max Hirsch	Granville	Jean Bart
1937	**WAR ADMIRAL**	1:58⅖	Chas.Kurtsinger	George Conway	Pompoon	Flying Scot
1938	**Dauber**	1:59⅘	Maurice Peters	Dick Handlen	Cravat	Menow
1939	**Challedon**	1:59⅘	George Seabo	Louis Schaefer	Gilded Knight	Volitant
1940	**Bimelech**	1:58⅗	F.A.Smith	Bill Hurley	Mioland	Gallahadion
1941	**WHIRLAWAY**	1:58⅘	Eddie Arcaro	Ben Jones	King Cole	Our Boots
1942	**Alsab**	1:57	Basil James	Sarge Swenke	Requested	Sun Again
1943	**COUNT FLEET**	1:57⅖	Johnny Longden	Don Cameron	Blue Swords	Vincentive
1944	**Pensive**	1:59⅕	Conn McCreary	Ben Jones	Platter	Stir Up
1945	**Polynesian**	1:58⅘	W.D.Wright	Morris Dixon	Hoop Jr.	Darby Dieppe
1946	**ASSAULT**	2:01⅖	Warren Mehrtens	Max Hirsch	Lord Boswell	Hampden
1947	**Faultless**	1:59	Doug Dobson	Ben Jones	On Trust	Phalanx
1948	**CITATION**	2:02⅖	Eddie Arcaro	Ben Jones	Vulcan's Forge	Boyard
1949	**Capot**	1:56	Ted Atkinson	J.M.Gaver	Palestinian	Noble Impulse
1950	**Hill Prince**	1:59⅕	Eddie Arcaro	Casey Hayes	Middleground	Dooley
1951	**Bold**	1:56⅖	Eddie Arcaro	Preston Burch	Counter Point	Alerted
1952	**Blue Man**	1:57⅖	Conn McCreary	Woody Stephens	Jampol	One Count
1953	**Native Dancer**	1:57⅘	Eric Guerin	Bill Winfrey	Jamie K.	Royal Bay Gem
1954	**Hasty Road**	1:57⅖	Johnny Adams	Harry Trotsek	Carrilation	Hasseyampa
1955	**Nashua**	1:54⅗	Eddie Arcaro	Jim Fitzsimmons	Saratoga	Traffic Judge
1956	**Fabius**	1:58⅖	Bill Hartack	Jimmy Jones	Needles	No Regrets
1957	**Bold Ruler**	1:56⅕	Eddie Arcaro	Jim Fitzsimmons	Iron Liege	Inside Tract
1958	**Tim Tam**	1:57⅕	I.Valenzuela	Jimmy Jones	Lincoln Road	Gone Fishin'
1959	**Royal Orbit**	1:57	Wm.Harmatz	R. Cornell	Sword Dancer	Dunce

Year	Winner	Time	Jockey	Trainer	2nd place	3rd place
1960	**Bally Ache**	1:57⅗	Bobby Ussery	Jimmy Pitt	Victoria Park	Celtic Ash
1961	**Carry Back**	1:57⅗	Johnny Sellers	Jack Price	Globemaster	Crozier
1962	**Greek Money**	1:56⅕	John Rotz	V.W.Raines	Ridan	Roman Line
1963	**Candy Spots**	1:56⅕	Bill Shoemaker	Mesh Tenney	Chateaugay	Never Bend
1964	**Northern Dancer**	1:56⅘	Bill Hartack	Horatio Luro	The Scoundrel	Hill Rise
1965	**Tom Rolfe**	1:56⅕	Ron Turcotte	Frank Whiteley	Dapper Dan	Hail To All
1966	**Kauai King**	1:55⅖	Don Brumfield	H. Forrest	Stupendous	Amberoid
1967	**Damascus**	1:55⅕	Bill Shoemaker	Frank Whiteley	In Reality	Proud Clarion
1968	**Forward Pass**	1:56⅘	I.Valenzuela	Henry Forrest	Out Of the Way	Nodouble
1969	**Majestic Prince**	1:55⅗	Bill Hartack	Johnny Longden	Arts & Letters	Jay Ray
1970	**Personality**	1:56⅕	Eddie Belmonte	John Jacobs	My Dad George	Silent Screen
1971	**Canonero II**	1:54	Gustavo Avila	Juan Arias	Eastern Fleet	Jim French
1972	**Bee Bee Bee**	1:55⅗	Eldon Nelson	Red Carroll	No Le Hace	Key To The Mint
1973	**SECRETARIAT**	1:54⅖	Ron Turcotte	Lucien Laurin	Sham	Our Native
1974	**Little Current**	1:54⅗	Miguel Rivera	Lou Rondinello	Neapolitan Way	Cannonade
1975	**Master Derby**	1:56⅖	Darrel McHargue	Smiley Adams	Foolish Pleasure	Diabolo
1976	**Elocutionist**	1:55	John Lively	Paul Adwell	Play The Red	Bold Forbes
1977	**SEATTLE SLEW**	1:54⅖	Jean Cruguet	Billy Turner	Iron Constitution	Run Dusty Run
1978	**AFFIRMED**	1:54⅖	Steve Cauthen	Laz Barrera	Alydar	Believe It
1979	**Spectacular Bid**	1:54⅕	Ron Franklin	Buddy Delp	Golden Act	Screen King
1980	**Codex**	1:54⅕	Angel Cordero	D.Wayne Lukas	Genuine Risk	Colonel Moran
1981	**Pleasant Colony**	1:54⅗	Jorge Velasquez	John Campo	Bold Ego	Paristo
1982	**Aloma's Ruler**	1:55⅖	Jack Kaenel	John Lensini	Linkage	Cut Away
1983	**Deputed Testamony**	1:55⅖	Donald Miller	Bill Boniface	Desert Wine	High Honors
1984	**Gate Dancer**	1:53⅗	Angel Cordero	Jack Van Berg	Play On	Fight Over
1985	**Tank's Prospect**	1:53⅖	Pat Day	D.Wayne Lukas	Chief's Crown	Eternal Prince
1986	**Snow Chief**	1:54⅘	Alex Solis	Melvin Stute	Ferdinand	Broad Brush
1987	**Alysheba**	1:55⅘	Chris McCarron	Jack Van Berg	Bet Twice	Cryptoclearance
1988	**Risen Star**	1:56⅕	E.Delahoussaye	Louie Roussel	Brian's Time	Winning Colors
1989	**Sunday Silence**	1:53⅘	Pat Valenzuela	Chas.Whittingham	Easy Goer	Rock Point

Belmont Stakes, 1867-89

For three-year-olds. Held three weeks after Preakness Stakes at Belmont Park in Elmont, N.Y. Inaugurated in 1867 at Jerome Park, moved to Morris Park in 1890 and Belmont Park in 1905.

Originally run at 1 mile and 5 furlongs (1867-89), then 1¼ miles (1890-1905), 1⅜ miles (1906-25), and the present 1½ miles since 1926.

Trainer with most wins: James Rowe, Sr.(8).

Jockey with most wins: Eddie Arcaro and Jim McLaughlin (6).

Winning fillies: Ruthless (1967) and Tanya (1925).

Year	Winner	Time	Jockey	Trainer	2nd place	3rd place
1867	**Ruthless**	3:05	J.Gilpatrick	A.J.Minor	De Courcy	Rivoli
1868	**General Duke**	3:02	Bobby Swim	A.Thompson	Northumberland	Fannie Ludlow
1869	**Fenian**	3:04¼	C.Miller	J.Pincus	Glenelg	Invercauld
1870	**Kingfisher**	2:59½	W.Dick	R.Colston	Foster	Midday
1871	**Harry Bassett**	2:56	W.Miller	D.McDaniel	Stockwood	By-the-Sea
1872	**Joe Daniels**	2:58½	James Rowe	D.McDaniel	Meteor	Shylock
1873	**Springbok**	3:01¾	James Rowe	D.McDaniel	Count d'Orsay	Strachino
1874	**Saxon**	2:39½	G.Barbee	W.Pryor	Grinstead	Aaron Pennington
1875	**Calvin**	2:42¼	Bobby Swim	A.Williams	Aristides	Milner
1876	**Algerine**	2:40½	Billy Donohue	T.B.Doswell	Fiddlestick	Barricade
1877	**Cloverbrook**	2:46	C.Holloway	J.Walden	Loiterer	Baden-Baden
1878	**Duke of Magenta**	2:42¾	L.Hughes	R.W.Walden	Bramble	Sparta
1879	**Spendthrift**	2:42¾	George Evans	T.Puryear	Monitor	Jericho
1880	**Grenada**	2:47	L.Hughes	R.W.Walden	Ferncliffe	Turenne
1881	**Saunterer**	2:47	T.Costello	R.W.Walden	Eole	Baltic
1882	**Forester**	2:43	Jim McLaughlin	L.Stuart	Babcock	Wyoming
1883	**George Kinney**	2:42½	Jim McLaughlin	James Rowe,Sr.	Trombone	Renegade
1884	**Panique**	2:42	Jim McLaughlin	James Rowe,Sr.	Knight of Ellerslie	Himalaya
1885	**Tyrant**	2:43	Paul Duffy	C.Claypool	St.Augustine	Tecumseh
1886	**Inspector B**	2:41	Jim McLaughlin	F.McCabe	The Bard	Linden
1887	**Hanover**	2:43½	Jim McLaughlin	F.McCabe	Oneko	—
1888	**Sir Dixon**	2:40¼	Jim McLaughlin	F.McCabe	Prince Royal	—
1889	**Eric**	2:47	W.Hayward	J.Huggins	Diable	Zephyrus
1890	**Burlington**	2:07¾	Pike Barnes	A.Cooper	Devotee	Padishah
1891	**Foxford**	2:08¾	Ed Garrison	M.Donovan	Montana	Laurestan
1892	**Patron**	2:17	W.Hayward	L.Stuart	Shellbark	—

Belmont Stakes (Continued)

Year	Winner	Time	Jockey	Trainer	2nd place	3rd place
1893	**Comanche**	1:53¼	Willie Simms	G.Hannon	Dr.Rice	Rainbow
1894	**Henry of Navarre**	1:56½	Willie Simms	B.McClelland	Prig	Assignee
1895	**Belmar**	2:11½	Fred Taral	E.Feakes	Counter Tenor	Nanki Pooh
1896	**Hastings**	2:24½	H.Griffin	J.J.Hyland	Handspring	Hamilton II
1897	**Scottish Chieftain**	2:23½	J.Scherrer	M.Byrnes	On Deck	Octagon
1898	**Bowling Brook**	2:32	F.Littlefield	R.W.Walden	Previous	Hamburg
1899	**Jean Bereaud**	2:23	R.Clawson	Sam Hildreth	Half Time	Glengar
1900	**Ildrim**	2:21½	Nash Turner	H.E.Leigh	Petrucio	Missionary
1901	**Commando**	2:21	H.Spencer	James Rowe,Sr.	The Parader	All Green
1902	**Masterman**	2:22½	John Bullman	J.J.Hyland	Ranald	King Hanover
1903	**Africander**	2:23⅕	John Bullman	R.Miller	Whorler	Red Knight
1904	**Delhi**	2:06⅖	George Odom	James Rowe,Sr.	Graziallo	Rapid Water
1905	**Tanya**	2:08	E.Hildebrand	J.W.Rogers	Blandy	Hot Shot
1906	**Burgomaster**	2:20	Lucien Lyne	J.W.Rogers	The Quail	Accountant
1907	**Peter Pan**	—	G.Mountain	James Rowe,Sr.	Superman	Frank Gill
1908	**Colin**	—	Joe Notter	James Rowe,Sr.	Fair Play	King James
1909	**Joe Madden**	2:21⅗	E.Dugan	Sam Hildreth	Wise Mason	Donald MacDonald
1910	**Sweep**	2:22	James Butwell	James Rowe,Sr.	Duke of Ormonde	—
1911	Not held					
1912	Not held					
1913	**Prince Eugene**	2:18	Roscoe Troxler	James Rowe,Sr.	Rock View	Flying Fairy
1914	**Luke McLuke**	2:20	Merritt Buxton	J.F.Schorr	Gainer	Charlestonian
1915	**The Finn**	2:18⅖	George Byrne	E.W.Heffner	Half Rock	Pebbles
1916	**Friar Rock**	2:22	E.Haynes	Sam Hildreth	Spur	Churchill
1917	**Hourless**	2:17⅘	James Butwell	Sam Hildreth	Skeptic	Wonderful
1918	**Johren**	2:20⅖	Frank Robinson	A.Simons	War Cloud	Cum Sah
1919	**SIR BARTON**	2:17⅖	John Loftus	H.Guy Bedwell	Sweep On	Natural Bridge
1920	**Man o'War**	2:14⅕	Clarence Kummer	L.Feustel	Donnacona	—
1921	**Grey Lag**	2:16⅘	Earl Sande	Sam Hildreth	Sporting Blood	Leonardo II
1922	**Pillory**	2:18⅘	C.H.Miller	T.J.Healey	Snob II	Hea
1923	**Zev**	2:19	Earl Sande	Sam Hildreth	Chickvale	Rialto
1924	**Mad Play**	2:18⅘	Earl Sande	Sam Hildreth	Mr.Mutt	Modest
1925	**American Flag**	2:16⅘	Albert Johnson	G.R.Tompkins	Dangerous	Swope
1926	**Crusader**	2:32⅕	Albert Johnson	George Conway	Espino	Haste
1927	**Chance Shot**	2:32⅖	Earl Sande	Pete Coyne	Bois de Rose	Flambino
1928	**Vito**	2:33⅕	Clarence Kummer	Max Hirsch	Genie	Diavolo
1929	**Blue Larkspur**	2:32⅘	Mack Garner	C.Hastings	African	Jack High
1930	**GALLANT FOX**	2:31⅗	Earl Sande	Jim Fitzsimmons	Whichone	Questionnaire
1931	**Twenty Grand**	2:29⅗	Chas.Kurtsinger	James Rowe,Jr.	Sun Meadow	Jamestown
1932	**Faireno**	2:32⅘	Tom Malley	Jim Fitzsimmons	Osculator	Flag Pole
1933	**Hurryoff**	2:32⅗	Mack Garner	H.McDaniel	Nimbus	Union
1934	**Peace Chance**	2:29⅕	W.D.Wright	Pete Coyne	High Quest	Good Goods
1935	**OMAHA**	2:30⅗	Willie Saunders	Jim Fitzsimmons	Firethorn	Rosemont
1936	**Granville**	2:30	James Stout	Jim Fitzsimmons	Mr.Bones	Hollyrood
1937	**WAR ADMIRAL**	2:28⅗	Chas.Kurtsinger	George Conway	Sceneshifter	Vamoose
1938	**Pasteurized**	2:29⅖	James Stout	George Odom	Dauber	Cravat
1939	**Johnstown**	2:29⅗	James Stout	Jim Fitzsimmons	Belay	Gilded Knight
1940	**Bimelech**	2:29⅗	Fred Smith	Bill Hurley	Your Chance	Andy K.
1941	**WHIRLAWAY**	2:31	Eddie Arcaro	Ben Jones	Robert Morris	Yankee Chance
1942	**Shut Out**	2:29⅕	Eddie Arcaro	John Gaver	Alsab	Lochinvar
1943	**COUNT FLEET**	2:28⅕	Johnny Longden	Don Cameron	Fairy Manhurst	Deseronto
1944	**Bounding Home**	2:32⅕	G.L.Smith	Matt Brady	Pensive	Bull Dandy
1945	**Pavot**	2:30⅕	Eddie Arcaro	Oscar White	Wildlife	Jeep
1946	**ASSAULT**	2:30⅘	Warren Mehrtens	Max Hirsch	Natchez	Cable
1947	**Phalanx**	2:29⅖	R.Donoso	Syl Veitch	Tide Rips	Tailspin
1948	**CITATION**	2:28⅕	Eddie Arcaro	Jimmy Jones	Better Self	Escadru
1949	**Capot**	2:30⅕	Ted Atkinson	John Gaver	Ponder	Palestinian
1950	**Middleground**	2:28⅗	William Boland	Max Hirsch	Lights Up	Mr.Trouble
1951	**Counterpoint**	2:29	David Gorman	Syl Veitch	Battlefield	Battle Morn
1952	**One Count**	2:30⅕	Eddie Arcaro	Oscar White	Blue Man	Armageddon
1953	**Native Dancer**	2:28⅗	Eric Guerin	Bill Winfrey	Jamie K.	Royal Bay Gem
1954	**High Gun**	2:30⅘	Eric Guerin	Max Hirsch	Fisherman	Limelight
1955	**Nashua**	2:29	Eddie Arcara	Jim Fitzsimmons	Blazing Count	Portersville
1956	**Needles**	2:29⅗	David Erb	Hugh Fontaine	Career Boy	Fabius
1957	**Gallant Man**	2:26⅗	Bill Shoemaker	John Nerud	Inside Tract	Bold Ruler
1958	**Cavan**	2:30⅕	Pete Anderson	Tom Barry	Tim Tam	Flamingo
1959	**Sword Dancer**	2:28⅖	Bill Shoemaker	Elliott Burch	Bagdad	Royal Orbit

Year	Winner	Time	Jockey	Trainer	2nd place	3rd place
1960	**Celtic Ash**	2:29⅗	Bill Hartack	Tom Barry	Venetian Way	Disperse
1961	**Sherluck**	2:29⅕	Braulio Baeza	Harold Young	Globemaster	Guadalcanal
1962	**Jaipur**	2:28⅘	Bill Shoemaker	B.Mulholland	Admiral's Voyage	Crimson Satan
1963	**Chateaugay**	2:30⅕	Braulio Baeza	James Conway	Candy Spots	Choker
1964	**Quadrangle**	2:28⅖	Manuel Ycaza	Elliott Burch	Roman Brother	Northern Dancer
1965	**Hail to All**	2:28⅖	John Sellers	Eddie Yowell	Tom Rolfe	First Family
1966	**Amberoid**	2:29⅗	William Boland	Lucien Laurin	Buffle	Advocator
1967	**Damascus**	2:28⅘	Bill Shoemaker	F.Y.Whiteley	Cool Reception	Gentleman James
1968	**Stage Door Johnny**	2:27⅕	Gus Gustines	John Gaver	Forward Pass	Call Me Prince
1969	**Arts And Letters**	2:28⅘	Braulio Baeza	Elliott Burch	Majestic Prince	Dike
1970	**High Echelon**	2:34	John Rotz	John Jacobs	Needles N Pins	Naskra
1971	**Pass Catcher**	2:30⅖	Walter Blum	Eddie Yowell	Jim French	Bold Reason
1972	**Riva Ridge**	2:28	Ron Turcotte	Lucien Laurin	Ruritania	Cloudy Dawn
1973	**SECRETARIAT**	2:24	Ron Turcotte	Lucien Laurin	Twice A Prince	My Gallant
1974	**Little Current**	2:29⅕	Miguel Rivera	Lou Rondinello	Jolly Johu	Cannonade
1975	**Avatar**	2:28⅕	Bill Shoemaker	Tommy Doyle	Foolish Pleasure	Master Derby
1976	**Bold Forbes**	2:29	Angel Cordero	Laz Barrera	McKenzie Bridge	Great Contractor
1977	**SEATTLE SLEW**	2:29⅗	Jean Cruguet	Billy Turner	Run Dusty Run	Sanhedrin
1978	**AFFIRMED**	2:26⅘	Steve Cauthen	Laz Barrera	Alydar	Darby Creek Road
1979	**Coastal**	2:28⅗	Ruben Hernandez	David Whiteley	Golden Act	Spectacular Bid
1980	**Temperence Hill**	2:29⅘	Eddie Maple	Joseph Cantey	Genuine Risk	Rockhill Native
1981	**Summing**	2:29	George Martens	Luis Barerra	Highland Blade	Pleasant Colony
1982	**Conquistador Cielo**	2:28⅕	Laffit Pincay	Woody Stephens	Gato Del Sol	Illuminate
1983	**Caveat**	2:27⅘	Laffit Pincay	Woody Stephens	Slew o'Gold	Barberstown
1984	**Swale**	2:27⅕	Laffit Pincay	Woody Stephens	Pine Circle	Morning Bob
1985	**Creme Fraiche**	2:27	Eddie Maple	Woody Stephens	Stephan's Odyssey	Chief's Crown
1986	**Danzig Connection**	2:29⅘	Chris McCarron	Woody Stephens	Johns Treasure	Ferdinand
1987	**Bet Twice**	2:28⅕	Craig Perret	Jimmy Croll	Cryptoclearance	Gulch
1988	**Risen Star**	2:26⅖	E.Delahoussaye	Louie Roussel	Kingpost	Brian's Time
1989	**Easy Goer**	2:26	Pat Day	Shug McGaughey	Sunday Silence	Le Voyageur

Breeders' Cup, 1984-88

Inaugurated on Nov. 10, 1984, the Breeders' Cup consists of seven races at one track on one day late in the year to determine thoroughbred racing's principal champions.

Breeders' Cup Day has been held at Hollywood Park (Calif.) in 1984, Aqueduct Racetrack (N.Y.) in 1985, Santa Anita Park (Calif.) in 1986, Hollywood Park in 1987, and Churchill Downs (Ky.) in 1988. It will be held this year on Nov. 4 at Gulfstream Park (Fla.).

The steeplechase was added to the Breeders' Cup championship roster in 1986, but has been held each year at Fair Hill Race Course (Md.)

Trainer with most wins: D. Wayne Lukas (9).
Jockeys with most wins: Pat Day and Laffit Pincay, Jr. (4).
Horse with most wins: Miesque (2).

Juvenile

Distances: one mile (1984-85, 87); 1$\frac{1}{16}$ miles (1986,88).

Year	Winner	Time	Jockey	Trainer	2nd place	3rd place
1984	**Chief's Crown**	1:36⅕	Don MacBeth	Roger Laurin	Tank's Prospect	Spend A Buck
1985	**Tasso**	1:36⅕	Laffit Pincay	Neil Drysdale	Storm Cat	Scat Dancer
1986	**Capote**	1:43⅘	Laffit Pincay	D.Wayne Lukas	Qualify	Alysheba
1987	**Success Express**	1:35⅕	Jose Santos	D.Wayne Lukas	Regal Classic	Tejano
1988	**Is It True**	1:46⅗	Laffit Pincay	D.Wayne Lukas	Easy Goer	Tagel

Juvenile Fillies

Distances: one mile (1984-85, 87); 1$\frac{1}{16}$ miles (1986, 88).

Year	Winner	Time	Jockey	Trainer	2nd place	3rd place
1984	**Outstandingly**	1:37⅘	Walter Guerra	Pancho Martin	Dusty Heart	Fine Spirit
1985	**Twilight Ridge**	1:35⅘	Jorge Velasquez	D.Wayne Lukas	Family Style	Steal A Kiss
1986	**Brave Raj**	1:43⅕	Pat Valenzuela	Melvin Stute	Tappiano	Saros Brig
1987	**Epitome**	1:36⅖	Pat Day	Phil Hauswald	Jeanne Jones	Dream Team
1988	**Open Mind**	1:46⅗	Angel Cordero	D.Wayne Lukas	Darby Shuffle	Lea Lucinda

Note: in 1984, winner **Fran's Valentine** was disqualified for interference in the stretch and placed 10th.

Breeders' Cup (Continued)

Sprint

Distance: six furlongs (1984-88).

Year	Winner	Time	Jockey	Trainer	2nd place	3rd place
1984	**Eillo**	1:10⅕	Craig Perret	Budd Lepman	Commemorate	Fighting Fit
1985	**Precisionist**	1:08⅖	Chris McCarron	R.Fenstermaker	Smile	Mt.Livermore
1986	**Smile**	1:08⅖	Jacinto Vasquez	S.Schulhofer	Pine Tree Lane	Bedside Promise
1987	**Very Subtle**	1:08⅘	Pat Valenzuela	Melvin Stute	Groovy	Exclusive Enough
1988	**Gulch**	1:10⅖	Angel Cordero	D.Wayne Lukas	Play The King	Afleet

Mile

Year	Winner	Time	Jockey	Trainer	2nd place	3rd place
1984	**Royal Heroine**	1:32⅗	Fernando Toro	John Gosden	Star Choice	Cozzene
1985	**Cozzene**	1:35	Walter Guerra	Jan Nerud	Al Mamoon	Shadeed
1986	**Last Tycoon**	1:35⅕	Yves St.-Martin	Robert Collet	Palace Music	Fred Astaire
1987	**Miesque**	1:32⅘	Freddie Head	Francois Boutin	Show Dancer	Sonic Lady
1988	**Miesque**	1:38⅗	Freddie Head	Francois Boutin	Steinlen	Simply Majestic

Note: in 1985, 2nd place finisher **Palace Music** was disqualified for interference and placed 9th.

Distaff

Distances: 1¼ miles (1984-87); 1⅛ miles (1988).

Year	Winner	Time	Jockey	Trainer	2nd place	3rd place
1984	**Princess Rooney**	2:02⅖	E.Delahoussaye	Neil Drysdale	Life's Magic	Adored
1985	**Life's Magic**	2:02	Angel Cordero	D.Wayne Lukas	Lady's Secret	DontstopThemusic
1986	**Lady's Secret**	2:01⅕	Pat Day	D.Wayne Lukas	Fran's Valentine	Outstandingly
1987	**Sacahuista**	2:02⅘	Randy Romero	D.Wayne Lukas	Clabber Girl	Oueee Bebe
1988	**Personal Ensign**	1:52	Randy Romero	Shug McGaughey	Winning Colors	Goodbye Halo

Turf

Distance: 1½ miles (1984-88).

Year	Winner	Time	Jockey	Trainer	2nd place	3rd place
1984	**Lashkari**	2:25⅕	Yves St-Martin	De Royer-Dupre	All Along	Raami
1985	**Pebbles**	2:27	Pat Eddery	Clive Brittain	Strawberry Rd.II	Mourjane
1986	**Manila**	2:25⅖	Jose Santos	Leroy Jolley	Theatrical	Estrapade
1987	**Theatrical**	2:24⅖	Pat Day	Bill Mott	Trempolino	Village Star II
1988	**Grt.Communicator**	2:35⅕	Ray Sibille	Thad Ackel	Sunshine Forever	Indian Skimmer

Classic

Distance: 1¼ miles (1984-88).

Year	Winner	Time	Jockey	Trainer	2nd place	3rd place
1984	**Wild Again**	2:03⅖	Pat Day	V.Timphony	Slew O'Gold	Gate Dancer
1985	**Proud Truth**	2:00⅘	Jorge Velasquez	John Veitch	Gate Dancer	Turkoman
1986	**Skywalker**	2:00⅖	Laffit Pincay	M.Whittingham	Turkoman	Precisionist
1987	**Ferdinand**	2:01⅖	Bill Shoemaker	C.Whittingham	Alysheba	Judge Angelucci
1988	**Alysheba**	2:04⅘	Chris McCarron	Jack Van Berg	Seeking the Gold	Waquoit

Note: in 1984, 2nd place finisher **Gate Dancer** was disqualified for interference and placed 3rd.

Steeplechase

Distances: 2⅜ miles (1986); 2⅝ miles (1987-88).

Year	Winner	Time	Jockey	Trainer	2nd place	3rd place
1986	**Census**	4:27⅗	Jeff Teter	Janet Elliott	Kesslin	Pont du Loup
1987	**Gacko**	5:15⅕	Roger Duchene	Xavier Guigand	Inlander	Gateshead
1988	**Jimmy Lorenzo**	5:12⅖	Graham McCourt	Jonathan Sheppard	Kalankoe	Polar Pleasure

Awards

Horse of the Year, 1936-70

In 1971, the **Daily Racing Form**, the Thoroughbred Racing Associations, and the National Turf Writers Assn. joined forces to create the Eclipse Awards. Before then, however, the **Racing Form** (1936-70) and the TRA (1950-70) issued separate selections for Horse of the Year. Their picks differed only four times from 1950-70 and are so noted. Horses listed in capital LETTERS are Triple Crown winners. Horses with an asterisk are fillies.

1936 Granville	1946 ASSAULT	1955 Nashua	1963 Kelso
1937 WAR ADMIRAL	1947 Armed	1956 Swaps	1964 Kelso
1938 Seabiscuit	1948 CITATION	1957 Bold Ruler (DRF)	1965 Roman Brother (DRF)
1939 Challedon	1949 Capot	Dedicate (TRA)	Moccasin (TRA)
1940 Challedon	1950 Hill Prince	1958 Round Table	1966 Buckpasser
1941 WHIRLAWAY	1951 Counterpoint	1959 Sword Dancer	1967 Damascus
1942 Whirlaway	1952 One Count (DRF)	1960 Kelso	1968 Dr. Fager
1943 COUNT FLEET	Native Dancer (TRA)	1961 Kelso	1969 Arts and Letters
1944 Twilight Tear*	1953 Tom Fool	1962 Kelso	1970 Fort Marcy (DRF)
1945 Busher*	1954 Native Dancer		Personality (TRA)

Eclipse Awards, 1971-88

The Eclipse Awards, honoring the Horse of the Year and other champions of the sport, are sponsored by the **Daily Racing Form**, the Thoroughbred Racing Associations and the National Turf Writers Assn.

The awards are named after the 18th century racehorse and sire, Eclipse, who began racing at age five and was unbeaten in 18 starts (eight wins were walkovers). As a stallion, Eclipse sired winners of 344 races, including three Epsom Derby champions.

Horses listed in capital LETTERS won the Triple Crown that year. Age of horse in parentheses where necessary.

Horse of the Year

1971 Ack Ack (5)	1975 Forego (5)	1980 Spectacular Bid (4)	1984 John Henry (9)
1972 Secretariat (2)	1976 Forego (6)	1981 John Henry (6)	1985 Spend A Buck (3)
1973 SECRETARIAT (3)	1977 SEATTLE SLEW (3)	1982 Conquistador	1986 Lady's Secret (4)
1974 Forego (4)	1978 AFFIRMED (3)	Cielo (3)	1987 Ferdinand (4)
	1979 Affirmed (4)	1983 All Along (4)	1988 Alysheba (4)

Older Colt, Horse or Gelding

1971 Ack Ack (5)	1975 Forego (5)	1980 Spectacular Bid (4)	1984 Slew o' Gold (4)
1972 Autobiography (4)	1976 Forego (6)	1981 John Henry (6)	1985 Vanlandingham (4)
1973 Riva Ridge (4)	1977 Forego (7)	1982 Lemhi Gold (4)	1986 Turkoman (4)
1974 Forego (4)	1978 SEATTLE SLEW (4)	1983 Bates Motel (4)	1987 Ferdinand (4)
	1979 AFFIRMED (4)		1988 Alysheba (4)

Older Filly or Mare

1971 Shuvee (5)	1975 Susan's Girl (6)	1980 Glorious Song (4)	1984 Princess Rooney (4)
1972 Typecast (6)	1976 Proud Delta (4)	1981 Relaxing (5)	1985 Life's Magic (4)
1973 Susan's Girl (4)	1977 Cascapedia (4)	1982 Track Robbery (6)	1986 Lady's Secret (4)
1974 Desert Vixen (4)	1978 Late Bloomer (4)	1983 Ambassador of	1987 North Sider (5)
	1979 Waya (5)	Luck (4)	1988 Personal Ensign (4)

3-Year-Old Colt

1971 Canonero II	1975 Wajima	1980 Temperence Hill	1984 Swale
1972 Key to the Mint	1976 Bold Forbes	1981 Pleasant Colony	1985 Spend A Buck
1973 SECRETARIAT	1977 SEATTLE SLEW	1982 Conquistador Cielo	1986 Snow Chief
1974 Little Currant	1978 AFFIRMED	1983 Slew o' Gold	1987 Alysheba
	1979 Spectacular Bid		1988 Risen Star

3-Year-Old Filly

1971 Turkish Trousers	1975 Ruffian	1980 Genuine Risk	1984 Life's Magic
1972 Susan's Girl	1976 Revidere	1981 Wayward Lass	1985 Mom's Command
1973 Desert Vixen	1977 Our Mims	1982 Christmas Past	1986 Tiffany Lass
1974 Chris Evert	1978 Tempest Queen	1983 Heartlight No. One	1987 Sacahuista
	1979 Davona Dale		1988 Winning Colors

2-Year-Old Colt

1971 Riva Ridge	1975 Honest Pleasure	1980 Lord Avie	1984 Chief's Crown
1972 Secretariat	1976 Seattle Slew	1981 Deputy Minister	1985 Tasso
1973 Protagonist	1977 Affirmed	1982 Roving Boy	1986 Capote
1974 Foolish Pleasure	1978 Spectacular Bid	1983 Devil's Bag	1987 Forty Niner
	1979 Rockhill Native		1988 Easy Goer

Eclipse Awards (Continued)

2-Year-Old Filly

1971 Numbered Account	1976 Sensational	1980 Heavenly Cause	1984 Outstandingly
1972 La Prevoyante	1977 Lakeville Miss	1981 Before Dawn	1985 Family Style
1973 Talking Picture	1978 Candy Eclair	1982 Landaluce	1986 Brave Raj
1974 Ruffian	It's in the Air	1983 Althea	1987 Epitome
1975 Dearly Precious	1979 Smart Angle		1988 Open Mind

Champion Turf Horse

1971 Run the Gantlet (3)	1973 Secretariat (3)	1975 Snow Knight (4)	1977 Johnny D (3)
1972 Cougar II (6)	1974 Dahlia (4)	1976 Youth (3)	1978 Mac Diarmida (3)

Champion Male Turf Horse

1979 Bowl Game (5)	1981 John Henry (6)	1984 John Henry (9)	1987 Theatrical (5)
1980 John Henry (5)	1982 Perrault (5)	1985 Cozzene (4)	1988 Sunshine Forever (3)
	1983 John Henry (8)	1986 Manila (3)	

Champion Female Turf Horse

1979 Trillion (5)	1981 De La Rose (3)	1984 Royal Heroine (4)	1987 Miesque (3)
1980 Just A Game II (4)	1982 April Run (4)	1985 Pebbles (4)	1988 Miesque (4)
	1983 All Along (4)	1986 Estrapade (6)	

Sprinter

1971 Ack Ack (5)	1976 My Juliet (4)	1980 Plugged Nickle (3)	1984 Eillo (4)
1972 Chou Croute (4)	1977 What A Summer (4)	1981 Guilty Conscience (5)	1985 Precisionist (4)
1973 Shecky Greene (3)	1978 Dr.Patches (4)	1982 Gold Beauty (4)	1986 Smile (4)
1974 Forego (4)	J.O.Tobin (4)	1983 Chinook Pass (4)	1987 Groovy (4)
1975 Gallant Bob (3)	1979 Star de Naskra (4)		1988 Gulch (4)

Steeplechase or Hurdle Horse

1971 Shadow Brook (7)	1975 Life's Illusion (4)	1980 Zaccio (4)	1984 Flatterer (5)
1972 Soothsayer (5)	1976 Straight & True (6)	1981 Zaccio (5)	1985 Flatterer (6)
1973 Athenian Idol (5)	1977 Cafe Prince (7)	1982 Zaccio (6)	1986 Flatterer (7)
1974 Gran Kan (8)	1978 Cafe Prince (8)	1983 Flatterer (4)	1987 Inlander (6)
	1979 Martie's Anger (4)		1988 Jimmy Lorenzo (6)

Outstanding Jockey

1971 Laffit Pincay,Jr.	1975 Braulio Baeza	1980 Chris McCarron	1984 Pat Day
1972 Braulio Baeza	1976 Sandy Hawley	1981 Bill Shoemaker	1985 Laffit Pincay,Jr.
1973 Laffit Pincay,Jr.	1977 Steve Cauthen	1982 Angel Cordero,Jr.	1986 Pat Day
1974 Laffit Pincay,Jr.	1978 Darrel McHargue	1983 Angel Cordero,Jr.	1987 Pat Day
	1979 Laffit Pincay,Jr.		1988 Jose Santos

Outstanding Apprentice Jockey

1971 Gene St. Leon	1975 Jimmy Edwards	1980 Grank Lovato,Jr.	1984 Wesley Ward
1972 Thomas Wallis	1976 George Martens	1981 Richard Migliore	1985 Art Madrid,Jr.
1973 Steve Valdez	1977 Steve Cauthen	1982 Alberto Delgado	1986 Allen Stacy
1974 Chris McCarron	1978 Ron Franklin	1983 Declan Murphy	1987 Kent Desormeaux
	1979 Cash Asmussen		1988 Steve Capanas

Outstanding Trainer

1971 Charlie Whittingham	1975 Steve DiMauro	1980 Bud Delp	1985 D.Wayne Lukas
1972 Lucien Laurin	1976 Laz Barrera	1981 Ron McAnally	1986 D.Wayne Lukas
1973 H.Allen Jerkens	1977 Laz Barrera	1982 Charlie Whittingham	1987 D.Wayne Lukas
1974 Sherrill Ward	1978 Laz Barrera	1983 Woody Stephens	1988 Shug McGaughey
	1979 Laz Barrera	1984 Jack Van Berg	

Outstanding Owner

1971 Mr.& Mrs.E.E.	1976 Dan Lasater	1981 Dotsam Stable	1986 Mr.& Mrs. Eugene
Fogleson	1977 Maxwell Gluck	1982 Viola Sommer	Klein
1972 No award	1978 Harbor View Farm	1983 John Franks	1987 Mr.& Mrs. Eugene
1973 No award	1979 Harbor View Farm	1984 John Franks	Klein
1974 Dan Lasater	1980 Mr.& Mrs. Bertram	1985 Mr.& Mrs. Eugene	1988 Ogden Phipps
1975 Dan Lasater	Firestone	Klein	

Outstanding Owner-Breeder

1971 Paul Mellon	1972 Meadow Stable/	1973 Meadow Stable/
	Meadow Stud	Meadow Stud

Outstanding Breeder

1974 John W.Galbreath	1977 Edward Plunket	1980 Mrs. Henry D.	1984 Claiborne Farm
1975 Fred W.Hooper	Taylor	Paxson	1985 Nelson Bunker Hunt
1976 Nelson Bunker Hunt	1978 Harbor View Farm	1981 Golden Chance Farm	1986 Paul Mellon
	1979 Claiborne Farm	1982 Fred W.Hooper	1987 Nelson Bunker Hunt
		1983 Edward P.Taylor	1988 Ogden Phipps

Man of the Year

1972 John W.Galbreath   1973 Edward P. Taylor   1974 William L.McKnight   1975 John A. Morris

Outstanding Achievement

1971* Charles Engelhard   1972* Arthur B.Hancock, Jr.
*Awarded posthumously

Award of Merit

1976 Jack J.Dreyfus	1978 Ogden Mills	1980 John D.Schapiro	1985 Keene Daingerfield
1977 Steve Cauthen	(Dinny) Phipps	1981 Bill Shoemaker	1986 Herman Cohen
	1979 Frank E.(Jimmy) Kilroe	1984 John Gaines	1987 J.B.Faulconer
			1988 John Forsythe

Special Award

1971 Robert J.Kleberg	1976 Bill Shoemaker	1984 C.V.Whitney	1987 Anheuser-Busch
1974 Charles Hatton	1980 John T.Landry	1985 Arlington Park	1988 Edward J.
	Pierre E. Bellocq (Peb)		DeBartolo, Sr.

Harness Racing

Triple Crown Winners

Trotters

Six 3-year-olds have won the Yonkers Trot, Hambletonian and Kentucky Futurity in the same year since the Trotting Triple Crown was established in 1955. Stanley Dancer is the only driver/trainer to win it twice.

Year	Horse	Driver/Trainer	Owner
1955	**Scott Frost**	Joe O'Brien	S.A. Camp Farms
1963	**Speedy Scot**	Ralph Baldwin	Castleton Farms
1964	**Ayres**	John Simpson, Sr.	Charlotte Sheppard
1968	**Nevele Pride**	Stanley Dancer	Nevele Acres & Lou Resnick
1969	**Lindy's Pride**	Howard Beissinger	Lindy Farms
1972	**Super Bowl**	Stanley Dancer	Rachel Dancer & Rose Hild Breeding Farm

Pacers

Seven 3-year-olds have won the Cane Pace, Little Brown Jug and Messenger Stakes in the same year since the Pacing Triple Crown was established in 1956. No trainer or driver has won it more than once.

Year	Horse	Driver	Trainer	Owner
1959	**Adios Butler**	Clint Hodgins	Paige West	Paige West & Angelo Pellillo
1965	**Bret Hanover**	Frank Ervin	Frank Ervin	Richard Downing
1966	**Romeo Hanover** .	Bill Myer & George Sholty*	Jerry Silverman	Lucky Star Stable & Morton Finder
1968	**Rum Customer** . . .	Billy Haughton	Billy Haughton	Kennilworth Farms & L.C. Mancuso
1970	**Most Happy Fella** .	Stanley Dancer	Stanley Dancer	Egyptian Acres Stable
1980	**Niatross**	Clint Galbraith	Clint Galbraith	Niagara Acres, Niatross Stables & Clint Galbraith
1983	**Ralph Hanover** . .	Ron Waples	Stan Firlotte	Waples Stable, Pointsetta Stable, Grant's Direct Stable & P.J. Baugh

*Myer drove Romeo Hanover in the Cane, Sholty in the other two races.

Triple Crown Near Misses

Trotters

Five horses have won the first two legs of the Triple Crown—the Yonkers Trot (YT) and the Hambletonian (Ham)—but not the third. The eventual winner of the Ky. Futurity (KF) is listed.

Year	Horse	YT	Ham	KF
1962	**AC's Viking**	won	won	Safe Mission
1976	**Steve Lobell**	won	won	Quick Pay
1977	**Green Speed**	won	won	Texas
1978	**Speedy Somolli** . . .	won	won	Doublemint
1987	**Mack Lobell**	won	won	Napoletano

Note: Green Speed (1977) was not eligible for Ky. Futurity.

Pacers

Five horses have won the first two legs of the Triple Crown, but not the third. The Cane Pace (CP), Little Brown Jug (LBJ), and Messenger Stakes (MS) have not always been run in the same order so numbers after races won indicate sequence for that year.

Year	Horse	CP	LBJ	MS
1957	**Torpid**	won,1	won,2	DNF
1960	**Countess Adios**	won,2	NE	won,1
1971	**Albatross**	won,2	2nd*	won,1
1976	**Keystone Ore**	won,1	won,2	2nd*
1986	**Barberry Spur**	won,1	won,2	2nd*

Winning horses: Nansemond (1971), Windshield Wiper (1976), Amity Chef (1986).

Note: Torpid (1957) was scratched before the final heat; and Countess Adios (1960) was not eligible for Messenger.

Harness Racing (Continued)
The Hambletonian, 1926-89

For three-year-old trotters. Inaugurated in 1926 and has been held in Syracuse, N.Y.; Lexington, Ky.; Goshen, N.Y, Yonkers, N.Y.; Du Quoin, Ill.; and, since 1981 at The Meadowlands in East Rutherford, N.J. Run at one mile since 1947. Winning horse must win two heats.
Drivers with most wins: Ben White, Stanley Dancer and Billy Haughton (4).

Year	Winner	Driver	Fastest Heat	Year	Winner	Driver	Fastest Heat
1926	Guy McKinney	Nat Ray	2:04¾	1958	Emily's Pride	Flave Nipe	1:59.4
1927	Iosola's Worthy	Marvin Childs	2:03¾	1959	Diller Hanover	Frank Ervin	2:01.1
1928	Spencer	W.H.Lessee	2:02½				
1929	Walter Dear	Walter Cox	2:02¾	1960	Blaze Hanover	Joe O'Brien	1:59.3
				1961	Harlan Dean	James Arthur	1:58.2
1930	Hanover's Bertha	Tom Berry	2:03	1962	A.C.'s Viking	Sanders Russell	1:59.3
1931	Calumet Butler	R.D.McMahon	2:03¼	1963	Speedy Scot	Ralph Baldwin	1:57.3
1932	The Marchioness	Wm. Caton	2:01¼	1964	Ayres	J.Simpson Sr.	1:56.4
1933	Mary Reynolds	Ben White	2:03¾	1965	Egyptian Candor	Del Cameron	2:03.4
1934	Lord Jim	Doc Parshall	2:02¾	1966	Kerry Way	Frank Ervin	1:58.4
1935	Greyhound	Sep Palin	2:02¼	1967	Speedy Streak	Del Cameron	2:00
1936	Rosalind	Ben White	2:01¾	1968	Nevele Pride	Stanley Dancer	1:59.2
1937	Shirley Hanover	H.Thomas	2:01½	1969	Lindys Pride	H.Beissinger	1:57.3
1938	McLin Hanover	Henry Tomas	2:02¼				
1939	Peter Astra	Doc Parshall	2:04¼	1970	Timothy T.	J.Simpson, Jr.	1:58.2
				1971	Speedy Crown	H.Beissinger	1:57.2
1940	Spencer Scott	Fred Egan	2:02	1972	Super Bowl	Stanley Dancer	1:56.2
1941	Bill Gallon	Lee Smith	2:05	1973	Flirth	Ralph Baldwin	1:57.1
1942	The Ambassador	Ben White	2:04	1974	Christopher T.	Bill Haughton	1:58.3
1943	Volo Song	Ben White	2:02½	1975	Bonefish	Stanley Dancer	1:59
1944	Yankee Maid	Henry Thomas	2:04	1976	Steve Lobell	Bill Haughton	1:56.2
1945	Titan Hanover	H.Pownall,Sr.	2:04	1977	Green Speed	Bill Haughton	1:55.3
1946	Chestertown	Thomas Berry	2:02½	1978	Speedy Somolli	H.Beissinger	1:55
1947	Hoot Mon	Sep Palin	2:00	1979	Legend Hanover	George Sholty	1:56.1
1948	Demon Hanover	Harrison Hoyt	2:02				
1949	Miss Tilly	Fred Egan	2:01.2	1980	Burgomeister	Bill Haughton	1:56.3
				1981	Shiaway St. Pat	Ray Remmen	2:01.1
1950	Lusty Song	Del Miller	2:02	1982	Speed Bowl	Tommy Haughton	1:56.4
1951	Mainliner	Guy Crippen	2:02.3	1983	Duenna	Stanley Dancer	1:57.2
1952	Sharp Note	Bion Shively	2:02.3	1984	Historic Freight	Ben Webster	1:56.2
1953	Helicopter	Harry Harvey	2:01.3	1985	Prakas	Bill O'Donnell	1:54.3
1954	Newport Dream	Del Cameron	2:02.4	1986	Nuclear Kosmos	Ulf Thoresen	1:55.2
1955	Scott Frost	Joe O'Brien	2:00.3	1987	Mack Lobell	John Campbell	1:53.3
1956	The Intruder	Ned Bower	2:01.2	1988	Armbro Goal	John Campbell	1:54.3
1957	Hickory Smoke	J.Simpson Sr.	2:00.1	1989	Park Avenue Joe*	Ron Waples	2:00.4

*Declared winner after dead heat with Probe in third race. Park Avenue Joe was 2nd in first heat and won the second heat. Probe won first heat, but placed 9th in the second heat. The time of 2:00.4 was the clocking of the dead heat.

Harness Horse of the Year

Chosen by U.S. Trotting Assn. and U.S. Harness Writers Assn. Trotters are noted with asterisk (*).

Year		Year		Year		Year	
1947	Victory Song*	1960	Adios Butler	1970	Fresh Yankee*	1980	Niatross
1948	Rodney*	1961	Adios Butler	1971	Albatross	1981	Fan Hanover
1949	Good Time	1962	Su Mac Lad*	1972	Albatross	1982	Cam Fella
		1963	Speedy Scot*	1973	Sir Dalrai	1983	Cam Fella
1950	Proximity*	1964	Bret Hanover	1974	Delmonica Hanover*	1984	Fancy Crown*
1951	Pronto Don*	1965	Bret Hanover	1975	Savoir*	1985	Nihilator
1952	Good Time	1966	Bret Hanover	1976	Keystone Ore	1986	Forrest Skipper
1953	Hi Lo's Forbes	1967	Nevele Pride*	1977	Green Speed*	1987	Mack Lobell*
1954	Stenographer*	1968	Nevele Pride*	1978	Abercrombie	1988	Mack Lobell*
1955	Scott Frost*	1969	Nevele Pride*	1979	Niatross		
1956	Scott Frost*						
1957	Torpid						
1958	Emily's Pride*						
1959	Bye Bye Byrd						

One Mile Track Records

Trotting
All-Age: 1:52.1—Mack Lobell, Springfield, Illinois; Aug. 21, 1987. **Two-Year Old:** 1:55.3—Mack Lobell, Lexington, Ky.; Oct. 3. 1986. **Three-Year Old:** 1:52.1—Mack Lobell, Springfield, Illinois; Aug. 21, 1985.

Pacing
All-Age: 1:48.2*—Matt's Scooter, Lexington, Ky. (Sept. 23,1988). **Two-Year Old:** 1:52.0—Raque Bogart, Lexington, Ky. (Sept.30,1988) and L Dees Trish, Lexington, Ky (Oct.1,1988). **Three-Year Old:** 1:48.2*—Matt's Scooter, Lexington, Ky. (Sept.25,1988).
*denotes record taken in time trial.

USA midfielder **Tab Ramos** reacts to scoring the go-ahead goal in America's 1-0 victory over Costa Rica in a World Cup qualifying match April 30 in St. Louis.

SOCCER

INSIDE

Elsewhere in Almanac
For related information refer to the following chapters: Sports Organizations and Updates.

*The U.S. chases a World Cup berth,
Italian clubs rule Europe,
Brazil wins Copa America,
and 95 die in Sheffield tragedy.*

SOCCER

1988-89 YEAR IN REVIEW

by Paul Gardner

The scenes at the United States Soccer Federation's 1989 Annual General Meeting in August were not quite what one might have expected.

After all, the biggest prize in international sports—the World Cup—was coming to America in 1994, plus the U.S. national team—not, it is true, without some difficulty—was on course to qualify for the 1990 finals in Italy.

Such achievements surely suggested that a sea of smiling, satisfied faces would welcome USSF president Werner Fricker. But that was not to be the case. There was much unrest among the membership, even the threat of a move to unseat Fricker.

At the roots of the discord lie the difficulties the USSF, a volunteer organization, has had in trying to move into the

Soccer journalist **Paul Gardner** has been a columnist for **Soccer America** since 1982. He has also written three books on the sport and served as a World Cup TV commentator for ABC in 1982 and NBC in 1986.

world of big-time sports promotions. Fricker, a dynamic but dour man, clearly has little patience for many of the USSF's elected officers. To get things done, he has simply bypassed them— leading to accusations that he is running the USSF like a dictator. "I am not dictatorial," is Fricker's reply, "I am demanding. I expect performance."

Fricker's main antagonist was Treasurer Paul Stiehl, who insisted that the USSF was in financial trouble, and that Fricker had repeatedly broken the Federation's bylaws by spending money without authorization. Fricker vehemently rejected the charges—but there was one area where all parties agreed that action was urgently needed: finding money to finance the national team program.

When it was decided in the fall of 1988 to pay grants (they averaged around $20,000) to 16 national team players, the program was initially financed by a $500,000 loan. The long-term plan was that sponsorship money would pay for it, but by August no sponsorship money had been found.

It was in this atmosphere of urgency that Fricker presented a comprehensive television deal—to run through the 1994 World Cup—involving NBC and its cable subsidiary SportsChannel America. The deal—which meant a minimum of $1 million a year to the USSF for the next five years—was approved, but many members were left wondering whether it was the best deal possible, and feeling that they were being pressured into approving it.

Fricker insisted that it was the best, indeed that it was the **only,** deal available: "There is no other guy to deal with, there is no other offer—it's this or nothing." Some doubt was thrown on this assertion by a later complaint from the TBS Network that it had not been provided with all the necessary information that would have enabled it to make a bid.

The stormy meeting ended with Fricker still firmly in charge. But a feeling persisted that, unless he changed his style and became more responsive to other USSF officers, he would face stiff opposition when he ran for re-election in 1990.

As elsewhere in sports, money seemed to dominate the U.S. soccer scene. The year's only major news from World Cup USA 1994—the body set up by the USSF to run the 1994 World Cup—revealed the granting of a "substantial" line of credit by Manufacturers Hanover Trust.

On the field, the USA's bid to qualify for the World Cup finals in Italy (it would be the USA's first appearance in the finals since 1950) continued. It needed to finish as winner or runner-up in a qualifying group that also included Costa Rica, El Salvador, Guatemala and Trinidad & Tobago. (These games also had a monetary value: qualification would mean a share—estimated to be at least $1.2 million—in the profits of the 1990 World Cup.)

In the spring, a loss on the road to Costa Rica was offset by home wins over the same opponent and Guatemala. But the inconsistency of the team was alarming. Coach Bob Gansler's laconic "Any time I win, I feel lucky" could not disguise the fact that the USA had been almost supernaturally fortunate to beat Costa Rica 1–0. The winning American goal had come on a deflected shot while the

Costa Ricans had two scores disallowed and missed a penalty kick. Such luck ran out in the next game, when the USA dropped a home point in a 1–1 tie with Trinidad & Tobago.

The Americans did not participate in any World Cup qualifying matches in July and August, but did manage to defeat Soviet Union club champion Dnepr, 1–0, in an Aug. 26 exhibition match before 43,356 in Philadelphia. Resuming Cup play on Sept. 17 the USA stayed in the chase by shutting out El Salvador, 1–0, on a goal by Hugo Perez (a native of El Salvador) at a neutral site in Honduras.

Two encouraging moments for U.S. soccer came earlier in the year. In March, Gansler coached the Under-20 team to a fourth place finish in the World Championship—the best performance ever by an American team at any age level. Best, that is, in the outdoor sport. In January, FIFA (the Federation Internationale de Football Association) had staged the first-ever world championship for 5-a-side (indoor) soccer, and the USA captured the bronze medal.

The Major Indoor Soccer League, which plays a version of indoor soccer that is markedly different from FIFA's, found the going difficult after 10 years. Reduced to seven teams (it had once boasted 14), the MISL turned back to its roots and enticed Earl Foreman, the league's first commissioner, to come out of retirement and take over again. Meanwhile, the San Diego Sockers defeated the regular season champion Baltimore Blast in seven games to win their second straight MISL title and fifth since 1983.

Outdoors, the two regional semi-pro leagues—the Western Soccer League and (in the East) the American Soccer League —completed modestly successful seasons in September when the two league champions met in San Jose. The ASL's Ft. Lauderdale Strikers beat the WSL's San Diego Nomads, 3-1, before 8,632. Both leagues drew crowds averaging around 2,000 during the regular season.

The small attendance figures underlined the essence of soccer's problem in America. Its explosive and impressive growth has vastly increased the number of participants, but soccer has yet to prove that it can be a spectator sport in the U.S.

Brazil gained its first major championship since the 1970 World Cup when **Romario** headed in this goal to beat Uruguay, 1-0, in the Copa America final July 16 in Rio de Janeiro.

The World

The money problem for international soccer was that there was too much of it in West Europe, and not enough anywhere else. The inevitable result: a mass migration of top stars from Latin America and, to a lesser extent, East Europe to clubs in Spain, West Germany, France and—in particular—Italy.

With apparently limitless billions of lire at their command, the 18 Italian first division clubs (each permitted to sign up to three foreign players) greedily devoured the world's talent. At the start of the 1989 season, over 50 of the game's top stars— from Latin America, from the USSR, even from West Germany and Holland—were playing in Italy.

For the players the rewards were staggering: salaries worth millions of dollars (Dutch midfielder Ruud Gullit signed a $6.4 million three-year contract with Milan) and huge performance bonuses (up to $380,000 per player). For the clubs, the payoff came in sold-out stadiums (at a time when soccer attendances else-

where were static or falling) and success in the lucrative European inter-club competitions. In 1989, Italian clubs came close to carrying off all three titles: AC Milan defeated Steaua Bucharest of Romania to win the European Cup and Napoli beat VBF Stuttgart of West Germany to win the UEFA Cup, while Sampdoria lost to Barcelona in the final of the Cup Winners' Cup.

But what was good for Italy was not nearly so wonderful for South America. Argentina, Brazil and Uruguay saw their best players whisked away—and had a lot of trouble getting them back to play for the national teams. The South American Championship (the ''Copa America''), played in the summer in Brazil, was bedeviled by arguments over the release of players.

Brazil took the Copa with a 1–0 victory over Uruguay, capping a solid performance in which it conceded only one goal in six games. Incredibly, it was the country's first major soccer trophy since winning the World Cup in 1970. The

Argentina's **Diego Maradona,** playing for his Italian team Napoli, moves past a fallen defender in a league match last January.

emphasis on defense was something new for Brazil, highlighted by coach Sebastiao Lazaroni's tactical use of a sweeper—a position hitherto unknown in Brazilian soccer.

Argentina, world champions and favorites, finished a feeble third. Coach Carlos Bilardo put the blame on the problems with overseas players, who made up over half his squad: "The players arrived late, they arrived injured, and they arrived exhausted."

One was the world's No. 1 player, Diego Maradona. His lethargic performance for Argentina was seen by many as a direct result of his deteriorating relationship with his Italian club, Napoli. Unhappy with the Napoli fans who had booed him when he limped off after only 17 minutes of a game in June, Maradona had said: "The people who jeered are ignorant cretins. I want to stay in Napoli, but if peace there depends on my leaving, then I'll go."

Evidently to emphasize his displeasure, Maradona did not report back to Italy by the pre-season deadline. Instead, he went off to the Andes to do the very thing that most European clubs specifically bar their players from doing: skiing.

Fan trouble in soccer was not restricted to Maradona. The curse of hooliganism continued, despite the banning of English clubs from Europe. Incidents were reported from Greece, West Germany, Hungary, Yugoslavia, Holland, and from China and the USSR. In Italy, an ominous new dimension arrived: a street brawl broke out in Genoa between fans of the local clubs Sampdoria and Genoa—even though no game was being played.

The English government pressed ahead with its scheme to make all soccer fans carry compulsory identity cards despite opposition from the soccer authorities. The Dutch government tried to put such a scheme into operation at the beginning of the 1989–90 season without much success. Of the two clubs ordered to carry out the plan, one defied the government and refused, while the other gave in to angry fans who threatened to storm the turnstiles.

Bad crowd control was responsible for 95 people being crushed to death at an F.A. Cup semifinal match April 15 in Sheffield, England.

The trauma of the 1985 Heysel Stadium disaster in Brussels dragged on. On that occasion, 39 Juventus (Italy) fans were crushed to death as a result of rioting by supporters of the English club Liverpool before the start of the European Cup final.

After four years of complicated legal maneuvering, 24 Liverpool fans were charged with violent behavior and tried before a Belgian court. The verdicts were announced in April. Fourteen of the accused were found guilty and sentenced to three years in jail, but half the sentence was suspended and all 14 were released pending appeals. The other 10 Liverpool fans were released as the case against them was not proven. Found guilty of criminal negligence, and given suspended jail sentences, were the former president of the Belgian soccer federation, and the police chief in charge of security at the game.

Heysel Stadium itself has been given the death sentence. It is to be demolished and replaced by a new one on the same site, tentatively named the King Baudouin Stadium.

It was left to England to provide the year's most tragic news—an incident that, perversely, had nothing to do with hooliganism. On April 15, at the Hillsborough Stadium in Sheffield, bad crowd control and overcrowding led to the crushing to death of 95 fans. An official report blamed police ineptitude for the tragedy. (Later in the year came an admission from the Soviet Union that a similar but much bigger disaster had occurred in Moscow in 1982, and had been hushed up for seven years: over 340 fans had been killed.)

Nevertheless, English soccer had its shining moment with what must surely be the most incredible finish ever to a league championship season. On May 26, after a season that had lasted nine months and featured 379 games, the result was still in doubt as Arsenal and Liverpool played the 380th and final game. Arsenal needed to win by a margin of at least two goals to take the title—any other result and Liverpool were champions. Leading by only 1–0 as the referee prepared to signal the end of the game, Arsenal appeared doomed.

But in the final seconds, unmarked midfielder Michael Thomas burst past the heavy-footed Liverpool defense to fire home the winner and win Arsenal's first championship since 1971. For Liverpool, the defeat came six days after winning the F.A.Cup with a 3–2 victory over Everton in overtime.

On the World Cup front, things also looked good for England, which led its qualifying group and looked certain to nail down a berth in Italy in 1990. France—semifinalists in both the 1982 and the 1986 World Cups—looked certain to be eliminated, despite the appointment of their former star Michel Platini as coach. He first announced that he'd quit if France didn't qualify, then changed his mind and said he'd like to stay on. That choice is often not available: poor results meant dismissal for the coaches of East Germany and Kuwait, and led Hungary's Gyorgy Mezey to resign. El Salvador changed coaches three times in three games—and lost all of them.

FIFA, which controls the World Cup, sent inspectors to Italy and declared that it was confident that all the stadia would be ready on time for the Italia-90 opening game on June 8, 1990.

In the other senior tournament under its control, soccer in the Olympic Games, FIFA stuck to its position that the Olympics should be a competition for players aged 24 years and under. The International Olympic Committee had been urging that the competition be opened to all players, amateurs and professionals, regardless of age.

Much more troublesome was the question of age in FIFA's Under-20 and Under-17 championships. After the U-20 World Cup (won by Portugal), Iraq was slapped with a two-year ban from age-group competition for using an over-age player. In the U-17 World Cup it was the winners, Saudi Arabia, and Nigeria

which were under investigation by FIFA.

Finally, in a breaking-down of one of soccer's longest-lasting and most offensive barriers, staunchly Protestant Glasgow Rangers announced their first major signing of a Catholic player— forward Mo Johnston. Said coach Graeme Souness: "If we've upset some people, that's too bad. All we want is the best team in Europe."

1989 World Cup Qualifying

CONCACAF Zone

Third and final round in North America-Central America-Caribbean Basin Zone qualifier. Five teams competing for two berths in World Cup in Italy, June 8-July 8, 1990.

Results

Mar.19 at Guatemala 1 . . . . . . Costa Rica 0

Apr.2   at Costa Rica 2 . . . . . . .Guatemala 1
Apr.16 at Costa Rica 1 . . . . .USA 0
Apr.30 at USA 1 . . . . .Costa Rica 0

May 13 at USA 1 . . . . .Trinidad/Tobago 1
May 28 at Trinidad/Tobago 1 . . .Costa Rica 1

June 11 at Costa Rica 1 . . .Trinidad/Tobago 0
June 17 at USA 2 . . . . .Guatemala 1
June 25 Costa Rica 4 . . . . . . .at El Salvador 2

July 16 at Costa Rica 1 . . . . . .El Salvador 0
July 30 at Trinidad/Tobago 2 . .El Salvador 0

Aug.13 at El Salvador 0 . .Trinidad/Tobago 0
Aug.20 Trinidad/Tobago 1 . .at Guatemala 0

Sept.3 Trinidad/Tobago 2 . . . . .Guatemala 1
Sept.17 USA 1, El Salvador 0 .(at Honduras)

Remaining Games

Oct.8   USA at Guatemala

Nov.5   El Salvador at USA
Nov.19 USA at Trinidad/Tobago
        El Salvador at Guatemala
Nov.26 Guatemala at El Salvador

CONCACAF Standings
(as of Sept. 18)

Each team plays a home-and-home series with the other four for a total of eight games. The Top 2 teams qualify for the World Cup.

	GP	W	L	T	Pts	GF	GA
Costa Rica	8	5	2	1	11	10	6
Trinidad/Tobago . . .	7	3	1	3	9	7	4
United States . .	5	3	1	1	7	5	3
x-Guatemala	5	1	4	0	2	4	7
x-El Salvador	5	0	4	1	1	2	8

x-Eliminated from contention.

1989 International Champions

National Team Competition

World Wide

Cup	Winner
Coca-Cola Cup (FIFA Under-20)	Portugal
JVC Cup (FIFA Under-17)	Saudi Arabia
Five-a-Side (FIFA Indoor)	Brazil

Continental

Cup	Winner
Copa America........................	Brazil

Club Team Competition

World Wide

Cup
Toyota Cup: AC Milan vs Nacional Medellin
Dec.17, 1989 at Tokyo

Europe

International

Cup	Winner
European Cup	AC Milan (Italy)
Cup Winners Cup	Barcelona (Spain)
UEFA Cup	Napoli (Italy)

South America

International

Cup	Winner
Copa Libertadores ...	Nacional Medellin (Colombia)

National

Country	League Champion
Argentina	Independiente
Brazil...........................	Bahia
Chile	Cobreloa
Uruguay........................	Danubio

National

Country	League Champion	Cup Winner
England	Arsenal	Liverpool
France	Olympique Marseille	Olym.Marseille
Holland	PSV Eindhoven	PSV Eindhoven
Italy	Inter-Milan	Sampdoria
Portugal....	Benfica	Belenenses
Scotland ...	Glasgow Rangers	Glasgow Celtic
Soviet Union	Dnepr	Torpedo Moscow
Spain	Real Madrid	Real Madrid
W.Germany	Bayern Munich	Borussia Dortmund
Yugoslavia..	Vojvodina	Partizan

United States Champions

Major Indoor Soccer League

Final 1988-89 Standings

	W	L	Pct	GB	GF	GA
Baltimore	29	19	.604	—	215	208
San Diego	27	21	.562	2	218	168
Dallas.................	24	24	.500	5	185	206
Tacoma	23	25	.479	6	208	207
Wichita	23	25	.479	6	213	208
Los Angeles	21	27	.438	8	218	222
Kansas City	21	27	.438	8	194	233

Playoffs

Wild Card Series (Best-of-5)
Wichita over Tacoma (3-2)

Semifinals (Best-of-7)
Baltimore over Wichita (4-2)
San Diego over Dallas (4-3)

Finals (Best-of-7)
San Diego over Baltimore (4-3)

Other Champions

American Soccer League: Ft. Lauderdale
Western Soccer Leage: San Diego
ASL-WSL Playoff: Ft. Lauderdale

NCAA Div.I Tournament

1988 NCAA Div.I Men's Tournament
(Nov. 12 – Dec. 4)

First Round: FDU-Teaneck 1, Penn St. 0; Phila.Textile 1, Navy 0; North Carolina 2, Wake Forest 0; SMU 2, Notre Dame 0; Brooklyn 4, Adelphi 1; Boston Univ. 3, Connecticut 1; UCLA 2, San Diego St. 1; Fresno St. 2, UNLV 1 (2 OT, penalty kicks).

Second Round: Virginia 1, FDU-Teaneck 0; Howard 2, Phila.Textile 1; South Carolina 3, North Carolina 1; SMU 2, St.Louis 1 (2 OT); Seton Hall 5, Brooklyn 2; Indiana 3, Boston Univ. 1; Portland 2, UCLA 0; Fresno St. 2, Evansville 1 (2 OT, penalty kicks).

Quarterfinals: Howard 3, Virginia 2 (2 OT); South Carolina 1, SMU 0; Indiana 3, Seton Hall 1; Portland 2, Fresno St. 0.

Semifinals: Howard 2, South Carolina 0; Indiana 1, Portland 0.

Championship: Indiana 1, Howard 0.

The World Cup

The Federation Internationale de Football Association (FIFA) began the World Cup championship tournament in 1930 with a 13-team field in Uruguay. Sixty years later, the 1990 World Cup in Italy marks the eighth time the competition has been held in Europe. Countries in South and Central America have hosted the Cup six times and the United States has been selected by FIFA as the tournament site for the first time in 1994.

Brazil retired the first World Cup (called the Jules Rimet Trophy after FIFA's first president) in 1970 after winning it for the third time. Since 1974, the award has been known as simply the FIFA World Cup.

Year	Winner	Manager	Score	Loser	Host	Leading Goal Scorers
1930	**Uruguay**	Alberto Suppici	4-2	Argentina	Uruguay	8—Guillermo Stabile, Arg.
1934	**Italy**	Vittorio Pozzo	2-1*	Czechoslovakia	Italy	4—Angelo Schiavio, Italy
						Oldrich Nejedly, Czech
						Edmund Conen, Germany
1938	**Italy**	Vittorio Pozzo	4-2	Hungary	France	8—Leonidas, Brazil
1942	Not held					
1946	Not held					
1950	**Uruguay**	Juan Lopez	2-1	Brazil	Brazil	7—Ademir, Brazil
1954	**W.Germany**	Sepp Herberger	3-2	Hungary	Switzerland	11—Sandor Kocsis, Hungary
1958	**Brazil**	Vicente Feola	5-2	Sweden	Sweden	11—Just Fontaine, France
1962	**Brazil**	Aymore Moreira	3-1	Czechoslovakia	Chile	5—Drazan Jerkovic, Yugo.
1966	**England**	Alf Ramsey	4-2*	W.Germany	England	9—Eusebio, Portugal
1970	**Brazil**	Mario Zagalo	4-1	Italy	Mexico	10—Gerd Muller, W.Germany
1974	**W.Germany**	Helmut Schoen	2-1	Holland	W.Germany	7—Grzegorz Lato, Poland
1978	**Argentina**	Cesar Menotti	3-1*	Holland	Argentina	6—Mario Kempes, Arg.
1982	**Italy**	Enzo Bearzot	3-1	W.Germany	Spain	6—Paolo Rossi, Italy
1986	**Argentina**	Carlos Bilardo	3-2	W.Germany	Mexico	6—Gary Lineker, England

*After overtime.

The United States in World Cup Competition

While the United States has fielded a team every year of the World Cup, from 1930-86 only three national sides were able to make it past the preliminary competition and qualify for the final World Cup tournament.

The U.S. has won only three World Cup tournament matches—two opening round games in 1930 (which enabled the Americans to reach the semifinals) and a stunning first round, 1-0, upset of England in 1950. Center forward Joe Gaetjens scored the goal.

1930 (at Uruguay)

1st Round Matches
United States 3 . . . . Belgium 0
United States 3 . . . . Paraguay 0

Semifinals
Argentina 6 . . . . United States 1
US Goals: Bert Patenaude (3), Bart McGhee (2), James Brown, Ed Florie.

1934 (at Italy)

1st Round Match
Italy 7 . . . . United States 1
US Goal: Buff Donelli (who later became a noted college and NFL football coach).

1950 (at Brazil)

1st Round Matches
Spain 3 . . . . United States 1
United States 1 . . . . England 0
Chile 5 . . . . United States 2
US Goals: John Souza (2), Joe Gaetjens, Gino Pariani.

World Cup Final Fours

1930 (at Uruguay)

Semifinals
Argentina 6 . . . . United States 1
Uruguay 6 . . . . Yugoslavia 1

Third Place
No game

Final
Uruguay 4 . . . . Argentina 2
Goals: Uruguay—Pablo Dorado, Pedro Cea, Santos Iriarte, Hector Castro; Argentina—Carlos Peucelle, Guillermo Stabile.
Halftime: Argentina led, 2-1.

1934 (at Italy)

Semifinals
Czechoslovakia 3 . . . . Germany 1
Italy 1 . . . . Austria 0

Third Place
Germany 3 . . . . Austria 2

Final
(After extra time)
Italy 2 . . . . Czechoslovakia 1
Goals: Italy—Raimondo Orsi, Angelo Schiavio; Czech.—Antonin Puc.
Halftime: 0-0.
Regulation: 1-1.

World Cup (Continued)

1938 (at France)

Semifinals
Italy 2 . . . . Brazil 1
Hungary 5 . . . . Sweden 1

Third Place
Brazil 4 . . . . Sweden 2

Final
Italy 4 . . . . Hungary 2
Goals: Italy—Gino Colaussi (2), Silvio Piola (2);
Hungary—Pal Titkos, Georges Sarosi.
Halftime: Italy led, 3-1.

1950 (at Brazil)

A 4-team, final pool determined the champion in 1950.
While there were no official Third Place or Final matches, the last two games happened to work out that
way. Uruguay beat Brazil for the Cup.

Final Pool Matches
Uruguay 2 . . . . Spain 2
Brazil 7 . . . . Sweden 1
Uruguay 3 . . . . Sweden 2
Brazil 6 . . . . Spain 1
Sweden 3 . . . . Spain 1
Uruguay 2 . . . . Brazil 1
Goals: Uruguay—Juan Schiaffino, Alcide Ghiggia;
Brazil—Friaca.
Halftime: 0-0.

Final Standings
	W	L	T	Pts	GF	GA
Uruguay	2	0	1	**5**	7	5
Brazil	2	1	0	**4**	14	4
Sweden	1	2	0	**2**	6	11
Spain	0	2	1	**1**	4	11

1954 (at Switzerland)

Semifinals
West Germany 6 . . . . Austria 1
Hungary 4 . . . . Uruguay 2

Third Place
Austria 3 . . . . Uruguay 1

Final
West Germany 3 . . . . Hungary 2
Goals: W.Germany—Max Morlock, Helmut Rahn (2);
Hungary—Ferenc Puskas, Zoltan Czibor.
Halftime: 2-2.

1958 (at Sweden)

Semifinals
Brazil 5 . . . . France 2
Sweden 3 . . . . West Germany 1

Third Place
France 6 . . . . West Germany 3

Final
Brazil 5 . . . . Sweden 2
Goals: Brazil—Vava (2), Pele (2), Mario Zagalo;
Sweden—Nils Liedholm, Agne Simonsson.
Halftime: Brazil led, 2-1.

1962 (at Chile)

Semifinals
Brazil 4 . . . . Chile 2
Czechoslovakia 3 . . . . Yugoslavia 1

Third Place
Chile 1 . . . . Yugoslavia 0

Final
Brazil 3 . . . . Czechoslovakia 1
Goals: Brazil—Amarildo, Zito, Vava; Czech.—Josef
Masopust.
Halftime: 1-1.

1966 (at England)

Semifinals
West Germany 2 . . . . USSR 1
England 2 . . . . Portugal 1

Third Place
Portugal 2 . . . . USSR 1

Final
(After extra time)
England 4 . . . . West Germany 2
Goals: England—Geoff Hurst (3), Martin Peters;
W.Germany—Helmut Haller, Wolfgang Weber.
Halftime: 1-1.
Regulation: 2-2.

1970 (at Mexico)

Semifinals
Italy 4 . . . . West Germany 3
Brazil 3 . . . . Uruguay 1

Third Place
West Germany 1 . . . . Uruguay 0

Final
Brazil 4 . . . . Italy 1
Goals: Brazil—Pele, Gerson, Jairzinho, Carlos Alber-
to; Italy—Roberto Boninsegna.
Halftime: 1-1.

1974 (at W.Germany)

Two 4-team, semifinal pools determined the finalists in
1974. The two second place teams met in the consolation game.

Semifinal Pool Standings
Group A	W	L	T	Pts	GF	GA
Holland	3	0	0	**6**	8	0
Brazil	2	1	0	**4**	3	3
East Germany	0	2	1	**1**	1	4
Argentina	0	2	1	**1**	2	7

Group B	W	L	T	Pts	GF	GA
West Germany	3	0	0	**6**	7	2
Poland	2	1	0	**4**	3	2
Sweden	1	2	0	**2**	4	6
Yugoslavia	0	3	0	**0**	2	6

Third Place
Poland 1 . . . . Brazil 0

Final
West Germany 2 . . . . Holland 1
Goals: W.Germany—Paul Breitner (penalty), Gerd
Muller; Holland—Johan Neeskens (penalty).
Halftime: W.Germany led, 2-1.

1978 (at Argentina)

Two 4-team, semifinal pools determined the finalists again in 1978. The two second place teams met in the consolation game.

Semifinal Pool Standings

Group A	W	L	T	Pts	GF	GA
Holland	2	0	1	5	9	4
Italy	1	1	1	3	2	2
West Germany	0	1	2	2	4	5
Austria	1	2	0	2	4	8

Group B	W	L	T	Pts	GF	GA
Argentina	2	0	1	5	8	0
Brazil	2	0	1	5	6	1
Poland	1	2	0	2	2	5
Peru	0	3	0	0	0	10

Third Place

Brazil 2 . . . . Italy 1

Final
(After extra time)

Argentina 3 . . . . Holland 1
Goals: Argentina—Mario Kempes (2), Daniel Bertoni; Holland—Dirk Nanninga,
Halftime: Argentina led, 1-0.
Regulation: 1-1.

Most Valuable Player

The Golden Ball Award has been presented to the Most Valuable Player in last two World Cups: Paolo Rossi of Italy in 1982, and Diego Maradona of Argentina in 1986.

All-Time Leading Scorers

The All-Time leading goal scorers in World Cup play.

No. Player
14— Gerd Muller, West Germany (1970,74)
13— Just Fontaine, France (1958)
12— Pele, Brazil (1958,70)
11— Sandor Kocsis, Hungary (1954)
10— Helmut Rahn, West Germany (1954,58)

1982 (at Spain)

Semifinals

Italy 2 . . . . Poland 0
West Germany 3* . . . . France 3
*After extra time, W.Germany won on penalty kicks, 5 to 4.

Third Place

Poland 3 . . . . France 2

Final

Italy 3 . . . . West Germany 1
Goals: Italy—Paolo Rossi, Marco Tardelli, Alessandro Altobelli; W.Germany—Paul Breitner.
Halftime: 0-0.

1986 (at Mexico)

Semifinals

Argentina 2 . . . . Belgium 0
West Germany 2 . . . . France 0

Third Place
(After extra time)

France 4 . . . . Belgium 2

Final

Argentina 3 . . . . West Germany 2
Goals: Argentina—Jose Brown, Jorge Valdano, Jorge Burruchaga; W.Germany—Karl-Heinz Rummenigge, Rudolf Voeller.
Halftime: Argentina led, 1-0.

World Cup Appearances

The number of teams eligible for the final round has grown from 13 (1930) to 16 (1934-78) to 24 (since 1982). Seven countries have sent teams to the World Cup at least nine times.

Country	App	Cups
Brazil	13	3 (1958,62,70)
Italy	11	3 (1934,38,82)
West Germany	11	2 (1954,74)
Argentina	9	2 (1978,86)
France	9	0
Hungary	9	0
Mexico	9	0

Other Worldwide Tournaments

Under-20 Championship

Held every two years since 1977. Officially called The World Youth Championship for the FIFA/Coca-Cola Cup.

Year	Winner
1977	USSR
1979	Argentina
1981	West Germany
1983	Brazil
1985	Brazil
1987	Yugoslavia
1989	Portugal

Under-17 Championship

Held every two years since 1985. Officially called The FIFA U-17 World Tournament for the JVC Cup.

Year	Winner
1985	Nigeria
1987	USSR
1989	Saudi Arabia

Five-A-Side Championship

Inaugurated in 1989. FIFA's only indoor tournament.

Year	Winner
1989	Brazil

Continental Competition

European Championship

Held every four years since 1960. Officially called the European Football Championship.

Year	Winner	Year	Winner	Year	Winner	Year	Winner
1960	USSR	1968	Italy	1976	Czechoslovakia	1984	France
1964	Spain	1972	West Germany	1980	West Germany	1988	Holland

Copa America (South American Champion)

Held irregularly since 1916. Officially called the Copa America.

Year	Winner	Year	Winner	Year	Winner	Year	Winner
1916	Uruguay	1925	Argentina	1942	Uruguay	1958	Argentina
1917	Uruguay	1926	Uruguay	1945	Argentina	1959	Uruguay
1919	Brazil	1927	Argentina	1946	Argentina	1963	Bolivia
1920	Uruguay	1929	Argentina	1947	Argentina	1967	Uruguay
1921	Argentina	1935	Uruguay	1949	Brazil	1975	Peru
1922	Brazil	1937	Argentina	1953	Paraguay	1979	Paraguay
1923	Uruguay	1939	Peru	1955	Argentina	1983	Uruguay
1924	Uruguay	1941	Argentina	1956	Uruguay	1987	Uruguay
				1957	Argentina	1989	Brazil

Club Competition

Toyota Cup

Contested annually between the winners of the previous year's European Cup and Libertadores Cup.
Originally the **Intercontinental Cup** (1960-79). Best-of-three game format until 1968, then two-game/total-goal format was used. Toyota became sponsor in 1980, changed the format to one-game championship and moved it to Tokyo.

Year	Winner	Year	Winner	Year	Winner
1960	Real Madrid (Spain)	1970	Feyenoord (Holland)	1980	Nacional (Uruguay)
1961	Penarol (Uruguay)	1971	Nacional (Uruguay)	1981	Flamengo (Brazil)
1962	Santos (Brazil)	1972	Ajax-Amsterdam (Holland)	1982	Penarol (Uruguay)
1963	Santos (Brazil)	1973	Independiente (Argentina)	1983	Gremio (Brazil)
1964	Inter-Milan (Italy)	1974	Atletico Madrid (Spain)	1984	Independiente (Argentina)
1965	Inter-Milan (Italy)	1975	Not held	1985	Juventus (Italy)
1966	Penarol (Uruguay)	1976	Bayern Munich (W.Germany)	1986	River Plate (Argentina)
1967	Racing Club (Argentina)	1977	Boca Juniors (Argentina)	1987	FC Porto (Portugal)
1968	Estudiantes (Argentina)	1978	Not held	1988	Nacional (Uruguay)
1969	AC Milan (Italy)	1979	Olimpia (Paraguay)		

European Cup

Contested annually since the 1955-56 season by the league champions of the member countries of the Union of European Football Associations (UEFA).

Year	Winner	Year	Winner	Year	Winner
1956	Real Madrid (Spain)	1968	Manchester United (England)	1980	Nottingham Forest (England)
1957	Real Madrid (Spain)	1969	AC Milan (Italy)	1981	Liverpool (England)
1958	Real Madrid (Spain)			1982	Aston Villa (England)
1959	Real Madrid (Spain)	1970	Feyenoord (Holland)	1983	SV Hamburg (W.Germany)
		1971	Ajax-Amsterdam (Holland)*	1984	Liverpool (England)
1960	Real Madrid (Spain)	1972	Ajax-Amsterdam (Holland)	1985	Juventus (Italy)
1961	Benfica (Portugal)	1973	Ajax-Amsterdam (Holland)*	1986	Steaua Bucharest (Romania)
1962	Benfica (Portugal)	1974	Bayern-Munich (W.Germany)*	1987	FC Porto (Portugal)
1963	AC Milan (Italy)	1975	Bayern-Munich (W.Germany)	1988	PSV Eindhoven (Holland)
1964	Inter-Milan (Italy)	1976	Bayern-Munich (W.Germany)	1989	AC Milan (Italy)
1965	Inter-Milan (Italy)	1977	Liverpool (England)		
1966	Real Madrid (Spain)	1978	Liverpool (England)		
1967	Glasgow Celtic (Scotland)	1979	Nottingham Forest (England)*		

*Four times the European Cup winner has refused to participate in the Intercontinental Cup (now Toyota Cup) against South America's Libertadores Cup winner. In each case, the European Cup runner-up went instead: Panathinaikos (Greece) in 1971, Juventus (Italy) in 1973, Atletico Madrid (Spain) in 1974, and Malmo (Sweden) in 1979.

European Cup Winners' Cup

Contested annually since the 1960-61 season by the cup winners of the members countries of the Union of European Football Associations (UEFA).

Year	Winner	Year	Winner	Year	Winner
1961	Fiorentina (Italy)	1970	Manchester City (England)	1980	Valencia (Spain)
1962	Atletico Madrid (Spain)	1971	Chelsea (England)	1981	Dynamo Tbilisi (USSR)
1963	Tottenham Hotspur (England)	1972	Glasgow Rangers (Scotland)	1982	Barcelona (Spain)
1964	Sporting Lisbon (Portugal)	1973	AC Milan (Italy)	1983	Aberdeen (Scotland)
1965	West Ham United (England)	1974	FC Magdeburg (E.Germany)	1984	Juventus (Italy)
1966	Borussia Dortmund (W.Ger.)	1975	Dynamo Kiev (USSR)	1985	Everton (England)
1967	Bayern Munich (W.Germany)	1976	Anderlecht (Belgium)	1986	Dynamo Kiev (USSR)
1968	AC Milan (Italy)	1977	SV Hamburg (W.Germany)	1987	Ajax-Amsterdam (Holland)
1969	Slovan Bratislava (Czech.)	1978	Anderlecht (Belgium)	1988	Mechelen (Belgium)
		1979	Barcelona (Spain)	1989	Barcelona (Spain)

UEFA Cup

Contested annually since the 1957-58 season by teams other than league champions and cup winners and selected by UEFA based on each country's previous performance in the tournament. Teams from England have been banned indefinitely from UEFA Cup play since 1985-86 for the criminal behavior of their supporters.

Year	Winner	Year	Winner	Year	Winner
1958	Barcelona (Spain)	1970	Arsenal (England)	1980	Eintracht Frankfurt
1959	Not held	1971	Leeds United (England)		(West Germany)
		1972	Tottenham Hotspur (England)	1981	Ipswich Town (England)
1960	Barcelona (Spain)	1973	Liverpool (England)	1982	IFK Gothenburg (Sweden)
1961	AS Roma (Italy)	1974	Feyenoord (Holland)	1983	Anderlecht (Belgium)
1962	Valencia (Spain)	1975	Borussia	1984	Tottenham Hotspur (England)
1963	Valencia (Spain)		Moenchengladbach (W.Ger.)	1985	Real Madrid (Spain)
1964	Real Zaragoza (Spain)	1976	Liverpool (England)	1986	Real Madrid (Spain)
1965	Ferencvaros (Hungary)	1977	Juventus (Italy)	1987	IFK Gothenburg (Sweden)
1966	Barcelona (Spain)	1978	PSV Eindhoven (Holland)	1988	Bayer Leverkusen
1967	Dynamo Zagreb (Yugoslavia)	1979	Borussia		(West Germany)
1968	Leeds United (England)		Moenchengladbach (W.Ger.)	1989	Napoli (Italy)
1969	Newcastle United (England)				

Copa Libertadores

Contested annually since the 1955-56 season by the league champions of South America's football union.

Year	Winner	Year	Winner	Year	Winner
1960	Penarol (Uruguay)	1970	Estudiantes (Argentina)	1980	Nacional (Uruguay)
1961	Penarol (Uruguay)	1971	Nacional (Uruguay)	1981	Flamengo (Brazil)
1962	Santos (Brazil)	1972	Independiente (Argentina)	1982	Penarol (Uruguay)
1963	Santos (Brazil)	1973	Independiente (Argentina)	1983	Gremio (Brazil)
1964	Independiente (Argentina)	1974	Independiente (Argentina)	1984	Independiente (Argentina)
1965	Independiente (Argentina)	1975	Independiente (Argentina)	1985	Argentinos Juniors (Argentina)
1966	Penarol (Uruguay)	1976	Cruzeiro (Brazil)	1986	River Plate (Argentina)
1967	Racing Club (Argentina)	1977	Boca Juniors (Argentina)	1987	Penarol (Uruguay)
1968	Estudiantes (Argentina)	1978	Boca Juniors (Argentina)	1988	Nacional (Uruguay)
1969	Estudiantes (Argentina)	1979	Olimpia (Paraguay)	1989	Nacional Medellin (Colombia)

Player of the Year Awards

Europe

Year	Player, Club	Nat'l Team	Year	Player, Club	Nat'l Team
1956	Stanley Matthews, Blackpool	England	1973	Johan Cruyff, Barcelona	Holland
1957	Alredo di Stefano, Real Madrid	Arg./Spain	1974	Johan Cruyff, Barcelona	Holland
1958	Raymond Kopa, Real Madrid	France	1975	Oleg Blokhin, Dynamo Kiev	Soviet Union
1959	Alfredo di Stefano, Real Madrid	Arg./Spain	1976	Franz Beckenbauer, Bayern Munich	W.Ger.
1960	Luis Suarez, Barcelona	Spain	1977	Allan Simonsen, B.M'chengladbach	Denmark
1961	Enrique Sivori, Juventus	Arg./Italy	1978	Kevin Keegan, SV Hamburg	England
1962	Josef Masopust, Dukla Praque	Czech.	1979	Kevin Keegan, SV Hamburg	England
1963	Lev Yachin, Dynamo Moscow	USSR			
1964	Denis Law, Manchester United	Scotland	1980	Karl-Heinz Rummenigge, B.Munich	W.Ger.
1965	Eusebio, Benfica	Portugal	1981	Karl-Heinz Rummenigge, B.Munich	W.Ger.
1966	Bobby Charlton, Manchester United	England	1982	Paolo Rossi, Juventus	Italy
1967	Florian Albert, Ferencvaros	Hungary	1983	Michel Platini, Juventus	France
1968	George Best, Manchester United	N.Ireland	1984	Michel Platini, Juventus	France
1969	Gianni Rivera, AC Milan	Italy	1985	Michel Platini, Juventus	France
			1986	Igor Belanov, Dynamo Kiev	Soviet Union
1970	Gerd Muller, Bayern Munich	W.Ger.	1987	Ruud Gullit, AC Milan	Holland
1971	Johan Cruyff, Ajax	Holland	1988	Marco Van Basten, AC Milan	Holland
1972	Franz Beckenbauer, Bayern Munich	W.Ger.			

South America

Year	Player, Club	Nat'l Team	Year	Player, Club	Nat'l Team
1971	Tostao, Cruzeiro	Brazil	1980	Diego Maradona, Boca Juniors	Argentina
1972	Teofilo Cubillas, Alianza Lima	Peru	1981	Zico, Flamengo	Brazil
1973	Pele, Santos	Brazil	1982	Zico, Flamengo	Brazil
1974	Elias Figueroa, Internacional	Chile	1983	Socrates, Corinthians	Brazil
1975	Elias Figueroa, Internacional	Chile	1984	Enzo Francescoli, River Plate	Uruguay
1976	Elias Figueroa, Internacional	Chile	1985	Julio Cesar Romero, Fluminense	Paraguay
1977	Zico, Flamengo	Brazil	1986	Antonio Alzamendi, River Plate	Uruguay
1978	Mario Kempes, Valencia	Argentina	1987	Carlos Valderrama, Deportivo Cali	Colombia
1979	Diego Maradona, Argentinos Jrs	Argentina	1988	Ruben Paz, Racing Buenos Aires	Uruguay

Soccer in the United States

MISL, 1979-89

Formed for the 1978-79 season, the Major Indoor Soccer League withstood a challenge by a NASL indoor league (1980-83) and remains the only major league soccer circuit in the country.

Year	Winner	Series	Loser	Year	Winner	Series	Loser
1979	New York Arrows	2-0	Philadelpia	1984	Baltimore Blast	4-1	St. Louis
				1985	San Diego Sockers	4-1	Baltimore
1980	New York Arrows	7-4*	Houston	1986	San Diego Sockers	4-3	Minnesota
1981	New York Arrows	6-5*	St. Louis	1987	Dallas Sidekicks	4-3	Tacoma
1982	New York Arrows	3-2	St. Louis	1988	San Diego Sockers	4-0	Cleveland
1983	San Diego Sockers	3-2	Baltimore	1989	San Diego Sockers	4-3	Baltimore

*MISL title was decided by a championship game in 1980 and '81.
Playoff MVPs: 1979—Shep Messing, NY; **1980**—Steve Zungul, NY; **1981**—Zungul, NY; **1982**—Zungul, NY; **1983**—Juli Veee, SD; **1984**—Scott Manning, Balt.; **1985**—Zungul, SD; **1986**—Brian Quinn, SD; **1987**—Tatu, Dallas; **1988**—Hugo Perez, SD; **1989**—Victor Nagueira, SD.

NASL, 1967-84

After competing as rival leagues in 1967, the National Professional Soccer League (NPSL) and United Soccer Association (USA) merged in 1968 to become the North American Soccer League. The NASL folded after the 1984 season. From 1975-84, the league's championship game was called the Soccer Bowl.

Year	Champion	Most Valuable Player	Year	Champion	Most Valuable Player
1967	Oak. Clippers (NPSL)	Robt. Boninsegna, Chi.	1976	Toronto Metros	Pele, New York
1968	LA Wolves (USA)	Ruben Navarro, Phila.	1977	New York Cosmos	Franz Beckenbauer, NY
			1978	New York Cosmos	Mike Flanagan, N.Eng.
1970	Rochester Lancers	Carlos Metidieri, Roch.	1979	Vanc. Whitecaps	Johan Cruyff, Los Ang.
1971	Dallas Tornado	Carlos Metidieri, Roch.			
1972	New York Cosmos	Randy Horton, N.Y.	1980	New York Cosmos	Roger Davis, Seattle
1973	Philadelphia Atoms	Warren Archibald, Miami	1981	Chicago Sting	Giorgio Chinaglia, NY
1974	Los Angeles Aztecs	Peter Silvester, Balt.	1982	New York Cosmos	Peter Ward, Seattle
1975	Tampa Bay Rowdies	Steven David, Miami	1983	Tulsa Roughnecks	Roberto Cabanas, NY
			1984	Chicago Sting	Steve Zungul, San Jose

College Soccer

NCAA Division I Champions

1959 St. Louis	1970 St. Louis	1980 San Francisco
	1971 Howard†	1981 Connecticut
1960 St. Louis	1972 St. Louis	1982 Indiana
1961 West Chester, PA	1973 St. Louis	1983 Indiana
1962 St. Louis	1974 Howard	1984 Clemson
1963 St. Louis	1975 San Francisco	1985 UCLA
1964 Navy	1976 San Francisco	1986 Duke
1965 St. Louis	1977 Hartwick	1987 Clemson
1966 San Francisco	1978 San Francisco †	1988 Indiana
1967 Mich. St. & St. Louis*	1979 SIU-Edwardsville	
1968 Mich. St. & Maryland**		
1969 St. Louis		

*Shared title after championship game called due to inclement weather.
**Shared title after 2-2, double overtime tie.
†Title vacated.

Hermann Award

Named after Robert Hermann of St.Louis, one of the founders of the North American Soccer League. First presented to the U.S. College Player of the Year in 1967. Voting done by Division I college coaches and selected sportswriters.

Year	Player, school	Year	Player, school
1967	Dov Markus, Long Island	1978	Angelo DiBernardo, Indiana
1968	Manuel Hernandez, S.Jose St.	1979	Jim Stamatis, Penn St.
1969	Al Trost, St.Louis		
		1980	Joe Morrone, Jr., Conn.
1970	Al Trost, St.Louis	1981	Armando Betancourt, Indiana
1971	Mike Seerey, St.Louis	1982	Joe Ulrich, Duke
1972	Mike Seerey, St.Louis	1983	Mike Jeffries, Duke
1973	Dan Counce, St.Louis	1984	Amr Aly, Columbia
1974	Farrukh Quraishi, Oneonta	1985	Tom Kain, Duke
1975	Steve Ralbovsky, Brown	1986	John Kerr, Duke
1976	Glenn Myernick, Hartwick	1987	Bruce Murray, Clemson
1977	Billy Gazonas, Hartwick	1988	Ken Snow, Indiana

Tour de France winner **Greg LeMond** (center) of the United States with runner-up **Laurent Fignon** (left) of France and third place finisher **Pedro Delgado** of Spain.

INTER-NATIONAL SPORTS

INSIDE

Elsewhere in Almanac

For related information refer to the following chapters: Halls of Fame & Awards, Business & Media, and Updates.

*LeMond wins 2nd Tour de France,
Sotomayor 1st to clear 8 feet,
but as several world records fall
drug revelations abound.*

INTERNATIONAL SPORTS

1988-89 YEAR IN REVIEW

by Phil Hersh

It was April 20, 1987. Greg LeMond lay waiting for help on an isolated farm near Sacramento, Calif., with 46 shotgun pellets in his body and blood pouring from some of the holes they had opened. The year before, LeMond had become the first American cyclist to win the Tour de France. Now, shot accidentally by his brother-in-law on a turkey hunt, he felt as if he were waiting to die.

It was July 23, 1989. Greg LeMond was waiting on a starting ramp at Versailles, France, with 15.4 miles of road between him and the finish of the 76th Tour de France. He was 50 seconds behind leader Laurent Fignon, a difference cycling experts said was unlikely to be erased in so short a time trial. LeMond had led the race for seven of its previous 20 stages, but his hopes of winning were literally all but dead.

Greg LeMond would cheat death in

1987 and the clock in 1989. His dramatic recovery from the hunting injury, which left 30-odd pellets still in his body, and his melodramatic triumph in the Tour de France, which he won by 8 seconds after 87 hours of riding, made one of the most compelling stories of this or any other year in sports.

There is no comparing life-and-death, the real thing, with do-or-die in sports. Let it be said then that LeMond at age 28 is simply a versatile sort of Lazarus, able to rise to whatever occasion presents itself.

Soaring above obstacles was the theme of the two most significant achievements in the world of international sports in 1989. They were, coincidentally, separated by less than a week.

The second involved Cuban high jumper Javier Sotomayor who is just 21 years old. On July 29 in San Juan, Puerto Rico, Sotomayor became the first person to jump 8 feet—officially, 2.44 meters, or 96.06299 inches. Call it a whisper over 8 feet, a statistical barrier that once screamed of impossibility.

Phil Hersh has been the **Chicago Tribune's** full-time Olympics reporter since 1986. He covered his first Olympic Games at Lake Placid in 1980 for the **Chicago Sun-Times.**

Wide World Photos

Canadian sprinter **Ben Johnson** admitted in June that he used steroids, then was stripped of his 100-meter world record in September.

It had been 33 years since a 19-year-old American, Charley Dumas, became the first to jump 7 feet. The record had crept up, ever so slowly, until Sotomayor moved it the final 3/4 inch in two increments—1/4 inch in 1988 in Spain, 1/2 inch on the final day of the Caribbean Zone Track and Field Championships in Puerto Rico.

Like LeMond, the 6-foot, 3-inch Sotomayor was an athlete trying to make up for lost time. His country's second straight Olympic boycott had deprived him of a chance to win the gold medal in Seoul.

Both LeMond and Sotomayor provided a singular response to long-held beliefs about the limits of man's willpower and physical ability. They provided a pleasant counterpoint to a year in which it was revealed all too clearly that surpassing such limits—and the opposition—is often a matter of chemical warfare.

A Canadian government inquiry, spurred by sprinter Ben Johnson's drug bust after winning the 1988 Olympic 100 meters, led to insider revelations about the most sordid side of international sports. The inquiry, which resulted in months of national self-flagellation by unnecessarily shamed Canadians, made headlines week after week, capped by Johnson's admission that steroids were an integral part of his training program.

After having the Olympic medal and world record of 9.79 seconds stripped

from him in Seoul, Johnson had denied ever using steroids. He stood silently by that statement even after his coach, Charlie Francis, testified to the contrary March 1 in Toronto, prompting the Toronto Star to headline, "BEN LIED!"

In 29 hours of testimony over eight days, Francis shook the foundations of the Olympic movement with his detailed evidence of illegal drug use by Johnson and 12 other athletes he had coached. He also implicated dozens of others, including U.S. sprinter Florence Griffith Joyner, by inference.

When Johnson took the stand June 12, before an audience including 200 reporters from Canada, the U.S. and Europe, he came clean, although he tried to shift the blame for his drug use to Francis. The next day, the 27-year-old Johnson accepted full responsibility for his steroid use, apologized to the Canadian people and advised young athletes not to cheat.

"If I get a chance to compete again, I want to say that drugs don't make you run faster and that Ben Johnson can beat anybody in the world," said Johnson, suspended until Sept. 24, 1990 by the International Track Federation but given a lifetime ban by Canadian sports officials.

The International Amateur Athletic Federation, meeting in Barcelona on Sept. 5, stripped Johnson of the 100-meter world record (9.83) he set at the 1987 World Championships in Rome. He also lost his 60-meter indoor mark (6.41) as the IAAF voted to nullify all world records by athletes who have admitted using banned drugs. Johnson confessed to steroid use as far back as 1981, but had passed all post-race drug tests until last year.

The Canadian inquiry provided only some of 1989s startling revelations about drug use.

Both the international and U.S. track governing bodies hastened their attempts to implement random, unannounced drug testing. Other international sports federations with doping problems, notably weightlifting, were on the same course. The International Ski Federation even tested for blood doping at its 1989 Nordic World Championships.

Two French women, heptathlete Chantal Beaugeant and skier Christelle

Guignard, were among the most prominent athletes caught for drug use in 1989. Beaugeant, 4th ranked in the world last year, tested positive for a steroid and was suspended two years. Guignard, bronze medalist in the giant slalom at the World Championships, got a one-year suspension after testing positive for a stimulant.

At a U.S. Senate hearing, sprinter Diane Williams of Los Angeles tearfully recounted how performance-enhancing drugs had taken over her life and body from 1981 to 1984. The result was not only fast times but also acne, psoriasis, enlargement of the clitoris, irregular or no menstrual periods, a deeper voice and aggressive behavior.

Two East German defectors, both formerly prominent in their country's sports program, told the West German newspaper **Bild** of rampant drug use on the other side of the wall. "All East German Stars Doped; Even Katarina Witt," **Bild** proclaimed, with the stories adding that it went undetected because East Germany devised ways to beat the tests. Witt,

the two-time Olympic champion in figure skating, was said to have taken steroids. East German officials and Witt's old coach predictably dismissed the allegations as ridiculous.

When Griffith Joyner, 29, announced her competitive retirement in late February, less than eight months after redefining all conceptions of fast women, it only increased speculation that she, too, had been using performance enhancers and wanted out before getting caught. The fact that Griffith Joyner had passed dozens of drug tests no longer seemed of consequence after testimony in Canada about how easy it was to beat the rap.

"You can't stop a person from thinking what they want," said Griffith Joyner, who won three Olympic gold medals and obliterated the old world records in Seoul, in the 100 and 200 meters and won the Sullivan Award as America's foremost amateur athlete of 1988. "You can't stop rumors and you can't stop jealousies."

Ironically, the Tour de France had been

Wide World Photos

Florence Griffith Joyner, the world's fastest woman, announced her retirement from competitive track and field Feb. 26. With her in New York was husband and coach **Al Joyner.**

living under a drug cloud since it was revealed that 1988 winner Pedro Delgado of Spain had tested positive for probenecid, a drug often used to mask the presence of performance-enhancing drugs. Probenecid was not banned by the International Professional Cycling Federation (FICP) until after the 1988 Tour.

And Greg LeMond, according to his attorney, had left his 1988 team, PDM of Holland, when it was suggested that a banned drug, testosterone, might speed his comeback.

It must have been tempting for Le-Mond, 28, to consider such a shortcut, so long did it take him to regain the form that won the 1986 Tour de France. The next two years were complicated by the near fatal shooting, a broken wrist, appendicitis, and an infected leg tendon that required surgery.

In 1987 and 1988, he would often lag so embarrassingly in races that teammates had to push him, and opponents laughed at him. After a late May mountain stage of the 1989 Tour of Italy, Le-Mond was so far behind he said, "I am in a tunnel, and I surely won't see the light until the end of the year." He couldn't count on much pathfinding from domestiques (helpers) on his relatively weak new team, ADR of Belgium, and he finished 39th in Italy.

So LeMond's aspirations for the 1989 Tour de France were modest: a finish in the top 20. That changed during the fifth stage, a 46-mile time trial, when LeMond suddenly emerged with the leader's yellow jersey for the first time since the end of his 1986 triumph. LeMond was then shooting for at least the top three.

He would trade that yellow jersey with Fignon twice in the next 12 stages, most of them raced across the Pyrenees and Alps. The Frenchman appeared to have regained it for good when he came out of the Alps with a 50-second lead. Only LeMond believed he could wipe that out in the downhill run from Versailles to the Champs Elysees.

LeMond beat Fignon by 58 seconds over the 15.4 miles of the final stage, by 8 seconds over the 2,023 miles of the race. It was the closest tour ever by 30 seconds. In the bicentennial of the French Revolution, this was the day that would shake the cycling world for years.

"UNFORGETTABLE!" bannered the French newspaper L'Equipe, the race's sponsor, in its account of the triumph "THE AMERICAN MIRACLE," it said a day later.

Neither was an exaggeration.

LeMond made more headlines on Aug. 27, when he won the pro men's road race at the World Cycling Championships in Chamberg, France. Despite hitting a fence with two laps to go, he came from behind to win the 162.5-mile race in the last 250 yards. LeMond became only the fifth rider to take both the Tour de France and the World Championship in the same year, joining Louison Bobet and Bernard Hinault of France, Eddy Merckx of Belgium and Stephen Roche of Ireland.

Other highlights from the year in international sports:

Winter Sports

Figure Skating: Katarina Witt's two Olympic titles became the golden brick road to financial wizardry previously unavailable for East German athletes, generally never seen again once their Olympic careers are over. Witt was given virtual freedom of travel and allowed to sign a multiyear contract (estimates of its value ran to $378 million) with the European tour of Holiday on Ice. Her take is said to be 20 percent, with the rest going to the state.

Witt was one of three Olympic gold medal skaters to move out of the amateur ranks. That is the usual progression, which makes the year after the Olympics transitional, with the pecking order for the next Games generally established in the middle year's World Championships.

At the 1989 Worlds in Paris, the competitors included just one of the 1988 Olympic gold medalists, Soviet pair Ekaterina Gordeeva and Sergei Grinkov, who won their fifth world title in six years.

Midori Ito, the Japanese skater who was a dazzling non-medalist in the Olympics, triple jumped her way to a world title over favored American Jill Trenary, who faltered badly in the long program and took the bronze, with Claudia Leistner of West Germany second. Canada's Kurt Browning, the first ever to land a clean quadruple jump the year

American speed skater **Bonnie Blair** (center) defeated East Germany's **Angela Hauck** and **Christa Luding** in February to win the World Sprint Championships in Holland.

before, hit another to beat U.S. champion Chris Bowman.

Kristi Yamaguchi was the story at February's U.S. nationals in Baltimore. The tiny 17-year-old Californian was a surprising second to Trenary in singles and teamed with Rudi Galindo to win the pairs, becoming the first senior woman to win more than one medal at nationals since 1953.

Speed Skating: Olympic gold medalist Bonnie Blair of Champaign, Ill., ended the nine-year reign of East German women over the world sprint title when she upset two-time world sprint winner Christa Luding in Heerenveen, Holland. "In the speedskating world, the sprint title is better (than an Olympic medal) because it isn't a one-shot deal," Blair said, referring to the meet's format of having the winner decided by a four-race total. Igor Zhelezovski of the Soviet Union took the men's title.

Eric Flaim of Pembroke, Mass., defending titlist in the World All-Around Championships, was a badly beaten fourth in 1989. Leo Visser of Holland took the title, while Constanze Moser of East Germany won the women's event.

Hockey: Despite continuing friction—nearly open rebellion—between star players and coach Viktor Tikhonov, the Soviet Union won its 21st world title since 1954 in Stockholm, beating silver medalist Canada 5-3 and defending champion Sweden 5-1 in the medal round. Czechoslovakia was third, and the U.S., sixth.

After the World Championships, four longtime Soviet mainstays, including two-thirds of the vaunted KLM line (Sergei

Switzerland's **Vreni Schneider** claimed a record 14 victories on the women's World Cup circuit as the Swiss again dominated in alpine skiing.

Makarov, 31, and Igor Larianov, 29) and defenseman Viacheslav Fetisov, 31, were allowed to sign with National Hockey League teams. A future star, 20-year-old right wing Alexander Mogilny, defected after the World Championships and was signed by the Buffalo Sabres.

Alpine Skiing: Led by Vreni Schneider's record-breaking 14 tour victories, Swiss skiers dominated the World Cup circuit for the seventh straight year. Schneider's record—7 for 7 in slaloms, 6 for 7 in giant slaloms, 1 for 1 in combined—was one more win than Ingemar Stenmark of Sweden had in 1979. Stenmark, 32, whose 86 World Cup wins are more than double the total of his closest pursuer, retired after 16 seasons in the "White Circus."

Marc Girardelli, an Austrian who lives in Switzerland and skis for Luxembourg, won his third overall title in five years and became the first skier to win in all five World Cup disciplines. Alberto Tomba, last year's playboy Olympic slalom and giant slalom champion, was out of shape and won only one race.

In the biennial World Championships at Vail, Colo., star-crossed Tamara McKinney of Lexington, Ky., filled in a noteworthy gap in her brilliant career by winning the combined over Schneider. It was the first Olympic or World Championship gold medal for McKinney, the best woman skier in U.S. history. She later added a bronze in slalom.

Nordic Skiing: The Finns dominated the World Championships on their home course in Lahti, winning twice as many gold medals (6) as runnerup Sweden and nearly doubling the total medal count (15 to 8) of the next countries, Norway and the Soviet Union. Marjo Matikainen of Finland, who retired after the season, won five medals, including two gold.

The British Ski Federation banned ski jumper Eddie "The Eagle" Edwards from competing in the World Championships. British officials said Edwards, clown prince of the 1988 Olympics where he was last in both events, "was jumping worse than ever." Edwards broke his collarbone in training Jan. 3, but the myopic ex-plasterer has still made a small commercial fortune from his ineptness.

Summer Sports

Archery: Denise Parker, 15, of South Jordan, Utah, the youngest U.S. Olympian in 1988 and youngest Pan Am Games gold medalist in 1987, won the bronze medal at the 1989 World Championships in Lausanne, Switzerland, with South Koreans taking 1-2-4, led by Olympic champion Kim Soo-Nyung. Parker was the first U.S. woman medalist at the worlds since LuAnn Ryon in 1977.

In the men's competition, Stanislav Zabrodsky of the Soviet Union not only won his first world title but his winning score of 1,342 points was one more than the 10-year-old total round world record set by Darrell Pace of the U.S.

Basketball: At a specially called congress April 6 in Munich, the International Amateur Basketball Federation (FIBA) opened the Olympics and World Championships to all professional players, including those from the National Basketball Association. The vote was 56-13, with the U.S. voting no.

The first event in which NBA players might participate is the 1990 Goodwill Games July 20-Aug. 5 in Seattle. Some may also play in the World Championships scheduled for Argentina just after the Goodwill Games.

Yugoslavia, led by Portland Trail Blazer draftee Drazen Petrovic, beat defending champion Greece 98-77 for the 1989 European Basketball Championship in Zagreb.

In Varna, Bulgaria, the Soviet women beat Czechoslovakia 64-61 for their 15th straight title in the biennial European Championships.

Boxing: Reacting to the chaos and scandal in the 1988 Olympic boxing tournament, the International Boxing Federation gave two-year suspensions to 23 officials and South Korean boxer Jon-Il Byun, whose ring sit-in after a defeat precipitated a minor riot. Also included were the officials who stole the superwelter title from American Roy Jones.

Cycling: Greg Lemond's dramatic victories in the Tour de France and World Cycling Championships (see above) should made him a serious Athlete of the Year candidate in 1989. Overshadowed by LeMond's heroics was the sport's **other** Tour de France and World Champion: Jeannie Longo of France, who actually outdid LeMond by winning three world titles—the road race, individual pursuit and 30-kilometer points race.

Elsewhere, Dag Otto Lauritzen of Norway won the inaugural Tour de Trump, sponsored by New York City megamogul Donald Trump; and Laurent Fignon of France won the Tour of Italy, with defending champ Any Hampton of the U.S. placing third.

Diving: Chinese divers, led by double Olympic champion Gao Min, took four of the six titles at the year's biggest meet, May's FINA World Cup in Indianapolis. Gao Min won both springboard events, while Wendy Williams of the U.S. took the platform. On the men's side, Tan Liangde and Xiong Ni of China won the 3-meter and platform, respectively, while Matt Lenzi was a surprise 1-meter champion.

At July's U.S. Olympic Festival in Oklahoma City, Lenzi became the first diver to perform a 4½ somersault from the 3-meter board, although his scores were only in the 3's.

Fencing: For the second straight time, West Germany dominated the World Championships, winning nine of a possible 20 medals in Denver. The Soviet Union was top gold medalist, with two individual and two team.

Gymnastics: America's top female gymnast of 1988, Phoebe Mills of Northfield, Ill., retired in June because of health and motivational problems. Mills, 16, was the only U.S. woman ever to win a gymnastics medal (bronze in balance beam) during a boycott-free Olympics. Brandy Johnson, 16, who left Bela Karolyi's Houston gym to return home to Florida, succeeded Mills as national all-around champion and was also the individual champion at the USA-USSR dual meet in Columbus, Ohio.

Quadruple Olympic medalist Dmitri Bilozerchev, 22, was thrown off the Soviet national team for alcohol abuse. Bilozerchev, youngest world champion in history in 1983, had made a celebrated recovery from a car wreck while driving drunk in 1985.

Rowing: Kris Karlson of Weston, Conn., won gold medals in both the women's lightweight single and double sculls at the World Championships in Bled, Yugoslavia, Sept. 9-10. Karlson, 25, who teamed with Carey Beth Sands to take the doubles title, became the first American since Jack Kelly Sr. at the 1924 Olympics to win two different international rowing championships.

The West German crew won the men's heavyweight eights in Bled, beating East Germany. Earlier in the summer at the 150th anniversary of the Henley Regatta, West Germany's Hansa Dortmund crew became the first crew to navigate the 1-mile, 550-yard course in less than six minutes, winning the Grand Cup in 5:58 by three lengths over Soviet Dynamo.

Swimming: On Aug. 3, U.S. breaststroker Mike Barrowman, 20, of Rockville, Md., and the University of Michigan became the first to break a long course world record since the 1988 Olympics. Seventeen days later, Barrowman was one of four U.S. swimmers to star in an unprecedented record-setting effort at the Pan Pacific Swimming Championships in Tokyo.

That ended a season in which Janet Evans of Placentia, Calif., the triple Olympic gold medalist who turned 18 Aug. 28, became the world's dominant woman swimmer. Her rival for that distinction, Kristin Otto of East Germany, won merely two gold medals at the European Swimming Championships in Bonn, exactly one-third Otto's haul at the 1988 Olympics. She was only third in the 200 backstroke.

At the Pan Pacifics, Evans set a world record in the 800 freestyle, won three individual events and was part of the win-

Wide World Photos

Mike Barrowman of the U.S. acknowledges the cheers of the crowd in Tokyo after breaking the world record in the 200-meter breaststroke. Barrowman was one of the four Americans who set new world marks on Aug. 20 at the Pan Pacific Championships.

ning 4 x 200 relay. A few weeks later, she began her freshman year at Stanford University.

Evans' world record was one of four set by U.S. swimmers in the final day of the Pan Pacifics, the first such one-day achievement in U.S. swimming history.

Swimming World Records Set in 1989

MEN

Event	Holder	Record	Old Mark	Former Holder
50-m freestyle	Tom Jager, USA	22.12	22.14	Matt Biondi, USA (118)
200-m freestyle	Giorgio Lamberti, Italy	1:46.69	1:47.25	Duncan Armstrong, AUS (1988)
100-m breaststroke	Adrian Moorhouse, Britain	1:01.49	1:01.65	Steve Lundquist, USA (1984)
200-m breaststroke	Mike Barrowman, USA	2:12.89	2:12.90	Mike Barrowman, USA (1989) & Nick Gillingham, GBR (1989)
200-m indiv. medley	Dave Wharton, USA	2:00.11	2:00.17	Tamas Darnyi, Hungary (1988)

WOMEN

Event	Holder	Record	Old Mark	Former Holder
800-m freestyle	Janet Evans, USA	8:16.22	8:17.12	Janet Evans, USA (1988)

For complete World Records List, see page 446.

Cuban high jumper **Javier Sotomayor** points out just how high eight feet is shortly after becoming the first man to clear the height without a pole on July 29.

The record swims:
• Evans, 8:16.22 in the 800 freestyle, breaking her own 1988 mark of 8:17.12.
• Barrowman, 2:12.89 in the 200 breaststroke, reclaiming by .01 sole posession of the record he had set earlier in the month, but which was later tied by Nick Gillingham of Great Britain in the European Swimming Championships.
• David Wharton, 2:00.11 in the 200 individual medley, breaking the 2:00.17 set by Tamas Daryni of Hungary in 1988.
• Tom Jager, 22.12 in the 50 free, breaking the 22.14 set in 1988 by Matt Biondi, who ended his brief post-Olympic retirement and swam in the U.S. nationals. Biondi, who had five gold and seven total Olympic medals, won the national title in the 50 free after the controversial disqualification of Jager for an alleged false start.

The U.S. dominated the Pan Pacifics, with 25 gold medals, followed by Canada, Australia, and China with three apiece.

Two men's world records were broken at the European Championships in August: Adrian Moorhouse of Britain reset the 100-meter breaststroke mark (1:01.49) and Giorgio Lamberti of Italy did the same in the 200 free (1:46.69). Hungary's Tamas Darnyi was the only wimmer to win threee individual events at the meet.

Moorhouse, who went on to win his fourth European title in the final, became the first British recordman in 13 years with a clocking of 1:01.49, beating the 1:01.65 established by Steve Lundquist of the U.S. at the 1984 Olympics. Lamberti clocked 1:46.69, bettering the 1:47.25 by Australia's Duncan Armstrong at the 1988 Olympics.

Lamberti also won the 100 free in European record time and anchored Italy's winning 4 x 200 relay. Darnyi, winner of both individual medleys at the Olympics, took those events and the 200 butterfly in the Europeans.

Even with a limited work load from Otto, East Germany won 14 of the 16 women's events at the European meet.

That total included two wins apiece by Daniela Hunger (200-400 IM) and Susanne Boernike (100-200 Breast). Meanwhile, Marianne Muis of the Netherlands collected six medals—four silvers and two bronzes, evenly divided between individual events and relays.

In the U.S. Nationals, which served as trials for the Pan Pacific Meet, Janet Evans of Placentia, Calif. won the limit of events she could enter—four. Evans won the 200 and 400-meter individual medleys and the 400 and 800 freestyles.

The star of the short-course season, Livia Copariu of Romania, defected while competing in France in April. Copariu, 16, had set world short course records in the 50 and 100 freestyles. After more than a month in hiding, she eventually rejoined a former coach who had settled in West Germany.

Table Tennis: China's decade-long dominance of the men's events was definitively ended at the 40th World Championships in Dortmund, West Germany, when Janove Waldner won the individual title, his Swedish teammates beat China 5-0 for the team crown, and no Chinese pair reached the doubles final, won by West Germany. China nevertheless swept the titles in the women's events.

Track & Field: Javier Sotomayor's 8-foot high jump (see above) was the highlight of a season in which the sport was muddied by the never-ending fallout of Ben Johnson's drug bust and Carl Lewis' battle with The Athletics Congress/ USA, governing body of U.S. track.

Lewis, 28, boycotted the national championships in protest over TAC policies involving direct support to athletes and what he felt was a lack of true commitment to the fight against performance-enhancing drugs. At the same time, the six-time Olympic gold medalist announced his intention to compete through the 1992 Olympics.

Sotomayor, who set an indoor world mark of 7-11½ while winning the World Indoor Championship in March, was among five men who had stunning world-record efforts during the 1989 outdoor season.

The other four came, not surprisingly, during the European Grad Prix circuit, and they broke the oldest two track records (the long jump is a field event) on the books, both held for 11 years by the ill-fated Kenyan, Henry Rono. Rono, who set world records in four events during a 91-day span in 1978, was denied an Olympic run by his country's 1976-80 boycotts and is trying to put his life back together after years of alcoholism.

The older of Rono's marks, 8:05.4 in the 3,000-meter steeplechase set May 13, 1978, fell July 3 in Stockholm to Peter Koech of Kenya. Koech, silver medalist at the Seoul Olympics, ran 8:05.35.

The second—and what many called the toughest track record to break—was Rono's 7:32.1 in the 3,000 meters, set June 17, 1978. It fell to Said Aouita's stunning 7:29.45, August 20 in Cologne,

Track & Field World Records set in 1989

MEN

Event	Holder	Record	Old Mark	Former Holder
3,000 meters	Said Aouita, Morocco	7:29.45	7:32.01	Henry Rono, Kenya (1978)
10,000 meters	Arturo Barrios, Mexico	27:08.23	27:13.81	Fernando Mamede, Por (1984)
110-meter hurdles	Roger Kingdom, USA	12.92	12.93	Renaldo Nehemiah, US (1981)
3,000-m steeplechase	Peter Koech, Kenya	8:05.35	8:05.40	Henry Rono, Kenya (1978)
4x200-meter relay	Santa Monica Track Club (Danny Everett, Leroy Burrell, Floyd Heard, Carl Lewis)	1:19.38	1:20.26	Southern Cal (1978)
High Jump	Javier Sotomayor, Cuba	8 ft-0	7 ft-11½	Sotomayor (1988,89)

WOMEN

Event	Holder	Record	Old Mark	Former Holder
Mile	Paula Ivan, Romania	4:15.61	4:16.71	Mary Slaney, USA (1985)
5-km walk	Ileana Salvador, Italy	20:27.59	20:32.75	Kerry Saxbe, Aus. (1989)
10-km walk	Ileana Salvador, Italy	42:39.2	43:26.12	Kerry Saxbe, Aus. (1989)
Triple Jump	Galina Chistyakova, USSR	47 ft-7¾	46 ft¾	Li Huirong, China (1987)

For complete World Records List, see page 448.

West Germany, giving the Moroccan world records at 1,500, 2,000, 3,000 and 5,000 meters.

The most significant other record was likely Roger Kingdom's 12.92 timing in the 110-meter hurdles at the Weltklasse Meet Aug. 16 in Zurich, where he knocked .01 off the mark Renaldo Nehemiah had established in the same meet eight years earlier. The record established Kingdom, who won the Olympic hurdles gold in 1984 and 1988, as arguably the greatest hurdler ever. Ironically, Nehemiah was a last-minute scratch from this year's Weltklasse because of a dispute over appearance fees.

Kingdom lowered the 110-meter hurdles record a second time at the World Cup meet in Barcelona, Sept. 10, but his 12.87 clocking was judged to be wind-aided.

The biggest slice off a record, occurred Aug.18 in West Berlin, where Anturo Barrios became the first Mexican runner to hold a world standard. Barrios, fifth in the 1988 Olympics, took more than five seconds off Fernando Mamede's 1984 record (27:13.81) in the 10,000 meters, clocking 27:08.23.

Another record-setter was Paula Ivan of Romania, 4:15.61 in the mile at Nice, who broke Mary Slaney's 1985 mark of 4:16.71.

Indoors, the major record-setters were: Sergei Bubka of the Soviet Union, who regained at 19-9¼ the world pole vault mark he briefly lost to countryman Rodion Gataullin; Paul Ereng of Kenya, whose 1:44.87 in the World Indoor Championships knocked .07 off Sebastian Coe's 6-year-old mark; and Randy Barnes of Texas A&M, who had a 74-4 in the shot, improving Werner Gunthor of Switzerland's mark by 15½ inches.

On the American scene, high jumper Hollis Conway was in the record spotlight. Conway, Olympic silver medalist, claimed U.S. records indoors (7-9¼) and outdoors (7-10). Dawn Sowell showed flashes as the next FloJo when she set collegiate 100 and 200-meter records of 10.78 and 22.04 seconds in the thin air of Provo, Utah.

In one April weekend, Ethiopian men established their dominance in world marathoning, reviving the tradition of barefoot Abebe Bikila, who won the 1960 and 1964 Olympic titles. That weekend saw Abebe Mekkonen win Boston in 2 hours, 9 minutes, 26 seconds; world record-holder Belainey Densimo win Rotterdam in 2:08:39; and Keleke Mefeteria win the IAAF World Marathon Cup in Milan in 2:10:28, as Ethiopia won the team title. A week later, reigning world champion Douglas Wakiihuri of Kenya won the London Marathon in 2:09:03.

Running her first marathon in four years, 1984 Olympic champion Joan Samuelson staggered painfully to a 9th place Boston finish in 2:37.52, the worst performance of her 10-year marathoning career and 13 minutes behind Ingrid Kristiansen of Norway. Crying at the

Said Aouita of Morocco, who already held world records in the 1,500, 2,000, and 5,000 meters, added the 3,000 meters to his collection on August 20 at a meet in Cologne.

post-race press conference, the oft-injured Samuelson said she would take an indefinite rest but "this is not it. I have it in me to come back for one more competitive effort."

Volleyball: An era ended in early July when Karch Kiraly, 28, the world's best all-around player, and Steve Timmons, 30, the ferocious spiker, left the U.S. volleyball team after winning the USA Cup for the sixth consecutive year. Before they joined the team in 1981, the U.S. had never won an Olympic medal or finished higher than sixth at the World Championships. Their efforts brought Olympic gold in 1984 and 1988, a world title in 1986 and a Pan Am Games gold in 1987. Their teams had a 209-32 record from 1984-88.

Wrestling: U.S. Olympic gold medal winners Kenny Monday (163 lbs) and John Smith (136 lbs) were the only American winners at September's World Freestyle Championships in Switzerland. The Soviet Union won eight medals in the tournament, including four gold.

Olympic Business: At its 95th session in San Juan, Puerto Rico, the International Olympic Committee voted unani-mously to give Juan Antonio Samaranch another 8-year term as president. Earlier in the year, the IOC executive committee approved several changes in the 1992 summer Olympic program, giving full medal status to baseball and women's judo and adding a total of 20 events, including the women's 10-kilometer walk in track and field.

The United States Olympic Committee denied Anchorage a third chance to represent the U.S. in bidding for the Winter Olympics. Anchorage, a loser internationally for the 1992 and 1994 events, was beaten as U.S. candidate by Salt Lake City. Other announced cities in the bidding, to take place at the 1991 IOC session, are favorite Nagano, Japan; Val d'Aosta, Italy; and Ostersund, Sweden.

The long-awaited Steinbrenner Commission report, the result of a year long review of USOC operations, proved underwhelming. Its emphasis was mainly on winning. "Winning medals must always be the primary goal," the report said, while also suggesting ways to improve marketing, streamline bureaucracy and better support athletes.

Swimming

World & American Records

Through Oct. 1, 1989

MEN

Freestyle

Distance	Record	Time	Record Holder	Date	Location
50 meters	World	22.12	**Tom Jager,** USA	Aug. 20, 1989	Tokyo
	American	same			
100 meters	World	48.42	**Matt Biondi,** USA	Aug. 10, 1988	Austin, Texas
	American	same			
200 meters	World	1:46.69	**Giorgio Lamberti,** Italy	Aug. 15, 1989	Bonn, W.Ger.
	American	1:47.72	**Matt Biondi**	Aug. 8, 1988	Austin, Texas
400 meters	World	3:46.95	**Uwe Dassler,** E.Germany	Sept. 23, 1988	Seoul
	American	3:48.06	**Matt Cetlinski**	Aug. 11, 1988	Austin, Texas
800 meters	World	7:50.64	**Vladimir Salnikov,** USSR	July 4, 1986	Moscow
	American	7:52.45	**Sean Killion**	July 27, 1987	Clovis, Calif.
1,500 meters	World	14:54.72	**Vladimir Salnikov,** USSR	Feb. 22, 1983	Moscow
	American	15:01.51	**George DiCarlo**	June 30, 1984	Indianapolis

Backstroke

Distance	Record	Time	Record Holder	Date	Location
100 meters	World	54.51	**David Berkoff,** USA	Sept. 24, 1988	Seoul
	American	same			
200 meters	World	1:58.14	**Igor Poliansky,** USSR	Mar. 3, 1985	Erfurt, E.Ger.
	American	1:58.86	**Rick Carey**	June 27, 1984	Indianapolis

Breaststroke

Distance	Record	Time	Record Holder	Date	Location
100 meters	World	1:01.49	**Adrian Moorhouse,** Britain	Aug. 15, 1989	Bonn, W.Ger.
	American	1:01.65	**Steve Lundquist**	July 29, 1984	Los Angeles
200 meters	World	2:12.89	**Mike Barrowman,** USA	Aug. 20, 1989	Tokyo
	American	same			

Butterfly

Distance	Record	Time	Record Holder	Date	Location
100 meters	World	52.84	**Pablo Morales,** USA	June 23, 1986	Orlando, Fla.
	American	same			
200 meters	World	1:56.24	**Michael Gross,** W.Germany	June 27, 1986	Bonn, W.Ger.
	American	1:57.75	**Pablo Morales**	Aug. 3, 1984	Los Angeles

Individual Medley

Distance	Record	Time	Record Holder	Date	Location
200 meters	World	2:00.11	**Dave Wharton,** USA	Aug. 20, 1989	Tokyo
	American	same			
400 meters	World	4:15.42	**Tamas Darnyi,** Hungary	Sept. 21, 1988	Seoul
	American	4:16.12	**Dave Wharton**	Aug. 14, 1987	Brisbane, Aus.

Relays

Event	Record	Time	Record Holder	Date	Location
400-m Free	World	3:16.53	**USA** (Chris Jacobs, Troy Dalbey, Tom Jager, Matt Biondi)	Sept. 23, 1988	Seoul
	American	same			
800-m Free	World	7:12.51	**USA** (Troy Dalbey, Matt Cetlinski, Doug Gjertsen, Matt Biondi)	Sept. 21, 1988	Seoul
	American	same			
400-m Medley	World	3:36.93	**USA** (David Berkoff, Rich Schroeder, Matt Biondi, Chris Jacobs)	Sept. 25, 1988	Seoul
	American	same			

WOMEN

Freestyle

Distance	Record	Time	Record Holder	Date	Location
50 meters	World.....	24.98	**Yang Wenyi,** China	Apr. 11, 1988	Canton, China
	American .	25.50	**Leigh Ann Fetter**	Aug. 13, 1988	Austin, Texas
100 meters	World....	54.73*	**Kristin Otto,** E.Germany	Aug. 19, 1986	Madrid, Spain
	American .	55.30*	**Dara Torres**	Mar. 25, 1988	Orlando, Fla.
200 meters	World.....	1:57.55	**Heike Friedrich,** E.Germany	June 18, 1986	Berlin
	American .	1:58.23	**Cynthia Woodhead**	Sept. 3, 1979	Tokyo
400 meters	World.....	4:03.85	**Janet Evans,** USA	Sept. 22, 1988	Seoul
	American .	same			
800 meters	World.....	8:16.22	**Janet Evans,** USA	Aug. 20, 1989	Tokyo
	American .	same			
1,500 meters	World.....	15:52.10	**Janet Evans,** USA	Mar. 26, 1988	Orlando, Fla.
	American .	same			

*Set on first leg of relay race.

Backstroke

Distance	Record	Time	Record Holder	Date	Location
100 meters	World.....	1:00.59*	**Ina Kleber,** E.Germany	Aug. 24, 1984	Moscow
	American .	1:01.20	**Betsy Mitchell**	June 24, 1986	Orlando, Fla
200 meters	World.....	2:08.60	**Betsy Mitchell,** USA	June 27, 1986	Orlando, Fla
	American .	same			

*Set on first leg of relay race.

Breaststroke

Distance	Record	Time	Record Holder	Date	Location
100 meters	World.....	1:07.91	**Silke Hoerner,** E.Germany	Aug. 21, 1987	Strasbourg, FRA
	American .	1:08.91	**Tracey McFarlane**	Aug. 11, 1988	Austin, Texas
200 meters	World.....	2:26.71	**Silke Hoerner,** E.Germany	Sept. 21, 1988	Seoul
	American .	2:29.58	**Amy Shaw**	Aug. 16, 1987	Brisbane, Aus.

Butterfly

Distance	Record	Time	Record Holder	Date	Location
100 meters	World.....	57.93	**Mary T.Meagher,** USA	Aug. 16, 1981	Brown Deer, WI
	American .	same			
200 meters	World.....	2:05.96	**Mary T.Meagher,** USA	Aug. 13, 1981	Brown Deer, WI
	American .	same			

Individual Medley

Distance	Record	Time	Record Holder	Date	Location
200 meters	World.....	2:11.73	**Uta Geweniger,** E.Germany	July 4, 1981	Berlin
	American .	2:12.64	**Tracy Caulkins**	Aug. 3, 1984	Los Angeles
400 meters	World.....	4:36.10	**Petra Schneider,** E.Germany	Aug. 1, 1982	Guayaquil, EQU
	American .	4:37.76	**Janet Evans**	Sept. 19, 1988	Seoul

Relays

Event	Record	Time	Record Holder	Date	Location
400-m Free	World.....	3:40.57	**E.Ger.** (Kristin Otto, Manuella Stellmach, Sabine Schulze, Heike Friedrich)	Aug. 19, 1986	Madrid, Spain
	American .	3:43.43	**USA** (Jenna Johnson, Carrie Steinseifer, Dara Torres, Nancy Hogshead)	July 31, 1984	Los Angeles
800-m Free	World.....	7:55.47	**E.Ger.** (Manuella Stellmach, Astrid Strauss, Anke Mohring, Heike Friedrich)	Aug. 18, 1987	Strasbourg, FRA
	American .	8:02.12	**USA** (Betsy Mitchell, Mary T. Meagher, Kim Brown, Mary Wayte)	Aug. 17, 1986	Madrid, Spain
400-m Medley	World.....	4:03.69	**E.Ger.** (Ina Kleber, Sylvia Gerasch, Ines Geissler, Birgit Meineke)	Aug. 24, 1984	Moscow
	American .	4:07.75	**USA** (Betsy Mitchell, Jenny Hau, Mary T.Meagher, Jenna Johnson)	Aug. 22, 1986	Madrid, Spain

Track & Field
World Records
Through Oct. 1, 1989

MEN

Running

Event	World Mark	Record Holder	Date	Location
100 meters	9.92	**Carl Lewis,** USA	Sept. 23, 1988	Seoul
200 meters	19.72	**Pietro Mennea,** Italy	Sept. 17, 1979	Mexico City
400 meters	43.29	**Butch Reynolds,** USA	Aug. 16, 1988	Zurich, Switzerland
800 meters	1:41.73	**Sebastian Coe,** Britain	June 10, 1981	Florence, Italy
1,000 meters	2:12.18	**Sebastian Coe,** Britain	July 11, 1981	Oslo, Norway
1,500 meters	3:29.46	**Said Aouita,** Morocco	Aug. 23, 1985	West Berlin
One Mile	3:46.32	**Steve Cram,** Britain	July 27, 1985	Oslo, Norway
2,000 meters	4:50.81	**Said Aouita,** Morocco	July 16, 1987	Paris
3,000 meters	7:29.45	**Said Aouita,** Morocco	Aug. 20, 1989	Cologne, W.Ger.
5,000 meters	12:58.39	**Said Aouita,** Morocco	July 22, 1987	Rome
10,000 meters	27:08.23	**Arturo Barrios,** Mexico	Aug. 18, 1989	West Berlin
20,000 meters	57:24.2	**Jos Hermens,** Holland.	May 1, 1976	Papandal, Holland
25,000 meters	1:13:55.8	**Toshihiko Seko,** Japan	Mar. 22, 1981	Christchurch,N.Zea.
30,000 meters	1:29:18.8	**Toshihiko Seko,** Japan	Mar. 22, 1981	Christchurch,N.Zea.
Marathon	2:06:50	**Belayneh Densimo,** Ethiopia	Apr. 17, 1988	Rotterdam, Holland

Note: The **One Mile** run is 1,609.344 meters and the **Marathon** is 42,194.988 meters (26 miles, 385 yards).

Hurdles

Event	World Mark	Record Holder	Date	Location
110-meter High	12.92	**Roger Kingdom,** USA	Aug. 16, 1989	Zurich, Switzerland
400-meter Low	47.02	**Edwin Moses,** USA	Aug. 31, 1983	Koblenz, W.Ger.

Note: The hurdles at 110 meters are 3 feet 6 inches high and the hurdles at 400 meters are 3 feet. There are 10 hurdles in each race.

Steeplechase

Event	World Mark	Record Holder	Date	Location
3,000m Steeplechase	8:05.35	**Peter Koech,** Kenya	July 3, 1989	Stockholm

Note: The steeplechase course consists of 28 hurdles (3 feet high) and seven water jumps (12 feet long).

Walking

Event	World Mark	Record Holder	Date	Location
20 kilometers	1:18:40.0	**Ernesto Canto,** Mexico	May 5, 1984	Bergen, Norway
30 kilometers	2:07:59.8	**Jose Marin,** Spain	Aug. 4, 1979	Barcelona
50 kilometers	3:41:38.4	**Raul Gonzalez,** Mexico	May 25, 1979	Bergen, Norway

Relays

Event	World Mark	Record Holder	Date	Location
4x100-meter Relay	37.83	**USA** (Sam Graddy, Ron Brown, Calvin Smith, Carl Lewis)	Aug. 11, 1984	Los Angeles
4x200-meter Relay	1:19.38	**USA** (Danny Everett, Leroy Burrell, Floyd Heard, Carl Lewis)	Aug. 23, 1989	Koblenz, W.Ger.
4x400-meter Relay	2:56.16	**USA** (Vince Matthews, Ron Freeman, Larry James, Lee Evans)	Oct. 20, 1968	Mexico City
		USA (Danny Everett, Steve Lewis, Kevin Robinzine, Butch Reynolds)	Oct. 1, 1988	Seoul
4x800-meter Relay	7:03.89	**Britain** (Peter Elliott, Garry Cook, Steve Cram, Sebastian Coe)	Aug. 30, 1982	London
4x1,500-meter Relay	14:38.8	**West Germany**	Aug. 14, 1977	Cologne, W.Ger.

Decathlon

Event	World Mark	Record Holder	Date	Location
Decathlon	8,847 Pts	**Daley Thompson,** Britain	Aug.8-9, 1984	Los Angeles

Note: the Decathlon consists of 10 events—100m, LJ, SP, HJ, 400m, 110m H, Discus, PV, Javelin, 1,500m (in that order) over 2 days.

Field Events

Event	World Mark	Record Holder	Date	Location
High Jump	8-0	**Javier Sotomayor,** Cuba	July 29, 1989	San Juan, Puerto Rico
Pole Vault	19-10½	**Sergei Bubka,** USSR	July 10, 1988	Nice, France
Long Jump	29-2½	**Bob Beamon,** USA	Oct. 18, 1968	Mexico City
Triple Jump	58-11½	**Willie Banks,** USA	June 16, 1985	Indianapolis
Shot Put	75-8	**Ulf Timmermann,** E.Germany	May 22, 1988	Canea, Crete
Discus	243-0	**Jurgen Schult,** E.Germany	June 6, 1986	Neubrandenburg, EG
Javelin (old)	343-10	**Uwe Hohn,** E.Germany	July 20, 1984	Oslo, Norway
Javelin (new)	287-7	**Jan Zelezny,** Czech.	May 31, 1987	Nitra, Czechoslovakia
Hammer	284-7	**Yuri Sedykh,** USSR	Aug. 30, 1986	Stuttgart, W.Germany

Note: The international weights for men—**Shot** (16 lb), **Discus** (4 lb/6.55 oz), **Hammer** (16 lb), new **Javelin** (minimum 1 lb/12¼ oz).

WOMEN

Running

Event	World Mark	Record Holder	Date	Location
100 meters	10.49	**Florence Griffith Joyner,** USA	July 16, 1988	Indianapolis
200 meters	21.34	**Florence Griffith Joyner,** USA	Sept. 29, 1988	Seoul
400 meters	47.60	**Marita Koch,** E.Germany	Oct. 6, 1985	Canberra, Australia
800 meters	1:53.28	**Jarmila Kratochvilova,** Czech.	July 26, 1983	Munich
1,000 meters	2:30.6	**Tatyana Providokhina,** USSR	Aug. 20, 1978	Podolsk, USSR
1,500 meters	3:52.47	**Tatyana Providokhina,** USSR	Aug. 13, 1980	Zurich
One Mile	4:15.61	**Paula Ivan,** Romania	July 10, 1989	Nice, France
2,000 meters	5:28.69	**Maricica Puica,** Romania	July 11, 1986	London
3,000 meters	8:22.62	**Tatyana Providokhina,** USSR	Aug. 26, 1984	Leningrad, USSR
5,000 meters	14:37.33	**Ingrid Kristiansen,** Norway	Aug. 5, 1986	Stockholm
10,000 meters	30:13.74	**Ingrid Kristiansen,** Norway	July 5, 1986	Oslo, Norway
Marathon	2:21:06	**Ingrid Kristiansen,** Norway	Apr. 21, 1985	London

Note: The **One Mile** run is 1,609.344 meters; and the **Marathon** is 42,194.988 meters (26 miles, 385 yards).

Hurdles

Event	World Mark	Record Holder	Date	Location
100-meter High	12.21	**Yordanka Donkova,** Bulgaria	Aug. 21, 1988	Stara Zagora, Bulg.
400-meter Low	52.94	**Marina Stepanova,** USSR	Sept. 17, 1986	Tashkent, USSR

Note: The hurdles at 100 meters are 2 feet 9 inches high and the hurdles at 400 meters are 2 feet 6 inches. There are 10 hurdles in each race.

Walking

Event	World Mark	Record Holder	Date	Location
5 kilometers	20:27.59	**Ileana Salvador,** Italy	June 3, 1989	Trent, Italy
10 kilometers	42:39.2	**Ileana Salvador,** Italy	June 18, 1989	Rome

Relays

Event	World Mark	Record Holder	Date	Location
4x100-meter Relay	41.37	**East Germany**	Oct. 6, 1985	Canberra, Australia
4x200-meter Relay	1:28.15	**East Germany**	Aug. 9, 1980	Jena, E.Germany
4x400-meter Relay	3:15.18	**USSR**	Oct. 1, 1988	Seoul
4x800-meter Relay	7:50.17	**USSR**	Aug. 5, 1984	Moscow

Heptathlon

Event	World Mark	Record Holder	Date	Location
Heptathlon	7,291 Pts	**Jackie Joyner-Kersee,** USA	Sept. 23, 1988	Seoul

Note: the Heptathlon consists of 7 events—100m, H, SP, HJ, 200m, LJ, Javelin, 800m (in that order) over 2 days.

Field Events

Event	World Mark	Record Holder	Date	Location
High Jump	6-10¼	**Stefka Kostadinova,** Bulgaria	Aug. 30, 1987	Rome
Long Jump	24-8¼	**Galina Chistyakova,** USSR	June 11, 1988	Leningrad, USSR
Triple Jump	47-7¾	**Galina Chistyakova,** USSR	July 3, 1989	Stockholm
Shot Put	74-3	**Natalya Lisovskaya,** USSR	June 7, 1987	Moscow
Discus	252-0	**Gabriele Reinsch,** E.Germany	July 9, 1988	Neubrandenburg, EG
Javelin	262-5	**Petra Felke,** E.Germany	Sept. 9, 1988	Potsdam, E.Germany

Note: The international weights for women—**Shot** (8 lb/13 oz), **Discus** (2 lb/3.27 oz), **Javelin** (minimum 1 lb/5.16 oz).

American Track & Field Records
Through Oct. 1, 1989

MEN

Running

Event	US Mark	Record Holder
100 m	9.92*	Carl Lewis (1988)
200 m	19.75	Carl Lewis (1983) & Joe DeLoach (1988)
400 m	43.29*	Butch Reynolds (1988)
800 m	1:42.60	Johnny Gray (1985)
1,000 m	2:13.9	Rick Wohlhuter (1974)
1,500 m	3:29.77	Sydney Maree (1985)
One Mile	3:47.69	Steve Scott (1982)
2,000 m	4:52.44	Jim Spivey (1987)
3,000 m	7:35.84	Doug Padilla (1983)
5,000 m	13:01.15	Sydney Maree (1985)
10,000 m	27:20.56	Mark Nenow (1986)
20,000 m	58:25.0	Bill Rodgers (1977)
25,000 m	1:14:11.8	Bill Rodgers (1979)
30,000 m	1:31:49	Bill Rodgers (1979)
Marathon	2:08:52	Alberto Salazar (1982)

Hurdles

Event	US Mark	Record Holder
110-m High	12.92*	Roger Kingdom (1989)
400-m Low	47.02*	Edwin Moses ((1983)

Steeplechase

Event	US Mark	Record Holder
3,000 m	8:09.17	Henry Marsh (1985)

Walking

Event	US Mark	Record Holder
20 km	1:24:50	Tim Lewis (1988)
30 km	2:23:14	Goetz Klopfer (1970)
50 km	3:56:55	Marco Evoniuk (1988)

Relays

Event	US Mark	Record Holder
4x100 m	37.83*	Olympic team (1984)
4x200 m	1:19.38*	Santa Monica Track Club (1989)
4x400 m	2:56.16*	Olympic Team (1968) & Olympic Team (1988)
4x800 m	7:06.5	Santa Monica Track Club (1988)
4x1,500 m	14:46.3	National Team (1979)

Decathlon

Event	US Mark	Record Holder
Decathlon	8,634 Pts	Bruce Jenner

Field Events

Event	US Mark	Record Holder
High Jump	7-10	Hollis Conway (1989)
Pole Vault	19-6½	Joe Dial (1987)
Long Jump	29-2½*	Bob Beamon (1968)
Triple Jump	58-11½*	Willie Banks (1985)
Shot Put	73-10¾	John Brenner (1987)
Discus	237-4	Ben Plucknett (1981)
Javelin (old)	327-2	Tom Petranoff (1983)
Javelin (new)	280-1	Tom Petranoff (1986)
Hammer	268-8	Jud Logan (1988)

WOMEN

Running

Event	US Mark	Record Holder
100 m	10.49*	F.Griffith Joyner (1988)
200 m	21.34*	F.Griffith Joyner (1988)
400 m	48.83	Valerie Brisco (1984)
800 m	1:56.90	Mary Slaney (1985)
1,000 m	2:34.65	Mary Slaney (1988)
1,500 m	3:57.12	Mary Slaney (1983)
One Mile	4:16.71	Mary Slaney (1985)
2,000 m	5:32.7	Mary Slaney (1984)
3,000 m	8:25.83	Mary Slaney (1985)
5,000 m	14:59.99	PattiSue Pulmer (1989)
10,000 m	31:35.3	Mary Slaney (1982)
Marathon	2:21:21	Joan Samuelson (1985)

Hurdles

Event	US Mark	Record Holder
100-m High	12.61	Gail Devers (1988) & Jackie Joyner-Kersee (1988)
400-m Low	53.37	Sandra Farmer-Patrick (1989)

Walking

Event	US Mark	Record Holder
5 km	22:38.0	Teresa Vaill (1989)
10 km	44:46.1	Lynn Weik (1989)

Relays

Event	US Mark	Record Holder
4x100 m	41.55	National team (1987)
4x200 m	1:32.57	Louisiana St. (1989)
4x400 m	3:15.51	Olympic Team (1988)
4x800 m	8:17.09	Athletics West (1983)

Heptathlon

Event	US Mark	Record Holder
Heptathlon	7,291 Pts*	J.Joyner-Kersee (1988)

Field Events

Event	US Mark	Record Holder
High Jump	6-8 (twice)	Louise Ritter (1988)
Long Jump	24- 5 1/2	J.Joyner-Kersee (1987)
Triple Jump	45- 7 1/2	Sheila Hudson (1989)
Shot Put	66- 2 1/2	Ramona Pagel (1988)
Discus	216-10	Carol Cady (1986)
Javelin	227- 5	Kate Schmidt (1977)

*indicates World Record.

*indicates World Record.

Olympic Games

First held in Athens in 1896, the modern Olympic Games were an attempt by French educator Pierre de Coubertin and others to revive the Greek tradition of a regularly scheduled athletic festival and to promote international
good will among the youth of the world.

The International Olympic Committee (IOC) expanded the Olympics in 1924 by adding the Winter Games for
cold weather sports. Both the Summer and Winter Games have been held at four-year intervals except during
the century's two world wars.

Summer Games

Year	No.	Location	Dates	Nations	Most Medals	USA Medals
1896	I	Athens, Greece	Apr 6-15	13	Greece (10-19-18–47)	11-7-1–19 (2nd)
1900	II	Paris, France	May 20-Oct 28	22	France(29-41-32–102)	21-16-16–53(2nd)
1904	III	St.Louis, Missouri	July 1-Nov 23	12	USA (80-86-72–238)	same
1906	—	Athens, Greece	Apr 22-May 2	20	France (15-9-16–40)	12-6-5–23 (4th)
1908	IV	London, Great Britain	Apr 27-Oct 31	23	Britain(56-50-39–145)	23-12-13–48(2nd)
1912	V	Stockholm, Sweden	May 5-Jul 22	28	Sweden(24-24-17–65)	25-18-19–62(2nd)
1916	VI	Not held†				
1920	VII	Antwerp, Belgium	Apr 20-Sept 12	29	USA (41-27-27–95)	same
1924	VIII	Paris, France	May 4-July 27	44	USA (45-27-27–99)	same
1928	IX	Amsterdam, Holland	May 17-Aug 12	46	USA (22-18-16–56)	same
1932	X	Los Angeles, California	July 30-Aug 14	37	USA (41-32-31–104)	same
1936	XI	Berlin, Germany	Aug 1-16	49	Ger. (33-26-30–89)	24-20-12–56(2nd)
1940	XII	Not held†				
1944	XIII	Not held†				
1948	XIV	London, Great Britain	July 29-Aug 14	59	USA (38-27-19–84)	same
1952	XV	Helsinki, Finland	July 19-Aug 3	69	USA (40-19-17–76)	same
1956	XVI	Melbourne, Australia‡	Nov 22-Dec 8	67	USSR (37-29-32–98)	32-25-17–74(2nd)
1960	XVII	Rome, Italy	Aug 25-Sept 11	83	USSR(43-29-31–103)	34-21-16–71(2nd)
1964	XVIII	Tokyo, Japan	Oct 10-24	93	USA (36-26-28–90)	same
1968	XIX	Mexico City, Mexico	Oct 12-17	112	USA (45-28-34–107)	same
1972	XX	Munich, West Germany	Aug 26-Sept 10	122	USSR (50-27-22–99)	33-31-30–94(2nd)
1976	XXI	Montreal, Canada	July 17-Aug 1	92	USSR(49-41-35–125)	34-35-25–94 (3rd)
1980	XXII	Moscow, USSR	July 19-Aug 3	81	USSR* (80-69-46–195)	Did not compete
1984	XXIII	Los Angeles, California	July 28-Aug 12	144	USA* (83-61-30–174)	same
1988	XXIV	Seoul, South Korea	Sept 17-Oct 2	159	USSR (55-31-46–132)	36-31-27–94 (3rd)
1992	XXV	Barcelona, Spain	TBA			

†The 1916 Games were scheduled for Berlin; the 1940 Games for Tokyo; and the 1944 Games for London. All were cancelled
due to world wars.
‡In 1956, the equestrian events were held in Stockholm, June 10-17.
*The USA was among 64 nations that boycotted the 1980 Summer Games in Moscow; while the USSR, East Germany and most
eastern bloc countries stayed away from the 1984 Summer Games in Los Angeles.

Winter Games

Year	No.	Location	Dates	Nations	Most Medals	USA Medals
1924	I	Chamonix, France	Jan 25-Feb 4	16	Norway (4-7-6—17)	1-2-1—4 (4th)
1928	II	St.Moritz, Switzerland	Feb 11-19	25	Norway (6-4-5—15)	2-2-2—6 (2nd)
1932	III	Lake Placid, New York	Feb 4-15	17	USA (6-4-2—12)	same
1936	IV	Garmisch-Partenkirchen, Germany	Feb 6-16	28	Norway (7-5-3—15)	1-0-3—4 (T-5th)
1940	—	Not held†				
1944	—	Not held†				
1948	V	St.Moritz, Switzerland	Jan 30-Feb 8	28	Norway (4-3-3—10) Sweden (4-3-3—10) Switz. (3-4-3—10)	3-4-2—9 (4th)
1952	VI	Oslo, Norway	Feb 14-25	30	Norway (7-3-6—16)	4-6-1—11 (2nd)
1956	VII	Cortina d'Ampezzo, Italy	Jan 26-Feb 5	32	USSR (7-3-6—16)	2-3-2—7 (T-4th)
1960	VIII	Squaw Valley, California	Feb 18-28	30	USSR (7-5-9—21)	3-4-3—10 (2nd)
1964	IX	Innsbruck, Austria	Jan 29-Feb 9	36	USSR (11-8-6—25)	1-2-3—6 (7th)
1968	X	Grenoble, France	Feb 6-18	37	Norway (6-6-2—14)	1-5-1—7 (T-7th)
1972	XI	Sapporo, Japan	Feb 3-13	35	USSR (8-5-3—16)	3-2-3—8 (6th)
1976	XII	Innsbruck, Austria‡	Feb 4-15	37	USSR (13-6-8—27)	3-3-4—10 (T-3rd)
1980	XIII	Lake Placid, New York	Feb 14-23	37	USSR (10-6-6—22)	6-4-2—12 (3rd)
1984	XIV	Sarajevo, Yugoslavia	Feb 7-19	49	USSR (6-10-9—25)	4-4-0—8 (T-5th)
1988	XV	Calgary, Canada	Feb 13-28	57	USSR (11-9-9—29)	2-1-3—6 (T-8th)
1992	XVI	Albertville, France	TBA			
1994	*XVII	Lillehammer, Norway	TBA			

†The 1940 Winter Games were scheduled first for Sapporo (Japan was stripped of the Games in 1937 when the Sino-Japanese
war broke out), then St.Moritz (the Swiss felt ski instructors should not be considered professionals, the IOC disagreed), then finally
Garmisch-Partenkirchen. The 1944 Games were scheduled for Cortina d'Ampezzo. Both were cancelled due to World War II.
‡The IOC originally granted the 1976 Winter games to Denver, but in 1972 Colorado voters rejected a $5 million bond issue to
finance the undertaking. Denver immediately withdrew as host and the IOC designated Innsbruck, the site of the 1964 Games.
*Starting in 1994, the Winter Games will no longer be held in the same year as the Summer Games, but rather two years before.

Summer Olympics, 1896-1988

Gold medal winners in the following events: basketball, boxing, diving, gymnastics, swimming, tennis, track & field, volleyball, water polo, and freestyle wrestling.

Basketball

MEN

Year	Champion, 2nd, 3rd	Year	Champion, 2nd, 3rd
1936	**United States**, Canada, Mexico	1968	**United States**, Yugoslavia, Soviet Union
1948	**United States**, France, Brazil	1972	**Soviet Union**, United States, Cuba
1952	**United States**, Soviet Union, Uruguay	1976	**United States**, Yugoslavia, Soviet Union
1956	**United States**, Soviet Union, Uruguay	1980	**Yugoslavia**, Italy, United States
1960	**United States**, Soviet Union, Brazil	1984	**United States**, Spain, Yugoslavia
1964	**United States**, Soviet Union, Brazil	1988	**Soviet Union**, Yugoslavia, United States

WOMEN

Year	Champion, 2nd, 3rd	Year	Champion, 2nd, 3rd
1976	**Soviet Union**, United States, Bulgaria	1984	**United States**, South Korea, China
1980	**Soviet Union**, Bulgaria, Yugoslavia	1988	**United States**, Yugoslavia, Soviet Union

Boxing

Light Flyweight (106 lbs)

Year	Champion	Final Match	Year	Champion	Final Match
1968	Francisco Rodriguez, VEN	Decision, 3-2	1980	Shamil Sabyrov, USSR	Decision, 3-2
1972	György Gedó, HUN	Decision, 5-0	1984	Paul Gonzales, USA	Default
1976	Jorge Hernandez, CUB	Decision, 4-1	1988	Ivailo Hristov, BUL	Decision, 5-0

Flyweight (112 lbs)

Year	Champion	Final Match	Year	Champion	Final Match
1904	George Finnegan, USA	Stopped in 1st	1960	Gyula Török, HUN	Decision, 3-2
1920	Frank DiGennara, USA	Decision	1964	Fernando Atzori, ITA	Decision, 4-1
1924	Fidel LaBarba, USA	Decision	1968	Ricardo Delgado, MEX	Decision, 5-0
1928	Antal Kocsis, HUN	Decision	1972	Georgi Kostadinov, BUL	Decision, 5-0
1932	István Énekes, HUN	Decision	1976	Leo Randolph, USA	Decision, 3-2
1936	Willi Kaiser, GER	Decision	1980	Peter Lessov, BUL	Stopped in 2nd
1948	Pascual Perez, ARG	Decision	1984	Steven McCrory, USA	Decision, 4-1
1952	Nathan Brooks, USA	Decision, 3-0	1988	Kim Swang-Sun, KOR	Decision, 4-1
1956	Terence Spinks, GBR	Decision			

Bantamweight (119 lbs)

Year	Champion	Final Match	Year	Champion	Final Match
1904	Oliver Kirk, USA	Stopped in 3rd	1956	Wolfgange Behrendt, E.Ger	Decision
1908	A. Henry Thomas, GBR	Decision	1960	Oleg Grigoryev, USSR	Decision
1920	Clarence Walker, SAF	Decision	1964	Takao Sakurai, JPN	Stopped in 2nd
1924	William Smith, SAF	Decision	1968	Valery Sokolov, USSR	Stopped in 2nd
1928	Vittorio Tamagnini, ITA	Decision	1972	Orlando Martinez, CUB	Decision, 5-0
1932	Horace Gwynne, CAN	Decision	1976	Yong-Jo Gu, PRK	Decision, 5-0
1936	Ulderico Sergo, ITA	Decision	1980	Juan Hernandez, CUB	Decision, 5-0
1948	Tibor Csik, HUN	Decision	1984	Maurizio Stecca, ITA	Decision, 4-1
1952	Pentti Hämäläinen, FIN	Decision, 2-1	1988	Kennedy McKinney, USA	Decision, 5-0

Featherweight (125 lbs)

Year	Champion	Final Match	Year	Champion	Final Match
1904	Oliver Kirk, USA	Decision	1956	Vladimir Safronov, USSR	Decision
1908	Richard Gunn, GBR	Decision	1960	Francesco Musso, ITA	Decision, 4-1
1920	Paul Fritsch, FRA	Decision	1964	Stanislav Stepashkin, USSR	Decision, 3-2
1924	John Fields, USA	Decision	1968	Antonio Roldan, MEX	Won on Disq.
1928	Lambertus van Klaveren, HOL	Decision	1972	Boris Kousnetsov, USSR	Decision, 3-2
1932	Carmelo Robledo, ARG	Decision	1976	Angel Herrera, CUB	KO in 2nd
1936	Oscar Casanovas, ARG	Decision	1980	Rudi Fink, E.Ger	Decision, 4-1
1948	Ernesto Formenti, ITA	Decision	1984	Meldrick Taylor, USA	Decision, 5-0
1952	Jan Zachara, CZE	Decision, 2-1	1988	Giovanni Parisi, ITA	Stopped in 1st

Lightweight (132 lbs)

Year	Champion	Final Match	Year	Champion	Final Match
1904	Harry Spanger, USA	Decision	1956	Richard McTaggart, GBR	Decision
1908	Frederick Grace, GBR	Decision	1960	Kazimierz Pazdzior, POL	Decision, 4-1
1920	Samuel Mosberg, USA	Decision	1964	Józef Grudzień, POL	Decision
1924	Hans Nielsen, DEN	Decision	1968	Ronnie Harris, USA	Decision, 5-0
1928	Carlo Orlandi, ITA	Decision	1972	Jan Szczepański, POL	Decision, 5-0
1932	Lawrence Stevens, SAF	Decision	1976	Howard Davis, USA	Decision, 5-0
1936	Imre Harangi, HUN	Decision	1980	Angel Herrera, CUB	Stopped in 3rd
1948	Gerald Dreyer, SAF	Decision	1984	Pernell Whitaker, USA	For retired in 2nd
1952	Aureliano Bolognesi, ITA	Decision, 2-1	1988	Andreas Zuelow, E.Ger	Decision, 5-0

Light Welterweight (139 lbs)

Year	Champion	Final Match	Year	Champion	Final Match
1952	Charles Adkins, USA	Decision, 2-1	1972	Ray Seales, USA	Decision, 3-2
1956	Vladimir Yengibaryan, USSR	Decision	1976	Ray Leonard, USA	Decision, 5-0
1960	Bohumil Nemeček CZE	Decision, 5-0	1980	Patrizio Oliva, ITA	Decision, 4-1
1964	Jerzy Kulej, POL	Decision, 5-0	1984	Jerry Page, USA	Decision, 5-0
1968	Jerzy Kulej, POL	Decision, 3-2	1988	Viatcheslav Janovski, USSR	Decision, 5-0

Welterweight (147 lbs)

Year	Champion	Final Match	Year	Champion	Final Match
1904	Albert Young, USA	Decision	1960	Nino Benvenuti, ITA	Decision, 4-1
1920	Albert Schneider, CAN	Decision	1964	Marian Kasprzki, POL	Decision, 4-1
1924	Jean Delarge, BEL	Decision	1968	Manfred Wolke, E.Ger	Decision, 4-1
1928	Edward Morgan, NZE	Decision	1972	Emilio Correa, CUB	Decision, 5-0
1932	Edward Flynn, USA	Decision	1976	Jochen Bachfeld, E.Ger	Decision, 3-2
1936	Sten Suvio, FIN	Decision	1980	Andrés Aldama, CUB	Decision, 4-1
1948	Julius Torma, CZE	Decision	1984	Mark Breland, USA	Decision, 5-0
1952	Zygmunt Chychla, POL	Decision, 3-0	1988	Robert Wangila, KEN	Stopped in 2nd
1956	Nicolae Linca, ROM	Decision, 3-2			

Light Middleweight (156 lbs)

Year	Champion	Final Match	Year	Champion	Final Match
1952	László Papp, HUN	Decision, 3-0	1972	Dieter Kottysch, W.Ger	Decision, 3-2
1956	László Papp, HUN	Decision	1976	Jerzy Rybicki, POL	Decision, 5-0
1960	Skeeter McClure, USA	Decision, 4-1	1980	Armando Martinez, CUB	Decision, 4-1
1964	Boris Lagutin, USSR	Decision, 4-1	1984	Frank Tate, USA	Decision, 5-0
1968	Boris Lagutin, USSR	Decision, 5-0	1988	Park Si-Hun, KOR	Decision, 3-2

Middleweight (165 lbs)

Year	Champion	Final Match	Year	Champion	Final Match
1904	Charles Mayer, USA	Stopped in 3rd	1956	Gennady Schatkov, USSR	KO in 1st
1908	John Douglas, GBR	Decision	1960	Edward Crook, USA	Decision, 3-2
1920	Harry Mallin, GBR	Decision	1964	Valery Popenchenko, USSR	Stopped in 1st
1924	Harry Mallin, GBR	Decision	1968	Christopher Finnegan, GBR	Decision, 3-2
1928	Piero Toscani, ITA	Decision	1972	Vyacheslav Lemechev, USSR	KO in 1st
1932	Carmen Barth, USA	Decision	1976	Michael Spinks, USA	Stopped in 3rd
1936	Jean Despeaux, FRA	Decision	1980	José Gomez, CUB	Decision, 4-1
1948	László Papp, HUN	Decision	1984	Joon-Sup Shin, KOR	Decision, 3-2
1952	Floyd Patterson, USA	KO in 1st	1988	Henry Maske, E.Ger	Decision, 5-0

Light Heavyweight (178 lbs)

Year	Champion	Final Match	Year	Champion	Final Match
1920	Eddie Eagan, USA	Decision	1960	Cassius Clay, USA	Decision, 5-0
1924	Harry Mitchell, GBR	Decision	1964	Cosimo Pinto, ITA	Decision, 3-2
1928	Victor Avendaño, ARG	Decision	1968	Dan Poznyak, USSR	Default
1932	David Carstens, SAF	Decision	1972	Mate Parlov, YUG	Stopped in 2nd
1936	Roger Michelot, FRA	Decision	1976	Leon Spinks, USA	Stopped in 3rd
1948	George Hunter, SAF	Decision	1980	Slobodan Kacar, YUG	Decision, 4-1
1952	Norvel Lee, USA	Decision, 3-0	1984	Anton Josipović, YUG	Default
1956	James Boyd, USA	Decision	1988	Andrew Maynard, USA	Decision, 5-0

Heavyweight (200 lbs)

Year	Champion	Final Match	Year	Champion	Final Match
1984	Henry Tillman, USA	Decision, 5-0	1988	Ray Mercer, USA	Stopped in 1st

Super Heavyweight (Unlimited)

Year	Champion	Final Match	Year	Champion	Final Match
1904	Samuel Berger, USA	Decision	1956	Pete Rademacher, USA	Stopped in 1st
1908	Albert Oldham, GBR	KO in 1st	1960	Franco De Piccoli, ITA	KO in 1st
1920	Ronald Rawson, GBR	Decision	1964	Joe Frazier, USA	Decision, 3-2
1924	Otto von Porat, NOR	Decision	1968	George Foreman, USA	Stopped in 2nd
1928	Arturo Rodriguez Jurado, ARG	Stopped in 1st	1972	Teófilo Stevenson, CUB	Default
1932	Santiago Lovell, ARG	Decision	1976	Teófilo Stevenson, CUB	KO in 3rd
1936	Herbert Runge, GER	Decision	1980	Teófilo Stevenson, CUB	Decision, 4-1
1948	Rafael Iglesias, ARG	KO in 2nd	1984	Tyrell Biggs, USA	Decision, 4-1
1952	Ed Sanders, USA	Won on Disq.	1988	Lennox Lewis, CAN	Stopped in 2nd

Diving

MEN

Springboard Diving

Year	Champion	Points	Year	Champion	Points
1908	Albert Zürner, W.Ger	85.5	1956	Bob Clotworthy, USA	159.56
1912	Paul Günther, W.Ger	79.23	1960	Gary Tobian, USA	170.00
1920	Louis Kuehn, USA	675.4	1964	Ken Sitzberger, USA	159.90
1924	Albert White, USA	696.4	1968	Bernie Wrightson, USA	170.15
1928	Pete DesJardins, USA	185.04	1972	Vladimir Vasin, USSR	594.09
1932	Michael Galitzen, USA	161.38	1976	Phil Boggs, USA	619.05
1936	Richard Degener, USA	163.57	1980	Aleksandr Portnov, USSR	905.025
1948	Bruce Harlan, USA	163.64	1984	Greg Louganis, USA	754.41
1952	David Browning, USA	205.29	1988	Greg Louganis, USA	730.80

Platform Diving

Year	Champion	Points	Year	Champion	Points
1904	George Sheldon, USA	12.66	1952	Sammy Lee, USA	156.28
1906	Gottlob Walz, W.Ger	156.0	1956	Joaquin Capilla Perez, MEX	152.44
1908	Hjalmar Johansson, SWE	83.75	1960	Bob Webster, USA	165.56
1912	Erik Adlerz, SWE	73.94	1964	Bob Webster, USA	148.58
1920	Clarence Pinkston, USA	100.67	1968	Klaus Dibiasi, ITA	164.18
1924	Albert White, USA	97.46	1972	Klaus Dibiasi, ITA	504.12
1928	Pete DesJardins, USA	98.74	1976	Klaus Dibiasi, ITA	600.51
1932	Harold Smith, USA	124.80	1980	Falk Hoffmann, E.Ger	835.650
1936	Marshall Wayne, USA	113.58	1984	Greg Louganis, USA	710.91
1948	Sammy Lee, USA	130.05	1988	Greg Louganis, USA	638.61

WOMEN

Springboard Diving

Year	Champion	Points	Year	Champion	Points
1920	Aileen Riggin, USA	539.9	1960	Ingrid Krämer, E.Ger	155.81
1924	Elizabeth Becker, USA	474.5	1964	Ingrid Engel-Krämer, E.Ger	145.00
1928	Helen Meany, USA	78.62	1968	Sue Gossick, USA	150.77
1932	Georgia Coleman, USA	87.52	1972	Micki King, USA	450.03
1936	Marjorie Gestring, USA	89.27	1976	Jennifer Chandler, USA	506.19
1948	Vicki Draves, USA	108.74	1980	Irina Kalinina, USSR	725.910
1952	Pat McCormick, USA	147.30	1984	Sylvie Bernier, CAN	530.70
1956	Pat McCormick, USA	142.36	1988	Gao Min, CHN	580.23

Platform Diving

Year	Champion	Points	Year	Champion	Points
1912	Greta Johansson, SWE	39.9	1960	Ingrid Krämer, E.Ger	91.28
1920	Stefani Fryland-Clausen, DEN	34.6	1964	Lesley Bush, USA	99.80
1924	Caroline Smith, USA	33.2	1968	Melina Duchkova, CZE	109.59
1928	Elizabeth Becker Pinkston, USA	31.6	1972	Ulrika Knape, SWE	390.00
1932	Dorothy Poynton, USA	40.26	1976	Elena Vaytsekhovskaya, USSR	406.59
1936	Dorothy Poynton Hill, USA	33.93	1980	Martina Jäschke, E.Ger	596.250
1948	Vicki Draves, USA	68.87	1984	Zhou Jihong, CHN	435.51
1952	Pat McCormick, USA	79.37	1988	Xu Yanmei, CHN	445.20
1956	Pat McCormick, USA	84.85			

Gymnastics

MEN

All-Around

Year	Champion	Points	Year	Champion	Points
1900	Gustave Sandras, FRA	302	1948	Veikko Huhtanen, FIN	229.7
1904	Julius Lenhart, AUT	69.80	1952	Viktor Chukarin, USSR	115.7
1906	Pierre Paysse, FRA	116	1956	Viktor Chukarin, USSR	114.25
1908	Alberto Braglia, ITA	317.0	1960	Boris Shakhlin, USSR	115.95
1912	Alberto Braglia, ITA	135.0	1964	Yukio Endo, JPN	115.95
1920	Giorgio Zampori, ITA	88.35	1968	Sawao Kato, JPN	115.9
1924	Leon Stukelj, YUG	110.340	1972	Sawao Kato, JPN	114.650
1928	Georges Miez, SWI	247.500	1976	Nikolai Andrianov, USSR	116.65
1932	Romeo Neri, ITA	140.625	1980	Aleksandr Dityatin, USSR	118.65
1936	Alfred Schwarzmann, GER	113.100	1984	Koji Gushiken, JPN	118.7
			1988	Vladimir Artemov, USSR	119.125

Horizontal Bar

Year Champion	Points	Year Champion	Points
1896 Hermann Weingartner, GER	—	1960 Takashi Ono, JPN	19.60
1904 Anton Heida, USA		1964 Boris Shakhlin, USSR	19.625
& Edward Hennig, USA	40	1968 Akinori Nakayama, JPN	19.55
1924 Leon Stukelj, YUG	19.73	1972 Mitsuo Tsukahara, JPN	19.725
1928 Georges Miez, SWI	19.17	1976 Mitsuo Tsukahara, JPN	19.675
1932 Dallas Bixler, USA	18.33	1980 Stoyan Deltchèv, BUL	19.825
1936 Aleksanteri Saarvala, FIN	19.367	1984 Shinji Morisue, JPN	20.00
1948 Josef Stalder, SWI	19.85	1988 Vladimir Artemov, USSR	
1952 Jack Günthard, SWI	19.55	& Valeri Lioukine, USSR	19.900
1956 Takashi Ono, JPN	19.60		

Parallel Bars

Year Champion	Points	Year Champion	Points
1896 Alfred Flatow, GER	—	1960 Boris Shakhlin, USSR	19.40
1904 George Eyser, USA	44	1964 Yukio Endo, JPN	19.675
1924 August Güttinger, SWI	21.63	1968 Akinori Nakayama, JPN	19.475
1928 Ladislav Vácha, CZE	18.83	1972 Sawao Kato, JPN	19.475
1932 Romeo Neri, ITA	18.97	1976 Sawao Kato, JPN	19.675
1936 Konrad Frey, GER	19.067	1980 Aleksandr Tkachyov, USSR	19.775
1948 Michael Reusch, SWI	19.75	1984 Bart Conner, USA	19.95
1952 Hans Eugster, SWI	19.65	1988 Vladimir Artemov, USSR	19.925
1956 Viktor Chukarin, USSR	19.20		

Vault

Year Champion	Points	Year Champion	Points
1896 Karl Schumann, GER	—	1956 Helmut Bantz, W.Ger	18.85
1904 George Eyser, USA		1960 Takashi Ono, JPN	19.35
& Anton Heida, USA	36	1964 Haruhiro Yamashita, JPN	19.60
1924 Frank Kriz, USA	9.98	1968 Makhail Voronin, USSR	19.00
1928 Eugen Mack, SWI	9.58	1972 Klaus Köste, E.Ger	18.85
1932 Savino Guglielmetti, ITA	18.03	1976 Nikolai Andrianov, USSR	19.45
1936 Alfred Schwarzmann, GER	19.20	1980 Nikolai Andrianov, USSR	19.825
1948 Paavo Aaltonen, FIN	19.55	1984 Lou Yun, CHN	19.95
1952 Viktor Chukarin, USSR	19.20	1988 Lou Yun, CHN	19.875

Pommel Horse

Year Champion	Points	Year Champion	Points
1896 Jules Zutter, SWI	—	1960 Eugen Ekman, FIN	19.375
1904 Anton Heida, USA	42	1964 Miroslav Cerar, YUG	19.525
1924 Josef Wilhelm, SWI	21.23	1968 Miroslav Cerar, YUG	19.325
1928 Hermann Hanggi, SWI	19.75	1972 Viktor Klimenko, SOV	19.125
1932 István Pelle, HUN	19.07	1976 Zoltán Magyar, HUN	19.70
1936 Konrad Frey, GER	19.333	1980 Zoltán Magyar, HUN	19.925
1948 Paavo Aaltonen, FIN	19.35	1984 Li Ning, CHN	19.95
1952 Viktor Chukarin, USSR	19.50	1988 Lyubomir Gueraskov, BUL	
1956 Boris Shakhlin, USSR	19.25	Dmitri Bilozertchev, USSR	
		& Zsolt Borkai, HUN	19.958

Rings

Year Champion	Points	Year Champion	Points
1896 Ioannis Mitropoulos, GRE	—	1960 Albert Azaryan, USSR	19.725
1904 Hermann Glass, USA	45	1964 Takuji Haytta, JPN	19.475
1924 Francesco Martino, ITA	21.553	1968 Akinori Nakayama, JPN	19.45
1928 Leon Stukelj, YUG	19.25	1972 Akinori Nakayama, JPN	19.35
1932 George Gulack, USA	18.97	1976 Nikolai Andrianov, USSR	19.65
1936 Alois Hudec, CZE	19.433	1980 Aleksandr Dityatin, USSR	19.875
1948 Karl Frei, SWI	19.80	1984 Koji Gushiken, JPN	19.85
1952 Grant Shaginyan, USSR	19.75	1988 Holger Behrendt, E.Ger	
1956 Albert Azaryan, USSR	19.35	& Dmitri Bilozertchev, USSR	19.925

Floor Exercise

Year Champion	Points	Year Champion	Points
1932 István Pelle, HUN	9.60	1968 Sawao Kato, JPN	19.475
1936 Georges Miez, SWI	18.666	1972 Nikolai Andrianov, USSR	19.175
1948 Ferenc Pataki, HUN	19.35	1976 Nikolai Andrianov, USSR	19.45
1952 William Thoresson, SWE	19.25	1980 Rolant Brückner, E.Ger	19.75
1956 Valentin Muratov, USSR	19.20	1984 Li Ning, CHN	19.925
1960 Nobuyuki Aihara, JPN	19.45	1988 Sergei Kharikov, USSR	19.925
1964 Franco Menichelli, ITA	19.45		

Men's Gymnastics (Continued)
Team Combined Exercises

Year	Champion	Points	Year	Champion	Points
1904	United States	374.43	1952	Soviet Union	574.40
1906	Norway	19.00	1956	Soviet Union	568.25
1908	Sweden	438	1960	Japan	575.20
1912	Italy	265.75	1964	Japan	577.95
1920	Italy	359.855	1968	Japan	575.90
1924	Italy	839.058	1972	Japan	571.25
1928	Switzerland	1718.625	1976	Japan	576.85
1932	Italy	541.850	1980	Soviet Union	598.60
1936	West Germany	657.430	1984	United States	591.40
1948	Finland	1358.30	1988	Soviet Union	593.35

WOMEN

All-Around

Year	Champion	Points	Year	Champion	Points
1952	Maria Gorokhovskaya, USSR	76.78	1972	Lyudmila Tourischeva, USSR	77.025
1956	Larissa Latynina, USSR	74.933	1976	Nadia Comaneci, ROM	79.275
1960	Larissa Latynina, USSR	77.031	1980	Yelena Davydova, USSR	79.15
1964	Vera Cáslavská, CZE	77.564	1984	Mary Lou Retton, USA	79.175
1968	Vera Cáslavská, CZE	78.25	1988	Elena Shushunova, USSR	79.662

Vault

Year	Champion	Points	Year	Champion	Points
1952	Yekaterina Kalinchuk, USSR	19.20	1972	Karin Janz, E.Ger	19.525
1956	Larissa Latynina, USSR	18.833	1976	Nelli Kim, USSR	19.80
1960	Margarita Nikolayeva, USSR	19.316	1980	Natalya Shaposhnikova, USSR	19.725
1964	Vera Cáslavská, CZE	19.483	1984	Ecaterina Szabó, ROM	19.875
1968	Vera Cáslavská, CZE	19.775	1988	Svetlana Boguinskaya, USSR	19.905

Uneven Bars

Year	Champion	Points	Year	Champion	Points
1952	Margit Korondi, HUN	19.40	1972	Karin Janz, E.Ger	19.675
1956	Agnes Keleti, HUN	18.966	1976	Nadia Comaneci, ROM	20.00
1960	Polina Astakhova, USSR	19.616	1980	Maxi Gnauck, E.Ger	19.875
1964	Polina Astakhova, USSR	19.332	1984	Ma Yanhong, CHN	19.95
1968	Vera Cáslavská, CZE	19.65	1988	Daniela Silivas, ROM	20.00

Balance Beam

Year	Champion	Points	Year	Champion	Points
1952	Nina Bocharova, USSR	19.22	1972	Olga Korbut, USSR	19.40
1956	Agnes Keleti, HUN	18.80	1976	Nadia Comaneci, ROM	19.95
1960	Eva Bosáková, CZE	19.283	1980	Nadia Comaneci, ROM,	19.80
1964	Vera Cástavská, CZE	19.449	1984	Simona Pauca, ROM	19.80
1968	Natalya Kuchinskaya, USSR	19.65	1988	Daniela Silivas, ROM	19.924

Floor Exercise

Year	Champion	Points	Year	Champion	Points
1952	Agnes Keleti, HUN	19.36	1972	Olga Korbut, USSR	19.575
1956	Agnes Keleti, HUN	18.733	1976	Nelli Kim, USSR	19.85
1960	Larissa Latynina, USSR	19.583	1980	Nadia Comaneci, ROM	19.875
1964	Larissa Latynina, USSR	19.599	1984	Ecaterina Szabó, ROM	19.975
1968	Vera Cáslavská, CZE	19.675	1988	Daniela Silivas, ROM	19.937

Team Combined Exercises

Year	Champion	Points	Year	Champion	Points
1928	Holland	316.75	1968	Soviet Union	382.85
1936	West Germany	506.50	1972	Soviet Union	380.50
1948	Czechoslovakia	445.45	1976	Soviet Union	466.00
1952	Soviet Union	527.03	1980	Soviet Union	394.90
1956	Soviet Union	444.800	1984	Romania	392.02
1960	Soviet Union	382.320	1988	Soviet Union	395.475
1964	Soviet Union	280.890			

Rhythmic All-Around

Year	Champion	Points	Year	Champion	Points
1984	Lori Fung, CAN	57.950	1988	Marina Lobatch, USSR	60.00

Soccer

Year	Champion, 2nd, 3rd	Year	Champion, 2nd, 3rd
1900	**Great Britain**, France, Belgium	1952	**Hungary**, Yugoslavia, Sweden
1904	**Canada**, USA I, USA II	1956	**Soviet Union**, Yugoslavia, Bulgaria
1906	**Denmark**, Smyrna (Int'l entry), Greece	1960	**Yugoslavia**, Denmark, Hungary
1908	**Great Britain**, Denmark, Holland	1964	**Hungary**, Czechoslovakia, E. Germany
1912	**Great Britain**, Denmark, Holland	1968	**Hungary**, Bulgaria, Japan
1920	**Belgium**, Spain, Holland	1972	**Poland**, Hungary, E. Germany
1924	**Uruguay**, Switzerland, Sweden	1976	**East Germany**, Poland, Soviet Union
1928	**Uruguay**, Argentina, Italy	1980	**Czechoslovakia**, E. Germany, Soviet Union
1936	**Italy**, Austria, Norway	1984	**France**, Brazil, Yugoslavia
1948	**Sweden**, Yugoslavia, Denmark	1988	**Soviet Union**, Brazil, W. Germany

Swimming
MEN
50-Meter Freestyle

Year	Champion	Time	Year	Champion	Time
1904	Zoltán Halmay, HUN	28.0	1988	Matt Biondi, USA	22.14 **(WR)**

100-Meter Freestyle

Year	Champion	Time	Year	Champion	Time
1896	Alfréd Hajós, HUN	1:22.2 **(OR)**	1952	Clarke Scholes, USA	57.4
1904	Zoltán Halmay, HUN	1:02.8	1956	Jon Henricks, AUS	55.4 **(OR)**
1906	Charles Daniels, USA	1:13.4	1960	John Devitt, AUS	55.2 **(OR)**
1908	Charles Daniels, USA	1:05.6 **(WR)**	1964	Don Schollander, USA	53.4 **(OR)**
1912	Duke Kahanamoku, USA	1:03.4	1968	Michael Wenden, AUS	52.2 **(WR)**
1920	Duke Kahanamoku, USA	1:00.4 **(WR)**	1972	Mark Spitz, USA	51.22 **(WR)**
1924	Johnny Weissmuller, USA	59.0 **(OR)**	1976	Jim Montgomery, USA	49.99 **(WR)**
1928	Johnny Weissmuller, USA	58.6 **(OR)**	1980	Jorg Woithe, E.Ger	50:40
1932	Yasuji Miyazaki, JPN	58.2	1984	Rowdy Gaines, USA	49.80 **(OR)**
1936	Ferenc Csik, HUN	57.6	1988	Matt Biondi, USA	48.63 **(OR)**
1948	Wally Ris, USA	57.3 **(OR)**			

200-Meter Freestyle

Year	Champion	Time	Year	Champion	Time
1900	Frederick Lane, AUS	2:25.2 **(OR)**	1976	Bruce Furniss, USA	1:50.29 **(WR)**
1904	Charles Daniels, USA	2:44.2	1980	Sergei Kopliakov, USSR	1:49.81 **(OR)**
1968	Michael Wenden, AUS	1:55.2 **(OR)**	1984	Michael Gross, W.Ger	1:47,44 **(WR)**
1972	Mark Spitz, USA	1:52.78 **(WR)**	1988	Duncan Armstrong, AUS	1:47.25 **(WR)**

400-Meter Freestyle

Year	Champion	Time	Year	Champion	Time
1896	Paul Neumann, AUT	8:12.6	1952	Jean Boiteux, FRA	4:30.7 **(OR)**
1904	Charles Daniels, USA	6:16.2	1956	Murray Rose, AUS	4:27.3 **(OR)**
1906	Otto Scheff, AUT	6:23.8	1960	Murray Rose, AUS	4:18.3 **(OR)**
1908	Henry Taylor, GBR	5:36.8	1964	Don Schollander, USA	4:12.2 **(WR)**
1912	George Hodgson, CAN	5:24.4	1968	Mike Burton, USA	4:09.0 **(OR)**
1920	Norman Ross, USA	5:26.8	1972	Bradford Cooper, USA*	4:00.27
1924	Johnny Weissmuller, USA	5:04.2 **(OR)**	1976	Brian Goodell, USA	3:51.93 **(WR)**
1928	Alberto Zorilla, ARG	5:01.6 **(OR)**	1980	Vladimir Salnikov, USSR	3:51.31 **(OR)**
1932	Buster Crabbe, USA	4:48.4 **(OR)**	1984	George DiCarlo, USA	3:51.23 **(OR)**
1936	Jack Medica, USA	4:44.5 **(OR)**	1988	Ewe Dassler, E.Ger	3:46.95 **(WR)**
1948	Bill Smith, USA	4:41.0 **(OR)**			

*Cooper finished second to Rick DeMont of the U.S. who was disqualified when he flunked the post-race drug test (his asthma medication was on the IOC's banned list).

1500-Meter Freestyle

Year	Champion	Time	Year	Champion	Time
1896	Alfred Hajos, HUN	18:22.2 **(OR)**	1948	James McLane, USA	19:18.5
1900	John Arthur Jarvis, GBR	13:40.2	1952	Ford Konno, USA	18:30.3 **(OR)**
1904	Emil Rausch, W.Ger	27:18.2	1956	Murray Rose, AUS	17:58.9
1906	Henry Taylor, GBR	28:28.0	1960	John Konrads, AUS	17:19.6 **(OR)**
1908	Henry Taylor, GBR	22:48.4 **(WR)**	1964	Robert Windle, AUS	17:01.7 **(OR)**
1912	George Hodgson, CAN	22:00.0 **(WR)**	1968	Mike Burton, USA	16:38.9 **(OR)**
1920	Norman Ross, USA	22:23.2	1972	Mike Burton, USA	15:52.58 **(WR)**
1924	Boy Charlton, AUS	20:06.6 **(WR)**	1976	Brian Goodell, USA	15:02.40 **(WR)**
1928	Arne Borge, SWE	19:51.8 **(OR)**	1980	Vladimir Salnikov, USSR	14:58.27 **(WR)**
1932	Kusuo Kitamura, JPN	19:12.4 **(OR)**	1984	Mike O'Brien, USA	15:05.20
1936	Noboru Terada, JPN	19:13.7	1988	Vladimir Salnikov, USSR	15:00.40

Men's Swimming (Continued)

100-Meter Backstroke

Year	Champion	Time	Year	Champion	Time
1904	Walter Brack, W.Ger	1:16.8	1952	Yoshinobu Oyakawa, USA	1:05.4 **(OR)**
1908	Arno Bieberstein, W.Ger	1:24.6 **(WR)**	1956	David Theile, AUS	1:02.2 **(OR)**
1912	Harry Hebner, USA	1:21.2	1960	David Theile, AUS	1:01.9 **(OR)**
1920	Warren Kealoha, USA	1:15.2	1968	Roland Matthes, E.Ger	58.7 **(OR)**
1924	Warren Kealoha, USA	1:13.2 **(OR)**	1972	Roland Matthes, E.Ger	56.58 **(OR)**
1928	George Kojac, USA	1:08.2 **(WR)**	1976	John Naber, USA	55.49 **(WR)**
1932	Masaji Kiyokawa, JPN	1:08.6	1980	Bengt Baron, SWE	56.33
1936	Adolf Kiefer, USA	1:05.9 **(OR)**	1984	Rick Carey, USA	55.79
1948	Allen Stack, USA	1:06.4	1988	Daichi Suzuki, JPN	55.05

200-Meter Backstroke

Year	Champion	Time	Year	Champion	Time
1900	Ernst Hoppenberg, W.Ger	2:47.0	1976	John Naber, USA	1:59.19 **(WR)**
1964	Jed Graef, USA	2:10.3 **(WR)**	1980	Sándor Wladár, HUN	2:01.93
1968	Roland Matthes, E.Ger	2:09.6 **(OR)**	1984	Rick Carey, USA	2:00.23
1972	Roland Matthes, E.Ger	2:02.82 **(EWR)**	1988	Igor Polianski, USSR	1:59.37

100-Meter Breaststroke

Year	Champion	Time	Year	Champion	Time
1968	Don McKenzie, USA	1:07.7 **(OR)**	1980	Duncan Goodhew, GBR	1:03.44
1972	Nobutaka Taguchi, JPN	1:04.94 **(WR)**	1984	Steve Lundquist, USA	1:01.65 **(WR)**
1976	John Hencken, USA	1:03.11 **(WR)**	1988	Adrian Moorhouse, GBR	1:02.04

200-Meter Breaststroke

Year	Champion	Time	Year	Champion	Time
1908	Frederick Holman, GBR	3:09.2 **(WR)**	1956	Masaru Furukawa, JPN	2:34.7 **(OR)**
1912	Walter Bathe, W.Ger	3:01.8 **(OR)**	1960	Bill Mulliken, USA	2:37.4
1920	Hakan Malmroth, SWE	3:04.4	1964	Ian O'Brien, AUS	2:27.8 **(WR)**
1924	Robert Skelton, USA	2:56.6	1968	Felipe Munoz, MEX	2:28.7
1928	Yoshiyuki Tsuruta, JPN	2:48.8 **(OR)**	1972	John Hencken, USA	2:21.55 **(WR)**
1932	Yoshiyuki Tsuruta, JPN	2:45.4	1976	David Wilkie, GBR	2:15.11 **(WR)**
1936	Tetsuo Hamuro, JPN	2:41.5 **(OR)**	1980	Robertas Zhulpa, USSR	2:15.85
1948	Joseph Verdeur, USA	2:39.3 **(OR)**	1984	Victor Davis, CAN	2:13.34 **(WR)**
1952	John Davies, AUS	2:34.4 **(OR)**	1988	Jozsef Szabo, HUN	2:13.52

100-Meter Butterfly

Year	Champion	Time	Year	Champion	Time
1968	Doug Russell, USA	55.9 **(OR)**	1980	Par Arvidsson, SWE	54.92
1972	Mark Spitz, USA	54.27 **(WR)**	1984	Michael Gross, W.Ger	53.08 **(WR)**
1976	Matt Vogel, USA	54.35	1988	Anthony Nesty, SUR	53.0 **(OR)**

200-Meter Butterfly

Year	Champion	Time	Year	Champion	Time
1956	Bill Yorzyk, USA	2:19.3 **(OR)**	1976	Mike Bruner, USA	1:59.23 **(WR)**
1960	Mike Troy, USA	2:12.8 **(WR)**	1980	Sergei Fesenko, USSR	1:59.76
1964	Kevin Berry, AUS	2:06.6 **(WR)**	1984	Jon Sieben, AUS	1:57.04 **(WR)**
1968	Carl Robie, USA	2:08.7	1988	Michael Gross, W.Ger	1:56.94 **(OR)**
1972	Mark Spitz, USA	2:00.70 **(WR)**			

200-Meter Individual Medley

Year	Champion	Time	Year	Champion	Time
1968	Charles Hickcox, USA	2:12.0 **(OR)**	1984	Alex Baumann, CAN	2:01.42 **(WR)**
1972	Gunnar Larsson, SWE	2:07.17 **(WR)**	1988	Tamas Darnyi, HUN	2:00.17 **(WR)**

400-Meter Individual Medley

Year	Champion	Time	Year	Champion	Time
1964	Richard Roth, USA	4:45.4 **(WR)**	1980	Aleksandr Sidorenko, USSR	4:22.89 **(OR)**
1968	Charles Hickcox, USA	4:48.4	1984	Alex Baumann, CAN	4:17.41 **(WR)**
1972	Gunnar Larsson, SWE	4:31.98 **(OR)**	1988	Tamas Darnyi, HUN	4:14.75 **WR)**
1976	Rod Strachan, USA	4:23.68 **(WR)**			

4x100-Meter Freestyle Relay

Year	Champion	Time	Year	Champion	Time
1964	United States	3:32.2 **(WR)**	1984	United States	3:19.03 **(WR)**
1968	United States	3:31.7 **(WR)**	1988	United States	3:16.53 **(WR)**
1972	United States	3:26.42 **(WR)**			

4x200-Meter Freestyle Relay

Year	Champion	Time	Year	Champion	Time
1906	Hungary	16:52.4	1956	Australia	8:23.6 (WR)
1908	Great Britain	10:55.6 (WR)	1960	United States	8:10.2 (WR)
1912	Australia/New Zealand	10:11.6 (WR)	1964	United States	7:52.1 (WR)
1920	United States	10:04.4 (WR)	1968	United States	7:52.33
1924	United States	9:53.4 (WR)	1972	United States	7:35.78 (WR)
1928	United States	9:36.2 (WR)	1976	United States	7:23.22 (WR)
1932	Japan	8:58.4 (WR)	1980	Soviet Union	7:23.50
1936	Japan	8:51.5 (WR)	1984	United States	7:15.69 (WR)
1948	United States	8:46.0 (WR)	1988	United States	7:12.51 (WR)
1952	United States	8:31.1 (OR)			

4x100-Meter Medley Relay

Year	Champion	Time	Year	Champion	Time
1960	United States	4:05.4 (WR)	1976	United States	3:42.22 (WR)
1964	United States	3:58.4 (WR)	1980	Australia	3:45.70
1968	United States	3:54.9 (WR)	1984	United States	3:39.30 (WR)
1972	United States	3:48.16 (WR)	1988	United States	3:36.93 (WR)

WOMEN

50-Meter Freestyle

Year	Champion	Time
1988	Kristin Otto, E.Ger	25.49 (OR)

100-Meter Freestyle

Year	Champion	Time	Year	Champion	Time
1912	Fanny Durack, AUS	1:22.2	1960	Dawn Fraser, AUS	1:01.2 (OR)
1920	Ethelda Bleibtrey, USA	1:13.6 (WR)	1964	Dawn Fraser, AUS	59.5 (OR)
1924	Ethel Lackie, USA	1:12.4	1968	Jan Henne, USA	1:00.0
1928	Albina Osipowich, USA	1:11.0 (OR)	1972	Sandra Neilson, USA	58.59 (OR)
1932	Helene Madison, USA	1:06.8 (OR)	1976	Kornelia Ender, E.Ger	55.65 (WR)
1936	Rie Mastenbroek, HOL	1:05.9 (OR)	1980	Barbara Krause, E.Ger	54.79 (WR)
1948	Greta Andersen, DEN	1:06.3	1984	Nancy Hogshead, USA	55.92
1952	Katalin Szöke, HUN	1:06.8		& Carrie Steinseifer, USA	55.92
1956	Dawn Fraser, AUS	1:02.0 (WR)	1988	Kristin Otto, E.Ger	54.93

200-Meter Freestyle

Year	Champion	Time	Year	Champion	Time
1968	Debbie Meyer, USA	2:10.5 (OR)	1980	Barbara Krause, E.Ger	1:58.33 (OR)
1972	Shane Gould, AUS	2:03.56 (WR)	1984	Mary Wayte, USA	1:59.23
1976	Kornelia Ender, E.Ger	1:59.26 (WR)	1988	Heike Friedrich, E.Ger	1:57.65 (OR)

400-Meter Freestyle

Year	Champion	Time	Year	Champion	Time
1920	Ethelda Bleibtrey, USA	4:34.0 (WR)	1960	Chris Von Saltza, USA	4:50.6 (OR)
1924	Martha Norelius, USA	6:02.2 (OR)	1964	Ginny Duenkel, USA	4:43.3 (OR)
1928	Martha Norelius, USA	5:42.8 (WR)	1968	Debbie Meyer, USA	4:31.8 (OR)
1932	Helene Madison, USA	5:28.5 (WR)	1972	Shane Gould, AUS	4:19.44 (WR)
1936	Rie Mastenbroek, HOL	5:26.4 (OR)	1976	Petra Thumer, E.Ger	4:09.89 (WR)
1948	Ann Curtis, USA	5:17.8 (OR)	1980	Ines Diers, E.Ger	4:08.76 (OR)
1952	Valeria Gyenge, HUN	5:12.1 (OR)	1984	Tiffany Cohen, USA	4:07.10 (OR)
1956	Lorraine Crapp, AUS	4:54.6 (OR)	1988	Janet Evans, USA	4:03.85 (WR)

800-Meter Freestyle Relay

Year	Champion	Time	Year	Champion	Time
1968	Debbie Meyer, USA	9:24.0 (OR)	1980	Michelle Ford, AUS	8:28.90 (OR)
1972	Keena Rothhammer, USA	8:53.68 (WR)	1984	Tiffany Cohen, USA	8:24.95 (OR)
1976	Petra Thümer, E.Ger	8:37.14 (WR)	1988	Janet Evans, USA	8:20.20 (OR)

100-Meter Backstroke

Year	Champion	Time	Year	Champion	Time
1924	Sybil Bauer, USA	1:23.2 (OR)	1964	Cathy Ferguson, USA	1:07.7 (WR)
1928	Maria Braun, HOL	1:22.0	1968	Kaye Hall, USA	1:06.2 (WR)
1932	Eleanor Holm, USA	1:19.4	1972	Melissa Belote, USA	1:05.78 (WR)
1936	Nida Senff, HOL	1:18.9	1976	Ulrike Richter, E.Ger	1:01.83 (OR)
1948	Karen-Margrete Harup, DEN	1:14.4 (OR)	1980	Rica Reinisch, E.Ger	1:00.86 (WR)
1952	Joan Harrison, SAF	1:14.3	1984	Theresa Andrews, USA	1:02.55
1956	Judith Grinham, GBR	1:12.9 (OR)	1988	Kristin Otto, E.Ger	1:00.89
1960	Lynn Burke, USA	1:09.3 (OR)			

Women's Swimming (Continued)

200-Meter Backstroke

Year Champion	Time	Year Champion	Time
1968 Lillian Watson, USA	2:24.8 (OR)	1980 Rica Reinisch, E.Ger	2:11.77 (WR)
1972 Melissa Belote, USA	2:19.19 (WR)	1984 Jolanda de Rover, HOL	2:12.38
1976 Ulrike Richter, E.Ger	2:13.43 (OR)	1988 Krisztina Egerszegi, HUN	2:09.29 (OR)

100-Meter Breaststroke

Year Champion	Time	Year Champion	Time
1968 Djurdjica Bjedov, YUG	1:15.8 (OR)	1980 Ute Geweniger, E.Ger	1:10.22
1972 Cathy Carr, USA	1:13.58 (WR)	1984 Petra van Staveren, HOL	1:09.88 (OR)
1976 Hannelore Anke, E.Ger	1:11.16	1988 Tania Dangalakova, BUL	1:07.95 (OR)

200-Meter Breaststroke

Year Champion	Time	Year Champion	Time
1924 Lucy Morton, GBR	3:33.2 (OR)	1964 Galina Prozumenshikova, USSR	2:46.4 (OR)
1928 Hilde Schrader, W.Ger	3:12.6	1968 Sharon Wichman, USA	2:44.4 (OR)
1932 Clare Dennis, AUS	3:06.3 (OR)	1972 Beverley Whitfield, AUS	2:41.71 (OR)
1936 Hideko Maehata, JPN	3:03.6	1976 Marina Koshevaia, USSR	2:33.35 (WR)
1948 Petronella van Vliet, HOL	2:57.2	1980 Lina Kaciusyte, USSR	2:29.54 (OR)
1952 Eva Szekely, HUN	2:51.7 (OR)	1984 Anne Ottenbrite, CAN	2:30.38
1956 Ursula Happe, W.Ger	2:53.1 (OR)	1988 Silke Hoerner, E.Ger	2:26.71 (WR)
1960 Anita Lonsbrough, GBR	2:49.5 (WR)		

100-Meter Butterfly

Year Champion	Time	Year Champion	Time
1956 Shelly Mann, USA	1:11.0 (OR)	1976 Kornelia Ender, E.Ger	1:00.13 (=WR)
1960 Carolyn Schuler, USA	1:09.5 (OR)	1980 Caren Metschuck, E.Ger	1:00.42
1964 Sharon Stouder, USA	1:04.7 (WR)	1984 Mary T. Meagher, USA	59.26
1968 Lyn McClements, AUS	1:05.5	1988 Kristin Otto, E.Ger	59.00 (OR)
1972 Mayumi Aoki, JPN	1:03.34 (WR)		

200-Meter Butterfly

Year Champion	Time	Year Champion	Time
1968 Ada Kok, HOL	2:24.7 (OR)	1980 Ines Geissler, E.Ger	2:10.44 (OR)
1972 Karen Moe, USA	2:15.57 (WR)	1984 Mary T. Meagher, USA	2:06.90 (OR)
1976 Andrea Pollack, E.Ger	2:11.41 (OR)	1988 Kathleen Nord, E.Ger	2:09.51

200-Meter Individual Medley

Year Champion	Time	Year Champion	Time
1968 Claudia Kolb, USA	2:24.7 (OR)	1984 Tracy Caulkins, USA	2:12.64 (OR)
1972 Shane Gould, AUS	2:23.07 (WR)	1988 Daniela Hunger, E.Ger	2:12.59 (OR)

400-Meter Individual Medley

Year Champion	Time	Year Champion	Time
1968 Donna De Varona, USA	5:18.7 (OR)	1980 Petra Schneider, E.Ger	4:36.29 (WR)
1968 Claudia Kolb, USA	5:08.5 (OR)	1984 Tracy Caulkins, USA	4:39.24
1972 Gail Neall, AUS	5:02.97 (WR)	1988 Janet Evans, USA	4:37.76
1976 Ulrike Tauber, E.Ger	4:42.77 (WR)		

4x100-Meter Freestyle Relay

Year Champion	Time	Year Champion	Time
1912 Great Britain	5:52.8 (WR)	1960 United States	4:08.9 (WR)
1920 United States	5:11.6 (WR)	1964 United States	4:03.8 (WR)
1924 United States	4:58.8 (WR)	1968 United States	4:02.5 (OR)
1928 United States	4:47.6 (WR)	1972 United States	3:55.19 (WR)
1932 United States	4:38.0 (WR)	1976 United States	3:44.82 (WR)
1936 Holland	4:36.0 (OR)	1980 East Germany	3:42.71 (WR)
1948 United States	4:29.2 (OR)	1984 United States	3:43.43
1952 Hungary	4:24.4 (WR)	1988 East Germany	3:40.63 (OR)
1956 Australia	4:17.1 (WR)		

4x100-Meter Medley Relay

Year	Champion	Time	Year	Champion	Time
1960	United States	4:41.1 (WR)	1976	East Germany	4:07.95 (WR)
1964	United States	4:33.9 (WR)	1980	East Germany	4:06.67 (WR)
1968	United States	4:28.3 (OR)	1984	United States	4:08.34
1972	United States	4:20.75 (WR)	1988	East Germany	4:03.74 (OR)

Synchronized Swimming — Solo

Year	Champion	Points	Year	Champion	Points
1984	Tracie Ruiz, USA	198.467	1988	Carolyn Waldo, CAN	200.15

Synchronized Swimming — Duet

Year	Champion	Points	Year	Champion	Points
1984	Tracie Ruiz & Candy Costie, USA	195.584	1988	Carolyn Waldo & Michelle Cameron, CAN	197.717

Tennis

MEN

Singles

Year	Champion		Year	Champion	
1896	John Boland	Great Britain/Ireland	1908	(Indoor) Arthur Gore	Great Britain
1900	Hugh Doherty,	Great Britain	1912	Charles Winslow	South Africa
1904	Beals Wright	United States	1912	(Indoor) André Gobert	France
1906	Max Decugis	France	1920	Louis Raymond	South Africa
1908	Josiah Ritchie	Great Britain	1924	Vincent Richards	United States
			1988	Miloslav Mecir	Czechoslovakia

Doubles

Year	Champions	Year	Champions
1896	John Boland, IRL & Fritz Traun, GER	1912	Charles Winslow & Harold Kitson, SAF
1900	Hugh and Reggie Doherty, GBR	1912	(Indoor) André Gobert & Maurice Germot, FRA
1904	Edgar Leonard & Beals Wright, USA	1920	Noel Turnbull & Max Woosnam, GBR
1906	Max Decugis & Maurice Germot, FRA	1924	Vincent Richards & Frank Hunter, USA
1908	George Hillyard & Reggie Doherty, GRB	1988	Ken Flach & Robert Seguso, USA
1908	(Indoor) Arthur Gore & Herbert Barrett, GBR		

WOMEN

Singles

Year	Champion		Year	Champion	
1900	Charlotte Cooper	Great Britain	1912	Edith Hannam	Great Britain
1906	Esmee Simiriotu	Greece	1920	Suzanne Lenglen	France
1908	Dorothy Chambers	Great Britain	1924	Helen Wills	United States
1908	Gwendoline Eastlake-Smith	Great Britain	1988	Steffi Graf	West Germany
1912	Marguerite Broquedis	France			

Doubles

Year	Champions	Year	Champions
1920	Winifred McNair & Kitty McKane, GBR	1988	Pam Shriver & Zina Garrison, USA
1924	Hazel Wightman & Helen Wills, USA		

Track and Field

MEN

100 Meters

Year	Champion	Time	Year	Champion	Time
1886	Thomas Burke, USA	12.0	1948	Harrison Dillard, USA	10.3 (=OR)
1900	Frank Jarvis, USA	11.0	1952	Lindy Remigino, USA	10.4
1904	Archie Hahn, USA	11.0	1956	Bobby Morrow, USA	10.5
1906	Archie Hahn, USA	11.2	1960	Armin Hary, GER	10.2 (OR)
1908	Reggie Walker, SAF	10.8 (=OR)	1964	Bob Hayes, USA	10.0 (=WR)
1912	Ralph Craig, USA	10.8	1968	Jim Hines, USA	9.95 (WR)
1920	Charley Paddock, USA	10.8	1972	Valery Borzov, USSR	10.14
1924	Harold Abrahams, GBR	10.6 (=OR)	1976	Hasely Crawford, TRI	10.06
1928	Percy Williams, CAN	10.8	1980	Allan Wells, GBR	10.25
1932	Eddie Tolan, USA	10.3 (OR)	1984	Carl Lewis, USA	9.99
1936	Jesse Owens, USA	10.3	1988	Carl Lewis, USA	9.92 (WR)

Men's Track and Field (Continued)

200 Meters

Year	Champion	Time		Year	Champion	Time
1900	John Walter Tewksbury, USA	22.2		1952	Andrew Stanfield, USA	20.7
1904	Archie Hahn, USA	21.6 (OR)		1956	Bobby Morrow, USA	20.6 (OR)
1908	Bobby Kerr, CAN	22.6		1960	Livio Berruti, ITA	20.5 (=WR)
1912	Ralph Craig, USA	21.7		1964	Henry Carr, USA	20.3 (OR)
1920	Allen Woodring, USA	22.0		1968	Tommie Smith, USA	19.83 (WR)
1924	Jackson Scholz, USA	21.6		1972	Valery Borzov, USSR	20.00
1928	Percy Williams, CAN	21.8		1976	Donald Quarrie, JAM	20.23
1932	Eddie Tolan, USA	21.2 (OR)		1980	Pietro Mennea, ITA	20.19
1936	Jesse Owens, USA	20.7 (OR)		1984	Carl Lewis, USA	19.80 (OR)
1948	Mel Patton, USA	21.1		1988	Joe DeLoach, USA	19.75 (OR)

400 Meters

Year	Champion	Time		Year	Champion	Time
1896	Tom Burke, USA	54.2		1948	Arthur Wint, JAM	46.2
1890	Maxey Long, USA	49.4 (OR)		1952	George Rhoden, JAM	45.9
1904	Harry Hillman, USA	49.2 (OR)		1956	Charley Jenkins, USA	46.7
1906	Paul Pilgrim, USA	53.2		1960	Otis Davis, USA	44.9 (WR)
1908	Wyndham Halswelle, GBR	50.0		1964	Mike Larrabee, USA	45.1
1912	Charlie Reidpath, USA	48.2 (OR)		1968	Lee Evans, USA	43.86 (WR)
1920	Bevil Rudd, SAF	49.6		1972	Vince Matthews, USA	44.66
1924	Eric Liddell, GBR	47.6 (OR)		1976	Alberto Juantorena, CUB	44.26
1928	Raymond Barbuti, USA	47.8		1980	Viktor Markin, USSR	44.60
1932	Bill Carr, USA	46.2 (WR)		1984	Alonzo Babers, USA	44.27
1936	Archie Williams, USA	46.5		1988	Steve Lewis, USA	43.87

800 Meters

Year	Champion	Time		Year	Champion	Time
1896	Teddy Flack, AUS	2:11.0		1948	Mal Whittfield, USA	1:49.2 (OR)
1900	Alfred Tysoe, BFR	2:01.2		1952	Mal Whittfield, USA	1:49.2 (=OR)
1904	James Lightbody, USA	1:56.0 (OR)		1956	Tom Courtney, USA	1:47.7 (OR)
1906	Paul Pilgrim, USA	2:01.5		1960	Peter Snell, NZE	1:46.3 (OR)
1908	Mel Sheppard, USA	1:52.8 (WR)		1964	Peter Snell, NZE	1:45.1 (OR)
1912	Ted Meredith, USA	1:51.9 (WR)		1968	Ralph Doubell, AUS	1:44.3 (=WR)
1920	Albert Hill, GBR	1:53.4		1972	Dave Wottle, USA	1:45.9
1924	Douglas Lowe, GRB	1:52.4		1976	Alberto Juantorena, CUB	1:43.50 (WR)
1928	Douglas Lowe, GRB	1:51.8 (OR)		1980	Steve Ovett, GBR	1:45.4
1932	Tommy Hampson, GBR	1:49.7 (WR)		1984	Joaquim Cruz, BRA	1:43.00 (OR)
1936	John Woodruff, USA	1:52.9		1988	Paul Ereng, KEN	1:43.45

1500 Meters

Year	Champion	Time		Year	Champion	Time
1896	Teddy Flack, AUS	4:33.2		1948	Henry Eriksson, SWE	3:49.8
1900	Charles Bennett, GBR	4:06.2 (WR)		1952	Josy Barthel, LUX	3:45.1 (OR)
1904	James Lightbody, USA	4:05.4 (WR)		1956	Ron Delany, IRL	3:41.2 (OR)
1906	James Lightbody, USA	4:12.0		1960	Herb Elliott, AUS	3:35.6 (WR)
1908	Mel Sheppard, USA	4:03.4 (OR)		1964	Peter Snell, NZE	3:38.1
1912	Arnold Jackson, GBR	3:56.8 (OR)		1968	Kip Keino, KEN	3:34.9 (OR)
1920	Albert Hill, GBR	4:01.8		1972	Pekkha Vasala, FIN	3:36.3
1924	Paavo Nurmi, FIN	3:53.6 (OR)		1976	John Walker, NZE	3:39.17
1928	Harry Larva, FIN	3:53.2 (OR)		1980	Sebastian Coe, GBR	3:38.4
1932	Luigi Beccali, ITA	3:51.2 (OR)		1984	Sebastian Coe, GBR	3:32.53 (OR)
1936	John Lovelock, NZE	3:47.8 (WR)		1988	Peter Rono, KEN	3:35.96

5,000 Meters

Year	Champion	Time		Year	Champion	Time
1912	Hannes Kolehmainen, FIN	14:36.6 (WR)		1960	Murray Halberg, NZE	13:43.4
1920	Joseph Guillemot, FRA	14:55.6		1964	Bob Schul, USA	13:48.8
1924	Paavo Nurmi, FIN	14:31.2 (OR)		1968	Mohamed Gammoudi, TUN	14:05.0
1928	Ville Ritola, FIN	14:38.0		1972	Lasse Viren, FIN	13:26.4 (OR)
1932	Lauri Lehtinen, FIN	14:30.0 (OR)		1976	Lasse Viren, FIN	13:24.76
1936	Gunnar Höckert, FIN	14:22.2 (OR)		1980	Miruts Yifter, ETH	13:21.0
1948	Gaston Reiff, BEL	14:17.6 (OR)		1984	Said Aouita, MOR	13:05.59 (OR)
1952	Emil Zátopek, CZE	14:06.6 (OR)		1988	John Ngugi, KEN	13:11.70
1956	Vladimir Kuts, USSR	13:39.6 (OR)				

10,000 Meters

Year	Champion	Time	Year	Champion	Time
1912	Hannes Kolehmainen, FIN	31:20.8	1960	Pyotr Bolotnikov, USSR	28:32.2 (OR)
1920	Paavo Nurmi, FIN	31:45.8	1964	Billy Mills, USA	28:24.4 (OR)
1924	Ville Ritola, FIN	30:23.2 (WR)	1968	Naftali Temu, KEN	29:27.4
1928	Paavo Nurmi, FIN	30:18.8 (OR)	1972	Lasse Viren, FIN	27:38.4 (WR)
1932	Janusz Kusocinski, POL	30:11.4 (OR)	1976	Lasse Viren, FIN	27:40.38
1936	Ilmari Salminen, FIN	30:15.4	1980	Miruts Yifter, ETH	27:42.7
1948	Emil Zátopek, CZE	29:59.6 (OR)	1984	Alberto Cova, ITA	27:47.54
1952	Emil Zátopek, CZE	29:17.0 (OR)	1988	Brahim Boutaib, MOR	27:21.46
1956	Vladimir Kuts, USSR	28:45.6 (OR)			

Marathon

Year	Champion	Time	Year	Champion	Time
1896	Spiridon Louis, GRE	2:58:50	1948	Delfo Cabrera, ARG	2:34:51.6
1900	Michel Théato, FRA	2:59:45	1952	Emil Zátopek, CZE	2:23:03.2 (OR)
1904	Thomas Hicks, USA	3:28:63	1956	Alain Mimoun, FRA	2:25:00.0
1906	Billy Sherring, CAN	2:51:23.6	1960	Abebe Bikila, ETH	2:15:16.2 (WB)
1908	John Hayes, USA	2:55:18.4 (OR)	1964	Abebe Bikila, ETH	2:12:11.2 (WB)
1912	Kenneth McArthur, SAF	2:36:54.8	1968	Mamo Wolde, ETH	2:20:26.4
1920	Hannes Kolehmainen, FIN	2:32:35.8 (WB)	1972	Frank Shorter, USA	2:12:19.8
1924	Albin Stenroos, FIN	2:41:22.6	1976	Waldemar Cierpinski, E.Ger	2:09:55.0 (OR)
1928	Boughêra El Ouafi, FRA	2:32:57.0	1980	Waldemar Cierpinski, E.Ger	2:11:03.0
1932	Juan Carlos Zabala, ARG	2:31:36.0 (OR)	1984	Carlos Lopes, POR	2:09:21.0 (OR)
1936	Kee-Chung Sohn,* JPN	2:29:19.2 (OR)	1988	Gelindo Bordin, ITA	2:10:32

*Sohn was a Korean, but forced to compete for Japan, which occupied Korea at the time.
Note: Marathon distances—40,000 meters (1896,1904); 40,260 meters (1900); 41,860 meters (1906); 42,195 meters (1908 and since 1924); 40,200 meters (1912); 42,750 meters (1920). Current distance of 42,195 meters measures 26 miles, 385 yards.

110-Meter Hurdles

Year	Champion	Time	Year	Champion	Time
1896	Thomas Curtis, USA	17.6	1948	William Porter, USA	13.9 (OR)
1900	Alvin Kraenzlein, USA	15.4 (OR)	1952	Harrison Dillard, USA	13.7 (OR)
1904	Frederick Schule, USA	16.0	1956	Lee Calhoun, USA	13.5 (OR)
1906	Robert Leavitt, USA	16.2	1960	Lee Calhoun, USA	13.8
1908	Forrest Smithson, USA	15.0 (WR)	1964	Hayes Jones, USA	13.6
1912	Frederick Kelly, USA	15.1	1968	Willie Davenport, USA	13.3 (OR)
1920	Earl Thomson, CAN	14.8 (WR)	1972	Rod Milburn, USA	13.24 (=WR)
1924	Daniel Kinsey, USA	15.0	1976	Guy Drut, FRA	13.30
1928	Syd Atkinson, SAF	14.8	1980	Thomas Munkelt, E.Ger	13.39
1932	George Saling, USA	14.6	1984	Roger Kingdom, USA	13.20 (OR)
1936	Forrest (Spec) Towns, USA	14.2	1988	Roger Kingdom, USA	12.98 (OR)

400-Meter Hurdles

Year	Champion	Time	Year	Champion	Time
1900	John Walter Tewksbury, USA	57.6	1956	Glenn Davis, USA	50.1 (=OR)
1904	Harry Hillman, USA	53.0	1960	Glenn Davis, USA	49.3 (=OR)
1908	Charles Bacon, USA	55.0 (WR)	1964	Rex Cawley, USA	49.6
1920	Frank Loomis, USA	54.0 (WR)	1968	David Hemery, GBR	48.12 (WR)
1924	Morgan Taylor, USA	52.6	1972	John Akii-Bua, UGA	47.82 (WR)
1928	David Burghley, GBR	53.4 (OR)	1976	Edwin Moses, USA	47.64 (WR)
1932	Bob Tisdall, IRL	51.7	1980	Volker Beck, E.Ger	48.70
1936	Glenn Hardin, USA	52.4	1984	Edwin Moses, USA	47.75
1948	Roy Cochran, USA	51.1 (OR)	1988	Andre Phillips, USA	47.19 (OR)
1952	Charles Moore, USA	50.8 (OR)			

3,000 Meter-Steeplechase

Year	Champion	Time	Year	Champion	Time
1900	George Orton, CAN/USA	7:34.4	1956	Chris Brasher, GBR	8:41.2 (OR)
1904	James Lightbody, USA	7:39.6	1960	Zdzislaw Krzyszkowiak, POL	8:34.2 (OR)
1908	Arthur Russell, GBR	10:47.8	1964	Gaston Roelants, BEL	8:30.8 (OR)
1920	Percy Hodge, GBR	10:00.4 (OR)	1968	Amos Biwott, KEN	8:51.0
1924	Ville Ritola, FIN	9:33.6 (OR)	1972	Kip Keino, KEN	8:23.6 (OR)
1928	Toivo Loukola, FIN	9:21.8 (WR)	1976	Anders Gärderud, SWE	8:08.2 (WR)
1932	Volmari Iso-Hollo, FIN*	10:33.4	1980	Bronislaw Malinowski, POL	8:09.7
1936	Volmari Iso-Hollo, FIN	9:03.8 (WR)	1984	Julius Korir, KEN	8:11.80
1948	Thore Sjöstrand, SWE	9:04.6	1988	Julius Kariuki, KEN	8:05.51 (OR)
1952	Horace Ashenfelter, USA	8:45.4 (WR)			

*Iso-Hollo ran one extra lap due to lap counter's mistake.

Men's Track & Field (Continued)
4x100-Meter Relay

Year	Champion	Time	Year	Champion	Time
1912	Great Britain	42.4 (OR)	1960	Germany	39.5 (=WR)
1920	United States	42.2 (WR)	1964	United States	39.0 (WR)
1924	United States	41.0 (=WR)	1968	United States	38.2 (WR)
1928	United States	41.0 (=WR)	1972	United States	38.19 (=WR)
1932	United States	40.0 (WR)	1976	United States	38.33
1936	United States	39.8 (WR)	1980	Soviet Union	38.26
1948	United States	40.6	1984	United States	37.83 (WR)
1952	United States	40.1	1988	Soviet Union	38.19
1956	United States	39.5 (WR)			

4x400-Meter Relay

Year	Champion	Time	Year	Champion	Time
1908	United States	3:29.4	1956	United States	3:04.8
1912	United States	3:16.6 (WR)	1960	United States	3:02.2 (WR)
1920	Great Britain	3:22.2	1964	United States	3:00.7 (WR)
1924	United States	3:16.0 (WR)	1968	United States	2:56.16 (WR)
1928	United States	3:14.2 (WR)	1972	Kenya	2:59.8
1932	United States	3:08.2 (WR)	1976	United States	2:58.65
1936	Great Britain	3:09.0	1980	Soviet Union	3:01.1
1948	United States	3:10.4 (WR)	1984	United States	2:57.91
1952	Jamaica	3:03.9 (WR)	1988	United States	2:56.16 (=WR)

20,000-Meter Walk

Year	Champion	Time	Year	Champion	Time
1956	Leonid Spirin, USSR	1:31:27.4	1976	Daniel Bautista Rocha, MEX	1:24:40.6 (OR)
1960	Vladimir Golubnichiy, USSR	1:34:07.2	1980	Maurizio Damilano, ITA	1:23:35.5 (OR)
1964	Kenneth Matthews, GBR	1:29:34.0 (OR)	1984	Ernesto Canto, MEX	1:23:13.0 (OR)
1968	Vladimir Golubnichiy, USSR	1:33:58.4	1988	Josef Pribilinec, CZE	1:19:57.0 OR)
1972	Peter Frenkel, E.Ger	1:26:42.4 (OR)			

50,000-Meter Walk

Year	Champion	Time	Year	Champion	Time
1932	Thomas Green, GBR	4:50:10	1964	Abdon Pamich, ITA	4:11:12.4 (OR)
1936	Harold Whitlock, GBR	4:30:41.4 (OR)	1968	Christoph Höhne, E.Ger	4:20:13.6
1948	John Ljunggren, SWE	4:41.52	1972	Bernd Kannenberg, W.Ger	3:56:11.6 (OR)
1952	Giuseppe Dordoni, ITA	4:28:07.8 (OR)	1980	Hartwig Gauder, E.Ger	3:49:24.0 (OR)
1956	Norman Read, NZE	4:30:42.8	1984	Raúl González, MEX	3:47:26 (OR)
1960	Don Thompson, GBR	4:25:30.0 (OR)	1988	Vyacheslav Ivanenko, USSR	3:38:29.0 (OR)

High Jump

Year	Winner	Height	Year	Winner	Height
1896	Ellery Clark, USA	5-11¼	1948	John Winter, AUS	6-6
1900	Irving Baxter, USA	6-2¾ (OR)	1952	Walter Davis, USA	6-8½ (OR)
1904	Sam Jones, USA	5-11	1956	Charley Dumas, USA	6-11½ (OR)
1906	Cornelius Leahy, GBR/IRL	5-10	1960	Robert Shavlakadze, USSR	7-1 (OR)
1908	Harry Porter, USA	6-3 (OR)	1964	Valery Brumel, USSR	7-1¾ (OR)
1912	Alma Richards, USA	6-4 (OR)	1968	Dick Fosbury, USA	7-4¼ (OR)
1920	Richmond Landon, USA	6-4 (=OR)	1972	Yuri Tarmak, USSR	7-3¾
1924	Harold Osborn, USA	6-6 (OR)	1976	Jacek Wszola, POL	7-4½ (OR)
1928	Robert King, USA	6-4½	1980	Gerd Wessig, E.Ger	7-8¾ (WR)
1932	Duncan McNaughton, CAN	6-5½	1984	Dietmar Mögenburg, W.Ger	7-8½
1936	Cornelius Johnson, USA	6-8 (OR)	1988	Guennadi Avdeenko, USSR	7-9½ (OR)

Pole Vault

Year	Champion	Height	Year	Champion	Height
1896	William Hoyt, USA	10-10	1948	Guinn Smith, USA	14-1¼
1900	Irving Baxter, USA	10-10	1952	Bob Richards, USA	14-11 (OR)
1904	Charles Dvorak, USA	11-5¾	1956	Bob Richards, USA	14-11½ (OR)
1906	Fernand Gonder, FRA	11-5¾	1960	Don Bragg, USA	15-5 (OR)
1908	Edward Cooke, USA.		1964	Fred Hansen, USA	16-8¾ (OR)
	& Alfred Gilbert, USA	12-2 (OR)	1968	Bob Seagren, USA	17-8½ (OR)
1912	Harry Babcock, USA	12-11½ (OR)	1972	Wolfgang Nordwig, E.Ger	18-½ (OR)
1920	Frank Foss, USA	13-5 (WR)	1976	Tadeusz Slusarski, POL	18-½ (=OR)
1924	Lee Barnes, USA	12-11½	1980	Wladyslaw Kozakiewicz, POL	18-11½ (WR)
1928	Sabin Carr, USA	13-9¼ (OR)	1984	Pierre Quinon, FRA	18-10¼
1932	Bill Miller, USA	14-1¾ (OR)	1988	Sergei Bubka, USSR	19-9¼ (OR)
1936	Earle Meadows, USA	14-3¼ (OR)			

Long Jump

Year	Champion	Distance	Year	Champion	Distance
1896	Ellery Clark, USA	20-10	1948	Willie Steele, USA	25-8
1900	Alvin Kraenzlein, USA	23-6¾ (OR)	1952	Jerome Biffle, USA	24-10
1904	Meyer Prinstein, USA	24-1 (OR)	1956	Gregory Bell, USA	25-8¼
1906	Meyer Prinstein, USA	23-7½	1960	Ralph Boston, USA	26-7¾ (OR)
1908	Frank Irons, USA	24-6½ (OR)	1964	Lynn Davies, GBR	26-5¾
1912	Albert Gutterson, USA	24-11¼ (OR)	1968	Bob Beamon, USA	29-2½ (WR)
1920	William Petersson, SWE	23-5½	1972	Randy Williams, USA	27-½
1924	DeHart Hubbard, USA	24-5	1976	Arnie Robinson, USA	27-4¾
1928	Edward Hamm, USA	25-4½ (OR)	1980	Lutz Dombrowski, E.Ger	28-¼
1932	Ed Gordon, USA	25-¾	1984	Carl Lewis, USA	28-¼
1936	Jesse Owens, USA	26-5½ (OR)	1988	Carl Lewis, USA	28-7¼

Triple Jump

Year	Champion	Distance	Year	Champion	Distance
1896	James Connolly, USA	44-11¾	1948	Arne Ahman, SWE	50-6¼
1900	Meyer Prinstein, USA	47-5¾ (OR)	1952	Adhemar daSilva, BRA	53-2¾ (WR)
1904	Meyer Prinstein, USA	47-1	1956	Adhemar daSilva, BRA	53-7¾ (OR)
1906	Peter O'Connor, GBR/IRL	46-2¼	1960	Józef Schmidt, POL	55-2
1908	Timothy Ahearne, GBR/IRL	48-11¼ (OR)	1964	Józef Schmidt, POL	55-3½ (OR)
1912	Gustaf Lindblom, SWE	48-5¼	1968	Viktor Saneyev, USSR	57-¾ (WR)
1920	Vilho Tuulos, FIN	47-7	1972	Viktor Saneyev, USSR	56-11¼
1924	Nick Winter, AUS	50-11¼	1976	Viktor Saneyev, USSR	56-8¾
1928	Mikio Oda, JPN	49-11	1980	Jaak Uudmäe, USSR	56-11¼
1932	Chuhei Nambu, JPN	51-7 (WR)	1984	Al Joyner, USA	56-7½
1936	Naoto Tajima, JPN	52-6 (WR)	1988	Hristo Markov, BUL	57-9¼ (OR)

Shot Put

Year	Champion	Distance	Year	Champion	Distance
1896	Robert Garrett, USA	36-9¾	1948	Wilbur Thompson, USA	56-2 (OR)
1900	Richard Sheldon, USA	46-3¼ (OR)	1952	Parry O'Brien, USA	57-1½ (OR)
1904	Ralph Rose, USA	48-7 (WR)	1956	Parry O'Brien, USA	60-11¼ (OR)
1906	Martin Sheridan, USA	40-5¼	1960	Bill Nieder, USA	64-6¾ (OR)
1908	Ralph Rose, USA	46-7½	1964	Dallas Long, USA	66-8½ (OR)
1912	Patrick McDonald, USA	50-4 (OR)	1968	Randy Matson, USA	67-4¾
1920	Ville Pörhölä, FIN	48-7¼	1972	Wladyslaw Komar, POL	69-6 (OR)
1924	Bud Houser, USA	49-2¼	1976	Udo Beyer, E.Ger	69-¾
1928	John Kuck, USA	52-¾ (WR)	1980	Vladimir Kiselyo, USSR	70-½ (OR)
1932	Leo Sexton, USA	52-6 (OR)	1984	Alessandro Andrei, ITA	69-9
1936	Hans Woellke, GER	53-1¾ (OR)	1988	Ulf Timmermann, E.Ger	73-8¾ (OR)

Discus Throw

Year	Champion	Distance	Year	Champion	Distance
1896	Robert Garrett, USA	95-7½	1948	Adolfo Consolini, ITA	173-2 (OR)
1900	Rodulf Bauer, HUN	118-3 (OR)	1952	Sim Iness, USA	180-6 (OR)
1904	Martin Sheridan, USA	128-10½ (OR)	1956	Al Oerter, USA	184-11 (OR)
1906	Martin Sheridan, USA	136 ft	1960	Al Oerter, USA	194-2 (OR)
1908	Martin Sheridan, USA	134-2 (OR)	1964	Al Oerter, USA	200-1 (OR)
1912	Armas Taipale, FIN	148-3 (OR)	1968	Al Oerter, USA	212-6 (OR)
1920	Elmer Niklander, FIN	146-7	1972	Ludvik Daněk, CZE	211-3
1924	Bud Houser, USA	151-4 (OR)	1976	Mac Wilkins, USA	221-5
1928	Bud Houser, USA	155-3 (OR)	1980	Viktor Rashchupkin, USSR	218-8
1932	John Anderson, USA	162-4 (OR)	1984	Rolf Danneberg, W.Ger	218-6
1936	Ken Carpenter, USA	165-7 (OR)	1988	Jergen Schult, E.Ger	225-9¼ (OR)

Hammer Throw

Year	Champion	Distance	Year	Champion	Distance
1900	John Flanagan, USA	163-1	1952	József Csérmák, HUN	197-11 (WR)
1904	John Flanagan, USA	168-1 (OR)	1956	Harold Connolly, USA	207-3 (OR)
1908	John Flanagan, USA	170-4 (OR)	1960	Vasily Rudenkov, USSR	220-2 (OR)
1912	Matt McGrath, USA	179-7 (OR)	1964	Romuald Klim, USSR	228-10 (OR)
1920	Pat Ryan, USA	173-5	1968	Gyula Zsivótzky, HUN	240-8 (OR)
1924	Fred Tootell, USA	174-10	1972	Anatoly Bondarchuk, USSR	247-8 (OR)
1928	Pat O'Callaghan, IRL	168-7	1976	Yuri Sedykh, USSR	254-4 (OR)
1932	Pat O'Callaghan, IRL	176-11	1980	Yuri Sedykh, USSR	268-4 (WR)
1936	Karl Hein, W.Ger	185-4 (OR)	1984	Juha Tiainen, FIN	256-2
1948	Imre Németh, HUN	183-11	1988	Sergei Litinov, USSR	278-2½ (OR)

Men's Track and Field (Continued)

Javelin Throw

Year	Champion	Distance
1908	Eric Lemming, SWE	179-10 (WR)
1912	Eric Lemming, SWE	198-11 (WR)
1920	Jonni Myyrä, FIN	215-10 (OR)
1924	Jonni Myyrä, FIN	206-7
1928	Erik Lundkvist, SWE	218-6 (OR)
1932	Matti Järvinen, FIN	238-6 (OR)
1936	Gerhard Stöck, W.Ger	235-8
1948	Kai Tapio Rautavaara, FIN	228-10
1952	Cy Young, USA	242-1 (OR)

Year	Champion	Distance
1956	Egil Danielson, NOR	281-2 (WR)
1960	Viktor Tsibulenko, USSR	277-8
1964	Pauli Nevala, FIN	271-2
1968	Jänis Lüsis, USSR	295-7 (OR)
1972	Klaus Wolfermann, W.Ger	296-10 (OR)
1976	Miklos Németh, HUN	310-4 (WR)
1980	Dainis Kula, USSR	299-2
1984	Arto Härkönen, FIN	284-8
1988	Tapio Korjus, FIN	276-6

Decathlon

Year	Champion	Points
1904	Thomas Kiely, IRL	6036
1912	Jim Thrope, USA	8412 (WR)
1920	Helge Lövland, NOR	6803
1924	Harold Osborn, USA	7711 (WR)
1928	Paavo Yrjölä, FIN	8053 (WR)
1932	Jim Bausch, USA	8462 (WR)
1936	Glenn Morris, USA	7900 (WR)
1948	Bob Mathias, USA	7139
1952	Bob Mathias, USA	7887 (WR)

Year	Champion	Points
1956	Milt Campbell, USA	7937 (OR)
1960	Rafer Johnson, USA	8392 (OR)
1964	Willi Holdorf, W.Ger	7887
1968	Bill Toomey, USA	8193 (OR)
1972	Nikolai Avilov, USSR	8454 (WR)
1976	Bruce Jenner, USA	8617 (WR)
1980	Daley Thompson, GBR	8495
1984	Daley Thompson, GBR	8798 (=WR)
1988	Christian Schenk, E.Ger	8488

WOMEN

100 Meters

Year	Champion	Time
1928	Elizabeth Robinson, USA	12.2 (=WR)
1932	Stella Walsh, POL*	11.9 (=WR)
1936	Helen Stephens, USA	11.5‡
1948	Fanny Blankers-Koen, HOL	11.9
1952	Marjorie Jackson, AUS	11.5 (=WR)
1956	Betty Cuthbert, AUS	11.5
1960	Wilma Rudolph, USA	11.0

Year	Champion	Time
1964	Wyomia Tyus, USA	11.4
1968	Wyomia Tyus, USA	11.0 (WR)
1972	Renate Stecher, E.Ger	11.07
1976	Annegret Richter, W.Ger	11.08
1980	Lyudmila Kondratyeva, USSR	11.06
1984	Evelyn Ashford, USA	10.97 (OR)
1988	Florence Griffith Joyner, USA	10.54 (OR)

*An autopsy performed after Walsh's death in 1980 revealed that she was a man.
‡Wind-aided.

200 Meters

Year	Champion	Time
1948	Fanny Blankers-Koen, HOL	24.4
1952	Marjorie Jackson, AUS	23.7
1956	Betty Cuthbert, AUS	23.4 (=OR)
1960	Wilma Rudolph, USA	24.0
1964	Edith McGuire, USA	23.0 (OR)

Year	Champion	Time
1968	Irena Szewinska, POL	22.5 (WR)
1972	Renate Stecher, E.Ger	22.40 (=WR)
1976	Bärbel Eckert, E.Ger	22.37 (OR)
1980	Bärbel Eckert Wöckel, E.Ger	22.03 (OR)
1984	Valerie Brisco-Hooks, USA	21.81 (OR)
1988	Florence Griffith Joyner, USA	21.34 (WR)

400 Meters

Year	Champion	Time
1964	Betty Cuthbert, AUS	52.0 (OR)
1968	Colette Besson, FRA	52.0 (=OR)
1972	Monika Zehrt, E.Ger	51.08 (OR)
1976	Irena Szewinska, POL	49.29 (WR)

Year	Champion	Time
1980	Marita Koch, E.Ger	48.88 (OR)
1984	Valerie Brisco-Hooks, USA	48.43 (OR)
1988	Olga Bryzgina, USSR	48.65

800 Meters

Year	Champion	Time
1928	Lina Radke, W.Ger	2:16.8 (WR)
1960	Lyudmila Shevtsova, USSR	2:04.3 (=WR)
1964	Ann Packer, GBR	2:01.1 (OR)
1968	Madeline Manning, USA	2:00.9 (OR)
1972	Hildegard Falck, W.Ger	1:58.55 (OR)

Year	Champion	Time
1976	Tatyana Kazankina, USSR	1:54.94 (WR)
1980	Nadezhda Olizarenko, USSR	1:53.42 (WR)
1984	Doina Melinte, ROM	1:57.60
1988	Sigrun Wodars, E.Ger	1:56.10

1500 Meters

Year	Champion	Time
1972	Lyudmila Bragina, USSR	4:01.4 (WR)
1976	Tatyana Kazankina, USSR	4:05.48
1980	Tatyana Kazankina, USSR	3:56.6 (OR)

Year	Champion	Time
1984	Gabriella Doria, ITA	4:03.25
1988	Paula Ivan, ROM	3:53.96 (OR)

3000 Meters

Year	Champion	Time	Year	Champion	Time
1984	Maricica Puică, ROM	8:35.96 (OR)	1988	Tatyana Samolenko, USSR	8:26.53 (OR)

10,000 Meters

Year	Champion	Time
1988	Olga Boldarenko, USSR	31:44.69 (OR)

Marathon

Year	Champion	Time	Year	Champion	Time
1984	Joan Benoit, USA	2:24:52	1988	Rosa Mota, POR	2:25:39

100-Meter Hurdles

Year	Champion	Time	Year	Champion	Time
1932	Babe Didriksen, USA	11.7 (WR)	1968	Maureen Caird, AUS	10.3 (OR)
1936	Trebisonda Valla, ITA	11.7	1972	Annelie Ehrhardt, E.Ger	12.59 (WR)
1948	Fanny Blankers-Koen, HOL	11.2 (OR)	1976	Johanna Schaller, E.Ger	12.77
1952	Shirley Strickland, AUS	10.9 (WR)	1980	Vera Komisova, USSR	12.56 (OR)
1956	Shirley Strickland, AUS	10.7 (OR)	1984	Benita Fitzgerald-Brown, USA	12.84
1960	Irina Press, USSR	10.8	1988	Jordanka Donkova, BUL	12.38 (OR)
1964	Karin Balzer, E.Ger	10.5			

400-Meter Hurdles

Year	Champion	Time	Year	Champion	Time
1984	Nawal El Moutawakel, MOR	54.61 (OR)	1988	Debra Flintoff-King, AUS	53.17 (OR)

4x100-Meter Relay

Year	Champion	Time	Year	Champion	Time
1928	Canada	48.4 (WR)	1964	Poland	43.6
1932	United States	46.9 (WR)	1968	United States	42.8 (WR)
1936	United States	46.9	1972	West Germany	42.81 (=WR)
1948	Holland	47.5	1976	East Germany	42.55 (OR)
1952	United States	45.9 (WR)	1980	East Germany	41.60 (WR)
1956	Australia	44.5 (WR)	1984	United States	41.65
1960	United States	44.5	1988	United States	41.98

4x400 Meter Relay

Year	Champion	Time	Year	Champion	Time
1972	East Germany	3:23.0 (WR)	1984	United States	3:18.29 (OR)
1976	East Germany	3:19.23 (WR)	1988	Soviet Union	3:15.18 (WR)
1980	Soviet Union	3:20.2			

High Jump

Year	Champion	Height	Year	Champion	Height
1928	Ethel Catherwood, CAN	5-2½	1964	Iolanda Balas, ROM	6-2¾ (OR)
1932	Jean Shiley, USA	5-5¼ (WR)	1972	Ulrike Meyfarth, W.Ger	6-3½ (=WR)
1936	Ibolya Csák, HUN	5-3	1976	Rosemarie Ackermann, E.Ger	6-4 (OR)
1948	Alice Coachman, USA	5-6 (OR)	1980	Sara Simeoni, ITA	6-5½ (OR)
1952	Esther Brand, SAF	5-5¾	1984	Ulrike Meyfarth, W.Ger	6-7½ (OR)
1956	Mildred McDaniel, USA	5-9¼ (WR)	1988	Louise Ritter, USA	6-8 (OR)
1960	Iolanda Balas, ROM	6-¾ (OR)			

Long Jump

Year	Champion	Distance	Year	Champion	Distance
1948	Olga Gyarmati, HUN	18-8¼	1972	Heidemarie Rosendahl, W.Ger	22-3
1952	Yvette Williams, NZE	20-5¾ (OR)	1976	Angela Voigt, E.Ger	22-¾
1956	Elzbieta Krzesinska, POL	20-10 (=WR)	1980	Tatiana Kolpakova, USSR	23-2 (OR)
1960	Vyera Krepkina, USSR	20-10¾ (OR)	1984	Anisoara Cusmir-Stanciu, ROM	22-10
1964	Mary Rand, GBR	22-2¼ (WR)	1988	Jackie Joyner-Kersee, USA	24-3½ (OR)
1968	Viorica Viscopoleanu, ROM	22-4½ (WR)			

Women's Track and Field (Continued)

Shot Put

Year	Champion	Distance
1948	Micheline Ostermeyer, FRA	. . . 45-1½
1952	Galina Zybina, USSR	. . . . 50-1¾ **(WR)**
1956	Tamara Tyshkevich, USSR	. . . 54-5 **(OR)**
1960	Tamara Press, USSR	. . . . 56-10 **(OR)**
1964	Tamara Press, USSR	. . . . 59-6¼ **(OR)**
1968	Margitta Gummel, E.Ger	. . . . . 64-4 **(WR)**

Year	Champion	Distance
1972	Nadezhda Chizhova, USSR	. . . 69-(WR)
1976	Ivanka Hristova, BUL	. . . . 69-5¼ **(OR)**
1980	Ilona Slupianek, E.Ger	. . . . 73-6¼ **(OR)**
1984	Claudia Losch, W.Ger	. . . . 67-2¼
1988	Natalya Lisovskaya, USSR	. . . . 72-11½

Discus Throw

Year	Champion	Distance
1928	Halina Konopacka, POL	. . . . . 129-11¾ **(WR)**
1932	Lillian Copeland, USA	. . . . 133-2 **(OR)**
1936	Gisela Mauermayer, W.Ger	. . 156-3 **(OR)**
1948	Micheline Ostermeyer, FRA	. . . 137-6
1952	Nina Romaschkova, USSR	. . . . 168-8 **(OR)**
1956	Olga Fikotová, CZE	. . . . 176-1 **(OR)**
1960	Nina Ponomaryeva, USSR	. . . . 180-9 **(OR)**

Year	Champion	Distance
1964	Tamara Press, USSR	. . . . 187-10 **(OR)**
1968	Lia Manoliu, ROM	. . . . 191-2 **(OR)**
1972	Faina Melnik, USSR	. . . . 218-7 **(OR)**
1976	Evelin Schlaak, E.Ger	. . . . 226-4 **(OR)**
1980	Evelin Schlaak, E.Ger	. . . . 229-6 **(OR)**
1984	Ria Stalman, HOL	 214-5
1988	Martina Hellmann, E.Ger	. . . 237-2¼ **(OR)**

Javelin Throw

Year	Champion	Distance
1932	Babe Didriksen, USA	. . . . 143-4 **(OR)**
1936	Tilly Fleischer, W.Ger	. . . . 148-3 **(OR)**
1948	Herma Bauma, AUT	 149-6
1952	Dana Zátopková, CZE	 165-7
1956	Inese Jaunzeme, USSR	 176-8
1960	Elvira Ozolina, USSR	. . . . 183-8 **(OR)**
1964	Mihaela Penes, ROM	 198-7

Year	Champion	Distance
1968	Angela Nemeth, HUN	. . . . 198 ft
1972	Ruth Fuchs, E.Ger	 209-7
1976	Ruth Fuchs, E.Ger	. . . . 216-4 **(OR)**
1980	Maria Colon Rueñes, CUB	. . . . 224-5 **(OR)**
1984	Tessa Sanderson, GBR	. . . . 228-2 **(OR)**
1988	Petra Felke, E.Ger	. . . . 245 ft **(OR)**

Heptathlon

Seven-event Heptathlon replaced five-event Pentathlon in 1984.

Year	Champion	Points
1964	Irina Press, USSR	. . . . 5246 **(WR)**
1968	Ingrid Becker, W.Ger	 5098
1972	Mary Peters, GBR	. . . . 4801 **(WR)**
1976	Siegrun Siegl, E.Ger	 4745

Year	Champion	Points
1980	Nadezhda Tkachenko, USSR	. . . . 5083 **(WR)**
1984	Glynis Nunn, AUS	. . . . 6390 **(OR)**
1988	Jackie Joyner-Kersee, USA	. . . . . 7215 **(WR)**

Volleyball

MEN

Year	Champion, 2nd, 3rd
1964	**Soviet Union**, Czechoslovakia, Japan
1968	**Soviet Union**, Japan, Czechoslovakia
1972	**Japan**, E. Germany, Soviet Union
1976	**Poland**, Soviet Union, Cuba

Year	Champion, 2nd, 3rd
1980	**Soviet Union**, Bulgaria, Romania
1984	**United States**, Brazil, Italy
1988	**United States**, Soviet Union, Argentina

WOMEN

Year	Champion, 2nd, 3rd
1964	**Japan**, Soviet Union, Poland
1968	**Soviet Union**, Japan, Poland
1972	**Soviet Union**, Japan, N. Korea
1976	**Japan**, Soviet Union, S. Korea

Year	Champion, 2nd, 3rd
1980	**Soviet Union**, E. Germany, Bulgaria
1984	**China**, United States, Japan
1988	**Soviet Union**, Peru, China

Water Polo

Year	Champion, 2nd, 3rd
1900	**Great Britain**, Belgium, France
1904	**USA (NY)**, USA (Chi.), USA (Mo.)
1908	**Great Britain**, Belgium, Sweden
1912	**Great Britain**, Sweden, Belgium
1920	**Great Britain**, Belgium, Sweden
1924	**France**, Belgium, United States
1928	**Germany**, Hungary, France
1932	**Hungary**, Germany, United States
1936	**Hungary**, Germany, Belgium
1948	**Italy**, Hungary, Holland

Year	Champion, 2nd, 3rd
1952	**Hungary**, Yugoslavia, Italy
1956	**Hungary**, Yugoslavia, Soviet Union
1960	**Italy**, Soviet Union, Hungary
1964	**Hungary**, Yugoslavia, Soviet Union
1968	**Yugoslavia**, Soviet Union, Hungary
1972	**Soviet Union**, Hungary, United States
1976	**Hungary**, Italy, Holland
1980	**Soviet Union**, Yugoslavia, Hungary
1984	**Yugoslavia**, United States, W. Germany
1988	**Yugoslavia**, United States, Soviet Union

Freestyle Wrestling

Light Flyweight (106 lbs)

Year	Champion		Year	Champion	
1904	Robert Curry	United States	1980	Claudio Pollio	Italy
1972	Roman Dmitriev	Soviet Union	1984	Bobby Weaver	United States
1976	Hasan Isaev	Bulgaria	1988	Takashi Kobayashi	Japan

Flyweight (115 lbs)

Year	Champion		Year	Champion	
1904	George Mehnert	United States	1968	Shigeo Nakata	Japan
1948	Lennart Viitala	Finland	1972	Kiyoma Kato	Japan
1952	Hasan Gemici	Turkey	1976	Yuji Takada	Japan
1956	Mirian Tsalkalamanidze	Soviet Union	1980	Anatoly Beloglazov	Soviet Union
1960	Ahmet Bilek	Turkey	1984	Saban Trstena	Yugoslavia
1964	Yoshikatsu Yoshida	Japan	1988	Mitsuru Sato	Japan

Bantamweight (126 lbs)

Year	Champion		Year	Champion	
1904	Isidor Niflot	United States	1960	Terry McCann	United States
1908	George Mehnert	United States	1964	Yojiro Uetake	Japan
1924	Kustaa Pihlajamäki	Finland	1968	Yojiro Uetake	Japan
1928	Kaarlo Mäkinen	Finland	1972	Hideaki Yanagida	Japan
1932	Robert Pearce	United States	1976	Vladimir Umin	Soviet Union
1936	Ödön Zombori	Hungary	1980	Sergei Beloglazov	Soviet Union
1948	Nasuh Akar	Turkey	1984	Hideaki Tomiyama	Japan
1952	Shohachi Ishii	Japan	1988	Sergei Beloglazov	Soviet Union
1956	Mustafa Dagistanli	Turkey			

Featherweight (137 lbs)

Year	Champion		Year	Champion	
1904	Benjamin Bradshaw	United States	1956	Shozo Sasahara	Japan
1908	George Dole	United States	1960	Mustafa Dagistanli	Turkey
1920	Charles Ackerly	United States	1964	Osamu Watanabe	Japan
1924	Robin Reed	United States	1968	Masaaki Kaneko	Japan
1928	Allie Morrison	United States	1972	Zagalav Abdulbekov	Soviet Union
1932	Hermanni Pihlajamäki	Finland	1978	Jung-Mo Yang	Korea
1936	Kustaa Pihlajamäki	Finland	1980	Magomedgasan Abushev	Soviet Union
1948	Gazanfer Bilge	Turkey	1984	Randy Lewis	United States
1952	Bayram Sit	Turkey	1988	John Smith	United States

Lightweight (150 lbs)

Year	Champion		Year	Champion	
1904	Otto Roehm	United States	1956	Emamali Habibi	Iran
1908	George de Relwyskow	Great Britain	1960	Shelby Wilson	United States
1920	Kalle Anttila	Finland	1964	Enyu Dimov	Bulgaria
1924	Russell Vis	United States	1968	Abdollah Movahhed	Iran
1928	Osvald Käpp	Estonia	1972	Dan Gable	United States
1932	Charles Pacôme	France	1976	Pavel Pinigin	Soviet Union
1936	Károly Kárpáti	Hungary	1980	Saipulla Absaidov	Soviet Union
1948	Celal Atik	Turkey	1984	In-Tak You	Korea
1952	Olle Anderberg	Sweden	1988	Arsen Fadzaev	Soviet Union

Welterweight (163 lbs)

Year	Champion		Year	Champion	
1904	Charles Erickson	United States	1960	Doug Blubaugh	United States
1924	Hermann Gehri	Switzerland	1964	Ismail Ogan	Turkey
1928	Arvo Haavisto	Finland	1968	Mahmut Atalay	Turkey
1932	Jack Van Bebber	United States	1972	Wayne Wells	United States
1936	Frank Lewis	United States	1976	Jiichiro Date	Japan
1948	Yasar Dogu	Turkey	1980	Valentin Angelov	Bulgaria
1952	Bill Smith	United States	1984	Dave Schultz	United States
1956	Mitsuo Ikeda	Japan	1988	Kenny Monday	United States

Freestyle Wrestling (Continued)

Middleweight (181 lbs)

Year	Champion		Year	Champion	
1908	Stanley Bacon	Great Britain	1960	Hasan Güngör	Turkey
1920	Eino Leino	Finland	1964	Prodan Gardzhev	Bulgaria
1924	Fritz Hagmann	Switzerland	1968	Boris Gurevitch	Soviet Union
1928	Ernst Kyburz	Switzerland	1972	Levan Tediashvili	Soviet Union
1932	Ivar Johansson	Sweden	1976	John Peterson	United States
1936	Emile Poilvé	France	1980	Ismail Abilov	Bulgaria
1948	Glen Brand	United States	1984	Mark Schultz	United States
1952	David Tsimakuridze	Soviet Union	1988	Han Myang-Woo	South Korea
1956	Nikola Stanchev	Bulgaria			

Light Heavyweight (198 lbs)

Year	Champion		Year	Champion	
1920	Anders Larsson	Sweden	1960	Ismet Atli	Turkey
1924	John Spellman	United States	1964	Aleksandr Medved	Soviet Union
1928	Thure Sjöstedt	Sweden	1968	Ahmet Ayik	Turkey
1932	Peter Mehringer	United States	1972	Ben Peterson	United States
1936	Knut Fridell	Sweden	1976	Levan Tediashvili	Soviet Union
1948	Henry Wittenberg	United States	1980	Sanasar Oganesyan	Soviet Union
1952	Wiking Palm	Sweden	1984	Ed Banach	United States
1956	Gholam Reza Takhti	Iran	1988	Makharbek Khadartsev	Soviet Union

Heavyweight (220 lbs)

Year	Champion		Year	Champion	
1972	Ivan Yarygin	Soviet Union	1984	Lou Banach	United States
1976	Ivan Yarygin	Soviet Union	1988	Vasile Puscasu	Romania
1980	Ilya Mate	Soviet Union			

Super Heavyweight (Unlimited)

Year	Champion		Year	Champion	
1904	Bernhuff Hansen	United States	1956	Hamit Kaplan	Turkey
1908	George Con O'Kelly	Great Britain/Ireland	1960	Wilfred Dietrich	West Germany
1920	Robert Roth	Switzerland	1964	Aleksandr Ivanitsky	Soviet Union
1924	Harry Steel	United States	1968	Aleksandr Medved	Soviet Union
1928	Johan Richthoff	Sweden	1972	Aleksandr Medved	Soviet Union
1932	Johan Richthoff	Sweden	1976	Soslan Andiev	Soviet Union
1936	Kristjan Palusalu	EST	1980	Soslan Andiev	Soviet Union
1948	Gyula Bóbis	Hungary	1984	Bruce Baumgartner	United States
1952	Arsen Mekokishvili	Soviet Union	1988	David Gobedjichvili	Soviet Union

Note: Current events not included in this summary: archery, canoeing, cycling, equestrian, fencing, field hockey, team handball, judo, modern pentathlon, rowing, shooting, table tennis, weightlifting, Greco-Roman wrestling and yachting.

Winter Olympics, 1924-88

Gold medal winners in all of the current events: alpine skiing, biathlon, bobsled, figure skating, ice hockey, luge, nordic skiing, and speed skating.

Alpine Skiing

MEN

Downhill

Year	Champion	Time	Year	Champion	Time
1948	Henri Oreiller, FRA	2:55.0	1972	Bernhard Russi, SWI	1:51.43
1952	Zeno Colo, ITA	2:30.8	1976	Franz Klammer AUT	1:45.73
1956	Toni Sailer, AUT	2:52.2	1980	Leonhard Stock, AUS	1:45.50
1960	Jean Vuarnet, FRA	2:06.0	1984	Bill Johnson, USA	1:45.59
1964	Egon Zimmermann, AUT	2:18.16	1988	Pirmin Zurbriggen, SWI	1:59.63
1968	Jean-Claude Killy, FRA	1:59.84			

Slalom

Year	Champion	Time	Year	Champion	Time
1948	Edi Reinalter, SWI	2:10.3	1972	Francisco Ochoa, SPA	1:49.27
1952	Othmar Schneider, AUT	2:00.0	1976	Piero Gros, ITA	2:03.29
1956	Toni Sailer, AUT	3:14.7	1980	Ingemar Stenmark, SWE	1:44.26
1960	Ernst Hinterseer, AUT	2:08.9	1984	Phil Mahre, USA	1:39.41
1964	Pepi Stiegler, AUT	2:11.13	1988	Alberto Tomba, ITA	1:39.47
1968	Jean-Claude Killy, FRA	1:39.73			

Giant Slalom

Year	Champion	Time	Year	Champion	Time
1952	Stein Eriksen, NOR	2:25.0	1972	Gustav Thöni, ITA	3:09.62
1956	Toni Sailer, AUS	3:00.1	1976	Heini Hemmi, SWI	3:26.97
1960	Roger Staub, SWI	1:48.3	1980	Ingemar Stenmark, SWE	2:40.74
1964	Francois Bonlieu, FRA	1:46.71	1984	Max Julen, SWI	2:41.18
1968	Jean-Claude Killy, FRA	3:29.28	1988	Alberto Tomba, ITA	2:06.37

Super Giant Slalom

Year	Champion	Time
1988	Frank Piccard, FRA	1:39.66

Alpine Combined

Year	Champion	Points	Year	Champion	Points
1936	Franz Pfnür, GER	99.25	1988	Hubert Strolz, AUT	36.55
1948	Henri Oreiller, FRA	3.27			

WOMEN

Downhill

Year	Champion	Time	Year	Champion	Time
1948	Hedy Schlunegger, SWI	2:28.3	1972	Marie-Theres Nadig, SWI	1:36.68
1952	Trude Jochum-Beiser, AUT	1:47.1	1976	Rosi Mittermaier, W.Ger	1:46.16
1956	Madeleine Berthod, SWI	1:40.7	1980	Annemarie Moser-Pröll, AUT	1:37.52
1960	Heidi Biebl, GER	1:37.6	1984	Michela Figini, SWI	1:13.36
1964	Christl Haas, AUT	1:55.39	1988	Marina Kiehl, W.Ger	1:25.86
1968	Olga Pall, AUT	1:40.87			

Slalom

Year	Champion	Time	Year	Champion	Time
1948	Gretchen Fraser, USA	1:57.2	1972	Barbara Cochran, USA	1:31.24
1952	Andrea Mead Lawrence, USA	2:10.6	1976	Rosi Mittermaier, W.Ger	1:30.54
1956	Renée Colliard, SWI	1:52.3	1980	Hanni Wenzel, LIE	1:25.09
1960	Anne Heggtveit, CAN	1:49.6	1984	Paoletta Magoni, ITA	1:36.47
1964	Christine Goitschel, FRA	1:29.86	1988	Vreni Schneider, SWI	1:36.69
1968	Marielle Goitschel, FRA	1:25.86			

Giant Slalom

Year	Champion	Time	Year	Champion	Time
1952	Andrea Mead Lawrence, USA	2:06.8	1972	Marie-Theres Nadig, SWI	1:29.90
1956	Ossi Reichert, GER	1:56.5	1976	Kathy Kreiner, CAN	1:29.13
1960	Yvonne Rüegg, SWI	1:39.9	1980	Hanni Wenzel, LIE	2:41.66
1964	Marielle Goitschel, FRA	1:52.24	1984	Debbie Armstrong, USA	2:20.98
1968	Nancy Greene, CAN	1:51.97	1988	Vreni Schneider, SWI	2:06.49

Women's Alpine Skiing (Continued)

Super Giant Slalom

Year	Champion	Time
1988	Sigrid Wolf, AUT	1:19.03

Alpine Combined

Year	Champion	Points	Year	Champion	Points
1936	Christl Cranz, GER	97.06	1988	Anita Wachter, AUT	29.25
1948	Trude Beiser, AUT	6.58			

Biathlon

10 Kilometers

Year	Champion	Time	Year	Champion	Time
1980	Frank Ullrich, E.Ger	32:10.69	1988	Frank-Peter Roetsch, E.Ger	25:08.1
1984	Erik Kvalfoss, NOR	30:53.8			

20 Kilometers

Year	Champion	Time	Year	Champion	Time
1960	Klas Lestander, SWE	1:33:21.6	1976	Nikolai Kruglov, USSR	1:14:12.26
1964	Vladimir Melanin, USSR	1:20:26.8	1980	Anatoly Alyabiev, USSR	1:08:16.31
1968	Magnar Solberg, NOR	1:13:45.9	1984	Peter Angerer, W.Ger	1:11:52.7
1972	Magnar Solberg, NOR	1:15:55.50	1988	Frank-Peter Roetsch, E.Ger	56:33.33

4x7.5-Kilometer Relay

Year	Champion	Time	Year	Champion	Time
1968	Soviet Union	2:13:02.4	1980	Soviet Union	1:34:03.27
1972	Soviet Union	1:51:44.92	1984	Soviet Union	1:38:51.7
1976	Soviet Union	1:57:55.64	1988	Soviet Union	1:22:30.0

Bobsled

Two-Man

Year	Champion (Driver)	Time	Year	Champion (Driver)	Time
1932	United States (Hubert Stevens)	8:14.74	1968	Italy (Eugenio Monti)	4:41.54
1936	United States (Ivan Brown)	5:29.29	1972	West Germany (Wolfgang Zimmerer)	4:57.07
1948	Switzerland (Felix Endrich)	5:29.2	1976	East Germany (Meinhard Nehmer)	3:44.42
1952	Germany (Andreas Ostler)	5:24.54	1980	Switzerland Erich Schärer)	4:09.36
1956	Italy (Lamberto Dalla Costa)	5:30.14	1984	East Germany (Wolfgang Hoppe)	3:25.56
1964	Great Britain (Anthony Nash)	4:21.90	1988	Soviet Union (Janis Kipours)	3:54.19

Four-Man

Year	Champion (Driver)	Time	Year	Champion (Driver)	Time
1924	Switzerland (Eduard Scherrer)	5:45.54	1964	Canada (Vic Emery)	4:14.46
1928	United States (Billy Fiske)	3:20.5	1968	Italy (Eugenio Monti)	2:17.39
1932	United States (Billy Fiske)	7:53.68	1972	Switzerland (Jean Wicki)	4:43.07
1936	Switzerland (Pierre Musy)	5:19.85	1976	East Germany (Meinhard Nehmer)	3:40.43
1948	United States (Francis Tyler)	5:20.1	1980	East Germany (Meinhard Nehmer)	3:59.92
1952	West Germany (Andreas Ostler)	5:07.84	1984	East Germany (Wolfgang Hoppe)	3:20.22
1956	Switzerland (Franz Kapus)	5:10.44	1988	Switzerland (Ekkehard Fasser)	3:47.51

Figure Skating

Men's

Year	Champion		Year	Champion	
1908	Ulrich Salchow	Sweden	1960	David Jenkins	United States
1920	Gillis Grafström	Sweden	1964	Manfred Schnelldorfer	West Germany
1924	Gillis Grafström	Sweden	1968	Wolfgang Schwarz	Austria
1928	Gillis Grafström	Sweden	1972	Ondrej Nepela	Czechoslovakia
1932	Karl Schäfer	Austria	1976	John Curry	Great Britain
1936	Karl Schäfer	Austria	1980	Robin Cousins	Great Britain
1948	Dick Button	United States	1984	Scott Hamilton	United States
1952	Dick Button	United States	1988	Brian Boitano	United States
1956	Hayes Alan Jenkins	United States			

Women's

Year	Champion		Year	Champion	
1908	Madge Syers	Great Britain	1960	Carol Heiss	United States
1920	Magda Julin	Sweden	1964	Sjoukje Dijkstra	Holland
1924	Herma Planck-Szabó	Austria	1968	Peggy Fleming	United States
1928	Sonja Henie	Norway	1972	Beatrix Schuba	Austria
1932	Sonja Henie	Norway	1976	Dorothy Hamill	United States
1936	Sonja Henie	Norway	1980	Anett Pötzsch	E.Germany
1948	Barbara Ann Scott	Canada	1984	Katarina Witt	E.Germany
1952	Jeanette Altwegg	Great Britain	1988	Katarina Witt	E.Germany
1956	Tenley Albright	United States			

Pairs

Year	Champion	Year	Champions
1908	Anna Hubler & Heinrich Burger, GER	1960	Barbara Wagner & Robert Paul, CAN
1920	Ludovika & Walter Jakobsson, FIN	1964	Lyudmila Belousova & Oleg Protopopov, USSR
1924	Helene Engelmann & Alfred Berger, AUT	1968	Lyudmila Belousova & Oleg Protopopov, USSR
1928	Andrée Joly & Pierre Brunet, FRA		
1932	Andrée & Pierre Brunet, FRA	1972	Irina Rodnina & Aleksei Ulanov, USSR
1936	Maxi Herber & Ernst Baier, GER	1976	Irina Rodnina & Aleksandr Zaitsev, USSR
1948	Micheline Lannoy & Pierre Baugniet, BEL	1980	Irina Rodnina & Aleksandr Zaitsev, USSR
1952	Ria & Paul Falk, W.Ger	1984	Elena Valova & Oleg Vasiliev, USSR
1956	Elisabeth Schwartz & Kurt Oppelt, AUT	1988	Ekaterina Gordeeva & Sergei Grinkov, USSR

Ice Dance

Year	Champions	Year	Champion
1976	Lyudmila Pakhomova & Aleksandr Gorshkov, USSR	1984	Jayne Torvill & Christopher Dean, GBR
1980	Natalia Linichuk & Gennady Karponosov, USSR	1988	Natalia Bestemianova &Andrei Bukin, USSR

Ice Hockey

Year	Champion, 2nd, 3rd	Year	Champion, 2nd, 3rd
1920	**Canada**, United States Czechoslovakia	1960	**United States**, Canada, Soviet Union
1924	**Canada**, United States, Great Britain	1964	**Soviet Union**, Sweden, Czechoslovakia
1928	**Canada**, Sweden, Switzerland	1968	**Soviet Union**, Czechoslovakia, Canada
1932	**Canada**, United States, Germany	1972	**Soviet Union**, United States, Czechoslovakia
1936	**Great Britain**, Canada, United States	1976	**Soviet Union**, Czechoslovakia, W.Germany
1948	**Canada**, Czechoslovakia, Switzerland	1980	**United States**, Soviet Union, Sweden
1952	**Canada**, United States, Sweden	1984	**Soviet Union**, Czechoslovakia, Sweden
1956	**Soviet Union**, United States, Canada	1988	**Soviet Union**, Finland, Sweden

Luge

MEN

Singles

Year	Champion	Time	Year	Champion	Time
1964	Thomas Köhler, E.Ger	3:26.77	1980	Bernhard Glass, E.Ger	2:54.796
1968	Manfred Schmid, AUT	2:52.48	1984	Paul Hildgartner, ITA	3:04.258
1972	Wolfgang Scheidel, E.Ger	3:27.58	1988	Jens Mueller, E.Ger	3:05.548
1976	Dettlef Günther, E.Ger	3:27.688			

Doubles

Year	Champion	Time	Year	Champion	Time
1964	Austria	1:41.62	1976	East Germany	1:25.604
1968	East Germany	1:35.85	1980	East Germany	1:19.331
1972	East Germany & Italy	1:28.35	1984	West Germany	1:23.620
			1988	East Germany	1:31.940

WOMEN

Singles

Year	Champion	Time	Year	Champion	Time
1964	Ortrun Enderlein, E.Ger	3:24.67	1980	Vera Zozulia, USSR	2:36.537
1968	Erica Lechner, ITA	2:28.66	1984	Steffi Martin, E.Ger	2:46.570
1972	Anna-Maria Müller, E.Ger	2:59.18	1988	Steffi Martin Walter, E.Ger	3:03.973
1976	Margit Schumann, E.Ger	2:50.621			

Nordic Skiing

CROSS-COUNTRY, MEN

15 Kilometers

Event was held over 18 kilometers from 1924-52.

Year	Champion	Time	Year	Champion	Time
1924	Thorleif Haug, NOR	1:14:31.0	1964	Eero Mäntyranta, FIN	50:54.1
1928	Johan Gröttumsbraten, NOR	1:37:01.0	1968	Harald Grönningen, NOR	47:54.2
1932	Sven Utterström, SWE	1:23:07.0	1972	Sven-Ake Lundbäck, SWE	45:28.24
1936	Erik-August Larsson, SWE	1:14:38.0	1976	Nikolai Bazhukov, USSR	43:58.47
1948	Martin Lundström, SWE	1:13:50.0	1980	Thomas Wassberg, SWE	41:57.63
1952	Hallgeir Brenden, NOR	1:01:34.0	1984	Gunde Svan, SWE	41:25.6
1956	Hallgeir Brenden, NOR	49:39.0	1988	Mikhail Deviatiarov, USSR	41:18.9
1960	Hakon Brusveen, NOR	51:55.5			

30 Kilometers

Year	Champion	Time	Year	Champion	Time
1956	Veikko Hakulinen, FIN	1:44:06.0	1976	Sergei Saveliev, USSR	1:30:29.38
1960	Sixten Jernberg, SWE	1:51:03.9	1980	Nikolai Zimyatov, USSR	1:27:02.80
1964	Eero Mäntyranta, FIN	1:30:50.7	1984	Nikolai Zimyatov, USSR	1:28:56.3
1968	Franco Nones, ITA	1:35:39.2	1988	Alexi Prokourorov, USSR	1:24:26.3
1972	Vyacheslav Vedenine, USSR	1:36:31.15			

50 Kilometers

Year	Champion	Time	Year	Champion	Time
1924	Thorleif Haug, NOR	3:44:32.0	1964	Sixten Jernberg, SWE	2:43:52.6
1928	Per Erik Hedlund, SWE	4:52:03.0	1968	Ole Ellefsaeter, NOR	2:28:45.8
1932	Veli Saarinen, FIN	4:28:00.0	1972	Pal Tyldum, NOR	2:43:14.75
1936	Elis Wiklund, SWE	3:30:11.0	1976	Ivar Formo, NOR	2:37:30.05
1948	Nils Karlsson, SWE	3:47:48.0	1980	Nikolai Zimyatov, USSR	2:27:24.60
1952	Veikko Hakulinen, FIN	3:33:33.0	1984	Thomas Wassberg, SWE	2:15:55.8
1956	Sixten Jernberg, SWE	2:50:27.0	1988	Gunde Svan, SWE	2:04:30.9
1960	Kalevi Hämäläinen, FIN	2:59:06.3			

4x10-Kilometer Relay

Year	Champion	Time	Year	Champion	Time
1936	Finland	2:41:33.0	1968	Norway	2:08:33.5
1948	Sweden	2:32:08.0	1972	Soviet Union	2:04:47.94
1952	Finland	2:20:16.0	1976	Finland	2:07:59.72
1956	Soviet Union	2:15.30.0	1980	Soviet Union	1:57.03.46
1960	Finland	2:18.45.6	1984	Sweden	1:55:06.3
1964	Sweden	2:18:34.6	1988	Sweden	1:43:58.6

CROSS-COUNTRY, WOMEN

5 Kilometers

Year	Champion	Time	Year	Champion	Time
1964	Claudia Boyarskikh, USSR	17:50.5	1980	Raisa Smetanina, SOV	15:06.92
1968	Toini Gustafsson, SWE	16:45.2	1984	Marja-Liisa Hämäläinen, FIN	17:04.0
1972	Galina Kulakova, USSR	17:00.50	1988	Marjo Matikainen, FIN	15:04.0
1976	Helena Takalo, FIN	15:48.69			

10 Kilometers

Year	Champion	Time	Year	Champion	Time
1952	Lydia Wideman, FIN	41:40.0	1972	Galina Kulakova, USSR	34:17.82
1956	Lyubov Kosyreva, USSR	38:11.0	1976	Raisa Smetanina, USSR	30:13.41
1960	Maria Gusakova, USSR	39:46.6	1980	Barbara Petzold, E.Ger	30:31.54
1964	Claudia Boyarskikh, USSR	40:24.3	1984	Marja-Liisa Mämäläinen, FIN	31:44.2
1968	Toini Gustafsson, SWE	36:46.5	1988	Vida Ventsene, USSR	30:08.3

20 Kilometers

Year	Champion	Time	Year	Champion	Time
1984	Marja-Liisa Hämäläinen, FIN	1:01.45.0	1988	Tamara Tikhonova, USSR	55:53.6

4x5-Kilometer Relay

Year	Champion	Time	Year	Champion	Time
1956	Finland	1:09:01.0	1976	Soviet Union	1:07:49.75
1960	Sweden	1:04:21.4	1980	East Germany	1:02:11.10
1964	Soviet Union	59:20.2	1984	Norway	1:06:49.7
1968	Norway	57:30.0	1988	Soviet Union	59:51.1
1972	Soviet Union	48:46.15			

SKI JUMPING
Individual 70-Meter

Year Champion	Points	Year Champion	Points
1964 Veikko Kankkonen, FIN	229.9	1980 Anton Innauer, AUT	266.3
1968 Jiri Raska, CZE	216.5	1984 Jens Weissflog, E.Ger	215.2
1972 Yukio Kasaya, JPN	244.2	1988 Matti Nykänen, FIN	229.1
1976 Hans-Georg Aschenbach, E.Ger	252.0		

Individual 90-Meter

Year Champion	Points	Year Champion	Points
1924 Jacob Tullin Thams, NOR	18.960	1964 Toralf Engan, NOR	230.7
1928 Alf Andersen, NOR	19.208	1968 Vladimir Beloussov, USSR	231.3
1932 Birger Rudd, NOR	228.1	1972 Wojciech Fortuna, POL	219.9
1936 Birger Ruud, NOR	232.0	1976 Karl Schnabl, AUT	234.8
1948 Petter Hugsted, NOR	228.1	1980 Jouko Törmänen, FIN	271.0
1952 Arnfinn Bergmann, NOR	226.0	1984 Matti Nykänen, FIN	231.2
1956 Antti Hyvärinen, FIN	227.0	1988 Matti Nykänen, FIN	224.0
1960 Helmut Rechnagel, E.Ger	227.2		

Team 90-Meter

Year Champion	Points
1988 Finland	634.4

NORDIC COMBINED (Ski Jump and Cross-Country)
Individual

Year Champion	Points	Year Champion	Points
1924 Thorleif Haug, NOR	18.906	1964 Tormod Knutsen, NOR	469.28
1928 Johan Gröttumsbraten, NOR	17.833	1968 Franz Keller, GER	449.04
1932 Johan Gröttumsbraten, NOR	446.00	1972 Ulrich Wehling, GDR	413.340
1936 Oddbjörn Hagen, NOR	430.3	1976 Ulrich Wehling, GDR	423.39
1948 Heikki Hasu, FIN	448.80	1980 Ulrich Wehling, GDR	432.200
1952 Simon Slattvik, NOR	451.621	1984 Tom Sandberg, NOR	422.595
1956 Sverre Stenersen, NOR	455.000	1988 Hippolyt Kempf, SWI	235.8
1960 Georg Thoma, GER	457.952		

Team

	Jump Pts	30-km Time
Year Champion		
1988 West Germany	629.8	1:20:46

Speed Skating
MEN
500 Meters

Year Champion	Time	Year Champion	Time
1924 Charles Jewtraw, USA	44.0	1960 Yevgeny Grishin, USSR	40.2 (=WR)
1928 Bernt Evensen, NOR	43.4 (OR)	1964 Terry McDermott, USA	40.1 (OR)
& Clas Thunberg, FIN	43.4 (OR)	1968 Erhard Keller, W.Ger	40.3
1932 John Shea, USA	43.4 (=OR)	1972 Erhard Keller, W.Ger	39.44 (OR)
1936 Ivar Ballangrud, NOR	43.4 (=OR)	1976 Yevgeny Kulikov, USSR	39.17 (OR)
1948 Finn Helgesen, NOR	43.1 (OR)	1980 Eric Heiden, USA	38.03 (OR)
1952 Kenneth Henry, USA	43.2	1984 Sergei Fokichev, USSR	38.19
1956 Yevgeny Grishin, USSR	40.2 (=WR)	1988 Jens-Uwe Mey, E.Ger	36.45 (WR)

1000 Meters

Year Champion	Time	Year Champion	Time
1976 Peter Mueller, USA	1:19.32	1984 Gaétan Boucher, CAN	1:15.80
1980 Eric Heiden, USA	1:15.18 (OR)	1988 Nikolai Guliaev, USSR	1:13.03 (OR)

1500 Meters

Year Champion	Time	Year Champion	Time
1924 Clas Thunberg, FIN	2:20.8	1964 Ants Antson, USSR	2:10.3
1928 Clas Thunberg, FIN	2:21.1	1968 Kees Verkerk, HOL	2:03.4 (OR)
1932 Jack Shea, USA	2:57.5	1972 Ard Schenk, HOL	2:02.96 (OR)
1936 Charles Mathisen, NOR	2:19.2 (OR)	1976 Jan Egil Storholt, NOR	1:59.38 (OR)
1948 Sverre Farstad, NOR	2:17.6 (OR)	1980 Eric Heiden, USA	1:55.44 (OR)
1952 Hjalmar Andersen, NOR	2:20.4	1984 Gaétan Boucher, CAN	1:58.36
1956 Yevgeny Grishin, USSR	2:08.6 (WR)	1988 Andre Hoffman, E.Ger	1:52.06 (WR)
1960 Roald Aas, NOR	2:10.4		

Men's Speed Skating (Continued)

5000 Meters

Year	Champion	Time
1924	Clas Thunberg, FIN	8:39.0
1928	Ivar Ballangrud, NOR	8:50.5
1932	Irving Jaffee, USA	9:40.8
1936	Ivar Ballangrud, NOR	8:19.6 (OR)
1948	Reidar Liaklev, NOR	8:29.4
1952	Hjalmar Andersen, NOR	8:10.6 (OR)
1956	Boris Shilkov, USSR	7:48.7 (OR)
1960	Viktor Kosichkin, USSR	7:51.3
1964	Knut Johannesen, NOR	7:38.4 (OR)
1968	Fred Anton Maier, NOR	7:22.4 (WR)
1972	Ard Schenk, HOL	7:23.61
1976	Sten Stensen, NOR	7:24.48
1980	Eric Heiden, USA	7:02.29 (OR)
1984	Tomas Gustafson, SWE	7:12.28
1988	Tomas Gustafson, SWE	6:44.63 (WR)

10,000 Meters

Year	Champion	Time
1924	Julius Skutnabb, FIN	18:04.8
1928	Ivar Ballangrud, NOR	18:36.5
1932	Irving Jaffee, USA	19:13.6
1936	Ivar Ballangrud, NOR	17:24.3 (OR)
1948	Ake Seyffarth, SWE	17:26.3
1952	Hjallis Andersen, NOR	16:45.8 (OR)
1956	Sigvard Ericsson, SWE	16:35.9 (OR)
1960	Knut Johannesen, NOR	15:46.6 (WR)
1964	Jonny Nilsson, SWE	15:50.1
1968	Johnny Höglin, SWE	15:23.6 (OR)
1972	Ard Schenk, HOL	15:01.35 (OR)
1976	Piet Kleine, HOL	14:50.59 (OR)
1980	Eric Heiden, USA	14:28.13 (WR)
1984	Igor Malkov, USSR	14:39.90
1988	Tomas Gustafson, SWE	13:48.20 (WR)

WOMEN

500 Meters

Year	Champion	Points
1960	Helga Haase, E.Ger	45.9
1964	Lydia Skoblikova, USSR	45.0 (OR)
1968	Lyudmila Titova, USSR	46.1
1972	Anne Henning, USA	43.33 (OR)

Year	Champion	Time
1976	Sheila Young, USA	42.76 (OR)
1980	Karin Enke, E.Ger	41.78 (OR)
1984	Christa Rothenburger, E.Ger	41.02 (OR)
1988	Bonnie Blair, USA	39.10 (WR)

1000 Meters

Year	Champion	Time
1960	Klara Guseva, USSR	1:34.1
1964	Lydia Skoblikova, USSR	1:33.2 (OR)
1968	Carolina Geijssen, HOL	1:32.6 (OR)
1972	Monika Pflug, W.Ger	1:31.40 (OR)
1976	Tatiana Averina, USSR	1:28.43 (OR)
1980	Natalia Petruseva, USSR	1:24.10 (OR)
1984	Karin Enke, E.Ger	1:21.61 (OR)
1988	Christa Rothenburger, E.Ger	1:17.65 (WR)

1500 Meters

Year	Champion	Time
1960	Lydia Skoblikova, USSR	2:25.2 (WR)
1964	Lydia Skoblikova, USSR	2:22.6 (OR)
1968	Kaija Mustonen, FIN	2:22.4 (OR)
1972	Dianne Holum, USA	2:20.85 (OR)
1976	Galina Stepanskaya, USSR	2:16.58 (OR)
1980	Annie Borckink, HOL	2:10.95 (OR)
1984	Karin Enke, E.Ger	2:03.42 (WR)
1988	Yvonne Van Gennip, HOL	2:00.68 (OR)

3000 Meters

Year	Champion	Time
1960	Lydia Skoblikova, USSR	5:14.3
1964	Lydia Skoblikova, USSR	5:14.9
1968	Johanna Schut, HOL	4:56.2 (OR)
1972	Christina Baas-Kaiser, HOL	4:52.14 (OR)
1976	Tatiana Averina, USSR	4:45.19 (OR)
1980	Bjorg Eva Jensen, NOR	4:32.13 (OR)
1984	Andrea Schöne, E.Ger	4:24.79 (OR)
1988	Yvonne Van Gennip, HOL	4:11.94 (WR)

5000 Meters

Year	Champion	Time
1988	Yvonne Van Gennip, HOL	7:14.13 (WR)

The America's Cup

International yacht racing was launched in 1851 when England's Royal Yacht Squadron staged a 60-mile regatta around the Isle of Wight and offered a silver trophy to the winner. The 101-foot schooner **America**, sent over by the New York Yacht Club, won the race and the prize. Originally called the Hundred-Guinea Cup, the trophy was renamed The America's Cup after the winning boat's owners deeded it to the NYYC with instructions to defend it whenever challenged.

From 1870-1980, the NYYC successfully defended the Cup 25 straight times; first in large schooners and J-class boats that measured up to 140 feet in overall length, then in 12-meter boats. A foreign yacht finally won the Cup in 1983 when **Australia II** beat defender **Liberty** in the seventh and deciding race off Newport, R.I. Four years later, the San Diego Yacht Club's **Stars & Stripes** won the Cup back, sweeping the four races of the final series off Fremantle, Australia.

Then in 1988, New Zealand's Mercury Bay Boating Club, unwilling to wait the usual three to four-year period between Cup defenses, challenged the SDYC to a match race, citing the Cup's 102-year-old Deed of Gift which clearly stated that every challenge had to be honored. Mercury Bay announced it would race a 133-foot monohull. San Diego countered with a 60-foot catamaran. The resulting best-of-three series (Sept.7-8) was a mismatch as the SDYC's catamaran **Stars & Stripes** won two straight by margins of better than 18 and 21 minutes.

Mercury Bay syndicate leader Michael Fay protested the outcome and took the SDYC to court in New York State (where the Deed of Gift was first filed) claiming San Diego had violated the spirit of the deed by racing a catamaran instead of a monohull. N.Y.State Supreme Court judge Carmen Ciparick agreed and on March 28, 1989, ordered the SDYC to hand the Cup over to Mercury Bay. The SDYC refused, but did consent to the court's appointment of the New York Yacht Club as custodian of the Cup until an appeal was ruled on.

On Sept.19, 1989, the Appellate Division of the N.Y.Supreme Court overturned Ciparick's decision and awarded the Cup back to the SDYC. Meanwhile, barring a successful appeal by Mercury Bay, the next America's Cup defense is expected to take place in May, 1992 off San Diego. To avoid the chaos of the last 12 months, a new class of boat—75-foot monohulls with 110-foot masts—has been agreed to by all potential challengers.

America's Cup Races, 1851-1988

Schooners and J-Class Boats

Year	Winner	Skipper	Series	Loser	Skipper
1851	America	Richard Brown	—	—	—
1870	Magic	Andrew Comstock	1-0	Cambria, GBR	J.Tannock
1871	Columbia	Nelson Comstock	4-1	Livonia, GBR	J.R.Woods
1876	Madeleine	Josephus Williams	2-0	Countess of Dufferin, CAN	Alexander Cuthbert
1881	Mischief	Nathanael Clock	2-0	Atalanta, CAN	Alex.Cuthbert
1885	Puritan	Aubrey Crocker	2-0	Genesta, GBR	John Carter
1886	Mayflower	Martin Stone	2-0	Galatea, GBR	Dan Bradford
1887	Volunteer	Hank Haff	2-0	Thistle, GBR	John Barr
1893	Vigilant	Nathanael Herreshoff	3-0	Valkyrie II, GBR	Wm.Granfield
1895	Defender	Hank Haff	3-0	Valkyrie III, GBR	Wm.Granfield & E.A.Sycamore
1899	Columbia	Charles Barr	3-0	Shamrock, GBR	Archibald Hogarth & Bob Wringe
1901	Columbia	Charles Barr	3-0	Shamrock II, GBR	E.A.Sycamore
1903	Reliance	Charles Barr	3-0	Shamrock III, GBR	Bob Wringe
1920	Resolute	Charles F.Adams III	3-2	Shamrock IV, GBR	William Burton & Alfred Turner
1930	Enterprise	Harold S.Vanderbilt	4-0	Shamrock V, GBR	Ernest Heard
1934	Rainbow	Harold S.Vanderbilt	4-2	Endeavour, GBR	T.O.M.Sopwith
1937	Ranger	Harold S.Vanderbilt	4-0	Endeavour II, GBR	T.O.M.Sopwith

12-Meter Boats

Year	Winner	Skipper	Series	Winner	Skipper
1958	Columbia	Briggs Cunningham	4-0	Sceptre, GBR	Graham Mann
1962	Weatherly	Emil (Bus) Mosbacher	4-1	Gretel, AUS	Alex.Sturrock
1964	Constellation	Eric Ridder & Bob Bavier	4-0	Sovereign, AUS	Peter Scott
1967	Intrepid	Emil (Bus) Mosbacher	4-0	Dame Pattie, AUS	Alex.Sturrock
1970	Intrepid	Bill Ficker	4-1	Gretel II, AUS	Jim Hardy
1974	Courageous	Ted Hood	4-0	Southern Cross, AUS	Jim Hardy
1977	Courageous	Ted Turner	4-0	Australia, AUS	Noel Robins
1980	Freedom	Dennis Conner	4-1	Australia, AUS	Jim Hardy
1983	Australia II	John Bertrand	4-3	Liberty	Dennis Conner
1987	Stars & Stripes	Dennis Conner	4-0	Kookaburra III, AUS	Ian Murray

60-ft Catamaran vs 133-ft Monohull

Year	Winner	Skipper	Series	Loser	Skipper
1988	Stars & Stripes	Dennis Conner	2-0	New Zealand, NZE	David Barnes

Cycling

1989 Tour de France

MEN

76th Tour de France: 27 stages covering 2,020 miles. Winning time—87 hours, 38 minutes, 35 seconds. Greg LeMond's 8-second margin of victory was the closest in race history.

	Behind			Behind
1 Greg LeMond, USA, (Coors Light-ADR)	—		6 Charly Mottet, France (RMO)	10:06
2 Laurent Fignon, France (Super-U)	0:08		7 Steven Rooks, Holland (PDM)	11:10
3 Pedro Delgalo, Spain (Reynolds)	3:34		8 Raul Alcala, Mexico (PDM)	14:21
4 Gert-Jan Theunisse, Holland (PDM)	7:30		9 Sean Kelly, Ireland (PDM)	18:25
5 Marino Lejarreta, Spain (Paternina)	9:39		10 Robert Millar, Britain (Z-Peugeot)	18:46

WOMEN

6th Tour de France: 11 stages covering 482 miles. Winning time—21 hours, 59 minutes, 38 seconds.

	Behind			Behind
1 Jeannie Longo, France	—		4 Susan Elias, USA	14:48
2 Maria Canins, Italy	8:44		5 Cecile Odin, France	15:28
3 Inga Thompson, USA	12:24			

Tour de France, 1903-89

France's premier sporting event since 1903, the Tour is staged throughout the country and sometimes in neighboring countries over four weeks.

Most wins: Jacques Anquetil of France, Eddy Merckx of Belgium and Bernard Hinault of France (5).

MEN

Year Winner	Year Winner	Year Winner
1903 Maurice Garin, France	1930 Andre Leducq, France	1960 Gastone Nencini, Italy
1904 Henri Cornet, France	1931 Antonin Magne, France	1961 Jacques Anquetil, France
1905 Louis Trousselier, France	1932 Andre Leducq, France	1962 Jacques Anquetil, France
1906 Rene Pottier, France	1933 Georges Speicher, France	1963 Jacques Anquetil, France
1907 Lucien Petit-Breton, France	1934 Antonin Magne, France	1964 Jacques Anquetil, France
1908 Lucien Petit-Breton, France	1935 Romain Maes, Belgium	1965 Felice Gimondi, Italy
1909 Francois Faber, Luxembourg	1936 Sylvere Maes, Belgium	1966 Lucien Aimar, France
	1937 Roger Lapebie, France	1967 Roger Pingeon, France
1910 Octave Lapize, France	1938 Gino Bartali, Italy	1968 Jan Janssen, Holland
1911 Gustave Garrigou, France	1939 Sylvere Maes, Belgium	1969 Eddy Merckx, Belgium
1912 Odile Defraye, Belgium		
1913 Philippe Thys, Belgium	1940 Not held	1970 Eddy Merckx, Belgium
1914 Philippe Thys, Belgium	1941 Not held	1971 Eddy Merckx, Belgium
1915 Not held	1942 Not held	1972 Eddy Merckx, Belgium
1916 Not held	1943 Not held	1973 Luis Ocana, Spain
1917 Not held	1944 Not held	1974 Eddy Merckx, Belgium
1918 Not held	1945 Not held	1975 Bernard Thevenet, France
1919 Firmin Lambot, Belgium	1946 Jean Lazarides, France*	1976 Lucien van Impe, Belgium
	1947 Jean Robic, France	1977 Bernard Thevenet, France
1920 Philippe Thys, Belgium	1948 Gino Bartali, Italy	1978 Bernard Hinault, France
1921 Leon Scieur, Belgium	1949 Fausto Coppi, Italy	1979 Bernard Hinault, France
1922 Firmin Lambot, Belgium		
1923 Henri Pelissier, France	1950 Ferdinand Kubler, Switz.	1980 Joop Zoetemilk, Holland
1924 Ottavio Bottecchia, Italy	1951 Hugo Koblet, Switzerland	1981 Bernard Hinault, France
1925 Ottavio Bottecchia, Italy	1952 Fausto Coppi, Italy	1982 Bernard Hinault, France
1926 Lucien Buysse, Belgium	1953 Louison Bobet, France	1983 Laurent Fignon, France
1927 Nicholas Frantz, Lux'bourg	1954 Louison Bobet, France	1984 Laurent Fignon, France
1928 Nicholas Frantz, Lux'bourg	1955 Louison Bobet, France	1985 Bernard Hinault, France
1929 Maurice Dewaele, Belgium	1956 Roger Walkowiak, France	1986 Greg LeMond, USA
	1957 Jacques Anquetil, France	1987 Stephen Roche, Ireland
	1958 Charly Gaul, Luxembourg	1988 Pedro Delgado, Spain
	1959 Federico Bahamontes, Spain	1989 Greg LeMond, USA

*The Tour de France was only a 5-day race in 1946.

WOMEN

Year	Year	Year
1984 Marianne Martin, USA	1986 Maria Canins, Italy	1988 Jeannie Longo, France
1985 Maria Canins, Italy	1987 Jeannie Longo, France	1989 Jeannie Longo, France

Boston Marathon, 1897-89

America's oldest regularly contested foot race, the Boston Marathon is held on Patriots' Day every April. It has been run at four different distances: 24 miles, 1232 yards (1897-1923); 26 miles, 209 yards (1924-26); 26 miles, 385 yards (1927-52); 25 miles, 958 yards (1953-56); and 26 miles, 385 yards (since 1957).

Most wins: Clarence DeMar (7), Gerard Cote and Bill Rodgers (4).

MEN

Year	Winner	Time	Year	Winner	Time
1897	John McDermott, New York	2:55:10	1943	Gerard Cote, Canada	2:28:25
1898	Ronald McDonald, Massachusetts	2:42:00	1944	Gerard Cote, Canada	2:31:50
1899	Lawrence Brignolia, Massachusetts	2:54:38	1945	John A.Kelley, Massachusetts	2:30:40
			1946	Stylianos Kyriakides, Greece	2:29:27
1900	Jim Caffrey, Canada	2:39:44	1947	Yun Bok Suh, Korea	2:25:39
1901	Jim Caffrey, Canada	2:29:23	1948	Gerard Cote, Canada	2:31:02
1902	Sam Mellor, New York	2:43:12	1949	Karle Leandersson, Sweden	2:31:50
1903	J.C. Lorden, Massachusetts	2:41:29			
1904	Mike Spring, New York	2:38:04	1950	Kee Yonh Ham, Korea	2:32:39
1905	Fred Lorz, New York	2:38:25	1951	Shigeki Tanaka, Japan	2:27:45
1906	Tim Ford, Massachusetts	2:45:45	1952	Doroteo Flores, Guatemala	2:31:53
1907	Tom Longboat, Canada	2:24:24	1953	Keizo Yamada, Japan	2:18:51
1908	Tom Morrissey, New York	2:25:43	1954	Veiko Karvonen, Finland	2:20:39
1909	Henri Renaud, New Hampshire	2:53:36	1955	Hideo Hamamura, Japan	2:18:22
			1956	Antti Viskari, Finland	2:14:14
1910	Fred Cameron, Nova Scotia	2:28:52	1957	John J.Kelley, Connecticut	2:20:05
1911	Clarence DeMar, Massachusetts	2:21:39	1958	Franjo Mihalic, Yugoslavia	2:25:54
1912	Mike Ryan, Illinois	2:21:18	1959	Eino Oksanen, Finland	2:22:42
1913	Fritz Carlson, Minnesota	2:25:14			
1914	James Duffy, Canada	2:25:01	1960	Paavo Kotila, Finland	2:20:54
1915	Edouard Fabre, Canada	2:31:41	1961	Eino Oksanen, Finland	2:23:39
1916	Arthur Roth, Massachusetts	2:27:16	1962	Eino Oksanen, Finland	2:23:48
1917	Bill Kennedy, New York	2:28:37	1963	Aurele Vandendriessche, Belgium	2:18:58
1918	World War relay race		1964	Aurele Vandendriessche, Belgium	2:19:59
1919	Carl Linder, Massachusetts	2:29:13	1965	Morio Shigematsu, Japan	2:16:33
			1966	Kenji Kimihara, Japan	2:17:11
1920	Peter Trivoulidas, New York	2:29:31	1967	David McKenzie, New Zealand	2:15:45
1921	Frank Zuna, New Jersey	2:18:57	1968	Amby Burfoot, Connecticut	2:22:17
1922	Clarence DeMar, Massachusetts	2:18:10	1969	Yoshiaki Unetani, Japan	2:13:49
1923	Clarence DeMar, Massachusetts	2:23:37			
1924	Clarence DeMar, Massachusetts	2:29:40	1970	Ron Hill, England	2:10:30
1925	Charles Mellor, Illinois	2:33:00	1971	Alvaro Mejia, Colombia	2:18:45
1926	John Miles, Nova Scotia	2:25:40	1972	Olavi Suomalainen, Finland	2:15:39
1927	Clarence DeMar, Massachusetts	2:40:22	1973	Jon Anderson, Oregon	2:16:03
1928	Clarence DeMar, Massachusetts	2:37:07	1974	Neil Cusack, Ireland	2:13:39
1929	John Miles, Nova Scotia	2:33:08	1975	Bill Rodgers, Massacusetts	2:09:55
			1976	Jack Fultz, Pennsylvania	2:20:19
1930	Clarence DeMar, Massachusetts	2:34:48	1977	Jerome Drayton, Canada	2:14:46
1931	James Henigan, Massachusetts	2:46:45	1978	Bill Rodgers, Massachusetts	2:10:13
1932	Paul deBruyn, Germany	2:33:36	1979	Bill Rodgers, Massachusetts	2:09:27
1933	Leslie Pawson, Rhode Island	2:31:01			
1934	Dave Komonen, Canada	2:32:53	1980	Bill Rodgers, Massachusetts	2:12:11
1935	John A. Kelley, Massachusetts	2:32:07	1981	Toshihiko Seko, Japan	2:09:26
1936	Ellison Brown, Rhode Island	2:33:40	1982	Alberto Salazar, Massachusetts	2:08:52
1937	Walter Young, Canada	2:33:20	1983	Greg Meyer, New Jersey	2:09:00
1938	Leslie Pawson, Rhode Island	2:35:34	1984	Geoff Smith, England	2:10:34
1939	Ellison (Tarzan) Brown, Rhode Is	2:28:51	1985	Geoff Smith, England	2:14:05
			1986	Rob de Castella, Australia	2:07:51*
1940	Gerard Cote, Canada	2:28:28	1987	Toshihiko Seko, Japan	2:11:50
1941	Leslie Pawson, Rhode Island	2:30:38	1988	Ibrahim Hussein, Kenya	2:08:43
1942	Joe Smith, Massachusetts	2:26:51	1989	Abebe Mekonnen, Ethiopia	2:09:06

*Record for distance.

WOMEN

Year	Winner	Time	Year	Winner	Time
1972	Nina Kuscsik, New York	3:08:58	1980	Jacqueline Gareau, Canada	2:34:28
1973	Jacqueline Hansen, California	3:05:59	1981	Allison Roe, New Zealand	2:26:46
1974	Miki Gorman, California	2:47:11	1982	Charlotte Teske, West Germany	2:29:33
1975	Liane Winter, West Germany	2:42:24	1983	Joan Benoit, Maine	2:22:43*
1976	Kim Merritt, Wisconsin	2:47:10	1984	Lorraine Moller, New Zealand	2:29:28
1977	Miki Gorman, California	2:48:33	1985	Lisa Larsen Weidenbach, Mass	2:34:06
1978	Gayle Barron, Georgia	2:44:52	1986	Ingrid Kristiansen, Norway	2:24:55
1979	Joan Benoit, Maine	2:35:15	1987	Rosa Mota, Portugal	2:25:21
			1988	Rosa Mota, Portugal	2:24:30
			1989	Ingrid Kristiansen, Norway	2:24:33

*Record for distance.

New York City Marathon, 1970-88

Started in 1970, the New York City Marathon is run in the fall, through all of the city's five boroughs and finishes in Central Park.

Most wins: Greta Waitz (9), Bill Rodgers (4).

MEN

Year	Winner	Time
1970	Gary Muhrcke, USA	2:31:38
1971	Norman Higgins, USA	2:22:54
1972	Sheldon Karlin, USA	2:27:52
1973	Tom Fleming, USA	2:21:54
1974	Norbert Sander, USA	2:26:30
1975	Tom Fleming, USA	2:19:27
1976	Bill Rodgers, USA	2:10:09
1977	Bill Rodgers, USA	2:11:28
1978	Bill Rodgers, USA	2:12:12
1979	Bill Rodgers, USA	2:11:42
1980	Alberto Salazar, USA	2:09:41
1981	Alberto Salazar, USA	2:08:13
1982	Alberto Salazar, USA	2:09:29
1983	Rod Dixon, New Zealand	2:08:59
1984	Orlando Pizzolato, Italy	2:14:53
1985	Orlando Pizzolato, Italy	2:11:34
1986	Gianni Poli, Italy	2:11:06
1987	Ibrahim Hussein, Kenya	2:11:01
1988	Steve Jones, Wales	2:08:20

WOMEN

Year	Winner	Time
1970	No Finisher	
1971	Beth Bonner, USA	2:55:22
1972	Nina Kuscsik, USA	3:08:41
1973	Nina Kuscsik, USA	2:57:07
1974	Katherine Switzer, USA	3:07:29
1975	Kim Merritt, USA	2:46:14
1976	Miki Gorman, USA	2:39:11
1977	Miki Gorman, USA	2:43:10
1978	Greta Waitz, Norway	2:32:30
1979	Greta Waitz, Norway	2:27:33
1980	Greta Waitz, Norway	2:25:41
1981	Allison Roe, New Zealand	2:25:29
1982	Greta Waitz, Norway	2:27:14
1983	Greta Waitz, Norway	2:27:00
1984	Greta Waitz, Norway	2:29:30
1985	Greta Waitz, Norway	2:28:34
1986	Greta Waitz, Norway	2:28:06
1987	Priscilla Welch, Britain	2:30:17
1988	Greta Waitz, Norway	2:28:07

Triathlon

1989 World Championship

Held for the first time Aug.6, 1989 in Avignon, France. The World Triathlon Championship included a 1,500-meter swim (0.9 miles), 40-km bike ride (24.9 miles), and 10-km run (6.2 miles).

MEN

	Time
1 Mark Allen, USA	1:58:46
2 Glenn Cook, Britain	1:59:64

WOMEN

	Time
1 Erin Baker, New Zealand	2:10:02
2 Jan Ripple, USA	2:38:02

Ironman Triathlon Championship, 1978-88

The race that created a new sport back in 1978 with a 2.4-mile swim, a 112-mile bike ride, and a 26.2-mile run. Held every October in Hawaii. Honolulu cab driver Gordon Haller won the first race in 11 hours and 46 minutes.

Most wins: Dave Scott (6), Paula Newby-Fraser (3).

MEN

Year	Date	Winner	Time	Runner-up	Margin	Start	Finish	Location
I	2/18/78	Gordon Haller	11:46	John Dunbar	34:00	15	12	Waikiki Beach
II	1/14/79	Tom Warren	11:15:56	John Dunbar	48:00	15	12	Waikiki Beach
III	1/10/80	Dave Scott	9:24:33	Chuck Neumann	1:08	108	95	Ala Moana Park
IV	2/14/81	John Howard	9:38:29	Tom Warren	26:00	326	299	Kailua-Kona
V	2/6/82	Scott Tinley	9:19:41	Dave Scott	17:16	580	541	Kailua-Kona
VI	10/9/82	Dave Scott	9:08:23	Scott Tinley	20:05	850	775	Kailua-Kona
VII	10/22/83	Dave Scott	9:05:57	Scott Tinley	0:33	964	835	Kailua-Kona
VIII	10/6/84	Dave Scott	8:54:20	Scott Tinley	24:25	1,036	903	Kailua-Kona
IX	10/25/85	Scott Tinley	8:50:54	Chris Hinshaw	25:46	1,018	965	Kailua-Kona
X	10/18/86	Dave Scott	8:28:37	Mark Allen	9:47	1,039	951	Kailua-Kona
XI	10/10/87	Dave Scott	8:34:13	Mark Allen	11:06	1,380	1,284	Kailua-Kona
XII	10/22/88	Scott Molina	8:31:00	Mike Pigg	2:11	1,277	1,189	Kailua-Kona
XIII	10/15/89	Mark Allen	8:09:15	Dave Scott	0:58	1,285	1,231	Kailua-Kona

WOMEN

Year	Winner	Time	Runner-up
1978	No finishers		
1979	Lyn Lemaire	12:55	None
1980	Robin Beck	11:21:24	Eve Anderson
1981	Linda Sweeney	12:00:32	Sally Edwards
1982	Kathleen McCartney	11:09:40	Julie Moss
1982	Julie Leach	10:54:08	Joann Dahlkoetter
1983	Sylviane Puntous	10:43:36	Patricia Puntous
1984	Sylviane Puntous	10:25:13	Patricia Puntous
1985	Joanne Ernst	10:25:22	Liz Bulman
1986	Paula Newby-Fraser	9:49:14	Sylviane Puntous
1987	Erin Baker	9:35:25	Sylviane Puntous
1988	Paula Newby-Fraser	9:01:01	Erin Baker
1989	Paul Newby-Fraser	9:00:56	Sylviane Puntous

Figure Skating

MEN

World Champions
Skaters who won world and Olympic championships in the same year are listed in **bold** type.

Year Winner
1896 Gilbert Fuchs, Germany
1897 Gustav Hugel, Austria
1898 Henning Grenander, Sweden
1899 Gustav Hugel, Austria

1900 Gustav Hugel, Austria
1901 Ulrich Salchow, Sweden
1902 Ulrich Salchow, Sweden
1903 Ulrich Salchow, Sweden
1904 Ulrich Salchow, Sweden
1905 Ulrich Salchow, Sweden
1906 Gilbert Fuchs, Germany
1907 Ulrich Salchow, Sweden
1908 **Ulrich Salchow**, Sweden
1909 Ulrich Salchow, Sweden

1910 Ulrich Salchow, Sweden
1911 Ulrich Salchow, Sweden
1912 Fritz Kachler, Austria
1913 Fritz Kachler, Austria
1914 Gosta Sandhal, Sweden
1915 Not held .
1916 Not held
1917 Not held
1918 Not held
1919 Not held

1920 Not held
1921 Not held
1922 Gillis Grafstrom, Sweden
1923 Fritz Kachler, Austria
1924 **Gillis Grafstrom**, Sweden
1925 Willy Bockl, Austria
1926 Willy Bockl, Austria
1927 Willy Bockl, Austria

Year Winner
1928 Willy Bockl, Austria
1929 Gillis Grafstrom, Sweden

1930 Karl Schafer, Austria
1931 Karl Schafer, Austria
1932 **Karl Schafer**, Austria
1933 Karl Schafer, Austria
1934 Karl Schafer, Austria
1935 Karl Schafer, Austria
1936 **Karl Schafer**, Austria
1937 Felix Kaspar, Austria
1938 Felix Kaspar, Austria
1939 Graham Sharp, Britain

1940 Not held
1941 Not held
1942 Not held
1943 Not held
1944 Not held
1945 Not held
1946 Not held
1947 Hans Gerschwiler, Switz.
1948 **Dick Button**, USA
1949 Dick Button, USA

1950 Dick Button, USA
1951 Dick Button, USA
1952 **Dick Button**, USA
1953 Hayes Jenkins, USA
1954 Hayes Jenkins, USA
1955 Hayes Jenkins, USA
1956 **Hayes Jenkins**, USA
1957 David Jenkins, USA
1958 David Jenkins, USA
1959 David Jenkins, USA

Year Winner
1960 Alan Giletti, France
1961 Not Held
1962 Donald Jackson, Canada
1963 Donald McPherson, Canada
1964 **Manfred Schneldorfer**,W.Ger
1965 Alain Calmat, France
1966 Emmerich Danzer, Austria
1967 Emmerich Danzer, Austria
1968 Emmerich Danzer, Austria
1969 Tim Wood, USA

1970 Tim Wood, USA
1971 Ondrej Nepela, Czech.
1972 **Ondrej Nepela**, Czech.
1973 Ondrej Nepela, Czech.
1974 Jan Hoffmann, E.Germany
1975 Sergie Volkov, USSR
1976 **John Curry**, Britain
1977 Vladimir Kovalev, USSR
1978 Charles Tickner, USA
1979 Vladimir Kovalev, USSR

1980 Jan Hoffmann, E.Germany
1981 Scott Hamilton, USA
1982 Scott Hamilton, USA
1983 Scott Hamilton, USA
1984 **Scott Hamilton**, USA
1985 Alexander Fadeev, USSR
1986 Brian Boitano, USA
1987 Brian Orser, Canada
1988 **Brian Boitano**, USA
1989 Kurt Browning, Canada

U.S. Champions

Year Winner
1914 Norman Scott
1915 Not held
1916 Not held
1917 Not held
1918 Nathaniel Niles
1919 Not held

1920 Sherwin Badger
1921 Sherwin Badger
1922 Sherwin Badger
1923 Sherwin Badger
1924 Sherwin Badger
1925 Nathaniel Niles
1926 Chris Christenson
1927 Nathaniel Niles
1928 Roger Turner
1929 Roger Turner

1930 Roger Turner
1931 Roger Turner
1932 Roger Turner
1933 Roger Turner
1934 Roger Turner
1935 Robin Lee
1936 Robin Lee
1937 Robin Lee
1938 Robin Lee
1939 Robin Lee

Year Winner
1940 Eugene Turner
1941 Eugene Turner
1942 Robert Specht
1943 Arthur Vaughn
1944 Not held
1945 Not held
1946 Dick Button
1947 Dick Button
1948 Dick Button
1949 Dick Button

1950 Dick Button
1951 Dick Button
1952 Dick Button
1953 Hayes Jenkins
1954 Hayes Jenkins
1955 Hayes Jenkins
1956 Hayes Jenkins
1957 David Jenkins
1958 David Jenkins
1959 David Jenkins

1960 David Jenkins
1961 Bradley Lord
1962 Monty Hoyt
1963 Thomas Litz
1964 Scott Allen

Year Winner
1965 Gary Visconti
1966 Scott Allen
1967 Gary Visconti
1968 Tim Wood
1969 Tim Wood

1970 Tim Wood
1971 John (Misha) Petkevich
1972 Ken Shelley
1973 Gordon McKellen
1974 Gordon McKellen
1975 Gordon McKelle
1976 Terry Kubicka
1977 Charles Tickner
1978 Charles Tickner
1979 Charles Tickner

1980 Charles Tickner
1981 Scott Hamilton
1982 Scott Hamilton
1983 Scott Hamilton
1984 Scott Hamilton
1985 Brian Boitano
1986 Brian Boitano
1987 Brian Boitano
1988 Brian Boitano
1989 Christopher Bowman

Figure Skating (Continued)

WOMEN

World Champions

Skaters who won World and Olympic championships in the same year are listed in **bold** type.

Year Winner	Year Winner	Year Winner
1906 Madge Syers, Britain	1934 Sonja Henie, Norway	1962 Sjoukje Dijkstra, Holland
1907 Madge Syers, Britian	1935 Sonja Henie, Norway	1963 Sjoukje Dijkstra, Holland
1908 Lily Kronberger, Hungary	1936 **Sonja Henie**, Norway	1964 **Sjoukje Dijkstra**, Holland
1909 Lily Kronberger, Hungary	1937 Cecilia Colledge, Britain	1965 Petra Burka, Canada
1910 Lily Kronberger, Hungary	1938 Megan Taylor, Britain	1966 Peggy Flemming, USA
1911 Lily Kronberger, Hungary	1939 Megan Taylor, Britain	1967 Peggy Flemming, USA
1912 Meray Horvath, Hungary		1968 **Peggy Flemming**, USA
1913 Meray Horvath, Hungary	1940 Not held	1969 Gabriele Seyfert, E.Germany
1914 Meray Horvath, Hungary	1941 Not held	
1915 Not held	1942 Not held	1970 Gabriele Seyfert, E.Germany
1916 Not held	1943 Not held	1971 Beatrix Schuba, Austria
1917 Not held	1944 Not held	1972 **Beatrix Schuba**, Austria
1918 Not held	1945 Not held	1973 Karen Magnussen, Canada
1919 Not held	1946 Not held	1974 Christine Errath, E.Germany
	1947 Barbara Ann Scott, Canada	1975 Dianne DeLeeuw, Holland
1920 Not held	1948 **Barbara Ann Scott**, Canada	1976 **Dorothy Hamill**, USA
1921 Not held	1949 Alena Vrzanova, Czech.	1977 Linda Fratianne, USA
1922 Herma Planck-Szabo, Austria		1978 Annette Poetzsch, E.Germany
1923 Herma Planck-Szabo, Austria	1950 Alena Vrzanova, Czech.	1979 Linda Fratianne, USA
1924 **Herma Planck-Szabo**, Austria	1951 Jeannette Altwegg, Britain	
1925 Herma Planck-Szabo, Austria	1952 Jacqueline Du Bief, France	1980 **Annett Poetzsch**, E.Germany
1926 Herma Planck-Szabo, Austria	1953 Tenley Albright, USA	1981 Denise Biellmann, Switz.
1927 Sonja Henie, Norway	1954 Gundi Busch, W.Germany	1982 Elaine Zayak, USA
1928 **Sonja Henie**, Norway	1955 Tenley Albright, USA	1983 Rosalyn Sumners, USA
1929 Sonja Henie, Norway	1956 Carol Heiss, USA	1984 **Katarina Witt**, E.Germany
1930 Sonja Henie, Norway	1957 Carol Heiss, USA	1985 Katarina Witt, E.Germany
1931 Sonja Henie, Norway	1958 Carol Heiss, USA	1986 Debi Thomas, USA
1932 **Sonja Henie**, Norway	1959 Carol Heiss, USA	1987 Katarina Witt, E.Germany
1933 Sonja Henie, Norway		1988 **Katarina Witt**, E.Germany
	1960 **Carol Heiss**, USA	1989 Midori Ito, Japan
	1961 Not Held	

U.S. Champions

Year Winner	Year Winner	Year Winner
1914 Theresa Weld	1940 Joan Tozzer	1965 Peggy Flemming
1915 Not held	1941 Jane Vaughn	1966 Peggy Flemming
1916 Not held	1942 Jane Sullivan	1967 Peggy Flemming
1917 Not held	1943 Gretchen Merrill	1968 Peggy Flemming
1918 Rosemary Beresford	1944 Gretchen Merrill	1969 Janet Lynn
1919 Not held	1945 Gretchen Merrill	
	1946 Gretchen Merrill	1970 Janet Lynn
1920 Theresa Weld	1947 Gretchen Merrill	1971 Janet Lynn
1921 Theresa W.Blanchard	1948 Gretchen Merrill	1972 Janet Lynn
1922 Theresa W.Blanchard	1949 Yvonne Sherman	1973 Janet Lynn
1923 Theresa W.Blanchard		1974 Dorothy Hamill
1924 Theresa W.Blanchard	1950 Yvonne Sherman	1975 Dorothy Hamill
1925 Beatrix Loughran	1951 Sonya Klopfer	1976 Dorothy Hamill
1926 Beatrix Loughran	1952 Tenley Albright	1977 Linda Fratianne
1927 Beatrix Loughran	1953 Tenley Albright	1978 Linda Fratianne
1928 Maribel Vinson	1954 Tenley Albright	1979 Linda Fratianne
1929 Maribel Vinson	1955 Tenley Albright	
	1956 Tenley Albright	1980 Linda Fratianne
1930 Maribel Vinson	1957 Carol Heiss	1981 Elaine Zayak
1931 Maribel Vinson	1958 Carol Heiss	1982 Rosalyn Sumners
1932 Maribel Vinson	1959 Carol Heiss	1983 Rosalyn Sumners
1933 Maribel Vinson		1984 Rosalyn Sumners
1934 Suzanne Davis	1960 Carol Heiss	1985 Tiffany Chin
1935 Maribel Vinson	1961 Laurence Owen	1986 Debi Thomas
1936 Maribel Vinson	1962 Barbara Pursley	1987 Jill Trenary
1937 Maribel Vinson	1963 Lorraine Hanlon	1988 Debi Thomas
1938 Joan Tozzer	1964 Peggy Flemming	1989 Jill Trenary
1939 Joan Tozzer		

Alpine Skiing
World Cup Champions, 1967-89

MEN

Year	Winner	Year	Winner	Year	Winner
1967	Jean-Claude Killy, France	1975	Gustavo Thoeni, Italy	1982	Phil Mahre, USA
1968	Jean Claude Killy, France	1976	Ingemar Stenmark, Sweden	1983	Phil Mahre, USA
1969	Karl Schranz, Austria	1977	Ingemar Stenmark, Sweden	1984	Pirmin Zurbriggen, Switz.
1970	Karl Schranz, Austria	1978	Ingemar Stenmark, Sweden	1985	Marc Girardelli, Lux'bourg
1971	Gustavo Thoeni, Italy	1979	Peter Luescher, Switz.	1986	Marc Girardelli, Lux'bourg
1972	Gustavo Thoeni, Italy			1987	Pirmin Zurbriggen, Switz.
1973	Gustavo Thoeni, Italy	1980	Andreas Wenzel, Lichten.	1988	Pirmin Zurbriggen, Switz.
1974	Piero Gros, Italy	1981	Phil Mahre, USA	1989	Marc Girardelli, Lux'bourg

WOMEN

Year	Winner	Year	Winner	Year	Winner
1967	Nancy Greene, Canada	1975	Annemarie Moser-Proell, Aust.	1982	Erika Hess, Switzerland
1968	Nancy Greene, Canada	1976	Rosi Mittermaier, W.Germany	1983	Tamara McKinney, USA
1969	Gertrud Gabi, Austria	1977	Lise-Marie Morerod, Switz.	1984	Erika Hess, Switzerland
1970	Michele Jacot, France	1978	Hanni Wenzel, Lichtenstein	1985	Michela Figini, Switz.
1971	Annemarie Proell, Austria	1979	Annemarie Moser-Proell, Aust.	1986	Maria Walliser, Switz.
1972	Annemarie Proell, Austria			1987	Maria Walliser, Switz.
1973	Annemarie Proell, Austria	1980	Hanni Wenzel, Lichtenstein	1988	Michela Figini, Switz.
1974	Annemarie Proell, Austria	1981	Marie-Theres Nadig, Switz.	1989	Vreni Schneider, Switz.

Sled Dog Racing
The Iditarod, 1973-89

The annual 1,160-mile race from Anchorage to Nome, Alaska. Begun in 1973, the race follows an old frozen river mail route and is named after a deserted mining town along the way. The Iditarod also commemorates a famous midwinter emergency mission to get medical supplies to Nome during a 1925 diptheria epidemic. Men and women mushers compete together. **Most wins:** Rick Svenson (4), Susan Butcher (3).

Year	Winner	Elapsed Time	Year	Winner	Elapsed Time
1973	Dick Wilmarth	20 days, 00:49:41	1982	Rick Swenson	16 days, 04:40:10
1974	Carl Huntington	20 days, 15:02:07	1983	Rick Mackey	12 days, 14:10:44
1975	Emmitt Peters	14 days, 14:43:45	1984	Dean Osmar	12 days, 15:07:33
1976	Gerald Riley	18 days, 22:58:17	1984	Libby Riddles	18 days, 00:20:17
1977	Rick Swenson	16 days, 16:27:13	1986	Susan Butcher	11 days, 15:06:00
1978	Dick Mackey	14 days, 18:52:24	1987	Susan Butcher	11 days, 02:05:13*
1979	Rick Swenson	15 days, 10:37:47	1988	Susan Butcher	11 days, 11:41:40
1980	Joe May	14 days, 07:11:51	1989	Joe Runyan	11 days, 05:24:34
1981	Rick Swenson	12 days, 08:45:02			

*Course record.

Pro Rodeo
All-Around Champion Cowboys, 1929-88

Sanctioned by the Professional Rodeo Cowboys Association.

Year	Champion	Year	Champion	Year	Champion
1929	Earl Thode	1934	Leonard Ward	1940	Fritz Truan
1930	Clay Carr	1935	Everett Bowman	1941	Homer Pettigrew
1931	John Schneider	1936	John Bowman	1942	Gerald Roberts
1932	Donald Nesbit	1937	Everett Bowman	1943	Louis Brooks
1933	Clay Carr	1938	Burel Mulkey	1944	Louis Brooks
		1939	Paul Carney		

Year	Champion	Earnings	Year	Champion	Earnings	Year	Champion	Earnings
1945	No award		1960	Harry Tompkins	$32,522	1975	Tom Ferguson	$50,300
1946	No award		1961	Benny Reynolds	31,309		& Leo Camarillo	50,300
1947	Todd Whatley	$18,642	1962	Tom Nesmith	32,611	1976	Tom Ferguson	87,908
1948	Gerald Roberts	21,766	1963	Dean Oliver	31,329	1977	Tom Ferguson	65,981
1949	Jim Shoulders	21,495	1964	Dean Oliver	31,150	1978	Tom Ferguson	83,734
1950	Bill Linderman	30,715	1965	Dean Oliver	33,163	1979	Tom Ferguson	96,272
1951	Casey Tibbs	29,104	1966	Larry Mahan	40,358	1980	Paul Tierney	105,568
1952	Harry Tompkins	30,934	1967	Larry Mahan	51,996	1981	Jimmie Cooper	105,861
1953	Bill Linderman	33,674	1968	Larry Mahan	49,129	1982	Chris Lybbert	123,709
1954	Buck Rutherford	40,404	1969	Larry Mahan	57,726	1983	Roy Cooper	153,391
1955	Casey Tibbs	42,065	1970	Larry Mahan	41,493	1984	Dee Picket	122,618
1956	Jim Shoulders	43,381	1971	Phil Lyne	49,245	1985	Lewis Feild	130,347
1957	Jim Shoulders	33,299	1972	Phil Lyne	60,852	1986	Lewis Feild	166,042
1958	Jim Shoulders	32,212	1973	Larry Mahan	64,447	1987	Lewis Feild	144,335
1959	Jim Shoulders	32,905	1974	Tom Ferguson	66,929	1988	Dave Appleton	121,546

Little League Baseball

Twelve-year-old Chris Drury pitched a six-hitter and first baseman Ken Martin had a home run and three runs batted in to lead Trumbull, Conn., to a 5-2 victory over Kaohsiung, Taiwan, Aug. 26 in the 1989 Little League World Series at Williamsport, Pa.

The win was only the third of the decade for an American team and the first since 1983. Since 1967, Asian ballclubs from Taiwan, Japan and South Korea have won 18 of 23 championships.

Little League World Series, 1947-89

Year	Winner	Score	Loser	Year	Winner	Score	Loser
1947	Williamsport, PA	16-7	Lock Haven, PA	1968	Osaka, Japan	1-0	Richmond, VA
1948	Lock Haven, PA	6-5	St. Petersburg, FL	1969	Taipei, Taiwan	5-0	Santa Clara, CA
1949	Hammonton, NJ	5-0	Pensacola, FL				
				1970	Wayne, NJ	2-0	Campbell, CA
1950	Houston, TX	2-1	Bridgeport, CT	1971	Tainan, Taiwan	12-3	Gary, IN
1951	Stamford, CT	3-0	Austin, TX	1972	Taipei, Taiwan	6-0	Hammond, IN
1952	Norwalk, CT	4-3	Monongahela, PA	1973	Tainan City, Taiwan	12-0	Tucson, AZ
1953	Birmingham, AL	1-0	Schenectady, NY	1974	Kao Hsiung, Taiwan	7-2	El Cajon, CA
1954	Schenectady, NY	7-5	Colton, CA	1975	Lakewood, NJ	4-3*	Tampa, FL
1955	Morrisville, PA	4-3	Merchantville, NJ	1976	Tokyo, Japan	10-3	Campbell, CA
1956	Roswell, NM	3-1	Merchantville, NJ	1977	Kao Hsiung, Taiwan	7-2	El Cajon, CA
1957	Monterrey, Mex.	4-0	LaMesa, CA	1978	Pin-Tung, Taiwan	11-1	Danville, CA
1958	Monterrey, Mex.	10-1	Kankakee, IL	1979	Hsien, Taiwan	2-1	Campbell, CA
1959	Hamtramck, MI	12-0	Auburn, CA				
				1980	Hua Lian, Taiwan	4-3	Tampa, FL
1960	Levittown, PA	5-0	Ft. Worth, TX	1981	Tai-Chung, Taiwan	4-2	Tampa, FL
1961	El Cajon, CA	4-2	El Campo, TX	1982	Kirkland, WA	6-0	Hsien, Taiwan
1962	San Jose, CA	3-0	Kankakee, IL	1983	Marietta, GA	3-1	Barahona, D.Rep.
1963	Granada Hills, CA	2-1	Stratford, CT	1984	Seoul, S.Korea	6-2	Altamonte Sgs, FL
1964	Staten Island, NY	4-0	Monterrey, Mex.	1985	Seoul, S.Korea	7-1	Mexicali, Mex.
1965	Windsor Locks, CT	3-1	Stoney Creek, Can.	1986	Tainan Park, Taiwan	12-0	Tucson, AZ
1966	Houston, TX	8-2	W.New York, NJ	1987	Hua Lian, Taiwan	21-1	Irvine, CA
1967	West Tokyo, Japan	4-1	Chicago, IL	1988	Tai-Chung, Taiwan	10-0	Pearl City, HI
				1989	Trumbull, CT	5-2	Kaohsiung, Taiwan

*Foreign teams were banned from the tournament in 1975. The ban was lifted the next year.

Softball

Men's and women's national champions since 1933 in Major Fast Pitch, Major Slow Pitch and Super Slow Pitch (men only). Sanctioned by the Amateur Softball Association of America.

MEN
Major Fast Pitch

Year Champion	Year Champion	Year Champion
1933 J.L.Gill Boosters, Chicago	1953 Briggs Beautyware	1972 Raybestos Cardinals
1934 Ke-Nash-A, Kenosha, WI	1954 Clearwater Bombers	1973 Clearwater Bombers
1935 Crimson Coaches, Toledo, OH	1955 Raybestos Cardinals, Stratford, CT	1974 Gianella Bros, Santa Rosa, CA
1936 Kodak Park, Rochester, NY		1975 Rising Sun Hotel, Reading, PA
1937 Briggs Body Team, Detroit	1956 Clearwater Bombers	1976 Raybestos Cardinals
1938 The Pohlers, Cincinnati	1957 Clearwater Bombers	1977 Billard Barbell, Reading, PA
1939 Carr's Boosters, Covington, KY	1958 Raybestos Cardinals	1978 Billard Barbell
	1959 Sealmasters, Aurora, IL	1979 McArdle Pontiac/Cadillac, Midland, MI
1940 Kodak Park, Rochester, NY		
1941 Bendix Brakes, South Bend, IN	1960 Clearwater Bombers	
1942 Deep Rock Oilers, Tulsa, OK	1961 Sealmasters	1980 Peterbilt Western, Seattle
1943 Hammer Air Field, Fresno, CA	1962 Clearwater Bombers	1981 Archer Daniels Midland, Decatur, IL
1944 Hammer Air Field	1963 Clearwater Bombers	
1945 Zollner Pistons, Ft.Wayne, IN	1964 Burch Tool, Detroit	1982 Peterbilt Western
1946 Zollner Pistons	1965 Sealmasters	1983 Franklin Cardinals, Stratford, CT
1947 Zollner Pistons	1966 Clearwater Bombers	
1948 Briggs Beautyware, Detroit	1967 Sealmasters	1984 California Kings, Merced, CA
1949 Tip Top Tailors, Toronto	1968 Clearwater Bombers	1985 Pay'n Pak, Seattle
	1969 Raybestos Cardinals	1986 Pay'n Pak
1950 Clearwater (FL) Bombers		1987 Pay'n Pak
1951 Dow Chemical, Midland, MI	1970 Raybestos Cardinals	1988 TransAire, Elkhart, IN
1952 Briggs Beautyware	1971 Welty Way, Cedar Rapids, IA	1989 Penn Corp, Sioux City, IA

Super Slow Pitch

Year Champion	Year Champion	Year Champion
1981 Howard's/Western Steer, Denver, NC	1984 Howard's/Western Steer	1988 Starpath, Monticello, KY
1982 Jerry's Catering, Miami	1985 Steele's Sports, Grafton, OH	1989 Ritch's Salvage, Harrisburg, NC
1983 Howard's/Western Steer	1986 Steele's Sports	
	1987 Steele's Sports	

Major Slow Pitch

Year	Champion
1953	Shields Construction, Newport, KY
1954	Waldneck's Tavern, Cincinnati
1955	Lang Pet Shop, Covington, KY
1956	Gatliff Auto Sales, Newport, KY
1957	Gatliff Auto Sales
1958	East Side Sports, Detroit
1959	Yorkshire Restaurant, Newport, KY
1960	Hamilton Tailoring, Cincinnati
1961	Hamilton Tailoring
1962	Skip Hogan A.C., Pittsburgh

Year	Champion
1963	Gatliff Auto Sales
1964	Skip Hogan A.C.
1965	Skip Hogan A.C.
1966	Michael's Lounge, Detroit
1967	Jim's Sport Shop, Pittsburgh
1968	County Sports, Levittown, NY
1969	Copper Hearth, Milwaukee
1970	Little Caesar's, Southgate, MI
1971	Pile Drivers, Va.Beach, VA
1972	Jiffy Club, Louisville, KY
1973	Howard's Furniture, Denver, NC
1974	Howard's Furniture
1975	Pyramid Cafe, Lakewood, OH
1976	Warren Motors, J'ville, FL

Year	Champion
1977	Nelson Painting, Okla.City
1978	Campbell Carpets, Concord, CA
1979	Nelco Mfg.Co., Okla.City
1980	Campbell Carpets
1981	Elite Coating, Gordon, CA
1982	Triangle Sports, Minneapolis
1983	No.1 Electric & Heating, Gastonia, NC
1984	Lilly Air Systems, Chicago
1985	Blanton's Fayetteville, NC
1986	Non-Ferrous Metals, Cleveland
1987	Stapath, Monticello, KY
1988	Bell Corp/FAF, Tampa, FL
1989	Ritch's Salvage, Harrisburg, NC

WOMEN

Major Fast Pitch

Year	Champion
1933	Great Northerns, Chicago
1934	Hart Motors, Chicago
1935	Bloomer Girls, Cleveland
1936	Nat'l Screw & Mfg., Cleveland
1937	Nat'l Screw & Mfg.
1938	J.J.Krieg's, Alameda, CA
1939	J.J.Krieg's
1940	Arizona Ramblers, Phoenix
1941	Higgins Midgets, Tulsa, OK
1942	Jax Maids, New Orleans
1943	Jax Maids
1944	Lind & Pomeroy, Portland, OR
1945	Jax Maids
1946	Jax Maids
1947	Jax Maids
1948	Arizona Ramblers
1949	Arizona Ramblers
1950	Orange (CA) Lionettes
1951	Orange Lionettes
1952	Orange Lionettes

Year	Champion
1953	Betsy Ross Rockets, Fresno, CA
1954	Leach Motor Rockets, Fresno, CA
1955	Orange Lionettes
1956	Orange Lionettes
1957	Hacienda Rockets, Fresno, CA
1958	Raybestos Brakettes, Stratford, CT
1959	Raybestos Brakettes
1960	Raybestos Brakettes
1961	Gold Sox, Whittier, CA
1962	Orange Lionettes
1963	Raybestos Brakettes
1964	Erv Lind Florists, Portland, OR
1965	Orange Lionettes
1966	Raybestos Brakettes
1967	Raybestos Brakettes
1968	Raybestos Brakettes
1969	Orange Lionettes
1970	Orange Lionettes
1971	Raybestos Brakettes

Year	Champion
1972	Raybestos Brakettes
1973	Raybestos Brakettes
1974	Raybestos Brakettes
1975	Raybestos Brakettes
1976	Raybestos Brakettes
1977	Raybestos Brakettes
1978	Raybestos Brakettes
1979	Sun City (AZ) Saints
1980	Raybestos Brakettes
1981	Orlando (FL) Rebels
1982	Raybestos Brakettes
1983	Raybestos Brakettes
1984	Los Angeles Diamonds
1985	Hi-Ho Brakettes, Stratford, CT
1986	So.California Invasion, LA
1987	Orange County Majestics, Anaheim, CA
1988	Hi-Ho Brakettes (CT)
1989	Whittier (CA) Raiders

Major Slow Pitch

Year	Champion
1959	Pearl Laundry, Richmond, VA
1960	Carolina Rockets, High Pt., NC
1961	Dairy Cottage, Covington, KY
1962	Dana Gardens, Cincinnati
1963	Dana Gardens
1964	Dana Gardens
1965	Art's Acres, Omaha, NE
1966	Dana Gardens
1967	Ridge Maintenance, Cleveland
1968	Escue Pontiac, Cincinnati
1969	Converse Dots, Hialeah, FL

Year	Champion
1970	Rutenschruder Floral, Cincinnati
1971	Gators, Ft.Lauderdale, FL
1972	Riverside Ford, Cincinnati
1973	Sweeney Chevrolet, Cincinnati
1974	Marks Brothers Dots, Miami
1975	Marks Brothers Dots
1976	Sorrento's Pizza, Cincinnati
1977	Fox Valley Lassies, St.Charles, IL
1978	Bob Hoffman's Dots, Miami
1979	Bob Hoffman's Dots

Year	Champion
1980	Howard's Rubi-Otts, Graham, NC
1981	Tifton (GA) Tomboys
1982	Richmond (VA) Stompers
1983	Spooks, Anoka, MN
1984	Spooks
1985	Key Ford Mustangs, Pensacola, FL
1986	Sur-Way Tomboys, Tifton, GA
1987	Key Ford Mustangs
1988	Spooks
1989	Canaan's Illusions, Houston

Wrestling

NCAA Division I Champions

Year	Champion	Year	Champion	Year	Champion	Year	Champion	Year	Champion
1928	Oklahoma St.*	1932	Indiana*	1936	Oklahoma	1940	Oklahoma St.	1945	Not Held
1929	Oklahoma St.	1933	Oklahoma St.* Iowa St.*	1937	Oklahoma St.*	1941	Oklahoma St.	1946	Oklahoma St.
1930	Oklahoma St.*	1934	Oklahoma St.	1938	Oklahoma St.	1942	Oklahoma St.	1947	Cornell College
1931	Oklahoma St.*	1935	Oklahoma St.	1939	Oklahoma St.	1943	Not Held	1948	Oklahoma St.
						1944	Not Held	1949	Oklahoma St.

Wrestling (Continued)

Year Champion	Year Champion	Year Champion	Year Champion	Year Champion
1950 Northern Iowa	1958 Oklahoma St.	1966 Oklahoma St.	1974 Oklahoma	1982 Iowa
1951 Oklahoma	1959 Oklahoma St.	1967 Michigan St.	1975 Iowa	1983 Iowa
1952 Oklahoma	1960 Oklahoma	1968 Oklahoma St.	1976 Iowa	1984 Iowa
1953 Penn St.	1961 Oklahoma St.	1969 Iowa St.	1977 Iowa St.	1985 Iowa
1954 Oklahoma St.	1962 Oklahoma St.		1978 Iowa	1986 Iowa
1955 Oklahoma St.	1963 Oklahoma	1970 Iowa St.	1979 Iowa	1987 Iowa St.
1956 Oklahoma St.	1964 Oklahoma St.	1971 Oklahoma St.		1988 Arizona St.
1957 Oklahoma	1965 Iowa St.	1972 Iowa St.	1980 Iowa	1989 Oklahoma St.
		1973 Iowa St.	1981 Iowa	

*Unofficial champions.

Lacrosse

NCAA Men's Champions

Division I

Year Champion	Year Champion	Year Champion	Year Champion	Year Champion
1971 Cornell	1975 Maryland	1979 Johns Hopkins	1983 Syracuse	1987 Johns Hopkins
1972 Virginia	1976 Cornell	1980 Johns Hopkins	1984 Johns Hopkins	1988 Syracuse
1973 Maryland	1977 Cornell	1981 North Carolina	1985 Johns Hopkins	1989 Syracuse
1974 Johns Hopkins	1978 Johns Hopkins	1982 North Carolina	1986 North Carolina	

Division III

Year Champion	Year Champion	Year Champion	Year Champion	Year Champion
1980 Hobart	1982 Hobart	1984 Hobart	1986 Hobart	1988 Hobart
1981 Hobart	1983 Hobart	1985 Hobart	1987 Hobart	1989 Hobart

Chess

World Champions

Years	Champion	Years	Champion	Years	Champion
1866-94	Wilhelm Steinits, Austria	1937-46	Dr. A. Alekhine, France	1961-63	Mikhail Botvinnik, USSR
1894-1921	Emanuel Lasker, Germany	1948-57	Mikhail Botvinnik, USSR	1963-69	Tigran Petrosian, USSR
1921-27	Jose Capablanca, Cuba	1957-58	Vassily Smyslov, USSR	1969-72	Boris Spassky,, USSR
1927-35	Dr. A. Alekhine, France	1958-59	Mikhail Botvinnik, USSR	1972-75	Bobby Fischer, USA
1935-37	Dr. Max Euwe, Holland	1969-61	Mikhail Tal, USSR	1975-85	Anatoly Karpov, USSR
				1985-	Bary Kasparov, USSR

Note: Fischer defaulted Championship in 1975.

U.S. Champions

Unofficial

Years	Champion	Years	Champion	Years	Champion
1857-71	Paul Morphy	1876-80	James Mason	1889-90	S. Lipschutz
1871-76	George Mackenzie	1880-89	George Mackenzie	1890	Jackson Showalter
				1890-91	Max Judd

Official

Years	Champion	Years	Champion	Years	Champion
1891-92	Jackson Showalter	1951-54	Larry Evans	1980-81	Larry Evans
1892-94	S. Lipshutz	1954-57	Arthur Bisguier		Larry Christiansen
1894	Jackson Showalter	1957-61	Bobby Fischer		Walter Browne
1894-95	Albert Hodges	1961-62	Larry Evans	1981-83	Walter Browne
1895-97	Jackson Showalter	1962-68	Bobby Fischer		Yasser Seirawan
1897-1906	Harry Pillsbury	1968-69	Larry Evans	1983	Walter Browne
1906-09	Vacant	1969-72	Samuel Reshevsky		Larry Christiansen
1909-36	Frank Marshall	1972-73	Robert Byrne		Roman Dzindzichashvili
1936-44	Samuel Reshevsky	1973-74	Lubomir Kavalek	1984-85	Lev Alburt
1944-46	Arnold Denker		John Grefe	1986	Yasser Seirawan
1946-48	Samuel Reshevsky	1974-77	Walter Browne	1987	Joel Benjamin
1948-51	Herman Steiner	1978-80	Lubomir Kabalek		Nick DeFirmian
				1988	Michael Wilder

Retiring six-time U.S. Open champion **Chris Evert** waves good-by to a New York crowd of 20,000 after losing her quarterfinal match to Zina Garrison, Sept. 5.

TENNIS

INSIDE

Elsewhere in Almanac
For related information refer to the following chapters: Halls of Fame & Awards, Sports Organizations, and Updates.

*C*hris Evert calls it a career;
Youth is served at French Open;
Becker and Graf sweep singles
at Wimbledon and U.S. Open.

TENNIS

1989 YEAR IN REVIEW

by Jim Martz

At Wimbledon, Chris Evert bid farewell with a ta-ta wave as she exited Center Court after losing to Steffi Graf in the semifinal. When she decided a few weeks later that the 1989 U.S. Open would be her last major tennis tournament, she wondered how she should say good-bye at the National Tennis Center in New York.

Raise her arms and do a football stadium wave? Give a peace sign? High-five the umpire?

When the moment finally came on Sept. 5, she did it in Chris Evert style. No fanfare, no schmaltz.

After plunking a forehand return of serve into the net, she shook hands with her surprise conqueror, Zina Garrison, stuffed her racquets into a bag, put on a turquoise warmup jacket, gave a so-long wave to the Stadium Court crowd of

Jim Martz is the Regional Sports Editor of the **Miami Herald** and has covered tennis for the paper since 1973. He is also the author of a new book, *Hurricane Warning: University of Miami Football*, which was published in October, 1989.

20,000 and gave a hug to Garrison as they walked off the court. It was Garrison, not Evert, who shed a few tears.

Evert saved hers for a meeting with her husband, former U.S. Olympic skier Andy Mill, and her parents, Jimmy and Colette Evert, behind closed doors in a small room underneath the stands.

"Everybody had a few tears," said Jimmy Evert, who first taught his daughter the game when she was five at Holiday Park in Fort Lauderdale, Fla.

The 20-year career of Chris America, as she was dubbed by commentator Bud Collins, was over except for a Federation Cup appearance and a few exhibitions. Her retirement was the major story in a year in which Boris Becker challenged Ivan Lendl for the No. 1 ranking, Steffi Graf continued her domination by winning three Grand Slam tournaments, and a pair of 17-year-olds, American Michael Chang and Spain's Arantxa Sanchez, stunned the tennis world by winning French Open titles.

At the start of the year, Evert, 34, told the Women's International Tennis

Association that this probably would be her last full season on tour. When she lost to 15-year-old Monica Seles of Yugoslavia in the Virginia Slims of Houston final and then lost in the first round of the European Open to Barbara Paulus, she knew the end was near.

"I don't have the heart to stay out there and fight all day," she said.

What was billed as Evert's Last Tango in Paris never came about. She withdrew from the French Open, a tournament she had won seven times. But she entered Wimbledon (which she had won three times) and the U.S. Open (six titles) and left indelible marks at both with vintage performances.

In the quarterfinals at Wimbledon, Evert surged back from a 2–5 third-set deficit to beat Italy's Laura Golarsa, 6–3, 2–6, 7–5. Then Graf beat her, 6–2, 6–1.

At the U.S. Open, the fourth-round Evert-Seles matchup became the talk of the tournament. Many figured this would be the changing of the guard match that would send Evert packing. But Evert, who played in three U.S. Opens before Seles was born, trounced her, 6–0, 6–2. Veteran observers said that probably the only time she surpassed that level of intensity in 19 Opens was when she stopped Tracy Austin, 4–6, 6–1, 6–1, in the 1980 semifinals.

"It was a huge match," Evert said. "The crowd helped me a lot."

Two days later, Evert squandered a 5–2 lead and lost to Garrison, 7–6, 6–2. "That's one of the reasons why I am retiring," Evert said. "Because you play a great match then two days later you're a bit flat. This has happened all year with me, and I think that's why it's time."

Evert departed with a 1,304–146 career match record. She won 157 singles tournaments, a record for women and men. That included 18 Grand Slam titles, ranking her third behind Margaret Court and Helen Wills Moody (see box). She also won seven doubles titles and $8.8 million in prize money.

Her fondest memories?

"The time when I started," she said, emphasizing the 7–6, 7–6 victory over Margaret Court in 1970 soon after Court won the Grand Slam.

The men and women wrapped up their

seemingly endless 1988 season at Madison Square Garden in New York. At the Virginia Slims Championships in November, Pam Shriver stunned Graf, 6–3, 7–6, in the semifinals. It was only the third loss in 75 matches that year for Graf (Gabriela Sabatini won the other two). In the final, which features the only best-of-five-sets match in women's tennis, Sabatini wore down Shriver, 7–5, 6–2, 6–2.

At the Masters in December, Becker prevailed in the fifth-set tiebreaker with Lendl, 5–7, 7–6, 3–6, 6–2, 7–6(7–5). The match ended with a dramatic exchange lasting 37 groundstrokes and ending on a Becker backhand that struck the net and, to Becker's relief, landed on Lendl's side of the net.

"The importance of this for me will be realized in the future," Becker said prophetically. "I am playing the very best tennis of my life."

Becker's heroics continued in the Davis Cup final round at Gothenburg, Sweden, where he led an inspired West German team to its first title. In a surprising reversal of form, coach Nikki Pilic's team upset defending champion Sweden, 4–1. And it happened on clay, the Swedes' choice of surface, at the Scandinavium Stadium.

Carl-Uwe Steeb, undaunted by the

Australian Open champion **Ivan Lendl** lost to Boris Becker at the Masters and the U.S. Open, but he was the computer's pick for No. 1 in 1989.

pressure and saving a match point, set the tone when he surprised the world's No.1-ranked player at the time, Mats Wilander, 8–10, 1–6, 6–2, 6–4, 8–6. That eased the pressure on Becker, who avenged his loss in the Wimbledon final to Stefan Edberg, 6–3, 6–1, 6–4. In doubles, Becker and Eric Jelen clinched the championship by overcoming Edberg and Anders Jarryd in five sets to the delight of the 1,500 German fans in the crowd of 12,000.

At the Australian Open in January, Lendl launched the 1989 season by winning his first championship Down Under, 6–2, 6–2, 6–2, over Miloslav Mecir. That vaulted Lendl back atop the computer rankings for the first time since his loss to Wilander in the '88 U.S. Open final. And Graf's domination of the Grand Slam tournaments continued as she didn't drop a set in seven matches and beat Helena Sukova, 6–4, 6–4, in the final. At age 19, Graf had now won six Grand Slam titles.

Back in the USA, Lendl and Sabatini won finals at the fifth Lipton International Players Championships at Key Biscayne, Fla. Graf skipped the tournament that follows a two-week Grand Slam tournament format, and Sabatini captured the final, 6–1, 4–6, 6–2, over Evert. Lendl took the men's championship in a walk-over after a freak accident cost upstart Thomas Muster a chance to play in the final.

Muster, from that coldbed of tennis, Austria, upset France's Yannick Noah in the semifinals. Two hours later, Muster suffered ligament damage to his left knee when he was struck by a car while he was going to a restaurant in downtown Miami.

"I was shocked and scared, but I thought, 'Thank God, I'm alive,'" said Muster, who moved into the top 10 rankings for the first time because of his play at Key Biscayne.

Meanwhile, not since Eisenhower was president and "I Love Lucy" was starting to capture America's fancy had a player from the United States won the French Open men's singles title. That was in 1955

Seventeen-year-olds **Arantxa Sanchez** of Spain (left) and **Michael Chang** of the U.S. were the talk of the French Open. Sanchez upset Steffi Graf in the women's final and Chang knocked off both Ivan Lendl and Stefan Edberg on his way to the men's title.

when Tony Trabert beat Sven Davidson.

Enter Michael Chang, an unlikely 17-year-old hero from Southern California. The Great American Hope was supposed to be 18-year-old Andre Agassi, the No. 5 seed. But it was Chang, a 5-8, 135-pound baseliner and 15th seed, who gave American tennis a shot in the arm.

In a dramatic fourth-round match with three-time champion Lendl, Chang endured severe leg cramps to win, 4–6, 4–6, 6–3, 6–3, 6–3. Chang barely could move in the final set, yet a befuddled Lendl couldn't put him away. At 4–3, 15–30, Chang flicked an underhand serve that stunned Lendl, who lost the point and his composure. At match point, Chang staggered to within a couple of feet of the service box to receive Lendl's second serve. Lendl's serve bounced off the net cord for a double fault. Chang, in tears, fell to his knees.

"I was trying to break his concentration," Chang said of his tactics. "I would do anything to stay out there."

In the final, Chang became the youngest man ever to win a Grand Slam title as he outlasted Sweden's Stefan Edberg, 6–1, 3–6, 4–6, 6–4, 6–2.

Arantxa Sanchez, inspired by Chang's effort against Lendl, upended an ailing Graf to win the women's title, 7–6, 3–6, 7–5. Sanchez hustled all over the court and played the match of her life. Graf, who said she was suffering from menstrual cramps and had been brought low by food poisoning earlier in the week, committed 68 backcourt errors.

"I fought to win the tournament of my life, the one I've been dreaming about," Sanchez said.

Two weeks later, Lendl won the first grass court title of his career (and 79th overall) at the Queen's Club in London. But that didn't translate into a championship at Wimbledon, the lone major title to elude him. He lost in the semifinals to eventual champion Becker, 7–5, 6–7, 2–6, 6–4, 6–3. Edberg, who beat Becker in the 1988 final, felt like he was "playing uphill" in the final as 21-year-old Becker won his third Wimbledon title in five years, 6–0, 7–6, 6–4.

"Last year I was too confident against Stefan," Becker said. "That defeat taught me a lot.

491

Wide World Photos

West Germany's **Steffi Graf** and **Boris Becker** won singles titles at both Wimbledon and the U.S. Open. The Wimbledon sweep was the first by a European country since Dorothy Round and Fred Perry of England did it in 1934.

Breakfast at Wimbledon became a doubleheader because the women's final, postponed by rain the previous day, was played just before the Becker-Edberg match. Graf, eager to atone for the loss to Sanchez in Paris, halted Martina Navratilova's pursuit of a record ninth Wimbledon singles title and won her second in a row, 6–2, 6–7, 6–1.

"I did everything I could, and I got beat," said Navratilova, who skipped the entire clay court season to prepare for Wimbledon. "She's so big and strong. They used to say I was tall, but I'm only 5-7½. I said to Virginia Wade, 'I'm going to have to grow three inches.'"

The Graf and Becker victories marked the first time since 1934 a single European nation had captured both Wimbledon singles titles.

A couple of weeks later in Munich, West Germany, the U.S. met the defending champions in semifinal Davis Cup play. The Americans were back in World Group competition after a year of zonal

play, but their hopes diminished when John McEnroe was forced to withdraw because of an ailing back.

Brad Gilbert, the last-minute replacement and one of the hottest players during the summer, gave the U.S. a lift in the opening match by outlasting Steeb, 6–2, 2–6, 2–6, 6–4, 6–4. Then in a match rated one of the finest in modern Davis Cup history, Agassi built a two set-lead and served for victory at 6–5 in the third before Becker staged a valiant comeback. The fifth set was halted by a midnight curfew and was resumed 14 hours later. Becker won the one-set shootout and the match, 6–7, 6–7, 7–6, 6–3, 6–4.

"I'm disappointed because I had my chances," Agassi said after losing for the first time in eight Davis Cup matches. "But I don't feel I lost it. I feel he beat me."

The Germans grabbed a 2–1 lead when Becker teamed with Jelen to hand Ken Flach and Robert Seguso their first loss in 11 Davis Cup doubles, 3–6, 7–6,

6–4, 7–6. Steeb ousted the U.S. with a surprisingly easy, 4–6, 6–4, 6–4, 6–2, triumph over Agassi. Meanwhile in the other Davis Cup semifinal, Sweden posted a 4–1 victory over visiting Yugoslavia.

At the U.S. Open, Evert wasn't the only Golden Oldie making headlines. Jimmy Connors, who celebrated his 37th birthday during his 20th appearance in the tournament, gave the New York crowd another fist-pumping performance as he upset Edberg, 6–2, 6–3, 6–1, in the fourth round.

"I enjoy it here probably more than any place in the world," said Connors, five-time U.S. Open champion. "The atmosphere, the people. You open the gates and the people flood in. Everybody's pushing and shoving.

"I've always said that New York people are the most sports-wise in the world . . . But they're also animals. I put myself in that group. To be put in a cage with these people is a lot of fun."

Agassi weathered a furious Connors comeback in the fifth set of the quarterfinals but lost to Lendl in the semifinals.

In the women's final, Graf overcame a 2–4 deficit in the second set to beat Navratilova, 3–6, 7–5, 6–1, and win her seventh Grand Slam title out of the last eight. "I just didn't tighten the screws enough," Navratilova said.

Becker, who survived two match points against 65th-ranked Derrick Rostagnoz in the second round, made it a second straight West German sweep of a Grand Slam tournament as he edged Lendl, 7–6, 1–6, 6–3, 7–6. And that raised the inevitable "Who's No. 1?" question.

"I won Wimbledon and the U.S. Open and the computer doesn't say I'm No. 1, but I'm quite close to it," Becker said. "Ivan has been very consistent this year. He won many smaller tournaments. But as I've learned, the Grand Slams are the most important tournaments. If you can do well there, that's what it's all about. Winning two Grand Slams is the best that I can be, almost."

As Evert was saying her farewells, a 13-year-old Evert protegée was being introduced. Jennifer Capriati, who originally took lessons from Jimmy Evert while growing up in the Fort Lauderdale suburb of Lauderhill, became the youngest ever to win a Grand Slam junior championship. She won the French Open singles, Wimbledon doubles and U.S. Open singles and doubles as well as the U.S. National 18s singles title.

Inevitably, the comparisons with Evert were heaped upon Capriati, who has practiced a few times with Chris. "I want to be known as Jennifer Capriati, my own game," she said. "She is my idol and she is a great person, but I don't really want to be known as the next Chris Evert."

The Pros Prefer ATP

For several years, tennis pros talked of emulating the pro golf tour and taking control of their own sport. On Nov. 2, 1988, the Association of Tennis Professionals backed that talk with action by breaking from the Men's Tennis Council and forming the ATP Tour, which will begin in 1990.

The players said the basic reason for the break from the MTC, which had been the governing body of the men's circuit, was the lack of a significant player voice in the organization, promotion and administration of the men's pro game. In meetings between several top pros and Hamilton Jordan, chief executive officer of the ATP and former Chief of Staff of the Carter White House, the ATP submitted suggestions for improvement to the International Tennis Federation. When those were rejected, the ATP bolted.

The new tour will feature a streamlined schedule of 75 tournaments on every continent and an off-season of eight weeks at the end of the year. The season-ending Masters in New York will move to Frankfurt, West Germany, and become the ATP Tour World Championship. Meanwhile, the ATP moved its headquarters from the Dallas area to a new $6 million facility at Ponte Vedra Beach near Jacksonville, Fla.

1989 Money Leaders

MEN
ATP Tour through Sept.24, 1989.

		Earnings
1	Boris Becker	$1,183,478
2	Ivan Lendl	1,117,054
3	Stefan Edberg	712,672
4	John McEnroe	602,156
5	Brad Gilbert	475,848
6	Michael Chang	450,152
7	Alberto Mancini	428,351
8	Miloslav Mecir	319,397
9	Aaron Krickstein	312,318
10	Andre Agassi	300,506
11	Tim Mayotte	298,424
12	Jakob Hlasek	271,832
13	Carl-Uwe Steeb	261,387
14	Martin Jaite	257,394
15	Jim Pugh	253,583

WOMEN
WITA Tour through Sept.24, 1989.

		Earnings
1	Steffi Graf	$1,338,905
2	Martina Navratilova	818,964
3	Gabriela Sabatini	489,301
4	Arantxa Sanchez	477,598
5	Zina Garrison	381,278
6	Helena Sukova	325,029
7	Jana Novotna	296,896
8	Chris Evert	231,683
9	Mary Joe Fernandez	199,955
10	Natalia Zvereva	193,033
11	Monica Seles	185,711
12	Hana Mandlikova	180,753
13	Larisa Savchenko	179,997
14	Pam Shriver	175,740
15	Manuela Maleeva	175,633

1989 Men's Singles Results

Finals	Tournament (Location)	Winner	Loser	Score
Jan. 15	New South Wales Open (Sydney)	Aaron Krickstein	Andrei Cherkasov	64 62
Jan. 29	**Australian Open** (Melbourne)	Ivan Lendl	Miloslav Mecir	62 62 62
Feb. 12	Rotterdam (Holland) Grand Prix	Jakob Hlasek	Andres Jarryd	61 75
Feb. 19	Volvo of Memphis, TN	Brad Gilbert	Johan Kriek	62 62 ret
Feb. 19	Stella Artois Indoor (Milan)	Boris Becker	Alexander Volkov	61 62
Feb. 26	U.S.Pro Indoor (Philadelphia)	Boris Becker	Tim Mayotte	76 61 63
Feb. 26	Lyon (France) Grand Prix	John McEnroe	Jakob Hlasek	63 76
Mar. 8	WCT Finals (Dallas)	John McEnroe	Brad Gilbert	63 63 76
Mar. 12	Scottsdale Open (Scottsdale, AZ)	Ivan Lendl	Stefan Edberg	62 63
Mar. 19	Champions Cup (Indian Wells, CA)	Miloslav Mecir	Yannick Noah	36 26 61 62 63
Apr. 2	Lipton International (Key Biscayne, FL)	Ivan Lendl	Thomas Muster	Walkover
Apr. 23	Japan Open (Tokyo)	Stefan Edberg	Ivan Lendl	63 26 64
Apr. 30	Monte Carlo Open	Alberto Mancini	Boris Becker	75 26 76 75
May 7	Bavarian Open (Munich)	Andrei Chesnokov	Martin Strelba	57 76 62
May 8	Tourn.of Champions (Forest Hills, NY)	Ivan Lendl	Jaime Yzaga	62 61
May 15	German Open (Hamburg)	Ivan Lendl	Horst Skoff	64 61 63
May 21	Italian Open (Rome)	Alberto Mancini	Andre Agassi	63 46 26 76 61
June 11	**French Open** (Paris)	Michael Chang	Stefan Edberg	61 36 46 64 62
June 18	Queen's Club Championship (London)	Ivan Lendl	Christo van Rensburg	46 63 64
July 9	**Wimbledon** (London)	Boris Becker	Stefan Edberg	60 76 64
July 16	Gunze World Tournament (Osaka)	Anders Jarryd	Pete Sampras	64 36 64
July 31	Sovran Bank Classic (Washington, DC)	Tim Mayotte	Brad Gilbert	36 64 75
Aug. 6	Volvo Int'l (Stratton Mt., VT)	Brad Gilbert	Jim Pugh	75 60
Aug. 9	U.S.Pro Championships (Boston)	Andres Gomez	Mats Wilander	61 64
Aug. 13	U.S.Hardcourt Champs.(Indianapolis)	John McEnroe	Jay Berger	64 46 64
Aug. 20	Canadian Open (Montreal)	Ivan Lendl	John McEnroe	61 63
Aug. 20	ATP Championship (Cincinnati)	Brad Gilbert	Stefan Edberg	64 26 76
Sep. 10	**U.S.Open** (Flushing, NY)	Boris Becker	Ivan Lendl	76 16 63 76
Sep. 24	Volvo of Los Angeles	Aaron Krickstein	Michael Chang	26 64 62

1989 Women's Singles Results

Finals	Tournament (Location)	Winner	Loser	Score
Jan. 15	New South Wales Open (Sydney)	Martina Navratilova	Catarina Lindqvist	62 64
Jan. 29	**Australian Open** (Melbourne)	Steffi Graf	Helena Sukova	64 64
Feb. 5	Pan Pacific Open (Tokyo)	Martina Navratilova	Lori McNeil	67 63 76
Feb. 19	Va.Slims of Washington, DC	Steffi Graf	Zina Garrison	61 75
Feb. 26	Va.Slims of California (Oakland)	Zina Garrison	Larisa Savchenko	61 61
Mar. 3	U.S.Hardcourts (San Antonio, TX)	Steffi Graf	Ann Henricksson	61 64
Mar. 12	Va.Slims of Indiana Wells, CA	Manuela Maleeva	Jenny Byrne	64 61
Mar. 19	Va.Slims of Florida (Boca Raton)	Steffi Graff	Chris Evert	46 62 63
Apr. 2	Lipton International (Key Biscayne, FL)	Gabriela Sabatini	Chris Evert	61 46 62
Apr. 9	Family Circle Cup (Hilton Head, SC)	Steffi Graf	Natalia Zvereva	61 61
Apr. 16	Bausch & Lomb (Amelia Island, FL)	Gabriela Sabatini	Steffi Graf	36 63 75
Apr. 23	Eckerd Open (Tampa, FL)	Conchita Martinez	Gabriela Sabatini	63 62
Apr. 30	Va.Slims of Houston	Monica Seles	Chris Evert	36 61 64
May 7	Citizen Cup (Hamburg)	Steffi Graf	Jana Novotna	Default
May 14	Italian Open (Rome)	Gabriela Sabatini	Arantxa Sanchez	62 57 64

Finals	Tournament (Location)	Winner	Loser	Score
May 21	Lufthansa Cup (Berlin)	Steffi Graf	Gabriela Sabatini	63 61
May 28	European Open (Geneva)	Manuela Maleeva	Conchita Martinez	64 60
June 10	**French Open** (Paris)	Arantxa Sanchez	Steffi Graf	76 36 75
June 18	Dow Classic (Birmingham, Eng.)	Martina Navratilova	Zina Garrison	76 63
June 25	Pilkington Champs. (Eastbourne, Eng.) ..	Martina Navratilova	Raffaella Reggi	76 62
July 9	**Wimbledon** (London)	Steffi Graf	Martina Navratilova	62 67 61
July 16	Gunze World Tournament (Osaka)	Gabriela Sabatini	Mary Joe Fernandez	61 62
July 23	Va.Slims of Newport, RI	Zina Garrison	Pam Shriver	60 61
Aug. 6	Great Amer.Bank Classic (San Diego) ...	Steffi Graf	Zina Garrison	64 75
Aug. 13	Va.Slims of Los Angeles	Martina Navratilova	Gabriela Sabatini	60 62
Aug. 20	United Jersey Bank Classic (Mahwah, NJ)	Steffi Graf	Andrea Temesvari	75 62
Aug. 27	Canadian Open (Toronto)	Martina Navratilova	Arantxa Sanchez	62 62
Sep. 9	**U.S.Open** (Flushing, NY)	Steffi Graf	Martina Navratilova	36 75 61
Sep. 24	Va.Slims of Dallas	Martina Navratilova	Monica Seles	76 63

1989 Grand Slam Champions

Australian Open

Men's Singles:	Ivan Lendl
Men's Doubles:	Jim Pugh & Rick Leach
Women's Singles:	Steffi Graf
Women's Doubles:	Martina Navratilova & Pam Shriver
Mixed Doubles:	Jana Novotna & Jim Pugh

French Open

Men's Singles:	Michael Chang
Men's Doubles:	Patrick McEnroe & Jim Grabb
Women's Singles:	Arantxa Sanchez
Women's Doubles:	Natalia Zvereva & Larisa Savchenko
Mixed Doubles:	Manon Bollegraf & Tom Nijssen

Wimbledon

Men's Singles:	Boris Becker
Men's Doubles:	John Fitzgerald & Anders Jarryd
Women's Singles:	Steffi Graf
Women's Doubles:	Jana Novotna & Helena Sukova
Mixed Doubles:	Jana Novotna & Jim Pugh

U.S. Open

Men's Singles:	Boris Becker
Men's Doubles:	John McEnroe & Mark Woodforde
Women's Singles:	Steffi Graf
Women's Doubles:	Hana Mandlikova & Martina Navratilova
Mixed Doubles:	Robin White & Shelby Cannon

1989 Davis Cup

West Germany is the defending champion after upsetting Sweden, 4-1, on Dec. 18, 1988 to win the Davis Cup for the first time.

Quarterfinals
(April 7-9)

United States 5	France 0
West Germany 3	Czechoslovakia 2
Sweden 3	Austria 2
Yugoslavia 4	Spain 1

Semifinals
West Germany 3, United States 2
(at Munich, July 21-23)

Day One—Brad Gilbert (US) def. Carl-Uwe Steeb (WG), 6-2,2-6,2-6,6-4,6-4; Boris Becker (WG) def. Andre Agassi (US), 7-6,7-6,6-7,3-6,6-4.

Day Two—Becker & Eric Jelen (WG) def. Ken Flach & Robert Seguso (US), 3-6,7-6,6-4,7-6.

Day Three—Steeb (WG) def. Agassi (US), 4-6,6-4,6-4, 6-2; Gilbert (US) def. Patrick Kuhnen (WG), 6-4,1-6,6-4.

Sweden 4, Yugoslavia 1
(at Bastad, Sweden, July 21-23)

Day 1—Jonas Svensson (S) def. Goran Ivanisevic (Y), 6-4,7-6,3-6,6-4; Mats Wilander (S) def. Goran Prpic (Y), 7-6,6-1,6-0.

Day 2—Ivanisevic & Prpic (Y) def. Stefan Edberg & Anders Jarryd (S), 4-6,6-4,6-4,6-3.

Day 3—Svensson (S) def. Prpic (Y), 6-7,6-4,7-6,3-6,6-3; Wilander (S) def. Ivanisevic (Y), 6-3,6-3.

Final
Sweden at West Germany (Dec.15-17)

1989 Federation Cup

The United States won its 13th Fed Cup on Oct. 9, beating Spain, 3-0, at Ariake Colosseum in Tokyo.

Thirty-two national teams participated in the 7-day best-of-three match event.

Quarterfinals

USA 3	Austria 0
Spain 2	USSR 1
Australia 2	Bulgaria 1
Czechoslovakia 2	West Germany 1

Semifinals
USA 2, Czechoslovakia 0

Singles—Chris Evert (US) def. Jana Novotna (Czech), 6-2, 6-3; Martina Navratilova (US) def. Helena Sukova (Czech), 4-6, 6-1, 6-4.

Doubles—Pam Shriver & Zina Garrison (US) def Novotna & Jana Pospisilova (Czech), 4-1, cancelled (rain).

Spain 2, Australia 0

Singles—Conchita Martinez (SPA) def. Elizabeth Smylie (AUS), 6-3, 6-2; Arantxa Sanchez (SPA) def. Anne Minter (AUS), 6-1, 4-6, 6-2.

Doubles—cancelled (rain).

Final
USA 3, Spain 0

Singles—Chris Evert (US) def. Conchita Martinez (SPA), 6-3, 6-2; Martina Navratilova (US) def. Arantxa Sanchez (SPA), 0-6, 6-3, 6-4.

Doubles—Pam Shriver & Zina Garrison (US) def. Martinez & Sanchez (SPA), 7-5, 6-1.

Grand Slam Events

MEN

Australian Open, 1920-89

Became an Open Championship in 1969. Two tournaments were held in 1977; the first in January, the second in December. Tournament moved back to January in 1987, so no championship was decided in 1986.
Surface: Synpave Rebound Ace (hardcourt surface composed of polyurethane and synthetic rubber).
First year: 1905. **Most wins:** Roy Emerson (6).

Year	Winner	Loser	Score	Year	Winner	Loser	Score
1920	Pat Wood	R.Thomas	63 46 68 61 63	1956	Lew Hoad	K.Rosewall	64 36 64 75
1921	Rhys Gemmell	A.Hedeman	75 61 64	1957	Ashley Cooper	N.Fraser	63 911 64 62
1922	Pat Wood	G.Patterson		1958	Ashley Cooper	M.Anderson	75 63 64
			60 36 36 63 62	1959	Alex Olmedo	N.Fraser	61 62 36 63
1923	Pat Wood	C.B.St.John	61 61 63				
1924	James Anderson	R.Schlesinger		1960	Rod Laver	N.Fraser	57 36 62 86 86
			63 64 36 57 63	1961	Roy Emerson	R.Laver	16 63 75 64
1925	James Anderson	G.Patterson	119 26 62 63	1962	Rod Laver	R.Emerson	86 06 64 64
1926	John Hawkes	J.Willard	61 63 61	1963	Roy Emerson	K.Fletcher	63 63 61
1927	Gerald Patterson	J.Hawkes		1964	Roy Emerson	F.Stolle	63 64 62
			36 64 36 18 16 63	1965	Roy Emerson	F.Stolle	79 26 64 75 61
1928	Jean Borotra	R.O.Cummings		1966	Roy Emerson	A.Ashe	64 68 62 63
			64 61 46 57 63	1967	Roy Emerson	A.Ashe	64 61 61
1929	John Gregory	R.Schlesinger	62 62 57 75	1968	Bill Bowrey	J.Gisbert	75 26 97 64
1930	Gar Moon	H.Hopman	63 61 63	1969	Rod Laver	A.Gimeno	63 64 75
1931	Jack Crawford	H.Hopman	64 62 26 61				
1932	Jack Crawford	H.Hopman	46 63 36 63 61	1970	Arthur Ashe	D.Crealy	64 97 62
1933	Jack Crawford	K.Gledhill	26 75 63 62	1971	Ken Rosewall	A.Ashe	61 75 63
1934	Fred Perry	J.Crawford	63 75 61	1972	Ken Rosewall	M.Anderson	76 63 75
1935	Jack Crawford	F.Perry	26 64 64 64	1973	John Newcombe	O.Parun	63 67 75 61
1936	Adrian Quist	J.Crawford	62 63 46 36 97	1974	Jimmy Connors	P.Dent	76 64 46 63
1937	V.B.McGrath	J.Bromwich	63 16 60 26 61	1975	John Newcombe	J.Connors	75 36 64 75
1938	Don Budge	J.Bromwich	64 62 61	1976	Mark Edmondson	J.Newcombe	67 63 76 61
1939	John Bromwich	A.Quist	64 61 63	1977	Roscoe Tanner	G.Vilas	63 63 63
1940	Adrian Quist	J.Crawford	63 61 62		Vitas Gerulaitis	J.Lloyd	63 76 57 36 62
1941-45	Not held			1978	Guillermo Vilas	J.Marks	64 64 36 63
1946	John Bromwich	D.Pails	57 63 75 36 62	1979	Guillermo Vilas	J.Sadri	76 63 62
1947	Dinny Pails	J.Bromwich	46 64 36 75 86				
1948	Adrian Quist	J.Bromwich	64 36 63 26 63	1980	Brian Teacher	K.Warwick	75 76 63
1949	Frank Sedgman	K.McGregor	63 63 62	1981	Johan Kriek	S.Denton	62 76 67 64
1950	Frank Sedgman	K.McGregor	63 64 46 61	1982	Johan Kriek	S.Denton	63 63 62
1951	Richard Savitt	K.McGregor	63 63 61	1983	Mats Wilander	I.Lendl	61 64 64
1952	Ken McGregor	F.Sedgman	75 1210 26 62	1984	Mats Wilander	K.Curran	67 64 76 62
1953	Ken Rosewall	M.Rose	60 63 64	1985	Stefan Edberg	M.Wilander	64 63 63
1954	Mervyn Rose	R.Hartwig	62 06 64 62	1986	Not held (moved to Jan.,1987)		
1955	Ken Rosewall	L.Hoad	97 64 64	1987	Stefan Edberg	P.Cash	63 64 36 57 63
				1988	Mats Wilander	P.Cash	63 67 36 61 86
				1989	Ivan Lendl	M.Mecir	62 62 62

French Open, 1925-89

Prior to 1925, entry was restricted to members of French clubs. From 1941-45, tournament was closed to all foreigners. Became an Open Championship in 1968, but closed to contract pros in 1972.
Surface: Red clay.
First year: 1891. **Most wins:** Max Decugis (8). **Most wins since 1925:** Bjorn Borg (6).

Year	Winner	Loser	Score	Year	Winner	Loser	Score
1925	Rene Lacoste	J.Borotra	75 61 64	1940	Not held		
1926	Henri Cochet	R.Lacoste		1941	Bernard Destremau	n/a	n/a
1927	Rene Lacoste	B.Tilden	64 46 57 63 119	1942	Bernard Destremau	n/a	n/a
1928	Henri Cochet	R.Lacoste	57 63 61 63	1943	Yvon Petra	n/a	n/a
1929	Rene Lacoste	J.Borotra	63 26 60 26 86	1944	Yvon Petra	n/a	n/a
				1945	Yvon Petra	B.Destremau	75 64 62
1930	Henri Cochet	B.Tilden	36 86 63 61	1946	Marcel Bernard	J.Drobny	36 26 61 64 63
1931	Jean Borotra	C.Boussus	26 64 75 64	1947	Joseph Asboth	E.Sturgess	86 75 64
1932	Henri Cochet	G.de Stefani	60 64 46 63	1948	Frank Parker	J.Drobny	64 75 57 86
1933	Jack Crawford	H.Cochet	86 61 63	1949	Frank Parker	Budge Patty	63 16 61 64
1934	Gottfried vonCramm	J.Crawford	64 79 36 75 63				
1935	Fred Perry	G.von Cramm	63 36 61 63	1950	Budge Patty	J.Drobny	61 62 36 57 75
1936	Gottfried vonCramm	F.Perry	60 26 62 26 60	1951	Jaroslav Drobny	E.Sturgess	63 63 63
1937	Henner Henkel	H.Austin	61 64 63	1952	Jaroslav Drobny	F.Sedgman	62 60 36 64
1938	Don Budge	R.Menzel	63 62 64	1953	Ken Rosewall	V.Seixas	63 64 16 62
1939	Don McNeill	B.Riggs	75 60 63	1954	Tony Trabert	A.Larsen	64 75 61

Year	Winner	Loser	Score	Year	Winner	Loser	Score
1955	Tony Trabert	S.Davidson	26 61 64 62	1972	Andres Gimeno	P.Proisy	46 63 61 61
1956	Lew Hoad	S.Davidson	64 86 63	1973	Ilie Nastase	N.Pilic	63 63 60
1957	Sven Davidson	H.Flam	63 64 64	1974	Bjorn Borg	M.Orantes	67 60 61 61
1958	Mervyn Rose	L.Ayala	63 64 64	1975	Bjorn Borg	G.Vilas	62 63 64
1959	Nicola Pietrangeli	I.Vermaak	36 63 64 61	1976	Adriano Panatta	H.Solomon	61 64 46 76
				1977	Guillermo Vilas	B.Gottfried	60 63 60
1960	Nicola Pietrangeli	L.Ayala	36 63 64 46 63	1978	Bjorn Borg	G.Vilas	61 61 63
1961	Manuel Santana	N.Pietrangeli	4661366062	1979	Bjorn Borg	V.Pecci	63 61 67 64
1962	Rod Laver	R.Emerson	36 26 63 97 62				
1963	Roy Emerson	P.Darmon	36 61 64 64	1980	Bjorn Borg	V.Gerulaitis	64 61 62
1964	Manuel Santana	N.Pietrangeli	63 61 46 75	1981	Bjorn Borg	I.Lendl	61 46 62 36 61
1965	Fred Stolle	T.Roche	36 60 62 63	1982	Mats Wilander	G.Vilas	16 76 60 64
1966	Tony Roche	I.Gulyas	61 64 75	1983	Yannick Noah	M.Wilander	62 75 76
1967	Roy Emerson	T.Roche	61 64 26 62	1984	Ivan Lendl	J.McEnroe	36 26 64 75 75
1968	Ken Rosewall	R.Laver	63 61 26 62	1985	Mats Wilander	I.Lendl	36 64 62 62
1969	Rod Laver	K.Rosewall	64 63 64	1986	Ivan Lendl	M.Pernfors	63 62 64
				1987	Ivan Lendl	M.Wilander	75 62 36 76
1970	Jan Kodes	Z.Franulovic	62 64 60	1988	Mats Wilander	H.Leconte	75 62 61
1971	Jan Kodes	I.Nastasi	86 62 26 75	1989	Michael Chang	S.Edberg	61 36 46 64 62

Wimbledon, 1920-89

Officially called "The Lawn Tennis Championships" at the All-England Club, Wimbledon. Challenge round system (defending champion automatically qualifies for following year's final) used from 1877-1921. Became an Open Championship in 1968, but closed to contract pros in 1972.

Surface: Grass.

First year: 1877. **Most wins:** William Renshaw (7). **Most wins since 1920:** Bjorn Borg (5).

Year	Winner	Loser	Score	Year	Winner	Loser	Score
1920	Bill Tilden	G.Patterson	26 63 62 64	1958	Ashley Cooper	N.Fraser	36 62 64 1311
1921	Bill Tilden	B.Norton	46 26 61 60 75	1959	Alex Olmedo	R.Laver	64 63 64
1922	Gerald Patterson	R.Lycett	63 64 62				
1923	Bill Johnston	F.Hunter	60 63 61	1960	Neale Fraser	R.Laver	64 36 97 75
1924	Jean Borotra	R.Lacoste	61 36 61 36 64	1961	Rod Laver	C.McKinley	63 61 64
1925	Rene Lacoste	J.Borotra	63 63 46 86	1962	Rod Laver	M.Mulligan	62 62 61
1926	Jean Borotra	H.Kinsey	86 61 63	1963	Chuck McKinley	F.Stolle	97 61 64
1927	Henri Cochet	J.Borotra	46 46 63 64 75	1964	Roy Emerson	F.Stolle	64 1210 46 63
1928	Rene Lacoste	H.Cochet	61 46 64 62	1965	Roy Emerson	F.Stolle	62 64 64
1929	Henri Cochet	J.Borotra	64 63 64	1966	Manuel Santana	D.Rolston	64 119 64
				1967	John Newcombe	W.Bungert	63 61 61
1930	Bill Tilden	W.Allison	63 97 64	1968	Rod Laver	T.Roche	63 64 62
1931	Sidney Wood	F.Shields	w.o.	1969	Rod Laver	J.Newcombe	64 57 64 64
1932	Ellsworth Vines	H.Austin	64 62 60				
1933	Jack Crawford	E.Vines	46 119 62 26 64	1970	John Newcombe	K.Rosewall	57 63 62 36 61
1934	Fred Perry	J.Crawford	63 60 75	1971	John Newcombe	S.Smith	63 57 26 64 64
1935	Fred Perry	G.von Cramm	62 64 64	1972	Stan Smith	I.Nastase	46 63 63 46 75
1936	Fred Perry	G.von Cramm	61 61 60	1973	Jan Kodes	A.Metreveli	61 98 63
1937	Don Budge	G.von Cramm	63 64 62	1974	Jimmy Connors	K.Rosewall	61 61 64
1938	Don Budge	H.Austin	61 60 63	1975	Arthur Ashe	J.Connors	61 61 57 64
1939	Bobby Riggs	E.Cooke	26 86 36 63 62	1976	Bjorn Borg	I.Nastase	64 62 97
				1977	Bjorn Borg	J.Connors	36 62 61 57 64
1940-45	Not held			1978	Bjorn Borg	J.Connors	62 62 63
1946	Yvon Petra	G.Brown	62 64 79 57 64	1979	Bjorn Borg	R.Tanner	67 61 36 63 64
1947	Jack Kramer	T.Brown	61 63 62				
1948	Bob Falkenburg	J.Bromwich	75 06 62 36 75	1980	Bjorn Borg	J.McEnroe	16 75 63 67 86
1949	Ted Schroeder	J.Drobny	36 60 63 46 64	1981	John McEnroe	B.Borg	46 76 76 64
				1982	Jimmy Connors	J.McEnroe	36 63 67 76 64
1950	Budge Patty	F.Sedgman	61 810 62 63	1983	John McEnroe	C.Lewis	62 62 62
1951	Dick Savitt	K.McGregor	64 64 64	1984	John McEnroe	J.Connors	61 61 62
1952	Frank Sedgman	J.Drobny	46 63 62 63	1985	Boris Becker	K.Curran	63 67 76 64
1953	Vic Seixas	K.Nielsen	97 63 64	1986	Boris Becker	I.Lendl	64 63 75
1954	Jaroslav Drobny	K.Rosewall	1311 46 62 97	1987	Pat Cash	I.Lendl	76 62 75
1955	Tony Trabert	K.Nielsen	63 75 61	1988	Stefan Edberg	B.Becker	46 76 64 62
1956	Lew Hoad	K.Rosewall	62 47 75 64	1989	Boris Becker	S.Edberg	60 76 64
1957	Lew Hoad	A.Cooper	62 62 62				

U.S. Open, 1920-89

Challenge round system (defending champion automatically qualifies for following year's final) used from 1884-1911. Amateur and Open championships held in 1968 and '69. Became an exclusively Open championship in 1970.
Surface: Decoturf II (acrylic cement).
First year: 1881. **Most wins:** Richard Sears (7), Bill Larned (7) and Bill Tilden (7). **Most wins since 1920:** Tilden (7).

Year	Winner	Loser	Score	Year	Winner	Loser	Score
1920	Bill Tilden	B.Johnston	61 16 75 57 63	1955	Tony Trabert	K.Rosewall	97 63 63
1921	Bill Tilden	W.Johnson	61 63 61	1956	Ken Rosewall	L.Hoad	46 62 63 63
1922	Bill Tilden	B.Johnston	46 36 62 63 64	1957	Mal Anderson	A.Cooper	108 75 64
1923	Bill Tilden	B.Johnston	64 61 64	1958	Ashley Cooper	M.Anderson	
1924	Bill Tilden	B.Johnston	61 97 62				62 36 46 108 86
1925	Bill Tilden	B.Johnston	46 119 63 46 63	1959	Neale Fraser	A.Olmedo	63 57 62 64
1926	Rene Lacoste	J.Borotra	64 60 64	1960	Neale Fraser	R.Laver	64 64 97
1927	Rene Lacoste	B.Tilton	110 63 119	1961	Roy Emerson	R.Laver	75 63 62
1928	Henri Cochet	F.Hunter	46 64 36 75 63	1962	Rod Laver	R.Emerson	62 64 57 64
1929	Bill Tilden	F.Hunter	36 63 46 62 64	1963	Rafael Osuna	F.Froehling	75 64 62
1930	John Doeg	F.Shields	108 16 64 1614	1964	Roy Emerson	F.Stolle	64 62 64
1931	Ellsworth Vines	G.Lott Jr.	79 63 97 75	1965	Manuel Santana	C.Drysdale	62 79 75 61
1932	Ellsworth Vines	H.Cochet	64 64 64	1966	Fred Stolle	J.Newcombe	42 1210 63 64
1933	Fred Perry	J.Crawford		1967	John Newcombe	C.Graebner	64 64 86
			63 1113 46 60 61	1968	Arthur Ashe	B.Lutz	46 63 810 60 64
1934	Fred Perry	W.Allison	64 63 16 86	1968	Arthur Ashe	T.Okker	1412 57 63 36 63
1935	Wilmer Allison	S.Wood	62 62 63	1969	Stan Smith	B.Lutz	97 63 61
1936	Fred Perry	D.Budge	26 62 86 16 108	1969	Rod Laver	T.Roche	79 61 63 62
1937	Don Budge	G.von Cramm					
			61 79 61 36 61	1970	Ken Rosewall	T.Roche	26 64 76 63
1938	Don Budge	G.Mako	63 68 62 61	1971	Stan Smith	J.Kodes	36 63 62 76
1939	Bobby Riggs	S.van Horn	64 62 64	1972	Ilie Nastase	A.Ashe	36 63 67 64 63
				1973	John Newcombe	J.Kodes	64 16 46 62 63
1940	Don McNeill	B.Riggs	46 68 63 63 75	1974	Jimmy Connors	K.Rosewall	61 60 61
1941	Bobby Riggs	F.Kovacs	57 61 63 63	1975	Manuel Orantes	J.Connors	64 63 63
1942	Fred Schroeder	F.Parker	86 75 36 46 62	1976	Jimmy Connors	B.Borg	64 36 76 64
1943	Joseph Hunt	J.Kramer	63 68 108 60	1977	Guillermo Vilas	J.Connors	26 63 76 60
1944	Frank Parker	B.Talbert	64 36 63 63	1978	Jimmy Connors	B.Borg	64 62 62
1945	Frank Parker	B.Talbert	1412 61 62	1979	John McEnroe	V.Gerulaitis	75 63 63
1946	John Kramer	T.Brown, Jr.	97 63 60	1980	John McEnroe	B.Borg	76 61 67 57 64
1947	John Kramer	F.Parker	46 26 61 60 63	1981	John McEnroe	B.Borg	46 62 64 63
1948	Pancho Gonzales	E.Sturgess	62 63 1412	1982	Jimmy Connors	I.Lendl	63 62 46 64
1949	Pancho Gonzales	F.Schroeder		1983	Jimmy Connors	I.Lendl	63 67 75 60
			1618 26 61 62 64	1984	John McEnroe	I.Lendl	63 64 61
1950	Arthur Larsen	H.Flam	63 46 57 64 63	1985	Ivan Lendl	J.McEnroe	76 63 64
1951	Frank Sedgman	V.Seixas	64 61 61	1986	Ivan Lendl	M.Mecir	64 62 60
1952	Frank Sedgman	G.Mulloy	61 62 63	1987	Ivan Lendl	M.Wilander	67 60 76 64
1953	Tony Trabert	V.Seixas	63 62 63	1988	Mats Wilander	I.Lendl	64 46 63 57 64
1954	Vic Seixas	R.Hartwig	36 62 64 64	1989	Boris Becker	I.Lendl	76 16 63 76

Grand Slam Winners

The following players have won the championships of Australia, France, Wimbledon and the United States in the same calendar year.

Men's Singles
1938 Don Budge, USA
1962 Rod Laver, Australia
1969 Rod Laver, Australia

Men's Doubles
1951 Frank Sedgman, Australia
　　 & Ken McGregor, Australia

Women's Singles
1953 Maureen Connolly, USA
1970 Margaret Smith Court, Australia
1988 Steffi Graf, West Germany

Women's Doubles
1960 Maria Bueno, Brazil & two partners
1984 Martina Navratilova, USA & Pam Shriver, USA

Mixed Doubles
1963 Ken Fletcher, Australia
　　 & Margaret Smith, Australia
1967 Owen Davidson, Australia & two partners

Notes: In Women's Doubles—Bueno won Australia with Christine Truman then took the French, Wimbledon and the US with Darlene Hard. In Mixed Doubles—Davidson won Australia with Lesley Turner then took the French, Wimbledon and the US with Billie Jean King.

WOMEN
Australian Open, 1920-89

Became an Open Championship in 1969. Two tournaments were held in 1977; the first in January, the second in Decemer. Tournament moved back to January in 1987, so no championship was decided in 1986.

First year: 1922. **Most wins:** Margaret Smith Court (11).

Year	Winner	Loser	Score	Year	Winner	Loser	Score
1922	Mall Molesworth	E.Boyd	63 108	1958	Angela Mortimer	L.Coghlan	63 64
1923	Mall Molesworth	E.Boyd	61 75	1959	Mary Reitano	T.Schuman	62 63
1924	Sylvia Lance	E.Boyd	63 36 64	1960	Margaret Smith	J.Lehane	75 62
1925	Daphne Akhurst	E.Boyd	16 86 64	1961	Margaret Smith	J.Lehane	61 64
1926	Daphne Akhurst	E.Boyd	61 63	1962	Margaret Smith	J.Lehane	60 62
1927	Esna Boyd	S.Harper	57 61 62	1963	Margaret Smith	J.Lehane	62 62
1928	Daphne Akhurst	E.Boyd	75 62	1964	Margaret Smith	L.Turner	63 62
1929	Daphne Akhurst	L.Bickerton	61 57 62	1965	Margaret Smith	M.Bueno	57 64 52(ret)
1930	Daphne Akhurst	S.Harper	108 26 75	1966	Margaret Smith	N.Richey	w.o.
1931	Coral Buttsworth	M.Crawford	16 63 64	1967	Nancy Richey	L.Turner	61 64
1932	Coral Buttsworth	K.LeMessurier	97 64	1968	Billie Jean King	M.Smith	61 62
1933	Joan Hartigan	C.Buttsworth	64 63	1969	Margaret S.Court	B.Jean King	64 61
1934	Joan Hartigan	M.Molesworth	61 64	1970	Margaret S.Court	K.Melville	63 61
1935	Dorothy Round	N.Bolton	16 61 63	1971	Margaret S.Court	E.Goolagong	26 76 75
1936	Joan Hartigan	N.Bolton	64 64	1972	Virginia Wade	E.Goolagong	64 64
1937	Nancye Wynne	E.Westacott	63 57 64	1973	Margaret S.Court	E.Goolagong	64 75
1938	Dorothy M.Bundy	D.Stevenson	63 62	1974	Evonne Goolagong	C.Evert	76 46 60
1939	Emily Westacott	N.Hopman	61 62	1975	Evonne Goolagong	M.Navratilova	63 62
1940	Nancye Wynne	T.Coyne	57 64 60	1976	E.Goolag.Cawley	R.Tomanova	62 62
1941-45 Not held				1977	K.Melville Reid	D.Balestrat	75 62
1946	Nancye W.Bolton	J.Fitch	64 64		E.Goolag.Cawley	H.Gourlay	63 60
1947	Nancye W.Bolton	N. Hopman	63 62	1978	Chris O'Neill	B.Nagelsen	63 76
1948	Nancye W.Bolton	M.Toomey	63 61	1979	Barbara Jordan	S.Walsh	63 63
1949	Doris Hart	N.Bolton	63 64	1980	Hana Mandlikova	W.Turnbull	60 75
1950	Louise Brough	D.Hart	64 36 64	1981	M.Navratilova	C.Evert Lloyd	67 64 75
1951	Nancye W.Bolton	T.Long	61 75	1982	Chris Evert Lloyd	M.Navratilova	63 26 63
1952	Thelma Long	H.Angwin	62 63	1983	M.Navratilova	K.Jordan	62 76
1953	Maureen Connelly	J.Sampson	63 62	1984	Chris Evert Lloyd	H.Sukova	67 61 63
1954	Thelma Long	J.Staley	63 64	1985	M.Navratilova	C.Evert Lloyd	62 46 62
1955	Beryl Pemrose	T.Long	64 63	1986	Not held (moved to Jan.,1987)		
1956	Mary Carter	T.Long	36 62 97	1987	Hana Mandlikova	M.Navratilova	75 76
1957	Shirley Fry	A.Gibson	63 64	1988	Steffi Graf	C.Evert	61 76
				1989	Steffi Graf	H.Sukova	64 64

French Open, 1925-89

Prior to 1925, entry was restricted to members of French clubs. Became an Open Championship in 1968, but closed to contract pros in 1972.

First year: 1897. **Most wins:** Chris Evert (7).

Year	Winner	Loser	Score	Year	Winner	Loser	Score
1925	Suzanne Lenglen	K.McKane	61 62	1960	Darlene Hard	Y.Ramirez	63 64
1926	Suzanne Lenglen	M.Browne	61 60	1961	Ann Hayden	Y.Ramirez	62 61
1927	Kea Bouman	I.Peacock	62 64	1962	Margaret Smith	L.Turner	63 36 75
1928	Helen Wills	E.Bennett	61 62	1963	Lesley Turner	A.Jones	26 63 75
1929	Helen Wills	S.Mathieu	63 64	1964	Margaret Smith	M.Bueno	57 61 62
1930	Helen W. Moody	H.Jacobs	62 61	1965	Lesley Turner	M.Smith	63 64
1931	Cilly Aussem	B.Nuthall	86 61	1966	Ann Jones	N.Richey	63 61
1932	Helen W. Moody	S.Mathieu	75 61	1967	Francoise Durr	L.Turner	46 63 64
1933	Margaret Scriven	S.Mathieu	62 46 64	1968	Nancy Richey	A.Jones	57 64 61
1934	Margaret Scriven	H.Jacobs	75 46 61	1969	Margaret S.Court	A.Jones	61 46 63
1935	Hilde Sperling	S.Mathieu	62 61	1970	Margaret S.Court	H.Niessen	62 64
1936	Hilde Sperling	S.Mathieu	63 64	1971	E.Goolagong	H.Gourlay	63 75
1937	Hilde Sperling	S.Mathieu	62 64	1972	Billie Jean King	E.Goolagong	63 63
1938	Simone Mathieu	N.Landry	60 63	1973	Margaret S.Court	C.Evert	67 76 64
1939	Simone Mathieu	J.Jedrzejowska	63 86	1974	Chris Evert	O.Morozova	61 62
1940-45 Not held				1975	Chris Evert	M.Navratilova	26 62 61
1946	Margaret Osborne	P.Betz	16 86 75	1976	Sue Barker	R.Tomanova	62 06 62
1947	Patricia Todd	D.Hart	63 36 64	1977	Mima Jausovec	F.Mihai	62 67 61
1948	Nelly Landry	S.Fry	62 06 60	1978	Virginia Ruzici	M.Jausovec	62 62
1949	M.Osborne duPont	N.Adamson	75 62	1979	Chris Evert Lloyd	W.Turnbull	62 60
1950	Doris Hart	P.Todd	64 46 62	1980	Chris Evert Lloyd	V.Ruzici	60 63
1951	Shirley Fry	D.Hart	63 36 63	1981	Hana Mandlikova	S.Hanika	62 64
1952	Doris Hart	S.Fry	64 64	1982	M.Navratilova	A.Jaeger	76 61
1953	Maureen Connelly	D.Hart	62 64	1983	Chris Evert Lloyd	M.Jausovec	61 62
1954	Maureen Connelly	G.Bucaille	62 64	1984	M.Navratilova	C.Evert Lloyd	63 61
1955	Angela Mortimer	D.Knode	26 75 108	1985	Chris Evert Lloyd	M.Navratilova	63 67 75
1956	Althea Gibson	A.Mortimer	62 1210	1986	Chris Evert Lloyd	M.Navratilova	26 63 63
1957	Shirley Bloomer	D.Knode	61 63	1987	Steffi Graf	M.Navratilova	64 46 86
1958	Zsuzsi Kormoczy	S.Bloomer	64 16 62	1988	Steffi Graf	N.Zvereva	60 60
1959	Christine Truman	Z.Kormoczy	64 75	1989	Arantxa Sanchez	S.Graf	76 36 75

Wimbledon, 1920-29

Officially called "The Lawn Tennis Championships" at the All-England Club, Wimbledon. Challenge round system (defending champion automatically qualifies for following year's final) used from 1886-1921. Became an Open Championship in 1968, but closed to contract pros in 1972.
First year: 1884. **Most wins:** Helen Wills Moody (8) and Martina Navratilova (8).

Year	Winner	Loser	Score
1920	Suzanne Lenglen	D.Chambers	63 60
1921	Suzanne Lenglen	E.Ryan	62 60
1922	Suzanne Lenglen	M.Mallory	62 60
1923	Suzanne Lenglen	K.McKane	62 62
1924	Kathleen McKane	H.Wills	46 64 64
1925	Suzanne Lenglen	J.Fry	62 60
1926	Kathleen Godfree	L.de Alvarez	62 46 63
1927	Helen Wills	L.de Alvarez	62 64
1928	Helen Wills	L.de Alvarez	62 63
1929	Helen Wills	H.Jacobs	61 62
1930	Helen W.Moody	E.Ryan	62 62
1931	Cilly Aussem	H.Kranwinkel	75 75
1932	Helen W.Moody	H.Jacobs	63 61
1933	Helen W.Moody	D.Round	64 68 63
1934	Dorothy Round	H.Jacobs	62 57 63
1935	Helen W.Moody	H.Jacobs	63 36 75
1936	Helen Jacobs	H.K.Sperling	62 46 75
1937	Dorothy Round	J.Jedrzejowska	62 26 75
1938	Helen W.Moody	H.Jacobs	64 60
1939	Alice Marble	K.Stammers	62 60
1940-45	Not held		
1946	Pauline Betz	L.Brough	62 64
1947	Margaret Osborne	D.Hart	62 64
1948	Louise Brough	D.Hart	63 86
1949	Louise Brough	M.Osb.duPont	108 16 108
1950	Louise Brough	M.Osb.duPont	61 36 61
1951	Doris Hart	S.Fry	61 60
1952	Maureen Connolly	L.Brough	64 63
1953	Maureen Connolly	D.Hart	86 75
1954	Maureen Connolly	L.Brough	62 75
1955	Louise Brough	B.Fleitz	75 86
1956	Shirley Fry	A.Buxton	63 61
1957	Althea Gibson	D.Hard	63 62
1958	Althea Gibson	A.Mortimer	86 62
1959	Maria Bueno	D.Hard	64 63
1960	Maria Bueno	S.Reynolds	86 60
1961	Angela Mortimer	C.Truman	46 64 75
1962	Karen H.Susman	V.Sukova	64 64
1963	Margaret Smith	B.Jean Moffit	63 64
1964	Maria Bueno	M.Smith	64 79 63
1965	Margaret Smith	M.Bueno	64 75
1966	Billie Jean King	M.Bueno	63 36 61
1967	Billie Jean King	A.Haydon Jones	63 64
1968	Billie Jean King	J.Tegart	97 75
1969	Ann Jones	B.Jean King	36 63 62
1970	Margaret S.Court	B.Jean King	1412 119
1971	Evonne Goolagong	M.S.Court	64 61
1972	Billie Jean King	E.Goolagong	63 63
1973	Billie Jean King	C.Evert	60 75
1974	Chris Evert	O.Morzova	60 64
1975	Billie Jean King	E.Goolag.Cawley	60 61
1976	Chris Evert	E.Goolag.Cawley	63 46 86
1977	Virginia Wade	B.Stove	46 63 61
1978	M.Navratilova	Chris Evert	26 64 75
1979	M.Navratilova	Chris Evert Lloyd	64 64
1980	E.Goolag.Cawley	Chris Evert Lloyd	61 76
1981	Chris Evert Lloyd	H.Mandlikova	62 62
1982	M.Navratilova	Chris Evert Lloyd	61 36 62
1983	M.Navratilova	Andrea Jaeger	60 63
1984	M.Navratilova	Chris Evert Lloyd	76 62
1985	M.Navratilova	Chris Evert Lloyd	46 63 62
1986	M.Navratilova	H.Mandlikova	76 63
1987	M.Navratilova	Steffi Graf	75 63
1988	Steffi Graf	M.Navratilova	57 62 61
1989	Steffi Graf	M.Navratilova	62 67 61

U.S. Open, 1920-89

Amateur and Open Championships held in 1968 and '69. Became an exclusively Open Championship in 1970.
First year: 1887. **Most wins:** Molla B.Mallory (8). **Most wins since 1920:** Helen Wills Moody (7).

Year	Winner	Loser	Score
1920	Molla B.Mallory	M.Zinderstein	63 61
1921	Molla B.Mallory	M.Browne	46 64 62
1922	Molla B.Mallory	H.Wills	63 61
1923	Helen Wills	M.B.Mallory	62 61
1924	Helen Wills	M.B.Mallory	61 63
1925	Helen Wills	K.McKane	36 60 62
1926	Molla B.Mallory	E.Ryan	46 64 97
1927	Helen Wills	B.Nuthall	61 64
1928	Helen Wills	H.Jacobs	62 61
1929	Helen Wills	P.Watson	64 62
1930	Betty Nuthall	A.Harper	61 64
1931	Helen W.Moody	E.Whitingstall	64 61
1932	Helen Jacobs	C.Babcock	62 62
1933	Helen Jacobs	H.W.Moody	86 36 30(ret)
1934	Helen Jacobs	S.Palfrey	61 64
1935	Helen Jacobs	S.Palfrey Fabyan	62 64
1936	Alice Marble	H.Jacobs	46 63 62
1937	Anita Lizane	J.Jedrzejowska	64 62
1938	Alice Marble	N.Wynne	60 63
1939	Alice Marble	H.Jacobs	60 810 64
1940	Alice Marble	H.Jacobs	62 63
1941	Sarah P.Cooke	P.Betz	75 62
1942	Pauline Betz	L.Brough	46 61 64
1943	Pauline Betz	L.Brough	63 57 63
1944	Pauline Betz	M.Osborne	63 86
1945	Sarah P.Cooke	P.Betz	36 86 64
1946	Pauline Betz	P.Canning	119 63
1947	Louise Brough	M.Osborne	86 46 61
1948	Margaret O.duPont	L.Brough	46 64 1513
1949	Margaret O.duPont	D.Hart	64 61
1950	Margaret O.duPont	D.Hart	64 63
1951	Maureen Connolly	S.Fry	63 16 64
1952	Maureen Connolly	D.Hart	63 75
1953	Maureen Connolly	D.Hart	62 64
1954	Doris Hart	L.Brough	68 61 86
1955	Doris Hart	P.Ward	64 62
1956	Shirley Fry	A.Gibson	63 64
1957	Althea Gibson	L.Brough	63 62
1958	Althea Gibson	D.Hard	36 61 62
1959	Maria Bueno	C.Truman	61 64
1960	Darlene Hard	M.Bueno	64 1012 64
1961	Darlene Hard	A.Haydon	63 64
1962	Margaret Smith	D.Hard	97 64
1963	Maria Bueno	M.Smith	75 64
1964	Maria Bueno	C.Graebner	61 60

Year	Winner	Loser	Score	Year	Winner	Loser	Score
1965	Margaret Smith	B.Jean Moffit	86 75	1976	Chris Evert	E.Goola.Cawley	63 60
1966	Maria Bueno	N.Richey	63 61	1977	Chris Evert	W.Turnbull	76 62
1967	Billie Jean King	A.Haydon Jones	119 64	1978	Chris Evert	P.Shriver	76 64
1968	Margaret S.Court	M.Bueno	62 62	1979	Tracy Austin	C.Evert Lloyd	64 63
1968	Virginia Wade	B.Jean King	64 62	1980	Chris Evert Lloyd	H.Mandlikova	57 61 61
1969	Margaret S.Court	V.Wade	46 63 60	1981	Tracy Austin	M.Navratilova	16 76 76
1969	Margaret S.Court	N.Richey	62 62	1982	Chris Evert Lloyd	H.Mandlikova	63 61
1970	Margaret S.Court	R.Casals	62 26 61	1983	M.Navratilova	C.Evert Lloyd	61 63
1971	Billie Jean King	R.Casals	64 76	1984	M.Navratilova	C.Evert Lloyd	46 64 64
1972	Billie Jean King	K.Melville	63 75	1985	Hana Mandlikova	M.Navratilova	76 16 76
1973	Margaret S.Court	E.Goolagong	76 57 62	1986	M.Navratilova	H.Sukova	63 62
1974	Billie Jean King	E.Goolagong	36 63 75	1987	M.Navratilova	S.Graf	76 61
1975	Chris Evert	E.Goola.Cawley	57 64 62	1988	Steffi Graf	G.Sabatini	63 36 61
				1989	Steffi Graf	M.Navratilova	36 75 61

Year-end Tournaments

MEN

Grand Prix Masters

The year-end championship of the Men's Tour. Competed for by the year's top eight players. Originally a round-robin, the Masters now uses a round-robin format to decide the four semifinalists then is single elimination in the semifinals and final. The event has been held at Madison Square Garden in New York since 1978.

Year	Winner	Runner-Up		Year	Winner	Loser	Score
1970	Stan Smith (4-1)*	Rod Laver (4-1)		1980	Bjorn Borg	V.Gerulaitis	62 62
1971	Ilie Nastase (6-0)	Stan Smith (4-2)		1981	Bjorn Borg	I.Lendl	64 62 62

Year	Winner	Loser	Score	Year	Winner	Loser	Score
1972	Ilie Nastase	S.Smith	63 62 36 26 63	1982	Ivan Lendl	V.Gerulaitis	67 26 76 62 64
1973	Ilie Nastase	T.Okker	63 75 46 63	1983	Ivan Lendl	J.McEnroe	64 64 62
1974	Guillermo Vilas	I.Nastase	76 62 36 36 64	1984	John McEnroe	I.Lendl	63 64 64
1975	Ilie Nastase	B.Borg	62 62 61	1985	John McEnroe	I.Lendl	75 60 64
1976	Manuel Orantes	W.Fibak	57 62 06 76 61	1986	Ivan Lendl	B.Becker	62 76 63
1978*	Jimmy Connors	B.Borg	64 16 64	1986*	Ivan Lendl	B.Becker	64 64 64
1979	John McEnroe	A.Ashe	67 63 75	1987	Ivan Lendl	M.Wilander	62 62 63
				1988	Boris Becker	I.Lendl	57 76 36 62 76

*Tournament switched from December to January in 1977-78, then back to December in 1986.
Note: In 1970, Smith was declared the winner because he beat Laver in their round robin match (46 63 64).

WOMEN

Virginia Slims Championships

The year-end championship of the Women's Tour. Competed for by the year's top 16 players. The tournament final changed from a best-of-three to best-of-five set format in 1983.

Year	Winner	Loser	Score	Year	Winner	Loser	Score
1977	Chris Evert	B.J.King	62 62	1983	Martina Navratilova	C.Evert Lloyd	63 75 64
1978	Chris Evert	M.Navratilova	63 63	1984	Martina Navratilova	H.Sukova	63 75 64
1979	Martina Navratilova	T.Austin	62 61	1985	Martina Navratilova	H.Mandlikova	62 60 36 61
1980	Tracy Austin	A.Jaeger	62 62	1986	Martina Navratilova	S.Graf	76 63 62
1981	Tracy Austin	M.Navratilova	26 64 62	1987	Steffi Graf	G.Sabatini	46 64 60 64
1982	Martina Navratilova	C.Evert Lloyd	46 61 62	1988	Gabriela Sabatini	P.Shriver	75 62 62

No. 1 Players, 1973-88

MEN

The yearly top-ranked player in the world since 1973, according to the Association of Tennis Professionals (ATP) computer.

Year		Year		Year		Year	
1973	Ilie Nastase	1977	Jimmy Connors	1981	John McEnroe	1985	Ivan Lendl
1974	Jimmy Connors	1978	Jimmy Connors	1982	John McEnroe	1986	Ivan Lendl
1975	Jimmy Connors	1979	Bjorn Borg	1983	John McEnroe	1987	Ivan Lendl
1976	Jimmy Connors	1980	Bjorn Borg	1984	John McEnroe	1988	Mats Wilander

WOMEN

The yearly top-ranked player in the world since 1973, according to the Women's International Tennis Asso. (WITA).

Year		Year		Year		Year	
1973	Margaret Smith Court	1977	Chris Evert	1981	Chris.Evert	1985	Martina Navratilova
1974	Billie Jean King	1978	Martina Navratilova	1982	Martina Navratilova	1986	Martina Navratilova
1975	Chris Evert	1979	Martina Navratilova	1983	Martina Navratilova	1987	Steffi Graf
1976	Chris Evert	1980	Chris Evert	1984	Martina Navratilova	1988	Steffi Graf

The Davis Cup

Established in 1900 as an annual international tournament by American player Dwight Davis. Originally called the International Lawn Tennis Challenge Trophy. Challenge round system until 1972. Since 1981, the top 16 nations in the world have played a straight knockout tournament over the course of a year. The format is a best-of-five match of two singles, one doubles and two singles over three days. **Most Wins:** USA (28), Australia (26).

Challenge Rounds

Year	Winner	Loser	Score	Site	Year	Winner	Loser	Score	Site
1900	USA	Brit.Isles	3-0	Boston	1935	Britain	USA	5-0	Wimbledon
1901	Not held				1936	Britain	Australia	3-2	Wimbledon
1902	USA	Brit.Isles	3-2	New York	1937	USA	Britain	4-1	Wimbledon
1903	Brit.Isles	USA	4-1	Boston	1938	USA	Australia	3-2	Philadelphia
1904	Brit.Isles	Belgium	5-0	Wimbledon	1939	Australia	USA	3-2	Philadelphia
1905	Brit.Isles	USA	5-0	Wimbledon	1940-1945	Not held			
1906	Brit.Isles	USA	5-0	Wimbledon	1946	USA	Australia	5-0	Melbourne
1907	Australasia	Brit.Isles	3-2	Wimbledon	1947	USA	Australia	4-1	New York
1908	Australasia	USA	5-0	Melbourne	1948	USA	Australia	5-0	New York
1909	Australasia	USA	5-0	Sydney	1949	USA	Australia	4-1	New York
1910	Not held				1950	Australia	USA	4-1	New York
1911	Australasia	USA	5-0	N.Zealand	1951	Australia	USA	3-2	Sydney
1912	Brit.Isles	Australasia	3-2	Melbourne	1952	Australia	USA	4-1	Adelaide
1913	USA	Brit. Isles	3-2	Wimbledon	1953	Australia	USA	3-2	Melbourne
1914	Australasia	USA	3-2	New York	1954	USA	Australia	3-2	Sydney
1915-18	Not held				1955	Australia	USA	5-0	New York
1919	Australasia	Brit.Isles	4-1	Sydney	1956	Australia	USA	5-0	Adelaide
1920	USA	Australasia	5-0	N.Zealand	1957	Australia	USA	3-2	Melbourne
1921	USA	Japan	5-0	New York	1958	USA	Australia	3-2	Brisbane
1922	USA	Australasia	4-1	New York	1959	Australia	USA	3-2	New York
1923	USA	Australasia	4-1	New York	1960	Australia	Italy	4-1	Sydney
1924	USA	Australia	5-0	Philadelphia	1961	Australia	Italy	5-0	Melbourne
1925	USA	France	5-0	Philadelphia	1962	Australia	Mexico	5-0	Brisbane
1926	USA	France	4-1	Philadelphia	1963	USA	Australia	3-2	Adelaide
1927	France	USA	3-2	Philadelphia	1964	Australia	USA	3-2	Cleveland
1928	France	USA	4-1	Paris	1965	Australia	Spain	4-1	Sydney
1929	France	USA	3-2	Paris	1966	Australia	India	4-1	Melbourne
1930	France	USA	4-1	Paris	1967	Australia	Spain	4-1	Brisbane
1931	France	Britain	3-2	Paris	1968	USA	Australia	4-1	Adelaide
1932	France	USA	3-2	Paris	1969	USA	Romania	5-0	Cleveland
1933	Britain	France	3-2	Paris	1970	USA	W.Germany	5-0	Cleveland
1934	Britain	USA	4-1	Wimbledon	1971	USA	Romania	3-2	Charlotte

Final Rounds

Year	Winner	Loser	Score	Site	Year	Winner	Loser	Score	Site
1972	USA	Romania	3-2	Bucharest	1980	Czech.	Italy	4-1	Prague
1973	Australia	USA	5-0	Cleveland	1981	USA	Argentina	3-1	Cincinnati
1974	So.Africa	India	w.o.	—	1982	USA	France	4-1	Grenoble
1975	Sweden	Czech.	3-2	Stockholm	1983	Australia	Sweden	3-2	Melbourne
1976	Italy	Chile	4-1	Santiago	1984	Sweden	USA	4-1	Gothenburg
1977	Australia	Italy	3-1	Sydney	1985	Sweden	W.Germany	3-2	Munich
1978	USA	Britain	4-1	Palm Springs	1986	Australia	Sweden	3-2	Melbourne
1979	USA	Italy	5-0	San Francisco	1987	Sweden	India	5-0	Gothenburg
					1988	W.Germany	Sweden	4-1	Gothenburg

The Federation Cup

Started in 1963 by the International Lawn Tennis Federation as the Davis Cup of women's tennis. The major difference is that all competing countries gather at one site to decide the Cup winner in one week. **Most Wins:** USA (13), Australia (7), Czechoslovakia (5).

Year	Winner	Loser	Score	Site	Year	Winner	Loser	Score	Site
1963	USA	Australia	2-1	London	1977	USA	Australia	2-1	Eastbourne
1964	Australia	USA	2-1	Philadelphia	1978	USA	Australia	2-1	Melbourne
1965	Australia	USA	2-1	Melbourne	1979	USA	Australia	3-0	Spain
1966	USA	Germany	3-0	Italy	1980	USA	Australia	3-0	W.Germany
1967	USA	Britain	2-0	W.Germany	1981	USA	Britain	3-0	Tokyo
1968	Australia	Holland	3-0	Paris	1982	USA	W.Germany	3-0	Santa Clara
1969	USA	Australia	2-1	Athens	1983	Czech.	W.Germany	2-1	Zurich
1970	Australia	Britain	3-0	W.Germany	1984	Czech.	Australia	2-1	Brazil
1971	Australia	Britain	3-0	Perth	1985	Czech.	USA	2-1	Japan
1972	So.Africa	Britain	2-1	Africa	1986	USA	Czech.	3-0	Prague
1973	Australia	So.Africa	3-0	W.Germany	1987	W.Germany	USA	2-1	Vancouver
1974	Australia	USA	2-1	Italy	1988	Czech.	USSR	2-1	Melbourne
1975	Czech.	Australia	3-0	France	1989	USA	Spain	3-0	Tokyo
1976	USA	Australia	2-1	Philadelphia					

Wide World Photos

Wide World Photos

Two of golf's most prized trophies stayed put in 1989. The Ryder Cup remained in the clutches of Europe's captain **Tony Jacklin** (left), while **Curtis Strange** became the first U.S. Open champion to hold on to the hardware since Ben Hogan in 1951.

GOLF

INSIDE

Elsewhere in Almanac

For related information refer to the following chapters: Halls of Fame & Awards, Sports Organizations, and Updates.

Golf enjoys a year and decade
of unprecedented popularity;
All four Majors are ''lost'';
Europe ''wins'' Ryder cup, 14-14

GOLF

1989 YEAR IN REVIEW

by Marino Parascenzo

The end of both the year and the decade found golf churning through the most dynamic period in its history. The game was booming in the United States, bigger than ever, and booming around the world like never before. It was even taking root in places where golf used to be just another dirty word for capitalism: the Peoples Republic of China and the Soviet Union.

For all of this, 1989 will also go down as the year when it wasn't who won, but who lost. In professional golf's four flagship events, recognized around the world, it was a spectacular year for losing.

In April, Scott Hoch was about to win the Masters. Just two holes to go. But he bogeyed the 17th and slipped into a tie. Nick Faldo earned a shot at him by coming out of the pack with a final-round 65. Faldo three-putted the first playoff hole (No. 10) for a bogey, and Hoch needed

just a two-footer for a par and the victory. He missed it. He didn't get another chance. Faldo dropped a 25-foot birdie putt at the second hole (No. 11) for the win.

Said Faldo, ''It's a tough feeling to handle—to think you're standing over a putt and the whole world is watching.''

Said Hoch, ''I'm glad I don't have a gun.''

Others who almost won at Augusta but didn't: Australian Greg Norman bogeyed No. 18 after a weak approach and a weak chip shot, and tied for third, a stroke behind. Ben Crenshaw bunkered his approach at the 18th, bogeyed, and tied with Norman. Mike Reid was leading through the 13th, was tied after a bogey at the 14th, and was out of it when he double-bogeyed the 15th.

Faldo's victory underlined the growing strength of European golf, which has thoroughly broken decades of American domination. He was the second straight Briton (Sandy Lyle, 1988) to win the Masters. This made three European winners in five years, five in the past 10—

Marino Parascenzo has been the **Pittsburgh Post-Gazette**'s golf writer since 1975. He is also a contributing editor to **Golf Digest**.

Spain's flamboyant Severiano Ballesteros won in 1980 and '83, and West Germany's Bernhard Langer won in '85. In the 43 Masters before 1980, only South African Gary Player (three times) was able to break the American stranglehold.

• At the U.S. Open in June, Curtis Strange resisted temptation and didn't try to force the issue in the last round at the tough Oak Hill Country Club in Rochester, N.Y. His patience was rewarded with a second straight title. He was the first in 38 years to win back-to-back Opens since Ben Hogan did it in 1950-51.

In April, England's **Nick Faldo** won the Masters with a 25-foot putt on the second hole of sudden death.

Wide World Photos

Strange was chasing gritty Tom Kite in the final round, and badly wanted to gamble somewhere. "But I told myself not to make any stupid mistakes," Strange said. "I just tried to make pars—put it on the fairway and put it on the green." Kite crashed at the par-4 No. 5. He found water with his tee shot and three-putted from 10 feet for a triple-bogey 7, thus keeping a reputation he'd rather shake: The Best Never To Win A Major.

• At the British Open in July, Mark Calcavecchia, 29, the rising U.S. star, became the first American to win since 1983. He came from four shots off the pace in the final round and never smelled the lead until he tied for it at the final hole. Then he won it in a first-ever four-hole playoff over Australians Wayne Grady, the leader at the start of the day, and Greg Norman, who had blistered Royal Troon for a final-round 64. Grady shot a 1-over 16 for the four holes. Norman led with birdies on the first two holes, but quit at the final hole after going into a bunker, then out of bounds, with Calcavecchia lying two just in front of the flag.

Calcavecchia had hit a breathtaking 5-iron shot some 200 yards out of scraggly rough to within six feet. "It's a shot I'll never forget," Calcavecchia said. "I watched it, and I said I don't care where it ends up, because that's the best shot I've ever hit." He holed the putt for a birdie he didn't need.

After five years of struggling, Calcavecchia finally started to click on the Tour in 1986. The British Open was his first victory in a major, and the crowning jewel in a season that began with wins in the Phoenix and Los Angeles Opens. The British Open will stick with him for another reason. His first child, a daughter, was born shortly afterward. But if she had come sooner, he wouldn't have been the British Open champion. His wife, Sheryl, was back home in Phoenix, Ariz., awaiting the arrival of the baby. "If I had got a phone call last night, that she went into labor," he said that championship Sunday, "I'd have been on a plane and out of here."

• In August, mild-mannered Mike Reid, who missed in the Masters, had the PGA Championship and his first major title all wrapped up—except for the last three holes. But he staggered home at Kemper Lakes, near Chicago. He bogeyed the 16th and double-bogeyed the 17th. His bid for a tying birdie at the 18th missed and Payne Stewart, who had already finished with 67-276, had his first major title and his second win of the year after the Heritage Classic. Reid tied for second, a stroke back.

Said Reid: "Where can you go around here to have a good cry?"

Beyond the four majors, Calcavecchia, one of the most colorful figures to hit the pro tour in years, was the big individual story of 1989. Few golfers have ever brought such pure exuberance and a combination of raw power and high talent to the game. Many were comparing him with a vintage Arnold Palmer for his daring play. Also big in '89: Steve Jones, who had one win in his previous five years on the tour, broke through for three early victories—the MONY Tournament of Champions, the Bob Hope Chrysler Classic, and the Canadian Open. Kite won the Nestle Invitational and The Players Championship back-to-back; Blaine McCallister, with one win in his previous five years, took the Honda Classic and the Bank of Boston Classic, and Norman added The International and the Greater Milwaukee Open to his growing bag of victories.

On the Senior PGA Tour, the phenomenal success story of the over-50 set, Orville Moody, 55, was the key figure. Moody, who had won only once on the regular tour, the 1969 U.S. Open, took two of the three big senior titles in '89— the U.S. Senior Open and the Senior Tournament Players Championship. Larry Mowry took the other, the Senior PGA Championship.

And on the Ladies Professional Golf Association Tour, the money record fell hard and fast. By late summer, Betsy King, 34, had won six tournaments, including the U.S. Women's Open. Her winnings at that point: $654,132, shattering Pat Bradley's 1986 record of $492,021. Beth Daniel also broke Bradley's record with over $500,000. Daniel, who joined the LPGA Tour in 1977, broke out of a 4½-year drought with four victories in a span of six starts through early October.

Wide World Photos

Mark Calcavecchia gives the winner's trophy a kiss, July 23, after capturing the British Open in a 3-way, 4-hole playoff at Royal Troon.

On the non-paying level, 300-pound Chris Patton, 21, of Fountain Inn, S.C., won the U.S. Amateur, and Vicki Goetze, 17, of Hull, Ga., won the U.S. Women's Amateur.

And on the European PGA Tour, Faldo went on a rampage. Except for the Masters, he had a so-so time on the U.S. tour. Then he went back to Europe and won three straight starts. Ballesteros and England's Mark James also won three each. The Slump of the Year title went to Britain's Sandy Lyle, the former Masters and British Open champ and formerly considered one of the top five players in the world. Lyle finished second twice early on the U.S. tour, then sank into a deep and mysterious slump. He missed the cut in eight of his last nine starts in the United States, and he was 63 over par in his last 22 rounds. Things didn't improve appreciably when he returned to Europe.

The 1989 season also ended a decade unparalleled in golf worldwide. These were the key points:

Wide World Photos

Betsy King won her first U.S. Women's Open and has taken home over $650,000 to set a new LPGA earnings record in 1989.

• The PGA Tour exploded in all directions. In 1980, the purses totalled just under $13.4 million. In 1989, $39.5 million. For 1990, it will break $40 million easily, including 22 tournaments worth $1 million each.

The clamor for spots on the Tour had grown so intense that Commissioner Deane Beman was able to add a farm-system circuit for 1990. The Ben Hogan Tour, sponsored by the golf equipment company of that name, will be a series of thirty $100,000 tournaments for aspiring pros.

• The Senior PGA Tour, which began informally in 1980 with two events worth a total of $250,000, had 41 events worth $18.5 million in 1989. It was destined to grow bigger faster. Among the big names coming of age: Lee Trevino, in December, 1989, and Jack Nicklaus, in January, 1990.

• The LPGA Tour, growing by about $1 million a year, reached 33 events and nearly $14 million in 1989. The women's tour also had its rich overseas mix, notably Britain's Laura Davies, Japan's Ayako Okamoto, and Sweden's Liselotte Neumann.

• The European Tour fairly erupted. In 1979, it had 23 events worth a total of some $2.4 million; in 1989, 40 events worth $18.6 million (both figures at the late-1989 exchange rate). Golf was also booming elsewhere in the world, most notably Japan, with its strong pro tour and cadre of top-grade players such as Tommy Nakajima. The European tour had probably the only Fiji Islander ever to win a big pro event, lanky Vijay Singh, who took the Volvo Open early in April.

The European Tour itself is a study in the geopolitical upheaval in golf. British golf had been so weak that when Sandy Lyle won the British Open in 1985, he was the first native to do so in 16 years, since Tony Jacklin in 1969. It was the Americans who dominated the British Open. In fact, world golf. Then came the revolution, beginning in the late 1970s. There's no known single starting point. Doubtless it was a combination of things, principally: The tour's decision to abandon the smaller British ball (1.62 inches in diameter) and use the larger American ball (1.68), which required more skill, and therefore made the Europeans better. Another was the emergence of the

Resplendent in livery of the nearby Chicago Bears, **Payne Stewart** won the PGA Championship in Hawthorn Hills, Ill., in August and led the PGA Tour in earnings.

electrifying Ballesteros. It seems the Europeans began to believe in themselves when he broke the American grip and won the British Open in 1979. Spain also produced other classy players, notably the youthful Jose-Maria Olazabal, and along came the first West German golfer of note, Gernhard Langer, who won the 1985 Masters.

Europe's new muscle has been seen most clearly in the biennial Ryder Cup match, established in the 1920s as a competition between pros from America on one team and Great Britain and Ireland on the other. Americans dominated it to the point of boredom—a 25-3-1 record through 1983. But at the suggestion

of Jack Nicklaus, GB-Ireland was expanded to include all of Europe in 1979, to take advantage of the emerging Ballesteros. Europe won in 1985 and 1987 and tied in 1989. Future European teams could reflect other emerging nations. Sweden is the strongest of the rest, but Denmark, France, and Italy are stirring.

The pros aside, golf in general was enjoying its biggest popularity explosion ever in the '80s, and it showed no signs of abating as it entered the 1990s.

The National Golf Foundation, an industry study and promotional organization, said that when all the figures for 1989 were in, some 200,000 more

U.S. Bats .500 at The Belfry

September's Ryder Cup matches at The Belfry in Sutton Coldfield, England, were exciting but the result was a big disappointment for the United States team. America had the defending champion Europeans on the run, but let them get away and were lucky to salvage a 14-14 tie.

"Some people say golf was the winner," said Tom Kite, "but I assure you nobody was happy with that outcome." Americans had turned the biennial goodwill event into a yawner almost from the time it began in 1927 as U.S.-vs-Britain. It became the European team in 1979 and Europe was on the rise. The Yanks lead the series, 21-5-2. But they're 0-2-1 in the last three.

The American team—sporting U.S. Open champion Curtis Strange, British Open champ Mark Calcavecchia, and PGA champ Payne Stewart—took a 3-1 lead in the opening alternate-shot matches. Then non-playing captain Raymond Floyd puzzled many observers. True to his word to play all 12 men on his squad, he re-paired his teams for the afternoon better-ball, benching four players and sending in four new ones. The Europeans swept, 4-0, for a 5-3 lead.

Asked why he switched his successful combinations, Floyd replied: "There's more to the Ryder Cup than winning or losing. It's the spirit of play." European captain Tony Jacklin took the other approach. "I'm going for points, period." Jacklin said. Floyd insisted he would play all 12 again the next day, but when the time came, he said some players asked to be sat out in favor of guys who were playing well.

In the final-day singles, the Americans shook off a two-point deficit and were cleaning house, led by rookie Paul Azinger beating Europe's big gun, Spain's Seve Ballesteros; Kite mauling England's Howard Clark, 8 and 7, and rookie Chip Beck topping West Germany's Bernhard Langer. But the middle of the lineup broke down, notably big-hitting Fred Couples falling to Ireland's Christy O'Connor, 41, who fired a 229-yard 2-iron to about three feet on the last hole, and Ken Green getting spilled by Spain's Jose-Maria Canizares, 42, also at the 18th. It came down to the final match. Strange birdied the last four holes to beat Wales' Ian Woosnam and get the tie. But Europe kept the Cup.

Americans would have taken up the game, bumping up the record 23.8 million of 1988. Why the boom? The favorite speculations: More Americans in the older age brackets, more spare time and disposable income, and women taking to the game as never before. Some 41 percent of all new golfers were women.

One dark cloud hung over the game as 1989 neared its end. It was the broadest, most controversial issue to hit golf in years, maybe ever. It was the battle of the Karsten Manufacturing Corp. of Phoenix, Ariz., over its hot-selling PING EYE2 irons.

The United States Golf Association and the Royal and Ancient Golf Club of St. Andrews, Scotland, the two amateur organizations that establish playing rules and equipment standards accepted around the world, banned the club from their competitions, effective Jan. 1, 1990.

They ruled that the Pings were illegal because the grooves were too close together. Both organizations sponsor national championships, notably the U.S. Open and the British Open, respectively. The Karsten company sued the two for $100 million, and also challenged their right to make the rules.

In a separate issue, the PGA Tour banned all "square groove" clubs, beginning Jan. 1, 1990. The Pings are the best-known of this kind. The Tour contended that the shape of the grooves put more backspin on the ball than did the conventional V-shaped groove, thus giving the golfer greater control through technology rather than skill. Of some 40 club manufacturers, Karsten was the only one fighting this issue. Company founder and president Karsten Solheim said in October that he was preparing to sue the Tour over this issue as well.

1989 Money Leaders
Through Oct. 1, 1989

MEN		SENIORS		WOMEN	
1 Payne Stewart	$823,292	1 Bob Charles	$470,037	1 Betsy King	$654,132
2 Tom Kite	764,614	2 Orville Moody	464,155	2 Beth Daniel	504,851
3 Greg Norman	723,930	3 Harold Henning	390,517	3 Nancy Lopez	482,661
4 Mark Calcavecchia	694,741	4 Al Geiberger	364,491	4 Pat Bradley	408,964
5 Steve Jones	660,178	5 Bruce Crampton	358,187	5 Patty Sheehan	253,605
6 Paul Azinger	630,999	6 Don Bies	333,453	6 Tammie Green	204,143
7 Curtis Strange	630,420	7 Miller Barber	320,258	7 Patti Rizzo	197,652
8 Chip Beck	586,091	8 Dave Hill	312,341	8 Sherri Turner	190,979
9 Scott Hoch	557,157	9 Larry Mowry	280,979	9 Colleen Walker	185,291
10 Tim Simpson	537,597	10 Mike Hill	276,268	10 Jane Geddes	183,793
11 David Frost	530,263	11 Charles Coody	262,780	11 Juli Inkster	180,848
12 Fred Couples	502,844	12 Gary Player	253,246	12 Ayako Okamoto	179,495

1989 PGA Tour Results

Through the Centel Classic (Oct.1). Multiple winners: Mark Calcavecchia and Steve Jones (3); Tom Kite, Blaine McCallister, Greg Norman and Payne Stewart (2).

January	Champion	Earnings	June	Champion	Earnings
Tourn.of Champions	Steve Jones	$135,000	Kemper Open	Tom Byrum	$162,000
Bob Hope Classic	Steve Jones*	180,000	Westchester Classic	Wayne Grady*	180,000
Phoenix Open	Mark Calcavecchia	126,000	U.S.Open	Curtis Strange	200,000
Pebble Beach Pro-Am	Mark O'Meara	180,000	Canadian Open	Steve Jones	162,000
February	**Champion**	**Earnings**	**July**	**Champion**	**Earnings**
Los Angeles Open	Mark Calcavecchia	$180,000	Western Open	Mark McCumber*	$180,000
Hawaiian Open	Gene Sauers	135,000	Grtr.Hartford Open	Paul Azinger	180,000
ShearsonLehmanHutton	Greg Twiggs	126,000	Anheuser-BuschClassic	Mike Donald*	153,000
Doral Ryder Open	Bill Glasson	234,000	British Open	Mark Calcavecchia*	128,000
March	**Champion**	**Earnings**	Hardee's Classic	Curt Byrum	126,000
Honda Classic	Blaine McCallister	$144,000	Buick Open	Leonard Thompson	180,000
Nestle Invitational	Tom Kite*	144,000	**August**	**Champion**	**Earnings**
Players Championship	Tom Kite	243,000	St.Jude Classic	John Mahaffey	$180,000
USF&G Classic	Tim Simpson	135,000	PGA Championship	Payne Stewart	200,000
April	**Champion**	**Earnings**	The International	Greg Norman	180,000
Insurance Agent Open	Mike Sullivan	$144,000	World Series of Golf	David Frost*	180,000
The Masters	Nick Faldo*	200,000	Chattanooga Classic	Stan Utley	90,000
Deposit Guaranty	Jim Booros*	36,000	**September**	**Champion**	**Earnings**
Heritage Classic	Payne Stewart	144,000	Grtr.Milwaukee Open	Greg Norman	$144,000
Grt.Greensboro Open	Ken Green	180,000	B.C.Open	Mike Hulbert*	90,000
Las Vegas Invitational	Scott Hoch*	225,000	Bank of Boston Classic	Blaine McCallister	126,000
May	**Champion**	**Earnings**	Southern Open	Ted Schulz	72,000
Byron Nelson Classic	Jodie Mudd	$180,000	**October**	**Champion**	**Earnings**
Memorial Tournament	Bob Tway	160,000	Centel Classic	Bill Britton	135,000
Colonial Invitational	Ian Baker-Finch	180,000			
Atlanta Classic	Scott Simpson	162,000	*Won playoff to win tournament.		

1989 Seniors Tour Results

Through the Space Coast Classic (Oct.1). Multiple winners: Bob Charles (5); Miller Barber, Don Bies, Bruce Crampton, Jim Dent, Al Geiberger, Dave Hill, Orville Moody, Larry Mowry and Chi Chi Rodriguez (2).

January	Champion	Earnings	June (Continued)	Champion	Earnings
Tourn.of Champions	Miller Barber	$ 50,000	Doug Sangers Classic	Orville Moody	$105,000
Senior Skins Game	Chi Chi Rodriguez	120,000	Northville Invit'l	Butch Baird*	52,500
February	**Champion**	**Earnings**	Syracuse Classic	Jim Dent	45,000
PGA Sr.Champ.	Larry Mowry	$72,000	**July**	**Champion**	**Earnings**
Suncoast Classic	Bob Charles*	45,000	U.S.Senior Open	Orville Moody	$80,000
Aetna Challenge	Gene Littler	45,000	Digital Classic	Bob Charles	45,000
March	**Champion**	**Earnings**	Grand Rapids Open	John Paul Cain	45,000
Vintage Invitational	Miller Barber	$55,500	Ameritech Open	Bruce Crampton	75,000
Arizona Classic	Bruce Crampton	45,000	Newport Cup	Jim Dent	41,500
April	**Champion**	**Earnings**	**August**	**Champion**	**Earnings**
Senior Reunion	Don Bies	$45,000	Showdown Classic	Tom Shaw	$52,400
The Tradition	Don Bies	90,000	Senior Gold Rush	Dave Hill	52,500
Legends of Golf	Al Geiberger		Northwest Classic	Al Geiberger	52,500
	& Harold Henning	120,000	Charley Pride Classic	Bob Charles	45,000
May	**Champion**	**Earnings**	**September**	**Champion**	**Earnings**
Senior's Premier	Larry Mowry	$37,500	Premier Bank Classic	Rives McBee	$45,000
St.Christopher's	Dave Hill*	60,000	North Classic	Gary Player	52,500
The Commemorative	Bob Charles	45,000	Crestar Classic	Chi Chi Rodriguez	52,500
S'western Bell Classic	Bobby Nichols*	45,000	Paine Webber Invit'l	Cancelled (Hurricane Hugo)	
June	**Champion**	**Earnings**	**October**	**Champion**	**Earnings**
Doug Sangers Classic	Homero Blancas	$45,000	Space Coast Classic	Bob Charles	$45,000

1989 LPGA Tour Results

Through the San Jose Classic (Oct.1). Multiple winners: Betsy King (6); Beth Daniel (4); Nancy Lopez (3); Juli Inkster (2).

January	Champion	Earnings
Jamaica Classic	Betsy King	$75,000
Oldsmobile Classic . . .	Dottie Mochrie*	45,000

February	Champion	Earnings
Hawaiian Open	Sherri Turner	$45,000
Kemper Open	Betsy King	60,000

March	Champion	Earnings
Tucson Open	Lori Garbacz	$45,000
Turquoise Classic	Allison Finney	60,000

April	Champion	Earnings
Nabisco Dinah Shore .	Juli Inkster	$80,000
Inamori Classic	Patti Rizzo	45,000
Centinela Classic	Pat Bradley	67,500
USX Classic	Betsy King*	37,500
Sara Lee Classic	Kathy Postlewait	63,750

May	Champion	Earnings
Crestar Classic	Juli Inkster	$45,000
Chrysler-Plym.Classic .	Cindy Rarick	41,250
LPGA Championship .	Nancy Lopez	75,000
Corning Classic	Ayako Okamoto	48,750

June	Champion	Earnings
Rochester Internat'l . .	Patty Sheehan*	$45,000
Pat Bradley Internat'l .	Robin Hood	62,500
Lady Keystone Open .	Laura Davies	45,000
McDonald's Champ . .	Betsy King	82,500

July	Champion	Earnings
du Maurier Classic . . .	Tammie Green	$90,000
Jamie Farr Toledo . . .	Penny Hammel	41,250
U.S.Women's Open . . .	Betsy King	80,000
Boston Five Classic . . .	Amy Alcott	52,500
Atlantic City Classic . .	Nancy Lopez	33,750

August	Champion	Earnings
Grtr.Wash.(DC) Open	Beth Daniel	$45,000
Nestle World Champ .	Betsy King	83,500
Ocean State Open . . .	Tina Barrett	22,500

September	Champion	Earnings
Rail Charity Classic . . .	Beth Daniel	$41,250
Cellular One-Ping	M.Spencer-Devlin	45,000
Safeco Classic	Beth Daniel	45,000
MBS Classic	Nancy Lopez	45,000

October	Champion	Earnings
San Jose Classic	Beth Daniel	$48,750

1989 Ryder Cup

Europe 14, USA 14

The 28th Ryder Cup matches, played Sept. 22-24, at The Belfry in Sutton-Coldfield, England. Captains: Ray Floyd for the US and Tony Jacklin for Europe. Draw allows Europe to retain Cup. US leads series, 21-5-2.

Day One (Europe takes 5-3 lead)

Foursomes—Curtis Strange & Tom Kite (US) halved with Nick Faldo & Ian Woosnam (E); Payne Stewart & Lanny Wadkins (US) def. Howard Clark & Mark James (E), 1 up; Mark Calcavecchia & Ken Green (US) def. Bernhard Langer & Ronan Rafferty (E), 2 and 1; Tom Watson & Chip Beck (US) halved with Seve Ballesteros & Jose-Maria Olazabal (E).
Four-ball—Ballesteros & Olazabal (E) def. Watson & Mark O'Meara (US), 6 and 5; Clark & James (E) def. Wadkins & Fred Couples (US), 3 and 2; Sam Torrance & Gordon Brand Jr.(E) def. Strange and Paul Azinger (US), 1 up; Faldo & Woosnam (E) def. Calcavecchia & Mark McCumber (US), 2 up.

Day Two (Europe holds lead, 9-7)

Foursomes—Beck & Azinger (US) def. Torrance & Brand (E), 4 and 3; Faldo & Woosnam (E) def. Stewart & Wadkins (US), 3 and 2; Calcavecchia and Green (US) def. Rafferty & Christy O'Connor Jr.(E), 3 and 2; Ballesteros & Olazabal (E) def. Strange & Kite (US), 1 up.
Four-ball—Beck & Azinger (US) def. Faldo & Woosnam (E), 2 and 1; Kite & McCumber (US) def. Langer & Jose-Maria Canizares (E), 2 and 1; Ballesteros & Olazabal (E) def. Calcavecchia & Green (US), 4 and 2; Clark & James (E) def. Strange & Stewart (US), 1 up.

Day Three (Europe retains Cup, 14-14)

Singles—Kite (US) def. Clark (E), 8 and 7; Beck (US) def. Langer (E), 3 and 1; Azinger (US) def. Ballesteros (E), 1 up; James (E) def. O'Meara (US), 3 and 2; Olazabal (E) def. Stewart (US), 1 up; Rafferty (E) def. Calcavecchia (US), 1 up.
O'Connor (E) def. Couples (US), 1 up; Canizares (E) def. Green (US), 1 up; Watson (US) def. Torrance (E), 3 and 1; McCumber (US) def. Brand (E), 1 up; Wadkins (US) def. Faldo (E), 1 up; Strange (US) def. Woosnam (E), 2 up.

Ryder Cup Matches, 1927-89

The Ryder Cup was presented by British businessman Samuel Ryder in 1927 for competition between professional golfers from Great Britain and the United States. Since 1979, the British have been joined by the rest of Europe in challenging the US. The US leads the series with a 21-6-1 record after 28 matches.

Year Winner		Year Winner		Year Winner	
1927	United States, 9½-2½	1951	United States, 9½-2½	1971	United States, 18½-13½
1929	Britain-Ireland, 7-5	1953	United States, 6½-5½	1973	United States, 19-13
1931	United States, 9-3	1955	United States, 8-4	1975	United States, 21-11
1933	Britain-Ireland, 6½-5½	1957	Britain-Ireland, 7½-4½	1977	United States, 12½-7½
1935	United States, 9-3	1959	United States, 8½-3½	1979	United States, 17-11
1937	United States, 8-4				
1939	Not held	1961	United States, 14½-9½	1981	United States, 18½-9½
		1963	United States, 23-9	1983	United States, 14½-13½
1941	Not held	1965	United States, 19½-12½	1985	Europe, 16½-11½
1943	Not held	1967	United States, 23½-8½	1987	Europe, 15-13
1945	Not held	1969	Draw, 16-16	1989	Draw, 14-14
1947	United States, 11-1			**Note:** Great Britain-Ireland became
1949	United States, 7-5			Europe in 1979.	

Major Tournaments

MEN

The only golfer to ever win a recognized Grand Slam—four major championships in a single season—was Bobby Jones in 1930. That year, Jones won the US and British Opens as well as the US and British Amateurs.

The men's professional Grand Slam—the Masters, US Open, British Open and PGA Championship—did not gain acceptance until 30 years later when Arnold Palmer won the 1960 Masters and US Open. The media wrote that the popular Palmer was chasing the "new" Grand Slam and would have to win the British Open and the PGA to claim it. He did not, but then nobody has before or since. In 1951, Ben Hogan came the closest, winning the first three, but he did not get back from Europe in time to play in the PGA.

Major Championship Leaders

Active players in **bold** type.

	US Open	British Open	PGA	Masters	US Am	British Am	Total
Jack Nicklaus ...	4	3	5	6	2	0	**20**
Bobby Jones	4	3	0	0	5	1	13
Walter Hagen ...	2	4	5	0	0	0	11
Ben Hogan	4	1	2	2	0	0	9
Gary Player	1	3	2	3	0	0	9
John Ball	0	1	0	0	0	8	9
Arnold Palmer ..	1	2	0	4	1	0	8
Tom Watson	1	5	0	2	0	0	8
Harold Hilton	0	2	0	0	1	4	7
Gene Sarazen ...	2	1	3	1	0	0	7
Sam Snead	0	1	3	3	0	0	7
Harry Vardon....	1	6	0	0	0	0	7
Lee Trevino	2	2	2	0	0	0	6

Tournaments: US Open, British Open, PGA Championship, Masters, US Amateur, and British Amateur.

Masters, 1934-89

The Masters has been played every year since 1934 at the Augusta National Golf Club in Augusta, GA. Both the course (6,905 yards, par 72) and the tournament were created by Bobby Jones.

Most wins: Jack Nicklaus (6) and Arnold Palmer (4).

Year	Winner	Year	Winner	Year	Winner	Year	Winner
1934	Horton Smith	1948	Claude Harmon	1962	Arnold Palmer*	1976	Ray Floyd
1935	Gene Sarazen*	1949	Sam Snead	1963	Jack Nicklaus	1977	Tom Watson
1936	Horton Smith	1950	Jimmy Demaret	1964	Arnold Palmer	1978	Gary Player
1937	Byron Nelson	1951	Ben Hogan	1965	Jack Nicklaus	1979	Fuzzy Zoeller*
1938	Henry Picard	1952	Sam Snead	1966	Jack Nicklaus*		
1939	Ralph Guldahl	1953	Ben Hogan	1967	Gary Brewer	1980	Seve Ballesteros
1940	Jimmy Demaret	1954	Sam Snead*	1968	Bob Goalby	1981	Tom Watson
1941	Craig Wood	1955	Cary Middlecoff	1969	George Archer	1982	Craig Stadler*
1942	Byron Nelson*	1956	Jack Burke, Jr.			1983	Seve Ballesteros
1943	Not held	1957	Doug Ford	1970	Billy Casper*	1984	Ben Crenshaw
1944	Not held	1958	Arnold Palmer	1971	Charles Coody	1985	Bernhard Langer
1945	Not held	1959	Art Wall, Jr.	1972	Jack Nicklaus	1986	Jack Nicklaus
1946	Herman Keiser			1973	Tommy Aaron	1987	Larry Mize*
1947	Jimmy Demaret	1960	Arnold Palmer	1974	Gary Player	1988	Sandy Lyle
		1961	Gary Player	1975	Jack Nicklaus	1989	Nick Faldo*

Playoffs

1935: Sarazen (144) def. Craig Wood (149) in 36 holes. **1942:** Nelson (69) def. Ben Hogan (70) in 18 holes. **1954:** Snead (70) def. Ben Hogan (71) in 18 holes. **1962:** Palmer (68) def. Gary Player (71) and Dow Finsterwald (77) in 18 holes. **1966:** Nicklaus (70) def. Tommy Jacobs (72) and Gay Brewer (78) in 18 holes. **1970:** Casper (69) def. Gene Littler (74) in 18 holes. **1979:** Zoeller (4-3) def. Ed Sneed (4-4) and Tom Watson (4-4) on 2nd hole of sudden death. **1982:** Stadler (4) def. Dan Pohl (5) on 1st hole of sudden death. **1987:** Mize (4-3) def. Greg Norman (4-4) and Seve Ballesteros (5) on 2nd hole of sudden death. **1989:** Faldo (5-3) def. Scott Hoch (5-4) on 2nd hole of sudden death.

U.S. Open, 1895-1989

Played at a different course each year, the US Open was launched by the new US Golf Association in 1895. The Open switched from a 3-day, 36-hole Saturday finish to 4 days of play in 1965.

Most wins: Willie Anderson, Bobby Jones, Ben Hogan and Jack Nicklaus (4).

Year	Winner	Year	Winner	Year	Winner	Year	Winner
1895	Horace Rawlins	1920	Edward Ray	1944	Not held	1970	Tony Jacklin
1896	James Foulis	1921	Jim Barnes	1945	Not held	1971	Lee Trevino*
1897	Joe Lloyd	1922	Gene Sarazen	1946	Lloyd Mangrum*	1972	Jack Nicklaus
1898	Fred Herd	1923	a-Bobby Jones*	1947	Lew Worsham*	1973	Johnny Miller
1899	Willie Smith	1924	Cyril Walker	1948	Ben Hogan	1974	Hale Irwin
		1925	Willie Macfarlane*	1949	Cary Middlecoff	1975	Lou Graham*
1900	Harry Vardon	1926	a-Bobby Jones			1976	Jerry Pate
1901	Willie Anderson*	1927	Tommy Armour*	1950	Ben Hogan*	1977	Hubert Green
1902	Laurie Auchterlonie	1928	Johnny Farrell*	1951	Ben Hogan	1978	Andy North
1903	Willie Anderson*	1929	a-Bobby Jones*	1952	Julius Boros	1979	Hale Irwin
1904	Willie Anderson			1953	Ben Hogan		
1905	Willie Anderson	1930	a-Bobby Jones	1954	Ed Furgol	1980	Jack Nicklaus
1906	Alex Smith	1931	Billy Burke*	1955	Jack Fleck*	1981	David Graham
1907	Alex Ross	1932	Gene Sarazen	1956	Cary Middlecoff	1982	Tom Watson
1908	Fred McLeod*	1933	a-John Goodman	1957	Dick Mayer*	1983	Larry Nelson
1909	George Sargent	1934	Olin Dutra	1958	Tommy Bolt	1984	Fuzzy Zoeller*
		1935	Sam Parks, Jr.	1959	Billy Casper	1985	Andy North
1910	Alex Smith*	1936	Tony Manero			1986	Ray Floyd
1911	John McDermott*	1937	Ralph Guldahl	1960	Arnold Palmer	1987	Scott Simpson
1912	John McDermott	1938	Ralph Guldahl	1961	Gene Littler	1988	Curtis Strange*
1913	a-Francis Ouimet*	1939	Byron Nelson*	1962	Jack Nicklaus*	1989	Curtis Strange
1914	Walter Hagen			1963	Julius Boros*		
1915	a-Jerry Travers	1940	Lawson Little*	1964	Ken Venturi		
1916	a-Chick Evans	1941	Craig Wood	1965	Gary Player*		
1917	Not held	1942	Not held	1966	Billy Casper*		
1918	Not held	1943	Not held	1967	Jack Nicklaus		
1919	Walter Hagen*			1968	Lee Trevino		
				1969	Orville Moody		

Playoffs

1901: Anderson (85) def. Alex Smith (86) in 18 holes. **1903:** Anderson (82) def. David Brown (84) in 18 holes. **1908:** McLeod (77) def. Willie Smith (83) in 18 holes. **1910:** A.Smith (71) def. John McDermott (75) & Macdonald Smith (77) in 18 holes. **1911:** McDermott (80) def. Mike Brady (82) & George Simpson (85) in 18 holes. **1913:** Ouimet (72) def. Harry Vardon (77) & Edward Ray (78) in 18 holes. **1919:** Hagen (77) def. Mike Brady (78) in 18 holes. **1923:** Jones (76) def. Bobby Cruickshank (78) in 18 holes. **1925:** Macfarlane (75-72) def. Bobby Jones (75-73) in 36 holes. **1927:** Armour (76) def. Harry Cooper (79) in 18 holes. **1928:** Farrell (143) def. Bobby Jones (144) in 36 holes. **1929:** Jones (141) def. Al Espinosa (164) in 36 holes. **1931:** Burke (149-148) def. George Von Elm (149-149) in 72 holes. **1939:** B.Nelson (68-70) def. Craig Wood (68-73) in 36 holes. **1940:** Little (70) def. Gene Sarazen (73) in 18 holes. **1946:** Mangrum (72-72) def. Byron Nelson (72-73) and Vic Ghezzi (72-73) in 36 holes. **1947:** Worsham (69) def. Sam Snead (70) in 18 holes. **1950:** Hogan (69) def. Lloyd Mangrum (73) & George Fazio (75) in 18 holes. **1955:** Fleck (69) def. Ben Hogan (72) in 18 holes. **1957:** Mayer (72) def. Cary Middlecoff (79) in 18 holes. **1962:** Nicklaus (71) def. Arnold Palmer (74) in 18 holes. **1963:** Boros (70) def. Jacky Cupit (73) & Arnold Palmer (76) in 18 holes. **1965:** Player (71) def. Kel Nagle (74) in 18 holes. **1966:** Casper (69) def. Arnold Palmer (73) in 18 holes. **1971:** Trevino (68) def. Jack Nicklaus (71) in 18 holes. **1975:** L.Graham (71) def. John Mahaffey (73) in 18 holes. **1984:** Zoeller (67) def. Greg Norman (75) in 18 holes. **1988:** Strange (71) def. Nick Faldo (75) in 18 holes.

British Open, 1860-1989

The oldest of the Majors, the British Open began play in 1860 to determine "the champion golfer of the world." Conducted by the Royal and Ancient Golf Club of St.Andrews, The Open is rotated among select golf courses in England.

Most wins: Harry Vardon (6); James Braid, J.H.Taylor, Peter Thomson and Tom Watson (5).

Year	Winner	Year	Winner	Year	Winner	Year	Winner
1860	Willie Park	1870	Tom Morris, Jr.	1880	Bob Ferguson	1890	a-John Ball
1861	Tom Morris, Sr.	1871	Not held	1881	Bob Ferguson	1891	Hugh Kirkaldy
1862	Tom Morris, Sr.	1872	Tom Morris, Jr.	1882	Bob Ferguson	1892	a-Harold Hilton
1863	Willie Park	1873	Tom Kidd	1883	Willie Fernie*	1893	Wm.Auchterlonie
1864	Tom Morris, Sr.	1874	Mungo Park	1884	Jack Simpson	1894	J.H.Taylor
1865	Andrew Strath	1875	Willie Park	1885	Bob Martin	1895	J.H.Taylor
1866	Willie Park	1876	Bob Martin*	1886	David Brown	1896	Harry Vardon*
1867	Tom Morris, Sr.	1877	Jamie Anderson	1887	Willie Park, Jr.	1897	a-Harold Hilton
1868	Tom Morris, Jr.	1878	Jamie Anderson	1888	Jack Burns	1898	Harry Vardon
1869	Tom Morris, Jr.	1879	Jamie Anderson	1889	Willie Park, Jr.*	1899	Harry Vardon

British Open (Continued)

Year	Winner	Year	Winner	Year	Winner	Year	Winner
1900	J.H.Taylor	1922	Walter Hagen	1944	Not held	1966	Jack Nicklaus
1901	James Braid	1923	Arthur Havers	1945	Not held	1967	Roberto de Vicenzo
1902	Sandy Herd	1924	Walter Hagen	1946	Sam Snead	1968	Gary Player
1903	Harry Vardon	1925	Jim Barnes	1947	Fred Daly	1969	Tony Jacklin
1904	Jack White	1926	a-Bobby Jones	1948	Henry Cotton		
1905	James Braid	1927	a-Bobby Jones	1949	Bobby Locke*	1970	Jack Nicklaus*
1906	James Braid	1928	Walter Hagen			1971	Lee Trevino
1907	Arnaud Massy	1929	Walter Hagen	1950	Bobby Locke	1972	Lee Trevino
1908	James Braid			1951	Max Faulkner	1973	Tom Weiskopf
1909	J.H.Taylor	1930	a-Bobby Jones	1952	Bobby Locke	1974	Gary Player
		1931	Tommy Armour	1953	Ben Hogan	1975	Tom Watson*
1910	James Braid	1932	Gene Sarazen	1954	Peter Thomson	1976	Johnny Miller
1911	Harry Vardon*	1933	Denny Shute*	1955	Peter Thomson	1977	Tom Watson
1912	Ted Ray	1934	Henry Cotton	1956	Peter Thomson	1978	Jack Nicklaus
1913	J.H.Taylor	1935	Alf Perry	1957	Bobby Locke	1979	Seve Balleteros
1914	Harry Vardon	1936	Alf Padgham	1958	Peter Thomson*		
1915	Not held	1937	Henry Cotton	1959	Gary Player	1980	Tom Watson
1916	Not held	1938	Reg Whitcombe			1981	Bill Rogers
1917	Not held	1939	Dick Burton	1960	Kel Nagle	1982	Tom Watson
1918	Not held			1961	Arnold Palmer	1983	Tom Watson
1919	Not held	1940	Not held	1962	Arnold Palmer	1984	Seve Ballesteros
		1941	Not held	1963	Bob Charles*	1985	Sandy Lyle
1920	George Duncan	1942	Not held	1964	Tony Lema	1986	Greg Norman
1921	Jock Hutchison*	1943	Not held	1965	Peter Thomson	1987	Nick Faldo
						1988	Seve Ballesteros
						1989	Mark Calcavecchia

Playoffs

1876: Martin awarded title when David Strath refused playoff. **1883:** Fernie (158) def. Robert Ferguson (159) in 36 holes. **1889:** Park (158) def. Andrew Kirkaldy (163) in 36 holes. **1896:** Vardon (157) def. John H.Taylor (161) in 36 holes. **1911:** Vardon won when Arnaud Massy conceded at 35th hole. **1921:** Hutchison (150) def. Roger Wethered (159) in 36 holes. **1933:** Shute (149) def. Craig Wood (154) in 36 holes. **1949:** Locke (135) def. Harry Bradshaw (147) in 36 holes. **1958:** Thomson (139) def. Dave Thomas (143) in 36 holes. **1963:** Charles (140) def. Phil Rodgers (148) in 36 holes. **1970:** Nicklaus (72) def. Doug Sanders (73) in 18 holes. **1975:** Watson (71) def. Jack Newton (72) in 18 holes. **1989:** Calcavecchia (4-3-3-3--13) def. Wayne Grady (4-4-4-4—16) and Greg Norman (3-3-4-x) in 4 holes.

PGA Championship, 1916-1989

The PGA Championship began in 1916 as a professional golfers match play tournament, but switched to stroke play in 1958. Conducted by the PGA of America, the tournament is played on a different course each year. **Most wins:** Walter Hagen and Jack Nicklaus (5).

Year	Winner	Year	Winner	Year	Winner	Year	Winner
1916	Jim Barnes	1930	Tommy Armour	1950	Chandler Harper	1970	Dave Stockton
1917	Not held	1931	Tom Creavy	1951	Sam Snead	1971	Jack Nicklaus
1918	Not held	1932	Olin Dutra	1952	Jim Turnesa	1972	Gary Player
1919	Jim Barnes	1933	Gene Sarazen	1953	Walter Burkemo	1973	Jack Nicklaus
		1934	Paul Runyan	1954	Chick Harbert	1974	Lee Trevino
1920	Jock Hutchison	1935	Johnny Revolta	1955	Doug Ford	1975	Jack Nicklaus
1921	Walter Hagen	1936	Denny Shute	1956	Jack Burke, Jr.	1976	Dave Stockton
1922	Gene Sarazen	1937	Denny Shute	1957	Lionel Hebert	1977	Lanny Wadkins
1923	Gene Sarazen	1938	Paul Runyan	1958	Dow Finsterwald	1978	John Mahaffey
1924	Walter Hagen	1939	Henry Picard	1959	Bob Rosburg	1979	David Graham*
1925	Walter Hagen			1960	Jay Hebert	1980	Jack Nicklaus
1926	Walter Hagen	1940	Byron Nelson	1961	Jerry Barber*	1981	Larry Nelson
1927	Walter Hagen	1941	Vic Ghezzi	1962	Gary Player	1982	Raymond Floyd
1928	Leo Diegel	1942	Sam Snead	1963	Jack Nicklaus	1983	Hal Sutton
1929	Leo Diegel	1943	Not held	1964	Bobby Nichols	1984	Lee Trevino
		1944	Bob Hamilton	1965	Dave Marr	1985	Hubert Green
		1945	Byron Nelson	1966	Al Geiberger	1986	Bob Tway
		1946	Ben Hogan	1967	Don January*	1987	Larry Nelson*
		1947	Jim Ferrier	1968	Julius Boros	1988	Jeff Sluman
		1948	Ben Hogan	1969	Ray Floyd	1989	Payne Stewart
		1949	Sam Snead				

Playoffs

1961: J.Barber (67) def. Don January (68) in 18 holes. **1967:** January (69) def. Don Massengale (71) in 18 holes. **1977:** L.Wadkins (4-4-4) def. Gene Littler (4-4-5) on 3rd hole of sudden death. **1978:** Mahaffey (4-3) def. Jerry Pate (4-4) and Tom Watson (4-5) on 2nd hole of sudden death. **1979:** D.Graham (4-4-2) def. Ben Crenshaw (4-4-4) on 3rd hole of sudden death. **1987:** Nelson (4) def. Lanny Wadkins (5) on 1st hole of sudden death.

U.S. Amateur, 1895-89

Match play from 1895-64, stroke play from 1965-72, match play since 1972. **Most wins:** Bobby Jones (5).

Year Winner	Year Winner	Year Winner	Year Winner
1895 Charles Macdonald	1920 Chick Evans	1945 Not held	1970 Lanny Wadkins
1896 H.J.Whigham	1921 Jesse Guilford	1946 Ted Bishop	1971 Gary Cowan
1897 H.J.Whigham	1922 Jess Sweetser	1947 Skee Riegel	1972 Vinny Giles
1898 Findlay Douglas	1923 Max Marston	1948 William Turnesa	1973 Craig Stadler
1899 H.M.Harriman	1924 Bobby Jones	1949 Charles Coe	1974 Jerry Pate
1900 Walter Travis	1925 Bobby Jones	1950 Sam Urzetta	1975 Fred Ridley
1901 Walter Travis	1926 George Von Elm	1951 Billy Maxwell	1976 Bill Sander
1902 Louis James	1927 Bobby Jones	1952 Jack Westland	1977 John Fought
1903 Walter Travis	1928 Bobby Jones	1953 Gene Littler	1978 John Cook
1904 H.Chandler Egan	1929 Harrison Johnston	1954 Arnold Palmer	1979 Mark O'Meara
1905 H.Chandler Egan	1930 Bobby Jones	1955 Harvie Ward	1980 Hal Sutton
1906 Eben Byers	1931 Francis Ouimet	1956 Harvie Ward	1981 Nathanial Crosby
1907 Jerry Travers	1932 Ross Somerville	1957 Hillman Robbins	1982 Jay Sigel
1908 Jerry Travers	1933 George Dunlap	1958 Charles Coe	1983 Jay Sigel
1909 Robert Gardner	1934 Lawson Little	1959 Jack Nicklaus	1984 Scott Verplank
1910 W.C.Fownes, Jr.	1935 Lawson Little	1960 Deane Beman	1985 Sam Randolph
1911 Harold Hilton	1936 John Fischer	1961 Jack Nicklaus	1986 Buddy Alexander
1912 Jerry Travers	1937 John Goodman	1962 Labron Harris	1987 Billy Mayfair
1913 Jerry Travers	1938 William Turnesa	1963 Deane Beman	1988 Eric Meeks
1914 Francis Ouimet	1939 Bud Ward	1964 Bill Campbell	1989 Chris Patton
1915 Robert Gardner	1940 Richard Chapman	1965 Bob Murphy	
1916 Chick Evans	1941 Bud Ward	1966 Gary Cowan	
1917 Not held	1942 Not held	1967 Bob Dickson	
1918 Not held	1943 Not held	1968 Bruce Fleisher	
1919 Davidson Herron	1944 Not held	1969 Steve Melnyk	

British Amateur, 1900-89

Match play since 1885. **Most wins:** John Ball (8). **Most wins since 1900:** Michael Bonallack (5).

Year Winner	Year Winner	Year Winner	Year Winner
1885 Allen MacFie	1910 John Ball	1935 Lawson Little	1960 Joe Carr
1886 Horace Hutchinson	1911 Harold Hilton	1936 Hector Thomson	1961 Michael Bonallack
1887 Horace Hutchinson	1912 John Ball	1937 Robert Sweeny, Jr.	1962 Richard Davies
1888 John Ball	1913 Harold Hilton	1938 Charles Yates	1963 Michael Lunt
1889 Johnny Laidley	1914 J.L.C. Jenkins	1939 Alexander Kyle	1964 Gordon Clark
1890 John Ball	1915 Not held	1940 Not held	1965 Michael Bonallack
1891 Johnny Laidlay	1916 Not held	1941 Not held	1966 Bobby Cole
1892 John Ball	1917 Not held	1942 Not held	1967 Bob Dickson
1893 Peter Anderson	1918 Not held	1943 Not held	1968 Michael Bonallack
1894 John Ball	1919 Not held	1944 Not held	1969 Michael Bonallack
1895 Leslie Balfour	1920 Cyril Tolley	1945 Not held	1970 Michael Bonallack
1896 Freddie Tait	1921 William Hunter	1946 James Bruen	1971 Steve Melnyk
1897 Jack Allen	1922 Ernest Holderness	1947 William Turnesa	1972 Trevor Homer
1898 Freddie Tait	1923 Roger Wethered	1948 Frank Stranahan	1973 Dick Siderowf
1899 John Ball	1924 Ernest Holderness	1949 Samuel McCready	1974 Trevor Homer
1900 Harold Hilton	1925 Robert Harris	1950 Frank Stranahan	1975 Vinny Giles
1901 Harold Hilton	1926 Jesse Sweetser	1951 Richard Chapman	1976 Dick Siderowf
1902 Charles Hutchings	1927 William Tweedell	1952 Harvie Ward	1977 Peter McEvoy
1903 Robert Maxwell	1928 Thomas Perkins	1953 Joe Carr	1978 Peter McEvoy
1904 Walter Travis	1929 Cyril Tolley	1954 Douglas Bachli	1979 Jay Sigel
1905 Arthur Barry	1930 Bobby Jones	1955 Joe Conrad	1980 Duncan Evans
1906 James Robb	1931 Eric Smith	1956 John Beharrell	1981 Phillipe Ploujoux
1907 John Ball	1932 John deForest	1957 Reid Jack	1982 Martin Thompson
1908 E.A.Lassen	1933 Michael Scott	1958 Joe Carr	1983 Philip Parkin
1909 Robert Maxwell	1934 Lawson Little	1959 Deane Beman	1984 Jose-Maria Olazabal
			1985 Garth McGimpsey
			1986 David Curry
			1987 Paul Mayo
			1988 Christian Hardin
			1989 Stephen Dodd

Walker Cup Matches

The Walker Cup was presented by American businessman George Herbert Walker in 1922 for competition between amateur golfers from Great Britain and the United States. The US leads the series with a 28-3-1 record after 32 matches.

Year	Winner	Year	Winner	Year	Winner
1922	United States, 8-4	1940	Not held	1961	United States, 11-1
1923	United States, 6-5	1942	Not held	1963	United States, 14-10
1924	United States, 9-3	1944	Not held	1965	Draw, 12-12
1926	United States, 6½-5½	1946	Not held	1967	United States, 15-9
1928	United States, 11-1	1947	United States, 8-4	1969	United States, 13-11
1930	United States, 10-2	1949	United States, 10-2	1971	Britain-Ireland, 13-11
1932	United States, 9½-2½	1951	United States, 7½-4½	1973	United States, 14-10
1934	United States, 9½-2½	1953	United States, 9-3	1975	United States, 15½-8½
1936	United States, 10½-1½	1955	United States, 10-2	1977	United States, 16-8
1938	Britain-Ireland, 7½-4½	1957	United States, 8½-3½	1979	United States, 15½-8½
		1959	United States, 9-3	1981	United States, 15-9
				1983	United States, 13½-10½
				1985	United States, 13-11
				1987	United States, 16½-7½
				1989	Britain-Ireland, 12½-11½

Major Tournaments

WOMEN

The women's Grand Slam has consisted of four tournaments only 19 years. From 1955-66, the US Open, LPGA Championship, Western Open and Titleholders tournaments served as the major events. Since 1983, the US Open, LPGA, du Maurier Classic in Canada and Nabisco Dinah Shore have been the major events. No one has won a four-event Grand Slam on the women's tour, but Mickey Wright won three (LPGA, US Open and Titleholders) in 1961.

Major Championship Leaders

WOMEN

	US Open	LPGA	duM	Dinah	Title-holders	Western	US Am	Brit Am	Total
Patty Berg	1	0	0	0	7	7	1	0	16
Mickey Wright	4	4	0	0	2	3	0	0	13
Louise Suggs	2	1	0	0	4	4	1	1	13
Babe Zaharias	3	0	0	0	3	4	1	1	12
Betsy Rawls	4	2	0	0	0	2	0	0	8
JoAnne Carner	2	0	0	0	0	0	5	0	7
Kathy Whitworth	0	3	0	0	2	1	0	0	6
Pat Bradley	1	1	3	1	0	0	0	0	6
Julie Inkster	0	0	1	2	0	0	3	0	6
Glenna C.Vare	0	0	0	0	0	0	6	0	6

Tournaments: US Open, LPGA Championship, du Maurier Classic, Nabisco Dinah Shore, Titleholders (1937-72), Western Open (1937-67), US Amateur, and British Amateur.

Titleholders Championship, 1937-72

The Titleholders was considered a major title on the women's tour until it was discontinued after the 1972 tournament. **Most wins:** Patty Berg (7) and Louise Suggs (4).

Year	Winner	Year	Winner	Year	Winner	Year	Winner
1937	Patty Berg	1946	Louise Suggs	1955	Patty Berg	1965	Kathy Whitworth
1938	Patty Berg	1947	Babe Zaharias	1956	Louise Suggs	1966	Kathy Whitworth
1939	Patty Berg	1948	Patty Berg	1957	Patty Berg	1967	Not held
1940	Betty Hicks	1949	Peggy Kirk	1958	Beverly Hanson	1968	Not held
1941	Dorothy Kirby			1959	Louise Suggs	1969	Not held
1942	Dorothy Kirby	1950	Babe Zaharias				
1943	Not held	1951	Pat O'Sullivan	1960	Fay Crocker	1970	Not held
1944	Not held	1952	Babe Zaharias	1961	Mickey Wright	1971	Not held
1945	Not held	1953	Patty Berg	1962	Mickey Wright	1972	Sandra Palmer
		1954	Louise Suggs	1963	Marilynn Smith	1973	Tourney
				1964	Marilynn Smith		discontinued

Western Open, 1937-67

The Western Open was considered a major title on the women's tour until it was discontinued after the 1967 tournament. **Most wins:** Patty Berg (7), Louise Suggs and Babe Zaharias (4).

Year	Winner	Year	Winner	Year	Winner	Year	Winner
1937	Betty Hicks	1945	Babe Zaharias	1953	Louise Suggs	1961	Mary Lena Faulk
1938	Bea Barrett	1946	Louise Suggs	1954	Betty Jameson	1962	Mickey Wright
1939	Helen Dettweiler	1947	Louise Suggs	1955	Patty Berg	1963	Mickey Wright
1940	Babe Zaharias	1948	Patty Berg	1956	Beverly Hanson	1964	Carol Mann
1941	Patty Berg	1949	Louise Suggs	1957	Patty Berg	1965	Susie Maxwell
1942	Betty Jameson	1950	Babe Zaharias	1958	Patty Berg	1966	Mickey Wright
1943	Patty Berg	1951	Patty Berg	1959	Betsy Rawls	1967	Kathy Whitworth
1944	Babe Zaharias	1952	Betsy Rawls	1960	Joyce Ziske	1968	Tourney discontinued

U.S. Women's Open, 1946-1989

The US Women's Open began under the direction of the defunct Women's Professional Golfers Assn in 1946, passed to the LPGA in 1949 and to the USGA in 1953. The tournament used a match play format its first year then switched to stroke play. **Most wins:** Mickey Wright and Betsy Rawls (4).

Year	Winner	Year	Winner	Year	Winner	Year	Winner
1946	Patty Berg	1957	Betsy Rawls	1968	Susie M.Berning	1979	Jerilyn Britz
1947	Betty Jameson	1958	Mickey Wright	1969	Donna Caponi	1980	Amy Alcott
1948	Babe Zaharias	1959	Mickey Wright	1970	Donna Caponi	1981	Pat Bradley
1949	Louise Suggs	1960	Betsy Rawls	1971	JoAnne Carner	1982	Janet Anderson
1950	Babe Zaharias	1961	Mickey Wright	1972	Susie M.Berning	1983	Jan Stephenson
1951	Betsy Rawls	1962	Murle Lindstrom	1973	Susie M.Berning	1984	Hollis Stacy
1952	Louise Suggs	1963	Mary Mills	1974	Sandra Haynie	1985	Kathy Baker
1953	Betsy Rawls*	1964	Mickey Wright*	1975	Sandra Palmer	1986	Jane Geddes*
1954	Babe Zaharias	1965	Carol Mann	1976	JoAnne Carner*	1987	Laura Davies*
1955	Fay Crocker	1966	Sandra Spuzich	1977	Hollis Stacy	1988	Liselotte Neumann
1956	Kathy Cornelius*	1967	a-Catherine Lacoste	1978	Hollis Stacy	1989	Betsy King

Playoffs

1953: Rawls (71) def. Jackie Pung (77) in 18 holes. **1956:** Cornelius (75) def. Barbara McIntire (82) in 18 holes.
1964: Wright (70) def. Ruth Jessen (72) in 18 holes. **1976:** Carner (76) def. Sandra Palmer (78) in 18 holes.
1986: Geddes (71) def. Sally Little (73) in 18 holes. **1987:** Davies (71) def. Ayako Okamoto (73) and JoAnne Carner (74) in 18 holes.

LPGA Championship, 1946-1989

Officially the Mazda LPGA Championship since 1987, the tournament began in 1955 and has had extended stays at the Stardust CC in Las Vegas (1961-66), Pleasant Valley CC in Sutton, MA (1967-68,70-74) and the Jack Nicklaus Sports Center at Kings Island, OH (1978-89). **Most wins:** Mickey Wright (4), Kathy Whitworth and Nancy Lopez (3).

Year	Winner	Year	Winner	Year	Winner	Year	Winner
1955	Beverly Hanson	1964	Mary Mills	1973	Mary Mills	1982	Jan Stephenson
1956	Marlene Hagge*	1965	Sandra Haynie	1974	Sandra Haynie	1983	Patty Sheehan
1957	Louise Suggs	1966	Gloria Ehret	1975	Kathy Whitworth	1984	Patty Sheehan
1958	Mickey Wright	1967	Kathy Whitworth	1976	Betty Burfeindt	1985	Nancy Lopez
1959	Betsy Rawls	1968	Sandra Post*	1977	Chako Higuchi	1986	Pat Bradley
1960	Mickey Wright	1969	Betsy Rawls	1978	Nancy Lopez	1987	Jane Geddes
1961	Mickey Wright	1970	Shirley Englehorn*	1979	Donna Caponi	1988	Sherri Turner
1962	Judy Kimball	1971	Kathy Whitworth	1980	Sally Little	1989	Nancy Lopez
1963	Mickey Wright	1972	Kathy Ahern	1981	Donna Caponi		

Playoffs

1956: Hagge def. Patti Berg in sudden death. **1968:** Post (68) def. Kathy Whitworth (75) in 18-holes. **1970:** Englehorn def. Kathy Whitworth in sudden death.

du Maurier Classic, 1973-1989

Formerly known as La Canadienne in 1973 and the Peter Jackson Classic from 1974-83, this Canadian stop on the LPGA Tour became the third designated major championship in 1979. **Most wins as major:** Pat Bradley (3).

Year	Winner	Year	Winner	Year	Winner	Year	Winner
1973	Jocelyne Bourassa	1977	Judy Rankin	1980	Pat Bradley	1985	Pat Bradley
1974	Carole Jo Skala	1978	JoAnne Carner	1981	Jan Stephenson	1986	Pat Bradley*
1975	JoAnne Carner	1979	Amy Alcott	1982	Sandra Haynie	1987	Jody Rosenthal
1976	Donna Caponi			1983	Hollis Stacy	1988	Sally Little
				1984	Juli Inkster	1989	Tammie Green

Playoff

1986: Bradley def. Ayako Okamoto in sudden death.

Nabisco Dinah Shore, 1972-1989

Formerly known as the Colgate Dinah Shore from 1972-81, the tournament become the LPGA's fourth designated major championship in 1983. Named after the entertainer, this tourney has been played at Mission Hills CC in Rancho Mirage, CA since it began. **Most wins as major:** Amy Alcott and Juli Inkster (2).

Year Winner	Year Winner	Year Winner	Year Winner
1972 Jane Blalock	1976 Judy Rankin	1980 Donna Caponi	1985 Alice Miller
1973 Mickey Wright	1977 Kathy Whitworth	1981 Nancy Lopez	1986 Pat Bradley
1974 Jo Ann Prentice	1978 Sandra Post	1982 Sally Little	1987 Betsy King*
1975 Sandra Palmer	1979 Sandra Post	1983 Amy Alcott	1988 Amy Alcott
		1984 Juli Inkster*	1989 Juli Inkster

Playoffs
1984: Inkster def. Pat Bradley in Sudden Death. **1987:** King def. Patty Sheehan in Sudden Death.

U.S. Amateur, 1895-89

Stroke play in 1895, match play since 1896. **Most wins:** Glenna Collett Vare (6), JoAnne Carner (5).

Year Winner	Year Winner	Year Winner
1895 Mrs. Chas. S. Brown	1926 Helen Stetson	1957 JoAnne Gunderson
1896 Beatrix Hoyt	1927 Miriam Burns Horn	1958 Anne Quast
1897 Beatrix Hoyt	1928 Glenna Collett	1959 Barbara McIntire
1898 Beatrix Hoyt	1929 Glenna Collett	1960 JoAnne Gunderson
1899 Ruth Underhill	1930 Glenna Collett	1961 Anne Quast Decker
1900 Frances Griscom	1931 Helen Hicks	1962 JoAnne Gunderson
1901 Genevieve Hecker	1932 Virginia Van Wie	1963 Anne Quast Welts
1902 Genevieve Hecker	1933 Virginia Van Wie	1964 Barbara McIntire
1903 Bessie Anthony	1934 Virginia Van Wie	1965 Jean Ashley
1904 Georgianna Bishop	1935 Glenna Collett Vare	1966 JoAnne Gunderson Carner
1905 Pauline Mackay	1936 Pamela Barton	1967 Mary Lou Dill
1906 Harriot Curtis	1937 Estelle Lawson	1968 JoAnne Gunderson Carner
1907 Margaret Curtis	1938 Patty Berg	1969 Catherine Lacoste
1908 Katherine Harley	1939 Betty Jameson	1970 Martha Wilkinson
1909 Dorothy Campbell	1940 Betty Jameson	1971 Laura Baugh
1910 Dorothy Campbell	1941 Elizabeth Hicks	1972 Mary Budke
1911 Margaret Curtis	1942 Not held	1973 Carol Semple
1912 Margaret Curtis	1943 Not held	1974 Cynthia Hill
1913 Gladys Ravenscroft	1944 Not held	1975 Beth Daniel
1914 Katherine Harley	1945 Not held	1976 Donna Horton
1915 Florence Vanderbeck	1946 Babe Didrikson Zaharias	1977 Beth Daniel
1916 Alexa Stirling	1947 Louise Suggs	1978 Cathy Sherk
1917 Not held	1948 Grace Lenczyk	1979 Carolyn Hill
1918 Not held	1949 Dorothy Porter	1980 Juli Inkster
1919 Alexa Stirling	1950 Beverly Hanson	1981 Juli Inkster
1920 Alexa Stirling	1951 Dorothy Kirby	1982 Juli Inkster
1921 Marion Hollins	1952 Jacqueline Pung	1983 Joanne Pacillo
1922 Glenna Collett	1953 Mary Lena Faulk	1984 Deb Richard
1923 Edith Cummings	1954 Barbara Romack	1985 Michiko Hattori
1924 Dorothy Campbell Hurd	1955 Patricia Lesser	1986 Kay Cockerill
1925 Glenna Collett	1956 Marlene Stewart	1987 Kay Cockerill
		1988 Pearl Sinn
		1989 Vicki Goetze

Curtis Cup Matches

Named after British golfing sisters Harriot and Margaret Curtis, the Curtis Cup was first contested in 1932 between teams of women amateurs from the US and the British Isles.

Competed for every other year since 1932 (except during World War II). The US leads the series with a 19-4-2 record after 25 matches.

Year Winner	Year Winner	Year Winner
1932 United States, 5½-3½	1950 United States, 7½-1½	1970 United States, 11½-6½
1934 United States, 6½-2½	1952 British Isles, 5-4	1972 United States, 10-8
1936 Draw, 4½-4½	1954 United States, 6-3	1974 United States, 13-5
1938 United States, 5½-3½	1956 British Isles, 5-4	1976 United States, 11½-6½
1940 Not held	1958 Draw 4½-4½	1978 United States, 12-6
1942 Not held		
1944 Not held	1960 United States, 6½-2½	1980 United States, 13-5
1946 Not held	1962 United States, 8-1	1982 United States, 14½-3½
1948 United States, 6½-2½	1964 United States, 10½-7½	1984 United States, 9½-8½
	1966 United States, 13-5	1986 British Isles, 13-5
	1968 United States, 10½-7½	1988 British Isles, 11-7

PGA Seniors Championship

First played in 1937. **Most wins:** Sam Snead (6).

Year	Winner	Year	Winner	Year	Winner	Year	Winner
1937	Jock Hutchison	1950	Al Watrous	1963	Herman Barron	1977	Julius Boros
1938	Fred McLeod	1951	Al Watrous*	1964	Sam Snead	1978	Joe Jiminez*
1939	Not held	1952	Ernest Newnham	1965	Sam Snead	1979	Jack Fleck*
1940	Otto Hackbarth	1953	Harry Schwab	1966	Fred Haas	1979†	Don January
1941	Jack Burke	1954	Gene Sarazen	1967	Sam Snead		
1942	Eddie Williams	1955	Mortie Dutra	1968	Chandler Harper	1980	Arnold Palmer*
1943	Not held	1956	Pete Burke	1969	Tommy Bolt	1981	Miller Barber
1944	Not held	1957	Al Watrous			1982	Don January
1945	Eddie Williams	1958	Gene Sarazen	1970	Sam Snead	1983	Not Held
1946	Eddie Williams	1959	Willie Goggin	1971	Julius Boros	1984	Arnold Palmer
1947	Jock Hutchison			1972	Sam Snead	1984†	Peter Thomson
1948	Charles McKenna	1960	Dick Metz	1973	Sam Snead	1985	Not Held
1949	Marshall Crichton*	1961	Paul Runyan	1974	Robert de Vicenzo	1986	Gary Player
		1962	Paul Runyan	1975	Charlie Sifford*	1987	Chi Chi Rodriguez
				1976	Pete Cooper	1988	Gary Player
						1989	Larry Mowry

*Won in playoff. †Two championships played in 1979 and '84.

U.S. Senior Open

Established in 1980 for senior players 55 years-old and over, the minimum age was dropped to 50 (the PGA Seniors Tour entry age) in 1981. Arnold Palmer, Billy Casper and Orville Moody are the only golfers who have won both the US Open and US Senior Open. **Most wins:** Miller Barber (3), Gary Player (2).

Year	Winner	Year	Winner	Year	Winner	Year	Winner
1980	Roberto deVicenzo	1983	Bill Casper*	1986	Dale Douglass	1988	Gary Player*
1981	Arnold Palmer*	1984	Miller Barber	1987	Gary Player	1989	Orville Moody
1982	Miller Barber	1985	Miller Barber				

Playoffs

1981: Palmer (70) def. Bob Stone (74) and Billy Casper (77) in 18 holes. **1983:** Tied at 75 after 18-hole playoff, Casper def. Rod Funseth with a birdie on the 1st extra hole. **1988:** Player (68) def. Bob Charles (70) in 18 holes.

Annual Money Leaders

MEN

Year		Earnings	Year		Earnings	Year		Earnings
1934	Paul Runyan	$6,767	1952	Julius Boros	$37,033	1970	Lee Trevino	$157,037
1935	Johnny Revolta	9,543	1953	Lew Worsham	34,002	1971	Jack Nicklaus	244,490
1936	Horton Smith	7,682	1954	Bob Toski	65,820	1972	Jack Nicklaus	320,542
1937	Harry Cooper	14,139	1955	Julius Boros	63,122	1973	Jack Nicklaus	308,362
1938	Sam Snead	19,534	1956	Ted Kroll	72,836	1974	Johnny Miller	353,021
1939	Henry Picard	10,303	1957	Dick Mayer	65,835	1975	Jack Nicklaus	298,149
1940	Ben Hogan	10,655	1958	Arnold Palmer	42,608	1976	Nack Nicklaus	266,438
1941	Ben Hogan	18,358	1959	Art Wall	53,168	1977	Tom Watson	310,653
1942	Ben Hogan	13,143	1960	Arnold Palmer	75,263	1978	Tom Watson	362,429
1943	No records kept		1961	Gary Player	64,540	1979	Tom Watson	462,636
1944	Byron Nelson	37,968	1962	Arnold Palmer	81,448	1980	Tom Watson	530,808
1945	Byron Nelson	63,336	1963	Arnold Palmer	128,230	1981	Tom Kite	365,699
1946	Ben Hogan	42,556	1964	Jack Nicklaus	113,285	1982	Craig Stadler	446,462
1947	Jimmy Demaret	27,937	1965	Jack Nicklaus	140,752	1983	Hal Sutton	426,668
1948	Ben Hogan	32,112	1966	Billy Casper	121,945	1984	Tom Watson	476,260
1949	Sam Snead	31,594	1967	Jack Nicklaus	188,998	1985	Curtis Strange	542,321
1950	Sam Snead	35,759	1968	Billy Casper	205,169	1986	Greg Norman	653,296
1951	Lloyd Mangrum	26,089	1969	Frank Beard	164,707	1987	Curtis Strange	925,941
						1988	Curtis Strange	1,147,644

Note: In 1944-45, Nelson's winnings were in War Bonds.

WOMEN

Year		Earnings	Year		Earnings	Year		Earnings
1950	Babe Zaharias	$14,800	1963	Mickey Wright	$31,269	1976	Judy Rankin	$150,734
1951	Babe Zaharias	15,087	1964	Mickey Wright	29,800	1977	Judy Rankin	122,890
1952	Betsy Rawls	14,505	1965	Kathy Whitworth	28,658	1978	Nancy Lopez	189,814
1953	Louise Suggs	19,816	1966	Kathy Whitworth	33,517	1979	Nancy Lopez	197,489
1954	Patty Berg	16,011	1967	Kathy Whitworth	32,937	1980	Beth Daniel	231,000
1955	Patty Berg	16,497	1968	Kathy Whitworth	48,379	1981	Beth Daniel	206,978
1956	Marlene Hagge	20,235	1969	Carol Mann	49,152	1982	JoAnne Carner	310,399
1957	Patty Berg	16,272	1970	Kathy Whitworth	30,235	1983	JoAnne Carner	291,404
1958	Beverly Hanson	12,639	1971	Kathy Whitworth	41,181	1984	Betsy King	266,771
1959	Betsy Rawls	26,774	1972	Kathy Whitworth	65,063	1985	Nancy Lopez	416,472
1960	Louise Suggs	16,892	1973	Kathy Whitworth	82,864	1986	Pat Bradley	492,021
1961	Mickey Wright	22,236	1974	JoAnne Carner	87,094	1987	Ayako Okamoto	466,034
1962	Mickey Wright	21,641	1975	Sandra Palmer	76,374	1988	Sherri Turner	350,851

SENIORS

Year		Earnings	Year		Earnings	Year		Earnings
1980	Don January	$ 44,100	1983	Don January	$237,571	1986	Bruce Crampton	$454,299
1981	Miller Barber	83,136	1984	Don January	328,597	1987	Chi Chi Rodriguez	509,145
1982	Miller Barber	106,890	1985	Peter Thomson	386,724	1988	Bob Charles	533,929

Awards

PGA Player of the Year
Awarded by the PGA of America.

Year	Player	Year	Player	Year	Player	Year	Player
1948	Ben Hogan	1960	Arnold Palmer	1970	Billy Casper	1980	Tom Watson
1949	Sam Snead	1961	Jerry Barber	1971	Lee Trevino	1981	Bill Rogers
1950	Ben Hogan	1962	Arnold Palmer	1972	Jack Nicklaus	1982	Tom Watson
1951	Ben Hogan	1963	Julius Boros	1973	Jack Nicklaus	1983	Hal Sutton
1952	Julius Boros	1964	Ken Venturi	1974	Johnny Miller	1984	Tom Watson
1953	Ben Hogan	1965	Dave Marr	1975	Jack Nicklaus	1985	Lanny Wadkins
1954	Ed Furgol	1966	Billy Casper	1976	Jack Nicklaus	1986	Bob Tway
1955	Doug Ford	1967	Jack Nicklaus	1977	Tom Watson	1987	Paul Azinger
1956	Jack Burke	1968	No award	1978	Tom Watson	1988	Curtis Strange
1957	Dick Mayer	1969	Orville Moody	1979	Tom Watson		
1958	Dow Finsterwald						
1959	Art Wall						

LPGA Player of the Year
Awarded by the LPGA.

Year	Player	Year	Player	Year	Player	Year	Player
1966	Kathy Whitworth	1972	Kathy Whitworth	1977	Judy Rankin	1982	JoAnne Carner
1967	Kathy Whitworth	1973	Kathy Whitworth	1978	Nancy Lopez	1983	Patty Sheehan
1968	Kathy Whitworth	1974	JoAnne Carner	1979	Nancy Lopez	1984	Betsy King
1969	Kathy Whitworth	1975	Sandra Palmer	1980	Beth Daniel	1985	Nancy Lopez
1970	Sandra Haynie	1976	Judy Rankin	1981	JoAnne Carner	1986	Pat Bradley
1971	Kathy Whitworth					1987	Ayako Okamoto
						1988	Nancy Lopez

GWAA Players of the Year
Awarded by the Golf Writers Assn. of America.

Year	Men's Tour	Year	Men's Tour	Year	Women's Tour	Year	Women's Tour
1968	Billy Casper	1980	Tom Watson	1972	Kathy Whitworth	1983	JoAnne Carner
1969	Orville Moody	1981	Tom Kite	1973	Kathy Whitworth	1984	Patty Sheehan
1970	Billy Casper	1982	Tom Watson	1974	JoAnne Carner	1985	Nancy Lopez
1971	Lee Trevino	1983	Hal Sutton	1975	Sandra Palmer	1986	Pat Bradley
1972	Jack Nicklaus	1984	Tom Watson	1976	Judy Rankin	1987	Betsy King
1973	Tom Weiskopf	1985	Curtis Strange	1977	Judy Rankin	1988	Sherri Turner
1974	Johnny Miller	1986	Greg Norman	1978	Nancy Lopez		
1975	Jack Nicklaus	1987	Curtis Strange	1979	Nancy Lopez	**Year**	**Seniors' Tour**
1976	Jack Nicklaus & Jerry Pate	1988	Curtis Strange	1980	Beth Daniel	1986	Bruce Crampton
1977	Tom Watson			1981	Donna Caponi	1987	Chi Chi Rodriguez
1978	Tom Watson			1982	JoAnne Carner	1988	Bob Charles
1979	Tom Watson						

Golf Digest Rookies of the Year

Year	Men's Tour	Year	Men's Tour	Year	Women's Tour	Year	Women's Tour
1957	Ken Venturi	1973	Tom Kite	1962	Mary Mills	1975	Amy Alcott
1958	Bob Goalby	1974	Ben Crenshaw	1963	Clifford Ann Creed	1976	Ai-Yu Tu
1959	Joe Campbell	1975	Roger Maltbie	1964	Susie Maxwell	1977	Nancy Lopez
1960	Mason Rudolph	1976	Jerry Pate	1965	Margie Masters	1978	Janet Anderson
1961	Jackie Cupit	1977	Graham Marsh	1966	Jan Ferrais	1979	Beth Daniel
1962	Jack Nicklaus	1978	Pat McGowan	1967	Sharon Moran	1980	Myra Van Hoose
1963	Raymond Floyd	1979	John Fought	1968	Sandra Post	1981	Kyle O'Brien
1964	R.H.Sikes	1980	Gary Hallberg	1969	Jane Blalock	1982	Patti Rizzo
1965	Homero Blancas	1981	Mark O'Meara	1970	JoAnne Carner	1983	Juli Inkster
1966	John Schlee	1982	Hal Sutton	1971	Sally Little	1984	Marla Figueras-Dotti
1967	Lee Trevino	1983	Nick Price	1972	Jocelyne Bourassa	1985	Penny Hammel
1968	Bob Murphy	1984	Corey Pavin	1973	Laura Baugh	1986	Jody Rosenthal
1969	Grier Jones	1985	Phil Blackmar	1974	Jan Stephenson	1987	Laura Davies
1970	Ted Hayes, Jr.	1986	Brian Claar			1988	Liselotte Neuman
1971	Hubert Green	1987	Keith Clearwater				
1972	Lanny Wadkins	1988	Jim Benepe				

Ben Hogan Award

Awarded by the GWAA to the individual who has overcome serious illness or injury to play golf again.

Year	Player
1954	Babe Didkirson Zaharias
1955	Ed Furgol
1956	Dwight Eisenhower
1957	Clint Russell
1958	Dale Bourisseau
1959	Charlie Boswell
1960	Skip Alexander
1961	Horton Smith
1962	Jimmy Nichols
1963	Bobby Nichols
1964	Bob Morgan

Year	Player
1965	Ernest Jones
1966	Ken Venturi
1967	Warren Pease
1968	Shirley Englehorn
1969	Curtis Person
1970	Joe Lazaro
1971	Larry Hinson
1972	Ruth Jessen
1973	Gene Littler
1974	Gay Brewer
1975	Patty Berg
1976	Paul Hahn

Year	Player
1977	Des Sullivan
1978	Dennis Walters
1979	John Mahaffey
1980	Lee Trevino
1981	Kathy Linney
1982	Al Geiberger
1983	Calvin Peete
1984	Jay Sigel
1985	Rod Funseth
1986	Fuzzy Zoeller
1987	Charles Owens
1988	Pat Browne
1989	Sally Little

Bobby Jones Award

Awarded by the USGA for distinguished sportsmanship.

Year	Player
1955	Francis Ouimet
1956	Bill Campbell
1957	Babe Zaharias
1958	Margaret Curtis
1959	Findlay Douglas
1960	Chick Evans
1961	Joe Carr
1962	Horton Smith
1963	Patty Berg
1964	Charles Coe
1965	Glenna Collett Vare

Year	Player
1966	Gary Player
1967	Richard Tutts
1968	Robert Dickson
1969	Gerald Micklem
1970	Roberto DeVicenzo
1971	Arnold Palmer
1972	Michael Bonallack
1973	Gene Littler
1974	Byron Nelson
1975	Jack Nicklaus
1976	Ben Hogan
1977	Joseph Dey

Year	Player
1978	Bob Hope & Bing Crosby
1979	Tom Kite
1980	Charles Yates
1981	JoAnne Carner
1982	Billy Joe Patton
1983	Maureen Garrett
1984	Jay Sigel
1985	Fuzzy Zoeller
1986	Jess Sweetser
1987	Tom Watson
1988	Isaac Grainger

Wm. Richardson Award

Awarded by the GWAA to the individual who has consistently made outstanding contributions to golf.

Year	Player
1948	Robert A. Hudson
1949	Scotty Fessenden
1950	Bing Crosby
1951	Richard Tufts
1952	Chick Evans
1953	Bob Hope
1954	Babe Didrikson Zaharias
1955	Dwight Eisenhower
1956	George May
1957	Francis Ouimet
1958	Bobby Jones
1959	Patty Berg

Year	Player
1960	Fred Corcoran
1961	Joseph Dey
1962	Walter Hagen
1963	Joe & Herb Graffis
1964	Cliff Roberts
1965	Gene Sarazen
1966	Robert Harlow
1967	Max Elbin
1968	Charles Bartlett
1969	Arnold Palmer
1970	Roberto de Vincenzo
1971	Lincoln Werden
1972	Leo Fraser
1973	Ben Hogan
1974	Byron Nelson

Year	Player
1975	Gary Player
1976	Herbert Warren Wind
1977	Mark Cox
1978	Jack Nicklaus
1979	Jin Gaquin
1980	Jack Tuthill
1981	Robert Trent Jones
1982	Chi Chi Rodriguez
1983	Bill Campbell
1984	Sam Snead
1985	Lee Trevino
1986	Kathy Whitworth
1987	Frank Hannigan
1988	Roger Barry
1989	Ben Crenshaw

College Golf

Fred Haskins Award

Awarded by the Fred Haskins Commission to the Outstanding male collegiate golfer of the year.

Year	Player
1971	Ben Crenshaw, Texas
1972	Ben Crenshaw, Texas
1973	Ben Crenshaw, Texas
1974	Curtis Strange, Wake Forest
1975	Jay Haas, Wake Forest
1976	Phil Hancock, Florida

Year	Player
1977	Scott Simpson, USC
1978	Lindy Miller,
1979	Bobby Clampett, BYU
1980	Bobby Clampett, BYU
1981	Bob Tway, Oklahoma St.
1982	Willie Wood, Oklahoma St.

Year	Player
1983	Brad Faxon, Furman
1984	John Inman, N. Carolina
1985	Sam Randolph, USC
1986	Scott Verplank, Okla. St.
1987	Billy Mayfair, Ariz. St.
1988	Bob Estes, Texas

NCAA Championships
Men's Division I

Match play from 1897-1964, stroke plays since 1965.

Year	Team winner	Individual champion	Year	Team winner	Individual champion
1897	Yale	Louis Bayard, Princeton	1943	Yale	Wallace Ulrich, Carleton
1898	Harvard (spring)	John Reid, Yale	1944	Notre Dame	Louis Lick, Minnesota
1898	Yale (fall)	James Curtis, Harvard	1945	Ohio State	John Lorms, Ohio St.
1899	Harvard	Percy Pyne, Princeton	1946	Stanford	George Hamer, Georgia
			1947	LSU	Dave Barclay, Michigan
1900	Not held	—	1948	San Jose St.	Bob Harris, San Jose St.
1901	Harvard	H.Lindsley, Harvard	1949	North Texas	Harvie Ward, North Caro.
1902	Yale (spring)	Chas.Hitchcock, Jr., Yale			
1902	Harvard (fall)	Chandler Egan, Harvard	1950	North Texas	Fred Wampler, Purdue
1903	Harvard	F.O.Reinhart, Princeton	1951	North Texas	Tom Nieporte, Ohio St.
1904	Harvard	A.L.White, Harvard	1952	North Texas	Jim Vichers, Oklahoma
1905	Yale	Robert Abbott, Yale	1953	Stanford	Earl Moeller, Oklahoma St.
1906	Yale	W.E.Clow Jr., Yale	1954	SMU	Hillman Robbins, Memphis St.
1907	Yale	Ellis Knowles, Yale	1955	LSU	Joe Campbell, Purdue
1908	Yale	H.H.Wilder, Harvard	1956	Houston	Rick Jones, Ohio St.
1909	Yale	Albert Seckel, Princeton	1957	Houston	Rex Baxter Jr., Houston
			1958	Houston	Phil Rodgers, Houston
1910	Yale	Robert Hunter, Yale	1959	Houston	Dick Crawford, Houston
1911	Yale	George Stanley, Yale			
1912	Yale	F.C.Davison, Harvard	1960	Houston	Dick Crawford, Houston
1913	Yale	Nathaniel Wheeler, Yale	1961	Purdue	Jack Nicklaus, Ohio St.
1914	Princeton	Edward Allis, Harvard	1962	Houston	Kermit Zarley, Houston
1915	Yale	Francis Blossom, Yale	1963	Oklahoma St.	R.H. Sikes, Arkansas
1916	Princeton	J.W.Hubbell, Harvard	1964	Houston	Terry Small, San Jose St.
1917	Not held	—	1965	Houston	Marty Fleckman, Houston
1918	Not held	—	1966	Houston	Bob Murphy, Florida
1919	Princeton	A.L.Walker, Jr., Columbia	1967	Houston	Hale Irwin, Colorado
			1968	Florida	Grier Jones, Oklahoma St.
1920	Princeton	Jess Sweetster, Yale	1969	Houston	Bob Clark, Cal St.-LA
1921	Dartmouth	Simpson Dean, Princeton			
1922	Princeton	Pollack Boyd, Dartmouth	1970	Houston	John Mahaffey, Houston
1923	Princeton	Dexter Cummings, Yale	1971	Texas	Ben Crenshaw, Texas
1924	Yale	Dexter Cummings, Yale	1972	Texas	Ben Crenshaw, Texas
1925	Yale	Fred Lamprecht, Tulane			& Tom Kite, Texas
1926	Yale	Fred Lamprecht, Tulane	1973	Florida	Ben Crenshaw, Texas
1927	Princeton	Watts Gunn, Georgia Tech	1974	Wake Forest	Curtis Strange, W.Forest
1928	Princeton	Maurice McCarthy, G'town	1975	Wake Forest	Jay Haas, Wake Forest
1929	Princeton	Tom Aycock, Yale	1976	Oklahoma St.	Scott Simpson, USC
			1977	Houston	Scott Simpson, USC
1930	Princeton	G.T. Dunlap Jr., Princeton	1978	Oklahoma St.	David Edwards, Okla.St.
1931	Yale	G.T. Dunlap Jr., Princeton	1979	Ohio St.	Gary Hallberg, Wake Forest
1932	Yale	J.W. Fischer, Michigan			
1933	Yale	Walter Emery, Oklahoma	1980	Oklahoma St.	Jay Don Blake, Utah St.
1934	Michigan	Charles Yates, Ga.Tech	1981	Brigham Young	Ron Commans, USC
1935	Michigan	Ed White, Texas	1982	Houston	Billy Ray Brown, Houston
1936	Yale	Charles Kocsis, Michigan	1983	Oklahoma St.	Jim Carter, Arizona St.
1937	Princeton	Fred Haas, Jr., LSU	1984	Houston	John Inman, N.Carolina
1938	Stanford	John Burke, Georgetown	1985	Houston	Clark Burroughs, Ohio St.
1939	Stanford	Vincent D'Antoni, Tulane	1986	Wake Forest	Scott Verplank, Okla.St.
			1987	Oklahoma St.	Brian Watts, Oklahoma St.
1940	Princeton & LSU	Dixon Brooke, Virginia	1988	UCLA	E.J.Pfister, Oklahoma St.
1941	Stanford	Earl Stewart, LSU	1989	Oklahoma	Phil Mickelson, Ariz.St.
1942	LSU & Stanford	Frank Tatum Jr., Stanford			

Women's Division I

Year	Team winner	Individual champion	Year	Team winner	Individual champion
1982	Tulsa	Kathy Baker, Tulsa	1986	Florida	Page Dunlap, Florida
1983	TCU	Penny Hammel, Miami	1987	San Jose St.	Caroline Keggi,
1984	Miami,FL	Cindy Schreyer, Georgia			New Mexico
1985	Florida	Danielle Ammaccapane,	1988	Tulsa	Melissa McNamara, Tulsa
		Ariz.St.	1989	San Jose St.	Pat Hurst, San Jose St.

Former Formula One world champion **Emerson Fittipaldi** won both the Indianapolis 500 and the CART driving title in 1989.

AUTO RACING

INSIDE

Elsewhere in Almanac
For related information refer to the following chapters: Halls of Fame & Awards, Sports Organizations and Updates.

*Vets Fittipaldi and Waltrip
win at Indy and Daytona;
Sullivan and Elliott recover;
Prost, Senna rule Formula One.*

AUTO RACING

1989 YEAR IN REVIEW

by Mike Harris

Emerson Fittipaldi and Darrell Waltrip, both of whom were thought by some to be seeing their best days through the rear-view mirror, helped make 1989 "The Year of the Veteran" in motorsports.

Fittipaldi, who once retired from racing after winning a pair of Formula One championships, proved that at age 42 neither his competitive drive nor his ability to drive a race car as if it was running on rails had diminished.

The wily Fittipaldi added an unofficial national holiday to the calendar of his native Brazil on May 28 by winning the richest and most prestigious race of them all—the Indianapolis 500.

Fittipaldi had to survive a 210 mph bumping incident with Al Unser Jr. less than two laps from the end, but came away with what he called "the biggest,

most important race of my career" and the first $1 million first prize in motorsports history.

Waltrip, also 42, failed in his mission to win a $1 million bonus in 1989. But he also won the biggest race of his career and appeared to kick-start a driving career that had slipped from awesome to adequate.

Waltrip could be forgiven if prior to the 1989 season he was thinking more about what he would do with the rest of his life than about his future as a racer.

The driver from Franklin, Tenn., once the most dominant on the racetrack and the most outspoken off of it, last won the NASCAR Winston Cup stock car championship in 1985. Despite 73 career victories heading into the '89 season, the sport's all-time leading money winner, with more than $9.5 million in earnings, had won only three races in the past two seasons.

But then the Daytona 500, stock car racing's biggest event and the opening race of its 1989 season, gave Waltrip new life, momentum and enthusiasm.

Mike Harris has been Motorsports Editor for the **Associated Press** since 1980. He has been covering the Indianapolis 500 since 1969 and covers more auto races during the year than any other writer in the country.

Indianapolis 500 winner **Emerson Fittipaldi** (foreground) takes the lead with two laps remaining as **Al Unser, Jr.** hits the wall after the two drivers bumped tires.

After 17 years of trying and failing due to accidents, errors, bad luck and not enough race car, Waltrip found Victory Lane in NASCAR's crown jewel, winning $186,000 and ending the countless repetitions of the question: "Why can't you win the Daytona?"

Those two big wins by two of the sport's most gracefully aging veterans were just the start of a return to the top echelon by each.

Fittipaldi, who was the youngest driver ever to win a Formula One title when he first did it in 1972, quit the glamorous world circuit following the 1980 season.

The reasons for his retirement at the age of 31 were as complicated as the man himself. He cites "the politics and tensions of Formula One" as the key. But there was also the fact that running and financing his own team had drained him physically, mentally and economically.

But Fittipaldi never lost his love of speed and his need for competition. He decided to try Indy-car racing in 1984 and was welcomed with open arms by the CART-PPG series.

"It's an honor just to be on the same track with him," Al Unser, Jr. has said.

The second-generation Indy-car star may not have felt that way after bumping tires with Fittipaldi as the two battled for the lead at Indianapolis.

Unser wound up in the wall and Fittipaldi on the victory podium.

That bump was just one of a series of such incidents that have involved many of the top drivers on the Indy-car circuit since the middle of the 1988 season. Among others who have made contact in the midst of a tight race and at high speeds are Mario and Michael Andretti, the first father-son team in Indy-car history; Bobby Rahal; Scott Pruett, and 1988 series champion Danny Sullivan.

"It's strictly a competitive situation," Fittipaldi said. "You have so many good cars out there, and everyone is trying very hard to win and drive so close, that suddenly you have situations where some kind of contact is just going to happen."

Unser, an aggressive driver who has also been involved in bumping incidents with the two Andrettis, as well as another with Fittipaldi, said, "Nobody is mad at anybody, at least not after everyone cools down. We don't want to get hurt or see anybody hurt, but the competition is just so much better now than it's ever been before."

Bump or no bump, the victory at Indy ignited Fittipaldi, who went on to win three of the next four races, then added a pair of second-place finishes as he built a big lead in the 1989 points race. A victory on Sept. 24 at Nazareth, Pa., clinched the Brazilian's first driving championship in 15 years. He also joined Mario Andretti as the only other driver to win championships in both Formula One and Indy-car racing.

While Fittipaldi may have won at Indianapolis in May, the other two 500-mile races on the CART circuit, which are both run in August, went to two other drivers.

Michael Andretti won the Marlboro 500 at Michigan International Speedway and, two weeks later, Sullivan came up the winner in the Quaker State 500 at Pocono International Raceway. In both cases, Fittipaldi ran off to early leads only to encounter mechanical problems that knocked him off the pace and eventually out of action.

The victory for Sullivan, the 1985 Indy winner, was a very big one. It showed he was 100 percent recovered from a broken right forearm that virtually snuffed out his chances of winning a second consecutive Indy-car title.

Sullivan broke the arm in a crash during practice at Indianapolis. He drove in the race with the help of a specially designed brace, but eventually had to take two races off in order to allow the healing process to run its course.

Rick Mears, Sullivan's teammate, also won banner headlines by smashing his own one- and four-lap qualifying records at the Indianapolis Motor Speedway. Mears had a sizzling fast single lap of 224.254 mph on the 2½-mile oval, and averaged 223.885 for his four-lap, 10-mile qualifying run. A clutch problem ended his hopes of a fourth Indy victory, but he did get early season wins at Phoenix and Milwaukee and continued to battle Fittipaldi for the season championship.

Waltrip's victory at Daytona, a very popular one among fans and competitors, set the tone for the stock car season,

Wide World Photos

It took him 17 years, but **Darrell Waltrip** finally got to say he was No. 1 at the Daytona 500.

with another three-time Winston Cup champion, Dale Earnhardt, taking control of the points race early and staying out front throughout the spring and summer.

But it was Waltrip who continued to be the big story—one way or another.

Davey Allison won the next big race, the Winston 500 at Talladega Superspeedway, but Waltrip gave himself a shot at the Winston Million—a $1 million bonus for any driver who can win three of NASCAR's Big Four—by taking the Coca-Cola 600 at Charlotte Motor Speedway on the same day Fittipaldi won at Indianapolis.

May had not been the brightest month for Waltrip. Just a week earlier, while battling with the very aggressive Rusty Wallace for a $200,000 payoff in The Winston, a stock car invitational race on the same track, Wallace ran into the rear of Waltrip's car, sending it spinning off the track and out of contention.

Wallace, whose searing-hot finish in 1988—winning four of the last five races—gave him a second-place finish to Winston Cup champion Bill Elliott, went on to win The Winston and the big money, drawing Waltrip's enmity and boos and catcalls from the Tennesseean's many fans.

But all was forgotten and forgiven as Waltrip won the Coca-Cola 600 and set up another personal challenge—winning the Southern 500 at Darlington International Raceway—another of the very few big events he never has won.

That one would also have given Waltrip the Winston Million bonus. Instead, however, he tagged the wall early in the race at the oldest of NASCAR's superspeedways and never was in the running.

Waltrip got a $100,000 bonus for winning two of the Big Four events, and Earnhardt solidified his hold on first place with his second Southern 500 victory.

Ironically, Elliott—the only driver to have won the Winston Million, taking the big bonus in its inaugural season of 1985—was struggling through a season similar to Sullivan's on the Indy-car trail.

Elliott came into the season one of the strong favorites to compete for the title, but a crash during practice at Daytona in February left him with a broken left wrist.

The Dawsonville, Ga., driver had to ask the services of fellow Georgian and journeyman driver Jody Ridley as a relief driver for several races and was virtually out of championship contention by the time his wrist had healed.

"We just lost too much time and fell too far behind," Elliott said. "We couldn't do the testing we really wanted to do and I couldn't get in there and do the work on the car that I normally do. By the time I could, we were so far behind that we were just playing catch-up."

Like Sullivan, Elliott eventually came all the way back, winning the Miller High Life 400 at Michigan on June 25.

Formula One, despite making the much-heralded switch from turbo-charged engines to normally-aspirated power plants, remained in the clutches of McLaren-Honda drivers Ayrton Senna, a countryman of Fittipaldi and the 1988 champion, and Frenchman Alain Prost, a two-time champion and the man who broke Jackie Stewart's all-time record of 27 Formula One victories.

Senna, 29, and Prost, 34, make no secret that they do not like each other, but the team continued to work like a well-oiled machine in 1989, despite Ferrari's Nigel Mansell of Great Britain winning the season opener.

The hard-charging Senna won most of the poles, breaking the Formula One record of 33 career poles compiled by the late Jim Clark. Senna and Prost combined to win most of the races, battling each other closely into the late season for another championship.

In the IMSA Camel GT series, Australian-born Geoff Brabham picked up where he and his powerful Nissan GT prototype left off after running away with the 1988 championship.

Although the Porsche 962 shared by Bob Wollek of France, John Andretti—Mario's nephew—and Derek Bell of Great Britain opened the IMSA season by winning the prestigious Daytona 24-Hours, Brabham's new Nissan was the car to beat the rest of the way.

The son of three-time Formula One champion Jack Brabham won eight of the first 11 Camel GT events and was being pressed for the 1989 series title only by teammate and sometimes co-driver Chip Robinson, the 1987 IMSA titlist.

Those two combined for victories in the other two of IMSA's three biggest events —the Miami Grand Prix and the 12 Hours of Sebring.

The other big sports car race of 1989—the tradition-laden 24 Hours of LeMans in France—was the site of a major triumph for Mercedes Benz.

The German car manufacturer dropped out of racing competition after the 1955 season, during which a Mercedes driven by Frenchman Pierre Levegh was launched into the air and off the road at LeMans by a crash with another car and plowed into the crowd, killing more than 80 spectators in the worst disaster in auto racing history.

Mercedes, which was a pioneer in the sport, did not return until 1988. Ironically, the 1989 survival test at LeMans became probably its biggest single day in racing, with the trio of Jochen Mass and Manuel Reuter of West Germany and Stanley Dickens of Sweden driving to an overpowering victory that re-established the company as a force to be reckoned with in the world of sports car racing.

1989 NASCAR Winston Cup Results

Date	Event (Location)	Winner (start pos.)	MPH	Runner-up
Feb. 19	Daytona 500 (Daytona Beach, FL)	Darrell Waltrip (2)	148.466	Ken Schrader
Mar. 5	Goodwrench 500 (Rockingham, NC)	Rusty Wallace (1)	115.122	Alan Kulwicki
Mar. 19	Motorcraft 500 (Atlanta, GA)	Darrell Waltrip (4)	139.864	Dale Earnhardt
Mar. 26	Pontiac 400 (Richmond, VA)	Rusty Wallace (2)	89.619	Alan Kulwicki
Apr. 2	TranSouth 500 (Darlington, SC)	Harry Gant (10)	115.312	Davey Allison
Apr. 9	Valleydale Meats 500 (Bristol, TN)	Rusty Wallace (8)	76.034	Darrell Waltrip
Apr. 16	First Union 400 (North Wilkesboro, NC)	Dale Earnhardt (3)	89.937	Alan Kulwicki
Apr. 23	Pannill Sweatshirts 500 (Martinsville, VA)	Darrell Waltrip (10)	79.025	Dale Earnhardt
May 7	Winston 500 (Talladega, AL)	Davey Allison (2)	155.869	Terry Labonte
May 21	The Winston (Charlotte, NC)	Rusty Wallace (3)	133.150	Ken Schrader
May 28	Coca-Cola 600 (Charlotte, NC)	Darrell Waltrip (4)	144.077	Sterling Marlin
June 4	Budweiser 500 (Dover, DE)	Dale Earnhardt (2)	121.712	Mark Martin
June 11	Banquet Foods 300 (Sears Point, CA)	Ricky Rudd (4)	76.088	Rusty Wallace
June 18	Miller High Life 500 (Pocono, PA)	Terry Labonte (23)	131.319	Harry Gant
June 25	Miller High Life 400 (Brooklyn, MI)	Bill Elliott (2)	139.023	Rusty Wallace
July 2	Pepsi 400 (Daytona Beach, FL)	Davey Allison (8)	132.207	Morgan Shepherd
July 23	AC Spark Plug 500 (Pocono, PA)	Bill Elliott (14)	117.870	Rusty Wallace
July 30	Diehard 500 (Talladega, AL)	Terry Labonte (5)	157.354	Darrell Waltrip
Aug. 13	Budweiser at the Glen (Watkins Glen, NY)	Rusty Wallace (14)	89.242	Mark Martin
Aug. 20	Champion Spark Plug 400 (Brooklyn, MI)	Rusty Wallace (2)	157.704	Morgan Shepherd
Aug. 26	Busch 500 (Bristol, TN)	Darrell Waltrip (9)	85.554	Alan Kulwicki
Sep. 3	Southern 500 (Darlington, SC)	Dale Earnhardt (10)	135.462	Mark Martin
Sep. 10	Miller High Life 400 (Richmond, VA)	Rusty Wallace (6)	88.380	Dale Earnhardt
Sep. 17	Peak Performance 500 (Dover, DE)	Dale Earnhardt (15)	122.942	Mark Martin
Sep. 24	Goody's 500 (Martinsville, VA)	Darrell Waltrip (2)	76.571	Harry Gant

Winning Cars: Ford Thunderbird (D.Allison, Elliott, Labonte); Chevrolet Lumina (Earnhardt, Schrader, Waltrip); Oldsmobile Cutlass (Gant); Buick Regal (Rudd); Pontiac Grand Prix (Wallace).
Upcoming Races: Oct. 8—Charlotte 500 (Charlotte, NC); Oct. 15—Holly Farms 400 (North Wilkesboro, NC); Oct. 22—AC Delco 500 (Rockingham, NC); Nov. 5—Autoworks 500 (Phoenix, AZ); Nov. 19—Atlanta Journal 500 (Atlanta, GA).

Point Standings

Twenty-five of 29 races on 1989 schedule completed, through Goody's 500 (Sept.24). The 30th race on the schedule, "The Winston" (May 21), is not a points race. NASCAR awards points for places 1-40 and lap leaders, however, only 1-2-3 finishes are listed below.

Driver	1st	2nd	3rd	Points
1 Dale Earnhardt	4	3	6	3,540
2 Rusty Wallace	7	3	0	3,465
3 Mark Martin	0	5	4	3,285
4 Darrell Waltrip	6	2	1	3,252
5 Ricky Rudd	1	0	2	3,079
6 Bill Elliott	2	0	1	3,074
7 Ken Schrader	0	2	3	3,028
8 Davey Allison	2	1	0	2,992
9 Terry Labonte	2	1	0	2,940
10 Harry Gant	1	2	1	2,940

Money Leaders
Through Sept. 24, 1989

Driver	Earnings
1 Darrell Waltrip	$ 1,027,595
2 Rusty Wallace	1,023,015
3 Dale Earnhardt	816,175
4 Ken Schrader	723,715
5 Terry Labonte	558,527
6 Bill Elliott	557,192
7 Davey Allison	527,914
8 Mark Martin	474,448
9 Geoff Bodine	437,205
10 Morgan Shepherd	435,577
11 Alan Kulwicki	406,910
12 Harry Gant	402,977

1989 CART Indy Car Results

Date	Event (Location)	Winner (start pos.)	MPH	Runner-up
Apr. 9	Autoworks 200 (Phoenix, AZ)	Rick Mears (1)	126.112	Al Unser Jr.
Apr. 16	Toyota Grand Prix of Long Beach	Al Unser Jr. (1)	85.503	Mike Andretti
May 28	Indianapolis 500	Emerson Fittipaldi (3)	167.581	Al Unser Jr.
June 4	Miller High Life 200 (West Allis, WI)	Rick Mears (1)	130.160	Mike Andretti
June 18	Detroit Grand Prix	Emerson Fittipaldi (3)	76.112	Scott Pruett
June 25	Budweiser/G.I.Joe's 200 (Portland, OR)	Emerson Fittipaldi (2)	103.980	Bobby Rahal
July 2	Budweiser Cleveland Grand Prix	Emerson Fittipaldi (2)	128.072	Mario Andretti
July 16	Marlboro Grand Prix (E.Rutherford, NJ)	Bobby Rahal (6)	81.860	E.Fittipaldi
July 23	Molson Indy Toronto	Michael Andretti (5)	90.900	E.Fittipaldi
Aug. 6	Marlboro 500 (Brooklyn, MI)	Michael Andretti (8)	160.210	Teo Fabi
Aug. 20	Pocono 500	Danny Sullivan (7)	170.720	Rick Mears
Sep. 3	Red Roof Inns 200 (Lexington, OH)	Teo Fabi (1)	104.820	Al Unser Jr.
Sep. 10	Texaco-Havoline 200 (Elkhart Lake, WI)	Danny Sullivan (1)	122.803	Teo Fabi
Sep. 24	Bosch Spark Plug Grand Prix (Nazareth, PA)	Emerson Fittipaldi (2)	134.767	Rick Mears
Oct. 15	Champion Spark Plug 300K (Monterey, CA)			

Winning Cars: Lola-Chevrolet (Michael Andretti, Rahal, Bobby Unser Jr.); March-Porsche (Fabi); Penske PC-18 Chevrolet (Fittipaldi, Mears, Sullivan).

CART

Point Leaders

Fourteen of 15 races on 1989 schedule completed, through Bosch Spark Plug Grand Prix (Sept.24). Points awarded each race to pole sitter (1) and lap leader (1) and for places 1st through 12th, although only 1-2-3 finishes are listed below.

Driver	1st	2nd	3rd	Points
1 Emerson Fittipaldi	5	2	1	186*
2 Rick Mears	2	2	1	164
3 Michael Andretti	2	2	2	144
4 Teo Fabi	1	2	1	141
5 Al Unser, Jr	1	3	0	122
6 Danny Sullivan	2	0	3	107
7 Mario Andretti	0	1	2	94
8 Scott Pruett	0	1	1	89
9 Bobby Rahal	1	1	1	80
10 Arie Luyendyk	0	0	1	71

*Clinched championship on Sept.24.

Money Leaders
Through Sept.24, 1989

Driver	Earnings
1 Emerson Fittipaldi	$1,681,488
2 Al Unser, Jr	838,571
3 Rick Mears	821,524
4 Michael Andretti	694,443
5 Raul Boesel	615,485
6 Mario Andretti	570,734
7 Teo Fabi	570,688
8 Scott Pruett	569,636
9 Danny Sullivan	536,494
10 Bobby Rahal	514,704
11 Arie Luyendyk	467,585
12 Scott Brayton	424,042

Note: Fittipaldi's total is a new CART single season record.

Formula One

Results

Date	G.Prix	Winner	Runner-Up
Mar. 26	Brazil	Nigel Mansell	Alain Prost
Apr. 23	San Marino	Aryton Senna	Alain Prost
May 7	Monaco	Aryton Senna	Alain Prost
May 28	Mexico	Aryton Senna	R.Patrese*
June 4	USA	Alain Prost	R.Patrese
June 18	Canada	Thierry Boutsen	R.Patrese
July 9	France	Alain Prost	Nigel Mansell
July 16	Britain	Alain Prost	Nigel Mansell
July 30	Germany	Aryton Senna	Alain Prost
Aug. 13	Hungary	Nigel Mansell	Aryton Senna
Aug. 27	Belgium	Aryton Senna	Alain Prost
Sep. 10	Italy	Alain Prost	Gerhard Berger
Sep. 24	Portugal	Gerhard Berger	Alain Prost
Oct. 1	Spain	Aryton Senna	Gerhard Berger
Oct. 22	Japan		
Nov. 5	Australia		

*R.Patrese is Riccardo Patrese.
Winning Constructors: McLaren-Honda, 10 (Senna, Prost); Ferrari, 3 (Mansell, Berger); Williams-Renault, 1 (Boutsen).

Point Leaders

Fourteen of 16 races on 1989 schedule completed, through Spanish Grand Prix (Oct.1). Points awarded for places 1st through 6th, although only 1-2-3 finishes are listed below.

Driver	1st	2nd	3rd	Total Pts
1 Alain Prost, France	4	6	1	81*
2 Ayrton Senna, Brazil	6	1	0	60
3 Nigel Mansell, Britain	2	2	2	38
4 Riccardo Patrese, Italy	0	3	1	30
5 Thierry Boutsen, Belgium	1	0	2	24
6 Gerhard Berger, Austria	1	2	0	21
7 Alessandro Nannini, Italy	0	0	2	17
7 Nelson Piquet, Brazil	0	0	0	9
8 Eddie Cheever, USA	0	0	1	6
Derek Warwick, Britain	0	0	0	6
Michele Alborete, Italy	0	0	1	6

*Final Formula One point totals are based on the driver's best 11 finishes out of the number of races entered. Points listed here are total points for the season.
Note: Formula One does not keep Money Leader standings.

Endurance Races

24 Hours of Daytona
Feb. 4-5 at Daytona Beach, FL

IMSA Camel GT sports car race at Daytona International Speedway. Listed are drivers, hometowns or countries, car, laps completed and winner's average speed. Starting positions in parentheses.

Top 5 Finishers

1. (12) John Andretti, Indianapolis; Drek Bell, Britain; and Bob Wollek, France, Porsche 962, 621 laps, 92.009.
2. (2) Price Cobb, Evergreen, Colo.; John Nielsen, Denmark; Jan Lammers, Netherlands; and Andy Wallace, Britain, Jaguar XJR-9, 621.
3. (4) Wlater Brun, Switzerland; Hans Stuck, West Germany; Oscar Larrauri, Argentina; and Doc Bundy, Gainesville, Ga., Porsche 962, 603.
4. (5) Klaus Ludwig, West Germany; James Weaver, Britain; and Sarel van der Merwe, South Africa, Porsche 962, 600.
5. (10) Yoshimi Katayama and Takashi Yorino, Japan; and Elliott Forbes-Robinson, Denver, N.C., Mazda 767B, 559.

24 Hours of Le Mans
June 10-11 at Le Mans, France

Listed are drivers, country, car, distance covered and winner's average speed.

Top 5 Finishers

1. Joachen Mass, West Germany; Manuel Reuter, West Germany, and Stanley Dickens, Sweden, Mercedes, 389 laps, 136.394 mph.
2. Mauro Baldi, Italy; Ken Acheson, Britain, and Gianfranco Brancatelli, Italy, Mercedes, 384.
3. Hans Stuck, West Germany, and Bob Wollek, France, Porsche 962, 382.
4. Johnny Lammers, Netherlands; Patrick Tambay, France, and Andrew Gilbert-Scott, Britain, Jaguar XJR9, 380.
5. Jean-Louis Schlesser, France; Jean-Pierre Jabouille, France, and Alain Cudini, France, Mercedes, 378.

Daytona 500

Held every February on 2.5-mile trioval at Daytona International Speedway in Daytona Beach, FL, since 1959. Stock car racing on Daytona Beach, however, dates back to 1936. Daytona 500 consists of 200 laps around track.
Multiple wins: Richard Petty (7); Cale Yarborough (4); Bobby Allison (3); Bill Elliott (2). **Multiple poles:** Buddy Baker and Cale Yarborough (4); Fireball Roberts and Bill Elliott (3), Donnie Allison (2).

Year	Winner	Car	Owner	MPH	Fastest Qualifier	MPH
1959	Lee Petty	Oldsmobile	Petty Enterprises	135.521	Cotton Owens	143.198
1960	Junior Johnson	Chevrolet	Ray Fox	124.740	Fireball Roberts	151.556
1961	Marvin Panch	Pontiac	Smokey Yunick	149.601	Fireball Roberts	155.709
1962	Fireball Roberts	Pontiac	Smokey Yunick	152.529	Fireball Roberts	156.999
1963	Tiny Lund	Ford	Wood Brothers	151.566	Johnny Rutherford	165.183
1964	Richard Petty	Plymouth	Petty Enterprises	154.344	Paul Goldsmith	174.910
1965a	Fred Lorenzen	Ford	Holman-Moody	141.539	Darel Dieringer	171.151
1966b	Richard Petty	Plymouth	Petty Enterprises	160.627	Richard Petty	175.165
1967	Mario Andretti	Ford	Holman-Moody	149.926	Curtis Turner	180.831
1968	Cale Yarbrough	Mercury	Wood Brothers	143.251	Cale Yarborough	189.222
1969	LeeRoy Yarbrough	Ford	Junior Johnson	157.950	David Pearson	190.029
1970	Pete Hamilton	Plymouth	Petty Enterprises	149.601	Cale Yarborough	194.015
1971	Richard Petty	Plymouth	Petty Enterprises	144.462	A.J.Foyt	182.744
1972	A.J.Foyt	Mercury	Wood Brothers	161.550	Bobby Issac	186.632
1973	Richard Petty	Dodge	Petty Enterprises	157.205	Buddy Baker	185.662
1974c	Richard Petty	Dodge	Petty Enterprises	140.894	David Pearson	185.017
1975	Benny Parsons	Chevrolet	L.G.DeWitt	153.649	Donnie Allison	185.827
1976	David Pearson	Mercury	Wood Brothers	152.181	A.J.Foyt	185.943
1977	Cale Yarborough	Chevrolet	Junior Johnson	153.218	Donnie Allison	188.048
1978	Bobby Allison	Ford	Bud Moore	159.730	Cale Yarborough	187.536
1979	Richard Petty	Oldsmobile	Petty Enterprises	143.977	Buddy Baker	196.049
1980	Buddy Baker	Oldsmobile	Ranier Racing	177.602*	A.J.Foyt	195.020
1981	Richard Petty	Buick	Petty Enterprises	169.651	Bobby Allison	194.624
1982	Bobby Allison	Buick	DiGard Racing	153.991	Benny Parsons	196.317
1983	Cale Yarborough	Pontiac	Ranier Racing	155.979	Ricky Rudd	198.864
1984	Cale Yarborough	Chevrolet	Ranier Racing	150.994	Cale Yarborough	201.848
1985	Bill Elliott	Ford	Melling Racing	172.265	Bill Elliott	205.114
1986	Geoff Bodine	Chevrolet	Hendrick Motorsports	148.124	Bill Elliott	205.039
1987	Bill Elliott	Ford	Melling Racing	176.263	Bill Elliott	210.364†
1988	Bobby Allison	Buick	Miller High Life Buick	137.531	Ken Schrader	193.823
1989	Darrell Waltrip	Chevrolet	Tide Chevrolet	148.466	Ken Schrader	196.996

*Track and race record for Winning Time
†Track and race record for Qualifying Time.
Notes: a — rain shortened 1965 to 332+ miles; **b** — rain shortened 1966 race to 495 miles; **c** — in 1974, race shortened 50 miles due to energy crisis.

NASCAR

National Champions, 1949-88

Officially called the Winston Cup Championship since 1971 and based on official NASCAR (National Assn. for Stock Car Auto Racing) records through the 1988 racing season.
Multiple winners: Richard Petty (7); Dale Earnhardt, David Pearson, Lee Petty, Darrell Waltrip and Cale Yarborough (3); Buck Baker, Tim Flock, Ned Jarrett, Herb Thomas and Joe Weatherly (2).

Year	Champion	Year	Champion	Year	Champion	Year	Champion
1949	Red Byron	1960	Rex White	1970	Bobby Issac	1980	Dale Earnhardt
1950	Bill Rexford	1961	Ned Jarrett	1971	Richard Petty	1981	Darrell Waltrip
1951	Herb Thomas	1962	Joe Weatherly	1972	Richard Petty	1982	Darrell Waltrip
1952	Tim Flock	1963	Joe Weatherly	1973	Benny Parsons	1983	Bobby Allison
1953	Herb Thomas	1964	Richard Petty	1974	Richard Petty	1984	Terry Labonte
1954	Lee Petty	1965	Ned Jarrett	1975	Richard Petty	1985	Darrell Waltrip
1955	Tim Flock	1966	David Pearson	1976	Cale Yarborough	1986	Dale Earnhardt
1956	Buck Baker	1967	Richard Petty	1977	Cale Yarborough	1987	Dale Earnhardt
1957	Buck Baker	1968	David Pearson	1978	Cale Yarborough	1988	Bill Elliott
1958	Lee Petty	1969	David Pearson	1979	Richard Petty		
1959	Lee Petty						

All-Time Leaders

Victories

Drivers who have won at least 25 stock car races through the 1988 NASCAR season. Active drivers in **bold** type.

		Wins
1	**Richard Petty**	200
2	David Pearson	105
3	**Bobby Allison**	84
4	Cale Yarborough	83
5	**Darrell Waltrip**	73
6	Lee Petty	54
7	Ned Jarrett	50
	Junior Johnson	50
9	Herb Thomas	48
10	Buck Baker	46
11	Tim Flock	40
12	Bobby Issac	37
13	**Dale Earnhardt**	34
	Fireball Roberts	34
15	**Bill Elliott**	29
16	Rex White	28
17	Fred Lorenzen	26
18	Jim Paschal	25

Pole Positions

Drivers who have won at least 25 poles through the 1988 NASCAR season. Active drivers in **bold** type.

		Poles
1	**Richard Petty**	127
2	David Pearson	113
3	Cale Yarborough	70
4	**Bobby Allison**	57
	Darrell Waltrip	57
6	Bobby Issac	51
7	Junior Johnson	47
8	Buck Baker	44
9	Buddy Baker	40
10	Herb Thomas	38
11	Tim Flock	37
	Fireball Roberts	37
13	Ned Jarrett	36
	Rex White	36
15	**Bill Elliott**	35
16	Fred Lorenzen	33
17	Fonty Flock	30
18	Marvin Panch	25

Money Winners

The Top 15 money winners in stock car history, through the 1988 NASCAR season. Active drivers in **bold** type.

		Earnings
1	**Darrell Waltrip**	$8,674,063
2	**Dale Earnhardt**	8,308,848
3	**Bill Elliott**	8,306,969
4	**Bobby Allison**	7,102,233
5	**Richard Petty**	6,838,444
6	**Terry Labonte**	5,134,143
7	**Cale Yarborough**	5,003,616
8	Benny Parsons	3,926,539
9	**Ricky Rudd**	3,892,116
10	**Harry Gant**	3,628,832
11	**Neil Bonnett**	3,512,918
12	**Buddy Baker**	3,486,776
13	**Geoff Bodine**	3,248,155
14	**Rusty Wallace**	3,132,480
15	**Dave Marcis**	2,936,484

Indianapolis 500

Held every Memorial Day weekend on 2.5-mile rectangular course at Indianapolis Motor Speedway since 1911. Race consists of 200 laps around track.

Multiple wins: A.J.Foyt and Al Unser (4); Rick Mears, Louis Meyer, Mauri Rose, Johnny Rutherford, Wilbur Shaw and Bobby Unser (3); Gordon Johncock, Tommy Milton, Bill Vukovich and Rodger Ward (2).

Year	Winner (Start Pos.)	Car	MPH	Fastest Qualifier	MPH
1911	Ray Harroun (28)	Marmon Wasp	74.602	Lewis Strang	—
1912	Joe Dawson (7)	National	78.719	David Bruce-Brown	88.45
1913	Jules Goux (7)	Peugeot	75.933	Jack Tower	88.33
1914	Rene Thomas (15)	Delage	82.474	Georges Boillot	99.86
1915	Ralph DePalma (2)	Mercedes	89.840	Howard Wilcox	98.90
1916a	Dario Resta (4)	Peugeot	84.001	John Aitken	96.69
1917	Not held				
1918	Not held				
1919	Howard Wilcox (2)	Peugeot	88.050	Rene Thomas	104.78
1920	Gaston Chevrolet (6)	Monroe	88.618	Ralph DePalma	99.15
1921	Tommy Milton (20)	Frontenac	89.621	Ralph DePalma	100.75
1922	Jimmy Murphy (1)	Murphy Special	94.484	Jimmy Murphy	100.50
1923	Tommy Milton (1)	H.C.S. Special	90.954	Tommy Milton	108.17
1924	L.L.Corum & Joe Boyer (21)	Duesenberg Special	98.234	Jimmy Murphy	108.037
1925	Peter DePaolo (2)	Duesenberg Special	101.127	Leon Duray	113.196
1926b	Frank Lockhart (20)	Miller Special	95.904	Earl Cooper	111.735
1927	George Souders (22)	Duesenberg	· 97.545	Frank Lockhart	120.100
1928	Louis Meyer (13)	Miller Special	99.482	Leon Duray	122.391
1929	Ray Keech (6)	Simplex Piston Ring Spl.	97.585	Cliff Woodbury	120.599
1930	Billy Arnold (1)	Miller-Hartz Special	100.448	Billy Arnold	113.268
1931	Louis Schneider (13)	Bowes Seal Fast Special	96.629	Billy Arnold	116.080
1932	Fred Frame (27)	Miller-Hartz Special	104.144	Lou Moore	117.363
1933	Louis Meyer (6)	Tydol Special	104.162	Bill Cummings	118.530
1934	William Cummings (10)	Boyle Products Special	104.863	Kelly Petillo	119.329
1935	Kelly Petillo (22)	Gilmore Speedway Special	106.240	Rex Mays	120.736
1936	Louis Meyer (28)	Ring-Free Special	109.069	Rex Mays	119.644
1937	Wilbur Shaw (2)	Shaw-Gilmore Special	113.580	Jimmy Snyder	125.287
1938	Floyd Roberts (1)	Burd Piston Ring Special	117.200	Ronney Householder	125.769
1939	Wilbur Shaw (3)	Boyle Special	115.035	Jimmy Snyder	130.138

Indianapolis 500 (Continued)

Year	Winner	Car	MPH	Fastest Qualifier	MPH
1940	Wilbur Shaw (2)	Boyle Special	114.277	Rex Mays	127.850
1941	Floyd Davis				
	& Mauri Rose (17)	Noc-Out Hose Clamp Special	115.117	Mauri Rose	128.691
1942	Not held				
1943	Not held				
1944	Not held				
1945	Not held				
1946	George Robson (15)	Thorne Engineering Special	114.820	Ralph Hepburn	133.944
1947	Mauri Rose (3)	Blue Crown Spark Plug Spl.	116.338	Bill Holland	128.755
1948	Mauri Rose (3)	Blue Crown Spark Plug Spl.	119.814	Duke Nalon	131.603
1949	Bill Holland (4)	Blue Crown Spark Plug Spl.	121.327	Duke Nalon	132.939
1950c	Johnnie Parsons (5)	Wynn's Friction Proofing	124.002	Walt Faulkner	134.343
1951	Lee Wallard (2)	Belanger Special	126.244	Walt Faulkner	136.872
1952	Troy Ruttman (7)	Agajanian Special	128.922	Chet Miller	139.034
1953	Bill Vukovich (1)	Fuel Injection Special	128.740	Bill Vukovich	138.392
1954	Bill Vukovich (19)	Fuel Injection Special	130.840	Jack McGrath	141.033
1955	Bob Sweikert (14)	John Zink Special	128.209	Jack McGrath	142.580
1956	Pat Flaherty (1)	John Zink Special	128.490	Pat Flaherty	145.596
1957	Sam Hanks (13)	Belond Exhaust Special	135.601	Paul Russo	144.817
1958	Jim Bryan (7)	Belond AP Parts Special	133.791	Dick Rathmann	145.974
1959	Rodger Ward (6)	Leader Card 500 Roadster	135.857	Johnny Thomson	145.908
1960	Jim Rathmann (2)	Ken-Paul Special	138.767	Jim Hurtubise	149.056
1961	A.J.Foyt (7)	Bowes Seal-Fast Special	139.131	Eddie Sachs	147.481
1962	Rodger Ward (2)	Leader Card 500 Roadster	140.293	Parnelli Jones	150.370
1963	Parnelli Jones (1)	Agajanian-Willard Special	143.137	Parnelli Jones	151.153
1964	A.J.Foyt (5)	Sheraton-Thompson Special	147.350	Jim Clark	158.828
1965	Jim Clark (2)	Lotus Ford	150.686	A.J.Foyt	161.233
1966	Graham Hill (15)	American Red Ball Special	144.317	Mario Andretti	165.899
1967d	A.J.Foyt (4)	Sheraton-Thompson Special	151.207	Mario Andretti	168.982
1968	Bobby Unser (3)	Rislone Special	152.882	Joe Leonard	171.559
1969	Mario Andretti (2)	STP Oil Treatment Special	156.867	A.J.Foyt	170.568
1970	Al Unser (1)	Johnny Lightning 500 Spl.	155.749	Al Unser	170.221
1971	Al Unser (5)	Johnny Lightning Special	157.735	Peter Revson	178.696
1972	Mark Donohue (3)	Sunoco McLaren	162.962	Bobby Unser	195.940
1973e	Gordon Johncock (11)	STP Double Oil Filters	159.036	Johnny Rutherford	198.413
1974	Johnny Rutherford (25)	McLaren	158.589	A.J.Foyt	191.632
1975f	Bobby Unser (3)	Jorgensen Eagle	149.213	A.J.Foyt	193.976
1976g	Johnny Rutherford (1)	Hy-Gain McLaren/Goodyear	148.725	Mario Andretti	189.404
1977	A.J.Foyt (4)	Gilmore Racing Team	161.331	•Tom Sneva	198.884
1978	Al Unser (5)	FNCTC Chaparral Lola	161.363	Tom Sneva	202.156
1979	Rick Mears (1)	The Gould Charge	158.899	Rick Mears	193.736
1980	Johnny Rutherford (1)	Pennzoil Chaparral	142.862	Johnny Rutherford	192.256
1981h	Bobby Unser (1)	Norton Spirit Penske PC-9B	139.084	Tom Sneva	200.691
1982	Gordon Johncock (5)	STP Oil Treatment	162.029	Rick Mears	207.004
1983	Tom Sneva (4)	Texaco Star	162.117	Teo Fabi	207.395
1984	Rick Mears (3)	Pennzoil Z-7	163.612	Tom Sneva	210.029
1985	Danny Sullivan (8)	Miller American Special	152.982	Pancho Carter	212.583
1986	Bobby Rahal (4)	Budweiser/Truesports/March	170.722*	Rick Mears	216.828
1987	Al Unser (20)	Cummins Holset Turbo	162.175	Mario Andretti	215.390
1988	Rick Mears (1)	Penske-Chevrolet V-8	149.809	Rick Mears	219.198
1989	Emerson Fittipaldi (3)	Penske-Chevrolet PC-18	167.581	Rick Mears	223.885†

*Track record for Winning Time
†Track record for Qualifying Time.
Notes: a — 1916 race scheduled for 300 miles; **b** — rain shortened 1926 race to 400 miles; **c** — rain shortened 1950 race to 345 miles; **d** — 1967 race postponed due to rain after 18 laps (May 30), resumed next day (May 31); **e** — rain shortened 1973 race to 332+ miles; **f** — rain shortened 1975 race to 435 miles; **g** — rain shortened 1976 race to 255 miles; **h** — in 1981, runner-up Mario Andretti was awarded 1st place when winner Bobby Unser was penalized a lap after the race was completed for passing cars illegally under the caution flag. Unser and car-owner Roger Penske appealed the race stewards' decision to the U.S.Auto Club. Four months later, USAC overturned the ruling, saying that the penalty was too harsh and Unser should be fined $40,000 rather than stripped of his championship.

Indy Cars

National Champions, 1909-89

Officially called the PPG Indy Car World Series championship since 1979 and based on official AAA (American Automobile Assn., 1909-55), USAC (U.S.Auto Club, 1956-79), and CART (Championship Auto Racing Teams, 1979-present) records through the 1988 racing season.

Multiple titles: A.J.Foyt (7); Mario Andretti (4); Jimmy Bryan, Earl Cooper, Ted Horn, Rick Mears, Louis Meyer and Al Unser (3); Tony Bettenhausen, Ralph DePalma, Peter DePaolo, Joe Leonard, Rex Mays, Tommy Milton, Jimmy Murphy, Bobby Rahal, Wilbur Shaw, Tom Sneva, Bobby Unser and Rodger Ward (2).

AAA

Year	Champion	Year	Champion	Year	Champion	Year	Champion
1909	George Robertson	1920	Tommy Milton	1932	Bob Carey	1944	No racing
		1921	Tommy Milton	1933	Louis Meyer	1945	No racing
1910	Ray Harroun	1922	Jimmy Murphy	1934	Bill Cummings	1946	Ted Horn
1911	Ralph Mulford	1923	Eddie Hearne	1935	Kelly Petillo	1947	Ted Horn
1912	Ralph DePalma	1924	Jimmy Murphy	1936	Mauri Rose	1948	Ted Horn
1913	Earl Cooper	1925	Peter DePaolo	1937	Wilbur Shaw	1949	Johnnie Parsons
1914	Ralph DePalma	1926	Harry Hartz	1938	Floyd Roberts		
1915	Earl Cooper	1927	Peter DePaolo	1939	Wilbur Shaw	1950	Henry Banks
1916	Dario Resta	1928	Louis Meyer			1951	Tony Bettenhausen
1917	Earl Cooper	1929	Louis Meyer	1940	Rex Mays	1952	Chuck Stevenson
1918	Ralph Mulford			1941	Rex Mays	1953	Sam Hanks
1919	Howard Wilcox	1930	Billy Arnold	1942	No racing	1954	Jimmy Bryan
		1931	Louis Schneider	1943	No racing	1955	Bob Sweikert

USAC

Year	Champion	Year	Champion	Year	Champion	Year	Champion
1956	Jimmy Bryan	1962	Rodger Ward	1968	Bobby Unser	1974	Bobby Unser
1957	Jimmy Bryan	1963	A.J.Foyt	1969	Mario Andretti	1975	A.J.Foyt
1958	Tony Bettenhausen	1964	A.J.Foyt			1976	Gordon Johncock
1959	Rodger Ward	1965	Mario Andretti	1970	Al Unser	1977	Tom Sneva
		1966	Mario Andretti	1971	Joe Leonard	1978	Tom Sneva
1960	A.J.Foyt	1967	A.J.Foyt	1972	Joe Leonard	1979	A.J.Foyt
1961	A.J.Foyt			1973	Roger McCluskey		

CART

Year	Champion	Year	Champion	Year	Champion	Year	Champion
1979	Rick Mears	1981	Rick Mears	1984	Mario Andretti	1987	Bobby Rahal
1980	Johnny Rutherford	1982	Rick Mears	1985	Al Unser	1988	Danny Sullivan
		1983	Al Unser	1986	Bobby Rahal	1989	Emerson Fittipaldi

All-Time Leaders

Victories

Drivers who have won at least 15 races through the 1988 CART season. Active drivers in **bold** type.

		Wins
1	**A.J.Foyt**	67
2	**Mario Andretti**	51
3	**Al Unser**	39
4	Bobby Unser	35
5	**Johnny Rutherford**	27
6	Rodger Ward	26
7	**Gordon Johncock**	25
8	Ralph DePalma	24
9	**Rick Mears**	23
	Tommy Milton	23
11	Tony Bettenhausen	22*
	Earl Cooper	21
13	Jimmy Bryan	19
	Jimmy Murphy	19
15	**Bobby Rahal**	18
16	Ralph Mulford	17

Note: Bettenhausen won one race (in Milwaukee on Aug.29, 1948) as Myron Fohr's relief driver.

Pole Positions

Drivers who have won at least 10 poles from 1930 through the 1988 CART season. Active drivers in **bold** type.

		Poles
1	**Mario Andretti**	64
2	**A.J.Foyt**	53
3	Bobby Unser	49
4	**Al Unser**	27
5	**Rick Mears**	26
6	**Johnny Rutherford**	23
7	**Gordon Johncock**	20
8	Rex Mays	19
9	Don Branson	15
9	Tony Bettenhausen	14
	Tom Sneva	14
	Danny Sullivan	14
13	**Bobby Rahal**	13
14	Parnelli Jones	12
15	Danny Ongais	11
	Rodger Ward	11
17	Dan Gurney	10
	Johnny Thomson	10

Money Winners

The Top 15 money winners in Indy Car history, through the 1988 CART season. Active drivers in **bold** type.

		Earnings
1	**Mario Andretti**	$6,178,551
2	**Al Unser**	5,791,768
3	**Rick Mears**	5,684,137
4	**Bobby Rahal**	5,266,925
5	**Danny Sullivan**	4,255,444
6	**Johnny Rutherford**	4,168,774
7	**Al Unser, Jr.**	3,927,780
8	Tom Sneva	3,923,323
9	**A.J.Foyt**	3,901,376
10	**Michael Andretti**	3,596,878
11	**Gordon Johncock**	2,868,664
12	**Emerson Fittipaldi**	2,859,638
13	Bobby Unser	2,674,516
14	**Roberto Guerrero**	2,434,955
15	**Kevin Cogan**	2,302,907

Formula One

World Champions, 1950-88

Officially called the World Championship of Drivers and based on Formula One (Grand Prix) records through the 1988 racing season.

Multiple winners: Juan-Manuel Fangio (5); Jack Brabham, Niki Lauda, Nelson Piquet and Jackie Stewart (3); Alberto Ascari, Jim Clark, Emerson Fittipaldi, Graham Hill, and Alain Prost (2).

Year	Champion	Car	Year	Champion	Car
1950	Guiseppe Farina, ITA	Alfa Romeo	1970	Jochen Rindt, AUT	Lotus Ford
1951	Juan-Manuel Fangio, ARG	Alfa Romeo	1971	Jackie Stewart, GBR	Tyrrell Ford
1952	Alberto Ascari, ITA	Ferrari	1972	Emerson Fittipaldi, BRA	Lotus Ford
1953	Alberto Ascari, ITA	Ferrari	1973	Jackie Stewart, GBR	Tyrrell Ford
1954	Juan-Manuel Fangio, ARG	Maserati & Mercedes	1974	Emerson Fittipaldi, BRA	McLaren Ford
			1975	Niki Lauda, AUT	Ferrari
1955	Juan-Manuel Fangio, ARG	Mercedes	1976	James Hunt, GBR	McLaren Ford
1956	Juan-Manuel Fangio, ARG	Ferrari	1977	Niki Lauda, AUT	Ferrari
1957	Juan-Manuel Fangio, ARG	Maserati	1978	Mario Andretti, USA	Lotus Ford
1958	Mike Hawthorn, GBR	Ferrari	1979	Jody Scheckter, SAF	Ferrari
1959	Jack Brabham, AUS	Cooper Climax			
			1980	Alan Jones, AUS	Williams Ford
1960	Jack Brabham, AUS	Cooper Climax	1981	Nelson Piquet, BRA	Brabham Ford
1961	Phil Hill, USA	Ferrari	1982	Keke Rosberg, FIN	Williams Ford
1962	Graham Hill, GBR	BRM	1983	Nelson Piquet, BRA	Brabham BMW Turbo
1963	Jim Clark, GBR	Lotus Climax	1984	Niki Lauda, AUT	McLaren TAG Porsche Turbo
1964	John Surtees, GBR	Ferrari	1985	Alain Prost, FRA	McLaren TAG Porsche Turbo
1965	Jim Clark, GBR	Lotus Climax	1986	Alain Prost, FRA	McLaren TAG Porsche Turbo
1966	Jack Brabham, AUS	Brabham Climax	1987	Nelson Piquet, BRA	Williams Honda Turbo
1967	Denis Hulme, NZE	Brabham Repco	1988	Ayrton Senna, BRA	McLaren-Honda Turbo
1968	Graham Hill, GBR	Lotus Ford			
1969	Jackie Stewart, GBR	Matra Ford			

All-Time Leaders

The All-Time Top 20 Grand Prix drivers with starts, poles and 1-2-3 finishes. Based on records through the 1988 racing season. Active drivers in **bold** type.

		Sts	Pole	1st	2nd	3rd			Sts	Pole	1st	2nd	3rd
1	**Alain Prost**	137	18	35	21	13	11	**Ayrton Senna**	78	29	14	14	8
2	Jackie Stewart	99	17	27	11	5	12	Alberto Ascari	32	13	13	4	0
3	Jim Clark	72	33	25	1	6	13	**Nigel Mansell**	118	12	13	5	8
	Niki Lauda	171	24	25	20	9	14	**Mario Andretti**	128	18	12	2	5
5	Juan-Manuel Fangio	51	28	24	11	1	15	Alan Jones	116	6	12	8	5
6	**Nelson Piquet**	157	24	20	19	14	16	Carlos Reutemann	146	6	12	13	20
7	Sterling Moss	66	16	16	5	2	17	James Hunt	92	14	10	6	7
8	Jack Brabham	126	13	14	10	8	18	Ronnie Peterson	123	14	10	10	6
9	**Emerson Fittipaldi**	144	6	14	13	8	19	Jody Scheckter	112	3	10	14	9
10	Graham Hill	176	13	14	15	7	20	Denis Hulme	112	1	8	9	17
								Jackie Ickx	116	13	8	7	10

Note #1: the following drivers either died or were killed in their final year of competition—Clark in a Formula Two race in W. Germany in 1968; Hill in a plane crash in 1975; Ascari in a private practice run in 1955; and Peterson following an accident in the 1978 Italian Grand Prix.

Note #2: Fittipaldi and Andretti are still active, but driving on the CART circuit.

Wide World Photos

Thomas Hearns (facing camera) had **Sugar Ray Leonard** on the ropes in the 3rd round of their 12-round draw June 12 in Las Vegas. Leonard-Hearns II was their first meeting since 1981.

BOXING

INSIDE

Elsewhere in Almanac

For related information refer to the following chapters: Halls of Fame & Awards, Sports Organizations, and Updates.

It was déjà vu all over again for professional boxing in '89; Tyson, Leonard-Hearns II headline the decade in review.

BOXING

1989 YEAR IN REVIEW

by Elmer Smith

Future chroniclers of this era in professional boxing may be tempted to sum up 1989 this way: "SEE 1988."

You **can** see a lot of '88 and '87 and of the last five or six years in the issues and events that carried boxing through 1989 and over the cusp of the 90s. It was a year of continued trends, of relative stability in a business better known for its volatility, a year of triumph for the tried and true.

Boxing consumers—ticket buyers on one end, promoters and media outlets on the other—opted for more of the same. And they got it.

More of the same from Mike Tyson meant a continuation of what could turn into boxing's longest running road show. It's like the wrestling bear vs. assorted rubes in the wayside watering holes where the old carnivals used to stop. By 1989, just two years into his championship reign, we were paying to see how

Elmer Smith has been the boxing writer for the **Philadelphia Daily News** since 1983. He is the 1987 recipient of the Nat Fleisher Memorial Award presented by the Boxing Writers Assn. of America.

long the rubes would last with the bruising bruin from Brooklyn.

Jamaican-born British heavyweight Frank Bruno delighted a casino crowd at the Las Vegas Hilton on Feb. 25 by lasting almost through the fifth round. It took Tyson all of 14 seconds of round one to put the beefy Brit on the canvas. But he got up swinging and gave a good account of himself until referee Richard Steele had to peel Tyson off the cornered Bruno with five seconds left in the fifth.

Bruno hadn't won a round. But the fact that he had lasted through the first barrage was viewed as a possible tear in Tyson's cloak of invincibility.

But Tyson was coming off an eight-month layoff since his 91-second annihilation of Michael Spinks. In the interim, he had gained 50 pounds, divorced his wife, fired his manager Bill Cayton and trainer Kevin Rooney and formed a partnership with mega-promotor Don King.

In July, a more typical Tyson quickly disposed of Carl "The Truth" Williams in Atlantic City's Convention Hall. The controversy concerned whether the fight had

Former cruiserweight champion **Evander Holyfield** (left) scored a 10th round TKO over **Michael Dokes** in March to boost his status as a challenger for the heavyweight championship.

been stopped too soon or whether Williams was entitled to be rendered senseless in keeping with boxing and Tyson tradition.

"I could have continued," a still groggy Williams claimed after referee Randy Newmann stopped his feeble challenge after 93 seconds of the first and final round.

"I thought he could have kept fighting," Tyson agreed. ". . . I wanted to hit him with a combination."

The theme for the 90s may be to find a gimmick for Tyson—something like the night George Foreman fought four guys or the time Muhammad Ali took on the Japanese wrestler. The number of empty seats at his fights is rising faster than the stacked bodies of his stunned opponents.

As the year closed, former cruiserweight champion Evander Holyfield was being rushed to readiness for a big-money showdown with Tyson. He looked impressive in stopping James "Quick" Tillis and even more so in stopping former WBC champion Michael Dokes in a toe-to-toe thriller.

Not nearly so impressive is George Foreman's curious comeback. Foreman, fat and 41, somehow retained a bit of credibility even though he has made mostly lateral moves on the comeback trail since ending an eight-year layoff in 1987. In 1989, Foreman KO'd six pre-starched stiffs, none of whom was actually down for the count.

What was an erupting groundswell for a Foreman-Tyson match subsided some when a large segment of the viewing public saw Foreman for themselves on cable TV. USA network televised five of Foreman's fights in 1989, but did not renew the contract for the coming year.

Nevertheless, Foreman's future will extend into the '90s thanks to his deal to fight Gerry Cooney, 33, on Jan. 15 in Atlantic City. A spectacular win for either fighter could earn a Top 10 rating and make him instantly eligible to challenge Tyson.

But Foreman and Holyfield are the only big money possibilities on the horizon. Tyson's new "advisor" Don King was talking about putting Tyson on the international circuit where people will still pack a soccer stadium to catch a glimpse of him making short work of some local lad. The World Boxing Association, however, takes a dim view of such a tour

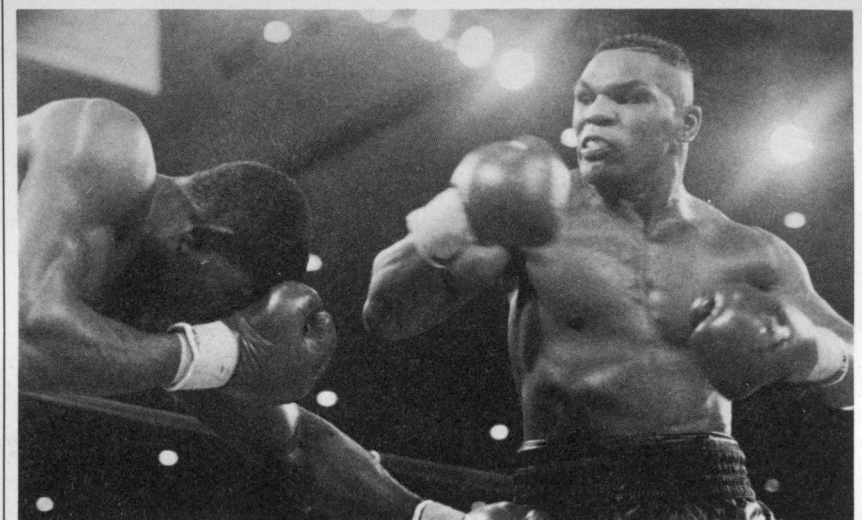

Wide World Photos

Meanwhile, heavyweight champion **Mike Tyson** (right) stopped **Frank Bruno** (left) in five rounds in February and then dispatched Carl "The Truth" Williams in 93 seconds in July.

and warned Tyson in October that if he didn't defend against Holyfield by February, he would lose the WBA third of his title.

Meanwhile Ray Leonard was having no trouble drawing a crowd in 1989. Seven years after his first retirement, and 21 pounds beyond his best fighting weight, 33-year-old Ray Charles Leonard was still the hottest ticket in all of boxing in 1989. At a time when not even the tried and true Tyson could command eight-figure paydays, Leonard could start a run on closed-circuit ticket offices all over the country just by announcing his next fight.

Leonard had stepped from the pages of boxing history and back into the hearts of an adoring public on April 6, 1987 with a flashdance in the desert that frustrated Marvelous Marvin Hagler and added Hagler's middleweight crown to the welterweight and junior middleweight titles Leonard had won before retiring to his counting room in 1982.

Leonard then ended another long lay-off on Nov. 7, 1988 when he rose from the Caesars Palace canvas to knock out World Boxing Council light heavyweight champion Donny Lalonde. Leonard won the vacant WBC super-middleweight (168 pounds) in the same fight, making him the first man in history to earn two world titles in one fight.

Three days earlier, Thomas "Hit Man" Hearns had headlined a championship triple-header down the Strip at the Las Vegas Hilton with a razor-thin unanimous decision over James "The Heat" Kinchen. An obviously faltering Hearns literally held on to win when referee Mills Lane failed to separate Kinchen and Hearns, who had been wobbled by a Kinchen punch.

Hearns, 31, who had lost the World Boxing Association middleweight title to Iran Barkley earlier in the year, won Kinchen's North American Boxing Federation supermiddleweight title and the newly-minted World Boxing Organization's world supermiddleweight crown. The tarnished WBO crown made Hearns, arguably at least, the first man in history to win world titles in five different weight classes.

The WBO, the fourth sanctioning organization, had been created a few months earlier by a splinter group that broke

broke away from the World Boxing Association at its convention in Caracas, Venezuela. Even Hearns, who had won the welterweight, junior middleweight, middleweight and light-heavyweight titles, had trouble taking the WBO crown seriously.

Leonard's dazzling performance at Caesars Palace a few days later was more than enough to dull the luster of Hearns new crown jewel. But the lure of a possible $15 million payday to fight a man who had stumbled through his last two fights and hadn't been able to beat Leonard when both were in their prime was more than the opportunistic Leonard could pass up.

The long-overdue rematch of the 1981 title showdown (which Leonard won with a 14th-round TKO) was signed a few weeks after their February fights. Promotor Bob Arum promised an $80 million gross and sent his combatants off in separate corporate jets to canvas the country selling the fight.

A star-studded crowd of 15,302 showed up at the Caesar's Palace Sports Arena June 12. There would have been more if there had been any more seats for them. Estimates ran as high as 2.5 million people who saw the fight at closed-circuit sites or by pay-per-view, which beamed the fight into their living rooms for an average of $40 per turn on.

They got their money's worth. To the casual viewer, both fighters looked to be in their prime. Leonard wobbled Hearns early and late in the fight. But Hearns somehow found the strength to stand up under the barrage.

And he toppled Leonard twice. The first knockdown, more of a push than a punch, came as Leonard slipped near the ropes. But a solid right hand put Leonard on the floor in the 11th.

The judges called it a draw to the satisfaction of almost no one. Most fans, noting the two knockdowns, thought Hearns had won clearly. But neither fighter had any complaint about the judges' call in the post-fight press conference.

If nothing else, the fight set up still another mega-payday for Leonard, who earned about $18 million and for Hearns, who grossed more than $15 million.

But Leonard had other options because 1989 also marked the return of Roberto Duran, the only man who has ever beaten Leonard. Leonard lost the WBC welterweight title to Duran by decision in Montreal in June 1980. He won it back in New Orleans five months later when Duran quit in the middle of the eighth in the famous "No Mas" fight.

Duran, now 38, burst back onto the scene on Feb. 24th with a calendar-defying performance that earned him a close but surprisingly undisputed win over Iran Barkley. Even Barkley, who had won at least six of the first eight rounds, was impressed.

"I was in there with a legend tonight," Barkley said. ". . . He took me to school."

The win energized Duran's legion of fans who have patiently awaited this latest return. With his large and loyal Hispanic following coupled with Leonard's proven drawing power, the potential is for a gross even larger than the $70-plus million collected for Leonard-Hearns II. Duran and Leonard are scheduled to meet Dec. 7th in Las Vegas.

Which tells you all you need to know about the business of boxing in 1989 and about what 1989s box office bonanzas portend for the 90s and beyond. Boxing fans who won't turn out in record numbers to buy the best of the current crop will pay a premium for a rematch of their most-revered legends, even if it promises to be an oldies but goodies night.

There is no logical reason for a fight fan to believe that Leonard/Duran III should be as good a fight as, say, Meldrick Taylor against Julio Cesar Chavez. But Duran and Leonard have always had fans who never go to see anyone else fight. It's more spectacle than sport and is not sold as much as presented.

"It's what people want," Arum said before the signing of Leonard/Duran III. "And it makes sense. These fighters have been involved in some of the great fights of the last 20 years. People know what to expect from them."

On the other hand, fans stayed away in droves on March 6 when Ray "Boom Boom" Mancini returned from a four-year layoff and lost a split decision to Hector "Macho" Camacho.

Sugar Ray Robinson (right), seen here as welterweight champion, pounding out a 10-round decision over Don Lee in 1949.

Sugar Ray Robinson (1921-1989)

He was born Walker Lee Smith in Detroit and may have remained as obscure as that name if he hadn't moved to New York as a teenager to turn pro.

Within a year, Walker Lee Smith changed his name to Sugar Ray Robinson and the sweetest practitioner of the sport A.J. Leibling once called "the sweet science" had begun perhaps the most illustrious career in boxing history.

Robinson, who had fought a long battle with Alzheimer's disease and related ailments, died of a massive heart attack on April 12. He was 67.

The legend of Sugar Ray Robinson began on Oct. 4, 1940 with a 2nd round knockout of someone named Joe Escheverria which started a winning streak of 40 straight that ended on Feb. 5, 1943 with a loss to Jake "The Raging Bull" LaMotta. Robinson had beaten LaMotta four months earlier and again just three weeks later. He went on to beat LaMotta four out of five times, including once for the middleweight title in 1951.

Even more incredible, Robinson didn't lose again for eight years until he was beaten by Randy Turpin on Jul.10, 1951. He reversed that loss, winning back the middleweight title from Turpin on Sep.12, 1951.

Nine months later, he built up a large lead against light-heavyweight champion Joey Maxim but lost his bid to rule a third weight class to heat exhaustion.

During the 8-year win streak that followed the LaMotta loss, Robinson won the world welterweight title from Tommy Bell and the middleweight title from LaMotta. And, on August 27, 1940, he defeated Henry Armstrong, one of the greatest fighters of any era.

Ironically, Armstrong died in Oct.1988, five months before Robinson. Hammerin' Henry, the first of the multiple champions, had held the featherweight, welterweight and lightweight titles at the same time, reigning as the best fighter within a 21-pound range.

Armstrong won 145 fights (98 by KO), lost 18, and fought nine draws. The record stood as the best of his time until Robinson's final tally of 174 wins (109 by KO), 19 losses, and six draws.

Wide World Photos

Former world lightweight and welterweight champion **Roberto Duran** reappeared in February to separate Iran Barkley from his WBC middleweight title.

The men most likely to make the big fights of the future continued to build box office profiles through 1989. Taylor came back from knee surgery after a long layoff to defend his IBF junior welterweight title in September with a decision over Courtney Hooper. Taylor's stablemate and 1984 Olympic teammate Pernell Whitaker took Greg Haughen's IBF lightweight title in February with a unanimous decision before a hometown crowd in Norfolk, Va., then retuned to Norfolk in April to defend it with a third-round KO of Louis Lomeli. He consolidated his claim as the best of the lightweights in August with a unanimous 12-round decision over veteran Jose Luis Ramirez. The Ramirez win reversed his only loss and gave Whitaker the WBC lightweight crown.

Undefeated Michael Nunn lost a little luster in August by returning to his safe style with a 12-round majority decision over Iran Barkley to retain his IBF middleweight crown. And John "The Beast"

Mugabi moved within challenging range of the safety-consious Nunn when he won the WBC super-welterweight (154 lb) title from Rene Jacquot. Mugabi won back his old titles in July when Jacquot twisted his ankle in a first-round knockdown and was unable to continue.

Welterweight champions Marlon Starling, Simon Brown and Mark Breland continued on a collision course in 1989. In a welterweight title doubleheader on Feb. 4 at Caesars Palace, Starling won the WBC title with a KO victory over Lloyd Honeyghan and Breland KO'd Lee Seung Soon in the first round to win the vacant WBA title. Two weeks later in Budapest, Brown knocked out Jorge Maysonet in three to retain the IBF title. But Starling has already beaten Brown and Breland.

Developing just outside the main spotlight in 1989 were the prospects from the 1988 U.S. Olympic team that the big-time promoters wooed shamelessly while their amateur status was still intact.

Dan and Lou Duva's Main Events/Monitor management promotion firm, Josephine Abercrombie's Houston Boxing Association and, most notably, Arum's Top Rank, Inc. set up their gold medal redemption booths in the boxing venue at the Chamsil Student Gymnasium in Seoul.

But none of the big-time promoters was able to sign the pick of the 1988 Olympic litter. Roy Jones, Jr., who won the Val Barker award as the best boxer of the Olympics, resisted overtures and offers for large signing bonuses from virtually every major promotor in the country.

Instead he has cast his lot with veteran trainer Pappy Gault and, in one of the strangest partnerships in boxing, Harold Rossfields Smith. Smith, the flamboyant manager and promotor of Muhammad Ali Professional Sports, Inc., was released from prison early in the year after serving a term for a multi-million dollar embezzlement scheme from the Wells Fargo Bank. Jones is trained by his father Roy Jones. But Smith and Gault are unofficial advisors.

It's working. Jones, who is 3–0, has already fought two eight rounders. He could be a contender in the middleweight division by the end of next year.

Major Bouts, 1988-89

November, 1988

Sugar Ray Leonard knocked out Donny Lalonde in 9th round to win WBC light heavyweight and super middleweight championships (Las Vegas, Nov. 7).

February, 1989

Marlon Starling knocked out Lloyd Honeyghan in 9th round to win WBC welterweight championship (Las Vegas, Feb. 4).

Mark Breland knocked out Lee Seung Soon in 1st round to win vacant WBA welterweight championship (Las Vegas, Feb. 4).

Rene Jacquot scored a unanimous 12-round decision over Donald Curry to win WBC super welterweight championship (Grenoble, France, Feb. 11).

Pernell Whitaker scored a unanimous 12-round decision over Greg Haugen to win IBF lightweight championship (Hampton, VA, Feb. 18).

Simon Brown stopped Jorge Maysonet in 3rd round to retain IBF welterweight title (Budapest, Hungary, Feb. 18).

Mike Tyson stopped Frank Bruno in 5th round to retain heavyweight title (Las Vegas, Feb. 25).

Roberto Duran scored a 12-round split decision over Iran Barkley to win WBC middleweight championship (Atlantic City, Feb. 24).

March, 1989

Virgil Hill scored a unanimous 12-round decision over Bobby Czyz to retain WBA light heavyweight title (Bismarck, ND, March 4).

Hector Camacho scored a 12-round split decision over Ray Mancini to win WBO junior welterweight championship (Reno, March 6).

Raul Perez scored a unanimous 12-round decision over Lucio Lopez to retain WBC bantamweight title (Los Angeles, March 9).

Evander Holyfield scored a 10th round TKO over Michael Dokes in heavyweight bout (Las Vegas, March 11).

Michael Nunn knocked out Sumbu Kalambay in 1st round to retain IBF middleweight title (Las Vegas, March 25).

Antonio Esparragoza knocked out Misuru Sugiya in 10th round to retain WBA featherweight title (Kawasaki, Japan, March 26).

April, 1989

Jeff Fenech retained WBC featherweight crown with a unanimous 12-round decision over Marcos Villasana (Melbourne, Australia, April 8).

Mark Breland retained WBA welterweight title by stopping Rafael Pineda in 5th round (Atlantic City, April 22).

Simon Brown retained IBF welterweight title by knocking out Al Long in 7th round (Washington, DC, April 27).

Pernell Whitaker knocked out Luis Lomeli in 3rd round to defend IBF lightweight crown (Norfolk, VA, April 30).

May, 1989

Julio Cesar Chavez, WBA and WBC lightweight champion, won WBC super lightweight championship when opponent Roger Mayweather quit after 10th round (Los Angeles, May 13).

Mike McCallum won vacant WBA middleweight championship with 12-round split decision over Herol Graham (London, May 13).

Jorge Paez fought Louis Espinoza to a 12-round draw; Paez retained IBF featherweight title (Phoenix, May 21).

Virgil Hill stopped Joe Lasisi in 7th round to retain WBA light heavyweight title (Bismarck, ND, May 27).

June, 1989

Sugar Ray Leonard fought Thomas Hearns to a 12-round draw; Leonard retained WBC super middleweight title (Las Vegas, June 12).

Jeff Harding knocked out Dennis Andries in 12th round to win WBC light heavyweight championship (Atlantic City, June 24).

Prince Charles Williams retained IBF light heavyweight title when opponent Bobby Czyz failed to answer bell for 11th round (Atlantic City, June 25).

Orlando Canizales scored a TKO in 11th round over Kelvin Seabrooks to defend IBF bantamweight title (Atlantic City, June 25).

July, 1989

John Mugabi stopped Rene Jacquot in 1st round to win WBC super welterweight championship (France, July 8).

Kaokor Galaxy scored a unanimous 12-round decision over Moon Sung Kil to win WBA bantamweight championship (Bangkok, July 8).

Edwin Rosario scored a 6th round TKO over Anthony Jones to win vacant WBA lightweight championship (Atlantic City, July 9).

Gianfranco Rosi scored a unanimous 12-round decision over Darrin Van Horn to win IBF junior middleweight championship (Atlantic City, July 15).

Mike Tyson stopped Carl (The Truth) Williams in 1st round to retain heavyweight title (Atlantic City, July 21).

Julian Jackson knocked out Terry Norris in 2nd round to retain WBA junior middleweight title (San Diego, July 30).

August, 1989

Jorge Paez scored a unanimous 12-round decision over Steve Cruz to retain IBF featherweight title (El Paso, Aug. 6).

Michael Nunn scored a 12-round split decision over Iran Barkley to retain IBF middleweight title (Reno, Aug. 14).

Pernell Whitaker scored a unanimous 12-round decision over Jose Luis Ramirez to defend IBF lightweight title and win vacant WBC lightweight championship (Norfolk, VA, Aug. 20).

September, 1989

Meldrick Taylor scored a unanimous 12-round decision over Courtney Hooper to retain IBF junior welterweight title (Atlantic City, Sept. 11).

Marlon Starling scored a unanimous 12-round decision over Chung Young Kil to retain WBC welterweight title (Hartford, Sept. 15).

Simon Brown knocked out Bobby Joe Young in 2nd round to retain IBF welterweight title (Rochester, NY, Sept. 20).

Antonio Esparragoza knocked out Eduardo Montoya in 5th round to retain WBA featherweight title (Mexicali, Mexico, Sept. 23).

October, 1989

John-John Molina stopped Tony Lopez in 10th round to win IBF junior lightweight championship (Sacramento, Oct. 7).

Current Champions

As of Oct.15, 1989 these are the champions of professional boxing's 17 principal weight divisions, as recognized by the World Boxing Assn.(WBA), World Boxing Council (WBC) and International Boxing Federation (IBF). Heavyweight champion Mike Tyson is the only fighter currently holding WBA, WBC and IBF titles.

	Weight Limit	WBA Champion	WBC Champion	IBF Champion
Heavyweight	—	Mike Tyson	Mike Tyson	Mike Tyson
Junior Heavyweight (Cruiserweight)	190 lbs	Vacant*	Carlos de Leon	Glenn McCrory
Light Heavyweight	175 lbs	Virgil Hill	Jeff Harding	Prince Charles Williams
Super Middleweight	168 lbs	Inchul Beak	Sugar Ray Leonard	Vacant†
Middleweight	160 lbs	Mike McCallum	Roberto Duran	Michael Nunn
Junior Middleweight (Super Welterweight)	154 lbs	Julian Jackson	John Mugabi	Gianfranco Rosi
Welterweight	147 lbs	Mark Breland	Marlon Starling	Simon Brown
Junior Welterweight (Super Lightweight)	140 lbs	Juan Coggi	Julio Cesar Chavez	Meldrick Taylor
Lightweight	135 lbs	Edwin Rosario	Pernell Whitaker	Pernell Whitaker
Junior Lightweight (Super Featherweight)	130 lbs	Brian Mitchell	Azumah Nelson	John-John Molina
Featherweight	126 lbs	Antonio Esparragoza	Jeff Fenech	Jorge Paez
Junior Featherweight (Super Bantamweight)	122 lbs	Juan Jose Estrada	Daniel Zaragoza	Fabrice Benichou
Bantamweight	118 lbs	Kaokor Galaxy	Raul Perez	Orlando Canizales
Junior Bantamweight (Super Flyweight)	115 lbs	Kaosai Galaxy	Gilberto Roman	Juan Polo
Flyweight	112 lbs	Jesus Rojas	Sot Chitalada	Dave McAuley
Junior Flyweight (Light Flyweight)	108 lbs	Myung Woo-yuh	Humberto Gonzalez	Muangshai Kittikasem
Mini-Flyweight (Strawweight)	105 lbs	Bong-jun Kim	Napa Katwanchai	Eric Chavez

*WBA Junior Heavyweight title became vacant in Sept.,1989 when champion Taoufik Belboull injured his knee and resigned.
†IBF Super Middleweight title became vacant in Sept.,1989 when champion Graciano Rocchigiani resigned and moved up to the light heavyweight division.

Mike Tyson's Career Record

Undisputed heavyweight champion Mike Tyson is 37-0 with 33 knockouts since turning pro in 1985.

1985

Date	Opponent, location	Result
Mar. 6	Hector Mercedes, Albany, NY	KO 1
Apr. 10	Trent Singleton, Albany, NY	KO 1
May 23	Donald Halpin, Atlantic City	KO 4
Jun. 20	Rick Spain, Atlantic City	KO 1
Jul. 11	John Anderson, Atlantic City	KO 1
Jul. 19	Larry Sims, Poughkeepsie, NY	KO 3
Aug. 15	Lorenzo Canady, Atlantic City	KO 1
Sep. 5	Michael Johnson, Atlantic City	KO 1
Oct. 9	Donnie Long, Atlantic City	KO 1
Oct. 25	Robert Colay, Atlantic City	KO 1
Nov. 1	Sterling Benjamin, Latham, NY	KO 1
Nov. 13	Eddie Richardson, Houston	KO 1
Nov. 22	Conroy Nelson, Albany, NY	KO 2
Dec. 6	Sam Scaff, New York	KO 1
Dec. 27	Mark Young, Colonie, NY	KO 1

1986

Date	Opponent, location	Result
Jan. 11	David Jaco, Albany, NY	KO 1
Jan. 24	Mike Jameson, Atlantic City	KO 5
Feb. 16	Jesse Ferguson, Troy, NY	KO 6
Mar. 10	Steve Zouski, Uniondale, NY	KO 3
May 3	Quick Tillis, Glens Falls, NY	W 10
May 20	Mitch Green, New York	W 10
Jun. 13	Reggie Gross, New York	KO 1
Jun. 28	William Mosea, Troy, NY	KO 1
Jul. 11	Lorenzo Boyd, Swan lake, NY	KO 2
Jul. 26	Marvis Frazier, Glens Falls, NY	KO 1

1986 (Continued)

Date	Opponent, location	Result
Aug. 17	Jose Ribalta, Atlantic City	KO 10
Sep. 6	Alfonso Ratliff, Las Vegas	KO 2
Nov. 22	Trevor Berbick, Las Vegas	TKO 2
	(Won WBC Heavyweight title)	

1987

Date	Opponent, location	Result
Mar. 7	Bonecrusher Smith, Las Vegas	W 12
	(Won WBA Heavyweight title)	
May 30	Pinklon Thomas, Las Vegas	TKO 6
Aug. 1	Tony Tucker, Las Vegas	W 12
	(Won IBF Heavyweight title)	
Oct. 16	Tyrell Biggs, Atlantic City	TKO 7

1988

Date	Opponent, location	Result
Jan. 22	Larry Holmes, Atlantic City	TKO 4
Mar. 20	Tony Tubbs, Tokyo	KO 2
Jun. 27	Michael Spinks, Atlantic City	KO 1

1989

Date	Opponent, location	Result
Feb. 25	Frank Bruno, Las Vegas	TKO 5
Jul. 21	Carl Williams, Atl.City	TKO 1

World Heavyweight Championship Fights

Widely accepted world champions in **bold** type. Note following result abbreviations: KO (knockout), TKO (technical knockout), Un (unanimous decision), Maj (majority decision), Split (split decision), Ref (referee's decision), ND (no decision), Disq (won on disqualification).

Year	Date		Winner	Age	Wgt	Loser	Wgt	Result		Location
1892	Sep.	7	James J.Corbett	26	178	**John L.Sullivan**	212	KO	21	New Orleans
1894	Jan.	25	**James J.Corbett**	27	184	Charley Mitchell	158	KO	3	Jacksonville, FL
1897	Mar.	17	Bob Fitzsimmons	24	167	**James J.Corbett**	183	KO	14	Carson City, NV
1899	Jun.	9	James J.Jeffries	24	206	**Bob Fitzsimmons**	167	KO	11	Coney Island, NY
1899	Nov.	3	**James J.Jeffries**	24	215	Tom Sharkey	183	Ref	25	Coney Island, NY
1900	Apr.	6	**James J.Jeffries**	24	NA	Jack Finnegan	NA	KO	1	Detroit
1900	May	11	**James J.Jeffries**	25	218	James J.Corbett	188	KO	23	Coney Island, NY
1901	Nov.	15	**James J.Jeffries**	26	211	Gus Ruhlin	194	TKO	6	San Francisco
1902	Jul.	25	**James J.Jeffries**	27	219	Bob Fitzsimmons	172	KO	8	San Francisco
1903	Aug.	14	**James J.Jeffries**	28	220	James J.Corbett	190	KO	10	San Francisco
1904	Aug.	25	**James J.Jeffries**	29	219	Jack Munroe	186	TKO	2	San Francisco
1905	Jul.	3	Marvin Hart	28	190	Jack Root	171	KO	12	Reno, NV
1906	Feb.	23	Tommy Burns	24	180	**Marvin Hart**	188	Ref	20	Los Angeles
1906	Oct.	2	**Tommy Burns**	25	NA	Jim Flynn	NA	KO	15	Los Angeles
1906	Nov.	28	**Tommy Burns**	25	172	Phila.Jack O'Brien	163½	Draw	20	Los Angeles
1907	May	8	**Tommy Burns**	25	180	Phila.Jack O'Brien	167	Ref	20	Los Angeles
1907	Jul.	4	**Tommy Burns**	26	181	Bill Squires	180	KO	1	Colma, Calif
1907	Dec.	2	**Tommy Burns**	26	177	Gunner Moir	204	KO	10	London
1908	Feb.	10	**Tommy Burns**	26	NA	Jack Palmer	NA	KO	4	London
1908	Mar.	17	**Tommy Burns**	26	NA	Jem Roche	NA	KO	1	Dublin
1908	Apr.	18	**Tommy Burns**	26	NA	Jewey Smith	NA	KO	5	Paris
1908	Jun.	13	**Tommy Burns**	26	184	Bill Squires	183	KO	8	Paris
1908	Aug.	24	**Tommy Burns**	27	181	Bill Squires	184	KO	13	Sydney
1908	Sep.	2	**Tommy Burns**	27	183	Bill Lang	187	KO	6	Melbourne
1908	Dec.	26	Jack Johnson	30	192	**Tommy Burns**	168	TKO	14	Sydney
1909	Mar.	10	**Jack Johnson**	30	NA	Victor McLaglen	NA	ND	6	Vancouver
1909	May	19	**Jack Johnson**	31	205	Phila.Jack O'Brien	161	ND	6	Philadelphia
1909	Jun.	30	**Jack Johnson**	31	207	Tony Ross	214	ND	6	Pittsburgh
1909	Sep.	9	**Jack Johnson**	31	209	Al Kaufman	191	ND	10	San Francisco
1909	Oct.	16	**Jack Johnson**	31	205½	Stanley Ketchel	170¼	KO	12	Colma, Calif.
1910	Jul.	4	**Jack Johnson**	32	208	James J.Jeffries	227	KO	15	Reno, Nev.
1912	Jul.	4	**Jack Johnson**	34	195½	Jim Flynn	175	TKO	9	Las Vegas, NM
1913	Dec.	19	**Jack Johnson**	35	NA	Jim Johnson	NA	Draw	10	Paris
1914	Jun.	27	**Jack Johnson**	36	221	Frank Moran	203	Ref	20	Paris
1915	Apr.	5	Jess Willard	33	230	**Jack Johnson**	205½	KO	26	Havana
1916	Mar.	25	**Jess Willard**	34	225	Frank Moran	203	ND	10	NYC (Mad.Sq.Garden)
1919	Jul.	4	Jack Dempsey	24	187	**Jess Willard**	245	TKO	4	Toledo, Ohio
1920	Sep.	6	**Jack Dempsey**	25	185	Billy Miske	187	KO	3	Benton Harbor, Mich.
1920	Dec.	14	**Jack Dempsey**	25	188¼	Bill Brennan	197	KO	12	NYC (Mad.Sq.Garden)
1921	Jul.	2	**Jack Dempsey**	26	188	Georges Carpentier	172	KO	4	Jersey City, N.J.
1923	Jul.	4	**Jack Dempsey**	28	188	Tommy Givvons	175½	Ref	15	Shelby, Montana
1923	Sep.	14	**Jack Dempsey**	28	192½	Luis Firpo	216½	KO	2	NYC (Polo Grounds)
1926	Sep.	23	Gene Tunney	29	189½	**Jack Dempsey**	190	Un	10	Philadelphia
1927	Sep.	22	**Gene Tunney**	30	189½	Jack Dempsey	192½	Un	10	Chicago
1928	Jul.	26	**Gene Tunney**	31	192	Tom Heeney	203½	TKO	11	NYC (Yankee Stadium)
1930	Jun.	12	Max Schmeling	24	188	Jack Sharkey	197	Foul	4	NYC (Yankee Stadium)
1931	Jul.	3	**Max Schmeling**	25	189	Young Stribling	186½	TKO	15	Cleveland
1932	Jun.	21	Jack Sharkey	29	205	**Max Schmeling**	188	Split	15	Long Island City, N.Y.
1933	Jun.	29	Primo Carnera	26	260½	**Jack Sharkey**	201	KO	6	Long Island City, N.Y.
1933	Oct.	22	**Primo Carnera**	26	259½	Paulino Uzcudun	229¼	Un	15	Rome

World Heavyweight Championship Fights (Continued)

Year Date	Winner	Age Wgt	Loser	Wgt	Result	Location
1934 Mar. 1	**Primo Carnera**	27 270	Tommy Loughran	184	Un 15	Miami
1934 Jun. 14	Max Baer	25 209½	**Primo Carnera**	263¼	TKO 11	Long Island City, N.Y.
1935 Jun. 13	James J.Braddock	29 193¾	**Max Baer**	209½	Un 15	Long Island City, N.Y.
1937 Jun. 22	**Joe Louis**	23 197¼	James J.Braddock	197	KO 8	Chicago
1937 Aug. 30	**Joe Louis**	23 197	Tommy Farr	204¼	Un 15	NYC (Yankee Stadium)
1938 Feb. 23	**Joe Louis**	23 200	Nathan Mann	193½	KO 3	NYC (Mad.Sq.Garden)
1938 Apr. 1	**Joe Louis**	23 202½	Harry Thomas	196	KO 5	Chicago
1938 Jun. 22	**Joe Louis**	24 198¼	Max Schmeling	193	KO 1	NYC (Yankee Stadium)
1939 Jan. 25	**Joe Louis**	24 200¼	John Henry Lewis	180¾	KO 1	NYC (Mad.Sq.Garden)
1939 Apr. 17	**Joe Louis**	24 201¼	Jack Roper	204¾	KO 1	Los Angeles
1939 Jun. 28	**Joe Louis**	25 200¾	Tony Galento	233¾	TKO 4	NYC (Yankee Stadium)
1939 Sep. 20	**Joe Louis**	25 200	Bob Pastor	183	KO 11	Detroit
1940 Feb. 9	**Joe Louis**	25 203	Arturo Godoy	202	Split 15	NYC (Mad.Sq.Garden)
1940 Mar. 29	**Joe Louis**	25 201½	Johnny Paychek	187½	KO 2	NYC (Mad.Sq.Garden)
1940 Jun. 20	**Joe Louis**	26 199	Arturo Godoy	201¼	TKO 8	NYC (Yankee Stad.)
1940 Dec. 16	**Joe Louis**	26 202¼	Al McCoy	180¾	TKO 6	Boston
1941 Jan. 31	**Joe Louis**	26 202½	Red Burman	188	KO 5	NYC (Mad.Sq.Garden)
1941 Feb. 17	**Joe Louis**	26 203½	Gus Dorazio	193½	KO 2	Philadelphia
1941 Mar. 21	**Joe Louis**	26 202	Abe Simon	254½	TKO 13	Detroit
1941 Apr. 8	**Joe Louis**	26 203½	Tony Musto	199½	TKO 9	St. Louis
1941 May 23	**Joe Louis**	27 201½	Buddy Baer	237½	Disq 7	Washington, DC
1941 Jun. 18	**Joe Louis**	27 199½	Billy Conn	174	KO 13	NYC (Polo Grounds)
1941 Sep. 29	**Joe Louis**	27 202¼	Lou Nova	202½	KO 6	NYC (Polo Grounds)
1942 Jan. 9	**Joe Louis**	27 206¾	Buddy Baer	250	KO 1	NYC (Mad.Sq.Garden)
1942 Mar. 27	**Joe Louis**	27 207½	Abe Simon	255½	KO 6	NYC (Mad.Sq.Garden)
1942 -45	World War II					
1946 Jun. 9	**Joe Louis**	32 207	Billy Conn	187	KO 8	NYC (Yankee Stadium)
1946 Sep. 18	**Joe Louis**	32 211	Tami Mauriello	198½	KO 1	NYC (Yankee Stadium)
1947 Dec. 5	**Joe Louis**	33 211½	Jersey Joe Walcott	194½	Split 15	NYC (Mad.Sq.Garden)
1948 Jun. 25	**Joe Louis**	34 213½	Jersey Joe Walcott	194¾	KO 11	NYC (Yankee Stadium)
1949 Jun. 22	Ezzard Charles	27 181¾	Jersey Joe Walcott	195½	Un 15	Chicago
1949 Aug. 10	Ezzard Charles	28 180	Gus Lesnevich	182	TKO 8	NYC (Yankee Stadium)
1949 Oct. 14	Ezzard Charles	28 182	Pat Valentino	188½	KO 8	San Francisco
1950 Aug. 15	Ezzard Charles	29 183¼	Freddie Beshore	184½	TKO 14	Buffalo
1950 Sep. 27	Ezzard Charles	29 184½	Joe Louis	218	Un 15	NYC (Yankee Stadium)
1950 Dec. 5	Ezzard Charles	29 185	Nick Barone	178½	KO 11	Cincinnati
1951 Jan. 12	Ezzard Charles	29 185	Lee Oma	193	TKO 10	NYC (Mad.Sq.Garden)
1951 Mar. 7	Ezzard Charles	29 186	Jersey Joe Walcott	193	Un 15	Detroit
1951 May 30	Ezzard Charles	29 182	Joey Maxim	181½	Un 15	Chicago
1951 Jul. 18	Jersey Joe Walcott	37 194	**Ezzard Charles**	182	KO 7	Pittsburgh
1952 Jun. 5	**Jersey Joe Walcott**	38 196	**Ezzard Charles**	191½	Un 15	Philadelphia
1952 Sep. 23	Rocky Marciano	29 184	**Jersey Joe Walcott**	196	KO 13	Philadelphia
1953 May 15	**Rocky Marciano**	29 184½	Jersey Joe Walcott	197¾	KO 1	Chicago
1953 Sep. 24	**Rocky Marciano**	30 185	Roland LaStarza	184¾	TKO 11	NYC (Polo Grounds)
1954 Jun. 17	**Rocky Marciano**	30 187½	Ezzard Charles	185½	Un 15	NYC (Yankee Stadium)
1954 Sep. 17	**Rocky Marciano**	31 187	Ezzard Charles	192½	KO 8	NYC (Yankee Stadium)
1955 May 16	**Rocky Marciano**	31 189	Don Cockell	205	TKO 9	San Francisco
1955 Sep. 21	**Rocky Marciano**	32 188¼	Archie Moore	188	KO 9	NYC (Yankee Stadium)
1956 Nov. 30	Floyd Patterson	21 182¼	Archie Moore	187¾	KO 5	Chicago
1957 Jul. 29	**Floyd Patterson**	22 184	Tommy Jackson	192½	TKO 10	NYC (Polo Grounds)
1957 Aug. 22	**Floyd Patterson**	22 187¼	Pete Rademacher	202	KO 6	Seattle
1958 Aug. 18	**Floyd Patterson**	23 184½	Roy Harris	194	TKO 13	Los Angeles
1959 May 1	**Floyd Patterson**	24 182½	Brian London	206	KO 11	Indianapolis
1959 Jun. 26	Ingemar Johansson	26 196	**Floyd Patterson**	182	TKO 3	NYC (Yankee Stadium)
1960 Jun. 20	Floyd Patterson	25 190	**Ingemar Johansson**	194¾	KO 5	NYC (Polo Grounds)

World Heavyweight Championship Fights (Continued)

Year	Date	Winner	Age	Wgt	Loser	Wgt	Result		Location
1961	Mar. 13	**Floyd Patterson**	26	194¾	Ingemar Johansson	206½	KO	6	Miami Beach
1961	Dec. 4	**Floyd Patterson**	26	188½	Tom McNeeley	197	KO	4	Toronto
1962	Sep. 25	Sonny Liston	30	214	**Floyd Patterson**	189	KO	1	Chicago
1963	Jul. 22	**Sonny Liston**	31	215	Floyd Patterson	194½	KO	1	Las Vegas
1964	Feb. 25	Cassius Clay	22	210½	**Sonny Liston**	218	TKO	7	Miami Beach
1965	Mar. 5	Ernie Terrell WBA	25	199	Eddie Machen	192	Un	15	Chicago
1965	May 25	**Muhammad Ali**	23	206	Sonny Liston	215¼	KO	1	Lewiston, Me.
1965	Nov. 1	Ernie Terrell WBA	26	206	George Chuvalo	209	Un	15	Toronto
1965	Nov. 22	**Muhammad Ali**	23	210	Floyd Patterson	196¾	TKO	12	Las Vegas
1966	Mar. 29	**Muhammad Ali**	24	214½	George Chuvalo	216	Un	15	Toronto
1966	May 21	**Muhammad Ali**	24	201½	Henry Cooper	188	TKO	6	London
1966	Jun. 28	Ernie Terrell WBA	27	209½	Doug Jones	187½	Un	15	Houston
1966	Aug. 6	**Muhammad Ali**	24	209½	Brian London	201½	KO	3	London
1966	Sep. 10	**Muhammad Ali**	24	203½	Karl Mildenberger	194¼	TKO	12	Frankfurt, W.Ger.
1966	Nov. 14	**Muhammad Ali**	24	212¾	Cleveland Williams	210½	TKO	3	Houston
1967	Feb. 6	**Muhammad Ali**	25	212¼	Ernie Terrell WBA	212½	Un	15	Houston
1967	Mar. 22	**Muhammad Ali**	25	211½	Zora Folley	202½	KO	7	NYC (Mad.Sq.Garden)
1968	Mar. 4	Joe Frazier	24	204½	Buster Mathis	243½	TKO	11	NYC (Mad.Sq.Garden)
1968	Apr. 27	Jimmy Ellis	28	197	Jerry Quarry	195	Maj	15	Oakland
1968	Jun. 24	Joe Frazier NY	24	203½	Manuel Ramos	208	TKO	2	NYC (Mad.Sq.Garden)
1968	Aug. 14	Jimmy Ellis WBA	28	198	Floyd Patterson	188	Ref	15	Stockholm
1968	Dec. 10	Joe Frazier NY	24	203	Oscar Bonavena	207	Un	15	Philadelphia
1969	Apr. 22	Joe Frazier NY	25	204½	Dave Zyglewicz	190½	KO	1	Houston
1969	Jun. 23	Joe Frazier NY	25	203½	Jerry Quarry	198½	TKO	8	NYC (Mad.Sq.Garden)
1970	Feb. 16	Joe Frazier NY	26	205	Jimmy Ellis WBA	201	TKO	5	NYC (Mad.Sq.Garden)
1970	Nov. 18	Joe Frazier	26	209	Bob Foster	188	KO	2	Detroit
1971	Mar. 8	Joe Frazier	27	205½	**Muhammad Ali**	215	Un	15	NYC (Mad.Sq.Garden)
1972	Jan. 15	**Joe Frazier**	28	215½	Terry Daniels	195	TKO	4	New Orleans
1972	May 26	**Joe Frazier**	28	217½	Ron Stander	218	TKO	5	Omaha, Neb.
1973	Jan. 22	George Foreman	25	217½	**Joe Frazier**	214	TKO	2	Kingston, Jamaica
1973	Sep. 1	**George Foreman**	25	219½	Jose (King) Roman	196½	KO	1	Tokyo
1974	Mar. 26	**George Foreman**	26	224¼	Ken Norton	212¼	TKO	2	Caracas, Venezuela
1974	Oct. 30	Muhammad Ali	32	216½	**George Foreman**	220	KO	8	Kinshasa, Zaire
1975	Mar. 24	**Muhammad Ali**	33	223½	Chuck Wepner	225	TKO	15	Cleveland
1975	May 16	**Muhammad Ali**	33	224½	Ron Lyle	219	TKO	11	Las Vegas
1975	Jul. 1	**Muhammad Ali**	33	224½	Joe Bugner	230	Un	15	Kuala Lumpur, Malaysia
1975	Oct. 1	**Muhammad Ali**	33	224½	Joe Frazier	215	TKO	15	Manila, Philippines
1976	Feb. 20	**Muhammad Ali**	34	226	Jean Pierre Coopman	206	KO	5	San Juan, P.R.
1976	Apr. 30	**Muhammad Ali**	34	230	Jimmy Young	209	Un	15	Landover, Md.
1976	May 24	**Muhammad Ali**	34	230	Richard Dunn	206½	TKO	5	Munich, W.Ger.
1976	Sep. 28	**Muhammad Ali**	34	221	Ken Norton	217½	Un	15	NYC (Yankee Stadium)
1977	May 16	**Muhammad Ali**	35	221¼	Alfredo Evangelista	209¼	Un	15	Landover, Md.
1977	Sep. 29	**Muhammad Ali**	35	225	Earnie Shavers	211¼	Un	15	NYC (Mad.Sq.Garden)
1978	Feb. 15	Leon Spinks	24	197¼	**Muhammad Ali**	224¼	Split	15	Las Vegas
1978	Jun. 9	Larry Holmes	28	209	Ken Norton WBC	220	Split	15	Las Vegas
1978	Sep. 15	Muhammad Ali	36	221	**Leon Spinks**	201	Un	15	New Orleans
1978	Nov. 10	Larry Holmes WBC	29	214	Alfredo Evangelista	208¼	KO	7	Las Vegas
1979	Mar. 23	Larry Holmes WBC	29	214	Osvaldo Ocasio	207	TKO	7	Las Vegas
1979	Jun. 22	Larry Holmes WBC	29	215	Mike Weaver	202	TKO	12	NYC (Mad.Sq.Garden)
1979	Sep. 28	Larry Holmes WBC	29	210	Earnie Shavers	211	TKO	11	Las Vegas
1979	Oct. 20	John Tate	24	240	Gerrie Coetzee	222	Un	15	Pretoria, S.Africa
1980	Feb. 3	Larry Holmes WBC	30	213½	Lorenzo Zanon	215	TKO	6	Las Vegas
1980	Mar. 31	Mike Weaver	27	232	John Tate WBA	232	KO	15	Knoxville, Tenn.
1980	Mar. 31	Larry Holmes WBC	30	211	Leroy Jones	254½	TKO	8	Las Vegas
1980	Jul. 7	Larry Holmes WBC	30	214¼	Scott LeDoux	226	TKO	7	Minneapolis
1980	Oct. 2	Larry Holmes WBC	30	211¼	Muhammad Ali	217½	TKO	11	Las Vegas
1980	Oct. 25	Mike Weaver WBA	28	210	Gerrie Coetzee	226½	KO	13	Sun City, Boph'swana

World Heavyweight Championship Fights (Continued)

Year	Date	Winner	Age	Wgt	Loser	Wgt	Result	Location
1981	Apr. 11	**Larry Holmes**	31	215	Trevor Berbick	215½	Un 15	Las Vegas
1981	Jun. 12	**Larry Holmes**	31	212¼	Leon Spinks	200¼	TKO 3	Detroit
1981	Oct. 3	Mike Weaver WBA	29	215	Quick Tillis	209	Un 15	Rosemont, Ill.
1981	Nov. 6	**Larry Holmes**	32	213¼	Renaldo Snipes	215¾	TKO 11	Pittsburgh
1982	Jun. 11	**Larry Holmes**	32	212½	Gerry Cooney	225½	TKO 13	Las Vegas
1982	Nov. 26	**Larry Holmes**	33	217½	Randall (Tex) Cobb	234¼	Un 15	Houston
1982	Dec. 10	Michael Dokes	24	216	Mike Weaver WBA	209¾	TKO 1	Las Vegas
1983	Mar. 27	**Larry Holmes**	33	221	Lucien Rodriguez	209	Un 12	Scranton, Pa.
1983	May 20	Michael Dokes WBA	24	223	Mike Weaver	218½	Draw 15	Las Vegas
1983	May 20	**Larry Holmes**	33	213	Tim Witherspoon	219½	Split 12	Las Vegas
1983	Sep. 10	**Larry Holmes**	33	223	Scott Frank	211¼	TKO 5	Atlantic City
1983	Sep. 23	Gerrie Coetzee	28	215	Michael Dokes WBA	217	KO 10	Richfield, Ohio
1983	Nov. 25	**Larry Holmes**	34	219	Marvis Frazier	200	TKO 1	Las Vegas
1984	Mar. 9	Tim Witherspoon	26	220¼	Greg Page	239½	Maj 12	Las Vegas
1984	Aug. 31	Pinklon Thomas	26	216	T. Witherspoon WBC	217	Maj 12	Las Vegas
1984	Nov. 9	**Larry Holmes** IBF	35	221½	Bonecrusher Smith	227	TKO 12	Las Vegas
1984	Dec. 1	Greg Page	26	236½	Gerrie Coetzee WBA	218	KO 8	Sun City, Boph'swana
1985	Mar. 15	**Larry Holmes**	35	223½	David Bey	233¼	TKO 10	Las Vegas
1985	Apr. 29	Tony Tubbs	26	229	Greg Page WBA	239½	Un 15	Buffalo
1985	May 20	**Larry Holmes**	35	222¼	Carl Williams	215	Un 15	Las Vegas
1985	Jun. 15	Pinklon Thomas	27	220¼	Mike Weaver	221¼	KO 8	Las Vegas
1985	Sep. 21	Michael Spinks	29	200	**Larry Holmes** IBF	221½	Un 15	Las Vegas
1986	Jan. 17	Tim Witherspoon	28	227	Tony Tubbs WBA	229	Maj 15	Atlanta
1986	Mar. 22	Trevor Berbick	33	218½	Pinklon Thomas WBC	222¾	Un 15	Las Vegas
1986	Apr. 19	**Michael Spinks**	29	205	Larry Holmes	223	Split 15	Las Vegas
1986	Jul. 19	Tim Witherspoon	28	234¾	Frank Bruno	228	TKO 11	Wembley, England
1986	Sep. 6	**Michael Spinks**	30	201	Steffen Tangstad	214¾	TKO 4	Las Vegas
1986	Nov. 22	Mike Tyson	20	221¼	Trevor Berbick WBC	218½	TKO 2	Las Vegas
1986	Dec. 12	Bonecrusher Smith	33	228½	T.Witherspoon WBA	233½	TKO 1	NYC (Mad.Sq.Garden)
1987	Mar. 7	Mike Tyson WBC	20	219	Bone Smith WBA	233	Un 12	Las Vegas
1987	May 30	Mike Tyson	20	218¾	Pinklon Thomas	217¾	TKO 6	Las Vegas
1987	May 30	Tony Tucker	28	222¼	Buster Douglas	227¼	TKO 10	Las Vegas
1987	Jun. 15	**Michael Spinks**	30	208¾	Gerry Cooney	238	TKO 5	Atlantic City
1987	Aug. 1	Mike Tyson	21	221	Tony Tucker IBF	221	Un 12	Las Vegas
1987	Oct. 16	Mike Tyson	21	216	Tyrell Biggs	228¾	TKO 7	Atlantic City
1988	Jan. 22	Mike Tyson	21	215¾	Larry Holmes	225¾	TKO 4	Atlantic City
1988	Mar. 20	Mike Tyson	21	216¼	Tony Tubbs	238¼	KO 2	Tokyo
1988	Jun. 27	Mike Tyson	21	218¼	**Michael Spinks**	212¼	KO 1	Atlantic City
1989	Feb. 25	**Mike Tyson**	22	218	Frank Bruno	228	TKO 5	Las Vegas
1989	Jul. 21	**Mike Tyson**	23	219¼	Carl Williams	218	TKO 1	Atlantic City

Notes

• Muhammad Ali was known as Cassius Clay when he stopped Sonny Liston on Feb. 25, 1964.

• WBC recognized Ken Norton as world champion when Leon Spinks refused to meet Norton before Spinks' rematch with Muhammad Ali. Norton had scored a 15-round split decision over Jimmy Young on Nov. 5, 1977 in Las Vegas.

• WBC recognized winner of Mar. 9, 1984 fight between Tim Witherspoon and Greg Page as world champion after Larry Holmes relinquished title in dispute. IBF then recognized Holmes.

• IBF recognized winner of May 30, 1987 fight between Tony Tucker and James (Buster) Douglas as world champion after Michael Spinks relinquished title in dispute.

Major Titleholders

Note the following sanctioning body abbreviations: NBA (National Boxing Association), WBA (World Boxing Association), WBC (World Boxing Council), GBR (Great Britain), IBF (International Boxing Federation), plus other national and state commissions.

Fighters who retired as champion are indicated by (*) and champions who abandoned or relinquished their titles are indicated by (†).

Heavyweights

Widely accepted champions in capital LETTERS. Current champions in **bold** type.

Champion	Held Title	Champion	Held Title
JOHN L.SULLIVAN	1885-92	Joe Frazier (NY)	1968-70
JAMES J.CORBETT	1892-97	Jimmy Ellis (WBA)	1968-70
BOB FITZSIMMONS	1897-99	JOE FRAZIER	1970-73
JAMES J.JEFFRIES	1899-1905*	GEORGE FOREMAN	1973-74
MARVIN HART	1905-06	MUHAMMAD ALI	1974-78*
TOMMY BURNS	1906-08	LEON SPINKS	1978
JACK JOHNSON	1908-15	Ken Norton (WBC)	1978
JESS WILLARD	1915-19	Larry Holmes (WBC)	1978-80
JACK DEMPSEY	1919-26	MUHAMMAD ALI	1978-79
GENE TUNNEY	1926-28*	John Tate (WBA)	1979-80
MAX SCHMELING	1930-32	Mike Weaver (WBA)	1980-82
JACK SHARKEY	1932-33	LARRY HOLMES	1980-85
PRIMO CARNERA	1933-34	Michael Dokes (WBA)	1982-83
MAX BAER	1934-35	Gerrie Coetzee (WBA)	1983-84
JAMES J.BRADDOCK	1935-37	Tim Witherspoon (WBC)	1984
JOE LOUIS	1937-49*	Pinklon Thomas (WBC)	1984-86
EZZARD CHARLES	1949-51	Greg Page (WBA)	1984-85
JERSEY JOE WALCOTT	1951-52	MICHAEL SPINKS	1985-87
ROCKY MARCIANO	1952-56*	Tim Witherspoon (WBA)	1986
FLOYD PATTERSON	1956-59	Trevor Berbick (WBC)	1986
INGEMAR JOHANSSON	1959-60	Mike Tyson (WBC)	1986-87
FLOYD PATTERSON	1960-62	James (Bonecrusher) Smith (WBA)	1986-87
SONNY LISTON	1962-64	Tony Tucker (IBF)	1987
CASSIUS CLAY (MUHAMMAD ALI)	1964-70	Mike Tyson (WBC,WBA,IBF)	1987-88
Ernie Terrell (WBA)	1965-67	**MIKE TYSON**	1988-

Note: John L.Sullivan held the Bare Knuckle championship from 1882-85.

Light Heavyweights

Widely accepted champions in capital LETTERS. Current champions in **bold** type.

Champion	Held Title	Champion	Held Title
JACK ROOT	1903	Eddie Cotton (Mich.)	1963-64
GEORGE GARDNER	1903	JOSE TORRES	1965-66
BOB FITZSIMMONS	1903-05	DICK TIGER	1966-68
PHILA.JACK O'BRIEN	1905-12*	BOB FOSTER	1968-74*
JACK DILLON	1914-16	Vicente Rondon (WBA)	1971-72
BATTLING LEVINSKY	1916-20	John Conteh (WBC)	1974-77
GEORGES CARPENTIER	1920-22	Victor Galindez (WBA)	1974-78
BATTLING SIKI	1922-23	Miguel A.Cuello (WBC)	1977-78
MIKE McTIGUE	1923-25	Mate Parlov (WBC)	1978
PAUL BERLENBACH	1925-26	Mike Rossman (WBA)	1978-79
JACK DELANEY	1926-27†	Marvin Johnson (WBC)	1978-79
Jimmy Slattery (NBA)	1927	Matthew (Franklin) Saad Muhammad (WBC)	1979-81
TOMMY LOUGHRAN	1927-29	Marvin Johnson (WBA)	1979-80
JIMMY SLATTERY	1930	Eddie (Gregory)	
MAXIE ROSENBLOOM	1930-34	Mustapha Muhammad (WBA)	1980-81
George Nichols (NBA)	1932	Michael Spinks (WBA)	1981-83
Bob Godwin (NBA)	1933	Dwight Braxton (WBC)	1981-83
BOB OLIN	1934-35	MICHAEL SPINKS	1983-85†
JOHN HENRY LEWIS	1935-38	J.B.Williamson (WBC)	1985-86
MELIO BETTINA (NY)	1939	Slobodan Kacar (IBF)	1985-86
Len Harvey (GBR)	1939-42	Marvin Johnson (WBA)	1986-87
BILLY CONN	1939-40†	Dennis Andries (WBC)	1986-87
ANTON CHRISTOFORIDIS (NBA)	1941	Bobby Czyz (IBF)	1986-87
GUS LESNEVICH	1941-48	Leslie Stewart (WBA)	1987
Freddie Mills (GBR)	1942-46	**Virgil Hill (WBA)**	1987-
FREDDIE MILLS	1948-50	**Prince Charles Williams (IBF)**	1987-
JOEY MAXIM	1950-52	Thomas Hearns (WBC)	1987
ARCHIE MOORE	1952-62	Donny Lalonde (WBC)	1987-88
Harold Johnson (NBA)	1961	Sugar Ray Leonard (WBC)	1988
HAROLD JOHNSON	1962-63	Dennis Andries (WBC)	1989
WILLIE PASTRANO	1963-65	**Jeff Harding (WBC)**	1989-

Middleweights

Widely accepted champions in capital LETTERS. Current champions in **bold** type.

Champion	Held Title	Champion	Held Title
JACK (NONPAREIL) DEMPSEY	1884-91	ROCKY GRAZIANO	1947-48
BOB FITZSIMMONS	1891-97	TONY ZALE	1948
CHARLES (KID) McCOY	1897-98	MARCEL CERDAN	1948-49
TOMMY RYAN	1898-1907	JAKE LA MOTTA	1949-51
STANLEY KETCHEL	1908	SUGAR RAY ROBINSON	1951
BILLY PAPKE	1908	RANDY TURPIN	1951
STANLEY KETCHEL	1908-10	SUGAR RAY ROBINSON	1951-52*
FRANK KLAUS	1913	CARL (BOBO) OLSON	1953-55
GEORGE CHIP	1913-14	SUGAR RAY ROBINSON	1955-57
AL McCOY	1914-17	GENE FULLMER	1957
Jeff Smith (AUS)	1914	SUGAR RAY ROBINSON	1957
Mick King (AUS)	1914	CARMEN BASILIO	1957-58
Jeff Smith (AUS)	1914-15	SUGAR RAY ROBINSON	1958-60
Lee Darcy (AUS)	1915-17	Gene Fullmer (NBA)	1959-62
MIKE O'DOWD	1917-20	PAUL PENDER	1960-61
JOHNNY WILSON	1920-23	TERRY DOWNES	1961-62
Wm.Bryan Downey (Ohio)	1921-22	PAUL PENDER	1962-63
Dave Rosenberg (NY)	1922	Dick Tiger (WBA)	1962-63
Jock Malone (Ohio)	1922-23	DICK TIGER	1963
Mike O'Dowd (NY)	1922	JOEY GIARDELLO	1963-65
Lou Bogash (NY)	1923	DICK TIGER	1965-66
HARRY GREB	1923-26	EMILE GRIFFITH	1966-67
TIGER FLOWERS	1926	NINO BENVENUTI	1967
MICKEY WALKER	1926-31†	EMILE GRIFFITH	1967-68
GORILLA JONES	1931-32	NINO BENVENUTI	1968-70
MARCEL THIL	1932-37	CARLOS MONZON	1970-77*
Ben Jeby (NY)	1932-33	Rodrigo Valdez (WBC)	1974-76
Lou Brouillard (NBA,NY)	1933	RODRIGO VALDEZ	1977-78
Vince Dundee (NBA,NY)	1933-34	HUGO CORRO	1978-79
Teddy Yarosz (NBA,NY)	1934-35	VITO ANTUOFERMO	1979-80
Babe Risko (NBA,NY)	1935-36	ALAN MINTER	1980
Freddie Steele (NBA,NY)	1936-38	MARVELOUS MARVIN HAGLER	1980-87
FRED APOSTOLI	1937-39	SUGAR RAY LEONARD	1987
Al Hostak (NBA)	1938	Frank Tate (IBF)	1987-88
Solly Krieger (NBA)	1938-39	Sumbu Kalambay (WBA)	1987-89
Al Hostak (NBA)	1939-40	Thomas Hearns (WBC)	1987-88
CEFERINO GARCIA	1939-40	Iran Barkley (WBC)	1988-89
KEN OVERLIN	1940-41	**Michael Nunn (IBF)**	1988-
Tony Zale (NBA)	1940-41	**Roberto Duran (WBC)**	1989-
BILLY SOOSE	1941	**Mike McCallum (WBA)**	1989-
TONY ZALE	1941-47		

Welterweights

Widely accepted champions in capital LETTERS. Current champions in **bold** type.

Champion	Held Title	Champion	Held Title
PADDY DUFFY	1888-90	JACK BRITTON	1915
MYSTERIOUS BILLY SMITH	1892-94	TED (KID) LEWIS	1915-16
TOMMY RYAN	1894-98	JACK BRITTON	1916-17
MYSTERIOUS BILLY SMITH	1898-1900	TED (KID) LEWIS	1917-19
MATTY MATTHEWS	1900	JACK BRITTON	1919-22
EDDIE CONNOLLY	1900	MICKEY WALKER	1922-26
JAMES (RUBE) FERNS	1900	PETE LATZO	1926-27
MATTY MATHEWS	1900-01	JOE DUNDEE	1927-29
JAMES (RUBE) FERNS	1901	JACKIE FIELDS	1929-30
JOE WALCOTT	1901-04	YOUNG JACK THOMPSON	1930
THE DIXIE KID	1904-05	TOMMY FREEMAN	1930-31
HONEY MELLODY	1906-07	YOUNG JACK THOMPSON	1931
Mike (Twin) Sullivan	1907-08	LOU BROUILLARD	1931-32
FRANK MANTELL	1907-08	JACKIE FIELDS	1932-33
HARRY LEWIS	1908-13	YOUNG CORBETT III	1933
Jimmy Gardner	1908-09	JIMMY McLARNIN	1933-34
Jimmy Clabby	1910-11	BARNEY ROSS	1934
WALDEMAR HOLBERG	1914	JIMMY McLARNIN	1934-35
TOM McCORMICK	1914	BARNEY ROSS	1935-38
MATT WELLS	1914-15	HENRY ARMSTRONG	1938-40
MIKE GLOVER	1915	FRITZIE ZIVIC	1940-41

Welterweights (Continued)

Champion	Held Title	Champion	Held Title
Izzy Jannazzo (Md.)	1940-41	JOSE NAPOLES	1971-75
Freddie (Red) Cochrane	1941-46	Hedgemon Lewis (NY)	1972-73
MARTY SERVO	1946*	Angel Espada (WBA)	1975-76
SUGAR RAY ROBINSON	1946-51†	JOHN H. STRACEY	1975-76
JOHNNY BRATTON	1951	CARLOS PALOMINO	1976-79
KID GAVILAN	1951-54	Pipino Cuevas (WBA)	1976-80
JOHNNY SAXTON	1954-55	WILFREDO BENITEZ	1979
TONY DeMARCO	1955	SUGAR RAY LEONARD	1979-80
CARMEN BASILIO	1955-56	ROBERTO DURAN	1980
JOHNNY SAXTON	1956	Thomas Hearns (WBA)	1980-81
CARMEN BASILIO	1956-57†	SUGAR RAY LEONARD	1980-82
VIRGIL AKINS	1958	Donald Curry (WBA)	1983-85
DON JORDAN	1958-60	Milton McCrory (WBC)	1983-85
BENNY (KID) PARET	1960-61	DONALD CURRY	1985-86
EMILE GRIFFITH	1961	LLOYD HONEYGHAN	1986-87
BENNY (KID) PARET	1961-62	JORGE VACA (WBC)	1987-88
EMILE GRIFFITH	1962-63	LLOYD HONEYGHAN (WBC)	1988-89
LUIS RODRIGUEZ	1963	Mark Breland (WBA)	1987
EMILE GRIFFITH	1963-66†	Marlon Starling (WBA)	1987-88
Charlie Shipes (Calif.)	1966-67	Thomas Molinares (WBA)	1988-89
CURTIS COKES	1966-69	**Simon Brown (IBF)**	1988-
JOSE NAPOLES	1969-70	**Mark Breland (WBA)**	1989-
BILLY BACKUS	1970-71	**MARLON STARLING (WBC)**	1989-

Lightweights

Widely accepted champions in capital LETTERS. Current champions in **bold** type.

Champion	Held Title	Champion	Held Title
JACK McAULIFFE	1886-94	Kenny Lane (Mich.)	1963-64
GEORGE (KID) LAVIGNE	1896-99	ISMAEL LAGUNA	1965
FRANK ERNE	1899-02	CARLOS ORTIZ	1965-68
JOE GANS	1902-04	CARLOS TEO CRUZ	1968-69
JIMMY BRITT	1904-05	MANDO RAMOS	1969-70
BATTLING NELSON	1905-06	ISMAEL LAGUNA	1970
JOE GANS	1906-08	KEN BUCHANAN	1970-72
BATTLING NELSON	1908-10	Pedro Carrasco (WBC)	1971-72
AD WOLGAST	1910-12	Mando Ramos (WBC)	1972
WILLIE RITCHIE	1912-14	ROBERTO DURAN	1972-79†
FREDDIE WELSH	1915-17	Chango Carmona (WBC)	1972
BENNY LEONARD	1917-25*	Rodolfo Gonzalez (WBC)	1972-74
JIMMY GOODRICH	1925	Ishimatsu Suzuki (WBC)	1974-76
ROCKY KANSAS	1925-26	Esteban DeJesus (WBC)	1976-78
SAMMY MANDELL	1926-30	Jim Watt (WBC)	1979-81
AL SINGER	1930	Ernesto Espana (WBA)	1979-80
TONY CANZONERI	1930-33	Hilmer Kenty (WBA)	1980-81
BARNEY ROSS	1933-35†	Sean O'Grady (WBA,WAA)	1981
TONY CANZONERI	1935-36	Alexis Arguello (WBC)	1981-82
LOU AMBERS	1936-38	Claude Noel (WBA)	1981
HENRY ARMSTRONG	1938-39	Andrew Ganigan (WAA)	1981-82
LOU AMBERS	1939-40	Arturo Frias (WBA)	1981-82
Sammy Angott (NBA)	1940-41	Ray Mancini (WBA)	1982-84
LEW JENKINS	1940-41	ALEXIS ARGUELLO	1982-83
SAMMY ANGOTT	1941-42*	Edwin Rosario (WBC)	1983-84
Beau Jack (NY)	1942-43	Choo Choo Brown (IBF)	1984
Slugger White (Md.)	1943	Livingstone Bramble (WBA)	1984-86
Bob Montgomery (NY)	1943	Harry Arroyo (IBF)	1984-85
Sammy Angott (NBA)	1943-44	Jose Luis Ramirez (WBC)	1984-85
Beau Jack (NY)	1943-44	Jimmy Paul (IBF)	1985-86
Bob Montgomery (NY)	1944-47	Hector Camacho (WBC)	1985-86
Juan Zurita (NBA)	1944-45	Edwin Rosario (WBA)	1986-87
IKE WILLIAMS	1947-51	Greg Haugen (IBF)	1986-87
JAMES CARTER	1951-52	Julio Cesar Chavez (WBA)	1987-88
LAURO SALAS	1952	Jose Luis Ramirez (WBC)	1987-88
JAMES CARTER	1952-54	JULIO CESAR CHAVEZ (WBC,WBA)	1988-89
PADDY DeMARCO	1954	Vinny Pazienza (IBF)	1987-88
JAMES CARTER	1954-55	Greg Haugen (IBF)	1988-89
WALLACE (BUD) SMITH	1955-56	**Pernell Whitaker (IBF,WBC)**	1989-
JOE BROWN	1956-62	**Edwin Rosario (WBA)**	1989-
CARLOS ORTIZ	1962-65		

Featherweights

Widely accepted champions in capital LETTERS. Current champions in **bold** type.

Champion	Held Title	Champion	Held Title
TORPEDO BILLY MURPHY	1890	Phil Terranova (NBA)	1943-44
YOUNG GRIFFO	1890-92	Sal Bartolo (NBA)	1944-46
GEORGE DIXON	1892-97	SANDY SADDLER	1948-49
SOLLY SMITH	1897-98	WILLIE PEP	1949-50
Ben Jordan (GBR)	1898-99	SANDY SADDLER	1950-57*
Eddie Santry (GBR)	1899-1900	HOGAN (KID) BASSEY	1957-59
DAVE SULLIVAN	1898	DAVEY MOORE	1959-63
GEORGE DIXON	1898-1900	ULTIMINIO (SUGAR) RAMOS	1963-64
TERRY McGOVERN	1900-01	VICENTE SALDIVAR	1964-67*
YOUNG CORBETT II	1901-03	Howard Winstone (GBR)	1968
ABE ATTELL	1903-04	Raul Rojas (WBA)	1968
BROOKLYN TOMMY SULLIVAN	1904-05	Jose Legra (WBC)	1968-69
ABE ATTELL	1906-12	Shozo Saijyo (WBA)	1968-71
JOHNNY KILBANE	1912-23	JOHNNY FAMECHON (WBC)	1969-70
Jim Driscoll (GBR)	1912-13	VICENTE SALDIVAR (WBC)	1970
EUGENE CRIQUI	1923	KUNIAKI SHIBATA (WBC)	1970-72
JOHNNY DUNDEE	1923-24†	Antonio Gomez (WBA)	1971-72
LOUIS (KID) KAPLAN	1925-26†	CLEMENTE SANCHEZ (WBC)	1972
Dick Finnegan (Mass.)	1926-27	Ernesto Marcel (WBA)	1972-74
BENNY BASS	1927-28	JOSE LEGRA (WBC)	1972-73
TONY CANZONERI	1928	EDER JOFRE (WBC)	1973-74
ANDRE ROUTIS	1928-29	Ruben Olivares (WBA)	1974
BATTLING BATTALINO	1929-32†	Bobby Chacon (WBC)	1974-75
Tommy Paul (NBA)	1932-33	ALEXIS ARGUELLO (WBA)	1974-76†
Kid Chocolate (NY)	1932-33	Ruben Olivares (WBC)	1975
Freddie Miller (NBA)	1933-36	David (Poison) Kotey (WBC)	1975-76
Baby Arizmendi (MEX)	1935-36	DANNY LOPEZ (WBC)	1976-80
Mike Belloise (NY)	1936-37	Rafael Ortega (WBA)	1977
Petey Sarron (NBA)	1936-37	Cecilio Lastra (WBA)	1977-78
HENRY ARMSTRONG	1937-38†	Eusebio Pedroza (WBA)	1978-85
Joey Archibald (NY)	1938-39	SALVADOR SANCHEZ (WBC)	1980-82
Leo Rodak (NBA)	1938-39	Juan LaPorte (WBC)	1982-84
JOEY ARCHIBALD	1939-40	Wilfredo Gomez (WBC)	1984
Petey Scalzo (NBA)	1940-41	Min-Keun Oh (IBF)	1984-85
Jimmy Perrin (La.)	1940-41	Azumah Nelson (WBC)	1984-88
HARRY JEFFRA	1940-41	Barry McGuigan (WBA)	1985-86
JOEY ARCHIBALD	1941	Ki-Young Chung (IBF)	1985-86
Richie Lemos (NBA)	1941	Steve Cruz (WBA)	1986-87
CHALKY WRIGHT	1941-42	Antonio Rivera (IBF)	1986-88
Jackie Wilson (NBA)	1941-43	**Antonio Esparragoza (WBA)**	1987-
WILLIE PEP	1942-48	Calvin Grove (IBF)	1988
Jackie Callura (NBA)	1943	**Jorge Paez (IBF)**	1988-
		Jeff Fenech (WBC)	1988-

Bantamweights

Widely accepted champions in capital LETTERS. Current champions in **bold** type.

Champion	Held Title	Champion	Held Title
HUGHEY BOYLE	1887-88	JOHNNY BUFF	1921-22
CHAPPIE MORAN	1889-90	JOE LYNCH	1922-24
TOMMY (SPIDER) KELLY	1890-92	ABE GOLDSTEIN	1924
BILLY PLIMMER	1892-95	CANNONBALL EDDIE MARTIN	1924-25
PEDLAR PALMER	1895-99	PHIL ROSENBERG	1925-27
TERRY McGOVERN	1899-1900	Teddy Baldock (GBR)	1927
DANNY DOUGHERTY	1900-01	BUD TAYLOR (NBA)	1927-28†
HARRY FORBES	1901-03	Willie Smith (GBR)	1927-28
FRANKIE NEIL	1903-04	Bushy Graham (NY)	1928-29
JOE BOWKER	1904-05	PANAMA AL BROWN	1929-35
JIMMY WALSH	1905-06†	Sixto Escobar (NBA)	1934-35
OWEN MORAN	1907-08	BALTAZAR SANGCHILLI	1935-36
MONTE ATTELL	1909-10	Lou Salica (NBA)	1935
FRANKIE CONLEY	1910-11	Sixto Escobar (NBA)	1935-36
JOHNNY COULON	1911-14	TONY MARINO	1936
Digger Stanley (GBR)	1910-12	SIXTO ESCOBAR	1936-37
Charles Ledoux (GBR)	1912-13	HARRY JEFFRA	1937-38
Eddie Campi (GBR)	1913-14	SIXTO ESCOBAR	1938-39*
KID WILLIAMS	1914-17	Georgie Pace (NBA)	1939-40
Johnny Ertle	1915-18	LOU SALICA	1940-42
PETE HERMAN	1917-20	MANUEL ORTIZ	1942-47
Memphis Pal Moore	1918-19	HAROLD DADE	1947
JOE LYNCH	1920-21	MANUEL ORTIZ	1947-50
PETE HERMAN	1921		

Bantamweights (Continued)

Champion	Held Title	Champion	Held Title
VIC TOWEEL	1950-52	ALFONSO ZAMORA	1975-77
JIMMY CARRUTHERS	1952-54*	Carlos Zarate (WBC)	1976-79
ROBERT COHEN	1954-56	JORGE LUJAN	1977-80
Raul Macias (NBA)	1955-57	Lupe Pintor (WBC)	1979-83
MARIO D'AGATA	1956-57	JULIAN SOLIS	1980
ALPHONSE HALIMI	1957-59	JEFF CHANDLER	1980-84
JOE BECERRA	1959-60*	Albert Davila (WBC)	1983-85
Johnny Caldwell (EBU)	1961-62	RICHARD SANDOVAL	1984-86
EDER JOFRE	1961-65	Satoshi Shingaki (IBF)	1984-85
MASAHIKO FIGHTING HARADA	1965-68	Jeff Fenech (IBF)	1985
LIONEL ROSE	1968-69	Daniel Zaragoza (WBC)	1985
RUBEN OLIVARES	1969-70	Miguel Lora (WBC)	1985-88
CHUCHO CASTILLO	1970-71	GABY CANIZALES	1986
RUBEN OLIVARES	1971-72	BERNARDO PINANGO	1986-87
RAFAEL HERRERA	1972	Wilfredo Vasquez (WBA)	1987-88
ENRIQUE PINDER	1972-73	Kevin Seabrooks (IBF)	1987-88
ROMEO ANAYA	1973	Kaokor Galaxy (WBA)	1988
Rafael Herrera (WBC)	1973-74	Moon Sung-Kil (WBA)	1988-89
ARNOLD TAYLOR	1973-74	**Kaokor Galaxy (WBA)**	1989-
SOO-HWAN HONG	1974-75	**Raul Perez (WBC)**	1988-
Rodolfo Martinez (WBC)	1974-76	**Orlando Canizales (IBF)**	1988-

Flyweights

Widely accepted champions in capital LETTERS. Current champions in **bold** type.

Champion	Held Title	Champion	Held Title
SID SMITH	1913	Betulio Gonzalez (WBC)	1972
BILL LADBURY	1913-14	Venice Borkorsor (WBC)	1972-73
PERCY JONES	1914	VENICE BORKORSOR	1973
JOE SYMONDS	1914-16	Chartchai Chionoi (WBA)	1973-74
JIMMY WILDE	1916-23	Betulio Gonzalez (WBA)	1973-74
PANCHO VILLA	1923-25	Shoji Oguma (WBC)	1974-75
FIDEL LaBARBA	1925-27*	Susumu Hanagata (WBA)	1974-75
FRENCHY BELANGER (NBA,IBU)	1927-28	Miguel Canto (WBC)	1975-79
Izzy Schwartz (NY)	1927-29	Erbito Salavarria (WBA)	1975-76
Johnny McCoy (Calif.)	1927-28	Alfonso Lopez (WBA)	1976
Newsboy Brown (Calif.)	1928	Guty Espadas (WBA)	1976-78
FRANKIE GENARO (NBA,IBU)	1928-29	Betulio Gonzalez (WBA)	1978-79
Johnny Hill (GBR)	1928-29	Chan-Hee Park (WBC)	1979-80
SPIDER PLADNER (NBA,IBU)	1929	Luis Ibarra (WBA)	1979-80
FRANKIE GENARO (NBA,IBU)	1929-31	Tae-Shik Kim (WBA)	1980
Willie LaMorte (NY)	1929-30	Shoji Oguma (WBC)	1980-81
Midget Wolgast (NY)	1930-35	Peter Mathebula (WBA)	1980-81
YOUNG PEREZ (NBA,IBU)	1931-32	Santos Laciar (WBA)	1981
JACKIE BROWN (NBA,IBU)	1932-35	Antonio Avelar (WBC)	1981-82
BENNY LYNCH	1935-38†	Luis Ibarra (WBA)	1981
Small Montana (NY,Calif.)	1935-37	Juan Herrera (WBA)	1981-82
PETER KANE	1938-43	Prudencio Cardona (WBC)	1982
Little Dado (NBA,Calif.)	1938-40	Santos Laciar (WBA)	1982-85
JACKIE PATERSON	1943-48	Freddie Castillo (WBC)	1982
RINTY MONAGHAN	1948-50*	Eleoncio Mercedes (WBC)	1982-83
TERRY ALLEN	1950	Charlie Magri (WBC)	1983
SALVADOR (DADO) MARINO	1950-52	Frank Cedeno (WBC)	1983-84
YOSHIO SHIRAI	1953-54	Soon-Chun Kwon (IBF)	1983-85
PASCUAL PEREZ	1954-60	Koji Kobayashi (WBC)	1984
PONE KINGPETCH	1960-62	Gabriel Bernal (WBC)	1984
HIROYUKI EBIHARA	1963-64	Sot Chitalada (WBC)	1984-88
PONE KINGPETCH	1964-65	Hilario Zapate (WBA)	1985-87
SALVATORE BURRINI	1965-66	Chong-Kwan Chung (IBF)	1985-86
Horacio Accavallo (WBA)	1966-68	Bi-Won Chung (IBF)	1986
WALTER McGOWAN	1966	Hi-Sup Shin (IBF)	1986-87
CHARTCHAI CHIONOI	1966-69	Dodie Penalosa (IBF)	1987
EFREN TORRES	1969-70	Fidel Bassa (WBA)	1987-89
Hiroyuki Ebihara (WBA)	1969	Choi Chang-Ho (IBF)	1987-88
Bernabe Villacampo (WBA)	1969-70	Rolando Bohol (IBF)	1988
CHARTCHAI CHIONOI	1970	Yong-Kang Kim (WBC)	1988-89
Berkrerk Chartvanchai (WBA)	1970	Duke McKenzie (IBF)	1988-89
Masao Ohba (WBA)	1970-73	**Dave McAuley (IBF)**	1989-
ERBITO SALAVARRIA	1970-73	**Sot Chitalada (WBC)**	1989-
		Jesus Rojas (WBA)	1989-

Wide World Photos

T.O.M. Sopwith
Aviator-Yachtsman

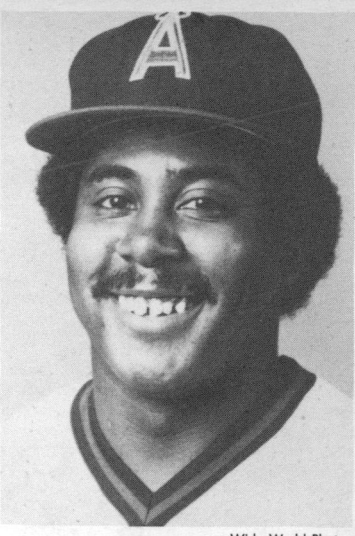

Wide World Photos

Donnie Moore
Pitcher

Wide World Photos

Larry Fleisher
Player Agent

Wide World Photos

Earl (Red) Blaik
Football Coach

DEATHS

Members of the national and international sports community who have died over the past year.

Deaths
November, 1988 through October, 1989

Craig Arfons, 39; speed racing enthusiast who was killed when his boat flipped several times at over 300 mph while attempting to break the world water speed record; father Walt and uncle Art each held world land speed records in the 1960s; in Sebring, Fla., July 9.

Sal Aunese, 21; former University of Colorado quarterback, who led the Buffaloes to an 8-3 record as a junior in 1988; set a school record of 92 passes without an interception from 1987-88; of stomach cancer; in Denver, Sept.23.

Ole Bardahl, 87; former U.S. and world speed boat champion whose Miss Bardahl boats won five Gold Cup titles in Unlimited hydroplane racing from 1963-68; in Seattle, Aug 13.

Rev. David Bauer, 64; priest and founder of Canada's national hockey team in 1963; coached Canada to 4th place in the 1964 Winter Olympics and was manager of the '68 bronze medal-winning team; in Goderich, Ontario, Nov.9, 1988.

Wally Berger, 83; former NL outfielder whose 38 HRs for the Boston Braves in 1930 was a rookie record until Oakland's Mark McGwire hit 49 in 1987; hit 242 homers and batted .300 in 11 years; in Redondo Beach, Calif., Dec.4, 1988.

Ricky Berry, 24; first round draft pick of the Sacramento Kings in 1988 and San Jose State's all-time leading scorer; of a self-inflicted gunshot wound; in Fair Oaks, Calif., Aug.14.

Earl (Red) Blaik, 92; former football coach at West Point who guided the Cadets to consecutive national championships in 1944 and '45; rebuilt program after 37 players were expelled in 1951 cribbing scandal; produced 33 first team All-America selections and three Heisman Trophy winners in 25 years as head coach at Dartmouth and Army; 19 former players and assistants under him went on to head coaching jobs in college or pro ranks; from complications following a fall that broke his hip; in Colorado Springs, May 6.

Tom Blackaller, 45; yachtsman and race car driver best known for his spirited but unsuccesful attempts to defeat Dennis Conner in the America's Cup trials of 1980, '83 and '87; of a heart attack while testing a Camel GT race car; in Sonoma, Calif., Sept.7.

Nick Bremigan, 43; an American League umpire since 1974; worked four playoff series, two All-Star games and the 1980 World Series; of a heart attack; in Garland, Texas, March 28.

Cliff Buck, 87; former president of both the Amateur Athletic Union (AAU) from 1964-65 and the U.S.Olympic Committee from 1969-73; in Carbondale, Colo., Feb.8.

August A.(Gussie) Busch Jr., 90; the last of the American beer barons, who built the Anheuser-Busch brewing company into the nation's largest; after buying the failing St.Louis Cardinals in 1953, Busch watched his team win five National League pennants and three World Series in 1964,'67 and '82; in suburban St.Louis, Sept.29.

Lee Calhoun, 56; former world record holder and two-time Olympic gold medalist in the 110-meter hurdles, setting an Olympic record (13.5) at Melbourne in 1956 and repeating as champion four years later in Rome; member of U.S. Olympic Hall of Fame; of complications resulting from a stroke; in Erie, Pa., June 22.

Betty Becker Pinkston Campbell, 86; two-time Olympic diving champion who won gold medals off the springboard at Paris in 1924 and off the platform at Amsterdam in 1928; of heart failure; in Detroit, April 6.

Eddie Cameron, 86; former basketball coach (1929-42), football coach (1942-45) and athletic director (1951-72) at Duke University; guided basketball team to 226-99 record and football to 25-11-1; one of the founders of the Atlantic Coast Conference in 1953; Duke's Cameron Indoor Stadium is named in his honor; in Durham, N.C., Nov.25, 1988.

Lou Campi, 84; member of the American Bowling Congress Hall of Fame, who won the first official PBA tournament in 1959; two-time winner of the national doubles championship; in Dumont, N.J.; Aug.31.

Henry Ciccarone, 50; former Johns Hopkins lacrosse coach, who guided the Blue Jays to three straight national championships from 1978-80; had a career record of 105-16 from 1975-80; in Cockeysville, Md., Nov. 16, 1988.

Joe Collins, 66; New York Yankees 1st baseman from 1948-57, who was a member of six World Series championship teams; in Union, N.J., Aug.30.

John F.X. Condon, 75; Madison Square Garden public adress announcer for N.Y.Knicks and college basketball from 1947-89; also served as Garden boxing executive and matchmaker; of cancer; in New York, Oct. 13.

Jocko Conlan, 89; National League umpire for 24 years, he became only the fifth arbiter selected for the Hall of Fame when he was elected in 1974; known for his numerous run-ins with manager Leo Durocher; an outfielder with the Chicago Cubs for two seasons (1934-35), he worked five World Series and six All-Star games as an ump; in Scottsdale, Ariz., April 16.

William Cox, 79; successful lumberman and entrepreneur who, at 33, bought the Philadelphia Phillies in 1943 but was banned from baseball later that year by commissioner Kenesaw Mountain Landis after Cox admitted he bet on Phillie games; following a long illness; in Mount Kisco, N.Y., Mar. 28.

Alfonso de Borbon, 52; first cousin of King Carlos of Spain and president of the Spanish Olympic Committee from 1984-87 and a member of the International Skiing Federation; killed in a skiing accident the day before the scheduled start of the World Alpine Skiing Championships at Beaver Creek, Colo., Jan. 30.

Frank DeFrancis, 62; international lawyer who was also part-owner of Laurel and Pimlico race tracks in Maryland; credited with saving the horse racing industry in the state by aggressively marketing the sport; of heart failure; in Miami, Aug. 18.

Esteban de Jesus, 37; former WBC lightweight champion who held the title from 1976-78, had a record of 57-5 with 32 knockouts, and was the only fighter to defeat Roberto Duran in the 1970s; convicted of murdering a motorist in a traffic dispute in 1981; of AIDS, contracted from longtime drug use; in San Juan, Puerto Rico, May 11.

Elvin (Ducky) Drake, 85; former head track coach and head trainer at UCLA; guided Bruins to first national track & field championship in 1956; UCLA track stadium named in his honor; of a heart attack; in Los Angeles, Dec.24, 1988.

Morley Drury, 85; All-American halfback at Southern Cal in the 1920s; first Trojan to gain 1,000 yards in a season and first to make the College Football Hall of Fame; of a stroke; in Long Beach, Calif., Jan. 22.

Nesuhi Ertegun, 71; record producer with an ear for rhythm and blues and jazz, who teamed with his brother Ahmet to make Atlantic Records one of the top labels in the country; an intense soccer fan, he bought the New York franchise in the North American Soccer League in 1971, named the team the Cosmos and signed stars like Pele and Franz Beckenbauer to play for him in front of sell-out crowds at Giants Stadium in the mid-1970s; of complications following cancer surgery; in New York, July 15.

Bibb Falk, 90; the player who replaced Shoeless Joe Jackson in the Chicago White Sox outfield after Jackson was banned from baseball in the wake of the 1919 Black Sox scandal; hit .314 in 12 seasons with Chicago and Cleveland; later coached the University of Texas to back-to-back national championships in 1949 and '50; after a long illness; in Austin, Texas, June 8.

Wes Fesler, 81; former three-time All-America at Ohio State (1928-30), who later coached the Buckeyes to a 21-13-3 record from 1947-50 and a 17-14 victory over Cal in the 1950 Rose Bowl; in Laguna Hills, Calif., July 30.

Larry Fleisher, 58; pro basketball player agent who founded and led the NBA Players Association from 1961-88 during which time player salaries rose from an average of $9,400 to over $600,000 without a strike; of a heart attack; in New York City, May 4. (See also Basketball.)

Lane Frost, 25; world champion bull rider of 1987; from injuries suffered when he was gored by the same bull that had thrown him during the Cheyenne (Wyo.) Frontier Days Rodeo, July 30.

Takeo Fujisawa, 78; co-founded Honda Motor Company with Soichiro Honda in 1948; directed Honda's development as the world's top motorcycle maker; later served as company's "supreme advisor" after his retirement in 1973; in Tokyo, Dec.30, 1988.

Carl Furillo, 66; former Brooklyn and Los Angeles Dodger rightfielder, who won the National League batting title in 1953 with .344 average; best remembered for his rifle arm and an uncanny knowledge of the rightfield wall at Ebbets Field in Brooklyn; in Stony Creek, Pa., Jan. 21.

A.Bartlett Giamatti, 51; baseball commissioner since April 1, 1989; banned Cincinnati legend and manager Pete Rose from baseball for life for betting on games involving the Reds; Renaissance scholar and president of Yale University from 1978-86; president of National League from 1986-89; of a heart attack; in Edgartown, Mass., Sept. 1. (See also Baseball.)

Vernon (Lefty) Gomez, 80; easy-going New York Yankee lefthanded pitcher, who posted six World Series wins in the 1930s and started the first three All-Star Games for the American League; had a record of 189-102 in 14 seasons; inducted into the Hall of Fame in 1972; of congestive heart failure and pneumonia; in Larkspur, Calif., Feb. 17.

Claude Harmon, 73; pro golfer who won the 1948 Masters, but was more celebrated as a teaching pro to four U.S. presidents and King Hassan II of Morocco; four days after undergoing heart surgery; in Houston, July 23.

Don Heffner, 78; former 2nd baseman with four AL teams in 11 seasons (1934-44); was oldest first-time manager ever (54) when named by Cincinnati Reds in 1966, but was fired after only 83 games; of complications from pneumonia; in Pasadena, Calif., Aug. 1.

Dan Hill, 72; All-American center on Duke's unbeaten, untied and unscored upon 1938 team that lost, 7-3, to Southern Cal in the '39 Rose Bowl; elected to College Football Hall of Fame in 1962; in Durham, N.C., Aug.24.

Clarke Hinkle, 79; former Green Bay fullback and linebacker (1932-41); a four-time All-Pro, he helped lead the Packers to NFL titles in 1936 and '39; inducted into the Pro Football Hall of Fame in 1964; in Toronto, Ohio, Nov.9,1988.

Carl Hubbell, 85; Hall of Fame lefthander and five-time 20-game winner, whose screwball helped fashion a record of 253-154 with a 2.97 ERA in 16 seasons with the New York Giants; named National League MVP twice (1935 and '36); fanned Babe Ruth, Lou Gehrig, Jimmie Foxx, Al Simmons and Joe Cronin in succession at 1934 All-Star Game; long-time director of S.F. Giants farm system; of injuries suffered in an automobile accident; in Scottsdale, Ariz., Nov. 22, 1988.

Buddy Jacobson, 58; a leading trainer of thoroughbred horses in New York state in the 1960s; convicted and sentenced to 25 years to life in 1980 for murdering the lover of a former girlfriend; of bone cancer; in Buffalo, May 16.

Judy Johnson, 89; outstanding 3rd baseman in the Negro Leagues from 1921-37; unofficial career batting average of .344; elected to Hall of Fame in 1975; in Wilmington, Del., June 13.

Dan Kelly, 52; hockey play-by-play broadcaster for the St. Louis Blues for two decades; named as a winner of the 1989 Lester Patrick Award for outstanding service to hockey in the U.S.; of cancer; in Chesterfield, Mo., Feb.10.

Augie Lio, 71; a guard and place kicker on Georgetown University's 1941 Orange Bowl team; inducted into the College Football Hall of Fame in 1979; former sportswriter and editor at the Passaic (N.J.) Herald & News; in Clifton, N.J., Sept.3.

Toni Matt, 69; Austrian immigrant who was a pioneer in American competitive skiing; set a record in April, 1939 that has never been broken when he skied down the treacherous Tuckerman's Ravine Headwall of Mt. Washington reaching speeds of up to 85 mph; of a heart attack; in Pawling, N.Y., May 17.

John Matuszak, 38; former defensive end who helped lead the Oakland Raiders to Super Bowl titles in 1977 and '81; Tampa University standout who was first overall pick (by Houston) in 1973 NFL draft; of heart failure; in Burbank, Calif., June 17.

John McCauley, 44; former NHL referee who became the league's director of officiating in 1986; from complications following surgery; in Georgetown, Ontario, June 2.

Jack McMahon, 60; former college basketball star at St.John's University where he helped lead the Redmen to the 1952 NCAA finals; later an NBA player and head coach who had become assistant coach and director of player personnel for the Golden State Warriors in 1986; died in his sleep; in Chicago, June 11. (See also Basketball.)

Donnie Moore, 35; former All-Star relief pitcher who had 31 saves for the California Angels in 1985; gave up Dave Henderson's dramatic two-out, two-strike ninth inning HR in 5th game of '86 AL playoffs against Boston; pitched for five major league teams in 13 years, but was released by Triple A Omaha on June 12; of a self-inflicted gunshot wound, after shooting his estranged wife; in Anaheim, Calif., July 18.

Wayne Moore, 44; offensive tackle for the Miami Dolphins in 1972 and '73 when they won consecutive Super Bowls; an All-Pro selection in '73; of a heart attack; in Miami, Aug.19.

Joe Morrison, 51; head football coach at the University of South Carolina and a former halfback and wide receiver for 14 years with the New York Giants (1959-72); college coach for 16 seasons at Tennessee-Chattanooga, New Mexico and South Carolina with a record of 101-72-7; of a heart attack; in Columbia, S.C., Feb.5.

Ondrej Nepela, 38; winner of five European men's figure skating championships and three straight world titles (1971-73); became the only Czechoslovakian skater to win an Olympic gold medal when he won the men's competition at the 1972 Winter Games in Sapporo, Japan; of throat cancer; in West Germany, Feb. 2.

Sherry O'Brien, 81; a Philadelphia public address announcer for the Phillies and A's at Shibe Park in the 1940s, who broke new ground in his field by personalizing player introductions with career and personal information as well as giving the full names of players; in Philadelphia, April 10.

Dominic (Ole) Olejniczak, 80; former mayor of Green Bay and president of the locally-owned Packers, who spearheaded the building of Lambeau Field in 1957 and hired Vince Lombardi as head coach a year later, decisions that put the Packers on a firm financial footing and led to five NFL championships from 1961-67; from complications following a series of strokes; in Green Bay, April 15.

Don Pratt, 45; a modified stock car driver from Lima, N.Y.; from injuries suffered after his car crashed into the wall at Pocono International Raceway during the running of the NASCAR Race of Champions; in Long Pond, Pa., Sept.17.

Joe Primeau, 83; Hockey Hall of Famer who centered the Toronto's "Kid Line" in the 1920s and '30s; only coach to win the Memorial, Allan and Stanley Cups at junior, senior and NHL levels of competition; following a long illness; in Toronto, May 15, 1989.

Katha Quinn, 34; sports information director at St. John's University since 1983; of liver cancer; in New York, March 17.

Jay Ramsdell, 25; commissioner of the Continental Basketball Association, who was among the 105 passengers confirmed dead after the crash of United Airlines Flight 232 at the Sioux Gateway Airport; in Sioux City, Iowa, July 19.

Joseph Raposo, 51; Grammy Award-winning composer and playwright and a creator of children's television show "Sesame Street"; one of his compositions was "There Used to Be a Ballpark"; of complications from lymphoma; in Bronxville, N.Y., Feb. 5.

Tim Richmond, 34; the Indianapolis 500 rookie-of-the-year in 1980, who switched to stock car racing and won 13 NASCAR events from 1980-87, including seven in 1986; of complications from AIDS; in West Palm Beach, Fla., Aug. 13.

Sugar Ray Robinson, 67; born Walker Smith Jr., took another fighter's name for an amateur bout and kept it; went on to become world welterweight and middleweight champion in a pro career that spanned three decades (1940-65) and resulted in a record of 174-19-6 with 109 knockouts; considered the best fighter "pound for pound" to ever step into the ring; of Alzheimer's disease and diabetes; in Culver City, Calif., April 12. (See also Boxing.)

Secretariat, 19; first Triple Crown winner since Citation in 1948 when he won the Kentucky Derby, Preakness and Belmont Stakes in 1973; set records at the Derby and Belmont that still stand and won the Belmont by an astonishing 31 lengths; Horse of the Year in 1972 and '73; widely acknowledged as the greatest race horse of the last 40 years; from a lethal injection (Secretariat suffered from laminitis, a painful and degenerative hoof disease that is usually incurable); in Paris, Ky., Oct. 4.

Rip Sewell, 82; Pittsburgh Pirates righthander from 1938-49, whose arching eephus pitch delighted fans and confounded NL hitters; also helped organize the baseball players pension fund in 1946; of kidney failure; in Plant City, Fla., Sept.2.

Hilda Strike Sisson, 78; Canadian runner who won the silver medal in the 100-meter dash at the 1932 Olympics in Los Angeles but who may have deserved the gold when it was discovered in 1980 that Stella Walsh, the winner of the race, was a man and should have been disqualified from competing as a woman; the IOC was petitioned to give Sisson the medal during the 1984 L.A. Olympics, but the effort was unsuccessful; of a heart attack; in Ottawa, March 9.

Sir Thomas (T.O.M.) Sopwith, 101; aviator and aircraft manufacturer whose companies built the famous Sopwith Camels of World War I; he also financed and skippered two unsuccessful attempts to win the America's Cup, losing with Endeavour in 1934 and Endeavour II in 1937; in Winchester, England, Jan.27.

Jesse Sweetser, 87; winner of U.S. Amateur golf championship as a 20-year-old in 1922 and first American to win British Amateur title when he did it in 1926; member of six Walker Cup teams as a player and two as non-playing captain; in Washington, D.C., May 27.

Edward Plunkett (E.P.) Taylor, 88; wealthy Canadian brewer and industrialist, whose 3-year-old colt Northern Dancer became the first Canadian-bred horse to win the Kentucky Derby in 1964; also won three Eclipse Awards as Man of the Year in 1973 and Outstanding Breeder in 1977 and '83; after a long illness; in the Bahamas, May 14.

Bill Terry, 90; the last National League player to hit .400 (.401 in 1930); player-manager of the New York Giants from 1932-36, led Giants to World Series championship in 1933; batted .341 during 14-year career and elected to Hall of Fame in 1954; in Jacksonville, Fla., Jan. 9.

John (Stumpy) Thomason, 83; the Georgia Tech halfback whose fumble in the 1929 Rose Bowl against California set up the famous wrong-way run of Cal's Roy Riegels; Riegels' 80-yard dash back to his own goal line resulted in a safety that enabled Tech to win the game, 8-7; the lone Tech touchdown was scored by Thomason; of Parkinson's disease; in Thomasville, N.C., April 20.

Tommy Thompson, 72; quarterback who led the Philadelphia Eagles to three straight NFL title games from 1947-49 and back-to-back championships in 1948 and '49; of cancer; in Calico Rock, Ark., April 21.

George (Specs) Toporcer, 90; first major leaguer other than a pitcher to wear eyeglasses on the playing field when the St.Louis Cardinals brought him up as a 22-year-old utility infielder in 1921; hit .279 over seven seasons and later managed in minor leagues; from injuries suffered in a fall at home in Huntington Station, N.Y., May 17.

Stacey Toran, 27; Los Angeles Raider strong safety and 1984 sixth round draft pick out of Notre Dame; of injuries suffered in an automobile accident; in Los Angeles, Aug.5.

William Thayer Tutt, 76; former president of the Amateur Hockey Assn. of the United States (AHAUS) for 14 years until his retirement in 1986; influential in making Colorado Springs the site of the NCAA Division I hockey tournament from 1948-57; after a long illness; in Colorado Springs, Feb.24.

Glenna Collett Vare, 86; winner of U.S. Women's Amateur championship six times from 1922-35 and a member of the World Golf Hall of Fame; the Vare Trophy, awarded to the player with the lowest average on the LPGA tour, is named for her; in Gulfstream, Fla., Feb.10.

Emil Verban, 73; former light-hitting NL 2nd baseman who batted .412 for the Cardinals in the All-St.Louis World Series of 1944; later played for Chicago and was immortalized in 1975 by Cub fans who picked him to represent the typical Cub—obscure but hard-working—and named their fan club, the Emil Verban Memorial Society, after him; in Lincoln, Ill., June 8.

Bob Walters, 51; former quarterback and defensive back with San Francisco 49ers, who coached Western Carolina to a 116-94-6 record from 1969-88; the third 49er from the early 1960's to die of amyotrophic lateral sclerosis (Lou Gehrig's Disease); in Cullowee, N.C., May 29.

Willie Wells, 82; nicknamed "Devil" for his relentless style of play, in 22 seasons in the Negro Leagues (1924-45) he batted .326 with 141 HRs; once called "the greatest living shortstop not in the Hall of Fame"; of heart failure; in Austin, Texas, Jan.22.

John Yovicsin, 70; Harvard football coach for 14 seasons, who retired in 1970 with a record of 78-42-5; the most memorable game of his tenure was a 29-29 tie with Yale in a battle of unbeaten teams in 1968; Harvard earned the draw by scoring 16 points in the last 42 seconds; of heart disease; in Hyannis, Mass., Sept.13.

Bibliography

Many sources were used in gathering information for this almanac. Day-to-day material was almost always found in copies of **USA Today, The Boston Globe**, and **The New York Times**.

Several weekly and bi-weekly periodicals were also used in the past year's pursuit of facts and figures, among them—**Sports Illustrated, The Sporting News, The Hockey News, The NCAA News, FIFA** (Soccer) **News, Track & Field News**, and **Baseball America**.

In addition, the following books provided a wealth of background material for one or more chapters of the almanac.

Baseball

The All-Star Game
(A Pictorial History, 1933 to Present)
By Donald Honig
The Sporting News Publishing Co. (1987)
St. Louis

The Baseball Encyclopedia
Fourth (1979) and Seventh (1988) Editions
Joseph L. Reichler, Editor
Macmillan Publishing Company
New York

The 1989 Baseball Encyclopedia Update
Collier Books
Macmillan Publishing Company
New York

Total Baseball
Edited by John Thorn and Pete Palmer
Warner Books (1989)
New York

The Sports Encyclopedia Baseball
Sixth Edition (1985)
Edited by David S. Neft and Richard M. Cohen
St. Martin's/Marek
New York

The Scrapbook History of Baseball
by Jordan A. Deutsch, Richard M. Cohen,
Roland T, Johnson, and David S. Neft
Bobbs-Merrill Company, Inc. (1975)
Indianapolis/New York

The Sporting News Official Baseball Guide, 1989
Edited by Dave Sloan
The Sporting News Publishing Co.
St. Louis

The Sporting News Official Baseball Register, 1989
Edited by Barry Siegel
The Sporting News Publishing Co.
St. Louis

The Complete Baseball Record Book, 1989
Edited by Craig Carter
The Sporting News Publishing Co.
St. Louis

College Football

Football: A College History
by Tom Perrin
McFarland & Company, Inc. (1987)
Jefferson, NC

Football: Facts & Figures
by Dr. L.H. Baker
Farrar & Rinehart, Inc. (1945)
New York

Great College Football Coaches of the Twenties and Thirties
by Tim Cohane
Arlington House (1973)
New Rochelle, NY

The Heisman, A Symbol of Excellence
by John T. Brady
Edited by John A. Walsh
Atheneum (1984)
New York

1988 NCAA Football
Compiled by Steve Boda, Jr. and
James M. Van Valkenburg
Edited by Michael V. Earle
NCAA Books
Mission, KA

Saturday Afternoon
by Richard Whittingham
Workman Publishing Co., Inc. (1985)
New York

Saturday's America
by Dan Jenkins
Sports Illustrated Books
Little, Brown & Company (1970)
Boston

You Have to Pay the Price
by Earl H. Blake with Tim Cohane
Holt, Rinehart and Winston (1960)
New York

Plus many college football guides, especially the 1988 guides compiled by Notre Dame, the Southeastern Conference and the Southwest Conference.

Pro Football

The Official NFL Encyclopedia
by Beau Riffenburgh
New American Library (1986)
New York

The Official 1988 NFL Record & Fact Book
Edited by Pete Abitante and Chuck Garrity, Jr.
Produced by NFL Properties, Inc.
New York

The Scrapbook History of Pro Football
by Richard M. Cohen, Jordan A. Deutsch,
Roland T, Johnson
and David S. Neft
Bobbs-Merrill Company, Inc. (1976)
Indianapolis/New York

CFL '88
(The Canadian Football League Facts
Figures & Records)
Editorial Director: John Iaboni
Toronto

College Basketball

All the Moves
(A History of College Basketball)
by Neil D. Isaacs
J.B. Lippincott Company (1975)
New York

Blue Ribbon College Basketball Yearbook
Edited by Chris Wallace
Christopher Publishing (1988)
Buckhannon, WV

The Final Four
Compiled by Billy Reed
Host Communications, Inc. (1988)
Lexington, KY

The Modern Encyclopedia of Basketball
(Second Revised Edition)
Edited by Zander Hollander
Dolphin Books (1979)
Doubleday & Company, Inc
Garden City, NY

1988 NCAA Basketball
Compiled by Gary K. Johnson, Richard M.
Campbell, Steve Boda, Jr., James F. Wright,
and James M. Van Valkenburg
Edited by Michelle A. Pond
NCAA Books
Mission, KS

College Sports

1988 NCAA Basketball
Compiled by Gary K. Johnson, Richard M.
Campbell, Steve Boda, Jr., James F. Wright,
and James M. Van Valkenburg
Edited by Michelle A. Pond
NCAA Books
Mission, KS

1988 NCAA Football
Compiled by Steve Boda, Jr. and
James M. Van Valkenburg
Edited by Michael V. Earle
NCAA Books
Mission, KS

1987-88 National Collegiate Championships
Edited by Theodore A. Breidenthal and
Michelle A. Pond
NCAA Books
Mission, KS

**NAIA Championship History and
Records Book, 1987-88**
National Assn. of Intercollegiate Athletics
NAIA Books
Kansas City, MO

Pro Basketball

**The 1988-89 Philadephia 76ers Statistical
Yearbook**
Edited by Harvey Pollack
Philadelphia 76ers
Philadelphia

From Peachbaskets to Slamdunks
(A Story of Professional Basketball)
by Robert D. Bole and Alfred C. Lawrence
B & L Publishers
Canaan, NH

The Pro Basketball Encyclopedia
Edited by Zander Hollander
Associated Features Inc. (1977)
Corwin Books
Los Angeles

**The Sporting News Official NBA Guide,
1988-89**
Edited by Alex Sachare and Dave Sloan
The Sporting News Publishing Co.
St. Louis

**The Sporting News Official NBA Register,
1988-89**
Edited by Alex Sachare and Dave Sloan
The Sporting News Publishing Co.
St. Louis

Hockey

Canada Cup '87—The Official History
No.1 Publications Ltd.
Toronto

Checking Back
(A History of the National Hockey League)
By Neil D. Isaacs
W.W.Norton & Company, Inc. (1977)
New York

The Hockey Encyclopedia
By Stan Fischler and Shirley Walton Fischler
Research Editor: Bob Duff
Macmillan Publishing Company (1983)
New York

Hockey Hall of Fame
(The Official History of the Game and
Its Greatest Stars)
By Dan Diamond and Joseph Romain
Doubleday (1988)
Dell Publishing Group, Inc.
New York

Hockey Twenty Years
(The NHL since 1967)
By Dan Diamond and Lew Stubbs
Doubleday & Company, Inc.
Garden City, NY

The National Hockey League
By Edward F Dolan Jr.
Bison Books Corp (1986)
W H Smith Publishers Inc.
New York

**The NHL Official Guide & Record Book,
1988-89**
The National Hockey League
New York/Montreal

Trail of the Stanley Cup
Volumes I-III
By Charles L. Coleman
Progressive Publications, Inc. (1969)
Sherbrooke, Quebec

Sports Personalities

Facts & Dates of American Sports
By Gorton Carruth & Eugene Ehrlich
Harper & Row, Publishers, Inc. (1988)
New York

101 Greatest Athletes of the Century
By Will Grimsley and the
   Associated Press Sports Staff
Bonanza Books (1987)
Crown Publishers, Inc.
New York

Superstars
By Frank Litsky
Vineyard Books, Inc. (1975)
Derbibooks Inc.
Secaucus, NJ

"The 40 Who Changed Sports, 1946-86"
Sport Magazine
December, 1986
New York

Arenas & Ballparks

Ballparks of North America
by Michael Benson
McFarland & Company, Inc. (1989)
Jefferson, NC

The Ballparks
by Bill Shannon and George Kalinsky
Hawthorn Books, Inc. (1975)
New York

Green Cathedrals
by Philip J. Lowry
Society for American Baseball Research (1986)
Manhattan, KS

The NFL's Encyclopedic History of Professional Football
Macmillan Publishing Co., Inc. (1977)
New York

Take Me Out to the Ball Park
by Lowell Reidenbaugh
The Sporting News Publishing Co. (1983)
St.Louis

24 Seconds to Shoot
(An Informal History of the NBA)
by Leonard Koppett
The Macmillan Company (1968)
New York

Plus many major league baseball, NBA, NFL, NHL league and team guides, and major college football and basketball guides.

Bowling

Bowlers Journal 1988 Annual
January, 1988
Chicago, IL

LPBT 1989 Guide
Ladies Pro Bowlers Tour
Rockford, IL

PBA 1989 Press-Radio-TV Guide
Professional Bowlers Association
Akron, OH

Horse Racing

1989 Directory and Record Book
The Thoroughbred Racing Associations
Lake Success, NY

The Trotting and Pacing Guide, 1989
Compiled and edited by John Pawlak
United States Trotting Association
Columbus, OH

Breeders' Cup 1988 Statistics
Breeders' Cup Limited
Lexington, KY

The Belmont Stakes Media Guide, 1988
The New York Racing Assn. Inc.
Jamaica, NY

The Kentucky Derby Media Guide, 1989
Churchill Downs Public Relations Dept.
Louisville, KY

The Preakness Stakes Media Guide, 1987
Compiled and edited by Lynda J. O'Dea
Maryland Jockey Club
Baltimore, MD

Soccer

The American Encyclopedia of Soccer
Edited by Zander Hollander
Everest House Publishers (1980)
New York

The Guinness Book of Soccer Facts & Feats
By Jack Rollin
Guinness Superlatives Ltd (1978)
Middlesex, England

The History of the World Cup
By Brian Glanville
Faber and Faber Limited (1984)
London/Boston

History of Soccer's World Cup
By Michael Archer
Chartwell Books, Inc. (1978)
Secaucus, NJ

MISL Official Guide, 1988-89
Major Indoor Soccer League
Overland Park, KA

International Sports

All That Glitters Is Not Gold
(An Irreverent Look at the Olympic Games)
By William O. Johnson, Jr.
G.P. Putnam's Sons (1972)
New York

An Illustrated History of the Olympics
Third Edition (1975)
By Dick Schaap
Alfred A. Knopf
New York

The Complete Book of the Olympics
Revised Edition (1988)
By David Wallechinsky
Penguin Books
New York

International Track and Field Annual, 1989
Assn. of Track & Field Statisticians
Edited by Peter Matthews
Simon & Schuster
London/New York

Pursuit of Excellence
(The Olympic Story)
By The Associated Press and Grolier
Grolier Enterprises Inc. (1979)
Danbury, CT

United States Olympic Books
Seven Editions: 1936,48,52,56,60,61-65,68
U.S. Olympic Association
New York

Miscellaneous

The Encyclopedia of Sports
Fifth Revised Edition (1975)
By Frank G. Menke
Revisions by Suzanne Treat
A.S. Barnes and Co., Inc.
Cranbury, NJ

The Great American Sports Book
By George Gipe
Doubleday & Company, Inc (1978)
Garden City, NY

Guinness Book of Sports Records, Winners & Champions
1982-83 Edition
By Norris McWhirter
Sterling Publishing Co., Inc.
New York

The World of Marathons
By Sandy Treadwell
Stewart, Tabori & Chang, Inc. (1987)
New York

"Ten Years of the Ironman"
Triathlete Magazine
October, 1988
Santa Monica, CA

Tennis

The Illustrated Encyclopedia of World Tennis
By John Haylett and Richard Evans
Exeter Books (1989)
New York

1988 Official USTA Yearbook and Tennis Guide
U.S. Tennis Association
New York

Official 1989 MTC Media Guide
Men's Tennis Council
New York

1989 WITA Media Guide
Women's International Tennis Association
Miami, FL

Golf

The PGA Tour Book, 1989
PGA Tour
Ponte Vedra, FL

LPGA 1989 Player Guide
Ladies Professional Golf Association
Sugar Land, TX

USGA Record Book
(1895-1959 and 1960-80)
U.S. Golf Association
Far Hills, NJ

The Golf Digest Almanac, 1989
Edited by Lois E. Hains
Golf Digest/Tennis, Inc.
Trumbull, CT

Guinness Golf Records, Facts and Champions
By Donald Steel
Guinness Superlatives Ltd (1987)
Middlesex, England

Auto Racing

CART 1989 Media Guide
Championship Auto Racing Teams
Bloomfield Hills, MI

1989 NASCAR Winston Cup Media Guide
Compiled and edited by Bob Kelly
Winston Cup Publicity
Winston-Salem, NC

Indianapolis 500 Media Fact Book, 1988
Indianapolis Motor Speedway
Indianapolis

Marlboro Grand Prix Guide, 1950-88
Compiled by Jacques Deschenaux
Charles Stewart & Company Ltd
Brebtford, England

Daytona Speedweeks 1989
Daytona International Speedway
Daytona Beach, FL

Boxing

The Ring 1987 Record Book & Boxing Encyclopedia
Edited by Herbert G. Goldman
The Ring Publishing Corp.
New York

Other Reference Books

The World Book Encyclopedia
1988 Edition
World Book, Inc.
Chicago

The World Book Yearbooks
Annual Supplements, 1954-89
World Book, Inc.
Chicago

Major League Cities & Teams

In 1989, there were 110 major league sports teams playing baseball, basketball, football and hockey in 61 cities and towns in the United States and Canada. Listed below are the cities and the teams that play there. If a team actually plays in a nearby suburb, that town is in parentheses. On the back cover to the right is a map with the principal cities pointed out.

Please note that the map includes four incorrect state abbreviations. **IOWA** should be **IA** (not IO), **KANSAS** should be **KS** (not KA), **NEBRASKA** should be **NE** (not NB), and **NEVADA** should be **NV** (not NE). Also, the LI under Uniondale, NY stands for Long Island.

Anaheim
AL California Angels
NFL L.A. Rams

Arlington
AL Texas Rangers

Atlanta
NL Braves
NBA Hawks
NFL Falcons

Baltimore
AL Orioles

Boston
AL Red Sox
NBA Celtics
NFL N.E.Patriots (Foxboro)
NHL Bruins

Buffalo
NFL Bills (Orchard Park)
NHL Sabres

Calgary
CFL Stampeders
NHL Flames

Charlotte
NBA Hornets

Chicago
AL White Sox
NL Cubs
NBA Bulls
NFL Bears
NHL Blackhawks

Cincinnati
NL Reds
NFL Bengals

Cleveland
AL Indians
NBA Cavaliers (Richfield)
NFL Browns

Dallas
NBA Mavericks
NHL Cowboys (Irving)

Denver
NBA Nuggets
NFL Broncos

Detroit
AL Tigers
NBA Pistons (Auburn Hills)
NFL Lions (Pontiac)
NHL Red Wings

East Rutherford
NBA New Jersey Nets
NFL New York Giants
NFL New York Jets
NHL New Jersey Devils

Edmonton
CFL Eskimos
NHL Oilers

Green Bay
NFL Packers

Hamilton
CFL Tiger-Cats

Hartford
NHL Whalers

Houston
NL Astros
NBA Rockets
NFL Oilers

Indianapolis
NBA Pacers
NFL Colts

Kansas City
AL Royals
NFL Chiefs

Los Angeles
NL Dodgers
NBA Clippers
NBA Lakers (Inglewood)
NFL Raiders
NHL Kings (Inglewood)

Miami
NBA Heat
NFL Dolphins

Milwaukee
AL Brewers
NBA Bucks

Minneapolis
AL Minn. Twins
NBA Minn. Timberwolves
NFL Minn. Vikings
NHL Minn. North Stars
   (Bloomington)

Montreal
NL Expos
NHL Canadiens

New Orleans
NFL Saints

New York
AL Yankees
NL Mets
NBA Knicks
NHL Rangers

Oakland
AL Athletics
NBA Golden St. Warriors

Orlando
NBA Magic

Ottawa
CFL Rough Riders

Philadelphia
NL Phillies
NBA 76ers
NFL Eagles
NHL Flyers

Phoenix
NBA Suns
NFL Cardinals (Tempe)

Pittsburgh
NL Pirates
NFL Steelers
NHL Penguins

Portland
NBA Trail Blazers

Quebec City
NHL Nordiques

Regina
CFL Saskatchewan Roughriders

Sacramento
NBA Kings

St.Louis
NL Cardinals
NHL Blues

Salt Lake City
NBA Jazz

San Antonio
NBA Spurs

San Diego
NL Padres
NFL Chargers

San Francisco
NL Giants
NFL 49ers

Seattle
AL Mariners
NBA SuperSonics
NFL Seahawks

Tampa
NFL Buccaneers

Toronto
AL Blue Jays
CFL Argos
NHL Maple Leafs

Uniondale
NHL N.Y.Islanders

Vancouver
CFL B.C. Lions
NHL Canucks

Washington
NBA Bullets (Landover, Md.)
NFL Redskins
NHL Capitals (Landover, Md.)

Winnipeg
NHL Jets
CFL Blue Bombers